The University of Chicago Spanish–English Dictionary

Diccionario Universidad de Chicago Inglés–Español

D1529684

The University of Chicago Spanish–English Dictionary

Diccionario Universidad de Chicago Inglés–Español

Originally Compiled by Carlos Castillo and Otto F. Bond
Compilación original de Carlos Castillo y Otto F. Bond

SIXTH EDITION · *SEXTA EDICIÓN*

David A. Pharies
Editor in Chief · *Director*

María Irene Moyna
Editor · *Editora*

Gary K. Baker
Assistant Editor · *Redactor*

Meagan M. Day
Editorial Assistant · *Redactora*

POCKET BOOKS
NEW YORK LONDON TORONTO SYDNEY NEW DELHI

Pocket Books
A Division of Simon & Schuster, Inc.
1230 Avenue of the Americas
New York, NY 10020

Copyright © 2012 by The University of Chicago

Published by arrangement with The University of Chicago Press

All rights reserved, including the right to reproduce this book or portions thereof in any form whatsoever. For information, address The University of Chicago Press, 1427 East 60th Street, Chicago, IL 60637.

This Pocket Books paperback edition May 2013

POCKET and colophon are registered trademarks of Simon & Schuster, Inc.

For information about special discounts for bulk purchases, please contact Simon & Schuster Special Sales at 1-866-506-1949 or business@simonandschuster.com.

The Simon & Schuster Speakers Bureau can bring authors to your live event. For more information or to book an event, contact the Simon & Schuster Speakers Bureau at 1-866-248-3049 or visit our website at www.simonspeakers.com.

Manufactured in the United States of America

10 9 8 7 6 5 4 3 2

ISBN 978-1-4516-6910-7

Contents

Preface to the Sixth Edition

The *University of Chicago Spanish–English Dictionary* has been compiled for the general use of Spanish-speaking learners of American English and American English-speaking learners of Spanish. In step with the rapid pace of cultural and linguistic change at the beginning of the twenty-first century, we have thoroughly revised the *Dictionary* for its sixth edition to reflect the most current vocabulary and usage in both languages.

Since our goal is to ensure that users will always find the words and phrases they seek, the greatest change for this new edition is the addition of some six thousand words and meanings. In choosing among possible additions, we have paid particular attention to frequency of use in written and spoken contexts, since a user is more likely to seek a word that appears frequently (e.g., *libertad* 'liberty', number 540 in frequency according to the extensive list available at www.wordfrequency.info) than one that appears infrequently (e.g., *verdolaga* 'purslane', number 19,705).

Frequency of use cannot serve as the sole criterion for new material, however, for three reasons. First, some words become current so quickly that no frequency list can possibly capture them. Digital terminology offers good examples of this trend, such as the word *app*, which has risen from obscurity to universal acceptance in very little time. Second, some of the changes that a dictionary should reflect occur at a semantic or phrasal level not captured by frequencies. Current expressions such as *to go off on* 'to scold' and *to be down with* 'to be in agreement with' consist of extremely frequent words used in novel ways. Finally, a word can be essential without being frequent. Medical terms, for example, can be vitally important to anyone negotiating another nation's health system, even if they are used infrequently outside of medical contexts.

Medicine is in fact one of four cultural and technical areas of increasing global importance for which we have specially enhanced our coverage for this edition. Along with the 600 new words and meanings that have been added in this field, the sixth edition incorporates 750 new items from the field of business, 500 relating to digital technology, and over 400 relating to the terminology of several globally popular sports, including basketball, baseball, soccer, tennis, and golf.

In many cases, the additions in these four areas warranted completely new entries, as in the case of *allergen* (Sp. *alérgeno*), *auditing* (*auditoría*), *adapter* (*adaptador*), and *unplayable* (*injugable*). In many others, we added a meaning or an equivalent to an existing entry, as in the case of *pinza* (to whose entry was added Eng. *[medical] clamp*), *fraudulento* (adding *bogus*), *descifrar* (*to decrypt*), and *abanicar* (*to swing and miss*). On the English side, many additions take the form of compounds attached to existing entries—for example, *clubfoot* (*pie zambo*), added to the *club* entry; *business agreement* (*con-*

venio comercial), added to the *business* entry; *copy protection* (*protección contra copias*) added to *copy*; and *corner kick* (*córner*) added to *corner*.

To further increase the utility of the *Dictionary* for beginning learners of both Spanish and English, we have added "blind" or reference entries for irregular verb forms that differ markedly from their citation forms. These entries take the following form: *quepa, quepo*: ver *caber* (Spanish–English) and *frozen*: see *freeze* (English–Spanish).

Finally, we have invested considerable effort in expanding and perfecting the already well-developed set of semantic delimiters or disambiguators whose purpose is to help users differentiate among meanings in polysemic words. The English word *easy*, for example, has different Spanish equivalents according to whether it means 'simple' (*fácil, sencillo*), 'compliant' (*fácil*), 'comfortable' (*cómodo*), 'informal' (*desenvuelto*), or 'unworried' (*tranquilo*). Similarly, the Spanish word *gusto* has different equivalents for its several meanings: 'sentido', 'sabor', 'sentido estético' (*taste*), 'agrado' (*pleasure*), and 'preferencia personal' (*like*).

Preámbulo a la sexta edición

El *Diccionario Universidad de Chicago Inglés-Español* se ha compilado para el uso general de estudiantes hispanoparlantes que aprenden el inglés de los Estados Unidos y para estudiantes angloparlantes de los Estados Unidos que estudian español. Para acompasarse a los rápidos cambios culturales y lingüísticos que se vienen sucediendo desde comienzos del siglo XXI, se ha hecho una revisión profunda del *Diccionario* con el fin de reflejar el vocabulario y los usos más actualizados en ambas lenguas.

Ya que nuestro propósito es asegurar que los usuarios siempre encuentren los términos y expresiones que buscan, el cambio más sustancial de esta nueva edición es la inclusión de unos seis mil términos y significados nuevos. Para elegir entre las muchas posibles adiciones, se le prestó mucha atención a la frecuencia de uso en el medio escrito y oral, ya que es más probable que un usuario se encuentre con una palabra que aparece con frecuencia (v.g., *libertad*, que ocupa el puesto 540 en frecuencia según la exhaustiva lista de frecuencias disponible en www.wordfrequency.info) que con otra palabra que aparece con baja frecuencia (v.g., *verdolaga*, que ocupa el puesto 19.705 en la misma lista).

Sin embargo, la frecuencia de uso no puede ser el único criterio empleado para incluir material nuevo, por tres razones. En primer lugar, algunas palabras se generalizan tan rápidamente que no alcanzan a ser incluidas en listas de frecuencia. Un buen ejemplo de esta tendencia lo constituye la terminología digital; considérese la palabra inglesa *app* 'aplicación informática', que en muy poco tiempo ha pasado de ser casi desconocida a tener aceptación general. En segundo lugar, algunos de los cambios que debe reflejar un diccionario suceden al nivel de la frase, y estos cambios no se pueden registrar meramente a partir de las frecuencias de los términos. Algunas expresiones actuales tales como *to go off on* 'regañar' y *to be down with* 'estar de acuerdo con' están constituidas por palabras de alta frecuencia empleadas en combinaciones novedosas. Por último, una palabra puede ser esencial sin por ello ser muy frecuente. Por ejemplo, la terminología médica puede ser de importancia vital para alguien que está tratando de resolver un problema de salud mientras se encuentra en un país extranjero. Por lo tanto, esas palabras deben figurar en el *Diccionario* aunque sean de poca frecuencia fuera de los contextos médicos.

De hecho, la medicina es una de las cuatro áreas culturales y técnicas cuya cobertura se ha aumentado en esta edición, debido a su importancia cada vez mayor en el contexto internacional. Además de 600 nuevos términos y significados del área médica, la presente edición incorpora 750 nuevos términos del campo de los negocios, 500 relacionados con el mundo de la informática y la tecnología digital y más de 400 relacionados con varios deportes de popularidad mundial, incluyendo el baloncesto, el béisbol, el fútbol, el tenis y el golf.

En muchos casos, las incorporaciones a estos cuatro campos nos llevaron a crear entradas completamente nuevas, como es el caso de *alérgeno* (ing. *allergen*), *auditoría* (*auditing*), *adaptador* (*adapter*) e *injugable* (*unplayable*). En muchos otros casos, se agregó un significado o un equivalente nuevo a una entrada preexistente. Tal es el caso de *pinza* (a cuya entrada se le agregó el significado inglés de [*medical*] *clamp*), *fraudulento* (*bogus*), *descifrar* (*decrypt*) y *abanicar* (con el significado en béisbol de *to swing and miss*). En el lado inglés, se incorporaron muchos términos compuestos a entradas ya existentes, tales como *clubfoot* (*pie zambo*), que fue agregado a la entrada de *club*; *business agreement* (*convenio comercial*), que fue agregado a la entrada de *business*; *copy protection* (*protección contra copias*) agregado a *copy*; y *corner kick* (*córner*) agregado a *corner*.

Para hacer todavía más útil el *Diccionario* para los estudiantes principiantes tanto de español como de inglés, se han agregado entradas "ciegas" o de referencia, para las formas verbales irregulares que son muy diferentes de sus formas infinitivas. Estas entradas tienen la siguiente estructura: *quepa*, *quepo*: ver *caber* (español–inglés) y *frozen*: see *freeze* (inglés–español).

Por último, se ha hecho un esfuerzo considerable para expandir y perfeccionar todavía más los delimitadores semánticos o desambiguadores, que tienen como propósito asistir a los usuarios a distinguir entre los diversos significados de palabras polisémicas. Por ejemplo, la palabra inglesa *easy* tiene diferentes equivalentes en español según signifique 'simple' (*fácil o sencillo*), 'compliant' (*fácil*), 'comfortable' (*cómodo*), 'informal' (*desenvuelto*) o 'unworried' (*tranquilo*). Del mismo modo, la palabra española *gusto* tiene diferentes equivalentes ingleses para sus múltiples significados: *taste* para 'sentido', 'sabor', 'sentido estético', *pleasure* para 'agrado' y *like* para 'preferencia personal'.

How to Use *The University of Chicago Spanish-English Dictionary*

Order of Entries

Alphabetical order is observed irrespective of hyphens or spaces, such that *air conditioner* precedes *aircraft* and *middle school* precedes *middle-sized*. Homographs are placed under a single entry (*lie* 'to prevaricate', *lie* 'to recline', both pronounced [laɪ]), unless they are pronounced differently (e.g., *bow* [baʊ] 'forward end of a vessel', *bow* [bo] 'bend, curve'). Regarding Spanish, according to the current policy of the Spanish Royal Academy,[1] *ch* and *ll* are no longer recognized as separate letters, such that *ch* now follows *ce* and precedes *ci*, and *ll* follows *li* and precedes *lo* in alphabetization.

Compounds listed within entries are also alphabetized. However, the need to list compounds under their first element sometimes interferes with alphabetization, as when *slumlord*, a compound listed under *slum*, comes before the next headword, *slumber*, even though strict alphabetization would require the reverse.

Spelling

Spelling of English words reflects common American usage, variants being noted where applicable (*ax*, *axe*; *sulfur*, *sulphur*; *stymie*, *stymy*). The spelling of Spanish words, where possible, follows the conventions of the Spanish Royal Academy. For the orthography of problematic Spanish words such as recent borrowings (*escáner*, *scooter*), country names (*Malí*, *Irak*) and adjectives of nationality (*zimbabuo*), a variety of authorities were consulted, including the *Diccionario del español actual*, the *Diccionario de dudas*, the *Libro de estilo* published by the Madrid newspaper *El País*, and various Internet sources.[2] It should be noted that there is vacillation in some cases, such as *Bahrain*, which is listed as *Bahrein* in the *Libro de estilo* and as *Bahráin* or *Bahréin* in the *Diccionario de dudas*. In these cases, we either opt for the form that appears to be most generally accepted or provide multiple equivalents.

---

1. Real Academia Española, *Ortografía de la lengua española* (Madrid: Espasa-Calpe, 1999), 2.

2. Manuel Seco, Olimpia Andrés, and Gabino Ramos, *Diccionario del español actual* (Madrid: Aguilar, 1999); Manuel Seco, *Diccionario de dudas y dificultades de la lengua española*, 10th ed. (Madrid: Espasa-Calpe, 1998); *El País: Libro de estilo*, 9th ed. (Madrid: Ediciones El País, 1990).

Omissions

Some categories of words are systematically omitted from the vocabulary entries. Adverbial forms ending in *-ly* (English) and *-mente* (Spanish) are included only when their usage and meaning are not transparently derivable from their adjectival bases. Thus, *clearly* is omitted, as its usage is predictable from its adjectival base ('in a clear way'), while *surely* is included, since in addition to 'in a sure way', it means 'undoubtedly' or 'without fail'. Similarly, *claramente* 'clearly' is omitted, while *atentamente* is retained, since the latter, in addition to meaning 'in an attentive manner', is used as a farewell, equivalent to 'yours truly'. Also, English nouns ending in *-ing* and adjectives in *-ed*, which may appear as glosses of Spanish words, are not always accorded separate entries on the English–Spanish side, due to their derivational regularity and to considerations of space.

Structure of Entries

1. HEADWORD. Spelling variants, if any, follow the most frequent form, which appears first. In Spanish, occupational designations, titles, and kinship terms are shown in both masculine and feminine forms, as in *abogado -da*.

2. PRONUNCIATION. Pronunciation of English words is indicated through a modified version of the International Phonetic Alphabet, whose conventions are explained on pp. 292–93. No individual transcription of Spanish words is required, given the simplicity and consistency of the Spanish orthographic system. See "The Spanish Spelling System and the Sounds Represented" (p. 2) for an explanation.

3. GRAMMATICAL CATEGORY. Meanings are marked according to whether they reflect usage as a noun (N), adjective (ADJ), adverb (ADV), conjunction (CONJ), preposition (PREP), pronoun (PRON), interjection (INTERJ), transitive verb (VT), or intransitive verb (VI). The exception to this rule is that nouns on the Spanish–English side are marked only by gender, M (masculine noun) or F (feminine noun).

   Order of meanings within an entry reflects frequency of usage. Where more than one grammatical category can be rendered by the same gloss, the two are listed together, cf. Eng. *red*, which can be glossed as Sp. *rojo* in both its adjective and noun meanings.

   Traditionally, Spanish adjectives are listed in their masculine form only. However, where the adjective normally functions as a noun as well, it is shown with both masculine and feminine forms if both are possible, cf. the case of *africano -na*, which can mean *African* in the adjectival sense as well as *African* (*man*) and *African* (*woman*).

   Special mention must be made of the combination "VI/VT." Occasionally, a single verb form may function both transitively and intransitively, e.g., both *to eat* and its Spanish equivalent *comer*. Not infrequently, however, Spanish glosses of English intransitives require the addition of the pronominal particle *-se*. Thus, in cases such as *to bathe*, marked "VI/VT" and glossed *bañar(se)*, it should be understood that the bare form is transitive and the *-se* form intransitive. Finally, where transitivity differs between a headword and its equivalent in the second language, particles must be added to reflect this, as in the case of the transitive English verb *to regret*, which is glossed in Spanish as *arrepentirse de*, since *arrepentirse* alone is intransitive. Where an English verb can be used both transitively and intransitively and its Spanish equivalent is only intransitive, the latter may sometimes be made transitive through the addition of a preposition, which appears in brackets. Thus, English *fight* is glossed as *pelear [con]* to show that its intransitive equivalent is *pelear*, whereas its transitive equivalent is *pelear con*.

Again for reasons of economy, pronominal forms of Spanish verbs are omitted in two cases: first, when the particle *-se* functions as a direct object, either reflexive or reciprocal, cf. *mirarse*, which can mean both *to look at oneself* and *to look at each other*, and second, when the addition of *-se* does not affect the English translation, cf. *bañar(se)*, glossed in both meanings as *to bathe*. In contrast, pronominal forms of verbs are included when they differ substantially in meaning from the bare forms, cf. *ir*, glossed as *to go*, vs. *irse*, which means *to leave*.

4. DELIMITERS. Whenever a word, within a grammatical category, is considered to have two or more meanings, these are differentiated by means of delimiters, that is, explanatory markers. Most commonly, synonyms are used, cf. *retort*, which in the meaning 'reply' is glossed as *réplica* and in the meaning 'vessel' as *retorta*. On occasion, however, other strategies may be adopted. Thus, transitive verbs are sometimes best differentiated according to the objects they take, cf. *to negotiate* (a contract), which is glossed *negociar*, while *to negotiate* (an obstacle) is glossed *salvar*. Similarly, adjectives may be most easily distinguished by showing the referents to which they regularly apply, cf. *refreshing*, which applied to drink is *refrescante*, to sleep is *reparador*, and to honesty is *amable*. Not infrequently, a single equivalent covers almost all meanings of a headword in a single grammatical category. In such cases, only the "exceptional" meaning, placed second, is delimited. For example, the equivalent of Eng. *net* in almost all its meanings is Sp. *red*, but when it refers specifically to a hairnet it is *redecilla*. Although delimiters typically precede the gloss they are meant to distinguish, occasionally they are placed afterward. In these cases they are meant to erase doubts about the applicability of a given gloss in a specific secondary context, cf. *site*, whose gloss *sitio* is followed by the delimiter "also Internet."

5. GLOSSES. Insofar as is possible, glosses are intended to match the headword in terms of meaning, register, and frequency. Thus, *cop* is glossed as *poli* rather than the more formal *policía*. Similarly, *orinar* is glossed as *to urinate* rather than the informal and vulgar *to pee*. Glosses separated by a comma are to be considered interchangeable, if not perfectly synonymous. Semicolons, on the other hand, indicate separate meanings.

6. REGIONAL USAGE. No systematic attempt has been made to reflect regional usage in either English or Spanish, since in the great majority of cases a word of more general currency is available as a gloss. Thus, among the many Spanish equivalents of Eng. *peasant*, Sp. *campesino* is understood everywhere, even where a local term also exists, such as Puerto Rican *jíbaro*, Cuban *guajiro*, and Chilean

guaso. However, Spanish regional usage is marked where any of the following conditions are met: (1) there is no term of international currency, or it might not be understood in a given location (cf. the various regional Spanish equivalents of Eng. *bean*) or (2) a specific regionalism is known throughout the Spanish-speaking world to be typical of a given dialect, cf. River Plate *che* 'hey!', Mexican *ándale* 'come on!', *cuate* 'pal'.

7. STYLISTIC MARKERS. Because, as mentioned earlier, equivalents are chosen in order to match headwords in all aspects of their meaning, including register and frequency, stylistic markers are only infrequently employed. For example, there is no need to mark the Spanish gloss *tonto* as familiar, since it is meant to be equivalent to the equally familiar Eng. *fool.* Only five register markers are employed: literary (*lit*), which also includes poetic and formal language; familiar (*fam*), which designates words used among family and friends; vulgar (*vulg*), for words whose use is socially censured; pejorative (*pej*), which implies a negative evaluation; and *offensive* (not abbreviated), for words meant to insult people.

8. COMPOUNDS. Ease of usage would dictate that each lexical item receive its own entry, but for reasons of economy this is not possible in a concise dictionary. This explains why compound words, which are composed of two or more preexisting words, are listed in almost all cases under the entry of their initial constituent, at the end of the corresponding grammatical category. Thus, *doghouse* is listed as —*house*, under *dog.* There are certain exceptions to this convention, however. First, compounds are listed under the headword of their second constituent when the first is extremely frequent, as are the so-called empty verbs such as Eng. *keep*, *take*, *turn*, Sp. *hacer*, *tener*, *tomar.* Thus, *to have a good time*, glossed *divertirse*, is listed under *time* rather than *have*, and *tener paciencia*, glossed *to be patient*, is under *paciencia* rather than *tener.* Second, English compounds whose first element is a preposition (*offsides*, *outcast*, *overcome*) are listed as separate headwords, chiefly because of their frequent grammatical complexity, cf. *overhead*, which can be an adverb (*it flew overhead*), an adjective (*overhead projector*), or a noun (*overhead from grant money*). Conversely, derived words, that is, words that contain one or more affixes (e.g., *antiabortion*, composed of the prefix *anti-* plus *abortion*, and *kingdom*, composed of *king* plus the suffix *-dom*), are listed as separate headwords.

9. ILLUSTRATIVE PHRASES. Appearing together with the compound words pertinent to any given grammatical category are illustrative phrases, a category defined so as to include idioms, collocations, proverbs, and, especially, sentences required to clarify usage in some way, as when the usage of *gustarle a uno* as a gloss of *to like* is illustrated by the phrase *he likes dogs*, with the translation *le gustan los perros.*

Cómo usar el *Diccionario Universidad de Chicago Inglés–Español*

Orden de las entradas

Se respeta el orden alfabético, independientemente de la presencia de guiones o espacios, de tal manera que *air conditioning* precede a *aircraft* y *middle school* precede a *middle-sized*. Los homógrafos se ubican en una sola entrada (*lie* 'mentir' y *lie* 'yacer', ambos con la pronunciación [laɪ]), a no ser que se pronuncien de forma diferente (e.g., *bow* [baʊ] 'proa' y *bow* [bo] 'curva'). En cuanto al español y siguiendo la política oficial de la Real Academia Española,[1] *ch* y *ll* ya no se reconocen como letras independientes, de tal manera que *ch* ahora sigue a *ce* y precede a *ci*, y *ll* sigue a *li* y precede a *lo* en el orden alfabético.

Asimismo, los compuestos incluidos dentro de una entrada determinada aparecen en orden alfabético a continuación de su primer elemento, lo cual a veces interfiere con el orden alfabético general. Así, por ejemplo, *rompeolas* aparece a continuación de *romper*, porque se trata de un compuesto de dicho verbo, si bien el orden alfabético requeriría lo contrario.

Ortografía

La ortografía de los vocablos ingleses refleja el uso general en inglés americano, y las variantes se incluyen en los casos pertinentes (*ax, axe; sulfur, sulphur; stymie, stymy*). La ortografía española sigue las convenciones de la Real Academia Española. Para la grafía española de palabras problemáticas, tales como préstamos recientes (*escáner, scooter*), nombres de países (*Malí, Irak*) y gentilicios (*zimbabuo*), se consultaron fuentes tales como el *Diccionario del español actual*, el *Diccionario de dudas*, el *Libro de estilo* de *El País* de Madrid y varios sitios en el internet.[2] Corresponde hacer notar que la grafía de algunos términos vacila entre varias posibles, cf. la versión española de *Bahrain*, que aparece como *Bahrein* en el *Libro de estilo* y como *Bahráin* o *Bahréin* en el *Diccionario de dudas*, en cuyo caso damos la forma que parece más generalmente aceptada u ofrecemos varias.

---

1. Real Academia Española, *Ortografía de la lengua española* (Madrid: Espasa-Calpe, 1999), 2.

2. Manuel Seco, Olimpia Andrés y Gabino Ramos, *Diccionario del español actual* (Madrid: Aguilar, 1999); Manuel Seco, *Diccionario de dudas y dificultades de la lengua española*, 10ª ed. (Madrid: Espasa-Calpe, 1998); *El País: Libro de estilo*, 9ª ed. (Madrid: Ediciones El País, 1990).

Omisiones

Algunas categorías de palabras se omiten sistemáticamente de las entradas del diccionario. Las formas adverbiales que terminan en *-mente* (español) y en *-ly* (inglés) se incluyen solamente cuando su uso y significado no pueden deducirse claramente de sus bases adjetivas. De esta forma, *claramente* se omite, ya que su significado es predecible a partir de su base adjetiva ('de manera clara'), mientras que *atentamente* se incluye, ya que además de significar 'de manera atenta', también se usa como fórmula de despedida epistolar. Del mismo modo, se omite *clearly*, porque su equivalente, 'de manera clara', se deduce de su base adjetiva, mientras que se incluye *surely* porque además de significar 'de forma segura' también quiere decir 'sin duda'. Debe notarse también que los sustantivos ingleses terminados en *-ing* y los adjetivos en *-ed*, que pueden aparecer como traducción de palabras españolas en la parte español–inglés, no figuran siempre como cabezas de artículo en la parte inglés–español debido a la total regularidad de su formación y a consideraciones de espacio.

Estructura de las entradas

1. PALABRAS CABEZA DE ARTÍCULO. Las variantes ortográficas, si las hay, siguen a la forma más frecuente, que aparece en primer término. En español, las designaciones de profesiones y oficios, los títulos y las relaciones de parentesco aparecen tanto en la forma masculina como en la femenina, como por ejemplo, *abogado -da*.

2. PRONUNCIACIÓN. La pronunciación de las palabras inglesas se indica mediante una versión modificada del Alfabético Fonético Internacional, cuyas convenciones se explican en las pgs. 292–93. No se requiere transcripción individual de las palabras españolas, gracias a la simplicidad y sistematicidad de la ortografía española. Para detalles, ver la sección titulada "The Spanish Spelling System" en la p. 2.

3. CATEGORÍA GRAMATICAL. Los significados se marcan según reflejen el uso de la palabra como sustantivo masculino (*m*), sustantivo femenino (*f*), adjetivo (*adj*), adverbio (*adv*), conjunción (*conj*), preposición (*prep*), pronombre (*pron*), interjección (*interj*), verbo transitivo (*vt*) o verbo intransitivo (*vi*). En inglés, en cambio, los sustantivos se marcan con *n*, abreviación de *noun*.

   Los significados dentro de una entrada aparecen ordenados de manera que el más frecuente figure primero. Cuando la misma traducción cubre el significado de dos categorías gramaticales, ambas aparecen juntas, cf. el inglés *red*, que puede traducirse como *rojo* tanto en su significado sustantivo como en el adjetivo.

   Siguiendo la tradición, los adjetivos españoles aparecen exclusivamente en su forma masculina. Sin embargo, cuando el adjetivo frecuentemente funciona además como sustantivo, se muestra tanto en la forma masculina como en la femenina si ambas son posibles, cf. el caso de *africano -na*, traducido al inglés como *African*, forma adecuada para todos sus usos.

   La combinación *vi/vt* merece mención especial. En ocasiones, una única forma verbal funciona tanto transitiva como intransitivamente, v.g., tanto *comer* como su equivalente inglés *to eat*. Sin embargo, es también frecuente que las traducciones españolas de verbos intransitivos ingleses requieran el agregado de una partícula pronominal -*se*. Así, en casos tales como *to bathe*, que se marca "vi/vt" y se traduce como *bañar(se)*, debe entenderse que la forma no pronominalizada es transitiva y la forma con -*se* es intransitiva. En aquellos casos cuando la palabra cabeza de artículo y su equivalente en la otra lengua difieren en transitividad, se deben agregar partículas para reflejar esta diferencia. Tal es el caso del verbo *aprobar*, que se traduce al inglés como *to approve of* en algunos de sus significados, ya que *to approve* es intransitivo si no va acompañado de preposición. Finalmente, en los casos en los que un verbo español puede usarse tanto intransitiva como transitivamente y su equivalente inglés es exclusivamente intransitivo, este último puede a veces volverse transitivo mediante el agregado de una preposición entre corchetes. Así, el esp. *chivar* se traduce como *to snitch* [*on*] para mostrar que su forma intransitiva en inglés es *to snitch* mientras que el equivalente transitivo es *to snitch on*.

Por razones de espacio se omiten las formas pronominales de los verbos españoles en dos casos. En primer lugar, se omiten si la partícula pronominal hace las veces de complemento directo reflexivo o recíproco, cf. *mirarse* (a sí mismo o el uno al otro). En segundo lugar no se incluyen tampoco si la partícula pronominal no afecta la traducción al inglés, como en el caso de *bañar* y *bañarse*, ambos *to bathe*. Sí se incluyen aquellas formas pronominales que difieren semánticamente de sus verbos de base, cf. *ir* vs. *irse*.

4. INDICADORES SEMÁNTICOS. En aquellos casos en los que una palabra, dentro de una misma categoría gramatical, tiene dos o más acepciones, estas se distinguen por medio de indicadores semánticos, o sea, explicaciones parentéticas. Lo más frecuente es que se empleen sinónimos, cf. *arco*, que se traduce *arc* cuando se trata de una curva, como *arch* cuando se refiere a una estructura arquitectónica, y como *bow* cuando se trata de un arma, aunque en otras ocasiones se adoptan otras estrategias. Así, los verbos transitivos a veces se distinguen con mayor facilidad mediante los tipos de complementos directos que los acompañan, cf. *acordonar* (un zapato) *to lace,* (un lugar) *to rope off,* (una moneda) *to mill*, mientras que la forma más sencilla de distinguir adjetivos es mostrar los tipos de referentes a los cuales se aplican con mayor frecuencia, cf. *inseguro*, que aplicado a una personalidad se traduce por *insecure*, a un vehículo por *unsafe*, y al andar por *unsteady*. Es frecuente que un único equivalente abarque casi todas las acepciones de una palabra cabeza de artículo dentro de una categoría gramatical determinada. En esos casos, solamente el significado "excepcional", que aparece en segundo lugar, se acompaña de un indicador semántico. Por ejemplo, el equivalente de *acceso* en casi todas sus acepciones es *access*, excepto cuando se refiere a un ataque de tos o rabia, en cuyo caso se traduce como *fit*. Aunque los indicadores semánticos normalmente preceden a la traducción que les corresponde, en ocasiones se ubican después. En estos casos tienen como objetivo eliminar dudas acerca del empleo de una traducción determinada en un contexto secundario específico, cf. *acompañar*, cuya traducción *to accompany* va seguida de un indicador semántico "también en música" para confirmar al lector su aplicación a ese contexto.

5. TRADUCCIONES. En la medida de lo posible, se ha tratado de que las traducciones sean equivalentes a la palabra cabeza de artículo en cuanto a su significado, registro y frecuencia. Así, *poli* se traduce como *cop* y no como *policeman*, palabra más formal. De la misma forma, *to urinate* se traduce como *orinar* y no como *hacer pipí*, palabra más familiar. Las traducciones separadas por una coma deben considerarse equivalentes, aunque no sean exactamente sinónimas. El uso del punto y coma indica acepciones distintas.

6. USO REGIONAL. No se ha hecho ningún esfuerzo sistemático por reflejar usos regionales, ni en inglés ni en español, ya que en la gran mayoría de los casos existe una palabra de uso general. Así, entre los muchos equivalentes españoles de la palabra inglesa *peasant*, su equivalente español *campesino* se entiende en todo el mundo de habla hispana, aun cuando existan términos locales, tales como *jíbaro* en Puerto Rico, *guajiro* en Cuba y *guaso* en Chile. Sin embargo, el uso regional se indica para el español en tres casos específicos. En primer lugar se encuentran los casos en los que una palabra determinada podría resultar desconocida en una región dada, como los varios equivalentes españoles del ingl. *bean*. En segundo término, se han incluido regionalismos que se reconocen en todo el mundo de habla hispana como típicos de un dialecto determinado, cf. español rioplatense *che*, mexicano *ándale*, *cuate*.

7. INDICADORES DE ESTILO. Ya que, como se mencionó anteriormente, los equivalentes se eligen para que correspondan a las palabras cabeza de artículo en todos los aspectos de su significado, incluyendo nivel de lengua y frecuencia, los indicadores de estilo se usan poco. Por ejemplo, no hay necesidad de indicar que la palabra inglesa *fool* es familiar, ya que figura como equivalente del español *tonto*. Se han empleado cinco indicadores de estilo: literario (*lit*), que incluye lenguaje poético y formal, familiar (*fam*), que designa palabras que se usan en situaciones de intimidad, vulgar (*vulg*), que designa términos cuyo uso está censurado socialmente, peyorativo (*pey*), que designa palabras que tienen una carga connotativa negativa hacia el referente, y ofensivo (sin abreviar), que designa insultos.

8. COMPUESTOS. El criterio de facilidad de uso requeriría que cada palabra recibiera su propia entrada, pero por razones de economía de espacio esto no es posible en un diccionario conciso. Por lo tanto, las palabras compuestas, formadas por dos o más vocablos preexistentes, aparecen en casi todos los casos en la entrada de su primer constituyente, al final de la categoría gramatical correspondiente. De tal forma, *hombre rana* aparece como — *rana*, en la entrada de *hombre*. Hay ciertas excepciones a esta regla, sin embargo. En primer lugar, los compuestos aparecen bajo la cabeza de artículo de su segundo constituyente cuando el primero es extremadamente frecuente, tal como lo son los verbos semánticamente "vacíos" como el español *hacer*, *tener*, *tomar* y el inglés *to keep*, *to take*, *to turn*. De este modo, *tener paciencia* aparece en la entrada de *paciencia* y no en la de *tener*, y *to have a good time* figura bajo *time* y no bajo *to have*. En segundo lugar, los compuestos ingleses cuyo primer elemento es una preposición (*offsides*, *overcome*, *outcast*) aparecen como cabezas de artículo independientes, sobre todo debido a su complejidad gramatical, cf. *overhead*, que puede ser adverbio (*it flew overhead*, que equivale a *voló en lo alto*), adjetivo (*overhead projector*, es decir, *retroproyector*) y sustantivo (*overhead from*

grant money, o sea, *gastos generales de una subvención*). No obstante, las palabras de-rivadas, i.e., aquellas que contienen uno o más afijos (e.g., *anticuerpo*, compuesta del prefijo *anti-* y *cuerpo*, y *cabezón*, compuesta por *cabeza* y el sufijo *-ón*), figuran como cabezas de artículo independientes.

9. FRASES ILUSTRATIVAS. Junto con las palabras compuestas de una determinada categoría gramatical figuran las frases ilustrativas, una categoría que incluye ex-presiones idiomáticas, colocaciones típicas, refranes y, especialmente, oraciones necesarias para aclarar el uso de alguna palabra, como cuando el uso de *like* como traducción de *gustar* se ilustra con la frase *he likes dogs*, que se traduce *le gustan los perros*.

Spanish–English · Español–Inglés

List of Abbreviations / Lista de abreviaturas

adj	adjective	adjetivo
adv	adverb, adverbial	adverbio, adverbial
Am	America	América
art	article	artículo
Carib	Caribbean	Caribe
conj	conjunction	conjunción
def	definite	definido
dem	demonstrative	demostrativo
Esp	Spain, Spanish	España, español
f	feminine	femenino
fam	familiar	familiar
indef	indefinite	indefinido
interj	interjection	interjección
interr	interrogative	interrogativo
inv	invariable	invariable
lit	literary	literario
loc	locution	locución
m	masculine	masculino
Méx	Mexico	México
num	numeral	numeral
pej, pey	pejorative	peyorativo
pers	personal	personal
pl	plural	plural
pos	possessive	posesivo
prep	preposition, prepositional	preposición, preposicional
pron	pronoun	pronombre
rel	relative	relativo
RP	River Plate	Río de la Plata
sg	singular	singular
Sp	Spain, Spanish	España, español
v aux	auxiliary verb	verbo auxiliar
vi	intransitive verb	verbo intransitivo
vt	transitive verb	verbo transitivo
vulg	vulgar	vulgar

Spanish Pronunciation

Spanish orthography very closely mirrors Spanish pronunciation, much more so than is the case in English. This explains why, in bilingual dictionaries such as this, each English entry must be accompanied by a phonetic representation, while Spanish pronunciation may be presented in synoptic form.

This synopsis is meant only as an introduction, however. In spite of the clarity of the orthographical system of Spanish, the individual sounds of the language are difficult for adult native speakers of English to pronounce, and this difficulty is compounded by the syllabic structure of the language. For these reasons, readers who wish to perfect their pronunciation of Spanish are strongly advised to seek the help of a competent teacher.

To say that orthography mirrors pronunciation means that there is a close correlation between letters and sounds. Thus, most Spanish letters correspond to a single sound, or to a single family of closely related sounds, as is the case for all vowels and the consonants *f, l, m, n, p, t,* and *s*. In a few cases a single letter represents two very different sounds, as *c*, which is pronounced as *k* before *a, o,* and *u*, but *th* (as in *thin*, in parts of Spain, or as *s* in America) before *e* or *i*. Rarely, two letters represent a single sound, as in the case of *ch*.

The overarching differences between Spanish and English pronunciation are tenseness of articulation and syllabification within the breath group. Due to the tenseness of their articulation, for example, all Spanish vowels have a clear nondiphthongal character, unlike English long vowels, which tend to be bipartite (e.g., *late*, pronounced [leⁱt]). Syllabification is a problem for English speakers because in Spanish, syllables are formed without respect to word boundaries, such that *el hado* 'fate' and *helado* 'ice cream' are both pronounced as e-la-do, and the phrase *tus otras hermanas* 'your other sisters' is syllabified as tu-so-tra-ser-ma-nas. In fast speech, vowels may combine, as in *lo ofendiste* 'you offended him', pronounced lo-fen-dis-te. Finally, when Spanish consonants occur in clusters, very often the articulation of the second influences that of the first, as when *un peso* 'one peso' is pronounced um-pe-so, and *en que* 'in which' is pronounced eŋ ke, where ŋ represents the sound of the letters *ng* in English.

The Spanish Spelling System and the Sounds Represented

I.   VOWELS

i as a single vowel always represents a sound similar to the second vowel of *police*. Examples: **hilo, camino, piso.** As a part of a diphthong, it sounds like the *y* of English *yes, year*. Examples: **bien, baile, reina.**

e is similar to the vowel of *late* ([leⁱt]), but without the diphthong. Examples: **mesa, hablé, tres.**

a is similar to the vowel of *pod*. Examples: **casa, mala, América.** Notably, **a** is always pronounced this way, even when not stressed. This contrasts with the English tendency to reduce unstressed vowels to schwa ([ə]), as in *America*, pronounced in English as [ə-mé-rɪ-kə].

o has a value similar to that of the vowel in Eng. *coat* [koʷt], but without the diphthong. Examples: **no, modo, amó.**

u has a value similar to that of English *oo*, as in *boot* [buʷt], but without the diphthong. Examples: **cura, agudo, uno.** Note that the letter **u** is not pronounced in the syllables **qui, que, gui,** and **gue** (unless spelled with dieresis, as in *bilingüe*). When **u** occurs in diphthongs such as those of **cuida, cuento, deuda,** it has the sound of *w* (as in *way*).

II. CONSONANTS

b and **v** represent the same sounds in Spanish. At the beginning of a breath group or when preceded by the *m* sound (which may be spelled *n*), they are both pronounced like English *b*. Examples: **bomba, en vez de, vine, invierno.** In other environments, especially between vowels, both letters are pronounced as a very relaxed *b*, in which the lips do not completely touch and the air is not completely stopped. This sound has no equivalent in English. Examples: **haba, uva, la vaca, la banda.**

c represents a *k* sound before **a, o, u, l,** and **r.** However, this sound is not accompanied by a puff of air as it is in Eng. *can* and *coat* (compare the *c* in *scan*, which is more similar to the Spanish sound). Examples: **casa, cosa, cuna, crudo, aclamar.** In contrast, when appearing before the vowels **e** and **i, c** is pronounced as *s* in Spanish America and the southwest of Spain, and as *th* (as in *thin*) in other parts of Spain (see **s** for more information).

ch is no longer considered to be a separate letter in the Spanish alphabet. However, it represents a single sound, which is similar to the English *ch* in *church* and *cheek*. Examples: **chato, chaleco, mucho.**

d is phonetically complex in Spanish. In terms of articulation, it is pronounced by the tongue touching the teeth rather than the alveolar ridge as in English. Second, it is represented by two variants. The first of these, which is similar to that of English *dame* and *did*, occurs at the beginning of breath groups or after **n** and **l.** Examples: **donde, falda, conde.** In all other situations the letter represents a sound similar to the *th* of English *then*. Examples: **hado, cuerda, cuadro, usted.** This sound tends to be very relaxed, to the point of disappearing in certain environments, such as word-final and intervocalic.

f is very similar to the English *f* sound. Examples: **faro, elefante, alfalfa.**

g is phonetically complex. Before the vowels **e** and **i,** it is pronounced as *h* in many American dialects, while in northern Spain it is realized like the *ch* in the German word *Bach.* Examples: **gente, giro.** At the beginning of breath groups and after nasals before the vowels **a, o, u,** and the consonants **l** and **r,** it is pronounced like the **g** of English *go.* Examples: **ganga, globo, grada.** In all other environments it is pronounced as a very relaxed *g.* Examples: **lago, la goma, agrado.**

h is silent. Examples: **hoja, humo, harto.**

j is realized in most American dialects as *h,* while in northern Spain it is pronounced like the *ch* in the German word *Bach.* Examples: **jamás, jugo, jota.**

k sounds like Eng. *k,* but without the accompanying puff of air. Examples: **kilo, keroseno.**

l is pronounced forward in the mouth, as the *l* in *leaf, leak,* never in the back, as in *bell, full.* Examples: **lado, ala, sol.**

ll is no longer considered to be a separate letter in the Spanish alphabet. However, it does represent a single sound, which differs widely in pronunciation throughout the Spanish-speaking world. In most areas, it is pronounced like the *y* of Eng. *yes,* though with greater tension. In extreme northern Spain and in parts of the Andes, it sounds like the *lli* in Eng. *million.* In the River Plate area it is pronounced like the *g* in *beige* or the *sh* in *ship.* Examples: **calle, llano, olla.**

m is essentially the same as in English. Examples: **madre, mano, cama.** However, in final position, as in **álbum** 'album', it is pronounced as [ŋ], the final sound of Eng. *sing.*

n is normally pronounced like Eng. *n.* Examples: **no, mano, hablan.** There are exceptions, however. For example, before **b, v, p,** and **m,** it is pronounced *m,* as in **en Barcelona, en vez de, un peso,** while before **k, g, j, ge-,** and **gi-,** it is realized as [ŋ], the final sound of Eng. *sing,* as in **anca, tengo, naranja, engendrar.**

ñ is similar to but more tense than the *ny* of Eng. *canyon.* Examples: **cañón, año, ñato.**

p is like English *p* except that it is not accompanied by a puff of air, as it is in Eng. *pill* and *papa* (compare the *p* in *spot,* which is more similar to the Spanish sound). Examples: **padre, capa, apuro.**

q combined with **u** has the sound of *k.* Examples: **queso, aquí, quien.**

r usually represents a sound similar to that of the *tt* in Eng. *kitty* and the *dd* in *ladder*. Examples: **caro, tren, comer.** In contrast, at the beginning of words and after **n, l, s,** the letter **r** is realized as a trill, as in **rosa, Enrique, alrededor, Israel.** The double letter **rr** always represents a trill, as in **carro, correr, guerrero.**

s is pronounced the same as in standard American English in most parts of Spanish America and in parts of southern Spain. In most of Spain, in contrast, it is realized with the tip of the tongue against the alveolar ridge, producing a whistling sound that is sometimes heard in southern dialects of American English. Examples: **solo, casa, es.** In the Caribbean and in coastal Spanish generally, there is a strong tendency to pronounce **s** in certain environments (usually preconsonantal) as *h*, or to eliminate it entirely. In these dialects, *esta* may be pronounced as *ehta* or *eta*.

t differs from English *t* in two respects: first, it is articulated by the tongue touching the teeth rather than the alveolar ridge, and second, it is not accompanied by a puff of air, as it is in English *too* and *titillate* (compare the *t* in *stop*, which is more similar to the Spanish sound). Examples: **tela, tino, tinta.**

x has a wide range of phonetic realizations. Between vowels, it is usually pronounced *ks* or *gs* (but never *gz*), as in **examen, próximo,** though in a few words it is pronounced as *s*, e.g., *exacto, auxilio.* Before a consonant, **x** is almost always pronounced *s*, as in **extranjero, experiencia.** In many Mexican and Central American words of indigenous origin, **x** represents *h*, as in **México.**

y varies regionally in its pronunciation. In most areas it is pronounced like the *y* of Eng. *yes*, though with greater tension. In the River Plate area it is pronounced like the *g* in *beige* or the *sh* in *ship*. Examples: **yo, ayer.**

z is subject to dialectal variation as well. In most parts of Spain, except the southwest, it is pronounced as the *th* in Eng. *thin, cloth*. In southwestern Spain and all of Spanish America, in contrast, it is pronounced *s*. Examples: **zagal, hallazgo, luz.**

Stress Assignment in Spanish and the Use of the Written Accent

Spanish words are normally stressed on the next-to-last syllable when they end in a vowel or the consonants **n** or **s.** Examples: **mesa, zapato, acontecimiento, hablan, mujeres.** Words whose pronunciation does not conform to this rule are considered exceptions, and their stressed syllable is indicated with an accent mark. Examples: **lámpara, estómago, género, acá, varón, además.**

Conversely, Spanish words are normally stressed on the final syllable when they end in a consonant other than **n** or **s.** Examples: **mujer, actualidad, pedal, voraz.** Words whose pronunciation does not conform to this rule are considered exceptions, and their stressed syllable is indicated with an accent mark. Examples: **nácar, volátil, lápiz.**

For the purposes of stress assignment, diphthongs are considered the same as simple vowels. Thus, **arduo** and **industria** are considered to have two and three syllables respectively, with regular stress on the penultimate syllable. However, some sequences of vowels are not considered diphthongs. For example, **alegría** and **continúo** are both considered to have four syllables, with the stress mark indicating the absence of a diphthong.

Until recently certain words received written accents in order to differentiate functions, even though they are pronounced identically (this is still true in certain cases, such as **de** 'of', **dé** 'give'). Thus, the orthography **esta** was assigned to the demonstrative adjective ('this', fem.), while the demonstrative pronoun ('this one', fem.) was written **ésta.** This convention is no longer observed by most writers.

Notes on Spanish Grammar

The Noun

Gender. All Spanish nouns, not just those that denote male or female beings, are assigned either masculine or feminine gender. As a general rule, male beings (**muchacho** 'boy', **toro** 'bull') and all nouns ending in -o (**lodo** 'mud') are assigned masculine gender (exceptions: **mano** 'hand', **foto** 'photo', both feminine). Similarly, female beings (**mujer** 'woman', **vaca** 'cow') and nouns ending in -a (**envidia** 'envy') tend to be assigned feminine gender (exceptions: **mapa** 'map', **drama** 'drama', **día** 'day', all masculine). In addition, nouns ending in **-ción, -tad, -dad, -tud,** and **-umbre** are always feminine: **canción** 'song', **facultad** 'college', **ciudad** 'city', **virtud** 'virtue', and **muchedumbre** 'crowd'. Otherwise, nouns ending in consonants and vowels other than -o and -a are of unpredictable gender. Some are feminine (**barbarie** 'savagery', **clase** 'class', **nariz** 'nose', **tribu** 'tribe'), while others are masculine (**antílope** 'antelope', **corte** 'cut', **mesón** 'lodge', **nácar** 'mother of pearl').

Nouns in -o that denote human beings (and to some extent, animals) form the feminine by replacing -o with -a, as in **tío** 'uncle' / **tía** 'aunt', **niño** 'boy' / **niña** 'girl', **oso** 'bear' / **osa** 'she-bear'. Where the masculine noun does not end in -o, the rules of formation are more complex. For example, nouns ending in **-ón, -or,** and **-án** require the addition of **-a,** as in the pairs **patrón / patrona** 'patron', **pastor / pastora** 'shepherd', **holgazán / holgazana** 'lazy person'. In other cases the difference is more unpredictable: **emperador** 'emperor' / **emperatriz** 'empress', **abad** 'abbot' / **abadesa** 'abbess'.

Some nouns have different genders according to their meanings: **corte** (m) 'cut', (f) 'court', **capital** (m) 'money capital', (f) 'capital city', while others have invariable endings which are used for both the masculine and the feminine: **artista** 'artist' (and all nouns ending in **-ista**), **amante** 'lover', **aristócrata** 'aristocrat', **homicida** 'murderer', **cliente** 'customer'. Finally, some words vacillate as to gender, e.g., **mar** 'sea', which is normally masculine but is feminine in certain expressions (**en alta mar** 'on the high seas') and in poetic contexts, and **arte,** which is masculine in the singular but feminine in the plural. Some words, such as **armazón** and **esperma,** can be both masculine and feminine.

Pluralization. Nouns ending in an unaccented vowel and -**é** add -**s** to form the plural: **libro / libros, casa / casas, café / cafés.** Nouns ending in a consonant, in -**y,** or in an accented vowel other than -**é** add -**es: papel / papeles, canción / canciones, ley / leyes, rubí / rubíes.** Exceptions to this rule include the words **papá / papás** and **mamá / mamás,** as well as the small group of nouns ending in unaccented -**es** or -**is,** which do not change in the plural: **lunes** 'Monday', 'Mondays', **tesis** 'thesis', 'theses'.

Articles

Definite Article. The equivalent of English **the** is as follows: masculine singular, **el;** feminine singular, **la;** masculine plural, **los;** feminine plural, **las.** Feminine words beginning with stressed **a** or **ha** take **el** in the singular and **las** in the plural: **el alma** 'the soul' / **las almas** 'the souls', **el hacha** 'the hatchet' / **las hachas** 'the hatchets'. In spite of this, these nouns remain feminine in the singular, as shown by adjective agreement: **el alma bendita** 'the blessed soul'. When preceded by the prepositions **a** and **de,** the masculine singular article **el** forms the contractions **al** and **del.**

Indefinite Article. The equivalent of English **a, an** is as follows: masculine singular, **un;** feminine singular, **una.** In the plural, masculine **unos** and feminine **unas** are equivalent to English **some.** Feminine words beginning with stressed **a** or **ha** take **un** in the singular and **unas** in the plural: **un alma** 'a soul' / **unas almas** 'some souls', **un hacha** 'a hatchet' / **unas hachas** 'some hatchets'.

Adjectives

Agreement. The adjective in Spanish agrees in gender and number with the noun it modifies: **el lápiz rojo** 'the red pencil', **la casa blanca** 'the white house', **los libros interesantes** 'the interesting books', **las flores hermosas** 'the beautiful flowers'.

Formation of the Plural. Adjectives follow the same rules as nouns for the formation of the plural: **pálido, pálidos** 'pale', **fácil, fáciles** 'easy', **cortés, corteses** 'courteous', **capaz, capaces** 'capable'.

Formation of the Feminine. Adjectives ending in -**o** change to -**a: blanco, blanca** 'white'. Adjectives ending in other vowels are invariable: **verde** 'green', **fuerte** 'strong', **indígena** 'indigenous, native', **pesimista** 'pessimistic', **baladí** 'trivial', as are adjectives ending in a consonant: **fácil** 'easy', **cortés** 'courteous', **mayor** 'older', 'larger'. Some cases are more complex: (a) adjectives ending in -**ón, -án, -or** (except comparatives like **mayor**) add -**a** to form the feminine: **holgazán, holgazana** 'lazy', **preguntón, preguntona** 'inquisitive', **hablador, habladora** 'talkative'; (b) adjectives of nationality ending in a consonant add **-a** to form the feminine: **francés, francesa** 'French', **español, española** 'Spanish', **alemán, alemana** 'German'.

Adverbs

Most adverbs are formed by adding **-mente** to the feminine form of the adjective: **clara** 'clear' / **claramente** 'clearly', **fácil** 'easy' / **fácilmente** 'easily'.

Comparison of Inequality in Adjectives and Adverbs

The comparative of inequality is formed by placing **más** or **menos** before the positive form of the adjective or adverb: **más rico que** 'richer than', **menos rico que** 'less rich than', **más tarde** 'later', **menos tarde** 'less late'. The superlative is formed by placing the definite article **el** before the comparative: **el más rico** 'the richest', **el menos rico** 'the least rich'.

The following adjectives and adverbs have irregular forms of comparison:

Positive	Comparative	Superlative
bueno	mejor	el (la) mejor
malo	peor	el (la) peor
grande	mayor	el (la) mayor
pequeño	menor	el (la) menor

Common Spanish Suffixes

-aco   is a pejorative suffix: **pajarraco** 'ugly bird' (from **pájaro** 'bird'), **libraco** 'large, bulky book' (**libro** 'book')

-ada *a.* attaches to verbal stems to indicate an action: **mirada** 'look' (**mirar** 'to look'), **empujada** 'push' (**empujar** 'to push')

     b. attaches to noun stems to indicate a blow: **cachetada** 'blow on the cheek' (**cachete** 'cheek'), **puñalada** 'stab with a dagger' (**puñal** 'dagger')

     c. attaches to nominal stems to indicate an action characteristic of a person or group: **bobada** 'foolish act' (**bobo** 'fool'), **niñada** 'childish act' (**niño** 'child')

-al, -ar   attach to nouns indicating trees to form nouns that denote a grove: **naranjal** 'orange grove' (from **naranjo** 'orange tree'), **pinar** 'pine grove' (**pino** 'pine tree')

-azo   attaches to noun stems, forming nouns that indicate
     a. augmentation: **hombrazo** 'big man' (**hombre** 'man'), **marranazo** 'large hog' (**marrano** 'hog')

8

b. a blow or explosion: **porrazo** 'blow with a club' (**porra** 'club'), **cañonazo** 'cannon shot' (**cañón** 'cannon')

cito is a diminutive suffix: **cochecito** 'a little car' (**coche** 'car'), **mujercita** 'little woman' (**mujer** 'woman')

dor forms agent nouns from verbs: **hablador** 'talker' (**hablar** 'to talk'), **regulador** 'regulator' (**regular** 'to regulate'), which are sometimes used as adjectives: **hablador** 'talkative', **regulador** 'regulating'

ejo is a pejorative suffix: **librejo** 'worthless book' (**libro** 'book'), **lugarejo** 'Podunk' (**lugar** 'place')

ería attaches to noun stems to denote
a. a place where something is made or sold: **zapatería** 'shoestore' (**zapato** 'shoe'), **pastelería** 'pastry shop' (**pastel** 'pastry')
b. a profession, business, or occupation: **carpintería** 'carpentry' (**carpintero** 'carpenter'), **ingeniería** 'engineering' (**ingeniero** 'engineer')
c. a group: **chiquillería** 'bunch of children' (**chiquillo** 'little kid')

ero a. attaches to nouns to indicate a person who makes, sells, or is in charge of something: **librero** 'bookseller' (**libro** 'book'), **zapatero** 'shoemaker' (**zapato** 'shoe'), **carcelero** 'jailer' (**cárcel** 'jail')
b. attaches to nominal stems to form adjectives: **guerrero** 'warlike' (**guerra** 'war'), **conejero** 'for hunting rabbits' (**conejo** 'rabbit')

ez, -eza are used to make abstract nouns from adjectival bases: **vejez** 'old age' (**viejo** 'old'), **niñez** 'childhood' (**niño** 'child'), **grandeza** 'greatness' (**grande** 'large, great'), **rareza** 'rarity' (**raro** 'rare')

ía forms abstract nouns from adjectival bases: **valentía** 'courage' (**valiente** 'brave'), **cobardía** 'cowardice' (**cobarde** 'coward')

ico is a diminutive suffix: **ratico** 'little while' (**rato** 'while'), **momentico** 'brief moment' (**momento** 'moment')

-(i)ento attaches to adjectives to indicate attenuation, as in **amarillento** 'yellowish' (**amarillo** 'yellow'), or an undesirable quality, as in **hambriento** 'hungry' (**hambre** 'hunger')

illo is sometimes a diminutive suffix: **politiquillo** 'insignificant politician' (**político** 'politician'), **chiquillo** 'little kid' (**chico** 'child')

ísimo attaches to adjectives to indicate an extreme degree of a quality: **hermosísimo** 'very beautiful' (**hermoso** 'beautiful')

-ito	is a diminutive suffix: **librito** 'small book' (**libro** 'book'), **casita** 'little house' (**casa** 'house')
-izo	forms adjectives from nominal stems, indicating a tendency or attenuation: **rojizo** 'reddish' (**rojo** 'red'), **olvidadizo** 'forgetful' (**olvidar** 'to forget')
-mente	is the adverbial ending attached to the feminine form of the adjective: **generosamente** 'generously' (**generoso** 'generous'), **claramente** 'clearly' (**claro** 'clear')
-ón *a.*	is an augmentative adjectival suffix: **barrigón** 'potbellied' (**barriga** 'belly'), **cabezón** 'large-headed' (**cabeza** 'head')
b.	attaches to verb stems to denote sudden actions: **tirón** 'pull, jerk' (**tirar** 'to pull'), **apretón** 'push' (**apretar** 'to push')
-oso	forms adjectives from nouns, indicating abundance or character: **rocoso** 'rocky' (**roca** 'rock'), **tormentoso** 'stormy' (**tormenta** 'storm')
-ote, -ota	is an augmentative and pejorative suffix attached to nouns: **discursote** 'long, boring speech' (**discurso** 'speech'), **narizota** 'big ugly nose' (**nariz** 'nose')
-udo	forms adjectives from nouns, indicating an excess: **peludo** 'hairy' (**pelo** 'hair'), **panzudo** 'big-bellied' (**panza** 'belly')
-ura	forms abstract nouns from adjectives: **negrura** 'blackness' (**negro** 'black'), **altura** 'height' (**alto** 'high')
-uzco	forms adjectives from other adjectives, indicating attenuation: **blancuzco** 'whitish' (**blanco** 'white'), **negruzco** 'blackish' (**negro** 'black')

Spanish Regular Verbs

First Conjugation

infinitive	**hablar**
pres. indic.	hablo, hablas, habla, hablamos, habláis, hablan
pres. subj.	hable, hables, hable, hablemos, habléis, hablen
pret. indic.	hablé, hablaste, habló, hablamos, hablasteis, hablaron
imp. indic.	hablaba, hablabas, hablaba, hablábamos, hablabais, hablaban

imp. subj.	hablara, hablaras, hablara, habláramos, hablarais, hablaran, *or*
	hablase, hablases, hablase, hablásemos, hablaseis, hablasen
fut. indic.	hablaré, hablarás, hablará, hablaremos, hablaréis, hablarán
cond.	hablaría, hablarías, hablaría, hablaríamos, hablaríais, hablarían
imper.	habla (tú), hable (usted), hablemos (nosotros), hablad (vosotros), hablen (ustedes)
pres. part.	hablando
past part.	hablado

Second Conjugation

infinitive	**comer**
pres. indic.	como, comes, come, comemos, coméis, comen
pres. subj.	coma, comas, coma, comamos, comáis, coman
pret. indic.	comí, comiste, comió, comimos, comisteis, comieron
imp. indic.	comía, comías, comía, comíamos, comíais, comían
imp. subj.	comiera, comieras, comiera, comiéramos, comierais, comieran, *or*
	comiese, comieses, comiese, comiésemos, comieseis, comiesen
fut. indic.	comeré, comerás, comerá, comeremos, comeréis, comerán
cond.	comería, comerías, comería, comeríamos, comeríais, comerían
imper.	come (tú), coma (usted), comamos (nosotros), comed (vosotros), coman (ustedes)
pres. part.	comiendo
past part.	comido

Third Conjugation

infinitive	**vivir**
pres. indic.	vivo, vives, vive, vivimos, vivís, viven
pres. subj.	viva, vivas, viva, vivamos, viváis, vivan
pret. indic.	viví, viviste, vivió, vivimos, vivisteis, vivieron
imp. indic.	vivía, vivías, vivía, vivíamos, vivíais, vivían
imp. subj.	viviera, vivieras, viviera, viviéramos, vivierais, vivieran, *or*
	viviese, vivieses, viviese, viviésemos, vivieseis, viviesen
fut. indic.	viviré, vivirás, vivirá, viviremos, viviréis, vivirán
cond.	viviría, vivirías, viviría, viviríamos, viviríais, vivirían
imper.	vive (tú), viva (usted), vivamos (nosotros), vivid (vosotros), vivan (ustedes)
pres. part.	viviendo
past part.	vivido

Spanish Irregular and Orthographic Changing Verbs

The superscript number or numbers listed as part of a verb entry indicate that the verb is to be conjugated like the model verb in this section that has the corresponding number. Only the tenses that have irregular forms or spelling changes are given, and these irregular forms and spelling changes are shown in boldface type.

1. **pensar**
   pres. indic. **pienso, piensas, piensa,** pensamos, pensáis, **piensan**
   pres. subj. **piense, pienses, piense,** pensemos, penséis, **piensen**
   imper. **piensa** (tú), **piense** (usted), pensemos (nosotros), pensad (vosotros), **piensen** (ustedes)

2. **perder**
   pres. indic. **pierdo, pierdes, pierde,** perdemos, perdéis, **pierden**
   pres. subj. **pierda, pierdas, pierda,** perdamos, perdáis, **pierdan**
   imper. **pierde** (tú), **pierda** (usted), perdamos (nosotros), perded (vosotros), **pierdan** (ustedes)

3. **discernir**
   pres. indic. **discierno, disciernes, discierne,** discernimos, discernís, **disciernen**
   pres. subj. **discierna, disciernas, discierna,** discernamos, discernáis, **disciernan**
   imper. **discierne** (tú), **discierna** (usted), discernamos (nosotros), discernid (vosotros), **disciernan** (ustedes)

4. **adquirir**
   pres. indic. **adquiero, adquieres, adquiere,** adquirimos, adquirís, **adquieren**
   pres. subj. **adquiera, adquieras, adquiera,** adquiramos, adquiráis, **adquieran**
   imper. **adquiere** (tú), **adquiera** (usted), adquiramos (nosotros), adquirid (vosotros), **adquieran** (ustedes)

5. **contar**
   pres. indic. **cuento, cuentas, cuenta,** contamos, contáis, **cuentan**
   pres. subj. **cuente, cuentes, cuente,** contemos, contéis, **cuenten**
   imper. **cuenta** (tú), **cuente** (usted), contemos (nosotros), contad (vosotros), **cuenten** (ustedes)

6. **volver**
   pres. indic. **vuelvo, vuelves, vuelve,** volvemos, volvéis, **vuelven**
   pres. subj. **vuelva, vuelvas, vuelva,** volvamos, volváis, **vuelvan**

imper.	**vuelve** (tú), **vuelva** (usted), volvamos (nosotros) volved (vosotros), **vuelvan** (ustedes)
past part.	**vuelto**

7. **dormir**

pres. indic.	**duermo, duermes, duerme,** dormimos, dormís, **duermen**
pres. subj.	**duerma, duermas, duerma, durmamos, durmáis, duerman**
pret. indic.	dormí, dormiste, **durmió,** dormimos, dormisteis, **durmieron**
imp. subj.	**durmiera, durmieras, durmiera, durmiéramos, durmierais, durmieran,** or **durmiese, durmieses, durmiese, durmiésemos, durmieseis, durmiesen**
imper.	**duerme** (tú), **duerma** (usted), **durmamos** (nosotros), dormid (vosotros), **duerman** (ustedes)
pres. part.	**durmiendo**

8. **sentir**

pres. indic.	**siento, sientes, siente,** sentimos, sentís, **sienten**
pres. subj.	**sienta, sientas, sienta, sintamos, sintáis, sientan**
pret. indic.	sentí, sentiste, **sintió,** sentimos, sentisteis, **sintieron**
imp. subj.	**sintiera, sintieras, sintiera, sintiéramos, sintierais, sintieran,** or **sintiese, sintieses, sintiese, sintiésemos, sintieseis, sintiesen**
imper.	**siente** (tú), **sienta** (usted), **sintamos** (nosotros), sentid (vosotros), **sientan** (ustedes)
pres. part.	**sintiendo**

9. **pedir**

pres. indic.	**pido, pides, pide,** pedimos, pedís, **piden**
pres. subj.	**pida, pidas, pida, pidamos, pidáis, pidan**
pret. indic.	pedí, pediste, **pidió,** pedimos, pedisteis, **pidieron**
imp. subj.	**pidiera, pidieras, pidiera, pidiéramos, pidierais, pidieran,** or **pidiese, pidieses, pidiese, pidiésemos, pidieseis, pidiesen**
imper.	**pide** (tú), **pida** (usted), **pidamos** (nosotros), pedid (vosotros), **pidan** (ustedes)
pres. part.	**pidiendo**

10. **reír**

pres. indic.	**río, ríes, ríe,** reímos, reís, **ríen**
pres. subj.	**ría, rías, ría, riamos, riáis, rían**
pret. indic.	reí, reíste, **rió,** reímos, reísteis, **rieron**

imp. subj.	**riera, rieras, riera, riéramos, rierais, rieran,** or **riese, rieses, riese, riésemos, rieseis, riesen**
imper.	**ríe** (tú), **ría** (usted), **riamos** (nosotros), reíd (vosotros), **rían** (ustedes)
pres. part.	**riendo**
past part.	**reído**

11. **reñir**

pres. indic.	**riño, riñes, riñe,** reñimos, reñís, **riñen**
pres. subj.	**riña, riñas, riña, riñamos, riñáis, riñan**
pret. indic.	reñí, reñiste, **riñó,** reñimos, reñisteis, **riñeron**
imp. subj.	**riñera, riñeras, riñera, riñéramos, riñerais, riñeran,** or **riñese, riñeses, riñese, riñésemos, riñeseis, riñesen**
imper.	**riñe** (tú), **riña** (usted), **riñamos** (nosotros), reñid (vosotros), **riñan** (ustedes)
pres. part.	**riñendo**

12. **seguir**

pres. indic.	**sigo, sigues, sigue,** seguimos, seguís, **siguen**
pres. subj.	**siga, sigas, siga, sigamos, sigáis, sigan**
pret. indic.	seguí, seguiste, **siguió,** seguimos, seguisteis, **siguieron**
imp. subj.	**siguiera, siguieras, siguiera, siguiéramos, siguierais, siguieran,** or **siguiese, siguieses, siguiese, siguiésemos, siguieses, siguiesen**
imper.	**sigue** (tú), **siga** (usted), **sigamos** (nosotros), seguid (vosotros), **sigan** (ustedes)
pres. part.	**siguiendo**

13. **erguir**

pres. indic.	**yergo, yergues, yergue,** erguimos, erguís, **yerguen** or **irgo, irgues, irgue,** erguimos, erguís, **irguen**
pres. subj.	**yerga, yergas, yerga, irgamos, irgáis, yergan** or **irga, irgas, irga, irgamos, irgáis, irgan**
pret. indic.	erguí, erguiste, **irguió,** erguimos, erguisteis, **irguieron**
imp. subj.	**irguiera, irguieras, irguiera, irguiéramos, irguierais, irguieran,** or **irguiese, irguieses, irguiese, irguiésemos, irguieseis, irguiesen**
imper.	**yergue** or **irgue** (tú), **yerga** or **irga** (usted), **irgamos** (nosotros), erguid (vosotros), **yergan** or **irgan** (ustedes)
pres. part.	**irguiendo**

14. **elegir**

pres. indic.	**elijo, eliges, elige,** elegimos, elegís, **eligen**
pres. subj.	**elija, elijas, elija, elijamos, elijáis, elijan**

pret. indic. elegí, elegiste, **eligió,** elegimos, elegisteis, **eligieron**
imp. subj. **eligiera, eligieras, eligiera, eligiéramos, eligierais, eligieran,** or **eligiese, eligieses, eligiese, eligiésemos, eligieseis, eligiesen**
imper. **elige** (tú), **elija** (usted), **elijamos** (nosotros), elegid (vosotros), **elijan** (ustedes)
pres. part. **eligiendo**

15. **tañer**
pret. indic. tañí, tañiste, **tañó,** tañimos, tañisteis, **tañeron**
imp. subj. **tañera, tañeras, tañera, tañéramos, tañerais, tañeran,** or **tañese, tañeses, tañese, tañésemos, tañeseis, tañesen**
pres. part. **tañendo**

16. **bullir**
pret. indic. bullí, bulliste, **bulló,** bullimos, bullisteis, **bulleron**
imp. subj. **bullera, bulleras, bullera, bulléramos, bullerais, bulleran,** or **bullese, bulleses, bullese, bullésemos, bulleseis, bullesen**
pres. part. **bullendo**

17. **gruñir**
pret. indic. gruñí, gruñiste, **gruñó,** gruñisteis, **gruñeron**
imp. subj. **gruñera, gruñeras, gruñera, gruñéramos, gruñerais, gruñeran,** or **gruñese, gruñeses, gruñese, gruñésemos, gruñeseis, gruñesen**
pres. part. **gruñendo**

18. **creer**
pret. indic. creí, creíste, **creyó,** creímos, creísteis, **creyeron**
imp. subj. **creyera, creyeras, creyera, creyéramos, creyerais, creyeran,** or **creyese, creyeses, creyese, creyésemos, creyeseis, creyesen**
pres. part. **creyendo**
past part. **creído**

19. **huir**
pres. indic. **huyo, huyes, huye,** huimos, huís, **huyen**
pres. subj. **huya, huyas, huya, huyamos, huyáis, huyan**
pret. indic. hui, huiste, **huyó,** huimos, huisteis, **huyeron**
imp. subj. **huyera, huyeras, huyera, huyéramos, huyerais, huyeran,** or **huyese, huyeses, huyese, huyésemos, huyeseis, huyesen**

imper.	**huye** (tú), **huya** (usted), **huyamos** (nosotros), huid (vosotros), **huyan** (ustedes)
pres. part.	**huyendo**

20. **argüir**

pres. indic.	**arguyo, arguyes, arguye,** argüimos, argüís, **arguyen**
pres. subj.	**arguya,arguyas, arguya, arguyamos, arguyáis, arguyan**
pret. indic.	argüí, argüiste, **arguyó,** argüimos, argüisteis, **arguyeron**
imp. subj.	**arguyera, arguyeras, arguyera, arguyéramos, arguyerais, arguyeran,** or **arguyese, arguyeses, arguyese, arguyésemos, arguyeseis, arguyesen**
imper.	**arguye** (tú), **arguya** (usted), **arguyamos** (nosotros), argüid (vosotros), **arguyan** (ustedes)
pres. part.	**arguyendo**

21. **errar**

pres. indic.	**yerro, yerras, yerra,** erramos, erráis, **yerran**
pres. subj.	**yerre, yerres, yerre,** erremos, erréis, **yerren**
imper.	**yerra** (tú), **yerre** (usted), erremos (nosotros), errad (vosotros), **yerren** (ustedes)

22. **oler**

pres. indic.	**huelo, hueles, huele,** olemos, oléis, **huelen**
pres. subj.	**huela, huelas, huela,** olamos, oláis, **huelan**
imper.	**huele** (tú), **huela** (usted), oled (vosotros), **huelan** (ustedes)

23. **avergonzar**

pres. indic.	**avergüenzo, avergüenzas, avergüenza,** avergonzamos, avergonzáis, **avergüenzan**
pres. subj.	**avergüence, avergüences, avergüence, avergoncemos, avergoncéis, avergüencen**
pret. indic.	**avergoncé,** avergonzaste, avergonzó, avergonzamos, avergonzasteis, avergonzaron
imper.	**avergüenza** (tú), **avergüence** (usted), **avergoncemos** (nosotros), avergonzad (vosotros), **avergüencen** (ustedes)

24. **degollar**

pres. indic.	**degüello, degüellas, degüella,** degollamos, degolláis, **degüellan**
pres. subj.	**degüelle, degüelles, degüelle,** degollemos, degolléis, **degüellen**
imper.	**degüella** (tú), **degüelle** (usted), degollemos (nosotros), degollad (vosotros), **degüellen** (ustedes)

25. **averiguar**
    pres. subj.   **averigüe, averigües, averigüe, averigüemos,
                        averigüéis, averigüen**
    pres. indic.   **averigüé,** averiguaste, averiguó, averiguamos,
                        averiguasteis, averiguaron
    imper.   averigua (tú), **averigüe** (usted), **averigüemos**
                        (nosotros), averiguad (vosotros), **averigüen** (ustedes)

26. **continuar**
    pres. indic.   **continúo, continúas, continúa,** continuamos,
                        continuáis, **continúan**
    pres. subj.   **continúe, continúes, continúe,** continuemos,
                        continuéis, **continúen**
    imper.   **continúa** (tú), **continúe** (usted), continuemos
                        (nosotros), continuad (vosotros), **continúen** (ustedes)

27. **reunir**
    pres. indic.   **reúno, reúnes, reúne,** reunimos, reunís, **reúnen**
    pres. subj.   **reúna, reúnas, reúna,** reunamos, reunáis, **reúnan**
    imper.   **reúne** (tú), **reúna** (usted), reunamos (nosotros), reunid
                        (vosotros), **reúnan** (ustedes)

28. **enviar**
    pres. indic.   **envío, envías, envía,** enviamos, enviáis, **envían**
    pres. subj.   **envíe, envíes, envíe,** enviemos, enviéis, **envíen**
    imper.   **envía** (tú), **envíe** (usted), enviemos (nosotros), enviad
                        (vosotros), **envíen** (ustedes)

29. **prohibir**
    pres. indic.   **prohíbo, prohíbes, prohíbe,** prohibimos, prohibís,
                        prohíben
    pres. subj.   **prohíba, prohíbas, prohíba,** prohibamos, prohibáis,
                        prohíban
    imper.   **prohíbe** (tú), **prohíba** (usted), prohibamos (nosotros),
                        prohibid (vosotros), **prohíban** (ustedes)

30. **buscar**
    pres. subj.   **busque, busques, busque, busquemos, busquéis,
                        busquen**
    pret. indic.   **busqué,** buscaste, buscó, buscamos, buscasteis, buscaron
    imper.   busca (tú), **busque** (usted), **busquemos** (nosotros),
                        buscad (vosotros), **busquen** (ustedes)

31. **trocar**

pres. indic.	**trueco, truecas, trueca,** trocamos, trocáis, **truecan**
pres. subj.	**trueque, trueques, trueque, troquemos, troquéis, truequen**
pret. indic.	**troqué,** trocaste, trocó, trocamos, trocasteis, trocaron
imper.	**trueca** (tú), **trueque** (usted), **troquemos** (nosotros), trocad (vosotros), **truequen** (ustedes)

32. **convencer**

pres. indic.	**convenzo,** convences, convence, convencemos, convencéis, convencen
pres. subj.	**convenza, convenzas, convenza, convenzamos, convenzáis, convenzan**
imper.	convence (tú), **convenza** (usted), **convenzamos** (nosotros), convenced (vosotros), **convenzan** (ustedes)

33. **esparcir**

pres. indic.	**esparzo,** esparces, esparce, esparcimos, esparcís, esparcen
pres. subj.	**esparza, esparzas, esparza, esparzamos, esparzáis, esparzan**
imper.	esparce (tú), **esparza** (usted), **esparzamos** (nosotros), esparcid (vosotros), **esparzan** (ustedes)

34. **cocer**

pres. indic.	**cuezo, cueces, cuece,** cocemos, cocéis, **cuecen**
pres. subj.	**cueza, cuezas, cueza, cozamos, cozáis, cuezan**
imper.	**cuece** (tú), **cueza** (usted), **cozamos** (nosotros), coced (vosotros), **cuezan** (ustedes)

35. **conocer**

pres. indic.	**conozco,** conoces, conoce, conocemos, conocéis, conocen
pres. subj.	**conozca, conozcas, conozca, conozcamos, conozcáis, conozcan**
imper.	conoce (tú), **conozca** (usted), **conozcamos** (nosotros), conoced (vosotros), **conozcan** (ustedes)

36. **placer**

pres. indic.	**plazco,** places, place, placemos, placéis, placen
pres. subj.	**plazca, plazcas, plazca, plazcamos, plazcáis, plazcan**
imper.	place (tú), **plazca** (usted), **plazcamos** (nosotros), placed (vosotros), **plazcan** (ustedes)

37. **yacer**
    - *pres. indic.* **yazco** or **yazgo** or **yago,** yaces, yace, yacemos, yacéis, yacen
    - *pres. subj.* **yazca, yazcas, yazca, yazcamos, yazcáis, yazcan,** or **yazga, yazgas, yazga, yazgamos, yazgáis, yazgan** or **yaga, yagas, yaga, yagamos, yagáis, yagan**
    - *imper.* yace or **yaz** (tú), **yazca** or **yazga** or **yaga** (usted), **yazcamos** or **yazgamos** or **yagamos** (nosotros), yaced (vosotros), **yazcan** or **yazgan** or **yagan** (ustedes)

38. **conducir**
    - *pres. indic.* **conduzco,** conduces, conduce, conducimos, conducís, conducen
    - *pres. subj.* **conduzca, conduzcas, conduzca, conduzcamos, conduzcáis, conduzcan**
    - *pret. indic.* **conduje, condujiste, condujo, condujimos, condujisteis, condujeron**
    - *imp. subj.* **condujera, condujeras, condujera, condujéramos, condujerais, condujeran,** or **condujese, condujeses, condujese, condujésemos, condujeseis, condujesen**
    - *imper.* conduce (tú), **conduzca** (usted), **conduzcamos** (nosotros), conducid (vosotros), **conduzcan** (ustedes)

39. **lucir**
    - *pres. indic.* **luzco,** luces, luce, lucimos, lucís, lucen
    - *pres. subj.* **luzca, luzcas, luzca, luzcamos, luzcáis, luzcan**
    - *imper.* luce (tú), **luzca** (usted), **luzcamos** (nosotros), lucid (vosotros), **luzcan** (ustedes)

40. **llegar**
    - *pres. subj.* **llegue, llegues, llegue, lleguemos, lleguéis, lleguen**
    - *pret. indic.* **llegué,** llegaste, llegó, llegamos, llegasteis, llegaron
    - *imper.* llega (tú), **llegue** (usted), **lleguemos** (nosotros), llegad (vosotros), **lleguen** (ustedes)

41. **negar**
    - *pres. indic.* **niego, niegas, niega,** negamos, negáis, **niegan**
    - *pres. subj.* **niegue, niegues, niegue, neguemos, neguéis, nieguen**
    - *pret. indic.* **negué,** negaste, negó, negamos, negasteis, negaron
    - *imper.* **niega** (tú), **niegue** (usted), **neguemos** (nosotros), negad (vosotros), **nieguen** (ustedes)

42. **colgar**
    pres. indic.   **cuelgo, cuelgas, cuelga,** colgamos, colgáis, **cuelgan**
    pres. subj.   **cuelgue, cuelgues, cuelgue, colguemos, colguéis,
                     cuelguen**
    pret. indic.   **colgué,** colgaste, colgó, colgamos, colgasteis, colgaron
    imper.   **cuelga** (tú), **cuelgue** (usted), **colguemos** (nosotros),
                     colgad (vosotros), **cuelguen** (ustedes)

43. **jugar**
    pres. indic.   **juego, juegas, juega,** jugamos, jugáis, **juegan**
    pres. subj.   **juegue, juegues, juegue, juguemos, juguéis,
                     jueguen**
    pret. indic.   **jugué,** jugaste, jugó, jugamos, jugasteis, jugaron
    imper.   **juega** (tú), **juegue** (usted), **juguemos** (nosotros), jugad
                     (vosotros), **jueguen** (ustedes)

44. **distinguir**
    pres. indic.   **distingo,** distingues, distingue, distinguimos, distinguís,
                     distinguen
    pres. subj.   **distinga, distingas, distinga, distingamos,
                     distingáis, distingan**
    imper.   distingue (tú), **distinga** (usted), **distingamos** (nosotros),
                     distinguid (vosotros), **distingan** (ustedes)

45. **coger**
    pres. indic.   **cojo,** coges, coge, cogemos, cogéis, cogen
    pres. subj.   **coja, cojas, coja, cojamos, cojáis, cojan**
    imper.   coge (tú), **coja** (usted), **cojamos** (nosotros), coged
                     (vosotros), **cojan** (ustedes)

46. **dirigir**
    pres. indic.   **dirijo,** diriges, dirige, dirigimos, dirigís, dirigen
    pres. subj.   **dirija, dirijas, dirija, dirijamos, dirijáis, dirijan**
    imper.   dirige (tú), **dirija** (usted), **dirijamos** (nosotros), dirigid
                     (vosotros), **dirijan** (ustedes)

47. **abrazar**
    pres. subj.   **abrace, abraces, abrace, abracemos, abracéis,
                     abracen**
    pret. indic.   **abracé,** abrazaste, abrazó, abrazamos, abrazasteis,
                     abrazaron
    imper.   abraza (tú), **abrace** (usted), **abracemos** (nosotros),
                     abrazad (vosotros), **abracen** (ustedes)

48. **empezar**
    pres. indic.   **empiezo, empiezas, empieza,** empezamos, empezáis, **empiezan**
    pres. subj.   **empiece, empieces, empiece, empecemos, empecéis, empiecen**
    pret. indic.   **empecé,** empezaste, empezó, empezamos, empezasteis, empezaron
    imper.   **empieza** (tú), **empiece** (usted), **empecemos** (nosotros), empezad (vosotros), **empiecen** (ustedes)

49. **forzar**
    pres. indic.   **fuerzo, fuerzas, fuerza,** forzamos, forzáis, **fuerzan**
    pres. subj.   **fuerce, fuerces, fuerce, forcemos, forcéis, fuercen**
    pret. indic.   **forcé,** forzaste, forzó, forzamos, forzasteis, forzaron
    imper.   **fuerza** (tú), **fuerce** (usted), **forcemos** (nosotros), forzad (vosotros), **fuercen** (ustedes)

50. **asir**
    pres. indic.   **asgo,** ases, ase, asimos, asís, asen
    pres. subj.   **asga, asgas, asga, asgamos, asgáis, asgan**
    imper.   ase (tú), **asga** (usted), **asgamos** (nosotros), asid (vosotros), **asgan** (ustedes)

51. **bendecir**
    pres. indic.   **bendigo, bendices, bendice,** bendecimos, bendecís, **bendicen**
    pres. subj.   **bendiga, bendigas, bendiga, bendigamos, bendigáis, bendigan**
    pret. indic..   **bendije, bendijiste, bendijo, bendijimos, bendijisteis, bendijeron**
    imp. subj.   **bendijera, bendijeras, bendijera, bendijéramos, bendijerais, bendijeran** or **bendijese, bendijeses, bendijese, bendijésemos, bendijeseis, bendijesen**
    fut. indic.   bendeciré, bendecirás, bendecirá, bendeciremos, bendeciréis, bendecirán
    cond.   bendeciría, bendecirías, bendeciría, bendeciríamos, bendeciríais, bendecirían
    imper.   **bendice** (tú), **bendiga** (usted), **bendigamos** (nosotros), bendecid (vosotros), **bendigan** (ustedes)
    pres. part.   **bendiciendo**
    past part.   bendecido

52. **caer**
    pres. indic.   **caigo,** caes, cae, caemos, caéis, caen
    pres. subj.   **caiga, caigas, caiga, caigamos, caigáis, caigan**

	pret. indic.	caí, caíste, **cayó,** caímos, caísteis, **cayeron**

pret. indic.   caí, caíste, **cayó,** caímos, caísteis, **cayeron**
imp. subj.   **cayera, cayeras, cayera, cayéramos, cayerais, cayeran,** or **cayese, cayeses, cayese, cayésemos, cayeseis, cayesen**
imper.   cae (tú), **caiga** (usted), **caigamos** (nosotros), caed (vosotros), **caigan** (ustedes)
pres. part.   **cayendo**
past part.   **caído**

53. decir[1]
pres. indic.   **digo, dices, dice,** decimos, decís, **dicen**
pres. subj.   **diga, digas, diga, digamos, digáis, digan**
pret. indic.   **dije, dijiste, dijo, dijimos, dijisteis, dijeron**
imp. subj.   **dijera, dijeras, dijera, dijéramos, dijerais, dijeran,** or **dijese, dijeses, dijese, dijésemos, dijeseis, dijesen**
fut. indic.   **diré, dirás, dirá, diremos, diréis, dirán**
cond.   **diría, dirías, diría, diríamos, diríais, dirían**
imper.   **di** (tú), **diga** (usted), **digamos** (nosotros), decid (vosotros), **digan** (ustedes)
pres. part.   **diciendo**
past part.   **dicho**

54. hacer
pres. indic.   **hago,** haces, hace, hacemos, hacéis, hacen
pres. subj.   **haga, hagas, haga, hagamos, hagáis, hagan**
pret. indic.   **hice, hiciste, hizo, hicimos, hicisteis, hicieron**
imp. subj.   **hiciera, hicieras, hiciera, hiciéramos, hicierais, hicieran,** or **hiciese, hicieses, hiciese, hiciésemos, hicieseis, hiciesen**
fut. indic.   **haré, harás, hará, haremos, haréis, harán**
cond.   **haría, harías, haría, haríamos, haríais, harían**
imper.   **haz** (tú), **haga** (usted), **hagamos** (nosotros), haced (vosotros), **hagan** (ustedes)
past part.   **hecho**

55. oír
pres. indic.   **oigo, oyes, oye,** oímos, oís, **oyen**
pres. subj.   **oiga, oigas, oiga, oigamos, oigáis, oigan**
pret. indic.   oí, oíste, **oyó,** oímos, oísteis, **oyeron**

[1]. The compound verbs of *decir* have the same irregularities with the exception of the following: The future and conditional forms of the compound verbs *contradecir, desdecir,* and *predecir* are used interchangeably in both their irregular and regular forms (see 51 **bendecir**). However, their past participles are always irregular (see 74 **Irregular Past Participles**).

imp. subj.	**oyera, oyeras, oyera, oyéramos, oyerais, oyeran,** or **oyese, oyeses, oyese, oyésemos, oyeseis, oyesen**
imper.	**oye** (tú), **oiga** (usted), **oigamos** (nosotros), oíd (vosotros), **oigan** (ustedes)
pres. part.	**oyendo**
past part.	**oído**

56. **poner**

pres. indic.	**pongo,** pones, pone, ponemos, ponéis, ponen
pres. subj.	**ponga, pongas, ponga, pongamos, pongáis, pongan**
pret. indic.	**puse, pusiste, puso, pusimos, pusisteis, pusieron**
imp. subj.	**pusiera, pusieras, pusiera, pusiéramos, pusierais, pusieran,** or **pusiese, pusieses, pusiese, pusiésemos, pusieseis, pusiesen**
fut. indic.	**pondré, pondrás, pondrá, pondremos, pondréis, pondrán**
cond.	**pondría, pondrías, pondría, pondríamos, pondríais, pondrían**
imper.	**pon** (tú), **ponga** (usted), **pongamos** (nosotros), poned (vosotros), **pongan** (ustedes)
past part.	**puesto**

57. **salir**

pres. indic.	**salgo,** sales, sale, salimos, salís, salen
pres. subj.	**salga, salgas, salga, salgamos, salgáis, salgan**
fut. indic.	**saldré, saldrás, saldrá, saldremos, saldréis, saldrán**
cond.	**saldría, saldrías, saldría, saldríamos, saldríais, saldrían**
imper.	**sal** (tú),[2] **salga** (usted), **salgamos** (nosotros), salid (vosotros), **salgan** (ustedes)

58. **tener**

pres. indic.	**tengo, tienes, tiene,** tenemos, tenéis, **tienen**
pres. subj.	**tenga, tengas, tenga, tengamos, tengáis, tengan**
pret. indic.	**tuve, tuviste, tuvo, tuvimos, tuvisteis, tuvieron**
imp. subj.	**tuviera, tuvieras, tuviera, tuviéramos, tuvierais, tuvieran,** or **tuviese, tuvieses, tuviese, tuviésemos, tuvieseis, tuviesen**
fut. indic.	**tendré, tendrás, tendrá, tendremos, tendréis, tendrán**

2. The compound *sobresalir* is regular in the familiar imperative: *sobresale.*

23

	cond.	**tendría, tendrías, tendría, tendríamos, tendríais, tendrían**
	imper.	**ten** (tú), **tenga** (usted), **tengamos** (nosotros), tened (vosotros), **tengan** (ustedes)

59. traer

pres. indic.	**traigo,** traes, trae, traemos, traéis, traen
pres. subj.	**traiga, traigas, traiga, traigamos, traigáis, traigan**
pret. indic.	**traje, trajiste, trajo, trajimos, trajisteis, trajeron**
imp. subj.	**trajera, trajeras, trajera, trajéramos, trajerais, trajeran,** or **trajese, trajeses, trajese, trajésemos, trajeseis, trajesen**
imper.	trae (tú), **traiga** (usted), **traigamos** (nosotros), traed (vosotros), **traigan** (ustedes)
pres. part.	**trayendo**
past part.	**traído**

60. valer

pres. indic.	**valgo,** vales, vale, valemos, valéis, valen
pres. subj.	**valga, valgas, valga, valgamos, valgáis, valgan**
fut. indic.	**valdré, valdrás, valdrá, valdremos, valdréis, valdrán**
cond.	**valdría, valdrías, valdría, valdríamos, valdríais, valdrían**
imper.	**val** or vale (tú), **valga** (usted), **valgamos** (nosotros), valed (vosotros), **valgan** (ustedes)

61. venir

pres. indic.	**vengo, vienes, viene,** venimos, venís, **vienen**
pres. subj.	**venga, vengas, venga, vengamos, vengáis, vengan**
pret. indic.	**vine, viniste, vino, vinimos, vinisteis, vinieron**
imp. subj.	**viniera, vinieras, viniera, viniéramos, vinierais, vinieran,** or **viniese, vinieses, viniese, viniésemos, vinieseis, viniesen**
fut. indic.	**vendré, vendrás, vendrá, vendremos, vendréis, vendrán**
cond.	**vendría, vendrías, vendría, vendríamos, vendríais, vendrían**
imper.	**ven** (tú), **venga** (usted), **vengamos** (nosotros), venid (vosotros), **vengan** (ustedes)
pres. part.	**viniendo**

62. dar

pres. indic.	**doy,** das, da, damos, dais, dan

pres. subj.	**dé**, des, **dé**, demos, deis, den
pret. indic.	**di, diste, dio, dimos, disteis, dieron**
imp. subj.	**diera, dieras, diera, diéramos, dierais, dieran**, or **diese, dieses, diese, diésemos, dieseis, diesen**
imper.	da (tú), **dé** (usted), demos (nosotros), dad (vosotros), den (ustedes)

63. **estar**

pres. indic.	**estoy, estás, está**, estamos, estáis, **están**
pres. subj.	**esté, estés, esté**, estemos, estéis, **estén**
pret. indic.	**estuve, estuviste, estuvo, estuvimos, estuvisteis, estuvieron**
imp. subj.	**estuviera, estuvieras, estuviera, estuviéramos, estuvierais, estuvieran**, or **estuviese, estuvieses, estuviese, estuviésemos, estuvieseis, estuviesen**
imper.	**está** (tú), **esté** (usted), estemos (nosotros), estad (vosotros), **estén** (ustedes)

64. **ir**

pres. indic.	**voy, vas, va, vamos, vais, van**
pres. subj.	**vaya, vayas, vaya, vayamos, vayáis, vayan**
imp. indic.	**iba, ibas, iba, íbamos, ibais, iban**
pret. indic.	**fui, fuiste, fue, fuimos, fuisteis, fueron**
imp. subj.	**fuera, fueras, fuera, fuéramos, fuerais, fueran**, or **fuese, fueses, fuese, fuésemos, fueseis, fuesen**
imper.	ve (tú), **vaya** (usted), **vayamos** (nosotros), id (vosotros), **vayan** (ustedes)
pres. part.	**yendo**

65. **ser**

pres. indic.	**soy, eres, es, somos, sois, son**
pres. subj.	**sea, seas, sea, seamos, seáis, sean**
imp. indic.	**era, eras, era, éramos, erais, eran**
pret. indic.	**fui, fuiste, fue, fuimos, fuisteis, fueron**
imp. subj.	**fuera, fueras, fuera, fuéramos, fuerais, fueran**, or **fuese, fueses, fuese, fuésemos, fueseis, fuesen**
imper.	**sé** (tú), **sea** (usted), **seamos** (nosotros), sed (vosotros), **sean** (ustedes)

66. **andar**

pret. indic.	**anduve, anduviste, anduvo, anduvimos, anduvisteis, anduvieron**

imp. subj.	**anduviera, anduvieras, anduviera, anduviéramos, anduvierais, anduvieran,** or **anduviese, anduvieses, anduviese, anduviésemos, anduvieseis, anduviesen**

67. **caber**

pres. indic.	**quepo,** cabes, cabe, cabemos, cabéis, caben
pres. subj.	**quepa, quepas, quepa, quepamos, quepáis, quepan**
pret. indic.	**cupe, cupiste, cupo, cupimos, cupisteis, cupieron**
imp. subj.	**cupiera, cupieras, cupiera, cupiéramos, cupierais, cupieran,** or **cupiese, cupieses, cupiese, cupiésemos, cupieseis, cupiesen**
fut. indic.	**cabré, cabrás, cabrá, cabremos, cabréis, cabrán**
cond.	**cabría, cabrías, cabría, cabríamos, cabríais, cabrían**
imper.	cabe (tú), **quepa** (usted), **quepamos** (nosotros), cabed (vosotros), **quepan** (ustedes)

68. **haber**

pres. indic.	**he, has, ha, hemos,** habéis, **han**
pres. subj.	**haya, hayas, haya, hayamos, hayáis, hayan**
pret. indic.	**hube, hubiste, hubo, hubimos, hubisteis, hubieron**
imp. subj.	**hubiera, hubieras, hubiera, hubiéramos, hubierais, hubieran,** or **hubiese, hubieses, hubiese, hubiésemos, hubieseis, hubiesen**
fut. indic.	**habré, habrás, habrá, habremos, habréis, habrán**
cond.	**habría, habrías, habría, habríamos, habríais, habrían**

69. **poder**

pres. indic.	**puedo, puedes, puede,** podemos, podéis, **pueden**
pres. subj.	**pueda, puedas, pueda,** podamos, podáis, **puedan**
pret. indic.	**pude, pudiste, pudo, pudimos, pudisteis, pudieron**
imp. subj.	**pudiera, pudieras, pudiera, pudiéramos, pudierais, pudieran,** or **pudiese, pudieses, pudiese, pudiésemos, pudieseis, pudiesen**
fut. indic.	**podré, podrás, podrá, podremos, podréis, podrán**
cond.	**podría, podrías, podría, podríamos, podríais, podrían**
pres. part.	**pudiendo**

70. **querer**

pres. indic.	**quiero, quieres, quiere,** queremos, queréis, **quieren**
pres. subj.	**quiera, quieras, quiera,** queramos, queráis, **quieran**
pret. indic.	**quise, quisiste, quiso, quisimos, quisisteis, quisieron**
imp. subj.	**quisiera, quisieras, quisiera, quisiéramos, quisierais, quisieran,** or **quisiese, quisieses, quisiese, quisiémos, quisieseis, quisiesen**
fut. indic.	**querré, querrás, querrá, querremos, querréis, querrán**
cond.	**querría, querrías, querría, querríamos, querríais, querrían**
imper.	**quiere** (tú), **quiera** (usted), queramos (nosotros), quered (vosotros), **quieran** (ustedes)

71. **saber**

pres. indic.	**sé,** sabes, sabe, sabemos, sabéis, saben
pres. subj.	**sepa, sepas, sepa, sepamos, sepáis, sepan**
pret. indic.	**supe, supiste, supo, supimos, supisteis, supieron**
imp. subj.	**supiera, supieras, supiera, supiéramos, supierais, supieran,** or **supiese, supieses, supiese, supiésemos, supieseis, supiesen**
fut. indic.	**sabré, sabrás, sabrá, sabremos, sabréis, sabrán**
cond.	**sabría, sabrías, sabría, sabríamos, sabríais, sabrían**
imper.	sabe (tú), **sepa** (usted), **sepamos** (nosotros), sabed (vosotros), **sepan** (ustedes)

72. **ver**[3]

pres. indic.	**veo, ves, ve, vemos, veis, ven**
pres. subj.	**vea, veas, vea, veamos, veáis, vean**
pret. indic.	**vi, viste, vio, vimos, visteis, vieron**
imp. indic.	**veía, veías, veía, veíamos, veíais, veían**
imp. subj.	**viera, vieras, viera, viéramos, vierais, vieran** or **viese, vieses, viese, viésemos, vieseis, viesen**
imper.	ve (tú), **vea** (usted), **veamos** (nosotros), ved (vosotros), **vean** (ustedes)
past part.	**visto**

---

3. The verb *prever* differs orthographically in the second- and third-person forms of the present indicative (*prevés, prevéis, prevé, prevén*), the first- and third-person singular forms of the preterit indicative (*preví, previó*), and the familiar imperative form (*prevé*).

73.   Defective Verbs

The following verbs are used only in the forms that have an **i** in the ending:
abolir, agredir, aterirse, empedernirse, transgredir.

The verb **atañer** is used only in the third person, most frequently in the present indicative: atañe, atañen.

The verb **concernir** is used only in the third person of the following tenses:

pres. indic.	**concierne, conciernen**
pres. subj.	**concierna, conciernan**
imp. indic.	concernía, concernían
imp. subj.	concerniera *or* concerniese, concernieran *or* concerniesen
fut. indic	concernirá, concernirán
cond.	concerniría, concernirían

The verb **roer** (also **corroer**) has three forms in the first person of the present indicative: **roo, royo, roigo,** all of which are infrequently used. In the present subjunctive the preferable form is **roa, roas, roa,** etc., although the forms **roya** and **roiga** are found.

The verb **soler** is used most frequently in the present and imperfect indicative. It is less frequently used in the present subjunctive.

pres. indic.	**suelo, sueles, suele,** solemos, soléis, **suelen**
pres. subj.	**suela, suelas, suela,** solamos, soláis, **suelan**
imp. indic.	solía, solías, solía, solíamos, solíais, solían

74.   Additional Irregular Past Participles
        absolver—**absuelto**
        abrir—**abierto**
        anteponer—**antepuesto**
        circunscribir—**circunscrito**
        componer—**compuesto**
        contradecir—**contradicho**
        cubrir—**cubierto**
        decir—**dicho**
        deponer—**depuesto**
        descomponer—**descompuesto**
        describir—**descrito**
        descubrir—**descubierto**
        desdecir—**desdicho**
        desenvolver—**desenvuelto**
        deshacer—**deshecho**
        devolver—**devuelto**
        disolver—**disuelto**

disponer—**dispuesto**
encubrir—**encubierto**
entreabrir—**entreabierto**
entrever—**entrevisto**
envolver—**envuelto**
escribir—**escrito**
exponer—**expuesto**
freír—**frito** (often regular, **freído**)
hacer—**hecho**
imponer—**impuesto**
imprimir—**impreso** (often regular, **imprimido**)
indisponer—**indispuesto**
inscribir—**inscrito**
interponer—**interpuesto**
morir—**muerto**
oponer—**opuesto**
poner—**puesto**
posponer—**pospuesto**
predecir—**predicho**
predisponer—**predispuesto**
prescribir—**prescrito**
presuponer—**presupuesto**
prever—**previsto**
proponer—**propuesto**
proscribir—**proscrito**
proveer—**provisto** (often regular, **proveído**)
pudrir—**podrido**
reabrir—**reabierto**
recubrir—**recubierto**
reescribir—**reescrito**
rehacer—**rehecho**
reponer—**repuesto**
resolver—**resuelto**
revolver—**revuelto**
romper—**roto**
satisfacer—**satisfecho**
sobreponer—**sobrepuesto**
suscribir—**suscrito**
superponer—**superpuesto**
suponer—**supuesto**
transcribir—**transcrito**
trasponer—**traspuesto**
ver—**visto**
volver—**vuelto**
yuxtaponer—**yuxtapuesto**

Aa

a PREP **voy — Londres** I'm going to London; **te lo doy — ti** I'm giving it to you; **se sentó — la sombra** she sat down in the shade; **tumbarse —l sol** to lie down in the sun; **una soga —l cuello** a rope around his neck; **lo miraba — la luz de una vela** she looked at him by the light of a candle; **— dos pesetas cada uno** at two pesetas each; **— las tres y media** at three-thirty; **sentarse — la mesa** to sit down at the table; **prestar dinero —l 15%** to lend money at 15%; **en grupos de — cinco** in groups of five; **cocina — gas** gas cooker; **fotos — todo color** full-color photos; **nadie le gana — testaruda** no one touches her for stubbornness; **terminaron — puñetazos** they ended up fighting; **¡— jugar!** let's play! **¿— qué vienen?** what are they coming for? **veo — mi mamá** I see my mother

AA [Alcohólicos Anónimos] F AA
abacá M manila
abad -esa ADJ abbot; F abbess
abadejo M cod
abadía F abbey
abajo ADV (dirección) down; (posición relativa) below; **mirar para —** to look down; **el piso de —** the apartment below; **véase —** see below; **— de** under, underneath; **Stefan está — del coche** Stefan is under/ underneath the car; **¡— el rey!** down with the king! **— firmante** undersigned; **echar —** to knock down; **río —** downstream; **venirse —** to go to ruin
abalanzarse[47] VI **— sobre** to lunge at, to swoop down upon
abanderado -da MF standard-bearer
abandonado ADJ abandoned; **es una persona muy abandonada** she's very unkempt
abandonar VT (a una persona, a una familia) to leave, to desert; (el hogar, un partido) to abandon; (una competencia, el poder) to give up; (una competencia, a un enamorado, el hábito de fumar) to quit; (en los naipes) to fold; (un curso) to drop out of
abandono M (descuido) neglect; (acción de abandonar, condición de abandonado) abandonment; **— de funciones** dereliction of duties
abanicar[30] VT (contra el calor) to fan; (en béisbol) to swing and miss
abanico M (accesorio) fan; (rango) array; (en béisbol) swing and a miss; **abrirse en —** to fan out

abaratar VT (bajar el precio) to lower the price of; (desprestigiar) to cheapen
abarcar[30] VT (categorías) to embrace, to encompass; (tiempo) to span
abarrotería F *Méx* grocery store
abarrotero -ra MF *Méx* grocer
abarrotes M PL *Méx* groceries; **tienda de —** *Méx* grocery store
abastecedor -ora MF supplier
abastecer[35] VT (un ejército, una ciudad) to supply; (una tienda) to stock
abastecimiento M supply
abasto M supply; **mercado de —s** farmers' market; **yo sola no doy —** I can't cope alone
abatido ADJ dejected, despondent, downcast
abatimiento M dejection, despondency
abatir VT (bajar) to lower; (derribar) to knock down; (desanimar) to depress; (matar a tiros) to shoot; **—se** to swoop down
abdicar[30] VI/VT to abdicate
abdomen M abdomen
abdominal ADJ abdominal; M sit-up
abecedario M alphabet
abedul M birch
abeja F bee; **— asesina** killer bee
abejón M bumblebee
abejorro M bumblebee
aberración F aberration
abertura F (acción) opening; (cualidad) openness
abeto M fir
abierto ADJ (no cerrado, no determinado, destapado) open; (franco) frank; **— de par en par** wide open
abierto *ver* abrir
abigarrado ADJ motley
abigeato M cattle rustling
abismal ADJ abysmal
abismo M abyss, chasm; **— generacional** generation gap
ablandar VT to soften
abnegación F self-denial
abobado ADJ silly
abocar[30] VI to turn onto; **—se a** to devote oneself to
abochornar VT (avergonzar) to embarrass; **—se** to become embarrassed
abocinar VT to flare
abofetear VT to slap
abogacía F legal profession; **estudiar —** to study law
abogado -da MF lawyer, attorney; **— tributarista** tax attorney, tax lawyer
abogar[40] VI **— por** to advocate, to plead for
abolengo M ancestry
abolición F abolition
abolir[73] VT to abolish
abollado ADJ dented
abolladura F dent

abollar VT to dent; **—se** to become dented

abolsarse VI to sag

abombar VT to make bulge

abominable ADJ abominable, loathsome

abominación F abomination

abominar VI to detest

abonado -da MF subscriber

abonar VT (suscribir) to subscribe; (pagar) to make a payment; (poner fertilizante) to fertilize; **—se** to subscribe; **— a una cuenta** credit an account

abono M (a una revista) subscription; (para una temporada deportiva) season ticket; (de autobús) pass; (para la tierra) fertilizer; (de dinero) payment

abordar VT (un avión, un buque) to board; (un problema) to tackle, to approach; (a una persona) to accost

aborigen ADJ aboriginal; MF native inhabitant; **— australiano** Australian aborigine

aborrascarse[30] VI to become stormy

aborrecer[35] VT to abhor, to loathe

aborrecible ADJ hateful, abhorrent

aborrecimiento M abhorrence

abortador -ora MF abortionist

abortar VI (naturalmente) to miscarry, to have a miscarriage; VI/VT (intencionadamente) to abort

abortero -ra MF abortionist

aborto M (espontáneo) miscarriage; (provocado) abortion; **— espontáneo** spontaneous abortion

abotargarse[40] VI to bloat

abotonar VT to button; **—se** to button up

abovedar VT (una iglesia) to vault, to cover with a vault; (una calle) to arch, to cover as a vault

abozalar VT to muzzle

abracadabra M abracadabra

abrasador ADJ burning

abrasar VT to burn; **—se** to be consumed

abrasión F abrasion; **— cutánea** dermabrasion

abrasivo ADJ abrasive

abrazadera F clamp

abrazar[47] VT (rodear con los brazos) to hug, to embrace; (rodear una cosa sujetando) to clasp; (una opinión) to espouse

abrazo M hug, embrace

abrevadero M trough

abrevar VT (dar de beber) to water; (beber) to drink

abreviación F abbreviation

abreviar VT to abbreviate, to abridge

abreviatura F abbreviation

abridor M opener

abrigado ADJ (ropa) warm; (lugar) sheltered

abrigar[40] VT (refugiados) to shelter; (emociones) to harbor; **—se** to bundle up

abrigo M (refugio) shelter; (prenda de vestir) coat, wrap; **— impositivo** tax shelter

abril M April

abrillantar VT to make shiny

abrir[74] VI/VT (una puerta) to open; VT (un candado) to unlock; (un grifo) to turn on; **— el apetito** to whet one's appetite; **— la sesión** call a meeting to order; **— paso** to make way; M SG **abrebotellas** bottle opener; M SG **abrelatas** can opener; VI (el cielo) to clear up; **—se** to open up; **—se paso** to press through; **en un — y cerrar de ojos** in the twinkle of an eye

abrochar VT to fasten; **—se** to buckle [up]

abrogación F repeal

abrogar[40] VT to repeal

abrojo M bur, sticker

abrumador ADJ overwhelming, overpowering

abrumar VT to overwhelm, to weigh down; **—se** to become foggy

abrupto ADJ abrupt

absceso M abscess

absolución F acquittal

absolutamente ADV, INTERJ absolutely

absoluto ADJ absolute; **en —** absolutely not

absolver[6,74] VT to absolve, to acquit

absorbente ADJ absorbent

absorber VT to absorb

absorción F absorption

absorto ADJ absorbed, engrossed

abstemio -mia ADJ abstemious; MF teetotaler

abstención F abstention

abstenerse[58] VI to abstain; **— de** to abstain from, to refrain from, to forego

abstinencia F abstinence

abstracción F abstraction

abstracto ADJ abstract

abstraer[59] VT to abstract

abstraído ADJ lost in thought

absurdo ADJ absurd, preposterous; M absurdity

abuchear VI/VT to boo, to jeer

abucheo M boo, jeer

abuelo -la M grandfather; F grandmother; **—s** grandparents

abulia F apathy

abultado ADJ bulgy

abultar VI to bulge

abundancia F abundance, plenty

abundante ADJ abundant, plentiful

abundar VI to abound; **— en** to abound in

aburrido ADJ (sin entretenimiento) bored; (pesado) boring, tiresome

aburrimiento M boredom

aburrir VT to bore; **—se** to become bored

abusar VT **— de** to abuse; (sexualmente) to molest

abuso M abuse; **— conyugal** spousal abuse; **— de confianza** breach of trust; **— de drogas** drug abuse; **— de sustancias** substance abuse

abyecto ADJ abject

acá ADV (en este lugar) here; (hacia este lugar) over here, *lit* hither; — **y allá** here and there

acabado ADJ finished; M finish

acabar VT to finish; VI to end; — **de comer** to have just eaten; — **por** to end up by; — **con** (la corrupción) to put an end to; (las cucarachas) to get rid of; **él y yo hemos acabado** he and I are through; **se acabaron los dulces** the candy is all gone; **se nos acabaron las ideas** we ran out of ideas; **y se acabó** and that's that

academia F (corporación, escuela militar) academy; (centro privado de enseñanza) private school

académico ADJ academic

acallar VT to silence, to quiet

acalorado ADJ heated

acaloramiento M **sufrió un —** he got too hot

acalorarse VI/VT (sofocarse) to overheat; (emocionarse) to get excited

acampada F camping trip

acampante MF camper

acampar VT to camp

acanalar VT to groove

acantilado ADJ sheer, steep; M bluff, cliff

acantonarse VT to be quartered

acaparar VT (productos) to hoard; (atención) to capture; (monopolizar) *fam* to hog; — **el mercado** to corner the market

acaramelar VT to candy

acariciar VT to caress; — **una esperanza** to harbor a hope

ácaro M mite

acarrear VT (transportar) to transport; (transportar en carro) to cart; (ocasionar) to bring about

acarreo M transport

acaso ADV perhaps; **por si —** just in case

acatamiento M compliance

acatar VT to abide by, to comply with

acatarrar VI to chill; **—se** to catch cold

acaudalado ADJ wealthy

acceder VI — **a** (un pedido) to accede to; VI (una invitación) to accept

accesibilidad F accessibility

accesible ADJ accessible, convenient

acceso M (entrada) access; (de ira) fit; — **a internet** Internet access; — **denegado** access denied; — **remoto** remote access, remote login; **de —** **prohibido** off limits

accesorio ADJ & M accessory

accidentado -da ADJ (viaje) eventful; (terreno) uneven; MF accident victim

accidental ADJ accidental

accidentarse VI to have an accident

accidente M (suceso imprevisto) accident; (del terreno) feature; (automovilístico) wreck; — **de tránsito** traffic accident; **por —** by accident

acción F (acto) action; (valor de bolsa) share of stock; — **de gracias** thanksgiving; **buenas acciones** good deeds; **acciones preferenciales** preferred stock; **acciones ordinarias** common stock

accionable ADJ actionable

accionar VT to operate

accionista MF shareholder, stockholder

acebo M holly

acechar VT (emboscar) to lie in ambush; (amenazar) to stalk

acecho M **rondar en —** to prowl; **estar al —** to lie in wait

aceitar VT to oil

aceite M oil; — **de linaza** linseed oil; — **de oliva** olive oil; — **de ricino** castor oil; — **vegetal** vegetable oil

aceitera F (recipiente) oilcan; (fábrica) oil factory

aceitoso ADJ oily

aceituna F olive

aceleración F acceleration

acelerador M accelerator

acelerar VT to accelerate, to speed up; VI to accelerate, to step on the gas; — **en vacío** to rev, to race; **—se** *Am* to get nervous

acémila F pack animal

acento M (pronunciación, signo) accent; (intensidad mayor, de voz) stress

acentuar[26] VT (aumentar) to accentuate; (poner tilde) to accent; (reforzar la voz) to stress; **—se** to accentuate

acepción F gloss, meaning

aceptable ADJ acceptable

aceptación F acceptance

aceptar VT to accept; — **entrega** to take delivery

acequia F irrigation ditch

acera F sidewalk

acerado ADJ made of steel

acerar VT to steel

acerca PREP — **de** about, concerning

acercamiento M approach

acercar[30] VT to bring near; **os acerco a la estación** I'll give you a ride to the station; **—se** to come near, to approach

acería F steel mill

acero M steel; — **inoxidable** stainless steel

acérrimo ADJ bitter

acertado ADJ right

acertar[1] VT to hit; VI to be right; — **con** to hit upon; — **a pasar** to happen to go by; **no —** to miss the mark

acertijo M riddle, conundrum

acervo M heritage

acetaminofén M acetaminophen

acetona F acetone

achacar[30] VI to blame

achacoso ADJ infirm, ailing

achaparrado ADJ (planta) stunted; (persona) squat

achaque M affliction, ailment; **—s** aches and pains

achicado ADJ weak-kneed

achicar[30] VT (de tamaño) to make small; (un vestido) to take in; (agua) to bail; **—se** (acobardarse) to feel intimidated; (empequeñecerse) to get smaller

achicoria F chicory

aciago ADJ unlucky

acicalado ADJ clean-cut

acicalarse VI to dress up

acicate M incentive

acidez F (de una solución) acidity; (del vinagre) sourness; **— de estómago** heartburn

ácido M acid; **—s grasos** fatty acids; ADJ (propio del ácido) acidic; (fruta) sour, tart

acierto M (contestación) right answer; (elección) felicitous choice

aclamación F acclamation, acclaim; **por —** by acclamation

aclamar VT to acclaim, to hail

aclaración F clarification

aclarar VT (con explicaciones) to clarify; (con agua) to rinse; (la voz) to clear; VI to dawn; **aclaró después de la tormenta** it cleared up after the storm; **—se** to lighten

aclimatar VT to acclimate

acné M acne

acobardar VT to intimidate

acogedor ADJ (persona) hospitable; (cuarto) cozy

acoger[45] VT (una sugerencia) to receive; (a un refugiado) to shelter; **—se** to take refuge; **—se a la ley** to have recourse to the law

acogida F reception

acogimiento M reception

acolchar VT to pad

acollarar VT to collar

acometer VT (atacar) to attack; (emprender) to undertake

acometida F attack

acomodado ADJ well-off

acomodador -ora MF usher

acomodar VT (arreglar) to arrange; (ajustar) to adjust; (adaptar) to adapt; **—se** (ponerse cómodo) to make oneself comfortable; (adaptarse) to adapt oneself

acomodo M position; **no tengo —** I can't find a comfortable position

acompañamiento M (acción, música) accompaniment; (grupo de personas que acompaña) retinue; (comida) side dish; (tenis) follow-through

acompañante ADJ accompanying; MF (compañero) companion; (en música) accompanist

acompañar VI/VT to accompany (también en

música); (escoltar) to escort; (en una carta) to enclose; **—se de** to be accompanied by; **esperemos que el tiempo acompañe** let's hope the weather cooperates; **te acompaño en el sentimiento** my thoughts are with you

acompasado ADJ (rítmico) rhythmical; (mesurado) measured

acomplejado ADJ self-conscious

acondicionar VT to prepare

acongojado ADJ grief-stricken

acongojar VT to distress; **—se** to become distressed

aconsejable ADJ advisable

aconsejar VT to advise, to counsel

acontecer[35] VI to take place

acontecimiento M event; **todo un —** quite a happening; **a esta altura de los —s** at this point in the proceedings

acopiar VT to stockpile

acopio M (acción de guardar) storing; (cosas guardadas) stockpile

acoplamiento M coupling; **— universal de cardán** universal joint

acoplar VT to couple; **—se** (piezas complementarias, partes) to couple, to join; (altavoces) to have feedback

acople M coupling, connection

acorazado ADJ armored; M battleship, warship

acorazar[47] VT to armor

acordado VI agreed-upon

acordar[5] VT to agree; VI **— en** to arrange to; **—se [de]** to remember

acorde M chord; ADJ in agreement; **en — con** in agreement with

acordeón M accordion

acordonar VT (un zapato) to lace; (un lugar) to rope off, to seal off; (una moneda) to mill

acorralar VT (meter en un corral) to corral; (arrinconar) to corner

acortamiento M shortening

acortar VT to shorten

acosar VT (perseguir) to harry; (atacar) to beset; (atormentar) to badger; (importunar sexualmente) to harass

acoso M (de presa) hunting down, pursuit; (de una persona) harassment, hounding

acostar[5] VT to put to bed; **—se** to go to bed; **—se con** to sleep with

acostumbrado ADJ (normal) accustomed; (habitual) customary; **estar — a** to be used / accustomed to

acostumbrar VT to accustom; (soler) to be accustomed to; **—se [a]** to get accustomed [to]; **acostumbraban ir al teatro** they used to go to the theater

acotación F (anotación) marginal note; (en una obra de teatro) stage directions

acotar VT (un terreno) to mark off; (un texto) to

make marginal notes on

acre ADJ acrid, pungent, sharp; M acre

acrecentamiento M growth, increase

acrecentar[1] VT to grow; **—se** to grow

acreditar VT (una cuenta) to credit; (a un profesional) to accredit; **— a una cuenta** to credit an account; **a quien pueda — ser el dueño de** to whoever can prove to be the owner of

acreedor -ora ADJ deserving; **saldo —** positive balance; MF creditor

acribillar VI (a balazos) to riddle [with]; (a pedradas) to pelt

acrílico ADJ & M acrylic

acritud F acrimony

acrobacia F (arte) acrobatics; (pirueta) stunt

acróbata MF acrobat

acrobático ADJ acrobatic

acrofobia F acrophobia

acrónimo M acronym

acta F (de nacimiento) certificate; (de una reunión) minutes; (de un congreso) proceedings

actitud F attitude, mind-set

activar VT to activate

actividad F activity

activismo M activism

activista MF activist

activo ADJ active; **en —** working; M assets; **— líquido** liquid assets; **— convertible** convertible assets

acto M (solemne, dramático) act; (acción) action; **— seguido** immediately after; **— fallido** Freudian slip; **en el —** on the spot; **hacer — de presencia** to show up

actor M actor, performer; **— de carácter** character actor

actriz F actor, actress, performer

actuación F (acción) acting; (rendimiento, desempeño) performance

actual ADJ current, present

actualidad F present time; **—es** latest news; **de —** up-to-date

actualización F (de información) update; (de ordenador) upgrade

actualizado ADJ (al día) up-to-date; (al minuto) up-to-the-minute

actualizar[47] VT to update; (programa de ordenador) to upgrade; (pantalla de ordenador) to refresh

actualmente ADV presently, currently

actuar[26] VI (comportarse) to act; (dar una representación) to perform

actuario -ria MF (judicial) clerk; (de seguros) actuary

acuarela F watercolor

acuario M aquarium

acuartelar VT to quarter

acuático ADJ aquatic

acuchillar VT (penetrar) to stab; (cortar) to slash

acuclillado ADJ squatting

acuclillarse VI to squat

acudir VI (ir) to go; (asistir) to attend; **— a** to turn to; **— al llamado** to respond to the call; **— al socorro de** to go to the rescue of; **— en masa** to flock

acueducto M aqueduct

acuerda, acuerde ver acordar

acuerdo M agreement; **— comercial** trade agreement; **— contractual** contractual agreement; **— global** package deal agreement; **estar de —** to be in agreement; **ponerse de —** to come to an agreement; **de — con** in accordance with

acumulación F (de dinero) accumulation; (de tensión) buildup

acumulador M storage battery

acumular VT (desperdicios) to accumulate; (fortuna) to amass; (deudas) to accumulate, to run up; **—se** to collect; **rabia acumulada** pent-up rage

acumulativo ADJ cumulative

acuñación F coinage, minting

acuñar VT (monedas, una expresión) to coin; (meter cuñas) to wedge

acuoso ADJ watery

acupuntor -ora MF acupuncturist

acupuntura F acupuncture

acurrucarse[30] VI to nestle, to huddle

acusación F accusation, charge

acusado -da MF accused; (en un juicio) defendant

acusador -ora MF accuser

acusar VT (culpabilizar) to accuse; (detectar) to detect; (revelar) to betray; (entre niños) to tattle, to tell; **— el golpe** to feel the blow; **— recibo** to acknowledge receipt

acuse M acknowledgment

acusetas MF SG tattletale

acusica MF tattletale

acústica F acoustics

acústico ADJ acoustic

adagio M adage

adaptabilidad F resilience, adaptability

adaptación F adaptation

adaptador M adapter

adaptar VT to adapt

adecuado ADJ appropriate

adecuar VT to adapt; **—se a** to be suitable for

adefesio M sight, hideous thing

adelantado ADJ (economía, alumno) advanced; (reloj) fast; (tren) ahead of time, ahead of schedule; **por —** in advance

adelantamiento M (de una fecha) bringing forward; (de un coche) overtaking

adelantar VT (una fecha, dinero) to advance; (la mano) to move forward; (un coche) to pass; (una noticia) to have a scoop; VI (un reloj) to

gain; — **en** to make progress in; —**se** (sacar
ventaja) to get ahead; (actuar antes) to go
first; (innovar) to be ahead; (hablar antes de
tiempo) to get ahead of oneself

adelante ADV forward; — **con los faroles** let's
get started; — **de mí** in front of me; **de aquí
en** — from now on; **hacia** — forward; **ir** —
to go ahead; **más** — later; **sacar** — to make
prosper; **seguir** — to go on; INTERJ go for it!

adelanto M (de la ciencia) advance,
breakthrough; (de un coche) passing; (pago)
advance; **el** — **de los relojes** setting the
clocks forward

adelfa F oleander

adelgazar[47] VI to lose weight; VT to lose; (hacer
perder peso) to make one lose weight; (hacer
menos espeso) to thin; (hacer parecer
delgado) to make one look thinner; — **cinco
kilos** to lose five kilos; —**se** to get thinner

ademán M gesture; **hacer un** — **a alguien** to
motion to someone

además ADV moreover, besides, in addition; —
de deberme dinero besides / in addition to
owing me money

adentrarse VI — **en** (un asunto) to go deeply
into; (un lugar) to go deep into, to penetrate
into; (una edad) to enter

adentro ADV inside; **ir para/hacia** — to go
inside; **hablar para sus** —**s** to talk to
oneself; **con lo de** — **para afuera** inside out

aderezar[47] VT (embellecer) to adorn;
(condimentar) to season, to garnish

aderezo M (adorno) adornment; (de un
alimento) seasoning; (de una ensalada)
dressing

adeudar VT (deber) to owe; — **una cuenta** to
debit an account

adeudo M (endeudamiento) indebtedness; (a
una cuenta) debit

adherencia F adhesion

adherir[8] VI to adhere; —**se a** (una cosa) to stick
to; (una huelga) to join; (una idea) to
subscribe to

adhesión F (a una cosa) adhesion; (a una
doctrina) adherence

adhesivo ADJ adhesive; M (pegamento) cement,
adhesive; (calcomanía) sticker

adicción F addiction

adición F addition

adicional ADJ additional

adictivo ADJ addictive, habit-forming

adicto -ta ADJ addicted; MF addict; — **al
trabajo** workaholic

adiestramiento M training

adiestrar VT to train

adinerado ADJ wealthy, well-to-do, moneyed

adiós INTERJ good-bye; **hacer** — **con la mano**
to wave good-bye

adiposo ADJ fatty

aditivo M additive

adivinanza F riddle

adivinar VT to guess

adivino -na MF fortune-teller

adjetivo ADJ & M adjective

adjudicación F award

adjudicar[30] VT to award; —**se** to be awarded

adjuntar VT (incluir en una carta) to enclose;
(añadir) to add, to attach, to append

adjunto ADJ (unido) attached; (incluido)
enclosed; (asistente) adjunct; ADV herewith;
M attachment

adminículo M gadget

administración F administration,
management; — **pública** civil service; —
intermedia middle management

administrador -ora MF administrator,
manager; — **de cuentas** account manager;
— **de un sitio web** webmaster

administrar VT (un medicamento) to
administer; (una empresa) to administer, to
manage; (justicia) to dispense; —**se** to budget

administrativo ADJ administrative

admirable ADJ admirable

admiración F admiration

admirador -ora MF admirer; (de una estrella de
cine) fan

admirar VT to admire; —**se** to be amazed; —**se
de** to wonder at

admisible ADJ admissible, allowable

admisión F (aceptación) admission;
(reconocimiento) acknowledgment

admitir VT (dejar entrar, reconocer) to admit;
(aceptar) to accept; (permitir) to allow

ADN [ácido desoxirribonucleico] M DNA

adobar VT (aderezar carne) to season; (curtir una
piel) to tan; (encurtir) to pickle

adobe M adobe

adobo M sauce for seasoning

adoctrinar VT to indoctrinate

adolecer[35] VI — **de** to suffer from

adolescencia F adolescence

adolescente ADJ adolescent; MF adolescent,
teenager

adonde ADV REL **esa es la casa** — **vamos** that's
the house [that] we're going to, that's the
house where we're going

adónde ADV INTERR & PRON where

adopción F adoption

adoptar VT to adopt

adoptivo ADJ adoptive

adoquín M cobblestone

adorable ADJ adorable

adoración F (a una persona) adoration; (a un
dios) worship

adorador -ora MF worshiper

adorar VT (a una persona) to adore; (a un dios) to
worship

adormecer[35] VT (dar sueño) to make drowsy;

(entumecer) to numb; **—se** (de sueño) to become drowsy; (de frío) to go numb

adormilado ADJ sleepy

adornar VT to adorn, to embellish

adorno M adornment, ornament, decoration

adquirir[4] VT (un bien) to acquire; (una característica) to take on

adquisición F (compra) acquisition; (nuevo miembro) addition; (compra de una compañía) takeover

adquisitivo ADJ purchasing

adrede ADV on purpose

adrenalina F adrenaline

aduana F (control) customs; (edificio) customshouse

aduanero -ra ADJ customs; **control —** customs control; MF customs officer

aducir[38] VT to adduce

adueñarse VI to take possession

adulación F flattery

adulador -ora ADJ flattering; MF flatterer

adular VI/VT to flatter

adulón -ona ADJ flattering; MF *fam* brown-noser

adulterar VT to adulterate

adulterio M adultery

adúltero -ra MF adulterer

adulto -ta ADJ & MF adult

adusto ADJ stern

advenedizo ADJ upstart

advenimiento M advent

adverbio M adverb

adversario -ria MF adversary, opponent

adversidad F adversity

adverso ADJ adverse

advertencia F (aviso) notice; (amonestación) warning, admonition

advertir[8] VT (avisar) to warn; (notar) to notice; (notificar) to advise, to tip off

Adviento M Advent

advierta, advierte *ver* advertir

adyacente ADJ adjacent

aéreo ADJ aerial; **correo —** airmail

aeróbico ADJ aerobic

aeróbic M aerobics

aerobio ADJ aerobic

aerodeslizador M hovercraft

aerodinámica F aerodynamics

aerodinámico ADJ aerodynamic, streamlined

aeródromo M airport

aeroespacial ADJ aerospace

aerolínea F airline

aeronáutica F aeronautics

aeronave F aircraft

aeropuerto M airport

aerosol M (suspensión) aerosol; (aparato) spray can

aerotransportado ADJ airborne

aerotransportar VT to airlift

afabilidad F affability, friendliness

afable ADJ affable, friendly

afamado ADJ famed

afán M eagerness

afanar VT *fam* to swipe; VI **—se** to work hard

afanoso ADJ hardworking

afasia F aphasia

afear VT to make ugly; **—se** to become ugly

afección F condition

afectación F affectation

afectado ADJ (dañado, lastimado) affected, stricken; (artificial) affected, unnatural

afectar VT to affect

afecto M affection, fondness; **— a** fond of

afectuoso ADJ affectionate, loving

afeitado -da ADJ clean-shaven; M shave

afeitadora F shaver

afeitar VT to shave

afelpado ADJ & M plush

afeminado ADJ effeminate

aferrado ADJ stubborn, obstinate

aferrar VT (agarrar) to grasp; (atar) to grapple; **—se** to cling

affaire M affair

Afganistán M Afghanistan

afgano -na ADJ & MF Afghan, Afghani

afianzado ADJ (garantizado) bonded; (apuntalado, amarrado) secured, firmed up

afianzar[47] VT (una pared) to secure; (un préstamo) to secure, to guarantee; (una amistad) to build up

afiche M poster

afición F (inclinación) inclination; (afecto) fondness; (hinchada) fans

aficionado -da ADJ **— a** fond of; MF (no profesional) amateur; (hincha) fan

aficionarse VI **— a** to become fond of

afilado ADJ sharp; M sharpening

afilador -ora MF grinder, sharpener

afilar VT to sharpen, to grind

afiliación F affiliation; **sin — política** nonpartisan

afiliarse VI **— con** to affiliate oneself with

afín ADJ kindred, related

afinación F tune-up

afinado ADJ in tune

afinador -ora MF tuner

afinar VT (una destreza) to perfect; (un plan) to fine-tune; (un piano) to tune; **—se** to become thinner

afinidad F (afecto) affinity; (parentesco) kinship

afirmación F (aseveración) assertion; (aseveración positiva) affirmation

afirmar VT (decir) to assert, to declare; (aseverar) to affirm; (sujetar) to secure; **—se** to steady oneself

afirmativa F affirmative answer

afirmativo ADJ affirmative

aflicción F affliction, woe

afligir[46] VT (dar dolor) to afflict; (entristecer) to distress

aflojar VT (una soga) to slacken, to loosen; (la vigilancia) to relax; — **el dinero** to hand over the money; VI to ease up, to slack off; —**se** to work loose, to loosen up

afluencia F influx

afluente M tributary

afluir[19] VI (río) to flow [into]; (turistas) to flock

afortunadamente ADV fortunately, luckily

afortunado ADJ fortunate, lucky

afrecho M bran

afrenta F affront

afrentar VT to offend

África F Africa

africano -na ADJ & MF African

afroamericano -na ADJ & MF African American

afrontar VT to face

afuera ADV (de un edificio) outdoors; (de un recipiente) outside; F PL **las —s** outskirts

agachar VT to lower; —**se** to crouch, to stoop

agalla F (de pez) gill; (de roble) gallnut; **tener —s** to have guts/spunk

agarrado ADJ tight-fisted

agarrar VT (sujetar) to seize, to grasp, to grab; (capturar) to catch; (adherirse) to grip; — **por sorpresa** to catch by surprise; **—le la onda a algo** to get the swing of something; —**se una neumonía** to catch a case of pneumonia; —**se** to hold on; —**se de** to latch onto; **agarré por la calle ocho** I took Eighth Street; **agarró y se fue** he up and went

agarre M (también golf) grip

agarrón M grab

agarrotarse VI (el cuerpo) to stiffen up; (un motor) to seize [up]

agasajar VT to entertain

agasajo M (acogida) welcome; (regalo) gift

agazaparse VI to crouch

agencia F agency, bureau; — **de empleo** employment agency; — **de publicidad** advertising agency; — **de viajes** travel agency; — **gubernamental** government agency

agenciar VT to wrangle

agenda F (cuaderno) daily planner; (orden del día) agenda

agente MF (representante) agent; (espía) operative; — **de policía** police officer; — **de compras** purchasing agent

ágil ADJ agile, nimble

agilidad F agility

agilizar VT to expedite

agitación F (acción de agitar, nerviosismo) agitation; (protesta) turmoil, unrest

agitado ADJ (estado) agitated; (vida) eventful, hectic; (mar) choppy; (sueño) uneasy

agitador -ora M (aparato) agitator; MF (rebelde) agitator, troublemaker

agitar VT (sacudir) to agitate, to shake up; (incitar a la protesta) to agitate; —**se** (ponerse nervioso) to get worked up; (moverse) to thrash around

aglomeración F crowd

aglomerado M particle board

aglomerarse VI to crowd together

agnóstico -ca ADJ & MF agnostic

agobiado ADJ (por los enemigos) embattled; (por el trabajo) overwhelmed

agobiante ADJ overwhelming

agobiar VT (con una carga excesiva) to weigh down; (con trabajo) to overwhelm; (con impuestos) to burden

agolparse VI to crowd together

agonía F throes of death; **ser un —s** to be a whiner

agonizante ADJ dying

agonizar[47] VI to be in the throes of death

agorafobia F agoraphobia

agorero -ra ADJ ominous; MF soothsayer

agosto M August; **hacer su —** to make hay while the sun shines

agotado ADJ (persona) worn-out, tired out; (libro) out-of-print; (mercancía) out-of-stock

agotador ADJ exhausting

agotamiento M (de una persona) exhaustion; (de un recurso) depletion

agotar VT (recurso) to exhaust, to use up, to deplete; (energía) to sap; (a una persona) to wear down; —**se** (acabarse) to be all gone; (venderse) to sell out; (secarse) to dry up; (libro) to go out of print

agraciado ADJ attractive

agraciar VT to grace

agradable ADJ (persona) agreeable, pleasant, congenial; (situación) pleasant, enjoyable

agradar VT to please

agradecer[35] VT (dar gracias) to thank; (sentir gratitud) to be grateful for; **se agradece** thank you

agradecido ADJ thankful, grateful

agradecimiento M thankfulness, appreciation; (en un libro) acknowledgment

agradezca, agradezco ver agradecer

agrado M pleasure; **de su —** to his liking

agrandamiento M enlargement

agrandar VT to enlarge

agrario ADJ agrarian

agravar VT to aggravate, to make worse; —**se** to get worse

agraviar VT to outrage

agravio M outrage

agredir[73] VT to assault

agregado -da MF (funcionario de embajada) attaché; (profesor) adjunct; M (mezcla) aggregate

agregar[40] VT to add

agresión F (violencia) aggression; (ataque) assault; — **con lesiones** assault and battery

agresividad F (actitud) aggressiveness; (propensión violenta) aggression

agresivo ADJ aggressive

agresor -ora MF aggressor, assailant

agreste ADJ (recio) rough; (silvestre) wild

agriar[28] VT to make sour; —**se** to go sour

agrícola ADJ agricultural

agricultor -ora MF agriculturist, farmer

agricultura F agriculture, farming

agridulce ADJ (sabor) sweet-and-sour; (memoria) bittersweet

agrietarse VI (cristales) to crack; (los labios) to chap

agrimensor -ora MF surveyor

agrimensura F surveying

agrio ADJ sour

agrisarse VI to gray

agropecuario ADJ agricultural

agrumarse VI to lump

agrupación F group

agrupamiento M grouping

agrupar VT (objetos, personas) to group; (documentos digitales) to queue

agua F water; — **con gas** sparkling water; — **corriente** running water; — **de colonia** cologne; — **de grifo** tap water; — **de manantial** spring water; — **dulce** fresh water; —**marina** aquamarine; — **mineral** mineral water; — **oxigenada** hydrogen peroxide; — **potable** drinking water; — **salada** salt water; —**s abajo** downstream; —**s arriba** upstream; —**s negras** sewer water; **hacer** —*fam* to take a leak; **se me hace** — **la boca** my mouth is watering

aguacate M avocado

aguacero M shower, cloudburst, downpour

aguada F watering hole

aguadero M watering hole

aguado ADJ (fruta) watery; (vino, sopa) watered-down

aguantar VT (miserias) to endure; (a una persona molesta) to bear, to stand; (un peso) to bear; (la respiración) to hold; VI (mantenerse) to stand; (durar) to last; (esperar) to wait; (no pudrirse) to keep; **aguántate** grin and bear it

aguante M (para el trabajo) endurance, stamina; (para el vino) tolerance

aguar[25] VT (añadir agua, despojar de fuerza) to water down; (estropear) to spoil; — **una fiesta** to ruin a party; —**se** to become diluted; MF SG **aguafiestas** killjoy, wet blanket

aguardar VI to wait; VT to wait for, to await

aguardentoso ADJ hoarse

aguardiente M brandy

aguarrás M turpentine

agudeza F (visual) sharpness, keenness; (del ingenio) quickness; (para los negocios) acumen; (dicho agudo) witticism

agudo ADJ (dolor, enfermedad, ángulo) acute; (vista, mente) sharp, keen; (mentón) pointed; (voz) high-pitched; (chiste) witty

agüero M portent, omen; **de mal** — portentous

aguijada F goad

aguijar VT to goad

aguijón M (de planta) spur; (de insecto) sting, stinger

aguijonear VT (a un buey) to goad, to prod; (insecto) to sting

águila F eagle; **es un** — he is sharp

aguilucho M eaglet

aguinaldo M Christmas bonus

aguja F (de coser, tejer, tocadiscos, pino, velocímetro) needle; (de reloj) hand; (riel móvil) railroad switch; (chapitel) steeple, spire; — **de croché** crochet hook; — **de punto** knitting needle; — **de zurcir** darning needle; — **hipodérmica** hypodermic needle; **como una** — **en un pajar** like a needle in a haystack

agujerear VT to pierce

agujero M (orificio) hole; (vacío legal) loophole; (déficit) shortfall; — **negro** black hole; **tapar** —**s** (reparar orificios) to plug holes; (pagar deudas) to pay debts

aguzar[47] VT to sharpen; — **el oído** to prick up one's ears

ahechaduras F PL chaff

ahí ADV there; **por** — over there, thereabouts; **de** — hence; — **te quiero ver** I want to see you in that situation

ahijado -da M godson; F goddaughter

ahínco M **trabajar con** — to work hard

ahogamiento M drowning

ahogar[40] VT (asfixiar en agua) to drown; (inundar con combustible) to flood; (asfixiar por falta de aire) to smother; (reprimir) to stifle; (asfixiar por presión al cuello) to throttle, to strangle, to choke; — **las penas bebiendo** to drown one's sorrows in drink; —**se** (en agua) to drown; (por falta de aire) to asphyxiate

ahogo M (por calor, falta de aire) suffocation; (por un esfuerzo) breathlessness; **vivir sin** —**s** to live a comfortable life

ahondar VT (hoyo) to deepen; (asunto) to dig deeper into; —**se** to become deeper

ahora ADV now; — **bien** now then; — **mismo** right now; — **sí** now we're cooking; **por** — for the present, for now; **hasta** — to date, up to now, so far

ahorcar[30] VT to hang; *fam* to string up

ahorita ADV (ahora mismo) right now; (dentro de poco) in a second

ahorrar VT (dinero) to save; (molestias) to spare

ahorrativo ADJ frugal, thrifty

ahorro M thriftiness; **—s** savings; **—s de toda la vida** life savings

ahuecar[30] VT to hollow out; **— la voz** to speak in a hollow voice

ahumado ADJ smoked; M smoking

ahumar VT to smoke

ahuyentar VT to drive away, to scare away; **—se** to get scared

airado ADJ irate

airarse VI to get angry

airbag M airbag

aire M air; (melodía) tune; (manera de ser) manner; **— acondicionado** air conditioning; **— libre** outdoors; **al — libre** outdoors; **cambiar de —s** to change surroundings; **darse —s** to posture; **en el —** up in the air; **estar en el —** to be on the air; **tener — de** to look like; **tomar —** to breathe in, to get some air

airear VT to air out

airoso ADJ graceful; **salir —** to come out smelling like a rose

aislacionismo M isolationism

aislado ADJ (persona) isolated; (lugar) secluded

aislador M insulator; ADJ insulating

aislamiento M (acción de aislarse) isolation; (cosa que aísla) insulation; (soledad) seclusion

aislante M insulator

aislar[28] VT (separar) to isolate; (envolver) to insulate; (rechazar socialmente) to ostracize

ajar VT (una planta) to wither; (las manos) to make rough; (la piel) to age

ajedrez M chess

ajeno ADJ (de otro) belonging to someone else; (extraño) alien; **— a un peligro** oblivious to a danger; **— a mi voluntad** beyond my control; **— a mi experiencia** foreign to my experience

ajetrearse VI to bustle about

ajetreo M bustle, hustle and bustle

ají M chile

ajo M garlic

ajonjolí M sesame

ajuar M (de novia) trousseau; (mobiliario) furnishings

ajustado ADJ tight, snug; **— a la ley** in accordance with the law

ajustar VT (una prenda) to adjust; (un contrato) to tweak; (una tuerca) to tighten; **— cuentas** to settle accounts; VI to fit tight; **—se a derecho** to be in accordance with the law

ajuste M (de horarios, planes) adjustment; (del cinturón) tightening; (de una máquina) fine-tuning; (de cuentas) settlement; (de una prenda) alteration; **hacer —s** to tinker with

ala F (de ave) wing; (de sombrero) brim; (en fútbol) winger; **cortarle las —s a alguien** to clip someone's wings

alabanza F praise

alabar VT to praise

alabeo M warp

alacena F pantry

alacrán M scorpion

alamar M (adorno) frog; (presilla) clasp

alambique M still

alambrada F wire fence

alambrado M (barrera) wire fence; (acción de alambrar) wiring

alambrar VT to wire

alambre M wire; **— de púas** barbed wire

alameda F poplar grove

álamo M poplar tree

alancear VT to wound with a lance, to spear

alano M mastiff

alarde M show; **hacer — de** to boast of, to show off

alardear VI **— de** to boast about

alargar[40] VT (hacer más largo) to lengthen; (un brazo, un guiso) to stretch [out]; **— la vista** to peer into the distance; **—se** to go on [longer than expected]

alargue M (fútbol) extra time

alarido M scream, howl

alarma F alarm; **— antirrobo** burglar alarm; **— contra incendios** fire alarm

alarmante ADJ alarming

alarmar VT to alarm

alba F dawn

albacea MF executor

albanés -esa ADJ & MF Albanian

Albania F Albania

albañal M sewer

albañil M mason, bricklayer

albañilería F masonry

albaricoque M apricot

albatros M albatross

alberca F (depósito) reservoir; (piscina) *Méx* swimming pool

albergar[40] VT (refugiar) to shelter; (hospedar) to lodge; (ser sede de) to house; (guardar rencor, un secreto) to harbor; **—se** (protegerse) to take shelter; (alojarse) to lodge

albergue M lodging; **dar —** (a un refugiado) to give refuge; (a un criminal) to harbor

albinismo M albinism

albino -na MF albino

albóndiga F meatball

albor M dawn

alborada F dawn

albornoz M bathrobe

alborotador -ora ADJ rowdy; MF troublemaker

alborotar VT (el pelo) to muss; (la casa) to mess up; (una turba) to rouse; (a los niños) to excite; **—se** to get excited

alboroto M hubbub, fuss

alborozado ADJ joyful

alborozar[47] VT to gladden; **—se** to rejoice

alborozo M joy

albricias F PL & INTERJ congratulations

álbum M album

alcachofa F artichoke

alcahuete -ta MF (soplón) tattletale; (mediador, encubridor) procurer

alcaide M warden

alcalde -esa MF mayor

alcaldía F (edificio) city hall; (oficio) mayoralty

álcali M alkali

alcalino ADJ alkaline

alcance M (de una persona) reach; (de los deseos) attainment; (de un misil) range; (de una ley) scope; **de corto[s] —[s]** of meager intellect; **al —** at hand, within reach; **a su —** within his reach; **al — del oído** within hearing; **dar — a** to catch up with; **de gran —** far-reaching; **de largo —** long-range

alcancía F piggybank

alcanfor M camphor

alcantarilla F (para agua sucia) sewer; (para lluvias) gully, gutter

alcantarillado M sewage system

alcanzar⁴⁷ VT (llegar, cumplir) to reach; (igualar) to catch up with; (pasar, poner en la mano) to pass; (herir a balazos) to get; **no alcanzo a verlo** I can't quite see it; **no me alcanza el dinero** I don't have enough money; **alcancé a conocer a mi abuela** I was born soon enough to meet my grandmother

alcaparra F caper

alcaucil M artichoke

alcázar M fortress

alce M (europeo, asiático) elk; (norteamericano) moose

alcoba F bedroom

alcohol M alcohol; **— etílico** ethyl alcohol; **— para fricciones** rubbing alcohol

alcohólico -ca ADJ & MF alcoholic

alcoholismo M alcoholism

alcornoque M (árbol) cork tree; (persona) blockhead

alcuza F oilcan

aldaba F (para llamar) knocker; (para cerrar) bolt

aldabón M large knocker

aldea F village, hamlet

aldeano -na MF villager; ADJ **joven aldeana** village girl

aleación F alloy

alear VT (metales) to alloy; VI (aves) to flap wings

aleatorio ADJ random

aleatorizar VT to randomize

aleccionar VT to teach a lesson

aledaños M PL vicinity

alegar⁴⁰ VT (aducir) to adduce; (pretender) to claim

alegato M (a favor de) plea; (en contra de) allegation

alegoría F allegory

alegrar VT (a una persona) to gladden; (una fiesta) to brighten up; **—se** to be glad; (por efecto del alcohol) to get tipsy

alegre ADJ (contento) joyful, cheerful, lighthearted; (ebrio) tipsy, lit

alegría F joy, merriment, cheer

alejamiento M (distanciamiento) withdrawal; (separacion de un cargo) dismissal

alejar VT (distanciar) to move away; (ahuyentar) to scare off; **—se** (físicamente) to move away; (emocionalmente) to withdraw

alelar VT to stupefy

alemán -ana ADJ & MF German; M (lengua) German

Alemania F Germany

alentador ADJ encouraging

alentar¹ VT (animar) to encourage, to cheer up; VI to breathe

alergeno/alérgeno M allergen

alergia F allergy

alérgico ADJ allergic

alergólogo -ga MF allergist

alero -ra MF (baloncesto) forward; M eaves

alerón M (de avión) aileron, flap; (de coche) spoiler

alerta ADJ & F alert

alertar VT to alert

aleta F (de pez) fin; (de ballena) fluke; (de buceador, delfín) flipper

aletargado ADJ sluggish, lethargic

aletargarse⁴⁰ VI to fall into lethargy, to become lethargic

aletazo M flap of a wing

aletear VI to flap, to flutter

aleteo M flapping, flutter

alevín M small fry

alevosía F treachery

alevoso ADJ treacherous

alfabetismo M literacy; **— digital** computer literacy

alfabetización F literacy; **— digital** computer literacy

alfabetizar⁴⁷ VI (enseñar) to teach to read and write; VT (ordenar) alphabetize

alfabeto M alphabet

alfalfa F alfalfa

alfanumérico ADJ alphanumeric

alfarería F pottery

alfarero -ra MF potter

alféizar M windowsill

alfeñique M (golosina) sugar paste; (persona) weakling

alférez MF second lieutenant; **— de fragata** ensign

alfil M bishop

alfiler M pin; **— de corbata** tie tack; **no cabe un —** it's totally full

alfiletero M pincushion

alfombra F (de pared a pared) carpet; (suelta) rug

alfombrar VT to carpet

alfombrilla F (en el suelo) mat; (para ordenador) mouse pad

alforja F saddlebag

alga F seaweed; **—s** algae

algarabía F uproar

algarrobo M locust tree

algazara F merriment

álgebra F algebra

algo PRON something; **— es —** something is better than nothing; **por — será** there must be reason; ADV somewhat, slightly

algodón M cotton; **— de azúcar** cotton candy; **se crió entre algodones** he had a protected childhood

algoritmo M algorithm

alguacil M (de policía) sheriff, marshal; (en un tribunal) bailiff

alguien PRON INDEF somebody, someone; **vino — a hablarte** someone came to talk to you; (en preguntas) anybody, anyone; **¿— lo vio?** did anyone see him?

alguno ADJ some; **—s** some, a few; **sin ruido —** without a sound; **en alguna parte** somewhere; **de alguna manera** somehow; **en algún momento** sometime; **¿lo has visto alguna vez?** have you ever seen him? **¿hay alguna forma de hacer esto?** is there any way to do this? PRON someone, something

alhaja F jewel (también persona); **—s** jewelry

alhajero M jewelry box

alharaca F fuss

alhelí M wallflower

aliado -da ADJ allied; MF ally

alianza F (con aliados, socios) alliance

aliar[28] VT to ally

alias M alias, assumed name; (uso policial) a k a

alicaído ADJ crestfallen

alicates M PL pliers

aliciente M inducement

aliento M (aire respirado) breath; (ánimo) encouragement; **cobrar —** to catch one's breath; **contener el —** to hold one's breath; **sin —** out of breath, breathless

aligerar VT to lighten; **— el paso** to quicken one's pace

alijo M cache, stash

alimentación F (comida) nourishment, food; (acción de dar de comer) feeding; **— intravenosa** intravenous feeding

alimentador M feeder; **— de hojas** paper feeder; **— de impresora** printer feeder

alimentar VT (a una persona) to feed, to nourish; (un fuego) to stoke

alimentario ADJ alimentary; **canal —** alimentary canal

alimenticio ADJ (nutritivo) nutritious, nourishing; (relativo a los alimentos) alimentary; **industria alimenticia** food industry; **pensión alimenticia** alimony

alimento M food, nourishment

alineación F (deportes) lineup; (coche) alignment; **— a la derecha** right justification; **— a la izquierda** left justification

alinear VT (objetos) to line up; (a un deportista) to put in the lineup; **—se con** to align oneself with

aliño M condiment, seasoning

alisar VT (tela) to smooth; (pelo) to straighten

alistamiento M enlistment

alistar VT to enlist

aliviar VT (aligerar) to lighten; (mitigar) to alleviate, to relieve; (tranquilizar) to relieve; **—se** (mejorarse) to get better; (hacer sus necesidades) to relieve oneself

alivio M relief (también golf); **— de la deuda** debt relief

aljaba F quiver

aljibe M cistern

allá ADV there, over there; **más —** farther, beyond; **el más —** the hereafter; **— tú** that's your problem

allanamiento M raid; **— de morada** forcible entry

allanar VT (la tierra) to level, to smooth; (una dificultad) to iron out; (una casa) to raid; **— el camino** to smooth the way

allegado -da ADJ close to; MF relative

allegar[40] VT to gather; **—se** to arrive

allí ADV (espacial) there; (temporal) then; **por —** through there

alma F soul; **con toda el —** from the bottom of one's heart; **hasta el —** to the bone; **ni un —** not a soul; **no me cabía el — en el cuerpo** was overjoyed; **se me fue el — al piso** my heart sank

almacén M (depósito) warehouse, storehouse, depot; (negocio) department store; **grandes almacenes** department store

almacenaje M storage

almacenamiento M storage; **— de datos** data storage; **— masivo** mass storage, bulk storage

almacenar VT to store, to stock up on; **— como** to save as

almacenista MF wholesaler

almáciga F nursery

almádena F sledgehammer

almanaque M (anuario) almanac; (calendario) calendar

almeja F clam

almendra F almond

almendro M almond tree

miar M haystack

míbar M syrup

midón M starch

midonado ADJ (persona) stiff; (camisa) starched

midonar VT to starch

mirante M admiral

mohada F pillow; **consultarlo con la —** to sleep on it

mohadilla F (para sellos) cushion; (en las patas de los perros) pad; **— eléctrica** heating pad

mohadón M cushion

mohaza F currycomb

mohazar[47] VT to groom

morranas F PL piles, hemorrhoids

morzar[49] VT to lunch, to eat lunch

muerzo M lunch

ocado ADJ wild

oe M aloe vera

ojamiento M (residencia) lodging, accommodations; (militar) quarters; **— web** web hosting

ojar VT (a un invitado) to lodge, to accommodate; (a unos huérfanos) to house; (a las tropas) to quarter; **—se** (una bala) to lodge; (una persona) to board, to room

ondra F lark

paca F alpaca

pinismo M mountain climbing

pinista MF mountain climber, mountaineer

pino ADJ alpine

piste M birdseed

quería F farmhouse

quilar VT to rent; **se alquila** for rent

quiler M (pago mensual) rent; (acción de alquilar) renting; **coche de —** rental car; **dar en —** to hire out

quitrán M tar

quitranar VT to tar

rededor ADV around; **— de la casa** around the house; M **—es** (de un área) surroundings; (de una ciudad) outskirts

ta F discharge; **dar de —** to discharge

tamente ADV highly

tanería F haughtiness

tanero ADJ haughty

tar M altar

teración F alteration; **alteraciones al orden público** public disturbances

terar VT to alter; **— el ánimo** to upset; **—se** to get upset

tercado M altercation

tercar[30] VT **— con** to quarrel with

ternador M alternator

ternancia F alternation

ternar VT to alternate; **— con** to rub elbows with

ternativa F alternative

alternativo ADJ (cambiante) alternating; (optativo) alternative

alterno ADJ alternate; **alterna y continua** AC/DC

alteza F highness

altibajos M PL ups and downs

altillo M attic

altímetro M altimeter

altiplano M high plateau

altisonante ADJ high-sounding

altitud F altitude

altivez F haughtiness

altivo ADJ haughty

alto ADJ (que está arriba) high; (que tiene altura vertical) tall; **altas finanzas** high finance; **— contraste** high contrast; **de alta calidad** high-quality; **de alta fidelidad** high-fidelity; **de — nivel** high-level; **de alta potencia** high-powered; **de — riesgo** high-risk; **de alta velocidad** high-speed; **en voz alta** aloud; **en — grado** to a great extent; **en alta mar** on the high seas; M **altavoz** loudspeaker; M **altoparlante** loudspeaker; M (altura) height; (piso) upper story; **— el fuego** cease-fire; ADV loud; **hablar —** to talk loud; **cotizarse —** to be set high; INTERJ halt!

altruismo M altruism

altura F (de persona, edificio, ola, epidemia) height; (de avión) altitude; (sobre el nivel del mar, lugar alto) elevation; **a estas —s** at this stage; **a la — de la calle ocho** at Eighth Street; **a la — de las circunstancias** equal to the circumstances

alubia F bean

alucinación F hallucination

alucinar VT (causar alucinaciones) to hallucinate; (fascinar) to fascinate; (deslumbrar) to bowl over; VI (sufrir alucinaciones) to hallucinate

alucinógeno M hallucinogen

alud M avalanche

aludir VI **— a** to allude to, to refer to

alumbrado M lighting; **— público** street lighting; ADJ lit

alumbramiento M childbirth

alumbrar VT encender, to light up; (dar a luz) to give birth to

aluminio M aluminum

alumnado M student body

alumno -na MF (de enseñanza primaria) pupil; (de enseñanza secundaria) student

alusión F allusion

aluvión M (de preguntas, pedidos) barrage; (de personas) flood

alza F appreciation; **— de precios** boost in prices

alzado ADJ elevated; MF insurgent

alzamiento M (acción de alzar) raising;

(insurrección) uprising

alzaprima F crowbar

alzar[47] VT (la mano, la voz, una casa) to raise; (a un niño) to lift up; — **la vista** to look up; —**se** to rise up in rebellion; —**se con** to make off with

amabilidad F kindness; ¿**tendría la** — **de . . . ?** would you mind . . . ?

amable ADJ kind, nice

amado -da MF beloved

amaestrador -ora MF trainer

amaestramiento M training

amaestrar VT to train

amagar[40] VI/VT threaten; **amagó que iba a llover** it looked like it was going to rain; **amagó con golpearla** he made as if he was going to hit her

amago M **hacer** — to make as if

amague M (baloncesto) fake, juke

amalgamar VT to amalgamate

amamantar VT to nurse, to breast-feed

amanecer[35] VI to dawn; — **enfermo** to wake up ill; **amanecí en Londres** I woke up in London; M dawn, sunrise, daybreak

amanerado ADJ effete

amansar VT to tame

amante MF lover; — **de** fond of

amañar VT (una elección) to rig; (un documento) to tamper with

amapola F poppy

amar VT to love

amargar[40] VT to embitter

amargo ADJ bitter

amargor M bitterness

amargura F bitterness

amarillear VI/VT to yellow, to turn yellow

amarillento ADJ yellowish

amarillo -lla ADJ yellow; MF (esquirol) scab

amarra F cable, rope; —**s** moorings; **soltar** —**s** to cast off

amarrar VT (un barco) to moor; (una cosa) to secure, to tie down

amartillar VT (pegar con martillo) to hammer; (un arma) to cock

amasar VT (masa) to knead; (una fortuna) to amass

amateur ADJ INV & MF amateur

amatista F amethyst

Amazonas M Amazon River

Amazonia M Amazon Forest

ambages M PL **hablar sin** — to not mince words, to speak plainly

ámbar M amber

ambición F ambition

ambicionar VT to have the ambition to

ambicioso ADJ (emprendedor) ambitious; (codicioso) overambitious

ambidiestro ADJ ambidextrous

ambiental ADJ (limpieza) environmental;

(temperatura) ambient

ambiente ADJ ambient; M (condiciones biológicas) environment; (atmósfera) atmosphere, ambience, ambiance; (sector social) milieu

ambigüedad F ambiguity

ambiguo ADJ ambiguous

ámbito M (ambiente) scene; (alcance) scope; (esfera) sphere

ambivalente ADJ ambivalent

ambos ADJ & PRON both

ambulancia F ambulance

ambulante ADJ itinerant

ambulatorio ADJ ambulatory

ameba F amoeba

amedrentar VT to scare

amén INTERJ amen; **decir** — to approve withou[t] discussion; — **de** besides

amenaza F threat, menace

amenazador ADJ threatening

amenazante ADJ threatening

amenazar[47] VT to threaten; — **con** to threaten to

amenidad F (cualidad de ameno) pleasantness

amenizar[47] VI to make entertaining

ameno ADJ enjoyable, entertaining

América F America

americano -na ADJ & MF American; F sport coa[t]

ametrallador -ora MF gunner; F machine gun

ametrallar VT to strafe, to machine-gun

amianto M asbestos

amigable ADJ friendly

amígdala F (faríngea) tonsil; (cerebral) amygdala

amigdalitis F tonsillitis

amigo -ga ADJ friendly; — **de** fond of; — **de lo ajeno** thieving; MF friend

amiguismo M cronyism

aminoácido M amino acid

aminorar VT to lessen

amistad F (relación) friendship; (amigo) friend **trabar** — to strike up a friendship

amistoso ADJ friendly, amicable

amnesia F amnesia

amniocentesis F amniocentesis

amnistía F amnesty

amo -ma M (de esclavo, sirviente) master; (de animal) owner; F (de esclavo, de sirviente) mistress; (de animal) owner; **ama de leche** wet nurse; **ama de llaves** housekeeper; **ama de casa** homemaker

amodorrado ADJ drowsy

amodorrar VI to make drowsy; —**se** to become drowsy

amolar[5] VT to annoy

amoldar VT to mold

amonestación F admonition, warning

amonestar VT to admonish, to warn

amoníaco M ammonia

amontonamiento M pile

amontonar VT to pile up

amor M love; **— propio** self-esteem; **de mil —es** gladly; **hacerle el — a** to make love to; **por el — de Dios** for God's sake; **por — al arte** unremunerated

amoral ADJ amoral

amoratado ADJ (de golpes) black-and-blue; (de frío, por falta de oxígeno) blue

amordazar[47] VT (a una persona) to gag; (a un perro, a los críticos) to muzzle

amorfo ADJ amorphous

amorío M love affair

amoroso ADJ loving, amorous

amortajar VT to shroud

amortiguador M shock absorber

amortiguar[25] VT (un sonido) to muffle, to absorb; (un golpe) to cushion, to absorb; (un dolor) to deaden, to dull

amortización F (desvalorización periódica) depreciation; (recuperación de una inversión) recovery; (reembolso gradual) amortization, paying off

amortizar[47] VT (recuperar a plazos) to amortize; (depreciar) to depreciate

amoscarse[30] VI to get peeved

amostazarse[47] VI to get peeved

amotinarse VI (en un barco) to mutiny; (en una cárcel) to riot

amparar VT (proteger) to protect; (refugiar) to shelter; **—se** to protect oneself

amparo M (protección) protection; (refugio) shelter; **al — de** under the protection of

amperio M ampere

ampicilina F ampicillin

ampliación F (de una foto) enlargement; (de una casa) extension

ampliar[28] VT (una foto) to enlarge; (una calle) to extend; (una explicación) to expand; (un volumen) to amplify; **— una imagen** to zoom in

amplificador M amplifier

amplificar[30] VT (un sonido) to amplify; (una imagen) to magnify

amplio ADJ (información, tiempo) ample; (piso) spacious, roomy; (región, resonancia, sonrisa) broad; (vestido) full; **de amplias miras** open-minded

amplitud F (de comprensión) breadth; (de onda) amplitude

ampolla F (de la epidermis) blister; (vasija) vial

ampollar VT to blister

ampuloso ADJ bombastic

amputar VT to amputate

amueblar VT to furnish

amuleto M amulet, charm

anacronismo M anachronism

ánade M duck

anadear VI to waddle

anadeo M waddle

anaerobio ADJ anaerobic

anal ADJ anal

anales M PL annals

analfabetismo M illiteracy

analfabeto -ta ADJ & MF illiterate

analgésico ADJ & M analgesic

análisis M analysis; **— costo-beneficio** cost-benefit analysis; **— de mercado** market analysis; **— de orina** urinalysis

analista MF analyst

anotación F (béisbol) run; (básquetbol) point; (fútbol americano) touchdown; (glosa) note

analítico ADJ analytical, analytic

analizador M parser

analizar[47] VT (datos) to analyze; (secuencia) to parse

analogía F analogy

analógico ADJ (relativo a la analogía) analogical; (no digital) analog

análogo ADJ analogous

ananá[s] M SG pineapple

anaquel M shelf

anaranjado ADJ & M (color) orange

anarquía F anarchy

anarquista MF anarchist

anatema M anathema

anatomía F anatomy

anatómico ADJ anatomical

anca F haunch, rump

ancho ADJ wide, broad; **a sus anchas** at his ease; **me viene —** it's too wide for me; M width, breadth; **a lo —** widthwise; **tiene un metro de —** it's one meter wide

anchoa F anchovy

anchura F width, breadth

ancianidad F old age

anciano -na ADJ elderly, aged; MF old person

ancla F anchor

anclar VI/VT to anchor

andada F **volver a las —s** to backslide

andador -ora MF walker

Andalucía F Andalusia

andaluz -za ADJ & MF Andalusian; M (dialecto) Andalusian

andamiaje M (para construcción) scaffolding; (fundamento) framework

andamio M scaffold

andanada F broadside; **una — de insultos** a barrage of insults

andante ADJ walking

andanzas F PL adventures

andar[66] VI to walk; (coche, motor, reloj) to run; (el tiempo) to pass; (un aparato) to work; **— con cuidado** to be careful; **— en coche** to travel by car, to ride in a car; **— mal** to be in bad shape, to be a mess; **— mal del corazón** to have heart trouble; **—se por las ramas / con vueltas** to beat around the bush; **no**

—**se con rodeos** to make no bones about it;
en eso ando that's what I'm up to;
¡andando! move on! **¿dónde anda a estas horas?** where is he at this hour? **¡ándale!**
Méx (apresúrate) come on! (de acuerdo) OK;
M gait
andariego ADJ fond of walking
andas F llevar en — *RP* to carry on one's shoulders
andén M (de tren) platform; (para peatones) sidewalk
Andes M PL Andes
andino ADJ Andean
Andorra F Andorra
andorrano-na ADJ & MF Andorran
andrajo M rag, tatter
andrajoso ADJ ragged, tattered
andrógino ADJ androgynous
anduve, anduviera, anduviese *ver* andar
anécdota F anecdote
anegar⁴⁰ VT to flood
anejo ADJ attached; M accompanying volume
anemia F anemia; — **falciforme** sickle cell anemia; — **por deficiencia de hierro** iron deficiency anemia
anémico ADJ anemic
anestesia F (acción de anestesiar) anesthesia; (sustancia) anesthetic
anestesiar VT to anesthetize
anestésico ADJ & M anesthetic
anestesiología F anesthesiology
anestesiólogo-ga MF anesthesiologist
anestesista MF anesthesiologist
aneurisma M aneurysm
anexar VT (un territorio) to annex; (con una carta) to enclose
anexión F annexation
anexo ADJ attached; M (de un edificio) annex, extension; (a una ley) rider
anfeta F *fam* speed
anfetamina F amphetamine
anfibio ADJ & M amphibian
anfiteatro M amphitheater
anfitrión-ona M host (también informático); F hostess
ángel M angel; — **de la guarda** guardian angel
angelical ADJ angelic
angélico ADJ angelic
angina F —**s** tonsillitis; — **del pecho** angina pectoris; — **laríngea** laryngeal angina
angiocardiografía F angiocardiography
angiograma M angiogram
angioplastia F angioplasty
anglosajón-ona ADJ & MF Anglo-Saxon
Angola F Angola
angolano-na, angoleño-ña, angolés-esa ADJ & MF Angolan
angostar VT to narrow, to contract
angosto ADJ narrow

angostura F (cualidad de angosto) narrowness; (desfiladero) narrows
anguila F eel; — **eléctrica** electric eel
angular ADJ angular
ángulo M (figura geométrica, enfoque) angle; (rincón, esquina) corner; — **muerto** blind spot; — **recto** right angle
anguloso ADJ angular
angustia F (desasosiego) anguish, anxiety, distress; (congoja) heartache; (desazón existencial) angst
angustiado ADJ (desasosegado) anguished, anxious; (acongojado) distraught
angustiante ADJ nerve-wracking
angustiar VT to distress; —**se** to feel distressed
angustioso ADJ distressing
anhelante ADJ longing
anhelar VT to long for, to yearn for
anhelo M longing, yearning
anidar VI to nest
anillas F PL gymnastics rings
anillo M ring; — **de boda** wedding ring; **me queda como** — **al dedo** it fits me like a glove
ánima F soul of the departed
animación F (viveza) animation, liveliness; (en películas) animation
animado ADJ (vivo) animate; (bullicioso) lively
animador-ora MF (de un espectáculo) host; (de un equipo) cheerleader
animal ADJ & M animal
animar VT (dar vida) to animate, to enliven; (incitar) to encourage, to urge on; (dar aliento) to cheer up; —**se** (alegrarse) to cheer up; (atreverse) to gather courage
ánimo M (espíritu) spirit; (aliento) encouragement; (humor) mood; (intención) intention; **no estoy de** — **para eso** I'm not in the mood for that; INTERJ hang in there!
animosidad F animosity
animoso ADJ spirited
aniñado ADJ childlike
aniquilar VT to annihilate, to wipe out
anís M anise
aniversario M anniversary
anoche ADV last night
anochecer³⁵ VI to get dark; **anochecimos en París** night found us in Paris; M nightfall, dusk
anomalía F anomaly
anómalo ADJ anomalous
anonadado ADJ dumbfounded
anonadar VT (aniquilar) to annihilate; (vencer) overwhelm; (desconcertar) to dumbfound; —**se** to become dumbfounded
anónimo ADJ anonymous, nameless; M anonymous letter
anorak M anorak
anorexia F anorexia

anoréxico ADJ anorexic

anormal ADJ abnormal; MF freak

anotación F (nota) annotation, notation; (en fútbol) goal

anotar VT (apuntar) to note; (marcar un tanto) to score; **—se** to sign up

anquilosarse VT (las articulaciones) to become stiff; (una institución) to become stagnant

ansia F (deseo) eagerness; (congoja) anguish

ansiar[28] VT to covet

ansiedad F anxiety

ansioso ADJ (ávido) anxious, eager; (inquieto) fretful

antagonismo M antagonism

antagonista MF antagonist

antagonizar[47] VT to antagonize

antaño ADV in the old days

antártico ADJ antarctic

Antártida F Antarctica

ante PREP before; **— este problema** in the face of this problem; **— todo** above all; M suede

anteanoche ADV night before last

anteayer ADV day before yesterday

antebrazo M forearm

antecedente ADJ & M antecedent; **—s** (profesionales) background; (criminales) record; **—s delictivos** criminal record

antecesor -ora MF (antepasado) ancestor; (predecesor) predecessor

antedatar VT to backdate

antedicho ADJ aforesaid

antelación LOC ADV **con —** beforehand

antemano LOC ADV **de —** beforehand

antena F (de radio) antenna, aerial; (de insecto) antenna, feeler

anteojera F blinder

anteojos M PL glasses, spectacles; **— de sol** sunglasses; **— bifocales** bifocals

antepasado -da MF ancestor, forebear

antepecho M sill

anteponer[56, 74] VT (poner delante, poner antes) to place before; (dar preferencia) to give priority to

anterior ADJ (en el tiempo) previous; (en el espacio) anterior, front; **— a** prior to

anterioridad F con **—** before

anteriormente ADV (antes) previously, formerly; (en la parte delantera) in front

antes ADV (previamente) before, formerly; (más temprano) sooner; **llegó —** he arrived sooner; **— de** before; **— la muerte** I'd rather die; **— bien** rather; **— de impuestos** pretax; **— del cierre** before closing; **lo — posible** ASAP, as soon as possible

antesala F (habitación) anteroom; (preludio) prelude; (béisbol) third base

antesalista MF third baseman

antiaborto ADJ INV antiabortion, right-to-life

antiácido ADJ & M antacid

antiaéreo ADJ antiaircraft

antialérgico ADJ antiallergic

antibacteriano ADJ antibacterial

antibalas ADJ INV bulletproof

antibalístico ADJ (misil) antiballistic; (chaqueta) bulletproof

antibiótico ADJ & M antibiotic; **— de amplio espectro** broad-spectrum antibiotic

antibloqueo ADJ INV antilock

anticipación LOC ADV **con —** in advance

anticipado LOC ADV **por —** in advance

anticipar VT (una fecha) to move up; (dinero) to advance; (el porvenir) to anticipate; **—se a los acontecimientos** to jump the gun

anticipo M advance, deposit

anticoagulante M anticoagulant

anticoncepción F contraception

anticonceptivo ADJ & M contraceptive

anticongelante M antifreeze

anticonvulsivo M anticonvulsant

anticuado ADJ antiquated, out-of-date

anticuerpo M antibody

antideportivo ADJ unsportsmanlike

antidepresivo ADJ & M antidepressant

antidiarreico M antidiarrheal

antidiurético M antidiuretic

antídoto M antidote

antieconómico ADJ wasteful

antiespasmódico M antispasmodic

antiestético ADJ unsightly

antígeno M antigen

antigualla F old piece of junk

antiguano -na ADJ & MF Antiguan

Antigua y Barbuda F Antigua and Barbuda

antigüedad F (cualidad de antiguo) antiquity; (objeto) antique; (tiempo en un cargo) seniority

antiguo ADJ (era, historia) ancient; (ropa) old; (mueble) antique; **a la antigua** in the old style; **la antigua capital** the former capital; **más —** with more seniority

antihigiénico ADJ unsanitary

antihistamínico M antihistamine

antiinflamatorio ADJ & M anti-inflammatory

Antillas F PL West Indies

antílope M antelope

antimonio M antimony

antimonopolio ADJ INV antitrust

antioxidante ADJ & M antioxidant

antiparras F PL goggles

antipatía F antipathy

antipático ADJ unfriendly, unkind

antipoliomielítico ADJ antipolio

antipsicótico M antipsychotic

antirreflejante ADJ anti-glare

antisemitismo M anti-Semitism

antiséptico ADJ & M antiseptic

antisocial ADJ antisocial

antítesis F antithesis

antitoxina F antitoxin

antitranspirante M antiperspirant

antitrust ADJ INV antitrust

antiviral M antiviral

antojadizo ADJ whimsical

antojarse VI **se le antojó comer salchicha** he took a notion to eat sausage; **esa tarea se me antoja difícil** that task seems hard to me

antojo M (deseo) whim, craving; (mancha de nacimiento) birthmark

antología F anthology, reader

antónimo M antonym

antorcha F torch

antracita F anthracite

ántrax M anthrax

antro M (bar) dive, joint; **— de perdición** den of iniquity

antropología F anthropology

antropólogo -ga MF anthropologist

anual ADJ annual, yearly

anualidad F annuity; **— variable** variable annuity

anuario ADJ annual; M yearbook

anudar VT to knot; **se le anudó la garganta** he got all choked up

anulación F (de un contrato) cancellation; (de un matrimonio) annulment

anular VT (un matrimonio) to annul; (un contrato, un evento) to cancel; (una sentencia) to overrule, to overturn; (un talón) to void; (un comando de computadora) to undo; **— una selección previa** to deselect; M ring finger

anunciador -ora MF announcer

anunciante MF advertiser

anunciar VT (información) to announce; (un producto) to advertise

anuncio M (de información) announcement; (de un producto) advertisement; **— clasificado** classified advertisement, want ad; **— publicitario** advertisement, ad; **poner un —** to place an ad

anzuelo M fishhook; **morder/picar el —** to take the bait

añadidura F addition; **por —** in addition

añadir VT to add

añejo ADJ aged, vintage

añicos M **hacerse —** to break into a thousand pieces

añil M indigo, bluing

año M year; (de la escuela) grade; (de vino) vintage; **— bisiesto** leap year; **— luz** light-year; **de cuarenta —s** aged forty; **del — hasta la fecha** year-to-date; **el — en curso** the current year; **el — pasado** last year; **en los —s veinte** in the 1920s; **entrado en —s** getting on in years; **¿cuántos —s tienes?** how old are you?

añojo -ja MF yearling

añoranza F longing; (del hogar) homesickness

añorar VT to long for, to be homesick for

añoso ADJ old

añublo M blight

aorta F aorta

apabullar VT (impresionar) to bowl over; (derrotar) to crush

apacentar[1] VI to graze, to pasture

apacible ADJ good-natured, laid-back

apaciguar[25] VT (pacificar) to pacify; (aplacar) to mollify, to appease; **—se** to calm down

apadrinar VT to sponsor; (en un bautismo) to act as godfather to; (en una boda) to act as best man for; (en un duelo) to second

apagado ADJ (no llamativo) flat; (no intenso) dull

apagar[40] VT (un fuego) to put out, to extinguish; (una luz) to turn off, to turn out; (motor) to turn off, to kill; (una computadora) to power down; (una vida) to kill, to snuff out; (la sed) to quench; **—se** (luz) to go out; (un color) to fade; (una voz) to trail off; (un volcán) to become extinct

apagón M blackout, outage

apalabrarse VI **— con** to make a verbal agreement with

apalancamiento M leverage

apalear VT to thrash

aparador M sideboard, buffet, cupboard

aparato M (de gimnasia artística) apparatus; (para ejercicio) machine; (de cocina) appliance; (de teléfono) telephone; (máquina, dirigencia política) machine; (boato) pomp; **— circulatorio** circulatory system; **— de televisión** television set; **— ortodóntico** braces; **— ortopédico** leg brace

aparatoso ADJ pompous

aparcamiento M (lugar para aparcar) parking lot; (acción de aparcar) parking

aparcar[30] VI/VT to park; MF SG **aparcacoches** valet

aparcero -ra MF sharecropper

aparear VT (animales) to mate; (calcetines) to match, to pair; **—se** (animales) to mate; (en un baile) to pair off

aparecer[35] VI (ponerse a la vista, publicarse) to appear; (hacer acto de presencia) to show up; **se me apareció un ángel** an angel appeared to me

aparejar VT (un cuarto, un ejército) to prepare; (problemas) to entail; (una embarcación) to rig

aparejo M (de caballo) harness; (de buque) rigging; (para pescar) tackle; **—s** equipment

aparentar VT to feign; VI to show off; **aparenta la edad que tiene** she looks her age

aparente ADJ apparent

aparezca, aparezco ver aparecer

aparición F (fantasma) apparition; (acción de aparecer) appearance

apariencia F (aspecto) appearance; (fingimiento) pretense, semblance; **las —s engañan** appearances are deceiving; **guardar las —s** to keep up appearances

apartado M section; **— postal** post office box; ADJ (recóndito) secluded; (distante) distant; **muy —** far apart

apartamento M apartment

apartamiento M separation

apartar VT (separar) sort out; **aparta las monedas de veinticinco centavos** set aside the quarters; (mover) to move away; **apartó la silla de la pared** he moved the chair away from the wall; (empujar) to push away/aside; **lo apartó de un empujón** she pushed him away; (aislar) to take aside; **lo aparté para hablarle** I took him aside to talk to him; (retirar) to take off; **apartó la cacerola del fuego** she took the pan off the fire; (alejar del cargo) to remove from office; **apartaron al ministro de su cargo** they removed the minister from his post; **apartó la vista** he looked away; VI **—se** to stray; **se apartaron del buen camino** they strayed from the straight and narrow; **los resultados se apartan de lo esperado** the results depart/deviate from the norm; **se apartó para que no lo atropellara el coche** he got out of the way so the car wouldn't hit him

aparte ADJ separate; ADV **bromas —** kidding aside; **dejar —** to exclude; **punto y —** new paragraph; M aside; PREP **— de** (además de) besides; (salvo) except for

apasionado ADJ (amor, hombre) passionate; (defensa, comentario) impassioned

apasionante ADJ exciting

apasionar VT **eso me apasiona** I love that; **—se por** to be passionate about

apatía F apathy

apático ADJ apathetic

apear VT to get down; **—se** to dismount

apechugar[40] VI **— con** to put up with

apedrear VT to stone

apegado ADJ attached

apegarse[40] VI to become attached

apego M attachment

apelación F appeal

apelar VI/VT to appeal

apellidarse VI to have the surname of

apellido M surname, last name

apelotonarse VI (una almohada) to ball up; (gente) to bunch together

apenado ADJ (dolorido) grieved; (avergonzado) embarrassed

apenar VT to grieve, to pain; **—se** to be grieved

apenas ADV hardly, scarcely, barely; **— llegó,**

se desmayó no sooner had he arrived than he fainted; **— comienza la reunión** the meeting is just starting

apéndice M (órgano, parte de un libro) appendix; (añadido) appendage

apendicectomía F appendectomy

apendicitis F appendicitis

apercibir VT to warn; **—se de** to notice

aperitivo M appetizer

apero M farm implement

apertura F (transparencia) openness; (oportunidad) opening; **a la —** at the opening

apesadumbrado ADJ doleful

apestar VT (hacer heder) to stink up; (causar la peste) to plague; VI to stink, to reek

apestoso ADJ (hediondo) smelly; (apestado) pestilent

apetecer[35] VI **no me apetece ir contigo** I don't feel like going with you

apetecible ADJ appetizing

apetito M appetite

apetitoso ADJ appetizing

apiadarse VI **— de** to pity, to take pity on

ápice M apex; (de la lengua) tip; **no apartarse ni un —** not to diverge a jot

apio M celery

apisonadora F steamroller

apisonar VT to pack down

aplacamiento M appeasement

aplacar[30] VT (a una persona) to appease, to mollify; (miedo) to allay; (sed, pasión) to quench; **—se** to relent

aplanadora F steamroller

aplanamiento M flattening, leveling

aplanar VT (un terreno) to level, to flatten; (con una aplanadora) to roll

aplastado ADJ flattened

aplastamiento M crushing

aplastante ADJ (derrota) crushing; (victoria) sweeping

aplastar VT (achatar) to squash, to crush; (derrotar) to plaster, to stomp; (una revolución) to squelch, to smash, to crush; **—se** to crumple

aplaudir VI/VT to applaud

aplauso[s] M SG/PL applause

aplazamiento M postponement, deferral; (de un proceso legal) continuance

aplazar[47] VT to postpone, to put off

aplicable ADJ applicable

aplicación F (acción de aplicarse) application; (de un castigo) administration; (de computadora) application, app; **— de fondo** background application

aplicado ADJ (conocimiento, ciencia) applied; (trabajador) industrious

aplicador M applicator

aplicar[30] VT to apply; **—se** to work hard, to apply oneself

aplomado ADJ (equilibrado) poised; (vertical) plumb

aplomar VT to plumb

aplomo M poise

apnea M apnea; — **obstructiva del sueño** sleep apnea

apocado ADJ timid

apocalipsis MF (desastre) apocalypse; (Biblia) Revelation

apocamiento M timidity

apocarse[30] VI to become intimidated

apodar VT to nickname

apoderado -da MF proxy, agent

apoderarse VI — **de** to take possession of, to seize

apodo M nickname

apogeo M apogee; **en su —** (una fiesta) in full swing; (un estilo) in its heyday, at its peak

apolillado ADJ (comido por las polillas) moth-eaten; (anticuado) antiquated

apología F apology

apoplejía F apoplexy

aporrear VT to club, to cudgel

aportación F contribution

aportar VT (evidencia) to provide; (dinero) to contribute

aporte M contribution

aposento M chamber

apostador -ora MF bettor

apostar[5] VI/VT (a los caballos) to bet, to wager; (a un centinela) to station, to post; — **por** (caballo) to bet on; (cambio) to commit to

apóstol M apostle

apóstrofe MF apostrophe, invocation

apóstrofo M (ortografía) apostrophe

apostura F bearing

apoyar VT (sostener) to rest; (respaldar) to support, to back; (votar por) to second; (respaldar un argumento) to buttress; —**se en** (recostarse contra) to lean on, to prop against; (basarse en) to be based on; M SG **apoyabrazos** armrest

apoyo M support

apreciable ADJ (digno de aprecio) esteemed; (perceptible) noticeable; (registrable) appreciable

apreciablemente ADV significantly

apreciación F appreciation

apreciado ADJ (amigo) dear; (tesoro) valued, prized

apreciar VT (valorar) to appreciate; (percibir) to notice; (registrar) to measure; (considerar) to take into consideration; (sentir afecto) to cherish; —**se** (un fenómeno) to be noticeable; (moneda) to appreciate

aprecio M appreciation

aprehender VT (a un delincuente) to apprehend; (contrabando) to seize; (una idea) to grasp

aprehensión F (arresto) apprehension; (incautación) seizure

apremiante ADJ pressing

apremiar VT to pressure

apremio M pressure

aprender VI/VT to learn; — **de memoria** to memorize, to learn by heart

aprendiz -za MF (de un oficio) apprentice, trainee; (de una lengua, canto) learner

aprendizaje M (de un oficio) apprenticeship; (acto de aprender) learning

aprensión F apprehension, misgivings

aprensivo ADJ apprehensive

apresar VT (aprisionar) to imprison; (incautar) to seize

aprestar VT to prepare; —**se a** to get ready to

apresurado ADJ hasty, hurried

apresurar VT to hurry, to hasten

apretado ADJ (zapato) tight; (beso) hard; (racimo) compact; (síntesis) succinct; (jornada) busy; (situación) difficult, dangerous

apretar[1] VT (un botón) to press; (un gatillo) to squeeze; (un tornillo) to tighten; (los dientes, puños) to clench; (a un bebé) to clasp; **me apretó para que le diera dinero** he pressured me to give him money; **ese profesor nos aprieta mucho** that teacher demands a lot of us; VI (zapatos) to be tight, to pinch; (sol) to be intense; (esforzarse) to try hard, to bear down; —**se** to crowd together

apretón M squeeze; — **de manos** handshake

aprieta, apriete ver apretar

aprieto M jam, fix, predicament; **en —s** in need, hard-pressed, in dire straits; **estar en un —** to be in a tight spot, to be in trouble, to be in a pickle; **poner en —s** to embarrass

aprisa ADV quickly

aprisco M (para el ganado) fold

aprisionar VT to trap

aprobación F (aceptación) approval; (adopción, promulgación) passage, adoption; (calificación) passing grade; — **de crédito** credit approval

aprobar[5] VT (una medida, una opinión) to approve of; (una ley) to pass, to approve; (un examen) to pass; (un crédito) to sign off on; VI to pass

aprontar VT to ready

apropiación F appropriation; — **indebida** embezzlement

apropiadamente ADV properly, appropriately

apropiado ADJ appropriate, suitable

apropiarse VT — **de** to appropriate

aprovechable ADJ usable

aprovechado ADJ opportunistic

aprovechamiento M use

aprovechar VT (una ocasión) to take advantage of; (el espacio) to utilize; (la enseñanza) to profit from; VI to be useful; **—se de** to take advantage of; INTERJ **¡que aproveche!** enjoy your meal!

aproximación F (acercamiento) approach; (estimado) rough estimate

aproximado ADJ approximate

aproximar VT to bring near; **—se** to approach; **— a** to approximate

aprueba, apruebe ver aprobar

aptitud F aptitude; **—es musicales** musical aptitude

apto ADJ apt, suitable; **— para menores** for general audiences

apuesta F bet, wager

apuesto ADJ good-looking

apuntalar VT to prop up, to shore up

apuntar VT (señalar) to point out; (dirigir sobre un blanco) to aim; (matricular) to enroll; (escribir) to write down, to note; (ayudar a un actor) to prompt; (marcar puntos) to score; VI (una flecha) to point; (canas) to sprout; **— a un blanco** to aim at a target; **me apunto para ir con vosotros** I'm game to go with you

apunte M notation; **—s** notes; **tomar —s** to take notes; **llevar el — a alguien** to pay attention to someone

apuñalar VT to stab

apurado ADJ (situación) difficult; (persona) in dire straits; (apresurado) in a hurry

apurar VT (consumir) to drink up; (apremiar) to put under pressure; **—se** Am to hurry

apuro M predicament, fix; (prisa) hurry; **estar en —s** to be in distress

aquejado ADJ stricken

aquejar VT to afflict, to trouble

aquel ADJ that; **aquella chica se llama María** that girl is named María; **aquellas ciudades son antiguas** those cities are old; PRON that one; **— es el mayor** that one is the oldest; **aquellos son mis hijos** those are my children; **de mis dos hijos, Juan y Pedro, este es gordo y — es flaco** of my two sons, Juan and Pedro, the latter is fat and the former is thin; **en/por — entonces** back then

aquí ADV here; **está por —** it is around here; **ven por —** come this way; **hasta —** this far; **de — a cuatro horas** four hours from now; **de — en adelante** from now on; **de — para allá** to and fro, back and forth; **— y ahora** here and now

aquietar VT to quiet; **—se** (los nervios) to calm down; (una tormenta) to subside

ara LOC ADV **en —s de** for the sake of

árabe MF (persona) Arab; M (caballo) Arabian; (lengua) Arabic; ADJ (caballo) Arabian; (costumbre, arte) Arab

Arabia Saudí, Arabia Saudita F Saudi Arabia

arácnido M arachnid

arado M plow

Aragón M Aragon

aragonés -esa ADJ Aragonese; MF (persona) Aragonese; M (dialecto) Aragonese

arancel M (impuesto) tariff; (lista de honorarios) list of fees

arancelario ADJ **acuerdo —** tariff agreement

arándano M blueberry; **— rojo** cranberry

arandela F washer

araña F (arácnido) spider; (candelabro) chandelier

arañar VT (rayar) to scratch; (herir con garras) to claw, to scratch; (raspar) to scrape, to score

arañazo M scratch

arañero M warbler

arar VI/VT to plow, to till

arbitraje M arbitration

arbitrar VT (un desacuerdo) to arbitrate; (un partido) to referee, to officiate; (un partido de béisbol) to umpire

arbitrariedad F (acción) arbitrary action; (cualidad) arbitrariness

arbitrario ADJ arbitrary

arbitrio M (libre albedrío) free will; (capricho) whim; (decisión) discretion; (deseos) wishes

árbitro -tra MF (del buen gusto) arbiter; (de conflictos) arbitrator; (de encuentros deportivos) referee

árbol M tree; (mástil) mast; **— de Navidad** Christmas tree; **— de levas** camshaft; **— genealógico** family tree

arbolado ADJ woody, wooded

arboleda F grove, clump

arbóreo ADJ arboreal

arbusto M shrub, bush

arca F ark; **— de Noé** Noah's ark; **las —s municipales** municipal coffers

arcada F arcade, archway; **tener/dar —s** to gag

arcaico ADJ archaic

arcaísmo M archaism

arcano ADJ arcane

arce M maple [tree]

arcén M shoulder of a road

archienemigo -ga MF archenemy

archipiélago M archipelago

archisabido ADJ very well-known

archivado ADJ on file

archivador M filing cabinet

archivar VT (guardar en un archivo) to file; (arrumbar) to shelve

archivo M (repositorio de documentos) archive; (fichero de ordenador) file; (acción de archivar) filing; **— comprimido** compressed file; **— cookie** cookie; **— corrupto** corrupted file; **— de datos** data file; **— de lectura/escritura** read/write file

arcilla F clay

arco M (geométrico, eléctrico) arc; (estructura

arquitectónica) arch; (arma, varilla de violín)
bow; **— iris** rainbow

arder VT to burn; **la cosa está que arde** things
are really getting hot; **el trigo se ardió** the
wheat spoiled

ardid M scheme, artifice

ardiente ADJ (deseo) ardent; (calor, fuego,
deseo) burning

ardilla F squirrel; **— de tierra** gopher; **—
listada** chipmunk

ardite M **no valer un —** not to be worth a
penny

ardor M (de pasión) ardor; (de fuego) heat; (por
ácido) burning; **— de estómago** heartburn

arduo ADJ arduous, grueling

área F area; **— de penales** (fútbol) penalty area,
box

arena F (tierra) sand; (plaza) arena; **—
movediza** quicksand

arenero M sandbox

arenga F harangue

arengar[40] VT to harangue

arenisca F sandstone

arenisco ADJ sandy

arenoso ADJ sandy

arenque M herring

arete M earring

argamasa F mortar

Argelia F Algeria

argelino -na ADJ & MF Algerian

Argentina F Argentina

argentino -na ADJ Argentine, Argentinian;
(como la plata) silvery; MF Argentine,
Argentinian

argolla F iron ring

argón M argon

argot M slang

argucias F PL trickery

argüir[20] VT to argue

argumentar VT to argue

argumento M (razonamiento) argument;
(conjunto de sucesos) plot

aridez F dryness

árido ADJ (seco) arid, dry, barren; (aburrido)
dry; **—s** dry goods

ariete M (militar) battering ram; (fútbol) center
forward

arisco ADJ surly

arista F (borde) edge; (de trigo) beard; **limar
—s** to overcome difficulties

aristocracia F aristocracy

aristócrata MF aristocrat

aristocrático ADJ aristocratic

aritmética F arithmetic

aritmético ADJ arithmetical

arma F (instrumento bélico) arm, weapon;
(división del ejército) branch; **— blanca**
sharp weapon; **— de fuego** firearm; **a las —s**
to arms; **de —s tomar** resolute; **tomar las**

—s to take up arms

armada F armada, fleet

armado ADJ armed; **a mano armada** at
gunpoint; M assembly, putting together

armador -ora MF (naviero) shipowner; (en
fútbol) playmaker; (en vóleibol) setter

armadura F (cobertura de hierro) armor; (de un
edificio) framework; (de gafas) frame; (de
música) key signature

armamento M armament

armar VT (proveer de armas) to arm; (abastecer
una embarcación) to equip; (reforzar) to
reinforce; (ensamblar) to assemble, to put
together; (levantar una tienda de campaña) to
pitch; **— jaleo** to whoop it up; **— relajo** to
make a mess; **—se de** to arm oneself with; **—
una pendencia** to pick a fight, to start a
quarrel

armario M (de ropa) wardrobe, closet; (de
cocina) cabinet, armoire

armatoste M unwieldy object

armazón MF framework, skeleton

Armenia F Armenia

armenio -nia ADJ & MF Armenian

armería F (depósito) armory; (tienda) gun shop

armiño M ermine

armisticio M armistice

armonía F harmony

armónico ADJ & M harmonic

armonioso ADJ harmonious

armonizar[47] VI/VT to harmonize, to blend

ARN [ácido ribonucleico] M RNA

arnés M harness

aro M (de rueda) rim; (de baloncesto) hoop; **no
tocó ni —** it was an airball

aroma M (olor agradable) aroma; (del vino)
bouquet

aromático ADJ aromatic

arpa F harp

arpía F shrew

arpillera F burlap

arpón M harpoon

arponear VT to harpoon

arqueado ADJ arched

arquear VT to arch

arqueología F archaeology

arqueológico ADJ archaeological

arquero -ra MF (tirador de flechas) archer;
(guardametas) goalkeeper

arquetipo M archetype

arquitecto -ta MF architect

arquitectónico ADJ architectural

arquitectura F architecture

arrabal M outlying slum

arraigar[40] VT to take root

arrancar[30] VT (una planta) to uproot; (el pelo) to
tear out; (un diente) to pull; (un vicio) to
eradicate; (una flor) to pick; (una confesión)
to extract; **— de** to wrest from; VI/VT (un

vehículo) to start; **arrancó para el valle** he took off for the valley; **arrancó a sudar** he began to sweat; **sus problemas arrancan de su niñez** his problems are rooted in his childhood; **—se los cabellos** to tear one's hair [out]

arranque M (proceso de arrancar) starting; (dispositivo para arrancar) starter; (decisión, empuje) gumption; **— de ira** fit of rage

arrasar VT (destruir) to level, to raze; (derrotar) to crush; **— con** to obliterate; VI to win

arrastrado ADJ wretched

arrastrar VT (mover por el suelo) to drag; (llevarse consigo) to sweep away; (atraer) to draw; (soportar) to bear; (pronunciar lentamente) to draw out; **— los pies** (moverse con dificultades) to shuffle; (ser renuente) to stall; VI (cortinas) to hang down to the floor; **—se** (una serpiente) to slither; (una lagartija, un insecto) to crawl; (una persona) to grovel; **— y soltar** to drag and drop, to drag and release; M SG **arrastrapiés** shuffle

array M array

arrayán M myrtle

arrear VT to drive, to herd

arrebatar VT (quitar) to snatch away, to wrest away; (quemar) to burn on the outside; **—se** to have a fit

arrebatiña F mad scramble

arrebato M fit, outburst

arreciar VI to increase in intensity

arrecife M reef

arreglar VT (poner en orden, concertar, adaptar música) to arrange; (ordenar) to tidy up; (reparar) to fix, to repair; (resolver) to settle; **— cuentas** to settle accounts; **ya te arreglo** I'll fix you; **—se** (embellecerse) to fix oneself up; (llevarse bien con) to get along with; (entablar relaciones amorosas) to start dating; (reconciliarse) to make up; (conformarse) to make do; (despejarse) to clear up; **arreglárselas** to cope, to manage

arreglo M arrangement; **con — a** in accordance with; **no tiene —** it can't be helped; **llegar a un —** to settle; **—s** alterations

arrellanarse VI to lounge, to loll

arremangado ADJ turned up, rolled up

arremangar[40] VT to roll up; **—se** to roll up one's sleeves, to knuckle down

arremeter VI to attack; **— contra** to lunge at

arremetida F thrust, lunge

arremolinarse VT (viento) to whirl around; (agua) to eddy

arrendajo M bluejay

arrendamiento M rental

arrendar VI/VT to rent, to lease; **se arrienda** for lease

arrendatario -ria MF tenant

arreo M adornment; **—s** tack, harness

arrepentido ADJ repentant, rueful

arrepentimiento M (contrición) repentance; (disgusto) regret

arrepentirse[8] VI (de los pecados) to repent; (de los errores) to regret

arrestar VT to arrest

arresto M arrest

arriar[28] VT (la bandera) to lower; (un cabo) to slacken

arriate M flower bed

arriba ADV above; **¡—! get up! ¡— las manos!** stick 'em up! **¡— Juan!** long live Juan! **de — abajo** from top to bottom; **lleno hasta —** full to the brim; **te vas para —** you are doing well; **viven—** they live upstairs

arribar VI LIT to arrive; (buque) to put into port

arribista MF social climber

arribo M LIT arrival

arriendo M leasing, rental

arriero -ra MF animal driver

arriesgado ADJ (peligroso) risky; (valiente) daring

arriesgar[40] VT to risk; **—se** to take a chance

arrimar VT (acercar) to bring near; (golpear) to strike; **—se a** (apoyarse) to lean on; (acercarse) to get near

arrinconar VT (acorralar) to corner; (poner en un rincón) to put in a corner; (abandonar) to abandon

arritmia F arrhythmia

arrobamiento M rapture

arrobarse VI to be enraptured

arrodillarse VI to kneel

arrogancia F arrogance

arrogante ADJ arrogant

arrogarse[40] VT to claim

arrojadizo ADJ for throwing

arrojar VT (lanzar) to throw, to hurl; (expulsar) to throw out; (botar) to throw away; (vomitar) to throw up, to vomit; (proyectar una luz) to shed, to throw; **— un saldo de** to show a balance of; **—se** to hurl oneself

arrojo M boldness, daring

arrollador ADJ overwhelming

arrollar VT (enrollar) to roll up; (arrastrar) to run over; (derrotar) to defeat

arropar VT (con ropa) to wrap up; (en la cama) to tuck in; **—se** to pull up the covers

arroyo M stream, creek

arroz M rice; **— integral** brown rice

arrozal M rice field

arruga F wrinkle

arrugar[40] VT to wrinkle; **— el ceño** to knit one's brow; **—se** (pasar a tener arrugas) to get wrinkles; (asustarse) to be afraid

arruinar VT (estropear) to ruin; (destruir) to destroy, to ravage; (aguar) to spoil; (dejar en la quiebra) to bankrupt, to ruin; **—se** to go to ruin

arrullar VI (una paloma) to coo; VT (a un enamorado) to whisper sweet nothings to; (a un niño) to rock to sleep, to lull to sleep

arrullo M (de la tórtola) cooing; (del agua) babbling

arrumbar VT (arrinconar) to put aside; (marginalizar) to marginalize

arsenal M (depósito) arsenal; (astillero) navy yard

arsénico M arsenic

arte M SG art; F PL arts; M (destreza) skill, ability; (actividad manual) craft; **bellas —s** fine arts; **el — por el —** art for art's sake; **malas —s** wiles; **no tener ni — ni parte en algo** to have nothing to do with something; **por — de** by means of; **por — de magia** by magic

artefacto M (aparato) contrivance, device; (bomba) bomb

arteria F artery

arterial ADJ arterial

arteriosclerosis F arteriosclerosis

artero ADJ artful, wily

artesanía F (trabajo, obra) craft; (habilidad) craftsmanship

artesano -na MF artisan; M craftsman; F craftswoman

ártico ADJ arctic

articulación F (acción de articular) articulation; (juntura) joint

articular VT (pronunciar) to articulate, to enunciate; (unir) to join

artículo M (de revista) article; (de diccionario) article, entry; **— de fondo** editorial; **— definido** definite article; **hacer el —** to give a sales pitch

artífice MF (autor) architect; M (artesano) craftsman; F craftswoman

artificial ADJ artificial

artificio M artifice

artificioso ADJ affected, contrived

artillería F artillery

artillero -ra MF (militar) gunner; (en fútbol) striker

artimaña F trick, wile

artista MF (plástica) artist; (drama, música) performer

artístico ADJ artistic

artritis F arthritis

artroscopia F arthroscopy

artroscópico ADJ arthroscopic

artrosis F degenerative joint disease

Aruba F Aruba

arveja F pea

arzobispo M archbishop

arzón M saddletree

as M ace (también atleta)

asa F handle

asado ADJ roasted; M (carne asada) roast; (carne

asada al aire libre) barbecue; (acción de asar) roasting

asador -ora M spit; MF barbecue cook

asalariado -da MF wage earner

asaltante MF mugger

asaltar VT (a una persona) to assault, to assail; (un banco) to hold up; (con preguntas) to assail; **—le a uno una idea** to be struck by an idea

asalto M (ataque) assault; (de un banco) holdup, stickup; **tomar por —** to storm

asamblea F assembly, gathering

asar VT to roast; **— a la parrilla** to grill; **— con adobo** to barbecue

asbesto M asbestos

ascendencia F ancestry

ascendente ADJ (que incrementa) ascending, rising; (que sube) upward

ascender² VT (a un empleado) to promote; (una montaña) to climb; VI to ascend; **— a** to amount to

ascendiente MF ancestor

ascenso M (acción de ascender) ascent; (en el trabajo) promotion

ascensor M elevator

asceta MF ascetic

ascético ADJ ascetic

ascienda, asciende *ver* ascender

asco M disgust, revulsion; **hacer —s a** to reject; **me da —** it makes me sick, it disgusts me; **ese hombre está hecho un —** that man is a mess; **su acné me da —** his acne is a turnoff

ascórbico ADJ ascorbic; **ácido —** ascorbic acid

ascua F ember; **estar en —s** to be on pins and needles; **tener a alguien en —s** to string someone along

aseado ADJ well-groomed

asear VT to clean up

asediar VT to besiege

asedio M siege

asegurable ADJ insurable

asegurador -ora MF underwriter

asegurar VT (una victoria) to assure; (una frontera, una cerradura) to secure; (con un contrato de seguros) to insure; **—se [de]** to make sure [of]; **te lo aseguro** I assure you

asemejarse VI **— a** to resemble

asentaderas F PL buttocks

asentamiento M (de una comunidad) settlement; (de un edificio) settling

asentar VT (datos) to enter; (una población) to establish; **—se** (posarse) to settle; (madurar) to settle down

asentimiento M assent, acquiescence

asentir⁸ VI to assent, to acquiesce; **— con la cabeza** to nod

aseo M (acción de asearse) cleaning; (cualidad de aseado) cleanliness; (cuarto de baño) bathroom; (servicio) toilet, restroom

aséptico ADJ aseptic

asequible ADJ (disponible) available; (barato, económico) affordable

aserción F assertion

aserradero M sawmill, lumber mill

aserrado ADJ serrated; M sawing

aserrar[1] VT to saw

aserrín M sawdust

aserto M assertion

asesinar VT to murder; (a una figura pública) to assassinate

asesinato M murder, killing; (de una figura pública) assassination

asesino -na ADJ murderous; MF killer, murderer; (de una figura pública) assassin; — **en serie** serial killer

asesor -ora MF consultant, advisor/adviser

asesoramiento M (profesional, legal) consulting, advising; (académico) counseling; — **de crédito** credit counseling

asesorar VT to advise

asesor -ora MF aide

asestar VT — **un golpe** to inflict/deal a blow

aseveración F assertion

aseverar VT to assert

asexual ADJ asexual

asfalto M asphalt

asfixia F suffocation, asphyxiation, asphyxia

asfixiar VT to suffocate, to smother

así ADV so, thus, like this; — — so-so; — **como** in the same way that; — **de grande** that big; — **que** so that; ¿— **que no vienes?** so you're not coming?

Asia F Asia

asiático -ca ADJ & MF Asian

asidero M hold; **eso no tiene — en la realidad** that has no basis in reality

asiduo ADJ (lector) assiduous; (cliente) steady

asiento M (lugar donde sentarse, parte de una silla, válvula) seat; (de nóminas) entry, record; **tomar —** to take a seat

asignación F (acción de asignar) assignment; (acción de dar fondos) appropriation; (lo asignado) allotment; (pago) allowance

asignar VT (una tarea) to assign; (fondos) to allot, to allocate, to earmark

asignatura F subject

asilado -da MF inmate; — **político -ca** political refugee

asilar VT (a un político) to give asylum to; (un animal) to shelter

asilo M (para los perseguidos) asylum; (para huérfanos, ancianos) home

asimétrico ADJ asymmetric, asymmetrical

asimilar VT (vitaminas, un grupo étnico) to assimilate; (información) to absorb

asimismo ADV likewise

asintomático ADJ asymptomatic

asir[50] VT to grasp, to grip; —**se a** to hold onto

asistencia F (presencia, personas presentes) attendance; (ayuda) assistance, aid; (servicio de averías) roadside assistance; (deporte) assist; — **médica** health care; — **social** (ayuda) welfare; (profesión) social work

asistente -ta ADJ assistant; MF assistant, helper; — **social** social worker

asistir VT — **a** (estar presente) to attend; (ayudar) to help, to assist

asma F asthma

asmático ADJ asthmatic

asno M ass, donkey

asociación F association; — **de propietarios** homeowners' association

asociado -da MF associate

asociar VT to associate; —**se** to join; —**se con** to fall in with

asolamiento M desolation

asolar VT to desolate, to devastate

asomar VI to show; VT to poke out, to stick out; —**se a** to look out

asombrar VT to astonish, to amaze, to astound; —**se** to be astonished

asombro M astonishment, amazement

asombroso ADJ astonishing, amazing

asomo LOC ADV **ni por —** by no means

asonancia F assonance

aspa F (de hélice) blade; (de ventilador) vane

aspartamo M aspartame

aspecto M (faceta) aspect, feature; (apariencia) looks

aspereza F roughness, harshness; **con —** sharply; **limar —s** to smooth over disagreements

áspero ADJ (terreno, mano) rough; (lucha) bitter; (tiempo, voz) harsh

aspiración F (ambición) aspiration, ambition; (respiración) breathing in; (succión) suction

aspiradora F vacuum cleaner

aspirante MF applicant, candidate

aspirar VT (inhalar) to breathe in, to inhale; (a un empleo) to apply for; — **a** to aspire to

aspirina F aspirin

asqueado ADJ disgusted

asquear VT to disgust

asquerosidad F nastiness; **¡estás hecho una —!** you're gross!

asqueroso ADJ nasty, disgusting, gross

asta F (de toro) horn; (de ciervo) antler; (de bandera) flagpole; (de lanza) shaft; **a media —** at half mast

asterisco M asterisk, star

asteroide M asteroid

astigmatismo M astigmatism

astilla F (de madera) chip, splinter; (de vidrio) sliver; —**s** kindling

astillar VT to chip, to splinter

astillero M shipyard

astringente ADJ & M astringent

astro M (del cielo) celestial body; (de cine) movie star

astrofísica F astrophysics

astrología F astrology

astronauta MF astronaut

astronáutica F astronautics

astronomía F astronomy

astronómico ADJ (relativo a las estrellas) astronomical; (muy elevado) astronomic, astronomical

astrónomo -ma MF astronomer

astucia F (listeza) cunning, guile; (treta) trick

asturiano -na ADJ & MF Asturian; (dialecto) Asturian

Asturias F SG Asturias

astuto ADJ shrewd, wily, cunning

asueto M (día libre) day off; (licencia) time off

asumir VT (una responsabilidad) to assume, to shoulder; (una mala noticia) to accept; — **un cargo** to take office

asunción F assumption; — **presidencial** presidential inauguration

asunto M (cuestión) matter; (tema de una obra) theme

asustadizo ADJ easily frightened, jumpy

asustado ADJ frightened, scared

asustar VT to frighten, to scare; —**se** to become frightened

atacante ADJ attacking; MF assailant

atacar[30] VT to attack, to assault; —**se de risa** to have a laughing fit

atado M bundle

atadura F **sin** —**s** with no strings attached

atajador M tackle

atajar VT (interrumpir) to cut off; VI (cortar camino) to take a shortcut

atajo M shortcut

atalaya F watchtower

atañer[15, 73] VI to concern, to pertain to

ataque M (de violencia, asma) attack; (de rabia, de tos) fit; (de epilepsia) seizure; (en fútbol americano) offensive series; — **cardíaco** heart attack; — **de nervios** nervous breakdown; — **relámpago** blitz

atar VT (sujetar) to tie, to bind; — **cabos** to put two and two together; —**se los zapatos** to tie one's shoes

atardecer[35] VI to get dark; M late afternoon, dusk, evening; **al** — at dusk

atareado ADJ busy

atarearse VI to busy oneself

atascadero M (lodazal) quagmire; (de tránsito) bottleneck

atascado ADJ stuck

atascar[30] VT (un tubo) to stop up; (una máquina) to jam; (el tráfico) to obstruct; —**se** (un vehículo) to get stuck; (una máquina) to get jammed

ataúd M coffin, casket

ataviar[28] VT to attire, to array; —**se** to dress up

atavío M attire, garb

ateísmo M atheism

atemorizar[47] VT to frighten

atención F attention; (médica) care; (acto de cortesía) courtesy; — **al cliente** customer care; — **médica a largo plazo** long-term care; — **prenatal** prenatal care; — **primaria** primary care; **a la** — **de** to the attention of; **llamar la** — (hacer notar) to call attention; (ser llamativo) to attract attention; (interesar) to interest; INTERJ watch out!

atender[2] VT (a un enfermo) to take care of, to look after; (una súplica) to heed; (a un cliente) to serve; (el trabajo) to attend to, to take care of; VI — **a** to pay attention to

atenerse[58] VI — **a los hechos** to bear the facts in mind, to limit oneself to the facts; — **a la ley** to abide by the law

atentado M (asesinato) assassination; (ataque fracasado) assassination attempt; (con bomba) bombing; **un** — **contra** an affront to

atentamente ADV (con atención) attentively; (despedida en cartas) yours truly / yours sincerely

atentar[1] VI — **contra la vida de alguien** to make an attempt on someone's life

atento ADJ (que presta atención) attentive; (amable) thoughtful

atenuar[26] VT (la violencia) to attenuate; (una luz) to dim; —**se** to abate

ateo -a MF atheist

aterciopelado ADJ velvety

aterido ADJ stiff with cold

aterirse[73] VI to become stiff with cold

aterrador ADJ terrifying

aterrar VT to terrify

aterrizaje M landing; — **forzoso** crash landing

aterrizar[47] VI/VT to land

aterrorizar[47] VT (intimidar) to terrorize; (dar miedo) to terrify

atesorar VT (memorias) to treasure; (dinero) to hoard

atestado ADJ crowded, crammed

atestar VT (certificar) to attest to; (llenar) to jam, to pack

atestiguar[25] VT to bear witness, to testify

atiborrar VT to stuff; —**se** to stuff one's face

atienda, atiende ver atender

atiesar VT to stiffen

atildado ADJ spruced up

atinar VT (acertar) to hit the mark; (adivinar) to guess right; **no** — **a decir palabra** not to manage to get a word out

atípico ADJ atypical

atisbar VT (mirar con disimulo) to peek at, to peep at; (vislumbrar) to catch a glimpse of; VI to peek

atisbo M glimpse, hint

atizar[47] VT (fuego) to poke, to stoke; (pasiones) to stir up, to stoke

atlántico ADJ Atlantic; M **Océano Atlántico** Atlantic Ocean

atlas M atlas

atleta MF athlete

atlético ADJ athletic

atletismo M track and field

atmósfera F atmosphere

atmosférico ADJ atmospheric

atolladero M quagmire

atolondrado ADJ scatterbrained; (muchacha) ditsy

atómico ADJ atomic

atomizador M atomizer

atomizar[47] VT to atomize

átomo M atom

atónito ADJ dumbfounded

atontado ADJ stupefied

atontar VT to stupefy

atorar VT to jam; —**se** to choke

atormentar VT to torment; —**se por** to agonize over

atornillar VT to bolt

atracadero M dock

atracar[30] VT (amarrar) to dock; (robar) to hold up, to mug; —**se** to gorge oneself

atracción F attraction

atraco M holdup, stickup

atracón M **darse un** — to gorge

atractivo ADJ attractive, fetching; M (capacidad de atraer) attractiveness, appeal; (cosa que atrae) attraction; — **sexual** sex appeal

atraer[59] VT to attract

atragantarse VI to choke

atraiga, atraigo, atrajo, atrajera, atrajese ver atraer

atrancar[30] VT to bolt, to bar

atrapada F catch

atrapar VT (en una trampa) to trap, to ensnare, to catch; (una pelota, el interés) to catch

atrás ADV — **de la casa** behind the house; **cuatro años** — four years back; **hacia** — backward; **para** — back/backwards; **quedarse** — to fall behind

atrasado ADJ (de tiempo) late; (en el pago) in arrears, behind; (país) backward; (un libro de biblioteca) overdue; **tengo sueño** — I'm behind in my sleep; **el reloj anda** — the clock is slow; **feliz cumpleaños** — belated happy birthday

atrasar VT (un plazo) to delay; (un objeto) to push back; (un reloj) to turn back; VI (un reloj) to run slow; —**se** to fall behind, to lag

atraso M (condición de atrasado) backwardness; (pago) back payment; (de trabajo) backlog; **con dos meses de** — two months in arrears

atravesar[1] VT (cruzar) to cross; (estar tendido) to span; (penetrar) to impale, to run through; — **un momento difícil** to go through a difficult moment; **se me atravesó un caballo** a horse crossed in front of me; —**se en la cama** to lie crossways in bed

atraviesa, atraviese ver atravesar

atrayendo ver atraer

atreverse VI to dare, to go for it; **¡atrévete!** go for it!

atrevido ADJ (audaz) bold, daring; (insolente) insolent

atrevimiento M (cualidad de atrevido) boldness, daring, audacity; (acción atrevida) daring act

atribución F attribution; **atribuciones** powers

atribuir[19] VT (imputar) to attribute, to ascribe; (conferir) to confer; VI —**se** to claim

atribular VT to distress; —**se** to be distressed

atributo M attribute

atribuya, atribuye, atribuyendo, atribuyera, atribuyese ver atribuir

atril M stand

atrincherar VT to entrench

atrio M atrium

atrocidad F atrocity

atrofia F atrophy

atrofiar VT to atrophy, to stunt

atronador ADJ thunderous, deafening

atronar[5] VI to make a racket

atropellar VT (a un peatón) to run over, to run down; (los derechos de alguien) to trample upon

atropello M (arrollamiento) running over; (ultraje) outrage; (abuso) trampling

atroz ADJ (modales, crimen) atrocious; (dolor) excruciating; (ofensa) grievous

atuendo M getup

atún M tuna

aturdido ADJ bewildered; **estar** — to be in a daze

aturdimiento M bewilderment

aturdir VT to bewilder, to daze

atusar VT to smooth, to fix

audacia F audacity, boldness

audaz ADJ audacious, bold

audible ADJ audible

audición F audition; — **radial** radio program

audiencia F (tribunal) court; (público) audience; (en un pleito, proceso legal) hearing

audífono M (para sordos) earphone; (para música) headphone

audio M audio; —**libro** audio book

audiología F audiology

audiovisual ADJ audiovisual; M audiovisual presentation

auditar VI/VT to audit

auditivo ADJ auditory

auditor -ora MF auditor

auditoría F (revisión) audit; (trabajo de auditor)

auditing

auditorio M (público) audience; (local) auditorium

auge M (del mercado) boom; (de una moda) heyday; (de una carrera) peak

augurar VT to foretell; **no — nada bueno** not to bode well

aula F (de clase) classroom; (de conferencia) lecture hall

aullar VI to howl

aullido M howl

aumentar VT to augment, to increase; **— los salarios** to raise pay; VI (precios) to rise, to escalate; (población) to grow; (violencia) to escalate

aumento M increase; (de expectativas) buildup; (de población) growth; (de precios) rise, upturn; (de peso) gain; **— por mérito** merit raise; **— salarial / de sueldo** pay raise

aun ADV even; **— así** even so; **— cuando** even though/if

aún ADV still

aunque CONJ though, although

aura F aura

áureo ADJ golden

aureola F halo

auricular M (de teléfono) receiver; **—es** headphones, earphones

aurora F dawn, aurora; **— boreal** aurora borealis, northern lights

auscultar VT to listen to with a stethoscope

ausencia F absence

ausentarse VT to absent oneself

ausente ADJ absent, missing

ausentismo M absenteeism

auspicios M PL auspices

austeridad F austerity

austero ADJ austere, stern

Australia F Australia

australiano -na ADJ & MF Australian

Austria F Austria

austríaco -ca ADJ & MF Austrian

autenticar[30] VT to authenticate

autenticidad F authenticity

auténtico ADJ authentic

autismo M autism

autista ADJ autistic

auto M (coche) auto; (orden judicial) writ; **— de choques** bumper car

autoadhesivo M decal; (para el parachoques) bumper sticker

autoayuda F self-help

autobiografía F autobiography

autobomba M *RP* fire engine

autobús M bus

autocine M drive-in movie theater

autocompasión F self-pity

autocontrol M self-control

autócrata MF autocrat

autóctono ADJ indigenous

autodestructivo ADJ self-destructive

autodeterminación F self-determination

autodisciplina F self-discipline

autoedición F desktop publishing

autoescuela F driving school

autoestima F self-esteem

autogobierno M self-government

autogol M own goal

autógrafo M autograph

autoimagen F self-image

automático ADJ automatic

automatización F automation

automatizar[47] VT (mecanizar) to automate; (hacer automáticamente) to do automatically

automóvil M automobile

automovilista MF motorist

automovilístico ADJ automotive

autonomía F autonomy; (de un vehículo) range

autonómico ADJ autonomic

autónomo ADJ (independiente) autonomous, independent; (que trabaja por su cuenta) self-employed; (que se presenta solo) stand-alone

autopista F freeway, turnpike; **— de la información** information superhighway

autopropulsado ADJ self-propelled

autopsia F autopsy

autor -ora MF author

autoridad F authority

autoritario ADJ (tiránico) authoritarian; (respetado) authoritative

autorización F authorization

autorizar[47] VT (permitir) to authorize; (dar propiedad intelectual) to license

autosatisfacción F self-satisfaction

autoservicio M (sistema de venta) self-service; (tienda) convenience store

autosuficiencia F self-reliance

autosuficiente ADJ (independiente) self-sufficient; (presumido) smug

autovía F freeway

auxiliar VT to help; ADJ auxiliary; MF assistant; **— de vuelo** flight attendant

auxilio M help

avalancha F avalanche

avalar VT to guarantee, to cosign

avaluar[26] VT to appraise

avalúo M appraisal

avance M (acción de avanzar, adelanto) advance, headway; (sinopsis de película) trailer

avanzada F scouting party

avanzado ADJ advanced

avanzar[47] VI (ir hacia adelante) to advance; (progresar) to make headway; **a medida que avanzaba la mañana** as the morning progressed; VT (un vehículo) to move forward; (una grabación) to fast-forward

avaricia F avarice

avariento ADJ avaricious, miserly

avaro ADJ miserly, avaricious

avasallar VT to subjugate

avatar M (vicisitud) vicissitude; (encarnación de un dios, personaje digital) avatar

ave F bird; **— de corral** poultry; **— de rapiña** bird of prey; **— canora** songbird; **— zancuda** wading bird

avecindarse VI to take up residence

avellana F hazelnut

avellano M hazel

avena F oats

avenencia F agreement

avenida F avenue

avenir⁶¹ VI to reconcile; **—se a** to come around to; **—se bien** to get along

aventadora F fan, blower

aventajar VT (ser mejor) to be superior to; (sobrepasar) to get ahead of

aventón M **dar un —** *Méx* to give a lift

aventura F (suceso) adventure; (relación amorosa) fling, affair

aventurado ADJ (arriesgado) risky; (atrevido) daring

aventurar VT (arriesgar) to risk; (sugerir) to venture; **—se a** to dare to

aventurero -ra ADJ adventurous; MF adventurer

avergonzado ADJ (tímido) abashed; (arrepentido) ashamed, embarrassed

avergonzar²³ VT to shame, to embarrass; **—se** to be ashamed/embarrassed

avería F (de frutas) damage, bruise; (de coche) breakdown, mechanical trouble

averiado ADJ (un coche) broken-down; (un televisor) on the blink; (un ascensor) out of service; (fruta) bruised, damaged

averiarse²⁸ VI (fruta) to become damaged; (un coche) to break down

averiguar²⁵ VT to find out, to ascertain

aversión F aversion, dislike

avestruz MF ostrich

avezado ADJ seasoned

aviación F aviation

aviador -ora MF aviator

aviar²⁸ VT to fix

avidez F eagerness

ávido ADJ eager, avid

avinagrado ADJ sour

avinagrar VT to sour; **—se** to become sour

avío M tidying up; **—s de pescar** fishing tackle

avión M (máquina) airplane; (ave) martin; **— comercial** airliner; **— a reacción** jet airplane; **— caza** fighter airplane

avisar VT (notificar) to advise; (alertar) to alert

aviso M notice; (publicitario) advertisement; **estar sobre —** to be forewarned; **poner sobre —** to forewarn; **sin previo —** without warning

avispa F wasp

avispado ADJ (despierto) lively; (inteligente) smart

avisparse VI to wise up

avispero M wasp's nest; **alborotar el —** to stir up a wasp's nest

avispón M hornet

avistar VT to catch sight of

avivar VT (una llama) to fan; (una fiesta) to enliven; (un fuego, un debate) to fuel

avizorar VT to spy on

axila F underarm

ay INTERJ (de dolor) ouch; (de decepción) oh, no; (de sorpresa desagradable) oh; **¡— de mí!** poor me; **¡ay, no!** oh, no!

ayer ADV yesterday

ayuda F (asistencia) help; (después de una catástrofe) relief; **— en línea** online help

ayudante -ta MF assistant, helper, aide; **— de médico** physician's assistant

ayudantía F assistantship

ayudar VT to help, to aid

ayunar VI to fast

ayunas F PL **en —** (antes de comer) without having eaten; (despistado) clueless; **estoy en —** I am fasting

ayuno M fast, fasting

ayuntamiento M (gobierno) municipal government; (edificio) city hall

azabache M jet; ADJ jet-black, raven

azada F hoe

azadón M hoe

azafato -ta MF (en aviones) flight attendant; (en ferias) host

azafrán M saffron

azahar M orange blossom

azar M chance; **al —** by chance, at random

azaroso ADJ (arriesgado) risky; (aleatorio) random

azerbaiyano -na, azerbaijano -na ADJ & MF Azerbaijani, Azerbaijanian

Azerbaiyán F Azerbaijan

azogar⁴⁰ VT to silver

azogue M (sustancia) quicksilver, mercury; (niño inquieto) restless child; **tener — en el cuerpo** to be restless

azorar VT (alarmar) to alarm; (avergonzar) to embarrass

azotaina F flogging

azotar VT (con azote) to whip, to lash, to flog; VI/ VT (el viento) to whip, to buffet; (el sol) to beat down; (la lluvia) to sting

azote M (instrumento) whip; (golpe) lash; (aflicción) scourge; (golpe de viento) buffet

azotea F flat roof

azteca ADJ, MF Aztec

azúcar MF sugar; **— moreno -na** brown sugar

azucarar VT to sugar

azucarera F (fábrica) sugar mill; *Am* (recipiente)

sugar bowl

azucarero M sugar bowl

azucena F white lily

azufre M sulfur, sulphur

azul ADJ blue; **— acero** steel blue; **— celeste** sky blue; **— claro** light blue; **— marino** navy blue

azulado ADJ bluish

azular VT to color blue

azulear VI (tener color azul) to be blue; (ponerse azul) to become blue; VT (dar color azul) to color blue

azulejar VT to tile

azulejo M tile

azuzar[47] VT (a un perro) to sic; (a una persona) to egg on

Bb

baba F drivel, drool, slobber; (de un caracol, de agua estancada) slime; **se le cae la — por el coche nuevo** he's drooling over the new car

babear VI to drivel, to drool

babero M bib

babor M portside

babosa F slug

babosear VI/VT to slobber [on]

baboso ADJ (caracol) slimy; (persona que babea) driveling; (persona tonta) idiotic; (adulador) fawning

babuino M baboon

baca F luggage rack

bacalao M cod

bache M (pozo) pothole; (momento) bad time; (de aire) air pocket

bacheado ADJ bumpy

bachiller -ra M (graduado) high school graduate; (alumno) high school student

bachillerato M baccalaureate

bacilo M bacillus

backgammon M backgammon

bacteria F bacteria

bacteriano ADJ bacterial

bacteriología F bacteriology

badajo M bell clapper

badana F sheepskin

bagaje M baggage

bagatela F trifle

bagazo M pulp

Bahamas F PL Bahamas

bahameño -ña ADJ & MF Bahamian

bahía F (geography) bay; (computer) slot

Bahrein M Bahrain

bahreiní ADJ & MF Bahraini

bailador -ora MF folk dancer; ADJ dancing

bailar VI/VT to dance; **me bailan los pantalones** my pants are falling off; **me tocó — con la más fea** I was left holding the bag; **que me quiten lo bailado** I enjoyed it anyway

bailarín -ina MF dancer

baile M (actividad) dance; (fiesta) dance, ball; **— aeróbico** aerobic dance; **— de máscaras** masked ball; **— folklórico** folk dance; **— zapateado** clog dance

bailongo M hop

bailotear VI to dance around

baivel M bevel

baja F (de temperatura, presión) drop; (de precios) decline; (de guerra) casualty; (del ejército) discharge, dismissal; (del trabajo) leave; **dar de —** to discharge; **darse de —** to call in sick

bajada F (acción de bajar, pendiente) descent; (de un caballo) dismount; **— contra-reloj** downhill ski race

bajar VI (descender) to go down; (correr) to run down; (de un árbol) to climb down; (de un caballo) to get down; (de un ómnibus) to step off, to get off; (en calidad) to worsen; (la marea) to ebb; (una creciente) to subside; VT (las escaleras) to go down; (un avión de un tiro) to shoot down; (comida con agua) to wash down; (la cabeza) to lower; (un cargamento) to let down; (el volumen) to turn down; (focos) to dim; (la voz) to lower, to soften; (los precios) to cut; **— de categoría** to demote; **— el cursor** to scroll down; **— en picado** to dive; **—se los pantalones** to pull down one's pants

bajeza F (cualidad) baseness; (acción) vile act

bajío M shoal

bajista ADJ (bolsa) bearish; MF (músico) bassist

bajo ADJ (nubes, estante, precio, voz grave) low; (persona) short; (voz débil) soft; (río) lower; (vista, persianas) lowered; (acto) base; **baja espalda** small of the back; **de baja calidad** low-end; **de baja ley** base; **de — precio** low-cost; **de — presupuesto** low-budget; **de —s ingresos** low-income; PREP under; **— contrato** under contract; **— control** under control, in hand; **— cuerda** under-the-table; **— fianza** on bail; **— fuego** under fire; **— sospecha** under a cloud; **— tierra** underground; **poner — llave** to lock up; **por lo —** under one's breath; M (en un coro, contrabajo) bass; (de pantalón) cuff; **hacer los —s** to cuff; ADV low

bala F (de pistola) bullet; (atletismo) shot; (de cañón) ball

balada F ballad

baladí ADJ trivial

balance M (cálculo) balance; (documento)

balance sheet; (número de víctimas) toll; (movimiento) sway; **hacer un** — to take stock

balancear VT to swing; VI to sway; **—se** to sway

balanceo M (de un cuerpo) swinging, swing; (de un barco) rolling, roll

balancín M seesaw

balanza F scale; **— comercial** balance of trade; **— de pagos** balance of payments

balar VI to bleat

balasto M ballast

balazo M (disparo) shot; (herida) bullet wound

balbucear VI (un adulto) to stammer; (un bebé) to babble

balbuceo M (tartamudeo) stammer; stammering; (de bebé) babble, babbling

balcón M balcony

balde M pail, bucket; **de** — gratis; **en** — in vain

baldear VT to flush

baldío ADJ (terreno) fallow; (acción) useless

baldosa F (en una casa) floor tile; (en una calle) flagstone

balido M bleat, bleating

balística F ballistics

balístico ADJ ballistic

ballena F (animal) whale; (para corsé) whalebone

ballenato M whale calf

ballet M ballet

balneario M (de veraneo) seaside resort; (con aguas medicinales) spa

balón M ball; **baloncesto** basketball; **balonmano** handball; **— de angioplastia** angioplasty balloon; **se le fue el** — (fútbol americano) he fumbled; (fútbol) he lost the ball; M **balonvolea** volleyball

balsa F (embarcación) raft, balsa; (lago) pond

bálsamo M balsam, balm

baluarte M bulwark, stronghold

bambolear VT to sway, to swing; **—se** to sway, to swing

bamboleo M swinging, swaying

bambú M bamboo

banal ADJ banal; **una respuesta** — a pat answer

banana F banana

banano M (tree) banana tree; (fruit) banana

banca F (industria) banking; (en el juego) bank; **— electrónica** e-banking; **— en línea** online banking; **— por internet** Internet banking

bancario-ria ADJ bank, banking; MF banker

bancarrota F bankruptcy

banco M (establecimiento) bank; (asiento) bench; (de peces) school; (de arena) shoal, spit; (de suplentes) bench; **— de datos** data bank; **— de niebla** fog bank; **Banco Mundial** World Bank

banda F (de músicos) band; (cinta ancha, también de computadora) band; (cinta de vestido) sash; (de delincuentes) gang, band, ring; (dibujo) stripe; (de neumático) tread; (lindero) side, edge, border; (de un barco) side; (en deporte) sideline; **— ancha** broadband; **— de frecuencia** frequency band; **— horaria** time slot; **— magnética** magnetic strip; **— sonora** soundtrack

bandada F (de aves) flock, flight; (de peces) school

bandeja F tray; **me lo sirvieron en** — [**de plata**] they served it to me on a silver platter

bandera F flag; **jurar la** — to pledge allegiance to the flag

banderín M pennant

banderola F pennant

bandido -da MF (delincuente) bandit, outlaw; (niño terrible) rascal

bando M (decreto) edict; (partido) camp

bandolero -ra MF bandit

Bangladesh M Bangladesh

bangladeshí, bangladesí ADJ & MF Bangladeshi

banjo M banjo

banquero -ra MF banker

banqueta F (taburete) stool; (acera) *Méx* sidewalk

banquete M banquet

banquetearse VI to feast

banquillo M bench (también en fútbol)

bañar VT (a un bebé) to bathe; (una torta) to ice, to frost; **—se** (en una bañera) to take a bath; (en el mar) to swim

bañera F bathtub

bañista MF bather

baño M (acción) bath; (cuarto) bathroom, lavatory; (de torta) icing, frosting; **darse un** — (bañarse) to take a bath; (nadar) to take a swim; **— de asiento** sitz bath; **— de esponja** sponge bath; **— [de] María** double boiler; **— de remolino** whirlpool bath; **— de sangre** bloodbath

bar M bar

barahúnda F ruckus, racket

baraja F pack/deck of cards

barajada F shuffle

barajar VI/VT (naipes) to shuffle; (alternativas) to weigh

baranda F railing, guard rail

barandal M banister

barandilla F rail, railing

barata F *Méx* sale

baratear VT to sell cheap

baratija F trinket, knickknack

barato ADJ cheap

baratura F cheapness

barba F beard; **—s** whiskers; **hacer algo en las —s de alguien** to do something right under someone's nose

barbacoa F barbecue
barbadense ADJ & MF Barbadian
barbado ADJ bearded
Barbados M Barbados
barbaridad F atrocity; **una — de** a lot of; **¡qué —!** what nonsense!
barbarie F savagery
bárbaro -ra ADJ (salvaje) barbarous, barbaric; (estupendo) cool, super; MF barbarian
barbecho M fallow land
barbería F barbershop
barbero -ra MF barber
barbilla F chin
barbitúrico M barbiturate
barbudo ADJ bearded
barca F rowboat
barcaza F barge
barco M boat; **— petrolero** oil tanker
bardo M bard
bario M barium
barítono M & M baritone
barlovento M windward
barniz M (para madera) varnish; (para cerámica) glaze; (de cultura) veneer
barnizar[47] VT (madera) to varnish; (cerámica) to glaze
barómetro M barometer
barón M baron
barquero -era M boatman; F boatwoman
barquillo M rolled wafer
barquinazo M **dar —s** to lurch
barra F (de hierro, arena, chocolate, en un bar) bar; (en gimnasia) crossbar; (signo ortográfico) slash; **— de estado** status bar; **— de herramientas** toolbar; **— de jabón** bar of soap; **— de menú** menu bar; **— de tareas** task bar; **— espaciadora** space bar; **— invertida** backslash
barrabasada F mischief
barraca F (de feria) stall, stand; (casucha) hovel; (depósito) shed
barracuda F barracuda
barranca F ravine
barranco M gully, ravine
barrena F (de un taladro) bit; (de un avión) tailspin; **entrar en —** to go into a tailspin
barrenar VT to drill
barredora F sweeper
barrendero -ra MF street sweeper
barrer VI/VT (pasar escoba) to sweep; (derrotar) to defeat decisively; M SG **barreminas** minesweeper
barrera F (protección) barrier; (valla) barrier, bar; **— arancelaria** tariff barrier; **— comercial** trade barrier; **— de coral** barrier reef; **— del sonido** sound barrier
barrica F vat
barricada F barricade
barrida F sweep

barrido M (acción de barrer) sweeping; (movimiento) sweep
barriga F (abdomen) belly; (panza) paunch; **rascarse la —** to do nothing
barrigón ADJ potbellied
barril M barrel, keg, drum
barrio M neighborhood, quarter; **— residencial** residential neighborhood; **—s bajos** slums
barritar VI to trumpet
barro M (lodo) mud; (arcilla) clay; (acné) pimple; **de —** earthen
barroco ADJ & M baroque
barroso ADJ muddy
barrote M bar
barruntar VT to suspect
barrunto M suspicion
bártulos M PL stuff
barullo M hubbub
basal ADJ basal
basalto M basalt
basar VT to base; **—se en** (depender de) to rely on; (fundamentar en) to be based on
basca F nausea
báscula F scale
base F (apoyo, área militar, en química, en béisbol) base; (punto de partida) basis; (de maquillaje) foundation; (de una campaña) plank; MF (baloncesto) point guard; **—s de concurso** contest rules; **— de datos** database; **— de lanzamiento** launching pad; **con — en** on the basis of; **en — a** on the basis of; **las —s** (de un partido) base, grass roots; (de un sindicato) rank and file; **salario — base** salary; **tener una — sólida** to be on a strong footing; **—s llenas** (béisbol) bases loaded; **— por bolas [intencional]** [intentional] base on balls
basic M (lenguaje de programación) BASIC
básico ADJ (fundamental) basic; (sin lujos) no-frills, bare-bones
básquet M basketball
básquetbol M basketball
bastante ADJ & PRON enough, sufficient; **tiene bastante dinero como para ser feliz** she has enough money to be happy; ADV (suficientemente) enough; **me lo has dicho bastante** you've told me that enough times; (mucho) quite a lot; **la herida me duele bastante** my injury is hurting a lot; (algo) quite, pretty; **la película estuvo bastante bien** the movie was quite good
bastar VI to be enough, to suffice; **¡basta!** enough!
bastardilla F italics
bastedad F coarseness
bastidor M (de teatro) wing; (para bordado) frame; (de coche) chassis; (de ventana) sash; **entre —es** (en teatro) offstage; (en privado)

behind the scenes

bastimentos M PL provisions

basto ADJ coarse, crude; M suit in the Spanish deck of cards

bastón M cane, walking stick; **— de esquí** ski pole

basura F rubbish, garbage, trash

basural M *Am* dump

basurero -ra MF (persona) garbage collector; M (lugar) dump

bata F (para llevar en casa) robe, housecoat; (de laboratorio) lab coat; (de pacientes) hospital gown; **— de baño** bathrobe

batahola F racket, din

batalla F battle; (un carro) wheelbase; **— naval** sea battle; **ropa de —** everyday clothing; **trabar —** to engage in battle

batallar VI to battle

batallón M battalion

batata F sweet potato

bate M baseball bat; **al —** at bat

batea F tray

bateador -ora MF batter; **— ambidiestro -ra** switch hitter; **— designado -da** designated hitter; **— emergente** pinch hitter

batear VT to bat, to hit; **— un jonrón** to hit a homerun; **— un sencillo** to hit a single

batería F (de coche, artillería, béisbol) battery; (de cocina) pots and pans; (musical) drums; **— de iones de litio** lithium-ion battery

baterista MF drummer

batiburrillo M hodgepodge

batido M shake, milk shake

batidor M whisk, beater

batidora F mixer

batintín M gong

batir VT (una alfombra) to beat; (un terreno) to comb; (mantequilla) to cream, to churn; (un récord) to break; (huevos) to beat; (crema) to whip; (alas) to flap, to beat; **— palmas** to clap, to applaud; **—se en duelo** to duel; **—se en retirada** to retreat

batuta F baton; **llevar la —** to call the shots

baudio M baud

baúl M trunk

bautismo M baptism, christening; **— de fuego** baptism of fire

bautizar[47] VT to baptize, to christen

bautizo M christening, baptism

baya F berry

bayeta F cleaning cloth

bayo ADJ bay

bayoneta F bayonet

baza F card trick; **meter — en una conversación** to participate in a conversation

bazar M bazaar

bazo M spleen

bazofia F slop

bazuca F bazooka

beagle M beagle

beato ADJ (bendito) blessed; (piadoso) beatified; (santurrón) overly pious

bebé M baby, infant

bebedero M (en un corral) drinking trough; (en el campo) watering hole; (para personas) water fountain

bebedor -ora MF drinker

beber VI/VT to drink

bebercio M *fam* booze

bebida F drink, beverage

beca F scholarship, fellowship

becario -ria MF scholar, fellow

becerro M (animal) calf; (piel) calfskin

becuadro M natural sign

befa F jeer

befar VT to jeer at

beicon M *Esp* bacon

beige ADJ & M beige

béisbol M baseball

beisbolista M baseball player

beldad F beauty

belga ADJ & MF Belgian

Bélgica F Belgium

Belice M Belize

beliceño -ña ADJ & MF Belizean

bélico ADJ warlike

belicoso ADJ (guerrero) bellicose; (peleador) feisty

beligerante ADJ & MF belligerent

bellaco M rascal, scoundrel

bellaquería F mischief

belleza F beauty

bello ADJ beautiful

bellota F acorn

bemol M (música) flat; **tener —es** to be tricky

bencina F benzine

bendecir[51] VT to bless

bendición F (parte de la misa) benediction; (acción de bendecir) blessing; (beneficio) boon, blessing

bendito ADJ (agua) holy; (alma) blessed; **— sea** may he be blessed; **dormir como un —** to sleep like a log; **es un —** he is a saint

benefactor -ora MF benefactor, patron

beneficencia F charity; **— pública** welfare

beneficiar VT to benefit; **—se de** to benefit from

beneficiario -ria MF (de una herencia, perdón, acto de bondad) beneficiary; (de un cheque) payee

beneficio M benefit (también espectáculo); **—s adicionales** perks; **—s por fallecimiento** death benefits

beneficioso ADJ beneficial

benéfico ADJ beneficent

benemérito ADJ worthy of esteem

benevolencia F benevolence

benévolo ADJ benevolent

bengala F flare

bengalés -esa ADJ & MF Bangladeshi

benigno ADJ benign

Benín M Benin

beninés -esa ADJ & MF Beninese

benjamín -ina MF youngest child

beodo ADJ drunk

berbiquí M carpenter's brace

berenjena F eggplant

bermejo ADJ reddish

bermellón M vermilion

berrear VI (animal) to bellow, to bawl; (bebé) to squall

berrido M (de animal) bellowing, bawling; (de bebé) squall, squalling

berrinche M tantrum

berro M watercress

berza F cabbage

besar VT to kiss

beso M kiss

bestia F beast

bestial ADJ bestial

best-seller M best seller

besuquear VT to kiss repeatedly; **—se** to make out

betabel M *Méx* beet

betabloqueador M beta blocker

betabloqueante M beta blocker

betún M shoe polish

Biblia F Bible

bíblico ADJ biblical

bibliografía F bibliography

biblioteca F (edificio) library; (anaquel) bookcase

bibliotecario -ria MF librarian

bicarbonato M bicarbonate; **— de sosa/soda** bicarbonate of soda

bíceps M SG bicep[s]

bicho M (insecto) bug (también en informática); (animal) *fam* critter; **— raro** odd bird; **mal —** creep; **¿qué — te ha picado?** what's gotten into you? **—s** vermin

bici F bike

bicicleta F bicycle; **— de montaña** mountain bike; **— estática** stationary bike

bicúspide ADJ bicuspid

biela F connecting rod

Bielorrusia F Belarus

bien ADV well; **—aventurado** blessed; **— arreglado** well-groomed; **— conocido** well-known; **— hecho** well-made, well-done; **— poco** very little; **agarrarse —** to hold on tight; **ahora —** now then; **apretar —** to press hard; **está —** she is fine; **más —** rather; **me doy — cuenta** I'm perfectly aware; **pues —** now; **qué —** how wonderful; **si —** although; **ya está —** that's enough; M good; **—es** property, assets; **—es**

consumibles consumable goods; **—es inmuebles** real estate; **—es muebles** personal property; **—es raíces** real estate; **—estar** well-being, welfare; **—hechor** benefactor; **persona de —** a good person; INTERJ OK!

bienio M biennium

bienvenida F welcome

bienvenido ADJ welcome

bifurcación F (en un camino) fork, forking; (en un programa de computadora) branch

bifurcarse[30] VI to fork, to branch off

bigamia F bigamy

bigote M (de hombre) mustache; (de animal) whisker

bikini M bikini

bilateral ADJ bilateral

bilingüe ADJ & MF bilingual

bilingüismo M bilingualism

bilis F bile

billar M (juego) billiards, pool; (mesa) pool table

billete M (de viaje, para espectáculos) ticket; (de banco) bill, banknote; (financiero) note; **— de ida solo** one-way ticket; **— de ida y vuelta** return ticket

billetera F billfold

billón M trillion

bimestral ADJ bimonthly

bimestre M two-month period

binario ADJ binary

bingo M bingo

binomial ADJ binomial

binomio M binomial

biodegradable ADJ biodegradable

biofeedback M biofeedback

biografía F biography

bioingeniería F bioengineering

biología F biology

biológico ADJ biological

biólogo -ga MF biologist

biombo M folding screen

biopsia F biopsy

bioquímica F biochemistry

biorritmo M biorhythm

biotecnología F biotechnology

bipartidista ADJ bipartisan

bipolar ADJ bipolar

birlar VT *fam* to pinch, to swipe

Birmania F Burma

birmano -na ADJ & MF Burmese, from Myanmar

birrete M mortarboard

bis M encore

bisabuelo -la M great-grandfather; F great-grandmother

bisagra F hinge

bisecar[30] VT to bisect

biselado ADJ beveled

biselar VT to bevel

bisemanal ADV biweekly

bisiesto ADJ **año**— leap year

bisnieto -ta M great-grandson; F great-granddaughter

bisonte M bison, buffalo

bistec M beefsteak

bisturí M scalpel

bisutería F costume jewelry

bit M bit

bizarría F gallantry

bizarro ADJ gallant

bizco ADJ cross-eyed

bizcocho M (pastel) sponge cake; (pastelillo) pastry

bizcochuelo M sponge cake

bizquear VI to be cross-eyed

black-jack M blackjack

blanca M half note

blanco ADJ (color) white; (tez) fair; M (color) white (también clara de huevos, ojos); (de tiro) target; **dar en el** — to hit the target; **en** — (hoja de papel, mente) blank; (sin dormir) sleepless; **en — y negro** in black and white

blancura F whiteness; (de tez) fairness

blancuzco ADJ whitish

blandir VT to brandish, to wield

blando ADJ (sin dureza, sin rigor) soft; (sensiblero) mushy

blandura F softness

blanqueador ADJ whitening; M bleach, whitener

blanquear VT (una pared) to whitewash; (dinero) to launder; (verduras) to blanch; **—se** to whiten

blanquecino ADJ whitish

blanqueo M whitening

blasfemar VI to blaspheme

blasfemia F blasphemy

blasón M coat of arms

blasonar VI to boast

blazer M blazer

blindado ADJ armored

blindaje M armor

blindar VT to armor

bloc M writing tablet, pad of paper

blog M blog

bloguear VI to blog

bloguero -ra MF blogger

bloque M block (también de motor, político); (edificio) building; **en** — together

bloquear VT (carretera, asalto, pase, virus digital) to block; (puerto) to blockade; (cuentas bancarias) to freeze; **—se** to choke

bloqueo M (deporte) block; (computadoras) block, blocking; (militar) blockade

blues M PL blues

bluff M bluff

blusa F blouse, top

boa F boa constrictor

boato M pomp

bobada F (tontería) foolish act; (fruslería) trifle

bobalicón -ona ADJ goofy; MF nincompoop

bobear VI to fool around, to monkey around

bobería F (cualidad) foolishness; (dicho) foolish remark; (hecho) foolish act

bobina F (de hilo) bobbin; (de alambre, de coche) coil; (de película) reel

bobinar VT to reel

bobo -ba ADJ (tonto) dumb, dimwitted, silly; (estupefacto) flabbergasted; MF dimwit, booby, fool

boca F mouth (también de río); (de un arma de fuego) muzzle; (del estómago) pit; (de una cueva) opening; **—calle** intersection; **— a —** mouth-to-mouth; **— abajo** face down; **— arriba** face up; **a — de jarro** at close range; **callarse la —** to shut up

bocadillo M snack; *Esp* sandwich

bocado M (de comida) bite, morsel, mouthful; (de una brida) bit

bocanada F (de líquido) mouthful; (de humo) puff; (de aire) sniff

bocazas MF SG loudmouth

boceto M sketch

bochorno M (calor) oppressive heat; (vergüenza) embarrassment

bochornoso ADJ (caluroso) sultry, oppressive, muggy; (vergonzoso) embarrassing

bocina F (de coche) horn; (megáfono) megaphone

bocinazo M honk, toot

bocio M goiter

boda F wedding; **—s de oro** golden anniversary; **—s de plata** silver anniversary

bodega F (despensa subterránea) cellar; (para vinos) wine cellar; (vinería) winery; (espacio en un barco, avión) hold; (tienda de comestibles) *Carib, Am Central* grocery store

bodeguero -ra MF (viñatero) wine producer; (almacenero) *Carib, Am Central* grocer

bofe M [de animal] lung; **echar los —s** to tire oneself out

bofetada F slap

boga LOC ADV **en —** in vogue, fashion

bogar⁴⁰ VI/VT to row

bogey M bogey

bohemio -mia ADJ & MF (nacionalidad) Bohemian; (estilo) bohemian

boicot M boycott

boicotear VT to boycott

boicoteo M boycott

boina F beret

bol M bowl

bola F (golf, tenis, béisbol) ball; (canica) marble; (de helado) dip; (de algodón) wad; (jugada de béisbol) ball; **— blanca** cue ball; **en —s** in the buff; **no dar pie con —** to be lost; **no**

dar ni — not to pay attention; **— de nudillos** knuckleball; **darle una base por** **—s** to walk someone; **sacar una base por** **—s** to walk; **— de break** break point; **— de partido** match-ball; **— de ruptura** break point

bolera F bowling alley

boleta F (de lotería) ticket; (de votación) *Méx* ballot

boletín M bulletin

boleto M ticket; **— de ida solo** one-way ticket; **— de ida y vuelta** return ticket

boliche M (juego) bowling; (bolera) bowling alley

bolígrafo M ballpoint pen; **— computadora portátil** pen computer; **— ordenador portátil** pen computer

bolita F pellet

Bolivia F Bolivia

boliviano -na ADJ & MF Bolivian

bollo M bun, roll

bolo M bowling pin; **jugar a los —s** to bowl

bolsa F (saco) bag; (cartera) purse; (órgano) sac; (marsupio) pouch; **— de valores** stock market; **— de aire** airbag; **— de estudio** scholarship; **— de miseria** pocket of poverty; **hace —s** it pooches out

bolsillo M pocket; **de —** pocket-sized

bolsista MF stockbroker

bolso M (grande) bag; (pequeño) purse

bomba F (para agua, gasolina) pump; (artefacto explosivo) bomb; (noticia, mujer) *fam* bombshell; **— atómica** atomic bomb; **— de hidrógeno** hydrogen bomb; **— de neutrones** neutron bomb; **— de tiempo** time bomb; **— fétida** stink bomb; **— incendiaria** incendiary bomb; **— inteligente** smart bomb; **lo pasamos —** we had a blast

bombacha F *RP* panties, underpants

bombardear VT to bombard

bombardeo M bombardment, bombing

bombardero -ra MF (tripulante) bombardier; M (avión) bomber

bombear VT to pump

bombero -ra MF firefighter

bombilla F lightbulb

bombo M (en música) bass drum; (en béisbol) fly ball; **dar —** to extol; **con —s y platillos** with great fanfare

bombón M (chocolate) bonbon; (mujer atractiva) *fam* dish

bombonería F candy store

bonachón ADJ (amable) good-natured; (inocente) naive

bonaerense ADJ from the city of Buenos Aires; MF person from Buenos Aires

bonanza F (buen tiempo) fair weather; (prosperidad) prosperity

bondad F goodness, kindness; **—es** virtues; **tenga la — de** would you please

bondadoso ADJ kind, kindly

boniato M sweet potato

bonito ADJ pretty; M tuna

bono M (título de deuda) bond; (vale) voucher

boñiga F dung

boqueada F gasp

boquear VI to gasp

boquete M opening

boquiabierto ADJ (de boca abierta) openmouthed; (asombrado) astonished

boquilla F (para cigarros) cigarette holder; (para trompeta) mouthpiece; **defender de —** to pay lip service to

bórax M borax

borbollar VI to bubble

borbollón M (burbujeo) bubbling; (alboroto) commotion; **a borbollones** bubbling over

borbotar VI to bubble, to gurgle

borboteo M bubbling, gurgling

bordado M embroidery, needlework

bordar VI/VT to embroider

borde M (de una superficie) edge, border; (de un vaso) rim, brim; (de un desastre) brink; (de una calle) *Méx* curb

bordear VT (rodear) to skirt, to go along the edge of; (adornar) to trim

bordillo M curb

bordo LOC ADV **a —** on board

bordó, bordeaux ADJ INV & M maroon

borla F (de birrete) tassel; (de algodón) powder puff

boro M boron

borra F dregs

borrachera F (estado) drunkenness; (juerga) drunken spree

borrachín -ina M drunkard

borracho -cha ADJ drunk, wasted; **no lo hago ni** — I would never do such a thing; MF drunkard, wino

borrado M erasure

borrador M (bosquejo) rough draft; (goma) eraser

borrar VT (texto escrito) to erase; (texto digital) to cut, to erase; **—se de un club** to withdraw from a club

borrasca F squall

borrego M lamb

borrico M donkey

borrón M blot, blotch, smudge; **hacer — y cuenta nueva** to start over at square one

borronear VT to smudge

borroso ADJ (imagen) blurry, blurred; (memoria) fuzzy

boscaje M thicket

Bosnia-Herzegovina F Bosnia and Herzegovina

bosnio -nia ADJ & MF Bosnian

bosque M forest, woods
bosquecillo M grove
bosquejar VT to sketch, to outline
bosquejo M sketch, outline
bosta F dung
bostezar[47] VI to yawn
bostezo M yawn
bota F (calzado) boot; (para vino) leather wine bag
botadura F launch
botánica F botany
botánico ADJ botanical
botar VT (una pelota) to bounce; (un buque) to launch; (basura) to throw out
botarate M fool
bote M (jarro) can; (embarcación) boat; (rebote) bounce; **— de basura** garbage can; **— de remos** rowboat; **— de salvamento** lifeboat; **de — en / a —** filled to overflowing; (tenis) **— pronto** half volley
botella F bottle
botero -ra M boatman; F boatwoman
botija F earthen jug
botijo M earthen jar
botín M (de guerra) booty, plunder; (de ladrón) loot, haul
botiquín M (en el baño) medicine cabinet; (de primeros auxilios) first-aid kit
botón M (de aparato, de camisa) button; (remache) stud; (de planta) bud; **botones** bellboy, page; **— de inicio** start button
bótox M botox
Botsuana F Botswana
botsuano -na MF Botswanan
botulismo M botulism
bouquet M bouquet
boutique F boutique
bóveda F (techo) arched roof, vault; **— celeste** the vault of heaven
bowling M bowling
box M (para coches de carrera) pit
boxeador -ora MF boxer, prizefighter
boxear VI/VT to box
boxeo M boxing
bóxer M boxer
boya F (en el mar) buoy; (corcho) float
boyante ADJ buoyant
boyar VI to buoy
bozal M muzzle
bozo M fuzz on the lip
bracear VI to move one's arms
bracero -ra MF migrant worker
bragas F PL underpants, panties
bragueta F fly
brainstorming M brainstorming
bramar VI (ciervo, cochino) to bellow; (león, viento) to roar
bramido M (de ciervo, cochino) bellow; (de león, viento) roar

brandy M brandy
brasa F ember
brasero M brazier
Brasil M Brazil
brasileño -ña ADJ & MF Brazilian
brasilero -ra ADJ & MF Brazilian
bravata F act of bravado
bravío ADJ wild
bravo ADJ (animal, río) wild; (terreno) rugged; (persona) brave; (barrio) tough; INTERJ bravo!
bravucón -ona ADJ bullying; MF bully
bravuconería F bullying
bravura F (de bestia) fierceness; (de persona) courage
braza F fathom
brazada F (cantidad) armful; (en natación) stroke
brazalete M bracelet
brazo M arm (también de silla); (de cornamenta) branch; (de balanza) beam; **— de mar** sound; **— derecho** right-hand man; **— s day laborers; con los —s abiertos** with open arms; **con los —s cruzados** with crossed arms; **ir del —** to go arm in arm; **luchar a — partido** to fight to the end
brea F pitch, tar
brecha F (en un muro) breach, gap; (entre generaciones) gap
brécol M broccoli
bregar[40] VI to struggle, to toil
breña F scrub
breve ADJ (cuento) brief, short; (bikini) scanty; **en —** shortly
brevedad F brevity, shortness; **a la —** as soon as possible
bribón -ona ADJ roguish; MF rascal, rogue, scoundrel
brida F bridle
brigada F brigade
brillante ADJ brilliant, bright; M diamond, gem
brillantez F brilliance
brillantina F glitter
brillar VI (oro) to shine; (ojos) to sparkle, to twinkle; (nieve) to glisten; **— por su ausencia** to be conspicuous by its absence
brillo M (de metal, piedras preciosas) shine, luster, sparkle; (de los ojos) twinkle; (de nieve) glistening; (del pelo, plumas) sheen; (de diamantes) sparkle; (de una pantalla) brightness; **dar —** to give luster; **sacar —** to polish
brilloso ADJ shiny
brincar[30] VI to hop, to skip
brinco M hop, skip
brindar VI (beber) to toast; (proporcionar) to provide; **— por alguien** to toast someone; **—se a hacer algo** to volunteer to do something
brindis M toast

brío M spirit
brioso ADJ spirited
brisa F breeze
británico ADJ British
brizna F blade of grass
broca F drill bit
brocado M brocade
brocal M (borde) rim; (boca de pozo) curb
brocha F paintbrush; **de — gorda** coarse
broche M (alhaja) brooch; (sujetador) clasp, clip;
(para el pelo) barrette; **— de oro** grand finale
brocheta F skewer
brócoli, bróculi M broccoli
broma F (chiste) joke; (réplica) jest, wisecrack; **—
pesada** practical joke; **—s aparte** kidding
aside; **en —** in jest; **gastar una —** to play a
joke; **ni en —** no way; **no estoy para —s** I'm
not in the mood for kidding
bromear VI to joke, to kid
bromista MF wag, joker
bromo M bromine
bromuro M bromide
bronca F row; **armar una —** to cause a
disturbance, to raise a rumpus; **echarle la —
a alguien** to bawl someone out; **tener —** to
be angry
bronce M bronze
bronceado ADJ (cubierto de bronce) bronzed;
(tostado) tanned; (de color bronce) bronze; M
suntan
broncear VT (un objeto) to bronze; **—se** to get a
tan
bronco ADJ (voz) gruff; (terreno) rough;
(caballo) wild
bronquial ADJ bronchial
bronquio M bronchial tube
bronquitis F bronchitis
brotar VI (planta) to sprout; (enfermedad
eruptiva) to break out; (agua) to gush, to flow,
to issue
brote M (de una enfermedad) outbreak; (retoño)
sprout, spear
broza F brushwood
bruces LOC ADV **de —** face down
brujería F witchcraft, devilry
brujo -ja M wizard, sorcerer; F witch
brújula F compass
bruma F mist
brumoso ADJ misty
brunch M brunch
bruneano -na ADJ & MF Bruneian
Brunéi M Brunei
bruñir[17] VT to burnish
bruscamente ADV (girar, responder) sharply;
(hablar) brusquely
brusco ADJ (descortés) brusque, curt;
(repentino) sudden
brusquedad F (descortesía) brusqueness; (lo
repentino) suddenness

brutal ADJ brutal
brutalidad F brutality
bruto -ta ADJ (ignorante) ignorant;
(maleducado, burdo) uncouth; (violento)
brutish; (sin descuentos) gross; **a lo —**
roughly; **en —** in the rough; **recaudar en —**
to gross; MF (ignorante) blockhead; (persona
violenta) brute; (mal educado) lout, brute
bucal ADJ oral
bucear VI (sumergirse) to scuba dive; (indagar)
to explore
buceo M scuba diving
buche M (en las aves) crop; (bocado) mouthful
bucle M (de pelo) curl, ringlet; (en informática)
loop
budín M pudding
budismo M Buddhism
budista ADJ, MF Buddhist
bueno ADJ good; **buena fe** good faith; **a la
buena de Dios** haphazardly; **de buenas a
primeras** out of the blue; **estar —** to be
sexy; **hace buen tiempo** it is fine weather;
lo — the good thing; **por las buenas o por
las malas** by hook or by crook; **ser — con
los números** to be good at figures; INTERJ
OK! **—s días** good day/morning; **buenas
noches** good night/evening; **buenas
tardes** good afternoon
buey M OX, steer
búfalo M buffalo, bison
bufanda F scarf, muffler
bufar VI to snort; **está que bufa** he is incensed
bufete M (despacho) lawyer's office; (negocio)
practice
buffet M buffet
bufido M snort
bufón -ona MF buffoon, jester
bufonear VI to clown
buhardilla F (desván) attic, garret
búho M owl
buhonero -ra MF peddler
buitre M vulture, buzzard
buje M bushing
bujía F spark plug
bulbo M bulb
bulldog M bulldog
bulevar M boulevard
Bulgaria F Bulgaria
búlgaro -ra ADJ & MF Bulgarian
bulimia F bulimia
bulla F uproar, fuss, bustle
bulldozer M bulldozer
bullicio M uproar, racket, bustle
bullicioso ADJ boisterous, rowdy
bullir[16] VI (hervir) to boil; (hacer burbujas) to
bubble; (ajetrearse) to bustle; (moverse) to
stir
bullón M puff
bullpen M bullpen

bulto M (paquete) bundle; (tumor) lump, growth; (silueta) shape; (saliente) bulge; **a —** approximately; **escurrir el —** to slack off

bungaló M bungalow

bungee M bungee jumping

búnker M bunker

buñuelo M fritter

buque M ship; **— de carga** freighter

burbuja F bubble

burdo ADJ coarse

burgués ADJ bourgeois

burguesía F bourgeoisie, middle class

burla F ridicule, mockery; **hacer — a alguien** to mock someone

burlar VT to mock; **—se de** to scoff at, to make fun of

burlesco ADJ burlesque

burlón ADJ mocking

burocracia F bureaucracy

burócrata MF bureaucrat

burrez F stupidity

burro M (animal) donkey, ass; (persona) dunce; ADJ dense

bursátil ADJ **mercado —** stock market

bursitis F bursitis

burundés -esa ADJ & MF Burundian

Burundi M Burundi

bus M bus; **— en serie** serial bus

busca LOC ADV **en — de** in search of

buscar[30] VT (objetos perdidos) to seek, to look for, to search for; (datos, palabras) to look up; (provocar) to provoke; (la verdad) to seek after; (minerales) to prospect for; (talento) to scout for; **—se problemas** to invite trouble; **— y reemplazar** to search and replace; **tú te lo buscaste** you asked for it; **ir a —** to fetch; M SG **buscapersonas** beeper, pager

búsqueda F search; **— del tesoro** treasure hunt; **— hacia atrás** backward search; **— por palabra clave** keyword search

busto M bust

butaca F (en la casa) armchair; (en el teatro) seat

Bután M Bhutan

butanés -esa ADJ & MF Bhutanese

butano M butane

buzo M diver

buzón M mailbox; **— de sugerencias** suggestion box

bypass M bypass operation, coronary bypass

byte M byte

Cc

cabal ADJ (completo) complete; (exacto) exact; (honrado) upright; **estar uno en sus —es** to be in one's right mind

cabalgar[40] VI to ride horseback

caballa F mackerel

caballada F herd of horses

caballejo M nag

caballeresco ADJ chivalrous

caballería F (tropas) cavalry; (equino) equine; (condición de caballero) knighthood

caballeriza F stable

caballerizo M groom

caballero M (señor) gentleman; (hidalgo) knight; **— andante** knight errant; ADJ gentlemanly

caballerosidad F chivalry

caballeroso ADJ chivalrous, gentlemanly

caballete M (soporte de madera) sawhorse; (de la nariz) bridge; (de pintor) easel; (de tejado) ridge

caballo M (animal) horse; (en ajedrez) knight; (heroína) *fam* smack; **a —** on horseback; **— de carreras** racehorse; **— de batalla** hobbyhorse; **— de fuerza** horsepower; **— de Troya** Trojan horse

cabaña F (casucha) hovel; (casa de campo) cabin, cottage; (conjunto de ganado) livestock

cabaret M cabaret

cabecear VI (mover la cabeza) to nod; (dormirse) to nod off; (un barco) to bob, to pitch; VT (balón) to head

cabeceo M (de la cabeza) nodding; (de un barco) pitching

cabecera F (de cama) headboard; (de mesa) head

cabecilla MF ringleader

cabellera F head of hair

cabello M hair; **traído por los —s** far-fetched

caber[67] VI to fit; **there is no doubt; no cabe nadie más** there is no room for anybody else; **no — uno en sí** to be puffed up with pride; **no cabe en lo posible** it is absolutely impossible; **¿en qué cabeza cabe?** who would believe that?

cabestrillo M sling

cabestro M halter

cabeza F head; **— de chorlito** scatterbrain, airhead; **— de playa** beachhead; **— de puente** bridgehead; **— de turco** scapegoat, fall guy; **— de serie** seed; **— rapada** skinhead; **a la —** at the forefront; **caerse de —** to fall head first; **echarse de —** to plunge headlong; **ir a la —** to lead the way; **por —** each; **romperse la —** to rack one's brains; **la fama se le fue a la —** fame went to his head; **sentar —** to settle down; **tiene la — cuadrada** she's a square

cabezada F nod; **dar —s** to nod off

cabezal M magnetic head

cabezazo M (golpe) head butt; (jugada de fútbol) header

cabezón ADJ (de cabeza grande) big-headed;

(testarudo) pig-headed; (con mucho alcohol) strong

cabezudo ADJ (de cabeza grande) big-headed; (testarudo) pig-headed

cabida F capacity; **dar** — to include; **tener** — **en** to fit in

cabina F (de pasajeros) cabin; (de piloto) cockpit; (de camión) cab; (de teléfono, control) booth

cabizbajo ADJ crestfallen, downcast

cable M cable; — **coaxial** coaxial cable; —**s del ordenador / de la computadora** media

cableado M wiring

cablevisión F cable television

cabo M (parte extrema) end; (hilo) thread; (cuerda) rope; (saliente de la costa) cape; MF (rango militar) corporal; — **suelto** loose end; **al** — **de** at the end of; **atar** —**s** to put two and two together; **de** — **a rabo** from beginning to end; **llevar a** — to carry out

cabotaje M coastal trade

Cabo Verde M Cape Verde

caboverdiano -na ADJ & MF Cape Verdean

cabra F goat; — **montés** mountain goat; [loco] **como una** — completely crazy

cabrá, cabría ver caber

cabrearse VI to get mad

cabrestante M winch

cabrillas F PL whitecaps

cabrio M rafter

cabrío ADJ **macho** — he-goat

cabriola F caper

cabriolar VI to cavort

cabritilla F kid [leather]

cabrito M kid [goat]

cabrón M (macho de cabra) he-goat; (cornudo) cuckold; MF (cobarde) wimp

caca F poop; **hacer** — to poop

cacahuate M Méx peanut

cacahuete M Esp peanut

cacao M cocoa

cacarear VI to cackle, to squawk

cacareo M cackling, squawking

cacatúa F cockatoo

cacería F hunt; — **de brujas** witch hunt

cacerola F saucepan

cacha F (de navaja) handle; (nalga) thigh, butt; **hasta la** — completely

cachalote M sperm whale

cacharro M (vasija) earthen pot; (coche viejo) clunker, jalopy

cachaza F slowness

cachazudo ADJ slow

caché M (en informática) cache; (distinción) cachet; — **de memoria** memory cache

cachear VT to body-search, to frisk

cachet M artist's fee

cachetada F slap

cachete M cheek

cachiporra F blackjack

cachivaches M PL stuff, odds and ends

cacho M hunk

cachorro M (de oso, lobo, tigre, león) cub; (de perro) puppy

cacique M (de indios) chief, chieftain; MF (caudillo) political boss

cacofonía F cacophony

cacto/cactus M cactus

cada ADJ each; — **uno** each one; — **vez más** more and more; — **vez menos gente** fewer and fewer people; — **vez menos harina** less and less flour; — **vez peor** worse and worse; **doscientas pesetas** — **una** two hundred pesetas each/apiece

cadalso M gallows

cadáver M (para enterrar) corpse; (para disecar) cadaver

cadavérico ADJ ghastly

caddie, caddy MF caddie

cadena F (serie de piezas) chain; (de televisión) network; (cordillera) mountain range; — **alimenticia** food chain; — **de montaje** assembly line; — **perpetua** life sentence; —**s** shackles; **tirar la** — to flush

cadencia F cadence

cadera F hip

cadete M cadet

cadmio M cadmium

caducar[30] VI to lapse, to expire

caducidad F expiration

caduco ADJ (deciduo) deciduous; (decrépito) decrepit

caer[52] VI to fall; (desplomarse) to fall down; (colgar) to hang; (ir a parar) to end up; **al** — **la noche** at nightfall; — **en desgracia** to fall into disfavor, to fall out of favor; — **en desuso** to fall into disuse; — **en cama** to fall ill; — **en cuenta** to catch on; — **en ruina** to fall into disrepair; —**le bien/mal a uno** (una persona) to make a good/bad impression; (una comida) to agree with; —**le en suerte a uno** to fall to one's lot; — **tan bajo** to fall so low; **caiga quien caiga** let fall who may; **dejar** — to drop; **está al** — he's about to show up; —**se** (persona) to fall down; (computadora, ordenador) to crash; **se cayó el sistema** the system crashed

café M (bebida) coffee; (color) brown; (establecimiento) coffee shop, café

cafeína F caffeine

cafetal M coffee plantation

cafetera F coffeepot

cafetería F snack bar, cafeteria, diner

cafetero -ra MF coffee dealer; ADJ **industria cafetera** coffee industry

cafeto M coffee bush

caída F (acción de caer) fall, tumble, spill; (de presión arterial) drop; (de un ordenador) crash; (de una cortina) hang; (de precios) drop; — **libre** free fall; — **del sol** sunset; — **en picado** nosedive; —**s del sistema** system crashes

caído ADJ (orejas) floppy; (arco del pie) fallen; **los** —**s** the fallen

caiga, caigo ver caer

caimán M alligator

caja F box; — **chica** petty cash; — **de ahorros** savings bank; — **de bateo** batter's box; — **de cambios** transmission; — **de escalera** stairwell; — **de fusibles** fuse box; — **de herramientas** toolkit; — **de jubilaciones** pension fund; — **de música** music box; — **de seguridad** safe deposit box; — **de reloj** watchcase; — **fuerte** safe; — **negra** flight recorder; — **registradora** (aparato) cash register, till; (mostrador) checkout counter; — **tonta** idiot box; — **torácica** rib cage; **entrar en** — (comenzar) to get going; (establecerse) to settle down

cajero -ra MF cashier; (en un banco) teller; — **automático** ATM

cajetilla F pack [of cigarettes]

cajilla F pack [of cigarettes]

cajón M (para transportes) crate; (parte de un mueble) drawer; **eso es de** — that's a foregone conclusion

cajuela F *Méx* car trunk

cal F lime; **cerrar a** — **y canto** to close hermetically

calabacín M zucchini

calabaza F (grande y redonda) pumpkin; (pequeña y/o alargada) squash; (vaciada) gourd; **dar**—**s** to turn down

calabozo M dungeon

calado M draft

calamar M squid

calambre M cramp

calamidad F calamity

calamina F calamine

calandria F lark

calar VT (agujerear) to perforate; (empapar) to soak, to drench; — **a alguien** to see through someone; — **hondo** to resonate; —**se** to get drenched

calavera F skull; M libertine

calcar³⁰ VT (sobre papel) to trace; (imitar) to copy

calcetería F hosiery

calcetín M sock

calcinar VT to bake

calcio M calcium

calco M (acción de calcar) tracing; **es el** — **de su padre** he's the spitting image of his father

calcomanía F decal

calculador ADJ calculating

calculadora F calculator

calcular VT (computar) to calculate, to figure; (sopesar) to weigh; (prever) to reckon

cálculo M (cómputo) calculation; (aritmética) arithmetic; (integral, diferencial) calculus; — **biliar** gallstone; — **renal** kidney stone

caldear VT to warm up; — **los ánimos** to get everyone upset

caldera F (en una máquina de vapor) boiler; (recipiente con asas) kettle; (de calefacción) furnace

calderón M hold

caldo M broth, stock; — **de cultivo** culture medium

calefacción F heat, heating; — **central** central heating

calendario M calendar

caléndula F marigold

calentador M heater; — **de agua** water heater

calentamiento M warming; (en deportes) warm-up; — **global** global warming

calentar¹ VI/VT (poner caliente) to warm, to heat; —**se** (ponerse caliente, prepararse para un partido) to warm up, to heat up

calentura F fever

calesa F buggy

caletre M **no tener** — to have no brains

calibrador M caliper

calibrar VT to gauge, to calibrate

calibre M (de pistola, tubo) caliber; (de alambre) gauge; (calibrador) caliper

calicó M calico

calidad F quality; **baja** — low quality; **de** — of good quality; **de** — **inferior** substandard; **estoy aquí en** — **de representante** I'm here in my capacity as representative

cálido ADJ warm

caliente ADJ (agradable) warm; (excesivo) hot

calificación F (nota) grade, mark; (acción de asignar notas) grading; (comparación) rating; — **crediticia** credit rating; **le dieron la** — **de genio** they called him a genius

calificar³⁰ VT (juzgar la calidad) to rate, to adjudge; (asignar nota) to grade; —**se como** to be characterized as

calificativo ADJ qualifying; M label

caligrafía F (letra) penmanship; (arte) calligraphy

calina F haze

callado ADJ silent, quiet; **estarse** — to keep quiet

callar VT (no manifestar, no dejar decir) to quiet; VI (no hablar) to remain silent; (dejar de hablar) to go quiet; —**se la boca** to shut up, to pipe down

calle F (de ciudad) street; (golf) fairway; — **abajo** down the street; — **arriba** up the street; — **de sentido único** one-way street; **no pisar la** — to stay home

calleja F narrow street

callejear VI to walk the streets

callejero ADJ **perro** — stray dog; **caos** — chaos

in the streets

callejón M alley; — **sin salida** blind alley, dead end

callo M callus, corn

calloso ADJ callous

calma F calm; — **chicha** absolute calm; **mantener la —** (no enojarse) to keep one's temper; (no ponerse nervioso) to stay calm; **tomar las cosas con —** to take things easy

calmante ADJ & M sedative

calmar VT (nervios) to calm; (dolor) to sooth; (miedo) to allay, to quell; (sed) to quench; **—se** (una persona) to calm down; (una tormenta, la ira) to subside, to abate

calmo ADJ calm

calmoso ADJ easygoing

calor M (temperatura alta) heat; (temperatura templada) warmth; (actitud acogedora) warmth; **hace — hoy** it's hot today; **los —es** hot flashes; **tengo —** I'm hot

caloría F calorie

calumnia F calumny, slander

calumniar VT to slander, to malign

calumnioso ADJ slanderous

caluroso ADJ (día) hot; (recepción) warm

calva F bald spot

calvario mi vida es un — *fam* my life is hell

calvicie F baldness

calvo ADJ bald, baldheaded; **ni tanto ni tan —** *fam* it ain't necessarily so; **quedarse —** to go bald

calza F long sock

calzada F pavement

calzado M footwear

calzador M shoehorn

calzar[47] VT (poner zapatos) to shoe; (hacer zapatos para) to make shoes for; **— a la familia** to buy shoes for the family; **calzo 42** I take size 10; **—se** to put on shoes

calzones M PL (de mujer) panties; (de hombre) shorts

calzonazos M SG henpecked man

calzoncillos M PL underpants, briefs; **— largos** long johns

cama F bed; **— de agua** waterbed; **— doble** double bed; **— elástica** trampoline; **— individual** twin bed; **guardar —** to be confined to bed; **meterse en la — con** to sleep with

camada F litter

camafeo M cameo

camaleón M chameleon

cámara F (espacio) chamber; (de neumático) inner tube; (fotográfica) camera; **— de comercio** chamber of commerce; **— de diputados** lower house; **— de gas** gas chamber; **— digital** digital camera; **— de oxígeno** oxygen tent; **— frigorífica** cold-storage locker; **— legislativa**

legislature; **— hiperbárica** hyperbaric chamber; **en — lenta** in slow motion; MF (persona que maneja una cámara) camera operator

camarada MF comrade

camarero -ra M (restaurante) waiter, server; (coche cama) steward; F (restaurante) waitress, server; (coche cama) stewardess; (hotel) maid; MF (béisbol) second baseman

camarilla F clique

camarógrafo -fa M cameraman; F camerawoman

camarón M shrimp

camarote M cabin, stateroom

cambalache M (intercambio) fraudulent swap; (tienda) secondhand store

cambalachear VI/VT to swap fraudulently

cambiante ADJ (que cambia) changing; (propenso a cambiar) changeable; (temperamento) volatile

cambiar VI/VT to change; VT (una cosa por otra) to exchange, to swap, to trade; **— de marcha** to shift gears; **— de opinión/parecer** to change one's mind; **— de sitio** to move places

cambiario ADJ **sistema —** foreign exchange system

cambio M (acción de cambiar) change; (marcha) gear; (cotización) exchange rate; (de ferrocarril) railway switch; (béisbol) changeup; **— de velocidad** (en béisbol) change-up; **— de lado** (tenis) changeover; **— de divisas** foreign exchange; **— para peor** a turn for the worse; **— y fuera** over and out; **a — [de]** in return [for]; **en —** on the other hand

cambista MF money changer

Camboya F Cambodia

camboyano -na ADJ & MF Cambodian

camellear VT to push [drugs]

camello -lla MF (animal) camel; (vendedor de droga) pusher

camerino M dressing room

Camerún M Cameroon

camerunés -esa ADJ & MF Cameroonian

camilla F stretcher, litter

camillero -ra MF hospital orderly

caminante MF walker, wayfarer

caminar VI/VT to walk; (baloncesto) to travel

caminata F long walk; (por un lugar agreste) hike

camino M (carretera) road; (itinerario, dirección a seguir) way; **— de** on the way to; **— de mesa** table runner; **— de rosas** bed of roses; **abrirse —** to make way; **a medio —** halfway; **en — [a]** on the way [to]; **llevar por mal —** to lead astray; **mostrar el —** to lead the way; **ponerse en —** to set out; **señalar el —** to show the way

camión M (de cargas) truck; (para transporte de personas) *Méx* bus; — **de la basura** garbage truck; — **de mudanzas** moving van; — **de remolque** tow truck, wrecker; — **de reparto** delivery truck; — **volteador** dump truck

camionero -ra MF truck driver; *Méx* bus driver

camioneta F (furgoneta) van, minivan; (camioncito) pickup truck; (coche sin maletero) station wagon

camisa F shirt; — **de fuerza** straitjacket; **meterse en — de once varas** to get into a jam

camiseta F (exterior) T-shirt; (interior) undershirt

camisón M nightgown

camorrista ADJ rowdy

campamento M (de refugiados, exploradores) camp; (recreativo) campground

campana F bell; **tocar una —** to ring a bell

campanario M belfry, bell tower

campanilla F (campana pequeña) small bell; (flor) bluebell; (órgano en la boca) uvula

campanilleo M ringing

campánula F bellflower

campaña F campaign; — **publicitaria** advertising campaign; **hacer —** to campaign; **el ejército estaba de —** the army was on the front

campechano ADJ straightforward

campeón -ona MF champion

campeonato M championship; — **Mundial de Fútbol** Soccer World Cup

campero ADJ **hombre —** a man from the country

campesino -na MF peasant; ADJ **casa campesina** peasant house

campestre ADJ rural

camping M (lugar) campground; (actividad) camping

campiña F open country

campista MF camper

campo M (fuera de la ciudad) country, countryside; (para cultivos, deportes, ámbito del saber) field; (grupo en un conflicto) camp; — **abierto** range; MF —**corto** (béisbol) shortstop; — **de acción** field of action; — **de batalla** battlefield; — **de concentración** concentration camp; — **de golf** golf course; — **de juego** athletic field; — **de tiro** shooting range; — **libre** free rein; — **magnético** magnetic field; — **minado** minefield; — **petrolífero** oil field; — **visual** visual field; **a — traviesa** cross-country; —**santo** churchyard

campus M campus

camuflaje M camouflage

camuflar VT to camouflage

can M dog

cana F white hair; **echar una — al aire** to go out for a good time

Canadá M Canada

canadiense ADJ & MF Canadian

canal M (cauce artificial de agua) canal; (estrecho marítimo, banda de frecuencia) channel; (emisora) station; — **de parto** birth canal; — **radicular** root canal

canalé M ribbed fabric

canalizar[47] VT to channel

canalón M spout

canana F cartridge belt

canapé M (mueble) divan; (aperitivo) canape, starter

canario -ria M canary; ADJ of/from the Canary Islands; MF Canary Islander

canasta F basket (también en baloncesto)

canasto M hamper

cancelación F cancellation

cancelar VT (contrato, sello) to cancel; (deuda) to pay off; (evento) to call off

cáncer M cancer; — **de mama** breast cancer; — **de colon** colorectal cancer

cancerígeno ADJ carcinogen

canceroso -sa MF cancer patient; ADJ cancerous

cancha F (de baloncesto, tenis) court; (de fútbol) field; **¡abran —!** gangway! **falta —** there's no room

canciller MF (de Alemania, de universidades) chancellor; (de EEUU) secretary of state

canción F song; — **de cuna** lullaby

candado M padlock

candela F (vela) candle; (fuego) fire

candelabro M candelabrum

candelero M candlestick; **en el —** in the limelight

candente ADJ red-hot

candidato -ta MF candidate

candidatura F (hecho de ser candidato) candidacy; (conjunto de candidatos) ticket

candidez F innocence

cándido ADJ naive

candil M oil lamp

candilejas F PL footlights

candor M innocence

canela F (especia) cinnamon; (árbol) cinnamon tree

canesú M yoke of a shirt

cangrejo M crab

canguro M kangaroo; MF *Esp* baby-sitter

caníbal ADJ & MF cannibal

canica F toy marble

caniche M poodle; — **enano** toy poodle

canilla F (espinilla) shin; (pantorrilla) calf; (grifo) faucet

canino ADJ canine; **tener un hambre canina** to be ravenous; M canine [tooth]

canje M exchange

canjear VT (prisioneros, libros) to exchange; (un

cupón) to redeem

cano ADJ gray-haired

canoa F canoe

canon M (regla, modelo) canon; (canción) round

canónigo M canon

canoso ADJ gray-haired

cansado ADJ (fatigado) tired, weary; (fatigoso) wearing, tiring

cansancio M weariness

cansar VT (fatigar) to tire, to tire out; (aburrir) to bore; **—se** to get tired

cantante MF singer

cantar VI/VT (hacer música) to sing; VT (anunciar) to call out; (revelar secretos) to squeal; **— a tono** to sing on key; **—le a alguien las cuarenta** to give someone a piece of one's mind; **— victoria** to declare victory; **en menos que canta un gallo** before you can say Jack Robinson; M epic poem; **eso es otro —** that's another story

cántaro M pitcher; **llover a —s** to rain cats and dogs

cantera F quarry

cantero M RP flower bed

cántico M chant

cantidad F quantity, amount; (de dinero) amount, sum; **— a pagar** amount payable; **— debida** amount due; **— pagada** amount paid; **— de gente** a lot of people

cantimplora F canteen, water bottle

cantina F (lugar donde comer) mess hall, mess, canteen; (bar) tavern

cantinela F chant

cantinero -ra MF bartender

canto M (cosa cantada) song; (piedra) pebble; **— de cisne** swan song; **— llano** chant; **— rodado** rounded pebble; **de —** on edge

cantor -ora MF singer

canturrear VI to hum

canturreo M hum, humming

caña F (planta gramínea) reed; (de azúcar) cane; (cerveza) *Esp* beer; (vaso) *Esp* beer glass; **— de pescar** fishing pole; **dale —** floor it

cañada F (barranco) ravine; (arroyo) brook

cáñamo M hemp

cañaveral M reed patch

cañería F (en la calle) piping; (en la casa) plumbing

caño M (tubo) pipe; (grifo) spout; (de arma) barrel; **de doble —** double-barreled

cañón M (arma) cannon; (pieza hueca) barrel; (cañada profunda) canyon; (de pluma, bolígrafo) shaft

cañonero M gunboat

caoba F mahogany

caos M chaos

caótico ADJ chaotic

capa F (prenda) cape, cloak; (de pintura, animal) coat; (de tierra) layer; (de hielo) sheet; **— de** **ozono** ozone layer; **— freática** water table; **de — y espada** cloak and dagger

capacidad F capacity; **—es** aptitude, ability, capability; **— de almacenamiento de disco** disk capacity

capacitación F training; **— para empleados** in-service training

capacitar VT (entrenar) to train; (habilitar) to qualify

capar VT to castrate

caparazón M shell

capataz -za MF boss, overseer

capaz ADJ (habilidoso) capable, able; (apto) apt; (espacioso) spacious, roomy; (competente) competent

capear VT to ride out, to weather

capellán M chaplain

caperuza F pointed hood

capilar ADJ & M capillary

capilla F chapel; **estar en —** (castigado) to be in the doghouse; (en ascuas) to be on pins and needles

capital M (dinero) capital; (de préstamo) principal; **— de riesgo** venture capital; **— inicial** start-up funds; **el gran —** big business; F capital [city]; ADJ main

capitalino ADJ **atmósfera capitalina** capital city atmosphere

capitalismo M capitalism

capitalista MF capitalist; ADJ capitalistic

capitalización F capitalization

capitalizar[47] VT (aportar capital) to capitalize; (aprovechar) to capitalize on

capitán -ana MF captain

capitanear VT to captain

capitel M capital

capitolio M capitol

capitulación F (militar) capitulation, surrender; **capitulaciones matrimoniales** prenuptial agreement

capitular VI to capitulate

capítulo M chapter

capó M hood [of a car]

capo M mafia boss

capota F top [of a car]

capote M cloak; (de coche) *Méx* hood; **decir para su —** to say under one's breath

capricho M caprice, whim, notion

caprichoso ADJ (impredecible) capricious; (impulsivo) whimsical, fanciful; (malcriado) willful

cápsula F capsule

captación F (de agua) collection; (de clientes) attraction; (de inversiones, fondos) raising

captar VT (un concepto) to grasp; (atención, interés) to capture; (una emisión) to receive; (una indirecta) to get; **— la onda** to get the drift

captor -ora MF captor

captura F (acción de capturar) capture; (pesca capturada) catch; (fútbol americano) sack; — **de video/vídeo** video capture

capturar VT to capture; (pescado) to catch

capucha F (de cabeza) hood, cowl; (de lapicero) cap

capuchina F nasturtium

capuchino M cappuccino

capullo M (de insecto) cocoon; (de flor) bud

caqui M khaki

cara F (rostro) face; (de cubo) surface; (de papel, moneda) side; (morro) nerve; — **a** — face to face; — **o cruz** heads or tails; **dar la** — to face up to things; **de** — **al sur** facing south; **decir en la** — to tell to one's face; **de dos** —**s** two-sided; **la otra** — **de la moneda** the other side of the coin; **poner buena** — to put on a good face; **se le ve en la** — it's written all over his face; **tener** — **[dura]** to have a lot of nerve; **un ojo de la** — an arm and a leg; **volverle la** — **a** to snub

carabinero -ra MF (oficial de aduana) border patrol officer; (agente de policía) police officer; M (crustáceo) red prawn

caracol M (molusco) snail; (concha) snail shell; INTERJ ¡—**es!** *fam* darn!

carácter M (temperamento, signo) character; (rasgo) characteristic; (índole) kind

característica F characteristic, feature; (en informática) feature

característico ADJ characteristic

caracterización F (descripción) characterization, description; (retrato) portrayal

caracterizar[47] VT to characterize

caramba INTERJ darn! good grief! heck!

carámbano M icicle

carambola F carom; **por** — indirectly

caramelo M (azúcar fundido) caramel; (dulce pequeño) bonbon

caramillo M reed pipe

carátula F (máscara) mask; (portada) title page

caravana F (en el desierto, convoy) caravan; (remolque) trailer

caray INTERJ *fam* shoot! darn!

carbohidrato M carbohydrate

carbón M (sustancia) coal; (pedazo) piece of coal; — **de leña** charcoal

carboncillo M charcoal drawing

carbonera F coal bin

carbono M carbon

carburador M carburetor

carburante M fuel

carca ADJ old-fashioned; MF *fam* fossil, old fogey

carcaj M quiver

carcajada F burst of laughter, guffaw

carcamal M *fam* fossil, old fogey

cárcel F jail, prison

carcelero -ra MF jailer

carcinógeno M carcinogen

carcinoma M carcinoma; — **de célula basal** basal cell carcinoma

carcomido ADJ worm-eaten

carda F card, comb

cardán M universal joint

cardar VT (lana) to card, to comb; (pelo) to rat, to tease

cardenal M (pájaro, prelado) cardinal; (moretón) bruise

cardíaco -ca ADJ cardiac; MF heart patient

cardinal ADJ cardinal

cardioangiograma M cardioangiogram

cardiograma M cardiogram

cardiología F cardiology

cardiólogo -ga MF cardiologist

cardiopulmonar ADJ cardiopulmonary

cardiovascular ADJ cardiovascular

cardo M thistle

cardumen M school of fish

carear VT to bring face to face; —**se** to meet face to face

carecer[35] VI — **de** to lack

carencia F (falta) lack; (deficiencia alimenticia) deficiency

carenciado ADJ disadvantaged

carente ADJ lacking; — **de** lacking in

carero ADJ expensive

carestía F (escasez) scarcity; (costo alto) high cost

careta F mask

carezca, carezco *ver* carecer

carga F (cosa cargada) load, freight; (de la prueba, impuesto) burden; (hipoteca) lien; (de encendedor) refill; (de explosivo, electricidad) charge; (de programas) upload; — **de municiones** round of ammunition; — **útil** payload; **volver a la** — to insist

cargado ADJ (bebida) stiff; (pausa) pregnant; (cartucho) live; — **de deudas** deep in debt; — **de espaldas** stooping

cargador M (de batería) charger; (de arma de fuego) clip, magazine

cargamento M cargo, load, shipment

cargar[40] VT (cargamentos, dados, arma, programa de ordenador) to load; (batería a una cuenta, en baloncesto) to charge; (de obligaciones) to burden with; (a un niño) to carry; (a un estudiante) *Esp* to flunk; (molestar) to bother; — **a alguien de responsabilidades** to saddle someone with responsibilities; — **al hombro** to shoulder; — **de combustible** to fuel; — **un programa** to upload; VI to charge; — **con la culpa** to be saddled with blame; — **sobre** to charge, to attack

cargo M (función en una empresa) position; (en una factura, a una cuenta) charge; (acusación) count, charge; — **de conciencia** guilt feelings; **—s atrasados** back charges; **— de tramitación** handling charges; **a mi —** under my charge; **hacerse — de** (responsabilizarse de) to take charge of; (ser consciente de) to understand; **investir de un —** to induct into office; **los niños están a — de la maestra** the children are under the care of the teacher; **la maestra está a[l] — de los niños** the teacher is in charge of the children

cargoso ADJ fussy

carguero ADJ freight-carrying

cariado ADJ decayed

caribeño ADJ Caribbean

caricatura F (dibujo) caricature; (con texto) cartoon

caricaturista MF cartoonist

caricaturizar[47] VT to caricature

caricia F caress

caridad F charity

caries F INV cavity, tooth decay

carillón M chimes

cariño M (amor) affection, fondness; (apodo) honey; **darle —s a alguien** to send love to someone; **ella y el perro se hacen —s** she and the dog nuzzle each other; **hacer algo con —** to do something with great care; **tenerle — a alguien** to be fond of someone

cariñoso ADJ affectionate, loving

carisma M charisma

caritativo ADJ charitable

cariz M complexion; **no me gusta el — que está tomando la situación** I don't like the look of this

carmesí ADJ INV & M crimson

carmín M (carmesí) crimson; (lápiz de labios) lipstick

carnal ADJ carnal

carnaval M carnival

carne F (para comer) meat; (de animal vivo, de persona, de tomate) flesh; **— de cañón** cannon fodder; **— de cerdo** pork; **— de cordero** mutton; **— de gallina** (comida) chicken; (reacción de la piel) goose bumps; **— de res** beef; **— de venado** venison; **— y hueso** flesh and blood; **como — y uña** fam thick as thieves; **en — viva** raw; **metido en —s** overweight

carnear VT to butcher

carnero M ram

carnet/carné M **— de conducir** driver's license; **— de identidad** ID

carnicería F (tienda) butcher's shop; (matanza) carnage, bloodbath

carnicero -ra MF butcher; ADJ (carnívoro) carnivorous; (cruel) cruel

carnívoro ADJ carnivorous

carnoso ADJ fleshy

caro ADJ expensive, high-priced, fam pricey; ADV

at a high price

carona F saddle pad

carótida F carotid artery

carozo M RP pit, stone

carpa F (pez) carp; (tienda) tent

carpeta F (para documentos, también de ordenador) folder; (cartera) portfolio

carpintería F (oficio) carpentry; (taller) carpenter's shop

carpintero -ra MF carpenter

carraspear VI to clear one's throat

carraspera F scratchy throat

carrera F (conjunto de estudios) major; (trayectoria profesional) career; (competición) race; (en las medias) run; (recorrido corto) run, dash; (en fútbol americano, béisbol) run; (de pistón) stroke; **— a pie** footrace; **— de caballos** horse race; **— de relevos** relay race; **a la —** running; **hacer —** to succeed in a profession; **tomar —** to get a running start; **— impulsada** (en béisbol) run batted in; **— limpia** (en béisbol) earned run; **— sucia** (en béisbol) unearned run

carreta F wagon

carrete M (de película) reel; (de hilo) bobbin; (de alambre) spool

carretera F highway; **— de circunvalación** bypass; **— de peaje** toll road

carretero ADJ **sistema —** highway system

carretilla F (de una rueda) wheelbarrow; (de más de una rueda) dolly; **de —** by memory

carretón M large wagon

carril M (de ferrocarril) rail; (de calle) lane

carrillo M cheek, jowl; **a dos/cuatro —s** voraciously

carrillón M chimes

carrizo M reed

carro M (automóvil) car; (vehículo de dos ruedas, de golf) cart; (de máquina de escribir) roll; **— alegórico** parade float; **— blindado** armored car; **— de guerra** chariot; **poner el — delante de los bueyes** to put the cart before the horse; **subirse al —** to get on the bandwagon

carrocería F auto body

carroña F carrion

carroza F (de caballos) coach; (de desfile) parade float; (fúnebre) hearse

carruaje M carriage, coach

carta F (misiva) letter; (naipe) card; (de restaurante) menu; (constitución) charter; (mapa) chart; **— blanca** freehand; **— con anexos** cover letter; **— de agradecimiento** thank-you letter; **— de remisión** cover letter; **— de renuncia** resignation letter; **a la —** à la carte; **echarle las —s a alguien** to do a card-reading for someone; **tomar —s en la situación** to take charge of a situation

cartearse VI to correspond

cartel M poster, placard; **en** — showing; **— de la droga** drug cartel

cartelera F (de periódico) entertainment section; (publicitaria) billboard; (tablón para anuncios) bulletin board

cárter M oil pan

cartera F (para dinero) wallet, billfold; (para papeles) briefcase; (escolar) satchel; (bolsa) handbag; (de valores) portfolio

carterista MF pickpocket

cartero -ra MF letter carrier; M mailman, postman

cartílago M cartilage

cartilla F (para aprender a leer) reader; (de información) booklet; **— de racionamiento** ration book; **— de examen de vista** eye chart

cartografiar[28] VT to chart

cartón M cardboard, pasteboard; **— de cigarrillos** carton of cigarettes

cartuchera F cartridge belt

cartucho M (de pistola) cartridge, shell; (de monedas) roll; (de dinamita) stick; **— de fogueo** blank cartridge; **— de tinta / tóner** toner cartridge; **quemar el último** — to exhaust one's resources

cartulina F thin cardboard

casa F (edificio) house; (hogar) home; (negocio) business firm; **— de ancianos** old folks' home; **— de citas** cheap motel for rendezvous; **— de empeños** pawnshop; **— de la moneda** mint; **— de muñecas** dollhouse; **— de pompas fúnebres** funeral home; **— de reposo** rest home; **— de rehabilitación** halfway house; **— de subastas** auction house; **— embrujada** haunted house; **— rodante** house trailer; **— solariega** manor house; **de — en —** from house to house; **en —** at home; **entró como Perico por su** — he made himself right at home; **estás en tu** — make yourself at home; **ir a** — to go home; **la — paga** on the house; **poner una** — to set up a household; **quedarse en** — to stay home; **tirar la — por la ventana** to live it up

casaca F riding jacket

casadero ADJ marriageable

casado ADJ married

casamentero -ra MF matchmaker

casamiento M wedding, marriage ceremony

casar VT to marry off; **—se** to get married, to wed; **—se con** to get married to; **no —se con nadie** to remain independent

cascabel M (campanita) jingle bell; (de víbora) rattle; **ser un** — to be lively; **ponerle el — al gato** to stick one's neck out

cascada F cascade, waterfall

cascajo M old wreck

cascar[30] VT (quebrar) to crack; (dar bofetadas) to slap around; **—se** to crack open; M SG

cascanueces nutcracker; MF SG

cascarrabias crab, grouch; ADJ INV grouchy

cáscara F (de huevo, fruto seco) shell; (de granos, arvejas) husk; (de fruto seco) hull; (de fruta) rind; (de naranja, manzana) peel

casco M (de ciclista, militar) helmet; (de obrero) hard hat; (de barco) hull; (de naranja) shell; (uña del pie de caballería) hoof; **— urbano** built-up area

cascote M rubble

caserío M (aldea) hamlet; (casa) *Esp* farmhouse

casero -ra ADJ (doméstico) domestic; (hecho en casa) homemade; MF (cuidador) caretaker; M (propietario) landlord; F landlady

caseta F (en un mercado) booth, stall; (de guardia) guardhouse; (de perro) doghouse

casete MF cassette

casi ADV almost, nearly; **— diez mil** almost/nearly ten thousand; **— lo hago** I almost did it; **— siempre** almost always; **— nadie** hardly anyone; **— nunca** hardly ever

casilla F (en el tablero de ajedrez) square; (en una tabla) box; (en un casillero) pigeonhole, cubbyhole; **— de perro** doghouse; **sacarle a alguien de sus —s** to drive someone up the wall

casino M (club) men's club; (lugar de apuestas) casino

caso M case; **— de fuerza mayor** act of God; **— perdido** (persona incapacitada) basket case; (persona incorregible) lost cause; **en — de** in the event of; **en — de que** in case that; **el — es que** the deal is that; **en todo** — in any case, at any rate; **en último** — as a last resort; **eso no viene al** — that is beside the point; **hacer — [de]** to pay attention [to]; **hacer — omiso de** to disregard; **no hay** — there's no point; **pongamos por** — let's suppose that; **venir al** — to come to the point

caspa F dandruff

casquillo M (de bala) case; (de lámpara) socket

cassette MF cassette

casta F caste

castaña F chestnut; **— de cajú** cashew

castañetear VI to chatter; **— con los dedos** to snap one's fingers

castañeteo M (de dientes) chattering; (de dedos) snapping

castaño M (árbol) chestnut tree; (color, madera) chestnut; ADJ chestnut-colored, brown

castañuela F castanet

castellano ADJ & MF Castilian; M (lengua) Castilian

castidad F chastity

castigar[40] VT to chastise, to punish

castigo M chastisement, punishment; **¡qué —!**

what a nuisance!

Castilla F Castile

castillo M castle; **— de arena** sandcastle; **—s en el aire** *fam* pie in the sky

casting M casting

castizo ADJ traditional

casto ADJ chaste

castor M beaver

castrar VT (a un hombre, animal) to castrate; (a una mascota) to neuter, to fix; (a mascotas hembras) to spay

casual ADJ chance, accidental

casualidad F chance, coincidence; **da la — que** it so happens that; **oír por —** to overhear; **por —** by chance

casucha F shack

cata F **— de vinos** wine-tasting

catalán-ana ADJ (del catalán) Catalan; (de Cataluña) Catalonian; MF Catalan; M (lengua) Catalan

catalejo M spyglass

catalizador M catalyst

catalogar[40] VT to catalog/catalogue

catálogo M catalog, catalogue

Cataluña F Catalonia

catar VT to taste

catarata F (cascada) cataract, waterfall; (de los ojos) cataract

catarí ADJ & MF Qatari

catarro M cold

catástrofe F catastrophe

catatonia F catatonia

catecismo M catechism

cátedra F (puesto de profesor) chair, professorship; (enseñanza) teaching; (división académica) department; **sentar —** to hold forth, to pontificate

catedral F cathedral

catedrático -ca MF [full] professor

categoría F category; **de —** important; **de — mundial** world-class; **de poca —** third-rate

caterpillar M caterpillar

catéter M catheter

cateterización F catheterization

cateterizar VT to catheterize

cátodo M cathode

catolicismo M Catholicism

católico -ca ADJ Catholic; MF Catholic

catorce NUM fourteen

catre M cot

cátsup M catsup, ketchup

cauce M channel; **— de río** riverbed

cauchero -ra MF rubber gatherer; ADJ **industria cauchera** rubber industry

caucho M rubber; **— sintético** synthetic rubber

caución F security payment

caudal M (de bienes) wealth; (de agua) volume of water

caudaloso ADJ mighty

caudillo M leader

causa F (motivo) cause; (proceso) case; **— noble** worthy cause; **— perdida** lost cause; **a — de** on account of, because of; **con conocimiento de —** wittingly; **hacer — común** to work together

causante ADJ causing; MF instigator

causar VT to cause; **— problemas** to make trouble

cáustico ADJ caustic

cautela F caution

cautelar ADJ preventive

cauteloso ADJ cautious, wary

cauterizar[47] VT to cauterize

cautivar VT (capturar) to capture; (atraer) to captivate

cautiverio M captivity

cautivo -va MF captive

cauto ADJ cautious, wary

cava F (acción de cavar) digging; (sótano) cellar; (vino) cava

cavar VT to dig

caverna F cavern, cave

cavidad F cavity

cavilar VI to muse

cayado M shepherd's crook, staff

cayendo, cayera, cayese, cayeron *ver* caer

cayo M key

caza F (acción de cazar) hunt, hunting; (conjunto de animales) wild game; **— mayor** big game; **— menor** small game; **andar a la — de** to hunt for; **dar — a** to hunt down; M (avión) fighter

cazador -ora ADJ hunting; MF hunter; F Windbreaker™

cazar[47] VI/VT (buscar presas) to hunt; (matar presas) to shoot, to bag; (atrapar presas) to trap; MF SG **cazatalentos** talent scout, headhunter; M **cazatorpedero** destroyer, torpedo boat

cazo M (cacerola) pan; (cucharón) ladle, dipper

cazoleta F pipe bowl

cazuela F (recipiente) casserole; (cazo) pan

CD M CD; **— ROM** CD-ROM

cebada F barley

cebador M pump primer

cebar VT (un animal) to fatten; (bombas) to prime; (anzuelos) to bait; **—se** to vent one's anger

cebo M (para peces) bait, lure; (para animales) feed

cebolla F onion

cebollar M onion patch

cebollino M scallion

cebra F (animal) zebra; (paso) crosswalk

cecear VI to lisp

ceceo M lisp

cecina F jerky

cedazo M sieve

ceder VT (propiedad) to cede, to assign; (un sitio) to yield, to give up; VI (el frío) to diminish; (la resistencia) to give way

cedro M cedar

cédula F document; **— de identidad** identification card

céfiro M zephyr

cegar[41] VT to blind

ceguera F blindness; **— cromática** color blindness

ceja F (sobre el ojo) eyebrow; (en una encuadernación) tab; **quemarse las —s** to cram for an exam; **cejijunto** with thick eyebrows

cejar VI to back down

celada F ambush

celador-ora MF (en una escuela) school monitor; (en un barrio) security officer

celar VT to guard

celda F cell

celebración F (fiesta) celebration; (acto solemne) performance

celebrar VT (una fiesta) to celebrate; (una reunión) to hold; (un rito) to perform

célebre ADJ famous, noted

celebridad F celebrity

celeste ADJ (relativo al firmamento) celestial; (del color del cielo) azure, light blue

celestial ADJ celestial, heavenly

célibe ADJ celibate; MF unmarried person

cellisca F sleet; **caer —** to sleet

celo M (diligencia) zeal; (excitación sexual) heat; **estar en —** to be in heat; **—s** jealousy; **tener —s** to be jealous

celofán M cellophane

celosía F window lattice

celoso ADJ (que tiene celos) jealous; (diligente) zealous

célula F cell; **— adiposa** fat cell; **— estaminal embrional** stem cell

celular ADJ cellular; M mobile phone

celulitis F cellulite

celuloide M celluloid

celulosa F cellulose

cementar VT to cement

cementerio M cemetery, graveyard

cemento M cement; **— armado** reinforced concrete

cena F supper, dinner

cenagal M quagmire, swamp

cenagoso ADJ marshy, swampy

cenar VI to eat supper, to eat dinner; **vamos a — pescado** we're having fish for dinner

cencerro M cowbell

cenicero M ashtray

ceniciento ADJ ashen

cenit M zenith

cenizas F PL ashes, cinders

censar VI/VT to take a census [of]

censo M census

censor-ora MF censor; **— de cuentas** auditor

censura F (reprobación) censure; (control) censorship

censurador ADJ censuring

censurar VT (criticar) to censure; (examinar) to censor

centavo M cent

centella F sparkle; **pasar como una —** to go by in a flash

centelleante ADJ sparkling

centellear VI to sparkle, to scintillate

centelleo M sparkle

centenar M group of a hundred; **—es** hundreds

centenario M centennial; ADJ centenarian

centeno M rye

centésimo ADJ & M hundredth

centígrado ADJ centigrade

centímetro M centimeter

céntimo M cent

centinela MF sentry, sentinel

centrado ADJ (un tablón) true; (un cuadro) centered; (una persona) focused; M truing

central ADJ central; F plant; **— de teléfonos** telephone exchange; **— eléctrica** power plant; **— lechera** milk processing plant; **— nuclear** nuclear power plant

centralita F switchboard

centralizar[47] VT to centralize; **—se** to become centralized

centrar VT to center; **—se** to focus, to be focused

céntrico ADJ central

centrífugo ADJ centrifugal

centrípeto ADJ centripetal

centro M center (también de baloncesto); (de ciudad) downtown; **— comercial** shopping center; **— de gravedad** center of gravity; **— de mesa** centerpiece; MF **—campista** (fútbol) midfield player

Centroamérica F Central America

centroamericano-na M Central American

ceñido ADJ tight

ceñir[11] VT (rodear) to gird; (abrazar) to encircle; **— la corona** to be crowned; VI (estar apretado) to be tight; **—se a** (limitarse) to limit oneself to; (arrimarse) to get close to

ceño M **fruncir el —** to frown, to scowl

cepa F (de árbol) stump; (de viña) stock; (de bacteria) strain; **de pura —** of good stock

cepillar VT (dientes, pelo) to brush; (madera) to plane, to shave

cepillo M (para pelo, dientes) brush; (para madera) carpenter's plane; **— de dientes** toothbrush

cepo M (para cazar) trap; (para inmovilizar coches) boot

cera F wax; **— de oídos** earwax; **— para muebles** polish

cerámica F (arte) ceramics; (conjunto de

artículos) pottery, earthenware
cerámico ADJ ceramic
cerbatana F blowpipe
cerca ADV near, nearby, close; — **de** near, close to; **de** — close up; F fence
cercado M (terreno cercado) enclosure; (cerca) fence
cercanía F proximity, nearness, closeness
cercano ADJ (lugar) near, nearby; (pariente) close; — **Oriente** Near East
cercar[30] VT (rodear con una cerca) to fence, to enclose; (sitiar) to besiege
cercenar VT (cortar) to chop off; (reducir) to curtail, to encroach upon
cerciorarse VI — **[de]** to make sure [of]
cerco M (sitio) siege; (cerca) fence
cerdo -da M (animal, persona sucia) hog, pig; (carne) pork; F (puerca) sow; (de cepillo) bristle
cerdoso ADJ bristly
cereal M cereal; —**es** breakfast cereal; **cultivo** — cereal crop
cerebral ADJ cerebral
cerebro M (órgano, genio) brain; (organizador de un plan) mastermind; **lavarle el** — **a** to brainwash
ceremonia F ceremony
ceremonial ADJ & M ceremonial
ceremonioso ADJ ceremonious
cereza F cherry
cerezo M cherry tree
cerilla F match
cerner[2] VT to sift; —**se** (un ave) to hover; (un desastre) to loom
cernícalo M kestrel
cero M (cifra) zero; (en deportes) nothing, goose egg, zip; (en tenis) love; — **absoluto** absolute zero; **partir de** — to start from scratch; **ser un** — **a la izquierda** to be a nobody
cerrado ADJ (no abierto) closed; (tonto) dense; (poco comunicativo) reserved; (intransigente) closed-minded; (anguloso) sharp; M enclosure
cerrador -ora MF closer
cerradura F lock; — **de combinación** combination lock
cerrajería F locksmith's shop
cerrajero -ra MF locksmith
cerrar[1] VT (la puerta, un cajón) to close, to shut; (un trato) to close, to clinch; (un terreno) to enclose; (el gas, un grifo) to turn off; (una fábrica) to shut down, to close; — **filas** to close ranks; — **el paso** to block passage; VI to close; —**se** (una flor, una tienda) to close; (un plazo) to end; —**se el cielo** to become overcast
cerrazón F (de la mente) closed-mindedness; (del cielo) stormy skies

cerro M hill
cerrojo M bolt
certamen M contest; — **de belleza** beauty contest
certero ADJ sure
certeza F certainty
certidumbre F certainty
certificación F certification
certificado ADJ certified; M certificate; — **de nacimiento** birth certificate
certificar[30] VT (la autenticidad) to certify; (una carta) to register
cervatillo M fawn
cervecera F brewery
cervecería F bar
cerveza F beer; — **de barril** draft beer
cervical ADJ cervical
cérvix M cervix
cerviz F cervix
cesar VI to cease; — **de trabajar** to stop working; — **en un cargo** to resign from a position; — **a** to dismiss
cesárea F cesarean [section]
cese M cessation; — **el fuego** ceasefire; — **de actividades** shutdown
cesión F (de propiedad) assignment; (de derechos) waiver
césped M (ante una casa) lawn; (hierba, también para tenis) grass
cesta F basket
cestería F basketry
cesto M (cesta) basket; (para ropa) hamper
cetrino ADJ olive-colored
chabacano ADJ (modales) crude; (gustos) tacky; M *Méx* apricot
chacal M jackal
chacha F servant girl
cháchara F small talk
chacota F joke; **tomarse algo a la** — to take lightly
chacra F (establecimiento agrícola) small farm; (terreno) small plot
Chad M Chad
chadiano -na ADJ & MF Chadian
chal M shawl, wrap
chala F *Am* husk; **quitar la** — to husk
chalán M horse trader
chalé M cottage
chaleco M waistcoat, vest; — **antibalas** bulletproof vest; — **de fuerza** straitjacket; — **salvavidas** life jacket
chalupa F small canoe; *Méx* tortilla with sauce
chamaco -ca M *Méx* boy; F *Méx* girl
chamarra F sheepskin jacket
chambergo M wide-brimmed hat
chambón ADJ clumsy
champán/champaña M champagne
champiñón M mushroom
champú M shampoo

chamuscadura F scorch

chamuscar[30] VT to scorch, to singe; **—se** to get scorched, to get singed

chamusquina F scorching, singeing

chance MF chance

chancearse VI **— de** to make fun of

chancho M hog

chanchullo M *fam* monkey business

chancleta F thong, flipflop; **tirar la —** to kick up one's heels

chanclo M galosh, overshoe; **—s** rubbers

chándal M sweatsuit

chantaje M blackmail

chantajear VT to blackmail

chanza F jest

chao INTERJ bye-bye

chapa F (de metal) sheet metal; (de policía) badge; (de botella) bottle top; (de madera) veneer; **— en la puerta** shingle on the door; **hacerle — y pintura a un coche** to fix the bodywork and paint of a car

chapado ADJ **— a la antigua** old-fashioned

chapalear VI to splash

chapar VT to plate

chaparral M dry rangeland, chaparral

chaparro M scrub oak; ADJ *Méx* short

chaparrón M cloudburst

chaperón -ona MF chaperon[e]; **ir de —** to chaperon[e]

chapitel M spire, steeple

chapotear VI to splash

chapoteo M splash, splashing

chapucear VT to botch, to bungle

chapucería F (trabajo, obra) botched job; (cualidad) sloppiness

chapucero ADJ shoddy, slipshod

chapurrear VT to speak a language poorly

chapuz M dive

chapuza F botched job

chapuzar[47] VI to dive

chaqueta F jacket; **— de sport** sport jacket

charada F charades

charca F pond

charco M puddle, pool; **cruzar el —** to cross the ocean

charcutería F (tienda) delicatessen; (industria) sausage-making

charla F chat, talk

charlar VI to chat, to gab

charlatán -ana ADJ talkative; MF (parlanchín) chatterbox, windbag; (curandero) charlatan, quack

charlotear VI to chatter, to jabber

charloteo M chatter, jabber

charol M (barniz) varnish; (cuero barnizado) patent leather

charolar VT to varnish

charqui M beef jerky

charro ADJ flashy, tawdry

chárter M charter flight

chascar VT (los nudillos, un hueso) to crack; (los labios) to smack; (la lengua) to click

chascarrillo M funny anecdote

chasco M (broma) prank, practical joke; (decepción) dud; **llevarse un —** to be disappointed

chasis M frame, chassis

chasquear VT (decepcionar) to disappoint; (una cerradura, la lengua) to click; (un látigo) to crack; (los labios) to smack; (los dedos) to snap; **—se** to be disappointed

chasquido M (de látigo, madera, articulaciones) crack; (de labios) smack; (de la lengua, una cerradura) click; (de los dedos) snap

chata F bedpan

chatarra F scrap iron

chatarrería F junkyard

chatear VI to chat

chato ADJ (nariz) snub-nosed; (zapatos, pecho) flat; **— como una tabla** as flat as a pancake

chaucha F green bean

chaval -la M *Esp* boy; F *Esp* girl

chaveta F cotter pin; **perder la —** *fam* to go bonkers

che INTERJ *RP* say! hey!

checo -ca ADJ & MF Czech

chef MF chef

cheque M check; **— de viajero** traveler's check; **— de caja** bank check; **— sin fondos** bad check, worthless check

chequear VT to check

checar VT to check

chequera F checkbook

chic ADJ INV & M chic

chicha F (bebida alcohólica) *Am* corn liquor; (carne) *Esp fam* meat; **de — y nabo** two-bit; **ni — ni limonada** neither fish nor fowl

chicharra F (insecto) cicada; (timbre) buzzer

chichón M bump, lump, knot

chicle M chewing gum; **— de globo** bubblegum

chico -ca ADJ small, little; M boy; F girl; **mis —s** my kids

chicote M *Am* whip

chicotear VT *Am* to whip

chicoteo M *Am* whipping

chiflado ADJ *fam* nuts, cuckoo, loony; MF (persona loca) *fam* basket case, loon

chifladura F craziness

chiflar VI (silbar) to whistle; VT (volver loco) to drive crazy; **—se** to go crazy

chiflido M whistle

chifón M chiffon

chile M chile

Chile M Chile

chileno -na ADJ & MF Chilean

chillar VI (persona) to shriek; (puerta, ratón) to squeak; (cerdo) to squeal

chillido M (de persona) shriek; (de puerta,

ratón) squeak; (de cerdo) squeal

chillón ADJ (sonido) shrill; (color) loud, gaudy, flashy

chimenea F (salida de humo) chimney; (hogar) fireplace; (de volcán, baño, mina) vent; (de fábrica) smokestack

chimpancé M chimpanzee

china F (porcelana) china; (piedra) pebble

China F China

chinche F (insecto) bedbug; (chincheta) thumbtack; MF (persona molesta) pain

chinchilla F chinchilla

chinchorro M rowboat

chino -na ADJ Chinese; M (lengua) Chinese; MF Chinese; **vi a un chino** I saw a Chinese person; **los chinos no están de acuerdo** the Chinese don't agree; **eso es** — that's Greek to me

chip M (de ordenador, en golf) chip; (de papa/patata) potato chip; — **de silicio** silicon chip

Chipre M Cyprus

chipriota ADJ & MF Cypriot[e]

chiquilín -ina M little boy; F little girl

chiquito ADJ tiny, wee

chiripa F stroke of good luck; **por/de** — by a fluke

chirivía F parsnip

chirona F jail

chirriante ADJ squeaky

chirriar[28] VI (puerta, freno) to squeak; (ave, freno) to screech

chirrido M (de puerta, freno) squeak; (de ave, freno) screech

chisgarabís M pipsqueak

chisguete M squirt

chisme M (rumor) gossip, piece of gossip; (objeto) *fam* gizmo, thingamajig

chismear VI to gossip

chismoso -sa ADJ gossipy; MF gossip

chispa F (partícula incandescente) spark; (ingenio) wit; **echar** —**s** to be furious; **pasar echando** —**s** to whiz by

chispeante ADJ (que echa chispas) sparkling; (ingenioso) witty

chispear VI (echar chispas) to spark; (lloviznar) to sprinkle

chisporrotear VI (fuego) to sputter; (cigarrillo) to fizzle; (carne) to sizzle

chisporroteo M (de fuego) sputter; (de carne) sizzle

chiste M (verbal) joke; (visual) cartoon; (ocurrencia) wisecrack; — **verde** dirty joke; **no le veo el** — I don't see the humor in it

chistera F top hat

chistoso -sa ADJ funny, amusing, humorous

chivar VI/VT to snitch [on], to rat [on]

chivatar VI/VT to squeal [on], to snitch [on]

chivato -ta MF (delator) informer, snitch, stool pigeon; (chivito) kid

chivo M kid; — **expiatorio** scapegoat; **estar como un** — to be crazy as a loon

chocante ADJ shocking, jarring

chocar[30] VI (golpearse) to bump, to collide; (antagonizar) to clash; VT (sorprender) to shock; (destrozar) to wreck; — **los cinco** to shake hands

chocarrería F coarseness

chochear VI to be in one's dotage

chochera F senility, dotage

chochez F senility, dotage

chocho ADJ senile; **estar** — to be in one's dotage; **estar** — **con** to dote on

choclo M ear of corn

chocolate M (planta, dulce) chocolate; (bebida) cocoa, drinking chocolate

chocolatera F chocolate pot

chocolatina F chocolate bar

chófer, chofer MF chauffeur, driver

cholo -la MF (mestizo) person of mixed race; (indio) Europeanized Indian

chopo M poplar

choque M (de objetos móviles) collision, bump, crash; (eléctrico, emocional, cultural) shock; — **insulínico** insulin shock

chorizo M sausage

chorlito M plover

chorrear VI/VT (poco) to drip; (mucho) to gush

chorro M spurt, jet; **a** —**s** in buckets

chotearse VI — **de** to make fun of

choteo M mocking

chovinismo M chauvinism

choza F hut, shack, hovel

chubasco M squall, shower

chuchería F trinket, knickknack

chueco ADJ *Am* crooked

chuleta F (papel para copiar) cheat sheet; (golf) divot; — **de cerdo** pork chop; — **de ternera** veal cutlet

chulo -la M (dandi) dandy, dude; (bravucón) tough guy; MF working-class resident of Madrid; ADJ (fanfarrón) boastful; (bonito) cute

chupada F (de cigarro) puff; (de bebida) sip

chupar VI/VT (succionar) to suck; (fumar) to puff [on]; VT (absorber) to absorb; (vivir a costa de) to sponge off; **chúpate esa** put that in your pipe and smoke it; M SG **chupasangre** leech

chupete M pacifier

chupetín M *RP* lollipop, sucker

churrasco M *Am* barbecued steak

churro M fritter

chusma F rabble, riffraff

chut M hard shot

chutar VI (drogas) to shoot up; VT (un balón) to shoot; **ir a — la bola** to kick the ball hard

chute M narcotic fix

chuzo M watchman's pike

CIA F CIA

cianotipo M blueprint
cianuro M cyanide
cibercafé M cybercafe
ciberespacio M cyberspace
cibernética F cybernetics
ciberpunk MF cyberpunk
cicatero ADJ stingy
cicatriz F scar
cicatrizar VI (formar cicatriz) to form a scar; (curarse) to heal up
cíclico ADJ cyclical
ciclista MF bicycle rider, cyclist, biker
ciclo M cycle; **—motor** moped; **— vital** life cycle; **— de auditoría** audit cycle; **— de facturación** billing cycle; **— presupuestario** budget cycle
ciclón M cyclone
ciclotrón M cyclotron
cicuta F hemlock
ciego ADJ (no vidente) blind; (por borrachera) plastered; (por drogas) high; **quedarse —** to go blind; **a ciegas** blindly
cielo M (firmamento) sky; (paraíso) heaven; **a — abierto** under the open sky; **minería a — abierto** open pit mining; **— raso** ceiling; **¡—s!** good heavens! **estar en el séptimo —** to be in seventh heaven; **me cayó del —** it's a godsend; **poner el grito en el —** fam to hit the ceiling
ciempiés M centipede
cien, ciento NUM hundred; **por ciento** percent
ciénaga F swamp, mire, marsh
ciencia F (campo de investigación) science; (conocimiento) knowledge; (arte) art; **— ficción** science fiction; **—s políticas** political science; **a — cierta** with certainty; **las —s ocultas** the occult; **no tiene —** there's nothing to it
cieno M mud, mire
científico -ca ADJ scientific; MF scientist
cierra, cierre ver cerrar
cierre M (traba) clasp, fastener; (cremallera) zipper; (acción de cerrar) closing, closure; **— patronal** lockout; **al —** (noticias) at press time; (acciones) at the close
ciertamente ADV certainly
cierto ADJ certain; (verdadero) true; (seguro) sure; **en — sentido** in a sense; **hasta — punto** to a certain extent; **por —** by the way; INTERJ you're right!
ciervo -va M (animal) deer; (macho) stag; **— volante** stag beetle; F (hembra) doe, hind
cierzo M north wind
cifra F (numeral) digit; (número) figure; (clave) cipher, key; **— aproximada** ballpark estimate; **poner en —** to encode
cifrado M encryption; **— de datos** data encryption
cifrar VT to write in code, to encrypt; **— las**

esperanzas en to place one's hopes on; **el monto se cifra en veinte millones de pesos** the figure amounts to twenty million pesos
cigarra F cicada
cigarrera F cigar case, cigarette case
cigarrillo M cigarette
cigarro M (cigarrillo) cigarette; (puro) cigar
cigoto M zygote
cigüeña F stork
cigüeñal M crankshaft
cilíndrico ADJ cylindrical
cilindro M cylinder
cima F summit
cimarrón -ona ADJ wild; MF runaway slave
címbalo M cymbal
cimbel M decoy
cimbrar VT to sway, to vibrate
cimentar VT (una casa) to lay the foundation of; (una victoria) to secure
cimiento M foundation
cinc M zinc
cincel M chisel
cincelar VT to chisel
cincha F cinch, girth
cinchar VT to cinch, to girth
cinco NUM five
cincuenta NUM fifty
cine M cinema, movies
cineasta MF filmmaker
cinematografía F cinematography, movie-making
cinematografiar[28] VI/VT to film
cinematográfico ADJ cinematographic; **industria cinematográfica** motion-picture industry
cinestesia F kinesthesia
cingalés -esa ADJ & MF Sri Lankan
cínico -ca ADJ cynical; MF cynic
cinismo M cynicism
cinta F (de adorno) ribbon; (adhesiva) tape; (cinematográfica) film; **— aislante** electrical tape; **— de vídeo** videotape; **— magnetofónica** recording tape; **— métrica** tape measure; **— rodante** treadmill; **— transportadora** conveyor belt
cinto M belt
cintura F (de persona) waist; (de cosa) middle
cinturón M belt; **— de seguridad** safety belt
ciprés M cypress
circo M circus
circonio M zirconium
circuitería F circuitry
circuito M circuit; **— cerrado** closed circuit; **— impreso** circuit board; **— integrado** integrated circuit
circulación F (de sangre, de bienes) circulation; (de vehículos) traffic; **poner en —** to circulate

circular VI to circulate; **hay que — por la derecha** you have to drive on the right; F circular letter

circulatorio ADJ circulatory; **problemas —s** cardiovascular problems; **atasco —** traffic jam

círculo M circle; **— vicioso** vicious circle

circuncidar VT to circumcise

circundante ADJ surrounding

circundar VT to surround

circunferencia F circumference

circunlocución F circumlocution

circunscribir[74] VT to circumscribe

circunspecto ADJ circumspect

circunstancia F circumstance

circunstancial ADJ circumstantial

cirio M candle

cirro M cirrus

cirrosis F cirrhosis

ciruela F plum; **— pasa** prune

ciruelo M plum tree

cirugía F surgery; **— de corazón abierto** open-heart surgery; **— plástica/estética** plastic surgery, cosmetic surgery

cirujano -na MF surgeon

cisne M swan

cisterna F cistern

cita F (romántica) date; (con el médico) appointment; (textual) quotation, quote; **— a ciegas** blind date; **darse —** to meet

citación F citation, summons

citar VT (a un testigo) to summon; (a un autor) to cite, to quote; **—se con** (el médico) to make an appointment with; (un amigo) to make a date with

citología F (ciencia) cell biology, cytology; (toma de células vaginales) pap smear

cítrico ADJ citric; M citrus

ciudad F city

ciudadanía F citizenship

ciudadano -na MF citizen

Ciudad del Vaticano F Vatican City

ciudadela F citadel

cívico ADJ civic

civil ADJ (no criminal, no religioso) civil; (no militar) civilian

civilidad F civility

civilización F civilization

civilizador ADJ civilizing

civilizar[47] VT to civilize; **—se** to become civilized

cizalla F metal shears

cizaña F **sembrar —** to sow discord

clamar VT/VI to demand; **— por** to clamor for

clamor M clamor, outcry

clamorear VI/VT to shout

clamoreo M shouting

clamoroso ADJ clamorous

clan M clan

clandestino ADJ clandestine

claqué M tap dance

clara F egg white; **— de huevo** egg white

claraboya F skylight

clarear VI (aclararse) to become clear; (amanecer) to grow light; (desenturbiarse) to thin; VT to illuminate; **—se** to grow light

claridad F (de ideas) clarity; (de la luz) brightness, lightness

clarificar[30] VT to clarify, to clear

clarín M bugle

clarinete M clarinet

clarividente MF & ADJ clairvoyant

claro ADJ clear; (franco) straightforward; (iluminado) light, bright; **azul —** light blue; **a las claras** clearly; ADV clearly; INTERJ of course! M (espacio) gap; (en un bosque) clearing; **— de luna** moonlight

clase F (tipo) kind, sort; (grupo social, sesión docente, alumnado) class; (aula) classroom; **— alta** upper class; **— media** middle class; **— obrera** working class; **— turista** economy class; **dar —** to teach a class; **toda — de** all sorts of

clasicismo M classicism

clásico ADJ (destacado, consabido) classic; (de un período histórico) classical; M classic

clasificación F (taxonómica) classification; (deportiva) qualification; **— descendiente** descending sort

clasificado M want ad

clasificar[30] VT (ordenar) to classify; (en deportes) to qualify; **—se para** to qualify for; **—se segundo** to come in second

claustro M cloister; **— de profesores** university faculty

claustrofobia F claustrophobia

claustrofóbico ADJ claustrophobic

cláusula F clause

clausura F closing

clausurar VT (una sesión) to bring to a close, to conclude; (una tienda) to close [down]

clavadista MF diver

clavado ADV exactly; M (de clavos) nailing; (en una piscina) dive; **tirarse un —** to dive

clavar VT (perforar con un clavo) to nail, to drive a nail into; (pinchar) to stick, to poke; **—le la mirada / los ojos a alguien** to stare at someone; **— los frenos** to stomp on the brakes; **me clavaron** I got a raw deal

clave F (sistema de signos) code; (tabla de correspondencias) key; (signo musical) clef; (clavicémbalo) harpsichord; (de mapa) legend; **— de fa** bass clef; **— de seguridad** password; **— de sol** treble clef; ADJ key

clavel M carnation

clavetear VT to put pegs on

clavicémbalo M harpsichord

clavícula F collarbone, clavicle

clavija F (de guitarra) peg; (de enchufe) pin

clavo M (pieza de metal) nail; (capullo) clove; (de zapato) spike; **dar en el —** to hit the nail on the head

claxon M car horn

clearing M clearing

clemencia F clemency, mercy

clemente ADJ forgiving, merciful

cleptomanía F kleptomania

cleptómano -na MF kleptomaniac

clerecía F (funciones) ministry; (clérigos) clergy

clerical ADJ clerical

clérigo M clergyman, minister

clero M clergy

clic M click; **hacer —** to click; **hacer doble —** to double-click

cliché M (placa fotográfica) photographic plate; (expresión muy usada) cliché

cliente MF, **clienta** F (de un profesional) client; (de un negocio) customer; (de un restaurante) patron; (de un hotel) guest

clientela F clientele, customer base

clientelismo M patronage

clima M climate

climático ADJ climatic; **cambio —** climate change

climatización F air conditioning

clímax M climax

clinch M clinch

clínica F clinic

clínico ADJ clinical

clip M paper clip

cloaca F sewer

clon M clone

clonación F cloning

clonaje M cloning

clonar VT to clone

cloquear VI to cluck

cloqueo M cluck, clucking

clorhidrato M hydrochloride; **— de Ritalina** Ritalin hydrochloride

cloro M chlorine

clorofila F chlorophyll

cloroformo M chloroform

cloruro M chloride

club M club (también palo de golf); **— nocturno** nightclub

coacción F compulsion, coercion; **bajo —** under duress

coagulación F (de sangre) clotting; (por productos químicos) coagulation

coagulante M coagulant

coagular VI (con productos químicos) to coagulate; (sangre) to clot

coágulo M clot

coalición F coalition

coartada F alibi

coartar VT (una libertad) to restrict; (a una persona) to inhibit; (la creatividad) to strangle

cobalto M cobalt

cobarde ADJ cowardly; MF coward

cobardía F cowardice

cobertizo M shed

cobertor M cover

cobertura F (de nieve, aérea) cover; (de seguros, noticias, televisión) coverage; **— extendida** extended coverage

cobija F (cubierta) cover; (manta) blanket

cobijar VT to shelter; **—se** to seek shelter

cobra F cobra

cobrador -ora MF (persona) collector; M (perro) retriever

cobranza F collection

cobrar VT (impuestos) to collect; (una factura) to charge; (un cheque) to cash; (el sueldo) to earn; (víctimas) to claim; **— al entregar** to collect on delivery; **— ánimo** to take heart; **— caro** to charge a lot; **— de más** to overcharge; **— de menos** to undercharge; **— valor** to gain importance; **a —** receivable; **vas a —** you're in for it

cobre M (elemento) copper; (utensilios) copper utensils

cobrizo ADJ copper-colored

cobro M collection, charge; **— excesivo** overcharge

coca F (planta, hoja) coca; (cocaína) *fam* coke

cocaína F cocaine

cóccix M coccyx

cocear VI/VT to kick

cocer[34] VI/VT (huevos) to boil; (verduras) to cook; (cerámica) to fire; **— al vapor** to steam; **a medio —** half-cooked; **romper a —** to break into a boil; **¿qué se cuece aquí?** what's up?

coche M (automóvil, vagón) car; (autobús) coach; (vehículo tirado por caballerías) carriage; **— bomba** car bomb; **— cama** sleeper; **—-comedor** dining car; **— de bebé** stroller, baby carriage; **— de bomberos** fire engine; **— de choque** bumper car; **— de golf** golf cart; **— de línea** city bus; **— deportivo** sports car; **— fúnebre** hearse; **ir en —** to go by car, to drive; **pasear en —** to go on a drive

cochera F carport

cochinada F (asquerosidad) filthy action; (maldad) dirty trick

cochinilla F woodlouse

cochino -na ADJ filthy; MF pig

cocido M stew

cociente M quotient; **— intelectual** IQ

cocina F (habitación) kitchen; (electrodoméstico) range, stove; (arte) cuisine, cookery

cocinar VI/VT to cook; (tramar) to cook up

cocinero -ra MF cook

cócker MF cocker spaniel

coco M (fruto) coconut; (cabeza) *fam* dome; (fantasma) bogeyman; **comerse el —** to get all worked up

cocodrilo M crocodile

cóctel M (bebida) cocktail, mixed drink; (fiesta) cocktail party

codazo M jab with the elbow; **dar —s** to elbow

codear VI/VT to elbow, to jab; **—se** to nudge one another; **—se con** to rub elbows with

codeína F codeine

codicia F (avaricia) greed; (deseo sexual) lust

codiciar VT (una cosa) to covet; (a una persona) to lust after

codicioso ADJ covetous, greedy

codificación F coding, encoding

codificar[30] VT (mensaje) to codify, to encrypt; (programa de computadora) to code

código M code; **— abierto** open code; **— de acceso** access code; **— de barras** bar code; **— de país** country code; **— fuente** source code; **— genético** genetic code; **— impositivo** tax code; **— postal** zip code

codo M elbow; **— a —** side by side; **— de tenista** tennis elbow; **empinar el —** to drink too much; **hablar por los —s** to talk one's head off; **hasta los —s** up to one's elbows

codorniz F quail

coeficiente M coefficient; **— de inteligencia** intelligence quotient

coerción F coercion

coetáneo ADJ contemporary

coexistencia F coexistence; **— pacífica** peaceful coexistence

cofre M coffer

coger[45] VT (a un criminal, una pelota) to catch; (con las manos) to grasp; (flores) to gather; to pick; (a un empleado) to hire; (una emisora) to receive; (cosas del suelo) to pick up; (espacio) to take up; (un pez) to land, to catch; (un camino, tren, curso) to take; **— por/de sorpresa** to catch by surprise; **— el sueño** to fall asleep; **— hacia el castillo** tó turn toward the castle; **—le miedo a algo** to become scared of something; **—le el tranquillo a algo** to get into the swing of things; **—se un resfriado** to come down with a cold; **coge y le dice** he up and says

cognado ADJ & M cognate

cognitivo ADJ cognitive

cogollo M heart

cogote M neck

cohabitar VI (amigos) to live [with]; (una pareja) to cohabitate

cohecho M bribe

coheredero -ra MF joint heir

coherencia F (consecuencia) consistency; (lógica) coherence

coherente ADJ (consecuente) consistent; (lógico) coherent; (con significado)

meaningful; **lo que dices no es —** you're not making any sense

cohesión F cohesion

cohesivo ADJ coherent

cohete M rocket

cohetería F rocketry

cohibición F inhibition

cohibido ADJ inhibited, self-conscious

cohibir VT to inhibit

coincidencia F coincidence

coincidir VI to coincide

coito M coitus

cojear VI to limp; **saber de qué pie cojea alguien** to know someone's weaknesses

cojera F limp

cojín M cushion

cojinete M bushing; **— de bolas** ball bearing

cojo ADJ lame, crippled

cok M coke

col F cabbage; **—es de Bruselas** Brussels sprouts

cola F (de perro, ave, avión) tail; (de vestido) train; (hilera de gente) line; (secuencia de datos o programas) queue; (pegamento) glue; **— de caballo** ponytail; **hacer —** to stand in line; **no pegar ni con —** not to go together; **traer —** to have consequences

colaboración F collaboration

colaborador -ora MF (con el gobierno) collaborator; (de periódico) contributor

colaborar VI to collaborate; (con un periódico) to contribute

colación F **sacar a —** to bring up

colacionar VT to collate

colador M (para té) strainer; (para verduras) colander

colágeno M collagen

colapso M (de puente, edificio) collapse; (de nervios) breakdown; (de mercado) crash

colar[5] VT (té) to strain; (metal líquido) to pour; VI to go through, to slip through; **esa excusa no va a —** that excuse won't wash; **—se en una fiesta** to crash a party

colateral ADJ collateral

colcha F bedspread

colchón M (para dormir) mattress; (para emergencias) cushion

colchoneta F mat

colear VI (un perro) to wag the tail; (un tema) to be pending; (un auto) to fishtail

colección F collection

coleccionar VT to collect

coleccionista MF collector

colecta F charity collection

colectividad F collective, community

colectivo M (grupo) collective; (autobús) *Am* bus

colector M (de aguas negras) sewer; (eléctrico) collector; (de coche) manifold

colega MF colleague

colegio M (escuela privada) private school; (escuela primaria) elementary school; (centro de educación secundaria) high school; (asociación profesional) association, college

colegir[14] VI to gather

cólera F rage, wrath; **montar en —** to fly into a rage; M cholera

colérico ADJ irritable, choleric

colesterol M cholesterol

coleta F pigtail

coletilla F tag

coleto M **decir para su —** to say to oneself

colgadero M hanger; ADJ hanging

colgado ADJ high and dry

colgadura F drapery; **—s** hangings

colgante ADJ hanging; M pendant

colgar[42] VT (suspender, ahorcar) to hang; (un teléfono, un abrigo) to hang up; VI (un espejo) to hang; (un andrajo) to dangle; (un asunto) to be pending; **esa falda te cuelga por atrás** that dress hangs down in the back; **—se [un ordenador]** to crash; **—se de** to get hooked on; **—se del teléfono** to tarry on the phone

colibrí M hummingbird

cólico M colic

coliflor F cauliflower

colilla F cigarette butt

colina F hill, knoll

colindante ADJ neighboring

colindar VI **— con** to border [on], to adjoin

colirio M eyedrops

coliseo M coliseum

colisión F collision

collage M collage

collar M (de perlas) necklace; (de perro) collar; **— antipulgas** flea collar

collera F horse collar

collie M collie

colmar VT (un vaso) to fill; (una demanda) to satisfy; **— de alabanzas** to lavish praise upon

colmena F beehive

colmillo M (de persona) eyetooth, cuspid; (de elefante) tusk; (de víbora) fang

colmo M **— de la locura** height of folly; **¡eso es el —!** that takes the cake; **para —** to top it all

colocación F (ubicación) placement; (puesto) position

colocar[30] VT (poner, encontrar lugar para) to place; (casar) to marry off; (invertir) to invest; **—se** (encontrar empleo) to get a job; (ubicarse) to place oneself

coloide M colloid

Colombia F Colombia

colombiano -na ADJ & MF Colombian

colon M colon

colón M (moneda) colon

colonia F (territorio, grupo de insectos) colony; (comunidad de inmigrantes) community, settlement; (vivienda) development; (perfume) cologne

colonial ADJ colonial

colonización F colonization

colonizador -ora MF colonist

colonizar[47] VT to colonize, to settle

colono -na MF (habitante de una colonia) colonist, settler; (arrendatario) tenant farmer

colonoscopia F colonoscopy

coloquial ADJ colloquial

coloquio M colloquium

color M (tono) color; (pintura) paint; (maquillaje) rouge; (de naipes) flush; **—es primarios** primary colors; **a todo —** full color; **persona de —** person of color

coloración F coloring

colorado ADJ & M red; **ponerse —** to blush

colorante ADJ & M coloring

coloreado ADJ colored; M coloring

colorear VT to color

colorete M rouge

colorido M (de un caballo) coloring; (de un comentario, paisaje) color; ADJ colorful

colosal ADJ (grande) colossal; (estupendo) wonderful

colostomía F colostomy

columbrar VT to glimpse

columna F column; **— de dirección** steering column; **— vertebral** spinal column, backbone

columnista MF columnist

columpiar VI/VT to swing

columpio M swing

colza F (planta) rape; (aceite) rapeseed oil

coma F (signo) comma; M (falta de conciencia) coma

comadre F (mujer chismosa) gossip; (partera) midwife; (parienta) godmother of one's child

comadreja F weasel

comadrona F (mujer chismosa) gossip; (partera) midwife

comandancia F command

comandante MF (rango militar) major; (militar que ejerce el mando) commander; **— en jefe** commander in chief

comandar VT to command; **— un avión** to pilot an airplane

comando M (grupo militar) commando; (orden dada al ordenador) command

comarca F district

comatoso ADJ comatose

comba F (de una pared) bulge; (de madera) warp; **saltar a la —** to jump rope

combar VI (una pared) to sag; (madera) to warp; (trayectoria de pelota) to curve

combate M combat, fight; **fuera de —** out of combat / the competition

combatiente MF combatant

combatir VI/VT to combat

combativo ADJ combative

combinación F (mezcla) combination; (billete) transfer ticket

combinar VT to combine; **—se para hacer algo** to agree to do something; **esos colores no combinan** those colors don't match

combo M combo

combustible ADJ combustible; M fuel

combustión F combustion

comedero M trough

comedia F (obra teatral) comedy; (farsa) farce; **— de situación** situation comedy, sitcom; **hacer la — de** to play the part of

comediante MF comedian

comedido ADJ moderate; *Am* obliging

comedirse[9] VI to show restraint; **— a hacer algo** *RP* to volunteer to do something

comedor M (habitación) dining room; (de empresa) cafeteria

comensal MF [fellow] diner

comentador -ora MF commentator

comentar VI/VT to comment [on], to remark [on]

comentario M (análisis) commentary; (observación) comment, remark

comentarista MF commentator

comenzar[48] VI/VT to begin, to start; **— a comer** to begin to eat; **— preguntando** to begin by asking

comer VI/VT to eat; (al mediodía) to have lunch; (en ajedrez) to take; (en el juego de damas) to jump; **dar de —** to feed; **sin —lo ni beberlo** through no fault of one's own; **—se** (corroer) to eat away; (terminar la comida) to eat up; **—se las eses** to drop one's esses; **—se las palabras** to eat one's words; **—se un semáforo en rojo** to run a red light

comercial ADJ & M commercial

comercialización F marketing, merchandising

comercializar[47] VT (volver comercial) to commercialize; (vender) to market, to merchandise

comerciante MF merchant, trader, dealer

comerciar VI to trade

comercio M commerce, trade; **— electrónico** e-business; **— exterior** foreign trade; **— minorista** retail trade; **— mayorista** wholesaler

comestible ADJ edible; M PL groceries

cometa M (cuerpo celeste) comet; F (juguete) kite

cometer VT to commit

cometido M purpose, objective

comezón F itch, itching; **tener —** to itch

cómic M comic book

comicios M PL polls

cómico -ca ADJ comic, comical; MF comedian

comida F (ocasión) meal; (alimento) food; (al mediodía) lunch; **— basura** junk food; **—**

macrobiótica health food; **— rápida** fast food

comience, comienza *ver* comenzar

comienzo M beginning; **a —s de** toward the beginning of; **al —** at first, initially; **desde un/el —** from the start

comilla F quotation mark; **entre —s** in quotes

comilón -ona MF big eater; F binge

comino M cumin; **me importa un —** *fam* I don't give a hoot; **no vale un —** *fam* it's not worth a hoot

comisaría F **— de policía** police station, precinct

comisario -ria MF (comisionado) commissioner; (jefe de policía) police chief

comisión F (acción de cometer, porcentaje ganado) commission; (comité) committee

comisionar VT to commission

comistrajo M bad food

comisura F **— de los labios** corner of the mouth

comité M committee

comitiva F retinue

como ADV (del mismo modo que) as, like; **ella pinta — yo** she paints like I do; (aproximadamente) about; **pesa — diez kilos** it weighs about ten kilos; CONJ (puesto que) since; **— no tenemos dinero** since we have no money; **— no me pagues** if you don't pay me; **era — que muy viejo** he was, like, real old; **— que te voy a permitir** as if I would let you; **— quieras** as you please; **— si** as if; **¡— si me lo fuera a creer!** a likely story!

cómo ADV INTERR & PRON (de qué manera) how; (¿perdón?) excuse me? what? **¡— brillan las estrellas!** how the stars are shining! **¡— no!** of course! **¿a — me lo vende?** what does that cost?

cómoda F chest of drawers, dresser, bureau

comodidad F (cualidad) comfort; (cosa cómoda) convenience; **—es** amenities

comodín M joker, wild card

cómodo ADJ (mueble) comfortable; (horario) convenient; (persona) lazy

Comoras F PL Comoros

compactar VT to compact

compacto ADJ compact

compadecer[35] VT to pity; **—se de** to take pity on

compadre M (amigo) pal, crony; (pariente) godfather of one's child

compañero -ra MF (camarada) companion; (de un zapato) mate; **— de clase** classmate; **— de cuarto** roommate; **— de equipo** teammate

compañía F company; **— de importación y exportación** import-export company; **— fantasma** bogus company; **— recién establecida** start-up; **en — de** in the company of

comparable ADJ comparable

comparación F comparison

comparar VI/VT to compare; **—se con** to compare [oneself] with

comparativo ADJ comparative

comparecencia F appearance

comparecer[35] VI to appear

compartimiento M compartment

compartir VT (bienes) to share; (tiempo) to divide

compás M (instrumento de geometría) compass; (ritmo) beat; (espacio entre barras) measure, bar; (división de música) time signature; **marcar el —** to beat time

compasión F compassion

compasivo ADJ compassionate, sympathetic

compatibilidad F compatibility

compatible ADJ compatible

compatriota MF compatriot

compeler VT to compel

compendiar VT to summarize

compendio M digest, condensation

compenetración F bonding

compensación F compensation

compensar VT (un daño) to compensate; (un gasto) to offset; **compensa su falta de inteligencia con mucha disciplina** he makes up for his lack of intelligence with a lot of discipline; **te voy a — por esto** I'll make it up to you

competencia F (pugna, competición, competidores) competition; (cualidad de competente) competence

competente ADJ competent

competición[36] F athletic competition, meet

competidor -ora ADJ competing; MF (comercial) competitor; (deportivo) athlete, participant

competir[9] VI to compete, to vie

competitividad F competitiveness

competitivo ADJ competitive

compilador M compiler

compilar VT to compile

compinche M chum, crony

compita, compite, compitiendo, compitiera, compitiese ver competir

complacencia F satisfaction

complacer[36] VT to please, to gratify; **—se [en]** to take pleasure [in]

complaciente ADJ (que complace) obliging; (que consiente) indulgent

complejidad F complexity

complejo ADJ complex; M complex; **— de inferioridad** inferiority complex

complementar VT to complement, to supplement

complementario ADJ complementary

complemento M complement; **— alimenticio**

dietary supplement; **— directo** direct object; **— indirecto** indirect object; **—s** fringe benefits

completar VT (terminar) to complete; (en fútbol americano) to complete [passes]; **—se** to be completed

completo ADJ (terminado) complete; (lleno) full; **hoy tenemos el —** today we have a full house; **por —** completely

complexión F build

complicación F complication

complicado ADJ complicated

complicar[30] VT to complicate; **—le a alguien la vida** to give someone trouble

cómplice MF accomplice

complicidad F complicity

complot M plot

compondrá, compondría ver componer

componenda F (arreglo provisional) quick fix; (arreglo ilegal) shady deal

componente ADJ & M component

componer[56, 74] VT (un grupo) to compose, to make up; (imprenta) to set; (un coche descompuesto) to fix; (música) to compose; **—se de** to be composed of; **componérselas** to deal with one's problems alone

componga, compongo ver componer

comportamiento M conduct, behavior

comportarse VI/VT to conduct oneself, to behave

composición F composition

compositor -ora MF composer

compostura F (arreglo) repair; (dignidad) composure

compra F purchase; **— apalancada** LBO; **ir de —s** to go shopping; **— hostil** hostile takeover

comprador -ora MF (comercial) buyer, purchaser; (en una tienda) shopper

comprar VT to buy, to purchase; **compró su silencio** he gave her hush money

comprender VT (entender) to understand, to comprehend; (abarcar) to cover, to include

comprensible ADJ comprehensible, understandable

comprensión F (intelectual) understanding, comprehension; (emocional) sympathy, understanding

comprensivo ADJ understanding

compresa F compress

compresión F compression; **— de archivos** file compression

comprimido ADJ compressed; M tablet

comprimir VT to compress

comprobación F verification, check

comprobante M proof; **— de compra** proof of purchase

comprobar[5] VT (verificar) to verify, to check; (probar) to prove; (darse cuenta) to realize

comprometer VT (obligar) to commit; (poner

en peligro) to jeopardize, to compromise; **—se** (prometer) to promise; (tomar partido) to commit oneself; (para casarse) to get engaged

comprometido ADJ (obligado) obligated; (arriesgado) risky; (implicado) compromised; (con planes de casarse) engaged; (entregado, dedicado) committed, engaged

compromiso M (ideología, obligación, promesa) commitment; (acuerdo) agreement; (cita) appointment, engagement; (de matrimonio) engagement; (solución negociada) compromise; **no me pongas en — don't** compromise me; **sin — de compra** without obligation to buy

comprueba, compruebe *ver* comprobar

compuerta F sluice gate, floodgate

compuesto ADJ (ojos, tiempo, interés) compound; **estar — de** to be composed of; M compound

compuesto *ver* componer

compulsión F compulsion

compulsivo ADJ compulsive

compungirse[46] VI to feel sorry

computación F computing

computadora F computer; **— personal** personal computer; **— de escritorio** desktop computer; **— de mano** palmtop, handheld computer; **— digital** digital computer; **— portátil** laptop computer; **— torre** tower model

computar VT to compute

computarizar[47] VT to computerize

cómputo M computation

comulgar[40] VI (recibir el sacramento) to take Communion; (estar de acuerdo) to agree

común ADJ common; **en —** in common; **por lo — generally; el — de las gentes** the majority of the people

comuna F commune

comunicable ADJ communicable

comunicación F (interacción) communication; (ponencia) presentation; **se nos cortó la —** we got disconnected

comunicado M communiqué, report

comunicar[30] VI/VT to communicate; **—se con** (entenderse) to communicate with; (ponerse en contacto con) to reach; (desembocar en) to open into

comunicativo ADJ communicative

comunidad F community; **— internauta** Internet community; **— virtual** virtual community

comunión F communion

comunismo M communism

comunista ADJ & MF communist

comunitario ADJ (en común) communal; **espíritu —** community spirit; **presupuesto —** European Union budget

con PREP with; **— lo que come, tendría que estar obesa** given what she eats, she should be obese; **— mucho** by far; **— que le digas alcanza** just telling him is enough; **— tal [de] que** provided that; **— todo** all things considered

conato M attempt

concavidad F hollow

cóncavo ADJ concave

concebible ADJ conceivable

concebir[9] VT (engendrar) to conceive; (entender) to conceive of

conceder VT (dar) to grant; (admitir) to concede, to allow

concejal MF councilor

concejo M council

concentración F (densidad, atención, cantidad) concentration; (manifestación) rally, demonstration

concentrar VT to concentrate; **—se** (prestar atención) to concentrate, to focus; (manifestar) to rally

concepción F conception

concepto M (idea) concept; (artificio) conceit

conceptual ADJ conceptual

concernir[73] VT to concern

concertación F agreement

concertar[1] VT (arreglar) to arrange; (concretar) to finalize; (planear) to concert; **—se** to agree

concesión F (admisión) concession; (otorgamiento) grant; (permiso comercial) franchise

concesionario M dealership

concha F shell

conchabarse VI to conspire

conciba, concibe, concibiendo, concibiera, concibiese *ver* concebir

conciencia F (moral) conscience; (mental) consciousness, awareness; **tomar — de** to come to grips with; **— de marca** brand awareness

concienzudo ADJ conscientious, thorough

concierto M (música) concert; (armonía) harmony; (acuerdo) agreement

conciliación F conciliation

conciliar VT (personas) to conciliate; (ideas) to reconcile; **— el sueño** to fall sleep

concilio M council

concisión F conciseness

conciso ADJ concise, brief

conciudadano -na MF fellow citizen

concluir[19] VI/VT to conclude

conclusión F conclusion

concluya, concluye, concluyendo, concluyera, concluyese *ver* concluir

concluyente ADJ conclusive

concomitante ADJ attendant

concordancia F agreement

concordar[5] VI to agree

concordia F concord

concretamente ADV specifically; **tiene un perro, — un chihuahua** he has a dog, a chihuahua, to be precise

concretar VT (cerrar) to finalize; (especificar) to be specific about; (realizar) to realize; **—se a** to focus on

concreto ADJ concrete; **en —** specifically; M *Am* concrete

concubina F concubine

concurrencia F (reunión) gathering; (asistencia) attendance

concurrido ADJ well-attended

concurrir VI (confluir) to come together; (asistir) to attend

concursante MF contestant

concurso M (para un premio) contest; (en una licitación) call for bids; (para un puesto de trabajo) competitive examination; **— de belleza** beauty pageant

concusión F graft

concusionario -ria MF grafter

condado M county

conde M count

condecoración F decoration

condecorar VT to decorate

condena F (castigo) sentence; (crítica) condemnation; **¡qué —!** what a pain!

condenación F condemnation

condenado ADJ (perdido) damned; (sentenciado) sentenced; **está — a muerte** he's on death row

condenar VT (criticar) to condemn; (sentenciar) to sentence; **eso le condenó al fracaso** that doomed him to failure; **—se** to go to hell

condensación F condensation

condensar VI to condense

condesa F countess

condescendencia F (tolerancia) acquiescence; (superioridad) condescension

condescender[2] VI (acomodarse) to acquiesce; (dignarse) to condescend

condición F condition; **— social** social station; **a — de que** on the condition that; **condiciones** (físicas) condition; (de un contrato) terms, provisos

condicional ADJ & M conditional

condicionamiento M conditioning

condicionar VT to condition

condimentar VT to season

condimento M condiment, seasoning

condiscípulo -la MF classmate

condolencias F PL condolences; **dar las —** to offer one's condolences

condolerse[6] VI to offer one's condolences

condominio M condominium

cóndor M condor

conducción F (de electricidad) conduction; (de un difunto o prisionero) transport

conducente ADJ conducive

conducir[38] VT (a un grupo) to lead; (una orquesta, electricidad) to conduct; (un coche) to drive, to steer; **—se** to behave

conducta F (moral) conduct, behavior; (biológica) behavior; **— de alto riesgo** high-risk behavior

conducto M (de agua) conduit; (anatómico) duct; **— de aire** airway; **por — de** through

conductor -ora ADJ (de electricidad) conductive; M (de electricidad) conductor; MF (de coches) driver; (en baloncesto) point guard

conductual ADJ behavioral

conduje, condujera, condujese *ver* conducir

conectar VI/VT to connect

conectividad F connectivity

conector M connector; **— en serie** serial connector

conejillo M **— de Indias** guinea pig

conejo M rabbit

conexión F connection

confabulación F collusion

confección F (fabricación de ropa) dressmaking, tailoring; (calidad) workmanship; **de —** ready-made

confeccionar VT (productos) to manufacture; (ropa) to tailor, to sew

confederación F confederation

confederado -da ADJ & MF confederate

confederar VI to form a confederacy

conferencia F (discurso) lecture; (reunión) conference; **— de prensa** press conference; **dar una —** to give a lecture

conferenciante MF lecturer, speaker

conferenciar VI to confer

conferencista MF lecturer, speaker

conferir[8] VT to confer, to bestow; (un título) to confer

confesar[1] VI/VT to confess

confesión F confession

confesionario M confessional

confesor -ora MF confessor

confiabilidad F reliability

confiable ADJ reliable

confiado ADJ (seguro de sí) confident; (crédulo) trusting

confianza F confidence, trust; **en —** in confidence; **tener —** to be confident; **tener — en** to have confidence in; **tomar —s** to be overly familiar with

confianzudo ADJ overfamiliar

confiar[28] VT (un secreto) to confide; (un valor, bien) to entrust; **— en** to rely on; **confío que Dios me proteja** I trust that God will protect me

confidencia F confidence

confidencial ADJ confidential; **altamente —** top-secret

confidente MF (amigo) confidant; M (mueble) love seat

confiesa, confiese *ver* confesar

configuración F configuration

configurar VT to configure (también computadoras); —**se** to take shape

confinamiento M confinement

confinar VT to confine

confines M PL bounds, confines

confirmación F confirmation

confirmar VT to confirm

confiscación F (de una propiedad) confiscation, seizure; (de un monto) forfeiture

confiscar³⁰ VT to confiscate

confitar VT to candy

confite M candy

confitería F confectionery

confitura F confection

conflictivo ADJ (persona, tema) contentious; (región) volatile

conflicto M conflict

confluencia F (de calles) junction; (de ríos) confluence

conformación F creation, establishment

conformar VT to adapt; —**se** to go along; —**se con** to settle for

conforme ADJ in agreement, content; — **a** in accordance with; CONJ — **amanece** as dawn breaks

conformidad F conformity, agreement; **estar de/en — con** to be in accordance with

conformismo M conformity

confort M comfort

confortable ADJ comfortable

confortar VT to comfort

confraternidad F fraternity, fellowship

confraternizar⁴⁷ VI to fraternize

confrontación F confrontation

confrontar VT (a un enemigo) to confront; (dos listas) to compare

confundido ADJ confused, mixed-up

confundir VT to confuse, to perplex, to baffle; —**se** (personas) to become confused; (cosas) to mingle

confusión F (mental) confusion; (de cosas) clutter, disarray

confuso ADJ (que no comprende, desordenado) confused; (difícil de comprender) confusing

congelación F freezing; — **salarial** pay freeze

congelado ADJ frozen

congelador M freezer

congelar VT to freeze

congeniar VI — **con** to get along with

congénito ADJ congenital

congestión F congestion

conglomeración F conglomeration

conglomerado M conglomeration

Congo M Congo

congoja F anguish, grief

congoleño -ña ADJ & MF Congolese

congregación F (feligreses) congregation; (orden) order

congregar⁴⁰ VI to congregate

congresista MF (legislador) member of Congress; (asistente a un congreso) conference attendee, conventioneer

congreso M (cuerpo legislativo, edificio) congress; (reunión periódica) conference, convention

congresual ADJ congressional

congruencia F congruence

conífera F conifer

conjetura F conjecture, surmise

conjeturar VT to conjecture, to surmise

conjugación F conjugation

conjugar⁴⁰ VT to conjugate

conjunción F conjunction

conjuntamente ADV jointly

conjuntivitis F conjunctivitis, pinkeye

conjunto M (grupo de cosas) set; (totalidad) total, aggregate; (de ropa) outfit; — **musical** ensemble; **en** — as a whole, all told; ADJ joint

conjuración F conspiracy

conjurado -da MF conspirator

conjurar VT (conspirar) to conspire, to plot; (evitar, cancelar) to ward off

conjuro M incantation, spell

conllevar VT to entail, to involve

conmemoración F commemoration

conmemorar VT to commemorate

conmemorativo ADJ commemorative, memorial

conmigo PRON with me

conmiseración F commiseration

conmoción F commotion; — **cerebral** brain concussion, cerebral concussion

conmovedor ADJ moving, touching

conmover⁶ VT to move, to touch

conmovido ADJ moved, touched

conmutador M switch

conmutar VT to commute

connatural ADJ inborn

connotación F connotation

cono M cone

conocedor -ora ADJ who know[s], aware; **muy — de la situación** well aware of the situation; MF connoisseur, expert

conocer³⁵ VT to know (también en sentido carnal); (reconocer) to recognize; (tratar por primera vez) to meet; — **el paño** to know the ropes; **se conoce que** it is clear that

conocido -da ADJ well-known; MF acquaintance

conocimiento M knowledge, acquaintance; — **de embarque** bill of lading; **perder el** — to lose consciousness; **poner en** — to inform; —**s** knowledge

conozca, conozco *ver* conocer

conque CONJ so

conquista F conquest
conquistador -ora MF conqueror; ADJ conquering
conquistar VT (un terreno) to conquer; (el amor de alguien) to win
consabido ADJ habitual
consagración F consecration
consagrar VT (declarar consagrado) to consecrate; (dedicar) to devote
consciente ADJ conscious; **— del problema** aware of the problem
conscribir VT to draft
consecución F attainment, achievement
consecuencia F (hecho que resulta de otro) consequence; (cualidad de consecuente) consistency; **a — de** as a result of
consecuente ADJ (que se sigue de) consequent, logical; (fiel en sus actos) consistent
consecutivo ADJ consecutive
conseguible ADJ obtainable
conseguir[12] VT (un derecho) to attain, to get; (un objetivo) to achieve; (un puesto de trabajo) to land, to get; **— hacer algo** to manage to do something
consejero -ra MF (asesor) adviser; (miembro del consejo) board member; **consejero -ra delegado -da** *Esp* CEO
consejo M (opinión) counsel, advice; (comité) council; **— de guerra** court-martial
consenso M consensus
consentimiento M consent, acquiescence
consentir[8] VT (permitir) to consent to, to acquiesce to; (mimar) to pamper, to indulge; **— en** to permit
conserje MF (limpiador) janitor; (portero) superintendent; (recepcionista) hotel clerk
conserva F canned food; **en —** canned
conservación F conservation, preservation
conservador -ora MF (en política) conservative; (de museo) curator; ADJ (de tradiciones) conservative; (de alimentos) preservative
conservadurismo M conservatism
conservante M preservative
conservar VT (guardar) to keep; (mantener) to retain; (preservar) to preserve; (ahorrar) to conserve
conservatorio M conservatory
considerable ADJ considerable
considerablemente ADV significantly
consideración F consideration; **de —** considerable; **tomar/tener en —** to take into consideration
considerado ADJ considerate, thoughtful
considerar VT to consider
consiga *ver* conseguir
consigna F (eslogan) motto, watchword; (orden) order
consignación F consignment; **a/en —** on

consignment
consignar VT to consign
consignatario -ria MF consignee
consigo PRON with oneself/himself/herself/ themselves
consigo, consiguiendo, consiguiera, consiguiese *ver* conseguir
consiguiente ADJ consequent; **por —** consequently
consistencia F consistency
consistente ADJ (firme) consistent; **— de** consisting of
consistir VI **— en** to consist of
consocio -cia MF fellow member
consola F console; **— de juegos** game console
consolación F consolation
consolar[5] VT to console
consolidación F consolidation
consolidar VT to consolidate
consonante ADJ & F consonant
consorcio M consortium
consorte MF consort
conspicuo ADJ conspicuous
conspiración F conspiracy, plot
conspirador -ora MF conspirator, plotter
conspirar VI to conspire, to plot
constancia F (en el amor) constancy; (en el esfuerzo) perseverance; (en el trabajo) steadiness; (prueba) documentary proof
constante ADJ & F constant; **—s vitales** vital signs
constar VI to be stated; **aquí consta que me debes cien dólares** here it states that you owe me a hundred dollars; **— de** to consist of, to be composed of; **hacer —** to mention; **me consta que** I am aware that; **que conste** let it be known
constatar VT to verify
constelación F constellation
consternación F consternation, dismay
consternar VT to dismay
constipación F constipation
constipado ADJ *Esp* (resfriado) suffering from a cold; *Am* (seco de vientre) constipated; M *Esp* head cold
constitución F constitution
constitucional ADJ constitutional
constituir[19] VT to constitute
constitutivo ADJ (constituyente) constituent; (inherente) inherent; **— de un delito** which constitutes a crime
constituya, constituye *ver* constituir
constituyente ADJ constituent
constreñimiento M constraint
constreñir[11] VT (limitar) to constrain; (apretar) to constrict, to constrain
constricción F constriction
construcción F (actividad de construir, cosa construida) construction, building;

(gramatical) construction

constructivo ADJ constructive

constructor -ora MF builder; F construction company

construir[19] VI/VT to construct, to build

construye, construyendo, construyera, construyese *ver* construir

consuelo M consolation, comfort, solace

consuetudinario ADJ (acción) habitual; (derecho) common

cónsul MF consul

consulado M consulate

consulta F (acción de consultar) consultation; (pregunta) question; (consultorio) doctor's office

consultar VT to consult; **—lo con la almohada** to sleep on it

consultivo ADJ consultative

consultor ADJ consulting

consultoría F consulting firm

consultorio M doctor's office

consumado ADJ consummate, accomplished

consumar VT to consummate

consumidor -ora MF consumer; ADJ consuming

consumir VT to consume; **—se** (agua) to boil off; (neumático) to wear out; **—se de** to be consumed by

consumismo M consumerism

consumo M consumption

consunción F consumption

contabilidad F accounting, bookkeeping

contable MF accountant, bookkeeper

contactar VI/VT to contact; **—[se] con** to get in contact/touch with

contacto M contact; **— visual** eye contact; **en — con** in touch with

contado M **al —** in cash; ADJ **—s** few

contador -ora ADJ counting; M (de dinero) counter; (de electricidad) meter; **— Geiger** Geiger counter; MF accountant; **— público -ca** CPA

contaduría F accountant's office

contagiar VT to infect

contagio M (de enfermedad) contagion; (de ordenador) infection

contagioso ADJ contagious, catching, infectious

contaminación F (del agua, de la comida) contamination; (del medio ambiente) pollution; **— sonora** noise pollution

contaminante M contaminate

contaminar VT (agua, alimentos, cultura) to contaminate; (el medio ambiente) to pollute; **—se** (agua) to become contaminated; (medio ambiente) to become polluted

contar[5] VI/VT (medir una cantidad) to count; (decir historias) to tell; **el hotel cuenta con una piscina** the hotel has a swimming pool; **cuento con mi hermano** I count on my brother; **esto no cuenta** this doesn't count; **¿me lo vas a contar a mí?** you can say that again; **tienes que — el tiempo** you have to watch the time; M SG **cuentakilómetros** (marcador de kilómetros) odometer; (velocímetro) speedometer

contemplación F contemplation

contemplar VT (mirar, tener en cuenta) to contemplate; (consentir) to spoil; VI to contemplate

contemporáneo ADJ contemporary

contención F containment

contender[2] VI to contend

contendrá, contendría *ver* contener

contenedor M container

contenedorizar VT containerize

contener[58] VT (un líquido) to contain; (risa, lágrimas) to hold back; (entusiasmo) to restrain; (el aliento) to hold

contenga, contengo *ver* contener

contenido ADJ restrained; M content[s]

contentar VT to satisfy; **—se** to be satisfied

contento ADJ (conforme) content, contented; (feliz) happy; M contentment

conteo M count

contera F (de paraguas) tip; (de bolígrafo) cap

contestación F answer, reply

contestador M answering machine

contestar VT to answer; VI to talk back, to mouth off

contexto M context

contextura F (de un objeto) makeup; (de persona) build

contienda F (guerra) conflict; (encuentro deportivo) competition

contiene, contienes *ver* contener

contigo PRON with you

contiguo ADJ contiguous; **estar — a** to adjoin

continental ADJ continental

continente M (masa geográfica) continent; (opuesto a isla) mainland; ADJ continent

contingencia F contingency

contingente ADJ & M contingent

continuación F (de una acción) continuation; (de una película) sequel; (tenis) follow-through; **a —** after that; **a — hubo una guerra** there ensued a war

continuado ADJ continuing

continuar[26] VI/VT to continue

continuidad F continuity

continuo ADJ (ininterrumpido) continuous; (repetido) continual

contonearse VI (mujer) to swing one's hips; (hombre) to swagger

contoneo M (de mujer) swinging of the hips; (de hombre) swagger

contorno M (forma) outline, contour; (tamaño de árbol, persona) girth

contorsión F contortion

contra PREP against; M **los pro y los** — the pros and cons; **en** — against; F drawback; **llevarle la** — **a alguien** to contradict someone

contraatacar[30] VI/VT to counterattack

contraataque M (militar) counterattack; (en baloncesto) fast break

contrabajo M double bass; MF double bass player

contrabandear VI/VT to smuggle

contrabandista MF smuggler

contrabando M (actividad) smuggling; (mercancías) contraband; **hacer** — to smuggle

contracción F contraction

contrachapado M plywood

contractual ADJ contractual

contracultura F counterculture

contradecir[53, 74] VI/VT to contradict

contradicción F contradiction

contradictorio ADJ contradictory

contraejemplo M counterexample

contraer[59] VT (enfermedad) to contract; (derechos) to limit; (deudas) to incur; — **matrimonio** to get married

contraespionaje M counterespionage

contrafuerte M (de muro) buttress; (de zapato) counter

contrahecho ADJ deformed

contralor M (control) comptroller, controller; (auditor) auditor

contralto M (voz) alto; MF (persona) alto

contramandar VT to countermand

contramedida F countermeasure

contraoferta F counteroffer

contraorden F countermand

contrapartida F compensation

contrapelo LOC ADV **a** — against the grain

contrapesar VT to counterbalance

contrapeso M counterbalance

contraproducente ADJ counterproductive

contrariar[28] VT to annoy; —**se** to get annoyed

contrariedad F (fastidio) annoyance; (dificultad) snag

contrario ADJ (opuesto) opposite; (discrepante) conflicting; **al** — on the contrary; **de lo** — otherwise; **llevar la contraria** to be contrary; **por el** — on the contrary; **soy** — **al doblaje de películas** I'm against the dubbing of films; **todo lo** — just the opposite

contrarrestar VT to counteract

contrarrevolución F counterrevolution

contraseña F password, watchword

contrastar VI/VT to contrast

contraste M contrast

contrata F contract

contratación F hiring; — **externa** outsourcing

contratar VT (a un empleado) to hire; (un servicio) to contract for; —**se** to be hired; — **y despedir** hire and fire

contratiempo M mishap

contratista MF contractor, builder

contrato M contract; — **de alquiler** rental agreement; **por** — by contract

contravenir[61] VT to contravene

contraventana F shutter

contribución F (regalo, participación) contribution; (impuesto) tax; — **alternativa mínima** alternative minimum tax

contribuir[19] VT to contribute

contribuya, contribuye, contribuyendo, contribuyera, contribuyese ver contribuir

contribuyente MF taxpayer

contrincante MF opponent

contrito ADJ contrite

control M (dominio, dirección) control; (contralor médico) checkup; (vigilancia) check; (puesto) checkpoint; — **de calidad** quality control; — **de daños** damage control; — **de la natalidad** birth control; — **fronterizo** border control; — **paternal** parental control; — **remoto** remote control; **bajo** — under control

controlador -ora MF comptroller; M driver; — **de impresora** printer driver

controlar VT (restringir) to control; (vigilar) to check on

controversia F controversy

controvertido ADJ controversial

contumacia F obstinacy

contumaz ADJ stubborn

contundente ADJ (argumento) forceful; (objeto) blunt; (prueba) convincing; (victoria) resounding

contusión F bruise, contusion

contuve, contuviera, contuviese ver contener

convalecencia F convalescence

convalecer[35] VI to convalesce

convaleciente MF convalescent

convección F convection

convencer[32] VT (por lógica) to convince; (por insistencia) to persuade

convencimiento M (creencia) conviction; (acción) convincing

convención F convention

convencional ADJ conventional

convendrá, convendría, convenga, convengo ver convenir

convenido ADJ agreed-upon

conveniencia F (algo cómodo) convenience; (algo aconsejable) desirability; **a su** — at your convenience

conveniente ADJ (cómodo) convenient; (aconsejable) advisable

convenio M agreement; — **colectivo** collective bargaining; — **comercial** business agreement

convenir[61] VI (ser apropiado) to be suitable; (llegar a un acuerdo) to agree

convento M convent

convergencia F convergence

converger[45] VI to converge

conversación F conversation; **trabar — con** to engage in a conversation with

conversar VI to converse

conversión F conversion; **— de dos puntos** two-point conversion

converso -sa MF convert

convertible ADJ convertible

convertidor M converter

convertir[8] VT to convert; **—se en** to become

convexo ADJ convex

convicción F conviction

convicto -ta ADJ convicted; MF convict

convidar VT to invite; *Am* to offer

convierta, convierte *ver* convertir

convincente ADJ convincing, compelling

convine, conviniendo, conviniera, conviniese *ver* convenir

convirtiendo, convirtiera, convirtiese *ver* convertir

convite M (invitación) invitation; (banquete) banquet

convivencia F (coexistencia) coexistence; (cohabitación) cohabitation, living together

convivir VI (coexistir) to coexist; (cohabitar) to cohabitate, to live together

convocación F convocation

convocar[30] VT to convoke, to call together; (una reunión, un concurso) to convene

convocatoria F (anuncio) announcement; (llamamiento) call

convoy M convoy

convoyar VT to convoy

convulsión F convulsion

conyugal ADJ conjugal, marital

cónyuge MF spouse

coñac M cognac, brandy

cooperación F cooperation

cooperar VI to cooperate

cooperativa F cooperative, co-op

cooperativista MF member of a cooperative

cooperativo ADJ cooperative

coordenada F coordinate

coordinación F coordination

coordinado ADJ coordinated

coordinador -ora MF coordinator; ADJ coordinating

coordinar VT to coordinate

copa F (vaso) goblet, wineglass; (de árbol) top; (de sombrero) crown; (palo de la baraja) card in the suit of *copas*; (trofeo, parte de un sujetador) cup; **ir de —s** to go for a drink; **— del Mundo** World Cup

copago M copayment

copete M (de pelo) tuft; (de plumas) crest; **estar hasta el —** to be fed up

copia F (réplica) copy; (de foto) print; **— de respaldo** backup copy; **— de respaldo automático** automatic backup copy; **— de seguridad** backup copy; **— en papel** hard copy; **— impresa** hard copy

copiadora F copy machine

copiar VT (reproducir) to copy; (en un examen) to cheat

copión -ona MF copycat

copioso ADJ copious, plentiful

copla F (canción) popular song; (estrofa) stanza

copo M (de nieve) snowflake; (de lana, algodón) wad; **—s de maíz** cornflakes

copropietario -ria MF joint owner

coprotagonista MF costar

cópula F copula

copulación F copulation

copular VI to copulate

copyright M copyright

coque M coke

coqueta F (mujer) coquette; (mueble) dressing table

coquetear VI to flirt, to dally

coquetería F flirtation

coqueto ADJ flirtatious

coraje M (valentía) courage; (enojo) anger

coral M (marino) coral; (musical) chorale

coralino ADJ coral

coraza F armor

corazón M (órgano) heart; (de manzana) core; (vocativo) honey; **con el — en la boca** (cansado) really tired; (nervioso) on edge; **de buen —** kindhearted; **de todo —** wholeheartedly; **romperle el — a alguien** to break someone's heart

corazonada F hunch

corbata F necktie, tie, cravat

corcel M charger, steed

corchea F eighth note; **— con puntillo** dotted eighth note

corchete M (en costura) hook and eye; (paréntesis recto) square bracket; (llave) brace

corcho M (para botella) cork; (para pescar) float

corcova F hump, hunchback

corcovear VI to buck

cordaje M strings

cordel M string

cordero M (animal) lamb; (piel, cuero) lambskin

cordial ADJ cordial

cordillera F mountain range

cordobés -esa ADJ from Cordoba; MF person from Cordoba

cordón M (cinta) cord; (al borde de la calle) *Am* curb; **— de apertura** ripcord; **— de zapatos** shoelace, shoestring; **— policial** police cordon; **— umbilical** umbilical cord

cordoncillo M ridge, rib

cordura F sanity

Corea F Korea; — **del Norte** North Korea; — **del Sur** South Korea
coreano -na ADJ & MF Korean
corear VI/VT to chant
coreografía F choreography
cornada F goring
cornear VT to gore
corneja F crow
córner M corner kick
corneta F cornet; MF bugler
cornisa F cornice, ledge
corno M horn; — **francés** French horn
cornudo ADJ horned; M cuckold
coro M (cantantes) choir, chorus; (música) chorus; (parte de la iglesia) loft; **cantar a —** to sing in unison
corolario M corollary
corona F crown
coronación F coronation
coronar VT to crown
coronario ADJ coronary
coronel M colonel
coronilla F crown of the head; **estar hasta la —** to be fed up
corpiño M (almilla) bodice; (sujetador) *Am* bra
corporación F guild
corporal ADJ corporal, bodily
corporativo ADJ corporate
corpulento ADJ stout, corpulent
corpus M corpus
corpúsculo M corpuscle
corral M (de granja) barnyard, farmyard; (para ganado) corral, pen
correa F (de cuero) leather strap; (de ventilador) belt; (de perro) leash
corrección F (acción de corregir) correction; (cualidad de correcto) correctness
correctamente ADV correctly, properly
correcto ADJ (apropiado) correct, proper; (acertado) right
corrector -ora MF editor; — **de pruebas** proofreader
corredizo ADJ sliding
corredor -ora ADJ running; MF (persona que corre, también en deportes) runner; (deportista automovilístico, ciclista) racer; (intermediario) broker, agent; M (pasillo) hallway, corridor
correduría F brokerage
corregir[14] VT (errores) to correct; (exámenes) to grade; **—se** (en lo moral) to mend one's ways; (en los errores) to correct oneself
correlación F correlation
correlacionar VT to correlate
correlato M correlate
correo M mail; (edificio) post office; — **aéreo** air mail; — **certificado** certified mail; — **de voz** voice mail; — **electrónico** e-mail; — **electrónico basura** junk e-mail, spam;

echar al — to mail
correoso ADJ tough
correr VI (persona, agua, calle) to run; (coche) to go fast; (una puerta) to slide; (dinero, tiempo) to pass; — **con los gastos** to take on the costs; VT (una cortina) to draw; (una carrera, un riesgo) to run; **—se** (moverse) to scoot over; (desteñir) to run, to bleed; (manchar) to smear
correría F foray
correspondencia F correspondence
corresponder VI (ser adecuado, estar en consonancia) to correspond; (pertenecer) to belong; VT (amor, favores) to reciprocate; **a mí me corresponde llamarla** it's up to me to call her, it behooves me to call her
correspondiente ADJ corresponding; MF correspondent
corresponsal MF correspondent
corretaje M broker's/agent's commission
corretear VI to run around
corrida F (acción de correr) running; (competición) race; (de banco) run; — **de toros** bullfight; **de —** without stopping
corrido ADJ (experimentado) worldly; (continuo) uninterrupted; **de —** without stopping; M ballad
corriente ADJ (que corre) running; (común) usual; (franco) frank; **el — mes** the current month; **estar al —** to be up to date; F (de agua, electricidad) current; (de dinero) flow; (de pesimismo) wave; (de aire) draft; (de computadora) streaming; — **alterna** alternating current; — **continua** direct current; — **del Golfo** Gulf Stream; **al —** in the loop; **dejarse llevar por la —** to conform; **llevarle la — a alguien** to humor someone
corrija, corrijo, corrigiendo, corrigiera, corrigiese, corrigió *ver* corregir
corrillo M group of gossips
corro M circle of people
corroborar VT to corroborate
corroer[73] VT to corrode
corromper VT (a una persona) to corrupt; (un alimento) to rot; **—se** (una persona) to become corrupt; (un alimento) to rot
corrompido ADJ corrupt
corrosión F corrosion
corrupción F corruption
corrupto ADJ corrupt
corsé M corset
cortada F shortcut
cortado ADJ (abreviado, sucinto) clipped; (tímido) shy; M (café) coffee with some milk; (desnivel) slope; (tenis) backspin, slice
cortador -ora MF (persona) cutter; F (aparato) cutter; **cortadora de césped** lawn mower
cortadura M cut

cortante ADJ (comentario, instrumento) cutting; (frío, viento) biting; (tono, instrumento) sharp

cortar VT to cut (también un texto digital); (un vestido, el uso de algo) to cut out; (a un locutor, una rama, el gas) to cut off; (un árbol) to cut down; (las uñas) to clip; (el césped) to mow; — **el paso** to block; — **por lo sano** to take drastic action; M SG **cortacésped** lawn mower; M SG **cortacircuitos** circuit breaker; (estilo) style; — **cortafuego** fire line; M SG **cortafuegos** firewall; M SG **cortapapeles** paper cutter; M SG **cortaplumas** penknife; M SG **cortauñas** nail clipper; VI (el frío) to bite; (la piel) to crack; —**se** (lastimarse) to cut oneself; (intimidarse) to be intimidated; (cuajarse) to curdle, to sour; —**se el pelo** to get a haircut; — **y pegar** cut and paste

corte M (de un traje, herida) cut; (acción de cortar) cutting; (de televisión) commercial break; (estilo) style; — **y confección** dressmaking; **eso me da** — that embarrasses me; F (real, judicial) court; (séquito) retinue; **las** —**s** Spanish parliament; **hacer la** — to court

cortedad F shortness

cortejar VT to court, to woo

cortejo M (séquito) entourage; (acción de cortejar) courtship

cortés ADJ courteous, polite

cortesano -na MF courtier

cortesía F courtesy, politeness

córtex M cortex

corteza F (de árbol) bark; (de pan, de la Tierra) crust; (de queso, fruta) rind; — **cerebral** cerebral cortex

corticoesteroide M corticosteriod

cortijo M country house

cortina F (de ventana) curtain; (de lluvia) sheet; — **de humo** smoke screen

cortisona F cortisone

corto ADJ (breve) short; (tonto) short on brains; (encogido) bashful; — **de vista** short-sighted; **a** — **plazo** in the short run, in the short term; **quedarse** — to come up short; **vestirse de** — to wear a short dress; M —**circuito** short circuit

cosa F thing; **como quien no quiere la** — without realizing it; **como si tal** — as cool as a cucumber; **¡cómo son las** —**s!** what a surprise; **decir una** — **por otra** to tell a lie; **esperamos** — **de cinco minutos** we waited about five minutes; **las** —**s como son** let's be honest; **las** —**s de la vida** that's life; **no es gran** — it's no big deal; **otra** — something else

cosecha F crop, harvest; **de su** — of his invention; **vino** — **1975** wine of 1975 vintage

cosechadora F combine

cosechar VT (cultivos) to harvest; (resultados) to reap

coser VI/VT to sew

cosignatario -ria MF cosigner

cosmético ADJ & M cosmetic

cósmico ADJ cosmic

cosmología F cosmology

cosmonauta MF cosmonaut

cosmopolita ADJ cosmopolitan

cosmos M cosmos

cosmovisión F worldview

coso M doodad

cosquillas F **hacer** — to tickle; **tener** — to be ticklish

cosquillear VT to tickle

cosquilleo M tickle

cosquilloso ADJ ticklish

costa F (del mar) coast, shore; **a toda** — at all costs; —**s** costs

Costa de Marfil F Ivory Coast

costado M side; **al** — alongside; **de** — edgewise; **por los cuatro** —**s** from all sides

costal M sack

costanero ADJ coastal

costar[5] VI/VT to cost; — **trabajo** to be difficult; — **un dineral** to cost a fortune; — **un ojo de la cara** to cost an arm and a leg

Costa Rica F Costa Rica

costarricense, costarriqueño -ña ADJ & MF Costa Rican

coste M cost; — **de [la] vida** cost of living; **al** — at cost

costear VT to defray costs; VI to sail along the coast

costero ADJ coastal

costilla F rib; **lo hizo a** —**s de su padre** he did it at his father's expense

costo M cost; — **adicional** added cost, extra cost; — **de [la] vida** cost of living; **al** — at cost; — **de mantenimiento** maintenance cost; — **de operación** operating cost

costoso ADJ costly

costra F (de pan) crust; (de herida) scab

costroso ADJ (pan) crusty; (heridas) scabby

costumbre F (hábito) habit; (tradición) custom; **de** — habitual; **tener la** — **de** to have the habit of; **está más cansado que de** — he's especially tired today

costura F (acción de coser) sewing; (línea de puntadas) stitching; (unión de dos piezas) seam; **alta** — high fashion, haute couture

costurero -ra M (caja) sewing box; (sastre) tailor; F seamstress

costurón M (puntada) large stitch; (cicatriz) large scar

cota F (nivel del agua) height above sea level; (estándar) benchmark

cotejar VT to check against

cotejo M comparison
cotidiano ADJ everyday
cotización F price quote, price quotation
cotizar[47] VT to quote
coto M — **de caza** game preserve; **poner** — **a** to put an end to
cotorra F (loro) parrot; (persona) chatterbox
cotorrear VI to chatter
covacha F small cave
coyote M coyote
coyuntura F (articulación) joint; (situación) juncture; **aprovechar la** — to take advantage of the situation
coz F kick; **dar coces** to kick
crack M (cocaína) crack; (deportista) ace
cráneo M cranium, skull
craso ADJ crass
cráter M crater
crayola® F crayon
creación F creation
creacionismo M creationism
creador -ora MF creator; ADJ creative
crear VI/VT to create
creatividad F creativity
creativo ADJ creative
crecer[35] VI (un niño) to grow; (masa, río) to rise; (madera, mar) to swell; (la luna) to wax
crecida F rise of a river
crecido ADJ (adulto) grown; (grande) large; (demasiado alto) overgrown
creciente ADJ (que crece) growing; (luna) crescent; M (luna) crescent; (marea) high tide; (de un río) flood
crecimiento M growth
credencial F credential
credibilidad F credibility
crédito M (solvencia, unidad de estudios) credit; (hecho de creer) credence; (fama) reputation; (préstamo) loan; — **al consumidor** consumer credit; — **rotativo** revolving credit; **dar** — **a** to believe; —**s** film credits; **vender a** — to sell on credit
credo M creed
crédulo ADJ credulous, gullible
creencia F belief
creer[18] VI/VT (tomar como cierto) to believe; (opinar) to think, to feel; —**se** to fall for; **¿quién se cree que es?** who does he think he is? **se cree artista** he fancies himself an artist; **¡ya lo creo!** I should say so!
creíble ADJ credible, believable
crema F cream (también cosmético); — **de espárragos** cream of asparagus; — **para [los] labios** lip balm, Chapstick®
cremallera F (de coche) rack; (de prenda) zipper; — **y piñón** rack and pinion
cremar VT to cremate
cremoso ADJ creamy
creosota F creosote

crepitación F crackle
crepitar VI to crackle
crepúsculo M twilight
crespo ADJ wiry, kinky
crespón M crepe
cresta F (de ola, montaña) crest; (de ave) tuft; (de gallo) comb
creyendo, creyera, creyese, creyó ver creer
creyente MF believer; ADJ believing
crezca, crezco ver crecer
cría F (acción de criar) breeding; (camada) litter; (animal joven) young
criada ver criado
criadero M — **de peces** hatchery; — **de pollos** chicken farm
criado -da MF servant; F maid
criador -ora MF breeder
crianza F (de animales) breeding; (de hijos) upbringing; (modales) manners
criar[28] VT (animales) to breed; (hijos) to bring up, to rear, to raise; **estar criando malvas** fam to be pushing up daisies; —**se** to grow up
criatura F (ser extraño) creature; (bebé) baby
criba F sieve
cribar VT to sift
crimen M (delito grave) serious crime, felony; (asesinato) murder; — **de guerra** war crime
criminal ADJ & MF criminal
criminalidad F serious crime
crin F mane
criogénico ADJ cryogenic
criollo ADJ (nacido en América) born in Spanish America; (tradicionalmente americano) traditionally Spanish American; M (lengua) creole
críquet M cricket
crisálida F chrysalis
crisantemo M chrysanthemum
crisis F crisis; — **de la edad madura** midlife crisis
crisma F crown of the head
crisol M crucible, melting pot
crisparse VI (un músculo) to contract; (los puños) to clench; (los nervios) to be on edge
cristal M (mineral, vidrio fino) crystal; (vidrio de ventana) Esp glass, pane; (lente) lens; — **labrado** cut glass
cristalería F (objetos) glassware; (establecimiento) glassware store; (fábrica) glassworks
cristalino ADJ (de cristal) crystalline; (transparente) crystal-clear; M lens of the eye
cristalizar[47] VI/VT to crystallize
cristiandad F Christendom
cristianismo M Christianity
cristiano -na ADJ & MF Christian; **hablar en** — (claramente) to speak clearly; (español) to speak Spanish
criterio M criterion

crítica F criticism; (de un libro) review

criticar[30] VT to criticize

crítico -ca ADJ critical; MF critic; (de un libro) reviewer

criticón -ona ADJ critical; MF faultfinder

Croacia F Croatia

croar VI to croak

croata ADJ & MF Croatian

crocante ADJ crisp, crunchy

croché, crochet M crochet; **hacer —** to crochet

croissant M croissant

crol M (estilo de natación) crawl, freestyle

cromado ADJ chroming

cromo M chromium, chrome

cromosoma M chromosome

crónica F (narración de eventos) chronicle; (reportaje) feature; **— policial** police report

crónico ADJ chronic

cronista MF (deportivo) reporter; (histórico) chronicler

cronología F chronology

cronológico ADJ chronological

cronometrador -ora MF timer, timekeeper

cronometraje M timing

cronometrar VT to time

cronómetro M chronometer, stopwatch

croquet M croquet

croquis M rough sketch

cross M cross-country race

cruasán M croissant

cruce M (acción, lugar) crossing; (de dos calles) crossroads, intersection; (de razas) crossbreeding; (de palabras) blend; (animal híbrido) cross; **— peatonal** crosswalk

crucero M (buque de guerra) cruiser; (viaje de placer) cruise

cruceta F crosspiece

crucial ADJ crucial

crucificar[30] VT to crucify

crucifijo M crucifix

crucigrama M crossword puzzle

crudo ADJ (comida, seda) raw; (tiempo, invierno, imágenes) harsh; (petróleo, lenguaje) crude; **agua cruda** hard water; **color —** yellowish white

cruel ADJ cruel, mean

crueldad F cruelty, meanness

cruento ADJ grisly, gruesome

crujido M (de puerta, piso) creak; (de un tallo al quebrarse) crack; (de hojas) rustle; (de fuego) crackle

crujiente ADJ (manzana, tocino) crisp, crispy; (nueces) crunchy

crujir VI (puerta, piso) to creak; (dientes) to grate; (hojas) to rustle; (nueces) to crunch; (fuego) to crackle

cruz F (cristiana) cross; (de moneda) tails; **hacerse cruces** to dread

cruzada F crusade

cruzado M (soldado) crusader; ADJ (tenis) crosscourt; (boxeo) cross; (traje) double-breasted

cruzamiento M (de piernas, razas) crossing; (de calles) crossroads; (de razas) cross

cruzar[47] VT (la calle) to cross; (un cheque) to write across; **—le la cara a alguien** to backhand someone's face; **cruzo los dedos** I'll keep my fingers crossed; **—se con alguien** to bump into someone; **—se de brazos** to fold one's arms; **se me cruzó un ciervo** a deer crossed in front of me

cuaderno M notebook; **— de bitácora** logbook; **— de espiral** spiral notebook

cuadra F (establo) stable; (distancia) *Am* block

cuadrado ADJ square; **estar —** to be fat; M square; **es [un] —** he's a square; **dos al —** two squared; **elevar al —** to square

cuadrangular ADJ (geometría) quadrangular; M (béisbol) home run

cuadrar VT (estar en ángulo recto) to square; VI (corresponder) to fit; (ser conveniente) to be convenient; (ser iguales) to balance, to add up; **— con** to be in agreement with

cuadricular VT to divide into squares

cuadrilátero ADJ quadrilateral; M (en boxeo) ring; (polígono) quadrilateral

cuadrilla F (de ladrones) gang; (de obreros) crew; (baile) square dance

cuadro M (cuadrado) square; (pintura) picture; (de bicicleta) frame; (de jardín) bed; (en tela) checker; (de fútbol) team; **— clínico** symptoms; **— interior** (béisbol) infield; **— sinóptico** summary table; **a/de —s** checked

cuadrúpedo ADJ & M quadruped

cuajada F curd

cuajar VI (leche) to curdle; (queso, cemento) to set; (gelatina) to jell; (un grupo, una organización) to come about; **—se** to curdle; **la cosa no cuajó** that didn't pan out

cuajarón M clot

cual PRON REL which; **el/la —** (cosa) which; (persona) who; **lo —** which; **sea —sea** whichever it may be; ADV like; **— hoja al viento** like a leaf in the wind

cuál PRON INTERR which; **¿cuáles son los tuyos?** which ones are yours?

cualidad F quality, trait

cualitativo ADJ qualitative

cualquiera ADJ INDEF any; **de cualquier manera/forma** anyhow; **en cualquier lado** anywhere; PRON INDEF (cosa) any; (persona) anyone; **— que sea su nacionalidad** whatever his nationality may be; **— que elijas** whichever one you choose; **— podría hacer eso** anyone could do that

cuando ADV REL when; **— menos** at least; **— mucho** at most; **se rompió — lo usaba** it broke while she was using it; PREP **— la**

guerra during the war
cuándo ADV INTERR & PRON when
cuantía F (cantidad) quantity; (importancia) importance
cuántico ADJ quantum
cuantificar[30] VT to quantify
cuantioso ADJ considerable
cuantitativo ADJ quantitative
cuanto ADJ REL any; **lee — libro ve** she reads any book she sees; PRON REL **unos —s** a few; CONJ **hice — pude** I did as much as I could; ADV **— antes** as soon as possible; **— más trabajo, menos consigo** the more I work, the less I accomplish; **en —** as soon as possible; **en — a** regarding; **en — que** as
cuánto ADJ, ADV & PRON INTERR (dinero, agua) how much; (personas, libros) how many; **¿cada —?** how often? **¿— piensas quedarte?** how long do you plan to stay?
cuarenta NUM forty; **cantarle las — a alguien** to bawl someone out; **— iguales** (tenis) deuce
cuarentena F quarantine; **una — de libros** forty-odd books
cuarentón -ona MF person in his or her forties
cuaresma F Lent
cuarta F (marcha) fourth gear; (palmo) span of a hand
cuartear VT (una res) to quarter; (los labios) to chap; **—se** to chap
cuartel M barracks; **— general** headquarters; **no dar —** to give no quarter
cuartelada F military coup
cuartelazo M military coup
cuarteto M quartet
cuartilla F sheet of paper
cuarto ADJ one-fourth, quarter; M (habitación) room; (cantidad) quarter, one-fourth; **— de baño** bathroom; **— de estar** living room; **— de final** quarter finals; **— oscuro** darkroom; **¡ni que ocho —s!** no way! **tres —s** three-fourths
cuarzo M quartz
cuásar M quasar
cuate M *Méx* pal, buddy
cuatrero -ra MF cattle rustler
cuatrillizo -za MF quadruplet
cuatro NUM four; **— ojos** four-eyes; **más de —** a good number
cuba F (barril) cask, barrel; (tina) tub, vat
Cuba F Cuba
cubano -na ADJ & MF Cuban
cubeta F (recipiente rectangular) tray; (balde) pail; **— de hielo** ice tray
cúbico ADJ cubic
cubículo M cubicle
cubierta F (de libro) cover; (cosa para cubrir) covering; (neumático) tire; (de buque) deck
cubierto M place setting; **— de plata**

silverware; **a —** sheltered
cubierto *ver* cubrir
cubismo M cubism
cúbito M ulna
cubo M (cuerpo geométrico, tercera potencia) cube; (balde) bucket; (de rueda) hub; (juguete) building block; **— de basura** trash can
cubrir[74] VT (con una manta) to cover; (con carteles) to plaster; (una vacante) to fill; (con pintura) to coat; (con crema batida) to smother; (de niebla) to shroud; **—se** (nublarse) to fog up; (ponerse el sombrero) to put on one's hat
cucaracha F cockroach
cuchara F (cubierto) spoon; (de excavadora) bucket; (para helado) scoop; **— sopera** soup spoon; **meter la —** to butt in
cucharada F (lo que cabe en una cuchara) spoonful; (medida) tablespoonful; (de helado) dip
cucharadita F teaspoonful
cucharear VT to spoon
cucharita F teaspoon
cucharón M (para helado) scoop, dipper; (para sopa) ladle
cuchichear VI/VT to whisper
cuchicheo M whisper
cuchilla F (cuchillo grande) large knife, cleaver; (de afeitar, de licuadora) blade; (de patín) runner
cuchillada F (golpe) stab, slash; (herida) stab wound, gash
cuchillería F (conjunto de cuchillos) cutlery; (tienda) cutlery store
cuchillo M knife; **pasar a —** to kill with a knife
cuclillas LOC ADV **en —** squatting; **sentarse en —** to squat
cuclillo M cuckoo
cuco ADJ cute
cucú INTERJ cuckoo
cucurucho M (de papel) paper cone; (para helado) ice-cream cone; (capirote) hood
cuelga, cuelgue *ver* colgar
cuello M (del cuerpo) neck; (de una prenda) collar; **— de botella** bottleneck; **— uterino** cervix; **— vuelto** turtleneck; **estoy hasta el — en deudas** I'm up to my neck in debts
cuenca F (de un río) basin; (del ojo) eye socket
cuenco M earthen bowl
cuenta F (cálculo) count, calculation; (factura) bill, check; (relación de ingresos y gastos) account; (bolita) bead; (depósito bancario) bank account; **— conjunta** joint account; **— corriente** checking account; **— de ahorros** savings account; **— de contrapartida** contra account; **— de crédito** charge account; **— de depósito en garantía** charge account; **— de gastos** expense account; **— de mercado monetario** escrow

account; — **en un paraíso fiscal** offshore account; —**s por/a cobrar** accounts receivable; —**s por/a pagar** accounts payable; — **regresiva/atrás** countdown; **abrir/cerrar una** — to open/close an account; **a fin de** —**s** when all is said and done; **ajustar** —**s** to settle old scores; **caí en [la]** — **de que** it just dawned on me that; **dar** — **de** to finish off; **dar** —**s** to give an accounting; **darse** — to realize; **en** — **de margen** on margin; **en resumidas** —**s** in short; **eso corre por mí** — that is my responsibility; **habida** — **de** bearing in mind; **más de la** — more than necessary; **pasar la** — to call in a favor; **tomar/tener en** — to take into account; **trabajar por** — **propia** to freelance; M SG **cuentagotas** eyedropper

cuenta, cuente *ver* contar

cuento M story, tale; — **chino** tall tale; — **de hadas** fairy tale; — **de nunca acabar** never-ending story; **déjese de** —**s** come to the point; **traer a** — to bring up; **venir a** — to be to the point

cuerda F (soga) cord, rope; (de arco) bowstring; (de guitarra) string; (de reloj) spring; — **floja** tightrope; —**s vocales** vocal cords; **bajo** — under the table; **contra las** —**s** on the ropes; **dar** — **a** to wind; **no le des** — don't get him started

cuerdo ADJ sane

cuerno M horn (también instrumento de viento); (de caracol) feeler; (de ciervo) antler; — **de la abundancia** horn of plenty; **coger el toro por los** —**s** to take the bull by the horns; **poner** —**s a** to be unfaithful to

cuero M (piel de animal) hide; (piel curtida) leather; — **cabelludo** scalp; **en** —**s** naked

cuerpo M body; (torso) torso; ¡— **a tierra!** hit the deck! — **de bomberos** fire department; — **de policía** police force; — **de prensa** press corps; — **docente** teaching staff; **a** — **de rey** in great luxury; — **extraño** foreign body; **dar** — **a** to flesh out; **de** — **entero** through and through; **ganó por tres** —**s de ventaja** he won by three lengths; **ir de** — to have a bowel movement

cuervo M crow, raven

cuesta F slope; — **abajo** downhill; — **arriba** uphill; **a** —**s** piggyback

cuesta, cueste *ver* costar

cuestión F question; **en** — **de segundos** in a matter of seconds; **poner en** — to question; **ser** — **de** to be a matter of

cuestionable ADJ questionable

cuestionador ADJ questioning

cuestionar VT to question

cuestionario M questionnaire

cueva F cave

cuidado M (atención) care; (preocupación) worry; — **con el perro** beware of the dog; — **de la casa** housekeeping; — **dental** dental care; — **posparto** postnatal care; — **prenatal** prenatal care; — **terminal** end-of-life care; **al** — **de** under the care of; **con** — carefully; **eso me trae sin** — I don't care about that; **tener** — to be careful; **un enfermo de** — a severely ill patient; INTERJ look out!

cuidador -ora MF caregiver, caretaker

cuidadoso ADJ careful

cuidar VT to take care of, to look after; — **de** to take care of; — **la casa** to keep house; — **niños** to babysit; —**se de** to beware of

culata F (anca) haunch; (de rifle) butt; (de motor) cylinder head

culatazo M (golpe) blow with the butt of a rifle; (rebote al disparar) recoil

culebra F snake

culebrear VI to slither

culebrilla F shingles

culinario ADJ culinary

culminación F (de carrera, ceremonia) culmination, high point; (de un sueño) fulfillment

culminante ADJ climactic

culminar VI to culminate

culpa F (responsabilidad) fault, blame; (sentimiento) guilt; **echar la** — **a** to blame; **por** — **de** because of; **tener la** — to be to blame

culpabilidad F guilt

culpable ADJ guilty; MF culprit

culpar VT to blame

cultivable ADJ (planta) cultivable; (tierra) arable

cultivado ADJ (tierra) cultivated; (perlas, persona) cultured

cultivador -ora MF (persona) cultivator; F (aparato) cultivator

cultivar VT (cosecha) to grow, to raise; (la tierra) to farm; (relaciones, inteligencia) to cultivate; (microbios) to culture

cultivo M (de plantas) growing; (de la tierra) farming; (de microbios) culture; (de relaciones) cultivation; **de** — cultured

culto ADJ educated, cultured; M worship; **libertad de** — freedom of religion

cultura F culture; — **general** general knowledge

cultural ADJ cultural

culturismo M body-building

cumbre F summit

cumpleaños M SG birthday

cumplido ADJ (cortés) polite; (perfecto) perfect; M compliment; **hacer algo de** — to do something out of duty; **hacer un** — to pay a compliment

cumplimiento M (de un contrato)

performance; (de una promesa, obligación) fulfillment; (de un plazo) expiration

cumplir VT (una obligación) to fulfill, to discharge; (una promesa) to keep, to honor; (una condena) to complete, to serve; — **diez años** to turn ten; **hacer** — to enforce; VI (vencer) to expire; — **con** to meet [a goal]; **me cumple informarle que** it is my duty to inform you that

cúmulo M (grupo) host; (tipo de nube) cumulus

cuna F (que se mece) cradle; (con barandas) crib

cundir VI (extenderse) to spread; (rendir) to go a long way

cuneta F roadside ditch; **en la** — out to pasture

cuña F (pieza para hender) wedge; (bacinilla) bedpan

cuñado -da M brother-in-law; F sister-in-law

cuño M die-stamp; **de** — **hispano** with a Hispanic stamp

cuota F (cantidad que le corresponde a uno) quota, allotment; (cantidad que hay que pagar) dues; (mensualidad) installment; —**s del coche** car payments; —**s sindicales** union dues

cupé M coupé

cupe, cupiera, cupiese ver caber

cupo M (cantidad) quota; (capacidad) Am room

cupón M coupon

cúpula F dome

cura F cure, remedy; M priest

curable ADJ curable

curación F cure

curanderismo M faith healing

curandero -ra MF healer

curar VT (una enfermedad, carne) to cure; (una herida) to heal; —**se** to heal; —**se en salud** to take precautionary measures

curiosear VI to look around; (en asuntos ajenos) to pry

curiosidad F curiosity

curioso ADJ curious

Curita® F Am adhesive bandage, Band-aid®

currículo/currículum M résumé; — **vitae** CV

curro M Esp job

curruca F warbler

curry M curry

cursar VT (estudios) to take; (mensaje, invitación) to send

cursi ADJ (afectado) affected; (de mal gusto) tacky

cursillo M (individual) tutorial; (corto) short course

cursivo ADJ cursive; **escribir en cursiva** to write in cursive

curso M (de río, enfermedad, acontecimientos, moneda) course; (período docente) academic year; (grupo de estudiantes) class; (libro) textbook; — **legal** legal currency; **el mes en** — the current month

cursor M cursor

curtiduría F tannery

curtiembre F tannery

curtir VT (cuero) to tan; (cutis) to weather; (el carácter) to harden; —**se** (envejecerse) to get weathered; (acostumbrarse) to become accustomed to hardships

curva F curve (también béisbol); — **de campana** bell curve

curvatura F curvature

curvo ADJ curved

cúspide F summit

custodia F custody, keeping; **en** — (un monto de dinero) in escrow; (un prisionero) in custody

custodiar VT to guard

custodio -dia MF guardian

cutáneo ADJ cutaneous

cutícula F cuticle

cutis M facial skin

cuyo ADJ REL whose

cyborg M cyborg

Dd

dádiva F gift

dadivoso ADJ generous

dado ADJ given; M die; **jugar a los** —**s** to throw dice

dador -ora MF giver; — **de sangre** blood donor

daga F dagger

dalia F dahlia

daltónico ADJ color-blind

dama F lady; (en el juego de mesa) king; **jugar a las** —**s** to play checkers; — **de honor** bridesmaid

damajuana F demijohn

damasco M (fruta) apricot; (árbol) apricot tree

damisela F damsel

dandi M dandy

danés -esa ADJ Danish; MF Dane; M (lengua) Danish

danza F dance; — **del vientre** belly dance; **en** — in action

danzante MF dancer

danzar[47] VI/VT to dance

dañar VT to harm, to damage; —**se** to suffer harm

dañino ADJ harmful

daño M damage, harm; — **colateral** collateral damage; — **emergente** actual damage; — **físico** bodily harm; —**s materiales** property damage; —**s y perjuicios** damages; **hacer** — to harm

dañoso ADJ harmful

dar[62] VT (un regalo) to give; (un golpe, naipes) to

deal; (sal) to add; (una fiesta) to throw; (la hora) to strike; (un olor) to give off; (la alarma) to raise; (un paseo) to take; — **a** (un edificio) to face; (una calle) to lead to; — **a conocer** to announce; — **a entender** to intimate; — **con** to hit upon, to find; — **de alta** to discharge, to release from the hospital; — **de baja** to discharge; — **de comer** to feed; — **de sí** to perform at capacity; **esta tela da de sí** this fabric gives; — **en la pared** to hit the wall; —**le con** to scrub with; **lo misma da** it makes no difference; **¿qué más da?** what difference does it make? **dale que dale** on and on; **hoy no doy una** today I can't get anything right; **le doy cincuenta años** he must be about fifty; **me da rabia/miedo** that makes me angry/afraid; **no me da el tiempo para ir al cine** I don't have time to go to the movies; **que no le dé el sol** don't let the sun shine on it; **y dale** enough already; —**se a la bebida** to indulge in drinking; —**se por conforme** to be satisfied; —**se prisa** to hurry; **dárselas de** to boast of being; **en este lugar se dan las flores silvestres** in this location wildflowers are found

dardo M dart

dársena F dock

datar VT to date; — **de** to date from

dátil M date

dato M piece of information; —**s** data

d.C. ADV AD

de PREP — **la familia** of the family; — **Madrid** from Madrid; **habló — la guerra** he talked about the war; **el hombre — gafas** the man with glasses; **el mejor estudiante — la clase** the best student in the class; **fácil — hacer** easy to do; **más — tres** more than three; **llevar — la mano** to lead by the hand; — **regreso a España** upon returning to Spain; — **venta en farmacias** on sale in pharmacies; **ancianos — respeto** older people to be respected; — **lo más lindo** really pretty; **tonto — mí** silly me

dé *ver* dar

deambular VI to amble, to saunter; — **por** (el bosque) to wander about; (el internet) to surf

deán M dean

debacle M debacle

debajo ADV under, underneath; PREP — **de** under, below; **por — de** under

debate M debate

debatir VT to debate; —**se** to struggle

debe M debit

deber VT **deben apoyarme** they should support me; **debe de ser** it must be; **deberías sentarte** you should sit down; VT to owe; **me debes una** you owe me one; **me debo a mis alumnos** I'm devoted to my

students; M duty; —**es** homework

debidamente ADV duly

debido ADJ due; — **a** due to, owing to; **a su — tiempo** in due time

débil ADJ (sin fuerza) weak; (endeble) frail, feeble; (sonido) faint

debilidad F (falta de fuerza) weakness; (cualidad de endeble) frailty; (de un sonido) faintness

debilitamiento M weakening

debilitante ADJ debilitating

debilitar VT to weaken, to debilitate

débito M debit

debutar VI to make a debut

década F decade

decadencia F (moral) decadence, decay; (cultural, económica) decline

decadente ADJ decadent

decaer[52] VI (fuerza) to weaken; (energía) to ebb; (salud) to fail; (ánimo) to flag

decaimiento M (decadencia) decline; (debilidad) weakness

decano-na ADJ senior; MF dean

decapitar VT to behead, to decapitate

decatlón M decathlon

decena F —**s de candidatos** tens of candidates

decencia F decency

decenio M decade

decente ADJ decent; **muy —** rather good

decepción F disappointment

decepcionante ADJ disappointing

decepcionar VT to disappoint

decibelio M decibel

decidido ADJ resolute, determined; **una decidida preferencia** a decided preference

decidir VI/VT to decide; —**se** to make up one's mind; —**se a** to resolve to

deciduo ADJ deciduous

décima F tenth

decimal ADJ decimal

décimo ADJ & M tenth

decir[53, 74] VT (palabras, oraciones) to say; (una mentira, un chiste, la verdad) to tell; — **tonterías** to talk nonsense; **con —te que** suffice it to say that; **este tipo no me dice nada** this guy leaves me cold; **¡que me lo digan a mí!** you're telling me that? VI to say; **diga** hello (al contestar el teléfono); **es — that** is to say; **he dicho** I have spoken; **no es prometedor que digamos** it's hardly promising; **no me digas** you don't say; **querer —** to mean; M saying

decisión F decision; **tomar una —** to make a decision

decisivo ADJ decisive

declaración F (de amor, independencia, guerra) declaration; (de un hecho) statement; (de un testigo) deposition; — **de derechos** bill of rights; — **de impuestos / de la renta** tax return; — **de impuestos sobre la renta**

income tax return; **— jurada** affidavit; **— de
la misión** mission statement; **— errónea/
falsa** misstatement; **— sobre la
privacidad** privacy statement

declarar VT (amor, independencia, ingresos) to
declare; (un hecho) to state; **— culpable** to
find guilty; **os declaro marido y mujer** I
pronounce you man and wife; VI (como
testigo) to testify; **—se** (un amante) to declare
one's love; **—se culpable** to plead guilty;
—se en huelga to go on strike; **—se en
quiebra** to declare bankruptcy

declinar VI/VT to decline

declive M (pendiente) slope, drop; (decadencia)
decline

decoración F decoration; **— de interiores**
interior decorating

decorado M (de casa) decoration; (de escenario)
scenery

decorar VT to decorate

decorativo ADJ decorative

decoro M decorum, propriety

decorosamente ADV decorously, properly

decoroso ADJ decorous, proper

decrépito ADJ decrepit

decrepitud F decrepitude

decretar VT to decree

decreto M (disposición ejecutiva) decree; (ley)
act

dedal M thimble

dedicación F dedication

dedicar[30] VT (la vida) to dedicate, to devote; (un
libro) to dedicate; **—se** to dedicate oneself; (a
los estudios) to apply oneself

dedicatoria F dedication

dedo M (de la mano) finger; (del pie) toe; **—
anular** ring finger; **— índice** index finger;
— mayor / del corazón middle finger; **—
meñique** little finger; **— pulgar** thumb;
chuparse el — to be a fool; **chuparse los
—s** to lick one's fingers; **cruzar los —s** to
keep one's fingers crossed; **elegir a —** to
appoint directly; **hacer —** to hitch a ride; **no
mover un —** not to lift a finger

deducción F deduction; **— impositiva** tax
deduction

deducible ADJ deductible

deducir[38] VT (concluir) to deduce, to conclude;
(descontar) to deduct

defecación F bowel movement

defecar[30] VI/VT to defecate

defección F defection

defecto M defect, flaw; **por —** by default

defectuoso ADJ defective, faulty

defender[2] VT (un fuerte) to defend; (una causa)
to champion; (los derechos) to stand up for,
to stick up for; **se defiende en francés** he
can hold his own in French

defendible ADJ defensible

defensa F defense (también deportes); MF
(fútbol) defender; **— individual**
man-to-man defense; **— en zonas** zone
defense; **aprende — personal** he's learning
self-defense; **lo dijo en — propia** he said it
in self-defense

defensivo ADJ defensive; **a la defensiva** on the
defensive

defensor -ora MF (en la guerra) defender; (de
una causa) champion

deferencia F deference

deficiencia F deficiency

deficiente ADJ deficient

déficit M deficit, shortfall; **— presupuestario**
budget deficit

defienda, defiende ver defender

definición F definition; **— por penales**
penalty shoot-out

definido ADJ definite

definir VT to define

definitivamente ADV definitely; once and for
all; **— voy a comprar una impresora** I am
definitely going to buy a printer; **lo
arreglaremos todo —** we will take care of
everything once and for all

definitivo ADJ (superior) definitive; (final) final;
en definitiva all things considered

deflación F deflation

deflector M baffle

deforestación F deforestation

deformación F deformation

deformar VT to deform; **—se** to become
deformed

deforme ADJ deformed, misshapen

deformidad F deformity

defraudar VT (cometer fraude) to defraud;
(decepcionar) to disappoint

defunción F death

degenerado -da ADJ & MF degenerate

degenerar VI to degenerate

degenerativo ADJ degenerative

deglución F swallowing

degollar[24] VT to slash someone's throat

degradación F degradation

degradar VT (envilecer) to degrade, to debase;
(rebajar el rango) to demote; **—se** to degrade

degüello M throat-slashing; **lucha a —** fight to
the death

dehesa F pasture

deidad F deity

dejada F **— de volea** drop shot, stop-volley

dejadez F slovenliness

dejado ADJ slovenly

dejar VT (abandonar, no comer, legar) to leave;
(a un enamorado) to leave, to dump;
(permitir) to let; (soltar) to let go; **— de** to
stop; **— caer** to drop; **— pasar** to pass up;
déjame en paz leave me alone; **me dejó
atónito** it left/rendered me speechless; **no**

dejes de venir don't fail to come; **te lo dejo en mil dólares** I'll sell it to you for one thousand dollars; **—se** to let oneself go; **—se crecer la barba** to grow a beard

deje M slight accent

dejo M (sabor) aftertaste; (acento) slight accent; (toque) hint; **tener un — de** to smack of

delantal M apron

delante ADV in front; **— de** in front of, ahead of

delantera F (de carrera) lead; (de vestido) front; **llevar la —** to be in the lead; **tomar la —** to take the lead

delantero -ra ADJ (pata) front; MF (línea, deportista) forward; M front

delatar VT to inform against, to squeal on; **— la edad** to betray one's age

delator -ora MF accuser, informer

delegación F delegation

delegado -da MF delegate

delegar[40] VT to delegate

deleitar VT to delight; **—se en algo** to revel in something; **—se la vista con** to feast one's eyes on

deleite M delight

deletrear VT to spell; **— mal** to misspell

deleznable ADJ despicable

delfín M dolphin

delgadez F thinness

delgado ADJ thin, slender, slim

deliberación F deliberation

deliberadamente ADV deliberately

deliberado ADJ deliberate

deliberar VI/VT to deliberate

delicadeza F (tacto) gentleness; (fineza) delicacy; **con —** gently; **tuvo la — de llamar** he was kind enough to call

delicado ADJ (suave, frágil, controvertido) delicate; (enfermizo) frail; (exquisito) dainty; (quisquilloso) squeamish

delicatessen F PL delicacies

delicia F delight

delicioso ADJ delicious, delectable

delimitar VT to delimit

delincuencia F crime

delincuente ADJ & MF delinquent, criminal; **— juvenil** juvenile delinquent

delineador M eyeliner

delinear VT to delineate, to outline

delirante ADJ delirious, raving

delirar VI to be delirious, to rave

delirio M delirium; **— paranoico** paranoid delusion; **—s de grandeza** delusions of grandeur

delito M crime, offense

deltoides M SG deltoids

demacrado ADJ drawn, gaunt, haggard

demagogo -ga MF demagogue

demanda F (de mercancías) demand; (de seguros) insurance claim; (pleito) lawsuit;

por — on demand; **entablar una —** to file a lawsuit

demandado -da MF (en un pleito) defendant; (en un arbitraje) respondent

demandante MF plaintiff

demandar VT (pedir) to ask for; (poner pleito) to sue, to file a suit against

demarcar[30] VT to demarcate

demás ADJ (restante) remaining; PRON the others, the rest; **lo —** the rest; **y —** and whatnot; ADV **por lo —** moreover; **por —** useless

demasía LOC ADV **en —** excessively

demasiado ADV too; too much; **eso es — para mí** that's too much for me; **él es — alto** he's too tall; ADJ too much; too many; **— dinero** too much money; **demasiadas cosas** too many things

demencia F (locura) insanity; (senilidad) senility; (enfermedad mental) dementia

demente ADJ demented, insane, deranged

democracia F democracy

demócrata MF democrat; **Partido —** Democratic Party

democrático ADJ democratic; (del Partido —) Democrat, Democratic

democratización F democratization

demografía F demographics

demográfico ADJ demographic

demoler[6] VT to demolish, to tear down

demonio M demon; **¿qué —s haces?** what the heck are you doing? **un frío del —** bitter cold

demora F delay

demorar VT to delay; **—se** to linger

demostración F (prueba) demonstration; (de un programa digital) demo; **— de fuerza** show of force

demostrar[5] VT (mostrar) to demonstrate, to show; (comprobar) to prove, to demonstrate

demostrativo ADJ demonstrative

demudar VT to change, to alter

demuestra, demuestre ver demostrar

denegación F (de una petición) denial

dengue M dengue fever

denigrar VT to denigrate, to disparage

denodado ADJ untiring

denominación F (valor) denomination; (nombre) designation

denominador M denominator; **— común** common denominator

denominar VT to designate, to term

denostar[5] VT to revile

denotación F denotation

denotar VT to denote

densidad F density; **alta —** high density

denso ADJ (sólido) dense; (líquido) heavy

dentado ADJ (rueda) toothed; (montaña) ragged

dentadura F set of teeth; **— postiza** false teeth

dental ADJ dental

dentellada F (mordedura) bite; (señal de diente) tooth mark; **a —s** biting

dentífrico M toothpaste, dentifrice

dentista MF dentist

dentro ADV inside; (tenis) in; PREP **— de la casa** inside the house; **— de la ley** within the law; **— de quince días** (en el plazo de) within two weeks; (al cabo de) in two weeks; **por —** within

denuncia F (acusación) denunciation; (de mina, de seguro) claim

denunciar VT (un hecho negativo) to denounce; (una mina) to claim; (un delito) to report

deparar VT (tener preparado) to have in store; (proporcionar) to afford; **el destino me deparaba una sorpresa** fate had a surprise in store for me

departamento M (división) department; (piso) small apartment; (provincia) province

departir VI *lit* to commune

dependencia F (hecho de depender) dependence; (habituación) dependency; (filial) branch office

depender VI to depend; **— de** to depend on

dependiente -ta ADJ dependent; MF sales clerk, salesperson

depilación F hair removal

depilar VT to remove hair; (con cera) to wax

depilatorio ADJ & M depilatory

deplorable ADJ deplorable

deplorar VT to deplore

deponer[56, 74] VT (las armas) to lay down; (a un ministro) to depose, to remove; VI to defecate

deportar VT to deport

deporte M sport; **me gusta el —** I like sports/ athletics

deportista ADJ athletic; MF athlete

deportivo ADJ athletic; **revista deportiva** sports magazine

deposición F (de un testigo) deposition; (de un ministro) removal; (movimiento de vientre) bowel movement

depositante MF depositor

depositar VT to deposit; **—se** to settle

depositario -ria MF repository

depósito M (en el banco) deposit; (de gasolina) tank; (de agua) reservoir; (de armas) depot, dump; (de mercancías) stock room, storehouse; **— de cadáveres** morgue; **— de garantía** security deposit; **hacer un —** to make a deposit; **en —** on consignment

depravado ADJ depraved

depreciar VI to depreciate

depredador -ora MF predator

depresión F depression

depresor M depressor; **— de lengua** tongue depressor

deprimente ADJ depressing

deprimido ADJ depressed

deprimir VT to depress

deprisa ADV quickly

depuración F (de agua) purification; (de un programa) debugging

depurador M debugger

depurar VT to purify; (un programa) to debug

derby M derby

derecha F (política) right wing; (tenis) forehand; **a la —** to the right; **de —s** right-wing

derechista ADJ right-wing; MF rightist

derecho ADJ (no izquierdo) right; (recto) straight; **ponerse —** to hold oneself erect, to stand up straight; ADV straight; **volver — a casa** to go straight home; **todo —** straight ahead; M (preceptos, disciplina) law; (prerrogativa) right; **— al trabajo** right to work; **— consuetudinario** common law; **— de admisión** fee; **—s del cliente** customer rights; **— internacional** international law; **—s** fees; **—s aduaneros** tax on imports; **—s civiles** civil rights; **—s de autor** royalties; **—s de la mujer** women's rights; **—s de los animales** animal rights; **estar en su —** to be entitled; **poner al —** to put on right side out; **registrar los —s** to copyright

derechura F straightness

deriva F drift; **ir a la —** to be adrift

derivación F derivation

derivado M (subproducto) by-product; (palabra) derivative

derivar VT to derive

dermabrasión F dermabrasion

dermatología F dermatology

dermatólogo -ga MF dermatologist

derogación F repeal

derogar[40] VT to repeal

derramamiento M spill, spilling; **— de sangre** bloodshed

derramar VT (un líquido) to spill; (sangre, lágrimas) to shed; **—se** to spill over, to run over

derrame M spill; **— cerebral** stroke, cerebral hemorrhage

derredor LOC ADV **en —** all around

derrengar[40] VT (dañar la espalda) to sprain one's back; (cansar) to exhaust

derretir[9] VT to melt; **—se por alguien** to be crazy about someone

derribar VT (un edificio) to demolish, to tear down; (a una persona) to knock down; (un gobierno) to topple, to overthrow; (un avión) to shoot down, to down

derrocamiento M overthrow

derrocar[30] VT (un gobierno) to overthrow, to topple; (a un dictador) to depose

derrochador -ora ADJ extravagant; MF (de dinero) spendthrift; (de recursos) squanderer

derrochar VT (dinero) to squander; (salud) to

radiate

derroche M (de recursos) waste, extravagance; (de color) profusion

derrota F defeat

derrotar VT to defeat

derrotero M course

derrubio M washout

derruido ADJ dilapidated

derrumbadero M precipice

derrumbamiento M collapse

derrumbar VT to demolish; **—se** (edificio) to collapse; (túnel, caverna) to cave in

derrumbe M (de tierra) landslide; (de un edificio) collapse

desabotonar VT to unbutton, to undo

desabrido ADJ (comida) tasteless; (persona) *Am* dull; *Esp* surly

desabrigado ADJ exposed; **no salgas tan —** put on some warm clothes before you go out

desabrochado ADJ undone, unfastened

desabrochar VT (botones) to undo; (ganchos) to unhook; (hebillas, cinturones) to unbuckle; (botones) to unbutton; **—se** to come undone

desacato M disrespect; **— al tribunal** contempt of court

desacelerar VI to decelerate

desacierto M mistake

desaconsejable ADJ inadvisable

desaconsejar VT to caution against

desacoplar VT to uncouple, to disconnect

desacostumbrado ADJ unusual

desacostumbrar VT to break of a habit; **—se** to lose a habit

desacreditar VT to discredit

desactivación F deactivation

desactivar VT (explosivo, situación) to defuse; (mecanismo) to disable; (virus) to deactivate

desacuerdo M disagreement; **estar en —** to be at odds

desafiante ADJ defiant

desafiar[28] VT (retar) to challenge, to dare; (enfrentar) to defy

desafilado ADJ dull

desafilar VT to dull; **—se** to become dull

desafinado ADJ out of tune, off-key

desafinar VT to be out of tune

desafío M (reto) challenge; (desobediencia) defiance

desafortunadamente ADV unfortunately

desafortunado ADJ unfortunate, unlucky

desafuero M (de un diputado) withdrawal of immunity; (atropello) outrage

desagradable ADJ disagreeable, unpleasant

desagradar VT to displease

desagradecido ADJ ungrateful

desagrado M displeasure

desagraviar VI to make amends, to redress

desagravio M redress

desaguadero M drainpipe

desaguar[25] VI to drain

desagüe M (acción de desaguar) drainage; (de lavabo) drain, drainpipe; (en la azotea) gutter

desaguisado M mess

desahogado ADJ (cómodo) comfortable; (espacioso) spacious

desahogar[40] VT (aliviar) to relieve; **—se** to pour out one's feelings

desahogo M relief; **vivir con —** to live an easy life

desairar VT to slight, to snub, to rebuff

desaire M slight, snub, rebuff

desajustar VT to loosen; **—se** to come loose

desalentado ADJ despondent

desalentador ADJ disheartening

desalentar[1] VT to discourage, to dishearten; **—se** to get discouraged

desaliento M discouragement, dismay

desaliñado ADJ disheveled, slovenly, unkempt

desaliño M slovenliness

desalmado ADJ heartless

desalojar VT (una piedra) to dislodge; (un tribunal) to clear; (un edificio) to evacuate; (a un inquilino) to evict; (una vivienda) to vacate

desamparado ADJ helpless, forlorn

desamparar VT to forsake

desamparo M abandonment, helplessness

desamueblado ADJ unfurnished

desangrar VT to bleed; **—se** to bleed to death

desanimado ADJ (persona) discouraged; (jornada) dull

desanimar VT to discourage

desánimo M discouragement

desaparecer[35] VI (perderse) to disappear, to vanish; (morir) to pass away

desaparezca, desaparezco *ver* desaparecer

desaparición F disappearance; (muerte) demise

desapasionado ADJ dispassionate

desapego M detachment

desapercibido ADJ unnoticed

desaprobación F disapproval

desaprobar[5] VT to disapprove of

desarmado ADJ unarmed

desarmar VT (quitar las armas) to disarm; (desmontar) to take apart

desarme M disarmament

desarraigar[40] VT to uproot

desarreglar VT to disturb, to mess up

desarreglo M (trastorno, enfermedad) disorder; (desorden) mess

desarrollador-ora MF developer

desarrollar VT (aumentar) to develop; (extender algo enrollado) to unroll; (llevar a cabo) to carry out; (aclarar) to elaborate, to flesh out; **—se** to unfold

desarrollo M development; (de una ecuación) expansion; **en —** developing

desarticulado ADJ disjointed

desaseado ADJ slovenly

desaseo M slovenliness

desasir[50] VT to let go of

desasosiego M uneasiness

desastrado ADJ (desaseado) untidy; (funesto) ill-fated

desastre M disaster

desastroso ADJ disastrous

desatado ADJ (ambición) unfettered; (zapatos) untied

desatar VT (un nudo) to untie, to loosen; (una ola de violencia) to unleash; **—se** to come untied; **—se en insultos** to let out a string of insults

desatascador M plunger

desatascar[30] VT (un inodoro) to unclog; (un objeto atrapado) to dislodge

desatención F lack of attention

desatender[2] VT (no ocuparse de algo) to neglect; (ignorar) to ignore

desatendido ADJ (descuidado) neglected; (ignorado) ignored

desatento ADJ inattentive

desatinado ADJ imprudent

desatornillar VT to unscrew

desatracar[30] VI/VT to cast off, to shove off

desavenencia F discord

desayunar VT **desayuné huevos** I had eggs for breakfast; **—se** to have breakfast; **—se [con que]** to find out [that]

desayuno M breakfast

desazón F uneasiness

desbandarse VI to disband

desbaratar VT (un plan) to disrupt; (un hechizo) to break; **—se** to break down

desbocado ADJ (caballo) runaway; (collar) loose

desbordamiento M overflow

desbordante ADJ overflowing

desbordar VI (derramar) to overflow; VT (abrumar) to overwhelm; **—se** to overflow, to spill over

desbravar VT to break

descabalgar[40] VI to dismount

descabellado ADJ harebrained

descabezar[47] VT to behead; **— un sueño** to take a nap

descafeinado ADJ decaffeinated

descalabrar VT (la cabeza) to split someone's head open; (a una persona) to hurt

descalabro M disaster

descalcificación F decalcification

descalificar VT to disqualify

descalzar[47] VT to take off someone's shoes; **—se** to take off one's shoes

descalzo ADJ barefoot

descaminado ADJ **andar/ir —** to be on the wrong track

descamisado ADJ (sin camisa) shirtless; (pobre) poor

descansar VI/VT to rest; **— en paz** to rest in peace; **—se en** to rely on

descanso M (acción de descansar) rest; (de escalera) landing; (intermisión, receso) break; (en fútbol) halftime; **en —** at ease

descapotable ADJ & M convertible

descarado ADJ shameless, impudent, brazen; **a la descarada** shamelessly

descarga F (de batería, agua, armas) discharge; (de buques) unloading; (emocional) outpouring; (de electricidad) shock; (de internet) download

descargar[40] VT (una batería, agua) to discharge; (un buque, un arma de fuego) to unload; (bomba) to drop; (un programa de computadora) to download; **—se** (una batería) to drain; (ira) to vent

descargo M **en su —** in his defense

descarnado ADJ (realidad) stark; (cara) emaciated

descaro M effrontery, impudence, nerve

descarriar[28] VT to lead astray; **—se** to go astray

descarrilarse VI to derail, to jump the track

descartar VT (un naipe) to discard; (una posibilidad) to dismiss, to discard

descarte M discard; **por —** by elimination

descascararse VI (en jirones) to peel; (en fragmentos) to chip, to flake

descendencia F (linaje) descent; (descendientes) descendants

descendente ADJ descending, downward

descender[2] VI to descend; **— de** to descend from

descendiente MF descendant

descenso M descent

descentralización F decentralization

descienda, desciende *ver* descender

descifrado M deciphering

descifrar VT to decipher

descodificación F decoding, decryption

descodificar[30] VT to decode, to decrypt

descolgar[42] VT (una cortina) to take down; (un teléfono) to pick up; **—se con** to come up with; **—se de** to come down from

descollar[5] VI to excel

descolorido ADJ (persona) pale; (cosa) colorless

descomponer[56, 74] VT (disgustar) to upset; (dar diarrea) to give diarrhea; (dar náuseas) to make nauseous; (separar) to break down; (cadáveres) to decompose; (un reloj) to break; **— en factores** to factor; **—se** (productos químicos) to break down; (cadáveres) to decompose; (un reloj) to break; (sentir náuseas) to be nauseous; (tener diarrea) to have diarrhea; (disgustarse) to go to pieces

descomposición F (de cadáveres) decomposition; (de productos químicos) breaking down; (diarrea) diarrhea

descomprimir VT to decompress

descompuesto ADJ (roto) broken; (caótico)

chaotic; (con diarrea) having diarrhea

descomunal ADJ enormous

desconcertado ADJ disconcerted

desconcertante ADJ disconcerting

desconcertar[1] VT to disconcert, to puzzle, to baffle; **—se** to become disconcerted

desconchar VT to chip

desconcierto M confusion

desconectado ADJ disconnected

desconectar VT to disconnect

desconexión F (acción de desconectar) disconnecting; (incomunicación) disconnect

desconfiado ADJ mistrustful, suspicious

desconfianza F mistrust

desconfiar[28] VT to distrust, to mistrust, to be wary of

descongelación F thawing

descongestionante M decongestant

descongestionar VT to decongest

desconocer[35] VT (no reconocer) to fail to recognize; (no saber) not to know; **te desconozco** you are not acting like yourself today

desconocido -da ADJ unknown; MF stranger

desconocimiento M ignorance

desconsideración F thoughtlessness

desconsiderado ADJ thoughtless, inconsiderate

desconsolado ADJ disconsolate, dejected

desconsolador ADJ disheartening

desconsolar[5] VT to dishearten; **—se** to become disheartened

desconsuelo M dejection

descontaminación F decontamination

descontaminar VT to decontaminate

descontar[5] VT (bajar el precio) to discount; (excluir) to exclude; (quitar) to dock

descontentadizo ADJ hard to please

descontentar VT to displease

descontento ADJ & M discontent

descorazonado ADJ disheartened

descortés ADJ discourteous, impolite

descortesía F discourtesy, impoliteness

descortezar[47] VT to strip the bark from

descoser VT to rip; **—se** to come unsewn

descosido ADJ unsewn; M unsewn place; **hablar como un —** to talk one's head off

descostrar VT to remove the crust from

descrédito M discredit

descreído -da ADJ unbelieving; MF unbeliever

descreimiento M unbelief

describir[74] VT to describe

descripción F description

descriptivo ADJ descriptive

descrito *ver* describir

descuartizar[47] VT to quarter

descubierto ADJ (destapado) uncovered; (sin sombrero) hatless; **al —** in the open; **estar al — to** be exposed; **poner al —** to expose, to lay bare; **en —** overdrawn; M overdraft

descubierto *ver* descubrir

descubridor -ora MF discoverer

descubrimiento M discovery

descubrir[74] VT (hallar) to discover; (destapar) to uncover; **—se** to take off one's hat; **— el pastel** to spill the beans

descuento M discount; **— por grupo** group discount; **con —** at a discount; **los —s** extra time, injury time

descuidado ADJ (en una tarea) careless, negligent; (en el aspecto personal) slovenly

descuidar VT to neglect; **descuida, yo me ocupo de eso** don't worry, I'll take care of that; **—se** to be negligent

descuido M (falta de cuidado) neglect; (acción descuidada) oversight; **al —** offhand; **por —** by chance

desde PREP (origen) from; (tiempo) since; **— Madrid** from Madrid; **— el martes** since Tuesday; **— luego** of course; **— el principio** from the start; **— el vamos** from the get-go; **— entonces** ever since

desdecirse[53, 74] VI (contradecirse) to contradict oneself; (retractarse) to retract

desdén M disdain, scorn

desdentado ADJ toothless

desdeñar VT to disdain, to scorn

desdeñoso ADJ disdainful, scornful

desdicha F misfortune; **por —** unfortunately

desdichado ADJ wretched

desdoblamiento M division

desdoblar VT (desplegar) to unfold; (dividir) to divide

deseabilidad F desirability

deseable ADJ desirable

desear VT to desire

desecación F drying

desecar[30] VT to dry, to desiccate; **—se** to dry up, to desiccate

desechable VT disposable, throwaway

desechar VT (ropa vieja) to discard; (una oferta) to refuse; (una posibilidad) to dismiss

desecho M waste material; **—s** refuse, waste

desembalar VT to unpack

desembarazar[47] VT to rid of; **—se** to get rid of

desembarcadero M dock

desembarcar[30] VI (de un buque) to disembark, to go ashore; (de un avión) to deplane

desembarco M landing

desembarque M landing

desembocadura F mouth

desembocar[30] VI to flow; **— en** to flow into; **la calle Ocho desemboca en la avenida A** Eighth Street feeds into Avenue A

desembolsar VT to disburse, to pay out

desembolso M disbursement, outlay
desembragar[40] VI/VT to disengage [the clutch]
desempacar[30] VT to unpack
desempañar VT to wipe clean
desempate M (tenis) tie-break; **[partido de] desempate** playoff [game]
desempeñar VT to redeem; — **un cargo** to perform the duties of a position; — **un papel** to play a part; —**se** to get out of debt
desempeño M (de un cargo o papel) performance; (de una cosa en prenda) redemption
desempleado ADJ unemployed
desempleo M unemployment
desempolvar VT to dust off
desencadenar VT (quitar las cadenas) to unchain; (provocar, causar) to trigger, to spark
desencajado ADJ (mandíbula) dislocated; (mirada) wild; **estaba — en el funeral** he was deeply disturbed at the funeral
desencajar VT (un cajón) to unstick; (la mandíbula) to dislocate
desencantar VT (desilusionar) to disillusion; (quitar un hechizo) to remove a spell from
desencanto M disillusion
desenchufar VI/VT to unplug
desenfadado ADJ uninhibited
desenfado M lack of inhibition
desenfrenadamente ADV with wild abandon
desenfrenado ADJ (sin moderación) unbridled, wanton, rampant; (muy rápido) reckless
desenganchar VT to unhook
desengañar VT to disabuse; —**se** (de un error) to become disabused; (de una ilusión) to become disillusioned
desengaño M disillusion
desengranar VT to take out of gear
desenlace M (de un libro) ending; (de un suceso) outcome
desenmarañar VT to disentangle
desenmascarar VT to unmask, to expose
desenredar VT (el cabello) to disentangle; (una historia) to disentangle
desenrollar VT to unroll
desenroscar VT to untwist
desentenderse[2] VI to pay no attention
desentendido ADJ **hacerse el —** to pretend not to notice/know
desenterrar[1] VT (un tesoro) to unearth, to dig up; (un cadáver) to disinter
desentonado ADJ out of tune
desentonar VI (cantar mal) to sing off key; (estar fuera de lugar) to be out of place
desentrañar VT to unravel
desenvoltura F self-assurance
desenvolver[6, 74] VT (desenrollar) to unroll; (quitar la envoltura) to unwrap; —**se** to behave

desenvuelto ADJ self-assured
deseo M desire, wish; (sexual) desire; **pedir un —** to make a wish
deseoso ADJ desirous
desequilibrado -da ADJ unbalanced; MF unbalanced person
desequilibrar VT to unbalance
desequilibrio M imbalance
deserción F desertion; — **escolar** school dropout rate
desertar VI/VT to desert; — **de** to defect from
desértico ADJ desert
desertor -ora MF (militar) deserter; (escolar) drop-out
desesperación F desperation
desesperadamente ADV desperately
desesperado ADJ desperate
desesperanza F despair, hopelessness
desesperanzado ADJ hopeless
desesperanzar[47] VT to discourage, to deprive of hope; —**se** to despair
desesperar VI to despair; VT to drive crazy
desestabilizar[47] VT to destabilize
desestimación F rejection
desestimar VT to reject
desfachatez F audacity
desfalcar[30] VT to embezzle
desfalco M embezzlement
desfallecer[35] VI (debilitarse) to grow weak; (desmayarse) to faint
desfallecimiento M (debilidad) weakness; (desmayo) faint
desfavorable ADJ unfavorable
desfibrilación F defibrillation
desfibrilador M defibrillator
desfibrilar VT to defibrillate
desfigurar VT (el rostro) to disfigure; (una estatua) to deface
desfiladero M narrow passage
desfilar VI (coches) to file by; (soldados, modelos) to parade
desfile M parade
desgana F (falta de apetito) lack of appetite; (falta de entusiasmo) lack of enthusiasm
desganado ADJ apathetic, without enthusiasm
desgarbado ADJ ungainly, gawky
desgarrado ADJ (prenda, músculo) torn; (grito) heartrending
desgarradura F tear
desgarrar VT (rasgar) to tear; (un escándalo) to dredge up; —**le el corazón a alguien** to break someone's heart; —**se** to tear, to pull
desgarro M muscle pull
desgarrón M tear
desgastar VT to wear away; —**se** to get worn away
desgaste M wear and tear
desglosar VT (una suma) to itemize; (un tema) to break down

desglose M (de una suma) itemization; (de un tema) breakdown

desgracia F (infortunio) misfortune; (infelicidad) unhappiness; —**s personales** casualties; **caer en** — to fall into disgrace/ disfavor

desgraciadamente ADV unfortunately

desgraciado -da ADJ (desafortunado) unfortunate; (infeliz) unhappy; MF (persona desafortunada) unfortunate person

desgranar VT (granos) to thrash, to thresh; (guisantes) to shell

desgravable ADJ tax-deductible

desgreñado ADJ disheveled, unkempt

desgreñar VT to dishevel; —**se** to muss up one's hair

desguazar[47] VT to scrap

deshabitado ADJ (territorio) uninhabited; (casa) vacant

deshacer[54, 74] VT (una acción, comando a la computadora) to undo; (una cama) to strip; (un plato, un jarrón) to destroy; (un sólido en un líquido) to dissolve; (un nudo) to untie; — **la maleta** to unpack the suitcase; —**se de** to get rid of; —**se en elogios** to rave about

deshaga, deshago, deshará, desharía ver deshacer

desharrapado ADJ ragged

deshecho ver deshacer

deshelar[1] VT to thaw

desheredar VT to disinherit

deshice, deshiciera, deshiciese ver deshacer

deshielo M thaw

deshierbar VT to weed

deshilachar VT to unravel, to fray

deshojado ADJ leafless

deshojar VT to strip of leaves; —**se** (un árbol) to shed leaves; (un libro) to lose pages

deshonestidad F (falta de honradez) dishonesty; (falta de recato) immodesty

deshonesto ADJ (no honrado) dishonest; (no modesto) immodest

deshonra F dishonor, disgrace

deshonrar VT to dishonor, to disgrace

deshonroso ADJ dishonorable

deshora LOC ADV **a** — at an inopportune time; **comer a** — to eat between meals

deshuesar VT (un fruto) to stone; (un animal) to bone

deshumanizar[47] VT to dehumanize

deshumidificador M dehumidifier

desidia F indolence

desierto ADJ (lugar) deserted; (prémio) unawarded; M (región árida) desert; (región poco fértil y no habitada) wilderness

designación F (acción de designar, nombre) designation; (nombramiento) appointment

designar VT to designate; (a un funcionario) to appoint

designio M design

desigual ADJ (pelea) one-sided; (actuación) uneven; (números) not equal; (rango) unequal; (terreno) uneven

desigualdad F inequality; (del terreno) roughness

desilusión F disillusion, disappointment

desilusionar VT to disillusion, to disappoint; —**se** to become disillusioned/disappointed

desinencia F ending

desinfección F disinfection

desinfectante ADJ & M disinfectant

desinfectar VT to disinfect

desinfestación F disinfestation

desinflado ADJ (globo, persona) deflated; (neumático) flat; M flat tire

desinflar VT to deflate

desinformación F (falta de información) disinformation; (mala información) misinformation

desinformar VT to misinform

desinhibido ADJ uninhibited

desinstalar VT to uninstall

desintegración F disintegration; — **atómica** atomic decay

desintegrarse VI to disintegrate; (material radiactivo) to decay

desinterés M (falta de interés) lack of interest; (generosidad) unselfishness

desinteresado ADJ (apático) disinterested; (generoso) unselfish, selfless

desistir VI to desist

deslavado ADJ faded

deslavar VT (quitar color) to fade; (lavar ligeramente) to wash superficially

desleal ADJ (persona) disloyal, faithless; (competencia) unfair

desleír[10] VT to mix with a liquid

deslindar VT to mark off

desliz M slipup

deslizamiento M slide, glide

deslizar[47] VT (un patín) to slip, to slide, to glide; (una tarjeta) to swipe; —**se** (un patín) to slide, to glide; (un error) to slip by

deslucido ADJ (actuación) dull; (color) dingy

deslucir[39] VT (un espectáculo) to tarnish; (color) to make dingy

deslumbramiento M dazzle

deslumbrante ADJ dazzling

deslumbrar VT to dazzle; —**se** to be dazzled

deslustrar VT to tarnish

deslustre M tarnish

desmadejado ADJ (fatigado) exhausted; (desgarbado) ungainly

desmadejar VT to exhaust

desmán M abuse

desmantelar VT to dismantle

desmañado ADJ awkward, clumsy

desmayar VI to lose courage; —**se** to faint, to

pass out

desmayo M faint, swoon; **peleó sin**— he fought unflaggingly

desmedido ADJ excessive

desmejorar VI (empeorar el aspecto) to look worse; (debilitarse) to get worse

desmembrar VT to dismember

desmentido M denial

desmentir[8] VT to deny

desmenuzar[47] VT (pan) to crumble; (zanahorias) to mince

desmerecer[35] VI — **en valor** to not do justice; **no** — **de** to compare favorably with

desmesurado ADJ (esfuerzo) inordinate; (orejas) too large

desmigajar VT to crumb, to crumble

desmitificar[30] VT to debunk

desmochar VT to top, to cut the top off of

desmontar VT (limpiar un monte) to clear; (desarmar) to dismantle, to take apart; (derribar de una caballería) to throw; —**se** to dismount

desmoralizar[47] VT to demoralize; —**se** to become demoralized

desmoronar VT to crumble

desmovilizar[47] VT to demobilize

desnatar VT to skim

desnaturalizado ADJ (madre) unnatural; (aceite) denatured

desnudar VT to undress; —**se** to get undressed

desnudez F nakedness

desnudo ADJ nude, naked

desnutrición F malnutrition

desnutrido ADJ underfed, undernourished

desobedecer[35] VT to disobey

desobediencia F disobedience; — **civil** civil disobedience

desobediente ADJ disobedient

desocupación F (paro) unemployment; (abandono de vivienda) vacating

desocupado ADJ (asiento, casa) unoccupied, empty; (tiempo) idle; (que no trabaja) unemployed

desocupar VT to vacate; —**se** to become free

desodorante M deodorant

desodorizar VT to deodorize

desoír[55] VT to turn a deaf ear to

desolación F desolation

desolado ADJ desolate, bleak

desolar VT to lay waste to, to desolate; —**se** to be desolated

desollar[5] VT to skin; — **vivo** to skin alive

desorbitado ADJ (precio, reacción) out of proportion; (ojos) bulging

desorden M disorder, disarray; — **público** public disturbance; **en** — in disarray

desordenado ADJ (persona, situación) messy; (persona, estilo de vida) wild; (cuarto) untidy, disorderly; (archivo) disorganized

desordenar VT to mess up

desorganización F disorganization

desorganizado ADJ disorganized

desorientar VT (marear, hacer perder) to disorient; (confundir) to confuse; —**se** to lose one's bearings, to become disoriented

desovar VT to spawn

desoxidar VT to deoxidize

despabilado ADJ (despierto) wide-awake; (listo) on the ball

despabilar VT (cortar el pabilo) to trim the wick of; (despertar) to awaken; —**se** to wake up

despachar VT (problemas) to dispatch; (una carta) to mail; (a un cliente) to take care of; (mercancías) to ship; (a una víctima) to bump off; (un pedido) to fill; — **al público** to sell to the public; —**se a su gusto** to speak one's mind

despacho M (oficina) office; (comunicación) dispatch; (envío de cartas) mailing; (envío de mercancías) shipping

despachurrar VT to squash

despacio ADV slow, slowly

desparasitar VT to worm

desparejo ADJ uneven

desparpajo M (desenvoltura) ease; (descaro) impudence

desparramar VT to scatter; —**se** to be scattered

desparramo M (lío) commotion; (de libros) clutter

despatarrarse VT (caerse) to sprawl; (abrirse de piernas) to spread one's legs

despecho M spite; **por**— out of spite

despectivo ADJ derogatory, pejorative

despedazar[47] VT to tear to pieces

despedida F farewell; — **de soltero** bachelor party

despedir[9] VT (decir adiós) to see off; (echar de un empleo) to fire, to dismiss; (emitir un dolor) to emit, to give off; **despídeme de tus padres** say good-bye to your parents for me; —**se [de]** to take leave [of], to say good-bye [to]

despegar[40] VT (dos cosas pegadas) to detach; VI (un avión) to take off; (un cohete) to blast off; —**se** to become detached

despegue M (de avión) takeoff; (de cohete) blastoff, liftoff

despeinado ADJ unkempt

despejado ADJ (el cielo) clear, cloudless; (un camino) clear; (la frente) with one's hair pulled back; (una persona) bright

despejador M (fútbol americano) punter

despejar VT (el campo, una pelota) to clear; (en fútbol americano) to punt; VI (una duda, el cielo) to clear up; —**se** to sober up

despellejar VT to skin

despensa F pantry

despeñadero M cliff

despeñar VT to push off a precipice; —**se** to fall down a precipice

despepitar VT (una granada) to seed; (una manzana) to core; —**se por una cosa** to be crazy about something

desperdiciar VT to waste; —**se** to go to waste

desperdicio M waste; —**s** scraps

desperdigar[40] VT to scatter; —**se** to be scattered

desperezarse[47] VI to stretch

desperezo M stretch

desperfecto M damage; — **mecánico** mechanical breakdown

despertador M alarm clock

despertar[1] VT (a una persona) to awaken, to wake up; (sospecha) to arouse; (interés, deseo) to kindle; —**se** to wake up

despiadado ADJ merciless, heartless, ruthless

despida, despide, despidiendo, despidiera, despidiese ver despedir

despido M dismissal, termination; — **temporal de un empleado** layoff

despierta, despierte ver despertar

despierto ADJ (no dormido) awake; (vivaracho) alert

despilfarrador ADJ wasteful

despilfarrar VT to squander

despilfarro M waste

despistado ADJ absent-minded, out of it

despistar VT (confundir) to throw off the track; (deshacerse de) to lose; —**se** to get confused

desplantador M trowel

desplante M rude remark

desplazado -da MF displaced person

desplazamiento M (de tropas) movement; (de refugiados) displacement

desplazar[47] VT to displace; —**se** to move

desplegar[41] VT (papel plegado) to unfold; (una bandera) to unfurl; (tropas) to deploy; (interés) to display

despliegue M display

desplomarse VI (edificio, precios) to collapse; (una persona) to slump; (esperanzas) to be dashed

desplome M collapse

desplumar VT (un ave) to pluck; (a un incauto) to fleece

despoblado ADJ uninhabited; — **de árboles** treeless; M open country

despojar VT to despoil; —**se** to shed leaves

despojos M PL (de batalla) spoils; (mortales) remains

desportilladura F chip

desportillar VT to chip

desposeer VT to dispossess

déspota MF despot

despótico ADJ despotic

despotismo M despotism

despotricar[30] VI to rant

despreciable ADJ (vil) contemptible, despicable, worthless; (insignificante) negligible

despreciar VT (menospreciar) to despise, to look down on; (rechazar) to snub

desprecio M (menosprecio) contempt, disdain; (rechazo) snub

desprender VT (un cierre) to unfasten; (algo prendido) to detach; (gases) to give off; —**se de algo** to part with something; —**se la ropa** to undo one's clothes; **de lo dicho se desprende que** from what has been said it follows that

desprendimiento M (de retina) detachment; (de energía) release; (de tierra) landslide; (generosidad) generosity

despreocupado ADJ carefree

desprestigiar VT to discredit; —**se** to lose one's prestige

desprestigio M loss of prestige

desprevenido ADJ unprepared; **tomar** — to take by surprise

desproporcionado ADJ disproportionate, out of proportion

despropósito M nonsense

desprovisto ADJ — **de** lacking in

después ADV after, afterward; — **de** after; — **de todo** after all; — **de horas hábiles** after hours

despuntar VI/VT to blunt; —**se** to become blunt

desquiciar VT to unhinge; —**se** to come unhinged

desquitarse VI to get even

desquite M getting even, revenge

desregular VT to deregulate

destacable ADJ notable, noteworthy

destacado ADJ outstanding

destacamento M military detachment, military detail

destacar[30] VT (tropas) to detach; (una cualidad) to highlight, to accentuate; VI to stand out; —**se** to stand out

destajo LOC ADV **a** — by the job

destapar VT (una cacerola) to take the top off; (un plan, a un niño en cama) to uncover; —**se** (en la cama) to uncover; (desnudarse) to bare all

destartalado ADJ dilapidated

destellar VI to flash

destello M flash

destemplado ADJ (persona) feverish; (sonido) out of tune

desteñido ADJ washed-out

desteñir[11] VI/VT to fade; VI to run; —**se** to fade

desternillarse VI — **de risa** to die laughing

desterrado -da ADJ exiled, banished; MF (persona) exile

desterrar[1] VT to exile, to banish

destetar VT to wean

destierro M exile, banishment
destilación F distillation
destilar VT to distill
destilería F distillery
destinar VT (determinar el destino) to destine; (dirigir) to address; (asignar) to commit
destinatario -ria MF addressee, recipient
destino M (hado) destiny, fate, lot; (uso) use; (final de viaje) destination
destitución F dismissal
destituir[19] VT to dismiss
destornillador M screwdriver
destoxificación F detoxification
destrabar VT to untie
destreza F dexterity, skill
destripar VT to gut
destronar VT to dethrone
destrozar[47] VT (estropear) to ruin; (causar grandes daños) to destroy; (derrotar) to rout
destrozo M damage
destrucción F destruction
destructible ADJ destructible
destructivo ADJ destructive
destructor -ra ADJ destructive; M (buque) destroyer; MF (persona) destroyer
destruir[19] VT (destrozar) to destroy, to obliterate; (estropear) to ruin
destruya, destruya, destruyendo, destruyera, destruyese ver destruir
desunir VT to divide; **—se** to come apart
desusado ADJ (no frecuente) unusual; (no usado) obsolete
desuso M disuse, obsolescence; **caer en —** to fall into disuse
desvaído ADJ faded
desvainar VT to hull, to husk
desvalido ADJ helpless
desvalijar VT (un cuarto) to ransack; (a una persona) to clean out
desvalimiento M helplessness
desván M attic
desvanecer[35] VT (un color) to fade; (un contorno) to blur; **—se** (una persona) to faint; (un color, arrugas) to fade; (un sonido) to trail off
desvanecido ADJ (una persona) fainted; (un color) faded; (un contorno) blurred
desvanecimiento M (de una persona) fainting; (de colores) fading; (de un contorno) blurring
desvariar[28] VI to rave
desvarío M raving
desvelado ADJ sleepless
desvelar VT to keep awake; **—se** to be sleepless
desvelo M (falta de sueño) sleeplessness; **—s** (esfuerzos) efforts
desvencijado ADJ dilapidated, rickety; **estoy —** I'm all beat up
desventaja F disadvantage; **estar en —** to be at a disadvantage

desventura F misfortune
desventurado ADJ unfortunate
desvergonzado ADJ shameless
desvergüenza F shamelessness
desvestir[9] VT to undress; **—se** to get undressed, to undress
desviación F (de una norma) deviation, divergence; (en ruta) detour; (de fondos) diversion; (de la columna vertebral) curvature; **— estándar** standard deviation
desviar[28] VT (la vista) to avert; (fondos, tráfico) to divert; (un golpe) to ward off; (una conversación) to steer; (un tren) to sidetrack; **—se de** (un camino) to stray from; (una norma) to deviate from
desvío M (camino secundario) side road; (desviación) detour
desvirtuar[26] VT to distort; **—se** to become distorted
desvivirse VI **— por hacer algo** to bend over backward to do something; **— por alguien** to go out of one's way for someone
detallado ADJ detailed
detallar VT to detail, to go into detail about
detalle M (pormenor) detail; (venta al por menor) retail; (lista) list; **¡qué —!** how thoughtful! **con/al/en —** in detail
detallista ADJ (cuidadoso) meticulous; (considerado) thoughtful; M (comercio) retail; MF retailer
detección F detection
detectar VT to detect
detective M detective; **— privado** private eye
detector M detector; **— de incendios** smoke detector; **— de mentiras** lie detector; **— de metales** metal detector
detención F (arresto) detention, arrest; (de un vehículo) stop; **— domiciliaria** house arrest; **— ilegal** false arrest
detendrá, detendría ver detener
detener[58] VT (arrestar) to detain, to arrest; (parar) to stop; **—se** to stop; **—se en** to linger on; **—se a pensar** to stop to think
detenga, detengo ver detener
detenidamente ADV closely
detenido ADJ thorough
detenimiento LOC ADV **con —** with care
detergente ADJ & M detergent
deteriorado ADJ in disrepair
deteriorar VT to deteriorate
deterioro M deterioration, disrepair
determinación F determination; **— del grupo sanguíneo** blood typing
determinado ADJ (cierto) certain; **es lo que suponen determinadas personas** that is what certain people suppose; (específico) definite, specific; **pidió una cantidad determinada** he asked for a specific amount
determinante ADJ determining; M determiner

determinar VT to determine
detestable ADJ detestable
detestar VT to detest
detiene, detienes ver detener
detonación F detonation; **hacer detonaciones** to backfire
detonar VI/VT to detonate
detrás ADV behind; **— de** (en el espacio) behind; (en el tiempo) after; **por —** behind
detritus M INV debris
detuve, detuviera, detuviese ver detener
deuce M deuce
deuda F debt; **— incobrable** bad debt
deudor -ora ADJ & MF debtor; **— hipotecario** mortgagor
devaluación F devaluation
devanar VT to spool; **—se los sesos** to rack one's brain
devaneo M (pasatiempo) idle pursuit; (amorío) fling
devastador ADJ devastating
devastar VT to devastate
devengar[40] VT to earn
devoción F devotion
devolución F (de un producto) return; (de poder político) devolution
devolver[6, 74] VT (dar al dueño) to return; (enviar por correo) to send back; **— al remitente** to return to sender; **— la llamada** to call back; VI (vomitar) to throw up
devorar VT to devour
devoto ADJ (pío) devout; (que muestra devoción) devoted
devuelto, devuelva, devuelve ver devolver
dextrosa F dextrose
di ver dar, decir
día M day; **— a —** day-to-day; **— tras —** day after day; **al —** up-to-date; **al otro —** on the next day; **de —** by day; **de todos los —s** everyday; **el — de mañana** in the future; **hoy —** nowadays; **no veo el —** I can't wait; **ponerse al —** to catch up; **por —** by the day; **todo el —** all day; **todos los —s** every day; **un — sí y otro no** every other day; **vivir al —** to live from hand to mouth
diabetes F SG diabetes
diablo M devil; **pobre —** poor devil; **¿por qué —s dices eso?** fam why the heck are you saying that?
diablura F devilry, mischief
diabólico ADJ (ritual) diabolic, devilish; (perverso) diabolical
diácono M deacon
diacrítico ADJ & M diacritic
diafragma M diaphragm
diagnosis F diagnosis
diagnosticar[30] VT to diagnose
diagnóstico ADJ diagnostic; M diagnosis
diagonal ADJ & F diagonal

diagrama M diagram; **— de flujo** flow chart; **— de pastel** pie chart
dial M dial
dialéctica F dialectic
dialéctico ADJ dialectic
dialecto M dialect
dialectología F dialectology
diálisis F dialysis
dialogar[40] VI to dialogue, to hold talks
diálogo M dialogue, conversation; **fue un — de sordos** they talked past each other
diamante M diamond; **— en bruto** diamond in the rough
diámetro M diameter
diana F bull's-eye
diapasón M tuning fork
diapositiva F slide
diario ADJ daily; M (periódico) newspaper; (de sucesos personales) journal, diary; (de navegación) log; **a —** every day; **de —** everyday; **llevar un —** to keep a diary
diarrea F diarrhea
diastólico ADJ diastolic
diatriba F diatribe
dibujante MF illustrator
dibujar VT to draw; **—se** to appear, to loom
dibujo M (arte de dibujar, cosa dibujada) drawing; (diseño) design; **— al carbón** charcoal drawing; **—s animados** animated cartoon
dicción F diction
diccionario M dictionary
dice, dicen ver decir
dicha F happiness
dicharachero ADJ witty
dicho ADJ aforementioned; M saying
dicho ver decir
dichoso ADJ happy; **todo el — día** the whole blessed day
diciembre M December
diciendo ver decir
dicotomía F dichotomy
dictado M (ejercicio) dictation; (orden) dictate; **escribir al —** to take dictation
dictador -ora MF dictator
dictadura F dictatorship
dictamen M (opinión) report; (judicial) ruling
dictaminar VI (dar una opinión) to report; (fallar) to rule
dictar VT to dictate; **— clase** to teach class; **— sentencia** to rule
diecinueve NUM nineteen
dieciocho NUM eighteen
dieciséis NUM sixteen
diecisiete NUM seventeen
diente M (de persona, sierra) tooth; (de víbora) fang; (de rueda dentada) cog; (de tenedor) prong; **— de león** dandelion; **— de leche** baby tooth; **—s postizos** false teeth; **entre**

—s under one's breath; **tener buen —** to have a good appetite

diera, diese *ver* dar

diesel M diesel

diestra F right hand

diestro -tra ADJ (habilidoso) skillful, deft; (no zurdo) right-handed; MF right-handed person; **a diestra y siniestra** on all sides

dieta F (ingesta) diet; (dinero para gastos) per diem; **estar a —** to be on a diet

dietético ADJ dietary

dietista MF dietitian

diez NUM ten

diezmar VT to decimate

diezmo M tithe; **pagar el —** to tithe

difamación F (oral) slander; (escrita) libel

difamar VT to defame, to malign; (oralmente) to slander; (por escrito) to libel

difamatorio ADJ slanderous

diferencia F difference; **a — de** unlike; **hacer —s entre** to treat differently; **partir la —** to split the difference

diferenciación F differentiation, distinction

diferencial ADJ & M (distancia, pieza de coche) differential; F (matemática) differential

diferenciar VT to differentiate; **—se de** to differ from

diferente ADJ different

diferir[8] VT (aplazar) to defer; VI (ser diferente) to differ

difícil ADJ difficult, hard

difícilmente ADV (apenas) hardly; (con dificultad) with difficulty

dificultad F difficulty

dificultar VT to make difficult

dificultoso ADJ difficult

difteria F diphtheria

difundir VT (luz) to diffuse; (noticias) to broadcast

difunto -ta ADJ & MF deceased

difusión F (de luz) diffusion; (de noticias) broadcasting

difuso ADJ diffuse

diga *ver* decir

digerible ADJ digestible

digerir[8] VT to digest

digestible ADJ digestible

digestión F digestion

digestivo ADJ digestive

digesto M digest

digital ADJ digital

digitalizar[47] VT to digitalize, to digitize

digitar VI/VT to type

dígito M digit

dignarse VI to deign

dignatario -ria MF dignitary

dignidad F dignity

digno ADJ (respetable) worthy; (orgulloso) dignified; **— de confianza** trustworthy; **— de elogio** praiseworthy

digo *ver* decir

digresión F digression

dije M charm

dije, dijera, dijese *ver* decir

dilación F delay; **sin —** without delay

dilatación F (de un metal, parte dilatada) expansion; (del ojo) dilation

dilatar VT (pupilas, capilares) to dilate; (metal, músculo) to expand; (tiempo, plazo) to defer; (prolongar) to prolong; **—se en un asunto** to dwell on a subject

dilema M dilemma

diletante MF dilettante

diligencia F (laboriosidad) diligence, industry; (vehículo) stagecoach; (tarea) errand; **— debida** due diligence

diligente ADJ diligent, industrious

dilucidar VT to elucidate

diluido ADJ dilute

diluir[19] VT (una solución) to dilute; (pintura, sopa) to thin

diluvio M deluge

dimensión F dimension

dimes M PL **— y diretes** gossip; **andar en — y diretes** to quibble

diminutivo ADJ & M diminutive

diminuto ADJ (tamaño) diminutive; (cantidad) minute

dimisión F resignation

dimitir VI to resign

Dinamarca F Denmark

dinámica F dynamics

dinámico ADJ dynamic

dinamismo M vigor

dinamita F dynamite

dinamitar VT to dynamite

dínamo M dynamo

dinastía F dynasty

dineral M fortune

dinero M money; **— contante y sonante** ready cash, hard cash; **— de plástico** plastic, credit card; **— sucio** dirty money

dinosaurio M dinosaur

diodo M diode; **— electroluminiscente** light-emitting diode

Dios M God; **dios — dirá** we'll see; **— los cría y ellos se juntan** birds of a feather flock together; **— mediante** God willing; **¡— mío!** my God! **— te lo pague** may God reward you; **— y su madre** everybody and their dog; **a la buena de —** any old way; **como — manda** as it should be; **¡por —!** oh, my! **que — te oiga** I hope you're right

diosa F goddess

diploma M diploma

diplomacia F diplomacy

diplomático -ca ADJ diplomatic; MF diplomat

diptongo M diphthong

diputación F council

diputado -da MF representative

dique M (presa) dike; (al lado de un río) levee; — **seco** dry dock

dirá ver decir

dirección F (sentido, rumbo) direction; (domicilio) address; (administración) management; (administración de una escuela) principal's office; (mecanismo, acción de conducir) steering; — **asistida** power steering; — **de correo electrónico** e-mail address

directiva F (orden) directive; (norma) guidelines; (junta de directores) board of directors

directrices F PL guidelines

directivo -va ADJ leadership; MF officer

directo ADJ (sin desviaciones, intermediarios) direct; (derecho) straight; **en** — live

director -ora MF (de una empresa) director, manager; (de una escuela) principal; (de orquesta) conductor; — **de correos** postmaster; — **general** CEO; — **técnico** coach

directorio M (índice) directory; (junta directiva) board of directors; — **[de] raíz** root directory; — **padre** parent directory

diría ver decir

dirigente MF leader; — **sindical** union leader

dirigible M dirigible

dirigir[46] VT (una obra teatral) to direct; (una empresa) to manage; (una orquesta) to conduct; (a un turista) to guide; (un saludo, una carta, una pregunta, una crítica) to address; —**se a** (hablar con) to address; (ir a) to go to; (tratar de) to be aimed at

discapacidad F disability

discapacitado ADJ disabled

discar[30] VI/VT Am to dial

discernimiento M discernment, insight

discernir[3] VT to discern

disciplina F discipline

disciplinar VT to discipline

discípulo -la MF disciple

disco M (cartílago, objeto plano y circular) disk; (fonográfico) record; — **compacto** compact disc; — **comprimido** compressed disk; — **de iniciación** boot disk; — **duro** hard disk; — **duro interno** internal hard disk; — **volador** Frisbee®; **es un** — **rayado** he's a broken record

díscolo ADJ unruly

disconforme ADJ dissatisfied

discontinuo ADJ discontinuous

discordancia F discord

discordia F discord

discoteca F (lugar donde bailar) discotheque; (colección de discos) record collection

discreción F discretion; **a** — at one's own discretion

discrepancia F discrepancy

discrepar VI to disagree; — **de** to take issue with

discreto ADJ (prudente) discreet; (separado) discrete; **un partido** — a sorry game

discriminación F discrimination; — **por edad** age discrimination; — **positiva** affirmative action; — **sexual** sexual discrimination

discriminar VI to discriminate; — **a** to discriminate against

disculpa F (excusa) excuse; (perdón) apology

disculpable ADJ excusable

disculpar VT (excusar) to excuse; (perdonar) to forgive, to pardon; —**se** to apologize

discurrir VI (transcurrir) to pass; (exponer) to discourse

discursear VI to make speeches

discurso M (enunciado) discourse; (disertacíon pública) speech, address; — **de apertura** keynote address

discusión F (charla) discussion; (riña) argument

discutible ADJ debatable, questionable

discutir VT (hablar sobre) to discuss; (oponerse a) to dispute; VI (reñir) to argue

disecar[30] VT (cortar) to dissect; (preparar para conservar) to stuff

diseminación F dissemination

diseminar VT to disseminate

disensión F dissension, dissent

disenso M dissent

disentería F dysentery

disentir[8] VI to dissent, to disagree

diseñador -ora MF designer

diseñar VT to design

diseño M design; — **de interiores** interior design; — **de página** page layout; — **gráfico** graphic design

disertación F lecture

disertar VI to lecture

disfraz M (para ocultarse) disguise; (de carnaval) costume

disfrazar[47] VT to disguise

disfrutar VI/VT to enjoy; — **de** to enjoy

disfrute M enjoyment

disfunción F dysfunction

disgustado ADJ (molesto) upset; (enojado) angry

disgustar VT to upset; —**se** (molestarse) to get upset; (enfadarse) to get angry

disgusto M (desagrado) unpleasantness; (discusión) quarrel; **a** — (con desgana) against one's will; (con incomodidad) uncomfortably; (en disconformidad) in conflict; **esa niña no da más que** —**s** that girl keeps us upset all the time

disidente ADJ & MF dissident

disimulado ADJ **hacerse el** — to pretend not to notice

disimular VI (fingir) to dissemble; (ocultar) to

conceal

disimulo M (fingimiento) dissimulation; (ocultamiento) concealment

disipación F dissipation

disipar VT (niebla, calor) to dissipate; (dudas) to dispel; (miedo) to allay; (dinero) to squander; **—se** to dissipate; (miedo, dudas) to allay, to lift

dislexia F dyslexia

dislocación F dislocation

dislocar[30] VT to dislocate; **—se** to get dislocated

disminución F (acción de disminuir) decrease, lessening; (desprecio) belittling; (de ventas) dip, decrease

disminuir[19] VT (menguar) to diminish, to decrease, to lessen; (despreciar) to belittle

disminuya, disminuye, disminuyendo, disminuyera, disminuyese ver disminuir

disolución F dissolution

disoluto ADJ dissolute, loose

disolvente M solvent; **— de pintura** paint thinner

disolver[6, 74] VT (sal) to dissolve; (reunión) to break up

disonancia F discord

dispar ADJ disparate

disparar VT (un arma de fuego) to shoot, to fire; (una cámara) to click; (la inflación) to trigger; VI (en fútbol) to shoot; **—le a alguien** to shoot at someone; **—se** (aumentar) to take off; (salir) to shoot out

disparatado ADJ absurd

disparatar VI to talk nonsense

disparate M absurdity, nonsense; **decir —s** to talk nonsense; **un — de plata** a ton of money

disparo M (acción de disparar) shooting; (tiro, herida) shot, gunshot; (tiro de fútbol) shot at goal

dispensa F dispensation

dispensación F dispensation

dispensar VT to dispense; **— de** to exempt from

dispensario M dispensary

dispersar VT to disperse

dispersión F dispersal

disperso ADJ (diseminado) dispersed, scattered; (distraído) absent-minded, distracted; (no concentrado) disperse

display M display

displicencia F flippancy

displicente ADJ (comportamiento) flippant; (actitud) cavalier

dispon, dispondrá, dispondría ver disponer

disponer[56, 74] VT (colocar) to arrange; (preparar) to prepare, to dispose; (mandar) to order; **— de** to have; **—se** to set about; **—se para** to get ready for

disponga, dispongo ver disponer

disponibilidad F availability

disponible ADJ (asiento, taxi) available; (dinero)

on hand; (inventario) in stock

disposición F (voluntad) disposition; (colocación) arrangement; (de ánimo) mood; **a — de** at the disposal of

dispositivo M device; **— analógico** analog device; **— de almacenamiento** storage device; **— de salida** output device; **— intrauterino** intrauterine device

dispuesto ADJ ready; **bien —** willing; **no estar — a** to be unwilling to

dispuesto, dispuse, dispusiera, dispusiese ver disponer

disputa F (controversia) dispute; (riña) argument

disputar VI/VT to dispute; **—se el poder** to vie/ challenge/contend for power; **—se la posición** to jockey for position

disquete M floppy disk; **— de iniciación** bootable diskette

disquetera F disk drive

distancia F distance; **a —** at arm's length; **guardar —s** to keep at a distance; **¿a qué — está?** how far away is it?

distanciarse VT to distance oneself

distante ADJ distant

distar VI **dista mucho de** it's a far cry from; **dista diez kilómetros de** it's ten kilometers from

distender[2] VT (aflojar) to relax; (dilatar) to expand

distensión F distension; **— muscular** muscle strain

distinción F distinction

distinguido ADJ distinguished

distinguir[44] VT to distinguish

distintivo ADJ distinctive, distinguishing; M distinguishing characteristic

distinto ADJ (diferente) different; (claro) distinct

distorsión F distortion

distorsionar VT to distort

distracción F distraction

distraer[59] VT (la atención) to distract; (fondos, mano de obra) to divert; **—se** (divertirse) to entertain oneself; (dispersarse) to become distracted, fam to space out

distraído ADJ distracted, absent-minded; **hacerse el —** to play dumb

distribución F distribution

distribuidor -ora MF (persona) distributor; M (pieza de un motor) distributor

distribuir[19] VT to distribute

distrito M district

Distrito de Columbia M District of Columbia

distrofia F dystrophy; **— muscular** muscular dystrophy

disturbio M disturbance, trouble

disuadir VT (mediante palabras) to dissuade; (mediante acciones) to deter

DIU [dispositivo intrauterino] M IUD

diurético ADJ & M diuretic

diurno ADJ (actividad) daytime; (animal) diurnal

divagación F rambling

divagar[40] VI to ramble on, to digress

diván M divan; (de psiquiatra) couch

divergencia F divergence

divergir[46] VI to diverge

diversidad F diversity

diversión F (pasatiempo) amusement, entertainment, fun; (hecho de distraer la atención) diversion

diverso ADJ diverse; —**s** various

diverticulitis F diverticulitis

divertido ADJ amusing, entertaining

divertir[8] VT to amuse, to entertain; —**se** to have a good time, to have fun

dividendo M dividend

dividir VT to divide; (un territorio) to partition

divierta, divierte ver divertir

divieso M boil

divinidad F divinity

divino ADJ divine; **estuvo** — it was heavenly; **lo pasé** — I had a wonderful time

divirtiendo, divirtiera, divirtiese, divirtió ver divertir

divisa F (señal) emblem; (moneda) currency; (moneda extranjera) foreign currency

divisar VT to make out, to catch sight of

división F division; (de un territorio) partition

divisorio ADJ dividing

divorciar VT to divorce; —**se** to get divorced

divorcio M divorce

divulgación F dissemination; — **financiera** financial disclosure

divulgar[40] VT (un secreto) to divulge; (información) to disseminate

dobladillo M hem; **hacer —s** to hem

doblado ADJ (hipócrita) hypocritical; M (de tela, papel) folding; (de tubos) bending

doblaje M dubbing

doblar VT (una sábana) to fold; (el capital) to double; (una esquina) to turn; (la voz de un actor) to dub; VI (un coche) to turn; (una campana) to knell; —**se** to bend over

doble ADJ double (también en tenis); — **agente** double agent; — **falta** double fault; — **indemnización** double indemnity; — **matanza** double play; — **pulsación** double click; — **personalidad** split personality; — **visión** double vision; **de** — **caño** double-barreled; **de** — **filo** double-edged; **de** — **sentido** two-way; MF (persona muy parecida, actor sustituto) double; M (repique) knell; —**s** doubles; —**s mixtos** mixed doubles; **el** — double

doblegar[40] VT to break

doblete M double

doblez M fold; F deceitfulness

doce NUM twelve

docena F dozen; — **del fraile** baker's dozen

docente ADJ teaching

dócil ADJ (persona, animal) docile, pliant; (pelo) manageable

docto ADJ learned

doctor-ora MF doctor; — **en medicina** MD

doctorado M doctorate

doctrina F doctrine

documentación F documentation (también para computadoras)

documental ADJ & M documentary

documentar VT to document

documento M document; — **de instrucciones previas** living will; — **de voluntad anticipada** living will

dogma M dogma

dogmático ADJ dogmatic

dogo M pug

dólar M dollar

dolencia F ailment

doler[6] VI to ache, to hurt; **me duele el brazo** my arm aches, my arm is sore; —**se de** (compadecerse) to feel sorry for; (arrepentirse) to regret

doliente ADJ aching; MF mourner

dolor M (físico) pain, ache; (espiritual) sorrow, pain; — **de barriga** bellyache; — **de cabeza** headache; — **de espalda** backache; — **de muela** toothache; — **de oídos** earache; — **de garganta** sore throat; —**es del crecimiento** growing pains; — **de garganta** sore throat; —**es de parto** labor pains

dolorido ADJ aching, sore

doloroso ADJ painful

doma F (de caballos) breaking; (de leones) taming

domado ADJ (caballo) broken; (león) tamed

domador-ora MF (de perros) trainer; (de leones) lion tamer

domar VT (caballos, personas) to break; (leones) to tame

domesticar[30] VT to domesticate, to tame

doméstico-ca ADJ domestic; MF servant

domiciliarse VI to take up residence; **¿dónde se domicilia usted?** where do you reside?

domicilio M (casa) dwelling; (dirección) address

dominación F domination

dominador-ora ADJ (predominante) dominant; (tiránico) domineering, overbearing

dominante ADJ (predominante) dominant; (tiránico) domineering, overbearing

dominar VT (tener bajo su autoridad, ser más alto) to dominate; (reprimir) to control, to rein in; (tener sometido a su voluntad) to domineer

domingo M Sunday; — **de Ramos** Palm Sunday; — **de Pascua** Easter Sunday

Dominica F Dominica

dominicano -na ADJ & MF Dominican [de la República Dominicana]

dominio M (sobre una tierra, derecho de usar una cosa) dominion; (de sí mismo) control; (de una lengua) mastery, command; (hecho de dominar) domination; (ámbito, campo) domain; **— público** public domain

dominiqués -esa ADJ & MF Dominican [de Dominica]

dominó M (pieza) domino; (juego) dominoes

domo M dome

don M (gracia) gift; (título, jefe mafioso) don; **un — nadie** a nobody

dona F *Méx* doughnut, donut

donación F donation

donador -ora MF donor

donaire M grace

donante MF donor; **— universal** universal donor

donar MF to donate

doncella F *lit* maiden

donde ADV REL where; **de —** whence, from which; **ir — el herrero** to go to the blacksmith's shop; **— no** otherwise; **—quiera** wherever; **donde no comas, no te dejo salir a jugar** if you don't eat, I won't let you go out to play

dónde ADV INTERR where

donoso ADJ graceful

donut M *Esp* doughnut, donut

doña F doña

dopamina F dopamine

dopar VT to dope

dorado ADJ (cubierto de oro) gilt; (de color oro) golden; M dolphin fish

dorar VT to gild; **— la píldora** to sweeten the pill

dormido ADJ asleep

dormir[7] VI/VT to sleep; **— a** to put to bed; **— a un paciente** to anesthetize a patient; **— la mona** to sleep it off; **— la siesta** to take a nap; **se me ha dormido el brazo** my arm has fallen asleep; **—se** to fall asleep

dormitar VI to doze, to snooze

dormitorio M bedroom

dorso M back, reverse

dos NUM two; **— puntos** colon; **— veces** twice; **cada — por tres** constantly; **en un — por tres** in a jiffy; **los —** both of them

DOS M DOS

doscientos NUM two hundred

dosel M canopy

dosificar[30] VT to dose

dosis F (de medicamento) dose; (de droga) hit

dotación F (de fondos) endowment; (de personal) complement

dotar VT to endow

dote F dowry; **—s** talents

doy *ver* dar

draga F dredge

dragado M dredging

dragar[40] VT (para limpiar) to dredge; (para buscar objetos) to drag; M SG **dragaminas** minesweeper

dragón M (animal fantástico) dragon; (planta) snapdragon

drama M drama

dramático ADJ dramatic

dramatizar[47] VT to dramatize

dramaturgo -ga MF playwright, dramatist

drapear VI to drape

drástico ADJ drastic

drenaje M drainage

drenar VI/VT to drain

dribbling M dribble, dribbling

driblar VI/VT to dribble

drible M dribble

dril M drill

drive M drive

drive-in M drive-in

driver M driver

droga F drug; **— anticancerosa** anticancer drug; **—s de diseño** designer drugs; **tomar —s** to do drugs; MF **drogadicto -ta** drug addict

drogar[40] VT to drug

drogata MF junkie

drogota MF junkie

droguería F (tienda) drugstore; (industria) drug industry

droguero -ra MF druggist

dropar VI to drop

ducado M dukedom

ducha F shower

ducharse VI to shower

ducho ADJ skillful

dúctil ADJ (metal) ductile; (persona) flexible, supple

duda F doubt; **en —** in doubt; **fuera de —** beyond doubt; **no cabe —** there's no doubt; **poner en —** to cast doubt on; **sin —** without a doubt, undoubtedly; **sin lugar a —s** without doubt; **tengo una —** I have a question

dudar VT (no creer) to doubt; (vacilar) to hesitate; **— de** to have doubts about

dudoso ADJ doubtful; **de dudosa honestidad** of dubious honesty

duela F stave

duela, duele *ver* doler

duelo M (combate) duel; (luto) mourning; (pena) grief; (dolientes) mourners; **estar de —** to be in mourning

duende M (gnomo) goblin, gremlin; (gracia) charm

dueño -ña MF owner; **me sentí — de la situación** I felt like I was in control of the situation; M landlord; F landlady

duerma, duerme *ver* dormir

dueto M duet

dulce ADJ (sabor, personalidad) sweet; (clima) pleasant; (agua) fresh; **—amargo** bittersweet; M (cosa dulce) sweet; (mermelada) preserves, conserve

dulcería F confectionery

dulcificar[30] VT to sweeten

dulzón ADJ unpleasantly sweet

dulzor M sweetness

dulzura F sweetness

duna F dune

dúo M duet; **decir a —** to say in unison

duodeno M duodenum

dúplex M duplex

duplicado ADJ & M duplicate; **por —** in duplicate

duplicar[30] VT to duplicate

duplicidad F duplicity

duque M duke

duquesa F duchess

durabilidad F durability

duración F duration; (de una película, vocal) length; **— de la vida** lifespan

duradero ADJ (ropa) durable, serviceable; (pilas) long-lasting

durante PREP during; **— el mandato de los Demócratas** under the Democrats; **— muchos años** for/over many years

durar VI/VT to last

duraznero M peach tree

durazno M (fruto) peach; (árbol) peach tree

dureza F (de metal) hardness; (del clima, de la expresión, de una tempestad) severity; (del invierno) harshness; (de un boxeador) toughness; (del cuero) stiffness

durmamos, durmiendo *ver* dormir

durmiente ADJ sleeping; M railroad tie, sleeper

durmiera, durmiese *ver* dormir

duro ADJ (metal, golpe, droga, agua) hard; (clima, tormenta) severe; (invierno, expresión, sonido) harsh; (soldado) tough; (grifo) stuck; (viento) strong; (autoridad) inflexible; (pan) stale; (cuero) stiff; **— de corazón** hard-hearted; **— de entendederas** slow on the uptake; **a duras penas** barely; M five-peseta coin; **no tengo un —** I'm flat broke

DVD M DVD

Ee

e CONJ and

ebanista MF cabinetmaker

ébano M ebony

ebrio ADJ drunk, inebriated

ebullición F boiling

eccema M eczema

echar VT (una pelota, redes) to throw, to cast; (yemas, hojas) to sprout; (a un empleado) to fire; (humo, olor) to give off; (un líquido) to pour; (a un borracho) to throw out; **— abajo** to knock down; **— a la basura** to throw away; **— al mar** to put to sea; **— al correo** to mail; **— anclas** to drop anchor; **— a pique** to sink; **— carnes** to get fat; **— de menos** to miss; **— de ver** to notice; **— mano de** to seize upon; **— la culpa** to blame; **— por la borda** to jettison; **— raíces** to take root; **— sangre** to bleed; **— suertes** to draw lots; **— una carta** to mail a letter; **— una siesta** to take a nap; **— un vistazo** to glance at, to take a look at; **te echo una carrera** I'll race you; **—le el muerto a alguien** to pass the buck to someone; **—se** to lie down; **—se a** to start to; **—se a correr** to bolt; **—se a perder** to spoil; **—se a reír** to burst out laughing; **—se a un lado** to dodge; **—se atrás** to back down/off; **—se para atrás** to lean back

ecléctico ADJ eclectic

eclesiástico ADJ & M ecclesiastic

eclipsar VT (ocultar) to eclipse; (superar) to eclipse, to outshine, to overshadow; **—se** to fade

eclipse M eclipse; **— de sol** solar eclipse; **— de luna** lunar eclipse

eco M echo; **hacer —** to echo; **hacerse — de** to repeat

ecocardiograma M echocardiogram

ecología F (medio ambiente) environment; (ciencia) ecology

ecológico ADJ (ambiental) environmental, ecological; (bueno para la naturaleza) eco-friendly

ecologista ADJ environmental; MF environmentalist

economato M commissary

economía F (actividades de producción) economy; (ciencia) economics; (familiar) finances; **— doméstica** home economics; **—s** savings; **hacer —s** to be thrifty

económico ADJ (relativo a la economía) economic; (frugal) frugal, thrifty; (barato) economical

economista MF economist

economizar[47] VT to economize, to save

ecosistema M ecosystem

ecuación F equation

ecuador M equator

Ecuador M Ecuador

ecualizar[47] VT to equalize

ecuatoriano -na ADJ & MF Ecuadorian

ecuménico ADJ ecumenical

edad F age; — **avanzada** ripe old age; — **de merecer** marriageable age; — **de Piedra** Stone Age; — **del consentimiento sexual** age of consent; — **Media** Middle Ages; — **mental** mental age

edición F (ejemplar) edition; (acción de editar) publication; — **de sobremesa** desktop publishing

edicto M edict

edificación F building

edificar[30] VT (construir) to build; (infundir sentimientos morales) to edify, to uplift

edificio M building

editar VT to edit, to publish

editor -ora ADJ publishing; MF editor

editorial ADJ publishing; F publishing house; M editorial

editorializar[47] VI to editorialize

edredón M comforter

educación F (escolar) education; (social) breeding; — **a distancia** distance learning; — **cívica** civics; — **especial** special education; — **en línea** e-learning; — **física** physical education; — **para adultos** continuing education; — **superior** higher education

educado ADJ (cortés) well-bred; (instruido) educated

educador -ora MF educator

educar[30] VT (desarrollar conocimientos) to educate; (entrenar) to train

educativo ADJ educational

edulcorante M sweetener

EEUU [Estados Unidos] M SG/PL USA

efectivamente ADV actually; **más de los que — encuentran** more than they actually find; INTERJ exactly

efectividad F effectiveness; **tener —** to be valid, to become valid

efectivo ADJ (eficaz) effective; (real) actual; **hacer —** (un cheque) to cash; (una deuda) to pay off; (una amenaza) to make good on; M cash; **en —** in cash; **—s** troops

efecto M (resultado) effect, result; (letra comercial) bill of exchange; (rotación) English, spin; **en —** in fact; **llevar a —** to carry out; **surtir —** to work; — **invernadero** greenhouse effect; **—s especiales** special effects; **—s personales** personal effects; **perder —** to wear off; **rebotar con —** to glance off; **a estos —s** to this effect; **para los —s** to all intents and purposes; **por — de** as a consequence of

efectuar[26] VT to effect; **—se** to be carried out

eficacia F efficacy, effectiveness; — **de una ley** force of law

eficaz ADJ effective

eficiencia F efficiency

eficiente ADJ efficient

efigie F effigy; **quemar en —** to burn in effigy

efímero ADJ ephemeral, fleeting

efusivo ADJ effusive

egipcio -cia ADJ & MF Egyptian

Egipto M Egypt

égloga F pastoral

ego M ego

egocéntrico ADJ egocentric, self-centered

egoísmo M selfishness

egoísta ADJ selfish; MF selfish person

egotismo M egotism

egresado -da MF graduate

eje M (de la Tierra) axis; (de un vehículo) axle; — **del pistón** piston rod; **eso me parte por el —** that messes up my plans

ejecución F (de un condenado) execution; (de un plan, una orden) carrying out, execution; (de una tarea) performance; (de una propiedad) foreclosure

ejecutable ADJ executable

ejecutar VT (a un condenado) to execute; (un plan, una orden) to carry out; (una tarea, música) to perform; (una propiedad) to foreclose on

ejecutivo -va ADJ & MF executive; — **de empresa** corporate officer

ejemplar ADJ exemplary, model; M (libro) copy; (individuo) specimen

ejemplario M handout

ejemplificar[30] VT to exemplify

ejemplo M (cosa típica) example; (modelo) model; **a — de** on the example of; **dar —** to set an example; **por —** for example

ejercer[32] VT (una profesión) to practice; (influencia, fuerza) to exert; (poder) to wield

ejercicio M exercise; (de una profesión) practice; **hacer —** to exercise; — **contable** accounting period; — **físico** physical exercise; **—s de Kegel** Kegel exercises; **en —** active

ejercitar VT (la vista, los músculos) to exercise; (a soldados) to drill; (a alumnos) to train; **—se** to train

ejército M army; **el —** the military

ejido M common

ejote M *Méx* green bean

el ART DEF M the; — **de la derecha** the one on the right; — **que** the one that; — **que sepa** whoever knows

él PRON PERS M SG (como sujeto) he; — **dijo** he said; (como objeto) him; **para —** for him; **le di el libro a —** I gave the book to him; **estamos hablando de —** we're talking about him; **el libro de —** his book

elaboración F (de miel, comida) making; (de un método) development; (de un informe) drafting

elaborado ADJ elaborate

elaborar VT (un método) to elaborate, to

develop; (comida) to make; (un informe) to draft

elasticidad F elasticity

elástico ADJ (sustancia) elastic; (cuerpo) supple; (horario) flexible; M elastic

elección F (votación) election; (selección) choice, selection; **no tuve —** I had no choice

electo ADJ elect

elector -ora ADJ electoral; MF elector

electoral ADJ electoral

electricidad F electricity; **— estática** static electricity

electricista MF electrician

eléctrico ADJ (aparato) electric; (instalación, corriente) electrical

electrificar[30] VT to electrify

electrizado ADJ electrified

electrizante ADJ electrifying

electrizar[47] VT (suministrar electricidad) to electrify; (emocionar) to galvanize, to electrify

electrocardiograma M electrocardiogram

electrocutar VT to electrocute

electrodo M electrode

electrodoméstico M electrical appliance

electroencefalograma M electroencephalogram

electroimán M electromagnet

electrólisis F electrolysis

electromagnético ADJ electromagnetic

electrón M electron

electrónica F electronics

electrónico ADJ electronic

elefante M elephant

elegancia F elegance

elegante ADJ (armonioso) elegant; (bien vestido) stylish, classy

elegibilidad F eligibility

elegible ADJ eligible

elegir[14] VT (seleccionar) to choose, to select; (votar) to elect

elemental ADJ (sencillo) elementary; (básico) elemental

elemento M element

elenco M cast

elevación F elevation; **tirar por —** to throw high in the air

elevado ADJ (pensamiento, estilo) elevated; (fiebre, montaña) high; (precios) high; M (béisbol) fly ball

elevador M elevator

elevar VT (en una jerarquía) to elevate; (precios, voz, objeto) to raise; (el espíritu) to uplift; **— la vista** to look up; **— al cuadrado** to square; **— al cubo** to cube; **—se a** to go up to, to rise to; **el rascacielos se eleva sobre la ciudad** the skyscraper towers over the city

elfo M elf

eliminación F elimination

eliminar VT to eliminate

eliminatoria F (atletismo, natación) heat; **—s** (fútbol) playoffs

elíptico ADJ elliptical

elite/élite F elite

elitista ADJ & MF elitist

ella PRON PERS F SG (como sujeto) she; **— dijo** she said; (como objeto) her; **para —** for her; **le di el libro a —** I gave the book to her; **el libro de —** her book

ellas PRON PERS F PL (como sujeto) they; **— dijeron** they said; (como objeto) them; **para — for them; les di el libro a —** I gave them the book; **el libro de —** their book

ello PRON NEUTRO IT; **— es que** the fact is that

ellos PRON M PL (como sujeto) they; **— dijeron** they said; (como objeto) them; **para —** for them; **les di el libro a —** I gave them the book; **el libro de —** their book

elocuencia F eloquence

elocuente ADJ eloquent; **las estadísticas son —s** the statistics speak for themselves

elogiar VT to praise

elogio M praise

elote M *Méx* corn on the cob

elucidación F elucidation

elucidar VT to elucidate

eludir VT to elude, to avoid, to dodge

emanación F emanation, flow

emanar VI/VT to emanate

emancipación F emancipation

emancipar VT to emancipate; **—se** to become free

emascular VT to emasculate

embadurnar VT to daub

embajada F embassy

embajador -ora MF ambassador

embalador -ora MF packer

embalaje M packing, packaging

embalar VT to pack; VI to accelerate

embaldosar VT to tile

embalsamar VT (a un muerto) to embalm; (un animal) to stuff

embalse M reservoir

embanderar VT to adorn with flags

embarazada ADJ pregnant

embarazar[47] VT (impedir) to hamper; (fecundar) to make pregnant; **—se** to get pregnant

embarazo M (obstáculo) impediment; (estado de embarazada) pregnancy

embarazoso ADJ embarrassing, awkward

embarcación F boat, embarkation, craft

embarcadero M wharf, pier

embarcar[30] VT (pasajeros) to embark; (mercancías) to load; **—se** to embark, to go aboard; **—se en** to embark upon

embargar[40] VT to seize; **estar embargado de emoción** to be overcome with emotion

embargo M embargo; **— judicial** seizure; **imponer un —** to embargo; **sin —** nevertheless, however

embarque M (de mercancías) loading; (de pasajeros) embarkation

embarrado ADJ smeared with mud

embarrar VT to smear with mud, to muddy

embate M lashing

embaucador M confidence man

embaucar[30] VT to dupe

embeber VT to soak up; **—se** to be absorbed

embelesar VT to enrapture

embeleso M rapture

embellecer[35] VI/VT to beautify

embestida F charge

embestir[9] VI/VT to charge

embetunar VT to polish

emblanquecer[35] VI/VT to whiten

emblema M emblem

embobar VT to amaze; **—se** to be amazed

embolia F embolism; **— cerebral** cerebral embolism

émbolo M piston, plunger

embolsar VT (dinero) to pocket; (una compra) to bag

emborrachar VT (a una persona) to intoxicate; (el carburador) to flood; **—se** to get drunk

emborronar VT (manchar) to blot; (hacer impreciso) to blur

emboscada F ambush; **tender una —** to lie in ambush

emboscar[30] VT to ambush; **—se** to lie in ambush

embotamiento M (efecto de embotar) dullness, bluntness; (acción de embotar) dulling

embotar VT to dull

embotelladora F bottling plant

embotellamiento M (de cerveza) bottling; (de tráfico) traffic jam, bottleneck

embotellar VT (cerveza) to bottle; (tráfico) to bottle up

embozar[47] VT to conceal

embragar[40] VI to engage the clutch

embrague M clutch

embriagado ADJ drunken

embriagar[40] VT to intoxicate; **—se** to become intoxicated

embriaguez F intoxication, drunkenness

embridar VT to bridle

embrión M embryo

embrionario ADJ embryonic

embriónico ADJ embryonic

embrollar VT (involucrar) to embroil; (confundir) to muddle

embrollo M muddle

embromar VT to kid

embrujar VT to bewitch

embrujo M spell

embrutecer[35] VT to stupefy

embudo M funnel

embuste M lie

embustero -ra MF liar, trickster

embutido M sausage

embutir VT to cram, to jam

emergencia F emergency

emergente ADJ emergent, emerging

emerger[45] VI (surgir) to emerge; (salir del agua) to surface

emigración F (de personas) emigration; (de animales) migration

emigrante ADJ & MF emigrant

emigrar VI (personas) to emigrate; (animales) to migrate

eminencia F eminence; **— gris** gray eminence

eminente ADJ eminent

emisario -ria MF emissary; M outlet

emisión F (de acciones, billetes) issue; (de un olor) discharge; (de programas) broadcast; (de gas) emission

emisor ADJ emitting; M transmitter

emisora F radio/television station

emitir VT (un olor, vapor) to emit; (juicios) to pronounce; (dinero, acciones) to issue; VI/VT (programas) to broadcast; **—se** to be on the air; **el programa se emite en horas de la mañana** the program airs in the morning

emoción F emotion; **¡qué —!** what a thrill!

emocional ADJ emotional

emocionante ADJ (conmovedor) touching; (apasionante) exciting

emocionar VT (apasionar) to excite; (conmover) to move, to touch; **—se** (estar ilusionado) to be excited; (estar conmovido) to be touched

emoticón M emoticon

emoticono M emoticon

emotivo ADJ emotional

empacador -ora MF packer

empacar[30] VT (regalos, mercancías) to pack; (algodón) to bale

empachar VI to cause indigestion; **—se** to suffer indigestion; **—se de** to get sick on, to stuff oneself with

empacho M (indigestión) indigestion; (cohibición) inhibition; **no tener — en** to have no qualms about

empalagar[40] VI/VT to cloy

empalagoso ADJ cloying, saccharine

empalar VT to impale

empalizada F stockade, palisade

empalmar VT to splice; **— con** to join

empalme M (de caminos) junction; (de cuerdas) splice; **— genético** gene splicing

empanada F turnover, pie

empanar VT to bread

empañado ADJ (vidrio) misty, foggy; (metal, reputación) tarnished

empañar VT (vidrio) to fog up; (metal, reputación) to tarnish

empapado ADJ soggy, sopping wet

empapamiento M soaking

empapar VT (mojar) to soak, to drench; (recoger con algo) to soak up; **—se** (mojarse) to get soaked; (enterarse) to find out all about

empapelado M wallpapering

empapelar VT to paper, to wallpaper; **— las calles** to plaster the streets

empaque M (acción de empacar) packing; (envoltorio) packaging

empaquetadura F gasket

empaquetar VT to pack, to package; **—se** to get dolled up

emparedado M sandwich

emparejar VT (una carga, un partido) to even up; VI/VT (los enamorados) to pair up; (calcetines, zapatos) to match up

emparentado ADJ akin, related

emparentar VT to relate by marriage; **—se** to become related by marriage

empastar VT to fill

empaste M filling

empatar VI to tie; **— una marca** to tie a record

empate M tie, draw

empatía F empathy

empecinado ADJ stubborn

empedernido ADJ (criminal) hardened; (mujeriego) incorrigible; (solterón) confirmed

empedernirse[73] VI to become hardened

empedrado M (acción) paving with stones; (cosa) cobblestone pavement; ADJ paved with stones

empedrar[1] VT to pave with stones

empeine M (del pie) instep; (del vientre) groin

empellón M shove; **a empellones** with shoves, shoving

empeñar VT to pawn; **— la palabra** to pledge; **—se** (endeudarse) to go into debt; (obstinarse) to insist; (esforzarse) to apply oneself; **—se en** to engage in

empeño M (prenda) pawn; (insistencia) insistence; (deseo) desire; (esfuerzo) exertion; **poner — en** to strive for

empeorar VT to make worse, to aggravate; VI to worsen; **—se** to get worse

empequeñecer[35] VT to make smaller; VI to get smaller

emperador -triz M emperor; F empress

emperifollarse VI to deck oneself out, to doll oneself up

empezar[48] VI/VT to begin, to start; **— a** to start to; **— de cero** to start from scratch; **para —** for starters; **no tengo ni para — con él** I can't touch him; **empezamos mal** we got off to a bad start; **un paquete sin —** an unopened box; **por algo se empieza** you have to start somewhere

empinado ADJ steep

empinar VT to raise; **— el codo** to drink; **—se** (una persona) to stand on tiptoes; (un caballo) to rear; (una torre) to tower

empírico ADJ empirical

empizarrar VT to cover with slate

emplastar VT to plaster

emplasto M plaster

emplazamiento M (colocación) placement; (lugar) location

empleado -da MF employee; **— temporal** temp

emplear VT (usar) to employ, to use; (dar trabajo) to employ; **—se en** to be employed in

empleo M (ocupación) employment, work; (puesto de trabajo) job; (utilización) use

emplumado ADJ feathery

emplumar VT (adornar) to adorn with feathers; (pegar plumas en el cuerpo) to tar and feather; VI (echar plumas) to grow feathers

empobrecer[35] VI/VT to impoverish

empollar VT (huevos) to hatch, to brood; VI/VT (para un examen) to cram

empollón -ona MF *fam* egghead, overachiever

empolvar VT to cover with dust; **—se** (con cosméticos) to powder oneself; (con polvo) to get dirty

emponzoñar VT to poison

empotrado ADJ built-in

emprendedor ADJ enterprising

emprender VT (una tarea) to undertake; (un viaje) to embark on; **—la con alguien** to attack someone

empresa F (cosa que se emprende) undertaking; (compañía) company, enterprise; **libre —** free enterprise; **— privada** private enterprise; **— pública** public company; **— tiburón** raider

empresarial ADJ **—es** business administration studies; **grupo —** business group

empresario -ria MF entrepreneur

empréstito M loan

empujar VT (mover) to push; (mover con violencia) to shove; (apresurar) to hurry

empuje M (ánimo) drive; (fuerza de propulsión) thrust; (fuerza hacia arriba) lift

empujón M shove, push; **dar empujones** to jostle

empuñadura F (espada) hilt; (cuchillo) handle; (palo de golf, raqueta) grip

empuñar VT to grasp

emular VT to emulate

en PREP in; **— Asturias** in Asturias; (sobre una superficie) on, upon; **— la mesa** on the table; **sentarse — el suelo** to sit down on the floor; **me lo vendió — mil pesetas** she sold it to me for a thousand pesetas; **— la parada del autobús** at the bus stop; **— la noche** at night; **ir — tren** to go by train

enaguas F PL petticoat

enajenación M (locura) insanity; (transferencia) transfer

enajenar VT (trasladar) to transfer; (alienar) to alienate; **—se** to become alienated

enaltecer[35] VT to extol

enamorado -da ADJ in love; MF lover

enamoramiento M crush

enamorar VT to make fall in love; **—se [de]** to fall in love [with]

enanismo M dwarfism

enano -na MF (personaje imaginario, persona deforme) dwarf; (persona pequeña bien proporcionada) midget

enarbolar VT (una bandera) to raise on high; (un garrote) to brandish

enardecer[35] VT to inflame; **—se** to become inflamed

enardecimiento M inflaming

encabezado M header

encabezamiento M heading

encabezar[47] VT (una carta, una obra, un gobierno) to head; (un desfile) to lead

encabritarse VI (un caballo) to rear [up]; (una persona) to get furious

encadenar VT (poner en cadenas) to chain; (unir) to link

encajar VI/VT (colocar) to fit; VI (un gol) to allow; **el policía me encajó una multa** the policeman stuck me with a fine; **tu historia no encaja** your story doesn't hold water

encaje M (tejido) lace; (reserva bancaria) reserve; (acción de encajar) fitting together

encajonar VT (meter en una caja) to box; (apretar) to squeeze in

encallar VI to run aground, to strand; (una ballena) to beach; VT to ground

encamarse VI **— con** to go to bed with, to sleep with

encaminar VT to direct; **—se hacia** to head for

encanecer[35] VI to go gray; VT to cause to go gray

encanijado ADJ sickly

encanijarse VI to become sickly

encantado ADJ (contento) delighted; (hechizado) enchanted; **— de conocerla** pleased to meet you

encantador -ora ADJ charming, delightful; MF charmer

encantamiento M enchantment

encantar VT to enchant; **eso me encanta** I love that

encanto M (encantamiento) enchantment; (atractivo) charm; **un — de persona** a delightful person; **como por —** as if by magic

encapotado ADJ overcast

encapotarse VI to become overcast

encapricharse VI **— con/de/por** to become infatuated with

encapuchar VT (a una persona) to hood; (un

bolígrafo) to put the top on

encaramar VT to raise; **—se** to climb up on; **—se al primer puesto** to rise to first place

encarar VT to face; **me encaró el fusil** he pointed the rifle at me; **—se con** to face

encarcelamiento M imprisonment

encarcelar VT to imprison, to jail, to incarcerate

encarecer[35] VI (subir de precio) to increase in price; VT (rogar) to beg

encarecidamente ADV earnestly

encargado -da ADJ on order; MF person in charge; **— de curso** lecturer

encargar[40] VT (responsabilizar) to put in charge; (pedir) to order; (mandar) to commission, to order; **— a alguien una tarea** to charge someone with a task; **—se de** to take care of

encargo M (pedido) order; (tarea) assignment, charge, errand; **construido por/de —** custom-built; **hecho por —** made to order

encariñarse VI **— de** to become fond of

encarnación F incarnation

encarnado ADJ (color) red; (uña) ingrown

encarnar VT (un ideal) to embody; (a un personaje) to play; **se me encarnó una uña** one of my nails got ingrown

encarnizado ADJ fierce

encarnizarse[47] VI **— con alguien** to attack someone viciously

encarte M insert

encasillar VT to pigeonhole

encauzamiento M channeling

encauzar[47] VT to channel

encefalitis F encephalitis; **— espongiforme bovina** mad cow disease

encendedor M cigarette lighter

encender[2] VT (un cigarro, fuego) to light; (un fósforo) to strike; (una luz, radio) to switch on, to turn on; (una computadora) to power on, to power up; (pasión) to arouse; VI **—se** (una persona, sexualmente) to become aroused; (una lámpara) to turn on

encendido ADJ (rojo) bright; (excitado) aroused; M ignition

encerado M (pizarrón) blackboard; (acción de encerar) waxing; (capa de cera) wax coating; ADJ waxed

encerar VT to wax, to polish

encerrar[1] VT (palabras entre paréntesis) to enclose; (una oveja) to pen; (a una persona) to lock up; (un contenido) to contain; (un peligro) to involve; **—se** (aislarse) to isolate oneself; (obstinarse) to become fixated

encestar VI to make a basket

enchapar VT (metal) to plate; (madera) to veneer

enchilada F enchilada

enchufar VT (un aparato eléctrico) to plug in; (a un protegido) to fix up; **— un tubo con otro** to fit one pipe into another

enchufe M (entrada eléctrica) socket, plug-in, electrical outlet; (situación ventajosa) connection

encías F PL gums

enciclopedia F encyclopedia

encienda, enciende ver encender

encierra, encierre ver encerrar

encierro M (confinamiento) confinement; (lugar) enclosure

encima ADV (arriba) on top; (además) in addition; — **de** on top of, atop; **por — de** above; **sacarse de** — to get rid of; **orinarse** — to urinate on oneself; **ya tenía el coche** — the car was already on top of me; **no lleves tanto dinero** — don't carry so much money on you; **se nos vienen — los exámenes** the exams are upon us; **mi madre siempre me está** — my mother is always on me; **lo leí por** — I scanned it

encimera F counter

encina F oak

encinta ADJ pregnant

enclaustrar VT to cloister

enclavarse VI to be located

enclave M enclave

enclenque ADJ (endeble) sickly; (desvencijado) rickety[5]

encoger[45] VI/VT to shrink; **—se** (una prenda) to shrink; (una persona) to be intimidated; **—se de hombros** to shrug one's shoulders

encogido ADJ (tímido) shy; M (encogimiento) shrinkage, shrinking

encogimiento M (acción de encoger) shrinkage, shrinking; **— de hombros** shrug

encolar VT to glue

encolerizar[47] VT to incense; **—se** to become incensed, to lose one's temper

encomendar[1] VT to entrust; **—se** to commend oneself

encomienda F (encargo) assignment, task; (colonial) encomienda [colonial land grant]

enconar VT to inflame; VI **—se** (discusión) to become inflamed; (herida) to fester

encono M animosity

encontrado ADJ contrary, opposing

encontrar[5] VT (hallar) to find; (verse con) to meet; **— a** to run into; **—se** (estar ubicado) to be located; (hallarse) to feel; **—se con** (verse por acuerdo) to meet with; (verse, por coincidencia) to run into; (enterarse) to find out; **vas a encontrarte la casa en obras** you'll find the house under construction

encontronazo M collision

encordado M strings

encordar[5] VT to string

encorvado ADJ stoop-shouldered

encorvamiento M slouch, stoop

encorvar VT to stoop; **—se** to bend over

encostrarse VI to scab

encrespar VT (el pelo) to curl; (el mar) to make choppy; **—se** (el pelo) to get curly; (el mar) to get choppy

encrucijada F crossroads

encuadernación F (oficio) bookbinding; (producto) binding

encuadernar VT to bind

encuadrar VT to frame; **la poesía de esta época se encuadra en tres tendencias** the poetry of this period can be classified into three tendencies

encubierto ADJ covert

encubrimiento ADJ (de un delincuente) concealment; (de un escándalo) cover-up

encubrir[74] VT (un secreto) to conceal; (un escándalo) to cover up, to hush up

encuentra, encuentre ver encontrar

encuentro M (casual) encounter; (planeado) meeting; (partido) game; (de atletismo) meet; **salir al — de** (ir a encontrar) to go out to meet; (contradecir) to counter

encuerar VT to strip

encuesta F survey, poll

encuestado -da MF respondent

encuestar VI/VT to survey, to poll

encumbrado ADJ elevated, lofty

encumbramiento M elevation

encumbrar VT to elevate

encurtido M pickle

encurtir VT to pickle

ende LOC ADV **por —** hence

endeble ADJ (persona) feeble; (material, argumento) flimsy; (mesa) rickety

endémico ADJ endemic

endemoniado ADJ (poseído por el diablo) possessed by the devil; (niño) devilish; (pregunta) tough

enderezar[47] VT to straighten; **enderézate** stand up straight; **la niña se enderezó con los años** the girl straightened out after a few years

endeudamiento M indebtedness

endeudarse VI to get into debt

endiablado ADJ devilish

endocrino ADJ endocrine

endocrinología F endocrinology

endodermo M endoderm

endomingado ADJ dressed in one's Sunday best

endorfina F endorphin

endosante MF endorser

endosar VT to endorse

endoso M endorsement

endrogar VT to drug

endulzante M sweetener

endulzar[47] VT to sweeten; **se endulzó el tiempo** the weather became milder

endurecer[35] VT to harden, to stiffen; VI **—se** (músculos) to get hard; (pegamento) to set

endurecimiento M hardening

enebro M juniper

eneldo M dill

enema MF enema

enemigo -ga ADJ & MF enemy; **buques — s** enemy ships; **ser — de algo** to dislike something

enemistad F enmity

enemistar VT to cause enmity between; **—se con** to become an enemy of

energético ADJ **política energética** energy policy

energía F energy; **— eólica** wind power; **— hidráulica** water power; **— nuclear** nuclear energy; **— solar** solar energy; **— térmica** thermal energy

enérgicamente ADV strongly

enérgico ADJ (persona) energetic; (protesta, medida, tono) forceful

enero M January

enervar VT (debilitar) to enervate; (irritar) to irritate

enfadado ADJ angry

enfadar VT to anger; *fam* to piss off; VI **—se** to get angry

enfado M anger

enfadoso ADJ annoying

enfardar VT to bale

énfasis M emphasis

enfático ADJ emphatic

enfatizar[47] VT to emphasize

enfermar VT to sicken; VI to become sick; **—se** to become ill

enfermedad F (malestar) sickness, illness; (cardiovascular, de Parkinson) disease; (social) ill; **— contagiosa** contagious disease; **— coronaria** heart disease; **— de altura** altitude sickness; **— de Alzheimer** Alzheimer's disease; **— de las vacas locas** mad cow disease; **— del legionario** legionnaire's disease; **— de Lou Gehrig** Lou Gehrig's disease; **— de Lyme** Lyme disease; **— de Parkinson** Parkinson's disease; **— degenerativa articular** degenerative joint disease; **— mental** mental illness; **— parasitaria** parasitic disease; **— por radiación** radiation sickness

enfermería F infirmary

enfermero -ra M male nurse; F nurse

enfermizo ADJ (persona) sickly, infirm; (obsesión, aspecto) unhealthy; (imaginación) sick

enfermo -ma ADJ sick, ill; **me tiene — que vengan tarde** I'm sick of them coming late; MF patient; **— del corazón** heart patient

enfisema M emphysema

enflaquecer[35] VI to get thin

enfocar[30] VT (los ojos) to focus; (un faro) to point; (una cámara) to train; (un tema) to approach

enfoque M (método) approach; (acción de enfocar) focusing

enfrentamiento M clash, confrontation

enfrentar VT (enemigos) to confront; (una dificultad) to face, to tackle; **— a dos personas** to pit two people against each other; **—se con** to clash with

enfrente ADV opposite; **— de** in front of, opposite

enfriamiento M (del aire) cooling; (de una persona) chill; (de la economía, las relaciones) cooling off

enfriar[28] VT to cool, to chill; VI **—se** to cool off

enfundar VT to sheathe

enfurecer[35] VT to infuriate, to enrage; VI **—se** to become enraged, to rage

enfurruñado ADJ sulky

enfurruñarse VI to sulk

engalanar VT (una mesa) to decorate; (a una muchacha) to dress up; **—se** to dress up

enganchar VT (bueyes) to hitch; (una red) to snag; (un teléfono) to hook up; (a los televidentes, a un adicto) to hook; VI **—se** to get hooked

enganche M (del gas, teléfono) connection, hookup; (de drogas) addictiveness; (de vagones) coupling; (de caballos) team; (primer pago) *Méx* down payment

enganchón M snag

engañador ADJ deceitful

engañar VT (mentir) to deceive; (ser infiel) to cheat on; **— el hambre** to ward off hunger; **—se** to deceive oneself

engaño M deceit, deception

engañoso ADJ (una persona) deceitful; (un hecho) misleading

engastar VT to set

engaste M setting

engatusar VT to coax, to cajole

engendrar VT (emociones) to engender; (hijos) to father

englobar VT to encompass

engomar VT to glue

engordar VI to get fat, to put on weight; VT to make fat, to fatten; **esta semana he engordado dos kilos** I gained two kilos this week

engorroso ADJ irksome

engoznar VT to hinge

engranado ADJ meshed, interlocking; **estar —** to be in gear

engranaje M gears, gearing; **el — del partido** the party apparatus

engranar VT (meter una marcha) to put in gear, to throw into gear; (encajar) to mesh; **— la marcha atrás** to put [the car] in reverse

engrandecer[35] VT (a una persona) to aggrandize; (un palacio) to make more grandiose

engrapar VT to staple, to cramp

engrasar VT (untar) to grease; (manchar) to make greasy; (sobornar) to grease someone's palm; **—se** to get greasy

engrase M grease job

engreído ADJ conceited

engreírse[10] VI to become conceited

engrillar VT to shackle

engrosar VT (una manifestación) to swell; (un volumen) to grow; (una persona) to get fat

engrudo M paste

engullir[16] VT to gobble

enhebrar VT (un hilo) to thread; (cuentas) to string; **— idioteces** to string together a bunch of idiocies

enhorabuena F congratulation; INTERJ congratulations

enigma M (misterio) enigma, conundrum; (adivinanza) riddle; (problema) puzzle

enjabonar VT (poner jabón) to soap, to lather; (adular) to flatter

enjaezar[47] VT to harness

enjalbegar[40] VT to whitewash

enjambre M swarm

enjaular VT (un animal) to cage; (a una persona) to jail

enjuagar[40] VT to rinse; (ropa) to rinse out; (platos) to rinse off

enjuague M (limpieza) rinse, rinsing; (trama) scheme; **— bucal** mouthwash

enjugar[40] VT (la frente) to wipe; (lágrimas) to wipe away

enjuiciar VT to prosecute, to try

enjuto ADJ dry; (delgado) thin

enlace M (de trenes, web) link; (químico) bond; (boda) marriage; (persona) liaison; **— muerto** dead link

enladrillado M brick pavement

enladrillar VT to brick, to pave with bricks

enlatar VT to can

enlazar[47] VT (unir) to link (también en la web); (sujetar con lazo) to rope, to lasso; VI to connect; **—se** to connect

enlodar VT to muddy; **—se** to get muddy

enloquecedor ADJ maddening

enloquecer[35] VT to drive crazy; VI to go crazy; **—se** to go crazy

enlosado M flagstone pavement

enlosar VT to pave with flagstones

enmantecar[30] VT to butter

enmarañar VT (pelo) to entangle; (problema) to complicate

enmarcar[30] VT (un cuadro) to frame; **se enmarca dentro de** it takes place in the context of

enmascarar VT to mask

enmendar[1] VT (una ley) to amend; (un texto) to revise; **— la situación** to mend matters; **no me enmiendes la plana** don't correct me;

VI **—se** to mend one's ways

enmienda F (de una ley) amendment; (de un texto) revision

enmohecer[35] VT to mold; **—se** to get moldy, to mold

enmudecer[35] VT to silence; VI to go silent

ennegrecer[35] VI/VT to blacken

ennoblecer[35] VT to ennoble

enojadizo ADJ hotheaded

enojado ADJ angry, mad

enojar VT to anger; **—se** to get angry

enojo M anger

enojoso ADJ bothersome

enorgullecer[35] VT to fill with pride; **—se de** to take pride in

enorme ADJ enormous

enormemente ADV vastly

enramada F bower

enrarecido ADJ thin, rare

enrarecimiento M rarity, thinness

enredadera F creeper

enredar VT (enmarañar) to entangle; (complicar) to complicate; (involucrar) to mix up; VI to cause trouble; **—se** to get tangled up; **—se con** to become involved with

enredijo M tangle, snarl

enredo M (enredijo) snarl; (lío) mess; (amancebamiento) affair

enredoso ADJ complicated

enrejado M (de metal) grating, grate; (de varillas) lattice

enrejar VT to install a grate on

enrevesado ADJ involved

enriquecer[35] VT to enrich; **—se** to become rich

enriquecimiento M enrichment

enrojecer[35] VI/VT to redden

enrollar VT (manga, alfombra) to roll up; (hilo, cuerda, cinta) to wind up; **—se con** to become involved with

enronquecer[35] VT to make hoarse; VI to become hoarse

enroscar[30] VT (soga) to coil, to roll up; (tuerca) to screw in; (tapa) to screw on; **—se** (vid) to twine; (serpiente) to coil up

ensacar[30] VT to sack

ensalada F salad

ensalzar[47] VT to extol

ensanchar VT to widen; **—se** (una calle) to widen; (una falda) to flare

ensanche M (de una calle) widening; (de una ciudad) expansion

ensangrentado ADJ gory, bloody

ensangrentar VT to smear blood on; **—se** to get covered with blood

ensartar VT (cuentas) to string; (aguja) to thread; (con un pincho) to pierce; (historias) to rattle off

ensayar VT (probar) to try out; (intentar) to try; (analizar un metal) to assay; (practicar una obra teatral) to rehearse

ensayo M (intento) trial, attempt; (de teatro) rehearsal; (obra literaria) essay; (nuclear) testing; (de un metal) assay; — **clínico** clinical trial; — **general** dress rehearsal; **por — y error** by trial and error

enseguida ADV at once, immediately

ensenada F cove

enseña F ensign, flag

enseñanza F teaching, education; —**s** teachings

enseñar VT (mostrar) to show; (instruir) to teach; — **a** to teach how to

enseres M PL household utensils

ensillar VT to saddle, to saddle up

ensimismarse VI to lose oneself in thought

ensoberbecer[35] VT to make haughty; —**se** to become haughty

ensombrecer[35] VT (oscurecer) to make shadowy; (entristecer) to sadden

ensoñación F dream

ensordecedor ADJ deafening

ensordecer[35] VT to deafen

ensortijar VT to curl

ensuciar VT to dirty, to sully; —**se** (mancharse) to get dirty; (defecar) to soil oneself

ensueño M reverie, dream

entablar VT (relaciones) to establish; (un conflicto) to start; (una conversación) to strike up; (una demanda) to file; (una pelea) to pick

entablillar VT to splint

entallar VT to take in

entarimar VT to floor with planks

ente M (ser) entity; (excéntrico) weirdo; (agencia) agency

enteco ADJ sickly

entender[2] VT (comprender) to understand; (oír) to hear; — **de** to know about; —**se con** (comunicar) to communicate with; (llevarse bien) to get along with; **dar a** — to intimate; **yo me entiendo** I know what I'm doing; **se entiende** of course

entendido -da ADJ (comprendido) understood; (experto) expert; **tengo — que** I understand that; **caridad mal entendida** misguided charity; MF expert

entendimiento M understanding

enterado ADJ informed; **darse por** — to acknowledge; **estar — de** to be privy to

enterar VT to inform; —**se** to find out [about]; **recién me entero** I just found out; **para que te enteres** just so you know

entereza F fortitude

enternecedor ADJ touching

enternecer[35] VT to touch; —**se** to be touched

entero ADJ (completo) entire, whole; (número) whole; **se mantuvo — durante el funeral** he held himself together during the funeral; M integer, whole number

enterramiento M (de un cable) burying; (de un difunto) burial

enterrar[1] VT (cable, muerto) to bury; (balón) to dunk

entibiar VT to make lukewarm; —**se** to become lukewarm

entidad F entity; **de** — significant; — **bancaria** banking institution

entienda, entiende ver entender

entierro M burial, funeral

entintar VT to stain with ink

entoldar VT to cover with an awning

entomología F entomology

entonación F intonation

entonar VT to sing; VI to sing in tune; — **con** to go well with; —**se** to get tipsy

entonces ADV then; **desde** — ever since; **hasta** — until then; **el — presidente** the then president; CONJ (así que) so

entornado ADJ half-open

entornar VT (una puerta) to leave ajar; (los ojos) to close partially

entorno M (lo que rodea) surroundings; (medio ambiente, informático) environment; — **de trabajo** work environment

entorpecer[35] VT (los sentidos) to dull; (el paso) to hinder; —**se** to become sluggish

entorpecimiento M (de los sentidos) dullness; (del paso) hindrance

entrada F (sitio por donde se entra, de un actor) entrance; (acción de entrar, artículo de diccionario) entry; (asistentes a un espectáculo) gate; (oportunidad para actuar) opening; (billete, derecho, precio de entrar) admission; (llegada) arrival; (primer plato) appetizer; (pago inicial) down payment; (tiempo en béisbol) inning; —**s** cash receipts; — **de coches** driveway; — **de datos** data input; — **por partida doble** double entry; **de** — from the start

entramado M lattice

entrante ADJ (alcalde) incoming; (año) next; M recess

entrañable ADJ (amistad) close; (persona) endearing

entrañas F PL (intestinos) entrails, *fam* guts; (sentimientos) heart, core; — **de la tierra** bowels of the earth; **de mis** — of my own flesh and blood

entrar VI (ir hacia adentro) to go in; (comenzar el día de trabajo) to come in; (caber) to fit; **dejar** — to let in; **hacer — en razón** to bring to reason; — **a medicina** to go into medicine; — **en calor** to warm up; — **en coma** to go into a coma; — **en/a un cuarto** to enter a room; — **en materia** to get to the meat of a matter; — **en vigencia/vigor** to go into effect; **me entró miedo** I became afraid; **me entró sueño** I got sleepy; **no sé**

cómo —le a esa chica I don't know how to approach that girl; **la física no me entra** I can't learn physics; **no entra entre mis favoritos** it is not included among my favorites; **la semana que entra** next week; **este vestido no me entra** this dress doesn't fit me; **seis entra dos veces en doce** six goes into twelve two times; **hazle —** show him in; VT (datos) to enter, to input

entre PREP (dos) between; (muchos) among; **— vaso y vaso** between glasses; **— dientes** under one's breath

entreabierto ADJ ajar, half-open

entreabrir[74] VT (puerta) to crack open; (los ojos) to half-open

entreacto M intermission

entrecano ADJ graying

entrecejo M space between the eyebrows

entrecortado ADJ (voz) faltering; (respiración) irregular

entrecortarse VI to falter

entrecruzar[47] VT to interlace; **—se** to cross

entredicho LOC ADV **en —** in doubt

entrega F (de un paquete) delivery; (de un manuscrito) submission; (al vicio) surrender; (de una novela) installment; (de revista) issue; **a la —** on delivery; **por —s** serial; **— a domicilio** home delivery; **— de premios** presentation of awards; **— el mismo día** same-day delivery; **— gratuita** free delivery; **— inicial** down payment

entregar[40] VT (un paquete) to deliver; (a un rehén, prisionero) to hand over; (a un delincuente) to turn in; (a una hija en matrimonio) to give; (premios) to hand out, to present; (tarea escolar) to hand in; (el coche) to trade in; **—se [a]** (la policía) to surrender [to]; (a una misión) to dedicate oneself to

entrelazar[47] VT to intertwine

entremés M (obra de teatro) interlude; (comida) hors d'oeuvre

entremeter VT to insert; **—se en** (meterse) to get mixed up in; (inmiscuirse) to meddle in

entremetido -da ADJ meddlesome, nosy; MF meddler, busybody

entremezclar VT to intermingle

entrenador -ora MF trainer, coach; **— en jefe** head coach

entrenamiento M training

entrenar VI/VT to train

entrepierna F (del cuerpo) crotch; (de pantalón) inseam

entrepiso M mezzanine

entresacar[30] VT (seleccionar) to cull; (adelgazar) to thin

entresuelo M (de hotel) mezzanine; (de cine) balcony

entretanto ADV meanwhile

entretejer VT (el pelo, una tela) to weave; (una historia) to weave together

entretener[58] VT (hacer atrasar) to delay; (distraer) to distract; (divertir) to entertain; **—se** (divertirse) to amuse oneself; (detenerse) to delay

entretenido ADJ entertaining

entretenimiento M entertainment, amusement

entrever[72, 74] VT (apenas) to catch a glimpse of; (a lo lejos) to make out

entreverar VT to mix, to intersperse; **—se** to meddle

entrevía F gauge

entrevista F interview; **— de salida** exit interview

entrevistar VT to interview; **—se con** to have an interview with

entristecer[35] VT to sadden; **—se** to become sad

entrometerse VI to meddle, to interfere

entrometido -da ADJ meddlesome, nosy; MF meddler, busybody

entronque M (ferroviario) junction; (parentesco) relationship

entropía F entropy

entumecido ADJ (dedo, diente) numb; (músculo) stiff

entumecimiento M (de los dedos, dientes) numbness; (de los músculos) stiffness

enturbiar VT (el agua) to muddy; (una decisión) to muddle; (el juicio, la alegría) to cloud; **—se** (agua) to get muddy; (alegría) to be marred

entusiasmado ADJ enthusiastic, excited

entusiasmar VT to excite; **—se** to be excited

entusiasmo M enthusiasm, excitement

entusiasta MF enthusiast; ADJ enthusiastic

enumerar VT to enumerate

enunciado M utterance

enunciar VT (palabras) to enunciate; (una teoría) to articulate, to enunciate

envainar VT to sheathe

envalentonar VT to embolden, to make bold; **—se** to become bold

envanecer[35] VT to make vain; **—se** to become vain

envarado ADJ stiff, staid

envaramiento M stiffness

envasar VT to package; **— al vacío** to vacuum-pack

envase M packaging

envejecer[35] VT to make old; **ese maquillaje te envejece** that makeup makes you look older; VI to grow old, to age

envejecimiento M aging

envenenamiento M poisoning

envenenar VT to poison

envergadura F (de un avión) wingspan; (de un ave) wingspread; (de un evento, proyecto) importance

envés M SG back

enviado -da MF (político) envoy; (periodístico) correspondent

enviar[28] VT to send; **— por fax** to fax

enviciar VT to corrupt; **—se con** to get hooked on

envidia F envy

envidiable ADJ enviable

envidiar VT to envy

envidioso ADJ envious, jealous

envilecer[35] VT to debase

envío M (acción) shipping; (mercancía) shipment; (manuscrito) submission; **— de anotación** touchdown pass; **— rápido** express delivery

envite M bet

envoltorio M (cosa envuelta) bundle; (envoltura) wrapper

envoltura F wrapping, wrapper; **— de plástico transparente** shrinkwrap

envolver[6, 74] VT (involucrar) to involve; (cubrir) to wrap; (atrapar) to entangle; (rodear) to surround; **—se** to become involved

envuelto, envuelva, envuelve ver envolver

enyesar VT (enlucir con yeso) to plaster; (escayolar) to put in a cast

enzima MF enzyme

épica F epic

epicentro M epicenter

épico ADJ epic

epidemia F epidemic

epidémico ADJ epidemic

epidermis F epidermis

epifanía F epiphany

epiglotis F epiglottis

epilepsia F epilepsy

epiléptico ADJ epileptic

epílogo M epilogue

episódico ADJ episodic

episodio M episode

epitafio M epitaph

epítome M epitome

época F (momento) time, period; (período histórico) age; (temporada) season; (período geológico) epoch

epopeya F epic poem

equidad F equity

equidistante ADJ equidistant

equilibrado ADJ balanced; M balancing

equilibrar VT to balance; **— un presupuesto** to balance a budget

equilibrio M equilibrium, balance; **perder el —** to lose one's balance; **hacer —s** to do a balancing act

equino ADJ & M equine

equinoccio M equinox

equipaje M baggage, luggage

equipamiento M equipment

equipar VT to equip, to outfit

equiparar VT to equate

equipo M (materiales) equipment; (grupo) team; **— de vida** life-support system; **— deportivo** sweatsuit; **— de esquí** ski gear

equitación F (arte) horsemanship; (actividad) riding

equitativo ADJ equitable

equivalente ADJ equivalent

equivaler[60] VI to be equivalent; **lo que equivale a decir** which amounts to saying

equivocación F mistake

equivocado ADJ mistaken, wrong; **estar —** to be wrong/mistaken

equivocar[30] VT to mistake; **—se** to be mistaken, to make a mistake, to miscalculate; **—se de sala** to choose the wrong room; **si no me equivoco** unless I'm mistaken; **me equivoqué de baño** I went into the wrong bathroom

equívoco ADJ (ambiguo) equivocal; (moralmente dudoso) questionable; M misunderstanding

era F (período) era, age; (lugar donde se trilla) threshing floor; (parcela) plot

era, eras ver ser

erario M treasury

erecto ADJ erect; (postura) upright

eres ver ser

ergonomía F ergonomics

ergonómico ADJ ergonomic

erguido ADJ erect, upright

erguir[13] VT to lift, to raise; **—se** to rise

erial M uncultivated land

erigir[46] VT (construir) to erect; (fundar) to found; **—se en** to set oneself up as

Eritrea F Eritrea

eritreo -a ADJ & MF Eritrean

erizado ADJ bristly; **— de** bristling with

erizar[47] VT to set on end; **—se** to bristle

erizo M hedgehog; **— de mar** sea urchin; **ser un —** to be a grouch

ermitaño -ña MF (persona) hermit; M (cangrejo) hermit crab

erógeno ADJ erogenous

erosión F erosion

erradicación F eradication

erradicar[30] VT to eradicate, to root out

errado ADJ erroneous, in error

errante ADJ wandering

errar[21] VT to miss; **— el cálculo** to miscalculate; VI (estar equivocado) to be mistaken; (vagar) to roam, to rove, to wander

errata F misprint, typographical error

errático ADJ erratic

erróneo ADJ erroneous

error M error, mistake; **— de hecho** factual error; **— de imprenta** misprint; **— no forzado** unforced error; **— tipográfico** typo

eructar VI to belch, to burp

eructo M belch, burp

erudición F erudition, learning, scholarship

erudito -ta ADJ (persona) erudite; (obra) scholarly, learned; MF scholar

erupción F eruption; **hacer —** to erupt

es *ver* ser

esbelto ADJ slender

esbozar[47] VT to outline; **— una sonrisa** to give a hint of a smile

esbozo M sketch, outline; **— de una sonrisa** hint of a smile

escabechar VT to pickle

escabroso ADJ (agreste) rugged; (espinoso) thorny; (sórdido) lurid, sordid

escabullirse[16] VI (ladrones) to slip away, to steal away; (lagartijas) to scurry away/off; **— de** to wriggle out of

escafandra F (para el agua) scuba gear; (para el espacio) spacesuit

escala F (escalera, escalafón) ladder; (serie de grados, notas, serie ascendente) scale; (parada) stopover; **— de sueldos** salary range, wage scale; **hacer — en** to stop over at; **— salarial** wage scale, pay scale; **a — nacional** nationwide; **a/de gran —** large-scale; **sin —s** nonstop

escalada F (de una montaña) climb; (de violencia) escalation

escalador -ora MF climber

escalar VT (subir) to scale, to climb; (cambiar de tamaño) scale

escaldadura F scald

escaldar VT (la piel) to scald; (las verduras) to blanch; **—se** to get scalded

escalera F (en un edificio) stairs, staircase; (portátil) ladder; (de naipes) straight; **— mecánica** escalator; **— de caracol** spiral/ winding staircase; **— de color** straight flush; **— de incendios** fire escape; **— real** royal flush

escalfar VT to poach

escalinata F grand staircase

escalofriante ADJ chilling, hair-raising

escalofrío M chill; **—s** the shivers

escalón M (peldaño) step, stair; (de escalera de mano, de escalafón) rung; (terraza) rung; (formación militar) echelon

escalonar VT (distribuir) to stagger; (aterrazar) to terrace

escalope M scallop

escama F (de animal) scale; (de piel, corteza) flake

escamar VT to scale

escamoso ADJ (animal) scaly; (piel) flaky

escamotear VT (esconder) to palm; (robar) to snatch; (eludir) to shirk

escampar VI to clear up

escandalizar[47] VT (chocar) to scandalize; (causar escándalo) to cause a scandal; **—se** to be shocked

escándalo M (suceso vergonzoso) scandal; (riña) uproar

escandaloso ADJ (chocante) scandalous, shocking; (ruidoso) raucous

escandir VT *lit* to scan

escaneado M scanning

escanear VT to scan

escáner M scanner; **— color** color scanner

escaño M seat in parliament

escapada F (escape) escape

escapar VI (de un lugar, una situación) to escape; (de alguien, de una responsabilidad) to run away; **—se** (persona) to escape; (gas) to leak; **se me escapó una sonrisa** I inadvertently smiled; **Matilde se me está escapando de las manos** Matilde is getting out of hand

escaparate M shop window

escapatoria F (de un lugar) escape, way out; (legal) loophole

escape M (fantasía, escapatoria) escape; (de coche) exhaust; (de gas, agua) leak

escápula F scapula

escarabajo M beetle

escaramuza F skirmish

escaramuzar[47] VI to skirmish

escarbar VI/VT to dig, to scratch; **— en los archivos** to dig around in the files; **—se los dientes** to pick one's teeth

escarcha F frost

escarchar VI to frost

escardar VT to weed

escarlata ADJ INV & M (color) scarlet; F (enfermedad) scarlet fever

escarlatina F scarlet fever

escarmentar[1] VI to learn one's lesson; VT to teach a lesson

escarmiento M lesson; **que te sirva de —** let that be a lesson to you

escarnecer[35] VT to deride

escarnio M derision

escarpa F steep slope

escarpado ADJ steep, precipitous; M steep slope

escasear VI to be scarce

escasez F (falta) shortage; (carestía) scarcity, want

escaso ADJ sparse, scarce; **una docena escasa** a scant dozen; **— de** short on; **— de personal** short-handed

escatimar VT to skimp on; **no — gastos** to spare no expense

escena F (fragmento de una obra de teatro, episodio) scene; (escenario) stage; **montar una —** to make a scene; **en —** on stage; **poner en —** to stage; **entrar en —** to go on stage

escenario M stage

escénico ADJ **pánico —** stage fright

escenificación F staging

escepticismo M skepticism

escéptico -ca ADJ skeptical; MF skeptic

escisión F split

esclarecer[35] VT to elucidate

esclavitud F slavery

esclavizar[47] VT to enslave

esclavo -va MF slave

esclerosis F sclerosis; **— múltiple** multiple sclerosis

esclusa F (de un canal) lock; (de una presa) floodgate, sluice gate

escoba F broom

escobilla F whisk broom

escocer[34] VI to sting

escocés -esa ADJ Scottish; **[cuadros] escoceses** plaid; MF Scot; M (whisky) Scotch; (lengua) Scots

Escocia F Scotland

escoger[45] VT to choose

escolar MF pupil; ADJ **año —** school year

escoliosis F scoliosis

escollo M (arrecife) reef; (obstáculo) obstacle

escolta F (policial) escort; MF (persona) escort; (baloncesto) shooting guard

escoltar VT to escort

escombros M PL rubble, debris

esconder VT to hide; VI **—se** to hide

escondidas LOC ADV **a —** on the sly; **entrar a —** to sneak in; **meter algo a —** to sneak something in; **jugar a las —** to play hide and seek

escondite M (en un juego) hiding place; (de ladrón) hideout; (de cazador) blind; **jugar al —** to play hide and seek

escondrijo M hiding place

escopeta F shotgun

escoplo M chisel

escora F listing

escorar VI to list

escorbuto M scurvy

escoria F (de metales) slag; (de la sociedad) scum, dregs

escorpión M scorpion

escotado ADJ low-cut

escote M (parte del vestido) neckline; (parte del cuerpo) cleavage; **pagar a —** to go Dutch

escotilla F hatch

escozor M smarting sensation; **— vaginal** vaginal itching

escribiente MF clerk

escribir[74] VI/VT to write; **¿cómo se escribe?** how do you spell it? **— a máquina** to type

escrito ADJ written; **— a máquina** typewritten; **no —** unwritten; **por —** in writing; M document

escrito *ver* escribir

escritor -ora MF writer, author

escritorio M (mueble) desk; (oficina) office

escritura F (acción de escribir) writing; (certificado de propiedad) deed; **— de traspaso** conveyance; **— de venta** bill of sale

escrúpulo M scruple, qualm; **sin —s** unscrupulous

escrupuloso ADJ scrupulous

escrutar VT (a una persona) to scrutinize; (el horizonte) to scan; (votos) to count

escrutinio M (examen) scrutiny; (recuento) vote count

escuadra F (de buques, soldados) squadron; (instrumento) square

escuadrilla F (de aviones) flight of aircraft; (de buques) squadron

escuadrón M squadron; **— de la muerte** death squad

escualidez F (delgadez) skinniness; (suciedad) squalor

escuálido ADJ (sucio) squalid; (delgado) thin

escuchar VT to listen to; (oír) to hear; VI to listen; **— a hurtadillas** to eavesdrop

escudar VT to shield

escudo M (arma defensiva) shield; (moneda de Portugal) escudo; **— de armas** coat of arms

escudriñar VT (a una persona) to scrutinize, to peer at; (el horizonte) to scan

escuela F school; **— industrial** trade school; **— normal** school of education; **— pública** public school; **— primaria** elementary school; **— secundaria** secondary school; **tener —** to have good technique

escueto ADJ (explicación) succinct; (verdad) simple

esculpir VI/VT to sculpture, to sculpt

escultor -ora MF sculptor

escultura F sculpture

escupir VI/VT to spit

escupitajo M spit

escurridizo ADJ (acera) slippery; (ladrón) elusive, slippery

escurrir VI/VT (platos, verduras) to drain; (ropa) to wring out; **—se** to slink away

ese ADJ DEM that, those; **esa chica se llama Matilde** that girl is called Matilde; **esas ciudades son antiguas** those cities are old; PRON that one, those; **ese es el mayor** that one is the oldest; **esos son mis hijos** those are my children

esencia F essence

esencial ADJ essential; **lo —** the gist, the bottom line, the name of the game

esfera F (cuerpo sólido) sphere; (espacio, ámbito) realm, sphere; (de reloj) face, dial; **— de influencia** sphere of influence

esférico ADJ spherical; M soccer ball

esfínter M sphincter

esforzado ADJ valiant

esforzarse[49] VI to try hard, to exert oneself; **—**

por to strive to, to make an effort to

esfuerzo M effort

esfumar VT to tone down; **—se** to vanish, to fizzle out

esgrima F fencing; **practicar —** to fence

esgrimir VT (armas) to brandish, to wield; (argumentos) to employ

eslabón M chain link; **— perdido** missing link

eslabonar VT to link

eslavo -va ADJ Slavic; MF Slav

eslogan M slogan

eslovaco M & MF Slovakian; M (lengua) Slovakian

Eslovaquia F Slovakia

Eslovenia F Slovenia

esloveno -na ADJ & MF Slovene; M (lengua) Slovéne

esmaltar VT to enamel

esmalte M enamel; **— de uñas** nail polish

esmeradamente ADV carefully

esmerado ADJ careful, painstaking

esmeralda F emerald

esmerarse VI to take pains

esmerilado ADJ frosted; M frosting

esmerilar VT to frost

esmero M care

esmirriado ADJ scrawny

esmoquin M tuxedo

esnifar VT to snort

esnob M snob

esnórquel M snorkel

eso PRON DEM that; **— es verdad** that's true; **— sí** granted; **a — de las tres** at about three o'clock; **de —, nada** no way! yeah, right! **en — llega y me dice** at that moment he arrives and says to me; **y — que le dije que viniese temprano** even when I told him to come early

esófago M esophagus

esotérico ADJ esoteric

espaciado M pitch, spacing; **— de palabras** word spacing

espacial ADJ spatial; **nave —** spaceship

espaciar VT to space; **—se** to space out

espacio M (capacidad) space, room; (superficie) expanse; (separación entre líneas) space, spacing; (en un formulario) blank space; (porción de tiempo) span; **— aéreo** aerospace; **— entre caracteres** letterspacing; **— exterior** outer space; **— noticioso** newscast; **a doble —** double-spaced; **a un —** single-spaced; **por — de una semana** for a week

espacioso ADJ spacious, roomy

espada F sword; **—s** (palo de naipes) swords; **— de doble filo** double-edged sword; **estar entre la — y la pared** to be between a rock and a hard place

espalda F back; **a —s de alguien** behind

someone's back; **caerse de —s** to fall on one's back; **nadar [de] —s** to do the backstroke; **tener las —s anchas** to take a lot of abuse; **volver las —s** to turn one's back

espaldar M chair back

espantadizo ADJ easily scared

espantado ADJ frightened

espantajo M scarecrow

espantar VT to frighten, to scare; (ahuyentar) to frighten away, to scare away; **—se** to get scared; M SG **espantapájaros** scarecrow

espanto M fright, dread; **estás hecho un —** you look a sight; **estoy curado de —** nothing surprises me anymore

espantoso ADJ frightful, dreadful

España F Spain

español -ola ADJ Spanish; MF Spaniard; M (lengua) Spanish

esparadrapo M surgical tape

esparcimiento M (recreo) relaxation; (reparto) spreading

esparcir[33] VT to scatter, to spread; **—se** to amuse oneself

espárrago M asparagus

espasmo M spasm, jerk

espasmódico ADJ spasmodic, jerky

espástico ADJ spastic

espátula F spatula

especia F spice

especial ADJ & M special; **en —** in particular, especially

especialidad F specialty, specialization

especialista MF specialist

especialización F specialization

especializar[47] VT to specialize; **—se en** to specialize in, to major in

especialmente ADV (de forma particular) specially; **esto lo hice — para ti** I made this specially for you; (en especial) especially; **este tipo es — bueno** this kind is especially good

especie F (clase) kind; (categoría biológica) species; **—s en peligro de extinción** endangered species; **pagar en —** to pay in kind; **una — de** a kind of

especiero M spice rack

especificar[30] VT to specify

específico ADJ & M specific

espécimen M specimen

espectacular ADJ spectacular

espectáculo M (escándalo) spectacle; (actuación pública) show; (vista) sight; **dar el —** to make a spectacle of oneself

espectador -ora MF (de un espectáculo) spectator; (de un suceso) onlooker

espectro M (fantasma) specter; (de la luz, de un antibiótico) spectrum

especulación F speculation

especulador -ora MF speculator

especular VT to speculate; ADJ mirror; **imagen —** mirror image

especulativo ADJ speculative

espejismo M (en el desierto) mirage; (ilusión) illusion

espejo M mirror; **— de cuerpo entero** full-length mirror; **— retrovisor** rearview mirror

espeluznante ADJ hair-raising

espeluznar VT to terrify; **—se** to be terrified

espera F (acción de esperar) wait; (aplazamiento) extension; **estar en — de** to be waiting for

esperanza F hope; **— de vida** life expectancy; **con una — de voto del 12,5%** expected to get 12.5% of the vote

esperanzado ADJ hopeful

esperanzador ADJ hopeful

esperanzar[47] VT to give hope to

esperar VT (tener esperanza) to hope; (estar embarazada, anticipar) to expect; (aguardar) to wait for; VI to wait; **como era de —** not surprisingly; **era de —** it was to be expected; **espera sentado** don't hold your breath; **estoy esperando un milagro** I'm hoping for a miracle; **todavía espera confirmación** it still awaits confirmation

esperma MF sperm

espermicida M spermicide

esperpento M fright, grotesque person or thing

espesar VT to thicken

espeso ADJ (pelo, sopa, niebla) thick; (cejas) bushy

espesor M thickness

espesura F (espesor) thickness; (lugar poblado de matorrales) thicket

espetar VT (decir bruscamente) to blurt out; (pinchar) to skewer

espeto, espetón M spit

espía MF spy

espiar[28] VI to spy; VT to spy on

espichar VI *fam* to croak, to bite the dust

espiga F spike

espigar[40] VT to glean; VI to grow spikes; **—se** to grow tall

espina F (de planta) thorn; (de pez) fish bone; **— dorsal** spinal column; **me quedé con la —** I was left wondering

espinaca F spinach

espinal ADJ spinal

espinazo M spine, backbone

espinilla F (en la pierna) shin; (de animal) shank; (acné, comedón) blackhead

espino M thorny shrub

espinoso ADJ thorny

espionaje M espionage

espiración F expiration

espiral ADJ & F spiral

espirar VI/VT to exhale, to breathe out, to expire

espíritu M (ánima, fantasma, intención de una ley) spirit; (alma) soul; **— fuerte** free spirit; **— deportivo** sportsmanship; **— emprendedor** can-do attitude, entrepreneurship; **— Santo** Holy Spirit

espiritual ADJ & M spiritual

espiritualidad F spirituality

espita F spigot

espléndido ADJ (estupendo) splendid; (dispendioso) lavish

esplendor M splendor

esplendoroso ADJ magnificent

espliego M lavender

espolear VT to spur

espoleta F bomb fuse

espolón M (de gallo, planta, estímulo) spur; (de buque) ram

espolvorear VT to dust, to sprinkle

esponja F (animal, utensilio) sponge; (borracho) souse

esponjado ADJ spongy

esponjar VT to make spongy; **—se** to become spongy

esponjoso ADJ spongy

esponsales M PL betrothal

espontaneidad F spontaneity

espontáneo ADJ spontaneous

espora F spore

esposar VT to handcuff

esposo -sa M husband; F wife; **esposas** handcuffs

espuela F spur

espulgar[40] VT to delouse

espuma F (de cerveza) froth; (de jabón) suds, lather; (de la boca) foam; (de colchón) foam rubber; (de mar) foam, spray; **echar — por la boca** to foam at the mouth; **hacer —** to make suds

espumar VT (quitar la espuma) to skim; (formar espuma) to foam

espumarajo M foam; **echar —s por la boca** to foam at the mouth

espumillón M tinsel

espumoso ADJ foamy

esputo M sputum

esquela F note; **— mortuoria** death notice

esquelético ADJ skeletal

esqueleto M (huesos) skeleton; (armazón) framework; **mover el —** (bailar) to dance; (moverse) to move

esquema M outline; **romperle los —s a alguien** (planes) to ruin one's plans; (conceptos) to shatter one's preconceptions

esquí M (tabla) ski; (deporte) skiing; **— acuático** (tabla) water ski; (deporte) waterskiing; **hacer — acuático** to water-ski

esquiar[28] VI to ski

esquila F (cencerro) cowbell; (acción de esquilar) shearing

esquilador -ora MF sheep shearer

esquilar VT to shear, to clip

esquileo M shearing

esquimal ADJ & MF Eskimo; M (lengua) Eskimo

esquina F corner; **en cada —** everywhere

esquinero ADJ **mesa esquinera** corner table; M cornerback

esquirol M strikebreaker

esquivar VT (a una persona) to avoid; (un golpe) to dodge

esquivo ADV (tímido) shy, coy; (huraño) aloof; (reservado) elusive; (indirecto) evasive

esquizofrenia F schizophrenia

estabilidad F stability

estabilización F stabilization

estabilizar[47] VT to stabilize

estable ADJ (mesa) stable; (precio) firm; (huésped) long-term

establecer[35] VT to establish; (averiguar) to ascertain; **— una cita** to set up an appointment; **—se** to settle

establecimiento M establishment

establezca, establezco ver establecer

establishment M establishment

establo M stable

estaca F (con punta) stake; (gruesa) club

estacada F stockade; **dejar en la —** to leave in the lurch

estacar[30] VT (atar) to stake; (delimitar) to stake off

estación F (de tren, autobús, radio) station; (del año) season; **— bípeda** bipedal stance; **— de bomberos** fire station; **— de esquí** ski resort; **— de servicio** gas/filling station; **— de trabajo** workstation; **— espacial** space station

estacional ADJ seasonal

estacionamiento M (acción) parking; (lugar) parking lot

estacionar VT (tropas) to station; (un vehículo) to park; **—se** (un coche) to park; (precios) to level off

estacionario ADJ stationary

estadía F stay

estadio M (recinto deportivo) stadium; (fase) stage

estadista M statesman; F stateswoman

estadística F (ciencia) statistics; **—s** (datos numéricos) statistics

estado M (situación, unidad política) state; **— civil** marital status; **— de cuenta** bank statement; **— de alarma** state of emergency; **— de ánimo** state of mind; **— de excepción** martial law; **— de guerra** state of war; **— de sitio** state of siege; **— mayor** chiefs of staff; **— policíaco** police state; **de — sólido** solid state; **en — interesante** expecting; **en — vegetativo** in a vegetative state, brain-dead

Estados Unidos M PL/SG United States

estadounidense ADJ & MF American

estafa F swindle, scam, racket

estafador -ora MF swindler, racketeer

estafar VT to swindle

estalactita F stalactite

estalagmita F stalagmite

estallar VI (una bomba) to explode; (un globo) to burst; (una guerra) to break out; (una persona) to snap; **— de risa** to burst out laughing; **— en una carcajada** to burst out laughing; **hacer —** to set off

estallido M (explosión) explosion; (ruido) bang, report

estampa F (de revista) illustration; (imagen) image; (apariencia) appearance; **de buena —** good-looking; **la viva — de la madre** the spitting image of her mother; **la viva — de la desolación** the very picture of desolation

estampado ADJ printed; M (tela) print; (acción) printing

estampar VT (en tela, papel) to print; (con un molde, en metal) to stamp; **—le un beso a alguien** to plant a kiss on someone

estampida F stampede

estampido M bang

estampilla F stamp

estampillar VT to stamp

estancado ADJ stagnant

estancamiento M stagnation (también económico)

estancar[30] VT to stem; to dam; to block; **—se** to stagnate

estancia F (estadía) stay; (habitación) hall; (hacienda) RP cattle ranch

estanco ADJ waterproof; M government store

estándar ADJ & M standard

estandarización F standardization

estandarizar[47] VT to standardize

estandarte M standard, banner

estanque M pond

estante M (tabla) shelf; (mueble) bookcase

estantería F (mueble) bookcase; (de biblioteca) stack

estañar VT to tin-plate

estaño M tin

estar[63] VI to be; **— a tres kilómetros de aquí** to be three kilometers from here; **— bien** to be all right; **— mal/enfermo del corazón** to have heart trouble; **— de más** to be unnecessary; **— para** to be about to; **— por** (a favor de) to be in favor of; (a punto de) to be about to; **— trabajando duro** to be working hard; **¿a cuántos estamos?** what day of the month is it? **ahí está** that's it; **¿está Alice?** is Alice there? **están muy buenos tus zapatos nuevos** your new shoes are nice; **estate tranquilo** don't worry; **no —** to be out; **cuarto de —** living room

estatal ADJ **compañía —** state-run company

estático ADJ static

estatua F statue

estatura F (importancia) stature; (altura física) height

estatutario ADJ statutory

estatuto M (ley) statute; (de una sociedad) bylaw; **— de quiebras** bankruptcy law

este ADJ DEM this, these; **esta chica se llama Hilary** this girl is called Hilary; **estas ciudades son antiguas** these cities are old; PRON DEM this one, these; **— es el mayor** this one is the oldest; **estos son mis hijos** these are my children; M & ADJ east; **hacia el — eastward**

estela F (de una embarcación) wake; (de humo, polvo) trail; **dejar una —** to leave a trail

estelar ADJ stellar

estenotipista MF court reporter

estentóreo ADJ booming

estepa F steppe

estera F mat

estercolar VT to fertilize with manure

estercolero M dunghill

estéreo ADJ & M stereo; **en —** in stereo

estereotipo M stereotype

estéril ADJ (gasa, esfuerzo) sterile; (mujer) barren

esterilidad F sterility

esterilizar[47] VT to sterilize

esternón M sternum, breastbone

esteroide M steroid; **— anabólico** anabolic steroid

estertor M death rattle

estética F aesthetics

estético ADJ aesthetic

estetoscopio M stethoscope

estibador M stevedore, longshoreman

estibar VT to stow

estiércol M manure

estigma M stigma

estigmatizar[47] VT to stigmatize

estilarse VI to be in style; **eso no se estila aquí** that's not done here

estilística F stylistics

estilístico ADJ stylistic

estilo M (literario, estético, caligráfico) style; (de natación) stroke; **— de vida** lifestyle; **— espalda** backstroke; **— indirecto** reported speech; **— libre** freestyle; **— mariposa** butterfly stroke; **— pecho** breaststroke; **— perrito** dog paddle; **cosas por el —** things like that

estima F esteem, regard

estimación F (cálculo) estimate; (estima) estimation

estimado ADJ esteemed; **— Sr.** Dear Sir

estimar VT (apreciar) to esteem; (determinar el valor) to estimate; (opinar) to think

estimulación F stimulation

estimulante ADJ stimulating; M stimulant

estimular VT (despertar, excitar) to stimulate; (alentar) to encourage

estímulo M stimulus

estío M *lit* summer

estipendio M stipend

estipulación F stipulation

estipular VT to stipulate

estirado ADJ stuck-up

estirar VT (alargar) to stretch; **— el cuello** to crane one's neck; **— la pata** *fam* to kick the bucket; (crecer) to grow; **—se** to stretch

estirón M growth spurt; **pegar un —** to have a growth spurt

estirpe F lineage

estival ADJ **vacaciones —es** summer vacation

esto PRON DEM this; **— es** that is to say; **a todo — meanwhile**; **en —** at this point

estocada F thrust; **lanzar una —** to thrust

estofa F type; **de baja —** low-class

estofado M stew

estofar VT to stew

estoico -ca ADJ & MF stoic

estolón M runner

estómago M stomach

Estonia F Estonia

estonio -nia ADJ & MF Estonian; M (lengua) Estonian

estopa F tow

estorbar VT (obstaculizar) to hinder, to impede; (molestar) to be a nuisance

estorbo M (obstáculo) hindrance, impediment; (molestia) nuisance

estornino M starling

estornudar VI to sneeze

estornudo M sneeze

estoy *ver* estar

estrado M bench

estrafalario ADJ bizarre, outlandish

estragar[40] VT (físicamente) to devastate; (moralmente) to corrupt

estrago M havoc; **hacer —s** to wreak havoc

estrangular VT to strangle

estratagema F stratagem

estrategia F strategy; (de negocios, deportes) game plan; **— de salida** exit strategy

estratégico ADJ strategic

estrato M stratum, layer; **— social** social class

estratosfera F stratosphere

estrechamente ADV closely

estrechamiento M constriction

estrechar VT (angostar) to narrow; (abrazar) to embrace; **la estrechó en sus brazos** he held her in his arms; **—se** to get narrower; **—se la mano** to shake hands

estrechez F (cualidad de estrecho) narrowness; (acción de estrechar) narrowing; (aprietos) dire straits

estrecho ADJ narrow; **la falda le quedaba estrecha** the skirt was too tight for her; M strait

estrella F star; **— binaria** binary star; **— de cine** movie star; **— de mar** starfish; **— fugaz** shooting star, falling star; **ver las —s** to see stars

estrellado ADJ (como una estrella) starlike; (cubierto de estrellas) starry

estrellar VT (aplastar) to smash; (romper) to crack; **—se** (avión) to crash; (intento) to fail; **—se contra** to smash into

estremecer[35] VT to make shudder; **el terremoto estremeció París** the earthquake rocked París; **—se** to shudder

estremecimiento M shudder

estrenar VT (un vestido) to wear for the first time; (una película, obra de teatro) to debut; (una bicicleta) to try out for the first time; (un título) to use for the first time; **—se** to debut

estreno M (de una película) premiere; (de un objeto) first use; (de una actividad) debut

estreñido ADJ (constipado) constipated; (antipático) uptight

estreñimiento M constipation

estreñir[11] VT to constipate; **—se** to become constipated

estrépito M racket, clatter; **causar —** to clatter

estrepitoso ADJ noisy

estrés M stress

estresante ADJ stressful, high-pressure

estresar VT to stress [out]

estría F (en la piel) stretch mark; (en una columna) flute; (en mármol) striation

estriado ADJ (piel) covered with stretch marks; (columna) fluted; (piedra) streaked

estriar[28] VT to flute; **—se** to get stretch marks

estribación F spur

estribar VI **— en** (apoyarse en) to lean on; (radicar en) to lie in

estribillo M refrain

estribo M (de silla, oído) stirrup; (de coche) running board; **perder los —s** to fly off the handle

estribor M starboard

estricnina F strychnine

estricto ADJ strict

estridente ADJ strident

estrofa F verse, stanza

estrógeno M estrogen

estropajo M scrubber; **tengo la boca que es un —** my mouth is as dry as a bone

estropajoso ADJ sinewy

estropear VT to ruin

estructura F structure

estructuración F structuring

estructural ADJ structural

estructurar VT to structure

estruendo M din, racket

estruendoso ADJ thunderous

estrujamiento M (para romper) crushing; (para sacar jugo) squeezing

estrujar VT (aplastar) to crush; (apretar) to squeeze

estrujón M squeeze

estuario M estuary

estucar[30] VT to stucco

estuche M (para joyas) jewelry box; (para pastillas) pill box; (para lentes) glasses case

estuco M stucco

estudiantado M student body

estudiante MF student

estudiantil ADJ **vida —** student life

estudiar VI/VT to study

estudio M (acción de estudiar, investigación, habitación) study; (taller de artista) studio; (apartamento pequeño) studio apartment; **en — ** under study; **— del impacto ambiental** environmental impact study

estudioso -sa ADJ studious; MF scholar

estufa F (para calentar) heater, stove; (para cocinar) stove

estupefaciente ADJ & M narcotic

estupefacto ADJ stunned, speechless

estupendo ADJ stupendous, terrific; **me la pasé — en la casa de Hilary** I had a great time at Hilary's house

estupidez F stupidity; **estupideces** nonsense

estúpido ADJ stupid

estupor M stupor

estupro M statutory rape

estuve, estuviera, estuviese ver estar

etanol M ethanol

etapa F stage; **por —s** by stages

etcétera CONJ et cetera, and so forth

éter M ether

eternidad F eternity

eternizarse[47] VI to drag on

eterno ADJ eternal, everlasting

ética F ethics

ético ADJ ethical

etimología F etymology

etíope ADJ & MF Ethiopian

Etiopía F Ethiopía

etiqueta F (de comportamiento) etiquette; (en una lata, botella) label; (en una prenda) tag; **— adhesiva** sticker; **— de identificación** name tag; **— de precio** price tag; **nos trataron con —** they treated us very formally; **vestirse de —** to dress formally

etiquetar VT (latas, botellas, personas) to label; (prendas) to tag

etnicidad F ethnicity

étnico ADJ ethnic

etnografía F ethnography

etnología F ethnology

eucalipto M eucalyptus

eufemismo M euphemism

euforia F euphoria

eunuco M eunuch

euro M euro
Europa F Europe
europeo -a ADJ & MF European
euskera M Basque [language]
eutanasia F euthanasia
evacuación F (de un lugar) evacuation; (del vientre) bowel movement; (de agua) drainage
evacuar VT (un lugar, a una persona) to evacuate; (el vientre) to void; (agua) to drain; VI to defecate
evadir VT to evade; **—se** to escape
evaluación F evaluation; **— del rendimiento** performance review
evaluar[26] VT (analizar) to evaluate, to assess; (tasar) to estimate; (calificar) to test
evangélico ADJ evangelical
evangelio M gospel
evaporación F evaporation
evaporar VT to evaporate; **—se** to vanish
evasión F (fiscal) evasion; (de prisioneros, de la realidad) escape; **— de capitales** capital flight; **— de impuestos** tax evasion
evasiva F **salirse con —s** to beat around the bush
evasivo ADJ evasive
evasor -ora MF evader
evento M event
eventual ADJ (posible) possible; (temporal) temporary
evidencia F evidence; **dejar/poner en — a alguien** to show someone up; **quedar/ponerse en —** to become apparent
evidenciar VT to make evident; **—se** to become evident
evidente ADJ evident, obvious
evidentemente ADV & INTERJ obviously
evitar VT (eludir) to avoid; (ahorrar) to spare
evocación F evocation
evocar[30] VT (una memoria) to evoke; (a los espíritus) to conjure up
evolución F evolution
evolucionar VI to evolve
evolutivo ADJ evolutionary
ex MF *fam* ex
exacerbar VT (intensificar) to exacerbate; (irritar) to aggravate
exactamente ADV & INTERJ exactly, precisely; **llegaron — a las tres** they arrived exactly at three
exactitud F accuracy, precision
exacto ADJ exact, precise, accurate; INTERJ exactly
exageración F exaggeration
exagerado ADJ exaggerated; **Jorge es un —** Jorge always exaggerates
exagerar VI/VT to exaggerate
exaltación F (elogio) praise; (excitación) excitement
exaltar VT to exalt; **—se** to get excited

examen M (inspección) examination; (prueba) examination, test, exam; **— de ingreso** entrance examination; **— dérmico de alergias** scratch test; **— final** final examination; **— físico** physical examination; **— médico** medical exam, checkup; **dar un —** to take a test; **poner un —** to give a test
examinar VT (inspeccionar) to examine; (someter a un examen) to test
exasperar VT to exasperate, to aggravate
excavación F (geológica) excavation; (arqueológica) dig
excavador -ora MF (persona) excavator; F (aparato) excavator, earthmover
excavar VT to excavate, to dig
excedente ADJ & M surplus
exceder VT (sobrepasar) to exceed; (superar) to surpass; **— de** to go beyond
excelencia F excellence; **por —** par excellence
excelente ADJ excellent, great
excentricidad F eccentricity
excéntrico ADJ eccentric
excepción F exception; **a — de** with the exception of
excepcional ADJ exceptional
excepto ADV & PREP except
exceptuar[26] VT to except
excesivo ADJ excessive
exceso M excess; **— de costos** overrun; **— de equipaje** excess baggage; **beber en —** to drink to excess; **comer en —** to overeat
excitación F (de músculos) excitement; (sexual) arousal
excitante ADJ stimulating
excitar VT (un nervio) to excite; (impulso sexual) to arouse; **—se** (sexualmente) to get aroused; (átomos) to be excited
exclamación F exclamation
exclamar VT to exclaim
excluir[19] VT to exclude
exclusión F exclusion
exclusivo ADJ exclusive
excomulgar[40] VT to excommunicate
excrecencia F excrescence
excreción F excretion
excremento M excrement
excretar VT to excrete
excursión F excursion, outing
excusa F excuse
excusable ADJ excusable
excusado M *Méx* toilet
excusar VT to excuse
exención F exemption
exento ADJ exempt; **— de impuestos** tax-exempt
exequias F PL funeral rites
exfoliación F exfoliation
exhalar VI/VT (aire) to exhale, to breathe out; (un olor) to give off; **— un suspiro** to sigh

exhaustivo ADJ exhaustive, thorough

exhausto ADJ exhausted

exhibición F (manifestación) exhibition; (despliegue) display

exhibicionismo M exhibitionism

exhibir VT (fotos) to exhibit; (mercancías) to display; (el carnet de identidad) to show; —**se** to show off; **le gusta exhibirse en traje de baño** she likes to show off in her bathing suit; **esa película ya no se exhibe** that movie is not showing anymore

exhortar VT to exhort, to urge

exhumación F exhumation

exigencia F demand

exigente ADJ demanding, exacting

exigir[46] VT to demand; **exigen a alguien que sepa inglés** they require someone who knows English

exiguo ADJ meager; **exigua mayoría** scant majority

exiliado-da MF exile

exiliar VT to exile

exilio M exile

eximido ADJ exempt; — **por la cláusula del abuelo** grandfathered

eximio ADJ illustrious

eximir VT (de impuestos) to exempt; (de sospecha) to clear; (de una responsabilidad) to excuse

existencia F existence; **complicarle la — a alguien** to cause someone trouble; **la lucha por la —** the fight for survival; —**s** stock on hand; **en —** in stock, on hand

existencial ADJ existential

existente ADJ extant, existing

existir VI to exist

éxito M success; (musical) hit; — **de taquilla** blockbuster; **tener —** to be successful; **tiene — con las mujeres** he's popular with women

exitoso ADJ successful

éxodo M exodus

exonerar VT to exonerate

exorbitante ADJ exorbitant

exorcisar VT to exorcise

exorcismo M exorcism

exótico ADJ exotic

expandir VT (dilatar) to expand, to spread; (propagar) to disseminate; —**se** to expand, to spread

expansión F (crecimiento) expansion; (diversión) relaxation

expansivo ADJ (que crece) expansive; (efusivo) effusive

expatriado-da MF expatriate

expatriar VT to expatriate, to exile

expectación F anticipation

expectativa F (esperanza) expectation; (posibilidad) prospect; **estar a la — de algo** to be on pins and needles; — **de vida** life expectancy

expectorante M expectorant

expectorar VI/VT to expectorate, to cough up

expedición F (viaje) expedition; (de documentos) issuing; (de mercancías) delivery

expedicionario-ria ADJ expeditionary; MF member of an expedition

expedidor-ora ADJ shipping; MF shipper

expediente M (administrativo) file, dossier; (policial, académico, médico) record

expedir[9] VT (enviar) to dispatch; (emitir) to issue

expeler VT to expel

expendedor-ora MF vendor; — **automático** vending machine

experiencia F experience

experimentación F experimentation

experimentado ADJ experienced

experimental ADJ experimental

experimentar VI (hacer experimentos) to experiment; VT (sufrir, tener experiencia) to experience

experimento M experiment

experto -ta ADJ & MF expert; — **en computación** wizard, *fam* techie

expiación F atonement

expiar[28] VT to atone for

expirar VI to expire

explanada F (terreno junto al mar) esplanade; (terreno nivelado) leveled area

explayarse VI to become extended; — **sobre** to enlarge upon

explicable ADJ explainable, explicable

explicación F explanation

explicar[30] VT to explain; —**se** to make oneself clear; **no me explico por qué** I can't figure out why

explicativo ADJ explanatory

explícito ADJ explicit

exploración F exploration

explorador-ora ADJ exploring; MF (expedicionario) explorer; (militar) scout

explorar VI/VT to explore; (con fines diagnósticos) to scan; (con fines militares) to scout

exploratorio ADJ exploratory

explosión F explosion; **hacer —** to explode

explosivo ADJ & M explosive

explotación F exploitation

explotar VT (sacar provecho) to exploit; (hacer explosión) to explode

expondrá, expondría *ver* exponer

exponente M exponent

exponer[56, 74] VT (al sol, al peligro) to expose; (al público) to exhibit, to display; (explicar) to state, to set forth; —**se al peligro** to expose oneself to danger

exponga, expongo *ver* exponer

exportación F (acción) exportation, export; (cosa) export

exportador -ora ADJ exporting; MF exporter

exportar VI/VT to export

exposición F (feria) exposition; (de arte) exhibition; (explicación) explanation; (al sol, a una influencia, al peligro) exposure

expresar VT to express

expresión F expression; **valga la —** so to speak

expresividad F expressiveness

expresivo ADJ expressive

expreso ADJ (explícito) express; (rápido) fast; M express train; **café —** espresso

exprimidor M juicer

exprimir VT (naranjas) to squeeze; (zumo) to squeeze out

expropiar VT to expropriate

expuesto ADJ exposed; **lo —** what has been said

expuesto *ver* exponer

expulsar VT to expel; (de un bar) to throw out; (de un partido) to eject

expulsión F expulsion

expuse, expusiera, expusiese *ver* exponer

exquisito -ta ADJ (arte) exquisite; (comida) delicious

extasiado ADJ rapt

extasiarse[28] VI to be enraptured

éxtasis M ecstasy (también droga)

extender[2] VT (el brazo, radio de acción, gratitud) to extend; (un tapete, una masa, un idioma) to spread; (un cheque) to draw up; **—se** to extend; **la fiesta se extendió hasta las 3** the party lasted until 3 o'clock

extendido ADJ (brazos) outstretched; (costumbre) widespread

extensión F (del antebrazo, de significado, telefónica) extension; (de terreno) expanse; (de un texto) length; (eléctrica) extension cord; **por —** by extension; **tener mucha —** to be widespread

extensivo ADJ extensive; **hacer —** to extend

extenso ADJ (calendario, plan, grupo) extensive; (narración, programa de radio) extended

extenuado ADJ exhausted

exterior ADJ (de fuera) exterior, outer; (mundo) outside; (política) foreign; M (parte de afuera) exterior, outside; (aspecto) outward appearance; (fútbol americano) end; **en —es** on location

exteriorizar[47] VT to externalize

exterminación F extermination

exterminar VT to exterminate

exterminio M extermination

externo ADJ external

extienda, extiende *ver* extender

extinción F extinction

extinguidor M fire extinguisher

extinguir[44] VT (un fuego) to extinguish, to put out; (una especie) to make extinct, to wipe out; **—se** (animal, volcán) to go extinct

extinto ADJ extinct

extintor M fire extinguisher

extirpación F removal

extirpar VT to remove

extorsión F extortion

extorsionar VT to extort money from

extorsionista MF racketeer

extra ADJ extra; **horas —s** overtime; MF (actor) extra; M (cosa accesoria) extra; F (pago extraordinario) bonus

extrabursátil ADJ over-the-counter

extracción F extraction

extracto M (resumen) abstract; (de café) extract

extradición F extradition

extraditar VT to extradite

extraer[59] VT (esencia) to extract; (minerales) to mine; (un diente) to pull

extraiga, extraigo, extraje, extrajera, extrajese *ver* extraer

extrajudicial ADJ out-of-court

extramarital ADJ extramarital

extranjero -ra ADJ foreign; MF foreigner; **en el — abroad**

extrañar VT (sorprender) to surprise; (echar de menos) to miss; **no es de — que** it's no wonder that; **no me extraña** it doesn't surprise me; **—se** to be surprised

extrañeza F surprise

extraño -ña ADJ (persona, costumbre) strange; (partícula) foreign; MF stranger

extraoficial ADJ unofficial

extraordinario ADJ extraordinary

extrapolar VI/VT to extrapolate

extrasensorial ADJ extrasensory

extraterrestre ADJ & M alien, extraterrestrial

extravagancia F (cualidad de extravagante) extravagance; (comportamiento extravagante) outrageous behavior

extravagante ADJ flamboyant, outrageous

extraviar[28] VT (perder) to misplace; (confundir) to lead astray; **—se** to lose one's way, to get lost

extravío M loss

extrayendo *ver* extraer

extremadamente ADV extremely

extremado ADJ extreme

extremar VT to maximize

extremidad F extremity

extremo ADJ (máximo, mínimo, extraordinario) extreme; (más lejano) farthest; **con — cuidado** with utmost care; M (punto más alejado) extreme; (de una región) end; **llegar al — de** to go so far as to; **— Oriente** Far East; **extrema izquierda** far left; F **extrema unción** last rites

extrovertido -da ADJ extroverted; MF extrovert

exuberante ADJ (vegetación, jóvenes)

exuberant; (mujer) voluptuous
exudar VI/VT to exude
exultante ADJ exhilarated, exultant
exultar VI to exult
eyacular VI/VT to ejaculate
eyectar VT to eject

Ff

fábrica F factory, plant; (de acero, textiles) mill
fabricación F manufacture, manufacturing
fabricante MF manufacturer; (de coches) maker
fabricar[30] VT (producir) to manufacture, to make; (construir) to build; (inventar) to concoct, to fabricate
fabril ADJ manufacturing
fábula F (relato) fable; (mentira) falsehood
fabuloso ADJ (imaginario) imaginary; (magnífico) awesome, fabulous
facción F faction; **facciones** facial features
faceta F facet
facha F **estaba hecho una —** he was a sight
fachada F facade
facial ADJ facial
fácil ADJ (sencillo) easy; (promiscuo) easy, loose; **— de entender** self-explanatory; **— de usar** user-friendly
facilidad F ease; (habilidad) facility, knack
facilitar VT (hacer más fácil) to facilitate; (proporcionar) to furnish
facsímil M fax
factible ADJ feasible
fáctico ADJ factual
factor M factor; **—es de riesgo** risk factors
factoría F trading post
factura F bill, invoice; **— detallada** itemized invoice
facturable ADJ billable
facturación F billing
facturar VT (importe) to invoice; (equipaje) to check
facultad F (habilidad) faculty; (autoridad) authority; (división de una universidad) college; **— de odontología** dental school
facundia F gift of gab
faena F (trabajo corporal) chore; (labor) task; (molestia) nuisance
fagot M bassoon
fairway M fairway
faisán M pheasant
faja F (cinta) sash; (prenda interior) girdle; (de tierra) ribbon, strip
fajar VT (ceñir) to gird; (envolver) to wrap up; (golpear) to thrash
fajo M (de dinero) wad; (de papel, paja) sheaf

falacia F fallacy
falaz ADJ fallacious
falda F (prenda de vestir) skirt (también mujeres); (de una montaña) slope
faldón M (de una camisa) tail, shirttail; (de un saco) coattail
falible ADJ fallible
falla F (en un argumento) flaw; (en un motor) miss; (de una máquina) failure; (geológica) fault; **las Fallas** Valencian holiday
fallar VI (no funcionar) to fail; (un motor) to miss; VI/VT (un juez) to find, to rule
fallecer[35] VI to pass away, to decease
fallecimiento M passing, decease
fallo M (de un programa) bug, glitch; (de la memoria) lapse; (de un juez) ruling, finding
falsear VT to falsify
falsedad F (dicho falso) falsehood; (condición de falso) falseness
falsificación F (de dinero) counterfeit; (de un documento) forgery
falsificar[30] VT (documento) to falsify, to fake; (dinero) to counterfeit; (una firma) to forge; (libros de contabilidad) to cook
falso ADJ (dato) false, untrue; (sentimientos) fake, phony; (dinero) counterfeit; (promesa) hollow; (amigo) faithless, two-faced; (excusa) made-up; **falsa alarma** false alarm; **jurar en —** to perjure oneself; **paso en —** a false step; **salida en —** false start
falta F (defecto) fault; (carencia) lack, want; (ausencia) absence, miss; (jugada ilícita) foul; (de ortografía) mistake; **— de aire** shortness of breath, breathlessness; **— de pago** default; **— de respeto** disrespect; **— personal** (baloncesto) personal foul; **— de pie** foot fault; **a — de** for want of, in the absence of; **cometer —** to commit a foul; **hacer —** to be necessary; **me haces —** I miss you; **sin —** without fail
faltar VI (ausentarse) to be absent; (no haber) to be lacking; **— a la palabra** to break a promise; **— a la verdad** to misstate oneself; **—le el respeto a** to disrespect; **— poco para las cinco** to be almost five o'clock; **me falta tiempo** I don't have enough time; **¡no faltaba más!** (con indignación) that's the last straw! (no hay de qué) don't mention it! (no te molestes) I wouldn't hear of it
falto ADJ lacking; **— de esperanza** devoid of hope
fama F (condición de conocido) fame; (reputación) reputation; **de — mundial** world-famous
famélico ADJ ravenous
familia F family; **— nuclear** nuclear family; **en — in** the family; **jefe de —** head of household; **la señora de Juan tuvo —** John's wife had a baby

familiar ADJ (muy conocido) familiar; (de familia) familial; **tamaño** — family-size; **coche** — family car; **vida** — family life; MF relative; —**es** next of kin

familiaridad F familiarity

familiarizar[47] VT to familiarize, to acquaint; —**se** to acquaint oneself, to become familiar with

famoso ADJ famous

fanático -ca ADJ fanatic; MF fanatic, zealot; (de deportes) freak

fanatismo M fanaticism

fanega F bushel

fanfarria F fanfare

fanfarrón -ona MF braggart, show-off; ADJ blustering

fanfarronear VI to bluster

fanfarronería F bluster, swagger

fango M mire

fangoso ADJ miry

fantasear VI to fantasize

fantasía F (imaginación) imagination; (imagen) fantasy; **de** — fake, artificial

fantasioso ADJ (niño) imaginative; (idea) fanciful

fantasma M ghost, phantom

fantasmagórico ADJ ghostly

fantástico ADJ fantastic

farándula F show business

fardo M (paquete) bundle; (de heno, algodón) bale

farfolla F husk

farfulla F jabber

farfullar VI to jabber

faringe F pharynx

faríngeo ADJ pharyngeal

farmacéutico -ca ADJ pharmaceutical; MF pharmacist, druggist

farmacia F pharmacy, drugstore

fármaco M medicine, pharmaceutical

farmacología F pharmacology

faro M (torre) lighthouse; (luz de alerta) beacon; (luz del coche) light; — **delantero** headlight

farol M (portátil) lantern; (del alumbrado público) street lamp, streetlight; (con pie de hierro) lamppost; (jactancia, envite) bluff; **darse** — to show off, to put on airs

farra F spree; **ir de** — to go on a spree

farsa F (engaño) sham, hoax; (obra teatral, imitación ridícula) farce, mockery

farsante MF fraud, fake

fascículo M installment

fascinación F fascination

fascinante ADJ fascinating, riveting

fascinar VI/VT to fascinate

fascismo M fascism

fascista ADJ & MF fascist

fase F phase

fastidiado ADJ irked

fastidiar VT to irk

fastidio M annoyance

fastidioso ADJ annoying, wearisome

fatal ADJ (mortal) fatal; (terrible) terrible; **mujer** — femme fatale; ADV very badly; **me fue** — **en el examen** I did very poorly on the exam

fatalidad F (desgracia) misfortune; (destino) destiny

fatídico ADJ ill-fated

fatiga F fatigue, exhaustion; — **ocular** eye strain; —**s** hardships

fatigado ADJ tired, weary

fatigar[40] VT to tire out

fatigoso ADJ (cansado) tiring; (aburrido) tiresome

fauces F PL jaws

faul M foul

fauna F fauna

favor M favor; **a** — **de** in favor of; **por** — please

favorable ADJ favorable

favorecer[35] VT to favor

favorezca, favorezco ver favorecer

favoritismo M favoritism

favorito -ta ADJ favorite; MF favorite; (en una elección) front-runner; (de la maestra) pet

fax M fax

faxear VT to fax

faz F face

FBI M FBI

fe F faith; — **de bautismo** baptismal certificate; — **de erratas** list of errors; — **de nacimiento** birth certificate; **buena** — good faith; **de buena** — in good faith; **dar** — **de** to vouch for

fealdad F ugliness

febrero M February

febril ADJ (con fiebre) feverish; (actividad) feverish, hectic

fecal ADJ fecal

fecha F date; — **de vencimiento** date due, due date

fechado ADJ dated

fechar VT to date

fechoría F misdeed

fecundación F fertilization

fecundar VT (un huevo) to fertilize; (una hembra) to impregnate

fecundo ADJ fertile

federación F federation

federal ADJ federal

felicidad F happiness; ¡—**es!** congratulations

felicitación F congratulation; ¡**felicitaciones!** congratulations!

felicitar VT to congratulate

feligrés -esa MF parishioner; **feligreses** congregation

felino ADJ feline; M cat

feliz ADJ happy

felizmente ADV happily

felpa F plush

felpudo M doormat

femenino ADJ (como una mujer, relativo al género gramatical) feminine; (de la mujer) female

feminidad F femininity

feminismo M feminism

feminista MF feminist

fémur M femur

fenómeno M phenomenon

feo ADJ (cara) ugly, homely; (dentadura) bad; (accidente) nasty

féretro M coffin

feria F (mercado) market; (exposición) fair; (espectáculo) carnival; (celebración) holiday

feriante MF trader at fairs, stallholder

fermentación F fermentation

fermentar VT (leche) to ferment; (cerveza) to brew

fermento M ferment

ferocidad F ferocity

feroz ADJ ferocious, fierce

férreo ADJ (puente) iron; (disciplina) harsh

ferretería F (tienda) hardware store; (artículos) hardware

ferrocarril M railroad, railway

ferroviario -ria ADJ railroad; MF railroad employee

ferry M ferryboat

fértil ADJ fertile

fertilidad F fertility

fertilización F fertilization

fertilizante M fertilizer

fertilizar[47] VT to fertilize

ferviente ADJ fervent

fervor M fervor, zeal

fervoroso ADJ zealous

festejar VT to celebrate

festejo M celebration

festín M feast; **darse un —** to treat oneself

festival M festival

festividad F festivity

festivo ADJ festive, celebratory; **día —** holiday

festón M scallop

festonear VT to scallop

fetal ADJ fetal

fetiche M fetish

fétido ADJ foul-smelling

feto M fetus

feudal ADJ feudal

feudo M manor

fiabilidad F reliability

fiable ADJ reliable

fiador -ora MF guarantor, voucher; (prestamista) backer; (de un preso) bondsman

fiambre M (carne) cold cut; (cadáver) fam stiff

fianza F (de un préstamo) security, guaranty; (de un preso) bail

fiar[28] VT (garantizar) to vouch for; **—se de** to trust

fiasco M fiasco

fibra F fiber; **— de vidrio** fiberglass; **— óptica** optical fiber

fibrosis F fibrosis; **— cística** cystic fibrosis

fibroso ADJ fibrous

ficción F fiction

ficha F (de teléfono) token; (de dominó) domino; (de damas) checker; (en poker, ruleta) chip; (tarjeta) index card; MF (delincuente) delinquent, criminal

fichar VT to open a file on; VI to punch in

fichero M (de computadora) file; (archivador) filing cabinet; **— de datos** data file

ficticio ADJ (no real) fictitious; (novelesco) fictional

fidedigno ADJ trustworthy

fideicomisario -ria MF trustee

fideicomiso M trusteeship

fidelidad F (de un amante) fidelity, faithfulness; (de una traducción) closeness; (a la bandera) allegiance

fideo M noodle

fiduciario -ria ADJ & MF fiduciary

fiebre F fever; **— aftosa** foot-and-mouth disease; **— amarilla** yellow fever; **— de candilejas** stage fright; **— del oro** gold rush; **— reumática** rheumatic fever; **— tifoidea** typhoid fever; **tener —** to run a fever

fiel ADJ (leal) faithful; (exacto) true, accurate; M pointer on a scale; **los —es** the congregation

fieltro M (tela) felt; (sombrero) felt hat

fiera F beast; **ponerse hecho una —** to go berserk

fiereza F ferocity

fiero ADJ (salvaje) fierce; (muy grande) huge

fiesta F (festejo) party; (día feriado) holiday; **aguar una —** to ruin a party

fiestero -ra ADJ fond of parties; MF merrymaker, party animal

figura F figure

figurado ADJ figurative

figurar VI (aparecer) to appear, to figure; (lucirse) to show off; **—se** to imagine; **¡figúrate!** imagine!

figurativo ADJ figurative

figurín M fashion plate

figurón M dummy

fijación F fixing; **— de precios** pricing

fijador M hairspray

fijar VT (un cartel) to fix, to fasten; (una fecha) to set; (precios) to peg; **—se en** (notar) to notice; (prestar atención) to pay attention to, to focus on

fijo ADJ (sujeto, incambiado) fixed; (inmóvil) fixed, stationary; (firme) firm; (definitivo) definite; (permanente) permanent

fila F (uno detrás del otro) row, file; (hombro a hombro) rank; (de espera) line; (de documentos) queue; **— india** single file; **cerrar —s** to close ranks; **romper —s** to break ranks

filamento M filament

filantropía F philanthropy

filarmónica F philharmonic

filarmónico ADJ philharmonic

fildear VT to field

fildeo M fielding

filete M (de carne) fillet; (de un plato) rim

filetear VT to fillet

filiación F (membresía) affiliation; (datos personales) personal information; (lazo de parentesco) filiation; **— política** political affiliation

filial ADJ filial; F affiliate, subsidiary

filibusterismo M filibustering

filigrana F filigree

Filipinas F Philippines

filipino -na ADJ & MF Filipino, Filipina

filme M film, movie

filmación F filming, shooting

filmar VT to film, to shoot

filo M (de una navaja) cutting edge; (biológico) phylum; **de doble —** two-edged; **al — de las dos** at around two o'clock

filón M seam, vein, pocket

filoso ADJ sharp

filosofía F philosophy

filosófico ADJ philosophical

filósofo -fa MF philosopher

filtración F (purificación) filtration; (pérdida) leak; (percolación) seepage

filtrar VT (purificar) to filter; (perder) to leak; (clasificar) to screen; **—se** (gotear) to leak through; (percolarse) to seep

filtro M filter; **— de aire** air filter; **— de amor** love potion

fin M (conclusión, objetivo) end; **— de año** New Year's Eve; **el — del mundo** (lugar apartado) boondocks; **— de semana** weekend; **— de siglo** turn of the century; **al —** at last; **al — y al cabo** at any rate; **a — de que** so that; **a — de mes** toward the end of the month; **de — de año** year-end; **en —** in conclusion; **poner — a** to put an end to; **por —** at last, finally; **sin —** (ilimitado) myriad; (continuo) endless

finado ADJ late

final ADJ final, last; F (deportiva) final; M (de una historia) ending; (de un terreno) end; (de una carrera) finish; (de una filmación) wrap

finalidad F objective, purpose

finalista MF finalist

finalización F completion

finalizar[47] VT to finish; **— una sesión** lo log off/out

finalmente ADV at last, finally

financiación F (para una compra) financing; (para un proyecto) funding

financiamiento M (para una compra) financing; (para un proyecto científico) funding; **— por el propietario** owner financing

financiar VT (una compra) to finance; (un proyecto) to underwrite, *fam* to bankroll

financiero -ra ADJ financial; MF financier

finanza F finance; **—s** finances

finca F (inmueble) property; (granja) farm, country estate

finés -esa MF Finn; M (lengua) Finnish; ADJ Finnish

fineza F (atención) courtesy; (suavidad) smoothness

fingir[46] VI/VT (sorpresa) to feign; (un ataque al corazón) to fake; **fingió que la quería** he pretended to love her

finiquito M settlement

finito ADJ finite

finlandés -esa MF Finn; M (lengua) Finnish; ADJ Finnish

Finlandia F Finland

fino ADJ (vino, arena, pelo, metal) fine; (sentidos) keen, sharp; (medias) sheer; (hielo, alambre, voz) thin; (modales) smooth, refined

finta F fake, juke

firma F (compañía) firm; (rúbrica) signature; **— consultora** consulting firm

firmamento M sky

firmante MF signer

firmar VI/VT (documento, carta) to sign; (contrato) to enter

firme ADJ (estructura) firm; (control) tight; (colores) fast; (amarras) secure; (mano) steady, sure; (resistencia) stiff; (apoyo, resistencia) strong, staunch, steadfast; **mantenerse —** to stand one's ground; **¡—s!** attention!

firmemente ADV firmly

firmeza F (de una estructura) firmness; (de la mano) steadiness; (de la resistencia) stiffness; (del apoyo) strength; **con —** firmly

fiscal ADJ fiscal; MF public prosecutor, district attorney

fiscalía F prosecution

fiscalización F (de comportamiento) supervision; (de gastos) oversight

fiscalizar[47] VT (comportamiento) to supervise; (gastos) to oversee

fisgar[40] VI to snoop

fisgón -ona ADJ snooping; MF snoop

fisgonear VI to snoop

físico -ca ADJ physical; MF (persona) physicist; M (cuerpo) physique; F physics

fisiología F physiology

fisiológico ADJ physiological

fisioterapia F physical therapy
fisonomía F features
fístula F fistula
fisura F fissure
fiyano ADJ Fijian
Fiyi M Fiji
flácido, fláccido ADJ (sin firmeza) limp, flaccid; (gordo) flabby
flaco ADJ thin, skinny; **su lado** — his weakness
flacura F thinness
flagrante ADJ gross; **en — delito** in the act
flamante ADJ brand-new
flamear VI (llamear) to flame; (ondear) to flap
flamenco -ca ADJ Flemish; MF Flemish person; M (lengua) Flemish; (ave) flamingo; (baile) flamenco
flamígero ADJ flaming
flan M caramel custard
flanco M (de un animal, ejército) flank; (de un neumático) sidewall
flanquear VT to flank
flaquear VI (intención) to waver; (salud) to wane
flaqueza F weakness
flash M (noticias, visión, memoria digital) flash; (lámpara) flashbulb, flash
flashback M flashback
flatulencia F flatulence
flauta F flute; **— dulce** recorder
flautín M piccolo
flecha F arrow
flechar VT to wound with an arrow
flechazo M (herida) wound from an arrow; (enamoramiento) love at first sight
fleco M (de una alfombra) fringe; (de pelo) bangs
flema F phlegm
flequillo M bangs
fletamento M charter
fletar VT to charter
flete M (contratación) charter; (envío) transport; (precio de transporte) freight
flexibilidad F (ductilidad) flexibility; (libertad) latitude
flexible ADJ (material) flexible; (cuerpo humano) limber, supple; (opinión) pliant, pliable
flojear VT to slacken
flojedad F laxity, looseness; (debilidad) weakness
flojera F (debilidad) weakness; (pereza) laziness
flojo ADJ (suelto) loose, slack; (holgazán) lazy; (inferior) crummy; (débil) weak; (sin fundamento) flimsy
floppy M floppy disk
flor F flower, blossom, bloom; (cumplido) compliment; **— de la edad** prime of life; **— de Pascua** poinsettia; **— y nata** the cream of the crop; **a — de** flush with; **en —** in bloom
flora F flora (también bacteriana); **— intestinal** intestinal flora

floración F blooming, blossoming
floral ADJ flowery
floreado ADJ flowery
florear VT (adornar con flores) to decorate with flowers; (adornar) to adorn
florecer[35] VI (echar flores) to flower, to bloom; (prosperar) to flourish, to thrive
floreciente ADJ (próspero) flourishing, prosperous; (florecido) blooming
florecimiento M flourishing
floreo M flourish
florería F florist's shop
florero M flower vase
florete M fencing foil
florido ADJ flowery
florista MF florist
floritura F flourish
flota F fleet
flotador M (para nadar) float; (de un avión) pontoon; ADJ floating
flotante ADJ floating, buoyant
flotar VI (estar suspendido, variar en valor) to float; (moverse en la superficie) to drift; (ir por el aire) to waft
flote M flotation; **a —** afloat; **poner a —** to set afloat
fluctuación F fluctuation; (amplitud de variación) range
fluctuar[26] VI to fluctuate
fluidez F (cualidad de fluido) fluency; (cualidad de diluido) thinness
fluido ADJ (que fluye) fluid, flowing; (no vacilante) fluent; M fluid
fluir[19] VI to flow
flujo M (de agua) flow; (vaginal) discharge; (de datos) streaming; **— continuo de datos de audio** audio streaming; **— continuo de datos de vídeo** video streaming; **— de caja** cash flow; **— de trabajo** work flow
flúor M (elemento gaseoso) fluorine; (sal) fluoride
fluorescente ADJ fluorescent
fluoruro M fluoride
fluvial ADJ **transporte —** river transportation
fluyente ADJ flowing
FMI [Fondo Monetario Internacional] M IMF
fobia F phobia
foca F seal
foco M (punto central) focus; (bombilla) bulb; (lámpara potente) spotlight
fofo ADJ mushy
fogata F (fuego abierto) bonfire; (en un campamento) campfire
fogonazo M flash
fogoso ADJ fiery, spirited
folclor, folclore M folklore
folclórico/folklórico ADJ folkloric; **cuento —** folktale

foliculitis F folliculitis

folículo M follicle

folio M folio

folíolo M leaflet

follaje M foliage

folleto M pamphlet, brochure

follón M (confusión) mess; (alboroto) ruckus

fomentar VT (estudio) to promote; (amistad) to foster; (discordia) to foment; (apoyo) to drum up

fomento M encouragement

fonda F inn

fondear VI to anchor

fondillos M PL seat of pants

fondista MF (posadero) innkeeper; (corredor) long-distance runner

fondo M (parte más profunda) bottom; (parte posterior) rear; (del mar) bed; (de un cuadro, foto) background; (de dinero) fund; (de una biblioteca) holdings; (de un jardín) backyard; — **común** pool; — **de contingencia** contingency fund; — **especulativo** hedge fund; — **físico** endurance; — **musical** background music; — **mutuo** mutual fund; —**s** funds; —**s administrados** managed funds; — **sin comisión de entrada** no-load fund; **a** — in depth; **carrera de** — long-distance race; **de cuatro en** — four abreast; **de** — (exhaustivo) in depth; (subyacente) underlying; **sin** — bottomless; **tocar** — to hit rock bottom

fonética F phonetics

fonético ADJ phonetic

fonógrafo M phonograph

fonología F phonology

fontanería F plumbing

fontanero -ra MF plumber

footing M jogging

forajido -da MF outlaw

foráneo ADJ foreign; **influencia foránea** outside influence

forastero -ra MF stranger, outsider

forcejear VI to struggle

forcejeo M struggle

fórceps M PL forceps

forense ADJ forensic; MF forensic scientist

forestal ADJ forest; **división** — forestry division

forja F (fogón) forge; (acción de forjar) forging; (taller) blacksmith's shop

forjado ADJ wrought

forjar VT (metales, un acuerdo) to forge; (un acuerdo) to hammer out; (un documento) to frame

forma F (figura) form, shape; (manera) manner; — **de pago** mode of payment; — **de pensar** mind-set; **ponerse en** — to get in shape; **no hay** — no way; **dar** — **a** to shape

formación F formation

formal ADJ (que atañe a la forma) formal, serious; (fiable) reliable

formaldehído M formaldehyde

formalidad F (convencionalidad) formality; (fiabilidad) reliability

formalismo M formality

formalizar⁴⁷ VT to make official; —**se** to settle down

formar VT (crear) to form; (reunir tropas) to muster; (entrenar) to train; —**se** (montañas) to form; (estudiantes) to be educated

formatear VT to format

formateo M formatting

formativo ADJ formative

formato M format; — **de archivo/fichero** file format; — **de texto enriquecido** rich text format

formidable ADJ formidable

formón M wood chisel

fórmula F formula

formulación F (acción de formular) formulation; (fórmula) formula; (redacción) wording

formular VT to formulate; (un plan, una pregunta) to frame; (un documento) to word

formulario M form

fornicar³⁰ VI to fornicate

fornido ADJ stout, sturdy

foro M forum; (de un escenario) back

forrado ADJ (con un forro) lined; (bien provisto) flush

forraje M forage, fodder

forrajear VI to forage

forrar VT (un saco) to line; —**se** to line one's pockets

forro M lining; (de un libro) jacket

fortalecer³⁵ VT to fortify, to strengthen

fortalecimiento M strengthening

fortaleza F (construcción) fortress, fort; (fuerza) fortitude

fortificación F fortification

fortificar³⁰ VT to fortify

fortuito ADJ fortuitous, accidental

fortuna F fortune; **por** — fortunately; **probar** — to try one's luck; **hacer** — to become rich

forúnculo M boil

forzar⁴⁹ VT to force, to coerce; — **la entrada** to break into

forzoso ADJ (por la fuerza) forcible; (inevitable) necessary; (aterrizaje) forced

fosa F (sepultura) grave; (de la nariz) cavity; (en el fondo del mar) trench

fosfato M phosphate

fósforo M (sustancia) phosphorus; (cerilla) match

fósil ADJ & M fossil

foso M (de un castillo) moat; (de un taller, teatro) pit

foto F snapshot, photo

fotocopia F photocopy
fotocopiadora F photocopier
fotocopiar VI/VT to photocopy
fotoeléctrico ADJ photoelectric
fotogénico ADJ photogenic
fotografía F (foto) photograph; (arte) photography; — **digital** digital photography
fotografiar[28] VT to photograph
fotógrafo -fa MF photographer
fotón M photon
fotosíntesis F photosynthesis
foul M foul
frac M tails
fracasar VI (un proyecto) to fail; (de una película) to bomb; (una embarcación) to break up
fracaso M (de un proyecto) failure; (de una película) flop, bomb
fracción F fraction
fractura F fracture, break; — **fina** hairline fracture
fracturar VT to fracture, to break; **se fracturó la cadera** she broke her hip
fragancia F fragrance
fragante ADJ fragrant; **en** — in the act
fragata F frigate
frágil ADJ (delicado) delicate; (quebradizo) fragile, brittle; (una paz) tenuous
fragilidad F (condición de quebradizo) brittleness, delicacy; (debilidad) frailty
fragmentación F fragmentation
fragmento M fragment; (de metal, piedra) scrap; (de una conversación) snatch; (de un texto) extract, excerpt
fragoso ADJ rugged
fragua F (fogón) forge; (taller) blacksmith's shop
fraguar[25] VT to forge; (una trama) to hatch; VI (cemento, yeso) to set
fraile M friar
frambuesa F raspberry
frambueso M raspberry bush
francamente ADV —, **me horroriza** frankly / to be honest, it horrifies me; **lo pasaban** — **bien** they were doing pretty well; —, **es ridículo** it is simply ridiculous
francés -esa ADJ French; M (lengua) French; (hombre) Frenchman; F (mujer) Frenchwoman
Francia F France
franco ADJ (sincero) frank, candid; (exento) free; **una franca mayoría** a clear majority; **un tratado** — -**americano** a Franco-American treaty
francotirador -ora MF sniper
franela F flannel
franja F ribbon
franquear VT (una frontera) to cross; (una carta) to frank; —**se** to be frank
franqueo M postage

franqueza F (personal) frankness; (institucional) openness
franquicia F (concesión) franchise; (exención) exemption
frasco M (recipiente de vidrio) flask; (de medicina, perfume) bottle; (de mermelada) jar
frase F phrase
frasear VI/VT to phrase
fraternal ADJ fraternal, brotherly
fraternidad F fraternity
fraternizar[47] VI fraternize
fraterno ADJ fraternal
fraude M fraud
fraudulento ADJ fraudulent
frazada F blanket
frecuencia F frequency; **con** — frequently
frecuentar VT to frequent; (una tienda) to patronize
frecuente ADJ frequent
fregadero M sink
fregado M scrubbing
fregar[41] VT to scour, to scrub
fregona F (persona) scrubwoman, drudge; (utensilio) mop
freír[10, 74] VI/VT to fry
frenar VT (un coche) to brake; (la inmigración) to restrain; (los impulsos) to bridle; VI to brake, to apply the brakes
frenesí M frenzy; (de actividad) flurry
frenético ADJ frantic
freno M (de coche) brake; (de caballo) bit; (contra el contrabando) curb
frente F forehead; **el sudor de la** — the sweat of one's brow; M (parte delantera, zona de combate, zona meteorológica) front; (de un edificio) face; — **a** (ante) in the face of; (al otro lado) facing; — **a** — face to face; **de** — head-on; **en** — **de** in front of; **hacer** — to face; **pasar al** — to come to the fore
fresa F (fruta) strawberry; (herramienta) mill
fresadora F milling machine
fresar VT to mill
fresco ADJ (reciente, descansado, insolente) fresh; (frío) cool, brisk; (poco abrigado) light; (no cocinado) raw; (pintura) wet; M (frío) coolness; (pintura) fresco
frescor M (de verduras) freshness; (del aire) coolness
frescura F (de verduras, de carácter) freshness; (del tiempo) coolness; (comentario) impudent remark
fresno M ash tree
friabilidad F looseness
frialdad F coldness, coolness
fricción F friction, rubbing
friccionar VT to rub
friega F rubbing, massage
frigorífico M (electrodoméstico) refrigerator;

(cámara) refrigeration chamber

frijol M bean

frío ADJ (de temperatura, de temperamento) cold; (helado) frigid; M cold; **tener —** to be cold

friolento ADJ sensitive to cold

friolera F **la — de $50,000** a trifling $50,000

fritada F dish of fried food

frito ADJ fried; M dish of fried food

fritura F (acción de freír) frying; (comida frita) dish of fried food

frivolidad F frivolity

frívolo ADJ frivolous

fronda F foliage

frondoso ADJ leafy

frontal ADJ (ataque) frontal; (colisión) head-on

frontera F frontier, border

fronterizo ADJ frontier

frontón M (juego) jai alai; (pista) jai alai court

frotación F rubbing

frotar VI/VT to rub

frote M rub

frotis M smear

fructífero ADJ fruitful

fructificar[30] VI to bear fruit

fructosa F fructose

frugal ADJ frugal

frunce M (volante) ruffle; (defecto) pucker

fruncir[33] VT to gather; **— el ceño** to frown, to knit one's brow; **— los labios** to purse one's lips

fruslería F trifle

frustración F frustration

frustrar VT (los planes) to frustrate, to thwart, to foil; (las esperanzas) to shatter, to dash; **—se** to fail, to miscarry

fruta F fruit

frutero -era MF fruit vendor; M fruit dish

fruto M fruit; **—s del mar** seafood

fue *ver* ser, ir

fuego M fire; (para un cigarro) light; **— antiaéreo** antiartillery fire; **—s artificiales** fireworks; **abrir el —** to begin to fire; **alto el —** cease-fire; **bajo —** under fire; **arma de —** firearm; **entre dos —s** between a rock and a hard place; **hacer —** to fire; **prender/poner/pegar — a** to set fire to

fuelle M bellows

fuel-oil M fuel oil

fuente F (surtidor) fountain; (manantial, referencia) spring; (caracteres de imprenta) font; **de buena —** from the horse's mouth

fuera ADV (en el exterior) outside; (tenis) out; **— de** outside of; **— de borda** outboard; **— de combate** out of commission; **— de juego** (fútbol) offside; **— de límites** (golf) out of bounds; **— de línea** offline; **— de serie** one of a kind; **— de servicio** out of service;

INTERJ out!

fuera, fuéramos *ver* ser, ir

fuero M (jurisdicción) jurisdiction; (privilegio) privilege, charter

fuerte ADJ (hombre, bebida) strong; (ruido) loud; (cuero) tough; (personalidad) forceful; (estantería) sturdy; (plato) hearty; M (castillo) fort; (talento especial) strong point; ADV (tirar) strongly; (respirar) heavily; (gritar) loud; **soplar —** to bluster; **pisar —** to stomp; **atar —** to tie tight

fuerza F (de una máquina) force; (de una persona, animal) strength; **— aérea** air force; **— bruta** brute force; **— de la naturaleza** force of nature; **— de tarea** task force; **— de voluntad** willpower; **—s armadas** armed forces; **a — de** by dint of; **con —** strongly; **hacer —** to press on; **por la —** by force; **sacar — de flaqueza** to pull oneself together

fuerza, fuerce *ver* forzar

fuese, fuésemos *ver* ser, ir

fuga F (escape) escape, flight; (de la cárcel) jailbreak; (de gas) leak; (de capitales) drain, flight

fugarse[40] VI to flee, to escape; **— con el dinero** to abscond with the money

fugaz ADJ fleeting

fugitivo -va ADJ fugitive; MF fugitive

fui, fuimos *ver* ser, ir

fulano -na MF so-and-so; **—, zutano y mengano** Tom, Dick, and Harry

fulgor M radiance

fulgurar VI to flash

full M full house

fullero -ra MF (tramposo) cheat; (en naipes) card sharp

fulminante M cap; ADJ devastating

fulminar VT to strike with lightning; to thunder; **lo fulminó con la mirada** she gave him a withering look

fumadero M crackhouse

fumador -ora MF smoker

fumar VI/VT to smoke; **—se mucho dinero** to blow a lot of money

fumigar[40] VT to fumigate, to fog

función F (uso) function; (representación) performance; (cargo) office; **— de búsqueda** search function

funcional ADJ functional; **una casa —** a practical/livable house

funcionamiento M operation, working

funcionar VI to function, to work; (motor) to run

funcionario -ria MF government employee, official; **— de préstamos** loan officer

funda F (de un mueble) cover; (de una almohada) pillowcase, slip; (de navaja) sheath

fundación F foundation

fundador -ora MF founder
fundamental ADJ (básico) fundamental; (importante) crucial
fundamentalmente ADV fundamentally, mainly
fundamentar VT to base, to support; **—se en/ sobre** to be based on, to be supported by
fundamento M foundation, basis; **—s** fundamentals
fundar VT (un instituto) to found, to establish; (un argumento) to base
fundición F (fábrica) foundry; (acción de fundirse) fusing
fundido ADJ molten; M (en cinematografía) fade-in/fade-out
fundidor -ora MF foundry worker
fundir VT (combinar) to fuse; (derretir) to melt; (moldear) to mold; **—se** (combinarse) to fuse; (romperse una bombilla) to burn out
fúnebre ADJ (relativo a funerales) funeral; (lúgubre) funereal
funeral ADJ & M funeral
funerario -ria ADJ funeral; F funeral parlor; MF funeral director
funesto ADJ ill-fated, unlucky
fungible ADJ fungible
fungicida M fungicide
funicular M cable car
funky ADJ funky
furgón M (vagón) boxcar; (camioneta de policía) police van; **— blindado** armored vehicle; **— de cola** caboose
furia F fury
furibundo ADJ furious, livid
furioso ADJ (persona) furious; (tempestad) fierce
furor M fury; **hacer —** to be all the rage
furtivo ADJ furtive, stealthy
fuselaje M fuselage
fusible M electric fuse
fusil M rifle
fusilamiento M execution by firing squad
fusilar VT to execute with firearms
fusión F (de hielo) melting; (nuclear) fusion; (empresarial) merger; (de documentos digitales) merge; **fusiones y adquisiciones** mergers and acquisitions
fusionar VT (metales) to fuse; (compañías, documentos digitales) to merge
fusta F crop
fustigar[40] VT (golpear) to lash, to whip; (criticar) to lash out at
fútbol M soccer; **— americano** football
futbolista MF soccer player
fútil ADJ futile, trivial
futilidad F triviality
futuro ADJ future; M future; **—s** futures

Gg

gabán M overcoat
gabardina F trench coat
gabinete M (ministerial) cabinet; (administrativo) office
Gabón M Gabon/Gabun
gabonés -esa ADJ & MF Gabonese
gacela F gazelle
gaceta F gazette
gacetilla F short news item
gachas F PL **— de avena** oatmeal
gacho ADJ (orejas) drooping; (cabeza) bowed; (ojos) lowered
gafar VT to jinx
gafas F PL glasses
gafe M jinx
gaffe M gaffe, faux pas
gag M gag
gaita F bagpipe
gaje M **—s del oficio** occupational hazards
gajo M (de planta) branch; (de naranja) section
gala F (cena) banquet; **—s** finery; **hacer — de** to boast of, to flaunt; **vestirse de —** to dress up
galán M (pretendiente) gallant, suitor; (en cine) leading man
galante ADJ gallant
galantear VT to court
galanteo M courting
galantería F (caballerosidad) gallantry; (cumplido) compliment
galardón M award
galaxia F galaxy
galera F galley (también prueba de imprenta); RP top hat
galerada F galley proof
galería F (salón) gallery; (pasillo) corridor; (tiendas) mall, gallery; (de coro) loft; (subterráneo) tunnel; **—s** Esp department store
Gales M Wales
galés -esa ADJ & MF Welsh
galgo M greyhound
Galicia F Galicia
gallardete M pennant
gallardía F (elegancia) elegance; (valentía) bravery
gallardo ADJ (elegante) elegant; (valiente) brave
gallego -ga ADJ Galician; M (lengua) Galician; MF Galician
gallera F cockpit
galleta F (salada) cracker; (dulce) cookie
gallina F (pollo) chicken; (hembra adulta) hen; MF coward; **— ciega** blind man's bluff; **la — de los huevos de oro** the goose that laid the

golden egg

gallinero M (de gallinas) chicken coop; (de teatro) gallery; **alborotar el —** to raise a ruckus

gallito ADJ cocksure, cocky; M braggart

gallo M cock, rooster; (de la voz) break; **tener —s en la garganta** to have a frog in one's throat; **en menos que canta un —** before you can say Jack Robinson

galón M (de líquido) gallon; (de tela) stripe

galopar VI/VT to gallop

galope M gallop; **al —** at a gallop

galvanizar[47] VT to galvanize

gama F gamut, range

gamba F large shrimp

gamberro -rra MF (rebelde, pandillero) punk, hoodlum; *Esp* (en fútbol) hooligan

Gambia F Gambia

gambiano -na ADJ & MF Gambian

gamo M buck

gamuza F (animal) chamois (también piel); (piel de venado) buckskin, deerskin; (piel de vaca) suede

gana F urge; **con —s** with a vengeance; **de buena —** willingly; **tener —s de** to feel like; **tengo —s [de ir al baño]** I have to go [to the bathroom]; **no me da la —** I just don't feel like it

ganadería F (cría) cattle breeding; (ganado) livestock

ganadero -ra M cattleman; F cattlewoman; ADJ **industria ganadera** cattle industry

ganado M livestock; **— ovino** sheep; **— porcino** swine; **— vacuno** cattle

ganador -ora MF winner; ADJ winning

ganancia F profit, gain, return; **—s** (recaudación de un evento) proceeds; (de un juego) winnings; (de un negocio) earnings; **—s pre-impositivas** before-tax earnings

ganapán M (obrero) menial worker; (trabajo) bread and butter

ganar VI/VT (una guerra, la lotería) to win; (kilos, eficacia) to gain; VT (un sueldo) to earn; (tiempo, espacio) to save; (tierra) to reclaim; **dejarse — por algo** to give in to something; **nos ganaron el partido** they beat us; **—se la vida** to make a living

ganchillo M crochet

gancho M hook (también en boxeo, baloncesto); (rama) snag; (para sujetar) clip; (atractivo) lure; **echar a uno el —** to hook someone; **tener —** to be attractive

gandul -la MF loafer

ganga F bargain, steal

gangoso ADJ twangy

gangrena F gangrene

gangrenarse VI to gangrene

gángster M gangster

ganguear VI to twang

ganso M (animal) goose; (macho) gander; (tonto) *fam* ding-a-ling

ganzúa F picklock

gañido M yelp

gañir[17] VI to yelp

garabatear VI/VT to scribble

garabato M scribble; **hacer —s** to scribble

garaje M garage

garante MF voucher

garantía F (de producto) guarantee, warranty; (de promesa) security, guaranty; (de un derecho) guarantee; (comercial) backing; **— de devolución de dinero** money-back guarantee; **— de préstamo** loan guarantee

garantizar[47] VT (producto) to guarantee, to warranty; (promesa) to warrant

garañón M stud, horse

garbanzo M chickpea

garbo M grace

garboso ADJ graceful

garfio M hook

garganta F (faringe) throat; (cuello) neck; (valle estrecho) gorge

gárgara F gargle; **hacer —s** to gargle

gargarismo M gargle

garita F sentry box

garito M gambling house

garra F (de ave) claw; (de león) paw with claws; **caer en las —s de alguien** to fall into someone's clutches

garrafa F decanter

garrapata F tick

garrapatear VI/VT to scribble

garrapiñar VT to candy

garrocha F pole

garrote M club

garrucha F pulley

gárrulo ADJ garrulous

garza F heron

gas M gas; **—es** (de motor) fumes; (de intestino) gas; **— ionizado** plasma; **— lacrimógeno** tear gas; **— mostaza** mustard gas; **— natural** natural gas; **— nervioso** nerve gas; **a todo —** at full speed

gasa F (tela) gauze; (para heridas) dressing

gaseosa F soda, soft drink

gaseoso ADJ gaseous

gasoducto M pipeline

gasolina F gasoline, gas

gasolinera F gas station

gastado ADJ (neumático) smooth; (ropa) worn-out, shabby

gastador -ora ADJ extravagant, wasteful; MF spendthrift

gastar VT (dinero, tiempo) to spend; (energía) to expend; (neumáticos, ropa) to wear out, to use up; **— una broma** to play a trick; **—se** to wear out

gasto M (desembolso) expense, expenditure;

(desgaste) wear; **—s de desplazamiento**
travel costs; **—s del hogar** household
expenses; **—s de subsistencia** living
expenses; **—s de viaje** travel expenses; **—s
menores** incidentals
gástrico ADJ gastric
gastritis F gastritis
gastroenteritis F gastroenteritis
gastrointestinal ADJ gastrointestinal
gastronomía F gastronomy
gatas LOC ADV **a —** on all fours
gatear VI to creep, to crawl
gatillo M (de arma de fuego) trigger; (de
dentista) forceps
gatito M kitten
gato M (felino) cat; (aparato para levantar) jack;
— montés wildcat, mountain lion; **aquí
hay — encerrado** I smell a rat; **a gatas** on
all fours; **dar — por liebre** to sell someone a
pig in a poke
gaucho M gaucho
gaveta F small drawer
gavilán M hawk
gavilla F (de maíz) sheaf; (de maleantes) gang
gaviota F seagull
gayola F *fam* big house
gazmoñería F prudery
gazmoño-ña MF prude; ADJ prudish
gaznate M gullet
gazpacho M *Esp* gazpacho
geco M gecko
géiser M geyser
gel M gel
gelatina F gelatin
gélido ADJ frigid
gema F gem, jewel
gemelo-la ADJ & MF identical twin; **—s**
(mellizos) identical twins; (binoculares)
binoculars, opera glasses; (botón) studs
gemido M (de dolor) moan, groan; (de queja)
whine
gemir[9] VI (gruñir) to moan, to groan;
(lloriquear) to whine
gen, gene M gene; **— recesivo** recessive gene
genealogía F genealogy
generación F generation
generador M generator
general ADJ & MF general; **por lo —** generally
generalidad F generality
generalización F (de un concepto)
generalization; (de una moda) spreading
generalizar[47] VI/VT to generalize; **—se** to
become widespread
generalmente ADV generally, usually
generar VT generate
genérico ADJ generic
género M (clase) kind; (gramatical) gender;
(tela) material; (literario) genre; (biológico)
genus; **— humano** human race; **—s** dry

goods
generosidad F generosity
generoso ADJ generous
genética F genetics
genético ADJ genetic
genial ADJ brilliant
genio MF (persona inteligente) genius; M
(inteligencia) genius, brilliance;
(temperamento) temperament, nature; (mal
humor) temper; **de mal —** mean; **de buen
—** good-natured
geniudo ADJ quick-tempered
genocidio M genocide
genoma M genome
gente F people; **— de campo** country folk; **—
de color** persons of color; **— en obra** men at
work; **— joven** young people; **— menuda**
small fry; **buena —** good person
gentil ADJ (cortés) gracious; (no judío) gentile;
MF gentile
gentileza F graciousness
gentío M crowd
gentuza F rabble, riffraff
genuino ADJ genuine
geocéntrico ADJ geocentric
geoestacionario ADJ geostationary
geofísica F geophysics
geografía F geography
geográfico ADJ geographical
geología F geology
geológico ADJ geological
geometría F geometry
geométrico ADJ geometric
geopolítico ADJ geopolitical
Georgia F Georgia
georgiano-na ADJ & MF Georgian
geotérmico ADJ geothermal
geranio M geranium
gerencia F management
gerente MF manager
geriatría F geriatrics
geriátrico ADJ geriatric
germánico ADJ Germanic
germen M germ
germinar VI to germinate, to sprout
gerundio M gerund, present participle
gestación F gestation
gesticular VI (con ademanes) to gesture; (con
movimientos exagerados) to gesticulate
gestión F (acción) step, measure; (dirección
empresarial, digital) management;
(administración política) administration;
—es negotiations; **— de datos** data
management; **hacer gestiones para** to take
steps to
gestionar VT (negociar) to negotiate;
(administrar) to administer, to manage
gesto M (con la cara) face; (con las manos)
gesture; **hacerle —s a alguien** to make

faces at someone
gestor -ora MF agent
Ghana F Ghana
ghanés -esa ADJ & MF Ghanaian
giba F hump, hunch
gibón M gibbon
Gibraltar M Gibraltar
gibraltareño -ña ADJ & MF Gibraltarian
giga F jig
gigabyte M gigabyte
gigahercio M gigahertz
gigante ADJ giant, gigantic; MF giant
gigantesco ADJ gigantic
gimnasia F gymnastics
gimnasio M gymnasium, gym
gimotear VI to whimper
gimoteo M whimper
ginebra F gin
ginecología F gynecology
ginecólogo -ga MF gynecologist
gingivitis F gingivitis
gira F tour
girar VI/VT (una llave, un volante, un coche, a la
    derecha) to turn; VI (un trompo, un disco) to
    revolve, to spin, to whirl; VT (dinero) to wire
girasol M sunflower
giratorio ADJ rotary, revolving
giro M (movimiento circular) rotation, spin;
    (cambio de dirección) turn; (expresión) turn
    of phrase; (monetario) draft, remittance; —
    de cheques sin fondos check kiting; —
    postal money order
giroscopio M gyroscope
gitano -na ADJ & MF gypsy
glacial ADJ glacial, bitter
glaciar M glacier
gladiador M gladiator
glamoroso ADJ glamorous
glamour M glamour
glándula F gland; **—s sudoríparas** sweat
    glands
glandular ADJ glandular
glaseado M (de torta) glaze; ADJ (papel) glossy
glasear VT to glaze
glaucoma M glaucoma
glicerina F glycerin
global ADJ (mundial) global; (de conjunto)
    blanket, overall
globalización F globalization
globo M (esfera) globe; (de árbol de Navidad)
    ball; (lleno de gas) balloon; (en tenis) lob; —
    ocular eyeball; **— terráqueo** globe
globulina F globulin
glóbulo M globule; **— rojo** red cell; **— blanco**
    white cell
gloria F glory
glorieta F (pérgola) arbor; (rotonda) traffic
    circle
glorificar[30] VT to glorify

glorioso M glorious
glosa F gloss
glosar VT to gloss
glosario M glossary
glotal ADJ glottal
glótico ADJ glottal
glotis F glottis
glotón -ona ADJ gluttonous; MF glutton
glotonería F gluttony
glucosa F glucose
gluglutear VI to gobble
gluten M gluten
gobernabilidad F governability
gobernación F (acción de gobernar) governing;
    (entidad gubernamental) government
gobernador -ora ADJ governing; MF governor
gobernante ADJ governing; MF ruler
gobernar[1] VI/VT to govern, to rule; (un buque)
    to steer
gobierno M government
goce M enjoyment
gofre M waffle
gol M goal; **— de campo** (fútbol americano)
    field goal; **— del empate** (fútbol) equalizer;
    — en contra (fútbol) own goal
goleador -ora MF (artillero) shooter; (máximo
    anotador) top scorer
goleta F schooner
golf M golf
golfo -fa M (mar) gulf; (sinvergüenza) rascal
gollería F delicacy
golondrina F swallow
golosina F sweet, goody, tidbit
goloso ADJ sweet-toothed
golpazo M bang, whack
golpe M (físico) blow, knock, whack;
    (emocional) blow; (estafa) sting; (robo)
    holdup; (golf) stroke; (de viento) buffet; (con
    el codo) jab; (con los nudillos) rap; **— bajo**
    low blow; **— cortado** (tenis) backspin, slice;
    — cruzado (tenis) crosscourt shot; **— de**
    aproximación (golf) approach shot; **— de**
    calor heat stroke; **— de derecha** (tenis)
    forehand; **— de estado** coup; **— de gracia**
    coup de grâce; **— de penalidad** (golf)
    penalty stroke; **— de sol** sunstroke; **de —**
    suddenly; **de un —** all at once
golpear VI/VT (pegar) to strike, to hit; (llamar) to
    knock, to rap; (dar una paliza) to beat, to
    batter; (patear) to kick; (codear) to jab
golpecito M tap
golpetear VI (dedos) to tap; (lluvia) to patter;
    (motor) to knock; (algo suelto) to rattle
golpeteo M (con los dedos) tap; (de lluvia)
    patter; (de un motor) knock; (de algo suelto)
    rattle
goma F (chicle) gum; (caucho) rubber;
    (neumático) tire; (en béisbol) home; **— de**
    borrar eraser; **— de mascar** chewing gum;

— **elástica** rubber band; **—espuma** foam

gomero M rubber tree

gomoso ADJ slimy

gónada F gonad

góndola F gondola

gong M gong

gonorrea F gonorrhea

gordinflón ADJ *pey* fatso

gordito ADJ chubby

gordo ADJ fat; **se armó la gorda** all hell broke loose; **hacer la vista gorda** to turn a blind eye

gordura F (cualidad) fatness; (sebo) fat

gorgojo M weevil

gorila M (primate) gorilla; (portero) bouncer; (guardaespaldas) bodyguard

gorjear VI (ave) to warble, to chirp, to twitter; (niño) to gurgle

gorjeo M (de ave) warble, twitter, chirp; (de niño) gurgle

gorra F cap; **de** — at someone else's expense; **vivir de** — to sponge

gorrino M piglet

gorrión M sparrow

gorro M cap

gorrón M sponge, sponger

gorronear VI/VT to mooch, to freeload

gospel M gospel

gota F (de líquido) drop; (de sudor) bead; (enfermedad) gout; **— a** — drop by drop; **—s oftálmicas** eyedrops; **ser dos —s de agua** to be like two peas in a pod; **sudar la — gorda** (transpirar) to sweat profusely; (trabajar) to work hard

gotear VI (caer gota a gota) to drip; (rápidamente) to dribble, to trickle; (salirse) to leak; (llover) to sprinkle

goteo M drip (también intravenoso); (rápido) dribble, trickle

gotera F leak

gotero M dropper

gótico ADJ Gothic; M (lengua) Gothic

gourmet ADJ & MF gourmet

gozar[47] VT to enjoy; **— de** to enjoy

gozne M hinge

gozo M pleasure, enjoyment

gozoso ADJ enjoyable

grabación F recording

grabado M (en piedra) engraving; (con ácido) etching

grabador -ora MF (persona) engraver; F (aparato) tape recorder; (empresa) recording company

grabar VI/VT (en piedra) to engrave; (con ácido) to etch; (en cinta magnetográfica) to record, to tape; (en computadora) to write; **— en la memoria** to etch/imprint on one's memory

gracejo M wit

gracia F (garbo, desenvoltura) grace,

gracefulness; (humor) humor; (monería) antic; (favor) favor; (indulto) pardon; **¡—s!** thanks! thank you! **—s a Dios** thank God; **caer en** — to please; **dar —s** to say the blessing; **dar las —s** to thank; **hacer** — to amuse; **tener** — to be funny

grácil ADJ supple, graceful

gracioso ADJ (chistoso) amusing, funny; (gentil) gracious

grada F step, bleachers

gradación F gradation

graderías F PL bleachers

grado M (de temperatura, de parentesco, de un ángulo, de universidad) degree; (militar) rank; (de alcohol) proof; **de buen** — willingly; **en alto** — to a great extent; **en mayor o menor** — to some extent; **quemadura de primer** — first-degree burn

graduación F (de una escuela) graduation, commencement; (militar) military rank; (de alcohol) proof; (de un lente óptico) correction

graduado -da MF graduate

gradual ADJ gradual

graduar[26] VT (ajustar) to adjust; (regular) to calibrate; **—se** to graduate, to get a degree

graffiti M graffiti

grafiar[28] VT to graph

gráfica F (arte) graphics; (representación) graph, chart; **— de pastel** pie graph

graficar[30] VT to chart

gráfico -ca ADJ graphic; **acento** — written accent; M (representación) graph, chart; MF (empleado) printer

grafito M graphite

grama F lawn

gramática F grammar

gramatical ADJ grammatical

gramo M gram

grana ADJ & F scarlet

granada F (fruta) pomegranate; (proyectil) grenade; **— de mano** hand grenade

Granada F Grenada

granadino -na ADJ & MF Grenadian

granado M pomegranate tree; ADJ notable

granate M garnet

Gran Bretaña F Great Britain

grande ADJ (de tamaño) large, big; (de importancia) great; **un gran poeta** a great poet; **divertirse en** — to have a whale of a time; **a —s alturas** at high altitudes; **de gran alcance** far-reaching; **de/a gran escala** large-scale; **en gran parte** in large measure, largely; **gran almacén** department store

grandeza F greatness; **delirios de** — delusions of grandeur

grandiosidad F grandeur

grandioso ADJ grandiose, grand

granero M (edificio) granary, grain barn; (recipiente) bin, crib; **el — de América** the breadbasket of America

granito M granite

granizada F hailstorm

granizar[47] VI to hail

granizo M hail

granja F farm

granjearse VI to win for oneself

granjero -ra MF farmer

grano M (de una foto, arena, semilla) grain; (cereal) cereal, grain; (barrito) pimple; **— de café** coffee bean; **ir al —** to come to the point

granuja MF ragamuffin

granular VT to granulate; **—se** to become granulated

granuloso ADJ granular

grapa F (para sujetar madera) clamp; (para sujetar papel) staple

grapadora F stapler

grasa F (aceite) grease; (animal) fat

grasiento ADJ greasy

graso ADJ (cutis) oily; (leche) fatty; (pelo) greasy

grasoso ADJ greasy

gratificación F bonus

gratificar[30] VT to gratify

gratis ADJ INV & ADV free

gratitud F gratitude, thankfulness

grato ADJ pleasant

gratuito ADJ (gratis) free; (arbitrario) wanton, gratuitous

grava F gravel

gravamen M (impuesto) tax, assessment; (carga sobre una propiedad) lien, encumbrance

gravar VT (con un impuesto) to tax, to assess; (con una carga) to encumber

grave ADJ (enfermedad, decisión) grave, serious; (sonido) low, deep; (injuria) grievous; (personalidad) earnest

gravedad F (fuerza de atracción) gravity; (de una situación) seriousness; (de una tormenta) severity; (de la voz) depth; (de una personalidad) earnestness

gravemente ADV (herido) seriously; (enfermo) seriously, gravely

gravitación F gravitation

gravitatorio ADJ gravitational

gravoso ADJ burdensome

graznar VI (cuervo) to caw, to croak; (pato) to quack; (ganso) to honk

graznido M (de cuervo) caw, croak; (de pato) quack; (de ganso) honk

Grecia F Greece

greda F clay

green M green

gregario ADJ gregarious

gremial ADJ **acuerdo —** union agreement

gremio M (conjunto de personas) trade; (asociación histórica) guild; (sindicato) trade union

greña F mop of hair

grey F flock, fold

griego -ga ADJ & MF Greek

grieta F crevice, crack

grifo M faucet, spigot, tap

grillete M fetter, shackle

grillo M (insecto) cricket; **—s** (grilletes) shackles

grima F uneasiness; **dar —** (disgustar) to be upsetting; (asquear) to be disgusting

gringo -ga ADJ & MF *pey* American

gripe, gripa F flu, influenza; **— asiática** Asiatic flu

gris ADJ & M gray

grisáceo ADJ grayish

gritar VI/VT (vociferar) to shout, to yell; (chillar) to scream

gritería F shouting

grito M (voz alta) shout, cry; (chillido) scream; **el último —** the last word; **estar en un —** to be in agony; **pedir a —s** to clamor for; **poner el — en el cielo** to hit the ceiling

grosella F currant

grosellero M currant

grosería F (cualidad) rudeness; (hecho, dicho) profanity, something rude

grosero ADJ (descortés) rude, ill-mannered; boorish; (vulgar) vulgar, profane; (sin arte) coarse, unrefined

grosor M thickness

grotesco ADJ grotesque

grúa F (máquina) crane; (guinche, remolcadora) wrecker, tow truck

grueso -sa ADJ (persona) thick-set, heavy; (tabla) thick; (palabra, arena) coarse; M (grosor) thickness; (mayoría) majority; F gross

grulla F crane

grumo M lump

grumoso ADJ lumpy

gruñido M (de perro) growl, snarl; (de cerdo) grunt; (humano) grumble

gruñir[17] VI (el cerdo) to grunt; (el perro) to growl, to snarl; (el ser humano) to grumble

gruñón -ona ADJ grumpy; MF grumpy person

grupa F rump; **volver —s** to turn around

grupo M group; **— de apoyo** support group; **— de presión** lobby; **— étnico** ethnicity; **— paritario** peer group; **— sanguíneo** blood type; **— de usuarios** user group

gruta F grotto, cavern

guacal M crate

guacamole M *Méx* guacamole

guacho M (cría de ave) chick; *Am* (animal huérfano) orphan

guadaña F scythe

guagua F (fruslería) trifle; *Carib* bus; *Chile* baby; LOC ADV **de —** for nothing, free

guaje -ja MF urchin

guano M guano, bird dung

guantada F slap

guante M glove (también en deporte); **arrojar el** — to challenge; **echarle el** — **a alguien** to capture someone; **te queda como un** — it fits you like a glove

guantelete M gauntlet

guantera F glove compartment

guapetón-ona MF *fam* fox

guapo ADJ (hombre) good-looking, handsome; (mujer) good-looking, pretty; (valiente) brave; **¡hola** —! hey, good-looking!

guarapo M cane syrup

guarda MF (guardián) guard; F (almacenamiento) storage

guardameta MF (fútbol) goalkeeper

guardar VT (almacenar) to keep, to store; (observar) to observe; (datos) to save; (proteger) to guard; — **como** to save as; — **rencor** to hold a grudge; — **un secreto** to keep a secret; —**se de** to guard against; M SG **guardabarros** fender; M SG **guardacostas** Coast Guard cutter; MF SG **guardaespaldas** bodyguard; M SG **guardafangos** fender; M SG **guardapelo** locket; M SG **guardarropa** (armario, ropa) wardrobe; (en un local) cloakroom; MF SG **guardabosque[s]** forest ranger, forester; MF SG **guardafrenos** brake operator; MF SG **guardagujas** switch operator; MF SG **guardameta** goalie

guardería F nursery, day-care center

guardia MF (vigilante) guard; (en baloncesto) point guard; — **civil** civil guard; F (vigilancia) guard; **bajar la** — to let down one's guard; **de** — (militar) on duty, on watch; (médico) on call; **en** — en garde; **hacer/montar** — to stand guard

guardián-ana MF guardian, keeper

guarecerse[35] VT to take shelter

guarida F den, lair

guarismo M cipher

guarnecer[35] VT (un plato) to garnish; (un vestido) to trim; (una fortaleza) to man, to garrison

guarnición F (de tropas) garrison; (de comida) trimmings; **guarniciones** harness

guarro ADJ filthy; M pig

guasa LOC ADV **de/a**— in jest, as a joke

guasón-ona MF joker

guata F padding

Guatemala F Guatemala

guatemalteco-ca ADJ & MF Guatemalan

guau INTERJ woof

guay ADJ *Esp* cool, great

guayaba F guava

guayabera F tropical pleated shirt

gubernamental ADJ governmental

gubernativo ADJ governmental

gubia F gouge

guedeja F shock of hair

guepardo M cheetah

guerra F war, warfare; **dar** — to aggravate; **en pie de** — at war; — **fría** cold war

guerrear VI to war

guerrero-ra MF warrior; **operación guerrera** war operation; **espíritu** — warrior spirit

guerrilla F guerrilla army

guerrillero-ra MF guerrilla

gueto M ghetto

guía MF (persona) guide, leader; F (cosa o animal) guide; — **para padres** parenting guide; — **telefónica** telephone directory

guiar[28] VT to guide, to lead; —**se por** to follow

guijarro M pebble

guinche M *Am* (grúa) winch; (remolque) tow truck

guinda F cherry

guindilla F *Esp* small hot pepper

Guinea F Guinea

guineano-na ADJ & MF Guinean

guingán M gingham

guiñada F wink

guiñapo M rag

guiñar VI/VT to wink

guiño M wink

guión M (ortografía) hyphen; (libreto) script, screenplay

guionista MF screenwriter

guirnalda F garland; (de Navidad) tinsel

guisa F a — **de** by way of

guisado M stew, hash

guisante M pea

guisar VI/VT (cocer) to cook; (en olla) to stew

guiso M stew, casserole

guitarra F guitar

gula F gluttony

gusano M worm; — **de seda** silkworm

gustar VT (agradar) to be pleasing to; **ella me gusta** I like her; **le gustan los perros** he likes dogs; **no me gustan las fiestas** I dislike parties; **te guste o no te guste** whether you like it or not; **cuando gustes** whenever you want; — **de** (preferir) to be fond of; (saborear) to taste

gusto M (sentido, sabor, sentido estético) taste; (agrado) pleasure; (preferencia personal) like; **a** — at ease; **a mi** — to my liking; **dar** — to be a pleasure; **darle el** — **a alguien** to humor someone; **darse el** — to indulge oneself; **de mal** — in bad taste; **el** — **es mío** the pleasure is mine; **estar a** — to be comfortable; **mucho** — nice to meet you; **por** — for fun; **tener el** — to have the pleasure of; **tomarle el** — **a una cosa** to become fond of something

gustoso ADJ (que gusta de) fond of; (agradable) pleasant; ADV willingly

Guyana F Guyana
guyanés -esa ADJ & MF Guyanese

Hh

ha, has *ver* haber
haba F (frijol) bean; (frijol verde) lima bean
habano M cigar
haber[68] V AUX to have; — **comido cuatro veces en un día** to have eaten four times in a day; **habérselas con** (un problema) to grapple with; (una persona) to have it out with; **ha de llegar mañana** he is to arrive tomorrow; **hay** there is, there are; **hay viento** it is windy; **hubo un problema** there was a problem; **había gente** there were people; **hay que** it is necessary to; **no hay de qué** don't mention it; **no hay forma** no way; **no hay problema** no problem; **¿qué hay?** what's up? **todo lo habido y por haber** everything possible; M (hacienda) assets; (columna en una cuenta) credit; —**es** earnings
habichuela F bean; — **verde** string bean
hábil ADJ adept, able; **día —** workday
habilidad F ability, skill
habilidoso ADJ deft, skillful
habilitar VT (equipar) to outfit; (autorizar) to authorize
habitación F (vivienda) dwelling; (cuarto) room
habitante MF (de un país, región) inhabitant; (de un barrio) resident
habitar VT to inhabit
hábitat M habitat
hábito M habit (también vestimenta religiosa); —**s de compra** buying habits
habitual ADJ habitual, usual
habituar[26] VT to accustom; —**se** to get used to
habla F (lenguaje) speech; (variedad local) dialect; — **infantil** baby talk; **al —** in communication with; **quedarse sin —** to be left speechless
hablador ADJ talkative
habladurías F idle talk, gossip
hablante ADJ speaking; **castellano—** Castilian-speaking; MF speaker; **castellano—** Castilian speaker
hablar VI/VT to talk; — **de política** to talk about politics; — **hasta por los codos** to talk one's head off; — **no cuesta nada** talk is cheap; — **por teléfono** to talk on the phone; — **solo / para sí** to talk to oneself; to speak; — **francés** to speak French; — **sin rodeos** to speak one's mind; — **por señas** to use sign language; **hablando mal y pronto** pardon

my French; **no —se** not to be on speaking terms; **no me hagas** — don't get me started on it; **hablando en serio, ¿qué es lo que quieres?** seriously, what do you want?
hablilla F malicious tale
habrá, habría *ver* haber
hacedor -ora MF maker
hacendado -da MF landowner
hacendoso ADJ industrious, diligent
hacer[54, 74] VT (crear) to do, to make; (causar) to make; (resolver) to do; (decir) to go; **la vaca hace 'mu'** the cow goes moo; — **clic** to click; — **economías** to scrimp; — **frío/calor/viento** to be cold/hot/windy; — **una oferta** make an offer; — **un pastel** to make a cake; — **un crucigrama** to do a crossword puzzle; — **un gol** to score a goal; **me hizo llorar** he made me cry; **hace mucho tiempo** a long time ago; **hace poco** a short while ago; **hizo como si estuvieras presente** he acted as if you were here; **a lo hecho, pecho** you've got to face the music; **la hiciste buena** you've really screwed up; **¿qué le vamos a hacer?** that's life; **¿qué se hizo de Juan?** whatever became of Juan? **haz el trabajo** do the work; **hecho a pedido** built to order; —**se rico** to become rich; —**se el tonto** to play the fool; —**se el listo** to pull a stunt; —**se pasar por el jefe** to pose as the boss; —**se a un lado** to step aside; —**se amigo de** to befriend; —**se a la oscuridad** to get used to the dark; —**se cargo** to take over; —**se [del] rogar** to play hard to get
hacha F (grande) ax[e]; (pequeña) hatchet
hachís M hashish
hacia PREP (en dirección a) toward; (aproximadamente) about; — **abajo** downward; — **adelante** forward; — **adentro** inward; — **afuera** outward; — **arriba** upward; — **atrás** backward; — **el este** eastward; — **la izquierda** to the left; **dar —** to face
hacienda F (bienes) estate; (establecimiento agropecuario) ranch; (impositiva) Internal Revenue Service
hacina F shock
hacinar VT (liar) to shock; (atestar) to crowd in
hada F fairy
hado M fate
haga, hago *ver* hacer
Haití M Haiti
haitiano -na ADJ & MF Haitian
halagar[40] VT to flatter, to compliment
halago M flattery, compliment
halagüeño ADJ (palabras) flattering; (perspectiva) promising
halcón M falcon
hálito M breath
halitosis F halitosis

hallar VT to find; **—se** to be; **—se en un aprieto** to be in a pickle; **—se mal de salud** to be in a bad way

hallazgo M finding; **ese documento fue un — sensacional** that document was a real find

halo M halo

halógeno ADJ & M halogen

halterofilia F weight training, weightlifting

hamaca F hammock

hambre F (deseo de comer) hunger; (hambruna) famine; **tener —** to be hungry; **pasar —** to go hungry; **morirse de —** to starve

hambrear VI/VT to starve

hambriento -a ADJ (con hambre) hungry; (famélico) famished, starving

hambruna F famine

hamburguesa F hamburger

hampa F underworld

hámster M hamster

hándicap M handicap

handicapar VT to handicap

hangar M hangar

hará, haría ver hacer

haragán -ana ADJ indolent; MF loafer

haraganear VI to loaf

haraganería F laziness

harapiento ADJ ragged, tattered

harapo M rag, tatter

hardware M hardware

harén M harem

harina F (fina) flour; (gruesa) meal; **— de avena** oat flour; **— de maíz** cornmeal; **es — de otro costal** that's another kettle of fish

hartar VT to satiate; **—se** (de comida) to have one's fill; (de aburrimiento) to get fed up

hartazgo M surfeit, excess

harto ADJ (satisfecho) full; **estar —** to be fed up; **ese asunto me tiene —** I'm sick and tired of the whole business

hasta PREP (temporal) till, until; (espacial) [up] to; **— ahora** to date / so far; **— cierto punto** to a certain extent; **— luego** good-bye, see you later; **— pronto** see you later; **caminó — la esquina** he walked to the corner; **lo llenó — el borde** he filled it up to brim; **estar — la coronilla** to be fed up; ADV even; **— mi madre lo notó** even my mother noticed it; **— que** until

hastiado ADJ jaded

hastial M gable

hastiar[28] VT to cloy, to tire; **—se** to grow weary of

hastío M tedium

hato M (envoltorio) bundle; (rebaño) herd

hay ver haber

haya F beech

haya, hayamos ver haber

hayuco M beechnut

haz[1] M (de leña) bundle; (de luz) beam; (de flechas) sheaf

haz[2] ver hacer

hazaña F deed, exploit, feat

hazmerreír M laughingstock

he VT IMPERSONAL **he aquí la lista** here's the list

he, hemos ver haber

hebilla F buckle

hebra F (de hilo) thread; (vegetal) fiber

hebreo -a ADJ & MF Hebrew

heces F PL (de vino, café) dregs; (excremento) feces

hechicería F enchantment

hechicero -ra ADJ bewitching; M sorcerer; F sorceress

hechizar[47] VT (embrujar) to bewitch, to enchant; (fascinar) to enthrall

hechizo M charm, spell

hecho M fact; **los —s de la noche del 17** the events of the night of the 17th; **de —** in fact

hecho ver hacer

hechura F cut

hectárea F hectare

heder[2] VI to stink, to reek

hediondez F stench

hediondo ADJ stinking, smelly

hedonismo M hedonism

hedor M stink, stench

hegemonía F hegemony

helada F (frente frío) freeze; (escarcha) frost

heladera F refrigerator

heladería F ice-cream parlor

helado ADJ (muy frío) frozen, freezing; (con hielo) icy; M ice cream

helar[1] VI/VT to freeze

helecho M fern

hélice F (espiral) helix; (de avión) propeller; (de barco) screw, propeller

helicóptero M helicopter

helio M helium

hematoma M hematoma

hembra F (de animal) female; (de venado) doe; (de ballena, foca) cow; (de ave) hen

hemisferio M hemisphere (también cerebral)

hemofilia F hemophilia

hemoglobina F hemoglobin

hemorragia F hemorrhage; **— cerebral** cerebral hemorrhage; **— vaginal** vaginal bleeding

hemorroide F hemorrhoid

henchir[9] VT to swell

hender[7] VI/VT to cleave, to split

hendido ADJ cleft, split

hendidura F (quebradura) crack; (geológica) fissure

henil M hayloft

heno M hay; **fiebre de —** hay fever

hepatitis F hepatitis

heraldo M herald

herbicida M weedkiller, herbicide
herbívoro ADJ herbivorous; M herbivore
herboso ADJ grassy
heredad F homestead
heredar VI/VT (recibir) to inherit; (dar) to bequeath
heredero -ra M heir; F heiress; **—s y cesionarios** heirs and assigns
hereditario ADJ hereditary
hereje MF heretic
herejía F heresy
herencia F (económica) inheritance; (cultural) heritage; (genética) heredity
herida F (lastimadura) injury; (abierta) wound; **— de bala** gunshot wound; **— perforada** puncture wound; **respirar por la —** to reopen an old wound
herido ADJ (lastimado) injured; (con herida abierta) wounded
herir[8] VI/VT (lastimar) to injure; (con herida abierta) to wound; (sentimientos) to hurt
hermafrodita MF hermaphrodite
hermanastro -tra M stepbrother; F stepsister
hermandad F (de hombres) brotherhood; (de mujeres) sisterhood
hermanito -ta M little brother; F little sister
hermano -na MF sibling; M brother (también religioso); **— mayor** older brother; **— menor** younger brother; F sister (también religiosa); **— mayor** older sister; **— menor** younger sister
herméticamente ADV tight, tightly
hermético ADJ hermetic, airtight; (a prueba de agua) watertight; (que no revela secretos) secretive
hermosear VT to beautify
hermoso ADJ beautiful, lovely
hermosura F beauty
hernia F hernia
héroe M hero
heroico ADJ heroic
heroína F (droga) heroin; (personaje) heroine
heroísmo M heroism
herpes M (erupción) herpes; (en la boca) cold sore; **— febril** fever blister
herradura F horseshoe
herraje M ironwork
herramienta F tool
herrar[1] VT (un caballo) to shoe; (una vaca) to brand
herrería F blacksmith's shop
herrero -ra MF blacksmith
herrumbre F rust
hervidero M swarm
hervidor M kettle
hervir[8] VI/VT to boil; **— a fuego lento** to simmer; **— de** to be swarming with; **me hervía la sangre** I was seething
hervor M boiling; **levantar el —** to come to a boil
heterodoxo ADJ unorthodox
heterogéneo ADJ heterogeneous
heterosexual ADJ heterosexual; *fam* straight
hexágono M hexagon
hiato M hiatus
hibernar VI to hibernate
hibridación F hybridization
híbrido ADJ & M hybrid
hice, hiciera *ver* hacer
hidalgo M nobleman
hidalguía F (nobleza) nobility; (generosidad) generosity
hidrato M hydrate
hidráulico ADJ hydraulic
hidroavión M hydroplane, seaplane
hidrocarburo M hydrocarbon
hidroeléctrico ADJ hydroelectric
hidrofobia F hydrophobia
hidrógeno M hydrogen
hiedra F ivy
hiel F gall
hielo M ice; **— seco** dry ice; **romper el —** to break the ice
hiena F hyena
hierba F (pasto) grass; (especia) herb; (marihuana) *fam* weed; **—buena** mint; **mala — weed; y otras —s** and so on
hierro M iron (también de golf); **— corrugado** corrugated iron; **— forjado** wrought iron; **— fundido** cast iron; **—s** handcuffs
hígado M liver; **malos —s** ill will
higiene F hygiene
higiénico ADJ hygienic
higienista MF hygienist
higo M fig; **me importa un —** I couldn't care less
higuera F fig tree
hijastro -tra M stepson; F stepdaughter
hijo -ja M son; **— de su madre** *fam* son of a gun; **John Smith —** John Smith Jr.; **sin —s** childless; F daughter
hilachas F loose threads
hilado M spinning
hilandería F (fábrica) spinning mill; (técnica) spinning
hilandero -ra MF spinner
hilar VI/VT to spin; **— fino** to split hairs
hilaridad F mirth
hilera F row, line
hilo M (para coser) thread; (para tejer, hilar) yarn; (alambre) filament; **— de agua** trickle; **— de pensamiento** train of thought; **— de perlas** string of pearls; **— de voz** thin voice; **— dental** floss; **al —** in a row; **mover —s** to pull strings; **seguir el — de** to keep track of; **pender de un —** to be hanging by a thread; **perder el —** to lose track
hilván M basting

hilvanar VT to baste, to tack

himen M hymen

himno M (religioso) hymn; (patriótico) anthem

hincapié M emphasis; **hacer** — to emphasize

hincar[30] VT — **los dientes en** to sink one's teeth into; **—se** to kneel

hincha MF (aficionado) supporter; F (antipatía) *Esp* grudge

hinchado ADJ (inflamado) swollen, bloated; (exagerado) inflated

hinchar VT (un río) to swell; (un globo) to blow up; — **por el equipo de Uruguay** to pull for the Uruguayan team; **—se** (cuerpo) to swell; (pulmones) to inflate; (mejillas) to bulge; (de orgullo) to puff up; (el pan) to rise

hinchazón F swelling

hindi M Hindi

hindú ADJ & MF Hindu

hinojos LOC ADV **de** — on one's knees

hipar VI hiccup

hiperactivo ADJ hyperactive, overactive

hiperdocumento M hyperdocument

hiperenlace M hyperlink

hipermedia M hypermedia

hipermercado M superstore

hipermétrope ADJ farsighted

hipersensible ADJ (a la luz) hypersensitive; (a la crítica) touchy

hipertensión F hypertension, high blood pressure

hiperventilar VI to hyperventilate

hipervínculo M hyperlink

hipnosis F hypnosis

hipnoterapia F hypnotherapy

hipnotizar VI/VT to hypnotize, to mesmerize

hipo M (espasmo) hiccup; (sollozo) sob; **tengo** — I have the hiccups

hipoalérgico ADJ hypoallergenic

hipocondríaco -ca, hipocondriaco -ca ADJ & MF hypochondriac

hipocresía F hypocrisy

hipócrita ADJ hypocritical, two-faced; MF hypocrite

hipódromo M racetrack

hipogloso M halibut

hipoglucemia F hypoglycemia

hipopótamo M hippopotamus

hipoteca F mortgage; — **con tasa de interés ajustable** adjustable-rate mortgage; — **de tasa fija** fixed-rate mortgage

hipotecar[30] VT to mortgage

hipotecario ADJ **banco** — mortgage bank

hipótesis F hypothesis

hipotiroidismo M hypothyroidism

hiriente ADJ (comentario) catty, hurtful

hirviente ADJ boiling

hisopo M swab

hispánico -ca ADJ Hispanic

hispano -na ADJ Hispanic, Spanish-speaking; MF (por su lengua) Spanish-speaking person; (por su etnia) Hispanic

Hispanoamérica F Spanish America

hispanoamericano ADJ Spanish-American

histamina F histamine

histerectomía F hysterectomy

histérico ADJ hysterical

historia F (el pasado, estudio del pasado) history; (relato) story; — **clínica** case history, medical history; **dejarse de —s** to stop fooling around; **esa es otra** — that's another story; **la — se repite** history repeats itself; **pasar a la** — to be a thing of the past

historiador -ora MF historian

historial M record; — **de crédito** credit history

histórico ADJ (de importancia histórica) historic; (pertinente a la historia) historical

historietas F PL funnies

histrionismo M histrionics

hito M landmark, milestone; **de** — **en** — fixedly; **marcar un** — to be a milestone

hobby M hobby

hocicar[30] VI/VT (un cerdo) to root; (un caballo) to nose

hocico M snout, muzzle

hockey M hockey

hogaño ADV *lit* nowadays

hogar M (lumbre) hearth, fireplace; (casa, asilo) home

hogareño ADJ domestic; **persona hogareña** homebody

hoguera F bonfire, campfire

hoja F (de planta) leaf; (de mesa plegable) flap; (de papel) sheet; (de libro) page; (de navaja) blade; — **clínica** medical chart; — **de afeitar** razor blade; — **de depósito** deposit slip; — **de ejercicios** worksheet; — **de metal** foil; **echar —s** to leaf; — **de servicio** record; F **—lata** tin plate

hojaldre M puff pastry

hojarasca F fallen leaves

hojear VT to page through, to flip through, to browse

hojuela F flake; **—s de maíz** cornflakes

hola INTERJ hello, hi

Holanda F Holland

holandés -esa ADJ Dutch; M (hombre) Dutchman; (lengua) Dutch; F Dutchwoman

holding M holding company

holgado ADJ (vida) comfortable; (pantalón) loose-fitting, baggy; (cuarto) roomy

holganza F (haraganería) idleness; (diversión) leisure

holgar[42] VI to loaf; **huelga decir** it is needless to say

holgazán -ana ADJ lazy, idle; MF idler, loafer, slouch

holgazanear VI to idle, to loaf

holgazanería F laziness

holgura F (de movimiento) ease; (financiera) comfort; (de la ropa) looseness

holístico ADJ holistic

hollejo M skin

hollín M soot, smut

holocausto M holocaust

hombre M man; — **anuncio** sandwich man; — **de bien** man of good will; — **de familia** family man; — **de las cavernas** caveman; — **de la calle** man on the street; — **de negocios** businessman; — **del saco** bogeyman; — **de paja** straw man; — **lobo** werewolf; — **orquesta** one-man band; — **rana** frogman; **es bien** — he's a real he-man; INTERJ come on!

hombrera F shoulder pad

hombro M shoulder; **encogerse de —s** to shrug; **cargar al** — to shoulder; **en/a —s** piggyback; **poner el** — to lend a hand

hombruno ADJ mannish

home M home

homenaje M homage, tribute

homeopatía F homeopathy

homeopático ADJ homeopathic

homicida MF murderer

homicidio M homicide, murder; — **culposo/ involuntario** manslaughter; — **sin premeditación** manslaughter

homofobia F homophobia

homofóbico ADJ homophobic

homogeneizar[47] VT to homogenize

homogéneo ADJ homogeneous

homólogo -ga MF counterpart

homóplato M shoulder blade

homosexual ADJ homosexual; *fam* gay

honda F sling, slingshot

hondo ADJ deep; M hollow

hondonada F hollow, dell

hondura F depth; **meterse en —s** to get in over one's head

Honduras F Honduras

hondureño -ña ADJ & MF Honduran

honestidad F (castidad) chastity, modesty; (honradez) honesty

honesto ADJ (casto) chaste, modest; (honrado) honest, straightforward

hongo M (seta) mushroom; (moho) fungus; **aburrirse como un** — to be bored stiff

honor M honor; **con —es** with honors; **tener el** — **de** to have the honor of; **hacerle los —es a** to be appreciative of

honorable ADJ honorable

honorario ADJ honorary; M PL fee

honra F honor

honradez F honesty

honrado ADJ honest

honrar VT (respetar) to honor; (dignificar) to do credit to

honroso ADJ honorable

hora F hour; — **de dormir** bedtime; — **oficial** standard time; — **punta** rush hour; —**s extra[s]** overtime; **a esta** — at this time; **¿a qué** —? at what time? **a todas** —**s** at all hours; **a última** — at the last minute; **decir la** — to tell time; **en** — on time; **es** — **de** it is time to; **es** — **de que me vaya** it's time for me to go; **kilómetros por** — kilometers per hour; **no ver la** — **de** to be dying to; **por** — by the hour; **¿qué** — **es?** what time is it? **ya era** — it was about time

horadar VT to bore

horario M (agenda) schedule, timetable; (manecilla del reloj) hour hand; — **de trabajo** work schedule

horca F (cadalso) gallows; (tridente) pitchfork; — **de ajos** string of garlic

horcajadas LOC ADV **a** — astraddle, astride

horda F horde

horizontal ADJ horizontal

horizonte M (del cielo) horizon; (de una ciudad) skyline

horma F (de zapato) shoe last; (de queso) wheel

hormiga F ant; — **blanca** termite

hormigón M concrete

hormigonera F cement mixer

hormiguear VI (moverse en grandes cantidades) to swarm; (dar sensación de hormigueo) to tingle

hormigueo M tingle

hormiguero M anthill

hormona F hormone; — **del crecimiento** growth hormone

hornada F batch

horneado M baking

hornear VI/VT to bake

hornilla F burner

horno M (industrial) furnace; (doméstico) oven; (para cerámica) kiln; — **de microondas** microwave oven; **alto** — blast furnace; **el** — **no está para bollos** it's not a good time; **recién salido del** — brand-new

horóscopo M horoscope

horquilla F (para el pelo) hairpin; (horca) pitchfork

horrendo ADJ (asesinato) horrific, ghastly; (vestido) hideous, ghastly

horrible ADJ horrible

horripilante ADJ gruesome, hair-raising

horror M (miedo, repulsión) horror; (monstruosidad) abomination; (espectáculo) sight; **tenerle** — **a** to be scared of

horrorizar[47] VT to horrify, to shock, to appall

horroroso ADJ appalling, awful

hortaliza F vegetable; —**s** produce

hortera ADJ tacky, uncool, cheesy

horticultura F horticulture

hosco ADJ sullen, surly

hospedaje M lodging

hospedar VT to lodge, to accommodate; **—se** to lodge, to room

hospicio M (para peregrinos) hospice; (para huérfanos) orphanage

hospital M hospital

hospitalario ADJ hospitable

hospitalidad F hospitality

hostal M hostel

hostería F inn, hostelry

hostia F (oblea) host, wafer; (golpe) whack

hostigamiento M harassment

hostigar[40] VT to harass, to harry

hostil ADJ hostile

hostilidad F hostility

hotel M hotel

hotelero -ra MF hotel keeper

hoy ADV today; **— [en] día** nowadays; **de — en adelante** from now on; **— por —** at present

hoya F river basin

hoyo M hole (también de golf); (muy profundo) pit; **— en uno** (golf) hole in one

hoyuelo M dimple

hoz F sickle

hozar[47] VI to root

HTML M HTML

hube, hubiera, hubo ver haber

hucha F piggy bank

hueco ADJ (vacío) hollow; (vanidoso) vain, affected; **palabras huecas** empty words; M (entre los dientes) gap; (cavidad) hollow; (de ascensor) shaft

huelga F strike, work stoppage; **— de hambre** hunger strike; **declararse en —** to strike; **en — on strike**

huelguista MF striker

huella F (rastro) trace, trail; (de pie) footprint, track; (de rueda) track; **— dactilar/digital** fingerprint; **seguir las —s de alguien** to follow in someone's footsteps

huérfano -na ADJ & MF orphan

huerta F (de verduras) large vegetable garden; (de árboles frutales) large orchard; **la — valenciana** the farming region of Valencia

huerto M (de verduras) vegetable garden; (de árboles frutales) orchard

hueso M (de animal) bone; (de fruta) stone, pit; **calado hasta los —s** soaked to the bone; **la sin —** the tongue; **no dejarle un — sano a alguien** to break someone's bones; **un — duro de roer** a hard pill to swallow

huésped MF (invitado) guest; (anfitrión) host (también de parásitos)

hueste F host

huesudo ADJ bony

hueva F spawn

huevo M egg; **— de Pascua** Easter egg; **— duro** hard-boiled egg; **— estrellado/frito** fried egg; **— pasado por agua** soft-boiled egg; **—s revueltos** scrambled eggs; **ir pisando**

—s to walk on eggshells

huida F flight

huir[19] VI to flee, to fly

hule M oilcloth

hulla F soft coal; **— blanca** hydroelectric power

humanidad F (cualidad y condición) humanity; (conjunto de los seres humanos) humankind; **—es** humanities

humanismo M humanism

humanitario ADJ (organización, ayuda) humanitarian; (generoso) humane

humano ADJ (del hombre) human; (generoso) humane; M human

humareda F cloud of smoke

humeante ADJ (hoguera) smoking; (sopa) steaming

humear VI (echar humo) to give off smoke; (echar vapor) to give off steam

humedad F (del aire) humidity; (de un paño) dampness; (en la tierra) moisture; (en una pared) moisture stain

humedal M wetland

humedecer[35] VT (sello, ojo) to moisten; (paño) to dampen; **se le humedecieron los ojos** his eyes grew teary

húmedo ADJ (trapo) damp; (aire) humid; (tierra) moist; (tiempo) wet, soggy

humero M flue, funnel

humidificar[30] VT to humidify

humildad F (actitud) humility; (condición) lowliness

humilde ADJ (actitud) humble; (condición) low, lowly, mean

humillación F humiliation

humillar VT (insultar) to humiliate; (disminuir) to humble; **—se** to grovel

humo M (de combustión) smoke; (de gases tóxicos) fume; (de agua) vapor, steam; **—s** conceitedness; **bajarle los —s a alguien** to cut someone down to size; **echar —** to put out smoke; **estar que echa —** to be fuming; **hacerse —** to vanish into thin air

humor M (actitud risueña) humor; (estado de ánimo) mood

humorada F witty remark

humorismo M (humor) humor; (profesión) comedy

humorista MF comedian

humorístico ADJ humorous

humoso ADJ smoky

hundimiento M (acción de hundirse) sinking; (hoyo) sinkhole

hundir VT (hacer naufragar) to sink, to scuttle; (arruinar) to destroy; (enterrar) to bury; **—se** (barco) to sink; (empresa, edificio, precios) to collapse; (tierra) to subside; (sol) to go down

húngaro -ra MF Hungarian

Hungría F Hungary

huracán M hurricane

huraño ADJ sullen, unsociable

hurgar[40] VI (en una bolsa) to rummage; (en la basura) to scavenge; **—se las narices** to pick one's nose

hurón M ferret

huronear VI to ferret out

hurra INTERJ hurrah

hurtadillas LOC ADV **a** — stealthily

hurtar VT to steal, to swipe; **— el cuerpo** to dodge; **—se** to hide

hurto M (robo) theft, larceny; (robo en tiendas) shoplifting; **— con escalo** break-in

husky M (perro) husky

husmear VT (un pedazo de carne) to sniff at; (a un delincuente) to smell out; (peligro) to smell; (en los asuntos ajenos) to nose around, to poke around

husmeo M sniff

huso M spindle; **— horario** time zone

huy INTERJ (de sorpresa) wow; (de pena) oh

huya, huye, huyendo, huyera, huyese *ver* huir

Ii

iba, ibas *ver* ir

ibérico ADJ Iberian

iberoamericano -na ADJ Ibero-American

ibuprofeno M ibuprofen

iceberg M iceberg

ictericia F jaundice

ictérico ADJ jaundiced

ID [investigación y desarrollo] F R&D

ida F outward journey; **—s y venidas** comings and goings

idea F (reflexión) idea, thought; (intuición) inkling

ideal ADJ & M ideal

idealismo M idealism

idealista ADJ idealistic; MF idealist

idear VT (un método) to devise, to think out, to plan; (un plan) to conceive; (una solución) to engineer; (un complot) to hatch

ídem PRON & ADV ditto

idéntico ADJ identical

identidad F identity

identificación F identification

identificar[30] VT to identify

ideología F ideology

ideológico ADJ ideological

idilio M idyll

idioma M language

idiosincrasia F idiosyncrasy

idiota ADJ idiotic, lamebrained; MF *fam* idiot

idiotez F idiocy

ido[1] ADJ out of it

ido[2] *ver* ir

idolatrar VT to idolize

idolatría F idolatry

ídolo M idol

idóneo ADJ (calificado) expert; (ideal) ideal

iglesia F church

iglú M igloo

ignición F ignition

ignifugar[40] VT to fireproof

ignorancia F ignorance

ignorante ADJ ignorant, uneducated; MF ignoramus

ignorar VT (no saber) to be unaware of; (hacer caso omiso de) to ignore, to disregard; (despreciar) to shrug off, to discount

igual ADJ (idéntico) equal; (semejante) same, alike; (derecho) even; **me da** — it's all the same to me; **al — que** just like; M equal sign

igualar VT (alisar) to level; (ser igual a) to equal; (hacer iguales) to equalize; (compararse con) to match

igualdad F equality

igualmente ADV (de manera igual) equally; **quedaron — sorprendidos** they were similarly surprised; **¡que te vaya bien!** — I hope things go well for you! likewise

ijada F loin

ijar M loin

ilegal ADJ illegal, unlawful, lawless

ilegítimo ADJ illegitimate

ileso ADJ unharmed, unhurt

ilícito ADJ illicit

ilimitado ADJ (crédito) unlimited; (energía) boundless; (horizonte) limitless

iluminación F (luz) illumination, lighting; (moral, académica) enlightenment

iluminado ADJ lit

iluminar VT (con luz) to illuminate, to brighten; (con conocimiento) to enlighten; **—se** to light up

ilusión F (idea o imagen falsa) illusion; (deseo) dream, fond hope; (entusiasmo) thrill; **— óptica** optical illusion; **me da** — I'm looking forward to

ilusionado ADJ excited

iluso ADJ naive

ilusorio ADJ illusory

ilustración F illustration; **la** — the Enlightenment

ilustrador -ora MF illustrator

ilustrar VT (dibujar) illustrate; (educar) to enlighten

ilustre ADJ illustrious

imagen F (representación, reputación) image; (foto, televisión) picture; (unidad de película fotográfica) frame; **— especular** mirror image; **la — del tacto** the soul of tact; **— por resonancia magnética** magnetic resonance imaging; **imágenes por**

ultrasonido ultrasound imaging
imaginable ADJ conceivable
imaginación F imagination
imaginar VT (crear una imagen mental) to imagine, to picture; (idear) to dream up
imaginario ADJ imaginary
imaginativo ADJ imaginative
imán M magnet
imantar VT to magnetize
imbatible ADJ unbeatable
imbécil ADJ idiotic
imbuir[19] VT to imbue
imitación F imitation
imitador -ora MF (copión) imitator; (mímico) mimic; **un — de Elvis** an Elvis impersonator
imitar VT (copiar) to imitate; (hacer mímica) to mimic; (representar a un personaje) to impersonate
impaciencia F impatience
impaciente ADJ impatient; *fam* antsy
impactar VI/VT to impact
impacto M impact
impagado ADJ unpaid
impala M impala
impar ADJ odd, uneven
imparcial ADJ (sin prejuicios) impartial, unbiased, neutral; (justo) evenhanded; (apartidario) nonpartisan
imparcialidad F impartiality
impartir VT to impart
impasible ADJ impassive
impasse M impasse
impávido ADJ undaunted
impeachment M impeachment
impecable ADJ (perfecto) flawless; (limpio) spick and span
impedimento M (obstáculo) impediment, hindrance; (incapacidad) handicap
impedir[9] VT to impede, to prevent, to hinder; (acceso) to bar
impeler VT (empujar) to impel; (inducir) to drive
impenetrable ADJ impenetrable
impensable ADJ unthinkable
imperante ADJ prevailing
imperar VI to prevail
imperativo ADJ & M imperative
imperceptible ADJ imperceptible
imperdible ADJ that shouldn't be missed; **una película —** a must-see movie; M safety pin
imperecedero ADJ undying
imperfecto ADJ & M imperfect
imperial ADJ imperial
imperialismo M imperialism
impericia F lack of skill
imperio M (organización política) empire; (gobierno) rule; **— industrial** manufacturing empire
imperioso ADJ (mandón) imperious; (necesario)

imperative
impermeabilizar[47] VT to waterproof
impermeable ADJ (al agua) waterproof; (a la crítica) impervious; M raincoat, slicker
impersonal ADJ impersonal
impertinencia F (actitud) impertinence, impudence; (réplica) backtalk
impertinente ADJ impertinent, impudent
impétigo M impetigo
ímpetu M impetus
impetuoso ADJ impetuous, brash
impida, impide, impidiendo, impidiera, impidiese *ver* impedir
impío ADJ godless
implacable ADJ implacable, relentless
implantación F (de un diente) implantation; (de una costumbre, sistema) establishment, introduction
implantar VT to implant
implante M implant; **— dental** dental implant
implementación F implementation
implementar VT to implement
implemento M implement
implicación F (lógica) implication; (en un delito) involvement
implicar[30] VT (involucrar) to implicate, to involve; (conllevar) to entail
implícitamente ADV implicitly, by implication
implícito ADJ implicit
implorar VI/VT to implore
impondrá, impondría *ver* imponer
imponente ADJ (impresionante) imposing; (espantoso) forbidding
imponer[56, 74] VT to impose, to force upon; (gravar) to assess; **—se** to get one's way
imponible ADJ taxable
impopular ADJ unpopular
importación F import
importancia F importance
importante ADJ (persona) important; (cantidad) substantial; (tema, asunto) weighty; (suceso, ocasión) momentous
importar VI (ser importante) to matter; **me importa un comino** I don't give a hoot; **no importa** it makes no difference; VT (introducir productos) to import
importe M amount
importunar VT to besiege
importuno ADJ inopportune
imposibilidad F impossibility
imposibilitar VT to make impossible
imposible ADJ impossible
imposición F (de ideas) imposition; (de impuestos) assessment
impositivo ADJ **sistema —** tax system
impostor -ora MF impostor, fraud
impotencia F impotence
impotente ADJ (sin poder) powerless; (sin libido) impotent

impreciso ADJ inaccurate

impredecible ADJ unpredictable

impregnar VT to impregnate

impremeditado ADJ unpremeditated

imprenta F (arte, oficio) printing; (máquina) press, printing press

imprescindible ADJ indispensable

impresión F (efecto en el ánimo) impression; (acción de imprimir) printing; (huella) imprint

impresionante ADJ (logro) impressive, imposing; (edificio) grand, imposing; (panorama) breathtaking

impresionar VT to impress; **—se** to be overwhelmed; **para** — for show

impreso M printed matter

impresor -ora MF (persona) printer; F (aparato) printer; **impresora de burbuja** bubble-jet printer; **impresora de inyección de tinta** ink-jet printer; **impresora en serie** serial printer; **impresora gráfica** plotter; **impresora láser** laser printer; **impresora local** local printer

imprevisible ADJ unpredictable

imprevisto ADJ unforeseen; M unforeseen event

imprimir[74] VI/VT (producir un impreso) to print; (marcar con presión) to imprint

improbable ADJ improbable, unlikely

improductivo ADJ unproductive

impromptu M impromptu

impropio ADJ (inadecuado) unbecoming; (atípico) atypical

improvisación F improvisation, role-playing

improvisado ADJ impromptu

improvisando ADV ad lib

improvisar VI/VT to improvise

improviso LOC ADV **de** — all of a sudden

imprudencia F (actitud) recklessness; (acción) reckless act

imprudente ADJ unwise, ill-advised

impublicable ADJ unprintable

impúdico ADJ immodest

impuesto M tax, duty; **—a la herencia** inheritance tax; **—s atrasados** back taxes; **— de tasa única** flat tax; **— de sucesión** inheritance tax; **—s** taxation; **— sobre ingresos** income tax; **— sobre las donaciones** gift tax; **— sobre las ventas** sales tax; **— sobre rentas** income tax

impuesto ver imponer

impugnar VT to contest, to dispute

impulsar VT (empujar) to propel, to drive; (estimular) to boost

impulsivo ADJ impulsive

impulso M (estímulo) boost; (deseo espontáneo) impulse, urge

impune ADJ unpunished

impunidad F impunity

impureza F impurity

impuro ADJ (sustancia) impure; (pensamiento) impure, unclean

impuse, impusiera, impusiese ver imponer

inacabado ADJ unfinished

inaccesible ADJ inaccessible

inaceptable ADJ (inadmisible) unacceptable; (insuficiente) inadequate

inacostumbrado ADJ unwonted

inactividad F inactivity

inactivo ADJ inactive

inadaptado -da ADJ maladjusted; MF misfit

inadecuado ADJ unsuitable

inadmisible ADJ (comportamiento) unacceptable; (pruebas) inadmissible

inadvertido ADJ unnoticed, unobserved

inagotable ADJ (recursos) inexhaustible; (optimismo) unfailing

inaguantable ADJ unbearable

inalámbrico ADJ cordless, wireless

inalterable ADJ unalterable, unchangeable

inalterado ADJ unchanged

inamovible ADJ immovable

inanición F starvation

inanimado ADJ inanimate

inapetencia F lack of appetite

inapreciable ADJ (invalorable) invaluable; (muy pequeño) too small to be seen

inapropiado ADJ unsuitable

inasequible ADJ inaccessible

inaudible ADJ inaudible

inaudito ADJ (historia, situación) unheard-of, unprecedented; (sufrimiento) untold

inauguración F (de un gobierno) inauguration; (de un monumento) dedication

inaugurar VT (un gobierno) to inaugurate; (un monumento) to dedicate

inca ADJ & MF Inca

incalculable ADJ untold

incandescencia F glow

incandescente ADJ incandescent, glowing

incansable ADJ untiring, tireless

incapacidad F inability

incapacitar VT to disable, to incapacitate

incapaz ADJ incapable

incautación F seizure

incauto ADJ unwary

incendiar VT to set fire to; VI/VT to burn; **—se** to catch fire, to burn down

incendiario -ria ADJ incendiary; MF arsonist

incendio M fire, blaze, conflagration; **— doloso** arson; **— forestal** forest fire

incentivo M incentive, inducement

incertidumbre F uncertainty, suspense

incesante ADJ incessant, ceaseless

incesto M incest

incestuoso ADJ incestuous

incidencia F incidence

incidental ADJ incidental

incidente M incident

incidir VI **—en un asunto** to affect/influence a situation

incienso M incense

incierto ADJ uncertain

incinerar VT to incinerate

incipiente ADJ incipient

incisión F incision

incisivo ADJ incisive; M incisor

incitar VT to incite, to whip up

incivilizado ADJ uncivilized

inclemencia F **las —s del tiempo** foul weather

inclemente ADJ inclement, foul

inclinación F (tendencia) inclination, bent, disposition; (acción de inclinar) tilting; (posición inclinada) tilt; (de un techo) slant; (del terreno) slope; (de opinión) bias

inclinar VT (ladear) to tilt; (bajar) to hang; **— la cabeza** to hang one's head; **—se** (doblarse en la cintura) to bend over; (tener tendencia a) to tend; (hacer una reverencia) to bow

incluido ADJ included; **con todo —** all-inclusive

incluir[19] VT (incorporar) to include; (abarcar) to include, to comprise; **incluyéndote a ti, somos cuatro** including you, there are four of us

inclusión F inclusion; **con — de** including

inclusive ADV even

inclusivo ADJ inclusive

incluso ADV even

incluya, incluye, incluyendo, incluyera, incluyese ver incluir

incobrable ADJ noncollectible, uncollectable

incógnita F unknown [quantity]

incógnito LOC ADV **de —** incognito

incoherente ADJ incoherent

incoloro ADJ colorless

incomestible ADJ inedible

incomformista ADJ & MF nonconformist

incomible ADJ inedible

incomodar VT to inconvenience

incomodidad F uneasiness

incómodo ADJ (silla) uncomfortable; (situación) awkward, inconvenient; (baúl) cumbersome; (silencio) uneasy; (que siente molestia) ill at ease

incomparable ADJ incomparable, peerless

incompatible ADJ incompatible

incompetente ADJ incompetent

incompleto ADJ incomplete

incomprensible ADJ incomprehensible

incomunicación F disconnect, miscommunication

inconcebible ADJ inconceivable

inconcluso ADJ unfinished

incondicional ADJ unconditional, unqualified

inconexo ADJ disconnected

inconformista MF nonconformist

inconfundible ADJ unmistakable

inconsciente ADJ (sin sentido) unconscious, senseless; (ignorante) unaware, oblivious

inconsecuencia F inconsistency

inconsecuente ADJ inconsistent

inconsolable ADJ heartbroken

inconstancia F inconstancy

inconstante ADJ inconstant, changeable

inconstitucional ADJ unconstitutional

incontable ADJ countless

incontenible ADJ uncontrollable

incontinente ADJ incontinent

incontrolable ADJ uncontrollable

incontrovertible ADJ incontrovertible

inconveniencia F inconvenience

inconveniente ADJ improper; M inconvenience, downside

incorporación F (inclusión) inclusion; (asimilación) incorporation

incorporado ADJ built-in

incorporar VT (incluir) to include; (asimilar) to incorporate; (agregar) to build into; **—se** (erguirse) to sit up

incorrectamente ADV incorrectly, wrongly

incorrecto ADJ incorrect, wrong

incorregible ADJ incorrigible

incredulidad F disbelief

incrédulo ADJ incredulous

increíble ADJ (inverosímil) incredible, unbelievable; (extraordinario) amazing

incrementar VT to augment

incremento M increment, increase

incriminar VT to incriminate

incrustación F inlay

incrustado ADJ (en piedra) embedded; (joyas) inlaid

incrustar VT (piedra) to embed; (oro) to inlay; **—se en** to become embedded in

incubadora F incubator

incuestionable ADJ unquestionable

inculcar[30] VT to inculcate, to instill

inculto ADJ (sin modales) uncultured, unrefined; (sin instrucción) uneducated

incumbencia F **no es de tu —** it's none of your business

incumplimiento M (de contrato) breach; (de deberes) nonperformance; (de deudas) default; (de metas) failure to accomplish; (de promesas) failure to keep

incumplir VT (contratos) to breach; (deberes) to fail to perform; (deudas) to default on; (metas) to fail to accomplish; (promesas) to renege on, to fail to keep

incurable ADJ incurable

incurrir VI **— en** (una deuda, un gasto) to incur; (un error) to fall into

incursión F raid, foray

incursionar VI to foray

indagación F investigation, probe

indagar[40] VI/VT to investigate, to inquire into

indebido ADJ improper

indecencia F indecency

indecente ADJ indecent

indecible ADJ unspeakable

indecisión F indecision

indeciso ADJ (que no ha decidido) undecided; (que suele vacilar) wishy-washy

indecoroso ADJ improper

indefendible ADJ indefensible

indefenso ADJ defenseless

indefinible ADJ indefinable

indefinido ADJ (plazo) indefinite; (silueta) undefined

indeleble ADJ indelible

indelicado ADJ indelicate

indemnización F (resarcimiento) indemnity; (de guerra) reparation; (de un pleito) recovery; **— por despido** severance pay

indemnizar[47] VT to indemnify

independencia F independence; (de un individuo) self-reliance

independiente ADJ independent

indescriptible ADJ indescribable

indeseable ADJ undesirable, unwelcome

indestructible ADJ indestructible

indeterminado ADJ indeterminate, undetermined

indexación F indexing

indexar VT to index

India F India

indicación F (señal) indication; (instrucción) instruction; **indicaciones** directions

indicador M pointer, indicator; **— clave** key indicator; **—es anticipados** leading indicators

indicar[30] VT (señalar) to indicate, to point out; (registrar) to read, to register; (mostrar) to show

indicativo ADJ & M indicative

índice M (lista alfabética) index; (tabla de materias) table of contents; (dedo) index finger; **— de confianza del consumidor** consumer confidence index; **— de mortalidad** mortality rate; **— de precios al consumidor** consumer price index

indicio M clue, sign

Índico M Océano **—** Indian Ocean

indiferencia F indifference; (frialdad) coolness

indiferente ADJ (apático) indifferent, unconcerned; (frío) cool; (sin entusiasmo) lukewarm; (no conmovido) unmoved; **esa chica me es —** I don't care about that girl

indígena ADJ indigenous; MF native

indigente ADJ destitute, indigent

indigestión F indigestion

indignación F indignation

indignado ADJ indignant

indignar VT to make indignant; **—se** to become indignant

indigno ADJ unworthy

índigo M indigo

indio -dia ADJ & MF Indian

indirecta F hint

indirecto ADJ (estilo, consecuencia) indirect; (ruta) roundabout

indisciplinado ADJ unruly

indiscreción F indiscretion

indiscreto ADJ indiscreet

indiscutible ADJ unquestionable

indispensable ADJ indispensable

indisponer[56, 74] VT to indispose; **—se** to become indisposed

indispuesto ADJ (disgustado) upset; (enfermo) indisposed

indistinto ADJ indistinct, vague

individual ADJ (derechos) individual; (habitación) single; **—es** singles

individualidad F individuality

individualismo M individualism

individualista ADJ & MF individualist

individuo ADJ & M individual

indivisible ADJ indivisible

indiviso ADJ undivided

indocumentado -da ADJ (carta) undocumented; (persona) without identity papers; MF illegal immigrant

índole F type

indolencia F indolence

indolente ADJ indolent

indoloro ADJ painless

indomable ADJ indomitable

indomado ADJ unbroken

Indonesia F Indonesia

indonesio -sia ADJ & MF Indonesian

inducción F induction

inducir[38] VT to induce, to prompt

indudable ADJ undeniable; unquestionable

indudablemente ADV undoubtedly

indulgencia F indulgence

indulgente ADJ indulgent, lenient

indultar VT to pardon

indulto M pardon

indumentaria F apparel

industria F industry, trade; **— petrolera** oil industry

industrial ADJ industrial; MF industrialist

industrialización F industrialization

industrioso ADJ industrious

inédito ADJ unpublished

inefable ADJ ineffable

ineficaz ADJ ineffective, ineffectual

ineficiente ADJ inefficient

inelegible ADJ ineligible

ineludible ADJ inescapable, unavoidable

inempleable ADJ unemployable

inepto ADJ inept

inequívoco ADJ unequivocal

inercia F inertia

inerte ADJ inert

inescrutable ADJ inscrutable

inesperado ADJ unexpected

inestabilidad F instability

inestable ADJ (personalidad, estructura) unstable; (andar) unsteady

inestimable ADJ inestimable, invaluable

inevitable ADJ (conclusión) inevitable; (accidente) unavoidable

inexacto ADJ inaccurate

inexcusable ADJ inexcusable

inexistente ADJ nonexistent

inexorable ADJ inexorable

inexperto ADJ (trabajador) inexperienced, unskilled; (ojo) untrained

inexplicable ADJ inexplicable

inexpresivo ADJ inexpressive, wooden

infalible ADJ (a toda prueba) infallible, foolproof; (confiable) unfailing

infame ADJ infamous

infamia F infamy

infancia F childhood

infante -ta MF (hijo -ja del rey) infante -ta; M (soldado) infantryman

infantería F infantry; **— de marina** marine corps

infantil ADJ (como niño) childlike; (aniñado) childish, infantile

infarto M infarction, heart attack; **— cardíaco** heart attack; **— cerebral** stroke, cerebral infarction; **— del miocardio** myocardial infarction

infección F infection; **— del tracto urinario** urinary tract infection; **— respiratoria alta** upper respiratory infection

infeccioso ADJ infectious

infectar VT to infect; **—se** to become infected

infecto ADJ foul, repugnant

infelicidad F misery

infeliz ADJ unhappy, wretched, miserable; MF poor wretch

inferencia F inference

inferior ADJ (en calidad) inferior, subpar; (en posición) lower

inferioridad F inferiority

inferir[8] VT to infer

infernal ADJ (calor) infernal; (ruido) unholy

infertilidad F infertility

infestación F infestation

infestar VT to infest

infiel ADJ unfaithful, faithless, untrue

infierno M (bíblico) hell; (lugar caliente) inferno; **en el quinto —** in the middle of nowhere

infinidad F infinity; **una — de** a large number of

infinitivo ADJ & M infinitive

infinito ADJ infinite; M infinity

inflación F inflation; **— básica** core inflation

inflado ADJ bloated; M pumping up

inflamable ADJ flammable

inflamación F inflammation

inflamar VT to inflame; **—se** to become inflamed

inflar VT (neumáticos) to inflate, to pump up; (globos) to blow up; (precios) to balloon

inflexible ADJ (rígido) inflexible; (testarudo) unbending, adamant

infligir[46] VT to inflict

influencia F influence, pull, clout; (sobre las masas) sway

influir[19] VI **— en/sobre** to influence; (las masas) to sway

influjo M influence

influya, influye, influyendo, influyera, influyese ver influir

influyente ADJ influential

infomercial M infomercial

información F information; (periodística) story

informal ADJ (no formal) informal, casual; (poco fiable) unreliable

informante MF (para un estudio) informant; (de la policía) informer

informar VT (enterar) to inform, to appraise; (un militar) to debrief; (un periodista) to report; (un abogado) to advise; **—se** to become informed

informática F computer science, information technology

informático -ca ADJ computing; MF computer specialist

informativo ADJ informative; M (televisión, radio) news program

informatizar[47] VT to computerize

informe M (de noticias) report; (militar) debriefing; **— de crédito** credit report; **—s de guía** information; ADJ shapeless

infortunio M misfortune

infracción F (de reglamentos) infraction, infringement; (de contrato) breach; (de tránsito) violation; (en deportes) penalty

infractor -ora MF lawbreaker

infraestructura F infrastructure

infrarrojo ADJ & M infrared

infrascrito -ta MF undersigned

infravalorado ADJ underrated, undervalued

infringir[46] VT to infringe, to breach, to violate

infructuoso ADJ fruitless, unsuccessful

ínfulas F PL airs; **darse —** to put on airs

infundado ADJ groundless, unfounded

infundir VT to infuse, to imbue

infusionar VT to steep

ingeniar VT to contrive; **ingeniárselas para** to contrive to

ingeniería F engineering; **— genética** genetic engineering; **— química** chemical engineering

ngeniero -ra MF engineer; **— civil** civil engineer; **— electricista** electrical engineer; **— en computación** computer engineer; **— informático** computer engineer

ngenio M (mental) ingenuity, cleverness; (verbal) wit; (artefacto) artifact; **— de azúcar** (refinería) sugar refinery, sugar mill; (plantación) sugar plantation

ngeniosidad F ingenuity

ngenioso ADJ ingenious, resourceful

ngenuidad F ingenuousness, naïveté

ngenuo -nua ADJ (inocente) naive, ingenuous; (crédulo) gullible; MF dupe

ngerir VI/VT to ingest

ngestión F ingestion

ngle F groin

nglés -esa ADJ English; M Englishman; (lengua) English; F Englishwoman

ngobernable ADJ unruly

ngratitud F ingratitude

ngrato -ta ADJ thankless, ungrateful; MF ingrate

ngrávido ADJ weightless

ngrediente M ingredient; **ese libro tiene todos los —s de un éxito** that book has all the makings of a best seller

ngresar VT (datos) to input; (dinero en una cuenta) to deposit; VI (a un hospital) to be admitted; (a un sistema) to log in

ngreso M (permiso para entrar) entrance, entry; (depósito bancario) deposit; (renta) income; **—s** (de una firma) earnings; (del estado) revenue; **— bruto** gross income; **— neto ajustado** adjusted net income; **—s discrecionales** discretionary income; **—s disponibles** disposable income

nhábil ADJ unskilled

nhabilidad F inability

nhabilitar VT to disqualify

nhalación F inhalation; **— de humo** smoke inhalation

nhalar VI/VT to breathe in, to inhale

nherente ADJ inherent

nhibición F inhibition

nhibidor ADJ inhibiting; M inhibitor

nhibir VT to inhibit

nhospitalario ADJ inhospitable

nhóspito ADJ inhospitable

nhumano ADJ inhuman

niciación M initiation, induction

nicial ADJ initial; (pago) up-front; F (letra) initial; (béisbol) first base

nicialista MF first baseman

nicializar[47] VT to initialize

nicialmente ADV initially

niciar VT (conversaciones) to initiate; (en un grupo) to induct; (software) to launch; (computadora) to boot up; (negociaciones) to enter

iniciativa F initiative

inicio M beginning, start

inimitable ADJ inimitable

inflamable ADJ fireproof

ininteligible ADJ unintelligible

ininterrumpido ADJ unbroken, uninterrupted

injerencia F interference

injertar VT to graft

injerto M graft; **— óseo** bone graft

injugable ADJ unplayable

injuria F (insulto) insult, verbal abuse; (daño) damage

injuriar VT to insult, to abuse verbally

injurioso ADJ insulting, injurious, verbally abusive

injustamente ADV unjustly, unfairly, wrongly

injusticia F (desigualdad) injustice; (acto injusto) wrong; (error judicial) miscarriage of justice

injustificable ADJ unjustifiable

injustificado ADJ uncalled-for, unwarranted

injusto ADJ unjust, unfair

inmaculado ADJ immaculate, spotless

inmaduro ADJ immature

inmanejable ADJ unmanageable

inmaterial ADJ immaterial

inmediaciones F PL vicinity

inmediato ADJ immediate, instant; **de —** at once

inmensidad F immensity, vastness

inmenso ADJ immense, vast

inmerso ADJ (en agua) submerged; (en el trabajo) absorbed; (en un tema, una situación) immersed

inmerecido ADJ unearned

inmigración F immigration

inmigrante ADJ & MF immigrant

inmigrar VI to immigrate

inminente ADJ imminent, impending

inmiscuir[19] VI to mix; **—se** to meddle

inmodestia F immodesty

inmodesto ADJ immodest

inmoral ADJ immoral

inmoralidad F immorality

inmortal ADJ & MF immortal

inmortalidad F immortality

inmóvil ADJ motionless, immobile

inmovilizar[47] VT (impedir los movimientos) to immobilize; (contra el suelo) to pin

inmueble M building

inmune ADJ immune

inmunidad F immunity

inmunodeficiencia F immunodeficiency

inmutable ADJ unchangeable, immutable

innato ADJ innate, inborn

innecesario ADJ unnecessary, needless

innegable ADJ undeniable

innoble ADJ ignoble

innocuo ADJ innocuous, harmless

innovación F innovation

innovador -ora ADJ innovating, innovative; MF innovator

innovar VI to innovate; VT to modernize

innumerable ADJ innumerable, countless

inocencia F innocence

inocente ADJ innocent, guiltless; MF dupe

inocuo ADJ innocuous, harmless

inodoro ADJ odorless; M toilet, commode

inofensivo ADJ inoffensive, harmless

inolvidable ADJ unforgettable

inoperable ADJ inoperable

inoportuno ADJ inopportune, untimely

inorgánico ADJ inorganic

inoxidable ADJ rustproof

inquietante ADJ distressing, worrisome

inquietar VT to worry

inquieto ADJ (movedizo) restless; (preocupado) uneasy

inquietud F (intranquilidad) restlessness; (preocupación) alarm, concern

inquilino -na MF (de un apartamento) tenant, renter; (de una pensión) lodger

inquina F spite

inquirir[4] VI/VT to inquire

inquisición F inquisition

inquisitivo ADJ inquisitive

insaciable ADJ insatiable

insalubre ADJ unhealthy, unsanitary

insatisfactorio ADJ unsatisfactory

insatisfecho ADJ dissatisfied, unhappy

inscribir[74] VT (grabar) to inscribe; (matricular) to register, to enroll; —**se** to register, to enroll

inscripción F (grabado) inscription; (matriculación) registration, enrollment

insecticida M insecticide

insectívoro ADJ insectivorous

insecto M insect

inseguridad F insecurity; **la — urbana** the lack of safety in cities / the city

inseguro ADJ (personalidad) insecure; (vehículo) unsafe; (andar) unsteady; (computadora) vulnerable to hacking

inseminación F insemination

insensato -ta ADJ foolish; MF fool

insensibilizar[47] VT to desensitize

insensible ADJ (cruel) insensitive, callous; (imperturbable) unfeeling, thick-skinned; (entumecido) numb

inseparable ADJ inseparable

inserción F insertion

insertar VT to insert

inservible ADJ useless

insidioso ADJ insidious

insigne ADJ famous

insignia F insignia, badge

insignificante ADJ insignificant, unimportant

insincero ADJ insincere

insinuación F (sugerencia) insinuation; (comentario sexual) innuendo

insinuante ADJ suggestive

insinuar[26] VT to insinuate, to suggest; —**se** to insinuate oneself

insípido ADJ insipid, flavorless

insistencia F (machaconería, testarudez) insistence; (perseverancia) persistence

insistente ADJ (testarudo, repetitivo) insistent; (perseverante) persistent

insistir VI/VT (repetir) to insist; (perseverar) to persist; — **en** to insist on; — **sobre** to harp o[n]

insolación F (por sol) sunstroke; (por calor) heatstroke

insolencia F (falta de respeto) insolence; (comentario) smart remark

insolente ADJ insolent, sassy

insólito ADJ (situación) unusual; (accidente) freak, freakish

insoluble ADJ insoluble

insolvente ADJ insolvent

insomne ADJ wakeful, unable to sleep

insomnio M insomnia

insoportable ADJ (persona, conducta) unbearable, impossible; (dolor) excruciating, unbearable

insospechado ADJ unsuspected

insostenible ADJ untenable

inspección F (revisación) inspection; (encuesta) canvass

inspeccionar VT to inspect, to survey

inspector -ora MF inspector

inspiración F (idea) inspiration; (inhalación) inhalation

inspirar VI/VT to inspire; VI to inhale, to breath[e] in

instalación F (de programas, fontanería) installation; (de aparatos electrónicos) setup; **instalaciones** fixtures

instalar VT (programas, fontanería) to install; (aparatos electrónicos) to set up; —**se** to take up residence

instancia LOC ADV **a —s de** at the request of

instantánea F snapshot

instantáneo ADJ instantaneous

instante M instant; **al —** right away

instar VT to enjoin

instauración F establishment

instigador -ra MF instigator

instigar[40] VT to instigate, to abet

instintivo ADJ instinctive

instinto M instinct; — **suicida** death wish

institución F institution; — **benéfica** charity

institucional ADJ institutional

instituir[19] VT to institute

instituto M (institución, agencia) institute; (escuela secundaria) high school

institutriz F governess

instrucción F instruction, schooling

instructivo ADJ instructive
instructor -ora MF instructor
instruir[19] VT to instruct, to school
instrumental ADJ instrumental
instrumentar VT (un plan) to implement; (música) to do the instrumentation for
instrumento M instrument; **— de cuerda** string instrument; **— de metal** brass instrument; **— de percusión** percussion instrument; **— de viento** wind instrument; **—s quirúrgicos** surgical instruments
insubordinado ADJ insubordinate
insuficiencia F (incapacidad) insufficiency; (falla de los órganos) failure; **— cardíaca congestiva** congestive heart failure; **— coronaria** coronary failure; **— renal** kidney failure, renal failure; **— respiratoria** respiratory failure
insuficiente ADJ insufficient, inadequate
insufrible ADJ insufferable
insulina F insulin
insulso ADJ bland
insultar VT to insult
insulto M insult; put-down
insuperable ADJ (resultado) insuperable; (obstáculo) insurmountable
insurgente ADJ & MF insurgent
insurrección F insurrection
insurrecto -ta ADJ rebellious; MF rebel
intachable ADJ blameless
intacto ADJ intact, unbroken
intangible ADJ intangible
integración F (de razas) integration; (de elementos) incorporation
integral ADJ (parte) integral; ADJ (harina) whole-grain
integrante ADJ integral
integrar VT (crear) to form; (ser miembro de) to be a member of
integridad F integrity
íntegro ADJ (objeto) whole; (texto) unabridged; (comportamiento) upright
intelecto M intellect
intelectual ADJ & MF intellectual
inteligencia F intelligence (también militar); (persona) mind; **— artificial** artificial intelligence
inteligente ADJ intelligent, bright, smart
inteligible ADJ intelligible
intemperie LOC ADV **a la —** exposed to the weather
intención F intention, intent
intencional ADJ intentional
intendente MF (civil) administrator; (militar) quartermaster general
intensidad F intensity
intensificar[30] VT to intensify; **—se** (frío) to intensify; (violencia) to escalate
intensivo ADJ intensive

intenso ADJ (actividad) intense; (debate) fierce; (calor) severe
intentar VI/VT to try; VT to attempt
intento M (tentativa) try, attempt; (propósito) intention
interacción F interaction
interactivo ADJ interactive
interactuar[26] VI to interact
intercalación F insertion
intercalar VT to insert
intercambiador M interchange
intercambiar VI/VT to exchange
intercambio M exchange
interceder VI to intercede
interceptación F interception (también en fútbol americano)
interceptar VT intercept (también en fútbol americano)
intercesión F intercession
intercesor -ora MF advocate
interés M (intelectual, financiero) interest; (preocupación) concern; (participación comercial) stake; **— compuesto** compound interest; **— mutuo** mutual interest; **intereses ocultos** hidden agenda
interesado ADJ (atento) interested; (preocupado) concerned; (egoísta) self-serving
interesante ADJ interesting
interesar VT to interest; **—se por** to become interested in
interestatal ADJ interstate
interestelar ADJ interstellar
interface MF interface
interfaz MF interface; **— digital de instrumentos musicales** musical instrument digital interface
interferencia F (en los negocios ajenos) interference; (en una transmisión) interference, static; **— externa** outside interference
interferir[8] VT to jam; VI to interfere
interferón M interferon
ínterin M interim; **en el —** meanwhile
interino ADJ acting, interim
interior ADJ (habitación) inside; (mundo, vida) inner; (zona geográfica) inland; (mercado, comercio) domestic; M (parte) inside part, interior; **el — de la caja** the inside of the box; (de un país) the country, the provinces; **una ciudad del —** a provincial town
interiorizar[47] VT to internalize
interjección F interjection
interlineal ADJ interlinear
interlock M interlock
interlocutor -ora MF interlocutor
interludio M interlude
intermediario -ria M middleman; MF (mensajero) go-between; ADJ intermediary

intermediarista MF second baseman

intermedio-a ADJ intermediate; M intermission; **por — de** through; F (béisbol) second base

interminable ADJ interminable, unending, endless

intermitente ADJ intermittent; M turn signal

internación F inpatient care

internacional ADJ international

internado-da M (escuela) boarding school; (práctica) internship; MF (alumno) boarding student; (en un hospital) patient

internalizar⁴⁷ VT to internalize

internar VT (en una cárcel) to intern; (en un hospital) to admit, to hospitalize; (en un hospital psiquiátrico) to commit

internauta MF Internet user

internet M Internet, web; **— inalámbrico** wireless Internet; **— móvil** mobile Internet

internista MF internist

interno-na ADJ (correo) internal; (mercado) domestic; MF (persona que vive internada) inmate; (residente médico) intern

interpersonal ADJ interpersonal

interponer⁵⁶,⁷⁴ VT to interpose; **—se** to intervene

interpretación F (de un texto) interpretation; (artística) performance, rendition

interpretar VT (ideas) to interpret; (música) to perform; (intenciones) to construe

intérprete MF (traductor, explicador) interpreter; (músico) artist, performer

interracial ADJ interracial

interrelacionado ADJ interrelated

interrogación F interrogation

interrogador-ora MF questioner; ADJ questioning

interrogar⁴⁰ VI/VT (la policía) to interrogate; (con intensidad) to grill; (a un testigo) to question, to cross-examine

interrogativo ADJ interrogative

interrogatorio M interrogation, questioning

interrumpir VI/VT (cortar) to interrupt; VT (servicios) to disrupt, to cut off; (producción de un modelo) to discontinue; (en una conversación) to intrude, to cut in; (software) to abort

interrupción F interruption; (en una conversación) intrusion; (de producción) stoppage; (software) abort

interruptor M switch

intersección F intersection

intersticio M interstice

intervalo M (período) interval; (en el teatro) intermission, interlude

intervención F intervention; **— de teléfono** wiretap

intervendrá, intervendría, intervenga, intervengo ver intervenir

intervenir⁶¹ VI to intervene; **— un teléfono** to wiretap

interventor-ora ADJ controlling, intervening; MF (en las elecciones) observer; (en lo fiscal) auditor

intervine, interviniendo, interviniera, interviniese ver intervenir

interviú F interview

intestino ADJ & M intestine; **— delgado** small intestine; **— grueso** large intestine; **—s** bowels

intimar VI to become friendly

intimidad F intimacy

intimidar VT (una persona) to intimidate; (una tarea) to daunt

íntimo ADJ intimate, close

intitular VT to entitle; **—se** to be entitled

intolerable ADJ intolerable

intolerancia F intolerance, bigotry; **— a la lactosa** lactose intolerance

intolerante ADJ intolerant, narrow-minded

intoxicación F intoxication, poisoning; **— con plomo** lead poisoning; **— por alimentos** food poisoning

intoxicar¹⁰ VT to poison, to intoxicate

intransigente ADJ intransigent, uncompromising

intransitivo ADJ intransitive

intravenoso ADJ IV [intravenous]

intrepidez F fearlessness

intrépido ADJ (sin miedo) intrepid, fearless; (aventurero) adventurous

intriga F intrigue

intrigante MF schemer; ADJ scheming

intrigar⁴⁰ VI/VT to intrigue, to scheme

intrincado ADJ intricate

intrínseco ADJ intrinsic

introducción F introduction

introducir³⁸ VT (incorporar) to introduce; (colocar) to put in, to insert

introduzca, introduzco ver introducir

introspección F introspection

introvertido-da ADJ introverted; MF introvert

intrusión F intrusion

intrusivo ADJ intrusive

intruso-sa ADJ intruding; MF intruder

intubación F intubation

intuición F intuition

intuir¹⁹ VT to sense

intuitivo ADJ intuitive

inundación F flood

inundar VI/VT (de agua, de pedidos) to inundate, to flood; (de regalos) to shower

inusitado ADJ unusual

inútil ADJ (medida) useless, pointless; (esfuerzo) futile; (persona) worthless, good-for-nothing

inutilidad F uselessness; (de un esfuerzo) futility

inutilizar⁴⁷ VT to render useless, to put out of

commission
invadir VI/VT to invade
invalidar VT to render invalid
inválido -da ADJ (discapacitado) invalid; (nulo) void; MF invalid
invalorable ADJ priceless, invaluable
invariable ADJ invariable
invasión F invasion
invasivo ADJ invasive
invasor -ora MF invader; ADJ invading
invencible ADJ invincible
invención F invention (también mentira); (mental) construct
inventar VT (un dispositivo) to invent; (una historia) to fabricate, to make up
inventariar[28] VT to inventory
inventario M inventory
inventiva F ingenuity
inventivo ADJ inventive
invento M invention
inventor -ora MF inventor
invernadero M greenhouse, hothouse; **efecto — ** greenhouse effect
invernal ADJ wintry
invernar[1] VI to winter
inverosímil ADJ unlikely, farfetched
inversión F (trasposición) inversion; (financiera) investment
inversionista MF investor
inverso ADJ inverse, reverse; **a la inversa** the other way around
inversor -ora MF investor
invertir[8] VT (dar vuelta) to invert, to reverse; VI/VT (dinero) to invest
investidura F inauguration, investment
investigación F (policial) investigation, inquiry; (científica) research
investigador -ora MF investigator; (científico) researcher
investigar[40] VI/VT (policía) to investigate, to look into; (científico) to research
investir[9] VI/VT to invest; **— de un cargo** to induct into office
invicto ADJ unbeaten
invierno M winter
invierta, invierte, invirtiendo, invirtiera, invirtiese, invirtió ver invertir
invisible ADJ (no visible) invisible; (oculto) unseen
invitación F invitation
invitado -da MF guest
invitar VI/VT to invite
invocación F invocation
invocar[30] VT (razones, argumentos) to invoke; (espíritu) to conjure
involucrar VT (implicar) to implicate; (consistir de) to involve
involuntario ADJ (automático) involuntary; (accidental) inadvertent

inyección F (en medicina) injection, shot; (en coches) fuel injection
inyectado ADJ **— de sangre** bloodshot
inyectar VT to inject
ion, ión M ion
ionizar[47] VT to ionize
ir[64] VI to go; **— a caballo** to ride horseback; **— a pie** to walk; **— [a] por** to fetch; **— aprendiendo** to learn gradually; **— corriendo** to run; **— de mal en peor** to go from bad to worse; **— en coche** to drive/ride in a car; **— tirando** to scrape along; **no me va ni me viene** it's all the same to me; **¿cómo te va?** how are you? **los platos no van aquí** the plates don't belong here; **¡vaya!** well now! **¡vaya a saber uno!** go figure! **¡vamos!** let's go! come on! **¡vaya hombre!** what a man! **¡ve a freír espárragos!** take a hike! **va por dos años que me casé** it's going on two years since I got married; **voy a comer** I'm going to eat; **va y se come un hongo venenoso** she goes and eats a poisonous mushroom; **en lo que va del año** since the beginning of the year; **ya van siete veces que me lo dice** that makes seven times that she's told me; **voy a ir de rojo** I'm going dressed in red; **para que no vayas a creer** lest you should think; **no vayas a caerte** don't fall; **¡qué va!** no way! **—se** to go away, to leave; **—se a la quiebra** to go broke; **—se a las manos** to come to blows; **—se a pique** to founder; **—se de vacaciones** to take a vacation
ira F ire, wrath
Irak M Iraq
Irán M Iran
iraní ADJ & MF Iranian
iraquí ADJ & MF Iraqi
irascible ADJ irascible, quick-tempered
iridiscente ADJ iridescent
iris M iris
Irlanda F Ireland
irlandés -esa MF Irish; ADJ Irish
IRM [imagen por resonancia magnética] F MRI
ironía F irony
irónico ADJ ironic, wry
irracional ADJ irrational, unreasonable
irradiar VT to radiate, to irradiate
irreal ADJ unreal
irreconocible ADJ unrecognizable
irrecuperable ADJ irretrievable
irreflexivo ADJ thoughtless
irrefutable ADJ irrefutable
irregular ADJ (situación) irregular; (borde, filo) ragged; (pulso) unsteady; (superficie) rough, uneven; (comportamiento) erratic, haphazard
irregularidad F irregularity

irremediable ADJ hopeless
irremplazable ADJ irreplaceable
irreparable ADJ irreparable
irreprochable ADJ irreproachable, flawless
irresistible ADJ irresistible
irrespetuoso ADJ disrespectful
irresponsabilidad F irresponsibility
irresponsable ADJ irresponsible
irreverente ADJ irreverent
irreversible ADJ irreversible
irrevocable ADJ irrevocable
irrigación F irrigation
irrigar[40] VI/VT to irrigate
irritable ADJ irritable
irritación F irritation
irritante ADJ (molesto) irritating, grating; (agresivo) abrasive
irritar VI/VT to irritate, to aggravate
irrumpir VI to burst into
isla F island, isle; **—s Fiyi** Fiji Islands; **—s Malvinas** Falkland Islands; **—s Marshall** Marshall Islands; **—s Salomón** Solomon Islands; **—s Vírgenes** Virgin Islands
islam, Islam M Islam
islámico ADJ Islamic
islamismo M Islam
islandés -esa MF Icelander; ADJ Icelandic
Islandia F Iceland
isleño -ña MF islander
isobara F isobar
isométrico ADJ isometric
isótopo M isotope
Israel M Israel
israelí ADJ & MF Israeli
istmo M isthmus
Italia F Italy
italiano -na ADJ & MF Italian
itálico ADJ italic; F **itálica** italics
ítem M item
itinerante ADJ itinerant
itinerario M itinerary
IVA [impuesto al valor añadido/agregado] M sales tax, VAT
izar[47] VT to hoist, to raise
izquierda F left (también política); (mano) left hand; **a la —** to the left
izquierdista ADJ & MF leftist
izquierdo ADJ left

Jj

jab M jab
jabalí M [wild] boar
jabalina F javelin
jabón M soap

jabonera F soap dish
jabonoso ADJ soapy
jaca F nag
jacinto M hyacinth
jactancia F boastfulness
jactancioso ADJ boastful, blustering
jactarse VI to boast, to brag
jacuzzi M Jacuzzi™, hot tub
jade M jade
jadear VI to pant, to gasp
jadeo M panting, gasping
jaez M harness
jaguar M jaguar
jalar VI/VT to pull, to tug
jalea F jelly
jaleo M (lío) mess; (barahúnda) ruckus
jam M jam session
Jamaica F Jamaica
jamaicano -na ADJ & MF Jamaican
jamaiquino -na ADJ & MF Jamaican
jamás ADV never
jamelgo M hack
jamón M ham
Japón M Japan
japonés -esa ADJ & MF Japanese
jaque M check; **— mate** checkmate; **tener a uno en —** fam to have someone by the short hairs
jaqueca F migraine
jarabe M syrup; **— de ipecacuana** ipecac syrup
jarana F revelry; **ir de —** to paint the town red
jarcia F rigging
jardín M (de flores) garden; (de césped) yard; (béisbol) outfield; **— de niños** kindergarten; **— infantil** nursery
jardinero -ra MF (de oficio) gardener; (en béisbol) outfielder
jarra F (cántaro) jug, pitcher; (taza) mug; **en —s** akimbo
jarro M pitcher, jug
jarrón M vase
jaspe M (piedra silícea) jasper; (mármol) veined marble
jaula F cage, coop
jauría F pack
jazmín M jasmine
jazz M jazz
jeans M PL jeans
jefatura F headquarters
jefe MF, **jefa** F (laboral) boss; (militar) commander; (departamental) chair, head; (policial) chief; **— del estado mayor** chief of staff; **— de departamento** department head
jején M gnat
jengibre M ginger
jerarquía F hierarchy
jerez M sherry
jerga F jargon, slang

jerigonza F (sinsentido) gibberish, gobbledygook; (juego lingüístico) pig Latin
jeringa F syringe
jeringar[40] VT to annoy
jeroglífico ADJ & M hieroglyphic
jersey M sweater
jesuita ADJ & M Jesuit
Jesús INTERJ God bless you! gesundheit!
jeta F (hocico) snout; (cara) mug
jet-set M jet set
jilguero M goldfinch
jinete M rider
jinetear VI to ride horseback
jingle M jingle
jirafa F giraffe
jobar INTERJ holy cow! holy Moses! holy mackerel!
jóckey M jockey
jocoso ADJ jocular
jofaina F basin
jogging M jogging
jolgorio M rumpus
jonrón M home run
Jordania F Jordan
jordano -na ADJ & MF Jordanian
jornada F (día laboral) workday; (coloquio) colloquium
jornal M daily wage
jornalero -ra MF day laborer
joroba F hump
jorobado -da ADJ & MF hunchback
jorobar VT (molestar) to hassle; (estropear) to gum up
jota F jay; **no saber ni —** to know zilch
joven ADJ young; MF young person
jovial ADJ jolly
joya F jewel; (persona apreciada) gem; **—s** jewelry
joyería F jewelry store, jeweler's
joyero -ra MF jeweler
joystick M joystick
juanete M bunion
jubilación F (retiro) retirement; (pagos) pension; **— anticipada** early retirement
jubilado ADJ retired; MF retiree
jubilar VT to pension, to retire; **—se** to retire
jubileo M jubilee
júbilo M glee
jubiloso ADJ jubilant, joyous
judaísmo M Judaism
judicial ADJ judicial
judío -ía ADJ Jewish; MF Jew; F bean; **judía blanca** navy bean; **judía pinta** pinto bean; **judía verde** green bean
juego M (actividad recreativa) play; (deporte) game; (conjunto de piezas) set; (muebles) suite; **— de apuestas** gambling; **— de damas** checkers; **— ofimático** office suite; **— de palabras** pun, play on words; **—s**

Olímpicos Olympic Games; **estar en —** to be at stake; **hacer —** to match
juerga F binge; **irse de —** to go on a binge, to party
juerguista MF merrymaker
jueves M Thursday
juez MF, **jueza** F (en un tribunal) judge; (en deportes) referee; **— de paz** justice of the peace; **— de línea** linesman; **— de silla** judge, umpire
jugada F play, move; **— de tres puntos** three-point play
jugador -ora MF (deportista) player; (apostador) gambler
jugar[43] VI to play; (apostar) to gamble; **— a la baraja / a los naipes** to play cards; **— con fuego** to play with fire; **— en casa** to play a home game; **— limpio** to play fair; **—se** to risk
jugarreta F bad turn
jugo M juice
jugoso ADJ juicy
juguete M plaything, toy
juguetear VI to toy with, to fiddle with
juguetón -ona ADJ playful
juicio M (criterio) judgment; (proceso) trial; **— por quiebra** bankruptcy proceedings; **perder el —** to lose one's mind; **a mi —** in my estimation
juicioso ADJ sensible, judicious
juke-box M jukebox
julio M July
jumbo ADJ jumbo; M jumbo jet
jumper M jumper
junco M (planta) rush, reed; (barco chino) junk
jungla F jungle
junio M June
junta F (reunión) meeting; (concejo) council; (juntura) joint; (pieza de motor) gasket; **— directiva** board of directors
juntar VT (tubos) to attach; (flores) to gather, to pick; (ganado) to round up, to wrangle; **— polvo** to gather dust; **— valor** to muster courage; **—se** (acumularse) to gather; (asociarse) to band together; (reunirse) to come together
junto ADJ together; LOC ADV **— a** next to; **— con** together with
juntura F (lugar) juncture; (articulación) joint
jurado -da MF (individuo) juror; M (grupo) jury
juramentar VI/VT to swear in; **—se** to be sworn in
juramento M oath; **— hipocrático** Hippocratic oath
jurar VI/VT to swear, to vow; **— en falso** to perjure oneself; **— la bandera** to pledge allegiance to the flag
jurídico ADJ legal
jurisdicción F jurisdiction

jurisprudencia F (doctrina) jurisprudence; (derecho) law

justa F joust, tilt

justamente ADV (exactamente) precisely; (con justicia) fairly

justicia F justice

justificación F justification

justificar[30] VT to justify

justo ADJ (ecuánime) just; (equitativo) equitable; (pío) righteous, upright; ADV exactly, right; **— después de** right after; **— en ese momento** exactly at that moment

juvenil ADJ (inmaduro) juvenile; (de apariencia joven) youthful

juventud F youth

juzgado M court

juzgar[40] VI/VT to judge, to pass judgment [on]; **— mal** to misjudge

Kk

kaki M khaki

kart M go-cart

kayak M kayak

Kazajstán M Kazakhstan

kazako -ka ADJ & MF Kazak[h]

Kenia F Kenya

keniata ADJ & MF Kenyan

kermés F bazaar

keroseno M kerosene

ketchup M catsup, ketchup

kg *ver* kilogramo

kilo M kilo

kilobyte M kilobyte

kilogramo M kilogram

kilometraje M mileage

kilómetro M kilometer

kilovatio M kilowatt; F **—-hora** kilowatt-hour

Kirguistán M Kyrgyzstan

Kiribati M Kiribati

kosher ADJ kosher

Kuwait M Kuwait

kuwaití ADJ & MF Kuwaiti

Ll

la ART DEF F the; **— del sombrero verde** the one with the green hat, that one with the green hat; PRON PERS it, her; PRON REL **— que** she who, the one that

laberinto M labyrinth, maze

labia F gift of gab

labial ADJ labial

labihendido N harelipped

labio M lip; **—s agrietados** chapped lips; **— leporino** cleft lip, harelip; **con — leporino** harelipped

labor F (trabajo) labor; (tarea) task; (manualidad) handiwork

laboral ADJ work-related; **legislación —** labor legislation

laboratorio M laboratory

laborioso ADJ (trabajoso) laborious; (trabajador) hardworking

laborterapia F occupational therapy

labrado ADJ carved

labrador -ora MF (persona) farmhand; M (perro) labrador

labranza F plowing

labrar VT to till; **—se una carrera** to carve out a career

laca F lacquer

lacar[30] VT to lacquer

lacayo M lackey, flunky

laciar VT RP to straighten

lacio ADJ straight

lacónico ADJ (persona) laconic; (comentario) terse

lacra F (física) scar; (moral) blight

lacre M sealing wax

lacrimógeno ADJ tear-producing

lactancia F lactation; **— materna** breast-feeding

lactar VT to nurse

lácteo ADJ (como la leche) milky; (hecho de leche) dairy

lactosa F lactose

LAD [lipoproteína de alta densidad] F HDL

ladeado ADJ (torcido) awry, askew; (asimétrico) lopsided

ladear VT (una superficie) to tilt; (la cabeza) to cock; (un avión) to bank; (ignorar) to snub, to ignore; **—se** to tilt, to lean

ladeo M tilt

ladera F hillside

ladilla F crab louse

ladillo M sidebar

ladino ADJ artful

lado M side; **— a —** side by side; **al —** nearby; **¡a un —!** gangway! **de —** sideways; **hacerse a un —** to move over

ladrar VI (perro) to bark; VI/VT (persona) to snap [at]

ladrido M bark, barking

ladrillo M brick

ladrón -ona MF (de casas) burglar; (con violencia) robber; (con astucia) thief; (de tiendas) shoplifter

lagartija F (animal) lizard; (ejercicio) push-up

lagarto M alligator; **— varano** monitor lizard

lago M lake

lágrima F tear, teardrop

lagrimear VI to weep

laguna F (de agua) lagoon; (de la memoria, conocimiento) gap; (legal) loophole

laico -ca MF layperson; ADJ lay

laja F slab

lamentable ADJ (desafortunado) lamentable, regrettable; (ruinoso) woeful

lamentablemente ADV unfortunately

lamentación F lamentation

lamentar VT (una acción) to lament, to regret; (una muerte) to grieve; **—se** to lament, to wail

lamento M lament, lamentation

lamer VT (pasar la lengua) to lick; (rozar) to lap

lamida F lick

lámina F (de vidrio, metal) sheet; (de metal) plate; (grabado) print

laminar VT to laminate

lámpara F lamp

lamparilla F night-light

lampiño ADJ (sin pelo) hairless; (sin barba) beardless

lana F wool; **— de acero** steel wool

lanar ADJ wool-bearing

lance M incident

lancear VT to lance, to spear

lanceta F lancet, lance

lancha F launch, boat; **— a motor** motorboat

langosta F (crustáceo) lobster; (insecto) locust

langostino M prawn

languidecer[35] VI to languish, to wilt

languidez F languor

lánguido ADJ languid, listless

lanilla F flannel

lanolina F lanolin

lanudo ADJ wooly, shaggy

lanza F lance, spear; **romper una — por alguien** to stick one's neck out for someone

lanzadera F shuttle

lanzador -ora MF (beisbol) pitcher

lanzamiento M (de un cohete, producto) launch; (de suministros) drop; (de una roca grande) heave; (de una pelota, en béisbol) pitch; (en tenis) toss

lanzar[47] VT (un cohete) to launch; (un producto) to launch, to roll out; (una pelota) to throw; (una bala) to fire; (algo pesado) to heave; (lodo) to sling; VI/VT (vomitar) to puke; **—se** to launch forth/out; **— un tiro libre** to shoot a free throw; M SG **—llamas** flamethrower

lanzazo M thrust with a lance

Laos M Laos

laosiano -na ADJ & MF Laotian

lápida F (piedra) stone tablet; (de sepultura) gravestone, tombstone

lapidar VT to stone

lapidario ADJ & M lapidary

lápiz M pencil; **— de color** crayon; **— de labios** lipstick

lapso M lapse, span

lapsus M lapse, slip of the tongue

laptop M laptop

laquear VT to lacquer

largar[40] VT (soltar) to cough up; **—se** *fam* to scram, to buzz off, to shove off

largo ADJ (camino, cuento) long; (discurso) lengthy; **de — alcance** long-range; **¡— de aquí!** scram! M **—metraje** feature film; **a la larga** in the long run; **a lo —** lengthwise; M length

larguero M crossbar

largueza F generosity

larguirucho ADJ lanky

largura F length

laringe F larynx

laringitis F laryngitis

larva F larva

láser M laser

lástima F pity; **¡qué —!** what a shame!

lastimadura F hurt

lastimar VT (herir) to hurt; (insultar) to hurt one's feelings; **—se** to get hurt

lastimoso ADJ pitiful

lastrar VT to ballast

lastre M ballast

lata F (envase) tin can, can; (con tapa) canister; (pesadez) bore; **dar la —** to be a nuisance

latente ADJ latent, dormant

lateral ADJ lateral, side

látex M latex

latido M (individual) beat, throb; (colectivo) beating; (del corazón) heartbeat

latifundio M large estate

latigazo M (golpe) lash; (chasquido) crack of a whip

látigo M whip

latín M Latin

latino -na ADJ (relativo a los hispanos) Latino; (relativo a la lengua latina) Latin; M Latino; F Latina

Latinoamérica F Latin America

latinoamericano ADJ Latin American

latir VI to beat, to throb

latitud F latitude (también flexibilidad)

latón M brass

latrocinio M larceny

laudable ADJ laudable

laurel M laurel; **dormirse sobre los —es** to rest on one's laurels

lava F lava

lavable ADJ washable

lavabo M (retrete) lavatory, toilet; (recipiente) sink

lavadero M laundry; **— automático** Laundromat™

lavado M wash, washing; **— de cerebro**

brainwashing; — **de dinero** money
laundering; — **en seco** dry cleaning
lavadora F washing machine
lavanda F lavender
lavandera F washerwoman
lavandería F laundry
lavar VI/VT to wash; (ropa) to launder; —**se** to
wash up; —**se las manos** to wash one's
hands; M SG **lavaplatos/lavavajillas**
dishwasher
lavativa F enema
lavatorio M washroom
laxante M laxative
laxitud F laxity
laxo ADJ lax
lazada F bowknot
lazar[47] VT to lasso
lazarillo M (persona) guide for the blind; (perro)
guide dog
lazo M (soga) lasso, rope; (vuelta) loop; (nudo
corredizo) noose; (relación) tie, bond
LBD [lipoproteína de baja densidad] F LDL
le PRON PERS — **dije** I told you/him/her; — **vi**
Esp I saw him/you; **se** — **murió el perro**
his/her dog died on him/her
leal ADJ loyal, trusty
lealtad F loyalty, allegiance; — **de marca** brand
loyalty
lección F lesson, assignment; **darle una** — **a**
alguien to teach someone a lesson
lechada F whitewash
leche F (de vaca) milk; — **desnatada** skim milk;
— **en polvo** powdered milk; — **entera**
whole milk; — **homogeneizada**
homogenized milk; — **malteada** malted
milk; **mala** — nasty disposition; **ir a toda** —
to barrel along; **ese tío es la** — that guy's a
case; **es un mala** — *fam* he's a nasty creep
lechería F dairy
lechero -ra ADJ dairy; M milkman; F milkmaid
lecho M bed (también de río)
lechón M suckling pig
lechoso ADJ milky
lechuga F lettuce
lechuza F screech owl, barn owl
lector -ora MF reader; — **de código de barras**
bar code reader; M — **de tarjetas** card reader
lectura F (acción) reading; (material) reading
matter
leer[18] VI/VT to read
legación F legation
legado M legacy, bequest
legajo M file
legal ADJ legal, lawful
legalidad F (conjunto de normas) law; (cualidad
de legal) legality
legalización F (de un documento)
authentication; (de una actividad)
legalization; — **de una validación**

testamentaria probate
legalizar[47] VT to legalize
legar[40] VT to will, to bequeath
legendario ADJ legendary
leggings M PL leggings
legible ADJ (descifrable) legible; (fácil de leer)
readable
legión F legion
legionario M legionnaire
legionelosis F legionnaire's disease
legislación F legislation
legislador -ora MF legislator, lawmaker
legislar VI/VT to legislate
legislativo ADJ legislative
legislatura F legislature
legitimidad F legitimacy
legítimo ADJ legitimate, lawful, rightful
lego -ga MF layperson; ADJ lay
legua F league
legumbre F legume
leído ADJ well-read
lejanía F distance
lejano ADJ (distancia) distant, faraway;
(parentesco) remote
lejía F (producto de limpieza) bleach; (de sosa)
lye
lejos ADV far away, far; **a lo** — in the distance; —
de far from; **desde** — from afar
lelo ADJ silly
lema M (frase típica) motto; (propaganda
política) slogan
lencería F lingerie
lengua F (órgano) tongue; (idioma) language; —
materna mother tongue
lenguado M sole
lenguaje M language (también en informática);
— **compilador** compiler language; —
corporal body language; — **[de] máquina**
machine language; — **de programación**
programming language; — **de signos** sign
language; — **ensamblador** assembly
language
lenguaraz ADJ gossipy
lengüeta F (de un instrumento de viento) reed;
(de un zapato) tongue
lengüetazo M lick
lentamente ADV slowly
lente MF lens; — **filtrador** filter lens; —**s**
eyeglasses; —**s de contacto** contact lenses;
—**s negros/oscuros** sunglasses, shades
lenteja F lentil
lentitud F slowness
lento ADJ (despacioso) slow; (tonto) dull;
(letárgico) sluggish; ADV slowly
leña F firewood
leñador -ora MF woodcutter, lumberjack
leñera F woodshed
leño M log
leñoso ADJ woody

león M lion; — **marino** sea lion
León M Leon
leona F lioness
leonés ADJ Leonese
leopardo M leopard
lepra F leprosy
lerdo ADJ slow
lesbiano -na ADJ lesbian; F lesbian
lesión F injury, lesion; — **ocular** eye injury
lesionar VT to injure; —**se** to get injured
Lesotho M Lesotho
letal ADJ lethal
letárgico ADJ lethargic
letargo M lethargy
letón -ona ADJ & MF Latvian
Letonia F Latvia
letra F (del alfabeto) letter; (caligrafía) handwriting; (de una canción) lyrics, words; — **bastardilla/cursiva** italics; — **chica** fine print; — **de cambio** bill of exchange; — **de imprenta** block letter; — **manuscrita** longhand; **sin** —**s** uneducated
letrado ADJ learned, literate
letrero M sign
letrina F latrine
leucemia F leukemia
leudar VI to rise; VT to leaven
leva F (de tropas) levy; (de motor) cam
levadura F leaven, yeast
levantamiento M (revuelta) uprising; (suspensión) suspension; — **de pesas** weight-lifting
levantar VT (la mano) to raise; (una caja) to lift; (un interruptor) to switch; (del piso) to pick up; (perdices) to flush; (a un dormido) to wake up, to rouse; (un edificio) to put up; — **el campamento** to break camp; — **falso testimonio** to bear false witness; — **la mesa** to clear the table; — **la sesión** to adjourn the meeting; — **vuelo** to take flight; —**se** (de la cama) to get up, to rise, to arise; (de una silla) to stand up, to get up; (un edificio) to go up
levar VT — **anclas** to weigh anchor
leve ADJ (brisa) light; (resfrío) mild; (problema) slight
levedad F (de una brisa) lightness; (de un resfrío) mildness
levemente ADV lightly
léxico M lexicon, dictionary; ADJ lexical
lexicografía F lexicography
ley F law, statute; — **de prescripción** statute of limitations; — **de [los] rendimientos decrecientes** law of diminishing returns; — **marcial** martial law; **de buena** — of good quality
leyenda F (mitología) legend; (texto que acompaña una figura) caption
leyendo, leyera, leyese, leyeron *ver* leer

liar[28] VT (paquetes) to bundle; (cigarros) to roll; —**se** to get involved
libanés -esa ADJ & MF Lebanese
Líbano M Lebanon
libelo M libel
libélula F dragonfly
liberación F (de un país ocupado) liberation; (de pecados) deliverance; (de presos) release
liberal ADJ & MF liberal
liberalidad F liberality
liberalismo M liberalism
liberalización F liberalization
liberar VT (de un deber) to relieve; (a un pueblo) to liberate; (del sufrimiento) to deliver; (a un preso) to free, to release
Liberia F Liberia
liberiano -na ADJ & MF Liberian
líbero M sweeper
libertad F liberty, freedom; — **condicional** parole; — **de expresión** free speech; **poner en** — to set free; **poner en** — **bajo fianza** to let out on bail; **poner en** — **condicional** to parole
libertador -ora MF liberator
libertar VT to liberate
libertinaje M licentiousness
libertino -na MF libertine
Libia F Libya
libidinoso ADJ libidinous
libido F libido
libio -bia ADJ & MF Libyan
libra F pound (también moneda)
librar VT (a un preso) to free, to set free; (de una obligación) to release; (un cheque) to write; (una letra de cambio) to draft; (una guerra) to wage; —**se de** to get rid of
libre ADJ (persona) free; (asiento) vacant; (camino) clear; (traducción) loose; (de una obligación) exempt; — **albedrío** free will; — **cambio/comercio** free trade; — **de cargos** toll-free; — **de gravámenes** free and clear; — **de intereses** interest-free; — **de impuestos** duty-free, tax-free; — **de virus** virus-free; — **pensador** freethinker
librería F bookstore
librero -ra MF bookseller
libresco ADJ bookish
libreta F small notebook; — **de direcciones** address book
libreto M libretto
libro M book; — **de bolsa** pocket book; — **de cocina** cookbook; — **de texto** textbook; — **electrónico** e-book; — **en rústica** paperback; — **mayor** ledger
licencia F (carnet de conducir, libertad poética) license; (permiso) leave; (permiso para ausentarse) leave of absence; — **de sitio** license; — **por maternidad** maternity leave
licenciado -da MF college graduate

licenciar VT to discharge; —**se** to graduate from college

licenciatura F bachelor's degree

licencioso ADJ licentious

liceo M high school

licitación F bid

lícito ADJ lawful, permissible

licor M liqueur, cordial

licuadora F blender

líder MF leader

liderar VT to head up

liderar VT to lead

liderazgo M (de una organización, condición de líder) leadership; (en una competencia) lead

lidiar VI/VT to contend, to grapple

liebre F hare; **levantar la** — to let the cat out of the bag

Liechtenstein M Liechtenstein

liechtensteiniano -na MF Liechtensteiner

lienzo M canvas

liftado M top spin

lifting M face-lift

liga F (alianza, grupo deportivo) league; (cinta elástica) garter; — **mayor** major league

ligado M slur

ligadura F ligature

ligamento M ligament

ligar[40] VT (atar) to bind; (conectar notas) to slur; VI (conquistar sexualmente) to score; —**se** to bind; —**se las trompas** to have one's tubes tied

ligeramente ADV lightly

ligereza F (de peso) lightness; (de temperamento) levity

ligero ADJ (poco pesado) light; (rápido) swift; (pequeño) slight; **a la ligera** lightly

liguero M garter belt

lija F sandpaper

lijar VI/VT to sandpaper, to sand

lila ADJ & MF lilac

lima F (fruta) lime; (árbol) lime tree; — **de uñas** nail file

limar VI/VT to file

limero M lime tree

limitación F (restricción) limitation; (defecto) shortcoming

limitar VT (restringir) to limit; (gastos) to curb; —**se a** to limit oneself to

límite M (restricción) limit; (de una región) boundary; (de la paciencia) bounds; — **de edad** age limit; — **de tiempo** time limit; — **de velocidad** speed limit

limítrofe ADJ bordering

limo M slime

limón M lemon

limonada F lemonade

limonero M lemon tree

limosna F alms, handout

limpiador M cleanser

limpiar VI/VT to clean; VT (una superficie) to wipe; (la piel) to cleanse; (un camino, una pantalla de computadora, la reputación) to clear; (animales) to dress; (zapatos) to shine; (un derrame) to mop up, to wipe up; (dejar sin dinero) to clean out; M SG

limpiaparabrisas windshield wiper; M SG

limpiavidrios squeegee

límpido ADJ limpid

limpieza F (pulcritud) cleanliness, neatness; (operación militar) mop-up; — **étnica** ethnic cleansing

limpio ADJ (casa) clean, neat; (piel, conciencia) clear; (juego) fair; (sin dinero) broke; **pasar en** — to make a clean copy

limusina F limousine

linaje M lineage, ancestry

linaza F linseed

lince M (animal) lynx; (persona astuta) sly fox; **con ojos de** — sharp-eyed

linchar VT to lynch

lindante ADJ neighboring

lindar VI to border, to adjoin

linde MF boundary

lindero ADJ adjoining; M boundary

lindo ADJ pretty; **un día** — a nice day; **de lo** — a lot

línea F (raya, cola) line; (en béisbol) line drive; — **aérea** airline; — **de banda** (fútbol) sideline; — **de conducta** course of action; — **de crédito** credit line; — **de fondo** baseline; — **de golpeo** line of scrimmage; — **de meta** goal line; — **de montaje** assembly line; — **ofensiva** offensive line; **batear una** — line out; **en** — online

lineal ADJ linear

linfa F lymph

linfocito M lymphocyte

linfoma M lymphoma

lingüista MF linguist

lingüística F linguistics

lingüístico ADJ linguistic

linimento M liniment

lino M (tela) linen; (fibra) flax

linóleo M linoleum

linterna F (a pilas, de bolsillo) flashlight; (de un faro) lantern

lío M (bulto) bundle; (enredo, molestia) mess, hassle; (amorío) affair, fling; **armar un** — to raise a ruckus; **meterse en un** — to get oneself into a mess

liofilizar VI/VT to freeze-dry

liposucción F liposuction

liquidación F (ajuste de cuentas, de bienes) settlement, liquidation; (rebaja) sale, clearance sale; (pago completo) payment in full

liquidar VT (bienes, mercancías) to liquidate, to sell off; (una cuenta, herencia) to settle; (a una persona) *fam* to waste, to off, to whack

liquidez F liquidity

líquido ADJ & M liquid; — **amniótico** amniotic fluid

lira F (moneda) lira

lírica F lyric poetry

lírico ADJ lyric, lyrical

lirio M iris, lily; — **de los valles** lily of the valley

lirismo M lyricism

lisiado ADJ (descapacitado) handicapped; (lesionado) injured

lisiar VT to handicap

liso ADJ (neumático) bald; (camino) even, smooth; (terreno) flat; (pelo) straight; **azul** — solid blue

lisonja F flattery

lisonjear VI/VT to flatter

lisonjero -ra MF flatterer; ADJ flattering

lista F (de palabras) list; (de miembros) roster; (de alumnos) roll; (banda) stripe; (de precios) schedule, list; — **de control** checklist; — **correo** mailing list; — **de espera** waiting list; — **negra** blacklist; **pasar** — to call the roll

listado ADJ striped; M listing, printout

listo ADJ (preparado) ready, set; (inteligente) clever, smart; **hacerse el** — to pull a stunt

listón M (tabla) board; (en salto de altura) crossbar

lisura F smoothness

litera F (cama en el tren, barco) berth; (cama superpuesta) bunk bed

literal ADJ literal

literario ADJ literary

literato -ta MF writer

literatura F literature

litigante MF litigant

litigio M (pleito) lawsuit; (acción de litigar) litigation

litio M lithium

litoral ADJ seaside; M seaboard, seacoast

litro M liter

Lituania F Lithuania

lituano -na ADJ & MF Lithuanian

liviano ADJ (leve) light; (promiscuo) promiscuous

lívido ADJ livid

living M living room

llaga F sore

llama F (fuego) flame; (animal) llama

llamada F (de teléfono, a la acción) call; (grito) hail; (nota al pie) footnote; — **de cobro revertido / por cobrar** collect call

llamado M (acción de convocar) call; (petición) appeal

llamador M knocker

llamamiento M (conversación) call; (exhortación) appeal; **hacer un** — to appeal

llamar VT (un nombre, una huelga, por teléfono) to call; (a la puerta) to knock; (gritar) to hail; — **la atención** to call attention; **me llamo Juan** my name is Juan

llamarada F blaze, flare

llamativo ADJ (impactante) striking, bold; (chabacano) gaudy, flashy

llameante ADJ flaming

llamear VI to flare, to flame

llana F trowel

llano ADJ (sencillo) plain; (liso) flat, smooth, level; (de poca profundidad) shallow; M plain

llanta F (reborde metálico) rim; (neumático) tire

llanto M crying, weeping

llanura F plain, prairie

llave F (para puertas) key; (de armas de fuego) lock; (en lucha libre) lock, hold; (grifo) faucet, tap; (interruptor) light switch; (de gas) cock; — **de tuercas** wrench; — **inglesa** pipe wrench; — **maestra** master key

llavero M key ring

llegada F arrival

llegar[40] VI (arribar) to arrive, to get there/here; (alcanzar) to reach; — **a las manos** to come to blows; — **a ser** to become; — **a un acuerdo** to strike a deal; — **a un arreglo** to cut a deal; — **tarde** to be late

llenar VT (un recipiente) to fill; (un formulario) to fill out; — **el tanque** to tank up, to gas up; —**se** to fill up; —**se de** to get filled with; —**se de oro** to make a killing

lleno ADJ full; — **de** full of; **de** — totally; M **un** — **completo** a full house

llevadero ADJ bearable

llevar VT (transportar) to carry, to take; (transportar en coche) to drive; (tener puesto) to wear; (contener) to hold; (inducir) to lead, to drive; — **a cabo** to carry out; — **la cuenta** to keep score; — **la ventaja** to have an advantage; — **los libros** to keep the books; — **un mes aquí** to have been here one month; **le llevo dos años a mi hermano** I'm two years older than my brother; **llevo las de perder** the odds are against me; —**se** to carry away, to take away; —**se bien con** to get along with

llorar VI (con ruido) to cry, to bawl; (con lágrimas) to weep; VT (una pérdida) to lament; (una muerte) to mourn

lloriquear VI to whimper

lloriqueo M whimper

llorón -ona ADJ weeping; MF crybaby, whiner

lloroso ADJ tearful, weeping

llovedizo ADJ **agua llovediza** rainwater

llover[6] VI/VT to rain; — **a cántaros** to rain cats and dogs; **llueva o truene** rain or shine

llovizna F drizzle

lloviznar VI to drizzle, to mist

lluvia F (precipitación) rain; (de preguntas,

críticas) barrage; (de protestas, flechas, piedras) volley; (de golpes, chispas) shower; — **ácida** acid rain; — **de ideas** brainstorming; — **torrencial** driving rain

lluvioso ADJ rainy

lo PRON PERS — **bueno** the good thing; — **de la protesta** the matter of the protest; — **que quiero** what I want; **sé** — **bueno que eres** I know how good you are; **yo** — **vi** I saw it/ him/you

loable ADJ laudable, praiseworthy

loar VT to laud

lobato M wolf cub

lobbista, lobista MF lobbyist

lobby M lobby

lobezno M wolf cub

lobo M wolf

lobotomía F lobotomy

lóbrego ADJ gloomy

lóbulo M lobe

local ADJ local; M premises

localidad F (pueblo) town, locality; (en un teatro) seat

localización F location

localizar[47] VT (encontrar) to locate; (limitar) to localize

loción F lotion

loco-ca ADJ insane, mad, crazy; — **de remate** stark raving mad; MF lunatic, insane person; M madman

locomotora F locomotive, train engine

locuaz ADJ garrulous, loquacious

locura F madness, insanity

locutor-ora MF radio announcer

lodazal M quagmire

lodo M mud

lodoso ADJ muddy

logaritmo M logarithm

logia F lodge

lógica F logic

lógicamente ADV logically

lógico ADJ (razonado) logical; (bien fundado) sound

logística F logistics

lograr VT to achieve, to accomplish; **logré convencerle** I managed to / succeeded in convincing him

logro M (lo conseguido) accomplishment, achievement; (hazaña) feat

loma F knoll

lombriz F (de tierra) earthworm; (de estómago) tapeworm

lomo M (de animal) back ridge; (corte de carne) loin

lona F canvas

longaniza F cured sausage

longevidad F longevity

longevo ADJ long-lived

longitud F (distancia angular) longitude; (largo) length; — **de onda** wavelength

lonja F (mercado) commodity exchange; (tajada) slice of meat

loquería F fam booby hatch, funny farm

loquero-ra MF (psiquiatra) fam shrink; M (manicomio) fam funny farm

lord M lord

loro M parrot

losa F (lápida) slab; (baldosa) flagstone

lote M lot

lotería F lottery

loza F (basta) crockery; (fina) china

lozanía F freshness, bloom

lozano ADJ fresh, blooming

LSD MF LSD

lubina F bass

lubricante ADJ & M lubricant

lubricar[30] VI/VT to lubricate

lucero M morning star; — **del alba** morning star

lucha F (pugna, contienda) struggle; (pelea) fight; — **libre** wrestling

luchador-ora MF fighter; (en lucha libre) wrestler

luchar VI/VT (contra un enemigo) to fight; (con un problema) to struggle; (en lucha libre) to wrestle; — **por** to strive for

lucidez F lucidity

lúcido ADJ lucid, clear-headed

luciérnaga F firefly, glowworm

lucio M pike

lucir[39] VI (mostrarse) to look; (favorecer, sentar bien) to look good on, to suit; VT (llevar) to model, to sport; (alardear de) to flaunt; —**se** (sobresalir) to excel; (ostentar) to show off

lucrativo ADJ lucrative, profitable

lucro M **sin fines de** — not for profit

luctuoso ADJ sad, mournful, dismal

luego ADV afterward, then, next; — **de** after; **desde** — of course; **hasta** — so long

lugar M place; — **común** platitude; — **de nacimiento** birthplace, place of birth; — **de trabajo** workplace; **dar** — **a** to give rise to; **no hay** — there's no room; **en** — **de** instead of

lúgubre ADJ mournful, gloomy

lujo M luxury; **darse un** — to indulge oneself; **con** — **de detalles** in great detail

lujoso ADJ (ropa) luxurious; (hotel) plush

lujuria F lust

lujurioso ADJ lustful

lumbago M lumbago

lumbar ADJ lumbar

lumbre F (fuego) fire; (luz) light

luminosidad F brilliance, luminosity

luminoso ADJ luminous

luna F (satélite) moon; (espejo) large mirror; — **de miel** honeymoon; **estar en la** — to be distracted; — **llena** full moon

lunar ADJ lunar; M (en la piel) mole; (en una tela) polka dot
lunático -ca ADJ & MF lunatic
lunes M Monday
lupa F magnifying glass
lúpulo M hops
lupus M lupus
lustrar VT to shine, to polish
lustre M luster, shine
lustroso ADJ (revista) glossy; (pelo) shiny, sleek
luto M mourning
luxación F dislocation
Luxemburgo M Luxembourg
luxemburgués -esa MF Luxembourger; ADJ Luxembourgian
luz F light (también aparato); (del sol) sunshine; (abertura) aperture; **— trasera** taillight; **— verde** green light; **dar a —** to give birth; **sacar a —** to disclose

Mm

macabro ADJ grim
macanudo ADJ cool
Macao M Macao
macarrones M PL macaroni
Macedonia F Macedonia
macedonio -nia ADJ & MF Macedonian
maceta F flower pot
machacar[30] VT (aplastar) to pound, to crush; (insistir) to harp on; (en baloncesto) to dunk
machacón ADJ persistent
machetazo M hack with a machete
machete M machete
machismo M [male] chauvinism
macho M (animal masculino) male; (mulo) he-mule; (varón) man; (hombre muy varonil) he-man; **— cabrío** he-goat; **— y hembra** hook and eye; ADJ (masculino) male; (fuerte) strong; INTERJ man!
machote ADJ butch
machucar[30] VT to bruise
macilento ADJ pale
macizo ADJ massive; M plateau
Madagascar M Madagascar
madeja F skein
madera F wood (también en golf); (árboles maderables) timber; (para construcción) lumber; **— contrachapada** plywood; **— flotante** driftwood; **— noble** hardwood; **—s** woodwinds; **tocar —** to knock on wood
maderaje M woodwork
madero M trunk
madrastra F stepmother
madre F mother; **— de alquiler** surrogate mother; **— patria** mother country; **—perla** mother-of-pearl; **— política** mother-in-law; **—selva** honeysuckle; **ciento y la —** everybody and their dog
madriguera F burrow, hole
madrileño -ña ADJ & MF [person] from Madrid
madrina F godmother
madrugada F early morning hours; **a las dos de la —** at two in the morning
madrugador -ra ADJ & MF early bird
madrugar VI to get up early; **— con gripe** to wake up with a cold
maduración F (animales, personas) maturation, maturing; (frutos) ripening; (vino) aging
madurar VI to mature, to grow up
madurez F (de persona) maturity; (de fruta) ripeness
maduro ADJ (persona) mature; (fruta) ripe
maestría F master's degree; **— en administración de empresas** master of business administration
maestro -tra MF (docente) [school]teacher; (artesano) master; (director) maestro
mafia F mafia
mafioso -sa MF mafioso
magia F magic
mágico ADJ magic, magical
magisterio M (actividad) teaching; (conjunto de los maestros) teachers; (profesión) teaching profession
magistrado -da MF magistrate
magistral ADJ masterful, masterly
magma M magma
magnánimo ADJ magnanimous
magnate MF magnate, tycoon
magnesia F magnesia
magnesio M magnesium
magnético ADJ magnetic
magnetismo M magnetism
magnetizar[47] VT to magnetize
magnificar[30] VT to magnify
magnificencia F magnificence
magnífico ADJ (palacio) magnificent; (día) glorious
magnitud F magnitude
magno ADJ great
magnolia F magnolia
magnolio M magnolia tree
mago M magician, wizard
magro ADJ lean
magulladura F bruise, contusion
magullar VI/VT (machucar) to bruise; (mutilar) to mangle
mahonesa F mayonnaise
maicena® F cornstarch
maíz M corn, maize
maizal M cornfield
majadería F stupidity

majadero ADJ stupid
majar VT to pound
majestad F majesty
majestuoso ADJ majestic, stately
majo ADJ (atractivo) good-looking; (agradable) charming
mal M (maldad) evil; (enfermedad) malady, affliction; (daño) harm; **— de altura** altitude sickness; **— de ojo** evil eye; ADV wrong, badly; **— aconsejado** misguided; **— adquirido** ill-gotten; **— hablado** foulmouthed; **hablar — de alguien** to speak ill of someone; **hacer —** to do wrong; **lo hice mal** I did it badly
malabarista MF juggler
malandanza F misfortune
malaria F malaria
Malasia F Malaysia
malasio -sia ADJ & MF Malaysian
Malawi M Malawi
malawiano -na ADJ & MF Malawian
malbaratar VT to undersell
malcontento ADJ discontented
malcriado ADJ spoiled
malcriar VT to spoil
maldad F evil, wickedness
maldecir[51] VI/VT to curse
maldición F curse
maldito ADJ accursed
Maldivas F PL Maldives
maldivo -va ADJ & MF Maldivian
maleable ADJ malleable
maleante MF gangster, hoodlum
malear VT to corrupt
maleducado ADJ ill-mannered, ill-bred
maleficio M evil spell
maléfico ADJ evil
malentendido M misunderstanding
malestar M (de estómago) upset; (físico) discomfort; (espiritual) malaise; (social) unrest
maleta F suitcase, bag; **hacer la —** to pack one's suitcase
maletero M car trunk
maletín M briefcase
malévolo ADJ (persona) malevolent; (comentario) snide
maleza F (en el monte) underbrush, scrub; (en un jardín) weeds
malformación F malformation
malgache ADJ & MF Madagascan
malgastar VI/VT to waste, to throw away
malgasto M waste
malhechor -ora MF evildoer, criminal
malhumorado ADJ grumpy, ill-humored
Mali, Malí M Mali
malí ADJ & MF Malian
malicia F malice
malicioso ADJ malicious, spiteful

malignidad F malignancy
maligno ADJ (persona) vicious, evil; (tumor) malignant
malinterpretar VI/VT to misunderstand
malla F (de armadura) mail; (de metal) mesh
malo ADJ bad; (calidad, letra) poor; (enfermo) ill; **mal estado** disrepair; **mal humor** bad mood; **mala fama** ill repute; **mala fe** bad faith; **mala hierba** weed; **mala pasada** bad turn; **mala racha** slump; **mala suerte** bad luck
malograr VT to spoil, to ruin; **—se** to fail, to miscarry
malpagar[40] VI/VT to underpay
malparto M miscarriage
malsano ADJ unhealthy, unwholesome
malta F malt
Malta F Malta
maltés -esa ADJ & MF Maltese
maltratar VT to mistreat, to abuse
maltrato M mistreatment, abuse
maltrecho ADJ battered
malvado ADJ wicked, evil
malvavisco M marshmallow
malversación F misuse, misappropriation
malversar VT to misuse, to embezzle
mamá F mama, mamma, mom
mamado ADJ drunk
mamar VI (un bebé) to suckle, to nurse; VI/VT to suck
mamario ADJ mammary
mamarracho M sight
mami F mommy
mamífero ADJ mammalian, mammal; M mammal
mamografía F mammography
mampara F partition
mamut M mammoth
manada F (de ballenas) pod; (de vacas) herd; (de lobos) pack
manantial M (naciente) spring; (fuente inagotable) wellspring
manar VI to stream out
mancha F (marca) stain, spot; (de tinta) blot; (cosa borrosa) blur; (aceitosa) smear, smudge; (menoscabo) tinge; (en la piel) blemish
manchado ADJ spotted
manchar VI/VT (ensuciar) to spot; (menoscabar) to stain, to blemish
manchón M large spot
mancilla F blemish
mancillar VT to defile, to sully
manco ADJ one-armed
mancuerna F dumbbell
mandado M errand
mandamás M *fam* big enchilada, big kahuna
mandamiento M commandment
mandante MF principal
mandar VI/VT (dar órdenes) to command, to

order; (enviar) to send; — **buscar a** to send for; — **decir** to send word; **¿quién manda?** who's in charge? —**se hacer un traje** to have a suit made; **¿mande?** (hola) hello; (perdón) excuse me? what?

mandarina F tangerine

mandatario -ria MF (mediante contrato) agent; (abogado) attorney; (de estado) head of state

mandato M (orden) command, order; (cargo político) term, mandate

mandíbula F (quijada) jaw; (hueso) jawbone

mandil M apron

mandioca F manioc

mando M (de un estado) rule; (de un aparato) control; — **a distancia** remote control

mandolina F mandolin

mandón -ona ADJ bossy, domineering; MF bossy person, control freak

mandonear VI/VT to domineer, to boss around

manea F hobble

manear VT to hobble

manecilla F clock hand

manejable ADJ manageable

manejar VT (un vehículo) to drive, to steer; (un negocio) to run, to manage; (una máquina) to operate

manejo M (de un negocio) running, management; (de asuntos) handling; (de una máquina) operation

manera F manner, way; **a — de** like; **de alguna — ** somehow; **de cualquier —** anyway; **de ninguna —** on no account; **de — que** so that

manga F (de una camisa) sleeve; (de una nave) beam; (de agua) hose; (tenis) set; — **de viento** windsock; **en —s de camisa** in shirtsleeves; **ser de — ancha** to be broad-minded; **sacar algo de la —** to pull something out of a hat

manganeso M manganese

mangle M mangrove

mango M (agarradera) handle, grip; (fruta, árbol) mango

mangosta F mongoose

manguera F hose

manguito M muff

maní M peanut

manía F (moda, estado patológico) mania; (hábito) bad habit; (tic) tic

maníaco -ca ADJ maniacal; MF maniac

maníaco-depresivo ADJ manic-depressive

maniatar VT to tie the hands; (manear) to hobble

maniático ADJ (que tiene manías) crotchety; (melindroso) fastidious

manicomio M *pey* insane asylum

manicura F manicure

manicurar VT to manicure

manido ADJ hackneyed

manifestación F (muestra) manifestation; (protesta) demonstration

manifestante MF demonstrator

manifestar[1] VI/VT to manifest, to show; (expresar) to air; (protestar en público) to demonstrate; (declarar) to state

manifiesta, manifieste *ver* manifestar

manifiesto ADJ & M manifest; **poner de —** to underscore; M (dogma) manifesto; **— de vuelo** manifest

manija F handle

maniobra F (militar) maneuver; (para llamar la atención) stunt; **— de Heimlich** Heimlich maneuver

maniobrar VI/VT to maneuver

manipulación F (de la opinión pública) manipulation; (de alimentos) handling

manipular VT (influir) to manipulate; (tocar con las manos) to handle

maniquí M (muñeco) mannequin; MF (modelo) model

manivela F crank

manjar M delicacy

mano F hand (también de naipes); (de pintura) coat; (fútbol) handball; — **de obra** workforce; **—s a la obra** let's get to work; **—s de mantequilla** butterfingers; **a — ** (presente) at hand; (con la mano) by hand; **a — armada** at gunpoint; **dar una —** to lend a hand; **dar una — de pintura** to put on a coat of paint; **darle una — a alguien** to lend someone a hand; **darse la —** (saludo) to shake hands; (señal de afecto) to hold hands; **de primera —** firsthand; **de segunda —** secondhand; **estar a — con alguien** to be even with someone; **hecho a —** handmade; **poner las —s en el fuego por alguien** to go out on a limb for someone; **quedar a —** to break even; **se le fue la —** he got carried away; **ser —** to lead [in a card game]; **tener buena — con/para algo** to have a knack for something; **tomarse de la —** to hold hands

manojo M (de monedas) handful; (de llaves) bunch

manómetro M pressure gauge

manopla F (guante) mitten; (en béisbol) glove

manosear VT to feel, to finger

manoseo M feel, grope

manotazo M swat; **tirarle un — a alguien** to take a swipe at someone

manotear VI to swat at

mansalva LOC ADV **a —** at will

mansedumbre F gentleness, meekness

mansión F mansion

manso ADJ (humilde) meek; (domesticado) tame; (apacible) gentle

manta F (gruesa) blanket, cover; (liviana) throw

manteca F lard, shortening; *RP* butter; **— de cacao** cocoa butter

mantecoso ADJ rich, buttery

mantel M tablecloth

mantendrá, mantendría *ver* mantener

mantener[58] VT (conservar, sostener) to maintain; (dejar prolongadamente) to keep; (alimentar, costear a alguien) to provide for; (apoyar a lo largo del tiempo) to sustain; **— a flote** to buoy up; **— el orden público** to keep the peace; **— en secreto** to keep under wraps; **— en suspenso** to keep in suspense; **— la calma** to remain calm, **—se** (quedarse) to remain; (ganarse la vida) to support oneself; **—se al corriente** to keep abreast; **—se al tanto** to stay informed; **—se en contacto** to keep in touch; **—se firme** to stand pat, to stick to one's guns

mantenga, mantengo *ver* mantener

mantenimiento M maintenance, upkeep

mantequera F (platillo) butter dish; (aparato para hacer mantequilla) churn

mantequilla F butter; **— de maní** peanut butter

mantiene, mantienes *ver* mantener

mantilla F mantilla

manto M mantle (también geológico); (de juez) robe

mantón M shawl

mantra M mantra

mantuve, mantuviera, mantuviese *ver* mantener

manual ADJ & M manual

manubrio M handlebar

manufactura F manufacture

manufacturar VT to manufacture

manufacturero-ra ADJ manufacturing; MF manufacturer

manuscrito ADJ written by hand; M manuscript

manutención F maintenance

manzana F (fruta) apple; (de ciudad) block; **— de la discordia** bone of contention

manzanar M apple orchard

manzano M apple tree

maña F (destreza) skill, knack; (artimaña) cunning

mañana F (división del día) morning; (futuro) tomorrow; ADV tomorrow; **— por la —** tomorrow morning

mañanero-ra MF early bird

mañoso ADJ tricky

mapa M map; **— de memoria** memory map; **— en relieve** relief map

mapache M raccoon

maple M maple

maqueta F mock-up

maquillaje M makeup

maquillar[se] VI/VT to put on makeup

máquina F (aparato) machine; (motor) engine; **— de búsqueda** search engine; **— de coser** sewing machine; **— de escribir** typewriter; **— de lavar** washing machine; **— de vapor** steam engine; **— expendedora** vending machine; **— fotográfica** camera

maquinación F scheming, plotting

maquinador-ora MF schemer

maquinal ADJ automatic

maquinar VI/VT to plot, to scheme

maquinaria F (aparato) machinery, apparatus; (del gobierno) machine

maquinilla F clipper; **— de afeitar** razor

maquinista M (de locomotora) locomotive engineer; (obrero) machinist

mar MF sea; **— de fondo** undercurrent; **llover a mares** to rain cats and dogs; **en alta —** on the high seas; **un — de cosas** a lot of things; **hacerse a la —** to put to sea

maraca F maraca

maraña F (de hilos) tangle, snarl; (de pelo) mat

marañón M cashew

maratón M marathon

maravilla F (portento) wonder, marvel; (flor) marigold; **a las mil —s** wonderfully

maravillar VT to amaze; **—se** to be amazed, to marvel

maravilloso ADJ marvelous, wonderful

marca F (récord) record; (de ganado) brand; (de producto) brand, brand name, label; (de coche) make; **— comercial** name brand; **— de nacimento** birthmark; **— de fábrica** trademark; **— genérica** generic brand; **— registrada** registered trademark; **de —** name-brand

marcadamente ADV sharply

marcado ADJ (acento) thick; (contraste) sharp, stark; (descenso) steep; (parecido) strong

marcador M (lapicero) marker; (en deporte) scoreboard; **— de libros** bookmark; **— genético** genetic marker; **¿cómo va el —?** what's the score?

marcar[30] VT (una respuesta) to mark; (ganado) to brand; (el ritmo) to beat; (la hora) to say; (un tanto) to score; (medida) to read, to show; (un número telefónico) to dial; **— para seleccionar** to highlight; **— un gol** to score a goal

marcha F (caminata, pieza musical) march; (partida) leaving; (progreso) course; (modo de andar) gait; (cambio en un coche) gear; (animación) nightlife; **— atrás** reverse; **ponerse en —** to get going; **puesta en —** beginning; **sobre la —** as you go

marchante MF (vendedor) art dealer; (cliente) customer

marchar VI (soldado) to march; (máquina, vehículo) to run; **—se** to go away

marchista MF walker

marchitar VT to wither; **—se** to wither, to shrivel up

marchito ADJ withered, shriveled up

marcial ADJ martial

marco M (de un cuadro, de una puerta, de referencia) frame; (moneda) mark

marea F tide; — **baja** low tide; — **alta** high tide

mareado ADJ (en un barco) seasick; (en un coche) carsick; (de alegría) giddy; (con vértigo) dizzy, lightheaded

marear VT (dar vértigo) to make dizzy; (en un barco) to make seasick; —**se** (tener vértigo) to get dizzy; (en un barco) to get seasick

marejada F tidal wave

maremoto M tidal wave

mareo M (en un barco) seasickness; (en un vehículo) motion sickness; (vértigo) dizziness

marfil M ivory

marfileño -ña ADJ & MF Ivorian

margarina F margarine

margarita F daisy; **echar —s a los cerdos** to cast pearls before swine

margen M (de un papel) margin; (de la sociedad) fringe; MF (de un río) bank; — **de error** margin of error; — **de ganancia** profit margin, markup; — **de seguridad** margin of safety; **al —** on the outside

marginación F (de un grupo) marginalization; (de un individuo) isolation; **hay cierta — entre entre los colegas** there is a certain distance among the colleagues; **la — de ciertos grupos minoritarios** the marginalization of certain minorities

marginado -da ADJ & MF outcast

marginal ADJ marginal

marginar VT to marginalize

mariachi M mariachi

marido M husband

mariguana, marihuana F marijuana; *fam* pot

marimba F marimba

marina F navy; — **mercante** merchant marine

marinar VT to marinate

marinero -ra ADJ (buque) seaworthy; (nación) seafaring; MF sailor

marino -na ADJ marine; MF sailor; (oficial) naval officer

marioneta F marionette

mariposa F (insecto) butterfly (también en natación); (tuerca) wing nut; — **nocturna** moth

mariquita F ladybug

mariscal M marshal; — **de campo** (militar) field marshal; (fútbol americano) quarterback

mariscos M PL shellfish

marítimo ADJ maritime

marketing M marketing

marmita F pot

mármol M marble

marmóreo ADJ marble

marmota F groundhog

maroma F rope

marqués M marquis

marquesa F marquise

marrano M hog

marrón ADJ brown

marroquí ADJ & MF Moroccan

Marruecos M Morocco

marshalés -esa ADJ & MF Marshallese

marsopa F porpoise

martes M Tuesday

martillar VI/VT to hammer

martillo M hammer (también hueso del oído, pieza de revólver); (de juez) gavel; — **neumático** jackhammer

martinete M (martillo grande) pile driver; (pieza de piano) piano hammer

martini M martini

mártir MF martyr

martirio M martyrdom

martirizar[47] VT to martyr, to torment

marxismo M Marxism

marzo M March

mas CONJ but

más ADJ more; PREP plus; ADV more; (más tiempo) longer; — **allá de** beyond; — **bien** rather; — **de tres** more than three; — **o menos** more or less; — **que nada** primarily; — **que nunca** more than ever; — **que tú** more than you; **a lo —** at best; **a — tardar** at the latest; **de —** extra; **el — allá** the hereafter; **es de lo — simpático** he's really nice; **es —** furthermore; **está de —** it is superfluous; **otro —** yet another; **por — que** no matter how much; **y — todavía** and then some

masa F mass; (de agua) body; (de harina) batter; (para amasar) dough; **en —** en masse, in large numbers; **las —s** the masses; — **de hojaldre** puff pastry

masacrar VT to massacre, to slaughter

masacre M massacre

masaje M massage

masajear VT to massage

masajista M masseur; F masseuse

mascar[30] VI/VT (chicle) to chew; (con ruido) to crunch

máscara F mask; — **de gas** gas mask

mascarada F masquerade

mascota F (animal doméstico) pet; (emblema de un equipo) mascot

masculino ADJ (como un hombre, género gramatical) masculine; (del hombre) male

mascullar VI/VT to mumble

masilla F putty

masivo ADJ massive

masón M mason

masonería F masonry

masoquismo M masochism

mastectomía F mastectomy

máster M master; — **en administración de empresas** master of business administration

masticar[30] VT to chew

mástil M (en un barco) mast; (para una bandera) flagpole, flagstaff

mastín M mastiff

masturbarse VI to masturbate

mata F bush; **— de pelo** head of hair

matadero M slaughterhouse

matador ADJ horrendous; M bullfighter

matanza F slaughter, killing

matar VT to kill; (animales) to butcher, to slaughter; **— a tiros** to gun down; **— de hambre** to starve; VT **matasellar** to cancel a stamp; M SG **matamoscas** flyswatter; M SG **matasellos** postmark; M SG **matasanos** quack [doctor]

mate M (en ajedrez) checkmate; (planta, bebida) mate; ADJ (pintura) flat; **hacer un —** (baloncesto) to dunk the ball

matemática, matemáticas F mathematics

matemático -ca ADJ mathematical; (exacto) precise; MF mathematician

materia F (sustancia) matter; (tema de estudio) school subject; (tema) topic; **— extraña** extraneous matter; **— fecal** fecal matter; **— gris** gray matter; **— prima** raw material

material ADJ (necesidades) material; (autor) real; M material

materialismo M materialism

maternal ADJ (instinto) maternal; (amor) motherly

maternidad F (relacionado con el nacimiento) maternity; (estado de ser madre) motherhood

materno ADJ maternal

matiné M matinee

matiz M (de un color) tint, shade, hue; (de ironía) tinge; (de sentido) nuance

matizar[47] VT (mezclar colores) to blend, to tinge; (moderar) to qualify

matón -ona MF (persona que intimida a los pequeños) bully; (pandillero, peleador) thug

matorral M (mata) thicket; (región) bush

matraz M flask

matriarca F matriarch

matrícula F (alumnado) enrollment, matriculation; (de un coche) registration; (placa) license plate; (costo de la universidad) tuition fees

matriculación F matriculation

matricular VT to matriculate, to enroll

matrilineal ADJ matrilineal

matrimonial ADJ marital

matrimonio M (estado civil) matrimony, marriage; (pareja) married couple

matriz F (en matemáticas) matrix; (bidimensional) array; (útero) womb; (plantilla) stencil; **casa —** main office

matrona ADJ frumpy, matronly; F matron

matutino ADJ of the morning

maullar VI to mew

maullido M mew

mauriciano -na ADJ & MF Mauritian

Mauricio M Mauritius

Mauritania F Mauritania

mauritano -na MF Mauritanian

maxilar M jawbone

máxima F maxim

maximizar VT to maximize

máximo ADJ & M maximum; (autoridad) ultimate; (cuidado) utmost; **— histórico** all-time high

maya ADJ & MF Maya, Mayan

mayo M (mes) May; (palo) maypole

mayonesa F mayonnaise

mayor ADJ (de tamaño) greater, larger; (de edad) older, elder; (rango, clave) major; **al por —** wholesale; **dedo —** middle finger; **el — número de votos** the most votes; M (adulto) adult

mayoral M boss

mayordomo M butler

mayoreo M wholesale

mayoría F majority; **— de edad** legal age, majority; **en su —** largely

mayorista MF wholesale dealer

mayoritario ADJ majority

mayúsculo -la ADJ (letra) capital; (problema) major; F capital letter

mazmorra F dungeon

mazo M mallet

mazorca F (con maíz) ear of corn; (sin maíz) corncob

me PRON PERS **él — vio** he saw me; **él — habló** he talked to me; **se — murió el perro** my dog died on me

mecánico -ca ADJ mechanical; MF mechanic; F mechanics

mecanismo M mechanism; **— de seguridad** safety device

mecanografía F typewriting

mecanografiar[28] VI/VT to type

mecanógrafo -fa MF typist

mecedora F rocking chair, rocker

mecenas MF SG/PL patron, sponsor

mecenazgo M patronage

mecer[32] VI/VT (cuna) to rock; (columpio) to swing

mecha F (de una vela) wick; (de explosivos) fuse; (de pelo) lock; **—s** (en el pelo) highlights

mechar VT (rellenar con tocino) to lard; (robar) to shoplift

mechero -ra MF shoplifter; M burner; **— Bunsen** Bunsen burner

mechón M lock, strand

medalla F medal

médano M dune

media F (hasta el muslo) stocking; (hasta la cintura) pantyhose; (calcetín) sock; (promedio) mean; M PL (medios de comunicación) media

mediación F mediation

mediador -ora MF mediator

mediados LOC ADV **a — de mayo** in mid-May

mediana F median

mediano ADJ (intermedio en tamaño) medium; (intermedio en calidad) average; **de tamaño — middle-sized; de mediana edad** middle-aged

medianoche F midnight

mediante PREP by means of

mediar VI (en un asunto) to mediate, to intervene; (tiempo) to intervene; **mediaba febrero** it was mid-February

medible ADJ measurable

medicación F medication

medicamento M medicine, drug

medicar VT to medicate; **—se** to self-medicate

medicina F medicine; **— defensiva** defensive medicine; **— familiar** family practice

medición F (de una cantidad) measurement; (de un terreno) survey

médico -ca MF doctor, physician; **— forense** coroner, medical examiner; **— general** general practitioner; **— tratante** attending physician; ADJ medical

medida F (dimensión) measure; (acto de medir) measurement; **— cautelar** restraining order; **— para áridos** dry measure; **a — que** as; **en la — en que** to the extent that; **hacer a la —** to make to measure; **hecho a la —** made-to-measure; **tomar —s** to take measures; **tomarle las —s a alguien** to measure someone

medidor M gauge, meter

medieval ADJ medieval

medio ADJ (la mitad) half; **— pastel** half a cake; (promedio) average; **el ciudadano —** the average man; **—día** (hora) noon, midday; (hora de comer) lunch hour, noon hour; (punto cardinal) south; (territorio) the south; **— hermano** half-brother; **a media asta** at half-mast; **a — camino** halfway; **clase media** middle class; **el americano —** the average American; **media hora** half an hour; **mi media naranja** my better half; **temperatura media** mean temperature; **— tiempo** (fútbol) halftime; **de — tiempo** part-time; **media volea** (tenis) half-volley; **hacer una cosa a medias** to do something halfway; **ir a medias** to go halves; M (centro) middle; (ambiente) medium; **—s** means, resources; **— ambiente** environment; **—s de comunicación** media; **— de transporte** means of transport; **en [el] — de** in the middle of; **en — de la calle** in the middle of the street; **meterse de por —** to intervene; **por — de** by means of; **por todos los —s** by all possible means; ADV half; **a — derretir** half-melted

medioambiental ADJ environmental

mediocre ADJ mediocre; (actuación) lackluster

mediocridad F mediocrity

medir[9] VI/VT to measure; VT (consecuencias) to gauge; (terreno) to survey; **— a pasos** to step off; **—se** to be moderate

meditación F meditation

meditar VI to meditate, to ponder

mediterráneo ADJ Mediterranean

médium MF medium, psychic

medroso ADJ fearful

médula F marrow, pith; **— espinal** spinal cord; **— ósea** bone marrow

medusa F jellyfish, man-of-war

megabyte M megabyte

megáfono M megaphone

megahercio, megahertz M megahertz

megalomanía F megalomania

mejilla F cheek

mejor ADJ better; **el —** the best; **en el — de los casos** at best; **te deseo lo —** I wish you the best; ADV better; **a lo —** maybe; **tanto — so** much the better

mejora F improvement

mejoramiento M improvement

mejorar VT to improve, to improve upon; (software, aparato) to upgrade; (las posibilidades de uno) to better; VI (ventas) to pick up; **—se** to get better/well

mejoría F improvement

melancolía F melancholy, gloom

melancólico ADJ melancholy, gloomy

melanoma M melanoma

melaza F molasses

melena F mane

melindre M affectation

melindroso ADJ affected, finicky

mella F notch; **hacer —** to make a dent

mellar VT to notch

mellizo -za ADJ & MF twin

melocotón M peach

melocotonero M peach tree

melodía F melody

melódico ADJ (agradable al oído) melodious; (relativo a la melodía) melodic

melodioso ADJ melodious

melodrama M melodrama

melómano -na ADJ music-loving; MF music lover

melón M melon, cantaloupe

membrana F (en un órgano) membrane; (en las patas de los patos) web

membrete M letterhead

membrillo M (fruta) quince; (árbol) quince tree

membrudo ADJ stout

memorable ADJ memorable

memorándum M memorandum

memoria F (facultad de recordar, recuerdo) memory; (obra autobiográfica) memoir;

(actas) proceedings; — **de acceso directo** random access memory [RAM]; — **de caché** cache memory; — **de ROM** read-only memory; — **de sólo lectura** read-only memory [ROM]; — **expandida** expanded memory; — **intermedia** buffer; — **residente** internal memory; **de** — by heart; **hacer** — to try to remember/recollect
memorial M memorial
memorizar[47] VI/VT to memorize
mención F mention
mencionar VT to mention
mendigar[40] VI to beg
mendigo -ga MF beggar
mendrugo M large crumb
menear VT (las caderas) to wiggle, to wriggle, to shake; (la cola) to wag
meneo M (de las caderas) wiggle; (de la cola) wag
menesteroso ADJ needy, destitute
mengua F diminution, waning
menguante ADJ waning
menguar[25] VI (luna) to wane; (energía) to flag; (provisiones) to dwindle
meningitis F meningitis
menjurje M concoction
menopausia F menopause
menor ADJ (de tamaño) smaller; (de cantidad) lesser, smaller; (de edad) younger; (de importancia, en música) minor; **el** — (de tamaño) the smallest; (de cantidad) the least, the smallest; (de edad) the youngest; MF — **de edad** minor; **al por** — retail
menos ADV (contables) less; (contables) fewer; — **de** less than, fewer than; — **de lo que se esperaba** less than expected, fewer than expected; — **mal** just as well; **a** — **que** unless; **al** — at least; **dar de** — to shortchange; **echar de** — to miss; **lo** — the least; **no es para** — there is good reason; **por lo** — at least; **signo de** — minus sign; **venir a** — to decline; **el que trabaja** — the one who works the least; **no puede** — **que hacerlo** he cannot help doing it; **tienes** — **que yo** you have less than I; **trabaja** — **que yo** she works less than I; PREP (salvo) except, but; **las cinco** — **cuarto** quarter to five; ADJ & PRON less, least; — **agua** less water; — **problemas** fewer problems; M minus
menoscabar VT to impair, to undermine
menoscabo M impairment
menospreciar VI/VT (despreciar) to despise; VT (burlarse de) to belittle, to demean
menosprecio M contempt
mensaje M message; — **de error** error message; — **de texto** text message
mensajería F carrier; — **instantánea** instant messaging
mensajero -ra MF messenger, courier
menstruación F menstruation

menstruar VI to menstruate
mensual ADJ monthly
mensualidad F (recibida) monthly allowance; (pagada) monthly installment
mensuario ADJ monthly
mensurable ADJ measurable
menta F mint, peppermint; — **verde** spearmint
mental ADJ mental
mentalidad F mentality
mente F mind
mentecato -ta ADJ foolish, simple; MF simpleton
mentir[8] VI to lie
mentira F lie, falsehood
mentirilla F fib, white lie
mentiroso -sa ADJ lying; MF liar
mentón M chin
mentor -ora MF mentor
menú M menu (también de computadoras); — **abatible** pull-down menu; — **del día** daily special; — **de inicio** start menu; — **emergente** pop-up menu
menudeo LOC ADV **al** — retail
menudo ADJ (pequeño) small; (insignificante) insignificant; **a** — often, frequently; **dinero** — small change; — **perro** that's some dog; M (entrañas) entrails
meñique ADJ & M little finger, *fam* pinkie; **dedo** — little finger
meollo M (médula) marrow; (parte sustancial de un asunto) marrow, pith, core; (seso) brain
mequetrefe M runt, pipsqueak
mercachifle M peddler, huckster
mercadear VT to market
mercadeo M merchandising; — **de nicho** niche marketing
mercader M merchant
mercadería F merchandise
mercado M market, marketplace; — **alcista** bull market; — **bajista** bear market; — **de divisas** currency exchange; — **de prueba** test market; — **de pulgas** flea market; — **de valores** stock market; — **extrabursátil** aftermarket; — **libre** free market; — **negro** black market; — **secundario** aftermarket
mercadotecnia F marketing
mercancía F merchandise, goods
mercante ADJ merchant
mercantil ADJ mercantile
merced LOC ADV — **a** thanks to; **a [la]** — **de** at the mercy of
mercenario -ria ADJ & MF mercenary
mercería F notions store
mercurio M mercury, quicksilver
merecedor ADJ deserving
merecer[35] VT to deserve, to merit
merecido M deserved punishment, due
merendar[1] VI to have a snack
merendero M picnic area

merezca, merezco *ver* merecer
meridiano ADJ & M meridian
meridional ADJ southern; MF southerner
merienda F afternoon snack
mérito M merit
meritorio ADJ meritorious, worthy
merluza F hake
merma F decrease
mermar VI/VT to decrease, to dwindle
mermelada F (de fresa, pera) jam; (de cítricos) marmalade
mero ADJ mere; **la mera idea** the very idea; M grouper
merodear VI to loiter
mes M month
mesa F (mueble) table; (consejo) board; (formación geológica) mesa; **— de noche** nightstand; **levantar la —** to clear the table; **poner la —** to set the table
mesada F monthly allowance
mesero -ra M waiter; F waitress
meseta F plateau
mesón M inn, lodge
mesonero -ra F innkeeper
mestizo -za ADJ (perros) mongrel; MF (mezcla de europeo e india) mestizo; (perro de raza mezclada) mongrel
mesura F moderation
mesurado ADJ (persona, opinión) moderate; (respuesta) measured
meta F (objetivo) goal; (en una carrera) finish line
metabólico ADJ metabolic
metabolismo M metabolism
metafísica F metaphysics
metafísico ADJ metaphysical
metáfora F metaphor
metafórico ADJ metaphorical
metal M metal; **— precioso** precious metal
metálico ADJ metallic; M cash
metalurgia F metallurgy
metamorfosis F metamorphosis
metano M methane
metástasis F metastasis
metastatizar VI to metastasize
meteorito M meteorite
meteoro M meteor
meteorología F meteorology
meteorológico ADJ meteorological; **parte —** weather report
meteorólogo -ga M weatherman; F weatherwoman
meter VT (en una bolsa) to put [into], to stick [into]; (un lío) to force [into]; (invertir) to invest; **— el estómago** to suck in one's stomach; **— la pata** to make a mistake; **— miedo** to scare; **— ruido** to make noise; **— un gol** to score a goal; **—se** to meddle; **—se a bailar** to begin to dance; **—se con** to mess

with; **—se en camisa de once varas** to get oneself into a fix
metódico ADJ methodical
método M method
metodología F methodology
metralleta F portable machine gun
métrico ADJ metric
metro M (medida, ritmo poético) meter; (cinta de medir) measuring tape; (tren subterráneo) subway, metro
metrónomo M metronome
metrópoli F metropolis
metropolitano ADJ metropolitan; M subway
mexicano -na ADJ & MF Mexican
México M Mexico
mezcla F (de ingredientes) mixture, mix; (en albañilería) mortar; (de café, especias) blend
mezclador -ora MF (persona) mixer; F (aparato) mixer
mezclar VT (ingredientes) to mix, to blend; (naipes) to shuffle; (números) to scramble; **—se** (combinarse) to mix; (tener trato con) to mingle; (entrometerse) to meddle
mezcolanza F hodgepodge
mezquindad F (crueldad) meanness; (tacañería) stinginess
mezquino ADJ (cruel) mean, mean-spirited, petty; (insignificante) small, petty; (tacaño) tight, stingy
mezquita F mosque
mi ADJ POS my
mí PRON PERS me; **es para —** it's for me; **me vio a —** he saw me; **me la dio a —** he gave it to me
miau M meow
mico M long-tailed monkey
micra F micron
micro M (autobús) bus; (micrófono) microphone
microbio M microbe, germ
microbiología F microbiology
microcirugía F microsurgery
microcomputadora F microcomputer
microeconomía F microeconomics
microficha F microfiche
microfilm M microfilm
micrófono M microphone
Micronesia F Micronesia
micronesio -sia ADJ & MF Micronesian
microonda F microwave; M SG **—s** microwave oven
microordenador M microcomputer
microorganismo M microorganism
microprocesador M microprocessor
microscópico ADJ microscopic
microscopio M microscope; **— electrónico** electron microscope
mida, mide, midiendo, midiera, midiese *ver* medir
miedo M fear; **— al escenario** stage fright;

tener — to be afraid
miedoso ADJ fearful
miel F honey
miembro M (integrante) member; (extremidad) limb
mienta, miente *ver* mentir
mientras CONJ (durante) while, as; (siempre y cuando) as long as; **— que** while; **— tanto** meanwhile; ADV in the meantime
miércoles M Wednesday
mies F grain; **—es** fields of grain
miga F crumb; **hacer buenas —s** to get along well
migaja F crumb
migración F migration
migrante ADJ migrant
migraña F migraine
migrar VI to migrate
migratorio ADJ migratory
mil NUM thousand; **— millones** billion; **llegamos a las — y quinientas** we got there very late
milagro M miracle, wonder
milagroso ADJ miraculous
milano M kite
milenio M millennium
milicia F militia
miligramo M milligram
mililitro M milliliter
milímetro M millimeter
militancia F (actitud) militance; (actitud) militancy
militante ADJ & MF militant
militar ADJ military; MF soldier; VI to militate
milla F mile
millaje M mileage
millar M thousand
millón M million
millonario-ria MF millionaire
millonésimo ADJ & M millionth
mimar VT to pamper, to spoil, to coddle
mimbre M wicker
mímico ADJ mimic; F mimicry
mimo M (trato cariñoso) caressing, cuddling; MF (actor) mime
mimoso ADJ cuddly
mina F (yacimiento) mine; (explosivo) [land] mine; (de un lápiz) lead; (fuente) storehouse
minado M mining
minar VT (sembrar minas) to mine; (socavar) to undermine; VI (cavar) to burrow
mineral M mineral; (de oro) ore; ADJ mineral
minería F mining
minero-ra MF miner; ADJ mining
mingitorio M urinal
miniatura F miniature
mini-break M (tenis) mini-break
minicomputadora F minicomputer
minifalda F miniskirt

minifundio M subsistence farm
minimizar[47] VT (gastos) to minimize; (a una persona) to belittle; VI (un incidente) to play down
mínimo ADJ (cantidad) least; (tamaño) smallest; M minimum; **como —** at least; **en lo más —** at all
minino M kitty
miniordenador M minicomputer
ministerial ADJ cabinet, ministerial
ministerio M (religioso) ministry; (gubernamental) ministry, department
ministro-tra MF minister, secretary; **— de justicia** attorney general
minoría F minority
minoridad F minority
minorista MF retailer
minoritario ADJ minority
mintiendo, mintiera, mintiese, mintió *ver* mentir
minucioso ADJ (detalle) minute; (trabajo) thorough; (persona) fastidious
minúsculo ADJ (tamaño) small, minuscule; (cantidad) negligible; **letra minúscula** lowercase letter
minusvalía F disability
minusválido-da ADJ disabled; MF disabled person
minutas F (honorarios) lawyers' fees; (actas) minutes
minutero M minute hand
minuto M minute
mío ADJ & PRON mine; **este libro es —** this book is mine; **un amigo —** a friend of mine
miope ADJ shortsighted, nearsighted
miopía F nearsightedness, myopia
mira F (dispositivo de arma) gun sight; (intención) intention; **con —s** with a view to
mirada F gaze, look; **— asesina** dirty look; **— de soslayo** side glance; **— fija** stare
mirador M vantage point, overlook
miramiento M consideration
mirar VI/VT to look [at]; (un partido, televisión) to watch; **— de soslayo** to look askance [at]; **— fijamente** to stare [at]; **¡mira [tú]!** you don't say!
miríada F myriad
mirilla F peephole
mirlo M blackbird
mirón M (curioso) onlooker; (erótico) voyeur
mirto M myrtle
misa F mass
misantropía F misanthropy
misántropo-pa MF misanthrope
misceláneo ADJ miscellaneous
miserable ADJ (vil, pobre) wretched, unhappy; (insignificante) paltry; (tacaño) miserly
miseria F (desgracia) misery; (pobreza) poverty,

squalor; (cantidad despreciable) trifle
misericordia F mercy
misericordioso ADJ merciful, gracious
mísero ADJ miserable
misil M missile; **— balístico** ballistic missile; **— crucero** cruise missile
misión F mission (también religiosa)
misionero -ra MF missionary
mismo ADJ same; **ese — día** that very day; **se nombró a sí —** he named himself; **lo —** the same thing; **me da lo —** it's all the same to me; **yo —** I myself
misoginia F misogyny
misterio M mystery
misterioso ADJ mysterious
místico -ca ADJ mystical; MF mystic
mitad F half; **por la —** in half; **en la — de** in the middle of; **a — de[l] camino** midway
mítico ADJ mythic, mythical
mitigar[40] VT to mitigate
mitin M political meeting
mito M myth
mitocondria F mitochondria
mitología F mythology
mitológico ADJ mythological
mixto ADJ mixed; **escuela mixta** coed school
mobiliario M furniture
mocasín M (zapatilla, culebra) moccasin; (zapato sin cordones) loafer
mochar VT to chop off
mochila F backpack, knapsack
moción F motion
moco M (interno) mucus
moda F fashion; **de —** fashionable, in style; **ponerse de —** to catch on
modales M PL manners
modalidad F form, variant; **ganó oro en la — de espalda** she won gold in the backstroke; **la — italiana es más conocida** the Italian form is better known
Moldavia F Moldova
modelar VI/VT to model
modelo ADJ & MF model
módem M modem
moderación F moderation, restraint
moderado -da ADJ (posición política) moderate; (invierno) mild; (precio) reasonable; (respuesta) measured; (clima) temperate; MF moderate
moderar VT (restringir) to moderate, to restrain; (presidir) to moderate
modernidad F (actualidad) modern age; (actualidad) modern world
modernismo M (cualidad de moderno) modernity, modernness; (tendencia artística) modernism
modernización F modernization
moderno ADJ modern
modestia F modesty

modesto ADJ modest
módico ADJ moderate, reasonable
modificación F modification
modificar[30] VT to modify
modismo M idiom
modista MF dressmaker
modo M (manera) mode, manner, way; (categoría gramatical) mood; (de computadora/ordenador) mode; **— a prueba de fallos/errores** safe mode; **— de ahorro** power-save mode; **— de dormir** sleep mode; **— de entrega** mode of delivery; **— de reescritura** overwrite mode; **a — de** by way of; **del mismo —** in like manner, similarly; **de ningún —** by no means; **de — que** so that; **de otro —** otherwise; **de ningún —** not at all; **de todos —s** anyway; **en cierto —** in a way; **ni —** no dice; **no hay —** no way
modorra F drowsiness
modulación F modulation
modular VT to modulate
módulo M (componente) module; (unidad) unit
mofa F jeer, ridicule
mofarse VI **— de** to make fun of, to scoff at
mofeta F skunk
moflete M fat cheek, jowl
mohair M mohair
mohín M grimace
moho M mold, mildew
mohoso ADJ moldy
mojado -da ADJ wet
mojadura F wetting
mojar VT (humedecer) to wet; (sumergir) to dip; **—se** to get wet
mojigatería F prudery
mojigato -ta ADJ prudish; MF prude
mojo M dip
mojón M landmark
molar ADJ molar
moldavo -va ADJ & MF Moldovan
molde M (norma) mold, cast; (tortera) cake pan; (patrón) pattern; (de imprenta) die; **letras de —** block letters
moldeado M molding
moldear VT to mold, to cast
moldura F molding
mole F mass
molécula F molecule
molecular ADJ molecular
moler[6] VI/VT to mill, to grind; **— a palos** to beat thoroughly
molestar VT to bother, to pester; **no te molestes** don't bother
molestia F bother, nuisance; **no te tomes la —** don't go to the trouble
molesto ADJ (que molesta) bothersome, irksome; (que está molesto) uneasy, uncomfortable
molibdeno M molybdenum

molienda F grinding
molinero -ra MF miller
molinete M (puerta) turnstile; (juguete) pinwheel
molinillo M mill, grinder
molino M mill; **— de viento** windmill
mollete M muffin
molusco M mollusk
momentáneo ADJ momentary
momento M (tiempo) moment; (impulso) momentum; **al —** immediately; **a cada —** continually; **en todo —** all the time; **no veo el —** I can't wait
momia F mummy
Mónaco M Monaco
monada F (acción graciosa) antic; (persona atractiva) *fam* peach
monarca MF monarch
monarquía F monarchy
monárquico -ca MF monarchist; ADJ monarchical
monasterio M monastery
mondar VT to pare; **—se los dientes** to pick one's teeth; M SG **mondadientes** toothpick
moneda F (dinero metálico) coin; (divisa) currency; **— corriente** common currency; **— de curso legal** legal tender; **— falsa** counterfeit money
monegasco -ca ADJ & MF Monegasque
monería F antic
monetario ADJ monetary
mongol -la ADJ & MF Mongolian
Mongolia F Mongolia
mongoloide ADJ mongoloid
monigote M puppet
monitor -ora M (aparato) monitor; **— [a] color** color monitor; MF (persona) monitor
monitorear VT to monitor
monitoreo M monitoring
monitorización F monitoring; **— fetal** fetal monitoring
monja F nun
monje M monk
mono -na MF (simio) monkey; **— araña** spider monkey; M (mimo) mimic; (prenda de trabajo) overalls, coverall; (síndrome de abstinencia) withdrawal symptoms; **dormir la mona** to sleep it off; ADJ cute
monogamia F monogamy
monokini M topless swimsuit
monólogo M monologue, monolog
mononucleosis F mononucleosis
monopatín M (tabla) skateboard; (con manillar) scooter; (de nieve) snowboard
monopolio M monopoly
monopolizar[47] VT (un producto) to monopolize; (un mercado) to corner
monotonía F monotony
monótono ADJ monotonous

monseñor M monsignor
monserga F nonsense
monstruo M (ser imaginario, persona perversa) monster; (persona grotesca) freak; ADJ INV monstrous
monstruosidad F monstrosity
monstruoso ADJ monstrous
monta F mount; **de poca —** of little value
montaje M (de un aparato) assembly, set up; (de una película) editing
montante M (total) total; (ventana de puerta) transom; (columna) upright
montaña F mountain; **— rusa** roller coaster
montañés -esa ADJ mountain; MF mountain dweller
montañismo M mountaineering
montañoso ADJ mountainous
montar VT (ir a caballo, en bicicleta) to ride; (un aparato) to assemble; (una película) to edit; (subirse al caballo) to mount, to get on; **— en cólera** to fly into a rage; **— una escena** to make a scene; **—se a caballo** to mount a horse
montaraz ADJ coarse
monte M (montaña) mount; (zona agreste) wilderness; **— de piedad** pawnshop
montés ADJ (salvaje) wild; (de la montaña) of the mountains
montículo M mound; (béisbol) pitcher's mound
monto M amount; **— debido** amount due; **— pagado** amount paid
montón M (pila) pile, heap; (de papel) stack; (de nieve) drift; (de flores) basketful; (de gente) bunch; **a montones** in abundance; **del —** run-of-the-mill
montura F (animal) mount; (silla) saddle; (armazón de gafas) frame, rim
monumental ADJ monumental
monumento M monument
moño M (de pelo) bun; (adorno) bow
mopa F mop
moquearse VI to become snotty
moquillo M distemper
MOR [movimientos oculares rápidos] M PL REM
mora F (fruta) blackberry, mulberry; (tardanza) delay, delinquency; **en —** in default, past due
morada F dwelling, abode
morado ADJ purple; **ojo —** black eye
morador -ora MF dweller
moral ADJ moral; F (principios éticos) morals; (estado de ánimo) morale; M mulberry tree
moraleja F moral
moralidad F morality
moralista MF moralist
moralizar[47] VI/VT to moralize
morar VI to dwell, to abide
mórbido ADJ morbid
morbilidad F (predisposición a la enfermedad)

morbidity

morbosidad F (que produce enfermedad) morbidity

morboso ADJ (mórbido) morbid; (atractivo) sexy

morcilla F blood sausage

mordacidad F sharpness

mordaz ADJ (comentario) cutting, sharp; (persona) sharp-tongued

mordaza F (de la boca) gag; (de un torno) vise jaw

mordedor ADJ biting, snappy

mordedura F bite

morder[6] VI/VT to bite; **—se la lengua** to bite one's tongue

mordida F (mordisco) bite; (soborno) bribe, kickback

mordiscar[30] VI/VT to nibble; to nip

mordisco M nibble, nip

mordisquear VI/VT to nip; to nibble

mordisqueo M nibble

moreno ADJ (piel) dark, dark-skinned, swarthy; (pelo) dark, brunette

moretón M bruise

morfina F morphine

morgue F morgue

moribundo ADJ dying, moribund

morir[7, 74] VI (persona, animal) to die; (calle) to end; **—se de envidia** to eat one's heart out; **—se de hambre** to starve; **—se de miedo** to die of fear; **—se de risa** to die laughing; **—se por algo** to crave something; **—se por alguien** to be crazy about someone

morisco ADJ Moorish

moro -ra ADJ Moorish; MF Moor; **—s y cristianos** (personas) Moors and Christians; (plato) beans and rice; **no hay —s en la costa** the coast is clear

morocho ADJ dark-haired, brunet, brunette

moroso ADJ delinquent, deadbeat

morrear VI to make out

morriña F homesickness

morro M (monte) knoll; (caradura) gall, nerve; (de un avión) nose; (de animal) snout

morrón M bell pepper

morsa F walrus

mortaja F shroud

mortal ADJ mortal, deadly; MF mortal

mortalidad F mortality

mortandad F death toll

mortecino ADJ fading

mortero M mortar

mortífero ADJ deadly

mortificación F mortification, chagrin

mortificar[30] VT to mortify, to chagrin

mortuorio ADJ mortuary; **casa mortuaria** funeral home

mosaico M mosaic

mosca F (insecto) fly; (dinero) dough; **—**

muerta hypocrite; **no se oía volar una —** you could have heard a pin drop

mosquear VT (crear desconfianza) to cause distrust; (hacer enfadar) to enrage; **—se** (desconfiar) to distrust; (enfadarse) to become enraged

mosquitero M (pantalla de ventana) window screen; (red) mosquito net

mosquito M mosquito

mostacho M mustache, moustache

mostaza F mustard

mostrador M counter

mostrar[5] VT to show; **—se reticente** to appear reticent

mostrenco ADJ stray

mota F speck, speckle

mote M nickname

moteado ADJ speckled, spotted

motear VT to speck, to speckle

motejar VI **— de** to brand as

motel M motel

motín M (en un barco) mutiny; (de prisioneros) riot

motivación F motivation

motivar VT (impulsar) to motivate; (causar) to cause

motivo M (causa) motive, reason; (figura repetida) motif, theme; **con — de** on the occasion of

moto F bike, motorcycle

motocicleta F motorcycle

motociclista MF biker, motorcyclist

motor ADJ of motion; M motor, engine; **— de reacción** jet engine; **— de búsqueda** search engine; **— de combustión interna** internal combustion engine; **— fuera de borda** outboard engine

motriz ADJ **fuerza —** motive power

movedizo ADJ restless

mover[6] VT to move; **— palancas** to pull strings; **—se** to move, to budge

movible ADJ movable

movido ADJ (vida, fiesta) eventful; (foto) blurred; **— por gas** powered by gas

móvil M (motivo) motive; (teléfono) mobile telephone; (adorno, juguete) mobile; ADJ (que se mueve) mobile; (que puede ser movido) movable; **un blanco —** a moving target

movilidad F mobility

movilización F mobilization

movilizar[47] VI/VT to mobilize

movimiento M (cambio de posición) movement, motion; (organización, pieza de reloj) movement; (comercial) traffic; **—s oculares rápidos** REM [rapid eye movements]; **los rojos tienen poco —** the red ones don't sell well; **un cuerpo en —** a moving body

Mozambique M Mozambique

mozambiqueño -ña ADJ & MF Mozambican

mozárabe ADJ Mozarabic

mozo -za ADJ young; **en mis años —s** in my youth; M (joven) young man; (sirviente) servant; F (joven) young woman; (sirvienta) servant; **— de cordel** porter; **buen —** handsome man

mucama F chambermaid

muchacho -cha M boy, youngster; F (chica) girl; (de servicio) maid

muchedumbre F crowd, throng

mucho ADJ a lot of; (cosas contables) many; (cosas incontables, en oraciones interrogativas y/o negativas) much; **¿tienes — tiempo?** do you have much time? **no tenemos — tiempo** we don't have much time; **tenemos —s problemas** we have many problems; ADV much; (demasiado) too much; **hace — que no lo veo** I haven't seen him for a long time; **ni con —** not by a long shot; **ni — menos** not by any means; **por — que** no matter how much; PRON a lot, many; (en preguntas y oraciones negativas) much; **¿había —s?** were there many?

mucoso ADJ mucous

muda F (de ropa, voz) change; (de plumas, piel de serpiente) molt

mudable ADJ fickle

mudanza F move

mudar VT (condiciones, clima) to change; (el pelo) to shed; (la piel, plumas) to molt; **—se [de casa]** to move [house]; **—se de ropa** to change clothes

mudez F dumbness, muteness

mudo -da ADJ (incapaz de hablar) mute, dumb; (por emoción) speechless; (película) silent; MF mute

mueble M piece of furniture; **—s** furniture

mueblería F (tienda) furniture store; (fábrica) furniture factory

mueca F grimace; **hacer —s** to grimace

muela F (diente) molar tooth; (piedra) grindstone; **— del juicio** wisdom tooth; **— impactada** impacted molar

muelle M (para embarcaciones) wharf, pier; (resorte) spring; **— en espiral** coil; **— real** mainspring

muera, muere ver morir

muérdago M mistletoe

muerte F death; **— cerebral** brain death; **— súbita** (fútbol) sudden death; (tenis) tie-break; **dar —** to kill; **sus clases son la —** his classes are unbearable; **de mala —** disreputable

muerto ADJ dead, lifeless; **— de cansancio** dead tired; **— de hambre** famished; **estoy — de sed** I'm parched; **echarle el — a uno** to pass the buck; **ni —** not in a million years

muerto ver morir

muesca F notch, indentation

muestra F (ejemplo) sample (también en computadoras); (señal) sign, token; **— de orina** urine specimen; **dar —s de impaciencia** to show impatience

muestra, muestre ver mostrar

muestrear VT to sample (también para computadoras)

muestreo M sampling

mueva, mueve ver mover

mugido M moo, lowing

mugir[46] VI to moo, to low

mugre F dirt, grime, crud

mugriento ADJ grimy, dirty

mujer F (género) woman; (esposa) wife; **— de negocios** businesswoman; **— de la vida** prostitute

mujeriego ADJ womanizing; M womanizer, *fam* player

mula ver mulo

mulato -ta ADJ & MF mulatto

muleta F crutch

muletilla F cliché

mullido ADJ fluffy

mullir[16] VT to fluff

mulo -la MF mule (también en el tráfico de drogas)

multa F fine, penalty; (de tránsito) ticket

multar VT to fine; (en tránsito) to ticket

multianual ADJ multiyear

multicultural ADJ multicultural

multilateral ADJ multilateral

multimedia M & ADJ INV multimedia

multipantalla ADJ multiscreen

múltiple ADJ multiple

multiplicación F multiplication

multiplicar[30] VI/VT to multiply; **—se** to breed

multiplicidad F multiplicity

múltiplo M multiple

multitarea F multitasking

multitud F multitude, throng

mundano ADJ mundane, worldly

mundial ADJ global, worldwide; **la guerra —** the world war

mundo M world; **todo el —** everybody; **tener — ** to be worldly; **el tercer —** the third world; **el — al revés** the world upside-down

munición F ammunition, munition

municipal ADJ municipal; **servicios —es** city services

municipalidad F municipality

municipio M municipality; (ayuntamiento) city hall

muñeca F (juguete) doll; (articulación del brazo) wrist; **— de trapo** ragdoll

muñeco M (juguete) boy doll; (de ventrílocuo) dummy; **— de nieve** snowman

muñón M stump

mural ADJ & M mural
muralla F wall
murciélago M bat
muriendo, muriera, muriese *ver* morir
murmullo M (voz baja) murmur; (ruido de agua) babble
murmuración F gossip
murmurar VI/VT (voz) to murmur; VI (agua) to babble
muro M wall; — **de contención** retaining wall
murria F the blues; **tener** — to have the blues
musa F muse
musaraña F shrew
muscular ADJ muscular
músculo M muscle
musculoso ADJ muscular
muselina F muslin
museo M museum
musgo M moss
musgoso ADJ mossy
música F music; — **de cámara** chamber music; — **folclórica** folk music; — **incidental** incidental music
musical ADJ & M musical
músico -ca ADJ musical; MF musician
musitar VI to mutter
muslo M thigh
mustio ADJ (triste) sad, humble; (marchito) limp; (deslucido) faded
musulmán -ana ADJ & MF Muslim, Moslem
mutación F mutation
mutante ADJ & MF mutant
mutilar VT to mutilate, to mangle; (a un ser vivo) to maim, to mutilate; (una estatua) to deface
mutuo ADJ mutual
muy ADV very; **estás** — **grande para eso** you're too big for that
Myanmar M Myanmar

Nn

nabo M turnip
nácar M mother-of-pearl
nacarado ADJ pearly
nacer[35] VI (un bebé) to be born; (una calle) to begin; — **de** (río) to spring from; — **de nuevo** to have a new lease on life
naciente ADJ (tendencia) incipient; (sol) rising; M (de río) origin
nacimiento M (alumbramiento) birth; (pesebre) nativity scene; (naciente) origin [of a river]; — **del pelo** hairline
nación F nation
nacional ADJ & MF national

nacionalidad F nationality
nacionalismo M nationalism
nacionalista ADJ & MF nationalist
nacionalizar[47] VT to nationalize
nada PRON nothing; *fam* squat, zilch; — **del otro mundo** nothing special; — **en absoluto** nothing at all; **como si** — as if nothing had happened; **de** — you are welcome, don't mention it; **no es por** —, **pero** I hope you don't mind my saying this, but; **no sirve para** — it's useless; **no tener** — **que ver con** to have nothing to do with; **no tengo** — **de dinero** I don't have any money; **para** — in the least; **quedar en la** — to fall through; **salir de la** — to come out of nowhere; ADV not at all; **no me gusta [para]** — I don't like it at all; (tenis) **quince a** — forty love; F (existencial) nothingness
nadador -ora MF swimmer
nadar VI/VT to swim; — **en la abundancia** to be in the lap of luxury
nadería F trifle, nothing
nadie PRON nobody; — **más** no one else; **no vi a** — **en el parque** I didn't see anyone in the park; **un don** — a nobody
nafta F gasoline
nailon M nylon
naipe M playing card
nalgada F smack on the bottom
nalgas F PL buttocks
Namibia F Namibia
namibio -bia ADJ & MF Namibian
nana F (canción de cuna) lullaby; (lastimadura) boo-boo; (niñera) babysitter
nanosegundo M nanosecond
nanotecnología F nanotechnology
napalm M napalm
napias F PL *fam* snout
naranja F (fruta) orange; ADJ INV & M (color) orange; — **de ombligo** navel orange; **mi media** — my better half
naranjal M orange grove
naranjo M orange tree
narcisismo M narcissism
narciso M narcissus, daffodil
narcolepsia F narcolepsy
narcótico ADJ & M narcotic
narcotizar[47] VT to drug
narcotraficante MF drug trafficker
narcotráfico M drug trafficking
nariz F nose; — **chata** pug nose; **sonarse la** — to blow one's nose; F PL **narices** nostrils; **se dio de narices contra la ventana** he bumped his nose on the window; **estoy hasta las narices** I've had it up to here
narración F narration
narrador -ora MF narrator
narrar VT to narrate, to recount
narrativa F narrative

narrativo ADJ narrative
NASA F NASA
nasal ADJ nasal
nata F skin of boiled milk; *Esp* cream
natación F swimming
natal ADJ (relativo al nacimiento) natal; (suelo) native; **mi ciudad —** my hometown
natalidad F birth rate
natilla[s] F SG/PL custard
nativo -va ADJ & MF native
nato ADJ **es un músico —** he's a born musician
natural ADJ (no artificial) natural; (nacido en un lugar) native; (nacido fuera del matrimonio) illegitimate; (sin afectación) unaffected; M nature; **al —** unprocessed
naturaleza F nature; **— muerta** still life
naturalidad F naturalness
naturalista MF naturalist
naturalización F naturalization
naturalizar[47] VT to naturalize; **—se** to become naturalized
naturalmente ADV (de forma natural) naturally; (desde luego) of course
naufragar[40] VI (un barco) to shipwreck; (una empresa) to fail
naufragio M shipwreck
náufrago -ga MF shipwrecked person
Nauru N Nauru
nauruano -na ADJ & MF Nauruan
náusea F nausea; **—s** morning sickness; **dar —s** to nauseate; **hasta la —** ad nauseam; **tener —s** to be nauseated, to be sick to one's stomach
nauseabundo ADJ nauseating
nauseoso ADJ (que siente náuseas) nauseous, queasy; (que provoca náuseas) nauseating
náutica F navigation
náutico ADJ nautical
navaja F (de explorador) jackknife, pocketknife; (de barbero) razor
navajazo M (golpe) stab with a jackknife; (herida) stab wound
naval ADJ naval
navarro -rra ADJ & MF Navarrese
nave F (embarcación) vessel; (parte de una catedral) nave; **— espacial** spaceship
navegable ADJ navigable
navegación F (de mar, río) navigation; (deportiva) boating; (en internet) surfing, browsing
navegador M browser; **— web** web browser
navegante MF navigator; ADJ navigating
navegar[40] VI/VT (buque) to navigate; (barco a vela) to sail; (en internet) to browse, to surf
Navidad F Christmas
navideño ADJ **fiesta navideña** Christmas party
navío M ship
nazi MF Nazi

neblina F mist
neblinoso ADJ misty
nebulosidad F cloudiness
nebuloso ADJ (poco claro) nebulous; (que tiene niebla) foggy
necesario ADJ necessary
neceser M toiletry bag
necesidad F (urgencia, sensación de falta) need; (cosa necesaria) necessity; **hacer sus —es** to relieve oneself; **de primera —** indispensable; **por —** out of necessity
necesitado ADJ needy
necesitar VT to need
necio -cia ADJ asinine, foolish
necrología F necrology
necrosis F necrosis
néctar M nectar
nectarina F nectarine
nefasto ADJ unholy
nefritis F nephritis
negación F (partícula gramatical) negation; (rechazo) denial
negar[41] VT (decir que no es verdad) to deny; (no consentir) to refuse; (no reconocer) to disavow; **—se [a]** to refuse [to]
negativa F (rechazo verbal) denial; (falta de cooperación) refusal
negativo ADJ negative; **signo —** minus sign; M [photographic] negative
negligencia F (falta de atención) negligence, neglect; (médica) malpractice
negligente ADJ negligent, neglectful
negociación F negotiation; **— laboral** collective bargaining
negociador -ora MF negotiator; ADJ negotiating
negociante MF businessperson
negociar VI/VT (acordar) to negotiate; (comerciar) to trade
negocio M (tienda, actividad comercial) business; (transacción) business deal, business transaction; **— de ventas por correo** mail-order business; **— principal** core business; **hombre de —s** businessman; **mujer de —s** businesswoman; **hacer —** to make a profit
negrear VI to appear black; VT to blacken
negrilla F boldface
negritas F PL boldface type
negro -ra ADJ black (también café sin leche); (futuro) bleak; **pasarlas negras** to undergo hardships; F (nota) quarter-note; MF (persona) person of color, black person
negrura F blackness
negruzco ADJ blackish
némesis F nemesis
nene -na M baby boy; F baby girl
nenúfar M water lily
neologismo M neologism

neón M neon
neonatal ADJ neonatal
neozelandés -esa MF New Zealander
Nepal M Nepal
nepalés -esa ADJ & MF Nepali
nepalí ADJ & MF Nepalese
nepotismo M nepotism
nervado ADJ veined
nervio M nerve; — **pellizcado** pinched nerve;
   — **pinzado** pinched nerve; **perder los —s**
   to lose one's cool; **tener los —s de punta** to
   be on edge
nerviosismo M nervousness
nervioso ADJ (relativo a los nervios) nervous;
   (inquieto) nervous, jumpy
nervudo ADJ sinewy, wiry
neto ADJ (mejoría) distinct; (ganancia) net
neumático M tire; ADJ pneumatic
neural ADJ neural
neuralgia F neuralgia
neurastenia F neurasthenia
neurocirugía F neurosurgery
neurocirujano -na MF neurosurgeon
neurólogo -ga MF neurologist
neurona F neuron, nerve cell
neurosis F neurosis
neurótico -ca ADJ & MF neurotic
neurotransmisor M neurotransmitter
neutral ADJ neutral
neutralidad F neutrality
neutralizar[47] VT to neutralize
neutro ADJ neutral; (género) neuter
neutrón M neutron
nevada F snowfall
nevado ADJ snowy
nevar[1] VI to snow
nevera F icebox, refrigerator
nevisca F snow flurry
ni CONJ & ADV — **con mucho** not by a long shot;
   — **hablar** forget it; — **habló conmigo** he
   didn't even talk to me; — **idea** [it] beats me;
   — **modo** no way; — **que esto fuera un**
   hotel it's not like this is a hotel; — **siquiera**
   not even; — **soñar** fat chance; — **trabaja** —
   estudia he neither works nor studies; — **una**
   palabra not a word; **no tiene amigos** —
   enemigos he has no friends nor enemies; **no**
   es rico — **mucho menos** he's not even close
   to being rich
Nicaragua F Nicaragua
nicaragüense ADJ & MF Nicaraguan
nicho M niche, recess
nicotina F nicotine
nidada F (huevos) nest of eggs; (crías) hatch,
   brood
nido M nest
niebla F fog
niega, niegue ver negar
nieto -ta M grandson; F granddaughter; —s
   grandchildren
nieve F snow (también droga en polvo)
Níger M Niger
Nigeria F Nigeria
nigeriano -na ADJ & MF Nigerian
nigerino -na ADJ & MF Nigerien
nigua F chigger
nihilismo M nihilism
nilón M nylon
nimio ADJ insignificant
ninguno ADJ & PRON **no tengo** — I have none /
   I don't have any; **ningún amigo mío** no
   friend of mine; **no tengo ningún libro** I
   don't have any books; — **de los dos** neither
   one; **de ningún modo** in no way
niñera F (ocasional) babysitter; (permanente)
   nanny
niñería F childish act
niñez F (infancia) childhood; (de niño) boyhood;
   (de niña) girlhood
niño -ña M child, kid, boy; F child, kid, girl;
   niña del ojo pupil [of the eye]; ADJ childish
níquel M nickel
niquelado ADJ nickel-plated
níspero M loquat
nitidez F sharpness
nítido ADJ sharp
nitrato M nitrate
nitrógeno M nitrogen
nitroglicerina F nitroglycerine
nivel M level (también herramienta); (grado
   jerárquico) echelon; — **de cobertura**
   coverage level; — **de mar** sea level; — **de**
   vida standard of living; **a** — straight; **a** — **de**
   level with
nivelar VT (emparejar) to level; (aplanar) to
   grade
níveo ADJ snowy
no ADV no; — **quiero** I don't want to; —
   acreditado unlicensed; — **afiliado**
   unaffiliated; — **ajustado** unadjusted; —
   autorizado unauthorized; — **comercial**
   noncommercial; — **confirmado**
   unconfirmed; — **conforme** nonconforming;
   — **declarado** undeclared; — **disponible**
   unavailable; — **divulgado** undisclosed; —
   esencial nonessential; — **especificado**
   unspecified; — **ético** unethical; —
   gubernamental nongovernmental; —
   negociable nonnegotiable; —
   reembolsable nonrefundable; —
   relacionado unrelated; — **residente**
   nonresident; — **restringido** unrestricted; —
   solicitado unsolicited; — **tributable**
   nontaxable; — **bien llegaron** no sooner had
   they arrived; — **sólo** not only; — **sea que**
   lest; **a** — **ser que** unless
noble ADJ noble; M nobleman; F noblewoman
nobleza F nobility

nocaut M knockout

noche F (período sin luz) night; (horas de la noche) nighttime; **—buena** Christmas Eve; **—vieja** New Year's Eve; **y día** day and night; **de —** at night; **de la — a la mañana** overnight; **esta —** tonight; **por la —** at night

noción F notion; **no tener ni —** to have no clue

nocivo ADJ harmful, noxious

nocturno ADJ (que actúa de noche) nocturnal; (que sucede todas las noches) nightly

nodo M node

nodriza F wet nurse

nódulo M node

nogal M walnut tree

nómada MF nomad

ningunear VT to dismiss

nomás ADV *Am* **aquí —** close by; **así —** just like that; **entre —** come right in

nombramiento M (civil) appointment; (militar) commission

nombrar VT (a un funcionario) to name, to appoint; (a un oficial militar) to commission

nombre M name; **— completo** full name; **— de acceso** login name; **— de pila** first name; **— de soltera** maiden name; **— del usuario** username; **en — de** on behalf of; **eso no tiene —** that's unheard of; **hacerse un —** to make a name for oneself

nomenclatura F nomenclature

nomeolvides M SG forget-me-not

nómina F payroll

nominación F nomination

nominal ADJ nominal

nominar VT to nominate

non ADJ odd; M odd number

nopal M prickly pear

noquear VT to knock out

norcoreano -na ADJ & MF North Korean

nordeste ADJ & M northeast

nórdico ADJ Nordic

noreste ADJ & M northeast

norma F norm, standard; **—s industriales** industry standards

normal ADJ (estándar, común) normal, standard; F (escuela) teacher's college; (línea) perpendicular line

normalidad F normalcy, normality; **con toda —** normally; **todo volvió a la —** everything returned to normal

normalizar[47] VT to normalize

normalmente ADV normally, usually

normativa F norm

noroeste ADJ & M northwest

norte ADJ & M north

norteamericano -na ADJ & MF (de América del Norte) North American; (de EEUU) American

norteño -ña ADJ northern; MF northerner

Noruega F Norway

noruego -ga ADJ & MF Norwegian; M (lengua) Norwegian

nos PRON us; **él — vio** he saw us; **— dio el libro** he gave us the book, he gave the book to us

nosotros -as PRON we; **para —** for us

nostalgia F nostalgia

nostálgico ADJ nostalgic

nota F (musical) note; (anotación) annotation; (calificación) grade, mark; **— al pie de página** footnote; **de — ** of note; **exagerar la —** to overdo something

notable ADJ notable, noteworthy, remarkable

notablemente ADV (destacadamente) notably; (visiblemente) noticeably

notación F notation

notar VT (percibir) to note, to notice; (señalar) to note

notariar VT to notarize

notario -ria MF notary

noticia F piece of news; **—s** news; **tener —s de alguien** to hear from someone

noticiario M newscast, news bulletin

noticiero M newscast

notificación F (informe) notification; (policial) summons; **— de despido** pink slip

notificar[30] VT to notify

notorio ADJ (conocido públicamente) well-known; (evidente) obvious

novato -ta MF (profesional) novice; (policía, atleta) rookie

novecientos NUM nine hundred

novedad F novelty; **—es** news; **sin —** all's well

novedoso ADJ novel

novela F novel; **— policial** detective novel

novelesco ADJ fictional

novelista MF novelist

noveno ADJ ninth

noventa NUM ninety

noviazgo M engagement

novicio -cia MF novice

noviembre M November

novillo -lla M steer; **hacer —s** to play hooky; F heifer

novio -via M (comprometido) fiancé; (no formal) boyfriend; (de boda) bridegroom; F (comprometida) fiancée; (no formal) girlfriend; (de boda) bride

novocaína F novocaine

nubarrón M thunderhead

nube F (atmosférica) cloud; (de humo) billow; **poner por las —s** to praise to the skies; **está en las —s** his head is in the clouds; **los precios están por las —s** prices have gone through the roof

nublado ADJ (cielo) cloudy, overcast; (los ojos, de emoción) misty; (los ojos, por falta de sueño) bleary

nublar VT to blur; **—se** (el cielo) to become overcast; (los ojos) to cloud over

nubosidad F (de un concepto) nebulousness;

(del cielo) cloudiness

nuboso ADJ cloudy

nuca F nape

nuclear ADJ nuclear

núcleo M (de célula, átomo) nucleus; (de reactor) core; (de sistema operativo) kernel

nudillo M knuckle

nudismo M nudism

nudista ADJ & MF nudist

nudo M knot (también en la madera, medida de velocidad); (de una obra teatral) turning point; (en el pelo) tangle; (en plantas) node; (en la garganta) lump; — **corredizo** slipknot; — **de rizo** square knot

nudoso ADJ knotty, gnarled

nuera F daughter-in-law

nuestro ADJ POS our; — **hijo** our son; PRON ours; **esto es** — this is ours

nuevamente ADV again

nueve NUM nine

nuevo ADV new; **de** — again; **¿qué hay de** — **?** what's new?

nuez F walnut; — **de Adán** Adam's apple; — **moscada** nutmeg

nulidad F (legal) nullity; (persona) nonentity

nulo ADJ null and void, invalid

numeral ADJ & M numeral

numerar VT to number

numérico ADJ numerical

número M (dígito) number; (en un espectáculo) act; (de una revista) issue; (cifra) figure; — **de serie** serial number

numeroso ADJ numerous

nunca ADV never, not ever; **no viene** — he never comes, he doesn't ever come; **más que** — more than ever; **casi** — hardly ever; **peor que** — worse than ever

nupcial ADJ nuptial, bridal

nupcias F PL nuptials

nutria F otter

nutrición F nutrition

nutrido ADJ **el congreso tuvo una nutrida concurrencia** the conference was well attended

nutriente M nutrient

nutrir VT to nourish

nutritivo ADJ nutritious, nourishing

Ññ

ñandú M rhea

ñato ADJ *Am* pug-nosed

ñoño ADJ bland

ñu M gnu

Oo

o CONJ or; — **se casa** — **lo mato** either he gets married or I'll kill him; — **sea** that is

oasis M oasis

obedecer[35] VI/VT to obey; **esto obedece a que** this is due to the fact that

obedezca, obedezco *ver* obedecer

obediencia F obedience

obediente ADJ obedient

obertura F musical overture

obesidad F obesity

obeso ADJ obese

obispo M bishop

obituario M obituary

objeción F objection

objetable ADJ objectionable

objetar VI/VT to object, to take exception [to]

objetividad F objectivity

objetivo ADJ objective; M (lente) objective; (meta) aim, objective

objeto M object

oblea F wafer

oblicuo ADJ (inclinado) oblique; (sesgado) biased

obligación F (deber) obligation, duty; (deuda) obligation; (título financiero) bond

obligado ADJ (forzado) forced; (obligatorio) compulsory, obligatory; **me vi** — **a comprar otro coche** I was forced / had to buy another car

obligar[40] VT to force, to compel, to oblige; —**se** [a] to obligate oneself [to]

obligatorio ADJ obligatory, compulsory

oboe M oboe

obra F (artística, literaria, de construcción) work; (lugar de construcción) construction site; — **maestra** masterpiece; **en** —**s** under construction

obrar VI to act; **obra en nuestro poder** we acknowledge receipt of

obrero -ra MF worker; ADJ working

obscenidad F obscenity; —**es** filth

obsceno ADJ obscene

obscuridad *ver* oscuridad

obsequiar VT to present, to give; **me obsequió perfume** he gave me perfume

obsequio M gift

obsequioso ADJ obsequious

observación F (mirada) observation; (comentario) remark

observador -ora MF observer; ADJ observant

observancia F observance

observar VI/VT (mirar) to observe; (hacer un comentario) to remark, to observe

observatorio M observatory

obsesión F obsession

obsesionado ADJ obsessed

obsesionar VT to obsess; **—se con** to obsess over, to be obsessed with

obsesivo-compulsivo ADJ obsessive-compulsive

obstaculizar VT to impede

obstáculo M (impedimento) obstacle, hindrance, impediment; (en carreras) hurdle

obstante LOC PREP **no — tu oposición** notwithstanding your opposition; LOC ADV **no —, voy a ir** nevertheless, I am going to go

obstar VT to preclude

obstetra MF obstetrician

obstetricia F obstetrics

obstinación F obstinacy

obstinado ADJ obstinate, bullheaded

obstinarse VI to be obstinate

obstrucción F (de justicia, de un caño) obstruction, blockage; (del intestino) obstruction, occlusion; **— intestinal** intestinal obstruction

obstruir[19] VT (un movimiento, procedimiento) to obstruct, to block; (un aparato) to jam; VI **—se** to get jammed

obtención F acquisition

obtendrá, obtendría ver obtener

obtener[58] VT (bienes) to obtain, to get; (permiso) to secure; (con dificultad) to procure

obtenga, obtengo, obtiene, obtienes ver obtener

obturador M (de una cámara fotográfica) shutter; (de un coche) choke

obtuve, obtuviera, obtuviese ver obtener

obviamente ADV obviously

obviar VT to obviate, to circumvent

obvio ADJ obvious

ocasión F (vez, instancia) occasion; (oportunidad) opportunity; (ganga) bargain; **de —** reduced

ocasional ADJ occasional

ocasionar VT to occasion, to cause

ocaso M sunset, twilight

occidental ADJ occidental, western; MF westerner

occidente M west

oceánico ADJ oceanic

océano M ocean

oceanografía F oceanography

ocelote M ocelot

ochenta NUM eighty

ocho NUM eight

ochocientos NUM eight hundred

ocio M (diversión) leisure; (inacción) idleness

ociosidad F idleness

ocioso ADJ (inactivo) idle; (no usado) unused

oclusión F occlusion

octágono M octagon

octano M octane

octava F octave

octavilla F tract

octavo ADJ & M eighth

octeto M byte

octógono M octagon

octubre M October

ocular M eyepiece; ADJ **infección —** eye infection

oculista MF oculist, eye doctor

ocultar VT to conceal; (información) to withhold

ocultismo M the occult

oculto ADJ (invisible) unseen; (sobrenatural) occult; (escondido) hidden, under wraps

ocupación F (trabajo) occupation; (capacidad) occupancy

ocupado ADJ (persona, teléfono) busy; (asiento, aseo) occupied

ocupante MF occupant

ocupar VT (usar) to occupy; (contratar) to employ; **—se de** to take care of, to address

ocurrencia F witticism, quip

ocurrente ADJ witty

ocurrir VI to occur

oda F ode

odiar VI/VT to hate

odio M hatred, hate

odioso ADJ (tarea) odious; (persona) hateful, obnoxious

odontología F dentistry

odre M wineskin

OEA [Organización de Estados Americanos] F OAS

oeste ADJ & M west

ofender VI/VT to offend; **—se** to get offended, to take offense

ofensa F offense

ofensiva F (militar) offensive; (deportiva) offense; (fútbol americano) offensive series

ofensivo ADJ offensive, obnoxious

oferta F (oportunidad) offer; (rebaja) special offer; **— de apertura** opening bid; **en —** on sale; **— de prueba** trial offer; **— pública inicial** initial public offering

offset M offset

oficial -la ADJ official; MF (militar) officer; (obrero calificado) skilled worker; **— general** high-ranking officer

oficialismo M party in power

oficialista ADJ in power

oficiar VI to officiate; **— de** to serve as

oficina F (despacho) office; (dependencia gubernamental) bureau; **— central** home office, headquarters; **— en el hogar** home office

oficinista MF office worker

oficio M (actividad laboral) trade, craft; (comunicación oficial) official communication; **tiene mucho —** he knows his stuff; **buenos —s** good offices

oficioso ADJ (entrometido) officious; (no oficial) unofficial, off-the-record

ofrecer[35] VT (un regalo) to offer; (en una subasta) to bid; (una cena) to give; **— resistencia** to put up resistance; **¿qué se le ofrece a usted?** how can I help you?

ofrecimiento M (acción de ofrecer) offering; (oferta) offer

ofrenda F offering

oftalmólogo -ga MF ophthalmologist

ofuscar[30] VT to bewilder

ogro M ogre

ohmio M ohm

oído M (facultad) hearing; (órgano) inner ear; (musical) ear; **— medio** middle ear; **al —** confidentially; **de —** by ear

oiga, oigo ver **oír**

oír[55] VI/VT (percibir) to hear; (atender) to listen; **— decir que** to hear that; **— hablar de** to hear about; **— misa** to attend mass; **¡oye!** listen! hey!

ojal M buttonhole

ojalá INTERJ **— estuviera aquí** I wish he were here; **— que venga** I hope that he comes

ojeada F glimpse

ojear VT to glimpse

ojera F dark circle under the eye

ojeriza F animosity

ojeroso ADJ with dark circles under the eyes

ojiva F (arco) pointed arch; (explosivo) warhead

ojo M (órgano, centro de huracán, instinto, yema de patata) eye; **¡—!** careful! look out! **a — de buen cubero** as a rule of thumb; **a —s vistas** clearly; **me costó un — de la cara** it cost me an arm and a leg; **¿no tienes —s en la cara?** are you blind? **dichosos los —s que te ven** you're a sight for sore eyes; **— de buey** porthole; **— de la cerradura** keyhole; **— de lince** eagle-eye; **— morado** black eye; **— por —** an eye for an eye

ola F wave; (de un olor) waft; (de protesta) storm

oleada F wave, surge

oleaje M swell, surge

óleo M oil painting

oleoducto M oil pipeline

oleoso ADJ oily

oler[22] VI/VT to smell (también sospechar); **— a** to smell of

olfatear VI/VT to scent, to sniff

olfateo M sniff, sniffing

olfato M (facultad) sense of smell; (instinto) nose

olfatorio ADJ olfactory

olimpíada F Olympiad; **—s** Olympic Games

olímpico ADJ Olympian

oliva F olive

olivar M olive grove

olivo M olive tree

olla F pot; **— de grillos** snake pit; **— podrida**

stew of mixed vegetables and meat

olmo M elm

olor M smell, odor

oloroso ADJ odorous

olvidadizo ADJ forgetful

olvidar VI/VT to forget; **—se [de]** to forget; **se me olvidó algo** I forgot something

olvido M oblivion; **caer en el —** to be forgotten; **echar al —** to cast into oblivion; **tus —s** your forgetfulness

Omán M Oman

omaní ADJ & MF Omani

ombligo M navel

OMC [Organización Mundial del Comercio] F WTO

omisión F omission; **por —** by default

omiso ADJ **hacer caso — [de]** to ignore

omitir VT (eliminar) to omit, to leave out; (no notar) to overlook

ómnibus M bus

omnipotente ADJ omnipotent

omnisciencia F omniscience

omnisciente ADJ omniscient

omnívoro ADJ omnivorous

omóplato M scapula

OMS [Organización Mundial de la Salud] F WHO

once NUM eleven

oncología F oncology

onda F wave; **— corta** shortwave; **— expansiva** shock wave; **— sonora** sound wave; **agarrarle la — a algo** to get in the swing of things; **captar la —** to get the drift

ondeado ADJ wavy

ondeante ADJ flying

ondear VI to wave

ondulación F ripple, ruffle, roll

ondulado ADJ (pelo) wavy; (paisaje) rolling

ondulante ADJ undulating

ondular VI to undulate; VI/VT to wave

ónix M onyx

omnipotencia F omnipotence

onomatopeya F onomatopoeia

ONU [Organización de las Naciones Unidas] F UN

onza F ounce

opacar[30] VT (oscurecer) to dull; (eclipsar) to overshadow

opaco ADJ (no transparente) opaque; (no brillante) dull

ópalo M opal

opción F option; **opciones** stock options; **— de venta** put option

opcional ADJ optional

OPEP [Organización de Países Exportadores de Petróleo] F OPEC

ópera F (composición) opera; (teatro) opera house

operable ADJ operable

operación F operation

operador -ora M (en matemáticas) operator; MF (de teléfono) operator

operar VI/VT (usar maquinaria) to operate; VT (intervenir quirúrgicamente) to operate on; (llevar a cabo) to carry out; VI (hacer cuentas) to do mathematical operations

operario -ria MF operator, operative

operativo ADJ (que funciona) operative; (vigente) in effect; M *Am* **— policial** police operation

opiáceo M opiate

opinar VI/VT to hold an opinion, to think

opinión F opinion, view, feeling; **cambiar de — ** to change one's mind

opio M opium

oponente MF (en un debate) opponent; (en una película) costar

oponer[56, 74] VT to oppose; **—se** to conflict; **—se a** to oppose, to be against

oponga, opongo *ver* oponer

oporto M port wine

oportunidad F (chance) opportunity, chance; (pretexto) opening; (fútbol americano) down

oportunista ADJ & MF opportunistic

oportuno ADJ (conveniente) opportune, timely; (adecuado) appropriate

oposición F opposition; **oposiciones** competitive examinations

opositor -ora MF opponent

opresión F oppression

opresivo ADJ oppressive

opresor -ora MF oppressor

oprimir VT (al pueblo) to oppress; (un botón) to press; (un enlace digital) to click

optar VI to choose; **— por** to choose

optativo ADJ optional

óptico -ca ADJ optical; MF optician; F optics

optimismo M optimism

optimista ADJ optimistic; MF optimist

optimizar VT to optimize

óptimo ADJ optimal

optometría F optometry

optometrista MF optometrist

opuesto ADJ opposite, contrary; **se mostró — al casamiento** he was against the marriage; **dos fuerzas opuestas** two opposing forces; **lo —** the opposite; **dirección opuesta** the opposite/reverse direction

opulencia F opulence

opulento ADJ (decoración) opulent; (sociedad) affluent

opuse, opusiera, opusiese *ver* oponer

oración F (frase) sentence; (plegaria) prayer

oráculo M oracle

orador -ora MF orator, speaker

oral ADJ oral

orangután M orangutan

orar VI/VT to pray

oratoria F oratory

oratorio M oratory

órbita F (de los cuerpos celestes) orbit; (de los ojos) eye socket

orbitador M orbiter

orbital ADJ orbital

orbitar VI/VT to orbit

orca F killer whale

orden M (limpieza, secuencia) order; **— ascendente** ascending order; **— de clasificación** sort order; **— del día** order of the day; **perturbar el — público** to disturb the peace; **sin — ni concierto** haphazard; F (mando) command, order; (grupo religioso) order; **— de cateo** warrant; **— de compra** purchase order; **— judicial** court order; **a sus órdenes** at your service

ordenación F (arreglo) ordering, organization; (de un cura) ordination; (informatización) computerization

ordenado ADJ orderly, neat

ordenador M *Esp* computer; **— de mano** palmtop; **— de sobremesa** desktop computer; **— digital** digital computer; **— portátil** laptop computer; **— torre** tower computer

ordenamiento M (arreglo) ordering, putting in order; (conjunto de leyes) legal code; **— territorial** land use

ordenanza F ordinance; MF orderly

ordenar VT (arreglar) to sort, to put in order; (mandar) to order, to command; (conferir órdenes religiosos) to ordain; **—se** to become ordained

ordeñar VT to milk

ordeño M milking

ordinal ADJ ordinal

ordinariez F vulgarity

ordinario ADJ (corriente) ordinary; (vulgar) vulgar

orear VT to air out

orégano M oregano

oreja F (outer) ear; (de un martillo) claw; (en un utensilio) flap; **aguzar la —** to prick up one's ears; **sonreír de — a —** to smile from ear to ear; **estar hasta las —s en algo** to be up to one's neck in something

orejera F earmuff

orfanato M orphanage

orfebre MF (con oro) goldsmith; (con plata) silversmith

orgánico ADJ organic

organigrama M organizational chart, flow chart

organismo M organism

organista MF organist

organización F organization

organizado ADJ organized

organizador -ora MF organizer

organizar[47] VT (una reunión, evento) to organize; (un ataque) to stage; (una fiesta) to give, to throw

organizativo ADJ organizational, organizing

órgano M organ

orgía F orgy

orgullo M pride; **es mi —** she's my pride and joy

orgulloso ADJ proud

orientación F (vocacional, psicológica) orientation, guidance; (de velas) trim; (de estudios) track; (de un objeto) lie; (del terreno) lay; **— horizontal** landscape; **— vertical** portrait

orientado ADJ oriented; **— al cliente** customer-oriented

oriental ADJ oriental, eastern; MF oriental

orientar VT to orient; **—se** to get one's bearings

oriente M Orient, east

orificio M orifice

origen M origin; (de un problema, conflicto) source; (antecedentes familiares) birth

original ADJ original; M (de una pintura) original; (de una cinta magnética) master

originalidad F originality

originar VT to originate, to give rise to; **—se** to originate, to arise

originario ADJ (original) original; **— de** (de cierto origen) coming from, native of

orilla F (de un lago, mar) shore, bank; (de una cama) edge; (de una prenda) hem

orillar VT (una calle) to border; (una prenda) to hem

orín M rust; M PL **orines** urine

orina F urine

orinal M chamber pot

orinar VI/VT to urinate

oriundo ADJ **ser — de** (persona) to hail from; (cosa) to originate in

orla F (de un uniforme) trimming; (de una alfombra) fringe

orlar VT to fringe

orlón™ M Orlon™

ornamentación F ornamentation

ornamental ADJ ornamental

ornamentar VT to ornament, to embellish

ornamento M ornament

ornar VT to adorn

ornitología F ornithology

oro M gold; **— blanco** white gold; **— en lingotes** gold bullion; **— negro** black gold; **— puro** solid gold; **prometer el — y el moro** to promise the moon

orondo ADJ self-satisfied

oropel M tinsel

oropéndola F oriole

orquesta F orchestra

orquestar VT to orchestrate

orquídea F orchid

ortiga F nettle

ortodoncia F orthodontics

ortodoxo ADJ orthodox

ortografía F orthography, spelling

oruga F caterpillar

orujo M rape

orzuelo M sty

osadía F boldness, daring

osado ADJ bold, daring

osamenta F skeleton

osar VI/VT to dare

oscilación F oscillation

oscilar VI to oscillate, to seesaw; **— entre** to range between

oscurecer VI (ponerse oscuro) to get dark; VT (poner oscuro) to darken; (volver poco inteligible, ocultar) to obscure; **—se** to get darker

oscuridad F (lugar sin luz) dark, darkness; (condición de oscuro) darkness; (falta de claridad conceptual, anonimato) obscurity

oscuro ADJ (sin luz) dark; (turbio) murky; (poco claro, poco conocido) obscure; **lentes —s** dark glasses; **gris —** dark gray; **a oscuras** in the dark

óseo ADJ bony

osezno M bear cub

osificarse VI to ossify

ósmosis F osmosis

oso -sa M bear; F she-bear; **— blanco/polar** polar bear; **— hormiguero** anteater

ostentación F ostentation, show, display; **hacer — de** to flaunt

ostentar VI/VT to display, to show off, to flaunt

ostentoso ADJ ostentatious, showy

osteoartritis F osteoarthritis

osteoporosis F osteoporosis

ostión M large oyster

ostra F oyster

OTAN [**Organización del Tratado del Atlántico Norte**] F NATO

otero M hillock

otitis F otitis; **— externa** swimmer's ear

otoñal ADJ autumnal

otoño M autumn, fall

otorgamiento M grant

otorgar[40] VT (permiso) to grant, to concede; (premio) to award

otro ADJ (uno adicional) another; (uno diferente) other; **otra vez** again; **otra cosa** something else; **— más** another one; **al — día** the next day; **de — modo** otherwise; **en otra parte** somewhere else; **la otra cara de la moneda** the flip side; **por otra parte** on the other hand; PRON (uno más) another one; (una persona diferente) someone else; (una cosa diferente) something else

out ADV & M out; **— forzado** force out

ovación F ovation, acclaim

oval ADJ oval

ovalado ADJ oval

óvalo M oval

ovárico ADJ ovarian

ovario M ovary

oveja F (ovino) sheep; (hembra) ewe

ovejero M sheepdog

overoles M PL overalls

ovillar VT to ball; **—se** to curl up into a ball

ovillo M ball of yarn; **hacerse un —** to curl up

OVNI [objeto volador no identificado] M UFO

ovoide N egg-shaped

ovulación F ovulation

ovular VI to ovulate

óvulo M egg

oxidación F oxidation, rusting

oxidado ADJ oxidized, rusty

oxidar VI/VT to oxidize, to rust

óxido M (compuesto químico) oxide; (herrumbre) rust

oxígeno M oxygen

oye, oyendo, oyera, oyese ver oír

oyente MF (que oye) listener, hearer; (alumno no oficial) auditor

ozono M ozone

Pp

pabellón M (puesto de feria) pavilion; (parte de un edificio) wing; (bandera) flag; (sección de hospital) ward; **— de la oreja** outer ear

pabilo M wick

paca F bale

pacana F (fruto) pecan; (árbol) pecan tree

pacer[35] VI to pasture, to graze; VT to crop, to graze

paciencia F patience; **con —** patiently; **tener —** to be patient

paciente ADJ & MF patient; **— ambulatorio -ria** outpatient; **— externo -na** outpatient; **— de alto riesgo** high-risk patient

pacificación F pacification

pacificar[30] VT to pacify

pacífico ADJ peaceful; M **Océano Pacífico** Pacific Ocean

pacifismo M pacifism

pactar VT (hacer un pacto) to make a pact / an agreement; (decidir de común acuerdo) to agree; VI **— con el diablo** to sell one's soul to the devil

pacto M pact, covenant

paddock M (de caballos) paddock; (de coches) pit

padecer[35] VI/VT to suffer; **— de cáncer** to suffer from cancer

padecimiento M suffering

padezca, padezco ver padecer

padrastro M (marido de la madre) stepfather; (uñero) hangnail

padre M father; **—s** parents, folks; **— de familia** male head of the household; **—nuestro** the Lord's Prayer; **John Smith, — John Smith Sr.; ser —** to become a father; ADJ **un lío** — a real mess

padrino M (de bautizo) godfather; (de boda) best man; (en un duelo) second

paella F paella

paga F (salario) pay; (para un niño) allowance; **— de tiempo y medio** time-and-a-half pay; **— por mérito** merit pay

pagadero ADJ payable, due

pagado ADJ paid; **— de sí mismo** self-satisfied

pagador -ora MF payer

paganismo M paganism

pagano -na ADJ & MF pagan

pagar[40] VT (cuentas, deudas) to pay; (préstamo) to pay off; (mercancías) to pay for; **—se de** to be proud of; **— el pato** to be left holding the bag; **pagan justos por pecadores** the just pay for the sins of others; **— a plazos** to pay in installments; **— al contado** to pay cash; **— con la misma moneda** to pay in kind; **— en especie** to pay in kind

pagaré M promissory note

página F page; **— de estilo** stylesheet; **— web** web page

paginar VT to paginate

pago M payment; **— en efectivo** cash payment; ADJ paid

paila F large pan

país M country; **— de origen** country of origin; **— en desarrollo** developing country; **— exportador de petróleo** oil-exporting country

paisaje M landscape, scenery

paisajismo M landscape architecture

paisano -na M countryman; F countrywoman

paja F straw (también para beber de un vaso); **a humo de —s** thoughtlessly; **por un quítame allá esas —s** for a trifle

pajar M hayloft

pájaro M bird; **— carpintero** woodpecker; **— pinto** cautious person; **un — francés** a French guy

paje M page

pajizo ADJ straw-colored

pajonal M *Am* grassland

pala F (para cavar) shovel; (para recoger basura) dustpan; (de hélice, remo) blade; (de zapato) upper; (para remar, de ping-pong) paddle; **— mecánica** power shovel; **lo tuvimos que recoger con —** he was exhausted

palabra F (unidad léxica) word; (facultad) speech; **— clave** key word; **—s mayores** a big deal; **cuatro —s** a few words; **cumplir**

con la — to keep one's word; **dejar con la — en la boca** to cut someone off in midsentence; **en pocas —s** in a nutshell; **faltar a la —** to break a promise; **la última —** the final say; **ni una —** not a word; **no dijo** — he didn't breathe a word; **un hombre de —** a man of his word; **tener la —** to have the floor; **tomar la —** to take the floor; **traducción — por —** word-for-word translation; **tragarse/comerse las propias —s** to eat one's words

palabrerío M verbiage
palabrero ADJ long-winded
palabrota F curse word, four-letter word; **—s** profanity
palacio M palace
paladar M palate; **— hendido** cleft palate; **— óseo** hard palate
paladear VT to relish
paladín M champion, crusader
palanca F (para levantar algo) lever; (para abrir algo) crowbar; (fuerza) leverage; **— de cambios** gearshift lever; **— de juegos** joystick; **— del regulador** throttle lever; **hacer —** to use leverage
palangana F basin
Paláu M Palau
palco M box
palenque M fence
paleontología F paleontology
Palestina F Palestine
palestino -na MF Palestinian; ADJ Palestinian
paleta F (de pintor) palette; (de albañil) trowel; (de ping-pong, para mezclar, batir) paddle; (hélice) blade; (de caramelo) lollipop, sucker; (de helado) Popsicle™
paletilla F shoulder
paleto -ta MF hayseed, hick
paliar VT to alleviate
paliativo M palliative
palidecer[35] VI to turn pale
palidez F pallor, paleness
pálido ADJ pallid, pale
palillo M (de dientes) toothpick; (de tambor) drumstick; (para comida china) chopstick; **tocar todos los —s** to try everything
palique M chitchat
paliza F beating, whipping; **dar una —** to beat, to whip
palma F (árbol) palm [tree]; (hoja) palm leaf; (de la mano) palm [of the hand]; **batir —s** to clap; **llevarse la —** to take the prize; **conocer como la — de la mano** to know like the back of one's hand
palmada F (en la espalda) slap; (aplauso) clap; (en el trasero) spank; **dar una —** (en la espalda) to slap; (en el trasero) to spank
palmear VT to slap on the back
palmera F palm tree

palmípedo M web-footed bird
palmo M span; **— a —** inch by inch
palmotear VT to slap on the back
palo M (de madera) stick; (de barco) mast; (de naipes) suit; (fútbol) goalpost; **—s** (fútbol americano) goalposts; **— de golf** golf club; **— de escoba** broomstick; **dar —s** to hit with a stick; **de tal — tal astilla** a chip off the old block
paloma F dove, pigeon
palomar M pigeon loft
palomilla F wing nut
palomita F (béisbol) fly ball; **—s** popcorn; **hacer —** to pop corn
palote M rolling pin
palpable ADJ palpable
palpar VT to feel
palpitación F palpitation
palpitante ADJ palpitating; **una cuestión —** a burning question
palpitar VI to palpitate
palta F Am avocado
paludismo M malaria
pampa F Am prairie
pamplinas F PL baloney, hogwash
pan M bread; (pieza) loaf of bread; **— comido** piece of cake, cinch; **— de cada día** everyday occurrence; **— rallado/molido** bread crumbs; **al —, — y al vino, vino** to call a spade a spade; **contigo, — y cebolla** love is all we need; **ganarse el —** to make a living
pana F corduroy
panacea F panacea, magic bullet
panadería F bakery
panadero -ra MF baker
panal M honeycomb
Panamá M Panama
panameño -ña ADJ & MF Panamanian
panamericano ADJ Pan-American
panceta F RP bacon
páncreas M SG pancreas
panda M panda bear
pandearse VT to buckle, to sag
pandemia F pandemic
pandémico M pandemic
pandeo M sag
pandereta F tambourine
pandilla F gang, band
panecillo M roll
panegírico M eulogy
panel M panel; **— de control** control panel
panera F breadbasket
panfleto M pamphlet
pánico ADJ & M panic
panoja F ear of corn
panorama M (paisaje) panorama; (horizonte) outlook
panorámico ADJ panoramic
panqueque M pancake

pantaletas F PL panties
pantalla F (de lámpara) lampshade; (para películas) screen; (de monitor) screen, display; (para actividades ilícitas) cover, front; **la — grande** the silver screen; **— dividida** split screen; **— táctil** touchscreen, touch-sensitive display
pantalón M pants, trousers; **— corto** shorts; **pantalones** pants, trousers; **llevar bien puestos los pantalones** to be master in one's own home
pantano M swamp, marsh
pantanoso ADJ swampy, marshy
panteón M vault
pantera F panther
pantomima F mime, pantomime
pantorrilla F calf
pantufla F slipper
panty M pantyhose
panza F paunch, belly
panzudo ADJ potbellied
pañal M diaper; **estar en —es** to be in its infancy
paño M (de tela) cloth; (de lana) woolen cloth; (para limpiar) rag; **— higiénico** sanitary napkin; **— mortuorio** pall; **— de manos** towel; **— de cocina** dishcloth; **— de mesa** tablecloth; **ella es mi — de lágrimas** I always cry on her shoulder; **—s menores** underwear
pañuelo M (de nariz) handkerchief; (de cuello) scarf
papa M pope; F *Am* potato; **no saber ni —** not to know a thing; **—s fritas** French fries
papá M papa, dad
papacito M (padre) daddy; (hombre apuesto) hunk
papada F double chin
papado M papacy
papagayo M parrot
papaíto M daddy
papal ADJ papal
papar VT to eat; MF SG **papamoscas** (pájaro) flycatcher; (tonto) half-wit; MF SG **papanatas** twerp
paparruchas F PL baloney, bull
papaya F papaya
papel M (para escribir) paper; (dramático) role, part; **— aluminio** aluminum foil; **— carbón** carbon paper; **— cuadriculado** graph paper; **— de cartas** stationery; **— de estaño** tinfoil; **— de estraza** brown paper; **— de lija** sandpaper; **— de seda** tissue paper; **— encerado** wax paper; **— higiénico** toilet paper; **— moneda** paper money; **— tisú** tissue paper; **desempeñar un —** to play a role; **en el —** on paper; **hacer buen —** to cut a good figure
papeleo M paperwork

papelera F (fábrica) paper factory; (cubo) wastepaper basket
papelería F stationery store
papeleta F (para escribir) slip of paper; (para votar) ballot
paperas F PL mumps
papito M daddy
páprika F paprika
papú ADJ & MF Papua New Guinean
paquete M (envuelto) package; (atado) bundle; (programas de ordenador) package; **— de programas de productividad** office suite; **— turístico** package tour.
Paquistán M Pakistan
paquistano -na ADJ & MF Pakistani
par ADJ even; M (de cosas idénticas) pair; (de cosas diferentes) couple; (título nobiliario) peer; (en golf) par; **a la —** at par; **sin —** peerless; **de — en —** wide-open
para PREP in order to, for; **lo hice —** ganar dinero I did it in order to earn money; **demasiado — mí** too much for me; **trabajo — mi padre** I work for my father; **— ser perro es inteligente** for a dog he's smart; **— mi sorpresa** to my surprise; **voy — Madrid** I'm going to Madrid; **— las dos** by two o'clock; **— atrás** backwards; **empezar** for starters; **— llevar** to go; **¿— qué?** what for? **— que** so that, so as to; **— siempre** forever; **— su información** FYI [for your information]; **habla — sí** he talks to himself; **— mis adentros** to myself; **— morirse de risa** hilarious; **no es — tanto** it's no big deal; **sin qué ni — qué** without rhyme or reason
parabién M congratulations; **dar el —** to congratulate
parada F (acción de parar) stop; (de perro de caza) point; (de taxis) stand; (militar) parade; (relevo de guardia) changing of the guard; (de balón) parry; (en fútbol americano) tackle
paradero M whereabouts
paradigma M paradigm
parado ADJ (inmóvil) stationary; (sin trabajo) unemployed, idle; **salir bien —** to come out on top
paradoja F paradox
paradójico ADJ paradoxical
parafernalia F paraphernalia
parafina F paraffin
parafrasear VI/VT to paraphrase
paráfrasis F paraphrase
paraguas M SG umbrella
Paraguay M Paraguay
paraguayo -ya ADJ & MF Paraguayan
paraíso M paradise
paraje M spot
paralelo -la ADJ & M parallel; F parallel line; **hacer —s** to draw parallels; **barras**

paralelas parallel bars

parálisis F (inmovilidad física, espiritual) paralysis; (condición médica) paralysis, palsy; **— cerebral** cerebral palsy

paralítico -ca ADJ & MF paralytic

paralización F (de tránsito) gridlock; (del cuerpo) paralysis

paralizar[47] VT (movimiento) to paralyze; (negociaciones) to stall; **—se** to gridlock

paramédico -ca ADJ & MF paramedic

parámetro M parameter

paramilitar ADJ & MF paramilitary

páramo M cold highland, moor

parangón M comparison; **sin —** incomparable

parangonar VT to compare

paraninfo M auditorium

paranoia F paranoia

paranoico -ca ADJ & MF paranoid

paranormal ADJ paranormal

parapléjico -ca MF paraplegic

parapsicología F parapsychology

parar VI/VT (detener) to stop; (motor) to stall; VT (un pase de pelota) to block; (un golpe) to parry; **— de hacer algo** to stop doing something; **y para de contar** and that's it; **— en seco** to stop short; **ir a —** to end up; **habló sin —** he talked nonstop; **—se** (detenerse) to stop; (erguirse) *Am* to stand up; **—se a pensar** to stop to think; M SG **parabrisas** windshield; M SG **paracaídas** parachute; M SG **paracaídas dorado** golden parachute; M **paracaidismo** parachuting; M SG **parachoques** bumper; M SG **pararrayos** lightning rod; M **parasol** parasol; MF **paracaidista** parachutist

parasítico ADJ parasitic

parásito M parasite

parcela F parcel, plot

parcelación F subdivision

parcelar VT to parcel [out]

parche M (para remendar, informático) patch; (de tambor) drumhead; (médico) Band-aid®; **— de ojo** eye patch

parcial ADJ partial

pardillo M linnet

pardo ADJ (color) gray-brown; (mulato) mulatto

pareado M couplet

parear VT to match

parecer[35] VI to seem; **— que** to seem like, to look like; **¿qué te parece?** what do you think? **—se a** to resemble, to look like; M (opinión) opinion; (aspecto) appearance; **al —** apparently; **a mi —** to my mind / way of thinking; **del mismo —** like-minded

parecido ADJ alike, similar; **bien —** good-looking; M similarity, resemblance

pared F wall; **poner a alguien contra la —** to corner; **subirse por las —es** to be furious; **de — a —** wall-to-wall; **reloj de —** wall clock

paredón M execution wall

pareja F (de personas) couple; (de cosas) [matching] pair; (compañero) partner

parejo ADJ (hermanos) alike; (carrera) even; (dientes) straight; **correr [al] —** to go hand in hand

parental ADJ parental

parentela F kin

parentesco M kinship, relation

paréntesis M parenthesis

parezca, parezco *ver* parecer

pargo M red snapper

paria MF pariah, outcast

paridad F parity

pariente MF, **parienta** F relative, relation; **— consanguíneo** blood relative

parir VI/VT to give birth [to]

parlamentar VI to parley

parlamentario -ria ADJ parliamentary; MF member of parliament

parlamento M (en una obra de teatro) speech; (negociación) parley; (cuerpo legislativo) parliament

parlanchín ADJ talkative; MF chatterbox

parlotear VI to chatter, to rattle on

parloteo M chatter

parodia F parody

parodiar VT to parody

parpadear VI (un ojo, pantalla) to blink; (una vela) to flicker; (una estrella) to twinkle

parpadeo M (del ojo) blink; (de una vela) flicker; (de una estrella) twinkle; (de una pantalla) blinking

párpado M eyelid

parque M park; **— automotor** fleet of cars; **— de atracciones** amusement park; **— zoológico** zoo

parra F grapevine

párrafo M paragraph; **echar un — con** to have a chat with

parral M grape arbor

parranda F binge, spree; **andar de —** to go out partying

parrandear VI to revel

parrandero -ra MF party animal

parrilla F (sobre el fuego) grill; (en el horno) broiler; (de calles) grid; (de coche) grille

parrillada F barbecue dish

párroco M parish priest

parroquia F (distrito) parish; (iglesia) parish church

parroquial ADJ parochial

parroquiano -na MF (de iglesia) parishioner; (de tienda) regular

parte F (sección) part; (lugar) place; (papel en

una obra teatral) lines; (persona legal) party; **— integrante** built-in part; **— interesada** interested party; **—s pudendas** private parts, *fam* privates; **a otra —** somewhere else; **a —s iguales** fifty-fifty; **de un tiempo a esta —** for some time; **de — de** on behalf of; **de — a —** completely; **echar a mala —** to take amiss; **en —** partly; **en gran —** in large measure; **en otra —** elsewhere; **en/por todas —s** everywhere; **formar — de** to be part of; **ir por —s** to proceed by steps; **la mayor — de** most of; **la — del león** the lion's share; **no está en ninguna —** it's nowhere to be found; **no va a ninguna —** it's going nowhere; **por otra —** on the other hand; **tomar — en** to take part in; M report; **dar —** to report; **dar — de enfermo** to call in sick; **dar — de un crimen** to report a crime

partera F midwife

partición F (of a country) partition; (of a cell) division

participación F (en un proyecto) participation, involvement; (en un negocio) interest; **— de nacimiento** birth announcement

participante MF (en un grupo) participant; (en una carrera) entrant; (en un concurso) contestant

participar VI to participate; VT to announce; **— de/en** to participate in, to share in

partícipe MF participant

participio M participle

partícula F particle

particular ADJ (específico) particular; (poco usual) peculiar; (privado) private; **en —** in particular; **clases —es** private lessons; M (detalle) particular; (asunto) matter; MF private citizen

partida F (fondos) appropriation; (grupo de personas) party; (cantidad de mercancía) parcel, lot; (de ajedrez) game; (acción de partir) departure; **— de nacimiento** birth record; **jugar una mala —** to play a mean trick; **por — doble** double-entry

partidario -ria MF (de una medida) supporter, advocate; (de un partido político) partisan

partidista ADJ & MF partisan

partido M (grupo político) party; (de golf) round; (de tenis, fútbol) game, match; **es un buen —** he's a good match; **sacar — de** to take advantage of; **tomar —** to take sides; **¿cómo va el —?** what's the score? ADJ split, cleft

partir VT (dividir) to divide; (repartir) to share; (quebrar) to break; **eso me parte por el eje** that screws me up; **que te parta un rayo** go jump in the lake; VI (salir) to depart, to leave; **a — de entonces** since then; **a — del lunes** starting Monday; **—se de risa** to die of

laughter

partisano -na MF partisan

partitura F musical score

parto M childbirth, delivery; **— prematuro** premature birth; **estar en trabajo de —** to be in labor

parvulario M kindergarten, nursery

párvulo -la MF nursery school child

pasa F raisin

pasable ADJ passable

pasada F (acción de pasar) passing; (con una máquina) pass; **una mala —** a mean trick; **de — by** the way

pasadizo M secret passage

pasado M past; ADJ (anterior) past; (demasiado maduro) overripe; **— mañana** day after tomorrow; **el año —** last year; **el — mes de septiembre** last September

pasador M (de un cierre) pin; (de la puerta) latch

pasaje M (sitio por donde se pasa, fragmento de texto) passage; (billete) ticket; (precio de un viaje) fare; (conjunto de los pasajeros) passengers

pasajero -ra ADJ fleeting, transitory; MF (en un coche, tren) passenger; (en un taxi) fare

pasante M (tenis) passing shot; MF (compañía) intern

pasaporte M passport

pasar VI (no querer jugar, ir de un lado a otro, seguir su proceso, transcurrir) to pass; (ocurrir) to happen; **— a ser** to become; **— de moda** to go out of style; **— hambre** to go hungry; **— por** to pass by; **— por alto** to pass over; **— una tarjeta por un lector** to swipe a card; **—le por la cabeza a alguien** to occur to someone; **pasan de los 80 años** they're over 80 years old; **te pasaste de la casa** you missed the house; **—se** to spoil; **—se de la raya** to cross the line; **—se de sol** to get too much sun; **—se de listo** to outsmart oneself; **se me pasó ir a buscarte** I totally forgot to pick you up; **me la paso bien** I have a good time; VT (la sal, una prueba, la plancha, una pelota) to pass; (un sofocón) to endure; (una tarde) to spend; **— las de Caín** to go through hell; **— en limpio** to make a new copy; **— por alto** to overlook; **— los 50 kmh** to exceed 50 kmh; **— revista** to pass in review; **nos pasó un Volvo** a Volvo passed us; **no lo paso** I can't stand him; M **tienen un buen —** they have a comfortable life; VT **pasamano** (de barco) guard rail, gangway; (de escalera) banister, railing; M **pasatiempo** pastime

pasarela F (en un barco) gangplank; (en un desfile de modas) runway

Pascua F (fiesta cristiana) Easter; (fiesta judía) Passover; **— Florida / de Resurrección** Easter Sunday; **— de Navidad** Christmas

pase M (deporte) pass; **— cruzado** cross; **— de anotación** touchdown pass; **— de cabeza** header; **— pantalla** screen pass

pasear VI (a pie) to take a walk; (en bici, a caballo) to go on a ride; (en coche) to go for a drive, to go on a ride; **—se** to parade, to take a walk; **—se a caballo** to go horseback riding; VT (un perro) to walk a dog

paseo M (a pie) walk, stroll; (a caballo, en bicicleta) ride; (en coche) drive, ride; (calle donde se pasea) mall; (recreativo) outing; **irse a —** to go jump in a lake; **dar un —** (a pie) to take a walk; (a caballo, en bicicleta) to go on a ride; (en coche) to go on a drive

pasillo M (de un teatro) aisle; (de un edificio) hallway, corridor; (para vuelo aéreo) corridor; **— de dobles** alley

pasión F passion

pasivo ADJ passive; **voz pasiva** passive voice; M (en un negocio) liabilities; (de una cuenta) debit side

pasmado ADJ astounded

pasmar VT to astound, to stun; **—se** to be astounded, to be stunned

pasmo M astonishment

pasmoso ADJ astonishing, stunning

paso M (acción de pasar, lugar donde pasar) pass; (de pie, de danza, distancia, de un proceso) step; (velocidad) pace; (de caballerías) walk; (de tornillo) pitch; (de coche) wheelbase; **— elevado** overpass; **— a nivel** grade crossing; **— de tortuga** snail's pace; **— a —** step by step; **dar —** (dejar pasar) to let pass; (dejar actuar) to make possible; **dar —s** to take steps; **hacer —s** to travel; **de —** by the way, in passing; **estar de —** to be passing through; **marcar el —** to set the pace; **al — que** while; **salir del —** to get out of a difficulty; **dicho sea de —** incidentally; **a cada —** at every turn; **— del tiempo** passage of time; **abrir — para** to make way for; **abrirse —** to plow through, to press through; ADJ dried

pasta F (de almidón) paste; (de harina) dough; (de fideos) pasta; (de libro) hard cover, binding; (dinero) *fam* dough; **de buena —** of good disposition; **— dentífrica/dental** toothpaste

pastar VI/VT to pasture, to graze

pastel M (torta) cake; (tarta) pie; (pintura, cuadro) pastel; **— de cumpleaños** birthday cake; **— de limón** lemon pie; **— de carne** meat pie; **descubrir el —** to spill the beans; ADJ pastel

pastelería F (establecimiento) pastry shop; (conjunto de pasteles) pastry

pastelero -ra M pastry cook

pasterizar, pasteurizar[9] VT to pasteurize

pastilla F (de medicina) tablet, pill; (para la tos) drop; (de jabón) bar

pastizal M grassland

pasto M (terreno) pasture, grassland; (hierba) grass; **ser — de** to be a victim of

pastor -ora MF (de ovejas) shepherd; (sacerdote protestante) pastor, minister; M **— alemán** German shepherd

pastoral ADJ pastoral; F pastoral letter

pastoril ADJ pastoral

pastoso ADJ pasty

pastura F feed

pat M putt

pata F (de animal, mueble) foot, leg; (de pollo) drumstick; (de un enchufe) pin; **— palmada** webfoot; **— de gallo** crow's feet; **en cuatro —s** on all fours; **a [la] — coja** skipping on one leg; **estirar la —** *fam* to kick the bucket; **mala —** bad luck; **metedura de —** faux pas; **meter la —** to slip up; **—s arriba** upside down; ADJ **patihendido** cloven-hoofed; **patitieso** dumbfounded; **patizambo** (hacia adentro) knock-kneed; (hacia afuera) bow-legged

patada F kick (también en deportes); **libros a —s** tons of books; **en dos —s** in a jiffy; **dar —s** to kick; **echar a —s** to kick out; **— lateral** (fútbol americano) onside kick

patalear VI (en el aire) to kick; (en el suelo) to stamp

pataleo M (en el aire) kick; (en el suelo) stamp

pataleta F fit; **tener una —** to throw a fit

patán M boor

patata F *Esp* potato; **—s fritas** French fries; **— caliente** hot potato

pateador M kicker

patear VT (algo, a alguien) to kick; (el suelo) to stamp; VI to tramp around; VI/VT (en golf) to putt; VI to kick; **— al arco** to shoot at goal

patentar VT to patent

patente ADJ & F patent; **se hizo — su ignorancia** he betrayed his ignorance; **— en trámite** patent pending

paternal ADJ (del padre) paternal; (como un padre) fatherly

paternidad F paternity, fatherhood; **prueba de —** paternity test

paterno ADJ paternal

patético ADJ moving

patetismo M pathos

patíbulo M gallows scaffold, gallows

patilla F (de gafas) arm; **—s** (de pelo) sideburns

patín M (tabla) skate; (de trineo) runner; **— de ruedas** roller skate; **— de cuchilla / de hielo** ice skate

patinaje M skating

patinar VI (una persona) to skate; (un coche sobre hielo) to skid; (un embrague) to slip; (en un examen) to blank out

patinazo M (de embrague) slip; (de coche) skid

patio M (de casa) patio, courtyard; (de escuela)

playground

pato M (ave) duck; (macho) drake; **pagar el** — to take the rap

patochada F blunder

patógeno M pathogen

patología F pathology

patológico ADJ pathological

patoso ADJ clumsy

patotero-ra MF *Am* hooligan

patraña F tall tale

patria F fatherland, homeland

patriarca M patriarch

patriarcal ADJ patriarchal

patrimonial ADJ inherited, patrimonial

patrimonio M patrimony; — **cultural** cultural heritage; — **neto** net worth; — **personal** personal assets

patriota MF patriot

patriótico ADJ patriotic

patriotismo M patriotism

patrocinador-ora MF sponsor

patrocinar VT to sponsor

patrocinio M sponsorship; — **empresarial** corporate backing

patrón-ona MF (protector) patron; (jefe) employer; (de navío) skipper; M (dueño de pensión) landlord; (de costura) pattern; (punto de referencia) yardstick, standard; (de planta) stock; (de un parásito) host; — **de oro** gold standard; F (dueña de pensión) landlady

patronal ADJ management; **asociación** — employers' association; F management

patronato M board of trustees

patrono-na MF patron

patrulla F (grupo de policías o soldados) patrol, squad; (coche) squad car

patrullar VI/VT to patrol

patrullero-ra M patrol car, squad car; MF patrol officer

pausa F (musical) pause, rest; **trabajar con** — to work slowly; **hacer** — to pause

pauta F guideline

pavimentar VT to pave

pavimento M pavement

pavo M turkey; — **real** peacock; ADJ silly

pavón M peacock

pavonearse VI to strut, to swagger

pavoneo M strut, swagger

pavor M dread

pavoroso ADJ frightful

payasada F clownish act or remark; —**s** antics, horseplay

payasear VI to clown around, to horse around

payaso M (de circo) clown; (persona poco seria) buffoon; **hacer el** — to clown around

paz F peace; **estamos en** — we are even; **[que] en** — **descanse** may she rest in peace; **hacer las paces** to make up; **dejar en** — to leave alone

PC M PC

peaje M (tasa) toll; (cabina donde se paga) tollbooth

peatón-ona MF pedestrian

peca F freckle

pecado M sin; — **mortal** mortal sin

pecador-ora MF sinner; ADJ sinful

pecaminoso ADJ sinful

pecar[30] VI to sin; — **contra** to transgress against; — **de bueno** to be too good; — **de generoso** to be generous to a fault; — **de oscuro** to be exceedingly unclear

pecera F (pequeña) fish tank, fishbowl; (grande) aquarium

pechera F (de camisa) front; (de delantal) bib

pecho M (parte del cuerpo) chest; (mama) breast; **dar el** — to nurse; **nadar** — to do the breaststroke; **tomar a** —**[s]** to take to heart; **sacar** — to puff out one's chest

pechuga F breast

pechugona ADJ buxom

pecio M flotsam and jetsam

pecoso ADJ freckled

pectoral ADJ & M pectoral

peculado M embezzlement

peculiar ADJ peculiar

peculiaridad F peculiarity

pedagogía F pedagogy, education

pedagógico ADJ pedagogical, teaching

pedagogo-ga MF pedagogue

pedal M pedal

pedalear VI/VT to pedal

pedante ADJ pedantic; MF pedant

pedazo M piece; — **de idiota** absolute idiot; **él es un** — **de pan** he's a saint; **hacer** —**s** to tear to pieces; **caerse a** —**s** to fall to pieces; — **por** — piece by piece

pederasta M pederast, pedophile

pedófilo-la MF pedophile

pederastia F pederasty

pedernal M flint

pedestal M pedestal

pedestre ADJ pedestrian

pediatra MF pediatrician

pediatría F pediatrics

pedido M (comercial) order; (petición) request; **hacer un** — to place an order; — **fijo** standing order; — **pendiente** back order; — **urgente** rush order

pedigrí M pedigree

pedigüeño-ña MF mooch, moocher; ADJ **no seas** — stop mooching

pedir[9] VT (requerir) to ask for, to request; (exigir) to demand; (encargar) to order, to requisition; — **limosna** to beg; — **prestado** to borrow; — **socorro** to cry for help; — **un deseo** to make a wish; — **que** to ask/pray that; — **la mano de una mujer** to ask a woman's hand in marriage; — **por alguien**

to ask to speak to someone

pedofilia F pedophilia

pedrada F **dar una** — to hit with a stone; **matar a —s** to stone to death

pedregal M rocky ground

pedregoso ADJ stony

pedrería F precious stones

pedrusco M boulder

pedúnculo M stem

pega F snag

pegadizo ADJ catchy

pegado ADJ (adherido) stuck; (contiguo) adjoining, contiguous; **quedarse** — to get an electric shock; **— al televisor** glued to the television

pegajoso ADJ sticky, tacky

pegamento M glue

pegar[40] VT (con el puño) to hit, to strike; (algo con pegamento) to stick, to glue; (botones) to sew on; **— con** to match; **— contra** to touch; **— un cuadrangular** to hit a homerun; **— un grito** to yell; **— un sencillo** to hit a single; **— un susto** to give a scare; **— un salto** to jump; **—le a la bola** to hit the ball; **—le un tiro a alguien** to shoot someone; **—se** (adherir) to stick together, to cling; (contagiarse) to be contagious; **—se a** to latch onto; **no — un ojo** not to sleep a wink

pegote M glob

pegotear VT to gum up

peinado M (estilo) coiffure, hairdo; (acción) combing

peinador-ora MF hairdresser

peinar VT to comb (también registrar); (en una peluquería) to style; **— a contrapelo** to rub the wrong way

peine M comb

pelada F bald spot

pelado ADJ (sin pelo) hairless; (pobre) poor; (sin cáscara) peeled; (sin árboles) treeless; (sin plumas) plucked; (sin dinero) broke

pelador M peeler

pelaje M coat, fur

pelar VT (el pelo) to cut the hair of; (las plumas) to pluck the feathers from; (frutas, verduras, huevo) to peel; (a un jugador) to fleece; **duro de —** hard to deal with; **el agua está que pela** the water is really hot; **—se** to peel; M SG **pelagatos** nobody

peldaño M step, stair

pelea F (de palabra) fight, quarrel; (de obra) fight, scrape; (de boxeo) fight; **— a puñetazos** fistfight; **— de perros** dogfight

pelear VI (con palabras) to fight, to quarrel; (con obras) to fight, to scuffle; **—se con alguien** to have a fight with someone

pelechar VI (perder la piel) to shed; (mejorar) to get better

pelele M (persona sin carácter) wimp; (muñeca) straw doll

peletería F (tienda) fur store; (comercio) fur trade

pelícano M pelican

película F film (también membrana); (obra cinematográfica) motion picture, film, movie; **de —** extraordinary; **dar una —** to show a film; **— muda** silent film

peligrar VI to be in danger

peligro M danger, peril; **ese muchacho es un —** that boy is dangerous; **en —** in danger; **poner en —** to imperil/endanger/jeopardize

peligroso ADJ dangerous, perilous

pellejo M (piel de animal) hide, pelt; (odre) wineskin; **salvar el —** to save one's skin; **ser todo —s** to be skin and bones; **jugarse el —** to risk one's life

pellizcar[30] VT to pinch

pellizco M pinching

pelma MF jerk

pelo M (de persona) hair; (de animal) fur; (de alfombra) pile; **con —s y señales** with every possible detail; **de medio —** low-class; **eso me viene al —** that suits me perfectly; **montar en —** to ride bareback; **ni un —** not at all; **no tener —s en la lengua** not to mince words; **se le ponen los —s de punta** his hair stands on end; **se salvó por un —** he was saved by the skin of his teeth; **tomarle el — a alguien** to tease someone, to pull someone's leg; **traído de los —s** far-fetched; ADJ **pelirrojo** redheaded

pelón ADJ bald

pelota F (objeto) ball; (juego) ballgame; **— vasca** jai-alai; **pasar la —** (dar el balón) to pass the ball; (dar la responsabilidad) to pass the buck

pelotear VI to rally

peloteo M rally

pelotera F brawl

pelotero-ra MF (jugador de béisbol) baseball player; (juego para niños) ball pit

pelotón M (pelota grande) large ball; (de tierra seca) clod; (de ciclistas) pack; (de soldados) platoon; (de fusilamiento) firing squad

peltre M pewter

peluca F wig

peludo ADJ (persona) hairy; (animal) furry; (perro) shaggy

peluquería F (para hombres) barbershop; (para mujeres) salon

peluquero-ra MF (de hombres) barber; (de mujeres) hairdresser

peluquín M toupee

pelusa F (de tela, ropa) lint, fluff; (de melocotón, de la piel) fuzz; (de plantas) hair; (de polvo) dust bunny

pelvis F pelvis

pena F (castigo) penalty; (tristeza) sorrow; (vergüenza) embarrassment; **— de muerte**

death penalty, capital punishment; **—s** hardships; **a duras —s** with great difficulty; **me da—** it grieves me; **hecho una—** looking like a mess; **¡qué—!** what a shame! **sería una— perder** it would be a shame to lose; **so— de** on pain of; **valer la—** to be worthwhile

penacho M (de plumas) tuft, crest; (de humo) plume

penal ADJ penal; M penitentiary

penalidad F (penuria) hardship; (castigo) penalty

penalizar[47] VT to penalize

penalti, penalty M penalty kick

penar VI to suffer; VT to punish

penco M plug, nag

pendencia F wrangle, fight

pendenciero ADJ quarrelsome

pender VI to hang, to dangle

pendiente F slope, incline; M *Esp* earring; ADJ (aretes) dangling; (negocio) pending, unfinished; (pago) outstanding; **quedo— de tu llamada** I look forward to your call

pendón M banner

péndulo M pendulum

pene M penis

penetración F penetration

penetrante ADJ (mirada, sonido) penetrating, piercing; (frío) biting; (comentario) cutting; (inteligencia) keen

penetrar VT (pasar al interior) to penetrate, to pierce; (comprender) to comprehend

penicilina F penicillin

península F peninsula

peninsular ADJ peninsular

penitencia F (religiosa) penance; (castigo) detention; **¡estás en—!** you're grounded!

penitenciaría F penitentiary

penitente ADJ & MF penitent

penoso ADJ (triste) painful, grievous; (difícil) trying; (que da vergüenza) embarrassing

pensador -ora MF thinker; ADJ reflective

pensamiento M (facultad, acción, efecto) thought; (flor) pansy

pensante ADJ thinking

pensar[1] VI/VT to think; **— en** to think about/ over; **— hacer algo** to intend to do something; **eso da que—** that seems questionable; **no lo pienses dos veces** don't think twice

pensativo ADJ pensive, thoughtful

pensión F (asignación periódica) pension, allowance; (comidas) board; (hostal) boardinghouse; **— completa** room and board; **tener en —** to have as a boarder

pensionado M boarding school

pensionar VT to pension

pensionista MF (que vive en una pensión) boarder; (que cobra una pensión) pensioner

pentágono M pentagon

pentagrama M musical staff

penthouse M penthouse

penúltimo ADJ next to the last, penultimate

penumbra F semi-darkness, dimness

penuria F (escasez) shortage; (pobreza) poverty

peña F boulder; **— folclórica** folklore club

peñasco M crag

peñascoso ADJ craggy

peñón M crag

peón -ona MF (obrero) unskilled laborer, farmhand; **— caminero** road worker; M (en ajedrez) pawn; (en damas) piece

peonada F gang of laborers

peonaje M gang of laborers

peonza F toy top

peor ADJ worse, worst; **este libro es—** this book is worse; **el— libro** the worst book; ADV worse; **trabaja—** he works worse; **—que** worse than; **— que nunca** worse than ever; **en el— de los casos** if worst comes to worst; **lo—** the worst [thing]; **tanto—** so much the worse

pepa F **es un viva la—** it's bedlam

pepino M cucumber

pepita F (simiente) seed; (tumor de gallina) pip; (masa de oro) nugget

pequeñez F (cualidad de pequeño) smallness; (cosa insignificante) trifle

pequeño -ña ADJ (de poco tamaño) small, little; (de corta edad) young; (de poca importancia) trivial

pera F pear; **pedirle —s al olmo** to ask the impossible

peral M pear tree

perca F perch; **— americana** black bass

percal M percale

percance M accident, mishap

percatarse VI (darse cuenta) to realize; (notar) to notice

percebe M barnacle

percepción F perception

perceptible ADJ perceptible, noticeable

perceptivo ADJ perceptive

percha F (para el armario) clothes hanger; (palo para colgar cosas) peg; (palo para aves) perch; (perchero) coat rack

perchero M coat rack

percibir VT (experimentar) to perceive, to sense; (recibir) to collect

percudir VT to make grimy; **—se** to get grimy

percusión F percussion

percutor M firing pin

perdedor -ora MF loser

perder[2] VT (dejar de tener algo, extraviar) to lose, to mislay, to misplace; (echar a perder) to spoil, to ruin; (ser derrotado) to lose; (no aprovechar) to waste; (no llegar a tiempo, no disfrutar) to miss; **— el conocimiento** to

lose consciousness; — **el tiempo** to waste
time; — **los estribos** to fly off the handle; —
hojas to shed leaves; — **pie** to lose one's
footing; — **terreno** to lose ground; **echarse
a** — to spoil; **el vaso pierde agua** the glass
leaks water; **llevo las de** — the odds are
against me; —**se** (extraviarse) to lose one's
way, to get lost; (apartarse del buen camino)
to go astray, to stray; **se han perdido las
llaves** the keys have gotten lost; —**se de
vista** to disappear; —[se] una
oportunidad to pass up / miss an
opportunity; — **el balón** (fútbol americano)
to fumble; (fútbol) to lose the ball
perdición F perdition, damnation
pérdida F (acción de perder, cosa perdida) loss;
(de dinero dado en prenda) forfeiture;
entrar en — to nosedive; — **de tiempo**
waste of time; — **de balón** (fútbol
americano) fumble, turnover; (fútbol) loss of
ball possession; —**s cubiertas** covered
losses; —**s totales** total loss
perdido -da ADJ (extraviado) lost, missing;
(aislado) isolated; (promiscuo) promiscuous;
un borracho — an utter drunkard; **estar —
por alguien** to be crazy about someone; M
degenerate
perdigón M (pollo de perdiz) young partridge;
(bolita de plomo) birdshot, buckshot
perdiz F partridge
perdón M (privado) forgiveness; (oficial)
pardon; **con — de los presentes** present
company excepted; **no tener** — to be
unforgivable; INTERJ excuse me
perdonar VT (en privado) to forgive;
(oficialmente) to pardon
perdurable ADJ lasting
perdurar VI to last
perecedero ADJ perishable
perecer[35] VI to perish
peregrinación F pilgrimage
peregrinar VI to go on a pilgrimage
peregrino -na MF pilgrim; ADJ far-fetched
perejil M parsley
perenne ADJ perennial
pereza F laziness, idleness, sloth
perezoso ADJ lazy, idle; M (animal) sloth
perfección F perfection; **a la** — to perfection,
perfectly
perfeccionamiento M perfecting
perfeccionar VT to perfect
perfeccionista MF perfectionist
perfectamente ADV perfectly; **tú hablas
español** — you speak Spanish quite well
perfecto ADJ perfect, flawless; **es un — tarado**
he's an utter idiot; **es un — desconocido**
he's a complete stranger
perfil M profile; **de** — from the side
perfilar VT to outline; —**se** (marcarse) to be

outlined; (definirse) to become clear
perforación F (de una superficie) perforation;
(de un pozo) drilling; (de la piel) piercing
perforar VT (agujerear) to perforate; (buscar
petróleo) to drill
perfumar VT to perfume, to scent
perfume M perfume, scent
perfumería F perfumery
pergamino M parchment
pérgola F arbor
pericia F expertness, know-how
perico M (loro) parakeet; (cocaína) *fam* snow
periferia F periphery, fringe
periférico ADJ & M peripheral
perilla F (adorno, remate) knob; (pelo de
barbilla) goatee; **me viene de** —**s** it's exactly
what I need
perímetro M perimeter
periódico M newspaper; — **mensual** monthly
periodical; ADJ periodic
periodismo M journalism
periodista MF journalist
periodístico ADJ journalistic
período M period (también menstruación); (de
materia radiactiva) half-life; — **de prueba**
(para un trabajo) probationary period; (para
una mercancía) trial period; — **glaciar** ice
age
peripecia F vicissitude
peripuesto ADJ dressed up, dolled up, decked
out
periquito M parakeet
periscopio M periscope
perista MF fence
perito -ta ADJ expert, practiced; MF technician
peritonitis F peritonitis
perjudicar[30] VT to harm
perjudicial ADJ harmful, detrimental
perjuicio M harm
perjurar VT to swear; VI to commit perjury;
—**se** to commit perjury
perjurio M perjury
perla F (de nácar) pearl; (persona) gem; (de
sudor) bead; (de sabiduría) nugget; (frase
inoportuna) blooper; **me viene de** —**s** it
suits me perfectly
perlado ADJ pearly
permanecer[35] VI to remain, to stay
permanencia F (carácter de permanente)
permanence; (acción de permanecer) stay
permanente ADJ permanent
permanezca, permanezco *ver* permanecer
permeable ADJ permeable
permear VT to permeate
permisible ADJ permissible
permisivo ADJ permissive
permiso M (para ir al baño) permission; (para
faltar al servicio militar) furlough; (para
faltar al trabajo) leave; (para casarse,

conducir) license, permit; **— de trabajo**
work permit; **con —** excuse me
permitir VT (dar permiso) to permit, to allow;
(posibilitar) to enable; **—se** (una libertad) to
take the liberty of; (un lujo) to allow oneself;
¿me permite? may I?
permuta F exchange
permutación F permutation
permutar VT to exchange
pernetas LOC ADV **en —** barelegged
pernicioso ADJ pernicious
pernicorto ADJ short-legged
perno M bolt, pin
pero CONJ but; ADV **muy — muy lindo** very,
very pretty; M objection; **no hay — que
valga** there are no buts about it
perogrullada F platitude
perorar VI to hold forth
perorata F lecture
peróxido M peroxide
perpendicular ADJ perpendicular
perpetrar VT to perpetrate
perpetuar[26] VT to perpetuate
perpetuo ADJ perpetual
perplejidad F perplexity, bewilderment
perplejo ADJ perplexed, bewildered; VT **dejar
—** to perplex
perrera F (lugar donde guardar perros) pound;
(rabieta) tantrum
perrero -ra MF dogcatcher; ADJ dog-loving
perro M dog; **— caliente** hot dog; **— callejero**
stray dog; **— cobrador** retriever; **— de caza**
hunting dog; **— de lanas** poodle; **—
esquimal** husky; **— faldero** lapdog; **—
guía** guide dog; **— guardián** watchdog,
guard dog; **— pastor** sheepdog; **— policía**
police dog; ADJ miserable; **en la perra vida**
never
perruno ADJ canine
persa ADJ & MF Persian; M (lengua) Persian
persecución F (religiosa) persecution; (policial)
pursuit, chase
perseguidor -ora MF (que sigue) pursuer; (que
acosa) persecutor
perseguir[12] VT (seguir para alcanzar) to pursue,
to chase; (seguir para encontrar) to track
down; (acosar) to hound; (tratar de destruir)
to persecute
perseverancia F perseverance
perseverar VI to persevere
Persia F Persia
persiana F blind, shade
**persiga, persigo, persigue, persiguiendo,
persiguiera, persiguiese** ver perseguir
persistencia F persistence
persistente ADJ persistent
persistir VI to persist
persona F person; **— influyente** player; **—
legal** legal entity; **en —** in person; **— mayor**

adult
personaje M (persona importante) personage;
(de obra literaria) character; **es todo un —**
he's quite a character
personal ADJ personal; M personnel, staff
personalidad F personality
personalmente ADV personally
personificar[30] VT to personify, to embody
perspectiva F (punto de vista, distancia, técnica
de dibujo) perspective; (panorama) view,
vista; (posibilidad) prospect; **tener en —** to
have planned
perspicacia F insight, sharpness
perspicaz ADJ perspicacious, perceptive
persuadir VT to persuade
persuasión F persuasion
persuasivo ADJ persuasive
pertenecer[35] VI to belong
perteneciente ADJ belonging
pertenencias F PL belongings
pertenezca, pertenezco ver pertenecer
pértiga F pole
pertinente ADJ pertinent, relevant
pertrechos M PL military supplies
perturbación F disturbance
perturbar VT to perturb, to disturb
Perú M Peru
peruano -na ADJ & MF Peruvian
perversidad F (distorsión) perversity; (maldad)
wickedness
perversión F perversion
perverso ADJ (distorsionante) perverse;
(malvado) wicked
pervertido -da MF pervert
pervertir[8] VT (enviciar) to pervert;
(distorsionar) to distort; **—se** to become
perverted
pesa F (para pesar) weight; (para hacer ejercicio)
dumbbell; **—s y medidas** weights and
measures
pesadez F (cualidad de pesado) heaviness;
(tedio) tiresomeness; (persona pesada)
tiresome person
pesadilla F nightmare
pesado -da ADJ (que pesa mucho, difícil de
digerir) heavy; (aburrido) tiresome; (robusto)
heavy-set; (tardo) slow; MF bore, pest
pesadumbre F grief, sorrow
pésame M condolence, expression of sympathy
pesar VT (apenar) to sadden; (medir el peso de)
to weigh; (recaer sobre) to weight down; VI
(tener peso, importancia) to weigh; M grief,
sorrow; LOC ADV **a — de** in spite of
pesaroso ADJ (triste) sad; (arrepentido)
repentant
pesca F (acción de pescar) fishing; (lo pescado)
catch; **ir de —** to go fishing
pescadería F fish market
pescado M fish

pescador-ora MF fisherman

pescar[30] VI/VT (capturar peces) to fish; (sacar del agua, coger, comprender, sorprender, pillar) to catch; (obtener) to land, to nail

pescozón M blow to the back of the head

pescuezo M neck

pesebre M (para pienso) manger, crib; (belén) nativity scene

peseta F peseta

pesimismo M pessimism

pesimista MF pessimist

pésimo ADJ dismal, wretched

peso M (fuerza, importancia) weight; (cosa opresiva) burden; (cosa pesada) load; **vender al —** to sell by weight; **levantar en —** to lift off the ground

pesquería F fishery

pesquero ADJ fishing; M fishing boat

pesquisa F inquiry

pestaña F (del ojo) eyelash; (en costura) fringe; (de papel, texto) tab; **quemarse las —s** to burn the midnight oil

pestañear VI to blink; **sin —** unflinchingly

pestañeo M blink

peste F (enfermedad) plague; (persona molesta) pest; (hedor) stench; **— bubónica** bubonic plague; **— negra** black death; **hablar —s de alguien** to speak badly of someone

pestilencia F pestilence

pestillo M deadbolt, latch

petaca F (para tabaco) tobacco pouch; (para whisky) flask

pétalo M petal

petardear VI to backfire

petardeo M backfire

petate M bundle; **liar el —** to pack up and go

petición F petition, request

peticionar VT to petition

petirrojo M robin

pétreo ADJ stony

petróleo M petroleum, oil; **— crudo** crude oil

petrolero-ra ADJ oil, petroleum; **plataforma —** oil rig; M oil tanker; F oil company

petrolífero ADJ (que contiene petróleo) oil-bearing; (que produce petróleo) oil-producing; (relativo al petróleo) oil

petulancia F smugness

petulante ADJ smug

petunia F petunia

peyorativo ADJ pejorative

peyote M peyote

pez M fish; **— dorado** goldfish; **— espada** swordfish; **— gordo** *fam* fat cat, big shot; **— vela** sailfish; **— volador** flying fish; **como — en el agua** perfectly at ease; F pitch

pezón M nipple

pezuña F hoof

phishing M phishing

piadoso ADJ pious, saintly

piafar VI to stamp

pianista MF pianist, piano player

piano M piano; **— de cola** grand piano; **— vertical** upright piano

pianola F player piano

piar[28] VI to peep, to chirp

pica F (lanza) pike; (palo de baraja) spade

picada F (de insecto) bite; (de avión) nosedive; **caer en —** to dive

picadillo M meat [and vegetable] hash

picado ADJ (mar) rough, choppy; (carne) chopped; (de viruela) poked; M (de avión) nosedive; **caer en —** to dive

picador M picador; ADJ stinging

picadora F grinder; **— de carne** meat grinder

picadura F (de serpiente) bite; (de insecto) sting, bite

picante ADJ (especia) spicy, hot; (queso) sharp; (obsceno) risqué; M (especia fuerte) strong seasoning; (cualidad) spiciness

picar[30] VI/VT (un pez) to bite; (un ave) to peck; (comer en pequeñas cantidades) to nibble; VT (tomates) to chop up; (carne) to mince; (una vaca) to goad, to poke; (la curiosidad) to pique; (con espuelas) to spur; VI (una comida picante) to sting; (el sol) to burn; (la piel) to itch, to smart; (un avión) to dive; **— alto** to aim high; **—se** to spoil; **se pica el mar** the sea is getting rough; **se me picó un diente** I got a cavity; M SG **picapleitos** *pey* shyster; M **picaporte** latch

picardía F mischief

picaresco ADJ picaresque

pícaro-ra MF rogue, rascal; ADJ roguish, mischievous

picazón F (en la piel) itch; (en la garganta) tickle; **provoca —** it causes itching

picea F spruce

pichi M jumper

pichón M (paloma) pigeon; (cría de ave) chick

picnic M picnic

pico M (de ave) beak, bill; (de montaña) peak; (herramienta) pick; (de tetera) spout; **cuarenta y —** forty-odd; **cerrar el —** to shut one's mouth; **tener el — de oro** to be very eloquent

pícolo M piccolo

picotazo M peck

picotear VI/VT (aves) to peck; (personas) to nibble

pictórico ADJ pictorial

pida, pide, pidiendo, pidiera, pidiese *ver* pedir

pídola F leapfrog

pie M (del cuerpo, de calcetín, de cama, medida) foot; (de foto) caption; (de copa) stem; (de lámpara) stand; (de página) bottom; (para un actor) cue; (de árbol) trunk; (de mueble) leg; **— de atleta** athlete's foot; **— de autor**

byline; **— de imprenta** printer's mark; **— zambo** clubfoot; **a —** on foot; **un soldado de a —** a footsoldier; **— de banco** silly remark; **a — juntillas** firmly; **al — de la letra** to the letter; **caer de —** to have good luck; **con un — en el estribo** with one foot out of the door; **dar —** (a una crítica) to give rise to; (a un actor) to cue; **de/en —** standing; **en — de guerra** (enojado) on the warpath; (belicoso) on a war footing; **estar de —** to be standing; **estar en — de igualdad con** to be on a par with; **esto no tiene ni —s ni cabeza** I can't make heads or tails of this; **ir a —** to walk; **perder —** to lose one's footing; **ponerse de —** to stand up

piedad F (cualidad de pío) piety; (misericordia) mercy; **tener —** to show mercy

piedra F stone; **— angular** cornerstone, keystone; **— caliza** limestone; **— de afilar** whetstone; **— de toque** touchstone; **— pómez** pumice; **— preciosa** gemstone; **ser — de escándalo** to be an object of scandal

piel F (humana) skin; (animal) hide, pelt; (para confección) fur; **— de gallina** goosebumps; **— de naranja** cellulite

piensa, piense ver pensar

pienso M feed; **ni por —** no way

pierda, pierde ver perder

pierna F leg; **— de ternera** leg of lamb; **dormir a — suelta** to sleep like a log

pieza F (de artillería, de tela, de música, de teatro) piece; (habitación) room; **— de repuesto** replacement part; **de una —** astonished; **menuda —** a piece of work

pífano M fife

pifia F goof, miscue

pifiar VT to goof up, to miscue

pigmento M pigment

pigmeo-a MF pygmy

pijama M pajamas

pila F (recipiente) basin; (bautismal) baptismal font; (cúmulo) pile, heap, stack; (generador) battery; **— atómica** atomic reactor

pilar M pillar

píldora F pill; **—s para dormir** sleeping pills

pillaje M pillage, plunder

pillar VT (saquear) to pillage, to plunder; (atrapar, coger) to catch; (en un juego infantil) to tag

pillo-lla ADJ (travieso) naughty; (taimado) sly; MF (adulto) scoundrel; (niño) scamp

pilluelo-la MF urchin

pilón M (fuente) large basin; (soporte) pylon

pilotar, pilotear VT to pilot, to fly

pilote M pile, stilt

piloto MF (conductor) pilot; (llama pequeña de gas) pilot light; **— automático** autopilot; **— de pruebas** test pilot

pimentar VT to pepper

pimentero M pepper shaker

pimentón M paprika

pimienta F pepper; **— blanca** white pepper; **— de cayena** red pepper; **— negra** black pepper

pimiento M pepper, bell pepper; **— verde** green pepper

pimpollo M (de rosa) rosebud; (de vid) shoot

PIN M PIN

pináculo M pinnacle

pinar M pine grove

pincel M artist's brush

pincelada F stroke; **dar las últimas —s** to put on the final touches

pinchadura F flat tire

pinchar VT (perforar) to prick, to puncture; (apuñalar) to poke; (inyectar) to inject; (intervenir un teléfono) to wiretap; (provocar) to needle; VI to have a flat; **ni corta ni pincha** he doesn't count; M SG **pinchadiscos** disk jockey, DJ

pinchazo M (acción de pinchar) puncture, prick; (neumático) flat tire; (puñalada) stab; (de teléfono) wiretap

pincho M (palo afilado) spike; (de rotisería) spit

pingajo M (harapo) tatter; (harapiento) person dressed in rags

ping-pong M ping-pong

pingüe ADJ abundant

pingüino M penguin

pino M (árbol) pine; (ejercicio) handstand; **en el quinto —** in the boondocks

pinta F (mancha) dot; (aspecto) looks; (medida de líquidos) pint

pintada F grafitti

pintado ADJ (animales, plantas) colorful; **ese traje te queda —** you look great in that suit

pintar VT (colorear) to paint; (describir) to depict; **este marcador no pinta** this marker won't write; **no — nada** to count for nothing; **las cosas no pintaban bien** things did not look well; **—se** to put on makeup

pintarrajear VT to daub, to smear with paint; **—se** to put on too much makeup

pinto ADJ paint, dapple[d]

pintor-ora MF painter; **— de brocha gorda** house painter

pintoresco ADJ picturesque, colorful

pintorrear VT to smear with paint

pintura F (acción de pintar, obra) painting; (sustancia) paint; **— al óleo** oil painting; **— en aerosol** spray paint; **— fresca** wet paint

pinza F (de cangrejo) claw; (de médico) clamp; (de vestido) dart; (instrumento) clothespin; **—s** tweezers

piña F (fruto del pino) pinecone; (ananás) pineapple; (bomba) hand grenade

piñata F piñata

piñón M (semilla del pino) pine nut; (rueda del engranaje) pinion; (de bicicleta) sprocket

pío ADJ pious; INTERJ peep; **ni** — not a word

piojo M louse; **como — s en costura** like sardines

piojoso ADJ lousy

pionero -ra MF pioneer

pipa F (para fumar) pipe; (semilla) sunflower seed; **pasarlo** — to have a great time

pipí M pee; **hacer** — *fam* to pee

pipiolo -la MF novice

pique M (rivalidad) rivalry; (desavenencia) falling-out; **echar a** — to sink; **irse a** — to capsize

piquete M picket (también de huelga)

piquetear M to picket

piragua F dugout canoe

pirámide F pyramid

pirata MF pirate; — **informático -ca** hacker

piratear VT to pirate

piratería F piracy

piromanía F pyromania

pirómano -na MF pyromaniac

piropo M compliment

pirotecnia F pyrotechnics

pirulí M sucker, lollipop

pisada F (paso) footstep; (huella) footprint; **seguir las — s de** to follow in the footsteps of

pisar VT (oprimir con el pie) to step on, to tread on; (apisonar) to mash; **jamás pisó una plaza de toros** he never set foot in a bullring; **ir pisando huevos** to walk on eggshells; VI to step on; — **fuerte** to throw one's weight around; M SG **pisapapeles** paperweight

piscifactoría F fishery, fish farm

piscina F swimming pool

piso M (suelo) floor; (planta) story; (vivienda) apartment; **de — a techo** from the ground up

pisotear VT to tramp on, to trample, to stomp on

pisotón M stamp; **dar un** — to stamp, to step on

pista F (rastro) track, scent; (noticia) clue; (de aterrizaje) runway; (de circo) arena, ring; (de patinaje) skating ring; (de tenis) court; (de baile) floor; (de carreras) track, racetrack; **seguir la** — to track; — **para bicicletas** bike lane

pistola F (revólver) pistol; (para pintura) gun

pistolera F holster

pistolero MF gunner; M gunman; F gun woman

pistón M (válvula) piston; (explosivo) cap

pitada F drag, puff

pitar VI to toot, to whistle; VI/VT (rechiflar) to boo

pitazo M honk

pitido M (silbido) whistle, toot; (en deportes) whistle

pitillo M cigarette

pito M whistle; **entre — s y flautas** when all is said and done; **¿qué — s toca?** what's his role here?

pitón M (serpiente) python; (punta de cuerno) tip of a bull's horn

pituitario ADJ pituitary

pivot MF *Am* (baloncesto) center

pivotar VI to pivot

pivote M pivot; — **central** kingpin

píxel M pixel

pizarra F (roca) slate; (pizarrón) blackboard, chalkboard

pizarrón M blackboard, chalkboard

pizca F (de sal) pinch, dash; (de evidencia) shred; (de verdad) grain; (de suciedad) speck; **no entiendo ni** — I don't understand a bit/jot

pizza F pizza

placa F (fotográfica) plate; (de policía) badge; (condecoración, sarro) plaque; (de coche) license plate; (de computadora/ordenador) board, card; — **lógica** logic board; — **madre** motherboard

placaje M tackle

placar[30] VI/VT to tackle

placebo M placebo

placenta F placenta, afterbirth

placentero ADJ pleasant

placer[36] M pleasure, enjoyment; VT *lit* to please

plácido ADJ placid

plaf INTERJ plop

plaga F (enfermedad) plague; (persona, insecto) pest

plagar[40] VT to infest; —**se de** to become infested with

plagio M plagiarism

plan M plan; — **de estudios** curriculum; — **de juego** game plan; — **de salud administrado** managed care; **se vistió en — de vampiresa** she was dressed to kill

plana F newspaper page; — **mayor** top brass; **enmendar la — a uno** to correct a person's mistakes

plancha F (electrodoméstico) iron; (lámina) metal plate; (parrilla) griddle; **hacer la** — to float; **tirarse una** — to fall flat on one's face

planchado M ironing

planchar VT to iron, to press; **me dejó planchado** it left me speechless

plancton M plankton

planeador M glider

planeamiento M planning

planear VI/VT to plan; VI (volar) to glide, to plane; VT (madera) to plane

planeo M gliding

planeta M planet

planetario M planetarium

planificación F organization, planning; —

familiar family planning; **— para contingencias** contingency planning

planificador M planner, scheduler; **— de rutas** trip planner

planificar[30] VI/VT to plan

planilla F (de sueldos) payroll; (digital) worksheet; *Am* **— de cálculo** spreadsheet

plano ADJ flat, even; M (superficie) plane; (de un edificio) plan; (de calles) map; **— inclinado** inclined plane; **caer de —** to fall flat; **de —** flatly; **primer —** foreground

planta F (vegetal) plant; (del pie) sole; **— baja** ground floor

plantación F plantation

plantar VT (una planta, cruz) to plant; (a un novio) to dump; (a un colega) to make wait; **—se** to stand firm, to refuse to move; **— una bofetada a alguien** to give someone a slap; **dejar plantado** to stand up

planteamiento M (enfoque) approach; (exposición) presentation; **es un — poco provechoso** it is not a very beneficial approach

plantear VT (presentar) to present; **me planteó sus planes** she explained her plans to me; (provocar) to give rise to; **eso plantea un problema** that gives rise to a problem; **—se** to occur to; **¿te has planteado lo que pasa si te quedas sin trabajo?** have you thought about what will happen if you become unemployed?

plantel M (personal) staff; (almáciga) nursery

plantilla F (pieza suelta) insole; (patrón para calcar) pattern, stencil; (digital) template

plantío M grove

plasma M plasma (también de pantalla)

plasmar VT (captar) to capture; (dar forma plástica o sensible) to mold, to shape; **—se** to materialize

plasta ADJ tiresome; F (cosa informe) lump; (persona) bore

plástico ADJ & M plastic

plata F (metal, color, objeto de plata) silver; *Am* (dinero) money; **hablar en —** to speak in plain language

plataforma F platform (también política y digital); **— de lanzamiento** launching pad; **— petrolífera** oil rig; **— continental** continental shelf

platanar M banana grove

plátano M (fruta) banana; (para cocinar) plantain; (bananero) banana tree; (árbol ornamental) plane tree

platea F main floor of a theater

plateado ADJ & M (color) silver; M (acción de platear) silver-plating

platear VT to silver-plate

platero -ra MF silversmith

plática F chat

platicar[30] VI to chat

platija F flounder

platillo M (plato pequeño) saucer; (instrumento musical) cymbal; **— volador** flying saucer

platino M platinum

plato M (recipiente) plate; (comida) dish; (béisbol) home plate; **— fuerte** main dish/ course; **— hondo** bowl; **— sopero** soup dish

plausible ADJ plausible

playa F beach

playboy M playboy

plaza F (espacio amplio) plaza, public square; (puesto de trabajo) job; **de cuatro —s** four-seater; **— de toros** bullring; **— mayor** main square

plazo M term; **a corto —** short-term; **a largo —** long-term, long-range; **a — fijo** fixed-term; **a —s** on credit; **cumplir un —** to meet a deadline

plazoleta F court

plazuela F court

pleamar M high tide

plebe F rabble

plebeyo -ya ADJ & MF plebeian

plegable ADJ folding

plegadera F paper folder

plegadizo ADJ folding

plegar[41] VT to fold; **—se [a]** (ceder) to yield [to]; (unirse) to join

pleitesía F compliance

pleito M (pelea) dispute; (demanda judicial) litigation, lawsuit; **poner —** to sue

plenamente ADV fully

plenario ADJ & M plenary

plenitud F **— de la vida** prime of life

pleno ADJ complete; **en — día** in broad daylight; **en — invierno** in the dead of winter; **en — rostro** right on the face; **en — verano** in midsummer; **en plena vista** in plain sight; M full session

pliego M leaflet

pliegue M (en papel) fold; (en tela) pleat

plomada F plumb

plomería F plumbing

plomero -ra MF plumber

plomizo ADJ leaden

plomo M (metal, color) lead; (pesa) lead weight; (perdigón) shot; **a —** plumb; **caer a —** to fall vertically; **sin —** unleaded; ADJ INV tiresome

pluma F (de ave) feather, quill; (para escribir) pen; **— fuente** fountain pen

plumaje M plumage

plumero M dust mop, duster

plumífero ADJ feathery

plumón M down

plural ADJ & M plural

pluralidad F plurality

pluriempleo M moonlighting

pluscuamperfecto ADJ & N pluperfect

plutonio M plutonium
pluvial ADJ **aguas —es** rainwater
pluviómetro M rain gauge
PNB [producto nacional bruto] M GNP
población F (conjunto de personas) population;
     (acción de poblar) settlement; (pueblo) town
poblado M hamlet
poblador -ora MF settler
poblar[5] VT (habitar) to populate; (colonizar) to
     settle; **—se de** to become covered with
pobre ADJ poor; MF **los —s** the poor
pobrecito -ta MF poor thing
pobreza F (miseria) poverty; (escasez) scarcity
pocilga F pigsty, pigpen
pocillo M cup
poción F potion
poco ADJ (no mucho) little; **poca paciencia**
     little patience; **al — rato** after a little while;
     (no muchos) few; **—s pasajeros** few
     passengers; **al — tiempo** shortly; **a los —s**
     meses after a few months; **de pocas luces**
     stupid; **en pocas palabras** in a nutshell;
     ADV little; **trabaja —** he works little; **—**
     caritativo not very charitable; **— conocido**
     little known; **— a —** little by little; **— más o**
     menos about; **hace —** a short while ago;
     por — me caigo I almost fell; **tener en — to**
     hold in low esteem; PRON a little, a bit; **un —**
     a little bit, a little while; **como —** at least;
     unos —s a few
poda F trim
podadera F pruning hook
podar VT to prune, to trim
poder[69] VI to be able to; **no puedo llegar**
     antes de las cinco I can't get there before
     five; **¿puedo sentarme?** may I be seated?
     puede que venga she may come; **a más no**
     — to the utmost; **no puedo más** I can't go
     on; **nadie puede con ella** nobody can deal
     with her; **no puede menos que venir** he
     can't help but come; **no puede menos que**
     hacerlo he cannot help doing it; M (fuerza)
     power; (escrito que da autoridad) proxy,
     power of attorney; **— ejecutivo** executive
     branch; **— judicial** judiciary branch; **—**
     legislativo legislative branch; **por —** by
     proxy
poderío M power, might
poderoso ADJ powerful, mighty
podiatra MF podiatrist
podiatría F podiatry
podio M podium
podólogo -ga MF podiatrist
podrá, podría ver poder
podredumbre F rot
podrido ADJ rotten
podrir ver pudrir
poema M poem
poesía F (género lírico) poetry; (poema) poem

poeta MF, **poetisa** F poet
poética F poetics
poético ADJ poetic
polaco -ca ADJ Polish; M (lengua) Polish; MF
     Pole
polaina F legging
polar ADJ polar
polaridad F polarity
polarización F polarization
polca F polka
polea F pulley
polémica F polemic, controversy
polémico ADJ polemic
polen M pollen
poli MF cop; F *fam* cops
policía F (en conjunto) police; (mujer)
     policewoman; M policeman; MF police officer
policíaco ADJ police
policial ADJ police; **parte —** police report
poliéster M polyester
poliestireno M Styrofoam™
poligamia F polygamy
políglota ADJ & MF polyglot
polígrafo M polygraph
poliinsaturado ADJ polyunsaturated
polilla F moth
polímero M polymer
polinizar[47] VT to pollinate
polio F polio
pólipo M polyp
política F (actividad relativa al gobierno)
     politics; (conjunto de orientaciones) policy;
     — exterior foreign policy
político -ca ADJ (relativo a la política) political;
     (diplomático) politic; MF politician
poliuretano M polyurethane
póliza F policy; **— de seguros** insurance policy
polizón -ona MF stowaway
polizonte M *pey* cop
polla F pullet
pollada F brood
pollera F (mujer) woman who raises and sells
     chickens; (falda) *Am* skirt
pollo M (cría de ave) young chicken; (carne)
     chicken
polo M (punto geográfico) pole; (juego) polo; **—**
     acuático water polo; **— de atención** focus
     of attention; **— Norte** North Pole
Polonia F Poland
poltrona F easy chair
polvareda F cloud of dust; **levantar una —**
     (causar escándalo) to raise a ruckus; (causar
     una nube de polvo) to kick up the dust
polvera F compact
polvo M (suciedad) dust; (partículas) powder; **—**
     de hornear baking powder; **juntar — to**
     gather dust; **limpio de — y paja** net
pólvora F gunpowder
polvoriento ADJ dusty

polvorín M (almacén de pólvora) magazine; (situación explosiva) powder keg

pomada F salve

pomelo M grapefruit

pómez F pumice

pomo M doorknob

pompa F (boato) pomp; (burbuja) soap bubble; **—s fúnebres** funeral ceremony

pomposo ADJ pompous

pómulo M cheekbone

pon *ver* poner

ponchado M (béisbol) strikeout

ponchar VT (un neumático) to puncture; **— a alguien** (en béisbol) to strike someone out; **—se** (un neumático) to become punctured; (en béisbol) to strike out

ponche M (bebida) punch; (en béisbol) strikeout

ponchera F punch bowl

poncho M poncho

ponderación F (acción de ponderar) pondering; (valor relativo) weighting

ponderar VT (considerar) to ponder, to consider; (exagerar) to exaggerate; (ajustar valores) to weight

pondrá, pondría *ver* poner

ponencia F presentation

poner[56, 74] VT to put, to place; (la mesa, un reloj) to set; (huevos) to lay; (azúcar) to add; (un examen) to give; (el televisor) to turn on; (un pleito) to file; **— a alguien a hacer algo** to assign someone to do something; **— en claro** to clarify; **— en limpio** to recopy, to make a clean copy; **— nombre a un niño** to name a child; **— sangre** to give a transfusion; **cada uno pone mil pesetas** each person contributes a thousand pesetas; **pongamos que** let us suppose that; **¿qué pone ahí?** what does it say there? **—se** (volverse) to become; (el sol) to set; (ropa) to put on; **—se a** to begin to; **—se al corriente** to become informed; **—se de acuerdo** to come to an agreement; **—se de pie** to stand up; **—se por delante en el marcador** (deporte) to take the lead

póney M pony

ponga, pongo *ver* poner

poniente M (oeste) west; (viento del oeste) west wind

pontón M pontoon

ponzoña F poison

ponzoñoso ADJ poisonous

pool M pool

popa F poop, stern

populacho M mob

popular ADJ (conocido y citado) popular; (del pueblo) folk

popularidad F popularity

populoso ADJ populous

popurrí M (de perfume) potpourri; (musical) medley

poquito *ver* poco

por PREP **— barco** by boat; **— casualidad** by chance; **— Dios** by God; **— etapas** by stages; **— las buenas o — las malas** by hook or by crook; **— litro** by the liter; **¿— qué?** why? for what reason? **multiplicar —** to multiply by; **lo agarró — la garganta** he grabbed him by the throat; **mi amor — ella** my love for her; **— poco tiempo** for a short time; **— primera vez** for the first time; **— vía de argumento** for the sake of argument; **— ejemplo** for instance; **— el momento** for the time being; **hazlo — mí** do it for my sake; **trabaja — mí** work on my behalf; **no me gustan — su olor** I don't like them because of their smell; **lo supe — él** I found out through him; **pasé — Londres** I passed through London; **un viaje — la costa** a trip along the coast; **— lo que cuentas** from what you're telling me; **— adelantado** in advance; **— escrito** in writing; **— la mañana** in the morning; **— lo general** in general; **— rachas** in spurts; **está — Badajoz** it's near Badajoz; **— fin** at last; **— el mes de marzo** around the month of March; **— ciento** percent; **— consiguiente** consequently; **— escrito** in writing; **— poco se muere** he almost died; **está — hacer** it is yet to be done; **él está — hacerlo** (a favor de) he is in favor of doing it; (a punto de) he is about to do it; **recibir — esposa** to take as a wife; **tener —** to consider, to think of as

porcelana F porcelain, china

porcentaje M percentage; **— de bateo** (béisbol) batting average

porche M porch, stoop

porcino ADJ **ganado —** swine; M pig

porción F (parte) portion, share; (de alimento) helping

pordiosear VT to panhandle

pordiosero -ra MF panhandler

porfía F obstinacy

porfiado ADJ willful

porfiar[28] VT to insist

pormenor M detail

pormenorizar[47] VT to detail, to go into detail about

porno M porn

pornografía F pornography

pornográfico ADJ pornographic

poro M pore

poroso ADJ porous

poroto M *Am* bean

porque CONJ because

porqué M reason; **el — de su tristeza** the reason for his sadness

porquería F (suciedad) filth; (acción despreciable) dirty trick; (cosa de mala

calidad) crud; (comida de mala calidad) junk
food

porra F club, cudgel

porrista MF cheerleader

portada F (de un libro) title page; (de una
revista) front cover

portador-ora MF (dé enfermedad) carrier; (de
cheque) bearer; **— del féretro** pallbearer

portal M portal, doorway; **— de videos/vídeos**
video portal

portar VT to carry; **—se** to behave; **—se mal** to
misbehave; M SG **portaaviones** aircraft
carrier; M SG **portaequipajes** luggage bin;
M **portaestandarte** standard-bearer; M
portafolio briefcase; M SG **portalámparas**
socket; M SG **portaligas** garter belt; M SG
portamonedas coin purse; M **portaobjeto**
slide; M SG **portapapeles** clipboard; MF
portavoz spokesperson

portátil ADJ portable

portazo M slam; **dar un —** to slam the door

porte M (envío) freight; (por correo) postage;
(aspecto) bearing, carriage; (capacidad de
carga) capacity; (tamaño) size; **— de armas**
the carrying of arms; **enviar — pagado** to
send prepaid

portear VT to carry

portentoso ADJ portentous

porteño -ña MF (de Buenos Aires) person from
Buenos Aires; (de un puerto) person from a
port city; ADJ (de Buenos Aires) from Buenos
Aires; (de un puerto) from a port city

portería F (de un edificio) entrance area; (en
fútbol) goal

portero -ra MF (de un edificio) doorkeeper,
superintendent; (en fútbol) goalkeeper; M **—
automático** intercom

portón M gate

portuario ADJ harbor, port; **trabajador —**
dockworker

Portugal M Portugal

portugués -esa ADJ & MF Portuguese; M
(lengua) Portuguese

porvenir M future

pos LOC PREP **en — de** after

posada F inn, lodge

posaderas F PL *fam* rear end

posadero -ra MF innkeeper

posar VT (la mano, los ojos) to rest; VI (en el
suelo) to sit down; (como modelo) to pose;
—se (partículas) to settle; (mariposa) to
alight; (pájaro) to perch

posdata F postscript

pose F pose

poseedor -ora MF possessor

poseer[18] VT to possess

poseído ADJ possessed

posesión F possession

posesivo ADJ & M possessive

poseyendo, poseyera, poseyese, poseyó *ver*
poseer

posfechar VT to postdate

posguerra F postwar period

posibilidad F possibility

posibilitar VT (hacer posible) to make possible;
(permitir) to allow, to permit

posible ADJ possible; **hacer lo —** to do one's
best; **es —** it's possible

posición F (ubicación) position; (opinión)
stance; (rango) standing; **— de negociación**
bargaining position; **— fetal** fetal position

posicionamiento M (acción de posicionar,
también de productos) placement,
positioning; (actitud política) position, stance

posicionarse VI to position oneself

positivo ADJ & M positive

poso M (de vino) dregs; (de café) grounds

posparto M postpartum

posponer[56, 74] VT (aplazar) to postpone, to
defer, to put off; (relegar) to put after

posta F (relevo) relay; (perdigón) buckshot

postal ADJ postal; F postcard

poste M (palo) post; (en fútbol) upright, goalpost

póster M poster

postergar[40] VT (para un ascenso) to pass over;
(posponer) to postpone

posteridad F posterity; **eso quedará para la
—** that will remain for all eternity

posterior ADJ (espacial) back, rear; (anatómico)
posterior; (temporal) later; **nuestro
divorcio fue — a la compra del negocio**
our divorce came after we purchased the
business

posterioridad LOC ADV **con —** later,
subsequently

posteriormente ADV (atrás) in the back;
(después) afterward[s]; **vocal pronunciada
—** vowel pronounced in the back [of the
mouth]

postigo M shutter

postizo ADJ false; **familia postiza** adoptive
family; M hairpiece

postnasal ADJ postnasal

postrado ADJ prostrate, prone

postrar VT to prostrate

postre M dessert; **a la —** at last

postulado M postulate

postulante MF candidate

postular VT to postulate

póstumo ADJ posthumous

postura F posture (también opinión)

potable ADJ drinkable, potable

potasio M potassium

pote M (cilíndrico) jar; (panzudo) jug

potear VI/VT to putt

potencia F (sexual) potency; (de una fuerza,
nación) power; **es un asesino en —** he's a
potential murderer; **— naval** sea power; **de**

alta — high-powered; **segunda** — the second power
potencial ADJ & M potential
potenciar VT (a una persona) to empower; (proyectos, relaciones) to promote, to support
potentado -da MF potentate
potente ADJ potent, powerful
potranco -ca M colt; F filly
potrero M pasture; *Am* cattle ranch, stock farm
potro M (caballo) colt; (en gimnasia) vaulting horse; **— de tormento** rack
pozo M (de agua, petróleo) well; (hoyo profundo) pit; (minero) mine shaft; **sacar del —** to rescue; **— negro** sink; **— sin fondo** bottomless pit; **— séptico** septic tank
práctica F (repetición, costumbre) practice; (destreza) skill; **en la —** in practice; **poner en —** to put into practice; **— comercial desleal** deceptive practice
prácticamente ADV (casi) practically, virtually; (de forma práctica) practically; (en la práctica) in practice
practicante ADJ practicing; MF (que practica) practitioner; (asistente de médico) physician's assistant
practicar[30] VI/VT (una habilidad) to practice; (un agujero) to make
práctico ADJ (sencillo) practical; (adiestrado) skillful; M **— de puerto** harbor pilot
pradera F prairie, grassland
prado M meadow, pasture
pragmático ADJ pragmatic
preadolescente ADJ & MF preteen, preadolescent
preámbulo M preamble
preaprobado ADJ preapproved
precalentamiento M warmup
precanceroso ADJ precancerous
precario ADJ precarious, *fam* touch-and-go
precaución F precaution
precaverse VT to take precautions
precavido ADJ cautious
precedencia F precedence
precedente ADJ preceding; M precedent; **sin —** unprecedented; **sentar —** to set a precedent
preceder VI/VT to precede
precepto M precept
preciado ADJ (estimado) prized; (valioso) valuable
preciarse VI **— de** to be proud of
precintar VT to seal
precinto M seal
precio M price; **poner — a** to put a price on; **no tener —** to be priceless; **— de compra** purchase price; **— de lista** list price; **— de mercado** market price; **— de referencia** bench price; **— justo en el mercado** fair market price; **— sugerido** suggested retail

price; **— sugerido por el fabricante** manufacturer's suggested retail price; **— vigente** going price
preciosista ADJ precious
precioso ADJ (metal, piedra, objeto de gran valor) precious; (muy bonito) beautiful, adorable
precipicio M precipice, cliff
precipitación F precipitation (también atolondramiento)
precipitado ADJ precipitate, hasty, rash; M precipitate
precipitar VI to precipitate; VT to hurl; **—se** (apresurarse) to be hasty; (arrojarse) to plunge, to plummet; (depositarse) to precipitate; (adelantarse) to come to a head
precisamente ADV precisely, exactly, just; **— de eso que quería hablar** that is just what I wanted to talk to you about; (de hecho) as a matter of fact; **—, se alojó en este hotel** as a matter of fact he stayed in this hotel
precisar VT (determinar) to determine precisely; (necesitar) to need
precisión F precision, accuracy; **precisiones** clarifications
preciso ADJ precise, accurate; **es — que vengas** you must come; **en este — instante** at this very moment
precoz ADJ (niño) precocious; (diagnóstico) early
precursor -ora MF precursor, forerunner
predecesor -ora MF predecessor
predecir[53, 74] VT to predict, to foretell
predestinar VT to predestine
predeterminado ADJ predetermined
predicación F preaching
predicado ADJ & M predicate
predicador -ora MF preacher
predicar[30] VI/VT to preach
predicción F prediction
predilección F predilection
predilecto ADJ favorite, pet
predio M piece of land
predisponer[56, 74] VT to predispose
predisposición F predisposition
predominante ADJ predominant, prevailing
predominar VI to predominate
predominio M predominance
preeclampsia F preeclampsia
preeminente ADJ foremost
preempacado ADJ prepacked
preescolar ADJ nursery; MF nursery school child
preestablecido ADJ preset
preestreno M preview
preexistente ADJ preexisting
prefacio M preface
preferencia F preference; (en el tráfico) right of way; **de —** predominantly
preferente ADJ (tratamiento) preferential;

(acciones) preferred
preferible ADJ preferable
preferido ADJ preferred, favorite
preferir[8] VT to prefer
prefiera, prefiere *ver* preferir
prefijar VT to prefix
prefijo M prefix
prefiriendo, prefiriera, prefiriese *ver* preferir
pregonar VT (noticias) to make public; (mercancías) to hawk
pregrabado ADJ prerecorded
pregunta F question; **hacer una —** to ask a question; **—s frecuentes** frequently asked questions
preguntar VI/VT to ask, to inquire; **— por** (pedir información) to inquire about; (pedir para hablar) to ask for; **—se** to wonder
preguntón ADJ inquisitive
prehistórico ADJ prehistoric
prejuicio M prejudice, bias
prejuzgar[40] VT to prejudge
preliminar ADJ & M preliminary
preludiar VT to prelude
preludio M prelude
prematrimonial ADJ premarital
prematuro ADJ (bebé) premature; (muerte) untimely
premeditado ADJ premeditated
premenstrual ADJ premenstrual
premiar VT to reward; **las obras premiadas** the award-winning works
première M premiere
premio M (galardón) prize, award; (de la moneda) appreciation; **Juan Pérez, — nacional de poesía** Juan Pérez, winner of the national poetry award; **— gordo** jackpot
premisa F premise
premonición F premonition
prenatal ADJ prenatal
prenda F (fianza) pawn, pledge; (de vestir) article of clothing, garment; **dejar en —** to pawn; **en — de** as a token of
prendar VT to charm; **—se de** to fall in love with
prendedor M brooch, pin
prender VT (agarrar) to grab; (sujetar) to clasp; (enganchar) to fasten; (detener) to arrest; (arraigar) to take root; (encender) to turn on, to switch on; **— fuego** to set on fire; **la vacuna no prendió** the vaccination didn't take
prensa F press; **tener mala —** to have bad press
prensar VT to press
prensil ADJ prehensile
prenupcial ADJ prenuptial
preñada ADJ pregnant
preñar VT to impregnate
preñez F pregnancy

preocupación F worry, concern
preocupado ADJ worried, concerned, anxious
preocupante ADJ worrisome
preocupar VT to worry, to concern; **—se de** to worry about; **—se por** to be concerned about
preocupón-ona MF worrywart
preparación F preparation
preparado ADJ ready; M preparation
preparar VT to prepare; **—se** to get ready, to brace oneself; **— el cuerpo de un difunto** to embalm a body
preparativo ADJ preparatory; M preparation
preparatorio ADJ preparatory; **escuela preparatoria** preparatory school
preponderancia F preponderance
preponderante ADJ preponderant
preponderar VI to predominate
preposición F preposition
prepucio M foreskin
prerrequisito M prerequisite
prerrogativa F prerogative
presa F (animal de caza) prey, quarry; (dique) dam
presagiar VT to forebode
presagio M omen, sign
présbita, présbite ADV & MF farsighted
prescindible ADJ dispensable
prescindir VI **— de** to dispense with, to do without
prescribir[74] VT to prescribe
prescripción F prescription
presencia F presence; **— de ánimo** presence of mind
presenciar VT to witness
presentable ADJ presentable
presentación F (de un tema) presentation; (de una persona) introduction
presentador-ora MF (de programa de televisión) host; (de noticiero) anchor
presentar VT (una idea) to present; (a una persona) to introduce; (la declaración de impuestos, una demanda) to file; (un informe) to submit; (documentos) to produce; (una queja) to lodge; (una renuncia) to tender; **—se** (aparecer) to appear; (hacerse conocer) to introduce oneself
presente ADJ present; M (tiempo) present; (regalo) present, gift; **al —** at the present time; **tener —** to bear in mind; **en el — [contrato]** herein; **por la — [carta]** hereby
presentimiento M presentiment, foreboding, hunch
presentir[8] VT to have a presentiment of
preservación F (protección) preservation; (ahorro) conservation
preservar VT (proteger) to preserve; (ahorrar) to conserve
presidencia F presidency
presidencial ADJ presidential

presidente MF, **presidenta** F (de un país) president; (de una reunión, junta) chair
presidiario-ria MF prisoner
presidio M prison
presidir VI to preside; VT to preside over
presilla F loop
presión F pressure; — **atmosférica** atmospheric pressure; — **arterial** blood pressure; — **arterial alta** high blood pressure, hypertension; — **de aire** air pressure
presionar VT (un botón) to press; (al gobierno) to lobby
preso-sa MF prisoner, inmate
prestación F provision; **prestaciones** benefits
prestador-ora MF lender
prestamista MF (de dinero) lender; (en un montepío) pawnbroker
préstamo M loan; — **convencional** conventional loan; — **garantizado** guaranteed loan
prestar VT to loan, to lend; — **ayuda** to give help; — **atención** to pay attention; — **juramento** to take an oath; — **servicio** to render service
prestatario-ria MF borrower
prestidigitación F sleight of hand
prestigio M prestige
prestigioso ADJ prestigious
presumido ADJ conceited, presumptuous
presumir VT (suponer) to presume; VI (ostentar) to show off; — **de valiente** to boast of one's valor
presunción F presumption
presuntamente ADV allegedly
presunto ADJ (dueño, autor de una obra) presumed; (autor de un crimen) alleged; — **heredero** heir apparent
presuntuoso ADJ presumptuous
presuponer[56, 74] VT to presuppose
presupuestación F budgeting
presupuestario ADJ budget, budgetary
presupuesto M (de gastos e ingresos) budget; (de costos) estimate; — **equilibrado** balanced budget
presuroso ADJ hasty
pretencioso ADJ pretentious
pretender VI (sostener) to claim, to purport; — **ser** to claim to be; — **al trono** to pretend to the throne; VT (intentar) to attempt
pretendiente MF, **pretendienta** F (al trono) pretender; (a un puesto) aspirant; M (de una mujer) suitor, admirer
pretensión F pretension
pretérito ADJ past; M past tense; — **perfecto** present perfect
pretexto M pretext, pretense; **so — de** under pretense of
pretil M railing

pretina F waistband
prevalecer[35] VI to prevail
prevaleciente ADJ prevalent
prevé, prevea, preveía ver prever
prevención F (protección) prevention; (recelo) caution
prevenido ADJ forewarned
prevenir[61] VT (precaver) to prevent; (prever) to foresee; (advertir) to warn; — **contra** to protect oneself against
preventivo ADJ preventive, precautionary
prever[72, 74] VT to foresee, to anticipate
previamente ADV previously
previo ADJ previous, prior; — **examen de salud** after undergoing a health examination
previsible ADJ foreseeable
previsión F foresight, anticipation
previsto ver prever
previsualización F previewing
prieto ADJ swarthy
prima F (cuota de seguro) premium; (recargo) surcharge; (pago extraordinario) bonus
primario ADJ primary
primate M primate
primavera F spring
primaveral ADJ springlike
primero ADJ & ADV first; **primer ministro** prime minister; **primer piso** second floor; **primer plano** foreground; **primera base** (posición) first base; (jugador) first baseman; **primera enseñanza** primary education; **primera persona** first person; **primer tiempo** first half; —**s auxilios** first aid; **a primera vista** at first sight; **de primer grado** first degree; **de primera** top-notch; **de primera mano** firsthand; **por primera vez** for the first time; — **del mes** first of the month; **Juan llegó —** Juan arrived first; F (marcha) first gear; (clase en un avión) first class
primicia F (fruto primero) first fruit; (noticia) scoop
primitivo ADJ primitive
primo-ma MF (hijo de tío) cousin; (persona incauta) sucker, dupe; — **hermano** first cousin; — **segundo** second cousin; ADJ prime
primogénito-ta ADJ & MF firstborn
primogenitura F birthright
primor M (esmero) care; (cosa fina) lovely thing
primordial ADJ primordial
primoroso ADJ exquisite
princesa F princess
principal ADJ principal, main; **la causa — de muerte** the leading cause of death; **el dormitorio —** the master bedroom
principalmente ADV mainly, principally
príncipe M prince
principesco ADJ princely

principiante MF beginner; ADJ beginning
principiar VT to commence
principio M (fundamento, regla de conducta) principle, tenet; (hecho de empezar, tiempo, lugar) beginning, start; **a —s de** toward the beginning of; **— activo** active ingredient; **al —** at the beginning, at first; **de — a fin** from beginning to end; **desde el —** from the beginning; **en —** in principle
pringar⁴⁰ VT (ensuciar) to get greasy; (mojar) to dip
pringoso ADJ greasy
pringue MF grease
prioridad F (autoridad, preferencia) priority, precedence; (en el tráfico) right of way
prioritario ADJ having priority, most important
prisa F haste, hurry; **a toda —** at full speed; **correr —** to be urgent; **darse —** to hurry; **las —s comienzan a la una** the rush starts at one; **tener —** to be in a hurry; **sin —** leisurely
prisión F prison; **— perpetua** life in prison
prisionero -ra MF prisoner; **— de guerra** prisoner of war
prisma M prism
prismáticos M PL binoculars
privacidad F privacy
privación F privation; **pasar privaciones** to suffer want
privado ADJ private; **en —** in private
privar VT to deprive; **—se de** to deprive oneself of
privativo ADJ exclusive
privatización F privatization
privatizar⁴⁷ VT to privatize
privilegiado ADJ privileged
privilegiar VT to favor, to give a privilege to
privilegio M privilege
pro M advantage; **en — de** in favor of; **en — y en contra** for and against
proa F prow, bow
proaborto ADJ INV pro-choice
probabilidad F (chance) likelihood; (en estadística) probability; **tienes pocas —es de ganar** you have little chance of winning; **¿qué —es tiene?** what are her odds?
probable ADJ probable, likely; **lo más —es que haya venido** in all likelihood he came
probador M dressing room
probar⁵ VT (alimento, bebida) to taste, to try, to sample; (una hipótesis) to prove; (una guitarra) to try out; (un coche) to test-drive; **—se un vestido** to try on a dress; **— fortuna** to try one's luck; **prueba a venir más temprano** try to come earlier; **no — bocado** not to eat a bite
probatorio ADJ probationary
probeta F test tube
problema M problem; **él sólo da —s** he's

nothing but trouble
problemático -ca ADJ problematic; F problems
procedencia F origin
procedente ADJ **— de** from
proceder VI to proceed; **— de** to come from; **— a** to proceed to; **— contra** to take action against
procedimiento M procedure; **—s** proceedings
procesable ADJ actionable
procesado -da MF accused; M processing
procesador ADJ processing; M processor; **— de textos** word processor
procesamiento M prosecution; **— de datos** data processing; **— de textos** word processing
procesar VT to prosecute, to try
procesión F procession; **la — va por dentro** he doesn't let it show
proceso M (etapas) process; (juicio) trial, legal proceedings
proclama F proclamation
proclamación F proclamation
proclamar VT to proclaim; **—se campeón** to be proclaimed winner
proclive ADJ prone
procrear VI/VT to procreate
proctología F proctology
procurador -ora MF attorney
procurar VT (intentar) to endeavor; (obtener) to procure, to obtain
prodigar⁴⁰ VT to lavish; **—se** to be lavish
prodigio M prodigy
prodigioso ADJ prodigious
pródigo -ga ADJ (derrochador) prodigal; (muy generoso) lavish; MF spendthrift
producción F (acción de producir) production; (cantidad producida) production, yield; **— masiva** mass production
producir³⁸ VT (efectos, mercancías, películas) to produce; (fruta, resultados) to yield, to bear; **—se** to happen
productividad F productivity
productivo ADJ (rendidor) productive; (exitoso) successful
producto M product; **— interno bruto** gross national product
productor -ora MF producer; ADJ **un país — de petróleo** an oil-producing country
produje, produjera, produjese ver producir
pro-elección ADJ INV pro-choice
proeza F exploit
profanación F desecration
profanar VT to profane, to desecrate
profano ADJ profane
profecía F prophecy
proferir⁸ VT to utter
profesar VT to profess
profesión F profession
profesional ADJ & MF professional; **— de la**

salud health care provider
profesionista MF *Méx* professional
profesor -ora MF (universitario) professor; (de enseñanza secundaria) teacher; (de tenis) instructor
profesorado M faculty
profeta MF prophet
profético ADJ prophetic
profetizar[47] VI/VT to prophesy
profilaxis F prevention
prófugo -ga ADJ & MF fugitive
profundidad F (del mar, de comprensión, de un armario) depth; (sabiduría) profundity
profundizar[47] VT to deepen; VI to go into deeply
profundo ADJ (idea, comentario, razonamiento) profound; (mar, pozo, armario, voz) deep
profuso ADJ profuse
progesterona F progesterone
programa M (de boxeo) card; (de televisión) show, program; (de un curso) syllabus; (de un congreso) program; **— antivirus** antivirus program, antivirus software; **— de protección contra virus** virus protection software; **— de instalación** setup program, install program; **— instalador** setup program, install program; **— para recuperar datos borrados** undelete utility; **—s almacenados en circuitos integrados** firmware
programable ADJ programmable
programación F programming
programador -ora MF programmer
programar VT (una computadora) to program; (un evento) to schedule
progresar VT to progress, to advance
progresión F progression
progresista ADJ & MF progressive
progresivo -va ADJ & MF progressive
progreso M progress
prohibición F prohibition, ban
prohibido ADJ forbidden; **prohibida la entrada** no admittance; **— el paso** no trespassing
prohibir[29] VT to prohibit, to ban; **se prohíbe fumar** no smoking
prohijar VT to adopt
prójimo -ma MF fellow human
prole F offspring
proletariado M proletariat
proletario -ria ADJ & MF proletarian
proliferación F proliferation, spread
prolífico ADJ prolific
prolijo ADJ (verboso) wordy; (esmerado) overly careful
prologar[40] VT to preface
prólogo M prologue, foreword, preface
prolongación F prolongation
prolongado ADJ extended

prolongar[40] VT to prolong; **—se** to wear on
promediar VT to average
promedio M average, mean; **de/en —** on average; **— de carreras limpias permitidas** earned run average
promesa F promise; **romper una —** to break a promise; **una joven —** a promising young player
prometedor ADJ promising
prometer VT to promise; VI to show promise
prometido -da ADJ engaged; M fiancé; F fiancée
prominente ADJ prominent
promiscuo ADJ promiscuous
promisorio ADJ promissory; **un futuro —** a promising future
promoción F (oferta comercial) promotion; (conjunto de personas) class
promocional ADJ promotional
promocionar VT to promote, to publicize
promontorio M promontory
promotor -ora MF (de un producto) promoter; (de bienes inmuebles) developer
promover[6] VT (ideas, producto, a un alumno) to promote; (la paz, una causa) to foster, to further
promulgación F enactment
promulgar[40] VT to promulgate, to enact
pronombre M pronoun
pronominal ADJ pronominal
pronosticar[30] VT to forecast
pronóstico M (del tiempo, de la economía) forecast; (de una enfermedad) prognosis
prontitud F promptness, dispatch
pronto ADJ (rápido) quick; (listo) ready; ADV soon, promptly; **de —** suddenly; **¡hasta —!** see you soon! **tan — como** as soon as
pronunciación F pronunciation
pronunciado ADJ pronounced
pronunciamiento M declaration, pronouncement
pronunciar VT (un sonido, una sentencia) to pronounce; (un discurso) to make, to deliver; **—se** (acusarse) to be pronounced; (expresarse) to declare one's opinion
propagación F propagation, spread
propaganda F (de ideas) propaganda; (de mercancías) advertising, publicity; **hacer —** to advertise
propagar[40] VT to propagate
propalar VT to spread
propano M propane
propasarse VI to go too far
propensión F propensity
propenso ADJ prone
propiciar VT to favor
propicio ADJ propitious, auspicious
propiedad F (cualidad, pertenencia, finca) property; (derecho de dueño) ownership; (corrección) precision; **— mayoritaria**

majority ownership; **— privada** private property; **—es** estate; **—es colindantes** adjoining properties

propietario -ria M (de una tienda) proprietor, owner; (de un apartamento) landlord; F (de una tienda) owner; (de un apartamento) landlady; **— ausente** absentee landlord

propina F tip, gratuity; **dar [una]** — to tip

propinar VT **— una paliza** to give a beating

propio ADJ (correcto) proper; **el significado** — the proper meaning; (típico) like; **no es — de él quejarse así** it's not like him to complain like that; (conveniente) appropriate; **una expresión propia** an appropriate expression; (que le pertenece) own; **su — hijo** his own son; **un hijo —** a son of his own; **por tu — bien** for your own good; (mismo) same; **al — tiempo** at the same time

propondrá, propondría *ver* proponer

proponente MF proponent

proponer[56,74] VT to propose; **—se** to set out to

proponga, propongo *ver* proponer

proporción F proportion, ratio; **proporciones** dimensions

proporcional ADJ proportional, proportionate

proporcionar VT (ajustar a proporción) to proportion; (brindar) to furnish, to provide

proposición F (lógica) proposition; (de matrimonio) proposal; **proposiciones deshonestas** indecent proposals

propósito M purpose, intent; **a —** (adecuado) apropos; (voluntariamente) on purpose, intentionally, deliberately; (además) by the way, incidentally; **a — de** apropos of

propuesta F proposal

propuesto *ver* proponer

propugnar VT to urge

propulsar VT to propel

propulsión F propulsion; **— a chorro** jet propulsion

propulsor -ora ADJ propelling; MF promoter

propuse, propusiera, propusiese *ver* proponer

prorratear VT to prorate

prórroga F (plazo) extension of time; (de un préstamo) renewal; (fútbol americano) overtime; (fútbol) extra time

prorrogar[40] VT (un pago) to put off, to defer; (un plazo) to extend; (un préstamo) to renew

prorrumpir VI to burst; **— en llanto** to burst into tears; **— en carcajadas** to burst out laughing

prosa F prose

prosaico ADJ prosaic

proscribir[74] VT to banish, to disenfranchise

proscripción F banishment

proseguir[12] VI to proceed

prosódico ADJ prosodic

prospectar VT to prospect

prospector -ora MF prospector

prosperar VI to prosper, to flourish, to thrive

prosperidad F prosperity

próspero ADJ prosperous

próstata F prostate [gland]

prostitución F prostitution

prostituir[19] VT to prostitute

prostituto -ta MF prostitute

protagonista MF protagonist

protagonizar[47] VT to star in

protección F protection; **— al consumidor** consumer protection; **— contra copias** copy protection; **— contra grabación** write protection; **— contra lectura** read protect; **— por contraseña** password protection

proteccionista ADJ & MF protectionist

protector -ora ADJ protective; MF protector; **— de pantalla** screen saver; **— de tensión** surge protector; **— sobrecargas de voltaje** surge protector; **— solar** sunblock

protectorado M protectorate

proteger[45] VT (a alguien vulnerable) to protect; (a un artista) to sponsor; **— contra grabación** to write-protect

protegido -da MF protégé[e]; **— por contraseña** password protected

proteína F protein

prótesis F prosthesis; **— de cadera** hip prosthesis

protesta F protest

protestante MF Protestant

protestar VI/VT to protest

protocolo M protocol

protón M proton

protoplasma M protoplasm

prototipo M prototype

protozoario M protozoan

protuberancia F protuberance, bulge, bump

protuberante ADJ bulging

provecho M (beneficio) benefit; (eructo) burp; **¡buen —!** bon appétit! **sacar — [de]** to benefit [from], to profit [from]

provechoso ADJ beneficial, advantageous

proveedor -ora MF (de un servicio) provider; (de un producto) supplier, vendor; **— de acceso** access provider; **— de acceso a internet** Internet access provider

proveer[18,74] VT to provide; **— de** to provide with; **—se de** to provide oneself with

provenga, provengo *ver* provenir

proveniente ADJ **— de** coming from

provenir[61] VI to arise; **— de** to stem from

proverbio M proverb

providencia F providence

providencial ADJ providential

provincia F province

provincial ADJ provincial

provinciano -na ADJ & MF provincial

provine, proviniendo, proviniera,

proviniese, provino *ver* provenir

provisión F provision, supply, store

provisional ADJ temporary, provisional

provisorio ADJ temporary

provocación F provocation

provocar[30] VT (ira) to provoke; (sexualmente) to excite; (un incendio) to start; (una respuesta) to elicit

provocativo ADJ provocative

proximidad F proximity, nearness; **en las —es** in the vicinity

próximo ADJ (posterior) next; (cercano) near, nearby; **el lunes — pasado** last Monday; **de próxima aparición** forthcoming

proyección F projection

proyectar VT (un plan) to project; (una película) to screen; (una sombra) to cast; **—se** to overhang, to jut

proyectil M projectile

proyecto M (idea) project; (arquitectónico) plan; **— de ley** bill

proyector M (para películas) projector; (en el teatro) spotlight

prudencia F prudence

prudente ADJ prudent

prueba F (de imprenta, argumento irrefutable) proof; (argumento parcial) evidence; (intento, dificultad) trial, test; (examen) test, examination; (de ropa) fitting; **— beta** beta test; **— de detección** screening test; **— de doble incógnita** double-blind test; **— de embarazo** pregnancy test; **— de esfuerzo** stress test; **— de esfuerzo máximo** exercise electrocardiogram; **— de fuego** trial by fire; **— de ingresos** means test; **— de paternidad** paternity test; **— de Rorschach** Rorschach test; **a —** on approval; **a — de fallos** foolproof; **a — de incendio** fireproof; **poner a —** to put to the test

prueba, pruebe *ver* probar

psicoanálisis M psychoanalysis

psicodélico ADJ & M psychedelic

psicología F psychology

psicológico ADJ psychological

psicólogo-ga MF psychologist

psicópata MF psychopath

psicosis F psychosis

psicosomático ADJ psychosomatic

psicoterapia F psychotherapy

psicótico ADJ psychotic

psiquiatra MF psychiatrist

psiquiatría F psychiatry

psíquico ADJ psychic

psoriasis F psoriasis

púa F (con punta aguda) spike; (de alambre) barb; (de guitarra) pick; (de erizo) quill; (de tridente) prong

puaf, puaj INTERJ yuck, ugh

pubertad F puberty

publicación F publication

publicar[30] VT to publish; (revelar) to divulge

publicidad F publicity, advertising; **— de cebo y anzuelo** bait-and-switch advertising; **— engañosa** false advertising; **— exterior** outdoor advertising; **hacer —** to advertise

publicitario-ria MF advertising agent; ADJ publicity

público ADJ public; M (testigo) public; (en un espectáculo) audience; **en —** in public

publirreportaje M infomercial

puchero M (vasija) pot; (guiso) stew; (gesto) pout; **hacer —s** to pout

puck M puck

pude, pudiendo, pudiera, pudiese *ver* poder

pudiente ADJ wealthy

pudín M pudding

pudor M (sexual) modesty; (emocional) reserve

pudrir[74] VI to rot

pueblerino ADJ provincial

pueblo M (población) town; (nación) people, folk

pueda, puede *ver* poder

puente M bridge (también dental, de gafas, de nariz); (fin de semana) long weekend; **— aéreo** (regular) shuttle; (de emergencia) airlift; **— cardiopulmonar** cardiopulmonary bypass, coronary bypass; **— colgante** suspension bridge; **— levadizo** drawbridge

puénting M bungee jumping

pueril ADJ childish

puerta F (de casa) door; (de aeropuerto, de ciudad) gate; (entrada) entrance; **— de acceso** gateway; **vender de — en —** to sell door to door; **dar a alguien con la — en las narices** to slam the door in someone's face; **llamar a la —** to knock on the door; **— trasera** back door; **a — cerrada** behind closed doors

puerto M port (también en informática); **— de acceso** gateway; **— de entrada** port of entry; **— de ratón** mouse port; **— paralelo** parallel port; **— serie/serial** serial port; **— USB** USB port; **llegar a buen —** to bring to a satisfactory conclusion

puertorriqueño-ña ADJ & MF Puerto Rican

pues CONJ (puesto que) since, for; ADV (entonces) then; **— bien** well then, now

puesta F **— al día** update; **— del sol** sunset, setting of the sun; **— en marcha** (de un proyecto) setting in motion; (de un coche) starting; **— en libertad** freeing

puestero-ra MF vendor, seller

puesto ADJ **bien —** (casa) well-appointed; (persona) well made-up; **llevar —** to have on; M (posición) place; (de venta) booth, stand; (de trabajo) post, position; **— de socorros** first-aid station; **quedarse con lo —** to be

left with only the clothes on one's back; CONJ
— que since

puesto *ver* poner

pugilato M boxing

pugilista MF boxer, prizefighter

pugna F struggle; **estar en — con** to be in
conflict with

pugnaz ADJ feisty

puja F (del viento) push; (en una subasta) bid

pujanza F vigor

pujar VI (para dar a luz) to push; (en una subasta)
to bid; **— por** to strive to

pujo M contraction

pulcritud F neatness

pulcro ADJ neat

pulga F flea; **tener malas —s** to be
ill-tempered

pulgada F inch

pulgar M thumb

pulido ADJ polished; M polishing

pulimento M (de modales) refinement; (de
metales) buffing; (polvo para pulir) scouring
powder

pulir VT (metal, un discurso) to polish; (madera)
to sand

pulla F taunt, dig

pulmón M lung; **— de acero** iron lung

pulmonar ADJ pulmonary; **capacidad —** lung
capacity

pulmonía F pneumonia

pulpa F pulp

púlpito M pulpit

pulpo M octopus

pulque M *Méx* pulque

pulquería F *Méx* pulque bar

pulsación F (de corazón) pulse; (de ratón de
computadora) click; (de tecla) keystroke

pulsar VT (una tecla) to press; (cuerdas de
guitarra) to pluck; (la opinión pública) to
gauge; **— y arrastrar** to click and drag

púlsar M pulsar

pulsera F (alhaja) bracelet; (de reloj) watchband;
reloj de — wristwatch

pulso M (pulsación) pulse; (firmeza de mano)
steadiness; **echar un —** to arm-wrestle;
tomar el — to take the pulse; **a —** with great
effort

pulular VI to swarm, to teem with

pulverizar[47] VT to pulverize

puma F mountain lion, cougar, puma

puna F cold, arid tableland of the Andes

punitivo ADJ punitive

punk ADJ & M punk

punkero -ra MF punk

punta F (de cuchillo) point; (de la lengua, de un
lápiz) tip; (de calcetín) toe; **— de lanza**
spearhead; **una — de** a bunch of; **a — de
cuchillo** at knifepoint; **— de flecha**
arrowhead; **de —** on end; **iba caminando**

de —s he was tiptoeing; **sacar — a un lápiz**
to sharpen a pencil; **en la — de la lengua** on
the tip of the tongue; **me pone los nervios
de —** it makes me nervous; M **—pié** kick; ADJ
puntiagudo sharp, pointed

puntada F stitch, prick

puntal M (de un edificio) prop; (de la economía)
mainstay

puntear VT (una guitarra) to pluck; (un mapa) to
make dots on; (una lista) to check off

puntería F aim; **tener buena —** to be a good
shot

puntero M pointer

puntilla F point lace; **de —s** on tiptoe

punto M (puntuación) period; (de cinturón)
notch; (marca, signo) point, dot; (anotación,
tema, lugar) point; (puntada) stitch; **—
álgido** fever pitch; **— culminante** (de una
carrera) peak; (de una historia) climax; (de
negociaciones) critical stage; **— de apoyo**
foothold; **— de condensación** dewpoint; **—
de congelación** freezing point; **— de
ebullición** boiling point; **— de juego** game
point; **— de manga** set point; **— de origen**
point of origin; **— de partida** point of
departure; **— de partido** match-point; **—
referencia** point of reference, benchmark;
— de vista viewpoint, point of view; **—
extra** (fútbol americano) point after
touchdown; **— muerto** (en un negocio)
stalemate, deadlock; (en un coche) neutral; **—
y coma** semicolon; **al —** at once; **a —** ready;
a — de on the point/verge of; **cogerle el —**
to figure out; **dos —s** colon; **el — medio** the
halfway mark; **en —** on the dot; **hacer —** to
knit; **hasta cierto —** to a certain extent;
poner los —s sobre las íes to dot one's i's
and cross one's t's

puntuación F punctuation

puntual ADJ (en hora) punctual, prompt;
(específico) specific

puntualidad F punctuality

puntualizar[47] VT to point out

puntuar[26] VT to punctuate

punzada F (de dolor) stab; (de remordimiento,
hambre) pang, twinge

punzante ADJ sharp, piercing

punzar[47] VT to prick

punzón M (en papel) hole punch; (en cuero) awl

puñado M handful; **a —s** by the handful

puñal M dagger

puñalada F stab; **coser a —s** to stab to death

puñetazo M punch, slug; **dar un —** to punch;
— en la mesa to bang on the table

puño M (mano cerrada) fist; (en una manga) cuff;
(de espada) handle; **arreglarlo con los —s**
to duke it out; **de mi — y letra** by my own
hand

pupa F *Esp* boo-boo

pupila F pupil

pupilo -la MF ward

pupitre M school desk

puré M purée; **— de patatas/papas** mashed potatoes; **hacer —** to smash

pureza F purity

purga F (política) purge; (medicinal) purgative

purgación F atonement

purgante ADJ & M purgative, laxative

purgar[40] VT (el vientre, a un rival) to purge; (frenos) to bleed; (pecados) to atone for

purgatorio M purgatory

purificar[30] VT to purify

purista ADJ & MF purist

puritano ADJ puritanical

puro ADJ pure; **lo hizo de — bueno** he did it out of sheer kindness; **a pura fuerza** by sheer force; **la pura verdad** the plain truth; **son puras mentiras** that's a lot of bull; **de purasangre** thoroughbred; M cigar

púrpura ADJ & M purple

pus M pus

puse, pusiera, pusiese ver poner

putrefacto ADJ putrid, decayed

putter M putter

Qq

Qatar M Qatar

quásar M quasar

que PRON REL that; (con antecedente no humano) which; (con antecedente humano) who, whom; **el/la —** the one that; **lo — tú dices** what you say; **vino la suegra, lo — complicó la visita** the mother-in-law came, which complicated the visit; CONJ that; **no creo — haya tiempo** I don't think [that] there's time; **estoy — me muero** I feel like I'm about to die; **Carlos es más alto — Luis** Carlos is taller than Luis; **más/menos —** more/less than; **déjalo aquí — lo voy a necesitar después** leave it here because I will need it later; **por mucho —** no matter how much; **a — gana** I bet he'll win; **— yo sepa** as far as I know

qué ADJ INTERR & PRON what, which; **¿— libro vas a usar?** what/which book are you going to use? **¿— dices?** what are you saying? **no sé — dijo** I don't know what he said; **¡— bonito!** how beautiful! **¡— de gente!** what a lot of people! **¿y eso —?** so what! **no hay de —** don't mention it; **¿— sé yo?** what do I know? **¿— tal?** how are you? **¡— más da!** what's the difference! **¡— va!** fam oh yeah? yeah right! **¡a mí —!** so what!

quebrada F (valle) ravine; (arroyo) creek

quebradizo ADJ breakable, brittle

quebrado ADJ (roto) broken; (rajado) cracked; (sin dinero) broke; M fraction

quebrantar VT (una casa, la salud) to weaken; (la ley) to violate

quebranto M weakening

quebrar[1] VT (romper) to break; (rajar) to crack; VI (irse a la bancarrota) to go bankrupt, to go under, to fail; **—se** to break [up]; **se quebró la muñeca** he broke his wrist; **—se uno la cabeza** to rack one's brain

queda F **toque de —** curfew

quedar VI (permanecer) to remain; (no haberse terminado) to be left; **queda leche en el vaso** there's milk in the glass; (estar ubicado) to be located; **la iglesia queda en la esquina** the church is located on the corner; (sentar bien la ropa) to suit; **— bien** to come out well; **— en** to agree to; **—se** to remain, to stay; **—se con una cosa** (comprar) to take/buy something; (llevarse) to take something

quehacer M chore, errand

queja F (protesta) complaint; (oficial) grievance

quejarse VI (protestar) to complain; (protestar ruidosamente) to gripe, to squawk; (protestar incesantemente) to whine

quejica ADJ whiny; MF nag, whiner

quejido M (de tono grave) moan, groan; (de tono agudo) squawk

quejoso ADJ whiny

quema F burning

quemado -da MF burn victim

quemador M burner

quemadura F (lugar quemado) burn; (sensación) burning; (enfermedad de plantas) blight

quemar VT to burn (también cedés); **—se** (un edificio) to burn up/down; (al sol) to sunburn

quemazón F burning sensation

quepa, quepamos ver caber

querella F lawsuit

querellante MF plaintiff

querellarse VI to file suit

querer[70] VI/VT (desear) to want; (amar) to love; **como quieras** as you please; **cuando quieras** whenever you want; **no quiso hacerlo** he refused to do it; **quiere llover** it is about to rain; **sin —** unwillingly; **— decir** to mean; **lo quiero mucho** I want it badly

querido -da ADJ beloved, dear; MF (enamorado) sweetheart; (como tratamiento) dear, darling

queroseno M kerosene

querrá, querría ver querer

quesería F dairy, cheese factory

queso M cheese; **— crema / de untar** cream cheese; **— suizo** swiss cheese

quiche M quiche

quicio M hinge; **sacar a uno de —** to drive someone up the wall

quiebra F bankruptcy (también moral); (de un mercado) crash; (de un comercio) failure; — **bancaria** bank failure

quiebra, quiebre ver quebrar

quiebre M break

quien PRON REL who, whom; **Juan, — recién cumplió cuarenta años** Juan, who just turned forty; — **hizo eso** whoever did that; **a — corresponda** to whom it may concern; **—quiera** whoever; **de —** whose; **con —** with whom

quién PRON INTERR & PRON who; **¿— es?** who is it? **no sé — entró** I don't know who came in; **¿a — se lo diste?** who did you give it to? to whom did you give it?

quiera, quiere ver querer

quieto ADJ still

quietud F stillness

quijada F jaw

quilate M carat

quilla F keel

química F chemistry

químico -ca ADJ chemical; MF chemist

quimioterapia F chemotherapy

quince NUM fifteen (también en tenis)

quincena F (de cosas) group of fifteen; (de días) two-week period

quincenal ADV biweekly

quincha F thatch

quinchar VT to thatch

quinesiología F kinesiology

quingombó M okra

quinientos NUM five hundred

quinina F quinine

quinqué M oil lamp

quinta F (casa) villa; (reclutamiento) draft

quinto ADJ, ADV, & M fifth

quiosco M kiosk, newsstand

quiquiriquí INTERJ cock-a-doodle-doo

quirófano M surgery, operating room

quiropráctico -ca ADJ chiropractic; MF chiropractor; F chiropractic

quirúrgico ADJ surgical

quise, quisiera, quisiese ver querer

quisquilloso ADJ particular, fussy

quiste M cyst

quitar VT (una mancha) to remove; (una prenda de vestir) to take off; (despojar de) to take away; M SG **quitaesmalte** nail polish remover; M SG **quitanieves** snowplow; M SG **quitamanchas** spot remover; VI **—se** to take off; **—se a alguien de encima** to get rid of someone; **quítate de ahí** move over

quite M **salir al — de** to go to the rescue of

quizá, quizás ADV perhaps, maybe

Rr

rabadilla F (coxis) tailbone; (de un ave) rump

rábano M radish; **me importa un —** I couldn't care less

rabia F (enfermedad) rabies; (enojo) rage; **me tiene —** he hates me; **dar —** to anger

rabiar VI to rage, to fume; **guapa a —** drop-dead beautiful

rabieta F tantrum

rabino -na MF rabbi

rabioso ADJ (hidrofóbico, apasionado) rabid, mad; (enojado) mad, furious

rabo M (cola) tail; (cabo) stem; **mirar con el — del ojo** to look out of the corner of one's eye; **con el — entre las piernas** with his tail between his legs

rabón ADJ bobtail

racha F (de suerte) streak; (de viento) gust

racial ADJ racial

racimo M (de plátanos, personas) bunch; (de uvas) cluster

raciocinio M reasoning

ración F (de guerra) ration, allowance; (de comida) portion

racional ADJ rational (también número)

racionalizado ADJ (justificado) rationalized; (reestructurado) streamlined

racionalizar[47] VT (una acción) to rationalize; (un negocio) to streamline

racionamiento M rationing

racionar VT to ration

racismo M racism

racista ADJ & MF racist

radar M radar

radiación F radiation

radiactivo ADJ radioactive

radiador M radiator

radial ADJ radial

radiante ADJ radiant

radiar VT (calor) to radiate; (por radio) to broadcast

radical ADJ (extremo) radical; (células) root; M (en química) radical; (en gramática) root

radicalismo M radicalism

radicar[30] VI to be located; **— en** to lie in; **—se** to take up residence

radio M (hueso, segmento de un círculo) radius; (elemento radiactivo) radium; F (aparato, difusión) radio; (emisora) radio station; **— de acción** sphere of influence

radiodifusión F broadcasting

radiodifusora F radio station

radioescucha MF radio listener

radiofónico ADJ radio

radiografía F x-ray
radiografiar[28] VT (hacer rayos x) to x-ray; (examinar con cuidado) to examine carefully
radiología F radiology
radiólogo -ga MF radiologist
radiotelescopio M radio telescope
radioterapia F radiation therapy
radiotransmisor M radio transmitter
radón M radon
raer[52] VI/VT to scrape [off]; (un artículo de ropa) to wear out
ráfaga F (de viento) gust, blast; (de luz) flash; (de ametralladora) burst
raído ADJ threadbare
raigón M stump
raíz F root; **— cuadrada** square root; **a — de** due to; **arrancar de —** to uproot; **cortar de —** to nip in the bud; **echar raíces** to take root
raja F (de melón) slice; (de falda) slit; (de leña) stick
rajadura F (en piedra, metal) crack; (en tela) rent, rip
rajar VT (una piedra) to crack; (un tronco) to split; **—se** (partir) to split open; (acobardarse) to chicken out, to blink; ADV **a rajatabla** strictly
ralea F ilk
ralear VI to thin out
ralentización F (de la economía) slump; (de un motor) idle
rallador M grater
rallar VT to grate, to shred
ralo ADJ sparse, thin
RAM M RAM
rama F branch, limb; (delgada) twig; **andarse por las —s** to beat around the bush; **algodón en —** raw cotton
ramaje M foliage
ramal M (de soga) strand; (de vía férrea) branch, spur
ramificarse[30] VI to divide into branches, to branch off
ramillete M bouquet, bunch, spray
ramo M (de flores) bouquet; (de una ciencia) branch; (de una actividad) line; **— de olivo** olive branch
rampa F ramp
ramplón ADJ vulgar
rana F frog
ranchero -ra MF rancher; **música ranchera** Mexican country music
rancho M (comida para soldados) mess; (comida mala) swill; (finca) ranch; (choza) hut; **hacer — aparte** to keep to oneself
rancio ADJ rancid; **de — abolengo** of ancient lineage
rango M (militar) rank; (categoría) standing
ranilla F frog [of a hoof]

ránking M (tenis) ranking
ranura F (corte) groove; (para insertar monedas, cartas) slot; **— para accesorios** accessory slot, expansion slot
rapar VT (pelo) to shave off; (cabeza) to shave
rapaz ADJ (animal) predatory; (destructivo) rapacious
rape M **cortar al —** to crop
rapé M snuff
rapear VI to rap
rápidamente ADV (con mucha velocidad) fast; (en poco tiempo) quickly
rapidez F (de un coche) speed; (de un movimiento) rapidity, quickness
rápido ADJ (con mucha velocidad) fast; (en poco tiempo) quick; M **—s** rapids; ADV (con mucha velocidad) fast; (en poco tiempo) quickly
rapiña F pillage
raptar VT to kidnap, to abduct
rapto M (secuestro) abduction, kidnapping; (arrebato) fit
raqueta F racket (también de tenis)
raquítico ADJ feeble, sickly
raramente ADV seldom, rarely
rareza F (escasez) rarity; (cosa rara) oddity; (cualidad de extraño) strangeness
raro ADJ (infrecuente) rare; (extraño) strange, funny; **rara vez** seldom, rarely; **sentirse —** to feel funny; **gas —** rare gas; **tierra rara** rare earth
ras LOC ADV **a — de la tierra** low to the ground
rascar[30] VT to scratch; M SG **rascacielos** skyscraper
rasgado ADJ **ojos —s** slit eyes
rasgadura F tear, rip
rasgar[40] VT to tear, to rip
rasgo M (propiedad) trait, feature; **a grandes —s** in broad strokes
rasgón M tear
rasguñar VT to scratch
rasguño M scratch
raso ADJ (superficie) smooth; (cucharada) level; **al —** in the open air; M satin
raspado M scrape
raspador M scraper
raspadura F scrape
raspar VT to scrape
raspón M scrape
rastra F harrow; **a —s** dragging, pulling
rastrear VT (a un animal) to trail, to track, to trace; (un terreno) to search
rastreo M sweep, search
rastrero ADJ (planta) creeping; (persona) contemptible
rastrillar VT to rake
rastrillo M rake
rastro M (huella) track, trail; (olor) scent; (mercado) flea market; **ni —s** no trace
rastrojo M stubble

rasurado M shave
rasurador -ora MF razor
rasurar VT to shave
rata F rat
ratear VT to pilfer
ratería F petty larceny, pilferage
ratero -ra MF pickpocket
ratificación F ratification
ratificar[30] VT to ratify
rato M while; **—s perdidos** leisure hours; **a cada —** frequently; **a —s** from time to time; **pasar el —** to kill time; **pasar un buen —** (divertirse) to have a pleasant time; (permanecer) to spend a long time; **un largo —** a great while
ratón M mouse (también de computadora); **— almizclero** muskrat; **— en serie** serial mouse
ratonera F mousetrap
raudal LOC ADV **a —es** in great quantities
raudo ADJ swift
raya F (línea) line; (linde) boundary; (lista) stripe; (en el pelo) part; (en un pantalón) crease; (de ortografía) dash; (en un zapato) scuff; (pez marino) stingray; **tener a —** to hold in check; **pasarse de la —** to be out of line, to cross the line
rayado ADJ (papel) lined; (vestido) striped; **hablaba como disco —** he talked like a broken record
rayar VT (papel) to rule, to make lines on; (disco, espejo) to scratch; (zapatos) to scuff; **— el alba** to dawn; **— en** to border on
rayo M (de luz) ray, beam, streak; (de relámpago) flash of lightning; (de rueda) spoke; (de esperanza) ray, flicker; **— láser** laser beam; **—s infrarrojos** infrared rays; **—s X** x-rays
rayón M rayon
raza F (de personas) race; (de animal) breed
razón F (facultad) reason; (proporción) ratio; **— social** company name; **a — de** at the rate of; **¡con —!** no wonder! **entrar en —** to listen to reason; **te doy la —** I admit you're right; **perder la —** to lose one's mind; **tener —** to be right
razonable ADJ reasonable
razonamiento M reasoning
razonar VI (pensar) to reason; (arguir) to argue
reabastecer[35] VT to replenish
reabrir[74] VT to reopen
reacción F reaction; **— en cadena** chain reaction; **— nuclear** nuclear reaction
reaccionar VI to react
reaccionario ADJ & MF reactionary
reacio ADJ averse, reluctant
reacondicionar VT to rebuild
reactivo M reagent
reactor M reactor; **— nuclear** nuclear reactor
readaptación F readjustment

readaptar VT to readjust
reafirmar VT to reaffirm; **—se** to reassert
reagrupar VT to regroup
reajustar VT to readjust
reajuste M readjustment
real ADJ (verdadero) real, actual; (del rey) royal; M fairground
realce M **dar —** to enhance
realeza F royalty
realidad F reality, actuality; **en —** really, actually; **en — no es abogado** he's not really a lawyer; **— virtual** virtual reality
realismo M realism
realista ADJ (auténtico) realistic; (partidario del rey) royalist; MF (no idealista) realist; (partidario del rey) royalist
realización F (de un sueño) realization, fulfillment; (de una tarea) completion; (de una película) production
realizador -ora MF (director) director; (productor) producer
realizar[47] VT (un sueño) to realize, to fulfill; (película) to produce
realmente ADV really
realzar[47] VT (mejorar) to enhance; (destacar) to accentuate; (intensificar) to heighten
reanimación F resuscitation; **— cardiopulmonar** cardiopulmonary resuscitation
reanimar VT (devolver fuerzas) to revive; (dar ánimos) to rally
reanudación F renewal; **— del juego** (fútbol) restart of play
reanudar VT (una amistad) to renew; (una reunión) to resume; (un partido del fútbol) to restart
reaparecer[35] VI to reappear
reasumir VT to resume
reata F lariat, lasso
reavivar VT to revive
rebaja F markdown, price cut; **con —** at a discount, on sale; **de —s** cut-rate
rebajado N on sale, reduced
rebajar VT (precios) to cut, to lower, to slash; (una bebida) to water down; (una crítica) to tone down; VI/VT (los cambios) to downshift; **—se** to lower oneself; **—se a** to stoop to
rebanada F slice
rebanar VT to slice
rebaño M flock, fold
rebasar VT (un coche) to overtake; (un límite) to exceed
rebatir VT to refute
rebato M alarm
rebelarse VI to rebel, to revolt
rebelde ADJ (niño) rebellious; (pelo) unruly; MF rebel
rebeldía F rebelliousness, defiance; (no comparecencia) default

rebelión F rebellion

rebenque M whip

rebobinar VT to rewind

reborde M edge

rebosante ADJ (de líquido) brimming, overflowing; (de salud) flush, glowing; — **de alegría** overjoyed

rebosar VI (líquido) to overflow, to brim over; (de alegría) to bubble over; (de salud) to glow

rebotar VI/VT (en baloncesto) to rebound, to bounce; (chocar) to bounce; (cambiar de dirección una bala) to ricochet; (cambiar de dirección una pelota) to carom

rebote M (en baloncesto) rebound, bounce; (de bala) ricochet

rebotear VI (en baloncesto) to rebound

rebozar[47] VT to cover with batter; —**se** to muffle up

rebozo M shawl; **sin** — frankly

rebullir[16] VI to stir

rebuscado ADJ (estilo) overly elaborate; (persona) affected

rebuscar[30] VT (espigar) to glean; VI — **en** (la memoria) to search through; (un cajón) to rummage in

rebuznar VI to bray

rebuzno M bray, braying

recabar VT to raise

recado M (mensaje) message; (quehacer) errand; — **de escribir** writing materials

recaer[52] VI to relapse; — **sobre** to fall to

recaída F relapse

recalar VI to make a stop at

recalcar[30] VT to accentuate

recalcitrante ADJ obstinate

recalentar[1] VT (volver a calentar) to warm over; (calentar en exceso) to overheat

recamar VT to embroider

recámara F (de un arma de fuego) chamber; *Méx* (dormitorio) bedroom

recapitular VI/VT to recapitulate, to sum up

recargado ADJ busy

recargar[40] VT to overload, to burden

recargo M (emocional) burden; (de precio) surcharge, premium; — **por mora** late fee

recatado ADJ (cauteloso) cautious; (modesto) modest

recato M (cautela) caution; (modestia) modesty

recaudación F collection, levy; — **de fondos** fundraising

recaudador -ora MF tax collector

recaudar VT (impuestos) to collect, to levy; (fondos) to raise; — **en bruto** to gross; — **fondos** to raise funds; **lo recaudado** proceeds

recaudo M **estar a buen** — to be in a safe place

rección F government

recelar VT to suspect; — **de** to be suspicious of

recelo M misgivings

receloso ADJ mistrustful

recepción F reception

receptáculo M receptacle, holder

receptor M receiver (también en fútbol americano); (en béisbol) catcher; — **abierto** wide receiver; — **cerrado** tight end

recesión F recession

receta F (de cocina) recipe; (de médico) prescription

recetar VT to prescribe

rechazar[47] VT (una propuesta, un plan) to reject; (un ataque) to repel, to repulse; (una invitación) to decline, to turn down, to refuse; (una acusación) to deny; (a un amante) to spurn, to reject

rechazo M (de un amante) rejection; (de un ataque) repulse; (de una oferta) refusal; (de una acusación) denial

rechifla F whistling, booing

rechiflar VT to whistle, to boo

rechinamiento M (de una puerta) creaking, squeaking; (de los dientes) grinding

rechinante ADJ squeaky

rechinar VI (una puerta) to squeak, to creak; VI/VT (los dientes) to grind; **eso me rechina** that grates on my nerves

rechoncho ADJ plump, chubby, roly-poly

recibidor -ora MF receiver; M reception room

recibimiento M reception

recibir VT (premio) to receive, to get; (visitas) to receive, to welcome; (una noticia trágica) to take; — **noticias de** to hear from; —**se** to graduate; —**se de médico** to graduate from medical school

recibo M receipt; **de** — acceptable; **al** — **de** upon receipt of; **acusar** — to acknowledge receipt; **acuse de** — acknowledgment of receipt

reciclaje M recycling

reciclar VI/VT to recycle

recidiva F relapse

recién ADV recently; — **casado** newlywed; — **comprado** brand-new; — **llegado** newly arrived; — **nacido** newborn; — **me entero** it's news to me

reciente ADJ recent

recinto M enclosure

recio ADJ strong, rugged

recipiente M container

recíproco ADJ reciprocal

recitación F recitation

recital M recital

recitar VT to recite, to speak

reclamación F (protesta) protest; (demanda) claim

reclamante MF claimant

reclamar VT (protestar) to protest; (demandar) to claim; VI (aves) to call

reclamo M (reclamación) claim; (queja) complaint; (voz de animal) call, cry;

(dispositivo) bird call; (señuelo) decoy

reclinar VT to lean; **—se** to recline

recluir[19] VT to confine; **—se** to be a recluse

recluso -sa MF (preso) inmate; (ermitaño) recluse

recluta F recruitment; MF (voluntario) recruit; (forzoso) conscript

reclutamiento M (voluntario) recruitment; (forzoso) conscription

reclutar VT (voluntariamente) to recruit; (por la fuerza) to draft, to conscript

recobrar VI to recover, to recuperate; VT to recover, to regain

recodo M bend, turn

recoger[45] VT (el cabello) to gather; (un cuarto) to tidy up; (citas en un texto) to collect; (la mesa) to clear; (polvo) to sweep up; (a un desamparado) to shelter; (los frutos del campo) to glean; **—se** (retirarse) to retire, to withdraw; (acumularse) to gather

recogida F (del cabello) gathering; (de un cuarto) tidying up; (de la mesa) clearing; (de un desamparado) sheltering

recogido ADJ (apartado) secluded; (tranquilo) peaceful, quiet

recogimiento M (aislamiento) seclusion; (meditación) meditation

recolección F (de frutos, datos) collecting, gathering; (de carga) pickup; (cosecha) harvest

recolectar VT to gather, to forage

recomendable ADJ advisable

recomendación F recommendation

recomendar[1] VT to recommend

recomienda, recomiende ver recomendar

recompensa F recompense, reward

recompensar VT to recompense, to reward

reconcentrar VI to concentrate intensely; **—se** to concentrate, to become absorbed in thought

reconciliación F reconciliation

reconciliar VT to reconcile

recóndito ADJ remote

reconfortante ADJ heartwarming, comforting

reconfortar VT to comfort

reconocer[35] VT (identificar) to recognize; (admitir) to admit, to acknowledge; (explorar) to reconnoiter

reconocible ADJ recognizable

reconocimiento M (identificación) recognition; (admisión, agradecimiento) acknowledgment; (exploración) scouting; **— de habla** speech recognition; **— de voz** voice recognition; **— visual** visual recognition; **hacer un —** to reconnoiter

reconozca, reconozco ver reconocer

reconsiderar VT to reconsider

reconstrucción F reconstruction

reconstruir[19] VT to reconstruct, to rebuild

reconstruya, reconstruye, reconstruyendo, reconstruyera, reconstruyese ver reconstruir

recopilación F collection, compilation

recopilar VT to compile

récord M record

recordar[5] VT (acordarse) to remember, to recollect, to recall; (hacer acordar) to remind

recordatorio M reminder

recorrer VT (andar una distancia) to cover; (examinar) to go over, to look over

recorrido M (ruta) run, route; (distancia) distance

recortado ADJ jagged

recortar VT (pelo, hilos, presupuesto) to trim; (uñas, periódicos) to clip; (una película) to shorten; **—se** to be outlined

recorte M (de pelos, hilos) trimming; (de uñas, periódicos) clipping; (de sueldo, de gastos) cut; (de recursos) cutback; (sobrante) trimming; **— salarial** pay cut

recostar[5] VT (sobre) to lay; (contra) to lean; **—se** to recline

recoveco M (en un camino) turn; (rincón) cranny

recreación F recreation

recrear VT to entertain; **—se** to amuse oneself

recreativo ADJ recreational; **actividades recreativas** leisure activities; **sala recreativa** game room

recreo M (recreación) recreation, relaxation; (tiempo de descanso) recess; (lugar de juego) playground

recriminar VT to recriminate

recrudecer[35] VI to flare up

recrudecimiento M flareup

recta F (de una pista) straight; (en béisbol) fastball; **— final** final stretch

rectangular ADJ rectangular

rectángulo M rectangle

rectificar[30] VT to rectify

rectitud F uprightness, righteousness

recto ADJ (no curvo) straight; (honrado) upright, righteous; (estricto) strict; **todo —** straight ahead; M rectum

rector -ora MF university president, chancellor

recua F herd

recubrir[74] VT to cover; **— con pintura** to coat with paint

recuento M account; **— sanguíneo** blood count

recuerda, recuerde ver recordar

recuerdo M (acción de recordar, cosa recordada) memory, recollection; (objeto que hace recordar) souvenir, token; **—s** regards; **dale —s a tu hermana** say hi to your sister

recular VI (retroceder) to move backward; (retroceder en un coche) to back up; (retroceder ante un desafío) to back down

recuperación F (salarial, de salud) recovery; (de datos, documentos guardados) retrieval; (de objetos, datos, documentos perdidos) recovery

recuperar VT (una cosa perdida) to recover; (datos, documentos guardados) to retrieve; (tiempo perdido) to make up for; (dinero perdido) to recoup; **—se** to recuperate

recurrente ADJ MF (que reclama) complainant; ADJ (repetitivo) recurring, recurrent

recurrir VT to appeal; **— a** to resort to, to have recourse to

recurso M (acción de recurrir) recourse; (reclamación) appeal; **—s** resources; **—s humanos** HR [human resources]; **—s naturales** natural resources

recusar VT (a una persona) to reject; (a un juez) to challenge

red F (para pescar, de tenis) net; (malla tejida) mesh; (de conexiones, para computadora) network; (para engañar) snare; (internet) World Wide Web, Internet; **— [de área] local** local area network

redacción F (ensayo) composition; (acción de redactar) drafting; (en un periódico) editorial department

redactar VT (un ensayo) to draft; (trabajo escolar) to compose

redactor-ora MF editor

redada F (de peces) catch, haul; (policial) raid

redar VT to throw a net

redecilla F hairnet

redención F redemption

redil M sheepfold, sheep pen; **volver al —** to come back into the fold

redimir VT (a un pecador) to redeem; (a un esclavo) to set free

rédito M (de ahorros) interest; (de acciones) yield

reditar[26] VT to yield

redoblar VT (esfuerzos) to double; VI/VT (un tambor) to roll

redoble M drumroll

redoma F flask

redonda F whole note; **a la —** all around

redondear VT (una figura) to make round; (una cifra) to round up

redondel M ring

redondez F roundness

redondo ADJ round; **en —** all around; **caer —** to collapse; **salir —** to turn out perfect

reducción F reduction, cutback; **— de sueldo** cut in salary; **hacer — de personal** to cut back on personnel

reducidor-ora MF *Am* fence

reducir[38] VT (una cantidad) to reduce; (un hueso) to set; (actividades) to curtail, to cut down on; (costos) to cut; (personal) to downsize, to cut back on; **—se a** to boil down to

reduje, redujera, redujese *ver* reducir

redundante ADJ redundant

reduzca, reduzco *ver* reducir

reedificar[30] VT to rebuild

reelección F reelection

reelegir[14] VT reelect

reembolsar VT to reimburse, to refund

reembolso M reimbursement, refund

reemplazable ADJ replaceable

reemplazar[47] VT to replace

reemplazo M replacement, substitute

reencarnación F reincarnation

reescribir[74] VT to rewrite

reestructuración F restructuring

reexpedir[9] VT to forward

referencia F reference

referéndum M referendum

referente LOC ADV **— a** a relative to

referir[8] VT (narrar) to narrate; **—se a** to refer to

refiera, refiere *ver* referir

refinación F refinement

refinado ADJ refined, genteel

refinamiento M refinement

refinanciar VI/VT to refinance

refinar VT to refine

refinería F refinery

refiriendo, refiriera, refiriese *ver* referir

reflector M (en una bicicleta) reflector; (en deportes) floodlight; (militar, policial) searchlight

reflejar VT (luz) to reflect; (imagen) to mirror; **—se** to be reflected

reflejo M (luz) reflection; (movimiento) reflex; **—s** frosting; ADJ reflex

reflexión F reflection

reflexionar VI to reflect; **— sobre** to think over

reflexivo ADJ (gramatical) reflexive; (pensativo) thoughtful

reflujo M (de agua) ebb; (gástrico) reflux

reforma F (política) reform; (religiosa) reformation

reformador-ora MF reformer

reformar VT (un gobierno, a un delincuente) to reform; (ropa) to make alterations in; **—se** to mend one's ways

reformatorio M reformatory

reformista MF reformer

reforzado ADJ reinforced; M reinforcement

reforzar[49] VT (una construcción) to reinforce; (las defensas) to beef up; (un argumento) to bolster, to buttress

refracción F refraction

refractario ADJ refractory

refrán M proverb, saying

refrenar VT (un caballo) to rein in; (emociones) to restrain, to check

refrendar VT (una sentencia) to uphold; (un documento) to countersign, to endorse

refrendario-ria MF endorser

refrendo M endorsement

refrescante ADJ refreshing

refrescar[30] VT to refresh (también pantalla de computadora); (el tiempo) to get cool; **—se** to cool off

refresco M (bebida) soft drink; (comida ligera) refreshment

refriega F fray, scuffle

refrigeración F refrigeration

refrigerador ADJ refrigerating; M refrigerator

refrigerante ADJ cooling; M coolant

refrigerar VT to cool, to refrigerate

refrigerio M refreshment

refrito ADJ (comida) refried; M (obra) rerun

refuerzo M (acción de reforzar) reinforcement; (de tela) backing; (de una vacuna) booster

refugiado-da MF refugee

refugiar VT to shelter; **—se** to take shelter

refugio M refuge, shelter; **— antiaéreo** bomb shelter; **— fiscal** tax shelter

refulgente ADJ resplendent

refundir VT to recast

refunfuñar VI to grumble, to mutter

refunfuño M grumbling, muttering

refunfuñón-ona ADJ grouchy, grumpy; MF grouch

refutar VT to refute

regadera F watering can

regadío M (tierra irrigada) irrigated land; (riego) irrigation

regalar VT (dar como presente) to give as a gift; (vender barato, donar) to give away; (agasajar) to regale

regaliz M licorice

regalo M (presente) present, gift; (para los sentidos) treat, delight

regañar VI (un perro) to snarl; VT (a un niño) to scold, to go off on; (constantemente) to nag; LOC ADV **a regañadientes** reluctantly

regaño M scolding, reprimand

regañón-ona ADJ nagging, scolding; MF scold

regar[41] VT (campos) to irrigate; (flores) to water

regate M dribble

regatear VI (precios) to haggle, to bargain; (fútbol) to dribble

regateo M bargaining

regazo M lap

regeneración F regeneration; **— audible** audible feedback

regente MF, **regenta** F regent; F regent's wife; ADJ ruling

reggae M reggae

régimen M (gobierno) regime; (dieta) diet; **— de vida** lifestyle

regimiento M regiment

regio ADJ (propio del rey) regal; (excelente) swell

región F region

regional ADJ regional

regir[14] VT to govern (también en sintaxis); VI to be in force; **—se por** to be guided by

registrador-ora MF (empleado) recorder, registrar; M **— de vuelo** flight recorder

registrar VT (examinar) to search; (dejar constancia) to record, to register; (inscribir) to log; **— al desnudo** to strip-search

registro M (de la voz, lingüístico) register; (de nacimientos) record, register; (del equipaje) search; (de un órgano) stop; (en la computadora) log; **— al desnudo** strip search

regla F (norma) rule; (utensilio para medir) ruler; (menstruación) period; **en —** in order; **por —** general as a general rule

reglamentación F (acción de reglamentar) regulation; (conjunto de reglas) regulations

reglamento M regulations; **—s y disposiciones administrativas** rules and regulations

regocijar VT to gladden; **—se** to rejoice

regocijo M joy, rejoicing

regodearse VI (en la desgracia propia) to wallow; (en la desgracia ajena) to gloat

regodeo M (en la desgracia propia) wallowing; (en la desgracia ajena) gloating

regordete ADJ plump

regresar VI to return

regreso M return; **estar de —** to be back

reguero M trail; **correr como un — de pólvora** to spread like wildfire

regulación F (acción de regular) regulation; (de una máquina) adjustment

regulador M regulator, governor, throttle; **— de voltaje** dimmer

regular VT (reglamentar) to regulate; (ajustar una máquina) to adjust; ADJ regular; **una paliza —** quite a beating; ADV so-so

regularidad F regularity

regularizar[47] VT (reglamentar) to regulate; (formalizar) to formalize; **—se** to become regular

regurgitar VI/VT to regurgitate

rehabilitación F rehabilitation

rehabilitador ADJ remedial

rehabilitar VT to rehabilitate

rehacer[54, 74] VT to remake; **—se** to recover

rehén MF hostage

rehuir[19] VT (a una persona) to shun; (responsabilidades) to shirk

rehusar[26] VT to refuse; **—se a** to refuse to

reimpresión F reprint

reina F queen

reinado M reign

reinante ADJ (política, opinión) prevailing; (monarca) ruling

reinar VI to reign

reincidencia F (episodio) relapse; (cualidad) recidivism

reincidir VI to relapse

reiniciar VT to reboot, to reset
reino M (territorio de un rey) kingdom, realm; (período de reinado) reign; (división biológica) kingdom; (ámbito) realm
reinserción F reinsertion; **— laboral** reemployment
reinstaurar VT to reinstate
reintegrar VT to rebate; **—se a** to return to
reintegro M rebate
reinvertir VI/VT to reinvest, to roll over
reír[10] VI to laugh; **—se de** to laugh at
reiterar VT to reiterate
reivindicación F (demanda) demand; (rehabilitación) vindication; (responsabilidad) responsibility; **la — del atentado** the responsibility for the act
reivindicar[30] VT (vengar) to vindicate; (responsabilizarse) to take responsibility, to claim
reja F (enrejado) grate, grating; (pieza de arado) plowshare; **entre —s** behind bars
rejilla F (para equipaje) luggage rack; (de coche) grille
rejuvenecer[35] VT to rejuvenate; VI to become rejuvenated
relación F (conocido) relation, connection; (trato) relationship, involvement; (relato) account, report; (lista) list; **relaciones** (conocidos) connections; (trato) dealings; **relaciones públicas** public relations; **con — a** in relation to
relacionado ADJ related, germane
relacionar VT to relate, to connect; **—se con** to relate to
relajación F relaxation
relajamiento M relaxation
relajante ADJ (actividad) relaxing; (droga) sedative; M **— muscular** muscle relaxant
relajar VT to relax; **—se** (abandonarse moralmente) to become lax; (tranquilizarse) to chill [out], to relax
relajo M (aflojamiento) relaxation; (desorden) mess
relamerse VI to lick one's lips
relámpago M lightning
relampaguear VI (el cielo) to lightning; (los ojos, cosa reluciente) to flash
relampagueo M flash of lightning
relatar VT to relate, to recount
relatividad F relativity
relativo ADJ relative; **— a** relative to
relato M (informe) account; (cuento) story, tale
relé M relay
relegar[40] VT to relegate
relevancia F importance
relevante ADJ important
relevar VT (a un trabajador, guardia) to relieve
relevista MF (atletismo) relay runner; (béisbol) reliever; **— de cierre** (béisbol) closer

relevo M (soldado) relief; **carrera de —s** relay race
relicario M reliquary, locket
relieve M relief; **de —** (mapa) relief; (persona) prominent; **poner de —** to emphasize; **letras en —** raised letters
religión F religion
religioso-sa ADJ religious; M monk; F nun
relinchar VI to neigh
relincho M neigh
reliquia F relic
rellenado M filling
rellenar VT (un vaso) to refill, to replenish; (un tanque de gasolina) to fill, to fill up; (un formulario) to fill out; (un hueco) to fill in; (una almohada) to stuff
relleno ADJ (un pimiento) stuffed; (la cara) full, round; (la figura, el cuerpo) plump; M (de comida) stuffing, dressing; (de un colchón) padding
reloj M (de pared) clock; (de muñeca, bolsillo) watch; (de horno) timer; **— de pulsera** wristwatch; **— de sol** sundial; **— despertador** alarm clock; **contra —** against the clock; **como un —** regularly, like clockwork
relojería F (tienda) watch shop; (actividad) clock-making
relojero-ra MF watchmaker
reluciente ADJ shining
relucir[39] VI to shine; **sacar a —** to bring up
relumbrar VI to glare
relumbre M glare
REM M REM
remachar VT (una victoria, un clavo) to clinch; (un remache) to rivet
remache M (acción de remachar) riveting; (clavo) clinching; (tachuela, clavija) rivet
remanente M remainder
remar VI/VT to row, to paddle
remarcado VT mark-up
rematador-ora MF auctioneer
rematar VT (acabar) to finish; (matar) to finish off; (perfeccionar) to give the finishing touches to; (subastar) to auction; VI (patear un balón) to take a shot
remate M (de una obra) finishing touch; (tiro) shot; (subasta) auction; (tenis) smash; **— de un chiste** punch line; **loco de —** stark raving mad
remedador-ora MF mimic
remedar VT to mimic, to ape, to mock
remediar VT to remedy
remedio M remedy, cure; **sin —** unavoidable; **no tiene —** it can't be helped; **no tengo más —** I can't help it; **el — es peor que la enfermedad** the remedy is worse than the disease
remedo M mockery

remendar[1] VT (ropa) to mend, to patch; (calcetines) to darn; (zapatos) to repair

remendón -ona MF cobbler

remero -ra MF rower

remesa F (de mercancías) shipment; (de dinero) remittance

remiendo M (de ropa) patch; (de zapatos) repair

remilgado ADJ fussy, prim

remilgo M fussiness, primness

reminiscencia F reminiscence

remisión F remission

remitente MF sender

remitir VT (enviar) to remit; (dirigir a otra parte de un texto) to refer; **—se** (ceder) to yield; **a las pruebas me remito** the evidence speaks for itself

remo M (pala) oar, paddle; (deporte) rowing

remodelación F (de una casa) remodeling; (de una ciudad) redevelopment, renewal; (de una organización) reorganization

remodelar VI/VT to remodel

remojar VT to soak

remojo M soaking; **poner en —** to soak

remojón M soaking

remolacha F beet

remolcador M tugboat

remolcar[30] VT to tow

remolino M (de viento) whirlwind; (de agua) whirlpool, eddy; (de pelo) cowlick; (juguete) pinwheel; **— de gente** throng, crowd

remolón -ona ADJ dallying; MF dallier

remolonear VI to dally

remolque M (acción de remolcar) tow; (vehículo remolcado) towed vehicle; (vehículo que remolca) tow truck; (caravana de camión) trailer; **llevar a —** to tow

remontada F (deporte) comeback

remontar VT (una cometa) to fly; (una pendiente, un río) to go up; **—se** to rise; **el globo se remonta** the balloon goes up; **el coche se remonta a los años 20** the car dates from the '20s; **para comprenderlo, debemos remontarnos a su juventud** in order to understand him, we must go back to his youth

remorder[6] VT to gnaw at

remordimiento M remorse

remoto ADJ remote, distant; **no tiene la más remota idea** he doesn't have the slightest idea

remover[6] VT (un cargo, un obstáculo) to remove; (un asunto problemático) to stir up

remuneración F remuneration, compensation

rémunerar VT remunerate, compensate

remunerado ADJ gainful

renacentista ADJ Renaissance

renacer[35] VI to be reborn

renacimiento M (resurgimiento) revival; (período histórico) Renaissance

renacuajo M (cría de rana) tadpole; (hombre esmirriado) shrimp

renal ADJ renal

rencilla F quarrel

rencor M rancor; **guardar —** to bear a grudge

rencoroso ADJ resentful

rendición F surrender

rendido ADJ exhausted

rendija F crack

rendimiento M (lo rendido) yield, output; (productividad) performance; **— previo** past performance

rendir[9] VT (someter) to subdue; (producir) to yield; (fatigar) to fatigue; **— homenaje** to pay homage; **— cuentas a** to answer to; VI (obtener buenos resultados) to perform well; **—se** (darse por vencido) to surrender, to give in; (fatigarse) to become fatigued

renegado -da MF renegade

renegar[41] VT (negar) to deny insistently; (repudiar) to renounce; **— de** to gripe about

renegociar VI/VT to renegotiate

renglón M line; **a — seguido** immediately following

rengo ADJ lame

renguear VI to limp

renguera F limp

reno M reindeer

renombrado ADJ renowned

renombre M renown; **de —** of note

renovable ADJ renewable

renovación F renewal; **— urbana** urban renewal

renovador -ora ADJ (artista) innovating; (baño) refreshing; MF innovator

renovar[5] VT (un edificio) to renovate; (ataques, temores) to renew

renquear VT to limp

renta F (de una persona) income; (de un gobierno) revenue; (alquiler) rent; **— anual** annuity; **—s internas** internal revenue; **vivir de la —** to live on the interest

rentabilidad F profitability; **cuentas y depósitos de alta —** high-return accounts and deposits

rentable ADJ (negocio, inversión) profitable; (idea) viable

renuencia F reluctance

renuente ADJ reluctant, loath; **ser — a** to be loath to

renueva, renueve ver renovar

renuevo M sprout

renuncia F (dimisión) resignation; (a un derecho) waiver; (a una herencia) renunciation

renunciar VI — a (un cargo) to resign; (la ciudadanía) to renounce; (un derecho) to relinquish, to waive

reñido ADJ contested

reñir[11] VI (discutir) to quarrel, to bicker, to argue; (pelear) to fight, to scuffle; (rezongar) to scold

reo -a MF defendant, accused

reojo M **mirar de —** to look out of the corner of one's eye

reorganización F reorganization

reorganizar[47] VT to reorganize, to regroup

repaginar VT to repaginate

repantigarse[40] VI to lounge

reparación F (compensación) reparation, redress; (arreglo) repair

reparador -ra ADJ refreshing; M serviceman; F service woman

reparar VT (arreglar) to repair; (compensar) to redress; **— en** to notice

reparo M **no tener —s en** to have no qualms about; **sin —s** freely; **hacer —s** to object

repartición F distribution

repartir VT (tierras, un botín) to distribute; (volantes) to hand out; (periódicos) to deliver; (naipes) to deal; (días libres) to space out

reparto M (de tierras) distribution; (de periódicos) delivery; (de naipes) dealing; (ruta de entrega) route; (lista de actores) cast; **— proporcional** apportionment

repasar VT (una lección) to review, to go over again; (en la memoria) to retrace; (leer por encima) to skim

repaso M review

repelente ADJ repellent

repeler VT to repel, to repulse

repente M **de —** suddenly

repentinamente ADV suddenly

repentino ADJ sudden

repercusión F repercussion

repercutir VI to have repercussions

repertorio M repertoire

repetición F (reiteración) repetition; (en tenis) let

repetido ADJ repeated; **repetidas veces** repeatedly

repetir[9] VI/VT (reiterar) to repeat; VI (eructar) to belch; (tomar una segunda ración) to have seconds; **— como loro** to parrot; **—se** to recur

repicar[30] VI/VT to ring

repique M ringing, ring

repiquetear VI/VT to ring

repiqueteo M ringing

repisa F shelf

repita, repitiendo, repitiera, repitiese, repito *ver* repetir

replegar[41] VT to fold; **—se** to retreat

repleto ADJ replete

réplica F (contestación) reply, comeback; (copia) replica; (temblor secundario) aftershock

replicación F replication

replicar[30] VI/VT (responder) to reply, to rejoin;

(reproducirse) to replicate

repliegue M (pliegue marcado) crease; (retirada) retreat

repollo M cabbage

reponer[56, 74] VT (reemplazar) to replace; (restituir) to restore; (replicar) to reply; (una obra de teatro) to revive; (una película) to show again; **—se** to recover one's health

reportaje M feature story

reportar VT (beneficios) to yield; VI (en una organización) to answer to; **—se enfermo** to call in sick

reportero -ra MF reporter

reposado ADJ quiet, calm

reposar VI to repose, to rest; **dejar —** to let steep; M SG **reposacabezas** headrest; M SG **reposapiés** footrest

reposición F (reemplazo) replacement; (de una obra de teatro) revival

reposo M (descanso) repose, rest; (sosiego) calm

repostería F (establecimiento) pastry shop; (actividad) baking

repostero -ra MF pastry cook

reprender VT to reprimand, to scold, to rebuke

reprensión F rebuke

represa F (dique) dam; (reservorio de agua) reservoir

represalia F reprisal

represar VT to dam

representación F (interpretación) representation; (delegación) delegation; (de un papel) portrayal; (de una obra de teatro) performance

representante MF (legislativo) representative; (comercial) agent

representar VT (una imagen) to represent, to depict; (una obra de teatro) to perform; (un personaje) to portray; **tiene treinta años, pero no los representa** he's thirty years old, but he doesn't look it; **tu presencia representa mucho para mí** your presence means a lot to me

representativo ADJ representative

represión F (psicológica) repression; (política) repression, suppression, crackdown

represivo ADJ repressive

reprimenda F reprimand, rebuke

reprimido ADJ repressed, pent-up

reprimir VT (impulsos) to repress; (una tendencia) to check; (enemigos políticos) to suppress, to crack down on; (una rebelión) to quell

reprobación F reproof

reprobar[5] VT to reprove; VI/VT (no aprobar un examen) to flunk, to fail

reprochar VT to reproach, to rebuke

reproche M reproach, rebuke

reproducción F reproduction

reproducir[38] VI/VT to reproduce; **—se** to

reproduce, to breed

reproductor-ora ADJ breeding; **aparato —** VCR; MF breeding animal

reproduje, reprodujera, reprodujese, reproduzca, reproduzco ver reproducir

reptar VI to crawl

reptil M reptile

república F republic

republicano-na ADJ & MF republican; (del Partido Republicano) Republican

repudiar VT (a la sociedad) to repudiate; (a un hijo) to disown; (una herencia) to renounce

repuesto M spare part; **de —** spare

repugnancia F repugnance, disgust, revulsion

repugnante ADJ repugnant, disgusting, loathsome

repugnar VI to be repugnant; VT to disgust, to cloy

repulir VT to polish up

repulsa F rebuff, repulse

repulsar VT to repulse

repulsivo ADJ repulsive, creepy

repuntar VI to rally

reputación F reputation

reputado ADJ reputable

requemar VT to burn

requerimiento M request

requerir[8] VT to require

requesón M cottage cheese

requiebros M PL advances

requisa F requisition

requisar VT (interceptar, incautar) to commandeer, to requisition; (registrar) to search

requisito M requirement, requisite

res F animal; **— lanar** sheep; **— vacuna** cow

resabio M (dejillo) aftertaste; (vicio) bad habit

resaca F (de mar) undertow; (malestar físico) hangover

resaltar VI (sobresalir) to stand out; (poner de relieve) to highlight

resarcir[33] VT to compensate for

resbaladizo ADJ slippery, slick

resbalar VI (deslizar) to slip; (ser/estar resbaladizo) to be slippery; **—se** to slip

resbalón M slip; **darse un —** to slip

resbaloso ADJ (que resbala) slippery; *Méx fam* (inmoral) sleazy

rescatar VT (a un secuestrado) to ransom; (a una persona en peligro) to rescue

rescate M (para un secuestrado) ransom; (de una persona en peligro) rescue

rescindir VT to rescind

rescoldo M embers

resecar[30] VT to dry; **—se** to dry out

reseco ADJ dried-up, parched

resentido ADJ resentful

resentimiento M resentment, grudge; **guardar —** to hold a grudge, to have hard feelings

resentirse[8] VI to hurt, to suffer; **— de** to resent

reseña F book review

reseñar VT to review

reserva F (de provisiones, de oro, de jugadores, del ejército) reserve; (de localidades, de hotel, de indios) reservation; (de animales) preserve; **sin —s** without reservations; **tener —s** to have reservations

reservación F *Am* reservation

reservado ADJ (distante) aloof; (discreto) reserved

reservar VT to reserve; **me reservo mi opinión** I'll spare you my opinion

resfriado M common cold; **estoy —** I've got a cold

resfriarse VI to catch cold

resfrío M cold, head cold

resguardar VT to shelter; **—se de** to seek shelter from

resguardo M (abrigo) shelter; (comprobante) deposit slip

residencia F residence

residencial ADJ (para vivir) residential; (en las afueras) suburban

residente ADJ & MF resident

residir VI to reside

residuo M residue

resignación F resignation

resignarse VI to resign oneself

resina F resin

resistencia F (fuerza opuesta) resistance; (de la calefacción) element; (aguante) endurance, stamina

resistente ADJ resistant, tough

resistir VT (una tentación) to resist; (un ataque) to withstand; **—se a un arresto** to resist arrest; VI to resist, to hold [up]

resollar[5] VI (por enfermedad) to wheeze; (después de un esfuerzo) to pant; (por alivio) to sigh

resolución F (acción de resolver) resolution; (ánimo) determination, resolve; **— óptica** optical resolution

resolver[6,74] VT (decidir) to decide; (solucionar) to solve; **—se a** to resolve to

resonancia F resonance

resonar[5] VI (sonidos) to resound, to boom; (una polémica) to resonate

resoplar VI (con enfado) to huff and puff; (un caballo) to snort

resoplido M (con enojo) puff; (de caballo) snort

resorte M spring

respaldar VT to back, to stand behind

respaldo M (parte de una silla) back; (apoyo) support, backing; **— automático** automatic backup; **— de archivos** backup; **— global** global backup

respectivo ADJ respective

respecto LOC ADV — **a/de** with respect to, concerning; **a ese** — on that score; **con** — **a** with regard to, regarding, vis-à-vis

respetable ADJ respectable

respetar VT to respect

respeto M respect, regard; **con todo** — with all due respect; **faltar el/al** — to slight, to disregard

respetuoso ADJ respectful

respingado M upturned

respingar[40] VI (dar respingos) to buck; (asustarse) to shy away

respingo M (salto) buck; (susto) start

respiración F respiration, breathing; — **boca a boca** mouth-to-mouth resuscitation

respirar VI/VT (inhalar y exhalar) to breathe; (sentir alivio) to breathe easy; **dejar** — to give a breather

respiratorio ADJ respiratory

respiro M (acto de respirar) breathing; (descanso) respite; **dame un** — I need a break

resplandecer[35] VI (brillar) to glare; (de felicidad) to glow

resplandeciente ADJ resplendent, radiant

resplandor M brilliance, radiance

responder VI (reaccionar) to respond; VT (contestar) to answer; (corresponder) to correspond

respondón ADJ saucy

responsabilidad F (obligación de aceptar consecuencias) responsibility; (obligación de informar) accountability

responsabilizar VT to hold liable, to hold responsible

responsable ADJ (que debe aceptar las consecuencias) responsible; (obligado legalmente) liable; (que tiene que informar) accountable

respuesta F response, answer

resquebrajadura F crack

resquebrajar VI to crack

resquicio M (rendija) crack; (laguna legal) loophole

resta F subtraction

restablecer[35] VT (un servicio) to reestablish; (una costumbre) to revive; —**se** to recover

restador -ora MF receiver

restante ADJ remaining

restañar/staunch VT to stanch/staunch

restar VT (sustraer) to subtract; (quitar) to take away from; (quedar) to remain; — **importancia a** to make light of

restauración F restoration

restaurante M restaurant

restaurar VT (el gobierno) to restore; (muebles) to refurbish

restitución F restitution

restituir[19] VT to pay back, to give back

resto M (lo demás) rest; (sobrante) remainder; (tenis) return of service; —**s** (de un edificio) remains; (de una comida) leftovers; **echar el** — to go all out

restorán M restaurant

restregar[41] VT to scrub, to scour

restricción F restriction

restringir[46] VT to restrict, to constrain

resucitación F resuscitation, revival

resucitar VT to resuscitate, to revive

resuello M (por enfermedad) wheeze; (por fatiga) panting

resuelto ADJ (de carácter decidido) resolute, strong-willed; (de actitud decidida) resolved

resuelvo, resuelva, resuelva ver resolver

resulta LOC ADV **de** —**s** as a result

resultado M (de una operación matemática) result; (de un suceso) outcome; (de un partido) score; — **final** (fútbol) final score; —**s científicos** findings; —**s electorales** returns; **como** — as a result; **dar buen** — to pan out; **dar por** — to result in

resultante ADJ resulting, consequent

resultar VI to result; — **de** to result from; **resulta que** it turns out that; **resultó ser un idiota** he turned out to be an idiot, he proved to be an idiot

resumen M summary, abstract; **en** — in sum, in brief

resumir VT to summarize, to sum up; —**se a** to be condensed to, to boil down to

resurgimiento M revival

resurgir[46] VI to arise again

resurrección F resurrection

retablo M altarpiece

retaguardia F rear guard

retal M remnant

retama F broom

retar VT to challenge

retardar VI/VT to retard

retardo M lag

retazo M remnant

retén M (aparato) retainer; (de vigilancia) checkpoint

retención F retention; — **de líquido** fluid retention; — **impositiva** tax withholding

retendrá, retendría ver retener

retener[58] VT (una pelota, la atención) to hold; (salarios, fondos) to garnish, to withhold

retenga, retengo ver retener

retina F retina

retintín M (en los oídos) ringing; (de cascabeles) jingle

retirada F (de tropas) retreat, withdrawal; (de un diplomático, producto) recall

retirar VT (apartar) to move away; (dinero) to withdraw; (algo dicho) to take back, withdraw; (un producto) to recall; —**se** (para dormir, de un empleo, de la carrera militar) to retire; (un ejército) to retreat, to pull back

retiro M (refugio) retreat; (jubilación) retirement; (de fondos) withdrawal; **— de deuda** debt retirement

reto M challenge

retocar[30] VT to retouch, to touch up

retomar VT to take up again

retoñar VI to sprout

retoño M sprout, shoot, bud

retoque M retouching

retorcer[34] VT (una toalla mojada) to wring out; (la muñeca) to wrench, to twist; **—se** (de dolor) to writhe; (de inquietud) to squirm

retorcido ADJ (persona) devious; (rama) gnarled

retorcimiento M (de dolor) writhing; (de inquietud) squirming

retórica F rhetoric

retornar VT to return

retorno M (de un viajero) return (también en un teclado); (de una costumbre, moda) revival; **— de línea automático** word wrap

retozar[47] VI (en juegos infantiles) to frolic, to romp; (en juegos eróticos) to cavort

retozo M frolic, romp

retractarse VI to take back one's words

retraer[59] VT (las garras) to retract; **—se** to withdraw

retraído ADJ shy

retraimiento M shyness

retrasado ADJ (falto de desarrollo) backward; (deficiente mental) retarded

retrasar VT (atrasar) to delay; (un reloj) to set back; **—se** to fall behind

retraso M delay, lag

retratar VT (describir) to portray; (pintar un retrato) to paint a portrait

retrato M (pintura) portrait; (descripción) portrayal

retreta F retreat

retrete M lavatory

retribución F (acción de retribuir) remuneration; (pago) salary

retro ADJ retro

retroactivo ADJ retroactive

retroalimentación F feedback

retroceder VI (recular) to step back; (por miedo) to recoil, to shrink back; (en un coche) to back up; (al mecanografiar) to backspace; (dar marcha atrás) to backtrack; (tropas) to retreat, to fall back; (una inundación) to recede

retroceso M (pérdida) step back; (de un arma de fuego) recoil; (económico) recession; (en un teclado) backspace

retrogradismo M backwardness

retrógrado ADJ backward

retroiluminación F backlighting

retroiluminado ADJ backlit

retroproyector M overhead projector

retrovirus M retrovirus

retrucar[30] VT to counter

retruécano M play on words

retumbar VI to rumble, to roll

retumbo M rumble

retuve, retuviera, retuviese *ver* retener

reubicar[30] VT to relocate

reuma M rheumatism

reumatismo M rheumatism

reumatoide ADJ rheumatoid

reunificación F reunification

reunión F (de negocios) meeting; (informal) get-together; (de ex-alumnos) reunion

reunir[27] VT (juntar) to gather; (convocar) to reunite, to bring together; (coleccionar) to collect; (juntar coraje) to muster; (juntar dinero) to raise; **—se** (formal) to meet; (informal) to get together; (un gentío) to gather

revancha F (venganza) revenge; (en deportes) return game

revelación F revelation

revelado M film development

revelador ADJ revealing

revelar VT (un secreto) to reveal; (película) to develop; (un escándalo) to expose; (información) to disclose; **—se** to show oneself

revendedor-ora MF (de mercadería) middleman; (de entradas) scalper

revender VT (vender de nuevo) to resell; (entradas) to scalp

reventar[1] VI/VT (estallar) to burst, to bust; (morir) to die; (fastidiar) to annoy

reventón M (acción de reventar) bursting; (de un neumático) blowout

reverberar VI to reverberate

reverdecer[35] VI (ponerse verde de nuevo) to become green again; (renovarse) to gain new strength

reverencia F (adoración) reverence; (gesto) bow

reverenciar VT to revere

reverendo -da ADJ & MF reverend

reverente ADJ reverent

reverso M reverse

revertir[8] VI to revert; **— en beneficio de** to be of benefit to

revés M (lado opuesto) reverse; (en tenis) backhand; (contratiempo) setback, downturn; **al —** (con lo de adelante hacia atrás) backwards; (con lo de arriba hacia abajo) upside down; (con lo de adentro hacia afuera) inside out; **dar vuelta al —** to turn inside out

revestimiento M overlay; (de piso) flooring; (de pared exterior) siding; (de pared interior) paneling

revestir[9] VT (un camino) to surface; (una pared) to cover; (conllevar) to be marked by

revisar VT (examinar) to review, to go over; (un

coche) to service
revisión F (de un libro) review; (de una película vieja) revival; (médica, mecánica) checkup
revisor-ora MF (en un tren, autobús) conductor; (de un texto) proofreader
revista F (inspección) inspection; (de tropas) muster; (publicación) magazine, journal, periodical; (espectáculo) revival; — **de historietas** comic book; — **electrónica** e-zine; **pasar** — to pass in review
revistar VT to inspect
revitalizar VT to revitalize
revivir VI/VT to revive
revocación F (de un derecho, de un fallo) revocation; (de una ley) repeal
revocar[30] VT (un fallo) to reverse; (una ley) to repeal; (una pared) to plaster
revolcar[31] VT (derribar) to knock over; —**se** (cerdos) to wallow; (niños) to roll around
revolear VT to roll
revolotear VI to flutter, to flit
revoltijo M (de cosas) jumble; (de pelo) muss
revoltoso-sa ADJ unruly, disorderly; MF troublemaker
revolución F (cambio radical) revolution; (giro) revolution, turn; **revoluciones por minuto** revolutions per minute
revolucionario-ria ADJ revolutionary, earthshaking; MF revolutionary
revolver[6, 74] VT (remover) to stir up; (registrar) to rummage in; (desordenar) to mess up; (huevos) to scramble; (ensalada) to toss; **eso me revuelve el estómago** that makes my stomach turn; —**se en la cama** to toss and turn in bed
revólver M revolver, pistol
revuelo M stir, commotion
revuelta F revolt
revuelto ADJ (el mar) rough; (el ánimo) restless; (el pelo) disheveled; **huevos —s** scrambled eggs
rey M king; **los —es Magos** the Wise Men
reyerta F melee, squabble
rezagarse[40] VI to straggle behind, to lag behind
rezar[47] VI/VT (a Dios) to pray; (un letrero) to say
rezo M prayer
rezongar[40] VI/VT (murmurar) to grumble; (quejarse) to gripe
rezongón-ona ADJ grumpy; MF grouch
rezumar VT to ooze
ría, ríe ver reír
riachuelo M brook
riada F flash flood
ribazo M steep bank
ribera F shore, bank; (de río) riverbank
ribereño ADJ on the bank
ribete M (de uniforme) trimming; (de alfombra) binding; (de ropa) piping; (de mosaico) border; **tener —s de** to have hints of

ribetear VT (un uniforme) to trim; (una alfombra) to bind; (un diseño) to border
ricacho ADJ very rich
rico ADJ (persona) rich, wealthy, affluent; (suelo) rich; (adorno) exquisite; (manjar) delicious; (niño) cute
ridiculizar[47] VT to ridicule, to deride
ridículo ADJ (sin sentido) ridiculous; (absurdo, risible) ludicrous; **hacer el** — to act the fool; **poner en** — to ridicule; **ponerse en** — to make a spectacle of oneself
riego M irrigation
riel M rail
rienda F rein; **dar — suelta** to give a free hand
riendo, riera, rieron, riese ver reír
riesgo M risk; — **ocupacional** occupational hazard/risk; **en** — at risk; **correr un** — to run a risk
rifa F raffle
rifar VT to raffle
rifirrafe M free-for-all
rifle M rifle
rigidez F rigidity
rígido ADJ rigid
rigor M (exactitud) rigor; (dureza) harshness; **en** — in reality; **de** — indispensable
riguroso ADJ (estricto) rigorous; (duro) harsh
rima F rhyme
rimar VI/VT to rhyme
rimbombante ADJ grandiose
rímel M mascara
rin M rim
rincón M (ángulo) corner; (lugar retirado) nook, alcove
rinconera F (estantería) corner cupboard; (mesa) corner table
rinda, rinde, rindiendo, rindiera, rindiese ver rendir
ring M boxing ring
ringlera F row
rinoceronte M rhinoceros
rinoplastia F rhinoplasty, fam nose job
rinovirus M rhinovirus
riña F (discusión) quarrel; (pelea) scrap, fight, spat
riñón M (órgano) kidney; (región lumbar) lower back
río M river; — **abajo** downstream
rió ver reír
ripio M rubble
riqueza F wealth; —**s** riches
risa F (carcajada) laugh; (acción, sonido de reír) laughter; **reventar/desternillarse de** — to burst with laughter; **morirse de** — to die laughing; **¡qué —!** what a joke!
risco M crag, bluff
risible ADJ laughable
risita F (burlona) snicker; (ahogada) chuckle
risotada F guffaw, gale of laughter

ristra F string

risueño ADJ (sonriente) smiling; (alegre) cheerful

rítmico ADJ rhythmical

ritmo M rhythm; **— cardíaco** heart rate; **— de vida** pace of life

rito M rite

ritual ADJ & M ritual

rival ADJ & MF rival

rivalidad F rivalry; **— entre hemanos** sibling rivalry

rivalizar[47] VI to rival; **— con** to compete with

rizado ADJ curly; M curling

rizar[47] VT (pelo) to curl, to crimp; (agua) to ripple

rizo M (en el pelo) curl, ringlet; (en el agua) ripple, ruffle; (pirueta de avión) loop

robar VT (a una persona) to rob; (un objeto, dinero) to steal; **—se una base** to steal a base

roble M oak tree

robledal M oak grove

robo M (violento) robbery; (furtivo) theft; **— a mano armada** armed robbery, holdup; **— con allanamiento** burglary; **— de base** base steal; **— de identidad** identity theft

robot M robot

robótica F robotics

robusto ADJ (fuerte) robust; (grueso) stout, stocky; (sólido) sturdy

roca F rock

roce M (de una bala) graze; (de dos superficies) rub, rubbing; (con la ley, la policía) brush

rociada F (acción de rociar) sprinkling, spraying; (de insultos) volley

rociar[28] VI/VT (con agua) to spray, to sprinkle; (con jugo, aliño) to baste

rocín M nag

rocío M (del alba) dew; (en aerosol) spray, mist

rock M rock

rocoso ADJ rocky

rodada F (superficial) track; (profunda) rut

rodadura F rolling

rodaja F flat round slice

rodaje M (de un coche) running; (de una película) shoot

rodante ADJ rolling

rodar[5] VI (girar) to roll; (caer) to tumble down; (vagar) to roam; (filmar) to shoot

rodear VT (cercar) to surround; (cubrir) to wrap around; (evitar) to go around

rodeo M (desvío) detour; (modo de expresarse) circumlocution; (espectáculo) rodeo

rodilla F knee; **de —s** on one's knees; **hincarse de —s** to kneel down

rodillo M (para pintar) roller; (para cocinar) rolling pin; (para caminos) road roller

rododendro M rhododendron

roedor M rodent

roer[73] VI/VT to gnaw

rogar[42] VT to pray, to beg, to beseech; **hacerse [del]** — to play hard to get; **se ruega no molestar** please do not disturb

rojez F redness

rojizo ADJ reddish

rojo ADJ & M red; **al — vivo** red-hot

rol M role

roletazo M ground ball; **lo sacaron con un —** he grounded out

rollizo ADJ plump; M log

rollo M (de papel, de película, de grasa) roll; (de árbol) log; (de cuerda) reel; (de tela) bolt; (discurso aburrido) long story; (mentira) lie; (lío) mess, hassle; (relación amorosa) affair; (manuscrito) scroll; (de alambre) coil; **dar el — to** hassle

ROM M ROM

romance ADJ Romance; M (lengua románica) Romance language; (español) Spanish language; (relación amorosa) romance; (composición métrica) ballad; **en buen —** in plain language

románico ADJ (arte) Romanesque; (lengua) Romance

romano -na ADJ & MF Roman

romanticismo M (corriente literaria) romanticism; (sentimentalismo) romance

romántico -ca ADJ & MF romantic

rombo M diamond

romería F pilgrimage

romero -ra MF (persona) pilgrim; M rosemary

romo ADJ (sin punta) blunt; (sin filo) dull

romper[74] VI/VT (un jarrón) to break; VT (relaciones) to sever; **— a** to start to; **— con** to break up with; **— el alba** to dawn; **— filas** to break ranks; **— un contrato** to break a contract; **rompió las aguas / la fuente** her water broke; **de rompe y rasga** coarse; M SG **rompecabezas** jigsaw puzzle; M SG **rompehuelgas** strikebreaker; M SG **rompeolas** breakwater

rompible ADJ breakable

rompientes M PL surf

rompimiento M (con el pasado) break; (de una promesa) breach

rompope M *Méx* eggnog

ron M rum

roncar[30] VI to snore

roncha F (de sarampión) spot; (de mosquito) bite

ronco ADJ hoarse, raspy

ronda F (de policía) patrol, beat; (de niños) circle; (de bebidas, de negociaciones, de golf) round

rondar VT (patrullar) to patrol; (acercarse) to hang around; (cantar serenatas) to serenade; **rondaba los cuarenta** she was around forty years old

ronquera F hoarseness

ronquido M snore

ronronear VI to purr

ronroneo M purr

ronzal M halter

roña F (enfermedad de plantas) scab; (sarna) mange; MF (tacaño) skinflint

roñoso ADJ (planta) scabby; (animal) mangy; (persona) stingy

ropa F clothing, clothes; — **blanca** linens; — **vieja** stew made from leftover meat

ropaje M apparel

ropería F checkroom

ropero M (armario) wardrobe; (cuarto) closet

roque M castle

rorro M baby

rosa F (flor) rose; (marca) blemish; — **de los vientos** mariner's compass; ADJ INV (rosado) rose-colored, pink

rosado ADJ (saludable) rosy; (de color de rosa) rose-colored, pink; M rosé wine

rosal M rosebush

rosario M rosary

rosbif M roast beef

rosca F (de tornillo) screw; (pan) ring-shaped roll; **pasarse de** — to go off the deep end

roséola F roseola

rostro M (cara) face; (morro) nerve

rotación F rotation

rotar VI/VT to rotate

rotativo ADJ (movimiento) rotary; (cultivos) rotating; M newspaper

rotatorio ADJ rotary

roto ADJ (averiado) broken; (cansado) exhausted; (ropa, voz) ragged

roto ver **romper**

rotor M rotor

rótula F kneecap

rotular VT to label

rótulo M (título) title; (etiqueta) label

rotundo ADJ resounding; **una negativa rotunda** a categorical denial

rotura F (de un aparato) break; (de un órgano, tubo) rupture; — **de servicio** (tenis) service break

roturar VT to plow

round M (en boxeo) round

rozadura F chafing

rozamiento M friction

rozar[47] VT (herir levemente) to graze; (arañar) to scrape; (irritar) to rub, to chafe; (limpiar un terreno) to clear; —**se con alguien** to have dealings with someone; **rozaba en los cuarenta** she was almost forty years old

Ruanda F Rwanda

ruandés -**esa** ADJ & MF Rwandan

rubéola/rubéola F rubella

rubí M (piedra preciosa) ruby; (en un reloj) jewel

rubicundo ADJ (permanente) ruddy; (temporal) flush

rubio -**a** ADJ & MF blond

rubor M (de la piel) blush, flush; (de las mejillas) bloom, glow

ruborizarse[47] VI to blush

rúbrica F (trazo) flourish; (título) title

rucio ADJ gray

rudeza F rudeness, coarseness

rudo ADJ rude, coarse; — **golpe** hard blow

rueca F spinning wheel

rueda F (de coche) wheel; (de personas) circle; (rodaja) slice; — **de prensa** news conference; **ir sobre** —**s** to be smooth sailing

ruedo M (de un circo) ring; (de vestido) hem

ruego M (plegaria) prayer; (petición) plea, entreaty

rufián M (matón) ruffian

rugby M rugby

rugido M roar

rugir[46] VI (animal) to roar; (estómago) to growl

rugoso ADJ rough

ruibarbo M rhubarb

ruido M noise; — **de fondo** background noise; **mucho** — **y pocas nueces** much ado about nothing

ruidoso ADJ noisy, loud

ruin ADJ (persona, cosa) vile; (animal) puny

ruina F (destrucción) destruction; (edificio derruido, estado de pobreza) ruin; (persona) wreck; (perjuicio) downfall; **en** —**s** in ruins

ruindad F (actitud) vileness; (acto) vile act

ruinoso ADJ ruinous

ruiseñor M nightingale

rulero M RP roller, curler

ruleta F roulette

rulo M roller, curler

Rumania F Romania, Rumania

rumano -**na** ADJ & MF Romanian, Rumanian

rumba F rumba

rumbear VI (dirigirse a) to head in a certain direction; (bailar) to dance the rumba

rumbo M course, route; — **a** toward

rumiar VI (meditar, comer el rumen) to ruminate; (reflexionar) to ruminate, to mull over, to brood over

rumor M rumor

runrún M (rumor) rumor; (sonido sordo) humming

ruptura F (de relaciones) break; (de órganos internos) rupture

rural ADJ rural

Rusia F Russia

ruso -**sa** ADJ & MF (persona) Russian; M (lengua) Russian

rústico ADJ (rural) rustic, rural; (tosco) coarse; **en rústica** paperback

ruta F (itinerario) route; (carretera) highway; (en informática) path

rutina F routine

Ss

sábado M Saturday

sábalo M shad

sábana F bed sheet

sabana F savannah

sabañón M chilblain

saber[71] VI/VT to know; (tener sabor) to taste; — **nadar** to know how to swim; **supo la verdad** he found out the truth; **las vacaciones me han sabido a poco** my vacation was too short; — **a ciencia cierta** to know for sure; — **de biología** to know all about biology; **a** — namely; **hacer** — to let know; **para que sepas** for your information; **sabérselas todas** to know the ropes; **vaya a** — who knows? **no sabe un comino** he doesn't know squat; — **a** to taste like; **sabe bien** it tastes good; M knowledge, learning; **a mi leal** — **y entender** as far as I know; M SG **sabelotodo** know-it-all

sabiduría F wisdom

sabiendas LOC ADV **a** — knowingly

sabiondo -da ADJ & MF wise guy; know-it-all

sabio -bia ADJ wise, sage; MF (estudioso) scholar; (sabedor) sage, wise person

sable M saber

sabor M taste, flavor

saborear VT to savor, to relish

sabotaje M sabotage

sabotear VT to sabotage

sabrá, sabría ver **saber**

sabroso ADJ (comida) savory, tasty; (cuento) juicy

sabueso M (perro) bloodhound; (detective) sleuth

sacador -ora MF (en deportes) server

sacar[30] VT (cosas de la maleta, a pasear) to take out; (manchas, dinero del banco) to get out; (los zapatos) to take off; (malas notas, carnet de conducir) to get; (una copia) to make; (una foto) to take; (una conclusión) to draw; (la lengua, la cabeza por la ventana) to stick out; (una pelota de tenis) to serve; (una asignatura escolar) *Esp* to pass; — **ampollas** to blister; — **brillo** to polish up; — **provecho [de]** to benefit [from]; — **a bailar** to ask to dance; — **a colación** to broach; — **a luz** to divulge; — **de un apuro** to bail out; **me saca de quicio** he gets my goat, he gets on my nerves; — **el cuerpo** to dodge; — **el mejor partido de** to make the best of; — **le el jugo a algo** to make the most of; — **en limpio** to deduce; —**se el sombrero** *Am* to take off one's hat; **¡sáquese de allí!** *Am* get out of there! — **punta** to sharpen; — **a alguien** (béisbol) to get someone out; M SG **sacabocados** punch; M SG **sacacorchos** corkscrew; M SG **sacamuelas** quack dentist; M SG **sacapuntas** pencil sharpener

sacarina F saccharine

sacarosa F sucrose

sacerdocio M priesthood

sacerdote M priest

saciar VT to satiate; —**se** to be satiated

saco M (bolsa) sack; (chaqueta) blazer, sport coat; (aparato de boxeo) punching bag; (parte de órgano interno) sac; — **de dormir** sleeping bag; — **de noche** overnight bag; **echar en** — **roto** to waste one's effort

sacramento M sacrament

sacrificar[30] VT (en un rito religioso) to sacrifice; (una mascota) to put to sleep

sacrificio M sacrifice (también en béisbol)

sacrilegio M sacrilege

sacrílego ADJ sacrilegious

sacristán M sexton

sacro M sacrum

sacudida F (sacudón) shake, jolt; (de terremoto) tremor; (de la cabeza) toss; (eléctrica) shock

sacudir VT (sarandear) to shake; (las alfombras) to beat; (el polvo) to dust; **ir sacudiéndose** to rattle along, to jolt along; —**se de alguien** to get rid of someone

sádico ADJ sadistic

sadismo M sadism

saeta F arrow

safari M safari

sagaz ADJ shrewd, astute

sagrado ADJ sacred, holy; **Sagradas Escrituras** Holy Scripture

sahumar VT to perfume with incense

sahumerio M burning of incense

sainete M one-act farce; **esa familia es un** — that family is a complete mess

sal F (mineral) salt; (gracia) wit; — **de Epsom** Epsom salt; — **gorda** cooking salt; — **yodada** iodized salt; — **de mesa** table salt; **dar** — to spice up; — **y pimienta** (condimentos) salt and pepper; (gracia) life, spark

sal ver **salir**

sala F (de estar) parlor, living room; (grande) hall, large room; — **de justicia** courtroom; — **de clase** classroom; — **de chat** chat room; — **de cuidados intensivos** intensive care unit; — **de espera** waiting room; — **de directorio** boardroom; — **de lectura** reading room; — **de operaciones** operating room; — **de recuperación** recovery room

salado ADJ (con sal) salty, savory; (gracioso) witty; *Am* (caro) expensive; M (acción) salting

salamandra F salamander

salar VT to salt; —**se** to become salty

salarial ADJ salary, wage
salario M pay, wages; — **base** base pay; — **bruto** gross pay; — **de subsistencia** living wage; — **mínimo** minimum wage
salchicha F sausage
saldar VT to settle
saldo M (resultado final) balance; (venta especial) sale; — **s** (restos) remnants; — **pendiente** balance due
saldrá, saldría ver salir
salegar[40] VT to give salt to; M salt lick
salero M (dispensador) salt cellar, salt shaker; (gracia) charm
saleroso ADJ charming
salga, salgo ver salir
salida F (partida) departure; (puerta) exit, way out; (comienzo de una carrera) start; (militar) sally; (eléctrica, de computadora) output; (de una crisis) way out; **este artículo tiene mucha** — this article sells well; **dar la** — to start a race; — **del sol** sunrise; — **de emergencia** emergency exit; — **en falso** false start
saliente ADJ (roca) salient, projecting; (gobierno) outgoing; M salient, projection, overhang
salina F salt mine
salino ADJ saline
salir[57] VI (del interior al exterior, para divertirse) to go out; (de un país) to depart, to leave; (del trabajo) to quit; (de un programa de computadora) to exit, to quit; (manchas de tinta) to come out; (un anillo del dedo) to come off; (el sol) to rise; (una publicación) to appear; (flores) to sprout; — **a bolsa** to go public; **trabajando no se puede** — **de pobre** you can't work your way out of poverty; **salió a su madre** she takes after her mother; — **a la luz** to surface; — **adelante** to overcome difficulties; — **bien** to turn out well; — **con** to date; — **ganando** to come out ahead; — **mal** to go wrong; **¿a cuánto sale?** how much is it? **no me sale ser amable con él** I can't bring myself to be nice to him; — **se** (gotear) to leak; (rebosar) to overflow; (proyectarse) to stick out
salitre F saltpeter
saliva F saliva
salmón M salmon
salmonela F salmonella
salmuera F brine
salobre ADJ salty
salomonense ADJ & MF Solomon Islander
salón M (de estar) living room, parlor; (de conferencias) hall; — **de belleza** beauty salon; — **de clase** classroom; — **de exposición y ventas** showroom; — **de exhibición** exhibition hall; — **de té** tearoom

salpicadero M dashboard
salpicadura F spatter, splash, splatter
salpicar[30] VI/VT (humedecer) to sprinkle, to spatter, to splash; (adornar) to punctuate; (dispersar) to intersperse
salpicón M meat salad
salpimentar[1] VT to salt and pepper
salsa F (blanca) sauce; (picante) salsa; **en su** — in her element; — **tártara** tartar sauce; — **de soya** soy sauce; — **de tomate** ketchup
saltar VI/VT (brincar) to jump, to leap; (una cerca) to jump over, to vault; (un renglón) to skip; (una ley) to ignore; VI (los fusibles) to trip; — **a la vista** to be obvious; — **sobre** to pounce on; **se le saltaron los ojos** his eyes bugged out; **se le saltó un botón** one of his buttons popped off; **se me saltaban las lágrimas** it brought tears to my eyes; M SG
saltamontes grasshopper
salteador -ora MF bandit
saltear VT to stir-fry
salto M jump, leap; — **alto** high jump; — **con esquí** ski jump; — **con pértiga** pole vault; — **de agua** waterfall; — **de cama** dressing gown; — **de línea** return; — **de línea forzado** hard return; — **de línea suave** soft return; — **de longitud** broad jump; — **de página** page break; — **de página forzado** forced page break, hard page break; — **de página suave/automático** soft page break; — **del ángel** swan dive; — **mortal** somersault; — **triple** triple jump; **a** — **de mata** from hand to mouth; **dar un** — (saltar) to jump; (el corazón) to skip a beat
saltón ADJ (que salta) jumping; (que resalta) bulging; M grasshopper
salubridad F sanitation
salud F health; — **mental** mental health; — **pública** public health; **curarse en** — to take precautions; INTERJ cheers!
saludable ADJ healthy, healthful
saludar VT (decir hola) to greet; (dar la bienvenida) to salute, to hail; (en el ejército) to salute; (hacer un gesto amistoso con la mano) to wave
saludo M (hola) greeting, salutation; (gesto) wave; (militar) salute; **retirar el** — **a alguien** to stop speaking to someone; — **s** best wishes, regards
salva F salvo
salvación F salvation
salvado M (harina) bran; (béisbol) save
salvador -ora MF savior; ADJ saving
salvadoreño -ña ADJ & MF Salvador[i]an
salvaguarda F safeguard
salvaguardar VT to safeguard
salvajada F (acción) savage act; (comentario) savage remark
salvaje ADJ (feroz) savage; (no domesticado)

wild; MF savage

salvajismo M savagery

salvamento M (de gente) rescue; (de bienes, propiedades) salvage; (béisbol) save

salvar VT (la vida, el alma) to save; (de un peligro) to rescue; (propiedad) to salvage; (un obstáculo) to clear; (un camino difícil) to negotiate; — **el pellejo** to save one's skin; **el puente salva el río** the bridge spans the river; —**se** to pull through; —**se por poco** to have a narrow escape; **sálvese quien pueda** every man for himself; M SG **salvapantallas** screen saver; M SG **salvavidas** (aparato) life preserver, life jacket; MF (persona) lifeguard

salvia F sage

salvo ADJ safe; **a**— safe; M —**conducto** safe-conduct; PREP save, except; — **en caso de desastre** barring a disaster

Samoa F Samoa

samoano -na ADJ & MF Samoan

sanar VI/VT to heal; M **sanalotodo** cure-all

sanatorio M (para convalecientes) sanatorium; (para enfermos) hospital

sanción F sanction

sancionar VT to sanction

sandalia F sandal

sandez F (acción) stupidity, foolishness; (dicho) foolish remark

sandía F watermelon

saneamiento M sanitation

sanear VT to drain

sangrar VI/VT to bleed; VT (un árbol) to tap; (un párrafo) to indent

sangre F blood; — **fría** coolness under pressure; **a** — **fría** in cold blood; **hacerse mala** — to get upset; **eso lo llevo en la** — that's in my blood; **de** — **caliente** warm-blooded; — **azul** blue blood; **sudar** — to sweat bullets; **de pura** — thoroughbred; **chupar la** — **a alguien** to be a parasite on someone

sangría F (bebida) wine punch; (acción de sangrar) bleeding; (espacio tipográfico) indentation; (pérdida) drain

sangriento ADJ (manchado de sangre, que provoca pérdida de sangre) bloody; (sanguinario) bloodthirsty

sanguijuela F leech

sanguinario ADJ bloody, vicious

sanguíneo ADJ blood; **grupo** — blood group

sanidad F public health

sanitario -ria ADJ sanitary; M —**s** bathroom fittings; MF public health worker

sanmarinense ADJ & MF San Marinese

sanmarinés -esa ADJ & MF San Marinese

sano ADJ (persona) healthy; (juicio) sound; (dieta) healthful; (vaso) unbroken; — **y salvo** safe and sound; **en su** — **juicio** of sound mind

sánscrito M Sanskrit

sanseacabó INTERJ **te quedas y**— you're staying and that's that

santalucense ADJ & MF St. Lucian

santiamén LOC ADV **en un**— in a jiffy, lickety-split

santidad F sanctity, holiness

santificar[30] VT to sanctify

santiguarse[25] VI to cross oneself

santo -ta ADJ saintly, holy; **esperar todo el** — **día** to wait the whole blessed day; MF saint; **día del** — saint's day; **quedarse para vestir** —**s** to be a spinster; **¿a** — **de qué?** for what reason? **¡por todos los** —**s!** my goodness!

santotomense ADJ & MF São Tomean

santuario M sanctuary

santurrón -ona ADJ & MF goody-goody

saña F fury

sañudo ADJ furious

sapo M toad (también hombre feo); **echar** —**s y culebras** to swear, to curse; **sentirse como un** — **de otro pozo** to feel like a fish out of water

saque M (tenis) service, serve; — **de inicio** (fútbol) kickoff; — **de banda** throw-in; — **de esquina** corner kick; — **de meta** goal kick; — **de puerta** goal kick; — **inicial** kick-off; — **ganador** ace; — **y volea** (tenis) serve and volley

saquear VT to sack, to plunder, to pillage

saqueo M sacking, plundering, pillaging

sarampión M measles; — **alemán** rubella

sarape M *Méx* serape

sarcasmo M sarcasm

sarcástico ADJ sarcastic

sarcófago M sarcophagus

sarcoma M sarcoma

sardina F sardine

sardo -da ADJ & MF Sardinian

sardónico ADJ sardonic

sargento -ta MF sergeant; F battle-ax[e]

sarmentoso ADJ gnarled

sarmiento M vine

sarna F mange

sarnoso ADJ mangy

sarpullido M rash

sarro M tartar, plaque

sarta F string; **una** — **de mentiras** a pack of lies; **una** — **de idiotas** a bunch of idiots

sartén F frying pan, skillet

sastre -tra MF tailor

sastrería F tailor shop

satánico ADJ satanic

satélite M satellite; — **artificial** man-made satellite

satén M satin

sátira F satire

satírico ADJ satirical

satirizar[47] VT to satirize

satisfacción F satisfaction

satisfacer[54, 74] VT (un deseo) to satisfy; (una deuda) to pay; **—se** to be satisfied

satisfactorio ADJ (aceptable) satisfactory; (exitoso) successful

satisfaga, satisfago, satisfará, satisfaría *ver* satisfacer

satisfecho ADJ contented, satisfied

satisfecho, satisfice, satisficiera, satisficiese *ver* satisfacer

saturar VT (una solución) to saturate; (un mercado) to glut; (líneas de teléfono) to overload

sauce M willow; **— llorón** weeping willow

saudí, saudita ADJ & MF Saudi Arabian

savia F sap

saxofón M saxophone

sazón F season; **a la —** at that time; **en —** ripe

sazonar VT (condimentar) to season, to flavor; (madurar) to ripen

scooter M scooter

scout MF scout

se PRON PERS **— coronó a sí mismo** he crowned himself; **— lavó la cara** he washed his face; **— besaron** they kissed each other; **— habla español** Spanish is spoken; **— lo puede combatir** it can be fought

sé *ver* saber

sea, seas *ver* ser

sebo M tallow, fat

seborrea F seborrhea

secador M hair dryer

secadora F clothes dryer

secante ADJ drying

secar[30] VT (la ropa) to dry; (las manos) to dry off; **—se** (planta) to dry up; (río) to run dry; (madera) to season

sección F (militar) platoon; (de un almacén) department; (un texto) section

seccionar VT to section

seco ADJ (ropa) dry; (río) dried-up; (planta) withered; (respuesta) curt, brief; **en —** on dry land; **parar en —** to stop short; **quedar —** to fall dead; **estar —** to be broke; **lavar en —** to dry-clean; **a secas** plain

secreción F secretion

secretar VT to secrete

secretaría F secretariat

secretariado M (profesión) secretarial profession; (secretaría) secretariat; (conjunto de secretarias) secretarial pool

secretario -ria MF secretary; **— general** secretary general

secretear VI to whisper

secreto ADJ (oculto) secret; (policía) undercover; M (cosa oculta) secret; (condición de oculto) secrecy; **— a voces** open secret; **en —** in secret; **— bancario** account holder confidentiality

secta F sect

sector M sector

sectorial ADJ sectorial

secuaz M henchman

secuela F consequence; **—s** aftermath

secuencia F (de acontecimientos) sequence; (de datos) string

secuenciar VT to sequence

secuestrador -ora MF kidnapper

secuestrar VT (a una persona) to kidnap, to abduct; (una propiedad) to seize; (un avión) to hijack

secuestro M (de una persona) kidnapping; (de propiedad) seizure; (de un avión) hijacking

secular ADJ secular

secundar VT (apoyar) to second; (imitar) to imitate; (seguir) to follow suit

secundaria F secondary school

secundario ADJ secondary

sed F thirst; **tener —** to be thirsty

seda F silk; **como una —** (suave) soft as silk; (afable) sweet-tempered

sedación F sedation

sedán M sedan

sedante ADJ & M sedative

sedar VT to sedate

sedativo ADJ & M sedative

sede F (gubernamental) seat; (religiosa) see; **— central** headquarters

sedentario ADJ sedentary

sedería F (conjunto de artículos de seda) silk goods; (tienda de sedas) silk shop

sedero -ra MF (que vende) silk dealer; (que fabrica) silk weaver; ADJ **industria sedera** silk industry

sedición F sedition

sediento ADJ thirsty; **estar — de** to thirst for

sedimento M sediment

sedoso ADJ silken, silky

seducción F seduction

seducir[38] VT (corromper) to seduce; (atraer) to entice; (persuadir con argucias) to lure

seductivo ADJ alluring

seductor -ora ADJ alluring; M seducer; F seductress

sefardí ADJ Sephardic; MF Sephardi; M (variedad del español) Sephardi

sefardita ADJ & MF Sephardi

segador -ora MF (persona) mower, reaper; F (máquina) mower, reaper

segar[41] VT (hierba) to mow; (mies) to reap

seglar ADJ secular; M layman; F laywoman

segmento M segment

segregar[40] VT (separar) to segregate; (producir secreciones) to secrete

seguido ADJ in a row; **dos horas seguidas** two hours in a row; ADV straight through; **trabajaron —** they worked continuously

seguidor -ora MF follower

seguimiento M (persecución) pursuit; (atención continuada) follow-up

seguir[12] VT (camino, instrucciones) to follow; (estudios) to pursue; (progreso de un avión) to track; **sigue trabajando** he keeps on working, he continues to work; **sigue allí** he is still there; **de lo anterior se sigue que** from the preceding it follows that; — **los pasos de** to follow in the footsteps of; —**le la corriente a alguien** to play along with someone; — **el tren** to keep up; — **el hilo de** to keep track of; — **la pista de** to trail

según PREP according to; — **se mire** depending on how you see it; — **pasa el tiempo** as time goes by; — **tus instrucciones** per your instructions; CONJ as; — **se informa** reportedly; **lo haré** — **me digas** I will do it as you tell me to

segundero M second hand

segundo -da ADJ & ADV second; MF second in command; — **tiempo** (fútbol) second half; — **servicio** (tenis) second serve; **segunda base** (posición en béisbol) second base; M (jugador) second baseman; **segunda hipoteca** second mortgage; **segunda intención** ulterior motive; **de segunda mano** secondhand, preowned; **de segunda** second-rate

segundón -ona MF (hijo) second-born child; (persona mediocre) also-ran

seguramente ADV certainly, surely; **lenta pero** — slowly but surely

seguridad F (contra el delito) security; (contra accidentes) safety; — **en sí mismo** self-confidence; — **social** social security

seguro ADJ (a prueba de delincuentes) secure; (que no ofrece o siente duda) sure, certain; (libre de peligro) safe; (firme) stable; **es** — **que** it is certain that; **su** — **servidor** yours truly; — **de sí mismo** self-assured; M (contrato contra riesgos) insurance; (dispositivo) safety device, restraint; — **contra accidentes** accident insurance; — **contra daños a terceros** liability insurance; — **contra incendios** fire insurance; — **contra inundaciones** flood insurance; — **contra todo riesgo** comprehensive insurance; — **de discapacidad** disability insurance; — **de vida** life insurance; — **de vida a término** term life insurance; — **de vida permanente** whole life insurance; — **médico** health insurance; **en** — in safety; **sobre** — without risk

seis NUM six

selección F selection, choice; — **de texto** highlighting; — **natural** natural selection; — **nacional** national team

seleccionado M — **nacional** national team

seleccionar VT to select, to choose

selectivo ADJ selective

selecto ADJ select, choice

sellar VT (poner sello) to stamp; (precintar) to seal

sello M (de correo) stamp; (de documento oficial) seal; (instrumento) seal, stamp; (de discos) label; — **de goma** rubber stamp; — **fiscal** revenue stamp

selva F (templada o fría) forest; (tropical) jungle; — **virgen** virgin forest

semáforo M traffic light

semana F week; **entre** — during the week

semanal ADJ weekly

semanario M weekly publication

semántica F semantics

semblante M countenance

semblanza F biographical sketch

sembrado M sown ground

sembradora F planting machine

sembrar[1] VT (plantar) to sow, to plant; (esparcir) to scatter; (minas) to lay; (pánico, alegría) to spread

semejante ADJ similar, like; — **afirmación** such a statement; **un tipo** — such a guy; M fellow human being

semejanza F resemblance, similarity; **a** — **de** in the manner of

semejar VT to resemble

semental ADJ stud; M stud, stallion

semestral ADJ biannual

semestre M semester

semianual ADJ biannual

semicírculo M semicircle

semiconductor M semiconductor

semifinal ADJ & F semifinal

semilla F seed

semillero M seedbed; — **de vicios** hotbed of vice

seminario M (religioso) seminary; (universitario) seminar

semítico ADJ Semitic

senado M senate

senador -ora MF senator

sencillez F simplicity; **con** — simply

sencillo ADJ (no complicado, humilde) simple; (fácil) easy, simple; (sin adornos) plain; (no afectado) straightforward; M (béisbol) single

senda F (construida) path, pathway; (natural) track, trail

sendero M (construido) path, pathway; (natural) track, trail

sendos ADJ **tenían** — **sombreros** each one had a hat

Senegal M Senegal

senegalés -esa ADJ & MF Senegalese

senil ADJ senile

senilidad F senility

seno M (pecho) breast; (hueco) sinus; (útero)

womb; (en matemática) sine; **— de la familia** bosom of the family

sensación F (física) sensation; (mental) feeling, impression; **tengo la — de que** I have the feeling that; **fue la — de la fiesta** she was the life of the party

sensacional ADJ sensational

sensatez F common sense

sensato ADJ sensible, level-headed

sensibilidad F (modo de pensar) sensibility; (percepción) sensitiveness

sensibilizar[47] VT to sensitize

sensible ADJ (que siente) sensitive; (notable) perceptible; **tengo el brazo muy — por el accidente** my arm is very tender because of the accident; **Juana es muy — en estas ocasiones** Juana is very emotional on these occasions

sensiblería F sentimentality

sensiblero ADJ sentimental, mushy

sensitivo ADJ sensitive

sensor M sensor

sensorial ADJ sensory

sensual ADJ (carnal) sensual; (de los sentidos) sensuous

sensualidad F sensuality

sentada F (acto de sentarse) sitting; (protesta) sit-in; **de una —** at one sitting

sentado ADJ **dar por —** to take for granted

sentar[1] VT to seat; **— bien** to agree with; **me sentó muy mal lo que dijo** what he said did not sit well with me; **este peinado te sienta** this hairdo becomes you; **no te sienta ese traje** that suit does not fit you; **— precedente** to set a precedent; **—se** to sit down

sentencia F (dicho) maxim; (fallo) ruling; (condena) sentence; (indemnización) award

sentenciar VT (condenar) to sentence; (fallar) to rule

sentido ADJ heartfelt; M (facultad) sense; (significado) meaning; (dirección) way; **— común** common sense; **— de la vista** sense of sight; **— del gusto** sense of taste; **— del humor** sense of humor; **— del oído** sense of hearing; **— del olfato** sense of smell; **— del tacto** sense of touch; **aguzar el —** to prick up one's ears; **de un solo —** one-way; **de dos —s** two-way; **dejar sin —** to render unconscious; **en cierto —** in a sense; **perder el —** to faint; **quedar —** to have one's feelings hurt; **sin —** meaningless; **tener —** to make sense

sentimental ADJ sentimental

sentimentalismo M sentimentality

sentimiento M feeling, sentiment

sentir[8] VT (percibir) to feel; (oír) to hear; (lamentar) to regret; **—se** to feel; **—se capaz de** to feel up to; **—se de los pies** to have pains in the feet

seña F (gesto) sign; (rasgo) trait; (marca) mark; **—s** name and address; **por más —s** as an additional proof; **—s de vida** life signs; **hablar por —s** to use sign language; **hacer —s** to signal

señal F (de tráfico, de violencia, de vida, de la cruz) sign; (de radio) signal; (pago anticipado) deposit; **en — de** in token of

señalar VT (marcar, señalar) to mark; (mostrar, mencionar) to point out; (fijar) to fix; **—se** to distinguish oneself

señor M (título) Mr.; (forma de tratamiento) sir; (dueño) *lit* master, lord; **el Señor** the Lord; **un gran —** a great man

señora F (dama) lady; (forma de tratamiento) madam, ma'am; (título) Mrs., Ms.; (esposa) wife

señorear VI to dominate

señoría F lordship; **su —** Your Honor

señorial ADJ lordly

señorío M (dominio) dominion; (dignidad) lordship

señorita F miss; **toda una —** quite a young lady

señorito M (joven) master; (dandi) dandy

señuelo M decoy, lure

sepa, sepamos *ver* saber

separación F separation

separado ADJ (apartado) separate; (estado civil) separated; **por —** separately

separar VT (apartar) to separate; (clasificar) to sort out; (despedir de un cargo) to remove; **—se** to separate, to part company

separata F offprint, reprint

septentrional ADJ northern

septicemia F blood poisoning

septiembre, setiembre M September

séptimo ADJ & M seventh

sepulcro M tomb

sepultar VT to bury, to inter

sepultura F (acción) burial; (lugar) grave, tomb; **dar —** to bury

sepulturero -ra MF gravedigger

sequedad F dryness

sequía F drought

séquito M retinue, entourage

ser[65] VI to be; **— de Valencia** to be from Valencia; **— de madera** to be made of wood; **a no — que** unless; **así es** that's right; **érase una vez** once upon a time; **es decir** that is to say; **es de esperar** it is to be expected; **es más** what's more; **la boda es hoy** the wedding takes place today; **son las nueve** it is nine o'clock; **somos cuatro** there are four of us; V AUX to be; **fue elegido presidente** he was elected president; M (entidad viviente) being; (esencia) essence; (existencia) existence; **un — humano** a human being

serbio-bia ADJ Serbian; MF (persona) Serb, Serbian; M (lengua) Serbian

serenar VI to quiet; **—se** (el alma) to become serene, to calm down; (el tiempo) to clear up

serenata F serenade; **dar—** to serenade

serenidad F serenity, peace of mind

sereno ADJ (mar, alma) serene; (cielo) clear; **al — in** the night air; M night watchman

serie F series; **— de instrucciones** (en un programa de computadora) macro; **en —** serial; **— ofensiva** offensive series

seriedad F seriousness, earnestness

serio ADJ (problema) serious; (persona) earnest, serious; **en —** seriously

sermón M (prédica) sermon; (reprimenda) lecture

sermonear VI/VT (predicar) to preach; (reprender) to lecture

serpentear VI to wind, to meander

serpiente F snake

serrado ADJ serrated

serranía F mountainous region

serrano-na M mountain man; F mountain woman; ADJ **zona serrana** mountain region

serrín M sawdust

serrucho M handsaw

servicial ADJ helpful

servicio M (también en tenis) service; (sirvientes) servants; (para un comensal) place setting; (aseo) restroom, facilities; **— a la habitación** room service; **— de ayuda al usuario** helpdesk; **— de contestador** answering service; **— de entrega** delivery service; **— directo** ace; **— militar** military service; **a su —** at your service; **de — pesado** heavy-duty; **estar en —** to be in commission; **poner en —** to commission, to put into service

servidor-ora MF (persona) servant; **un —** yours truly; **su seguro —** yours truly; M (ordenador) server; **— remoto** remote server

servidumbre F servitude

servil ADJ (personalidad) servile; (trabajo) menial

servilleta F napkin

servir[9] VI to serve; **— de** to serve as; **— para** to be used for; **para —le** at your service; **no — para nada** to be of no use; **¿en qué le puedo —?** how can I help you? **—se de** to make use of; **sírvase usted hacerlo** please do it

sésamo M sesame; **¡ábrete —!** open sesame!

sesenta NUM sixty

sesgado ADJ biased

sesgar[40] VT (una tela) to cut on the bias; (una opinión) to slant; (las estadísticas) to skew

sesgo M (en la tela) bias; (de los ojos, de orientación) slant; **al —** obliquely

sesión F (reunión, período) session; (de fotografía) sitting; (de una película) showing; **— de ejercicio** workout

seso M brain; **de poco —** foolish; **devanarse los —s** to rack one's brain

sestear VI to take a nap

sesudo ADJ (persona) brainy; (explicación) intelligent; (testarudo) *Méx* stubborn

set M set

seta F mushroom

setenta NUM seventy

seto M hedge

sétter M setter

seudónimo M pseudonym, pen name

severidad F severity, harshness

severo ADJ severe, stern, harsh

sevillano-na ADJ & MF Sevillian; F PL Sevillian dances

sexar VT to sex

sexismo M sexism

sexista MF sexist

sexo M (género) sex; **el bello —** the fair sex

sexto ADV, ADJ & M sixth

sexual ADJ sexual

sexualidad F sexuality

sexy ADJ sexy

Seychelles F PL Seychelles

SFA [Sistema de frenos antibloqueo] M ABS

shock M shock

short, shorts M shorts

si CONJ if; **yo voy — tú vas** I'm going if you're going; **no sé — viene o no** I don't know whether she's coming or not; **¡— ya te lo dije!** but I already told you! **— bien** although; **por — acaso** just in case; **— Dios quiere** God willing; **— no me equivoco** unless I'm mistaken

sí ADV yes; *fam* yeah; **¿—?** really? **— que fui** I did go; **creo que —** I think so; M consent; **me dio el —** she said yes; PRON himself, herself, itself, oneself, themselves; **de por —** in itself; **estar sobre —** to be on the alert; **volver en — to** come to; **pagado de —** self-satisfied; **estar fuera de —** to be beside oneself; **hablar para —** to talk to oneself; **dio todo de —** she gave her all; **cada cual para —** every man for himself

sicario M hitman

sicomoro M sycamore

SIDA [síndrome de inmunodeficiencia adquirida] M AIDS

siderurgia F steel industry

sidra F cider

siega F (de la hierba) mowing; (de las mieses) reaping

siembra F (acción de sembrar) sowing; (época) sowing time

siempre ADV always; **— nos has apoyado** you've always been very supportive of us; **desde —** since forever; **para/por —** forever;

por — jamás forevermore; **— que** (en cualquier momento) whenever; (con tal que) provided that; **— y cuando** provided that; **como —** as usual; **hoy no eres el mismo de —** you're not yourself today

sien F temple

sienta, siente ver sentar, sentir

sierpe F *lit* serpent

sierra F (herramienta) saw; (cordillera) small mountain range; **— de cadena** chainsaw

siesta F siesta, afternoon nap; **dormir la —** to take an afternoon nap

siete NUM seven

sífilis F syphilis

sifón M (para líquidos) siphon; (tubo) trap

siga, sigamos ver seguir

sigilo M stealth

sigla F acronym

siglo M century

signatario -ria MF signer

significación F (sentido) meaning; (importancia) significance

significado M meaning, sense

significar[30] VT to mean, to signify

significativo ADJ significant, meaningful

signo M sign; **— de admiración** exclamation point; **— de igual** equal sign; **— de interrogación** question mark; **— de más** plus sign; **— de menos** minus sign; **— de multiplicación** multiplication sign; **—s vitales** vital signs

sigo, siguiendo ver seguir

siguiente ADJ following; **al día —** the next day

siguiera, siguiese ver seguir

sílaba F syllable

silbar VI (soplar aire) to whistle; (rechiflar) to hiss

silbato M whistle (también en fútbol)

silbido M whistle

silenciador M (de arma) silencer; (de coche) muffler

silenciar VT to silence

silencio M silence, quiet; **guardar —** to keep quiet

silenciosamente ADV quietly

silencioso ADJ silent, quiet

silicio M silicon

silla F chair; (de montar) saddle; **— de ruedas** wheelchair; **— eléctrica** electric chair; **— plegadiza** folding chair

sillín M saddle, seat

sillón M (mueble) armchair

silo M silo

silogismo M syllogism

silueta F silhouette

siluro M catfish

silvestre ADJ wild

silvicultura F forestry

sima F chasm

simbiosis F symbiosis

simbólico ADJ symbolic

simbolismo M symbolism

simbolizar[47] VT to symbolize

símbolo M symbol; **— de status** status symbol; **— sexual** sex symbol

simetría F symmetry

simétrico ADJ symmetrical

simiente F seed

símil M simile

similar ADJ similar

similitud F resemblance, similarity

simio M ape

simpatía F friendliness; **no le tengo mucha —** I don't like him much

simpático ADJ (amistoso) nice, friendly, congenial; (sistema nervioso) sympathetic

simpatizante ADJ supporting, sympathizing; MF supporter, sympathizer

simpatizar[47] VI (con alguien) to like; (con una idea) to be sympathetic toward

simple ADJ (no complicado) simple; (mero) mere; (tonto) simpleminded

simplemente ADV simply, merely

simpleza F (sencillez) simplicity; (estupidez) stupidity

simplicidad F simplicity

simplificar[30] VT to simplify

simplista ADJ (inteptación) simplistic; (explicación) glib, simplistic

simplón -ona ADJ simpleminded; MF simpleton

simposio M symposium

simulación F simulation

simulacro M **— de batalla** mock battle; **— de incendio** fire drill

simulador -ora MF simulator; M **— de vuelo** flight simulator

simular VT to simulate, to feign

simultanear VI perform simultaneously

simultáneo ADJ simultaneous

sin PREP without; **— aliento** out of breath; **— amueblar** unfurnished; **— azúcar** sugar-free; **— comentarios** no comment; **— compromiso** without obligation; **— condiciones** unconditionally, with no strings attached; **— culpa** no-fault; **— declarar** unreported; **— derecho** nonvoting; **— duda** without doubt, undoubtedly; **— embargo** nevertheless; **— escrúpulos** unscrupulous; **— excepciones** across the board; **— falta** without fail; **— garantía** unsecured; **— intereses** interest-free; **— lujos** no-frills; **— marcar** unmarked; **— peligro** safely; **— percances** safely; **— problemas** trouble-free; **— receta** over-the-counter; **— riesgo** risk-free; **— seguro médico** uninsured; **— sentido** meaningless

sinagoga F synagogue

sincerarse VI to clear the air, to come clean

sinceridad F sincerity

sincero ADJ (personalidad) sincere; (opinión) candid; (agradecimiento) heartfelt, wholehearted

sincrónico ADJ (proceso) synchronous; (enfoque lingüístico) synchronic

sincronización F timing

sincronizar[47] VT to synchronize

sindical ADJ (relativo al síndico) trustee; (relativo al sindicato) union; **dirigente —** union leader

sindicar[30] VT to unionize, to syndicate

sindicato M (de trabajadores) syndicate, trade union, labor union; (de bancos) syndicate

síndico -ca MF receiver, trustee

síndrome M syndrome; **— de abstinencia** withdrawal symptoms; **— de choque tóxico** toxic shock syndrome; **— de Down** Down's syndrome; **— de muerte infantil súbita** crib death, sudden infant death syndrome

sinergia F synergy

sinfín M **un — de cosas** a lot of things

sinfonía F symphony

Singapur M Singapore

singapurense ADJ & MF Singaporean

singular ADJ (número) singular; (excepcional) unique

siniestro ADJ sinister; M disaster

sinnúmero M myriad

sino CONJ but; **no vino — que llamó** she didn't come but instead called; **no tengo dos — tres** I have not two but three; **no es — madera** it's only wood

sinónimo ADJ synonymous; M synonym

sinopsis F synopsis

sinrazón F injustice

sinsabor M trouble

sinsonte M mockingbird

sintamos ver sentir

sintaxis F syntax

síntesis F synthesis; **— de habla** speech synthesis; **— de habla** voice synthesis

sintético ADJ (producto) synthetic; (fibras) man-made

sintetizador M synthesizer

sintetizar[47] VT to synthesize

sintiendo, sintiera, sintiese ver sentir

síntoma M symptom

sintonía F tuning; **en —** on the same wavelength

sintonizador M tuner

sintonizar[47] VT (una emisora) to tune in; (un sintonizador) to fine-tune; **los dos sintonizan bien** the two are on the same wavelength

sinuoso ADJ (camino) sinuous, winding; (comportamiento) devious

sinusitis F sinusitis

sinvergüenza MF creep

siquiera ADV at least; **dame — unos días** give me a few days at least; **ni —** not even

sirena F (ninfa, bocina) siren; (mitad mujer, mitad pez) mermaid

Siria F Syria

sirio -ria ADJ & MF Syrian

sirve, sirviendo, sirviera, sirviese ver servir

sirviente MF, **sirvienta** F servant

sisar VT to pilfer, to swipe

sisear VI to hiss

siseo M hiss, hissing

sísmico ADJ seismic

sistema M system; **— binario** binary system; **— de asistencia de salud** health care system; **— de cifrado** encryption system; **— de reconocimiento óptico de caracteres** optical character recognition; **— experto** expert system; **— inmune** immune system; **— mundial de posicionamiento** global positioning system; **— nervioso central** central nervous system; **— operativo** operating system; **— solar** solar system

sistemático ADJ systematic

sistematizar[47] VI/VT to systematize

sistémico ADJ systemic

sistólico ADJ systolic

sitial M **— de honor** seat of honor

sitiar VT to besiege

sitio M (espacio vacío) room; (ubicación) place, site; (asedio) siege; **no hay —** there's no room; **esto no está en su —** this is out of place; **— web** website; **poner — a** to lay siege to; **poner a alguien en su —** to put someone in his place

sito ADJ situated

situación F (circunstancia) situation; (legal, financiera, social) status

situado ADJ situated; **estar —** to be located

situar[26] VT to locate, to place; **—se** to be located

sketch M sketch, skit

slalom M slalom

smog M smog

smoking M dinner jacket

so PREP **— pena de** under penalty of; **— pretexto de** under the pretext of; INTERJ whoa; ADV **— tonto** you stupid idiot!

sobaco M armpit

sobar VT (la masa) to knead; (a una persona) to fondle; (un traje) to wear out

soberanía F sovereignty

soberano -na ADJ & MF sovereign

soberbia F pride, haughtiness

soberbio ADJ (orgulloso) proud, haughty; (magnífico) magnificent

sobornar VT to bribe

soborno M (acción) bribery; (mordida) bribe, *fam* payola

sobra F surplus; **—s** leftovers, leavings; **de —**

sabes you know full well; **está de** — it is
superfluous; **las piezas de** — spare parts
sobrado ADJ more than enough
sobrante ADJ leftover, remaining; surplus
sobrar VI (dinero, libros) to be left over, to
remain; (personas) to be in the way
sobre PREP (encima de) above, over; (en contacto
con) on, upon; (acerca de) about; **un
préstamo — su coche** a loan on his car; —
todo above all, especially; — **las 9:30** at
about 9:30; **marchar — Madrid** to march
toward Madrid; M (para cartas) envelope; (de
sopa) packet; — **manila** manila envelope;
irse al — to hit the sack
sobreactuar[26] VI to ham it up
sobrealimentador M supercharger
sobrecalificado ADJ overqualified
sobrecarga F overload; — **de voltaje** power
surge; — **sensorial** sensory overload
sobrecargar[40] VT to overload
sobrecogedor ADJ awesome
sobrecoger[45] VI/VT to awe; —**se** to be in awe;
—**se de pánico** to be panic-stricken
sobrecogimiento M awe
sobrecompensar VI to overcompensate
sobrecorrección F overcorrection
sobredosis F overdose
sobreendeudado N debt-ridden
sobreentenderse[2] VI to be understood
sobreentendido ADJ understood; M
assumption
sobreestimar VT to overestimate
sobreexcitado ADJ overexcited, wired
sobreexcitar VT to overexcite
sobreextendido ADJ overextended
sobregirar VT to overdraw
sobregiro M overdraft
sobrehumano ADJ superhuman
sobrellevar VT to bear, to endure
sobremanera ADV beyond measure
sobremesa F after-dinner conversation
sobrenadar VI to float
sobrenatural ADJ supernatural
sobrenombre M nickname
sobrepasar VT to exceed
sobrepeso M overweight
sobreponerse[56, 74] VT to superimpose; VI — **a**
(valer más que) to outweigh; (recuperarse) to
get over
sobreproteger[45] VT to overprotect, to smother
sobrepujar VT to surpass
sobresaliente ADJ outstanding; MF understudy
sobresalir[57] VI (ser notable) to stand out; (estar
en un plano más saliente) to project, to jut
out; (ser excelente) to excel
sobresaltar VT to startle, frighten; —**se** to be
startled, to start
sobresalto M start, scare
sobrestante M foreman

sobresueldo M extra pay
sobretasa F surtax
sobretodo M overcoat
sobrevenir[61] VI to happen unexpectedly
sobrevivencia F survival
sobreviviente MF survivor; ADJ surviving
sobrevivir VI/VT to survive
sobriedad F sobriety
sobrino -na M nephew; F niece; — **nieto**
great-nephew; **sobrina nieta** great-niece
sobrio ADJ sober
socarrar VT to singe
socarrón ADJ sarcastic
socarronería F sarcasm
socavar VT (excavar por debajo) to dig under;
(debilitar) to undermine, to undercut
socavón M sinkhole; shaft, tunnel
sociable ADJ sociable, gregarious
social ADJ social
socialismo M socialism
socialista ADJ & MF socialist
socializar[47] VT to socialize
sociedad F (grupo humano) society; (firma)
company, partnership; — **anónima**
corporation; — **de consumo** consumer
society; **alta —** high society
socio -cia MF (de una firma) partner; (de un
club) member; — **minoritario** minority
partner; — **principal** senior partner; —
comercial trading partner
socioeconómico ADJ socioeconomic
sociología F sociology
sociópata MF sociopath
socorrer VT to help
socorro INTERJ & M help; **acudir al — de** to go
to the rescue of; **pedir —** to cry out for help
soda F soda
sodio M sodium
sodomía F sodomy
soez ADJ vulgar
sofá M sofa, couch; —**-cama** sleeper, sofa bed
sofisma M fallacy
sofisticado ADJ sophisticated
sofocante ADJ suffocating, oppressive
sofocar[30] VI/VT (ahogar) to suffocate; (una
rebelión) to quash, to quell, to suppress; (un
incendio) to put out
sofoco M suffocation
softball M softball
software M software; — **de fuente abierta**
open source software
soga F rope; **estar con la — al cuello** to have a
rope around one's neck
sois *ver* ser
soja F (planta) soy; (semilla) soybean
sojuzgar[40] VT to subjugate, to subdue
sol M sun; **de — a —** from sunrise to sunset;
hace — it is sunny; **tomar el —** to sunbathe;
ella es un — she's a gem; **arrimarse al —**

que más calienta to know which side one's bread is buttered on

solamente ADV only, solely

solana F sunny place

solapa F lapel

solapado ADJ underhanded

solar M (terreno) lot; (casa ancestral) manor; ADJ solar

solaz M *lit* recreation

soldado -da MF soldier; **— raso** private; **— de línea** regular soldier

soldador M soldering iron

soldadura F (acción de adherir con estaño) soldering; (resultado) solder; (acción de adherir sin estaño) welding; (resultado) weld; **— autógena** arc welding

soldar[5] VI/VT (con estaño) to solder; (sin estaño) to weld; **—se** to mend

soleado ADJ sunny

solear VT to put in the sun; **—se** to sun oneself

soledad F solitude, loneliness

solemne ADJ solemn; **— disparate** downright foolishness

solemnidad F solemnity

solenoide M solenoid

soler[6,73] VI **suelo levantarme a las siete** I usually get up at seven; **solía acostarme tarde** I used to go to bed late; **no suele importarle** he usually doesn't mind

solferino ADJ reddish-purple

solicitante MF applicant

solicitar VT (permiso) to request; (un puesto, una beca) to apply for

solícito ADJ solicitous

solicitud F (para beca, puesto) application; (de información, permiso) request; **— de préstamo** loan application; **a — de** at the request of

solidaridad F solidarity

solidario ADJ supportive, sympathetic

solidez F solidity

solidificar[10] VT to solidify

sólido ADJ (materia) solid; (mueble) sturdy; (argumento) strong; M solid

solista MF soloist

solitario -ria ADJ solitary; MF (persona) recluse; M (juego de cartas, brillante) solitaire; F tapeworm

sollozar[47] VI to sob

sollozo M sob

solo ADJ (desamparado) lonely, lonesome; (no acompañado) alone; **tengo un — coche** I have only one car; **a solas** alone; **habla solo** he talks to himself; **ni una sola palabra** not a single word; ADV just, only; **— quiero saber** I just/only want to know; M solo

solomillo M sirloin

solsticio M solstice

soltar[5] VT (a un prisionero) to let go, to release;

(el vientre) to loosen; (una carcajada) to let out; (bombas) to drop; (un disparate) to say; **— amarras** to cast off; **— el hervor** to come to a boil; **— tacos** to swear; **—se** to loosen up; **—se el pelo** to kick up one's heels

soltero -ra ADJ single, unmarried; M bachelor; F unmarried woman

solterón -ona M old bachelor; F *pey* spinster

soltura F ease; **hablar con —** to speak fluently

soluble ADJ soluble

solución F solution; **— salina** saline solution

solucionar VT to solve

solventar VT to settle

solvente ADJ & M solvent

somalí ADJ & MF Somalian

Somalia F Somalia

sombra F (de una figura) shadow; (protección del sol) shade; (para ojos) eye shadow; **hacer —** to overshadow; **dar —** to shade; **no fiarse ni de su propia —** to be scared of one's own shadow; **a la —** in the shade; **sin — de duda** without a shadow of a doubt

sombreado ADJ (protegido del sol) shady; (oscuro) shadowy

sombrear VT to shade

sombrerería F millinery

sombrerero -ra MF milliner

sombrero M hat; **— de copa** top hat; **— hongo** derby

sombrilla F parasol

sombrío ADJ (oscuro) dark; (triste) somber, gloomy

somero ADJ (agua) shallow; (discusión) superficial

someter VT (proponer algo) to submit; (poner bajo dominio) to subject; **—se a** to undergo

sometimiento M (propuesta) submission; (dominio) subjection

somnífero M sleeping pill

somnolencia F drowsiness, sleepiness

somnoliento ADJ drowsy

somos *ver* ser

son M sound; LOC ADV **al — de** to the sound of; **venimos en — de paz** we come in peace

son *ver* ser

sonaja F rattle

sonajero M rattle

sonámbulo -la MF sleepwalker

sonar[5] VI (hacer un sonido) to sound; (mencionarse) to be mentioned; (ser familiar) to sound familiar; **— a** to sound like; VT (bocina) to sound; (tambor) to beat; (campana, timbre) to ring; **—se la nariz / los mocos** to blow one's nose; **suena que** it is rumored that; M sonar

sonda F (de médico) catheter; (cohete) probe; **— de alimentación** feeding tube; **tirar una —** to sound

sondear VT (medir la oportunidad) to sound, to

fathom; (investigar la opinión) to sound out
sondeo M survey
soneto M sonnet
sonido M sound
sonoridad F (de la voz) sonority; (de un instrumento) tone; (de un sonido lingüístico) voicing
sonoro ADJ sonorous
sonreír[10] VI to smile
sonriente ADJ smiling
sonrisa F smile
sonrojarse VI to blush
sonrojo M blush, flush
sonrosado ADJ rosy
sonsacar[30] VT to extract
soñador -ora MF dreamer
soñar[5] VI/VT to dream; — **con** to dream of; — **despierto** to daydream; — **que** to dream that; **ni** — *fam* fat chance
soñoliento ADJ sleepy
sopa F (líquido) soup; (pan mojado) sop; **estar hecho una** — to be sopping wet; — **crema** cream soup
sopapo M smack
sopera F soup tureen
sopesar VT to weigh
sopetón LOC ADV **de** — all of a sudden
soplador -ora MF blower
soplar VI/VT (el viento) to blow; (la sopa) to blow on; (en un examen) to whisper the answers
soplete M blowtorch
soplo M breath, puff; **en un** — in a jiffy; — **cardíaco** heart murmur
soplón -ona MF informer, snitch, stool pigeon
sopor M lethargy
soportar VT (un peso) to support, to bear; (una molestia, a una persona) to stand, to bear; (un programa de computadora) to support
soporte M (de un peso, de un programa) support; (de una bicicleta) kickstand; — **técnico** technical support
soprano M (voz) soprano; F (cantante) soprano
sorber VI/VT to sip; —**se los mocos** to sniffle
sorbete M sherbet
sorbo M sip; **de un** — in one gulp
sordera F deafness
sórdido ADJ sordid, tawdry, sleazy
sordina F mute
sordo -da ADJ (persona) deaf; (dolor) dull; (sonido) dull, muffled; **hacer oídos** —**s** to turn a deaf ear; MF deaf person; **hacerse el** — to pretend not to hear
sordomudo -da ADJ deaf and dumb; MF deaf-mute
sorna F irony
sorprendente ADJ surprising, startling
sorprendentemente ADV surprisingly
sorprender VT to surprise; —**se** to be surprised
sorpresa F surprise; — **de cumpleaños** party

favor; **para mí** — to my surprise; **pillar por** — to catch by surprise
sortear VT (elegir al azar) to draw lots, to raffle; (esquivar) to dodge
sorteo M drawing, raffle
sortija F (anillo) ring; (de pelo) ringlet
sortilegio M spell, charm
SOS M SOS
sosa F soda
sosegado ADJ composed, sedate
sosegar[41] VT to calm, to quiet; —**se** to quiet down, to compose oneself
sosiego M quiet, calm
soslayo LOC ADV **de** — oblique, slanting; **mirar de** — to look out of the corner of one's eye
soso ADJ (comida) tasteless, insipid; (persona) dull
sospecha F suspicion
sospechar VT to suspect
sospechoso -sa ADJ suspicious; MF suspect
sostén M (apoyo, sustento) support, prop; (persona que sostiene) supporter, provider; (prenda) brassiere; — **de la familia** breadwinner
sostendrá, sostendría *ver* sostener
sostener[58] VT (una nota musical) to hold, to sustain; (una familia) to support; (un peso) to support, to hold; (una opinión) to claim, to uphold
sostenga, sostengo *ver* sostener
sostenible ADJ sustainable
sostenido ADJ sustained; M sharp
sostiene, sostienes, sostuve, sostuviera, sostuviese *ver* sostener
sota F jack, knave
sótano M cellar, basement
soto M thicket
soy *ver* ser
soya F (semilla) soybean; (planta) soy
squash M squash
Sr. M Mr.
Sra. F (casada) Mrs.; (sin indicación de estado civil) Ms.
S.R.C. [se ruega contestar] LOC RSVP
status M status
stop M stop sign
su ADJ POS (de él) his; (de ella) her; (de usted, ustedes) your; (de ellos, ellas) their
suave ADJ (pelo, piel) soft; (tiempo, droga) mild; (brisa, persona, animal) gentle; (coñac) smooth; **hablan** — they speak gently
suavemente ADV lightly, gently
suavidad F (de pelo, piel) softness; (de coñac) smoothness; (de tiempo, droga) mildness; (de brisa, persona, animal) gentleness
suavizante M fabric softener
suavizar[47] VT to soften
suazi ADJ & MF Swazi
Suazilandia F Swaziland

subalterno -na ADJ & MF subordinate
subarrendar VI/VT to sublet
subasta F auction
subastador -ora MF auctioneer
subastar VT to sell at auction, to auction
subcomité M subcommittee
subconsciente ADJ subconscious
subcontratar VT to subcontract, to contract out, to farm out
subdesarrollado ADJ underdeveloped
súbdito -ta MF subject
subdividir VT subdivide
subdivisión F subdivision
subempleado ADJ underemployed
subestimar VT to underestimate
subgerente MF assistant manager
subida F (de precios, de río) rise; (de montaña) climb; (de drogas) high; (cuesta) slope; **—s y bajadas** ups and downs
subido ADJ (color) bright; **— de tono** risqué
subíndice M subscript
subir VI (los precios) to rise, to go up; (la marea) to surge; (a un tren) to board; (a un autobús, coche) to get into; VT (algo del sótano) to bring up; (una montaña) to climb; (precios) to raise; **— a la red** to upload; **—se** to ride up; **el vino se me sube a la cabeza** wine goes to my head; M **subibaja** seesaw
súbitamente ADV suddenly
súbito ADJ sudden
subjetividad F subjectivity
subjetivo ADJ subjective
subjuntivo ADJ & M subjunctive
sublevación F revolt
sublevar VT (instigar) to incite to rebellion; (indignar) to infuriate; **—se** to revolt
sublime ADJ sublime
submarino ADJ underwater; M submarine
suboficial M noncommissioned officer
subordinado -da ADJ & MF subordinate
subordinar VT to subordinate
subproducto M by-product
subproletariado M underclass
subrayado ADJ underlined; M underscore, underlining
subrayar VT (con una línea) to underline, to underscore; (enfatizar) to emphasize, to underscore
subrepticio ADJ surreptitious
subrutina F subroutine
subsanar VT (una deficiencia) to remedy; (un error) to correct
subsecretario -ia MF undersecretary; **— de justicia** solicitor general
subsidiar VT to subsidize
subsidiario ADJ subsidiary
subsidio M subsidy
subsiguiente ADJ subsequent
subsistencia F survival

subsistir VI to subsist, to survive
subteniente MF second lieutenant
subterfugio M subterfuge
subterráneo ADJ subterranean, underground; M subway
subtítulo M (de un capítulo, película) subtitle; (pie de foto) caption
subtotal M subtotal
suburbano -na ADJ of shantytowns; MF shantytown resident
suburbio M shantytown
subvaluar[26] VT to underestimate
subvención F subsidy
subvencionar VT to subsidize
subversivo ADJ subversive
subyacente ADJ underlying
subyacer[37] VI to underlie
subyugar[40] VT (dominar) to subjugate; (hechizar) to charm
succión F suction
sucedáneo -a ADJ & MF substitute
suceder VI to happen, to occur; **— al trono** to succeed to the throne; VT to succeed
sucesión F (herencia, secuencia) succession; (heredero) descendant
sucesivo ADJ successive; **en lo —** in the future
suceso M (evento) event, occurrence; (incidente) incident
sucesor -ora MF successor
suciedad F (porquería) dirt, filth; (cualidad de sucio) filthiness
sucinto ADJ concise
sucio ADJ (baño, ropa) dirty, filthy; (trabajo, chiste) dirty; (conciencia) guilty; **blanco —** off-white; **este traje es —** this suit gets dirty easily
sucumbir VI to succumb
sucursal F branch, subsidiary
sudadera F sweatshirt
sudado ADJ sweaty
Sudáfrica F South Africa
sudafricano -na ADJ & MF South African
Sudamérica F South America
sudamericano -na ADJ & MF South American
Sudán M Sudan
sudanés -esa ADJ & MF Sudanese
sudar VT to sweat; **— la gota gorda** to sweat blood
sudeste ADJ southeast, southeastern; M southeast
sudoeste ADJ southwest, southwestern; M southwest
sudor M sweat
sudoración F sweating
sudoroso ADJ sweaty
Suecia F Sweden
sueco -ca ADJ Swedish; M (lengua) Swedish; MF Swede; **hacerse el —** to pretend not to understand

suegro -a M father-in-law; F mother-in-law

suela F (de zapato) sole; (pez) flounder

suela, suele ver soler

sueldo M salary

suelo M (tierra) soil, ground; (piso) floor; **arrastrar por el —** to drag; **por los —s** at rock-bottom

suelta, suelte ver soltar

suelto ADJ (no atado) loose, unattached; (flojo) loose; (libre) free; M loose change

suena, suene ver sonar

sueña, sueñe ver soñar

sueño M (acto de dormir) sleep; (acto de soñar) dream; (ganas de dormir) sleepiness; **en —s** dreaming; **conciliar el —** to get to sleep; **tener —** to be sleepy; **ni en —[s]** never; **perder el —** to lose sleep; **— profundo** sound sleep; **estar en el séptimo —** to be deeply asleep

suero M serum; **— de leche** buttermilk; **— fisiológico** saline solution

suerte F (destino) fate; (fortuna) luck; (clase) kind; **de —** in luck; **dejar a su —** to leave to his own devices; **echar —s** to cast lots; **mala —** (desgracia) bad luck; (lo siento) too bad; **tener —** to be lucky; **tentar a la —** to court danger; **tocarle algo en — a alguien** to be one's lot

suertudo -da ADJ lucky; MF lucky devil

suéter M sweater

suficiencia F adequacy; **¡tiene una —!** she's so arrogant!

suficiente ADJ (adecuado) sufficient, adequate; (arrogante) smug; M (calificación mínima) lowest passing grade; PRON enough; **ser —** to be enough; **tiempo más que —** ample time

sufijo M suffix

sufragar[40] VT to defray; **— los gastos** to meet the expenses

sufragio M suffrage

sufrido ADJ (madre) long-suffering; (tela) durable

sufrimiento M suffering

sufrir VI/VT (pasar apremios) to suffer; VT (soportar) to stand; (una lesión) to sustain; (un cambio) to undergo; (una pena) to grieve; **— de** to suffer from; **— de los pies** to have foot pains

sugerencia F suggestion

sugerir[8] VT to suggest

sugestión F suggestion

sugiere, sugirió, sugiriendo, sugiriera, sugiriese ver sugerir

suicida MF suicide [victim]

suicidarse VI to commit suicide

suicidio M suicide

suite F suite

Suiza F Switzerland

suizo -za ADJ & MF Swiss; M sweet roll

sujeción LOC ADV **con — a** subject to

sujetar VT (fijar) to attach; (unir) to hold; (someter) to subdue, to hold down; **—se** to hold on; M SG **sujetalibros** bookend; M SG **sujetapapeles** paper clip

sujeto ADJ held by; **— a** subject to; M (de oración, de experimento) subject; (individuo) individual

sulfato M sulfate

sulfurarse VI to hit the roof

sulfúrico ADJ sulfuric

sulfuro M sulfide

suma F (resultado aritmético) sum; (operación aritmética) addition; (cantidad) amount, sum; **en — in short**

sumadora F adding machine

sumamente ADV extremely

sumar VT to add, to add up; **—se a** to join

sumario M brief; ADJ summary

sumergible ADJ waterproof

sumergir[46] VT to submerge, to dip; **—se** to dive; **—se en** to immerse oneself in

sumidero M (socavón) sinkhole; (desagüe) drain

suministrar VT to furnish, to supply with

suministro M provision, supply; **— de energía** power supply; **—s** supplies, provisions

sumir VT to immerse

sumisión F submission

sumiso ADJ submissive

súmmum M ultimate, acme; **el — de la moda** the cat's meow

sumo ADJ utmost, paramount; **a lo —** at the most

suntuoso ADJ sumptuous, luxurious

supe, supiera, supiese ver saber

súper ADJ & ADV super; F (gasolina) high-octane gasoline; M (supermercado) supermarket

superabundancia F overabundance, glut

superación F (de expectativas) surpassing; (de límites) exceeding; (de un récord) breaking; (de una dificultad) overcoming

superar VT (las expectativas) to surpass; (un límite) to exceed; (una dificultad) to overcome, to surmount; (una prueba) to pass; (a un rival) to outdo; **—se** to improve oneself

superávit M surplus

supercomputadora F supercomputer

superdirecta F overdrive

superdotado ADJ gifted

superego M superego

superestrella F superstar

superficial ADJ (conocimiento, herida, persona) superficial; (persona) shallow

superficialidad F shallowness

superficie F (parte exterior) surface; (de una figura geométrica) area

superfluo ADJ superfluous

superíndice M superscript

superintendente MF superintendent
superior ADJ (mejor) superior; (más alto) higher; (más grande, intenso) greater; MF superior
superioridad F superiority
superlativo ADJ & M superlative
supermercado M supermarket
superordenador M supercomputer
superponer[56,74] VT to superimpose
superpotencia F superpower
superproducción F overproduction
supersónico ADJ supersonic
superstición F superstition
supersticioso ADJ superstitious
supervisar VT to supervise
supervisión F supervision
supervisor -ora MF supervisor
supervivencia F survival; **la — del más apto** the survival of the fittest
superviviente ADJ surviving; MF survivor
superyó M superego
supino ADJ supine
suplantar VT to supplant
suplementar VT to supplement
suplementario ADJ supplemental
suplemento M supplement
suplente ADJ & MF substitute
súplica F entreaty, plea
suplicar[30] VT to plead, to beseech
suplicio M ordeal
suplir VT (sustituir) to substitute for; (compensar) to make up for
supondrá, supondría ver suponer
suponer[56,74] VT (dar por sentado) to suppose, to presume, to surmise; (implicar) to involve; **es de — que ya esté preparado** presumably he's already prepared
suponga, supongo ver suponer
suposición F supposition, surmise
supositorio M suppository
supremacía F supremacy
supremo ADJ supreme
supresión F (de una idea) suppression; (de una palabra) deletion
suprimir VT (una idea) to suppress; (la esclavitud) to abolish; (una palabra) to delete
supuestamente ADV supposedly, allegedly
supuesto ADJ (hipotético) supposed; (alegado) alleged, ostensible; **dar por —** to assume; **por —** of course; M supposition, assumption
supuesto ver suponer
supuración F discharge
supurante ADJ festering, running
supurar VI to fester, to discharge
supuse, supusiera, supusiese ver suponer
sur ADJ & M south; **hacia el —** southward; **rumbo al —** southward
surcar[30] VT to plow
surco M (en la tierra) furrow; (en un camino) rut;

(en un disco) groove; (en el rostro) wrinkle
surcoreano -na ADJ & MF South Korean
sureño -ña ADJ southern; MF southerner
sureste ADJ southeast, southeastern; M southeast
surfear VI/VT to surf (también en el internet)
surfing M surfing; **hacer —** to surf
surgimiento M rise
surgir[46] VI (situación) to arise; (manantial) to rise; (problema) to emerge, to crop up
Surinam M Surinam, Suriname
surinamés -esa ADJ & MF Surinamer
surmenage M burnout
suroeste ADJ southwest, southwestern; M southwest
surrealismo M surrealism
surrealista ADJ surreal, surrealistic; MF surrealist
surtido M stock, assortment; ADJ assorted
surtidor M (bomba) pump; (chorro, pieza de carburador) jet
surtir VT to provide; **— efecto** to produce the desired effect; **— un pedido** to fill an order
susceptible ADJ susceptible
suscitar VT to stir up
suscribir[74] VT (una opinión) to subscribe to, to endorse; (un seguro) to underwrite; **—se a** to subscribe to
suscripción F subscription
suscriptor -ora F (de un revista) subscriber; (en el mercado de acciones) underwriter
susodicho ADJ above-mentioned
suspender VT (colgar) to suspend, to hang; (interrumpir) to suspend, to stop; (cancelar) to cancel; (castigar) to suspend; VI/VT (no aprobar) to fail, to flunk
suspense M suspense
suspensión F suspension
suspenso ADJ hanging; **quedarse —** to freeze; M (en un examen) failure; (en una película) suspense; **en —** in suspense
suspensorio M jock [strap]
suspicaz ADJ suspicious
suspirar VT to sigh; **— por** to yearn for
suspiro M sigh
sustancia F substance; **— peligrosa** hazardous substance
sustancial ADJ substantial
sustancioso ADJ substantial
sustantivo M noun; ADJ substantive
sustentable ADJ sustainable
sustentar VT to sustain
sustento M (alimento) sustenance; (apoyo) support; **ganarse el —** to earn a living
sustitución F substitution; **— protésica de la cadera** hip replacement
sustituible ADJ replaceable
sustituir[19] VI/VT to substitute for, to replace; **Juan sustituyó a María** John substituted

for Mary; **sustituí la leche por agua** I
replaced the milk with water
sustituto -ta MF substitute
sustituya, sustituye, sustituyendo,
sustituyera, sustituyese *ver* sustituir
susto M scare, fright
sustracción F subtraction
sustraer[59] VT to take away; **—se a** to avoid
susurrar VI/VT (una persona, el viento) to
whisper; (agua) to murmur, to ripple; (hojas)
to rustle
susurro M (de una persona, del viento) whisper;
(del agua) murmur; (de las hojas) rustle
sutil ADJ subtle
sutileza F (delicadeza) subtlety; (fineza excesiva)
nicety, quibble
sutilizar[47] VT to quibble over
sutura F suture
suyo ADJ & PRON POS (de él) his; (de ella) her; (de
usted, de ustedes) your; (de ellos, de ellas)
their; PRON (de él) his; (de ella) hers; (de
usted, de ustedes) yours; (de ellos, de ellas)
theirs; **salirse con la suya** to get one's own
way; **hacer de las suyas** to be up to one's
tricks; **los —s** his/her/your/their family
swing M swing

Tt

tabaco M tobacco
tábano M horsefly
tabaquismo M smoking
taberna F tavern, saloon
tabernero -ra MF bartender
tabicar[30] VT to partition
tabique M partition
tabla F (madera) board, plank; (teatro) stage;
(pliegue) pleat; (gráfica) table, chart; **— de**
surf surfboard; **— de planchar** ironing
board; **—s** (escenario) stage; **—s de la ley**
the tables of the law; **—s de multiplicar**
multiplication tables; **— periódica** periodic
table; **— de contenidos** table of contents; **—**
de cortar cutting board; **hacer —s** to tie
tablado M stage
tablero M (para juegos de mesa) board; (de
instrumentos) panel, instrument panel; (de
coche) dashboard; (pizarra) blackboard; (para
noticias) bulletin board; **— de mando**
control panel
tableta F (de aspirina) tablet; (de chocolate) bar
tablilla F (de arcilla) tablet; (de cama) slat; (para
fracturas) splint
tabloide M tabloid
tablón M plank

tabú M taboo
tabulador M tab
tabular VT (en una tabla, planilla) to tabulate, to
chart; (en la computadora) to tab
taburete M stool, footstool
TAC [tomografía axial computarizada] F
CAT scan
tacañería F stinginess, tightness
tacaño -ña ADJ stingy, miserly; MF miser,
penny-pincher
tacha F (mancha visible) blemish; (al honor) blot
tachado M strikethrough
tachar VT (borrar) to cross out, to delete;
(acusar) to accuse of
tachón M crossing out
tachonar VT to stud
tachuela F tack, thumbtack
tácito ADJ tacit
taciturno ADJ taciturn
taco M (de artillería) wad; (palo de billar) billiard
cue; (comida ligera) snack; (palabrota) swear
word; (comida) *Méx* taco; **—s** (en el zapato)
cleats; **soltar —s** *Esp* to swear
tacómetro M tachometer
tacón M heel
taconear VI to click one's heels
taconeo M clicking
táctica F tactic
táctil ADJ tactile
tacto M (acción de tocar) touch; (sentido) sense
of touch; (diplomacia) tact; **con mucho —**
gently
TAE [tasa anual equivalente] F APR
tahúr -ura MF gambler
tailandés -esa ADJ & MF Thai, Thailander
Tailandia F Thailand
taimado ADJ sly, devious
Taiwán M Taiwan
taiwanés -esa ADJ & MF Taiwanese
tajada F (de pan, jamón) slice; (de carne) slab;
sacar — to take one's cut
tajante ADJ (inequívoco) unequivocal; (cortante)
sharp
tajar VT to slice
tajear VI/VT to slash
tajo M (corte) slash, hack; (cañón) gorge;
(separación) gap
tal ADJ such; **— cual** just so; **— vez** perhaps; **un**
— García a certain García; **a — grado** to
such an extent; **de — palo — astilla** a chip
off the old block; **en — caso** in such a case;
CONJ **— como** like, just as; **con — [de] que**
provided that; ADV **¿qué —?** how is it going?
PRON **y —** and so on; **como si —** as if nothing
had happened
taladrar VT to bore, to drill
taladro M drill
talante M temperament
talar VT (un árbol) to chop down; (un bosque) to

lumber

talco M talcum

talento M talent

talentoso ADJ talented, gifted

talismán M charm

talla F (altura) height; (moral, intelectual) stature; (de ropa) size; (de madera) carving

tallado M carving

tallar VT (piedra) to carve; (madera) to whittle, to carve; (naipes) to deal

tallarín M noodle

talle M (cintura) waist, waistline; **tiene buen —** she has a good figure; **corto de —** short-waisted

taller M (para trabajo manual, enseñanza artística, congresos) workshop; (de artista plástico) studio; (de mecánico) garage, shop

tallo M stalk, stem

talón M (de pie, calcetín) heel; (de cheque) stub; **— de Aquiles** Achilles' heel; **girar sobre los talones** to turn on one's heels; **pisarle los talones a alguien** to be hot on someone's heels

talonario M checkbook

talonear VI to walk briskly

tamal M tamale

tamaño M size; **de — mediano** medium-sized; **de — natural** life-sized; ADJ such a big, so big a; **tamaña injusticia** such a big injustice

tambalearse VI (un borracho) to stagger; (un boxeador) to reel; (un viejo) to dodder; (un objeto) to wobble

tambaleo M stagger

también ADV also, too, as well; **este — me gusta** I like this one too, I like this one as well, I also like this one

tambor M (instrumento musical, pieza de máquina) drum; (músico) drummer; (cilindro) cylinder; **a — batiente** with fanfare

tamborilear VI to drum, to tap

tamborilero -ra MF drummer

tamiz M sieve

tamizar[47] VT to sift

tampoco CONJ either; **no lo hizo —** he did not do it either; **ni yo —** me either/neither

tampón M tampon

tan ADV **es — rica** she is so rich; **— alto como Juan** as tall as Juan; **— pronto como** as soon as; **es — idiota** he's such an idiot; **vecinos — simpáticos** such nice neighbors

tanda F (de personas) group; (de galletas) batch; (de ejercicios) set

tándem M tandem

tanga F thong

tangente ADJ & F tangent; **salirse por la —** (irse de tema) to go off on a tangent; (evadir) to beat around the bush

tangerina F tangerine

tangible ADJ tangible

tango M tango

tanque M tank

tantán M African drum

tantear VT (calcular) to estimate roughly; (averiguar) to sound out, to feel out; (apuntar) to score; (palpar) to grope

tanteo M (cálculo) estimate; (número de tantos) score; **al —** approximately

tanto ADJ, PRON, & ADV **lloró — que se le enrojecieron los ojos** he cried so much his eyes got red; **yo tengo — como tú** I have as much as you do; **me quiere —** he loves me so; **no te quiero —** I don't love you that much; **a cada —s pasos** every so many steps; **cuarenta y —s** forty-odd; **a — el kilo** at so much per kilo; **el — por ciento** at such and such a percentage; **estar al —** to be in the know; **no es para —** it's not such a big deal; **— da** it's all the same; **— como** as much as; **— en la ciudad como en el campo** both in the city and in the country; **entre/mientras —** meanwhile; **mantenerse al —** to stay informed; **otros —s** just so many more; **por lo —** therefore; **a las tantas** until late at night; M (en los deportes) point

Tanzania F Tanzania

tanzano -na ADJ & MF Tanzanian

tañer[15] VT *lit* (una guitarra) to play; VI (una campana) to ring, to toll

tañido M (de guitarra) twang; (de campanas) toll

tapa F (de botella) cap; (de libro) cover; (de coche) hood; (de olla, bote) lid, top; *Esp* (comida) bar snack

tapadera F (de recipiente) lid; (de un fraude) cover

tapado ADJ stuffy

tapar VT (una olla) to cover; (una salida) to block; (un caño) to plug up, to stop up; (encubrir) to cover up for; M SG **tapacubos** hubcap; M SG **tapajuntas** flashing; M SG **taparrabos** loincloth

tapete M runner

tapia F garden wall

tapiar VT to board up

tapicería F (para paredes) tapestry; (para muebles) upholstery; (tienda de textiles de decoración) tapestry shop; (arte) tapestry making; (tienda de textiles para muebles) upholstery shop

tapioca F tapioca

tapir M tapir

tapiz M (para pared) tapestry, wall hanging; (para muebles) upholstery

tapizar[47] VT to upholster

tapón M (de botella) stopper; (de lavabo) plug; (de corcho) cork; (en baloncesto) block; **— de oído** earplug; **tapones** (en el zapato de fútbol) cleats

taponar VT (baloncesto) to block
taponazo M pop of a cork
taquigrafía F shorthand
taquígrafo -fa MF stenographer
taquilla F ticket office, box office
tarambana MF knucklehead
tarántula F tarantula
tararear VI/VT to hum
tarareo M hum, humming
tarascada F (mordedura) snap, bite; (réplica) rude answer
tardanza F lateness
tardar VI to take time; **¿cuánto tarda el trámite de divorcio?** how long does it take to get divorced? **—se** to take a long time; **tu padre se tarda** your father is taking a long time; **a más —** at the latest
tarde F (después del almuerzo) afternoon; (hacia el anochecer) evening; **buenas —s** good afternoon; ADV late; **ya es —** it is late; **— o temprano** sooner o later; **más —** later on; **llegar —** to be late
tardío ADJ late
tardo ADJ *lit* slow
tarea F (trabajo) task, chore; (escolar) homework
tarifa F (impuesto) tariff; (lista de precios) list of prices; (de transporte) fare; (precio estipulado) rate
tarima F platform
tarjeta F card (también dispositivo de computadora); **— amarilla** yellow card; **— bancaria** bank card; **— comercial** business card; **— de circuito integrado** smart card; **— de sonido** sound card; **— gráfica** graphics card; **— inteligente** smart card; **— postal** postcard; **— de cobro automático / — de débito** debit card; **— de crédito** credit card; **— de Navidad** Christmas card; **— roja** red card; **marcar —** to punch in
tarro M jar
tarta F tart, pie
tartajear VI to stutter
tartamudear VI to stutter, to stammer
tartamudeo M stammer, stutter
tartamudez F stuttering
tartamudo -da MF stutterer, stammerer; ADJ stuttering, stammering
tártaro M tartar
tartera F round baking pan
tarugo M (trozo de madera) piece of wood; (tonto) blockhead
tasa F (índice) rate; (impuesto) tax; **— de desempleo** unemployment rate; **— de interés** interest rate; **— de mortalidad** death rate; **— de natalidad** birth rate; **— de ocupación** occupancy rate; **— de paro** unemployment rate; **— prima** prime rate
tasación F valuation, appraisal
tasajo M jerky

tasar VT to appraise, to assess
tatarabuelo -la M great-great-grandfather; F great-great-grandmother
tataranieto -ta M great-great-grandson; F great-great-granddaughter
tatuaje M tattoo
tatuar[26] VT to tattoo
tauromaquia F bullfighting
taxi M taxi, taxicab
taxidermia F taxidermy
taxista MF taxi driver, cab driver
taxonomía F taxonomy
Tayikistán M Tajikistan
tayiko -ka ADJ & MF Tajik
taza F (de té, café) cup; (del inodoro) bowl
tazón M (para beber) mug; (para comer) bowl
té M (bebida) tea; (fiesta) tea party
te PRON PERS you; **yo — amo** I love you; **— digo mañana** I'll tell you tomorrow; **no — mires en el espejo** don't look at yourself in the mirror
teatral ADJ theatrical
teatro M theater; **— de títeres** puppet show; **no hagas —** don't make such a production
techado M (techo) roof; (acción de techar) roofing
techar VT to roof
techo M (exterior) roof; (interior) ceiling; **— de cristal** glass ceiling
techumbre F roof
tecla F key; **— de alt** alt key; **— de alternativa gráfica** alt gr key; **— de borrado** delete key; **— de cambio** shift key; **— de comando** command key; **— de control** control key; **— de escape** escape key; **— de fin** end key; **— de función** function key; **— de mayúsculas** shift key; **— de ordenación** sort key; **— de reinicio** reset key; **— de retorno** return key; **— de retroceso** backspace key, return key; **— de tabulación** tab key; **— fin** end key; **dar uno en la —** to hit the nail on the head
teclado M keyboard; **— numérico** keypad
teclear VT (pulsar las teclas) to key in, to type; (hacer ruido) to click
tecleo M keying in, clicking
técnica F (método) technique; (tecnología) technology
técnico -ca ADJ technical; MF (en mecánica) technician; (de fútbol) coach
tecnología F technology; **— de punta** cutting-edge technology
tecnológico ADJ technological
tectónica F tectonics
tedio M boredom
tedioso ADJ tedious
tee M tee
teja F (de cerámica) tile; (de madera u otros materiales) shingle

tejado M roof

tejar M tile factory; VT to cover with tiles

tejedor-ora MF weaver

tejer VI/VT (cesta, tela) to weave; (suéter) to knit; M **tejemaneje** (fraude) hanky-panky; (actividad) goings-on

tejido M (tela) textile, fabric; (de células) tissue; (acción de hilar) weaving; (acción y efecto de tejer) knitting

tejo M disk

tejón M badger

tela F (paño) cloth, fabric; (lienzo para pintar) canvas; (de araña) web; (dinero) money; — **adhesiva** adhesive tape; — **de cebolla** onion skin; **en** — hardbound; **poner en** — **de juicio** to call into question

telar M loom

telaraña F cobweb, spider's web

tele F TV

telebobo-ba MF couch potato

telecomunicación F telecommunication

teleconferencia F teleconference

teledifusión F telecast

teledirección F remote guidance

teleférico M cable car

telefonazo M buzz, ring

telefonear VI/VT to telephone, to phone

telefónico ADJ **llamada telefónica** telephone call

telefonista MF telephone operator

teléfono M (aparato) telephone, phone; (número) telephone number

telegrafiar[28] VI/VT to telegraph, to wire

telegráfico ADJ telegraphic

telégrafo M telegraph

telegrama M telegram

telemarketing M telemarketing

telemercadeo M telemarketing

telémetro M range finder

telenovela F soap opera

teleobjetivo M zoom lens

telepatía F telepathy

telescopio M telescope

telespectador-ora MF viewer

telesquí M ski lift

teletipo M Teletype™

teletrabajo M telecommuting

televidente MF television viewer

televisar VT to televise

televisión F television; — **de alta definición** high-definition television

televisivo ADJ (apto para la televisión) televisable; (relativo a la televisión) television

televisor M television set; — **a/en color** color television

telón M theater curtain; — **de acero** iron curtain

tema M (de una obra literaria, musical) theme; (de conversación) topic, subject; (de un CD) song, track

temario M agenda

temático ADJ thematic

temblar[1] VI (la mano, la tierra) to tremble; (la voz) to shake, to quaver; (de frío) to shiver; (de miedo) to shudder; (la luz) to flicker

temblequear VI to dodder

temblón ADJ trembling

temblor M (acción de temblar) trembling; (de tierra) tremor; (de una llama) flicker; (de la voz) quaver; (de frío) shiver; (de miedo) shudder; — **de tierra** earthquake

tembloroso ADJ (mano) shaky; (llama) flickering; (voz) quavering; (de miedo) shuddering; (de frío) shivering

temer VI/VT to fear, to be afraid [of]; — **por** to fear for; **mucho me temo que** I fear that

temerario ADJ rash, reckless

temeridad F temerity, recklessness

temeroso ADJ fearful

temible ADJ dreadful, dread

temor M fear

témpano M (bloque de hielo) block of ice; (persona fría) cold fish

temperamento M temperament, disposition

temperancia F temperance

temperatura F temperature

tempestad F tempest, storm; **una** — **en un vaso de agua** a tempest in a teapot

tempestuoso ADJ tempestuous, stormy

templado ADJ (clima) moderate, temperate; (ánimo) serene; (actitud) moderate

templanza F temperance

templar VT (moderar, dar fuerza) to temper; (calentar) to warm up; (una guitarra) to tune

temple M (dureza) temper; (coraje) mettle; **de mal** — in a bad mood

templo M temple

temporada F season (también de fútbol); — **baja** off-season; — **de caza** hunting season

temporal ADJ (relativo al tiempo) temporal; (secular) worldly; (no permanente) temporary; M storm; **capear el** — to weather the storm

tempranero-ra ADJ early rising; MF early riser

temprano ADJ & ADV early

tenacidad F tenacity

tenaz ADJ tenacious

tenazas F PL (de cangrejo) pincers; (de mecánico) pliers; (de dentista) forceps; (para hielo) tongs

tendedero M clothesline

tendencia F tendency; (orientación) orientation; (de la moda) trend; **de** — **mayoritaria** mainstream; — **a la baja** downturn; — **al alza** upturn, upward trend

tender[2] VT (un mantel) to spread out; (la ropa) to hang out; (la mano) to extend; (un cable) to lay; (una trampa) to set; VI — **a** to tend to;

—**se** to stretch out

tendero -ra MF (de una tienda) storekeeper; (de una tienda de comestibles) grocer

tendido M (de cables) laying; (de ropa mojada) hanging out; (conjunto de cables) cables

tendinitis F tendonitis

tendón M tendon, sinew; — **de Aquiles** Achilles' tendon

tendrá, tendría ver tener

tenebroso ADJ (oscuro) dark; (sombrío) gloomy

tenedor -ora M table fork; MF holder, payee; — **de libros** bookkeeper

teneduría F — **de libros** bookkeeping

tener[58] VT to have; **tiene el pelo castaño** she has brown hair, her hair is brown; — **en cuenta** to bear in mind; — **en mucho** to esteem highly; — **por** to consider; — **que** to have to; — **ganas** to feel like; **tengo escrita la carta** I have the letter written; — **éxito** to be successful; — **miedo** to be afraid; — **sueño** to be sleepy; — **frío** to be cold; — **hambre** to be hungry; **tiene cinco años** she is five years old; —**se** to stand straight; **no** — **más remedio** to have no other choice; — **que ver con** to have to do with

tenería F tannery

tenga, tengo ver tener

tenia F tapeworm

teniente MF lieutenant

tenis M (juego) tennis; M PL (zapatos) sneakers, tennis shoes

tenista MF tennis player

tenor M (voz, estilo) tenor; (tono) tone, tenor; ADJ **saxofón** — tenor saxophone

tensión F tension

tenso ADJ (nervioso) tense; (extendido) taut

tentación F temptation

tentáculo M tentacle

tentador ADJ tempting

tentar[1] VT to tempt; — **a la suerte** to court danger; — **por todos los medios** to try everything

tentativa F attempt, try

tentativo ADJ tentative

tentempié M snack

tenue ADJ (tela) delicate; (luz) tenuous, dim, faint; (sonido) feeble

tenuidad F faintness, softness

teñir[11] VT (de color) to dye; (de emoción) to tinge

teología F theology

teológico ADJ theological

teólogo -ga MF theologian

teoría F theory; **en** — in theory

teórico ADJ theoretical

tepe M sod

tequila M tequila

terabyte M terabyte

terapeuta MF therapist

terapéutico ADJ therapeutic

terapia F (médica) therapy; (psicológica, marital) counseling; — **de electroshock** shock therapy; — **electroconvulsiva** shock therapy; — **hormonal** hormone therapy; — **ocupacional** occupational therapy

tercero ADJ third; **tercera base** third base; **tercera persona** third person; **tercera edad** old age; **tercer mundo** third world; M (en un contrato) third party; (en béisbol) third baseman

terciar VI/VT to arbitrate

tercio M third

terciopelo M velvet

terco ADJ obstinate, stubborn

tergiversación F distortion, misrepresentation

tergiversar VT (palabras) to distort; (datos) to skew

termal ADJ thermal

térmico ADJ heat, thermal

terminación F (de un proyecto) termination, completion; (de una palabra, cuento) ending; (de un piso) finish

terminal ADJ terminal; MF (de aeropuerto, de omnibus) terminal; M (de computadora, eléctrica) terminal

terminante ADJ (negativa) flat; (prohibición) absolute

terminar VI/VT (completar) to finish, to conclude; VI (tener como final) to end; — **por** to end up; **no termino de entender** I still can't understand; **terminó con las ratas** he got rid of the rats; **sin** — unfinished

término M (final) end; (período de tiempo) period; (límite) boundary; (palabra) term; — **medio** medium; **a** — (trabajo) with a deadline; (embarazo) full-term; **en primer** — first of all; **en** —**s generales** in general terms; **en último** — as a last resort; **estar en buenos** —**s** to be on good terms; **por** — **medio** on average; **poner** — to end

terminología F terminology

termita F termite

termo M thermos

termodinámico ADJ thermodynamic

termómetro M thermometer

termonuclear ADJ thermonuclear

termostato M thermostat

ternero -ra MF (animal) calf; F (carne) veal

terneza F tenderness

terno M three-piece suit

ternura F tenderness

terquedad F obstinacy, stubbornness

terraplén M embankment

terrateniente MF landholder

terraza F (terreno) terrace; (de casa) veranda; (delante de un bar) deck; (azotea) flat roof

terremoto M earthquake

terrenal ADJ earthly

terreno M (campo) piece of land, tract of land;

(lote) lot; (formación geológica) terrain; (campo científico) field; **— de juego parejo** level playing field; **ganarle — a alguien** to gain on someone; **perder —** to lose ground; **tantear el —** to put out feelers; **todo —** with four-wheel drive

terrestre ADJ terrestrial, earthly

terrible ADJ terrible, awful

terrier M terrier

territorio M territory

terrón M (de tierra) clod; (de azúcar) lump

terror M terror, dread

terrorismo M terrorism

terrorista ADJ & MF terrorist

terso ADJ (liso) smooth; (pulido) polished

tersura F smoothness

tertulia F social gathering

tesis F thesis; **— doctoral** dissertation

tesón M determination

tesonero ADJ determined

tesorería F treasury

tesorero-ra MF treasurer

tesoro M (riqueza) treasure; (tesorería) treasury

test M test

testaferro M straw man

testamentaria F (gestiones) execution; (bienes) estate

testamento M testament, will

testarudez F stubbornness

testarudo ADJ stubborn, headstrong

testículo M testicle

testificar[30] VI to testify

testigo MF witness; **— de cargo** witness for the prosecution; **— ocular** eyewitness; M proof

testimoniar VI to give testimony

testimonio M testimony, proof, evidence; **levantar falso —** to bear false witness; **en — de su amor** as a testament to his love

testosterona F testosterone

teta F teat

tétanos M SG tetanus, lockjaw

tetera F teapot, teakettle

tetilla F nipple

tetina F nipple

tetraciclina F tetracycline

tetrapléjico-ca ADJ & MF quadriplegic

tétrico ADJ gloomy

teutónico ADJ Teutonic

textear VT to text

textil ADJ & M textile

texto M (algo escrito) text; (libro escolar) textbook; **— listo para cámara** camera-ready copy

textual ADJ verbatim

textura F texture

tez F complexion

ti PRON PERS you; **para —** for you; **te lo doy a —** I give it to you

tía F (pariente) aunt; *fam* (mujer) woman, chick;

— abuela great-aunt

tibieza F (poco fervor, afecto) lukewarmness; (calor) warmth

tibio ADJ (ni caliente ni frío) tepid, lukewarm; (templado) warm

tiburón M shark

tic M twitch, tic

tictac M **hacer —** to tick

tiempo M (cronológico) time; (climático) weather; (gramatical) tense; (de un partido de cuatro tiempos) quarter; (de un partido de dos tiempos) half; **— compartido** timeshare; **— completo** full-time; **— de descuento** extra time; **— extra** overtime; **— libre** leisure hours, free time; **— parcial** part-time; **— pretérito** past tense; **— real** real time; **— suplementario** (fútbol americano) overtime; (fútbol) extra time; **— y medio** time and a half; **a —** on time; **al mismo —** at the same time; **antes de —** ahead of time; **a su —** in due course; **a un —** at the same time; **con —** in advance; **de medio —** half-time; **en aquel —** back then; **en mis —s** in my day; **hace buen —** the weather is nice; **hace mucho —** a long time ago; **mal —** rough weather; **motor de dos —s** two-stroke motor; **perder el —** to goof off, to waste time; **tener — de sobra** to have time to spare; **todo el —** all the time; **tomar el —** to clock

tienda F (de venta) store; (de campaña) tent; **— minorista** retail store; **— virtual** online store

tienda, tiende *ver* tender

tiene, tienes *ver* tener

tientas LOC ADV **a —** blindly; **andar a —** to feel one's way

tiento M care; **coger el —** to get the hang of something

tierno ADJ (fácil de cortar) tender; (joven) young; (cariñoso) affectionate

tierra F (planeta) earth; (superficie) land; (país) country; (suelo) soil; **— adentro** inland; **—s altas** highlands; **—s bajas** lowlands; **— batida** clay; **— de cultivo** farmland; **— de nadie** no-man's-land; **— firme** mainland; **—s raras** rare earths; **bajo —** underground; **caer a —** to fall to the ground; **dar en — con alguien** to overthrow someone; **echar por —** to knock down; **por —** overland

tieso ADJ stiff; **quedarse —** *fam* to kick the bucket

tiesto M flowerpot

tiesura F stiffness

tifoideo-a ADJ & F typhoid

tifón M typhoon

tifus M (causado por salmonella) typhoid fever; (causado por rickettsia) typhus

tigre M tiger

tijera[s] F SG/PL (instrumento para cortar) scissors; (patada de fútbol) scissor kick

tijereta F scissor kick

tijeretada F snip

tijeretazo M snip

tijeretear VT to snip

tildar VT to brand

tilde F (en la ñ) tilde; (en las vocales) accent [mark]

tilín M *fam* ding-a-ling

timador M confidence man

timbrar VT to stamp

timbrazo M ring

timbre M (aparato) buzzer, doorbell; (cualidad de la voz) timbre; (sello) stamp; (impuesto) stamp tax; (insignia heráldica) crest

timidez F timidity, shyness

tímido ADJ timid, shy, bashful

timo M confidence game, scam; — **en pirámide** Ponzi scheme

timón M helm, rudder

timonear VT to steer

timonel M pilot

timorato ADJ timorous, faint-hearted

tímpano M eardrum

tina F (bañera) tub; (de tintorero) vat

tinaja F large earthen jar

tinglado M (armazón) shed; (plataforma) platform

tinieblas F PL darkness; **en —** in the dark

tinitus M tinnitus

tino M (buen juicio) good judgment; (puntería) marksmanship

tinta F ink; **medias —s** wishy-washiness

tinte M (sustancia) dye, stain; (matiz) tint

tintero M inkwell; **eso se me quedó en el —** I never got to that

tintín M clink

tintinear VI to tinkle, to clink

tintineo M tinkle, tinkling

tinto ADJ red

tintorería F dry cleaner

tintorero -ra MF dry cleaner

tintura F (en medicina) tincture; (tinte) dye, tint

tiñoso ADJ scabby

tío -a M (hermano de la madre o el padre) uncle; **— abuelo** great-uncle; (tipo) guy; F (hermana de la madre o el padre) aunt; (tipa) woman, gal

tiovivo M merry-go-round

tipear, tipiar VI/VT to type

típico ADJ typical

tiple M treble

tipo -pa M (especie, imprenta) type; (tío) *fam* guy, dude; *Am* rate of interest; **— de cambio** rate of exchange; **— de interés** interest rate; **— de letra** typeface, font; **— de letra por omisión** base font; **un buen —** (hombre guapo) a good-looking fellow; (buena

persona) a regular guy; **tiene buen —** he's good looking; F (tía) *pey* woman, broad

tipografía F printing

tipología F typology

tira F (de papel, tocino, tela) strip; (de cuero, zapato) strap; **— cómica** comic strip

tirada F (de una pelota) throw; (de una publicación) issue, print run; (distancia) stretch; **de una —** all at once

tirador -ora MF (persona que dispara) shooter; M (tirachinas) slingshot; (pomo de la puerta) knob

tiranía F tyranny

tiránico ADJ tyrannical

tirano -na ADJ tyrannical; MF tyrant

tirante ADJ (cable) taut; (relaciones) strained; M (de caballería) trace; (de vestido) strap; (apoyo) brace, strut; **—s** suspenders

tirantez F tension, strain

tirar VT (pelota) to throw, to toss, to pitch; (derechos, dinero) to throw away; (una bala) to shoot; (una moneda) to flip, to toss; (dados) to cast; (una cuerda) to pull, to tug; VI/VT (en baloncesto) to shoot; VI **— a puerta** to shoot at goal; **—se** (echarse) to lie down; (en fútbol) to fake a foul; **— al suelo** to throw down; **— a** to tend toward; **— abajo** to knock over; **— de** to tug at; **— la cadena** to flush; **—se la casa por la ventana** to live it up; **— la chancleta** to kick up one's heels; **—se solo** to go it alone; **tirárselas de** to pretend to be; **no me tira la política** I'm not attracted to politics; **el coche tira a un lado** the car pulls to one side; **ir tirando** to get along; **trabajar con él es un constante tira y afloja** working with him is a roller-coaster; M **tirabuzón** (sacacorchos) corkscrew; (espiral) coil; M SG **tirachinas** slingshot

tiritar VI (de frío) to shiver; (de miedo) to shudder

tiro M (lanzamiento) throw; (disparo) shot; (deporte) shooting; (de cocaína) hit; (de dados) roll; (de caballos) team; (de chimenea) draft; (fútbol) shot; **— al arco** archery; **— al blanco** target practice; **— de esquina** corner kick; **— de penalidad** penalty kick; **— en suspensión** jump shot; **— libre** (baloncesto) free throw; (fútbol) free kick; **errar el —** to miss the mark; **matar a —s** to gun down; **ni a —s** absolutely not; **pegarle un — a alguien** to shoot someone; **me salió el — por la culata** the plan backfired on me

tiroides ADJ & M thyroid

tirón M (tironeo) jerk, tug, pull; (atracción fuerte, lesión de un músculo) pull; **de un —** all at once; **un — de orejas** a slap on the wrist

tironear VI/VT to jerk, to tug at

tirotear VI to shoot; **—se** to exchange shots

tiroteo M (tiros) shooting, gunfire; (entre bandos) shootout

tirria F dislike; **tenerle — a una persona** to have a strong dislike for someone

tisana F herbal tea

tísico ADJ consumptive

tisis F consumption

titánico ADJ titanic

titanio M titanium

títere M (marioneta) puppet; (persona) puppet, dupe; **—s** puppet show; **no dejar — con cabeza** to leave no one standing

titilación F flicker

titilar VI to flicker, to twinkle

titileo M twinkle

titubear VI (vacilar) to hesitate, to waver; (oscilar) to totter, to dodder

titubeo M hesitation

titular VT to entitle; **—se** to graduate; ADJ permanent; M (de periódico) headline; MF (de cargo) incumbent

titularidad F tenure

título M (de una obra, persona, liga) title; (derecho) claim, legal right; (universitario) degree, diploma; **— de propiedad** title deed; **—s de crédito** credits; **a — de** by way of

tiza F chalk

tiznado ADJ sooty

tiznar VT to smear with soot

tizne M soot

tizón M (leña) burning log; (parásito) smut

TNT M TNT

toalla F towel; **tirar la —** to throw in the towel

toallero M towel rack

tobillo M ankle

tobogán M slide

tocado M headdress; ADJ touched

tocador M (mueble) dressing table, vanity table; (habitación) *lit* boudoir

tocante a PREP concerning

tocar[30] VT (con los dedos) to touch; (un instrumento musical) to play; (una campana) to ring; (un timbre) to buzz; (a la puerta) to knock; (la bocina) to honk, to blast; (una alarma) to sound; (mencionar) to touch upon; **— en** to stop over in; **—le a uno** to be one's turn; **— fondo** to hit bottom; **— la pelota** (béisbol) bunt; M SG **tocadiscos** record player

tocayo -ya MF namesake

tocino M bacon

tocón M stump

todavía ADV still, as yet, yet; **— está aquí** she's still here; **¿— no has comido?** have you not eaten yet? **— no ha llegado** she still has not arrived, as yet she has not arrived; **me dio — más** she gave me even more

todo ADJ all; (cada uno) every, each; **— hombre** every man; **—s los días** every day; **a — correr** at top speed; **a toda costa** at all costs; **a toda marcha** in high gear; **a toda vela** under full sail; **a toda velocidad** at full speed; **a — volumen** at full blast; **de — corazón** wholeheartedly; **de —s modos** still, anyway, all the same; **del — entirely; en — caso** in any case, at any rate, in any event; **es — un personaje** he's quite a character; **por — lados** everywhere; **— el día** all day; **— el tiempo** all the time; **— el mundo** everyone; **todas las noches** nightly; **toda la noche** all through the night; **toda clase de** all sorts of; **en/por todas partes** everywhere, far and wide; **con toda el alma** from the bottom of one's heart; **con toda sinceridad** in all earnestness; PRON **de una vez por todas** once and for all; **— se vale** anything goes; **—s** everybody; **—s juntos** all together; ADV **— derecho** straight ahead; **— lo contrario** quite the opposite; **— recto** straight ahead; **— sucio** all dirty; **— o nada** all or nothing; **ante —** first of all; **así y —** in spite of that; **con —** in spite of that; **del —** completely; **sobre —** especially; M whole; **—poderoso** almighty; **el — es más que la suma de las partes** the whole is more than the sum of its parts

toga F (de catedrático) gown; (de juez) robe

Togo M Togo

togolés -esa ADJ & MF Togolese

toldería F Indian village

toldo M awning, canopy

tolerancia F tolerance

tolerante ADJ tolerant, broad-minded

tolerar VT to tolerate; **no lo puedo —** I can't stand it

tolete M oarlock

toma F (de una ciudad) taking; (cinematográfica) take; (de juramento) administration; (de teléfono) jack; **— de agua** faucet; **— de corriente** electric outlet; **— de poder** takeover; **— y daca** give-and-take

tomar VT (una pastilla) to take; (un juramento) to administer; (un vestido) to take in; (a un empleado) to hire; (una bebida) to drink; **— a pecho** to take to heart; **— asiento** to take a seat; **— desprevenido** to take by surprise; **— el sol** to sunbathe; **— lo a mal** to take the wrong way; **— el pelo a** to make fun of, to kid, to pull someone's leg; **— medidas** to take action; **— posesión** to take possession; **— una decisión** to make a decision; **—le las medidas a alguien** to measure someone for clothes; **—se de la mano** to hold hands; **—se la molestia** to bother to

tomate M tomato

tomillo M thyme

tomo M volume

tomografía F scan; **— axial computarizada** CAT scan; **— cerebral** brain scan

ton LOC ADV **sin — ni son** for no reason

tonada F tune

tonel M (barril) barrel; (persona) *pey* fatso

tonelada F ton

tóner M toner

Tonga F Tonga

tongano -na ADJ & MF Tongan

tongo M setup

tonicidad F tone; **— muscular** muscle tone

tónico -ca ADJ & M tonic; F (tono) tone; (agua) tonic [water]

tono M (al hablar) tone; (musical) pitch; (intervalo musical) step; **— de ocupado** busy signal; **— menor** minor key; **— muscular** muscle tone; **a —** on key; **bajar el —** to lower the volume; **darse —** to put on airs; **de buen —** in good taste; **fuera de —** out of place; **subido de —** risqué

tontear VI to fool around

tontería F (cualidad de tonto) stupidity; (hecho o dicho tonto) foolishness, nonsense

tonto -ta ADJ (ingenuo) foolish; (de poca inteligencia) stupid, dumb; **a tontas y a locas** haphazardly; MF (persona ingenua) fool; (persona de poca inteligencia) *fam* dummy, blockhead, dimwit; **— de capirote** dunce; **hacer[se] el —** to play the fool

topacio M topaz

topar VT to butt; **—se con** to bump into

tope M (de precios) ceiling, cap; (de tren) bumper; (de puerta) doorstop; **a — a** lot; **hasta el —** to the maximum; **estar hasta el —** to be completely full

topetazo M butt

tópico M (lugar común) cliché; (tema) topic; ADJ topical

topless ADJ topless

topo M mole (también espía)

toque M (con la mano) touch; (de campana) ringing; (de tambor) beat; (de trompeta) blare; (de pintura) dab; **— de queda** curfew; **— de pelota** (béisbol) bunt; **dar los últimos —s** to put the finishing touches; **dar —s** to dab; **un — femenino** a woman's touch

toquetear VI/VT to finger

toqueteo M feel

tórax M thorax

torbellino M whirlwind

torcedura F twist, sprain, strain

torcer[34] VT (el cuello) to twist; (una articulación) to sprain, to strain; (tergiversar) to distort; **—le el pescuezo a alguien** to wring someone's neck; VI (un río) to bend

torcido ADJ crooked, bent

tordo M thrush

torear VT (lidiar) to fight a bull; (provocar) to provoke

torero -ra MF bullfighter

tormenta F storm; **— de arena** sandstorm; **— eléctrica** electrical storm

tormento M torment

tormentoso ADJ stormy

tornadizo ADJ changeable

tornado M tornado, twister

tornar VI (regresar) to return; VT (cambiar) to turn; **— a hacer algo** to do something again

tornasolado ADJ iridescent

tornear VT to turn on a lathe

torneo M tournament

tornillo M screw; **— de banco** vise; **faltarle a uno un —** to have a screw loose

torniquete M (eje giratorio) turnstile; (contra hemorragia) tourniquet

torno M (para levantar cosas pesadas) hoist, winch; (para cerámica) lathe, pottery wheel; **en — [a]** around

toro M bull; **coger/agarrar el — por los cuernos** to take the bull by the horns

toronja F grapefruit

torpe ADJ (poco habilidoso) clumsy, awkward; (lento) slow, sluggish

torpedear VT to torpedo

torpedero -ra MF (en béisbol) shortstop; (barco) torpedo boat; (avión) torpedo plane

torpedo M torpedo

torpeza F (falta de habilidad) clumsiness; (lentitud) slowness, sluggishness

torpor M torpor

torrar VT to roast

torre F (de castillo) tower; (de buque de guerra) turret; (en ajedrez) castle; **— de control** control tower; **— de marfil** ivory tower; **— de perforación** oil derrick; **— de vigilancia** watchtower

torrencial ADJ torrential

torrente M torrent; **— de lágrimas** flood of tears; **— sanguíneo** bloodstream

torreón M large tower

torreta F turret

tórrido ADJ torrid

torsión F torsion

torso M torso

torta F (postre) cake; (bofetada) slap

tortícolis F kink

tortilla F (de huevo) omelet; (de harina) *Méx* tortilla; **se dio vuelta la —** the tables have turned

tórtola F turtledove

tortuga F tortoise, turtle; **— marina** sea turtle; **a paso de —** at a snail's pace

tortuoso ADJ (camino) tortuous; (carácter) devious

tortura F torture

torturante ADJ torturous

torturar VT to torture

torvo ADJ fierce

tos F cough; — **ferina** whooping cough

tosco ADJ coarse, crude

toser VI to cough

tosquedad F coarseness, crudeness

tostada F toast

tostado ADJ (pan) toasted; (café) roasted; M (acción de tostar pan) toasting; (color, bronceado) tan; (acción de tostar café) roasting

tostador -ora MF toaster

tostar[5] VT (pan) to toast; (piel) to tan; (café) to roast

total ADJ & M total; **en** — all together; —, **a mí no me importa** anyway, I don't care

totalidad F **la** — **del dinero** all the money; **en su** — as a whole

totalitario ADJ totalitarian

totalmente ADV totally, perfectly

tour M tour

tóxico ADJ toxic

toxina F toxin

traba F (estorbo) hindrance; (de caballo) hobble

trabajador -ora ADJ (esforzado) hardworking; (proletario) working; MF worker

trabajar VI/VT to work; — **un taxi** to drive a taxi; VI (una tienda) to be open; — **duro** to work hard; — **horas extras** to work overtime

trabajo M (actividad) work; (acción de trabajar) working; (empleo) job; (informe académico) paper; — **manual** manual labor; **da mucho** — it's a lot of work; **sin** — unemployed

trabajoso ADJ laborious

trabar VT (una puerta) to jam; (un caballo) to hobble; (a un boxeador) to clinch; (una salsa) to thicken; (negociaciones) to impede; — **amistad con alguien** to strike up a friendship with someone; — **batalla** to join battle; — **conversación** to strike up a conversation; M SG **trabalenguas** tongue twister

tracción F traction

tractocamión M tractor-trailer

tractor M tractor

tradición F tradition

tradicional ADJ traditional

traducción F translation

traducir[38] VI/VT to translate

traductor -ora MF translator

traduje, tradujera, tradujese, traduzca, traduzco ver traducir

traer[59] VT (venir con) to bring; (llevar puesto) to have on; (contener) to feature; — **a colación** to bring up; — **a mal a alguien** to mistreat someone; **este niño se las trae** this child is something else; **¿qué te traes entre manos?** what are you up to? **—se secretos** to have secrets

tráfago M bustle

traficante MF dealer

traficar[30] VI to traffic, to trade

tráfico M traffic

tragar[40] VI/VT (ingerir) to swallow; (comer) *fam* to stuff one's face; (consumir gasolina) to guzzle; (aguantar) to stand; (hacer desaparecer) to engulf; **—se algo** to swallow [accidentally]; **no me lo trago** I don't buy that; M **tragaluz** skylight; M/F SG **tragamonedas/tragaperras** slot machine

tragedia F tragedy

trágico ADJ tragic

trago M (lo tragado) swallow; (bebida alcohólica) shot, slug; **a —s** (beber) in sips; (poco a poco) little by little; **echar/tomar un** — to take a drink; **pasar un mal** — to suffer a difficulty

traición F (política) treason; (personal) betrayal; (acto desleal) treachery; **a** — by treachery

traicionar VT to double-cross

traicionero ADJ treacherous

traidor -ora ADJ treacherous; MF (político) traitor; (personal) betrayer

traiga, traigo ver traer

trailer M trailer

traílla F leash

traje M (conjunto) suit; (de fiesta) gown; — **de baño** swimsuit

traje, trajera, trajese ver traer

trajeado ADJ **bien** — well-dressed

trajín M hustle and bustle

trajinar VI to rush around

trama F (argumento) plot; (intriga) scheme; (conjunto de hilos) woof

tramador -ora MF plotter

tramar VT (con hilos) to weave; (intrigar) to plot, to scheme

tramitación F processing

tramitar VT to take steps to obtain

trámite M procedure, paperwork

tramo M (de carretera) stretch; (de puente) span; (de hielo) patch; (de escalera) flight

tramoyista MF stagehand

trampa F (de caza) trap, snare; (engaño) trick; — **de arena** (golf) sand trap; **hacer** — to cheat, to trick; **tender una** — to set a trap

trampear VI to cheat

trampilla F trapdoor

trampolín M (de piscina) springboard; (de circo) trampoline

tramposo -sa ADJ deceitful; MF cheat

tranca F crossbar

trance M (momento difícil) pass, difficult moment; (estado mental) trance; **el último** — the last moment of life; **a todo** — at any cost

tranco M stride; **a —s** hurriedly; **en dos —s** in a jiffy

tranquera F wooden fence
tranquilidad F tranquillity, calm, quiet
tranquilizante M tranquilizer
tranquilizar[47] VT to quiet, to calm down; —**se** to calm down, to wind down
tranquilo ADJ (silencioso) quiet, peaceful; (apacible) calm, cool; (despreocupado) calm, at ease; (no excitable) sedate, laid-back; (sin olas) smooth, tranquil
transacción F transaction; — **comercial** business transaction; **transacciones** trading; **transacciones a precio de mercado** arm's-length transactions
transar VI to compromise
transatlántico ADJ transatlantic; M transatlantic liner
transbordar VI to transfer
transbordo M transfer
transcribir[74] VT to transcribe
transcripción F transcript
transcultural ADJ cross-cultural
transcurrir VI to elapse
transcurso M passing, passage; **en el — de un año** in the course of a year
transeúnte MF passerby, transient
transferencia F transfer; — **electrónica** wire transfer
transferible ADJ transferable
transferir[8] VT to transfer (también en computadora)
transformación F transformation
transformador M transformer
transformar VT to transform
transfusión F transfusion; **dar una — de sangre** to give a transfusion
transgénico ADV genetically modified
transgredir[73] VT to transgress
transgresión F transgression
transgresor -ora MF lawbreaker
transición F transition
transigir[46] VI to compromise
transistor M transistor
transitable ADJ passable
transitar VI/VT to travel
transitivo ADJ transitive
tránsito M (acción de viajar) transit, passage; (tráfico) traffic; **de/en —** in transit
transitorio ADJ transitory
transmisible ADJ communicable
transmisión F transmission; — **automática** automatic transmission; — **por la web** webcast
transmisor M transmitter; ADJ transmitting
transmitir VI/VT (enviar) to transmit; (una enfermedad) to communicate; (por radio o televisión) to broadcast; — **por la web** to webcast
transnacional ADJ transnational
transparencia F (visual) transparency;

(institucional) openness
transparente ADJ transparent
transpiración F perspiration, sweating
transpirar VI/VT to transpire, to perspire
transportación F transportation, transport
transportar VT (mercancías, gente) to transport; (mercancías) to ship, to haul
transporte M (acción) transport, transportation; (vehículo de transporte) transport [vessel]; — **de locura** fit of madness; — **público** mass transit
transportista MF teamster, trucker
transversal ADJ transverse; F transversal
transverso ADJ transverse
tranvía M (transporte urbano) streetcar, trolley; (tren de cercanías) local train
trapacería F racket
trapacero -ra MF racketeer
trapeador M mop
trapear VI/VT *Am* to mop
trapecio M trapeze
trapezoide ADJ & M trapezoid
trapiche M sugar mill
trapisonda F trick
trapo M rag; —**s** *fam* duds; **a todo —** at full speed; **tratar a alguien como un —** to treat someone like dirt; —**s sucios** dirty laundry
tráquea F trachea, windpipe
traqueotomía F tracheotomy
traquetear VI (hacer sonido) to rattle, to clatter; (llevar a todos lados) to drag from place to place
traqueteo M rattle, clatter
tras PREP (temporal) after; (espacial) after, behind, in back of; **correr —** to run after; **día — día** day after day; **una vez — otra** time after time
trascendencia F (concepto filosófico) transcendence; (importancia) importance
trascendental ADJ (que sobrepasa la realidad) transcendental; (importante) important
trascendente ADJ (que sobrepasa la realidad) transcendental; (importante) important
trascender VT (sobrepasar) to transcend; VI (surgir) to emerge; (extender) to extend
trasegar[41] VT (vino) to pour from one container to another; (objetos) to move around; (papeles) to shuffle
trasero ADJ (punto, asiento) rear, back; (pata) hind; M (de persona) *fam* rear, rear end, bottom
traslación F transfer
trasladar VT (a un empleado) to transfer; (una reunión) to postpone; —**se** to travel
traslado M transfer
traslapo M overlap
trasnochar VI to stay up late
traspapelar VT to mislay, to misplace; —**se** to become mislaid

traspasar VT (pasar por) to transfix; (ir más allá de) to go beyond; (pasar un límite) to transgress, to cross over; (una propiedad) to transfer

traspaso M transfer

traspié M stumble, slip; **dar un—** to stumble

trasplantar VT to transplant

trasplante M transplant

trasponer[56, 74] VT to transpose

trasquilar VT (una oveja) to shear; (a una persona) to fleece

trastabillar VI to stumble

trastazo M bump

traste M (de guitarra) fret, stop; (trasero) buttocks; **dar al — con** to destroy; **irse al —** to go down the drain

trasto M piece of junk; **—s** stuff

trastocar[30] VT to disrupt

trastornar VT (alterar psíquicamente) to disturb; (alterar el funcionamiento) to disrupt; **—se** to go crazy

trastorno M (molestia) trouble; (patología) disorder; **— bipolar** bipolar disorder; **— de Asperger** Asperger's syndrome; **— de déficit de atención** attention deficit disorder; **— de la alimentación** eating disorder; **— de la personalidad** personality disorder; **— de personalidad múltiple** multiple personality disorder; **— del sueño** sleep disorder

trasudar VI/VT to perspire

trata F trade; **— de blancas** white slave trade

tratable ADJ (curable) treatable; (amistoso) approachable

tratado M (acuerdo) treaty; (libro) treatise

tratamiento M (acción de tratar) treatment; (fórmula de cortesía) form of address; **— de canal** root canal; **— de convalecencia** aftercare; **— de residuos** waste treatment; **— de textos** *Esp* word processing; **— postoperatorio** aftercare

tratante MF dealer, trader

tratar VT (una enfermedad, a un paciente, un asunto) to treat; VI (intentar) to try; **— como** to treat like; **— con** to have dealings with; **— de** to try to, to attempt; **— sobre** to be about; **lo trató de imbécil** she called him an idiot; **—le a uno de** to address someone as; **— en** to deal in; **—se con** to have to do with; **—se de** to be a question of, to be about

trato M (acuerdo) treatment; (acción de tratar) dealings; (convenio) deal; (comercio) trade; (modales) manners; **¡— hecho!** it's a deal! **tener buen—** to have good manners; **cerrar un—** to strike a bargain

trauma M trauma

traumático ADJ traumatic

traumatismo M trauma

través LOC ADV **a/al — de** through, across; **a —**

de las declaraciones throughout the declarations; **de —** across; **mirar de —** to look askance [at]

travesaño M crossbar (también en fútbol)

travesía F crossing, sea voyage, passage

travesura F mischief, prank; **—s** naughtiness; **hacer —s** to play pranks

traviesa F railway tie

travieso ADJ mischievous, naughty

trayecto M course, route

trayectoria F (de proyectil) trajectory, path; (profesional) career, track record

trayendo *ver* traer

traza F (huella) trace; (aspecto) appearance; **tiene —s de no acabar nunca** it looks as if it will never end

trazado M (de ciudad) layout; (de edificio) blueprint; (de un plan) outline

trazador M **— gráfico** plotter

trazar[47] VT (un dibujo) to trace, to sketch; (un plan) to outline; (un edificio) to blueprint; **— el curso** to plot a course

trazo M stroke

trébol M clover

trece NUM thirteen

trecho M stretch; **a —s** at intervals; **de — en —** at intervals

tregua F (de guerra) truce; (descanso) lull, respite

treinta NUM thirty (también en tenis)

treintañero -ra MF thirtysomething

tremendo ADJ (extraordinario) tremendous; (terrible) terrible

trementina F turpentine

tremolar VI (bandera) to flutter; (voz) to trill

trémolo M quaver

trémulo ADJ tremulous, trembling

tren M train; **— de aterrizaje** landing gear; **— de carga / de mercancías** freight train; **— de cercanías** local train; **— de vida** lifestyle; **— expreso** express train; **a todo —** at top speed; **perder el —** to miss the boat; **seguir el —** to keep up

trenza F braid

trenzar[47] VT to braid

trepador -ora ADJ (planta) climbing; (ciclista) climber; MF social climber; F climbing plant

trepar VI to climb

trepidar VI to tremble

tres NUM three

trescientos NUM three hundred

treta F trick, wile

triaje M triage

triangular ADJ triangular

triángulo M triangle; **— recto** right triangle

tribu F tribe

tribulación F tribulation

tribuna F (de orador) rostrum; (para el público) grandstand

tribunal M (sala del juez) court, courtroom; (cuerpo de jueces) panel of judges
tributable ADJ taxable
tributar VT to pay tribute with; VI to pay taxes
tributario ADJ & M tributary
tributo M (pago obligatorio) tribute; (impuesto) tax
triceps M triceps
triciclo M tricycle
tridimensional ADJ three-dimensional
trifulca F fight
trigo M wheat
trigueño ADJ (tez) swarthy; (pelo) dark-blond
trillado ADJ trite
trilladora F threshing machine
trillar VT to thresh
trillizo -za ADJ & MF triplet
trilogía F trilogy
trimestral ADJ quarterly
trimestre M quarter
trinar VI to trill; **está que trina** she is furious
trinchante M carving knife
trinchar VT to carve
trinche M pitchfork
trinchera F (fosa) trench; (gabardina) trench coat
trinchero M carving table
trineo M sleigh, sled
trinitense ADJ & MF Trinidadian
trino M trill
trinquete M ratchet
trío M trio
tripas F PL guts; **hacer de — corazón** to pluck up one's courage
triple ADJ triple; M (también en béisbol) triple; (baloncesto) three-point basket
triplicar[30] VT to triple, to treble
trípode M tripod
triptongo M triphthong
tripulación F crew
tripulante MF crew member
tripular VT to man
triquiñuela F caper
triquitraque M firecracker
triscar[30] VI to frisk
triste ADJ sad, sorrowful
tristeza F sadness, sorrow
tristón ADJ glum
tritón M newt
trituradora F (para desechos) garbage disposal unit; (para papel) paper shredder
triturar VI/VT (documentos) to shred; (granos) to grind
triunfador -ora MF winner; ADJ triumphant
triunfal ADJ triumphal
triunfante ADJ triumphant
triunfar VT to triumph
triunfo M triumph
trivial ADJ trivial, commonplace, trite

trizas F PL **hacer —** to tear into shreds
trocar[31] VT (transformar) to change into; (cambiar una cosa por otra) to exchange
trocear VT to divide into pieces
trocha F trail
trofeo M trophy
troje M granary
trola F whopper
trole M trolley
trolebús M trolley bus
tromba F waterspout; **salir en —** to storm out
trombón M trombone
trombosis F thrombosis; **— coronaria** coronary thrombosis
trompa F (de elefante) trunk; (instrumento musical) horn; **— de Eustaquio** eustachian tube; **— de Falopio** fallopian tube
trompada F blow with the fist
trompeta F trumpet
trompetazo M trumpet blast
trompetear VI to trumpet
trompo M spinning top
tronada F thunderstorm
tronar[5] VI to thunder
tronchar VT to chop off
tronco M (de árbol) trunk, log; (del cuerpo) trunk, torso; **— del encéfalo** brain stem; **dormir como un —** to sleep like a log
tronera F (de buque) gun port; (de mesa de billar) pocket
trono M throne (también wáter)
tropa F (en el ejército) troop; (oficiales) rank and file; **—s de asalto** storm troops; **—s de choque** shock troops
tropel LOC ADV **en —** in droves
tropezar[48] VI to stumble, to trip; **—[se] con alguien** to run into someone; **— con algo** to come across something
tropezón M stumble, trip; **salir a tropezones** to stumble out; **darse un —** to stumble
tropical ADJ tropical
trópico M tropic
tropiezo M stumble
troquel M die
trotar VI to trot, to jog
trote M trot; **al —** at a trot; **no estoy para estos —s** I'm too old for this
troza F log
trozar[47] VT to cut up
trozo M (de roca, madera, torta) piece; (de un texto) section; (de carbón) lump; (de carne) slab
trucha F trout
truco M clever trick
truculento ADJ gruesome
trueno M thunder
trueque M (intercambio) exchange; (transacción sin dinero) bartering
truhán -ana MF scoundrel

truja F cigarette
trust M trust
tu ADJ POS your
tú PRON PERS you
tuba F tuba
tuberculosis F tuberculosis
tubería F (tubo) pipe; (conjunto de tubos) piping
tubo M (cilindro hueco) tube; (de agua, órgano) pipe; (digestivo) tract; **— de ensayo** test tube; **— de escape** tailpipe; **— digestivo** gastrointestinal tract
tubular ADJ tubular
tuerca F nut
tuerto ADJ one-eyed
tuétano M marrow; **hasta los —s** through and through
tufillo M whiff
tufo M (humo) fumes; (hedor) stench
tugurio M hovel; **—s** slums
tulipán M tulip
tullido -da ADJ crippled; MF pey cripple
tullir VT to cripple; **—se** to become crippled
tumba F (panteón) tomb; (sepultura) grave; **soy una** — my lips are sealed
tumbar VT to knock down, to flatten; **—se** to lie down, to stretch out
tumbo M tumble, somersault; **dar —s** (persona) to stagger; (coche) to bump along
tumor M tumor; **— cerebral** brain tumor; **— maligno** malignancy
tumorectomía F lumpectomy
tumulto M (alboroto) tumult, uproar; (muchedumbre) mob
tumultuoso ADJ tumultuous
tuna F (fruta) prickly pear; Esp (grupo de cantantes) minstrel group
tunante -ta MF scamp
tunda F thrashing
túnel M tunnel
tunesino -na ADJ & MF Tunisian
Túnez M Tunisia
tungsteno M tungsten
túnica F tunic; **— de laboratorio** lab gown
tupido ADJ dense, compact
tupir VT (hacer tupido) to compact; (cubrir) to cover; **—se** to stuff oneself
turba F (muchedumbre) mob; (carbón fósil) peat
turbación F confusion
turbamulta F throng
turbante M turban
turbar VT to disturb; **—se** to become disturbed
turbina F turbine
turbio ADJ (pasado, secreto) dark; (agua, materia) murky
turbocompresor M turbocharger
turborreactor M turbojet
turbulencia F turbulence
turbulento ADJ turbulent
turco -ca ADJ Turkish; MF Turk; M (lengua) Turkish
turcomano -na ADJ & MF Turkmen
turismo M (actividad) tourism; (conjunto de turistas) tourists; **hacer —** to go sightseeing
turista MF tourist
turístico ADJ (relativo al turismo) tourist; **atracción turística** tourist attraction; **clase turística** coach class
Turkmenistán M Turkmenistan
turnarse VI to take turns
turno M (vuelta) turn; (de trabajo) shift; (en béisbol) at bat
turquesa F turquoise
Turquía F Turkey
turrón M nougat
tutear VT to address as "tú"
tutela F guardianship
tutelar VT to have charge of
tutor -ora MF (de un menor) guardian; M (de planta) prop
tutorial M tutorial
Tuvalu M Tuvalu
tuvaluano -na ADJ & MF Tuvaluan
tuve, tuviera, tuviese ver tener
tuyo ADJ & PRON POS your, yours; **el amigo —** your friend; **esto es —** this is yours
tweed M tweed

Uu

u CONJ or
ubicación F location
ubicar[30] VT (situar) to locate; (identificar) to place; **—se** to be located
ubicuo ADJ ubiquitous
ubre F udder
UCP [unidad central de proceso] F CPU
Ucrania F Ukraine
ucraniano -na ADJ & MF Ukrainian
UE [Unión Europea] F EU
ufanarse VI to glory [in], to be proud [of]
ufano ADJ proud
Uganda F Uganda
ugandés -esa ADJ & MF Ugandan
ujier M bailiff
úlcera F (lesión superficial) sore; (en el estómago) ulcer; (en la boca) canker, canker sore
ulcerar VI to ulcerate
ulceroso ADJ ulcerous
ulterior ADJ ulterior
últimamente ADV of late
ultimar VT to finalize
ultimátum M ultimatum
último ADJ (palabra, capítulo) last, final;

(destino) ultimate; (más reciente) latest; **estar en las últimas** to be on one's last legs; **la última palabra** the last word; **en los —s tiempos** lately; **en última instancia** ultimately; **a última hora** at the last moment; **por —** finally

ultrajante ADJ outrageous

ultrajar VT to outrage

ultraje M outrage, indignity

ultraligero M ultralight

ultramar LOC ADV **de —** overseas

ultramoderno ADJ ultramodern

ultrasonido M ultrasound

ultratumba LOC ADV **de —** from beyond the grave

ultravioleta ADJ & M ultraviolet

ulular VI (viento) to howl; (búho) to hoot

ululato M (viento) howling; (búho) hooting

umbral M threshold, doorstep; **— de rentabilidad** breakeven point

umbrío ADJ shady

un, uno, una ART INDEF a, an; **un hombre** a man; **un actor** an actor; **una mujer** a woman; **una manzana** an apple; NUM one; **de a —** one at a time; **es la una** it is one o'clock; PRON one; **uno por uno** one by one; **—s** some; **unos cuantos** some; **uno tiene que cuidarse** you've got to take care of yourself; **yo tengo uno** I have one; **uno tras otro** one after the other; **uno más** (tenis) let; **uno al lado del otro** side by side; **los unos a los otros / el uno al otro** one another / each other

unánime ADJ unanimous

unanimidad F unanimity

uncir³³ VT (a un buey) to yoke; (a un carro) to hitch

ungüento M ointment, salve

único ADJ (solo) only; **una única vez** a single time; (extraordinario) unique; **eres —** you're one of a kind

unidad F (indivisibilidad) unity; (ejemplar) unit; (fracción militar) unit, outfit; (de computadora) drive; **— central de proceso/procesamiento** central processing unit; **— de cuidado coronario** coronary care unit; **— de cuidados intensivos** intensive care unit; **— de disco duro** hard disk drive; **— de disquete** diskette drive; **— monetaria** currency unit

unido ADJ united; **una familia unida** a close-knit family

unificar³⁰ VT to unify

uniformar VT (estandarizar) to standardize; (dar uniformes) to furnish with uniforms

uniforme ADJ & M uniform

uniformidad F uniformity

unilateral ADJ unilateral

unión F (acción de unir, cosas unidas) union;

(lugar en que se unen dos cosas) junction; (indivisibilidad) unity

unir VT (una nación) to unite; (dos construcciones) to join; (cinta magnética, genes) to splice; (caños) to couple; VI/VT (con lazos) to bind

unisex ADJ INV unisex

unísono ADJ unison; **al —** in unison

unitario ADJ (partidario de la unidad) unitarian; (que tiene unidad) unitary

universal ADJ universal

universidad F (de enseñanza e investigación) university; (de enseñanza) college

universitario -ria ADJ university; (relativo a los deportes) collegiate; MF college student

universo M universe

untar VT (la piel con crema) to oil; (el pan con mantequilla) to spread on; (la cara con pintura) to smear; **—le la mano a alguien** to grease someone's palm

untuoso ADJ (graso) oily; (zalamero) slick, unctuous

uña F (de dedo) fingernail; (de gato) claw; **— encarnada** hangnail; **como — y carne** thick as thieves; **con — s y dientes** tooth and nail

uñero M hangnail

uranio M uranium

urbanidad F refinement, polish

urbanismo M (modo de vida) urbanism; (planificación) city planning

urbanización F development

urbanizar⁴⁷ VT to build up

urbano ADJ (relativo a la ciudad) urban; (refinado) suave; **autobús —** city bus

urbe F metropolis

urdimbre F warp

urdir VT (una tela) to weave; (una historia) to concoct; (un plan) to devise, to work out

uretra F urethra

urgencia F (prisa) urgency; (crisis médica) emergency; **con —** urgently; **—s** emergency room

urgente ADJ urgent, pressing

urgir⁴⁶ VT to urge; VI to be urgent

úrico ADJ uric

urinario ADJ urinary; M urinal

URL M URL

urna F (para cenizas) urn; (electoral) ballot box; **acudir a las —s** to go to the polls

urólogo -ga MF urologist

urraca F (ave) magpie; (persona acaparadora) packrat

urticaria F hives

Uruguay M Uruguay

uruguayo -ya ADJ & MF Uruguayan

usado ADJ (utilizado) used; (desgastado) worn

usar VT (emplear) to use; (ponerse) to wear; **—se** to be in use; **sin —** unused

USB M USB

uso M (empleo) use; (costumbre) usage, custom;
   al — de la época according to the custom of
   the time

usted PRON PERS you; **—es** you, you all, y'all

usual ADJ usual

usuario -ria MF (de un servicio) user; (en una
   biblioteca) borrower

usufructo M enjoyment

usufructuar[26] VT to enjoy the use of

usura F usury

usurero -ra MF usurer, loan shark

usurpar VT to encroach upon, to usurp

utensilio M utensil

uterino ADJ uterine

útero M uterus, womb

útil ADJ useful, helpful; M PL **—es** utensils

utilidad F usefulness, utility

utilitario ADJ utilitarian

utilización F use, utilization

utilizar[47] VT (emplear) to utilize; (explotar) to
   use

utopía F utopia

uva F grape

úvula F uvula

uvular ADJ uvular

Uzbekistán M Uzbekistan

uzbeko -ka ADJ & MF Uzbek

Vv

va, vamos *ver* ir

vaca F cow; **— marina** sea cow

vacación F vacation; **de vacaciones** on
   vacation

vacante ADJ vacant; F vacancy, opening

vaciar[28] VT (una botella) to empty; (una naranja)
   to hollow out; (una estatua) to cast; (una
   computadora) to dump

vacilación F hesitation

vacilante ADJ (dudoso) vacillating, hesitating;
   (tembloroso) shaky

vacilar VI to vacillate, to hesitate, to waver; **—
   [con]** *fam* to make fun [of]

vacío ADJ (envase) empty; (casa) vacant;
   (comentarios) idle; (expresión) blank; M
   (condición) emptiness; (lugar) void; (espacio
   sin aire) vacuum; **envasado al —**
   vacuum-packed; **hacer el —** to give the cold
   shoulder

vacuna F (inoculación) vaccine; (enfermedad)
   cowpox

vacunación F vaccination

vacunar VI/VT to vaccinate

vacuno ADJ bovine

vadear VT to ford

vado M ford, crossing

vagabundear VI to wander idly

vagabundo -da ADJ vagabond, vagrant; MF
   (pordiosero) tramp, bum; (trabajador
   errante) drifter, transient; (en la playa)
   beachcomber

vagancia F vagrancy

vagar[40] VI to wander, to roam

vagina F vagina

vaginal ADJ vaginal

vaginitis F vaginitis

vago -ga ADJ (idea) vague; (silueta) shadowy;
   (impresión) faint, vague; (persona) lazy; MF
   vagrant, tramp

vagón M railway car; **— restaurante** dining car

vaguedad F faintness

vahído M dizzy spell

vaho M steam

vaina F (de una espada) sheath; (de legumbres)
   pod, shell; (molestia) nuisance; (cosa mal
   recordada) thing

vainilla F vanilla

vaivén M swaying, swinging; **vaivenes** ups and
   downs

vajilla F tableware, dishes; **— de barro**
   earthenware; **— de porcelana** chinaware

vale M voucher; INTERJ oh well, OK

valedero ADJ valid

valenciano -na ADJ & MF Valencian

valentía F courage, valor, bravery

valentón -ona ADJ cocky; MF cocky person

valer[60] VT (tener un determinado valor) to be
   worth; VI (ser válido) to be valid; (estar
   permitido) to be allowed; (ser de utilidad) to
   be useful; **— la pena** to be worthwhile; **—
   más que** to outweigh; **—se de** to avail
   oneself of; **—se por sí mismo** to be
   self-sufficient; **¿cuánto vale?** how much is
   it? **hacer — los derechos** to assert one's
   rights; **hacerse —** to stand up for oneself; **le
   valió una paliza** that earned him a beating;
   más vale solo que mal acompañado
   better alone than in poor company; **no hay
   pero que valga** no buts about it; **más vale
   tarde que nunca** better late than never; **no
   vale ni un comino** it's not worth a hoot; **no
   vale** that's not fair; **¡vale!** OK! **¡válgame
   Dios!** gracious! **todo vale** anything goes

valeroso ADJ valorous, brave

valga, valgo *ver* valer

valía F worth

validez F validity

válido ADJ (entrada, cupón) valid; (cheque)
   good; (argumento) solid

valiente ADJ valiant, brave, courageous

valija F (para viajes) valise, suitcase; (para el
   correo) pouch

valioso ADJ valuable

valla F (en un jardín) fence; (en carreras) hurdle

vallar VT to fence

valle M valley, vale

valor M (precio) value, worth; (valentía) valor, mettle; **— contable** book value; **—es** securities; **—es en cartera** holdings; **— nominal** face value, par value; **—es respaldados por hipoteca** mortgage-backed securities; **armarse de —** to muster up one's courage

valoración F valuation

valorar VT (apreciar) to value; (determinar el valor) to appraise; (aumentar el valor) to make more valuable

valorizar[47] VT to make more valuable; **—se** to become more valuable

vals M waltz

valsar VI to waltz

valuación F valuation, appraisal

valuar[26] VT to appraise

valva F valve

válvula F valve; **— reguladora de aceleración** throttle

vampiresa F vamp

vampiro M vampire

vanagloria F boastfulness

vanagloriarse VI to boast

vanaglorioso ADJ boastful

vándalo -la MF vandal

vanguardia F vanguard; **a la —** at the forefront

vanidad F vanity, conceit

vanidoso ADJ vain

vano ADJ vain; **en —** in vain

Vanuatu M Vanuatu

vanuatuense ADJ & MF Vanuatuan

vapor M (de agua) vapor, steam; (buque) steamship; **—es** fumes; **cocer al —** to steam; **echar —** to give off steam

vapulear VT to thrash

vapuleo M thrashing

vaquería F cowshed

vaqueriza F cowshed

vaquero -ra M cowboy; **—s** blue jeans; F cowgirl; ADJ **botas vaqueras** cowboy boots

vaqueta F cowhide

vaquilla F heifer

vara F (rama) stick; (palo) rod

varadero M dry dock

varar VT to beach, to strand; VI to run aground

varear VT to whip with a stick

variable ADJ variable, changeable; F variable

variación F variation

variado ADJ varied

variante F variant

variar[28] VI/VT to vary

varicela F chicken pox

várices, varices F PL varicose veins

varicoso ADJ varicose

variedad F variety, assortment

varilla F (palo delgado) small rod; (para azotar) switch; (de paraguas) rib

vario ADJ varied; **—s** various, several

variopinto ADJ variegated

varita F wand

varón M male [person]

varonil ADJ (masculino) manly; (hombruno) mannish

vasco -ca ADJ & MF Basque; M (lengua) Basque

vascuence ADJ Basque; M (lengua) Basque

vascular ADJ vascular

vasectomía F vasectomy

vaselina F Vaseline™

vasija F vessel

vaso M (de vidrio) glass; (de papel, plástico) cup; (corto y grueso) tumbler; (sanguíneo) vessel; **— de precipitado** beaker

vástago M (de planta) shoot, sprout; (de persona) offspring; (de motor) rod

vasto ADJ vast

vataje M wattage

vaticinar VT to foretell

vaticinio M prediction

vatio M watt

vaya, vayamos, ve ver ir

vea, veamos ver ver

vecindad F (cercanía) vicinity; (barrio) neighborhood

vecindario M neighborhood

vecino -na MF (cercano, contiguo) neighbor; (residente de una zona) resident; ADJ neighboring

vector M vector

vedar VT to prohibit

vega F fertile plain

vegan ADJ & MF vegan

vegetación F vegetation

vegetal ADJ vegetable; M vegetable, plant

vegetar VI to vegetate

vegetariano -na ADJ & MF vegetarian

vehemencia F vehemence

vehemente ADJ vehement

vehículo M vehicle

veía, veíamos ver ver

veinte NUM twenty

veintena F (aproximadamente) group of [about] twenty; (exactamente) score

veinticinco NUM twenty-five

veintiuno NUM twenty-one; M (juego de naipes) blackjack

vejancón -ona M codger; F old woman

vejar VT to humiliate

vejestorio -ria M codger; F old woman

vejete M codger

vejez F old age

vejiga F (órgano) bladder; (ampolla) blister

vela F (período de vigilancia) vigil, watch; (de cera) candle; (de un navío) sail; **a toda —** under full sail; **en —** without sleep; **hacerse**

a la — to set sail
velada F (noche) evening; (fiesta) evening party
velador M nightstand
velar VI (no dormir) to keep vigil, to stay awake; (cubrir con velo) to veil; (exponer a la luz una película fotográfica) to expose; **— por** to look after
velatorio M wake
veleidoso ADJ fickle
velero M sailboat; ADJ swift-sailing
veleta F weathervane; MF fickle person
vello M (del cuerpo) body hair; (de frutas) fuzz
vellón M fleece
velloso ADJ fuzzy
velludo ADJ hairy
velo M veil; **— del paladar** soft palate
velocidad F velocity, speed; **— de transferencia** transfer rate; **a toda** — at full speed
velocímetro M speedometer
velorio M wake
veloz ADJ swift, fast
ven *ver* venir
vena F (vaso sanguíneo, veta) vein; (estado de ánimo) mood; (de locura) streak; **estar en** — to be in the mood, to be inspired
venado M (animal) deer; (macho) stag; (carne) venison
vencedor -ora ADJ winning; MF winner, victor
vencer[32] VT (a un enemigo) to conquer, to vanquish; (a un equipo) to defeat, to beat; (obstáculos) to overcome; (en valor, inteligencia) to surpass; VI **—se** (un plazo) to expire; (un colchón) to cave in
vencido ADJ (derrotado) defeated; (a pagar) due, overdue, past due; **darse por** — to give up, to surrender
vencimiento M (de una deuda) maturity; (de un contrato) expiration
venda F (para una herida) bandage; (sobre los ojos) blindfold
vendaje M bandage; **— quirúrgico** surgical dressing
vendar VT (una herida) to bandage; (los ojos) to blindfold
vendaval M gale
vendedor -ora MF vendor, seller, salesperson; **— mayorista** wholesaler
vender VI/VT (comercializar) to sell; (traicionar) to betray; **—se a** to go over to; **se vende** for sale
vendetta F vendetta
vendible ADJ marketable
vendimia F vintage
vendrá, vendría *ver* venir
veneciana F venetian blind
veneno M (sustancia dañina) poison; (ponzoña de víbora) venom
venenoso ADJ (planta) poisonous; (víbora)

venomous
venerable ADJ venerable
veneración F veneration, reverence
venerar VT (a una persona) to venerate, to revere; (a Dios) to worship
venezolano -na ADJ & MF Venezuelan
Venezuela F Venezuela
venga, vengamos *ver* venir
vengador -ora ADJ avenging; MF avenger
venganza F vengeance, revenge, payback
vengar[40] VT to avenge; **—se de** to retaliate for, to avenge, to take revenge
vengativo ADJ vindictive, vengeful
venida F coming
venidero ADJ forthcoming
venir[61] VI to come; **— a colación** to come up [in conversation]; **— al caso / a cuento** to be relevant; **— bien** to be convenient; **—le a uno bien** to be suitable to someone; **—se abajo** to collapse; **¿a qué viene eso?** what is the point of that? **el año que viene** next year; **lo mejor está por** — the best is yet to come; **no me vengas con excusas** no excuses; **venga lo que venga** come what may
venta F sale; **— al por mayor** wholesale; **— al por menor** retail; **— de liquidación** fire sale; **en** — for sale; **poner a la** — to put up for sale
ventaja F (también en tenis) advantage; (en una carrera) head start; **— al resto** ad out; **— al saque** ad in; **— al servicio** ad in
ventajoso ADJ advantageous
ventana F window (también digital); **tirar por la** — to throw out the window
ventanal M large window
ventanilla F [de coche, avión] window; (de la nariz) nostril
ventarrón M gale, high wind
ventear VI to sniff the wind
ventilación F (aireado) ventilation; (hueco para el aire) vent
ventilado ADJ airy
ventilador M (abertura) ventilator; (aparato) electrical fan
ventilar VT to ventilate, to air out; (una cuestión) to air
ventisca F blizzard
ventisquero M (lugar ventoso) place prone to blizzards; (lugar nevado) snowfield
ventolera F gust of wind; **darle a uno la — de** to take a notion to
ventosear VI to break wind
ventoso ADJ windy, breezy
ventrículo M ventricle
venturoso ADJ fortunate; **futuro** — bright future
veo *ver* ver
ver[72, 74] VI/VT (un paisaje) to see; (televisión,

espectáculos) to watch; (un programa de computadora) to view; **a** — let's see; **eso aún está por —se** that is still to be seen; **no lo puedo** — I can't stand him; **no veo la hora de terminar** I'm dying / I can't wait to finish; **no tener nada que** — **con** not to have anything to do with; **te veo preocupado** you look worried; **a mi modo de** — in my opinion; **—se obligado a** to be obliged to; **vérselas con algo** to confront something; **vérselas negras** to have a hard time

vera LOC ADV **a la** — beside

veracidad F truthfulness

veranear VI to spend the summer

veraneo M summer vacation

veraniego ADJ summer

verano M summer

veras LOC ADV **de** — really; **¿de —?** oh really? oh yeah?

veraz ADJ truthful

verbal ADJ verbal

verbena F carnival

verbo M verb

verborrágico ADJ long-winded

verboso ADJ verbose, wordy

verdad F truth; **¿—?** really? — **a medias** half-truth; **de** — indeed; **una pistola de** — a real pistol; **faltar a la** — to fib

verdaderamente ADV really, truly

verdadero ADJ true, real

verde ADJ green (también inmaduro, sin experiencia, ecologista); (chiste) off-color; — **oliva** olive-green; **ponerse** — to stuff oneself; M green; **poner** — **a alguien** to run someone down

verdear VI/VT to turn green

verdín M scum

verdor M greenness

verdoso ADJ greenish

verdugo M executioner, hangman

verdugón M welt

verdulero -ra MF vegetable vendor

verdura F (hortaliza) vegetable; (verdor) *lit* verdure; —**s** produce

vereda F (en el campo) path; (para peatones) *Am* sidewalk; **entrar en** — to toe the line

veredicto M verdict

verga F yard

vergonzoso ADJ (que da vergüenza) shameful, disgraceful; (que siente vergüenza) sheepish, bashful

vergüenza F (humillación) shame; (incomodidad) embarrassment; (escándalo) disgrace; **tener** — to be ashamed; **tener** — **ajena** to cringe; **es una** — it's a shame; **me dan** — **mis dientes** I'm embarrassed about my teeth; **me da** — **decírtelo** I'm embarrassed to tell you

vericueto M twists and turns

verídico ADJ truthful, true

verificación F verification, cross-check

verificar[30] VT to verify, to check; **—se** to take place

verja F grate

vermú M vermouth

vernáculo ADJ & M vernacular

verruga F wart

versado ADJ versed

versalillas F PL small caps

versalitas F PL small caps

versar VI — **sobre** to deal [with], to treat

versátil ADJ versatile

versículo M Bible verse

versión F (de un texto) version; (traducción) translation; (de una canción) rendition; — **beta** beta version; — **impresa** printout; — **original** original [of a film]

verso M line [of poetry]; — **libre** free verse; — **suelto/blanco** blank verse

versus PREP versus

vértebra F vertebra

vertebrado ADJ & M vertebrate

vertebral ADJ spinal

vertedero M dump, landfill

verter[2] VT (echar líquido) to pour; (vaciar) to pour out; (derramar) to spill; — **en** to empty into; **—se** to spill

vertical ADJ (en ángulo recto) vertical; (erguido) upright; (empinado) sheer

vertido M (acción) dumping; (lo vertido) waste; — **de petróleo** oil spill

vertiente F (pendiente) slope; (cuenca) watershed; ADJ flowing

vertiginoso ADJ dizzy, giddy

vértigo M (falta de equilibrio) vertigo; (frenesí) hectic pace

vertigoso ADJ dizzy, giddy

vesícula F gall bladder

vestíbulo M (de un edificio) vestibule, lobby; (de una casa) hallway

vestido M dress; — **de noche** evening gown; — **de novia** bridal dress

vestidura F attire

vestigio M vestige, trace, remnant

vestimenta F attire, dress; (estrafalaria) getup

vestir[9] VT to dress, to clothe; **—se** to get dressed; **—se de gala** to dress up

vestuario M (ropa) wardrobe; (en el teatro) costumes; (lugar para vestirse) changing room

veta F (de minerales) vein, seam; (de madera) grain; (de humor) strain

vetar VT to veto

veteado ADJ veined

veterano -na ADJ & MF veteran

veterinario -ria MF veterinarian; ADJ veterinary; F veterinary medicine

veto M veto

vetusto ADJ ancient

vez F time; **a la —** at the same time; **a su —** in turn; **a veces** sometimes; **cada — más** more and more; **cada — que** whenever; **de — en cuando** from time to time; **de una —** (por entero) all at once; (por fin) one and for all; **de una — por todas** once and for all; **en — de** instead of, in lieu of; **por primera —** for the first time; **otra —** again; **una — [que]** once; **una — tras otra** over and over; **una y otra —** over and over again; **raras veces** seldom; **hacer las veces de** to take the place of

vía F (camino) road; (de ferrocarril) track; (medio de acceso) avenue; **— de transmisión local** local bus; **— Láctea** Milky Way; **— navegable** waterway; **— respiratoria** airway; **—s urinarias** urinary tract; **por — de** by means of; **en —s de** in the process of; PREP via

viabilidad F viability

viable ADJ viable

viaducto M tunnel

viajante MF traveler; **— de comercio** ; M traveling salesman; F saleswoman

viajar VI (por tierra, aire) to travel, to journey; (por mar) to voyage; (con drogas) to trip

viaje M (por tierra, aire) trip, journey; (por mar) voyage; (en coche, caballo) ride; (por efecto de las drogas) trip; **— de ida y vuelta** round trip; **buen —** have a nice trip; **de —** out of town

viajero -ra MF traveler

viandante MF passerby

viático M (de viaje) per diem; (religioso) last rites

víbora F viper; **— de cascabel** rattlesnake

vibración F (de una cuerda) vibration; (de la lengua) trill

vibrador M vibrator

vibrante ADJ vibrating

vibrar VI/VT to vibrate

vicegobernador -ora MF lieutenant governor

vicepresidente MF, **vicepresidenta** F vice president

vicerrector -ora MF provost

viceversa ADV vice versa

viciado ADJ (aire) stale; (costumbre) stuffy; (corrupto) foul

viciar VT (estropear) to foul; (corromper) to corrupt

vicio M (mala costumbre) vice, bad habit; **de —** unjustifiably; **quitarse el — de** to wean oneself of

vicioso ADJ (persona) dissolute; (gasto) unjustifiable; (gramática) faulty

vicisitud F vicissitude

víctima F (de un crimen) victim; (en un accidente) casualty, victim

victimizar[47] VT to victimize

victoria F victory

victorioso ADJ victorious

vid F vine, grapevine

vida F life; **— media** half-life; **— mía** sweetheart; **— nocturna** nightlife; **— sentimental** love life; **así es la —** that's life; **de toda la —** lifelong; **de — o muerte** life-and-death; **en la — voy a hacer eso** I would never do that; **esto es —** this is the life; **ganarse la —** to earn a living; **sin —** lifeless

vidente MF seer; ADJ seeing

vídeo, video M (aparato) VCR; (técnica) video; (cinta) videocassette

videocámara F camcorder

videocasete F videocassette

videoclip M videoclip

videoconferencia F videoconference

videoconsola F video console

videojuego M video game

vidriado M glaze; ADJ glazed

vidriar VT to glaze

vidriera F show window

vidriero -ra MF glazier, glassmaker

vidrio M (sustancia) glass; (en una ventana) pane; **pagar los —s rotos** to be left holding the bag

vidrioso ADJ glassy

vieira F scallop

viejo -ja ADJ old; (chiste) stale; M (anciano) old man; (padre) father; **— amigo** longtime friend; **— verde** dirty old man; **los —s** the old folks; F (anciana) old woman; (madre) mother

viento M wind; **hace —** it is windy; **a los cuatro —s** in all directions

vientre M (abdomen) abdomen; (barriga) belly; (útero) womb

viernes M Friday

Vietnam M Vietnam

vietnamita ADJ & MF INV Vietnamese

viga F (de madera) beam, rafter; (de metal) girder

vigencia F **entrar en —** to go into effect; **estar en —** to be in force

vigente ADJ effective, in force

vigésimo NUM twentieth

vigía F lookout, reef; MF lookout

vigilancia F (cuidado) vigilance; (en una tienda) surveillance

vigilante ADJ vigilant; M watchman; F watchwoman

vigilar VI/VT to keep watch [over]; VT to keep an eye on; (policía) to stake out

vigilia F vigil, wake

vigor M vigor; **en —** in force; **entrar en —** to become effective

vigorizar[47] VT to invigorate

vigoroso ADJ vigorous
VIH [virus de inmunodeficiencia humana] M HIV
vil ADJ vile, base, low
vileza F villainy, baseness
vilipendiar VT to revile
villa F (aldea) village; (casa) country house
villancico M Christmas carol
villanía F villainy
villano -na ADJ villainous; MF villain
vilo LOC ADV **en —** (en el aire) suspended; (en ascuas) in suspense
vinagre M vinegar
vinculación F connection
vincular VT to link (también para páginas web); **—se** to link up
vínculo M link, tie; (en la web) link
vindicar[30] VT to vindicate
vine, viniendo, viniera, viniese ver venir
vinilo M vinyl
vino M wine; **— blanco** white wine; **— espumoso** sparkling wine; **— rosado** rosé wine; **— tinto** red wine
viña F vineyard
viñatero -ra MF winegrower
viñedo M vineyard
viola F viola
violación F (de la ley) violation, infringement; (sexual) rape
violado ADJ & M violet
violar VT (una ley) to violate, to break; (una mujer) to rape, to ravish; (una promesa) to breach; (una cerradura) to pick; (derechos) to infringe upon; (mandamientos) to trespass against
violencia F violence; **— doméstica** domestic violence
violentar VT (a una persona) to manhandle; (una casa) to break into; **—se** to get mortified
violento ADJ (deporte, tratamiento) violent, rough; (marido) abusive; (entrada) forcible; (ataque) vicious
violeta ADJ & M violet
violín M (para música clásica) violin; (para música folclórica) fiddle
violinista MF violinist
violonchelo M cello
VIP M VIP
virada F veer
viraje M swerve
viral ADJ viral
virar VI/VT (vehículo) to swerve, to veer; VI (barco) to tack
virgen ADJ & MF virgin; ADJ (cassette) blank; (selva) undisturbed
virginal ADJ virginal
viril ADJ virile, manly
virilidad F virility, manliness
virología F virology

virreinato M viceroyalty
virrey M viceroy
virtual ADJ virtual
virtud F (moral) virtue; (práctica) asset
virtuosismo M virtuosity
virtuoso -sa ADJ (moral) virtuous; ADJ & MF (artístico) virtuoso
viruela F smallpox
virulento ADJ virulent
virus M virus (también de computadoras); **— de inmunodeficiencia humana** human immunodeficiency virus
viruta F wood shaving
visa F visa
visado M visa
visar VT to endorse
visceral ADJ visceral
viscoso ADJ viscous
visera F visor
visibilidad F visibility
visible ADJ visible
visigodo -da ADJ Visigothic; MF Visigoth
visillo M window shade
visión F (capacidad de ver, lo visto) vision; (persona fea) sight; **— en túnel** tunnel vision
visionario -ria ADJ & MF visionary
visita F (acción de visitar) visit; (persona) visitor, caller; (a un edificio) tour; (en una página web) hit; **— de médico** house call
visitación F visitation
visitador -ora MF visitor, caller; (inspector) inspector; (vendedor de medicamentos) pharmaceutical sales representative
visitante MF caller, visitor; ADJ visiting (también en fútbol)
visitar VT (a un amigo, país) to visit; (a un paciente) to make a house call
vislumbrar VT to make out
viso M slip
visón M mink
víspera LOC ADV **en —s de** on the eve of
vista F (panorama) view, vista; (visión) eyesight; **a la —** in sight; **— cansada** eye strain; **a primera —** at first sight; **a simple —** with the naked eye; **bajar la —** to lower one's eyes; **conocer de —** to know by sight; **con —s a** with a view to; **en — de** considering; **hacer la — gorda** to look the other way; **¡hasta la —!** good-bye; **perder de —** to lose sight of; **tener a la —** to have before one's eyes; **tener — a** to look out on
vistazo M glance, glimpse, look; **dar/echar un — a** to glance over
visto ADJ **bien —** well thought of; **mal —** looked down upon; **— que** whereas; M **— bueno** approval; **dar el —bueno** to approve
visto ver ver
vistoso ADJ showy
visual ADJ visual

visualizador M display

visualizar[47] VT (en la imaginación) to visualize; (en pantalla) to display

vital ADJ vital; **fuerzas —es** life force

vitalicio ADJ life, for life; M lifetime pension

vitalidad F vitality

vitamina F vitamin

viticultor -ora MF winegrower

vítor M cheer

vitorear VI/VT to cheer

vitral M stained-glass window

vitrina F (ventana) shop window; (armario) showcase

vituperación F vituperation

vituperar VT to revile

vituperio M vituperation

viudo -da M widower; F widow; **viuda negra** black widow spider

vivacidad F vivacity

vivaracho ADJ vivacious

vivaz ADJ vivacious, lively

víveres M PL provisions

vivero M nursery

viveza F (vivacidad) liveliness; (inteligencia) cleverness

vívido ADJ vivid

vivienda F (casa) dwelling; (alojamiento) housing; — **unifamiliar** single-family home

viviente ADJ living

vivir VI/VT to live; **vive una vida normal** he leads a normal life; **vivieron felices y comieron perdices** they lived happily ever after; **¡viva!** hurrah! **¡viva el rey!** long live the king!

vivisección F vivisection

vivo ADJ (viviente) alive, living; (ágil) lively; (vistoso, intenso) vivid; (listo) clever; **en —** before a live audience; **en — y en directo** live; **de viva voz** by word of mouth

vocablo M word

vocabulario M vocabulary

vocación F (profesional) vocation, calling; (religioso) call

vocal ADJ (de la voz) vocal; (no consonántico) vowel; F vowel; MF member

vocálico ADJ vocalic

vocear VI/VT (gritar) to cry out; (anunciar) to page

vocerío M clamor

vocero -ra MF spokesperson

vociferante ADJ vociferous

vociferar VI to clamor

vodevil M vaudeville

vodka M vodka

volado ADJ (drogado) high; (escrito arriba) superscript

volador ADJ flying

volante ADJ flying; M (en un vestido) ruffle, frill; (en un coche) steering wheel; (en un motor) flywheel; (folleto) leaflet, handbill

volar[5] VI/VT to fly; **— por su cuenta** to fly solo; **ir volando** to hurry; VT (un puente) to blow up; VI (hojas) to blow; **—se** (hacer explosión) to blow up; (enojarse) to lose one's temper; (irse volando) to fly away

volátil ADJ volatile

volcada F **hacer una —** (baloncesto) to dunk the ball

volcán M volcano

volcánico ADJ volcanic

volcar[31] VT (voltear) to tip over, to knock over; (derramar) to spill; (vaciar) to empty; VI to roll over; **—se** (un coche) to tip over, to overturn; (en baloncesto) to dunk

volea F (en vóleibol) volley; (en béisbol) fly ball; (en tenis) volley

volear VI/VT to volley

voleibol, vóleibol M volleyball

volición F volition

volqueta F *Am* dump truck

volquete M dump truck

voltaje M voltage

voltear VT (una lámpara) to knock over, to turn over; (la cara) to turn away

voltereta F somersault, tumble; **dar una —** to somersault; **dar —s** to tumble

voltio M volt

voluble ADJ (malhumorado) moody; (mercado de valores) volatile

volumen M volume

voluminoso ADJ voluminous, bulky

voluntad F will; **a —** at will; **buena —** good will, willingness; **mala —** ill will; **por su propia —** of his own volition

voluntario -ria ADJ voluntary; MF volunteer

voluntarioso ADJ (bien dispuesto) willing; (testarudo) willful

voluptuoso ADJ voluptuous

voluta F scroll; **—s de humo** spirals of smoke

volver[6, 74] VT (regresar al punto de partida) to return, to come back; (ir de nuevo) to return, to go back, to go again; **— a comer** to eat again; **— del revés** to turn inside out; **— en sí** to regain consciousness; **—se** (regresar) to go back; (ponerse) to become; **—se contra** to turn against; **—se atrás** to turn back; **—se hacia** to go toward; **—se loco** to go crazy; VT (la cara) to turn away; (la página) to turn; **— las espaldas** to turn one's back

vomitar VI/VT to vomit, to throw up

vómito M vomit

voraz ADJ voracious, ravenous

vórtice M vortex

vos PRON *fam RP, Am Central* you

vosotros -as PRON PERS *Esp* you, you guys; (sur de EEUU) you all, y'all

votación F voting

votante MF voter
votar VI (emitir el voto) to vote; VT (elegir) to vote for; (aprobar) to vote into law; **— a/por** to vote for; **— a favor** to vote in favor; **— en contra** to vote against; **— es un deber importante** voting is an important duty
voto M (opinión) vote; (promesa) vow; **— de confianza** vote of confidence
voy *ver* ir
voz F (sonido, aptitud, voto) voice; (en un diccionario) headword; **a — en cuello** at the top of one's lungs; **alzar la —** to raise one's voice; **correr la —** to be rumored; **en — alta** aloud; **en — baja** quietly, softly; **a voces** shouting; **dar voces** to shout
vozarrón M loud voice
vudú M voodoo
vuela, vuele *ver* volar
vuelco M **dar un —** to overturn, to turn over; **todo daría un —** everything would change radically; **me dio un — el corazón** my heart skipped a beat
vuelo M (en avión) flight; (de una falda) flare; **al —** on the fly; **de alto —** prestigious; **levantar/alzar el —** to fly away
vuelta F (movimiento circular) turn; (regreso, devolución) return; (carrera ciclista) tour; (en una pista) lap; (curva) twist; (de un collar) loop; (en deportes) round; (dinero) change; **— de tuerca** unforeseen event; **a la — de la esquina** around the corner; **a — de correo** by return mail; **dar —** to turn upside down; **dar — al revés** to turn inside out; **dar — a una página / una llave** to turn a page / a key; **dar —s** to spin; **dar —s en la cama** to toss and turn; **dar — a algo** to turn something upside down; **dar la —** to turn around; **dar una —** to take a walk, to take a spin; **darse —** to roll over; **estar de — (de regreso)** to be back; (desencantado) to be jaded; **me da —s la cabeza** my head is spinning; **no tiene — de hoja** there are no two ways about it
vuelto M *Am* change
vuelto, vuelva, vuelve *ver* volver
vuestro ADJ POS *Esp* **— hermano** your brother; **un amigo —** a friend of yours; PRON **el —** yours
vulgar ADJ (común) ordinary; (tosco) vulgar
vulgaridad F vulgarity
vulgo M common people
vulnerable ADJ vulnerable

Ww

wafle M waffle
waflera F waffle iron

wáter M toilet
web F web, Internet, World Wide Web
whisky M whisk[e]y; **— escocés** scotch
wifi [fidelidad inalámbrica] F Wi-Fi™
windsurf M windsurfing
wok M wok

Xx

xenofobia F xenophobia
xilofón, xilófono M xylophone

Yy

y CONJ and
ya ADV (desde antes) already; (ahora) now; (pronto) soon; **¡—!** enough! **— era hora** it was about time; **¡— lo creo!** I should say so! **— no** no longer; **— que** since; **— sea que** whether; **— te arreglo** I'll fix you; **— verás** mark my words; **— voy** I am coming
yacer[37] VI to lie
yacimiento M (de minerales) deposit; (de petróleo) field
yanqui ADJ & MF *pey* American
yapa F freebie
yarda F yard (también en fútbol americano)
yate M yacht
yegua F mare
yelmo M helmet
yema F (de huevo) egg yolk; (de una planta) bud, shoot; **— de huevo** egg yolk; **— del dedo** fingertip
Yemen M Yemen
yemení ADJ & MF Yemeni
yen M yen
yendo *ver* ir
yerba *ver* hierba
yermo ADJ (estéril) barren; (desolado) bleak, stark
yerno M son-in-law
yesca F tinder
yeso M (mineral) gypsum; (en construcción, medicina) plaster [of Paris]; (escayola) cast
Yibuti M Djibouti
yibutiano -na ADJ & MF Djiboutian
yo PRON PERS I; M (ego) ego
yodo M iodine
yoduro M iodide
yoga M yoga
yogur M yogurt

yo-yo M yo-yo
yuan M yuan
yuca F (ornamental) yucca; (comestible) manioc
yudo M judo
yugo M yoke
Yugoslavia F Yugoslavia
yugoslavo -va ADJ & MF Yugoslavian
yugular ADJ & F jugular
yunque M anvil
yunta F yoke
yuppie MF yuppie
yuxtaponer[56, 74] VT juxtapose

Zz

zacate M grass (también en tenis)
zafar VT to release; **—se** (soltarse) to slip off; (no cumplir) to cop out; **—se de un aprieto** to squirm out of a difficulty
zafio ADJ boorish
zafiro M sapphire
zafra F [sugar] harvest
zaga LOC ADV **a la —** behind; F **ir a la —** to be behind; **quedar a la —** to fall behind
zaguán M vestibule, hall
zaino ADJ chestnut-colored
zalamería F (tacto) smoothness; (lisonja) flattery
zalamero -ra MF flatterer; ADJ (empalagoso) smooth, unctuous; (lisonjero) flattering
Zambia F Zambia
zambiano -na ADJ & MF Zambian
zambo ADJ knock-kneed
zambullida F dive, plunge
zambullir[16] VT to plunge, to dip; **—se** to dive, to plunge
zanahoria F carrot
zanca F leg of a wading bird
zancada F stride; **dar —s** to stride
zancadilla F intentional tripping; **hacer una —** to trip
zanco M stilt
zancudo ADJ long-legged, lanky; M *Am* mosquito
zángano M drone (también holgazán)
zangolotear VI/VT to jiggle
zangoloteo M jiggle
zanja F ditch, trench
zanjar VT to settle
zapapico M pickax[e]
zapata F brake shoe
zapatear VI to tap the feet in dancing
zapateo M tapping with the feet in dance
zapatería F shoe store
zapatero -ra MF (fabricante) shoemaker;

(vendedor) shoe dealer; (remendón) cobbler
zapatilla F (pantufla) slipper; (de vestir) pump; **—s** sneakers
zapato M shoe; **—s con tacos** (fútbol americano) cleats; **—s con tapones** (fútbol) cleats; **—s del mismo par** matching shoes
zar M czar
zarandear VT to jiggle; **—se** to flop around
zarandeo M jiggle
zarcillo M (arete) earring; (de planta) tendril
zarigüeya F opossum
zarpa F claw
zarpar VI to sail, to set sail
zarpazo M blow with a claw; **dar —s** to claw
zarza F bramble, briar
zarzamora F blackberry
zepelín M blimp, zeppelin
zigoto M zygote
zigzag M zigzag
zigzaguear VI to zigzag, to weave one's way
Zimbabue M Zimbabwe
zimbabuo -bua ADJ & MF Zimbabwean
zirconio M zirconium
zócalo M baseboard; *Méx* main square
zodíaco M zodiac
zombi M zombie
zona F (área) zone; (culebrilla) shingles; **— de anotación/ensayo** (fútbol americano) end zone; **— de calentamiento** (béisbol) bullpen; **— de strike** (béisbol) strike zone; **— gris** gray area; **— tampón** buffer zone
zonificación F zoning
zonzo ADJ silly, foolish
zoo M zoo
zoología F zoology
zoológico ADJ zoological; M zoo
zoom M (de cámara fotográfica) zoom lens; (de computadora) zoom
zopenco -ca MF dolt, numbskull
zorrillo M skunk
zorro -a MF (animal) fox; F (hembra) vixen; ADJ (astuto) foxy, cunning
zorzal M thrush
zozobra F anxiety, worry
zozobrar VI to founder
zueco M clog
zumbar VI (hacer sonidos los insectos) to buzz, to drone, to hum; (hacer ruido las máquinas) to whir, to whiz; (tintinear los oídos) to ring; (dar golpe) to sock
zumbido M (sonido de insectos) buzz, drone, hum; (sonido de máquina) whir, whiz; (sonido en los oídos) ring
zumo M fruit juice
zurcido M (remiendo) darn; (acción de remendar) darning
zurcir[33] VT to darn
zurdo -da ADJ left-handed, southpaw; MF *fam* southpaw

zuro M corncob
zurra F whipping
zurrar VT to whip, to thrash
zutano -na M so-and-so, what's-his-name; F
so-and-so, what's-her-name

Inglés–Español · English–Spanish

Lista de abreviaturas / List of Abbreviations

adj	adjetivo	adjective
adv	adverbio, adverbial	adverb, adverbial
Am	América	America
art	artículo	article
Carib	Caribe	Caribbean
conj	conjunción	conjunction
def	definido	definite
dem	demostrativo	demonstrative
f	femenino	feminine
fam	familiar	familiar
indef	indefinido	indefinite
interj	interjección	interjection
interr	interrogativo	interrogative
inv	invariable	invariable
lit	literario	literary
loc	locución	locution
m	masculino	masculine
Mex	México	Mexico
n	sustantivo	noun
num	numeral	numeral
pej, pey	peyorativo	pejorative
pl	plural	plural
poss	posesivo	possessive
prep	preposición, preposicional	preposition, prepositional
pron	pronombre	pronoun
rel	relativo	relative
RP	Río de la Plata	River Plate
sg	singular	singular
Sp	España, español	Spain, Spanish
v aux	verbo auxiliar	auxiliary verb
vi	verbo intransitivo	intransitive verb
vt	verbo transitivo	transitive verb
vulg	vulgar	vulgar

Pronunciación inglesa

I. VOCALES

Símbolo fonético	Ortografía inglesa	Explicación
[i]	see, pea	como la *i* en *hilo*
[ɪ]	bit	el sonido más aproximado es la *i* en *virtud*, pero la [ɪ] inglesa es más abierta, tirando a *e*
[e]	late, they	equivale aproximadamente a *ei*
[ɛ]	set	semejante a la *e* de *perro*, pero más abierta
[ɝ]	work, bird	como la *u* de *cud* (ver abajo) pero articulada simultáneamente con una *r*
[æ]	sat	sonido intermedio entre *e* y *a*
[ɑ]	hot	como la vocal de *pan*
[ɔ]	saw, laud	sonido intermedio entre *a* y *o*
[o]	low, mode	equivale aproximadamente a *ou*
[ʊ]	book, pull	como la *u* de *turrón*, pero más abierta
[u]	June, moon	como la *u* de *uno*
[ʌ]	cud	una *e* muy relajada
[ə]	<u>a</u>dept	una *e* muy relajada y átona
[ɚ]	teach<u>er</u>	una *e* átona relajada articulada simultáneamente con una *r*

II. DIPTONGOS

Símbolo fonético	Ortografía inglesa	Explicación
[aɪ]	pie, aisle	como *ai* en *aire*
[aʊ]	now, foul	como *au* en *causa*
[ɔɪ]	boy	como *oy* en *hoy*
[ju]	use	como *iu* en *ciudad*

III. CONSONANTES

Símbolo fonético	Ortografía inglesa	Explicación
[b]	bat	semejante a la *b* española
[d]	day	semejante a la *d* española, pero articulada en los alvéolos y con más tensión
[f]	fun, photo	como la *f* española

[g]	go	como la *g* de *goma*, pero con más tensión
[h]	hat	muy suave como la *j* de los dialectos caribeños del español
[j]	year	como la *i* del diptongo de *hielo*
[k]	cat, kill	como la *c* de *carro*, pero seguida de aspiración en posición inicial de sílaba (sobre todo tónica)
[l]	let	como la *l* de *lado*
[ł]	ball	como la *l* final catalana
[m]	much	como la *m* española
[n]	no	como la *n* española
[p]	pea	como la *p* española, pero seguida de aspiración en posición inicial de sílaba (sobre todo tónica)
[r]	red	no tiene equivalente en español; se pronuncia con la punta de la lengua enrollada hacia arriba, sin tocar el paladar
[s]	sea	como la *s* hispanoamericana (no la castellana)
[t]	tea	como la *t* española pero articulada en los alvéolos y seguida de aspiración en posición inicial de sílaba (sobre todo tónica)
[v]	very	se articula con los dientes incisivos superiores colocados en el labio inferior
[w]	weed	equivale a la *u* del diptongo de *fui*
[z]	zero, rose	como la *s* de *mismo* cuando se sonoriza, pero aun más sonora
[ɒ]	latter, ladder	como la *r* de *para*
[θ]	thin	como la *z* del español castellano en *zagal*
[ð]	this	como la *d* de *cada*
[ʃ]	sheet, machine, notation	una *s* muy palatal como en francés *chapeau* o italiano *lasciare*
[ʒ]	measure, beige	como la *ll* argentina en *valle*, cuando es sonora
[tʃ]	church	como la *ch* de *charla*
[dʒ]	judge	como la *y* de *inyectar*
[n̩]	eaten, button	representa la *n* silábica, articulada sin la vocal anterior
[ŋ]	ring	como la *n* española en *mango* y *banco*
[l̩]	rental	representa la *l* silábica, articulada como la *l* final catalana
[hw]	where	combinación de los sonidos [h] y [w] arriba descritos

Notas sobre gramática inglesa

El sustantivo

Género. En la gramática inglesa el género solo desempeña un papel importante en el sistema pronominal, p. ej. **he runs** 'él corre', **she runs** 'ella corre', **I see him** 'lo veo', **I see her** 'la veo'. En los sustantivos que designan a personas, se emplean varios métodos para distinguir entre los sexos, v. gr. el agregado de un sufijo, como en **actor** 'actor', **actress** 'actriz', el agregado de una palabra, como en **baby boy** 'niño', **baby girl** 'niña', **she-bear** 'osa', **male nurse** 'enfermero', o el uso de palabras completamente distintas, como en **uncle** 'tío', **aunt** 'tía'.

Número. Generalmente se forma el plural añadiendo **-s** al singular: **paper, papers** 'papel, papeles', **book, books** 'libro, libros', **chief, chiefs** 'jefe, jefes'.

Los sustantivos que terminan en **-ss, -x, -sh, -z** y **-o** añaden **-es** para formar el plural: **kiss, kisses** 'beso, besos', **box, boxes** 'caja, cajas', **dish, dishes** 'plato, platos', **buzz, buzzes** 'zumbido, zumbidos', **hero, heroes** 'héroe, héroes' (excepción: **piano, pianos**). Esto vale también para **-ch** cuando se pronuncia [č], como en **arch, arches** 'arco, arcos', pero no cuando se pronuncia [k], como en **monarch, monarchs** 'monarca, monarcas'.

Los sustantivos que terminan en **-fe,** y ciertos sustantivos que terminan en **-f,** cambian estas letras en **v** y añaden **-es** en el plural: **leaf, leaves** 'hoja, hojas', **life, lives** 'vida, vidas', **wife, wives** 'esposa, esposas', **knife, knives** 'cuchillo, cuchillos' (pero **reef, reefs** 'arrecife, arrecifes').

Para formar el plural de los sustantivos terminados en **-y** precedida de consonante se cambia la **-y** en **-ies: fly, flies** 'mosca, moscas', **family, families** 'familia, familias'. En cambio, los sustantivos terminados en **-y** precedida de vocal forman el plural añadiendo **-s** al singular: **day, days** 'día, días'.

Ciertos sustantivos forman el plural de una manera irregular: **man, men** 'hombre, hombres', **woman, women** 'mujer, mujeres', **mouse, mice** 'ratón, ratones', **louse, lice** 'piojo, piojos', **goose, geese** 'ganso, gansos', **tooth, teeth** 'diente, dientes', **foot, feet** 'pie, pies', **ox, oxen** 'buey, bueyes'.

Ciertos sustantivos que terminan en **-is** forman el plural cambiando la **i** de la terminación en **e: axis, axes** 'eje, ejes', **crisis, crises** 'crisis' (sg., pl.).

El adjetivo

El adjetivo inglés es invariable en cuanto a género y número. Normalmente se coloca delante del sustantivo: **an interesting woman** 'una mujer interesante', **a large man** 'un hombre grande', **beautiful birds** 'aves hermosas'.

Los comparativos y superlativos. Aunque no hay una regla general, por lo común los adjetivos monosílabos, los adjetivos acentuados en la última sílaba y algunos bisílabos comunes forman el comparativo de aumento y el superlativo añadiendo **-er** y **-est** (como **tall**). Los demás adjetivos van precedidos de **more** (para el comparativo) y **most** (para el superlativo) (como **careful**). Nótese que (1) si la palabra termina en **-e** muda, se añaden **-r** y **-st** en vez de **-er** y **-est** (ver **wise**), (2) los adjetivos terminados en **-y** cambian esta letra en **i** (ver **happy**), (3) los adjetivos terminados en consonante (menos **r**) precedida de vocal doblan la consonante (ver **fat**):

Positivo	Comparativo	Superlativo
tall alto	**taller** más alto	**the tallest** el más alto
careful cuidadoso	**more careful** más cuidadoso	**the most careful** el más cuidadoso
wise sabio	**wiser** más sabio	**the wisest** el más sabio
happy feliz	**happier** más feliz	**the happiest** el más feliz
fat gordo	**fatter** más gordo	**the fattest** el más gordo

Los adjetivos siguientes forman el comparativo y el superlativo de una manera irregular:

good	**better**	**best**
bad, ill	**worse**	**worst**
much	**more**	**most**

El adverbio

Muchos adverbios se forman añadiendo **-ly** al adjetivo: **courteous** 'cortés', **courteously** 'cortésmente', **bold** 'atrevido', **boldly** 'atrevidamente'. Existen las irregularidades ortográficas siguientes en la formación de los adverbios que terminan en **-ly**: (1) los adjetivos terminados en **-ble** cambian la **-e** en **-y: possible, possibly,** (2) los terminados en **-ic** añaden **-ally: poetic, poetically,** (3) los terminados en **-ll** añaden solo **-y: full, fully,** (4) los terminados en **-ue** pierden la **-e** final: **true, truly,** (5) los terminados en **-y** cambian la **-y** en **i: happy, happily.**

La mayor parte de los adverbios forman el comparativo y el superlativo con los adverbios **more** 'más' y **most** 'el/la más'. Asimismo los adverbios monosílabos añaden **-er** y **-est:**

Positivo	Comparativo	Superlativo
boldly	**more boldly**	**most boldly**
generously	**more generously**	**most generously**
soon	**sooner**	**soonest**
early	**earlier**	**earliest**
late	**later**	**latest**
fast	**faster**	**fastest**

Los adverbios siguientes forman el comparativo y el superlativo de una manera irregular:

well	better	best
badly	worse	worst
little	less	least
far	farther, further	farthest, furthest

Sufijos comunes del inglés

-dom   a partir de bases nominales, forma sustantivos con los sentidos de dominio, jurisdicción, estado, condición: **kingdom** 'reino' (**king** 'rey'), **martyrdom** 'martirio' (**martyr** 'mártir'), **freedom** 'libertad' (**free** 'libre')

-ee   a partir de verbos, forma sustantivos indicando a la persona que recibe una acción: **addressee** 'destinatario' (**to address** 'dirigir'), **employee** 'empleado' (**to employ** 'emplear').

-eer   a partir de bases diversas, forma sustantivos que denotan oficio u ocupación: **auctioneer** 'subastador' (**to auction** 'subastar'), **puppeteer** 'titiritero' (**puppet** 'títere')

-en   *a.*   forma adjetivos que denotan la sustancia de que está hecha una cosa: **golden** 'dorado' (**gold** 'oro'), **wooden** 'de madera' (**wood** 'madera')
       b.   forma verbos a partir de adjetivos: **to whiten** 'blanquear' (**white** 'blanco'), **to darken** 'oscurecer' (**dark** 'oscuro')

-er   *a.*   forma sustantivos a partir de verbos para indicar agente: **player** 'jugador' (**to play** 'jugar'), **speaker** 'hablante' (**to speak** 'hablar'), **baker** 'panadero' (**to bake** 'hornear')
       b.   forma sustantivos a partir de sustantivos para denominar al residente de un lugar: **New Yorker** 'neoyorquino' (**New York** 'Nueva York'), **islander** 'isleño' (**island** 'isla')

-ess   se usa para formar el género femenino de ciertos sustantivos: **princess** 'princesa' (**prince** 'príncipe'), **countess** 'condesa' (**count** 'conde')

-fold   indica el número de veces que se repite algo: **twofold** 'dos veces' (**two** 'dos'), **hundredfold** 'cien veces' (**hundred** 'cien')

-ful   *a.*   forma adjetivos a partir de sustantivos para indicar la presencia de una cualidad: **hopeful** 'esperanzado' (**hope** 'esperanza'), **careful** 'cuidadoso' (**care** 'cuidado'), **willful** 'voluntarioso' (**will** 'voluntad')
       b.   forma adjetivos a partir de verbos para indicar tendencia: **forgetful** 'olvidadizo' (**to forget** 'olvidar')

    c. forma sustantivos a partir de sustantivos indicando la capacidad: **handful** 'puñado' (**hand** 'mano'), **spoonful** 'cucharada' (**spoon** 'cuchara')

-hood forma abstractos a partir de sustantivos concretos: **motherhood** 'maternidad' (**mother** 'madre'), **childhood** 'niñez' (**child** 'niño'), **likelihood** 'probabilidad' (**likely** 'probable')

-ing *a.* forma adjetivos a partir de verbos: **running water** 'agua corriente' (**to run** 'correr'), **drinking water** 'agua potable' (**to drink** 'beber'), **waiting room** 'sala de espera' (**to wait** 'esperar'), **washing machine** 'máquina lavadora' (**to wash** 'lavar')

    b. se usa para formar sustantivos que expresan la acción de un verbo: **understanding** 'entendimiento' (**to understand** 'entender'), **supplying** 'abastecimiento' (**to supply** 'abastecer')

    c. se usa para formar sustantivos que denominan una cosa que desempeña una acción: **clothing** 'ropa' (**to clothe** 'vestir'), **covering** 'cobertura' (**to cover** 'cubrir')

-ish forma adjetivos a partir de sustantivos indicando semejanza o atenuación: **boyish** 'como un niño' (**boy** 'niño'), **womanish** 'como mujer, mujeril' (**woman** 'mujer'), **whitish** 'blancuzco' (**white** 'blanco')

-less se agrega a sustantivos para indicar falta de algo: **childless** 'sin hijos' (**child** 'hijo'), **penniless** 'sin dinero' (**penny** 'centavo'), **endless** 'interminable, sin fin' (**end** 'fin')

-like se añade a sustantivos para indicar semejanza: **lifelike** 'que parece vivo' (**life** 'vida'), **childlike** 'infantil' (**child** 'niño'), **tigerlike** 'como un tigre' (**tiger** 'tigre')

-ly *a.* se añade a adjetivos para formar adverbios: **slowly** 'lentamente' (**slow** 'lento'), **happily** 'felizmente' (**feliz** 'happy')

    b. deriva adjetivos a partir de sustantivos indicando una cualidad: **motherly** 'maternal' (**mother** 'madre'), **gentlemanly** 'caballeroso' (**gentleman** 'caballero'), **friendly** 'amistoso' (**friend** 'amigo')

    c. deriva adjetivos o adverbios de tiempo a partir de sustantivos: **daily** 'diario', 'diariamente' (**day** 'día'), **weekly** 'semanal', 'semanalmente' (**week** 'semana')

-ness forma nombres de cualidades a partir de adjetivos: **goodness** 'bondad' (**good** 'bueno'), **darkness** 'oscuridad' (**dark** 'oscuro'), **foolishness** 'tontería' (**fool** 'tonto')

-ship		se emplea para derivar sustantivos a partir de sustantivos y verbos para denotar
	a.	cualidades abstractas: **friendship** 'amistad' (**friend** 'amigo')
	b.	arte o destreza: **horsemanship** 'equitación' (**horseman** 'jinete')
	c.	dignidad, oficio, cargo o título: **professorship** 'cátedra' (**professor** 'catedrático'), **lordship** 'señoría' (**lord** 'señor')
	d.	la duración de una acción: **courtship** 'cortejo' (**to court** 'cortejar')

-some se añade a verbos para formar adjetivos que expresan tendencia excesiva: **tiresome** 'aburrido' (**to tire** 'aburrir'), **quarrelsome** 'pendenciero' (**to quarrel** 'discutir')

-th es el sufijo que forma números ordinales a partir de los cardinales: **fifth** 'quinto' (**five** 'cinco'), **tenth** 'décimo' (**ten** 'diez')

-ward se añade a sustantivos y adverbios para indicar movimiento hacia un lugar: **homeward** 'hacia casa' (**home** 'casa'), **downward** 'hacia abajo' (**down** 'abajo')

-wise, se añaden a sustantivos para indicar dirección o posición: **edgewise** 'de
-ways lado' (**edge** 'borde'), **lengthwise** 'a lo largo' (**length** 'largo'), **sideways** 'de lado' (**side** 'lado')

-y	*a.*	es un sufijo diminutivo: **doggy** 'perrito' (**dog** 'perro'), **Johnny** 'Juanito' (**John** 'Juan')
	b.	se añade a sustantivos para formar adjetivos que indican abundancia: **rocky** 'rocoso' (**rock** 'roca'), **rainy** 'lluvioso' (**rain** 'lluvia'), **hairy** 'peludo' (**hair** 'pelo'), **angry** 'enojado' (**anger** 'enojo')
	c.	se añade a sustantivos para formar adjetivos que expresan semejanza: **rosy** 'rosado' (**rose** 'rosa')

Verbos irregulares de la lengua inglesa

Se denominan verbos irregulares los que no forman el pretérito o el participio pasivo con la adición de **-d** o **-ed** al presente. Obsérvese que en ciertos verbos (aquí señalados con asterisco) coexiste la forma regular al lado de la irregular. Las formas poco usadas aparecen entre paréntesis.

Presente	*Pretérito*	*Participio pasivo*
*abide	(abode)	abided
am, is, are	was, were	been
arise	arose	arisen
*awake	awoke	awoken

Presente	*Pretérito*	*Participio pasivo*
bear	bore	borne
beat	beat	beaten
become	became	become
befall	befell	befallen
beget	begat	begotten
begin	began	begun
behold	beheld	beheld
bend	bent	bent
*beseech	(besought)	(besought)
beset	beset	beset
bet	bet	bet
bid 'ofrecer'	bid	bid
bid 'mandar'	bade	bidden
bind	bound	bound
bite	bit	bitten, bit
bleed	bled	bled
blow	blew	blown
break	broke	broken
breed	bred	bred
bring	brought	brought
build	built	built
*burn	burnt	burnt
burst	burst	burst
buy	bought	bought
cast	cast	cast
catch	caught	caught
choose	chose	chosen
cling	clung	clung
*clothe	(clad)	(clad)
come	came	come
cost	cost	cost
creep	crept	crept
cut	cut	cut
deal	dealt	dealt
dig	dug	dug
*dive	dove	dived
do	did	done
draw	drew	drawn
*dream	dreamt	dreamt
drink	drank	drunk
drive	drove	driven
*dwell	dwelt	dwelt
eat	ate	eaten
fall	fell	fallen

Verbos irregulares

Presente	Pretérito	Participio pasivo
feed	fed	fed
feel	felt	felt
fight	fought	fought
find	found	found
*fit	fit	fit
flee	fled	fled
fling	flung	flung
fly	flew	flown
forbear	(forbore)	(forborne)
forbid	forbade	forbidden
foresee	foresaw	foreseen
foretell	foretold	foretold
forget	forgot	forgotten
forgive	forgave	forgiven
forsake	forsook	forsaken
freeze	froze	frozen
get	got	got, gotten
give	gave	given
go	went	gone
grind	ground	ground
grow	grew	grown
hang[1]	hung	hung
have, has	had	had
hear	heard	heard
*hew	hewed	hewn
hide	hid	hidden, hid
hit	hit	hit
hold	held	held
hurt	hurt	hurt
keep	kept	kept
*kneel	knelt	knelt
*knit	knit	knit
know	knew	known
lay	laid	laid
lead	led	led
*lean	(leant)	(leant)
*leap	leapt	leapt
*learn	(learnt)	(learnt)
leave	left	left
lend	lent	lent
let	let	let

1. Es regular cuando significa 'ahorcar'.

Presente	Pretérito	Participio pasivo
lie[2]	lay	lain
*light	lit	lit
lose	lost	lost
make	made	made
mean	meant	meant
meet	met	met
mistake	mistook	mistaken
*mow	mowed	mown
pay	paid	paid
*plead	pled	pled
put	put	put
quit	quit	quit
read [rid]	read [rɛd]	read [rɛd]
rend	rent	rent
*rid	rid	rid
ride	rode	ridden
ring	rang	rung
rise	rose	risen
run	ran	run
*saw	sawed	sawn
say	said	said
see	saw	seen
seek	sought	sought
sell	sold	sold
send	sent	sent
set	set	set
*sew	sewed	sewn
shake	shook	shaken
*shave	shaved	shaven
*shear	sheared	shorn
shed	shed	shed
shine[3]	shone	shone
shoe	shod	shod
shoot	shot	shot
*show	showed	shown
shrink	shrank (shrunk)	shrunk (shrunken)
shut	shut	shut
sing	sang	sung
sink	sank	sunk
sit	sat	sat
slay	slew	slain

2. Es regular cuando significa 'mentir'.
3. Suele ser regular cuando es transitivo, en el sentido 'pulir, dar brillo'.

Presente	Pretérito	Participio pasivo
sleep	slept	slept
slide	slid	slid
sling	slung	slung
slink	slunk	slunk
slit	slit	slit
*smell	(smelt)	(smelt)
smite	smote	smitten
*sow	sowed	sown
speak	spoke	spoken
*speed	sped	sped
*spell	(spelt)	(spelt)
spend	spent	spent
*spill	(spilt)	(spilt)
spin	spun	spun
spit	spat, spit	spat, spit
split	split	split
*spoil	(spoilt)	(spoilt)
spread	spread	spread
spring	sprang, sprung	sprung
stand	stood	stood
*stave	(stove)	(stove)
steal	stole	stolen
stick	stuck	stuck
sting	stung	stung
stink	stank	stunk
*strew	strewed	strewn
stride	strode	stridden
strike	struck	struck, stricken
string	strung	strung
*strive	strove	striven
swear	swore	sworn
*sweat	sweat	sweat
sweep	swept	swept
*swell	swelled	swollen
swim	swam	swum
swing	swung	swung
take	took	taken
teach	taught	taught
tear	tore	torn
tell	told	told
think	thought	thought
throw	threw	thrown
thrust	thrust	thrust
tread	trod	trodden

Presente	Pretérito	Participio pasivo
understand	understood	understood
undertake	undertook	undertaken
undo	undid	undone
uphold	upheld	upheld
upset	upset	upset
*wake	woke	woken
wear	wore	worn
weave	wove	woven
*wed	wed	wed
weep	wept	wept
*wet	wet	wet
win	won	won
wind	wound	wound
withdraw	withdrew	withdrawn
withhold	withheld	withheld
withstand	withstood	withstood
wring	wrung	wrung
write	wrote	written

Aa

a [ə, e] INDEF ART un *m*, una *f*; **what — fool!** ¡qué tonto! **such — fool** tan tonto; **I'm — teacher / Catholic** soy maestro / católico

AA [Alcoholics Anonymous] [éé] N AA *f*

aback [əbǽk] ADV **to be taken —** estar desconcertado

abandon [əbǽndən] VT abandonar; N **with wild —** desenfrenadamente

abandonment [əbǽndənmənt] N abandono *m*, desamparo *m*

abashed [əbǽʃt] ADJ humillado, avergonzado

abate [əbét] VI/VT (trend, payments) disminuir, mitigar[se]; (storm) calmarse, atenuarse

abbey [ǽbi] N abadía *f*

abbot [ǽbət] N abad *m*

abbreviate [əbríviet] VT abreviar

abbreviation [əbriviéʃən] N (act of abbreviating) abreviación *f*; (short form) abreviatura *f*

abdicate [ǽbdɪket] VI/VT abdicar

abdomen [ǽbdəmən] N abdomen *m*, vientre *m*

abdominal [æbdámənl] ADJ abdominal; **— distension** distensión abdominal *f*

abduct [æbdʌ́kt] VT secuestrar, raptar

abduction [æbdʌ́kʃən] N secuestro *m*, rapto *m*

aberration [æbəréʃən] N anomalía *f*, aberración *f*

abet [əbét] VT instigar

abeyance [əbéəns] ADV LOC **in —** pendiente, en suspenso

abhor [əbhór] VT aborrecer

abhorrence [əbhórəns] N aborrecimiento *m*

abhorrent [əbhórənt] ADJ aborrecible

abide [əbáɪd] VT (tolerate) soportar; VI (dwell) morar, permanecer; **to — by** acatar, atenerse a

ability [əbílɪɖi] N (skill) habilidad *f*; (aptitude) capacidad *f*

abject [ǽbdʒɛkt] ADJ abyecto; **in — poverty** en extrema miseria

ablaze [əbléz] ADV en llamas

able [ébəl] ADJ hábil, capaz; **—-bodied** de cuerpo sano; **to be — to** (be capable of) poder; (have an acquired skill) saber

abnegate [ǽbnɪgɛt] VT renunciar

abnormal [æbnórməl] ADJ anormal

aboard [əbórd] ADV a bordo; **all —!** (train) ¡viajeros al tren! (ship) ¡pasajeros a bordo! **to go —** embarcarse, abordar

abode [əbód] N morada *f*

abode [əbód] *see* abide

abolish [əbálɪʃ] VT abolir, suprimir

abolition [æbəlíʃən] N abolición *f*

abominable [əbámənəbəl] ADJ abominable

abomination [əbamənéʃən] N (action, thing) abominación *f*; (condition, vice) horror *m*

aboriginal [æbərídʒənəl] ADJ aborigen

aborigine [æbərídʒəni] N aborigen *mf*; **Australian —** aborigen australiano -na *mf*

abort [əbórt] VT (fetus) abortar; VI/VT (mission) suspender; (software) interrumpir; N (software) interrupción *f*

abortion [əbórʃən] N aborto *m*

abortionist [əbórʃɪnɪst] N abortador -ora *mf*, abortero -ra *mf*

abortive [əbórdɪv] ADJ frustrado

abound [əbáund] VI abundar; **to — with** abundar en

about [əbáut] PREP (concerning) acerca de, tocante a; (near, surrounding) alrededor de, por; **to be — one's business** atender a su negocio; ADV más o menos, alrededor de; **at — ten o'clock** a eso de las diez, sobre las diez; **to be — to do something** estar por / para hacer algo, estar a punto de hacer algo; **I'm all — transparency** insisto en la transparencia

above [əbʌ́v] PREP **you could see the towers — the buildings** se veían las torres sobre los edificios; **everyone — five years of age** todos los de más de cinco años; **he's — me in the company** es mi superior en la compañía; **to be — suspicion** estar libre de toda sospecha; **I thought you were — such things** no pensaba que te rebajarías a eso; ADV **the apartment —** el apartamento de arriba; **books of fifty pages and —** libros de cincuenta páginas y más; **the remark quoted —** la observación anteriormente citada; **— all** sobre todo; **—-mentioned** susodicho, ya mencionado

abrasion [əbréʒən] N abrasión *f*

abrasive [əbrésɪv] ADJ (material) abrasivo; (person, tone) irritante

abreast [əbrést] ADV al lado; **to keep —** mantenerse al corriente; **four —** de cuatro en fondo

abridge [əbrídʒ] VT abreviar

abroad [əbród] ADV en el extranjero; **to go —** ir al extranjero

abrupt [əbrʌ́pt] ADJ abrupto

ABS [antilock braking system] [ébíés] N SFA *m*

abscess [ǽbsɛs] N absceso *m*

abscond [æbskánd] VI fugarse

absence [ǽbsəns] N (nonpresence) ausencia *f*; (lack) falta *f*; **in the — of** a falta de

absent [ǽbsənt] ADJ ausente; **—-minded** distraído, despistado; **to be — from school** faltar a la escuela

absentee [æbsəntí] N ausente *mf*; **— landlord** propietario -ria ausente *mf*

absenteeism [æbsəntízəm] N ausentismo *m*

absolute [ǽbsəlút] ADJ (ruler, certainty)

absoluto; (prohibition) terminante

absolutely [æbsəlútli] ADV absolutamente; —
not en absoluto; INTERJ —! ¡sí, señor! ¡claro!

absolve [æbzálv] VT absolver

absorb [əbzɔ́rb] VT (liquid) absorber; (shock)
amortiguar; (people, information) asimilar;
he is —ed in his work está absorto en su
trabajo

absorption [əbzɔ́rpʃən] N absorción f

abstain [æbstén] VI abstenerse; — **from**
abstenerse de

abstention [æbsténʃən] N abstención f

abstinence [ǽbstənəns] N abstinencia f

abstract [ǽbstrækt] ADJ abstracto; N (summary)
resumen m, extracto m; **in the** — en
abstracto

abstraction [æbstrǽkʃən] N abstracción f

absurd [əbsɚ́d] ADJ absurdo, disparatado

absurdity [əbsɚ́DIDi] N (quality) absurdo m;
(action) disparate m

abundance [əbʌ́ndəns] N abundancia f

abundant [əbʌ́ndənt] ADJ abundante

abuse[1] [əbjús] N (of privileges) abuso m; (of
authority) abuso m, desmán m; (physical)
maltrato m; (verbal) injuria f

abuse[2] [əbjúz] VT (privileges) abusar de;
(physically) maltratar; (verbally) injuriar

abusive [əbjúsiv] ADJ (physically) violento;
(verbally) injurioso

abysmal [əbízməl] ADJ abismal; — **results**
resultados desastrosos m pl

abyss [əbís] N abismo m

A/C [air conditioning] [ésí] N aire
acondicionado m

academic [ækədémik] ADJ (university)
académico; (school) escolar; N profesor -ora
universitario -ria mf

academy [əkǽdəmi] N academia f

accede [æksíd] VI acceder; **to** — **to** acceder a

accelerate [æksélərət] VI/VT acelerar

acceleration [ækselərérən] N aceleración f

accelerator [ækséləreɾə‑] N acelerador m

accent[1] [ǽksent] N (pronunciation) acento m;
(written) tilde f, acento escrito/ortográfico m

accent[2] [æksént] VT (syllable) acentuar

accentuate [æksént∫uet] VT (differences, facts,
syllables) acentuar, recalcar; (beauty) realzar

accept [æksépt] VT aceptar

acceptable [ækséptəbəl] ADJ aceptable

acceptance [ækséptəns] N (action) aceptación f;
(approval) aprobación f

access [ǽkses] N acceso m; — **code** código de
acceso m; — **provider** proveedor -ora de
acceso mf; — **denied** acceso denegado m; VT
acceder a

accessibility [æksesəbíliDi] N accesibilidad f

accessible [æksésəbəl] ADJ accesible

accessory [æksésəri] ADJ accesorio; N (to
clothes, to gadgets) accesorio m; (to a crime)

cómplice mf; — **slot** ranura para accesorios f

accident [ǽksiDənt] N accidente m; (mishap)
percance m; — **insurance** seguro contra
accidentes m; **by** — por casualidad

accidental [æksidéntl] ADJ (injury) accidental;
(discovery, meeting) casual, fortuito

acclaim [əklém] VT aclamar; N aclamación f,
ovación f

acclamation [ækləméʃən] N aclamación f

acclimate [ǽkləmet] VI/VT (to physical
conditions) aclimatar[se]; (to an ambience)
acostumbrar[se]

accolade [ǽkəled] N elogio m

accommodate [əkámədet] VT (adjust) tener en
cuenta; (lodge) hospedar, alojar; (contain)
tener capacidad para; VI **to** — **oneself**
adaptarse

accommodation [əkamədéʃən] N (adjustment)
acomodación f, adaptación f; —**s** (lodging)
alojamiento m; (facilities) comodidades f pl

accompaniment [əkʌ́mpənimənt] N
acompañamiento m

accompanist [əkʌ́mpənist] N acompañante mf

accompany [əkʌ́mpəni] VI/VT acompañar

accomplice [əkʌ́mplis] N cómplice mf

accomplish [əkʌ́mpliʃ] VT (objective) lograr;
(mission) completar

accomplished [əkʌ́mpliʃt] ADJ (actor, athlete)
consumado; (musician) talentoso

accomplishment [əkʌ́mpliʃmənt] N
(achievement) logro m; (skill) habilidad f;
(completion) realización f

accord [əkɔ́rd] N acuerdo m, convenio m; **of
one's own** — voluntariamente; VT otorgar,
conceder

accordance [əkɔ́rdns] ADV LOC **in** — **with** de
acuerdo con, de conformidad con

according to [əkɔ́rDiŋ] ADV LOC según

accordingly [əkɔ́rDiŋli] ADV (therefore) por
consiguiente; (correspondingly) como
corresponde

accordion [əkɔ́rDiən] N acordeón m

accost [əkɔ́st] VT abordar

account [əkáunt] N (bill) cuenta f; (story) relato
m, relación f; — **manager** administrador
-ora de cuentas mf; —**s payable** cuentas por/
a pagar f pl; —**s receivable** cuentas por/a
cobrar f pl; **to open [close] an** — abrir
[cerrar] una cuenta; **on** — **of** a causa de,
debido a; **on my** — por mí; **on one's own** —
por cuenta propia; **on no** — de ninguna
manera; **of no** — de ningún valor; **to take
into** — tener en cuenta; VI **to** — **for** dar
cuenta de; **how do you** — **for that?** ¿cómo
se explica eso?

accountability [əkauntəbíliDi] N
responsabilidad f

accountable [əkáuntəbəl] ADJ responsable

accountant [əkáuntnt] N Am contador -ra mf; Sp

contable *mf*

accounting [əkáuntıŋ] N contabilidad *f*; — **firm** empresa de contadores públicos *f*; — **period** ejercicio contable *m*

accredit [əkrédɪt] VT acreditar

acculturate [əkʌ́ltʃəret] VI/VT aculturar[se]

accumulate [əkjúmjəlet] VI/VT acumular[se]

accumulation [əkjumjəléʃən] N acumulación *f*

accuracy [ǽkjəəsi] N (of measure, instrument) precisión *f*, exactitud *f*; (of a translation) fidelidad *f*

accurate [ǽkjə·ıt] ADJ (measure, instrument) preciso, exacto; (translation) fiel

accursed [əkʌ́sɪd] ADJ maldito

accusation [ǽkjuzéʃən] N acusación *f*

accuse [əkjúz] VT acusar

accused [əkjúzd] ADJ acusado; N acusado -da *mf*, reo -a *mf*, procesado -da *mf*

accuser [əkjúzə·] N acusador -ra *mf*

accustom [əkʌ́stəm] VT acostumbrar, habituar; **to — oneself** acostumbrarse, habituarse; **to be —ed to** tener la costumbre de, estar acostumbrado a

AC/DC [alternating current / direct current] [ésídísí] ADJ alterna y continua

ace [es] N (cards, athlete, aviator) as *m*; (tennis) saque ganador *m*, servicio directo *m*; VT (a test) sacarse la máxima nota en

acetaminophen [əseDəmínəfən] N acetaminofén *m*

acetone [ǽsəton] N acetona *f*

ache [ek] N dolor *m*; **—s and pains** achaques *m pl*; VI doler; **my stomach —s** me duele el estómago

achieve [ətʃív] VT (a goal) conseguir, lograr; (a level) alcanzar

achievement [ətʃívmənt] N (attainment) consecución *f*; (success) logro *m*, realización *f*

Achilles tendon [əkıliz téndən] N tendón de Aquiles *m*

aching [ékıŋ] ADJ doliente, dolorido

achy [éki] ADJ dolorido

acid [ǽsɪd] ADJ ácido; N ácido *m*; (hallucinogen) LSD *m*; — **rain** lluvia ácida *f*; — **test** prueba de fuego *f*

acidic [əsídık] ADJ ácido

acidity [əsídıDi] N acidez *f*

acknowledge [æknálıʤ] VT (merits) reconocer; (faults) admitir, reconocer; (help) agradecer; **to — receipt** acusar recibo

acknowledgment [æknálıʤmənt] N (of merits) reconocimiento *m*; (of merits, faults) reconocimiento *m*, admisión *f*; (gratefulness) agradecimiento *m*; — **of receipt** acuse de recibo *m*

acme [ǽkmi] N súmmum *m*

acne [ǽkni] N acné *m*

acorn [ékɔrn] N bellota *f*

acoustics [əkústıks] N acústica *f*

acquaint [əkwént] VT informar, familiarizar; **to — oneself with** informarse de, familiarizarse con; **to be —ed with** (a person, city, country) conocer; (a piece of news) estar enterado de

acquaintance [əkwéntns] N (with facts) conocimiento *m*; (a person) conocido -a *mf*

acquiesce [ǽkwiés] VT asentir, condescender; (unwillingly) consentir

acquiescence [ǽkwiésəns] N asentimiento *m*, consentimiento *m*, condescendencia *f*

acquire [əkwáır] VT (knowledge, skill, purchase) adquirir; (fortune, information) obtener; (disease) contraer

acquisition [ǽkwəzíʃən] N (knowledge, skill, purchase) adquisición *f*; (fortune, information) obtención *f*

acquisitive [əkwízıDıv] ADJ codicioso

acquit [əkwít] VT absolver

acquittal [əkwídl] N absolución *f*

acre [ékə·] N acre [0.405 hectares] *m*

acrid [ǽkrıd] ADJ acre

acrimony [ǽkrəmoni] N acritud *f*

acrobat [ǽkrəbæt] N acróbata *mf*

acrobatic [ǽkrəbǽDık] ADJ acrobático; N **—s** acrobacia *f*

acronym [ǽkrənım] N acrónimo *m*, sigla *f*

acrophobia [ǽkrəfóbiə] N acrofobia *f*

across [əkrɔ́s] PREP **to lay one stick — the other** poner dos palos cruzados; **there's a bridge — that river** hay un puente sobre ese río; **he came — his old love letters** encontró sus viejas cartas de amor; **the library is — the street** la biblioteca está al otro lado de la calle; — **the board** de manera uniforme, sin excepciones; ADV **cut the boards** — corta los tablones a lo ancho; **five hundred miles** — de quinientas millas de ancho; **the meaning doesn't come** — el significado no se entiende

acrylic [əkrílık] ADJ & N acrílico *m*

act [ækt] N (deed, part of play) acto *m*; (part of show) número *m*; (law) ley *f*, decreto *m*; — **of God** caso de fuerza mayor *m*; VI (behave) actuar, comportarse; (take measures) obrar; (play a part, chemical process) actuar; (represent) representar; (function) funcionar; **to — up** (child) portarse mal; (car) funcionar mal; **to — out** (event) representar; (feelings) exteriorizar

acting [ǽktıŋ] N actuación *f*; (in a drama) representación *f*; ADJ (interim) interino; (substitute) suplente

action [ǽkʃən] N (practical measure, plot of a play) acción *f*; (deed) acto *m*; (functioning) funcionamiento *m*; **to take** — tomar medidas

actionable [ǽkʃənəbəl] ADJ accionable, procesable

activate [ǽktıvet] VT activar

active [æktɪv] ADJ activo

activism [æktɪvɪzəm] N activismo *m*

activist [æktɪvɪst] N activista *mf*

activity [æktívɪdi] N actividad *f*

actor [æktə] N actor *m*

actress [æktrɪs] N actriz *f*

actual [æktʃuəl] ADJ verdadero, real

actually [æktʃuəli] ADV en realidad, efectivamente

actuary [æktʃueri] N actuario -ria *mf*

acuity [əkjúɪdi] N agudeza *f*

acumen [ækjəmən] N perspicacia *f*, agudeza *f*

acupuncture [ækjʊpʌŋktʃə] N acupuntura *f*

acupuncturist [ækjʊpʌŋktʃə-ɪst] N acupuntor -ora *mf*

acute [əkjút] ADJ (pain, illness) agudo; (observation) perspicaz, penetrante

AD [édí] ADV d.C.

ad [æd] N anuncio publicitario *m*; — in (tennis) ventaja al saque *f*, ventaja al servicio *f*; — out (tennis) ventaja al resto *f*; — lib ADJ improvisado; ADV improvisando; to — lib VI improvisar

adamant [ædəmənt] ADJ inflexible, firme

Adam's apple [ædəmz æpəl] N nuez de Adán *f*

adapt [ədæpt] VT adaptar; VI to — to adaptar[se] a, acomodar[se] a

adaptation [ædəptéʃən] N adaptación *f*

adapter [ədæptə] N adaptador *m*

add [æd] VT añadir, agregar; (find sum) sumar; —ed cost costo adicional *m*; to — to aumentar; to — up (find sum) sumar; (make sense) cuadrar; N —-on accesorio *m*

addict [ǽdɪkt] N adicto -ta *mf*

addicted [ədíktɪd] ADJ adicto

addiction [ədíkʃən] N adicción *f*

addition [ədíʃən] N (of numbers) suma *f*; (to a collection, staff) adición *f*, adquisición *f*; (to a building) anexo *m*; in — [to] además [de]

additional [ədíʃənəł] ADJ adicional

additive [ǽdɪtɪv] N aditivo *m*

address¹ [ədrés] N (street) dirección *f*, domicilio *m*; (speech) discurso *m*; — book libreta de direcciones *f*; form of — tratamiento *m*

address² [ədrés] VT (write the address) dirigir; (speak to) dirigirse a; (deal with) ocuparse de

addressee [ædresí] N destinatario -ria *mf*

adduce [ədús] VT aducir

adept [ədépt] ADJ hábil

adequacy [ǽdɪkwəsi] N suficiencia *f*

adequate [ǽdɪkwɪt] ADJ (sufficient) suficiente; (acceptable) aceptable

adhere [ædhír] VI adherirse; to — to adherirse a

adherence [ædhírəns] N adhesión *f*

adhesion [ædhíʒən] N (thing or tissue that adheres) adherencia *f*; (act of sticking together) adhesión *f*

adhesive [ædhísɪv] ADJ adhesivo; — tape cinta adhesiva *f*

adjacent [ədʒésənt] ADJ adyacente

adjective [ædʒɪktɪv] ADJ & N adjetivo *m*

adjoin [ədʒɔ́ɪn] VT lindar con, colindar con; —ing colindante; VI estar contiguo a

adjourn [ədʒɚ́n] VT to — the meeting levantar la sesión; meeting —ed se levanta la sesión

adjournment [ədʒɚ́nmənt] N levantamiento de la sesión *m*

adjudge [ədʒʌ́dʒ] VT (declare) declarar; (deem) calificar

adjudicate [ədʒúdɪket] VI arbitrar; VT declarar

adjunct [ædʒʌŋkt] ADJ adjunto; N agregado -da *mf*

adjust [ədʒʌ́st] VT (fix) ajustar, graduar; (adapt a machine) regular; —ed net income ingreso neto ajustado *m*; VI ajustarse, adaptarse

adjustable [ədʒʌ́stəbəł] ADJ ajustable; —-rate mortgage hipoteca con tasa de interés ajustable *f*

adjustment [ədʒʌ́stmənt] N ajuste *m*; (to a machine) regulación *f*

administer [ædmínɪstə] VT (a business) administrar, gestionar; (a punishment) aplicar; (an oath) tomar[le]

administration [ædmɪnɪstréʃən] N administración *f*; (period in power) gestión *f*; (of punishment) aplicación *f*; (of an oath) toma *f*

administrative [ædmínɪstreɪdɪv] ADJ administrativo

administrator [ædmínɪstreɪdə] N administrador -ra *mf*; (civil) intendente *mf*

admirable [ædmə-əbəł] ADJ admirable

admiral [ædmə-əł] N almirante *m*

admiration [ædmə-éʃən] N admiración *f*

admire [ædmáɪr] VT admirar

admirer [ædmáɪrə] N admirador -ora *mf*; (suitor) pretendiente *mf*

admissible [ædmísəbəł] ADJ admisible

admission [ædmíʃən] N (acceptance) admisión *f*; (access, ticket price) entrada *f*; (confession) confesión *f*

admit [ædmít] VT (allow entry) admitir; (to a hospital) internar; (acknowledge) reconocer, admitir

admittance [ædmítns] N entrada *f*; no — prohibida la entrada

admonish [ædmánɪʃ] VT amonestar

admonition [ædmənɪʃən] N (warning) advertencia *f*; (reproof) amonestación *f*

adobe [ədóbi] N (mud) adobe *m*; (house) casa de adobe *f*

adolescence [ædlésəns] N adolescencia *f*

adolescent [ædlésənt] ADJ & N adolescente *mf*

adopt [ədápt] VT (child, custom) adoptar; (suggestion) aprobar

adoption [ədápʃən] N (of a child, custom) adopción *f*; (of a suggestion) aprobación *f*

adoptive [ədáptɪv] ADJ adoptivo

adorable [ədɔ́rəbəl] ADJ adorable, precioso

adoration [ædəréʃən] N adoración f

adore [ədɔ́r] VT adorar; **I — playing tennis** me encanta jugar al tenis

adorn [ədɔ́rn] VT adornar, ornar

adornment [ədɔ́rnmənt] N adorno m

adrenal [ədrínl] ADJ suprarrenal

adrenaline [ədrénəlin] N adrenalina f

adrift [ədríft] ADJ & ADV a la deriva

adult [ədált] ADJ & N adulto -ta mf

adulterate [ədáltəret] VT adulterar

adulterer [ədáltərɚ] N adúltero -ra mf

adultery [ədáltəri] N adulterio m

advance [ædvǽns] VI (move forward) avanzar; (make progress) avanzar, progresar; (bring forward) adelantar; VT (promote) promover; (propose) proponer; (pay beforehand) adelantar, anticipar; N (movement) avance m; (progress) adelanto m; (loan) adelanto m, anticipo m; **—s** (sexual) requiebros m pl; **in —** por adelantado, con anticipación

advanced [ædvǽnst] ADJ (idea, stage) avanzado; (country) adelantado

advancement [ædvǽnsmənt] N (movement) avance m; (rank) ascenso m; (knowledge) progreso m

advantage [ædvǽntɪdʒ] N ventaja f (also tennis); **it would be to your —** te convendría; **to take — of** aprovecharse de

advantageous [ædvæntédʒəs] ADJ ventajoso, provechoso

advent [ǽdvɛnt] N advenimiento m

adventure [ædvɛ́ntʃɚ] N aventura f

adventurer [ædvɛ́ntʃərɚ] N aventurero -ra mf

adventuresome [ædvɛ́ntʃɚsəm] ADJ atrevido, osado

adventurous [ædvɛ́ntʃɚəs] ADJ (seeking adventure) aventurero, intrépido; (daring) atrevido, audaz

adverb [ǽdvɚb] N adverbio m

adversary [ǽdvɚseri] N adversario -ria mf

adverse [ædvɝ́s] ADJ adverso

adversity [ædvɝ́sɪdi] N adversidad f

advertise [ǽdvɚtaiz] VT anunciar, hacer publicidad/propaganda para; VI hacer propaganda/publicidad; **to — for a cook** poner un anuncio buscando cocinero

advertisement [ædvɚtáizmənt] N anuncio publicitario m, aviso m

advertiser [ǽdvɚtaizɚ] N anunciante mf

advertising [ǽdvɚtaiziŋ] N publicidad f; **— agency** agencia de publicidad f; **— campaign** campaña publicitaria f; **— agent** agente publicitario -ria mf

advice [ædváis] N consejo m; (expert) asesoramiento m

advisable [ædváizəbəl] ADJ aconsejable, recomendable

advise [ædváiz] VI/VT (counsel) aconsejar, advertir; VT (inform) avisar, informar; (expertly) asesorar

adviser, advisor [ædváizɚ] N consejero -ra mf, asesor -ora mf

advocacy [ǽdvəkasi] N defensa f

advocate[1] [ǽdvəkɪt] N (promoter) partidario -ria mf; (defender) defensor -ora mf, intercesor -ora mf; (lawyer) abogado -da mf

advocate[2] [ǽdvəket] VT abogar por, defender

aerial [ériəł] ADJ aéreo; N antena f

aerobic [eróbɪk] ADJ (exercise) aeróbico; (air-breathing) aerobio; N **—s** aeróbic m

aerodynamic [erodaɪnǽmɪk] ADJ aerodinámico; N **—s** aerodinámica f

aeronautics [erənɔ́dɪks] N aeronáutica f

aerosol [érəsɑł] N aerosol m

aerospace [érospes] N espacio aéreo m; ADJ aeroespacial

aesthetic [esθέdɪk] ADJ estético; N **—s** estética f

affable [ǽfəbəł] ADJ afable

affair [əfér] N (social) acontecimiento social m; (business) asunto m, negocio m; (love) aventura amorosa f, affaire m

affect [əfɛ́kt] VT (have effect on) afectar; (move) conmover; (feign) fingir

affectation [æfɛktéʃən] N afectación f, melindre m

affected [əfɛ́ktɪd] ADJ (moved) afectado, conmovido; (feigned) fingido, artificioso, melindroso

affection [əfɛ́kʃən] N afecto m, cariño m

affectionate [əfɛ́kʃənɪt] ADJ afectuoso, cariñoso

affidavit [æfɪdévɪt] N declaración jurada f

affiliate[1] [əflliet] VT afiliar; VI afiliarse, asociarse

affiliate[2] [əflliit] N filial f

affiliation [əfɪliéʃən] N (relation) afiliación f; (membership) filiación f; **political —** filiación política f

affinity [əfínɪdi] N afinidad f

affirm [əfɝ́m] VT afirmar

affirmation [æfɚméʃən] N afirmación f

affirmative [əfɝ́mədɪv] ADJ afirmativo; **— action** discriminación positiva f; N **reply in the —** dar una respuesta afirmativa

affix[1] [əfíks] VT fijar; **to — one's signature** poner su firma, firmar

affix[2] [ǽfɪks] N afijo m

afflict [əflíkt] VT aquejar; **to be —ed with** padecer de, sufrir de

affliction [əflíkʃən] N (misery) aflicción f; (ailment) achaque m, mal m

affluent [ǽfluənt] ADJ (society) opulento; (person) rico

afford [əfɔ́rd] VT **I cannot — a car** no me alcanza el dinero para un coche; **he cannot — to waste time** no puede darse el lujo de perder tiempo; **I cannot — the risk** no me puedo permitir ese riesgo; **we will — you every opportunity** se te darán todas las oportunidades

affordable [əfɔ́rdəbəl] ADJ asequible

affront [əfránt] N afrenta f

Afghan, Afghani [ǽfgæn/æfgǽni] ADJ & N afgano -na mf

Afghanistan [æfgǽnɪstæn] N Afganistán m

afire [əfáɪr] ADJ & ADV en llamas

afloat [əflót] ADJ & ADV flotando, a flote

afraid [əfréd] ADJ asustado; **to be — [of]** temer, tener miedo [a]

afresh [əfréʃ] ADV de nuevo, desde el principio

Africa [ǽfrɪkə] N África f

African [ǽfrɪkən] ADJ & N africano -na mf

African American [ǽfrɪkənəmérɪkən] ADJ & N afroamericano -na mf

after [ǽftə] PREP (temporal) después de, tras; (spatial) detrás de; **— all** después de todo; ADV después; CONJ después [de] que

afterbirth [ǽftəbɜθ] N placenta f

aftercare [ǽftəker] N (post-illness) tratamiento de convalecencia m; (postoperative) tratamiento post-operatorio m

after-hours [ǽftə áurz] ADV después de horas hábiles

afterlife [ǽftəlaɪf] N el más allá m

aftermarket [ǽftəmarkɪt] ADJ de mercado secundario; N (for merchandise) mercado secundario m; (for stocks) mercado extrabursátil m

aftermath [ǽftəmæθ] N secuelas f pl

afternoon [ǽftənún] N tarde f; INTERJ **good —!** ¡buenas tardes!

aftershave [ǽftəʃev] N loción para después del afeitado f

aftershock [ǽftəʃak] N réplica f

aftertaste [ǽftətest] N (in the mouth) dejo m; (bad memory) resabio m

aftertax profit [ǽftətæksprófɪt] N ganancia neta f

afterthought [ǽftəθɔt] N **it was just an —** se nos ocurrió después

afterward, afterwards [ǽftəwəd[z]] ADV después, posteriormente

again [əgén] ADV otra vez, de nuevo; **— and —** repetidas veces; **to fall —** volver a caerse

against [əgénst] PREP contra; **— the grain** a contrapelo; **— all odds** a pesar de todo

age [edʒ] N (of a person) edad f; (era) era f, época f; **— of consent** edad de consentimiento sexual f; **— discrimination** discriminación por edad f; **— limit** límite de edad m; **old —** vejez f; **of —** mayor de edad; **to come of —** llegar a la mayoría de edad; **under —** menor de edad; VI/VT envejecer

aged[1] [edʒd] ADJ (wine) añejo; **— forty** de cuarenta años

aged[2] [édʒɪd] ADJ anciano

ageless [édʒlɪs] ADJ (everlasting) eterno; (not showing age) siempre joven; (classic) clásico

agency [édʒənsi] N agencia f; **through the — of** por mediación de

agenda [ədʒéndə] N orden del día m, agenda f

agent [édʒənt] N agente mf; (commercial) representante mf, gestor -ora mf; (legal) apoderado -da mf

aggrandize [əgrǽndaɪz] VT engrandecer

aggravate [ǽgrəvet] VT (worsen) exacerbar, agravar; (annoy) irritar, exasperar, exacerbar

aggregate [ǽgrɪgɪt] N conjunto m; (rock) agregado m; ADJ total, global

aggression [əgréʃən] N (attack) agresión f; (propensity to violence) agresividad f

aggressive [əgrésɪv] ADJ (violent) agresivo; (dynamic) emprendedor

aggressiveness [əgrésɪvnɪs] N agresividad f

aggressor [əgrésə] N agresor -ra mf

aghast [əgǽst] ADJ horrorizado

agile [ǽdʒəl] ADJ ágil

agility [ədʒílɪti] N agilidad f

aging [édʒɪŋ] N (of a person) envejecimiento m; (of wine) maduración f

agitate [ǽdʒɪtet] VT (shake) agitar; (perturb) turbar; (campaign) alborotar

agitation [ædʒɪtéʃən] N agitación f

agitator [ǽdʒɪtedə] N agitador -ra mf

agnostic [ægnástɪk] ADJ & N agnóstico -ca mf

ago [əgó] ADV **many years —** hace muchos años; **long —** hace mucho tiempo

agog [əgág] ADJ planchado, boquiabierto

agonize [ǽgənaɪz] VI sufrir angustiosamente; **to — over** atormentarse por

agony [ǽgəni] N (pain) dolor m, tormento m; (anguish) angustia f

agoraphobia [ægəəfóbiə] N agorafobia f

agrarian [əgrériən] ADJ agrario

agree [əgrí] VI (be in agreement) estar de acuerdo; (in grammar, mathematics) concordar; (color, food) sentarle bien; **to — upon** acordar, convenir, pactar; **they —d to meet the next day** quedaron en reunirse al día siguiente, acordaron reunirse al día siguiente; **the two sides —d to a truce** los dos bandos pactaron una tregua

agreeable [əgríəbəl] ADJ (nice) agradable; (willing) conforme

agreement [əgrímənt] N (concord, document) acuerdo m, concertación f, convenio m; (grammatical) concordancia f; **to be in —** estar de acuerdo; **to come to an —** ponerse de acuerdo, pactar

agricultural [ægrɪkʌ́ltʃəəl] ADJ (related to crops) agrícola; (related to crops and cattle) agropecuario

agriculture [ǽgrɪkʌltʃə] N agricultura f

aground [əgráund] ADV **to run —** encallar, varar

ahead [əhéd] ADV delante; **— of time** adelantado, con antelación; **to go —** ir

adelante, adelantarse; **to get** — prosperar;
our team is — nuestro equipo va primero;
the years — los años venideros

aid [ed] N (help) asistencia f; (assistant) ayudante
m f; VT ayudar; **to — and abet** instigar

aide [ed] N (high-ranking) asesor -ora m f;
(low-ranking) ayudante m f

**AIDS [acquired immune deficiency
syndrome]** [edz] N SIDA m

ail [el] VI/VT **what —s you?** ¿qué tienes? ¿qué te
aflige? **he's —ing** está enfermo

aileron [élərən] N alerón m

ailing [élɪŋ] ADJ (person) achacoso, enfermizo;
(economy) debilitado

ailment [élmənt] N achaque m, dolencia f

aim [em] N (with a weapon) puntería f;
(objective) objetivo m; VT (a weapon) apuntar;
(a question, blow) dirigir; **to — to please**
tratar de agradar

aimless [émlɪs] ADJ (purposeless) sin propósito;
(directionless) sin rumbo

air [ɛr] N aire m; **—bag** airbag m, bolsa de aire f;
—brake freno neumático m; **to —
condition** poner aire condicionado; **—
conditioner** acondicionador de aire m; **—
conditioning** aire acondicionado m,
climatización f; **—craft** aeronave f; **—craft
carrier** portaaviones m sg; **—field**
aeródromo m; **— force** fuerza aérea f;
—head cabeza de chorlito m f; **—lift** puente
aéreo m; **—line** línea aérea f, areolínea f; **—
mail** correo aéreo m; **—plane** avión m; **—
piracy** piratería aérea f; **—port** aeropuerto
m; **— power** fuerza aérea f; **— pressure**
presión de aire f; **— raid** ataque aéreo m; **—
rifle** escopeta de aire comprimido f; **—ship**
dirigible m; **— strike** bombardeo aéreo m;
—strip pista de aterrizaje f; **—-to-—**
aire-aire; **— traffic control** control del
tráfico aéreo m; **—way** conducto de aire m,
vía respiratoria f; **up in the** — en el aire,
incierto; **in the open** — al aire libre; **to be
on the** — estar en el aire, emitirse; **to put on
—s** presumir, darse ínfulas; **to vanish into
thin** — evaporarse; VT (an opinion)
manifestar; **to —lift** aerotransportar; **to —
out** orear, ventilar; ADJ aéreo; **—borne**
(troops) aerotransportado; (particles)
transportado por el aire; **— conditioned** con
aire acondicionado, climatizado; **—tight**
hermético

aisle [aɪl] N pasillo m; (of a church) nave lateral f

ajar [ədʒár] ADJ entornado, entreabierto

aka [ékéé] ADV (also called) también conocido
como; (in police usage) alias

akin [əkín] ADJ (related) emparentado; (similar)
semejante

à la mode [alɑmód] ADV con helado

alarm [əlárm] N (warning) alarma f; (worry)

inquietud f; **— clock** despertador m; **to
sound an** — tocar a rebato; VT (worry)
alarmar; (frighten) asustar

alarming [əlórmɪŋ] ADJ alarmante

Albania [ælbénɪə] N Albania f

Albanian [ælbénɪən] ADJ & N albanés -esa m f

albatross [ǽlbətrɔs] N albatros m

albinism [ǽlbɪnɪzəm] N albinismo m

albino [ælbáɪno] N albino -na m f

album [ǽlbəm] N álbum m

alcohol [ǽlkəhɔl] N alcohol m

alcoholic [ælkəhɔ́lɪk] ADJ & N alcohólico -ca m f

alcoholism [ǽlkəhɔlɪzəm] N alcoholismo m

alcove [ǽlkov] N rincón m

ale [el] N cerveza inglesa f

alert [əlɜ́t] ADJ (vigilant) alerta; (awake)
despierto; **to be** — (on guard) estar alerta;
(lively) ser despierto; N alerta f; VT alertar,
avisar

alfalfa [ælfǽlfə] N alfalfa f

algae [ǽldʒi] N algas f pl

algebra [ǽldʒəbrə] N álgebra f

Algeria [ældʒírɪə] N Argelia f

Algerian [ældʒírɪən] ADJ & N argelino -na m f

algorithm [ǽlgərɪðəm] N algoritmo m

alias [élɪəs] N alias m sg

alibi [ǽləbaɪ] N coartada f

alien [élɪən] N (visitor from space) extraterrestre
m f; (foreigner) extranjero -ra m f; ADJ ajeno

alienate [élɪənet] VT (people) alienar, alejar;
(property) enajenar

alight [əláɪt] VI (rider) apearse; (bird, insect)
posarse

align [əláɪn] VI/VT alinear[se]

alignment [əláɪnmənt] N alineación f

alike [əláɪk] ADJ parecido, igual; **to be** —
parecerse, ser iguales; ADV del mismo modo

alimentary [ælimɛ́ntəri] ADJ alimenticio; **—
canal** canal alimentario m

alimony [ǽləmoni] N pensión alimenticia f

alive [əláɪv] ADJ (living) vivo; **— with** lleno de;
the symphony came — **under his
direction** la sinfonía cobró vida bajo su
dirección

alkali [ǽlkəlaɪ] N álcali m

alkaline [ǽlkəlɪn] ADJ alcalino

all [ɔl] ADJ todo; **— the time** todo el tiempo; N
todo m; **to give one's** — dar todo de sí; PRON
todo; **is that —?** ¿eso es todo? — **or nothing**
todo o nada; ADV completamente, todo; **— at
once** (uninterrupted) de una vez; (sudden) de
repente; **—-inclusive** con todo incluido; **—-
time high** máximo histórico m; **— told** en
conjunto; **he's — dirty** está todo sucio; **it is
— over** se acabó; **not at** — de ninguna
manera; **nothing at** — nada en absoluto;
once [and] for — de una vez por todas;
she's — right está bien; INTERJ — **right**
bueno

allay [əlé] VT (fear, doubt) calmar, disipar; (anger) aplacar

allegation [ӕligéʃən] N acusación *f*

allege [əléʤ] VT (state) afirmar; (claim) alegar

alleged [əléʤd] ADJ (event) supuesto; (perpetrator) presunto

allegedly [əléʤɪdli] ADV supuestamente, presuntamente

allegiance [əlíʤəns] N lealtad *f*, fidelidad *f*; **to pledge — to the flag** jurar la bandera

allegory [ӕlɪɡɔri] N alegoría *f*

allergen [ӕlɚʤɪn] N alergeno/alérgeno *m*

allergic [əlɚ́ʤɪk] ADJ alérgico

allergist [ӕlɚʤɪst] N alergólogo -ga *mf*

allergy [ӕlɚʤi] N alergia *f*

alleviate [əlíviet] VT (suffering) aliviar; (hunger) paliar

alley [ӕli] N callejón *m*; (tennis) pasillo de dobles *m*; **right up her —** ideal para ella

alliance [əláiəns] N alianza *f*

allied [əláid, ӕlaid] ADJ aliado

alligator [ӕligeɾɚ] N caimán *m*; *Am* lagarto *m*

alliterate [əlíɾəret] VI hacer aliteración

allocate [ӕləket] VT asignar

allot [əlát] VT asignar

allotment [əlátmənt] N asignación *f*, cuota *f*

allow [əláu] VI/VT (permit) permitir; (make possible) posibilitar; (admit) admitir; **to — for** tener en cuenta

allowable [əláuəbəl] ADJ admisible, permisible

allowance [əláuəns] N (regular payment) asignación *f*, pensión *f*; (monthly payment) mensualidad *f*; (for a child) paga *f*, mesada *f*; (payment for a particular purpose) pago *m*; (food) ración *f*; **to make — for** tener en cuenta

alloy[1] [ӕlɔi] N aleación *f*

alloy[2] [əlɔ́i] VT alear

allude [əlúd] VI aludir; **to — to** aludir a

allure [əlúr] VI/VT seducir, atraer; N atractivo *m*

alluring [əlúrɪŋ] ADJ seductivo, atractivo

allusion [əlúʒən] N alusión *f*

ally[1] [ӕlai] N aliado -da *mf*

ally[2] [əlái] VT **to — oneself with** aliarse con

almanac [ɔ́lmənӕk] N almanaque *m*

almighty [ɔlmáiɖi] ADJ todopoderoso

almond [ɔ́mənd] N almendra *f*; **— tree** almendro *m*

almost [ɔ́lmost] ADV casi; **I — fell down** por poco me caigo

alms [ɔmz] N limosna *f*

aloe vera [ӕlovírə] N áloe *m*

alone [əlón] ADJ solo; **— among his contemporaries** único entre sus contemporáneos; ADV solo, solamente; **she — knew that** solo ella sabía eso; **all — a** solas; **to leave —** no tocar, dejar en paz

along [əlɔ́ŋ] PREP **he was walking — the street** andaba por la calle; **all — the coast** a

lo largo de toda la costa; **— with** junto con; **all —** desde el principio; **to carry — with oneself** llevar consigo; **to go — with** acceder a, conformarse con; **to get — with** llevarse bien con

alongside [əlɔ́ŋsáid] PREP al lado de; **— the boat** al lado del bote; ADV al lado, al costado; **the dog ran —** el perro corría al costado

aloof [əlúf] ADJ reservado, esquivo; ADV apartado

aloud [əláud] ADV en voz alta

alphabet [ӕlfəbet] N alfabeto *m*, abecedario *m*

alphanumeric [ӕlfənumérik] ADJ alfanumérico

alpine [ӕlpain] ADJ alpino

already [ɔlrédi] ADV ya

also [ɔ́lso] ADV también, además; **—-ran** (horse, candidate) caballo/candidato vencido *m*

alt [ӕlt] *see* alternate[1]

altar [ɔ́ltɚ] N altar *m*; **—piece** retablo *m*

alter [ɔ́ltɚ] VI/VT (change) alterar; (neuter) capar, castrar

alteration [ɔltɚréʃən] N (change) alteración *f*, cambio *m*; **—s** arreglos *m pl*, reformas *f pl*

altercation [ɔltɚkéʃən] N altercado *m*

alternate[1] [ɔ́ltɚnɪt] ADJ alternativo, alterno; **— route** ruta alternativa *f*; **— spelling** ortografía alterna *f*; **he visits us on — Mondays** nos visita un lunes sí y otro no; **alt key** tecla de alt *f*; **alt gr key** tecla de alternativa gráfica *f*; N suplente *mf*

alternate[2] [ɔ́ltɚnet] VI/VT alternar

alternation [ɔltɚnéʃən] N alternancia *f*

alternative [ɔltɚ́nəɖɪv] ADJ alternativo; **— minimum tax** contribución alternativa mínima *f*; N alternativa *f*

alternator [ɔ́ltɚneɖɚ] N alternador *m*

although [ɔlðó] CONJ aunque, si bien

altimeter [ӕltímiɖɚ] N altímetro *m*

altitude [ӕltitud] N altura *f*, altitud *f*; **— sickness** mal de altura *m*

alto [ӕlto] N contralto *mf*; ADJ alto

altogether [ɔltəɡéðɚ] ADV (completely) completamente; (all included) en total

altruism [ӕltruizəm] N altruismo *m*

aluminum [əlúmənəm] N aluminio *m*; **— foil** papel de aluminio *m*

always [ɔ́lwez] ADV siempre

Alzheimer's disease [ɔ́ltshaimɚz dizíz] N enfermedad de Alzheimer *f*

a.m. [éém] ADV de la mañana

am [ӕm] *see* be

amalgamate [əmӕlɡəmet] VI/VT (metals) amalgamar[se]; (companies) fusionar[se]

amass [əmӕs] VT acumular, amasar

amateur [ӕməʧɚ] ADJ amateur; N amateur *mf*; aficionado -da *mf*

amaze [əméz] VT maravillar, asombrar

amazement [əmézmənt] N asombro *m*

amazing [əmézɪŋ] ADJ asombroso, increíble

Amazon [ǽməzɑn] N (region) Amazonia *f*; (river) Amazonas *m sg*

ambassador [æmbǽsəDə-] N embajador -ora *mf*

amber [ǽmbə-] N ámbar *m*; ADJ (quality) ambarino; (material) de ámbar; (color) [de] color ámbar

ambidextrous [æmbɪdékstrəs] ADJ ambidiestro

ambience, ambiance [ǽmbiəns] N ambiente *m*

ambient [ǽmbiənt] ADJ ambiental; — **temperature** temperatura ambiente *f*

ambiguity [æmbɪgjúɪDi] N ambigüedad *f*

ambiguous [æmbígjuəs] ADJ ambiguo

ambition [æmbíʃən] N ambición *f*, aspiración *f*

ambitious [æmbíʃəs] ADJ ambicioso

ambivalent [æmbívələnt] ADJ ambivalente

amble [ǽmbəl] VI deambular

ambulance [ǽmbjələns] N ambulancia *f*

ambulatory [ǽmbjələtɔri] ADJ ambulatorio

ambush [ǽmbuʃ] N emboscada *f*, celada *f*; **to lie in** — tender una emboscada; VT emboscar

ameliorate [əmíliəret] VI/VT mejorar

amen [ámén] INTERJ amén

amenable [əménəbəl] ADJ bien dispuesto

amend [əménd] VT enmendar; **to make —s [for]** compensar [por]

amendment [əméndmənt] N enmienda *f*

amenities [əménɪDiz] N PL comodidades *f pl*

America [əmérɪkə] N América *f*

American [əmérɪkən] ADJ & N (continental) americano -na *mf*; (USA) americano -na *mf*, norteamericano -na *mf*, estadounidense *mf*

amethyst [ǽməθɪst] N amatista *f*

amiable [émiəbəl] ADJ amable

amicable [ǽmɪkəbəl] ADJ amistoso, amigable

amid [əmíd] PREP en medio de, entre

amino acid [əmínoǽsɪd] N aminoácido *m*

amiss [əmís] ADV **something is** — algo anda mal

ammonia [əmónjə] N amoníaco *m*

ammunition [æmjəníʃən] N munición *f*

amnesia [æmníʒə] N amnesia *f*

amnesty [ǽmnɪsti] N amnistía *f*

amniocentesis [æmniosɪntísɪs] N amniocentesis *f*

amniotic [æmniɑDɪk] ADJ amniótico; — **fluid** líquido amniótico *m*

amoeba [əmíbə] N ameba *f*

among [əmʌ́ŋ] PREP entre

amoral [emɔ́rəl] ADJ amoral

amorous [ǽmərəs] ADJ (sexually aroused) excitado; (in love) enamorado

amorphous [əmɔ́rfəs] ADJ amorfo

amortization [æmə-DIzéʃən] N amortización *f*

amortize [ǽmə-taɪz] VT amortizar

amount [əmáunt] N (of a substance) cantidad *f*; (of money) suma *f*, importe *m*; — **due** cantidad debida *f*, monto debido *m*; — **paid** cantidad pagada *f*, monto pagado *m*; — **payable** cantidad a pagar *f*; VI (add up to)

ascender [a]; **that —s to stealing** eso equivale a robar

ampere [æmpír] N amperio *m*

amphetamine [æmfétəmin] N anfetamina *f*

amphibian [æmfíbiən] N anfibio *m*

amphibious [æmfíbiəs] ADJ anfibio

amphitheater [ǽmfəθiəDə-] N anfiteatro *m*

ampicillin [æmpɪsílɪn] N ampicilina *f*

ample [ǽmpəl] ADJ (in quantity) suficiente; (in size) amplio

amplifier [ǽmpləfaɪə-] N amplificador *m*

amplify [ǽmpləfaɪ] VT (an explanation) ampliar; (a sound) amplificar

amplitude [ǽmplɪtud] N amplitud *f*

amputate [ǽmpjətet] VT amputar

amuck, amok [əmʌ́k] ADV **to run** — (kill people) perpetrar un ataque homicida; (go crazy) volverse loco

amulet [ǽmjəlɪt] N amuleto *m*

amuse [əmjúz] VT (make laugh) divertir; (help pass time) entretener; **to — oneself** divertirse, entretenerse

amusement [əmjúzmənt] N diversión *f*, entretenimiento *m*

amusing [əmjúzɪŋ] ADJ (entertaining) divertido; (funny) gracioso, chistoso

amygdala [əmígdələ] N amígdala *f*

an [ən, æn] INDEF ART un *m*, una *f*

anabolic [ænəbɑ́lɪk] ADJ anabólico; — **steroid** esteroide anabólico *m*

anachronism [ənǽkrənɪzəm] N anacronismo *m*

anaerobic [ænəróbɪk] ADJ anaerobio

anal [énl] ADJ anal; (neurotic) rígido, neurótico

analgesic [ænldʒízɪk] N & ADJ analgésico *m*

analogical [ænəlɑ́dʒɪkəl] ADJ analógico

analogous [ənǽləgəs] ADJ análogo

analogue, analog [ǽnəlɔg] ADJ analógico; — **device** dispositivo analógico *m*

analogy [ənǽlədʒi] N analogía *f*

analysis [ənǽlɪsɪs] N análisis *m*

analyst [ǽnəlɪst] N analista *mf*

analytic, analytical [ænəlíDɪk[əl]] ADJ (approach) analítico; (person) analítico, analista

analyze [ǽnəlaɪz] VT analizar

anarchist [ǽnə-kɪst] N anarquista *mf*

anarchy [ǽnə-ki] N anarquía *f*

anathema [ənǽθəmə] N anatema *m*

anatomical [ænətɑ́mɪkəl] ADJ anatómico

anatomy [ənǽDəmi] N anatomía *f*

ancestor [ǽnsestə-] N antepasado -da *mf*, ascendiente *mf*

ancestral [ænséstrəl] ADJ ancestral, de los antepasados; — **home** casa solariega *f*

ancestry [ǽnsestri] N linaje *m*, ascendencia *f*, abolengo *m*

anchor [ǽŋkə-] N ancla *f*; —**man** presentador *m*; —**woman** presentadora *f*; **to drop** — anclar, echar anclas; VT (a boat) anclar; (an argument) basar; VI echar anclas, fondear

anchovy [ǽntʃovi] N anchoa f

ancient [énʃənt] ADJ antiguo; pej vetusto

and [ænd] CONJ y; (before i, hi) e; — **so forth** etcétera, y así sucesivamente

Andalusia [ændəlúʒə] N Andalucía f

Andalusian [ændəlúʒən] ADJ & N andaluz -za mf

Andes [ǽndiz] N Andes m pl

Andorra [ændɔ́rə] N Andorra f

Andorran [ændɔ́rən] ADJ & N andorrano -na mf

androgynous [ændrádʒənəs] ADJ andrógino

anecdote [ǽnɪkdot] N anécdota f

anemia [əním(i)ə] N anemia f

anemic [əním(i)k] ADJ anémico

anesthesia [ænɪsθíʒə] N anestesia f

anesthesiologist [ænəsθiziáləʤɪst] N anestesiólogo -ga mf, anestesista mf

anesthesiology [ænɪsθiziáləʤi] N anestesiología f

anesthetic [ænɪsθédɪk] ADJ anestésico; N (substance) anestesia f

anesthetize [ənésθətaɪz] VT anestesiar

aneurysm [ǽnjʊrɪzəm] N aneurisma m

anew [ənú] ADV de nuevo, otra vez

angel [énʤəl] N ángel m

angelic [ænʤélɪk] ADJ angélico, angelical

anger [ǽŋgə] N enojo m, enfado m; VT enojar, enfadar

angina pectoris [ænʤáɪnəpéktə˞ɪs] N angina de pecho f

angiocardiography [ænʤiokɑrDiágrəfi] N angiocardiografía f

angiogram [ǽnʤiogræm] N angiograma m

angioplasty [ǽnʤiəplæsti] N angioplastia f; — **balloon** balón de angioplastia m

angle [ǽŋgəl] N (geometrical) ángulo m; (point of view) punto de vista m, perspectiva f; VI pescar

Anglo-Saxon [ǽnglosǽksən] ADJ & N anglosajón -ona mf

Angola [æŋgólə] N Angola f

Angolan [æŋgólən] ADJ & N angolano -na mf, angoleño -ña mf

angry [ǽngri] ADJ enojado, enfadado

angst [áŋkst] N angustia f

anguish [ǽŋgwɪʃ] N angustia f, ansia f, congoja f

angular [ǽŋgjələ] ADJ angular; (face) anguloso

animal [ǽnəməl] ADJ & N animal m; — **rights** derechos de los animales m pl

animate[1] [ǽnəmɪt] ADJ animado

animate[2] [ǽnəmet] VT (enliven) animar; (encourage) alentar; —**d cartoon** dibujo animado m

animation [ænəméʃən] N animación f

animosity [ænəmásɪDi] N animosidad f, ojeriza f, encono m

anise [ǽnɪs] N anís m

ankle [ǽŋkəl] N tobillo m

annals [ǽnlz] N anales m pl

annex[1] [ǽnɛks] N anexo m

annex[2] [ənéks] VT anexar

annexation [ænɛkséʃən] N anexión f

annihilate [ənáɪələt] VT aniquilar

anniversary [ænəvɝ́səri] N aniversario m

annotate [ǽnətet] VT anotar

annotation [ænətéʃən] N (action, result) anotación f; (result) nota f

announce [ənáʊns] VT (make known) anunciar, dar a conocer; (declare) anunciar

announcement [ənáʊnsmənt] N (of an engagement, birth, candidacy) anuncio m; (of a conference or competition) convocatoria f

announcer [ənáʊnsə] N anunciador -ra mf; (on radio) locutor -ora mf

annoy [ənɔ́ɪ] VI/VT fastidiar, contrariar

annoyance [ənɔ́ɪəns] N fastidio m, contrariedad f

annual [ǽnjuəl] ADJ anual; N (book) anuario m; (plant) planta anual f

annuity [ənjúɪDi] N anualidad f, renta anual f

annul [ənʌ́l] VT anular

annulment [ənʌ́lmənt] N anulación f

anomalous [ənámələs] ADJ anómalo

anomaly [ənáməli] N anomalía f

anonymous [ənánəməs] ADJ anónimo

anorak [ǽnəræk] N anorak m

anorexia [ænərɛ́ksiə] N anorexia f

anorexic [ænərɛ́ksɪk] ADJ anoréxico

another [ənʌ́ðə] ADJ otro; — **day** otro día; PRON otro; **I want** — quiero otro; **one** — el uno al otro, los unos a los otros

answer [ǽnsə] N (to a question) respuesta f, contestación f; (to a problem) solución f; VI contestar, responder; **to** — **for** ser responsable de/por; VT contestar

answering [ǽnsə-ɪŋ] ADJ — **machine** contestador automático m; — **service** servicio telefónico contratado m, servicio de contestador m

ant [ænt] N hormiga f; —**eater** oso hormiguero m; —**hill** hormiguero m

antacid [ǽntǽsɪd] N & ADJ antiácido m

antagonism [æntǽgənɪzəm] N antagonismo m

antagonist [æntǽgənɪst] N antagonista mf

antagonize [æntǽgənaɪz] VT antagonizar

antarctic [æntárktɪk] ADJ antártico

Antarctica [æntárktɪkə] N Antártida f

antecedent [æntəsídnt] ADJ & N antecedente m

antelope [ǽntəlop] N antílope m

antenna [ænténə] N antena f

anterior [æntíriə] ADJ anterior

anthem [ǽnθəm] N himno m

anthology [ænθáləʤi] N antología f

anthracite [ǽnθrəsaɪt] N antracita f

anthrax [ǽnθræks] N ántrax m

anthropologist [ænθrəpáləʤɪst] N antropólogo -ga mf

anthropology [ænθrəpáləʤi] N antropología f

anthropomorphize [ǽnθrəpəmɔ́rfaɪz] VI/VT antropomorfizar

antiabortion [ǽntiəbɔ́rʃən] ADJ antiaborto *inv*

antiaircraft [ǽntiérkræft] ADJ antiaéreo

antiallergic [ǽntiəlɝ́dʒɪk] ADJ antialérgico

antibacterial [ǽntibæktíriəl] ADJ antibacteriano

antiballistic [ǽntibəlístɪk] ADJ antibalístico

antibiotic [ǽntibaɪátɪk] N & ADJ antibiótico *m*

antibody [ǽntibaɒi] N anticuerpo *m*

anticancer [ǽntikǽnsɚ] ADJ anticanceroso *f*

anticipate [æntísəpət] VI/VT (foresee) prever; (jump the gun) anticiparse [a]

anticipation [æntisəpéʃən] N previsión *f*; **with great** — con gran expectación

anticlimactic [ǽntikləmǽktɪk] ADJ decepcionante

anticoagulant [ǽntikoǽgjələnt] ADJ & N anticoagulante *m*

anticonvulsant [ǽntikənvʌ́lsənt] ADJ & N anticonvulsivo *m*

antics [ǽntɪks] N payasadas *f pl*, monerías *f pl*, monadas *f pl*

antidepressant [ǽntidɪprésənt] ADJ & N antidepresivo *m*

antidiarrheal [ǽntidaɪəríəl] ADJ & N antidiarreico *m*

antidiuretic [ǽntidaɪərɛ́dɪk] ADJ & N antidiurético *m*

antidote [ǽntidot] N antídoto *m*

antifreeze [ǽntifriz] N anticongelante *m*

antigen [ǽntidʒən] N antígeno *m*

anti-glare [ǽntiglér] ADJ antireflejante

Antigua and Barbuda [æntígəændbarbúdə] N Antigua y Barbuda *f*

Antiguan [æntígən] ADJ & N antiguano -ana *mf*

antihistamine [æntihístəmin] N & ADJ antihistamínico *m*

anti-inflammatory [æntiɪnflǽmətɔri] ADJ & N antiinflamatorio *m*

antilock [ǽntilak] ADJ antibloqueo; — **brakes** frenos antibloqueo *mpl*

antimony [ǽntəmoni] N antimonio *m*

antioxidant [æntiáksɪdənt] N antioxidante *m*

antipathy [æntípəθi] N antipatía *f*

antiperspirant [æntipɝ́spəənt] N antitranspirante *m*

antipsychotic [æntisaɪkádɪk] ADJ & N antipsicótico *m*

antiquated [ǽntɪkweɒɪd] ADJ (custom) anticuado; (word) desusado

antique [æntík] ADJ antiguo; N antigüedad *f*

antiquity [æntíkwɪɒi] N antigüedad *f*

anti-Semitism [æntisémɪtizəm] N antisemitismo *m*

antiseptic [æntiséptɪk] ADJ & N antiséptico *m*

antisocial [æntisóʃəl] ADJ antisocial

antispasmodic [æntispæzmádɪk] ADJ & N antiespasmódico *m*

antithesis [æntíθəsɪs] N antítesis *f*

antitoxin [æntitáksɪn] N antitoxina *f*

antitrust [æntitrást] ADJ antimonopolio, antitrust

antiviral [æntiváɪrəl] ADJ & N antiviral *m*

antivirus [ǽntivaɪrəs] ADJ antivirus

antler [ǽntlɚ] N asta *f*, cuerno *m*

antonym [ǽntənɪm] N antónimo *m*

antsy [ǽntsi] ADJ (impatient) impaciente; (anxious) ansioso

anvil [ǽnvəl] N yunque *m*

anxiety [æŋzáɪɪɒi] N ansiedad *f*, angustia *f*

anxious [ǽŋkʃəs] ADJ (worried) ansioso, preocupado; (desirous) ansioso, deseoso

any [éni] ADJ & PRON cualquier[a], cualesquier[a], alguno; — **woman** cualquier mujer, una mujer cualquiera; — **houses** unas casas cualesquiera; *lit* cualesquiera casas; **in** — **case** en todo caso; **do you have** — **money?** ¿tienes dinero? **I don't have** — no tengo; **do you like** — **of these?** ¿te gusta alguno de estos?

anybody [énibaɒi] PRON alguien, cualquiera; — **could do that** cualquiera podría hacer eso; **is** — **here?** ¿hay alguien aquí? **he does not know** — no conoce a nadie

anyhow [énihaʊ] ADV de todos modos, en todo caso

anymore [énimɔ́r] ADV **he doesn't work** — ya no trabaja, no trabaja más

anyone [éniwʌn] PRON alguien, cualquiera; — **could do that** cualquiera podría hacer eso; **is** — **here?** ¿hay alguien aquí? **he does not know** — no conoce a nadie

anyplace [éniples] ADV en cualquier parte/lugar; **you can buy it** — se puede comprar en cualquier lugar; **he's not going** — no va a ninguna parte

anything [éniθɪŋ] PRON cualquier cosa, algo; — **is fine** cualquier cosa me viene bien; — **you wish** todo lo que quieras; **do you have** — **for a cough?** ¿tienes algo para la tos? **I don't know** — no sé nada

anytime [énitaɪm] ADV en cualquier momento

anyway [éniwe] ADV de todos modos, de cualquier manera, en todo caso

anywhere [énihwɛr] ADV en cualquier parte / lugar; **you can buy it** — se puede comprar en cualquier lugar; **he's not going** — no va a ninguna parte

aorta [eɔ́rɒə] N aorta *f*

apart [əpárt] ADV **they are three miles** — están a tres millas de distancia; **they kept him** — **from the group** lo apartaron del grupo; **each factor viewed** — cada factor visto por separado; **to take** — desarmar, desmontar; **to tear** — despedazar, hacer pedazos; **to tell** — distinguir

apartment [əpártmənt] N apartamento *m*; *Sp*

piso *m*
apathetic [æpəθέDIk] ADJ apático
apathy [ǽpəθi] N apatía *f*, abulia *f*
ape [ep] N simio *m*; VT remedar
aperture [ǽpɚtʃɚ] N abertura *f*; (of a pipe) luz *f*
apex [épɛks] N (of tongue) ápice *m*; (of a mountain) cumbre *f*
aphasia [əféʒə] N afasia *f*
apiece [əpís] ADV cada uno
apnea [ǽpniə] N apnea *f*
apocalypse [əpákəlɪps] N apocalipsis *mf*
apogee [ǽpədʒi] N apogeo *m*
apologetic [əpaləʤέDIk] ADJ lleno de disculpas
apologize [əpálədʒaɪz] VI disculparse
apology [əpálədʒi] N (expression of regret) disculpa[s] *f* [pl]; (justification) apología *f*
apoplexy [ǽpəplɛksi] N apoplejía *f*
apostle [əpásəl] N apóstol *m*
apostrophe [əpástrəfi] N (punctuation) apóstrofo *m*; (invocation) apóstrofe *m*
app [æp] N (computer software) aplicación *f*
appall [əpɔ́l] VT horrorizar
appalling [əpɔ́lɪŋ] ADJ horroroso
apparatus [æpɚǽbəs] N (single) aparato *m*; (group) maquinaria *f*
apparel [əpǽrəl] N indumentaria *f*, ropa *f*; (fine) ropaje *m*
apparent [əpǽrənt] ADJ (visible) visible; (clear) obvio, evidente; (seeming) aparente
apparition [æpɚíʃən] N aparición *f*, fantasma *m*
appeal [əpíl] N (legal) apelación *f*, recurso *m*; (request) llamamiento *m*, llamado *m*; (attraction) atractivo *m*; VT apelar, recurrir [contra]; VI **to — to** atraer
appear [əpír] VI (show up) aparecer[se]; (seem) parecer, aparentar; (be published) salir; (come before a judge) comparecer
appearance [əpírəns] N (looks) apariencia *f*, traza *f*, estampa *f*; (act of appearing) aparición *f*; (coming before a judge) comparecencia *f*
appease [əpíz] VT aplacar, apaciguar
appeasement [əpízmənt] N aplacamiento *m*, apaciguamiento *m*
appellate [əpέlɪt] N **— court** tribunal de apelaciones *m*
append [əpέnd] VT adjuntar
appendage [əpέndɪʤ] N apéndice *m*
appendectomy [æpɪndέktəmi] N apendicectomía *f*
appendicitis [əpɛndəsáɪDɪs] N apendicitis *f*
appendix [əpέndɪks] N apéndice *m*
appetite [ǽpɪtaɪt] N apetito *m*
appetizer [ǽpɪtaɪzɚ] N aperitivo *m*
appetizing [ǽpɪtaɪzɪŋ] ADJ apetecible, apetitoso
applaud [əplɔ́d] VI/VT aplaudir
applause [əplɔ́z] N aplauso[s] *m* [pl]
apple [ǽpəl] N manzana *f*; **— grove** manzanar *m*; **— of my eye** niña de mis ojos *f*; **—sauce** compota de manzana *f*; **— tree** manzano *m*;

Adam's — nuez de Adán *f*
appliance [əpláɪəns] N aparato *m*; (electric) aparato electrodoméstico *m*, electrodoméstico *m*
applicable [ǽplɪkəbəl] ADJ aplicable
applicant [ǽplɪkənt] N aspirante *mf*, solicitante *mf*
application [æplɪkéʃən] N (act of applying, computer software) aplicación *f*; (form) solicitud *f*, formulario *f*
applicator [ǽplɪkebɚ] N aplicador *m*
apply [əpláɪ] VT aplicar; **to — for** solicitar, pedir; **are you —ing for the scholarship?** ¿te presentas para la beca? ¿estás solicitando la beca? **to — oneself** aplicarse, dedicarse
appoint [əpɔ́ɪnt] VT (designate) nombrar, designar; (furnish) amueblar, equipar; **a well —ed house** una casa bien amueblada
appointee [əpɔɪntí] N persona nombrada *f*
appointment [əpɔ́ɪntmənt] N (designation) nombramiento *m*, designación *f*; (engagement) cita *f*; **doctor's —** cita/hora con el médico *f*; **—s** mobiliario *m sg*, accesorios *m pl*
apportion [əpɔ́rʃən] VT repartir proporcionalmente
apportionment [əpɔ́rʃənmənt] N reparto proporcional *m*
appraisal [əpɚézəl] N (of a property) tasación *f*, valuación *f*; (of a situation) evaluación *f*
appraise [əpɚéz] VT (a property) avaluar, valorar, tasar; (a situation) evaluar
appreciable [əpríʃəbəl] ADJ apreciable
appreciate [əpríʃiet] VT (value) apreciar, estimar; (recognize) darse cuenta, percibir; (thank) agradecer; **to — in value** apreciarse
appreciation [əprɪʃiéʃən] N (esteem) aprecio *m*; (thanks) agradecimiento *m*; (monetary value) apreciación *f*, alza *f*
apprehend [æprɪhénd] VT (arrest) aprehender; (understand) comprender
apprehension [æprɪhénʃən] N (arrest) aprehensión *f*; (worry) aprensión *f*
apprehensive [æprɪhénsɪv] ADJ aprensivo
apprentice [əpréntɪs] N aprendiz -iza *mf*; VT poner de aprendiz
apprenticeship [əpréntɪsʃɪp] N aprendizaje *m*
apprise [əpráɪz] VT informar
approach [əprótʃ] N (act of approaching) aproximación *f*; (method) enfoque *m*, acercamiento *m*; (means of access) acceso *m*, entrada *f*; **— shot** golpe de aproximación *m*; VI (go nearer) acercarse, aproximarse; (in golf) aprochar; VT (a problem) abordar, enfocar; **to — someone about a problem** plantearle a alguien un problema
approachable [əprótʃəbəl] ADJ tratable
approbation [æprəbéʃən] N aprobación *f*
appropriate[1] [əprópriit] ADJ apropiado,

adecuado

appropriate² [əprópriet] VT apropiarse; (funds) asignar

appropriation [əpropriéʃən] N (act of seizing) apropiación f; (assignment of funds) asignación f; (assigned funds) partida f

approval [əprúvəl] N aprobación f; **on —** a prueba

approve [əprúv] VI/VT aprobar

approximate¹ [əpráksəmɪt] ADJ aproximado

approximate² [əpráksəmet] VT aproximarse a

approximately [əpráksəmɪtli] ADV aproximadamente

APR [annual percentage rate] [épiár] N TAE f

apricot [éprɪkat] N albaricoque m; *Am* damasco m; *Mex* chabacano m

April [éprəl] N abril m

apron [éprən] N (for a cook) delantal m; (for a workman) mandil m

apropos [æprəpó] ADV a propósito; ADJ oportuno, pertinente; **— of** a propósito de

apt [æpt] ADJ (prone, able) capaz; (suited) pertinente; **is he — to be at home?** ¿estará en casa?

aptitude [æptɪtud] N aptitud f, capacidad f

aquamarine [akwəmərín] N aguamarina f

aquarium [əkwériəm] N (tank) acuario m, pecera f; (building) acuario m

aquatic [əkwápɪk] ADJ acuático

aqueduct [ækwɪdəkt] N acueducto m

Arab [ǽrəb] ADJ & N árabe mf

Arabic [ǽrəbɪk] ADJ árabe, arábigo; N (language) árabe m

arable [ǽrəbəl] ADJ cultivable

Aragonese [ærəgəníz] ADJ & N aragonés -esa m

arbiter [árbɪɒə] N árbitro -ra mf

arbitrariness [árbɪtrɛrɪnɪs] N arbitrariedad f

arbitrary [árbɪtrɛri] ADJ arbitrario; **— action** arbitrariedad f

arbitrate [árbɪtret] VI/VT (mediate) arbitrar [en], terciar [en]; (submit to mediation) someter al arbitraje

arbitration [arbɪtréʃən] N arbitraje m

arbitrator [árbɪtrɛɒə] N árbitro -tra mf

arbor [árbə] N pérgola f, glorieta f

arboreal [arbóriəl] ADJ arbóreo

arc [ark] N arco m

arcade [arkéd] N (series of arcs) arcada f; (shops) galería f; (video game center) sala de juegos electrónicos f

arcane [arkén] ADJ arcano

arch [artʃ] N arco m; (curved roof) bóveda f; **—way** arcada f; VI/VT arquear[se]

archaeological [arkiəládʒɪkəl] ADJ arqueológico

archaeology, archeology [arkiáɭədʒi] N arqueología f

archaic [arkéɪk] ADJ arcaico

archaism [árkeɪzəm] N arcaísmo m

archbishop [artʃbíʃəp] N arzobispo m

archenemy [artʃénəmi] N archienemigo -ga mf

archer [ártʃə] N arquero -ra mf

archery [ártʃəri] N tiro al arco m

archetype [árkɪtaɪp] N arquetipo m

archipelago [arkəpéləgo] N archipiélago m

architect [árkɪtɛkt] N arquitecto -ta mf; (creator) artífice mf

architectural [arkɪtɛktʃəəl] ADJ arquitectónico

architecture [árkɪtɛktʃə] N arquitectura f

archive [árkaɪv] N archivo m

arctic [árktɪk] ADJ ártico

ardent [árdn̩t] ADJ ardiente

ardor [árdə] N ardor m, fervor m

arduous [árdʒuəs] ADJ arduo

are [ar] *see* be

area [ériə] N (space) área f; (region) zona f; (of a geometric figure) superficie f, área f

arena [ərínə] N (for sports) estadio m; (in a circus) pista f

Argentina [ardʒəntínə] N Argentina f

Argentinian [ardʒəntíniən] ADJ & N argentino -na mf

argon [árgan] N argón m

argue [árgju] VT (reason) argüir, argumentar; VI (bicker) discutir, reñir

argument [árgjəmənt] N (reason) argumento m; (altercation) disputa f, discusión f

arid [ǽrɪd] ADJ árido

arise [əráɪz] VI (get up) levantarse; (appear) surgir; (result) provenir, resultar

arisen [ərízən] *see* arise

aristocracy [ærɪstákrəsi] N aristocracia f

aristocrat [ərístəkræt] N aristócrata mf

aristocratic [ərɪstəkrǽdɪk] ADJ aristocrático

arithmetic¹ [əríθmətɪk] N aritmética f

arithmetic² [ærɪθmɛ́dɪk] ADJ aritmético

ark [ark] N arca f; **Noah's —** arca de Noé f

arm [arm] N brazo m; **—chair** sillón m, butaca f; **—pit** sobaco m, axila f; **—rest** in a car apoyabrazos m sg; (on a sofa) brazo m; **— in —** del brazo; **at —'s length** a distancia; **—'s-length transactions** transacciones a precio de mercado f pl; **with open —s** con los brazos abiertos; **—s** armas f pl; VT armar; **—ed forces** fuerzas armadas f pl; **—ed robbery** robo a mano armada m

armada [armádə] N armada f, flota f

armament [árməmənt] N armamento m

Armenia [armíniə] N Armenia f

Armenian [armíniən] ADJ & N armenio -nia mf

armful [ármfʊl] N brazada f

armistice [ármɪstɪs] N armisticio m

armoire [armwár] N armario m

armor [ármə] N (of a knight) armadura f; (on a vehicle) blindaje m; (on insects) coraza f; VT (a car) blindar; (a tank) acorazar

armored [árməd] ADJ (van) blindado; (tank) acorazado

armory [árməri] N armería f

army [ármi] N ejército m; (multitude) muchedumbre f

aroma [ərómə] N aroma m

aromatic [ærəmǽdɪk] ADJ aromático

arose [əróz] *see* arise

around [əráund] ADV **there were books all —** había libros por todos lados; **there is a supermarket — here** hay un supermercado por aquí; **it was the only farm for miles —** era la única granja en millas a la redonda; **the tree is forty centimeters —** el árbol tiene cuarenta centímetros de circunferencia; **I'll show you —** te enseño el lugar; **the wheels turned —** las ruedas giraban; **turn —** date la vuelta; **she finally came —** al final la convencimos; **he hasn't been —** no ha estado por aquí; — **five o'clock** a eso de las cinco; PREP **a ribbon — her wrist** una cinta alrededor de su muñeca; **tie a string — your finger** átate un hilo al dedo; **the stay — the house** quédate cerca de la casa; **we drove — the block** dimos vuelta a la manzana; **he wandered — the park** deambuló por el parque; **the church — the corner** la iglesia a la vuelta de la esquina; **a town with mountains — it** un pueblo rodeado de montañas; **motion — its axis** movimiento en torno a su eje; —**-the-clock** veinticuatro horas al día; **we walked — town** dimos una vuelta por el pueblo

arouse [əráUz] VI despertar; VT (suspicion) despertar; (sexual response) excitar

arraign [ərén] VT hacer comparecer ante un juez

arrange [ərénʤ] VT arreglar

arrangement [ərénʤmənt] N (array) arreglo m; (placement) disposición f; (agreement) acuerdo m; **to make —s [for]** hacer arreglos [para]

array [əré] N (arrangement) abanico m, selección f; (placement of troops) orden m, formación f; (attire) gala f; (in software) vector m; VT (troops) formar; (attire) ataviar

arrears [ərírz] ADV LOC **in —** atrasado; N atrasos m pl

arrest [ərést] N arresto m, detención f; VI/VT arrestar, detener

arrhythmia [əríðmiə] N arritmia f

arrival [əráɪvəl] N llegada f; *lit* arribo m; **the new —s** los recién llegados

arrive [əráɪv] VI llegar; *lit* arribar

arrogance [ǽrəgəns] N arrogancia f

arrogant [ǽrəgənt] ADJ arrogante

arrow [ǽro] N flecha f; *lit* saeta f; —**head** punta de flecha f

arsenal [ársənl] N arsenal m

arsenic [ársənɪk] N arsénico m

arson [ársən] N incendio doloso m

art [art] N arte m [sg] f [pl]; (works) obras f pl; (skill) destreza f; **fine —s** bellas artes f pl; **master of —s** maestría en humanidades f; — **deco** art déco m

arterial [artíriəl] ADJ arterial

arteriosclerosis [artiriosklərósɪs] N arteriosclerosis f

artery [árðəri] N arteria f

artful [ártfəl] ADJ (aesthetic) artístico; (deceitful) artero, astuto

arthritis [arθráɪdɪs] N artritis f

arthroscopic [arθrəskápɪk] ADJ artroscópico

arthroscopy [árθrəskapi] N artroscopia f

artichoke [árdɪtʃok] N alcachofa f

article [árdɪkəl] N artículo m; — **of clothing** prenda de vestir f

articulate[1] [artíkjəlɪt] ADJ (clear) claro; (eloquent) elocuente; **he's very —** se expresa muy bien

articulate[2] [artíkjəlet] VI/VT (pronounce, join) articular; (express) enunciar

articulation [artikjəléʃən] N articulación f

artifact [árdəfækt] N artefacto m, ingenio m

artifice [árdəfɪs] N artificio m

artificial [ardəfíʃəl] ADJ artificial; (affected) afectado; — **insemination** inseminación artificial f; — **intelligence** inteligencia artificial f

artillery [artíləri] N artillería f

artisan [árdɪzən] N artesano -na mf, artífice mf

artist [árdɪst] N (painter, sculptor) artista mf; (performer) intérprete mf

artistic [artístɪk] ADJ artístico

Aruba [ərúbə] N Aruba f

as [æz] CONJ **— for me** en lo que a mí respecta; — **if** como si; **— is** en la condición en que está; **— it were** por decirlo así; **— of** a partir de; **— per** según; **— the illness worsened** a medida que empeoraba la enfermedad; **— yet** hasta ahora, todavía; **the same —** lo mismo que; **it broke — I was using it** se rompió cuando lo usaba; **she knitted — we talked** tejía mientras conversábamos; **he played — never before** jugó como nunca; PREP **— a child, I always felt loved** de niño, siempre me sentí querido; **— a teacher, I must be tough** como maestro, tengo que ser estricto; ADV **tan, tanto; — large —** tan grande como; **— long — you wish** todo el tiempo que quieras; **— much —** tanto como; **— well** también; **it's not — important** no es tan importante

ASAP [as soon as possible] [ésæp] ADV lo antes posible

asbestos [æzbéstəs] N asbesto m, amianto m

ascend [əsénd] VI ascender; —**ing order** orden ascendente m

ascent [əsént] N ascenso m

ascertain [æsə·tén] VT averiguar, establecer

ascetic [əsɛ́dɪk] ADJ ascético; N asceta *mf*

ascorbic [əskɔ́rbɪk] ADJ ascórbico

ascribe [əskráɪb] VT atribuir, imputar

aseptic [əsɛ́ptɪk] ADJ aséptico

asexual [esɛ́kʃuəl] ADJ asexual

ash [æʃ] N (residue, remains) ceniza *f*; (species of tree) fresno *m*; **—tray** cenicero *m*; **— Wednesday** miércoles de ceniza *m*

ashamed [əʃémd] ADJ avergonzado; **to be —** tener vergüenza, avergonzarse

ashen [ǽʃən] ADJ ceniciento

ashore [əʃɔ́r] ADV (movement) a tierra; (location) en tierra; **to go —** desembarcar

Asia [éʒə] N Asia *f*

Asian [éʒən] ADJ & N asiático -ca *mf*

Asiatic [eʒiǽdɪk] ADJ **— flu** gripe asiática *f*

aside [əsáɪd] ADV **all kidding —** bromas aparte; **his father took him —** su padre lo llamó aparte; **he threw his coat —** tiró su saco a un lado; PREP **— from** aparte de, además de; N (theater) aparte *m*

asinine [ǽsənaɪn] ADJ necio

ask [æsk] VT (inquire) preguntar; (request) pedir; **to — a question** hacer una pregunta; **to — about** preguntar por; **to — for** pedir; **to — for someone** pedir para hablar con alguien; **to — a woman's hand in marriage** pedir la mano de una mujer; **to — out** invitar a salir; **what's your —ing price?** ¿cuánto pides? **you —ed for it** te lo has buscado

askance [əskǽns] ADV **to look —** (obliquely) mirar de soslayo/través/reojo; (suspiciously) mirar con recelo

askew [əskjú] ADJ ladeado, torcido

asleep [əslíp] ADJ dormido; **to fall —** dormirse; **my arm is —** se me ha dormido/entumecido el brazo

asparagus [əspǽrəgəs] N espárrago *m*

aspartame [ǽspə·tem] N aspartamo *m*

aspect [ǽspekt] N aspecto *m*

aspen [ǽspɪn] N álamo temblón *m*

Asperger's disorder [ǽspə·gə·zdɪsɔ́rdə·] N trastorno de Asperger *m*

asphalt [ǽsfɑlt] N asfalto *m*

asphyxia [æsfíksiə] N asfixia *f*

aspiration [æspəréʃən] N aspiración *f*

aspire [əspáɪr] VI aspirar

aspirin [ǽsprɪn] N aspirina *f*

ass [æs] N asno *m*, burro *m*, borrico *m*

assail [əsél] VT (physically) asaltar, atacar; (verbally) atacar

assailant [əsélənt] N atacante *mf*, agresor -ora *mf*

assassin [əsǽsɪn] N asesino -na *mf*

assassinate [əsǽsənet] VT asesinar

assassination [əsæsənéʃən] N asesinato *m*

assault [əsɑ́lt] N asalto *m*, agresión *f*; **— rifle** rifle de asalto *m*; **— and battery** agresión con lesiones *f*; VT asaltar, agredir; (sexually)

violar

assay¹ [æsé] VT (situation) examinar, analizar; (metal) ensayar

assay² [ǽse] N ensayo *m*

assemble [əsɛ́mbəl] VI/VT (call together) reunir[se], congregar[se]; VT (put together) armar, montar

assembly [əsɛ́mbli] N (meeting) asamblea *f*, reunión *f*; (putting together) montaje *m*, armado *m*; **— language** lenguaje ensamblador *m*; **— line** cadena de producción *f*, línea de montaje *f*

assent [əsɛ́nt] N asentimiento *m*; VI asentir

assert [əsɝ́t] VT (declare) aseverar, afirmar; **to — one's rights** hacer valer los derechos de uno; **to — oneself** obrar con firmeza

assertion [əsɝ́ʃən] N (declaration) aseveración *f*, afirmación *f*, aserto *m*; **— of ownership** una afirmación de los derechos de propiedad

assess [əsɛ́s] VT (evaluate for tax purposes) tasar; (impose tax) gravar, imponer; (measure performance) evaluar

assessment [əsɛ́smənt] N (estimate) avalúo *m*, tasación *f*; (tax) imposición *f*, gravamen *m*; (testing) evaluación *f*

asset [ǽset] N (useful thing) ventaja *f*; (useful quality) virtud *f*; **—s** activo *m*, bienes *m pl*; (on balance sheet) haber *m*, activo *m*; **personal —s** bienes muebles *m pl*; **real —s** bienes inmuebles *m pl*

assiduous [əsíʤuəs] ADJ (constant) asiduo; (industrious) diligente

assign [əsáɪn] VT (allot) asignar; (appoint, designate) designar; (transfer property) ceder

assignment [əsáɪnmənt] N (act of assigning) asignación *f*; (task) encargo *m*, encomienda *f*; (mission) misión *f*; (transfer of property) cesión [de bienes] *f*; (homework) tarea *f*; (lesson) lección *f*

assimilate [əsíməlet] VI/VT asimilar[se]

assist [əsíst] VI/VT ayudar, asistir; N (in sports) asistencia *f*

assistance [əsístəns] N ayuda *f*, asistencia *f*

assistant [əsístənt] N ayudante *mf*, asistente -ta *mf*; ADJ auxiliar; **— manager** subgerente *mf*

assistantship [əsístəntʃɪp] N ayudantía *f*

associate¹ [əsóʃiɪt] ADJ asociado; N (acquaintance) compañero -ra *mf*; (co-worker) colega *mf*; (employee) empleado -da *mf*

associate² [əsóʃiet] VI/VT asociar[se]; **to be —d with** asociarse con

association [əsosiéʃən] N asociación *f*

assonance [ǽsənəns] N asonancia *f*

assorted [əsɔ́rdɪd] ADJ variado, surtido

assortment [əsɔ́rtmənt] N (act of assorting) clasificación *f*; (selection of wares) surtido *m*; (selection of tools, etc.) colección *f*

assume [əsúm] VT (responsibility, role) asumir;

(right) arrogarse; (suppose) dar por sentado, suponer; **—d name** alias *m*

assumption [əsámpʃən] N (premise) suposición *f*, supuesto *m*; (unstated belief) sobreentendido *m*; (seizure) toma *f*; (acceptance of duties) asunción *f*

assurance [əʃúrəns] N (promise) promesa *f*, palabra *f*; (reassurance) palabras de apoyo *f pl*; (certainty) certeza *f*; (confidence) confianza *f*

assure [əʃúr] VT (give confidence) asegurar; (encourage) infundir confianza

assuredly [əʃúrıdli] ADV seguramente, sin duda

asterisk [ǽstərɪsk] N asterisco *m*

asteroid [ǽstərɔɪd] N asteroide *m*

asthma [ǽzmə] N asma *m*

asthmatic [æzmǽdɪk] ADJ asmático

astigmatism [əstígmətɪzəm] N astigmatismo *m*

astonish [əstánɪʃ] VT asombrar, pasmar

astonishing [əstánɪʃɪŋ] ADJ asombroso, pasmoso

astonishment [əstánɪʃmənt] M asombro *m*, pasmo *m*

astound [əstáund] VT pasmar, asombrar

astraddle [əstrǽdl] ADV a horcajadas

astray [əstré] ADV **to go —** perderse, extraviarse; **to lead —** (seduce) llevar por mal camino, seducir; (perplex) confundir

astride [əstráıd] ADV a horcajadas

astringent [əstríndʒənt] ADJ & N astringente *m*

astrology [əstrálədʒi] N astrología *f*

astronaut [ǽstrɔnɔt] M astronauta *mf*

astronautics [æstrɔnɔ́dɪks] N astronáutica *f*

astronomer [əstránəmə] N astrónomo -ma *mf*

astronomic [æstrənámık] ADJ astronómico

astronomical [æstrənámıkəl] ADJ astronómico

astronomy [əstránəmi] N astronomía *f*

astrophysics [æstrofízıks] N astrofísica *f*

Asturian [æstúriən] ADJ & N asturiano -na *mf*

Asturias [æstúrias] N Asturias *f sg*

astute [əstút] ADJ astuto, sagaz

asylum [əsáıləm] N asilo *m*

asymmetric, asymmetrical [esımétrık[əl]] ADJ; asimétrico

asymptomatic [esımptəmǽdɪk] ADJ asintomático

at [æt] PREP **— the end of the story** al final de la historia; **— five o'clock** a las cinco; **— high altitude** a grandes alturas; **— last** por fin, al fin; **— once** enseguida; **— the table** a/ en la mesa; **— five dollars a kilo** a cinco dólares el kilo; **— Easter** en Pascua; **— home** en casa; **— war** en guerra; **wait — the door** espera en la puerta; **he is — peace with himself** está en paz consigo mismo; **the children are — play** los niños están jugando; **look — that** mira eso; **amazed —** pasmado por; **he laughed — me** se rió de mí

ate [et] *see* eat

atheism [éθiızəm] N ateísmo *m*

atheist [éθiıst] N ateo -a *mf*

athlete [ǽθlit] N deportista *mf*; (track and field) atleta *mf*; **—'s foot** pie de atleta *m*

athletic [æθlédɪk] ADJ deportivo; (concerning track and field; well-built) atlético

athletics [æθlédɪks] N deporte *m*; (track and field) atletismo *m*

Atlantic [ætlǽntık] ADJ atlántico; **— Ocean** Océano Atlántico *m*

atlas [ǽtləs] N atlas *m*

ATM [automatic teller machine] [étiém] N cajero automático *m*

atmosphere [ǽtməsfir] N (air) atmósfera *f*; (mood) ambiente *m*

atmospheric [ǽtməsfirık] ADJ atmosférico

atom [ǽdəm] N átomo *m*; **— bomb** bomba atómica *f*

atomic [ətámık] ADJ atómico; **— age** era atómica *f*; **— energy** energía atómica *f*; **— number** número atómico *m*; **— weight** peso atómico *m*

atomize [ǽdəmaız] VT atomizar

atomizer [ǽdəmaızə] N atomizador *m*

atone [ətón] VI **to — for** expiar, purgar

atonement [ətónmənt] N expiación *f*, purgación *f*

atop [ətáp] PREP encima de

atrium [étriəm] N (of office building, hotel) vestíbulo *m*, patio central *m*; (of church) atrio *m*

atrocious [ətrófəs] ADJ atroz

atrocity [ətrásıDi] N atrocidad *f*, barbaridad *f*

atrophy [ǽtrəfi] N atrofia *f*; VI/VT atrofiar[se]

attach [ətǽtʃ] VI/VT (pipe, cable) unir[se], juntar; (paper) sujetar; (wages) retener; (significance) atribuir; (an electronic file) adjuntar; **to be —ed to someone** estar apegado a alguien

attaché [ætæʃé] N agregado -da *mf*

attachment [ətǽtʃmənt] N (act of attaching) unión *f*; (pipe, cable) conexión *f*; (of wages) retención *f*; (significance) atribución *f*; (to an e-mail) adjunto *m*; (affection) apego *m*, cariño *m*; (accessory) accesorio *m*

attack [ətǽk] N ataque *m*, acometida *f*; VI/VT atacar, acometer

attain [ətén] VT (rank) alcanzar; (ambition) lograr *m*, realizar *f*; VI (age) llegar a

attainment [əténmənt] N (rank) alcance *m*; (ambition) logro *m*, realización *f*

attempt [ətémpt] N tentativa *f*, intento *m*; (murder) atentado *m*; VT tratar [de], intentar

attend [əténd] VT (meeting) asistir a, acudir a; VI **to — to** (a sick person) atender, cuidar; (a speaker) prestar atención; **—ing physician** médico -ca tratante *mf*

attendance [əténdəns] N asistencia *f*

attendant [əténdənt] N (at a gas station) encargado -da *mf*; (servant) sirviente -ta *mf*; ADJ concomitante

attention [əténʃən] N atención f; (courtesy) atenciones f pl; — **deficit disorder** trastorno de déficit de atención m; **to pay** — prestar atención; **to pay** — **to** atender a; **to call** — llamar la atención; INTERJ —! ¡firmes!

attentive [əténtɪv] ADJ (focused) atento; (courteous) cortés

attenuate [əténjuet] VT atenuar

attest [ətést] VT (bear witness to) atestiguar; (manifest) demostrar; VI certificar, dar fe, atestar

attic [ǽdɪk] N desván m, altillo m

attire [ətáɪr] N atavío m, vestidura f; VT ataviar

attitude [ǽdɪtud] N (mental) actitud f; (physical) postura f; (insolence) insolencia f, descaro m

attorney [ət³ni] N abogado -da mf, mandatario -ria mf; — **General** Ministro -tra de Justicia mf

attract [ətrǽkt] VT atraer; **to** — **attention** llamar la atención

attraction [ətrǽkʃən] N (act, power) atracción f; (charm) atractivo m; (of customers) captación f

attractive [ətrǽktɪv] ADJ atractivo; (beautiful) atractivo, agraciado

attractiveness [ətrǽktɪvnɪs] N atractivo m

attribute[1] [ǽtrəbjut] N atributo m

attribute[2] [ətríbjut] VT atribuir

attribution [ætrəbjúʃən] N atribución f

attrition [ətríʃən] N (wearing out) desgaste m; (casualties) bajas f pl; **war of** — guerra de agotamiento f

atypical [etípɪkəl] ADJ atípico

auburn [ɔ́bə·n] N & ADJ castaño rojizo m

auction [ɔ́kʃən] N subasta f, remate m; — **house** casa de subastas f; VI/VT subastar, rematar

auctioneer [ɔkʃəníɾ] N subastador -ra mf, rematador -ra mf

audacious [ɔdéʃəs] ADJ audaz, atrevido

audacity [ɔdǽsɪdi] N audacia f, desfachatez f, atrevimiento m

audible [ɔ́dəbəl] ADJ audible; — **feedback** regeneración audible f

audience [ɔ́diəns] N público m, auditorio m; (TV, radio) audiencia f

audio [ɔ́dio] ADJ de audio; — **book** audiolibro m; — **frequency** audiofrecuencia f; —**visual** audiovisual; —**visuals** audiovisuales m pl; N audio m

audiology [ɔdiáləʤi] N audiología f

audit [ɔ́dɪt] VI/VT (class) asistir de oyente; (accounts) auditar; N auditoría f; — **cycle** ciclo de auditoría m

auditing [ɔ́dɪtɪŋ] N auditoría f

audition [ɔdíʃən] N audición f; VI dar una audición [para]

auditor [ɔ́dɪdə·] N (of accounts) auditor -ora mf, contralor -ora mf; (of a class) oyente mf

auditorium [ɔdɪtɔ́riəm] N auditorio m,

paraninfo m

auditory [ɔ́dɪtɔri] ADJ auditivo

augment [ɔgmént] VT incrementar, aumentar

August [ɔ́gəst] N agosto m

aunt [ænt] N tía f

aura [ɔ́rə] N aura f

aurora [ərɔ́rə] N aurora f; — **borealis** aurora boreal f

auspices [ɔ́spɪsɪz] N auspicios m pl

auspicious [ɔspíʃəs] ADJ propicio

austere [ɔstír] ADJ austero

austerity [ɔstérɪdi] N austeridad f

Australia [ɔstréljə] N Australia f

Australian [ɔstréljən] ADJ & N australiano -na mf

Austria [ɔ́striə] N Austria f

Austrian [ɔ́striən] ADJ & N austríaco -ca mf

authentic [əθéntɪk] ADJ auténtico

authenticate [əθéntɪket] VT autenticar

authentication [əθentɪkéʃən] N legalización f

authenticity [əθentísɪdi] N autenticidad f

author [ɔ́θə·] N (professional) escritor -ra mf; (creator) autor -ora mf

authoritarian [əθɔritériən] ADJ autoritario

authoritative [əθɔ́riteDɪv] ADJ (official) autorizado; (dictatorial) autoritario

authority [əθɔ́rɪdi] N autoridad f; (permission) autorización f; **to have on good** — saber de buena fuente; **it's not within your** — no está dentro de tus facultades

authorization [ɔθ³izéʃən] N autorización f

authorize [ɔ́θəraɪz] VT autorizar, habilitar

autism [ɔ́tɪzəm] N autismo m

autistic [ɔtístɪk] ADJ autista

auto [ɔ́Do] see automobile, automatic

autobiography [ɔDobaɪógrəfi] N autobiografía f

autocrat [ɔ́Dəkræt] N autócrata mf

autograph [ɔ́Dəgræf] N autógrafo m

autoimmune [ɔDoɪmjún] ADJ autoinmune

automated [ɔ́DəmeDɪd] ADJ automatizado

automatic [ɔDəmǽDɪk] ADJ automático; (response) maquinal; — **backup** (copy) copia de respaldo automático f; (process) respaldo automático m; — **pilot** piloto automático m; — **transmission** transmisión automática f

automation [ɔDəméʃən] N automatización f

automobile [ɔ́Dəməbil] N automóvil m

automotive [ɔDəmóDɪv] ADJ (sport) automovilístico; (industry) automotor, automotriz

autonomic [ɔDənámɪk] ADJ autonómico

autonomous [ɔtánəməs] ADJ autónomo

autonomy [ɔtánəmi] N autonomía f

autopilot [ɔ́Dopaɪlət] N piloto automático m

autopsy [ɔ́tapsi] N autopsia f

autumn [ɔ́Dəm] N otoño m

autumnal [ɔtʌ́mnəl] ADJ otoñal

auxiliary [ɔgzíləri] ADJ & N auxiliar mf

avail [əvél] VI/VT servir; **to** — **oneself of**

aprovecharse de; N utilidad f; **of no** — de ninguna utilidad; **to no** — en vano

availability [əvelədfílɪdɪ] N (of a person, taxicab, funds) disponibilidad f; (of merchandise) existencias f pl

available [əvéləbəl] ADJ disponible, asequible

avalanche [ǽvəlæntʃ] N avalancha f, alud m

avarice [ǽvərɪs] N avaricia f

avaricious [ævərísəs] ADJ avaro, avariento

avatar [ǽvətɑr] N avatar m

avenge [əvéndʒ] VT vengar

avenger [əvéndʒə] N vengador -ra mf

avenue [ǽvənu] N avenida f; (means of access) vía f

aver [əvɚ] VT afirmar

average [ǽvrɪdʒ] N promedio m; **on** — de promedio; ADJ medio, mediano; **just** — (person) del montón; (thing) nada del otro mundo; VT promediar; **he —s 20 miles an hour** hace un promedio de 20 millas por hora

averse [əvɚs] ADJ reacio; **he's not** — **to a glass of wine** no se opone a una copa de vino

aversion [əvɚʒən] N aversión f

avert [əvɚt] VT (eyes) desviar, apartar; (danger) evitar

aviation [eviéʃən] N aviación f

aviator [évienə] N aviador -ra mf

avid [ǽvɪd] ADJ ávido

avocado [ævəkáɗo] N aguacate m; Am palta f

avocation [ævəkéʃən] N pasatiempo m

avoid [əvɔ́ɪd] VI/VT (stay away from) evitar; (dodge) esquivar

avow [əváu] VT confesar

avowal [əváuəl] N confesión f

avuncular [əvʌ́ŋkjələ] ADJ propio de un tío; — **attitude** actitud paternal y amistosa

await [əwét] VT aguardar

awake [əwék] ADJ despierto; VI/VT despertar[se]

awaken [əwékən] VI/VT despertar[se]

award [əwɔ́rd] N premio m, galardón m; (judicial) adjudicación f; VT otorgar, adjudicar

aware [əwér] ADJ consciente, enterado; **I'm** — **of that** eso me consta

awareness [əwérnɪs] N conciencia f

away [əwé] ADV **far** — lejos; — **from his family** lejos de su familia; **she looked** — apartó la vista; **she's** — no está; **he's been painting** — **all day** se ha pasado todo el día pintando; **right** — ahora mismo, ahorita; **ten miles** — a diez millas de distancia; **to give** — regalar; **to go** — irse; **to take** — quitar; **to blow** — (destroy) [hacer] volar; (astonish) dejar atónito

awe [ɔ] N sobrecogimiento m; **to be in** — sobrecogerse; VT sobrecoger

awesome [ɔ́səm] ADJ (awe-inspiring) sobrecogedor; (impressive) fabuloso

awestruck [ɔ́strʌk] ADJ pasmado

awful [ɔ́fəl] ADJ terrible, horroroso; ADV espantoso

awhile [əhwáɪl] ADV un rato

awkward [ɔ́kwəd] ADJ (clumsy) torpe, desmañado; (embarrassing) embarazoso; (unwieldy) incómodo

awl [ɔl] N punzón m

awning [ɔ́nɪŋ] N toldo m

awoke [əwók] see wake

awoken [əwókn] see wake

awry [ərái] ADJ (clothes) mal puesto; (hat) ladeado; **my plans went** — mis planes fracasaron rotundamente

ax, axe [æks] N hacha f; VT eliminar

axis [ǽksɪs] N eje m

axle [ǽksəl] N eje m

Azerbaijan [æzə-baɪdʒɑ́n] N Azerbaiyán m

Azerbaijani, Azerbaijanian [æzə-baɪdʒɑ́ni[ən]] ADJ & N azerbaijano -na mf, azerbaiyano -na mf

Aztec [ǽztɛk] ADJ & N azteca mf

azure [ǽʒə] ADJ [azul] celeste; N azul celeste m

Bb

babble [bǽbəl] N (baby talk) balbuceo m; (chatter) parloteo m; (murmur) murmullo m; VI (to talk like a baby) balbucear; (to chatter) parlotear; (to murmur) murmurar

baboon [bæbún] N babuino m

baby [bébi] N bebé mf; **who's the** — **in your family?** ¿quién es el menor/benjamín en tu familia? — **blue** celeste m; — **boomer** persona nacida entre 1946 y 1965 f; — **carriage** cochecito de bebé m; — **food** comida para bebés f; — **girl** nena f; — **sister** hermanita f; — **sitter** niñera f; — **talk** habla infantil f; — **tooth** diente de leche m; **to** — **sit** cuidar niños; **she had a** — dio a luz; VT mimar

baccalaureate [bækəlɔ́riət] N bachillerato m

bachelor [bǽtʃələ] N soltero m; —**'s degree** licenciatura f; — **of Arts** (degree) licenciatura en filosofía y letras f; (person) licenciado -da en filosofía y letras mf

bacillus [bəsíləs] N bacilo m

back [bæk] N (human body part) espalda f; (animal body part) lomo m; (opposite side) dorso m; (of chair) respaldo m, espaldar m; —**ache** dolor de espalda m; —**bone** columna vertebral f, espinazo m; —**pack** mochila f; **behind one's** — a espaldas de uno; **he has no** —**bone** no tiene carácter; **in** — **of** detrás de, tras; **in the** — **of the house** atrás de la casa; **to fall on one's** — caer de espaldas; **to**

turn one's — volver las espaldas; ADJ — **charges** cargos atrasados *m pl*; — **door** puerta trasera *f*; — **issues** números atrasados *m pl*; — **order** pedido pendiente *m*; — **taxes** impuestos atrasados *m pl*; **on the** — **burner** en suspenso; —**-and-forth movement** movimiento de vaivén *m*; VT respaldar, apoyar; VI dar marcha atrás; **to** — **down** echarse [para] atrás, recular; **to** — **up** (in a car) dar marcha atrás; (a file) hacer una copia de seguridad de; ADV (look) atrás / para atrás; (fall) de espaldas; **to** — **off** echarse atrás; — **and forth** de aquí para allá; **he ran** — **to the house** volvió corriendo a la casa; **he's** — **from work** está de vuelta del trabajo

backbite [bǽkbaɪt] VI/VT difamar

back date [bǽk det] VT antedatar

backer [bǽkɚ] N (financial) fiador -ra *mf*; (political) partidario -ria *mf*

backfire [bǽkfaɪr] VI (automobile) petardear, hacer detonaciones; (plan) ser contraproducente; N petardeo *m*

backgammon [bǽkgæmən] N backgammon *m*

background [bǽkgraʊnd] N (of a picture) fondo *m*; (experience) antecedentes *m pl*; (software) — **application** aplicación de fondo *f*; — **noise** ruido de fondo *m*; **I have a** — **in computers** tengo conocimientos de informática; **I know what goes on in the** — sé lo que pasa entre bastidores; **a humble** — orígenes humildes *m pl*

backhand [bǽkhænd] N revés *m*

backing [bǽkɪŋ] N (support) respaldo *m*, apoyo *m*; (guarantee) garantía *f*; (fabric) refuerzo *m*

backlash [bǽklæʃ] N reacción violenta *f*

backlighting [bǽklaɪdɪŋ] N retroiluminación *f*

backlit [bǽklɪt] ADJ retroiluminado

backlog [bǽklɔg] N atraso *m*

backpack [bǽklɔg] N mochila *f*; VI viajar con mochila

backseat [bǽksít] N asiento trasero *m*

backslash [bǽkslæʃ] N barra invertida *f*

backslide [bǽkslaɪd] VI volver a las andadas, reincidir

backspace [bǽkspes] N (action) retroceso *m*; (key) tecla de retroceso *f*; VI apretar la tecla de retroceso

backspin [bǽkspɪn] N efecto *m*, cortado *m*

backstage [bækstédʒ] ADV entre bastidores

backtrack [bǽktræk] VI retroceder, dar marcha atrás

backup [bǽkʌp] N (support) respaldo *m*; (copy) copia de seguridad *f*

backward [bǽkwəd] ADV hacia atrás, para atrás; — **search** búsqueda hacia atrás *f*; **to go** — recular; ADJ (underdeveloped) atrasado; (reactionary) retrógrado

backwardness [bǽkwədnɪs] N (underdevelopment) atraso *m*; (conservatism) retrogradismo *m*; (timidity) timidez *f*

backyard [bǽkjárd] N patio trasero *m*

bacon [békən] N tocino *m*, *Sp* beicon *m*

bacteria [bæktíriə] N bacteria[s] *f* [*pl*]

bacterial [bæktíriəl] ADJ bacteriano

bacteriology [bæktiriálədʒi] N bacteriología *f*

bad [bæd] ADJ malo; (man) perverso; (teeth) feo; (drug) dañoso; (flood) grave; (fruit) podrido; — **blood** enemistad *f*; — **check** cheque sin fondos *m*; — **debt** deuda incobrable *f*; — **faith** mala fe *f*; **to go from** — **to worse** ir de mal en peor; **he has a** — **heart** está enfermo del corazón; **to look** — tener mal aspecto; *fam* quedar mal; ADV mal; **not** — no está nada mal; **too** — ¡qué pena! VT **to** —**mouth** difamar [a]

bade [bed] *see* bid

badge [bædʒ] N insignia *f*, chapa *f*

badger [bædʒɚ] N tejón *m*; VT acosar

badly [bǽdli] ADV (do) mal; (want) mucho; (hurt) gravemente

baffle [bǽfəl] VT (confuse) confundir; (frustrate) desconcertar; N deflector *m*

bag [bæg] N bolsa *f*, bolso *m*; (suitcase) maleta *f*; (under eyes) ojera *f*; — **lady** vagabunda *f*; —**pipe** gaita *f*; VT (groceries) empacar, embolsar; (prey) cazar

baggage [bǽgɪdʒ] N (suitcases) equipaje *m*; (impediments) bagaje *m*; — **car** vagón de equipajes *m*; — **check** contraseña de equipajes *f*; — **claim** recogida de equipaje *f*; — **tag** etiqueta *f*; — **inspection** revisión de equipaje *f*

baggy [bǽgi] ADJ flojo, holgado

Bahamas [bəháməz] N Bahamas *f pl*

Bahamian [bəhémiən] ADJ & N bahameño -ña *mf*

Bahrain [barén] N Bahréin *m*

Bahraini [baréni] ADJ & N bahreiní *mf*

bail [bel] N fianza *f*; —**out** rescate financiero *m*; **to let out on** — poner en libertad bajo fianza; VT pagar la fianza; **to** — **someone out** pagarle la fianza a alguien; **to** — **someone out of a predicament** sacar a alguien de un apuro; **to** — **out water** achicar, vaciar; VI **to** — **out** (of a plane) tirarse con paracaídas de un avión; (of a situation) abandonar

bailiff [bélɪf] N ujier *mf*

bait [bet] N cebo *m*; VT (prepare hook) cebar; (attract customers) seducir; (harass) acosar; — **and switch advertising** publicidad de cebo y anzuelo *f*

bake [bek] VI/VT (in an oven) hornear; (in the sun) calcinar, abrasar; **I'm baking in this heat** me estoy asando, me muero de calor

baker [békɚ] N panadero -ra *mf*; —**'s dozen** la docena del fraile *f*

bakery [békəri] N panadería *f*

baking [békɪŋ] N (act of baking) horneado m;
(activity) repostería f; — **powder** polvo de
hornear m; — **soda** bicarbonato de sodio m
balance [bǽləns] N (instrument) balanza f;
(equilibrium) equilibrio m; (debit, credit)
saldo m, balance m; — **due** saldo pendiente
m; — **sheet** balance m; — **of payments**
balanza de pagos f; — **of trade** balanza
comercial f; **to lose one's** — perder el
equilibrio; VT equilibrar, hacer equilibrio
con; **to** — **the risks with the benefits**
sopesar los riesgos y los beneficios; VI
(accounts) cuadrar; —**ed budget**
presupuesto equilibrado m; **to** — **a budget**
equilibrar un presupuesto
balanced [bǽlənst] ADJ equilibrado
balancing [bǽlənsɪŋ] N equilibrado m
balcony [bǽlkəni] N balcón m; (in a theater)
palco m, entresuelo m
bald [bɔld] ADJ (person) calvo, pelón; (mountain)
pelón; (tire) liso; — **eagle** águila americana
de cabeza blanca f; —**headed** calvo; — **spot**
calva f; **he went** — se quedó calvo
baldness [bɔ́ldnɪs] N calvicie f
bale [beł] N paca f, fardo m; VT empacar, enfardar
balk [bɔk] VI oponerse, rehusarse a
ball [bɔł] N (tennis, baseball, golf) pelota f, bola f;
(baseball, opposite of strike) bola f;
(basketball, football, soccer) balón m;
(billiards) bola f; (of string, thread) ovillo m;
(cannon) bala [de cañón] f; (dance) baile m; —
and chain grillete m; — **bearing** cojinete de
bolas m; — **game** juego de pelota m;
(baseball) partido de béisbol m; —**park
estimate** cifra aproximada f; VT ovillar
ballad [bǽləd] N balada f; (historical) romance m
ballast [bǽləst] N lastre m; (railroad) balasto m;
VT lastrar
ballerina [bælərínə] N bailarina de ballet f
ballet [bælé] N ballet m
ballistic [bəlístɪk] ADJ balístico; — **missile**
misil balístico m; N —**s** balística f
balloon [bəlún] N globo m; — **mortgage**
hipoteca con pago final mayor f; VI (travel in a
balloon) pasear en globo; VI/VT (grow)
inflar[se]
ballot [bǽlət] N (system of voting) votación f;
(paper) papeleta f; Mex boleta f; — **box** urna f
balm [bɑm] N bálsamo m
balmy [bámi] ADJ templado
baloney [bəlóni] N pamplinas f pl, paparruchas f
pl
balsa [bɔ́łsə] N (wood) madera balsa f; (raft)
balsa f
balsam [bɔ́łsəm] N (resin) bálsamo m; (tree)
especie de abeto m
bamboo [bæmbú] N bambú m
ban [bæn] N prohibición f; (church) excomunión
f; VT prohibir

banal [bénl] ADJ banal
banana [bənǽnə] N plátano m, banana f; —
grove platanar m; — **split** banana split m; —
tree plátano m, banano m
band [bænd] N (group) banda f, pandilla f;
(group of musicians) banda f, conjunto m;
(cloth) banda f; (ribbon) cinta f; (leather) tira
f; **to join the** —**wagon** subirse al carro/tren;
—**width** amplitud de banda f; VI/VT **to** —
together unirse, juntarse
bandage [bǽndɪdʒ] N venda f, vendaje m; VT
vendar
Band-aid® [bǽnded] N Curita® f, parche m
bandit [bǽndɪt] N bandido -da mf, bandolero -ra
mf, salteador -ora f
bang [bæŋ] N (blow) golpe m, golpazo m; (sound)
estampido m, estallido m; —**s** fleco m,
flequillo m; **I get a** — **out of seeing my
grandkids** me emociona ver a mis nietos;
VI/VT (hit) golpear; (make noise) hacer
estrépito
Bangladesh [bæŋglədéʃ] N Bangladesh m
Bangladeshi [bæŋglədéʃi] ADJ & N bangladeshí
mf, bangladesí mf, bengalés -esa
banish [bǽnɪʃ] VT desterrar
banishment [bǽnɪʃmənt] N destierro m,
proscripción f
banister [bǽnɪstə] N barandal m, pasamano[s]
m, balaustrada f
banjo [bǽndʒo] N banjo m
bank [bæŋk] N (financial institution) banco m;
(in gambling) banca f; (of a body of water)
orilla f, ribera f, margen m; (slope) escarpa f;
— **card** tarjeta bancaria f; — **account** cuenta
bancaria f; — **check** cheque de caja m; —
failure quiebra bancaria f; —**note** billete m;
— **statement** estado de cuenta m; —**vault**
cámara f; ADJ bancario, de banco; VT (money)
depositar en un banco; VI (snow, sand)
amontonar; (airplane) ladear; **to** — **on** contar
con; **to** —**roll** financiar
banker [bǽŋkə] N (bank owner) banquero -ra
mf; (bank employee) bancario -ria mf
banking [bǽŋkɪŋ] N (activity) actividad bancaria
f; (industry) banca f; ADJ bancario, de banco
bankrupt [bǽŋkrʌpt] ADJ en bancarrota, en
quiebra; VT arruinar, quebrar
bankruptcy [bǽŋkrʌptsi] N bancarrota f,
quiebra f; — **law** estatuto de quiebras m; —
proceedings juicio por quiebra m; **to go
into** — declararse en quiebra
banner [bǽnə] N estandarte m, pendón m; ADJ
sobresaliente
banquet [bǽŋkwɪt] N banquete m, gala f
baptism [bǽptɪzəm] N (sacrament) bautismo m;
(action) bautizo m
baptize [bǽptaɪz] VT bautizar
bar [bɑr] N (of iron, sand, soap, of a tavern) barra
f; (of chocolate) barra f, tableta f; (vertical

rod) barrote *m*; (obstacle) barrera *f*, obstáculo *m*; (in music) compás *m*; (saloon) bar *m*; **—bell** barra para pesas *f*; **—code** código de barras *m*; **—code reader** lector de código de barras *m*; **— graph** gráfica de barras *f*; **—keeper/tender** tabernero -ra *mf*, cantinero -ra *mf*; **—room** bar *m*; **—room brawl** pelea de borrachos *f*; **behind —s** tras las rejas; **to be admitted to the —** recibirse de abogado; *vt* (door, exit) atrancar; (access) impedir; (from membership) excluir; **— none** sin excepción; **—ring a disaster** salvo en caso de desastre

barb [barb] N púa *f*; **—ed wire** alambre de púas *m*; *Sp* alambre de espino *m*

Barbadian [barbéɪɒiən] ADJ & N barbadense *mf*

Barbados [barbéɒos] N Barbados *m*

barbarian [barbérian] ADJ & N bárbaro -ra *mf*

barbaric [barbǽrɪk] ADJ bárbaro

barbarous [bárbəəs] ADJ bárbaro

barbecue [bárbɪkju] N (meat dish) barbacoa *f*, asado *m*, parrillada *f*; **— sauce** adobo de barbacoa *m*; *vi/vt* asar con adobo

barber [bárbə] N peluquero *m*, barbero *m*; **—shop** peluquería *f*, barbería *f*

barbiturate [barbítʃəɪt] N barbitúrico *m*

bard [bard] N bardo *m*

bare [ber] ADJ (legs, walls) desnudo; (pantry) vacío; **—back** a pelo; **—-bones** básico; **—faced** descarado; **—foot** descalzo; **the — necessities** lo imprescindible; **—headed** con la cabeza descubierta; **—legged** con las piernas desnudas; **— majority** escasa mayoría *f*; **to lay —** poner al descubierto; **with his — hands** con las propias manos

barely [bérli] ADV apenas

bargain [bárgɪn] N (agreement) trato *m*; (inexpensive purchase) ganga *f*, ocasión *f*; **— basement** sección de ofertas *f*; **into the —** por añadidura; **to strike a —** cerrar un trato; *vi* (haggle) regatear; (expect) contar con

bargaining [bárgənɪŋ] N (haggling) regateo *m*; (negotiation) negociación *f*; **—ing position** posición de negociación *f*

barge [bardʒ] N barcaza *f*; *vi* **to — into a room** irrumpir en un cuarto

baritone [bǽrɪton] N & ADJ barítono *m*

barium [bǽriəm] N bario *m*

bark [bark] N (of a dog) ladrido *m*; (on a tree) corteza *f*; *vi/vt* ladrar

barley [bárli] N cebada *f*

barn [barn] N (for animals) establo *m*; (for grain) granero *m*; **— owl** lechuza *f*; **—yard** corral *m*

barnacle [bárnəkəɫ] N percebe *m*

barometer [bərámɪɒə] N barómetro *m*

baron [bǽrən] N barón *m*

baroque [bərók] ADJ & N barroco *m*

barracks [bǽrəks] N cuartel *m*

barracuda [bǽrəkúɒə] N barracuda *f*

barrage [bəráʒ] N (of artillery fire) barrera de fuego *f*; (of questions) lluvia *f*, aluvión *m*

barrel [bǽrəɫ] N barril *m*, tonel *m*; (gun) cañón *m*, caño *m*; **he's a — of laughs** es un payaso; **he is scraping the bottom of the —** está desesperado; *vi* **to — along** ir disparado

barren [bǽrən] ADJ (land) árido, yermo; (female) estéril

barrette [bərét] N broche *m*

barricade [bǽrɪkéd] N barricada *f*; *vt* cerrar con barricadas; *vi* atrincherarse

barrier [bǽriə] N barrera *f*; **— reef** barrera de coral *f*

barrio [bário] N barrio hispano *m*

barter [bárɒə] *vi* hacer trueque; *vt* trocar; N trueque *m*

bartering [bárɒə-ɪŋ] N trueque *m*

basal cell carcinoma [bésəɫsɛɫkɑrsɪnómə] N carcinoma de célula basal *m*

basalt [bésɔɫt] N basalto *m*

base [bes] N base *f*; **—ball** béisbol *m*; **—ball player** beisbolista *m*, pelotero -ra *mf*; **—board** zócalo *m*; ADJ bajo, vil; (metal) de baja ley; **— font** tipo de letra por omisión *m*; **—line** línea de fondo *f*; **— on balls** base por bolas *f*; **— pay** salario base *m*; **—s loaded** bases llenas *f pl*; **— steal** robo de base *m*; *vi/vt* basar, fundamentar; **to be —d on** fundamentarse en; **the general is —d in Berlin** el general está estacionado en Berlín

baseless [bésɫɪs] ADJ sin fundamento

basement [bésmənt] N sótano *m*

baseness [bésnɪs] N bajeza *f*, vileza *f*

bash [bæʃ] *vt* golpear; N (party) fiesta *f*

bashful [bǽʃfəɫ] ADJ tímido, vergonzoso

bashfulness [bǽʃfəɫnɪs] N timidez *f*

basic [bésɪk] ADJ básico

basin [bésɪn] N (bowl) palangana *f*, jofaina *f*; (of a fountain) pilón *m*; (geographical formation) cuenca *f*; (pond) estanque *m*

basis [bésɪs] N fundamento *m*, base *f*; **on the — of** en base a, con base en; **on a regular —** regularmente

bask [bæsk] *vi* (in the sun) asolearse; (in praise) deleitarse

basket [bǽskɪt] N canasta *f*, cesta *f*, cesto *m*; (in basketball) canasta *f*; **—ball** (game) baloncesto *m*, básquetbol *m*, básquet *m*; (ball) balón de baloncesto *m*; **— case** (crazy person) chiflado -da *mf*; (helpless person) caso perdido *m*; **to make a —** (in basketball) encestar

basketful [bǽskɪtfəɫ] N (contents of a basket) canasto *m*; (large amount) montón *m*

basketry [bǽskɪtri] N cestería *f*

Basque [bæsk] ADJ & N (person) vasco -ca *mf*; (language) vascuence *m*, vasco *m*, euskera *m*

bass[1] [bes] N (voice, bass guitar) bajo *m*; (double bass) contrabajo *m*; **— clef** clave de fa *f*; **—**

drum bombo m; **— horn** tuba f

bass[2] [bæs] (marine fish) lubina f; (freshwater fish) perca f

bassist [bésɪst] N bajista mf

bassoon [bæsún] N fagot m

bastard [bǽstəd] N & ADJ bastardo -da mf

baste [best] VT (fabric) hilvanar; (meat) rociar

bat [bæt] N (baseball, cricket) bate m; (animal) murciélago m; VT golpear; **he is at —** está al bate; **it was his first at- —** fue su primer turno; VI (baseball) batear; **not to — an eye** no pestañear

batch [bætʃ] N (of cookies) hornada f; (of cement, files) tanda f; (of data) colección f

bath [bæθ] N baño m; **—robe** bata (de baño) f; Sp albornoz m; **—room** (in a house) baño m, cuarto de baño m; (public) Sp aseo m; Am servicio m, baño m; **—tub** bañera f

bathe [beð] VI/VT bañar[se]; **bathing suit** traje de baño m

bather [béðə] N bañista mf

baton [bətán] N batuta f

battalion [bətǽljən] N batallón m

batter [bǽDə] N (in baking) pasta f, masa f; (in baseball) bateador -ora mf; **—'s box** caja de bateo f; VT golpear

battery [bǽDəri] N (of car, artillery, in baseball) batería f; (of electronic devices) pila f; (of tests) serie f; (assault) asalto m

batting [bǽDɪŋ] N bateo m; **— average** porcentaje de bateo m

battle [bǽdl] N batalla f; **—-ax[e]** (weapon) hacha de guerra f; (woman) pej sargenta f; **— cry** grito de guerra m; **—field** campo de batalla m; **—ship** acorazado m; VI batallar; **to — cancer** luchar contra el cáncer

bawl [bɔl] VI berrear; **to — somebody out** echarle la bronca a uno

bay [be] N (body of water) bahía f; (howl) aullido m; **— leaf** hoja de laurel f; **— window** ventana saliente f; **to hold at —** tener a raya; ADJ bayo; VI aullar

bayonet [béənɛt] N bayoneta f

bazaar [bəzár] N (market place) bazar m; (benefit) kermés f

bazooka [bəzúka] N bazuca f

be [bi] VI ser, estar; **I am from Uruguay** soy de Uruguay; **there were four of us** éramos cuatro; **he is a doctor** es médico; **it's her** es ella; **sugar is sweet** el azúcar es dulce; **London is in England** Londres está en Inglaterra; **this water is cold** esta agua está fría; **the windows were open** las ventanas estaban abiertas; **there is a problem** hay un problema; **to — cold/warm/hungry/right / in a hurry** tener frío/calor/hambre/razón/prisa; **to be cold/hot/windy** hacer frío/calor/viento

beach [bitʃ] N playa f; **—comber** vagabundo -da

mf; **—head** cabeza de playa f; VT varar, encallar

beacon [bíkən] N faro m

bead [bid] N (of glass) cuenta f; (of sweat) gota f, perla f; **to get a — on somebody** apuntarle a alguien; VT (string) enhebrar/ensartar cuentas; (decorate) adornar con cuentas

beagle [bígəl] N beagle m

beak [bik] N pico m

beaker [bíkə] N vaso de precipitados m

beam [bim] N (of light) rayo m, haz m; (of a building) viga f; (of a ship) manga f; (of a scale) brazo m; **broad in the —** ancho de caderas; VI/VT (light, radio) emitir; (smile) estar radiante

bean [bin] N judía f, habichuela f; Sp alubia f; Am frijol m, Am poroto m; **Lima —** haba f; **—stalk** tallo de habas / frijol m; **Jack and the —stalk** Juanito y las habichuelas; **I don't know —s about that** no sé ni papa / ni jota de eso

bear [ber] N oso m; **— hug** abrazo fuerte m; **— market** mercado bajista m; VT (hold up, tolerate) soportar, aguantar; (suffer) sobrellevar; (have a child) dar a luz; (produce young) parir; (produce fruit) producir; **to — down** (mash) apretar; (push) pujar; **to — a grudge** guardar rencor; **to — in mind** tener en cuenta; **to — oneself with dignity** portarse con dignidad; **to — out** confirmar; **to — testimony** dar testimonio; **to — interest** devengar interés; **to — gifts** traer regalos; **to — a resemblance** parecerse; **to — the cost of something** asumir el costo de algo; **it doesn't — repeating** no merece repetirse

bearable [bérəbəl] ADJ llevadero, soportable

beard [bird] N (on a man) barba f; (of wheat) aristas f pl

bearded [bírdɪd] ADJ barbado, barbudo

bearer [bérə] N portador -ora mf

bearing [bérɪŋ] N porte m; **to lose one's —s** perder el rumbo, desorientarse; **it has no — on our situation** no tiene relación con nuestra situación

bearish [bérɪʃ] ADJ (of bears) osuno; (of stock market) bajista

beast [bist] N bestia f

beat [bit] VT (wings, eggs) batir; (a person) golpear; (a drum) tocar; (an opponent) vencer; (tempo) marcar; VI (heart) latir; (drum) sonar; **to — around the bush** andarse por las ramas; **to — off** rechazar; **to — up** dar una paliza; **—s me!** ¡ni idea! N (blow) golpe m; (drum) toque m; (heart) latido m; (tempo) compás m; (policeman's territory) ronda f; ADJ cansado

beaten [bítn] ADJ (mixed) batido; (defeated) vencido; **— path** camino trillado m

beaten [bítn] *see* beat
beater [bídɚ] N batidor *m*
beating [bíDɪŋ] N (whipping) paliza *f*; (pulsation) latido *m*
beau [bo] N pretendiente *m*
beautiful [bjúDəfɪl] ADJ hermoso; — **people** jet set *m*
beautify [bjúDəfaɪ] VT embellecer, hermosear
beauty [bjúDi] N belleza *f*, hermosura *f*; (woman) beldad *f*; — **contest/pageant** concurso/ certamen de belleza *m*; — **parlor** salón de belleza *m*
beaver [bívɚ] N castor *m*
became [bikém] *see* become
because [bikʌz] CONJ porque; — **of** por, a causa de, debido a
beckon [békən] VT llamar por señas
become [bikʌ́m] VI (turn into) convertirse en; **the water became ice** el agua se convirtió en hielo; **he became a doctor** llegó a ser médico; (suit) sentar bien; **that suit —s you** ese traje te luce bien; VI (change emotional or physical condition) ponerse; **she became ill** se puso enferma; (undergo a drastic change) volverse; **he became crazy** se volvió loco; **to — angry** enojarse; **to — frightened** asustarse; **to — old** envejecer; **what has — of him?** ¿qué ha sido de él?
becoming [bikʌ́mɪŋ] ADJ (appropriate) propio; **that dress is — to you** te sienta bien ese vestido
bed [bed] N (furniture) cama *f*; *lit* lecho *m*; (of a river) cauce *m*; (of the sea) fondo *m*; (in a garden) cuadro *m*; —**bug** chinche *mf*; —**clothes** ropa de cama *f*; —**pan** cuña *f*, chata *f*; —**ridden** postrado en cama; —**rest** reposo *m*; —**rock** lecho de roca *m*; —**room** alcoba *f*, dormitorio *m*; *Mex* recámara *f*; **at the —side** al lado de la cama; —**side table** mesita de noche *f*; —**side manner** manera de tratar a los pacientes *f*; —**sore** llaga *f*; —**spread** colcha *f*; —**spring** resorte del colchón *m*; —**time** hora de dormir *f*; —**wetting** enuresis nocturna *f*; **to go to —** acostarse; **to put to —** acostar
bedding [béDɪŋ] N ropa de cama *f*
bee [bi] N (insect) abeja *f*; (social gathering) tertulia *f*; **to have a — in one's bonnet** tener una idea metida en la cabeza; —**hive** colmena *f*; —**sting** picadura de abeja *f*
beech [bitʃ] N haya *f*; —**nut** hayuco *m*
beef [bif] N (meat) carne de vaca/res *f*; (complaint) queja *f*; — **jerky** cecina *f*; —**steak** bistec *m*; VI quejarse; **to — up** reforzar
been [bɪn] *see* be
beep [bip] N pitazo *m*; VI/VT (alarm) sonar; (horn) tocar
beeper [bípɚ] N buscapersonas *m sg*

beer [bir] N cerveza *f*
beet [bit] N remolacha *f*
beetle [bídl] N escarabajo *m*
befall [bɪfɔ́l] VT acontecerle a
befallen [bɪfɔ́lən] *see* befall
befell [bɪfɛ́l] *see* befall
befit [bɪfít] VT convenir
before [bɪfɔ́r] ADV (temporal) antes, con anterioridad; (spatial) delante; PREP (temporal) antes de; (spatial) delante de; *lit* ante; CONJ antes [de] que, antes de; — **beginning** antes de que comiences, antes de comenzar; —**-tax earnings** ganancias pre-impositivas *f pl*
beforehand [bɪfɔ́rhænd] ADV de antemano, con anterioridad
befriend [bɪfrénd] VT hacerse amigo de
beg [bɛg] VI (ask for alms) mendigar, pedir limosna; VI/VT (implore) rogar; **to — for mercy** pedir misericordia; **she —ged me to do it** me rogó que lo hiciera; **to — the question** dar por sentado lo mismo que se arguye
began [bɪgǽn] *see* begin
begat [bɪgǽt] *see* beget
beget [bɪgɛ́t] VT engendrar
beggar [bégɚ] N mendigo -ga *mf*
begin [bɪgín] VI/VT comenzar, empezar; **the ten dollars won't — to cover the expense** los diez dólares ni siquiera cubren los gastos
beginner [bɪgínɚ] N principiante *mf*
beginning [bɪgínɪŋ] N principio *m*; (temporal only) comienzo *m*; — **with** comenzando con/ por; **at the —** al/por el principio
begotten [bɪgátn] *see* beget
begrudge [bɪgrʌ́ʤ] VT aceptar de mala gana
begun [bɪgʌ́n] *see* begin
behalf [bɪhǽf] PREP LOC **on — of** (in place of) por, en nombre de, de parte de; (in favor of) a favor de
behave [bɪhév] VI portarse, comportarse; — **yourself!** ¡pórtate bien!
behavior [bɪhévjɚ] N comportamiento *m*, conducta *f*
behavioral [bɪhévjərəl] ADJ conductual, relativo a la conducta / al comportamiento
behead [bɪhéd] VT decapitar, descabezar
beheld [bɪhɛ́ld] *see* behold
behind [bɪháɪnd] ADV detrás; (in payments, schedule) atrasado; **he fell — his competitors** quedó a la zaga de sus competidores; **an hour —** una hora de retraso; **from —** desde atrás; **to fall —** atrasarse; **to leave something —** dejar atrás algo; PREP detrás de, tras; **we're all — you** todos te apoyamos; **who's — this evil plot?** ¿quién está detrás de este plan macabro? **one's back** a espaldas de uno; N trasero *m*
behold [bɪhóld] VT contemplar; — **the future**

king! ¡he aquí el futuro rey!
behoove [bɪhúv] VI **it behooves [one]** le corresponde [a uno]
beige [beʒ] ADJ & N beige *m*
being [bíɪŋ] N ser *m*; **for the time —** por ahora
Belarus [belərús] N Bielorrusia *f*
belated [bɪlédɪd] ADJ atrasado, tardío
belch [beltʃ] VI eructar, repetir; N eructo *m*
belfry [bélfri] N campanario *m*
Belgian [béldʒən] ADJ & N belga *mf*
Belgium [béldʒəm] N Bélgica *f*
belief [bɪlíf] N creencia *f*; (strong opinion) convicción *f*
believable [bɪlívəbəl] ADJ creíble
believe [bɪlív] VI/VT creer
believer [bɪlívə-] N creyente *mf*; (proponent) partidario -ria *mf*
belittle [bɪlídl̩] VT (a person) menospreciar, disminuir; (a situation) minimizar
belittling [bɪlídl̩ɪŋ] N menosprecio *m*, disminución *f*
Belize [bəlíz] N Belice *m*
Belizean [bəlízian] ADJ & N beliceño -ña *mf*
bell [bel] N campana *f*; (small) campanilla *f*; **—boy/hop** botones *m sg*; **— curve** curva de campana *f*; **—flower** campanilla *f*, campánula *f*; **— jar** campana de cristal *f*; **— pepper** pimiento *m*, morrón *m*; **— tower** campanario *m*; **with all the —s and whistles** con todos los accesorios
bellicose [bélikos] ADJ belicoso
belligerent [bəlídʒə-ənt] ADJ & N beligerante *mf*
bellow [bélo] VI/VT bramar, berrear; N bramido *m*; **—s fuelle** *m*
belly [béli] N barriga *f*, vientre *m*, panza *f*; **—ache** dolor de barriga *m*; **— button** ombligo *m*; **— dance** danza del vientre *f*; **— laugh** carcajada *f*
belong [bɪlɔ́ŋ] VI (ownership) pertenecer; **this car —s to me** este coche me pertenece; (correspondence) corresponder; **this key —s to this door** esta llave corresponde a esta puerta; (placement) ir; **this —s on the shelf** esto va en el estante
belongings [bɪlɔ́ŋɪŋz] N pertenencias *f pl*
beloved [bɪlávɪd] ADJ querido; N amado -da *mf*
below [bɪló] ADV abajo; **five — [zero]** cinco bajo cero; PREP bajo, debajo de, abajo de
belt [belt] N (for the waist) cinturón *m*, cinto *m*; (for a machine) correa *f*; (region) zona *f*; **— line** cintura *f*; VT pegar; **to — out a song** cantar una canción a voz en cuello
bemoan [bɪmón] VT lamentarse de, quejarse de
bench [bentʃ] N banco *m*; (without a back) banqueta *f*; (in sports) banco *m*, banquillo *m*; (in court) estrado *m*; **—mark** (upper limit) cota *f*; (parameter) punto de referencia *m*; **— price** precio de referencia *m*; **opinion of the —** opinión del tribunal *f*

bend [bend] VI/VT (make curved) doblar[se]; (force) someter; **to — over** inclinarse; **to — over backward** desvivirse; **to — the rules** hacer una excepción; N (road) curva *f*, recodo *m*; **—s** enfermedad de los buzos *f*
bending [béndɪŋ] N doblado *m*
beneath [bɪníθ] ADV abajo; PREP debajo de, bajo; (in rank) inferior a; **— contempt** totalmente despreciable; **that's — me** no es digno de mí
benediction [benɪdíkʃən] N bendición *f*
benefactor [bénəfæktə-] N benefactor -ora *mf*; *lit* bienhechor -ora *mf*
beneficent [bənéfɪsənt] ADJ benéfico
beneficial [benəfíʃəl] ADJ beneficioso
beneficiary [benəfíʃieri] N beneficiario -ria *mf*
benefit [bénəfɪt] N beneficio *m*, provecho *m*; **— performance** función de beneficencia *f*; VI/VT beneficiar[se], sacar provecho
benevolence [bənévələns] N benevolencia *f*
benevolent [bənévələnt] ADJ benévolo
benign [bɪnáin] ADJ benigno
Benin [benín] N Benín *m*
Beninese [beniníz] ADJ & N beninés -esa *mf*
bent [bent] N inclinación *f*; **to be — on** estar resuelto a
bent [bent] *see* bend
benzine [bénzin] N bencina *f*
bequeath [bɪkwíð] VT legar, heredar
bequest [bɪkwést] N legado *m*
berate [bɪrét] VT reprender
bereaved [bɪrívd] ADJ de luto
beret [bəré] N boina *f*
berry [béri] N baya *f*
berserk [bə-rzɚ́k] ADJ fuera de sí; **he went —** se puso hecho una fiera, se enfureció
berth [bɚθ] N litera *f*; **to give a wide — to** mantener una distancia prudencial de
beseech [bɪsítʃ] VT suplicar, rogar
beset [bɪsét] VT (attack) acosar; (surround) rodear
beside [bɪsáid] PREP al lado de; **sit down — me** siéntate a mi lado; **to be — oneself** estar fuera de sí; **that is — the point** eso no viene al caso; ADV al lado
besides [bɪsáidz] ADV además; **they have a table but not much —** tienen una mesa pero poca cosa más; PREP además de, aparte de
besiege [bɪsídʒ] VT (lay siege) sitiar, cercar; (importune) importunar, asediar
best [best] ADJ mejor; **—-case scenario** la mejor situación; **— man** padrino de boda *m*; **— seller** bestseller *m*; **she's the —** ella es la mejor; ADV mejor; **at — a** lo más, en el mejor de los casos; N **the — is still to come** lo mejor está por venir; **to do one's —** hacer lo mejor posible; **to get the — of a person** ganarle a una persona; **to make the — of** sacar el mejor partido de; VT vencer

bestial [béstʃəl] ADJ bestial

bestow [bɪstó] VT conferir; **to — gifts upon** dar regalos a

bet [bɛt] N apuesta f; VI/VT apostar; **to — on** apostar por

beta [bédə] N — **blocker** betabloqueador m, betabloqueante m; — **test** prueba beta f; — **version** versión beta f

betray [bɪtré] VT (a person) traicionar; (a secret) revelar; (a feeling) traslucir, delatar; **to — one's ignorance** hacer patente su ignorancia

betrayal [bɪtréəl] N traición f

betrayer [bɪtréə] N traidor -ra mf

betrothal [bɪtróðəl] N esponsales f pl

better [bédə] ADJ mejor; — **half** media naranja f; **the — part of a year** la mayor parte de un año; ADV mejor; **he lives — than a mile away** vive a más de una milla; **so much the — tanto mejor; —-off** en mejor posición económica; **to be — off** estar mejor así; **to change for the —** cambiar para bien; **to get — mejorar[se]**, aliviarse; VT mejorar; **to — oneself** mejorarse, mejorar de situación; N **the — of the two** el/la mejor de los dos

better, bettor [bédə] N apostador -ra mf

between [bɪtwín] PREP entre; ADV en medio

bevel [bévəl] N bisel m; VT biselar

beverage [bévrɪdʒ] N bebida f

bevy [bévi] N (of birds, people) bandada f; (of deer) manada f

beware [bɪwér] VI cuidarse [de]; — **of the dog** cuidado con el perro

bewilder [bɪwíldə] VT dejar perplejo, aturdir; **to be —ed** estar perplejo

bewilderment [bɪwíldəmənt] N perplejidad f, aturdimiento m

bewitch [bɪwítʃ] VT hechizar, embrujar

beyond [bɪjánd] ADV más allá; PREP más allá de; — **my reach** fuera de mi alcance; N **the great —** el más allá

Bhutan [butǽn] N Bután m

Bhutanese [butníz] ADJ & N butanés -esa mf

biannual [baɪǽnjuəl] ADJ bianual, semestral, semianual

bias [báɪəs] N (prejudice) prejuicio m; (in fabric) sesgo m; ADJ sesgado, oblicuo; VT predisponer; **—ed** parcial

bib [bɪb] N babero m; (of an apron) pechera f

Bible [báɪbəl] N Biblia f

biblical [bíblɪkəl] ADJ bíblico

bibliography [bɪbliágrəfi] N bibliografía f

bicarbonate [baɪkárbənɪt] N bicarbonato m

bicep, biceps [báɪsɛp[s]] N bíceps m sg

bicker [bíkə] VI reñir

bicuspid [baɪkáspɪd] ADJ bicúspide

bicycle [báɪsɪkəl] N bicicleta f; VI andar en bicicleta

bid [bɪd] N (in an auction, contest) licitación f,

puja f; (in card games) apuesta f; (attempt) tentativa f; VI/VT (offer) pujar; (command) mandar; (invite) rogar; (enter a bid in cards) apostar; **to — good-bye** despedirse; **to — up** pujar el precio

bidden [bídn] see bid

bidding [bídɪŋ] N (in auction) puja f; **at someone's —** por orden de alguien; **to do someone's —** cumplir con los deseos de alguien

bide [baɪd] VI/VT **to — one's time** esperar una oportunidad

biennium [baɪéniəm] N bienio m

bifurcate [báɪfəket] VI/VT bifurcar[se]

big [bɪg] ADJ grande; — **Bang Theory** Teoría del Big Bang f; — **brother** hermano mayor m; — **bucks** mucha plata f; — **business** el gran capital m; — **deal** asunto importante m; — **deal!** ¡no es para tanto! — **Dipper** Osa Mayor f; — **enchilada** fam mandamás m, fam pez gordo m; —-**headed** cabezón, cabezudo; —-**hearted** magnánimo; — **house** fam gayola f; — **kahuna** fam mandamás m, fam pez gordo m; — **name** personalidad prominente f; — **picture** panorama general m; — **shot** fam pez gordo m; — **sister** hermana mayor f; —-**ticket** caro; —-**wig** fam pez gordo m; — **with child** embarazada; **jazz was — in the 1920s** el jazz era popular en los años veinte; **she's a — deal** es una persona importante; ADV **she wants to go —time** se muere por ir; **to talk — jactarse**, fanfarronear; Am lucirse; **to go over — tener éxito; to be — on** ser entusiasta de

bigamy [bígəmi] N bigamia f

bigot [bígət] N intolerante m

bigotry [bígətri] N intolerancia f

bike [baɪk] N (bicycle) bici f; (motorcycle) moto f

biker [báɪkə] N (bicyclist) ciclista mf; (motorcyclist) motociclista mf

bikini [bɪkíni] N bikini m

bilateral [baɪlǽdəəl] ADJ bilateral

bile [baɪl] N (secretion) bilis f; (ill temper) mal genio m; — **duct** conducto biliar m

bilingual [baɪlíŋgwəl] ADJ & N bilingüe mf

bilingualism [baɪlíŋgwəlɪzm] N bilingüismo m

bill [bɪl] N (statement) factura f; (in a restaurant) cuenta f; (poster) cartel m; (bank note) billete m; (for movies, theater) programa m; (of a bird) pico m; (legislative) proyecto de ley m; —**board** cartelera f; —**fold** cartera f, billetera f; — **of exchange** letra de cambio f; — **of lading** conocimiento de embarque m; — **of rights** declaración de derechos f; — **of sale** escritura de venta f; VT cobrar, mandar la factura a

billable [bíləbəl] ADJ facturable

billiards [bíljədz] N billar m

billing [bílɪŋ] N (theater) orden de importancia en espectáculos m; (business) facturación f; — **cycle** ciclo de facturación m

billion [bíljən] NUM mil millones m pl

billow [bílo] N (of smoke) nube f; (of water) ola f; VI ondular, hacer olas

bimonthly [baɪmánθli] ADV bimestral

bin [bɪn] N (for clothes, food) cajón m, recipiente m; (on an airplane) portaequipajes m sg; (for coal) carbonera f; (for grain) granero m

binary [báɪneri] ADJ binario; — **star** estrella binaria f

bind [baɪnd] VI/VT (unite) unir; (connect) ligar; (tie) atar; (put a cover on a book) encuadernar; (press tightly) apretar; (oblige by contract) obligar

binding [báɪndɪŋ] N (of a book) encuadernación f; (on a rug) ribete m; ADJ obligatorio

binge [bɪndʒ] N (alcoholic) juerga f, parranda f; (food) comilona f; VI (on alcohol) emborracharse; (on food) atiborrarse

bingo [bíŋgo] N bingo m

binoculars [bənákjələz] N gemelos m pl, prismáticos m pl

binomial [baɪnómiəl] N binomio m; ADJ binomial

biochemistry [baɪokémɪstri] N bioquímica f

biodegradable [baɪodɪgrédəbəl] ADJ biodegradable

bioengineering [baɪoɛndʒənírɪŋ] N bioingeniería f

biofeedback [baɪofidbæk] N biofeedback m, retroalimentación biológica f

biography [baɪágrəfi] N biografía f

biological [baɪəládʒɪkəl] ADJ biológico

biologist [baɪálədʒɪst] N biólogo -ga mf

biology [baɪálədʒi] N biología f

biopsy [báɪapsi] N biopsia f

biorhythm [báɪorɪðəm] N biorritmo m

biotechnology [baɪoteknálədʒi] N biotecnología f

bipartisan [baɪpártɪzən] ADJ bipartidista

bipolar [baɪpólə] ADJ bipolar; — **disorder** trastorno bipolar m

birch [bɜtʃ] N abedul m

bird [bɜd] N ave f; (small) pájaro m; — **of prey** ave de rapiña f; — **seed** alpiste m; **odd** — persona peculiar f

birth [bɜθ] N (act of being born) nacimiento m; (act of giving birth) parto m; (lineage) linaje m; (origin) origen m; — **canal** canal de parto m; — **certificate** certificado de nacimiento m, fe/acta de nacimiento f; — **control** (policy) control de la natalidad m; (devices) anticonceptivos m pl; —**day** cumpleaños m sg; **in his / her** —**day suit** como Dios lo/la trajo al mundo; —**mark** antojo m, marca de nacimiento f; —**place** lugar de nacimiento m; —**rate** natalidad f, tasa de natalidad f;

—**right** derechos de nacimiento m pl; (of oldest child) primogenitura f; **to give** — dar a luz, parir, alumbrar; **by** — de nacimiento

biscuit [bískɪt] N panecillo m

bisect [báɪsɛkt] VT bisecar

bishop [bíʃəp] N obispo m; (in chess) alfil m

bison [báɪsən] N bisonte m, búfalo m

bit [bɪt] N (small piece) pedacito m, trocito m; (some) poquito m; (of a bridle) bocado m, freno m; (of a drill) broca f, barrena f; (computer) bit m; **I don't care a** — no me importa en absoluto

bit [bɪt] see bite

bitch [bɪtʃ] N perra f

bite [baɪt] VI/VT morder; (be duped) dejarse engañar; (insect, fish, snake) picar; **to** — **off** arrancar de un mordisco; N (act, wound) mordedura f, dentellada f; (morsel, small meal) bocado m, bocadito m; (of an insect) picadura f, roncha f

bitten [bɪtn] see bite

bitter [bídə] ADJ (taste) amargo; (cold) glacial; (enemy) acérrimo; (person) resentido; —**sweet** dulceamargo, agridulce; **to fight to the** — **end** luchar hasta morir; N —**s** cerveza amarga f

bitterness [bídə-nɪs] N (taste) amargor m; (feelings) amargura f; (anger) rencor m, resentimiento m

biweekly [baɪwíkli] ADV (every two weeks) quincenal; (twice a week) bisemanal

bizarre [bɪzár] ADJ (event) extraño; (appearance) estrafalario

blab [blæb] VI parlotear; VT descubrir el pastel

black [blæk] ADJ (color, ethnicity) negro; (night) oscuro; —**-and-blue** lleno de moretones, amoratado; N negro -a mf; — **bean** frijol negro m; —**berry** zarzamora f, mora f; —**bird** mirlo m; —**board** pizarrón m, pizarra f; — **death** peste negra f; — **eye** ojo amoratado/morado m; —**head** espinilla f; —**hole** agujero negro m; —**jack** (weapon) cachiporra f; (card game) black-jack m, veintiuno m; —**list** lista negra f; — **magic** magia negra f; — **mail** chantaje m; — **mark** mancha f; — **market** mercado negro m; —**out** apagón m; — **pepper** pimienta negra f; — **pudding** morcilla f; — **sheep** oveja negra f; —**smith** herrero m; —**smith's shop** herrería f, forja f; —**top** asfalto m; **to put down in** — **and white** poner por escrito; VI **to** — **out** (faint) desmayarse, perder el conocimiento; VT **to** —**mail** chantajear

blacken [blǽkən] VT ennegrecer, negrear; VI (sky) oscurecerse

blackness [blǽknɪs] N negrura f

bladder [blǽdə] N vejiga f

blade [bled] N (of a knife) hoja f; (of grass) brizna

f; (of an oar) pala *f*, paleta *f*; (of a propeller) aspa *f*

blame [blem] VT culpar, echar la culpa a, achacar la culpa a; **to be to —** tener la culpa; N (responsibility) culpa *f*; (reproof) reproche *m*

blameless [blémlɪs] ADJ intachable

blanch [blæntʃ] VI palidecer; VT (whiten) blanquear; (scald) escaldar

bland [blænd] ADJ insulso

blank [blæŋk] ADJ (not written on) en blanco; (not recorded on) virgen; (unadorned, expressionless) vacío; (confused) desconcertado; **— cartridge** cartucho de fogueo *m*; **— check** cheque en blanco *m*; **— verse** verso blanco *m*; N (place to be filled in on a form) espacio [en blanco] *m*; (gap) vacío *m*; VI **to — out** quedarse en blanco

blanket [blǽŋkɪt] N manta *f*, frazada *f*; *Am* cobija *f*; ADJ global; VT cubrir

blare [blɛr] VI hacer un ruido estruendoso; N estruendo *m*; (of a trumpet) toque *m*

blaspheme [blæsfím] VI/VT blasfemar [contra]

blasphemy [blǽsfəmi] N blasfemia *f*

blast [blæst] N (of wind) ráfaga *f*; (of criticism) lluvia *f*; (of a trumpet) trompetazo *m*; (explosive charge) carga *f*; (explosion) explosión *f*; **— furnace** alto horno *m*; **—off** despegue *m*; **we had a —** lo pasamos bomba; **at full —** a todo volumen; VI/VT (blow a horn) pitar, tocar; (shatter) volar; (criticize) criticar duramente; (blow hard) azotar; **to — off** despegar

blatant [blétnt] ADJ descarado

blaze [blez] N (flame) llamarada *f*; (fire) incendio *m*; (glow) resplandor *m*; (mark) señal *f*; **— of anger** arranque de ira *m*; VI (burn) arder; (shine) resplandecer; **to — a trail** marcar una senda

blazer [blézɚ] N blazer *m*, saco *m*

bleach [blitʃ] VI/VT (intentional) blanquear[se]; (accidental) desteñir[se]; N blanqueador *m*; *Sp* lejía *f*

bleachers [blítʃɚz] N gradas *f pl*

bleak [blik] ADJ (terrain) yermo, desolado; (winter) crudo; (wind) helado; (future) negro

bleary [blíri] ADJ nublado

bleat [blit] N balido *m*; VI balar

bled [blɛd] *see* bleed

bleed [blid] VI (lose blood) sangrar; (run, as in colors) correrse, desteñir[se]; **my heart —s for the poor** los pobres me dan lástima; VT (let blood) desangrar; (extort) extorsionar; (clean brakes) purgar

blemish [blémɪʃ] N mancha *f*, tacha *f*; VT manchar

blend [blɛnd] VI/VT (tea, paint) mezclar, entremezclar; (sea and sky) fundirse; (voices) armonizar; N mezcla *f*

blender [blɛ́ndɚ] N licuadora *f*

bless [blɛs] VT bendecir; INTERJ **— you!** ¡salud! ¡Jesús!

blessed[1] [blésɪd] ADJ (beatified) beato; (happy) bienaventurado, feliz; **— event** feliz acontecimiento *m*; **the whole — day** todo el santo día; **not a — drop of rain** ni una bendita gota de agua

blessed[2] [blɛst] ADJ **— with** dotado de

blessing [blésɪŋ] N bendición *f*; **to say the —** dar gracias

blew [blu] *see* blow

blight [blaɪt] N (plant disease) quemadura *f*, añublo *m*; (scourge) lacra *f*; VT (cause to wither) marchitar; (ruin) arruinar

blimp [blɪmp] N zepelín *m*

blind [blaɪnd] ADJ ciego; **— alley** callejón sin salida *m*; **— date** cita a ciegas *f*; **—fold** venda para los ojos *f*; **to —fold** vendar los ojos a; **— man's bluff** juego de la gallina ciega *m*; **— spot** ángulo muerto *m*; **to fly —** volar a ciegas; **to go —** quedarse ciego; N (shade) persiana *f*; (hunter's hiding place) escondite *m*; VT (make blind) cegar; (darken) oscurecer

blinder [bláɪndɚ] N anteojera *f*

blindly [bláɪndli] ADV a ciegas

blindness [bláɪndnɪs] N ceguera *f*

blink [blɪŋk] VI/VT (move eyelids) pestañear, parpadear; (go on and off, as of a light) parpadear; (ignore) pasar por alto; (flee a challenge) rajarse; N parpadeo *m*, pestañeo *m*; **on the —** averiado

blinker [blíŋkɚ] N intermitente *m*

blinking [blíŋkɪŋ] N parpadeo *m*

blip [blɪp] N (on radar) punto *m*; (moment) bache *m*

bliss [blɪs] N dicha *f*, felicidad absoluta *f*

blister [blístɚ] N ampolla *f*; (small) vejiga *f*; VT sacar ampollas; VI ampollarse

blitz [blɪts] N ataque relámpago *m*

blizzard [blízɚd] N ventisca *f*

bloat [blot] VI hinchar[se], abotagar[se]

bloated [blóDɪd] ADJ hinchado, inflado

blob [blɑb] N pedazo de algo sin forma *m*

block [blɑk] N (piece of stone, cement) bloque *m*; (piece of wood) trozo de madera *m*; (toy) cubo *m*; (in sports) bloqueo *m*; (in basketball) tapón *m*; (length from one street to the next) cuadra *f*; (square block) manzana *f*; (obstacle) obstáculo *m*; (group of tickets) sección *f*; **—buster** éxito de taquilla *m*; **—head** tarugo -ga *mf*, alcornoque *m*; VT (obstruct, also in sports) bloquear, tapar; (in basketball) taponar; (stop a pass) parar; **to — out** (an essay) esbozar, bosquejar; (the sun) ocultar

blockade [blɑkéd] N bloqueo *m*; VT bloquear

blockage [blákɪdʒ] N obstrucción *f*

blocking [blákɪŋ] N bloqueo *m*

blog [blɑg] N blog *m*; VI bloguear; **—ging** blogueo *m*

blogger [blágə] N bloguero -ra *mf*
blond [bland] ADJ & N rubio -a *mf*
blood [blʌd] N sangre *f*; **—bank** banco de sangre *m*; **—bath** carnicería *f*, baño de sangre *m*; **— count** recuento sanguíneo *m*; **— group** grupo sanguíneo *m*; **—hound** sabueso *m*; **— plasma** plasma sanguíneo *m*; **— poisoning** septicemia *f*; **— pressure** presión arterial *f*; **— relative** pariente consanguíneo *mf*; **—shed** derramamiento de sangre *m*; **—shot** inyectado de sangre; **—thirsty** sanguinario, sangriento; **— type** grupo sanguíneo *m*; **— vessel** vaso sanguíneo *m*; **in cold — a** sangre fría
bloody [blʌ́di] ADJ (violent) sangriento; (smeared) ensangrentado
bloom [blum] N (flower) flor *f*; (flowering) floración *f*; (youthfulness) lozanía *f*; (flush) rubor *m*; **in —** en flor; VI florecer
blooming [blúmɪŋ] ADJ (flowering) floreciente; (thriving) lozano
blooper [blúpə] N perla *f*
blossom [blásəm] N (flower) flor *f*; VI florecer
blot [blat] N (on paper) mancha *f*, borrón *m*; (on honor) tacha *f*; VI/VT manchar[se], emborronar[se]; **to — out** (obscure) borrar, tachar
blotch [blatʃ] VT borronear, manchar, cubrir con manchas; N mancha *f*, borrón *m*
blouse [blaʊs] N blusa *f*
blow [blo] VI (wind) soplar; (leaf) volar; (siren) sonar; (horse) resoplar; VT (play a horn) sonar; **to — a fuse** quemar un fusible; **to — away** (amaze) dejar atónito; (carry away on the wind) llevarse el viento; **to — down** tirar abajo; **to —-dry** secar con secador; **to — off** (ignore) ignorar; **to — one's nose** sonarse las narices / la nariz; **to — on the soup** soplar la sopa; **to — one's brains out** levantarse la tapa de los sesos; **to — out** reventar[se]; **to — over** (knock down) derribar; (dissipate) disiparse; **to — up** (a balloon) inflar, hinchar; (a bridge) volar; **this party —s** esta fiesta es pésima; N (stroke, shock) golpe *m*; (wind) tempestad *f*; (breath) soplo *m*; **—out** (tire failure) reventón *m*; (party) fiestón *m*; **—pipe** cerbatana *f*; **—torch** soplete *m*; **—up** (fight) pelea *f*, riña *f*; (photo) ampliación *f*; **to come to —s** irse a las manos
blower [blóə] N (artisan) soplador *m*; (machine) aventadora *f*
blown [blon] *see* blow
blue [blu] ADJ azul; (sad) triste, melancólico; (from cold) amoratado; N azul *m*; **—bell** campanilla *f*; **—berry** arándano *m*; **—bird** pájaro azul *m*; **—blood** sangre azul *f*; **— book** lista de precios de mercado *f*; **—chip** de primera línea; **—-collar** de clase obrera; **—jay** arrendajo *m*; **— jeans** vaqueros *m pl*;

—print (of a building) cianotipo *m*; (of a project) plan *m*, trazado *m*; **—-ribbon** distinguido; **— whale** ballena azul *f*; **light —** [azul] celeste *m*; **the —s** (sadness) melancolía *f*, murria *f*; (genre of music) blues *m pl*; VI ponerse azul, azulear; VT azular, teñir de azul; **to —print** trazar
bluff [blʌf] N (cliff) acantilado *m*, risco *m*; (false boast) bluff *m*; (in poker) farol *m*; VT hacer un bluff; **to call a —** poner en evidencia
bluffer [blʌ́fə] N bluff *m*
bluing [blúɪŋ] N añil *m*
bluish [blúɪʃ] ADJ azulado
blunder [blʌ́ndə] N disparate *m*, patochada *f*; VI meter la pata; **to — upon/into** tropezar con
blunt [blʌnt] ADJ (not sharp) romo; (rounded) contundente; (frank) directo, franco; VT despuntar
blur [blɜ] VT (to obscure) emborronar, desvanecer; (to make vision blurry) nublar; VI empañarse, nublarse; N [indistinct sight] mancha *f*; **it's a — in my mind** sólo tengo un recuerdo vago de eso
blurred [blɜd] ADJ borroso
blurry [blɜ́i] ADJ borroso
blurt [blɜt] VT **to — [out]** espetar
blush [blʌʃ] VI sonrojarse, ponerse colorado, ruborizarse; N (act of blushing) sonrojo *m*; (effect of blushing) rubor *m*; **at first — a** primera vista
bluster [blʌ́stə] VI (blow hard) soplar fuerte, rugir; (boast) fanfarronear; N (sound of wind) ventarrón *m*; (attitude) fanfarronería *f*
blustering [blʌ́stəɪŋ] ADJ fanfarrón, jactancioso; **— wind** ventarrón *m*
BM [**bowel movement**] [bíém] N defecación *f*
boa constrictor [bóəkənstríktə] N boa *f*
boar [bɔr] N jabalí *m*
board [bɔrd] N (wood) tabla *f*, listón *m*; (for a game) tablero *m*; (meals) pensión *f*; (for bulletins) cartelera *f*; **— of directors** junta directiva *f*; **—ing school** pensionado *m*, internado *m*; **—inghouse** pensión *f*; **— of trustees** patronato *m*; **—room** sala de directorio *f*; **on — a** bordo; **to go by the —** irse por la borda; VI (lodge) alojarse; **to — up** tapiar, cerrar con tablas; VT (boat, plane, train) abordar; (provide lodging) alojar
boarder [bɔ́rdə] N pensionista *mf*
boast [bost] N alarde *m*; VI jactarse, vanagloriarse, blasonar; VT **the town —s two new schools** el pueblo ostenta dos escuelas nuevas
boastful [bóstfəl] ADJ jactancioso, vanaglorioso
boastfulness [bóstfəlnɪs] N jactancia *f*, vanagloria *f*
boat [bot] N (any water vessel) embarcación *f*; (open and small) bote *m*, lancha *f*; (closed, larger) barco *m*; **—house** cobertizo para

botes m; —**man** barquero m, botero m

boating [bóɪɪŋ] N navegación f; **to go —** navegar

bob [bab] N (horsetail) cola cortada f; (of the head) sacudida f; (haircut) melena corta f; (of a pendulum) pesa f, plomada f; —**tail** rabón m; VI sacudirse; (a ship) cabecear; VT **to — one's hair** cortarse el pelo en melena

bobbin [bábɪn] N carrete m, bobina f

bobcat [bábkæt] N lince rojo m

bode [bod] VI **that doesn't — well** eso no augura nada bueno

bodice [báɪɪs] N corpiño m

bodily [bádʒli] ADJ corporal; —**harm** daño físico m

body [bádi] N (of a person, animal, wine, fabric) cuerpo m; (torso) tronco m; (corpse) cuerpo m, cadáver m; (of a text, army, etc.) parte principal f; (of water) masa f; (of a car) carrocería f; (of an airplane) fuselaje m; —**armor** armadura corporal f, armadura de cuerpo f; —**bag** bolsa para cadáveres f; —**building** culturismo m; —**count** número de muertos m; —**guard** guardaespaldas m sg; —**language** lenguaje corporal m; —**temperature** temperatura f; —**shop** taller de carrocería m; VT **to —search** cachear

bog [bag] N pantano m; VI hundir[se]; **to get —ged down** atascarse

bogey [bógi] N (golf) bogey m

bogeyman [búgimæn] N coco m; RP cuco m

bogus [bógəs] ADJ falso, fraudulento; —**company** compañía fantasma f

Bohemian [bohímiən] ADJ & N bohemio -a mf

boil [bɔɪl] VI/VT (water) hervir; (eggs) cocer; (ocean) bullir; (angry person) echar chispas; **to — down** to reducirse a; **to — over** derramarse; N (inflammation) forúnculo m, divieso m; (act of boiling) hervor m; —**ing point** punto de ebullición m; **to come to a —** soltar/romper el hervor

boiler [bɔ́ɪlə] N caldera f

boisterous [bɔ́ɪstə-əs] ADJ bullicioso

bold [bold] ADJ (not fearful) atrevido, osado; (unconventional) audaz; (visually striking) llamativo; —**faced** descarado; —**face type** negrita f, negrilla m

boldness [bódnɪs] N (courage) atrevimiento m, osadía f; (unconventional attitude) audacia f

Bolivia [balívia] N Bolivia f

Bolivian [balívian] ADJ & N boliviano -na mf

bolster [bólstə] N cojín cilíndrico m; VT reforzar; **to — someone's courage** alentar a alguien

bolt [bolt] N (door lock) pestillo m, cerrojo m; (crossbar) aldaba f; (pin) perno m, tornillo grande m; (of cloth) rollo m; **it came as a — from the blue** cayó como bomba; VT (fasten) atornillar; (lock door) cerrar con

tranca, atrancar; (devour) engullir; (break with) romper con; VI echarse a correr

bomb [bam] N bomba f; —**shell** bomba f; —**shelter** refugio antiaéreo m; VT (attack with bombs) bombardear; VI (fail) fracasar

bombard [bambárd] VT bombardear

bombardier [bambə-dír] N bombardero -ra mf

bombardment [bambárdmənt] N bombardeo m

bombastic [bambǽstɪk] ADJ grandilocuente, ampuloso

bomber [bámə] N bombardero m, avión de bombardeo m

bombing [bámɪŋ] N (from airplanes) bombardeo m; (terrorist) atentado m

bona fide [bónəfaɪd] ADJ genuino; —**offer** oferta seria f

bonbon [bánban] N caramelo m; (chocolate) bombón m

bond [band] N (tie) lazo m; (fetter) cadenas f pl; (financial instrument) bono m, obligación f; (adhesion) adherencia f; (chemical) enlace m; VI/VT (stick to) adherirse; (connect) establecer vínculos

bondage [bándɪdʒ] N servidumbre f, esclavitud f

bonded [bándɪd] ADJ afianzado

bonding [bándɪŋ] N (mother-child) lazos afectivos m pl; (male) compenetración f

bondsman [bándzmən] N fiador m

bone [bon] N hueso m; (of fish) espina f; —**china** porcelana fina f; —**graft** injerto óseo m; —**head** estúpido -da mf; —**marrow** médula ósea f; —**yard** cementerio m; —**of contention** manzana de la discordia f; **to make no —s about it** no andarse con rodeos; VT deshuesar; (fish) quitar las espinas; **to — up on something** estudiar algo

bonfire [bánfaɪr] N hoguera f, fogata f

bonnet [bánɪt] N gorro m

bonus [bónəs] N (extra salary) gratificación f, prima f; (at Christmas) aguinaldo m

bony [bóni] ADJ (with large bones) huesudo; (made of bones) óseo

boo [bu] VI/VT abuchear, rechiflar; INTERJ ¡bu! N rechifla f, abucheo m

boo-boo [búbu] N (minor injury) lastimadura f; Sp fam pupa f; Am nana f; **to make a —** meter la pata

booby [búbi] N (fool) bobo -a mf; (bird) bobo m; —**hatch** fam loquería f; —**prize** premio al peor competidor m; —**trap** trampa explosiva f

booger [búgə] N moco [seco] m

book [buk] N libro m; —**binding** encuadernación f; —**case** estante m, estantería f, biblioteca f; —**end** sujetalibros m sg; —**keeper** tenedor -ra de libros mf; Sp contable mf; —**keeping** teneduría de libros f, contabilidad f; —**mark** marcador de libros *m*; —**mobile** biblioteca móvil *f*; — **review** reseña *f*; —**seller** librero -ra *mf*; —**shelf** estante *m*; —**store** librería *f*; — **value** valor contable *m*; **by the** — siguiendo las reglas; **on the** —**s** registrado en los libros; **to keep** —**s** llevar los libros; VT (reserve) reservar; (hire) contratar; (record charges against) fichar

bookish [búkɪʃ] ADJ (person) estudioso; (allusion) libresco

booklet [búklɪt] N cartilla *f*

boom [bum] VI (resound) resonar; (prosper) prosperar; N (noise) explosión *f*; (increase) auge *m*

boon [bun] N (blessing) bendición *f*; (favor) favor *m*

boondocks [búndaks] ADV LOC **[out] in the** — *fam* en los quintos infiernos, en el quinto pino

boondoggle [búndagəl] N despilfarro *m*

boor [bur] N patán -ana *mf*

boorish [búrɪʃ] ADJ grosero, zafio

boost [bust] VT (to shove) empujar [desde abajo o detrás]; (to promote) estimular, impulsar; N (shove) empujón [desde abajo] *m*; (aid) estímulo *m*, impulso *m*; — **in prices** alza de precios *f*

booster [bústə] N (person) animador -ra *mf*; (rocket) acelerador *m*; (electronic device) amplificador *m*; (vaccination) refuerzo *m*

boot [but] N (shoe) bota *f*; (trunk of a car) cajuela *f*; (clamp for cars) cepo *m*; —**black** limpiabotas *m sg*; — **disk** disco de iniciación *m*; —**legger** contrabandista de licores *m*; —**able diskette** disquete de iniciación *f*; **to give the** — poner de patitas en la calle; **to** — por añadidura; VT dar una patada a; **to** — **[out]** echar a patadas; **to** — **up** (a computer) iniciar

booth [buθ] N (telephone) cabina *f*; (sales) puesto *m*; (ticket) taquilla *f*

booty [búdi] N (loot) botín *m*; (buttocks) trasero *m*

booze [buz] N *fam* bebercio *m*, bebida alcohólica *f*

borax [bóræks] N bórax *m*

border [bɔ́rdə] N (line between countries) frontera *f*; (edge, brink) borde *m*; (bed of flowers) ariete *m*; (design) ribete *m*; — **control** control fronterizo *m*; — **patrol officer** carabinero -ra *mf*; ADJ —**line** (on a border) fronterizo; (not up to standards) dudoso; VI/VT (make a design) ribetear; **to** — **on** colindar con; **it** —**s on madness** raya en la locura

bordering [bɔ́rdərɪŋ] ADJ limítrofe

bore [bɔr] N (hole) agujero *m*; (of a gun, cylinder) calibre *m*; (uninteresting person) aburrido -da *mf*, pesado -da *mf*; (uninteresting thing) lata *f*; VT (make a hole) taladrar, horadar; (fail to interest) aburrir

bore [bɔr] *see* bear

bored [bɔrd] ADJ aburrido; **I'm** — estoy aburrido

boredom [bɔ́rdəm] N aburrimiento *m*, tedio *m*

boric acid [bɔ́rɪk ǽsɪd] N ácido bórico *m*

boring [bɔ́rɪŋ] ADJ aburrido; **he's** — es aburrido

born [bɔrn] ADJ nacido; **he's a** — **dancer** es un bailarín nato; **she's a** — **liar** es una mentirosa de nacimiento; **to be** — nacer

borne [bɔrn] *see* bear

boron [bɔ́ran] N boro *m*

borrow [bɔ́ro] VT pedir prestado; **I** —**ed money from Fred** le pedí dinero prestado a Fred; **may I** — **your car?** ¿me prestas tu coche? **I** —**ed these books from the library** saqué estos libros de la biblioteca

borrower [bɔ́roə] N (of money) prestatario -ria *mf*; (of library books) usuario -ria *mf*

Bosnia and Herzegovina [bázniənhɜ́tsəgovínə] N Bosnia-Herzegovina *f*

Bosnian [báznian] ADJ & N bosnio -nia *mf*

bosom [búzəm] N pecho *m*, seno *m*; **in the** — **of the family** en el seno de la familia; — **buddy** amigo íntimo *m*

boss [bɔs] N jefe -fa *mf*; (on a plantation) mayoral *m*, capataz *m*; (political) dirigente *m*; (mafia) capo *m*; VT **to** — **around** mandonear

bossy [bɔ́si] ADJ mandón

botanical [bətǽnɪkəl] ADJ botánico

botany [bátni] N botánica *f*

botch [bátʃ] VT chapucear, estropear; N chapucería *f*, chapuza *f*

both [boθ] ADJ & PRON ambos, los dos

bother [báðə] VT molestar, fastidiar; VI molestarse, tomarse la molestia; N molestia *f*

bothersome [báðəsəm] ADJ (activity) molesto, enojoso; (person) enfadoso, molesto

botox [bótaks] N bótox *m*

Botswana [batswánə] N Botsuana *f*

bottle [bádl] N botella *f*; (for medicine, perfume) frasco *m*; —**neck** atascadero *m*, embotellamiento *m*; — **top** chapa de botella *f*; VT embotellar; **to** — **up** atascar, embotellar

bottom [bádəm] N (of a hole) fondo *m*; (of a pile, page, bed) pie *m*; (lower part) base *f*, parte de abajo *f*; (buttocks) trasero *m*; **to be at the** — **of the class** ser el último de la clase; **to hit** — tocar fondo; **who is at the** — **of all this?** ¿quién está detrás de todo esto? ADJ de abajo; — **line** (business) balance final *m*; (essential element) lo esencial; VI **to** — **out** tocar fondo

bottomless [bádəmlɪs] ADJ sin fondo; — **supply** recursos ilimitados *m pl*; — **accusation** acusación infundada *f*; **he's a** — **pit** es un barril sin fondo

botulism [bátʃəlɪzəm] N botulismo *m*

boudoir [búdwar] N tocador *m*

bough [bau] N rama *f*

bought [bɔt] *see* buy

bouillon [búljan] N caldo *m*

boulder [bóldə-] N peña f, pedrusco m

boulevard [búləvard] N bulevar m

bounce [bauns] N (of a ball) bote m, rebote m; (vitality) vitalidad f; VT echar, botar; **to — a check** rebotar un cheque; VI rebotar; **to — back** recuperarse

bouncer [baunsə-] N gorila m

bound [baund] N (jump) salto m; **—s** límite m, confín m; ADJ (tied up) atado; (confined) confinado; (obliged) obligado; (as a book) encuadernado; **to be — for** ir rumbo a; **to be — up in one's work** estar absorto en su trabajo; **it is — to happen** es seguro que pasará; **I am — to do it** estoy resuelto a hacerlo; VI (jump) saltar; (be contiguous) lindar

bound [baund] *see* bind

boundary [báundri] N (of a country, city) límite m, término m; (of a property) linde mf, lindero m

boundless [báundlɪs] ADJ ilimitado, sin límites

bountiful [báuntəfəl] ADJ abundante

bounty [báunti] N (abundance) abundancia f; (reward) recompensa f

bouquet [buké] N (of flowers, large) ramo m; (of flowers, small) ramillete m; (of wine) aroma m, bouquet m

bourgeois [burʒwá] ADJ & N burgués -sa mf

bourgeoisie [burʒwazí] N burguesía f

bout [baut] N [sports] encuentro m; **a — of flu** una gripe

boutique [butík] N boutique f

bovine [bóvaɪn] ADJ vacuno

bow[1] [bau] N (gesture) reverencia f; (prow) proa f; VI (bend at the waist) hacer una reverencia; (yield) someterse; **to — out** retirarse; VT inclinar

bow[2] [bo] N (for arrows, violin) arco m; (curve) curva f; (decoration) moño m; **—knot** lazada f; **—string** cuerda de arco f; ADJ **—legged** patizambo; VI/VT (bend) arquear[se]; (play a violin with a bow) tocar con arco

bowel [báuəl] N **—s** intestinos m pl; **—s of the earth** entrañas de la tierra f pl; **— movement** evacuación del vientre f

bower [báuə-] N enramada f

bowl [bol] N (container) bol m, tazón m; (dish) plato hondo m, (depression) cuenco m; (of a toilet) taza f; (of a pipe) cazoleta f; VT **to — over** apabullar, deslumbrar

bowling [bólɪŋ] N boliche m, bowling m; **let's go —** vamos al boliche; **— alley** boliche m, bolera f

box [baks] N (container) caja f; (for jewelry) estuche m; (in the theater) palco de teatro m; (for the jury) tribuna f; (on a page) cuadro m; (in soccer) área de penales f; **— car** vagón de carga m; **— office** taquilla f; **— seat** asiento de palco m; VT (put in a box) meter en una caja; (hit)

abofetear; (engage in sport) boxear

boxer [báksə-] N (fighter) boxeador -ra mf, pugilista mf; (breed of dog) bóxer m; **— shorts** calzoncillo[s] m

boxing [báksɪŋ] N boxeo m, pugilato m; **— glove** guante de boxeo m; **— ring** ring m, cuadrilátero m

boy [bɔɪ] N (baby) niño m; (young man) muchacho m, chico m; **— scout** boy scout m; **—friend** novio m

boycott [bɔ́ɪkat] VT boicotear; N boicoteo m, boicot m

boyhood [bɔ́ɪhʊd] N niñez f, juventud f

boyish [bɔ́ɪɪʃ] ADJ de muchacho

brace [bres] N (in construction) tirante m; (pair) par m; (printed character) corchete m; (of a carpenter) berbiquí m; **—s** (for teeth) aparato ortodóntico m; (for a leg) aparato ortopédico m; VT (against a shock) agarrarse; (support) asegurar

bracelet [bréslɪt] N brazalete m, pulsera f

bracket [brǽkɪt] N (support) soporte m, sostén m; (typographic sign) paréntesis recto m, corchete m; (division) banda f; VT (fix with brackets) fijar con soportes; (write in brackets) colocar entre paréntesis rectos; (associate) agrupar

brag [bræg] VI jactarse [de], hacer alarde [de]

braggart [brǽgə-t] ADJ & N fanfarrón -na mf

braid [bred] N trenza f; VT trenzar

brain [bren] N cerebro m; (food) seso m; **she blew out his —s** le levantó la tapa de los sesos; **he's short on —s** es corto de inteligencia; **he is the —s in this operation** él es el cerebro en esta operación; **to rack one's —s** devanarse los sesos, romperse la cabeza; **— death** muerte cerebral f; **— drain** fuga de cerebros f; **— scan** tomografía cerebral f; **— trust** grupo de expertos m; **— stem** tronco del encéfalo m; **—storming** lluvia de ideas f; **— tumor** tumor cerebral m; VT **to — someone** romperle la crisma a alguien; **to —wash** lavarle el cerebro a; ADJ **—dead** clínicamente muerto, en estado vegetativo

brainy [bréni] ADJ sesudo

brake [brek] N freno m; **— drum** tambor del freno m; **— fluid** líquido para frenos m; **—man** guardafrenos m sg; **— shoe** zapata f; **to apply the —s** frenar; VI/VT frenar

bramble [brǽmbəl] N zarza f

bran [bræn] N salvado m; (for birds) afrecho m

branch [bræntʃ] N (of a plant, of a family) rama f; (of a train track) ramal m; (of antlers) brazo m; (of a science) ramo m; (of a business) sucursal f; (of the armed forces) arma f; (in a computer program) bifurcación f; (of a river) tributario m; VI/VT ramificar[se]

brand [brænd] N (make, mark) marca f; (of

humor, etc.) tipo *m*; (mark of disgrace) estigma *m*; — **awareness** conciencia de marca *f*; — **loyalty** lealtad de marca *f*; — **name** marca *f*; ADJ —**-new** flamante, recién comprado; VT (burn) herrar, marcar; (stigmatize) estigmatizar; **to — as** tildar de, tachar de

brandish [brǽndɪʃ] VT blandir, esgrimir

brandy [brǽndi] N (fine) brandy *m*; (cheap) aguardiente *m*

brash [bræʃ] ADJ (impudent) descarado; (impetuous) impetuoso

brass [bræs] N (metal) latón *m*; (attitude) descaro *m*; (high-ranking officers) la plana mayor; — **instrument** instrumento de metal *m*; **to get down to — tacks** ir al grano; ADJ de latón

brassiere [brəzír] N sostén *m*

brat [bræt] N mocoso -sa *mf*

bravado [brəvádo] N alarde *m*

brave [brev] ADJ valiente, gallardo; N guerrero indio *m*; VT desafiar

bravery [brévari] N valentía *f*, gallardía *f*

brawl [brɔl] N reyerta *f*, riña *f*, pelotera *f*; VI reñir

bray [bre] N rebuzno *m*; VI rebuznar

brazen [brézən] ADJ (impudent) descarado; (made of brass) de latón

brazier [bréʒɚ] N brasero *m*

Brazil [brəzíl] N Brasil *m*

Brazilian [brəzíljən] ADJ & N brasileño -ña *mf*, brasilero -ra *mf*

breach [britʃ] N (opening) brecha *f*; (infraction) infracción *f*; (severance) ruptura *f*; — **of contract** incumplimiento de contrato *m*; — **of faith** abuso de confianza *m*; VT (make an opening) abrir una brecha en; (violate a law) violar, infringir

bread [brɛd] N pan *m*; —**basket** panera *f*; — **box** panera *f*; —**winner** sostén de la familia *m*; ADJ —**-and-butter** básico; VT empanar

breadth [brɛdθ] N anchura *f*, ancho *m*; (size) extensión *f*; (perspective) amplitud *f*

break [brek] VI (fracture) romperse; (pause) parar; VT (a record) batir; (a code) descifrar; (a law) violar; (news) dar, divulgar; (a bone) fracturar; (a horse) domar, desbravar; (a habit) quitar[se]; (a contract, promise) romper; (one's spirit) quebrar, doblegar; (one's heart) desgarrar; (cause to go bankrupt) arruinar; **to — a ten-dollar bill** conseguir cambio para un billete de diez dólares; **to — away** escaparse; **to — down** (a person) descomponerse; (a car) averiarse; (resistance) vencer; (continuity) interrumpir; **to — even** quedar a mano; **to — into** violentar; **to — loose** liberarse; **to — out** (war) estallar; (one's face) brotarse; (from prison) escaparse; **to — up** (into pieces) quebrarse; (a relationship) romper con; N (weather) cambio

m; (from work) descanso *m*; (with tradition) quiebre *m*, rompimiento *m*; (of a bone) fractura *f*; (from prison) fuga *f*; (opportunity) oportunidad *f*; —**-in** hurto con escalo *m*; —**down** (analysis) análisis *m*; (automotive) avería *f*; (nervous) colapso *m*; —**down of charges** desglose de cargos *m*; —**even point** umbral de rentabilidad *m*; — **point** (in tennis) bola de break *f*, bola de ruptura *f*; —**through** adelanto *m*; (military) penetración *f*; —**water** rompeolas *m sg*; **lucky** — golpe de suerte *m*

breakable [brékəbəl] ADJ quebradizo, rompible

breaker [brékɚ] N rompiente *f*

breakfast [brékfəst] N desayuno *m*; VI desayunar

breast [brɛst] N (of a woman) seno *m*, pecho *m*; (of a bird) pechuga *f*; —**bone** esternón *m*; — **cancer** cáncer de mama *m*; —**-feeding** lactancia materna *f*; —**stroke** (estilo de natación) pecho *m*; VI/VT **to —-feed** amamantar, dar de mamar

breath [brɛθ] N aliento *m*; *lit* hálito *m*; (current of air) soplo *m*; **in the same —** al mismo tiempo; **out of —** sin aliento; **to catch one's —** recobrar el aliento; **to hold one's —** aguantar la respiración; **to take a —** inhalar; **to take a deep —** respirar hondo; **under one's —** entre dientes, por lo bajo; ADJ —**taking** impresionante

breathe [brið] VI/VT respirar; **to — in** inspirar, aspirar; **to — into** infundir; **to — out** exhalar, espirar; **he did not — a word** no dijo palabra

breathing [bríðɪŋ] N respiración *f*

breathless [bréθlɪs] ADJ sin aliento

breathlessness [bréθlɪsnɪs] N falta de aire *f*

bred [brɛd] *see* breed

breed [brid] VT (mate) criar; (bring up) educar; (give rise to) engendrar; VI reproducirse, multiplicarse; N (species) raza *f*; (type) clase *f*

breeder [brídɚ] N (person who breeds) criador -ora *mf*; (animal used for breeding) [animal] reproductor *m*

breeding [brídɪŋ] N (of animals) cría *f*; (of people) educación *f*, modales *m pl*

breeze [briz] N brisa *f*

breezy [brízi] ADJ (windy) ventoso; (jaunty) ameno

brevity [brévɪdi] N brevedad *f*

brew [bru] VT (coffee) hacer; (mischief) fomentar, tramar; (beer) fabricar; VI (storm) armarse una tormenta; **let the tea —** deja reposar el té; N (mixture) mezcla *f*; (beer) cerveza *f*

brewery [brúari] N cervecera *f*, fábrica de cerveza *f*

briar [brátɚ] N zarza *f*

bribe [braɪb] N soborno *m*, cohecho *m*; *Mex* mordida *f*; VT sobornar

bribery [bráɪbəri] N soborno *m*

brick [brɪk] N ladrillo *m*; —**bat** (piece of brick) pedazo de ladrillo *m*; (insult) insulto *m*; —**layer** albañil *m*; —**laying** albañilería *f*; VT (adorn with bricks) revestir de ladrillo; (pave with bricks) enladrillar

bridal [bráɪdl̩] ADJ nupcial; — **dress** vestido de novia *m*

bride [braɪd] N novia *f*; —**groom** novio *m*; —**smaid** dama de honor *f*

bridge [brɪdʒ] N puente *m*; (of the nose) caballete *m*; (card game) bridge *m*; VT (a river) tender un puente sobre; (a gap) llenar, salvar

bridle [bráɪdl̩] N (harness) brida *f*; (restraint) freno *m*; VT (put on a bridle) poner una brida; (restrain) frenar; VI (be insulted) ofenderse

brief [brif] ADJ (short) breve, escueto; (concise) conciso, escueto; (curt) seco; N sumario *m*, resumen *m*; (report) expediente *m*; —**case** portafolio[s] *m sg*, maletín *m*; —**s** calzoncillos *m pl*; **in** — en suma; VT informar

briefing [brífɪŋ] N reunión para dar instrucciones *f*

brigade [brɪgéd] N brigada *f*

bright [braɪt] ADJ (shining) brillante; (full of light) iluminado; (smart) inteligente; (promising) venturoso, prometedor; (radiant) radiante; (colorful) subido

brighten [bráɪtn̩] VT (a room) iluminar; VI **to** — **up** (person) animar[se]; (sky) despejarse

brightness [bráɪtnɪs] N (light) claridad *f*; (cheerfulness) viveza *f*; (intelligence) inteligencia *f*

brilliance [bríljəns] N (of hair, of a historical period) brillantez *f*; (of intellect) genio *m*

brilliant [bríljənt] ADJ (shining) brillante; (intelligent) genial; (splendid) espléndido; N brillante *m*, diamante *m*

brim [brɪm] N borde *m*; (of a hat) ala *f*; **to fill to the** — llenar hasta el borde; **to be filled to the** — estar de bote en bote; VI **to** — **over** rebosar; **to be** —**ming with** estar rebosante de

brine [braɪn] N salmuera *f*

bring [brɪŋ] VT traer; (cause) ocasionar, causar; **to** — **about** producir, ocasionar; **to** — **down** (kill) bajar; (depress) deprimir; **to** — **forth** (give birth) dar a luz; (produce) producir; **to** — **to a stop** parar; **to** — **a session to a close** clausurar una sesión; **to** — **together** reunir, juntar; **to** — **oneself to do something** poder hacer algo; **to** — **a good price** redituar una buena ganancia; **to** — **up** (raise children) criar, educar; (mention) mencionar

brink [brɪŋk] N borde *m*; **on the** — **of** al borde de

brisk [brɪsk] ADJ (walk) rápido; (weather) fresco; (trading) activo

bristle [brɪsl̩] N cerda *f*; VI erizar[se]; **to** — **with** estar erizado de

bristly [brísli] ADJ (with bristles) erizado, cerdoso; (irascible) irascible

Britain [brítn̩] N Gran Bretaña *f*

British [brídɪʃ] ADJ británico

brittle [brídl̩] ADJ quebradizo, frágil

brittleness [brídl̩nɪs] N fragilidad *f*

broach [brotʃ] VT sacar a colación

broad [brɔd] ADJ (wide) ancho; (vast) vasto; (ample) amplio; —**band** banda ancha *f*; —**cast** emisión *f*; (on TV) transmisión por televisión *f*; —**cast station** emisora *f*; — **hint** insinuación clara *f*; — **jump** salto de longitud *m*; —**minded** tolerante; —**side** andanada *f*; — **spectrum antibiotic** antibiótico de amplio espectro *m*; **in** — **daylight** en pleno día; N *pej* tipa *f*; VT **to** —**cast** (communicate electronically) transmitir, emitir, radiar

broadcasting [brɔ́dkæstɪŋ] N (radio) radiodifusión *f*; (TV) transmisión por televisión *f*

brocade [brokéd] N brocado *m*

broccoli [brákəli] N brócoli *m*, brécol *m*

brochure [broʃúr] N folleto *m*

broil [brɔɪl] VI/VT asar[se] [a la parrilla]

broiler [brɔ́ɪlɚ] N (oven) parrilla *f*; (chicken) pollo [para asar] *m*

broke [brok] ADJ **to be** — estar limpio, estar pelado; **to go** — irse a la quiebra

broke [brok] *see* break

broken [brókən] ADJ (fragmented) roto, quebrado; (tamed) domado; (not functioning) descompuesto; (not continuous) interrumpido; —**down** averiado, descompuesto; — **English** inglés chapurrado/chapurreado *m*; —**hearted** deshecho, con el corazón destrozado

broken [brókən] *see* break

broker [brókɚ] N (intermediary) agente *mf*; (stock salesperson) corredor -ora de bolsa *mf*

brokerage [brókɚɪdʒ] N correduría *f*

bromide [brómaɪd] N bromuro *m*

bromine [brómin] N bromo *m*

bronchial [bráŋkiəl] ADJ bronquial; — **tube** bronquio *m*

bronchitis [brɑŋkáɪdɪs] N bronquitis *f*

bronco [bráŋko] N caballo no domado *m*

bronze [brɑnz] N bronce *m*; VT broncear

brooch [brutʃ] N broche *m*, prendedor *m*

brood [brud] N pollada *f*, nidada *f*; VI/VT empollar; **to** — **over** rumiar

brook [bruk] N riachuelo *m*, cañada *f*; VT tolerar

broom [brum] N (tool) escoba *f*; (plant) retama *f*; —**stick** palo de escoba *m*

broth [brɔθ] N caldo *m*

brothel [brɑ́θəl] N burdel *m*

brother [brʌ́ðɚ] N hermano *m*; —**in-law**

cuñado *m*; **oh —**! ¡caray!

brotherhood [brʌ́ðə·hud] N hermandad *f*

brotherly [brʌ́ðə·li] ADJ fraternal

brought [brɔt] *see* bring

brow [braʊ] N (eyebrow) ceja *f*; (ridge of eye) arco superciliar *m*; (forehead) frente *f*

brown [braʊn] ADJ (skin) moreno; (eyes, shoes, clothes) café, marrón; (hair) castaño; (dun) pardo; (tanned) bronceado; **— bear** oso pardo *m*; **— rice** arroz integral *m*; **— sugar** azúcar moreno -na *mf*; VI/VT (food) dorar[se]; N (color) café *m*, castaño *m*, moreno *m*, pardo *m*

brownie [braʊni] N bizcocho de chocolate *m*; **— points** méritos *m pl*

browse [braʊz] VT (a book) hojear; VI (grass) pacer, pastar; (Internet) navegar

browser [braʊzə·] N navegador *m*

browsing [braʊzɪŋ] N navegación *f*

bruise [bruz] N (on skin) moretón *m*, cardenal *m*, contusión *f*; (on fruit) magulladura *f*, cardenal *m*; VI/VT magullar[se], machucar[se]

brunch [brʌntʃ] N brunch *m*, desayuno tardío *m*

Brunei [brunái] N Brunéi *m*

Bruneian [brunáiən] ADJ & N bruneano -na *mf*

brunette, brunet [brunét] ADJ & N moreno -na *mf*, morocho -cha *mf*; *Cuba* trigueño -ña *mf*

brunt [brʌnt] N impacto *m*

brush [brʌʃ] N (for teeth, clothes) cepillo *m*; (for paint, shaving) brocha *f*; (artist's) pincel *m*; (vegetation) maleza *f*; (contact) roce *m*; **—off** despedida brusca *f*; **—wood** (dead) broza *f*; (live) maleza *f*; VT (clean with a brush) cepillar; (touch lightly) rozar; **to — aside** echar a un lado; **to — up on** repasar; **to — off** (clean) quitar con cepillo; (reject) despedir bruscamente a alguien

brusque [brʌsk] ADJ brusco

Brussels sprouts [brʌ́səlspraʊts] N coles de Bruselas *f pl*, repollitos de Bruselas *m pl*

brutal [brúdl] ADJ brutal

brutality [brutǽlɪDi] N brutalidad *f*

brute [brut] N (animal) bestia *f*; (person) bruto -ta *mf*; ADJ bruto

bubble [bʌ́bəl] N burbuja *f*; (in soap) pompa *f*; (in boiling water) borbollón *m*; (illusion) encanto *m*; **— bath** baño de burbujas *m*; **—gum** chicle de globo *m*; **—-jet printer** impresora de burbuja *f*; VI (make bubbles) borbotar, borbollar; (boil) bullir, hervir; **to — over with joy** rebosar de alegría

bubonic plague [bubánɪkplég] N plaga bubónica *f*

buck [bʌk] N (deer) gamo *m*; (male of other animals) macho *m*; (leap of horse) respingo *m*; **— private** soldado raso *m*; **—shot** posta *f*, perdigón *m*; **—skin** gamuza *f*; **—wheat** trigo sarraceno *m*; **to pass the —** echarle el muerto a uno; ADJ **—toothed** de dientes

salidos; VI (horse) respingar, corcovear; **to — a trend** oponerse; **to — up** cobrar ánimo

bucket [bʌ́kɪt] N cubo *m*, balde *m*; (of a loader) cuchara *f*; **— seat** asiento delantero individual *m*

buckle [bʌ́kəl] N (clasp) hebilla *f*; (kink in a board) torcedura *f*; VT (to clasp) abrocharse; (to bend) torcerse, pandearse; **to — down** esforzarse; **to — up** abrocharse

bud [bʌd] N botón *m*, retoño *m*; VI (make buds) echar retoños

Buddhism [búdɪzəm] N budismo *m*

Buddhist [búdɪst] ADJ & N budista *mf*

buddy [bʌ́di] N camarada *mf*

budge [bʌdʒ] VI moverse

budget [bʌ́dʒɪt] N presupuesto *m*; VT (money) presupuestar; (time, personal resources) administrar; **— cycle** ciclo presupuestario *m*; **— deficit** déficit presupuestario *m*

budgetary [bʌ́dʒɪteri] ADJ presupuestario

budgeting [bʌ́dʒɪdɪŋ] N presupuestación *f*

buff [bʌf] N (leather) gamuza *f*; (tan color) color beige *m*; (wheel for polishing) pulidor *m*; (devotee) aficionado *m*; **in the —** en cueros; ADJ (beige) de color beige; (muscular) musculoso; VT pulir

buffalo [bʌ́fəlo] N bisonte *m*, búfalo *m*; **— wings** alitas *f pl*

buffer [bʌ́fə·] N (in a computer) memoria intermedia *f*; (shock absorber) amortiguador *m*; (polishing device) pulidor -ra *mf*; **— zone** zona tampón *f*

buffet[1] [bʌ́fɪt] N (blow) golpe *m*, puñetazo *m*; (shock) azote *m*; VT (hit) golpear; (hit repeatedly) azotar

buffet[2] [bəfé] N (cabinet) aparador *m*; (meal) buffet *m*

buffoon [bəfún] N payaso -a *mf*, bufón -ona *mf*

bug [bʌg] N bicho *m*; (disease-causing) microbio *m*, virus *m*; (for eavesdropping) micrófono oculto *m*; (in a computer program) fallo *m*, bicho *m*; VT (bother) molestar; (install microphones) colocar micrófonos ocultos; **his eyes — ged out** se le saltaron los ojos

buggy [bʌ́gi] N (cart) calesa *f*; (baby carriage) cochecillo *m*

bugle [bjúgəl] N clarín *m*; VI tocar el clarín

build [bɪld] VT (construct) construir, edificar; (manufacture) fabricar; **to — into** incorporar; **to — up** (make stronger) fortalecer; (accumulate) acumular; (enhance) desarrollar; (urbanize) urbanizar; N **—-up** (of military forces) concentración *f*; (of substance) acumulación *f*; (of anticipation) aumento *m*; N (of human body) complexión *f*

builder [bɪ́ldə·] N contratista *mf*, constructor -ora *m*

building [bɪ́ldɪŋ] N (thing built) edificio *m*; (act of building) construcción *f*, edificación *f*;

(unit in a housing complex) bloque *m*; —
block (solid mass) bloque [de construcción]
m; (toy) cubo *m*; (essential element) elemento
fundamental *m*

built [bɪlt] ADJ —-**in** (furniture appliance)
empotrado; (feature) incorporado; —-**in
part** parte integrante *f*; —-**to-order** hecho a
pedido; —-**up** urbanizado

built [bɪlt] *see* build

bulb [bʌlb] N (plant) bulbo *m*; (light) bombilla *f*;
Am foco *m*

bulbous [bʌ́lbəs] ADJ bulboso

Bulgaria [bʌlɡériə] N Bulgaria *f*

Bulgarian [bʌlɡériən] ADJ & N búlgaro -ra *mf*

bulge [bʌldʒ] N bulto *m*, protuberancia *f*; VI
abultar, hincharse

bulgy [bʌ́ldʒi] ADJ abultado

bulimia [bjulímiə] N bulimia *f*

bulk [bʌlk] N (mass) cantidad *f*, volumen *m*;
(greater part) mayor parte *f*; —**storage**
almacenamiento masivo *m*; **in** — a granel; VI
to — **up** echar músculos

bulky [bʌ́lki] ADJ voluminoso

bull [bʊl] N toro *m*; —**dog** buldog *m*; —**dozer**
bulldozer *m*; —**fight** corrida de toros *f*;
—**fighter** torero *m*; —**fighting**
tauromaquia *f*; —**frog** rana grande *f*; —
market mercado alcista *m*; —**pen** (baseball)
zona de calentamiento *f*; —'**s eye** diana *f*; **to
hit the** —'**s-eye** dar en el blanco; ADJ
—**headed** terco, obstinado

bullet [bʊ́lɪt] N bala *f*; ADJ —**proof** antibalas *inv*,
antibalístico

bulletin [bʊ́lɪtn] N boletín *m*; —**board** tablero
m, cartelera *f*

bullion [bʊ́ljən] N oro en lingotes *m*

bully [bʊ́li] N matón -ona *mf*, bravucón -ona *mf*;
VT intimidar

bulwark [bʊ́lwək] N baluarte *m*

bum [bʌm] N (lazy person) holgazán -ana *mf*;
(hobo) vagabundo -da *mf*; (sports fan)
fanático -ca *mf*; ADJ falso; VI **to** — **around**
holgazanear; VT **to** — **something from
someone** gorronearle algo a alguien

bumblebee [bʌ́mbəlbi] N abejorro *m*, abejón *m*

bump [bʌmp] VT chocar; **to** — **along** ir dando
tumbos; **to** — **off** despachar; **to** — **into**
toparse con; N (blow) choque *m*, trastazo *m*;
(lump) protuberancia *f*; (lump on a person)
chichón *m*

bumper [bʌ́mpə-] N parachoques *m sg*, tope *m*;
— **car** coche de choque *m*, autito chocador *m*;
— **crop** cosecha abundante *f*; —-**to-
traffic** caravana de autos *f*; —**sticker**
autoadhesivo *m*

bumpy [bʌ́mpi] ADJ bacheado, lleno de baches

bun [bʌn] N (bread) bollo *m*; (in hair) moño *m*

bunch [bʌntʃ] N (of things) manojo *m*; (of
people) montón *m*, grupo *m*; (of grapes,

bananas) racimo *m*; (of flowers) ramillete *m*;
VI/VT juntar[se], agrupar[se]

bundle [bʌ́ndl] N (of things) paquete *m*, fardo *m*,
envoltorio *m*; (of clothes) lío *m*, atado *m*; (of
belongings) hato *m*, petate *m*; (of firewood)
haz *m*; VT (tie together) liar, atar; **to** — **up**
abrigarse; **to** — **off** despachar

bungalow [bʌ́ŋɡəlo] N bungaló *m*

bungee jumping [bʌ́ndʒidʒʌ́mpɪŋ] N bungee *m*,
puénting *m*

bungle [bʌ́ŋɡəl] VT estropear; VI chapucear

bunion [bʌ́njən] N juanete *m*

bunk [bʌŋk] N (place to sleep) litera *f*; (nonsense)
tonterías *f pl*; — **bed** litera *f*; VI dormir en una
litera

bunker [bʌ́ŋkə-] N búnker *m*

bunny [bʌ́ni] N conejito *m*

bunt [bʌnt] N (baseball) toque de pelota *m*; VI
tocar la pelota

buoy [búi] N boya *f*; VI boyar; **to** — **up** mantener
a flote, animar

buoyant [bɔ́iənt] ADJ (floating) boyante,
flotante; (optimistic) optimista

burden [bɝ́dn] N (load) carga *f*; (responsibility)
peso *m*; — **of proof** peso de la prueba *m*; VT
(heavily) recargar; (oppressively) agobiar

burdensome [bɝ́dnsəm] ADJ agobiante, gravoso

bureau [bjúro] N (government department)
oficina *f*, agencia *f*; (chest of drawers)
cómoda *f*

bureaucracy [bjurákrəsi] N burocracia *f*

bureaucrat [bjúrəkræt] N burócrata *mf*

burglar [bɝ́ɡlə-] N ladrón -ona *mf*; — **alarm**
alarma antirrobo *f*; — **proof** a prueba de
robos

burglary [bɝ́ɡləri] N robo con allanamiento *m*

burial [bériəl] N entierro *m*, enterramiento *m*;
— **ground** enterramiento *m*; — **place** lugar de
sepultura *m*

Burkina Faso [bəkínəfáso] N Burkina Faso *m*

burlap [bɝ́læp] N arpillera *f*

burlesque [bəlésk] ADJ burlesco; N espectáculo
de variedades *m*

burly [bɝ́li] ADJ corpulento

Burma [bɝ́mə] N Birmania *f*

Burmese [bɝmíz] ADJ & N birmano -na *mf*

burn [bɝn] VI/VT quemar[se], abrasar[se]; (a
house) incendiar[se]; (a CD) quemar[se]; (food)
quemar[se], requemar[se]; **he got** —**ed in
the transaction** lo estafaron en el negocio;
the bulb is still —**ing** la bombilla sigue
prendida; **the iodine** —**ed his skin** el yodo
le quemó la piel; VI (with heat, passion) arder,
abrasar; **my skin** —**s** me arde la piel; **he's**
—**ing with desire** arde en deseos; **to** —
down incendiarse; **to** — **off** (fog) disiparse;
to — **out** (bulb) fundirse; (worker) agotarse;
to — **up** quemarse completamente; N
quemadura *f*; —**out** surmenage *m*

burner [bɜ́nə-] N (person or thing that burns something) quemador -ra *mf*; (on stove) hornilla *f*; **Bunsen** — mechero Bunsen *m*

burning [bɜ́nɪŋ] ADJ (desire) ardiente, abrasador; (question) urgente; N (caused by acid) ardor *m*; (caused by fire) quemadura *f*

burnish [bɜ́nɪʃ] VT bruñir

burnt [bɜ́rnt] *see* burn

burp [bɜ·p] N eructo *m*; VI eructar, repetir

burr, bur [bɜ·] N abrojo *m*

burrow [bɜ́·o] N madriguera *f*; VI (dig) hacer madrigueras; (live) vivir en una madriguera

bursitis [bə·sáɪDɪs] N bursitis *f*

burst [bɜ·st] VI reventar[se]; **to — into a room** irrumpir en un cuarto; **to — into tears** romper en llanto; **to — out** salir disparado; **to — with laughter** estallar/reventar de risa; N (of activity) explosión *f*; (of laughter) carcajada *f*; (of machine-gun fire) ráfaga *f*; (of speed) aceleración *f*

Burundi [burúndi] N Burundi *m*

Burundian [burúndiən] ADJ & N burundés -esa *mf*

bury [béri] VT (body, treasure) enterrar; (body) sepultar; **to be buried in thought** estar absorto/meditabundo

bus [bʌs] N autobús *m*, ómnibus *m*; *Mex* camión *m*; *RP* colectivo *m*; *Chile* micro *m*; *Cuba* guagua *f*; (in a computer) bus *m*; VT transportar en autobús

bush [buʃ] N (plant) arbusto *m*, mata *f*; (region) matorral *m*; **to beat around the —** andarse por las ramas

bushed [buʃt] ADJ fatigado

bushel [búʃəl] N fanega *f*

bushing [búʃɪŋ] N buje *m*, cojinete *m*

bushy [búʃi] ADJ (whiskers) espeso; (plants) poblado de arbustos

business [bíznɪs] N (trade, store) negocio *m*; (occupation) ocupación *f*; (commercial activity) comercio *m*; **— acumen** buen sentido para los negocios *m*; **— agreement** convenio comercial *m*; **— card** tarjeta comercial *f*; **— day** día hábil *m*; **— group** grupo empresarial *m*; **— hours** horas hábiles *f pl*, horario de atención al público *m*; **— is booming** el negocio florece; **—like** (efficient) eficiente; (cold) impersonal; **—man** hombre de negocios *m*, negociante *m*; **— suit** traje *m*; **— transaction** negocio *m*, transacción comercial *f*; **—woman** mujer de negocios *f*, negociante *f*; **I'm tired of the whole —** este asunto me tiene harto; **I mean — hablo** en serio; **to do — with** comerciar con; **he has no — doing it** no tiene derecho a hacerlo; **it's none of your —** no es asunto tuyo; **mind your own —** no te metas en lo que no te importa

bust [bʌst] N (statue, body part) busto *m*; VI/VT (burst, hit, break) reventar; (force into bankruptcy) hacer quebrar; (lower in rank) degradar

bustle [bʌ́səl] N (noise) bullicio *m*; (movement) ajetreo *m*, tráfago *m*; VI (move busily) ajetrear[se]; (be crowded) bullir

busy [bízi] ADJ ocupado, atareado; (overdecorated) recargado; **—body** entrometido -da *mf*; **— signal** señal de ocupado *f*; VI **to — oneself** ocuparse

but [bʌt] CONJ (on the contrary) pero; (excepting) sino; PREP menos; **any day — today** cualquier día menos hoy; **he's nothing — trouble** sólo da problemas; ADV **— for you** si no fuera por ti

butane [bjútén] N butano *m*

butch [butʃ] ADJ machote

butcher [bútʃə-] N carnicero -ra *mf*; **—'s shop** carnicería *f*; VT (cattle) matar; (people) masacrar; (performance) estropear

butchery [bútʃəri] N carnicería *f*

butler [bʌ́tlə-] N mayordomo *m*

butt [bʌt] N; (of a rifle) culata *f*; (of a cigarette) colilla *f*; (blow with head) topetazo *m*, cabezada *f*, cabezazo *m*; **the — of ridicule** el blanco de las burlas; VT embestir, topar; **to — in** entrometerse; **to — into a conversation** meter baza; *Am* meter la cuchara

butter [bʌ́Də] N mantequilla *f*; **—cup** botón de oro *m*; **— dish** mantequera *f*; **—fingers** manos de mantequilla *mf sg*; **—milk** suero de leche *m*; **—scotch** dulce de azúcar y mantequilla *m*; VT (bread) untar con mantequilla; (a cakepan) enmantecar

butterfly [bʌ́Də-flaɪ] N mariposa *f*; **— stroke** estilo mariposa *m*

buttery [bʌ́Də·i] ADJ mantecoso

buttocks [bʌ́Dəks] N nalgas *f pl*, asentaderas *f pl*, cachas *f pl*

button [bʌ́tn] N botón *m*; **—hole** ojal *m*; VI/VT abotonar[se]; VI **to —hole** hacer ojales; VT **to —hole someone** detener a alguien

buttress [bʌ́trɪs] N apoyo *m*, sostén *m*; (of a building) contrafuerte *m*; VT apoyar, reforzar

buy [baɪ] VT comprar; **to — on credit** comprar a crédito; **to — in installments** comprar a plazos; **to — off** sobornar; **to — out** comprar la parte de; **to — up** acaparar; **I don't — that** no me lo trago; N (purchase) compra *f*; (bargain) ganga *f*

buyer [báɪə·] N comprador -ra *mf*

buying [báɪɪŋ] N **— frenzy** frenesí de compras *m*; **— habits** hábitos de compras *m pl*

buzz [bʌz] N zumbido *m*; (feeling of intoxication) borrachera *f*; (phone call) telefonazo *m*; **—word** palabra de moda *f*; **— saw** sierra circular *f*; VI (insect, ears) zumbar; (group) murmurar; VT hacer zumbar; **to — the bell** tocar el timbre; **to give someone a —**

pegarle/echarle un telefonazo a alguien; **to —
off** largarse
buzzard [bázɚd] N buitre m
buzzer [bázɚ] N timbre m, chicharra f
by [baɪ] PREP por; **— and —** a la larga; **— chance**
por casualidad; **— dint of** a fuerza de; **— far**
con mucho; **— night** de noche; **— the way** a
propósito; **— the liter** por litro; **— this
time tomorrow** mañana a esta hora; **— two
o'clock** para las dos; **we drove — the
church** pasamos por la iglesia; **a 4 — 3
room** un cuarto de 4 por 3; **multiply 2 — 2**
multiplica 2 por 2; **we live — the church**
vivimos al lado de la iglesia; **she had a son
— him** tuvo un hijo con él; **piece — piece**
pedazo a/por pedazo; ADV **the factory is
close —** la fábrica está cerca; **the bus drove
—** pasó el autobús
bye-bye [bátbát] INTERJ ¡adiós! ¡chaucito!
bygones [báɪgɔnz] N **let — be —** lo pasado
pisado
bylaw [bátlɔ] N estatuto m
by-line [báɪlaɪn] N pie de autor m
bypass [báɪpæs] VT evitar; N desvío m; **—
operation** bypass m
by-product [báɪprɑdɔkt] N subproducto m;
(chemical) derivado m
bystander [báɪstændɚ] N persona presente f
byte [baɪt] N byte m, octeto m

Cc

cab [kæb] N (of a truck) cabina f; (taxi) taxi m; **—
driver** taxista mf
cabaret [kæbɚé] N cabaret m
cabbage [kæbɪʤ] N col f, repollo m, berza f
cabin [kæbɪn] N (hut) cabaña f; (in an airplane)
cabina f; (in a ship) camarote m
cabinet [kæbnɪt] N (for dishes) armario m; (for
medicines) botiquín m; (for display) vitrina f;
(of ministers) gabinete m; **—level
appointment** nombramiento ministerial m;
—maker ebanista m
cable [kébɔl] N cable m; (on ships) amarra f;
(telegram) telegrama m; **— car** funicular m,
teleférico m; **— television** televisión por
cable f, cablevisión f; VI/VT telegrafiar
caboose [kɔbús] N furgón de cola m
cache [kæʃ] N (of weapons) alijo m; (in a
computer) caché m; **— memory** memoria de
caché f
cachet [kæʃé] N caché m
cackle [kǽkɔl] VI (hen) cacarear; (people)
parlotear; N (hen) cacareo m; (people)
parloteo m

cacophony [kɔkáfɔni] N cacofonía f
cactus [kǽktɔs] N cacto m, cactus m
cad [kæd] N pej canalla mf
cadaver [kɔdǽvɚ] N cadáver m
caddie [kǽɒi] N caddy m, caddie m
cadence [kédn̩s] N cadencia f
cadet [kɔdét] N cadete mf
cadmium [kǽdmiɔm] N cadmio m
café [kæfé] N (coffee only) café m; (coffee and
food) cafetería f
cafeteria [kæfɪtíriɔ] N cafetería f
caffeine [kǽfin] N cafeína f
cage [keʤ] N jaula f; VT enjaular
cahoots [kɔhúts] ADV LOC **in —** arreglados
cajole [kɔʤól] VI/VT engatusar, persuadir con
halagos
cake [kek] N pastel m, torta f; (sponge) bizcocho
m; (soap) pastilla f; **a piece of —** pan comido;
to take the — ser el colmo; VI/VT
apelmazar[se]
calamine [kǽlɔmaɪn] N calamina f
calamity [kɔlǽmɪɒi] N calamidad f
calcium [kǽlsiɔm] N calcio m
calculate [kǽlkjɔlet] VI/VT calcular; **his
actions were — d to fool us** con sus
acciones trataba de engañarnos
calculating [kǽlkjɔleɒɪŋ] ADJ calculador
calculation [kælkjɔléʃɔn] N cálculo m
calculator [kǽlkjɔleɒɚ] calculadora f
calculus [kǽlkjɔlɔs] N cálculo m
calendar [kǽlɪndɚ] N calendario m; **— year** año
civil m
calf [kæf] N (of leg) pantorrilla f, canilla f;
(animal) ternero -ra mf, becerro -rra mf; **—
skin** piel de becerro f
caliber [kǽlɔbɚ] N calibre m
calibrate [kǽlɔbret] VT calibrar, graduar
calico [kǽlɪko] N calicó m
caliper [kǽlɔpɚ] N (on brakes) calibrador m; (for
measuring) calibre m
call [kɔl] VT (summon, by telephone, a name, a
strike) llamar; (cry out) gritar; (a meeting)
convocar; **she — ed me a liar** me llamó
mentiroso; **— me back** llámame tú,
devuélveme la llamada; VI/VT (birds)
reclamar; **to — roll** pasar lista; VI (call out)
gritar; **to — a meeting to order** abrir la
sesión; **to — at a port** hacer escala en un
puerto; **to — for** pedir; **to — off** cancelar; **to
— on** (visit) visitar; (depend on) acudir a; **to
— together** convocar; **to — up** llamar por
teléfono; N (by telephone) llamada f;
(summons) llamamiento m, llamado m; (to
the ministry) vocación f; (for conference
papers) convocatoria f; (device for calling
birds) reclamo m; **to be on —** estar de
guardia; **there's no — for panic** no hay
motivo de alarma; **it's your —** tú decides;
within — al alcance de la voz

caller [kɔ́lə-] N visita f, visitante mf; (by telephone) persona que llama f; **— ID** identificador de llamadas m

calligraphy [kəlígrəfi] N caligrafía f

calling [kɔ́lɪŋ] N vocación f

callous [kǽləs] ADJ (having calluses) calloso; (insensitive) insensible

callus [kǽləs] N callo m

calm [kɑm] ADJ tranquilo, reposado, calmo; N calma f, tranquilidad f, sosiego m; VT calmar, tranquilizar, sosegar; **to — down** calmar[se]

calmness [kɑ́mnɪs] N calma f, tranquilidad f

calorie [kǽləri] N caloría f

calumny [kǽləmni] N calumnia f

cam [kæm] N leva f

Cambodia [kæmbódiə] N Camboya f

Cambodian [kæmbódiən] ADJ & N camboyano -na mf

camcorder [kǽmkɔrdə-] N videocámara f

came [kem] see come

camel [kǽməl] N camello m

cameo [kǽmio] N camafeo m; **— appearance** actuación especial f

camera [kǽmrə] N cámara f, cámara fotográfica f; **—man** cámara m, camarógrafo m; **—-ready copy** texto listo para cámara f; **—woman** cámara f, camarógrafa f

Cameroon [kæmərún] N Camerún m

Cameroonian [kæmərúniən] ADJ & N camerunés -esa mf

camouflage [kǽməflɑʒ] N camuflaje m; VT camuflar

camp [kæmp] N (campsite) campamento m; (faction) bando m; **—fire** fogata f, hoguera f; **—ground** campamento m, cámping m; **—site** campamento m; VI/VT acampar

campaign [kæmpén] N campaña f; VI hacer campaña

camper [kǽmpə-] N acampante mf, campista mf

camphor [kǽmfə-] N alcanfor m

camping [kǽmpɪŋ] N cámping m, acampada f; **let's go —** vamos de camping / de acampada

campus [kǽmpəs] N campus m

can [kæn] N lata f, bote m; **— of worms** caja de Pandora f; **— opener** abrelatas m sg; VT enlatar; V AUX **— you come tomorrow?** ¿puedes venir mañana? **— you see me?** ¿me ves? **I — ride a bicycle** sé andar en bicicleta; **a —-do attitude** un espíritu emprendedor

Canada [kǽnədə] N Canadá m

Canadian [kənédiən] ADJ & N canadiense mf

canal [kənǽl] N canal m

canary [kənέri] N canario m; **Canary Islands** Islas Canarias f pl

Canary Islands [kənériáilənz] N Islas Canarias f pl

cancel [kǽnsəl] VT cancelar; (a stamp) matasellar; (an order) anular

cancellation [kænsəléʃən] N (of a flight, performance) cancelación f; (of an order) anulación f

cancer [kǽnsə-] N cáncer m; **— patient** canceroso -sa mf; ADJ **—-causing** cancerígeno

cancerous [kǽnsəəs] ADJ canceroso

candelabrum, candelabra [kændəlábrəm -brə] N candelabro m

candid [kǽndɪd] ADJ franco, sincero

candidacy [kǽndɪdəsi] N candidatura f

candidate [kǽndɪdɪt] N (for office) candidato -ta mf; (for a job) aspirante mf, postulante mf

candle [kǽndl] N vela f, candela f; (on the altar) cirio m; **—stick** candelero m

candor [kǽndə-] N franqueza f

candy [kǽndi] N dulce m, caramelo m, confite m; (with chocolate) bombón m; **— store** bombonería f; VT confitar, acaramelar; (nuts) garapiñar; VI (syrup) cristalizarse

cane [ken] N (sugar) caña f; (walking) bastón m; **— chair** silla de mimbre f

canine [kénaɪn] ADJ canino, perruno; N (dog) can m, perro m; (tooth) canino m

canister [kǽnɪstə-] N lata f

canker [kǽŋkə-] N úlcera f

cannery [kǽnəri] N fábrica de conservas f

cannibal [kǽnəbəl] N caníbal m

cannon [kǽnən] N cañón m; **— fodder** carne de cañón f

canny [kǽni] ADJ sagaz, astuto

canoe [kənú] N canoa f

canon [kǽnən] N (rule, melody, body of works) canon m; (priest) canónigo m

canopy [kǽnəpi] N (of a bed) dosel m; (of a building) toldo m

cantaloupe [kǽntlop] N melón m

canteen [kæntín] N (snack bar) cantina f; (container) cantimplora f

canvas [kǽnvəs] N (fabric) lona f; (for painting) lienzo m

canvass [kǽnvəs] VI/VT (poll) encuestar; (solicit votes) solicitar votos en; (solicit sales) buscar pedidos comerciales en; N solicitud f

canyon [kǽnjən] N cañón m

cap [kæp] N (head covering without visor) gorro m; (head covering with visor) gorra f; (of a bottle) tapa f; (of a pen) capucha f, contera f; (limit) tope m; (for capgun) fulminante m, pistón m; VT (to cover, put a cap on) tapar; (to complete) rematar; (to limit) limitar

capability [kepəbíljtí] N capacidad f

capable [képəbəl] ADJ capaz

capacious [kəpéʃəs] ADJ amplio

capacity [kəpǽsɪdi] N capacidad f

cape [kep] N (clothing) capa f; (promontory) cabo m

caper [képə-] N (skipping) cabriola f; (prank) treta f, triquiñuela f; (crime) delito m; (food) alcaparra f; VI retozar

Cape Verde [kepvɜ́·d] N Cabo Verde *m*

Cape Verdean [kepvɜ́·ðiən] ADJ & N caboverdiano -na *mf*

capillary [kǽpəleri] N & ADJ [vaso] capilar *m*

capital [kǽpɪdl] N (city) capital *f*; (wealth) capital *m*; (of a column) capitel *m*; (letter) mayúscula *f*; **to make — of** sacar partido de, aprovecharse de; ADJ (city) capital; (financial) de capital; **— gains** ganancias en bienes de capital *f pl*; **— investment** inversión de capital *f*; **— punishment** pena de muerte *f*

capitalism [kǽpɪdlɪzəm] N capitalismo *m*

capitalist [kǽpɪdlɪst] N capitalista *mf*

capitalistic [kæpɪdlístɪk] ADJ capitalista

capitalization [kæpɪdlɪzéɪʃən] N capitalización *f*

capitalize [kǽpɪdlaɪz] VT (finance) capitalizar; (write) escribir con mayúscula; **to — on** sacar provecho de

capitol [kǽpɪdl] N capitolio *m*

capitulate [kəpítʃəlet] VI capitular

cappuccino [kæpətʃíno] N capuchino *m*

caprice [kəprís] N capricho *m*

capricious [kəpríʃəs] ADJ caprichoso

capsize [kǽpsaɪz] VI/VT volcar[se]

capsule [kǽpsəl] N cápsula *f*

captain [kǽptɪn] N capitán *m*; VT capitanear

caption [kǽpʃən] N (with illustration) pie *m*; (subtitle) subtítulo *m*

captivate [kǽptəvet] VT cautivar

captive [kǽptɪv] ADJ & N cautivo -va *mf*; **— animals** animales en cautiverio *m pl*

captivity [kæptívɪdi] N cautiverio *m*

captor [kǽptə] N captor -ra *mf*

capture [kǽptʃə] VT (apprehend, record data) capturar; (give expression to) plasmar; (attract) cautivar; (conquer) tomar; N captura *f*

car [kɑr] N (automobile) coche *m*, automóvil *m*; *Am* carro *m*, auto *m*; (railroad) vagón *m*, coche *m*; (elevator) cabina *f*; *Am* elevador *m*; **— bomb** coche bomba *m*; **—fare** pasaje *m*; **—jacking** secuestro de vehículo *m*; **—load** carga de un coche *f*; **—port** cochera *f*; **— wash** túnel de lavado *m*; ADJ **—sick** mareado; **to get —sick** marearse en el coche

caramel [kǽrəməl] N caramelo *m*

carat [kǽrət] N quilate *m*

caravan [kǽrəvæn] N caravana *f*

carbohydrate [kɑrbəháɪdret] N carbohidrato *m*, hidrato de carbono *m*

carbon [kɑ́rbən] N carbono *m*; **— copy** copia en papel carbón *f*; **— dioxide** dióxido de carbono *m*; **— monoxide** monóxido de carbono *m*; **— paper** papel carbón *m*

carburetor [kɑ́rbəredə·] N carburador *m*

carcass [kɑ́rkəs] N (of an animal) cuerpo muerto *m*; (of a ship) casco *m*

carcinogen [kɑrsínədʒən] N cancerígeno *m*, carcinógeno *m*

carcinoma [kɑrsənómə] N carcinoma *m*

card [kɑrd] N (piece of stiff paper) tarjeta *f*; (for games) naipe *m*, carta *f*; (for boxing events) programa *m*; (for textiles) carda *f*; (witty person) gracioso -sa *mf*; (in a computer) tarjeta *f*, placa *f*; **—board** (thick) cartón *m*; (thin) cartulina *f*; **— reader** lector de tarjetas *m*; **— sharp** fullero -ra *mf*; **pack of —s** baraja *f*; **to play —s** jugar a la baraja, jugar a los naipes; **he's holding all the —s** tiene todas las ventajas; VT (comb) cardar; (ask for identification) pedir identificación

cardiac [kɑ́rDiæk] ADJ cardiaco, cardíaco

cardinal [kɑ́rdnəl] ADJ (number, main) cardinal; (colored red) rojo, bermellón; N (bishop, bird) cardenal *m*

cardioangiogram [kɑrDioǽndʒiəgræm] N cardioangiograma *m*

cardiogram [kɑ́rDiogræm] N cardiograma *m*

cardiologist [kɑrDiáləḍʒist] N cardiólogo -ga *mf*

cardiology [kɑrDiáləḍʒi] N cardiología *f*

cardiopulmonary [kɑrDiopúlməneri] ADJ cardiopulmonar; **— bypass** puente cardiopulmonar *m*

cardiovascular [kɑrDiovǽskjələ·] ADJ cardiovascular

care [ker] N (worry) preocupación *f*; (attention) cuidado *m*, atención *f*, tiento *m*; (extreme attention) esmero *m*, primor *m*; **—giver** cuidador -ra de enfermos *mf*; **—taker** (of a house) casero -ra *mf*; **to be under the — of** estar al cuidado de; **to take — of** cuidar de, atender; ADJ **—free** despreocupado; VI (be concerned) importarle a uno; **to — about** interesarle a uno, importarle a uno; **to — for** (look after) cuidar de; (love) tenerle cariño a; **to — to** tener ganas de; **I couldn't — less** me importa un rábano; **what does he —?** ¿a él qué le importa? **would you — for a drink?** ¿te puedo ofrecer algo?

careen [kərín] VI ladearse a toda velocidad

career [kərír] N carrera *f*, trayectoria *f*

careful [kérfəl] ADJ (cautious) cuidadoso, cauteloso; (painstaking) esmerado; **to be —** tener cuidado

carefully [kérfəli] ADV (safely) con cuidado; (painstakingly) esmeradamente

carefulness [kérfəlnɪs] N cuidado *m*

careless [kérlɪs] ADJ descuidado

caress [kərés] N caricia *f*; VT acariciar

cargo [kɑ́rgo] N cargamento *m*

Caribbean [kærəbíən] N Caribe *m*; ADJ caribeño

caricature [kǽrɪkətʃə] N caricatura *f*; VT caricaturizar

caries [kériz] N caries *f*

carnage [kɑ́rnɪdʒ] N carnicería *f*

carnal [kɑ́rnl] ADJ carnal

carnation [kɑrnéʃən] N (flower) clavel *m*; (color) rosado *m*

carnival [kárnəvəl] N carnaval m; (traveling) feria f

carnivorous [karnívə·əs] ADJ carnívoro, carnicero

carol [kérəl] N villancico m; VI cantar villancicos

carom [kérəm] N carambola f; VI rebotar

carotid artery [kərádɪdárdəri] N [arteria] carótida f

carouse [kəráUz] VI andar de parranda

carp [karp] N carpa f; VI (complain) quejarse

carpenter [kárpəntə·] N carpintero -ra mf

carpentry [kárpəntri] N carpintería f

carpet [kárpɪt] N alfombra f; **—bagger** político -ca oportunista mf; VT alfombrar

carriage [kérɪdʒ] N (wheeled vehicle) carruaje m, coche m; (posture) porte m

carrier [kériə·] N (one who carries) portador -ra mf; (postal worker) cartero -ra mf; (transport company) mensajería f

carrion [kériən] N carroña f

carrot [kérət] N zanahoria f

carry [kéri] VT llevar; **do you — Italian wine?** ¿venden vino italiano? **the bill carried** se aprobó el proyecto de ley; **you — yourself well** te comportas bien; **he can't — a tune** no puede seguir una tonada; **this suitcase will — a lot** esta maleta es espaciosa; **to — away** llevarse; **he got carried away** se le fue la mano; **to — on** continuar; **to — out** (complete) llevar a cabo, ejecutar; (take out) sacar; N **—on** maleta de mano f

cart [kart] N (also golf) carro m; VT acarrear

cartilage [kárdlɪdʒ] N cartílago m

carton [kártṇ] N caja de cartón f

cartoon [kartún] N (drawing) caricatura f; (strip) tira cómica f; (film) dibujo animado m

cartoonist [kartúnɪst] N caricaturista mf

cartridge [kártrɪdʒ] N cartucho m; **— belt** cartuchera f, canana f

carve [karv] VI/VT (a piece of wood) tallar; (a turkey) trinchar; **to — out a career** labrarse una carrera

carving [kárvɪŋ] N (action) tallado m; (figure) talla f; **— knife** trinchante m

cascade [kæskéd] N cascada f

case [kes] N caso m; (box) caja f; (of a pillow) funda f; **— history** historia clínica f; **in — [that]** en caso de [que]; **in — it rains** por si llueve; **in any —** en todo caso; **just in —** por si acaso; **get off my —!** ¡déjame en paz! **— sensitive** sensible a la diferencia entre mayúsculas y minúsculas

cash [kæʃ] N efectivo m; **— advance** anticipo en efectivo m; **— and carry** al contado y sin entrega a domicilio; **— flow** corriente en efectivo f; **— on delivery** entrega contra reembolso f; **— payment** pago en efectivo m; **— register** caja registradora f; **to pay —** pagar al contado; VT cobrar

cashew [kéʃu] N marañón m, castaña de cajú f, Sp anacardo m

cashier [kæʃír] N cajero -ra mf; **—'s check** cheque de caja m

casino [kəsíno] N casino m

cask [kæsk] N tonel grande m

casket [kæskɪt] N ataúd m

casserole [kǽsəroʊl] N (container) cazuela f; (food) guiso m

cassette [kəsét] N cassette mf, casete mf

cast [kæst] VT (throw) tirar, echar; (form an object) moldear, vaciar; (give out dramatic roles) repartir papeles; **to — a ballot** votar; **to — about** buscar; **to — a glance** echar un vistazo; **to — aside** desechar; **to — doubt** poner en duda; **to — light on** aclarar; **to — lots** echar suertes; **to — off** (a ship) soltar amarras; (something rejected) deshacerse de; **to — out** exiliar; **to be — down** estar abatido; N (form) molde m; (in theater) reparto m, elenco m; (for broken bones) yeso; **to put in a —** enyesar; **— iron** hierro fundido m

castanet [kǽstənet] N castañuela f

caste [kæst] N casta f

castigate [kǽstɪget] VT (criticize) criticar, reprender; (punish) castigar

Castile [kæstíl] N Castilla f

Castilian [kæstíljən] N & ADJ castellano -na mf; **— speaker** castellanohablante mf; ADJ **— speaking** castellanohablante

casting [kǽstɪŋ] N (throwing) tiro m; (piece of metal) pieza fundida f; (selection of actors) cásting m

castle [kǽsəl] N castillo m; (chess piece) torre f, roque m

castor oil [kǽstə·ɔɪl] N aceite de ricino m

castrate [kǽstret] VT castrar; (animals) capar

casual [kǽʒuəl] ADJ (informal) informal; (offhand) al pasar

casualty [kǽʒuəlti] N (of war) baja f; (in an accident) víctima f

cat [kæt] N (domestic) gato -ta mf; (others) felino m; **—'s meow** súmmum m; **—fish** siluro m

Catalan [kǽdlæn] ADJ & N catalán -ana mf; (language) catalán m

catalog, catalogue [kǽdlɔg] N catálogo m; VT catalogar

Catalonia [kædlóniə] N Cataluña f

Catalonian [kædlóniən] ADJ catalán

catalyst [kǽdlɪst] N catalizador m

cataract [kǽdə·ækt] N catarata f

catastrophe [kətǽstrofi] N catástrofe f

catatonia [kædətóniə] N catatonia f

catch [kætʃ] VT (a criminal, ball) atrapar; Sp, Cuba coger; (a fish) pescar, capturar; (someone in an act) pillar; (a bus) agarrar; (what someone said) comprender, agarrar; **to — a glimpse of** vislumbrar; **to — cold**

resfriarse; **to — fire** prenderse fuego; **to — on** (understand) caer en cuenta; (become popular) ponerse de moda; **to — oneself** contenerse; **to — one's eye** llamarle a uno la atención; **to — sight of** avistar; **to — unawares** sorprender; **to — up** (with a person) alcanzar; (on work) ponerse al día, actualizarse; VI (get entangled) enredarse; (snap into place) agarrar; N (act of catching prey, quantity caught) captura f, redada f, pesca f; (prey) presa f; (device) pestillo m; (act of catching a ball) atrapada f; **—phrase** eslogan m; **— twenty-two** paradoja f; **he is a good —** es un buen partido; **to play —** jugar a la pelota; **what's the —?** ¿cuál es la treta?

catcher [kǽtʃə-] N (baseball) receptor -ora mf

catching [kǽtʃɪŋ] ADJ contagioso

catchy [kǽtʃi] ADJ pegadizo

catechism [kǽdɪkɪzəm] N catecismo m

category [kǽdɪgɔri] N categoría f

cater [kédə-] VI/VT abastecer de alimentos [banquetes, fiestas, etc.]; **to — to** atender a

caterpillar [kǽdəpɪlə-] N (insect) oruga f; (tractor) tractor oruga m, caterpillar m

cathedral [kəθídrəł] N catedral f

catheter [kǽθɪdə-] N catéter m, sonda f

catheterization [kæθədə-ɪzéʃən] N cateterización f

catheterize [kǽθədə-aɪz] VT cateterizar

cathode [kǽθod] N cátodo m; **— rays** rayos catódicos m pl

Catholic [kǽθlɪk] N & ADJ católico -ca mf

Catholicism [kəθálɪsɪzəm] N catolicismo m

CAT [computerized axial tomography] scan [kǽtskæn] N TAC f

catsup [kǽtʃəp] N cátsup m, ketchup m, salsa de tomate f

cattle [kǽdł] N ganado [vacuno] m; **—breeding** ganadería f; **—man** ganadero m; **— rustler** cuatrero m; **— rustling** abigeato m

catty [kǽdi] ADJ malicioso

caught [kɔt] see catch

cauliflower [kɔ́lɪflauə-] N coliflor f

cause [kɔz] N causa f, causante f; **— for celebration** motivo de celebración m; **the democratic —** la causa democrática f; **without —** sin motivo; VT (make happen) causar, ocasionar; (motivate) motivar; **to — to flee** hacer huir; **the heat —d her to faint** el calor la hizo desmayar

caustic [kɔ́stɪk] ADJ cáustico

cauterize [kɔ́dəraɪz] VT cauterizar

caution [kɔ́ʃən] N (prudence) cautela f, recato m; (warning) advertencia f; **—!** ¡cuidado! ¡atención! VT advertir; **to — against** desaconsejar

cautious [kɔ́ʃəs] ADJ cauto, cauteloso, precavido

cava [kávə] N (wine) cava f

cavalier [kævəlír] N caballero m, galán m; ADJ (disdainful) desdeñoso; (overly casual) displicente

cavalry [kǽvəlri] N caballería f

cave [kev] N cueva f, caverna f; **—man** hombre de las cavernas m; VI **to — in** (yield) ceder; (collapse) derrumbarse, desplomarse

cavern [kǽvə-n] N caverna f, gruta f

cavity [kǽvɪdi] N cavidad f; (in a tooth) caries f; (nasal) fosa f

cavort [kəvɔ́rt] VI cabriolar, retozar

caw [kɔ] N graznido m; VI graznar

CD [compact disc] [sídí] N CD m, disco compacto m; **— player** reproductor de discos compactos m; **—-ROM** CD-ROM m

cease [sis] VI cesar; VT interrumpir; N **—-fire** alto el fuego m; Am cese el fuego m

ceaseless [síslɪs] ADJ incesante

cedar [sídə-] N cedro m

cede [sid] VT ceder

ceiling [sílɪŋ] N techo m, cielo raso m; (cap) tope m; (sky) altura máxima f

celebrate [séləbret] VI/VT celebrar, festejar

celebrated [séləbredɪd] ADJ célebre

celebration [sɛləbréʃən] N (action) celebración f, festejo m; (festivities) fiesta f

celebratory [səlébrətori] ADJ festivo

celebrity [səlébrɪdi] N celebridad f

celery [sélɚi] N apio m

celestial [səléstʃəł] ADJ celeste; (heavenly) celestial; **— body** astro m

celibate [séləbɪt] ADJ célibe

cell [sɛł] N (room) celda f; (structural) célula f; **— biology** citología f

cellar [sélə-] N sótano m; (for wine) bodega f, cava f

cello [tʃélo] N violonchelo m

cellophane [sélafen] N celofán m

cellular [séljələ-] ADJ celular; **— phone** celular m; Sp móvil m

cellulite [séljəlait] N celulitis f

celluloid [séljəlɔɪd] N celuloide m

cellulose [séljəlos] N celulosa f

cement [sɪmént] N cemento m; (glue) adhesivo m; **— mixer** hormigonera f; VI/VT cementar

cemetery [sémɪteri] N cementerio m

censor [sénsə-] N censor -ora mf; VT censurar

censorship [sénsə-ʃɪp] N censura f

censure [sénʃə-] N censura f; VT censurar

census [sénsəs] N censo m; **to take a —** censar

cent [sɛnt] N centavo m, céntimo m

centennial [sɛténiəł] ADJ & N centenario m

center [sɛntə-] N centro m; (in basketball) centro m, Am pivot m; **— forward** (soccer) ariete mf; **— of gravity** centro de gravedad m; VI/VT centrar[se]

centigrade [sɛ́ntɪgred] ADJ centígrado

centimeter [sɛ́ntəmidə-] N centímetro m

centipede [sɛ́ntəpid] N ciempiés m

central [séntrəł] ADJ central; (downtown) céntrico; N central de teléfonos f; **— heating** calefacción central f; **— nervous system** sistema nervioso central m; **— processing unit** unidad central de proceso/ procesamiento f

Central [séntrəł] ADJ **— African Republic** República Centroafricana f; **— America** Centroamérica f; **— American** centroamericano

centralize [séntrəlaɪz] VI/VT centralizar[se]; **to be/become —d** centralizarse

centrifugal [sɛntrífəgəł] ADJ centrífugo

centripetal [sɛntrípɪdł] ADJ centrípeto

century [séntʃəri] N siglo m

CEO [chief executive officer] [síió] N Am director -ora general mf, Sp consejero -ra, delegado -da mf

ceramic [sərǽmɪk] ADJ cerámico; N **—s** cerámica f

cereal [síriəł] N (breakfast food) cereal m; (the grain itself) grano m; ADJ cereal

cerebral [səríbrəł] ADJ cerebral; **— concussion** conmoción cerebral f; **— cortex** corteza cerebral f; **— embolism** embolia cerebral f; **— hemorrhage** hemorragia cerebral f; **— palsy** parálisis cerebral f

ceremonial [sɛrəmóuniəł] ADJ & N ceremonial m

ceremonious [sɛrəmóunias] ADJ ceremonioso

ceremony [sérəmoni] N ceremonia f

certain [sɚtn] ADJ seguro; **— people** determinadas personas f pl; **— rules are inviolable** ciertas/determinadas reglas son inviolables; **death and taxes are —** lo único seguro son los impuestos y la muerte; **he's — to come** seguro que viene; **it is — that it rained** seguro que llovió

certainly [sɚtnli] ADV seguramente, sin duda; **she — gets her way** no cabe duda de que se sale con la suya; INTERJ ¡cómo no!

certainty [sɚtnti] N certeza f, certidumbre f

certificate [sətífɪkɪt] N certificado m; **— of baptism** fe de bautismo f; **— of deposit** certificado de depósito m

certification [sɚtəfɪkéʃən] N certificación f

certify [sɚdəfaɪ] VT certificar; **certified check** cheque certificado m; **certified mail** correo certificado m; **certified public accountant** contador -ora público -ca mf

cervical [sɚvɪkəł] ADJ cervical

cervix [sɚvɪks] N (neck) cerviz f; (uterine) cérvix m, cuello uterino m

cesarean section [sɪzériansékʃən] N cesárea f

cessation [sɛséʃən] N cese m

cesspool [séspuł] N pozo séptico m, fosa séptica f

Chad [tʃæd] N Chad m

Chadian [tʃǽdiən] ADJ & N chadiano -na mf

chafe [tʃef] VI/VT rozar[se]; N rozadura f

chaff [tʃæf] N ahechaduras f pl

chagrin [ʃəgrín] N mortificación f; VT mortificar

chain [tʃen] N cadena f; **— reaction** reacción en cadena f; **— saw** sierra f; **— smoker** persona que fuma como una chimenea f; **— store** tienda de cadena f; VI/VT encadenar[se]

chair [tʃer] N silla f; (academic) cátedra f; (of a meeting) presidente -ta mf; (of a department) jefe -fa mf; **—man** presidente m, director m, jefe m; **—manship** dirección f; **—person** presidente -ta mf, jefe -fa mf; **—woman** presidenta f, jefa f

chalk [tʃɔk] N (substance) caliza f; (piece) tiza f; **—board** pizarrón m, pizarra f, tablero m; VT marcar con tiza; **to — up** (attribute) atribuir; (score) marcar

chalky [tʃɔki] ADJ de/con/como tiza

challenge [tʃǽlɪndʒ] N desafío m, reto m; (of a jury) recusación f; VT (defy) desafiar, retar; (take exception) cuestionar, disputar; (recuse) recusar; **to be vertically —d** ser muy bajito

chamber [tʃémbɚ] N (legislative) cámara f; (in a palace) aposento m; (of a cannon) recámara f; **—maid** camarera f, mucama f; **— music** música de cámara f; **— of commerce** cámara de comercio f; **— pot** orinal m; **—s** (of a judge) despacho m

chameleon [kəmíljən] N camaleón m

chamois [ʃǽmi] N gamuza f

champagne [ʃæmpén] N champán m, champaña mf

champion [tʃǽmpiən] N campeón -ona mf; (of a cause) defensor -ora mf, paladín m; VT defender

championship [tʃǽmpiənʃɪp] N campeonato m

chance [tʃæns] N (opportunity) oportunidad f; (probability) probabilidad f; (unpredictable element) casualidad f, azar m; **by —** por casualidad; **game of —** juego de azar m; **to take a —** correr riesgo, arriesgarse; ADJ casual; VI arriesgarse; **we —d to meet him at the bar** nos encontramos con él en el bar por casualidad

chancellor [tʃǽnsələ-] N (chief minister) canciller m; (of a university) rector -ora de universidad mf

chandelier [ʃǽndəlír] N araña de luces f

change [tʃendʒ] VT cambiar; **to — clothes** cambiarse de ropa; **to — into** transformar[se] en; **to — trains** cambiar de tren; N cambio m; (money returned) vuelta f; Am vuelto m; (fresh clothes) muda de ropa f; **— of heart** cambio de opinión m; **— over** (tennis) cambio de lado m; **—-up** (baseball) cambio m, cambio de velocidad m

changeable [tʃéndʒəbəł] ADJ (variable) cambiante, variable; (fickle) inconstante, tornadizo; **— silk** seda tornasolada f

channel [tʃǽnł] N canal m; (bed of stream) cauce m; VT canalizar, encauzar

chant [tʃænt] N (plain song) canto llano m; (hymn) cántico m; (repeated slogan) cantinela f; VI/VT (sing) cantar; (repeat a slogan) corear

chaos [kéas] N caos m

chaotic [keáɪk] ADJ caótico

chap [tʃæp] VI/VT cuartear[se], agrietar[se]; —**ped lips** labios agrietados m pl; —**stick**® crema para los labios f; N (fellow) tipo m

chaparral [ʃæpəɹǽl] N chaparral m

chapel [tʃǽpəɫ] N capilla f

chaperon, chaperone [ʃǽpəɹon] N chaperón -ona f; VI ir de chaperón -ona

chaplain [tʃǽplɪn] N capellán m

chapter [tʃǽptə] N capítulo m

char [tʃɑɹ] VI/VT (reduce to ashes) carbonizar[se]; (scorch) chamuscar[se]

character [kǽɹɪktə] N carácter m; (of a novel) personaje m; — **actor** actor de carácter m; **Chinese** —**s** caracteres chinos m pl; **he's quite a** — es todo un personaje; **that's out of** — **for him** eso no es característico de él

characteristic [kæɹɪktəɹístɪk] ADJ característico; N característica f; (genetic) carácter m

characterization [kæɹɪktəɪzéʃən] N caracterización f

characterize [kǽɹɪktəɹaɪz] VT (describe) caracterizar; (attribute) calificar

charade [ʃəɹéd] N farsa f; —**s** charada f

charcoal [tʃɑɹkoɫ] N carbón de leña m; — **drawing** dibujo al carbón m

charge [tʃɑɹdʒ] VT (demand money) cobrar; (load) cargar; (buy on credit) cargar a cuenta; (attack) embestir; (in basketball) cargar; **to** —**off a loss** restar una pérdida; **to** —**someone with a task** encargarle a alguien una tarea; **to** — **with murder** acusar de homicidio; N (mission) misión f, encargo m; (accusation) cargo m, acusación f; (charge in account) cargo m, débito m; (explosives, electricity) carga f; (attack) embestida f; — **account** cuenta de crédito f; — **card** tarjeta de crédito f; **there will be a** — **for delivery** se cobra entrega a domicilio; **to be in** — **of** estar a cargo de; **under my** — a mi cargo

charger [tʃɑɹdʒə] N (for a battery) cargador m; (horse) corcel m

chariot [tʃǽɹiət] N carro de guerra m

charisma [kəɹízmə] N carisma m

charitable [tʃǽɹɪDəbəɫ] ADJ caritativo

charity [tʃǽɹɪDi] N (virtue, aid to the poor) caridad f; (institution) institución benéfica f, institución de beneficencia f; **to give to** — dar dinero a las instituciones benéficas; **to live on** — vivir de la caridad

charlatan [ʃɑ́ɹlətən] N charlatán -ana mf

charm [tʃɑɹm] N (attractiveness) encanto m, saleroso m; (trinket) dije m; (spell) sortilegio m, hechizo m; (amulet) talismán m, amuleto

m; VT (delight) encantar; (influence) hechizar, subyugar

charming [tʃɑ́ɹmɪŋ] ADJ encantador, saleroso; Sp majo

chart [tʃɑɹt] N (table) tabla f; (graph) gráfica f; (marine map) carta f; (of musical hits) lista de éxitos f; VT (in a table) tabular; (in a graph) graficar; (a region) cartografiar; **to** — **a course** trazar una ruta

charter [tʃɑ́ɹtə] N (of a city) fuero m; (of an organization) estatuto m; (document granting rights) constitución f, carta f; (hire) flete m; — **flight** [vuelo] chárter m; — **member** socio -cia fundador -ora mf; VT (a corporation) aprobar los estatutos; (a flight) fletar

chase [tʃes] VT (hunt) cazar; (follow rapidly) perseguir; **to** — **after** correr tras; **to** — **away** ahuyentar; N caza f, persecución f

chasm [kǽzəm] N sima f

chassis [tʃǽsi] N chasis m, bastidor m

chaste [tʃest] ADJ casto, honesto

chastise [tʃæstaɪz] VT (punish) castigar; (criticize) criticar

chastisement [tʃæstáɪzmənt] N (punishment) castigo m; (criticism) crítica f

chastity [tʃǽstɪDi] N castidad f, honestidad f

chat [tʃæt] N charla f; Mex plática f; — **room** sala de chat f; VI charlar; Mex platicar; VI chatear

chattel [tʃǽdɫ] N (movable property) bien mueble m; (slave) esclavo -va mf

chatter [tʃǽDə] VI (jabber) cotorrear, parlotear; VT (click rapidly) castañetear; N (of speech) cotorreo m, parloteo m; (of teeth) castañeteo m; —**box** charlatán -ana mf, cotorra f

chauffeur [ʃofə] N chófer m

chauvinism [ʃóvənɪzəm] N (nationalist) chovinismo m; (sexist) machismo m

cheap [tʃip] ADJ (economical) barato; (stingy) avaro; **life is** — **there** la vida no vale nada allí; **talk is** — hablar no cuesta nada; **to feel** — sentirse despreciable; N — **shot** golpe bajo m; —**skate** tacaño -ña mf

cheapen [tʃípən] VI/VT (lower in price) abaratar[se]; VT (lower in esteem) desvalorizar

cheapness [tʃípnɪs] N (low price) baratura f; (stinginess) avaricia f

cheat [tʃit] N tramposo -sa mf, fullero -ra mf; VT engañar; **to** — **at cards** hacer trampa en/a las cartas, trampear; **to** — **on a test** copiar; **to** — **on one's spouse** engañar a la pareja de uno

check [tʃek] VT (stop) refrenar; (restrain) reprimir; (leave luggage) facturar; (leave a coat) dejar; (verify) comprobar, verificar; Am chequear; Mex checar; (in chess) dar jaque; **to** — **against** cotejar con; **to** — **into a hotel** registrarse; **to** — **into something** averiguar algo; **to** — **off** puntear; **to** — **out a book** sacar [prestado] un libro; **to** — **up on**

controlar; **that —s out** lo hemos comprobado; N (bank) cheque *m*; (means of restraint) control *m*; (ticket) ficha *f*; (mark) marca *f*; (in a restaurant) cuenta *f*; (in fabric) cuadro *m*; (checked fabric) tela a cuadros *f*; (examination) comprobación *f*; (in chess) jaque *m*; **—book** chequera *f*, talonario *m*; **—ing account** cuenta corriente *f*; **— kiting** giro de cheques sin fondos *m*; **—list** lista de control *f*; **—mate** jaque mate *m*; **—out counter** caja *f*; **—point** control *m*, retén *m*; **—room** guardarropa *m*; **— stub** talón *m*; **—up** examen físico *m*

checker [tʃékɚ] N (on a fabric) cuadro *m*; (on a checkerboard) casilla *f*; (game piece) ficha *f*; (cashier) cajero -ra *mf*; (person who checks) verificador -ora *mf*; **—board** tablero *m*; **—ed cloth** tela a cuadros *f*; **—ed past** pasado oscuro *m*; **—s** juego de damas *m*; VT cuadricular

cheek [tʃik] N (on face) mejilla *f*; *Am* cachete *m*; (impudence) descaro *m*; (of buttocks) nalga *f*; **—bone** pómulo *m*

cheer [tʃɪr] N (shout) viva *m*, vítor *m*; (applause) aplausos *m pl*; (encouragement) ánimo *m*; (joy) alegría *f*; **—leader** animador -ora *mf*; *Am* porrista *mf*; INTERJ **—s!** ¡salud! VI/VT vitorear; **to — on** dar ánimo; **to — up** animar[se]

cheerful [tʃírfəl] ADJ (person) risueño, alegre; (room) alegre

cheerfulness [tʃírfəlnɪs] N alegría *f*

cheerless [tʃírlɪs] ADJ triste, sombrío

cheese [tʃiz] N queso *m*; **—burger** hamburguesa con queso *f*; **—cake** tarta de queso *f*

cheesy [tʃízi] ADJ (of cheese) de queso; (cheap) barato, (uncool) *Sp* hortera

cheetah [tʃíɾə] N guepardo *m*

chef [ʃef] N chef *mf*

chemical [kémɪkəl] ADJ químico; **— engineering** ingeniería química *f*; **— warfare** guerra química *f*; N producto químico *m*

chemist [kémɪst] N químico -ca *f*

chemistry [kémɪstri] N química *f*

chemotheraphy [kimoθérəpi] N quimioterapia *f*

cherish [tʃérɪʃ] VT apreciar; **I — the memory of him** tengo muy buenos recuerdos de él

cherry [tʃéri] N cereza *f*; **— tree** cerezo *m*

chess [tʃes] N ajedrez *m*; **—board** tablero de ajedrez *m*

chest [tʃest] N (body part) pecho *m*; (box) arca *f*; **— of drawers** cómoda *f*

chestnut [tʃésnʌt] N castaña *f*; **— tree** castaño *m*; ADJ castaño; (horse) zaino

chew [tʃu] VT (food) masticar; (nonfood) mascar; **—ing gum** goma de mascar *f*; *Am* chicle *m*; **to — a hole** hacer un agujero a mordiscos; **to — out** reprender; **to — over** meditar

sobre; **to — up** romper a mordiscos; N mascada *f*, bocado *m*

chewy [tʃúi] ADJ correoso

chic [ʃik] ADJ & N chic *m*

chick [tʃɪk] N (young chicken) pollito *m*; (young bird) pichón *m*; (young woman) *fam* chavala *f*, tía *f*; **—pea** garbanzo *m*

chicken [tʃíkɪn] N gallina *f*; (flesh) pollo *m*; **— coop** gallinero *m*; **—-hearted** cobarde; **— pox** varicela *f*

chicory [tʃíkori] N achicoria *f*

chide [tʃaɪd] VT regañar

chief [tʃif] N jefe *m*; (of a tribe) cacique *m*; **— of staff** (military) jefe del estado mayor *m*; (of a division) secretario -ria general *mf*; ADJ principal; **— justice** presidente de la Suprema Corte de los Estados Unidos *m*

chieftain [tʃíftən] N cacique *m*

chiffon [ʃɪfán] N chifón *m*

chigger [tʃígɚ] N nigua *f*

chilblain [tʃílblen] N sabañón *m*

child [tʃaɪld] N (young person) niño -ña *mf*; (offspring) hijo -ja *mf*; **—birth** parto *m*, alumbramiento *m*; **—like** infantil, aniñado; **—proof** a prueba de niños; **—'s play** cosa de niños *f*; **to be with —** estar embarazada; ADJ **of —bearing age** en edad de procrear

childhood [tʃáɪldhud] N niñez *f*, infancia *f*

childish [tʃáɪldɪʃ] ADJ infantil, pueril

childless [tʃáɪldlɪs] ADJ sin hijos

Chile [tʃíli] N Chile *m*

Chilean [tʃíliən] ADJ & N chileno -na *mf*

chili, chile [tʃíli] N (pepper) chile *m*, ají *m*; (meat dish) chile con carne *m*

chill [tʃɪl] N (coldness) frío *m*; (fear, cold with shivering) escalofrío *m*; **it had a —ing effect on the group** le cayó al grupo como un baldazo de agua fría; VI/VT enfriar[se]; **to — out** tranquilizarse, relajarse

chilly [tʃíli] ADJ frío

chime [tʃaɪm] N (sound) repique *m*; (instrument) carillón *m*, carrillón *m*; VI repicar; VT tañer; **to — in** intervenir [en una conversación]

chimney [tʃímni] N chimenea *f*

chimpanzee [tʃɪmpænzí] N chimpancé *m*

chin [tʃɪn] N barbilla *f*, mentón *m*

china [tʃáɪnə] N (material) porcelana *f*, china *f*; (dishes) vajilla de porcelana *f*, china *f*; **—ware** vajilla de porcelana *f*

China [tʃáɪnə] N China *f*

Chinese [tʃaɪníz] ADJ chino; N (inhabitant of China) chino -na *mf*; (language) chino *m*

chink [tʃɪŋk] N grieta *f*

chip [tʃɪp] N (of wood) astilla *f*; (in glass) desportilladura *f*; (in gambling) ficha *f*; (in computers) chip *m*; **he's a — off the old block** de tal palo, tal astilla; **he has a — on his shoulder** guarda resentimientos; VI/VT (wood) astillar[se]; (glass, plaster) desportillarse, desconchar[se]; (paint) descascarar[se]; (in golf) chipear; **to — in** contribuir; **to — a tooth** romperse un diente

chipmunk [tʃípmʌŋk] N ardilla listada f

chiropractic [kaɪrəpræktɪk] ADJ quiropráctico; N quiropráctica f

chiropractor [káɪrəpræktɚ] N quiropráctico -ca mf

chirp [tʃɚp] N pío m, gorjeo m; VI/VT piar, gorjear

chisel [tʃízəl] N escoplo m; (for stone) cincel m; (for wood) formón m; VT cincelar; (swindle) estafar

chiseler [tʃízlɚ] N estafador -ra mf

chit-chat [tʃíttʃæt] N palique m; VI charlar

chivalrous [ʃívəlrəs] ADJ (of knights) caballeresco; (courteous to women) caballeroso

chivalry [ʃívəlri] N caballerosidad f

chloride [klɔ́raɪd] N cloruro m

chlorine [klɔ́rin] N cloro m

chloroform [klɔ́rəfɔrm] N cloroformo m

chlorophyl, chlorophyll [klɔ́rəfɪl] N clorofila f

chocolate [tʃáklɪt] N chocolate m; (bar) chocolatina f; **— pot** chocolatera f

choice [tʃɔɪs] N (act of selecting, thing selected) selección f; (alternative) opción f; **to have no other —** no tener más remedio; ADJ selecto

choir [kwaɪr] N coro m

choke [tʃok] VI/VT (suffocate) ahogar[se]; (strangle) estrangular[se]; (on food) atragantarse, atorarse; (obstruct) tapar[se]; VI (in sports) bloquearse; **I'm all —d up** estoy muy conmovido; **to — back/down** contener; N (act of choking on something) atragantamiento m; (act of choking someone) estrangulación f; (device in cars) obturador m; (in sports) bloqueo m

cholera [kálɚə] N cólera m

choleric [kálɚɪk] ADJ colérico

cholesterol [kəléstɚɔl] N colesterol m

choose [tʃuz] VI/VT elegir, seleccionar, escoger; **to —** optar por

choosy [tʃúzi] ADJ quisquilloso

chop [tʃap] VI/VT cortar; **to — down** talar; **to — off** mochar, tronchar; **to — up** picar; N (act of chopping) golpe m; (cut of meat) chuleta f; **—s** morro m; **—stick** palillo m

choppy [tʃápi] ADJ picado, agitado

choral [kɔ́rəl] ADJ coral

chord [kɔrd] N (mathematical) cuerda f; (musical) acorde m; **it struck a — with me** me conmovió

chore [tʃɔr] N tarea f, faena f, quehacer m; **it's such a —** es un trabajo horrible

choreography [kɔriágrəfi] N coreografía f

chorus [kɔ́rəs] N coro m

chose [tʃoz] see choose

chosen [tʃózən] ADJ **my — profession** la

profesión de mi preferencia; **the — one** el elegido, la elegida

chosen [tʃózən] see choose

christen [krísən] VT bautizar

Christendom [krísəndəm] N cristianismo m

christening [krísənɪŋ] N bautizo m, bautismo m

Christian [krístʃən] ADJ & N cristiano -na mf; **— name** nombre de pila m

Christianity [krɪstʃiǽnɪɖi] N cristianismo m

Christmas [krísməs] N Navidad f, Pascua de Navidad f; **— card** tarjeta de Navidad f; **— Eve** Nochebuena f; **— gift** regalo de Navidad m; **— tree** árbol de Navidad m; ADJ navideño

chrome [krom] N cromo m; ADJ cromado

chromium [krómiəm] N cromo m

chromosome [króməsom] N cromosoma m

chronic [kránɪk] ADJ crónico

chronicle [kránɪkəl] N crónica f; VT registrar

chronicler [kránɪklɚ] N cronista mf

chronological [kranládʒɪkəl] ADJ cronológico

chronology [kranálədʒi] N cronología f

chronometer [kranámɪɖɚ] N cronómetro m

chrysalis [krísəlɪs] N crisálida f

chrysanthemum [krɪsǽnθəməm] N crisantemo m

chubby [tʃábi] ADJ rechoncho, gordito

chuck [tʃʌk] N (cut of meat) paletilla f; VT (to throw) lanzar; (to discard) tirar, botar

chuckle [tʃʌkəl] N risita f; VI reírse levemente

chum [tʃʌm] N compinche mf

chunk [tʃʌŋk] N trozo m, pedazo m; **a — of cash** un montón de plata

church [tʃɚtʃ] N iglesia f; **—man** clérigo m

churn [tʃɚn] N mantequera f; VI/VT (make butter) batir; (agitate) agitar, revolver

CIA [Central Intelligence Agency] [síáié] N CIA f

cicada [sɪkéɖə] N chicharra f

cider [sáɪɖɚ] N (alcoholic) sidra f; (non-alcoholic) Am jugo de manzana m; Sp zumo de manzana m

cigar [sɪgár] N puro m, habano m; **— store** tabaquería f; **close, but no —** bien, pero te quedaste corto

cigarette [sɪgɚét] N cigarrillo m; Sp pitillo m; Am cigarro m; **— case** cigarrera f; Sp pitillera f; **— holder** boquilla f; **— lighter** encendedor m

cinch [sɪntʃ] N (for a saddle) cincha f; (something easy) pan comido m; (favorite) favorito -ta mf; VT cinchar

cinder [sínɖɚ] N ceniza f, rescoldo m

cinema [sínəmə] N cine m

cinematography [sɪnəmətágrəfi] N cinematografía f

cinnamon [sínəmən] N canela f; **— tree** canelo f

cipher [sáɪfɚ] N cifra f, guarismo m; VI/VT cifrar[se]

circle [sɚ́kəl] N círculo m; (literary) ámbito m,

círculo m; VT (draw a circle) encerrar en un círculo; VI (go around) dar una vuelta

circuit [sɝ́kɪt] N circuito m; — **board** circuito impreso m; — **breaker** cortacircuitos m sg

circuitry [sɝ́kɪtri] N circuitería f

circular [sɝ́kjələ] ADJ circular; — **saw** sierra circular f; N circular f

circulate [sɝ́kjəlet] VI circular; VT (distribute) poner en circulación

circulation [sɝkjəléʃən] N circulación f

circulatory [sɝ́kjələtɔri] ADJ circulatorio; — **system** aparato circulatorio m

circumcise [sɝ́kəmsaɪz] VT circuncidar

circumference [səkə́mfəəns] N circunferencia f

circumlocution [sɝkəmlokjúʃən] N circunlocución f, rodeo m

circumscribe [sɝkəmskráɪb] VT circunscribir

circumspect [sɝ́kəmspɛkt] ADJ circunspecto

circumstance [sɝ́kəmstæns] N circunstancia f; — **s** condiciones financieras f pl

circumstantial [sɝkəmstǽnʃəl] ADJ circunstancial; — **evidence** pruebas circunstanciales f pl

circumvent [sɝkəmvɛ́nt] VT evitar, obviar

circus [sɝ́kəs] N circo m

cirrhosis [sɪrósɪs] N cirrosis f

cirrus [sírəs] N cirro m

cistern [sístən] N cisterna f, aljibe m

citadel [sídədɛl] N ciudadela f

citation [saɪtéʃən] N (summons) citación f; (quote, quotation) cita f; (commendation for bravery) mención f

cite [saɪt] VT (quote, summon) citar; (comment on) mencionar

citizen [sídɪzən] N (of a nation) ciudadano -na mf; (of a city or region) habitante mf

citizenship [sídɪzənʃɪp] N ciudadanía f

citrus [sítrəs] ADJ & N cítrico m

city [síɾi] N ciudad f; — **council** concejo m; — **hall** ayuntamiento m, alcaldía f; — **planning** urbanismo m; ADJ municipal, urbano

civic [sívɪk] ADJ cívico; N — **s** educación cívica f

civil [sívəl] ADJ (civilian) civil; (polite) cortés; — **disobedience** desobediencia civil f; — **engineer** ingeniero -ra civil mf; — **rights** derechos civiles m pl; — **service** administración pública f; — **war** guerra civil f

civilian [sɪvíljən] ADJ & N civil mf

civility [sɪvílɪti] N civilidad f, cortesía f

civilization [sɪvəlɪzéʃən] N civilización f

civilize [sívəlaɪz] VT civilizar

clad [klæd] ADJ vestido

claim [klem] VT (demand) reclamar, reivindicar; (assert) sostener, pretender; **to — to be** pretender ser; **to — responsibility** atribuirse la responsabilidad; **to — a mine** denunciar una mina; N (demand) reclamación f, reclamo m; (assertion)

afirmación f; (right) derecho m, título m; (on insurance) demanda f, denuncia f

claimant [klémənt] N demandante mf, reclamante mf; (to the throne) pretendiente mf

clairvoyant [klɛrvɔ́ɪənt] ADJ & N clarividente mf

clam [klæm] N almeja f; VI **to — up** callarse

clamber [klǽmbə] VI/VT (climb with effort) trepar con dificultad; (climb on all fours) subir gateando

clammy [klǽmi] ADJ frío y húmedo

clamor [klǽmə] N clamor m, vocerío m; VI clamar, vociferar

clamorous [klǽməəs] ADJ clamoroso

clamp [klæmp] N (support) grapa f; (vice) tornillo m; (wrap-around) abrazadera f; (medical) pinza f; VT sujetar; **to — down on** reprimir

clan [klæn] N clan m

clandestine [klændéstɪn] ADJ clandestino

clang [klæŋ] VI sonar; N sonido metálico m

clap [klæp] N (tap) palmada f; (blow) golpe seco m; — **of thunder** trueno m; VT (on the back) palmear; (in approval) aplaudir; (a book) cerrar de golpe

clapper [klǽpə] N badajo m

clarification [klærəfɪkéʃən] N aclaración f

clarify [klǽrəfaɪ] VT aclarar, clarificar

clarinet [klærənɛ́t] N clarinete m

clarity [klǽrɪti] N claridad f

clash [klæʃ] N (noise) estruendo metálico m; (collision) choque m; (conflict) conflicto m, enfrentamiento m; VI/VT (collide) chocar; (oppose, fight) enfrentarse a; (not go with) no combinar, no pegar

clasp [klæsp] N (fastener) broche m, cierre m; (grip) apretón m; VT (fasten) abrochar; (grip) apretar; (embrace) abrazar, prender

class [klæs] N clase f; (graduation class) promoción f, graduación f; **in a — by itself** único; — **mate** compañero -ra de clase mf, condiscípulo -la mf; — **room** salón de clase m, aula f; — **struggle** lucha de clases f; VI/VT clasificar[se]

classic [klǽsɪk] ADJ & N clásico -ca mf

classical [klǽsɪkəl] ADJ clásico

classicism [klǽsɪsɪzəm] N clasicismo m

classification [klæsəfɪkéʃən] N clasificación f

classify [klǽsəfaɪ] VT clasificar; **classified ad** anuncio clasificado m

classy [klǽsi] ADJ elegante

clatter [klǽɾə] N (noise) estrépito m; (movement) traqueteo m; VI (make noise) causar estrépito; (move) traquetear

clause [klɔz] N cláusula f

claustrophobia [klɔstrəfóbiə] N claustrofobia f

claustrophobic [klɔstrəfóbɪk] ADJ claustrofóbico

clavicle [klǽvɪkəl] N clavícula f

claw [klɔ] N (of a bear) garra f, zarpa f; (of a cat) uña f; (of a crab) pinza f; (of a hammer) orejas f pl; VI/VT arañar; **they —ed their way through** se abrieron paso con las uñas

clay [kle] N arcilla f; (for ceramics) greda f; (in tennis) tierra batida f

clean [klin] ADJ limpio; (free from impurities, not ornate) puro; (honorable) decente; **—-cut** (person) acicalado; (concept) bien definido; **— joke** broma inocente f; **—-shaven** afeitado; **he has a — record** no tiene antecedentes; **you'd better come —** deberías confesar; VI/VT limpiar; **he —ed me out** me limpió, me desvalijó; **to — up** (a room) limpiar, asear; (a document) pasar en limpio; (get rich) forrarse; N **—up** limpieza f

cleaner [klínə] N limpiador -ra mf; **—s** tintorería f

cleanliness [klénlinis] N limpieza f; (personal) aseo m

cleanse [klɛnz] VT limpiar

cleanser [klénzə] N limpiador m

clear [klir] ADJ claro; (skin, conscience) limpio; (sky) despejado; (path) libre; **—-cut** (clearly defined) bien definido; (obvious) claro; **—-headed** lúcido; **— profit** ganancia neta f; **to keep — of someone** evitar a alguien; **to pass — through** pasar de lado a lado; N **to be in the —** estar libre de culpa; VT (the mind, confusion, voice) aclarar[se]; (a road, one's reputation, computer screen) limpiar; (of criminal charges) absolver; (of suspicion) eximir; (liquid) clarificar; (a legislative bill, plan) aprobar, obtener autorización para; (land for farming) desmontar; (a hurdle) salvar; (a net gain) sacar; **to — the air** sincerarse; **to — the table** levantar la mesa; **to — up** (a mystery) aclarar[se]; (the sky) despejar[se]

clearance [klírəns] N (space) espacio libre m; (vertical) margen de altura m; (permission) autorización f; **— sale** liquidación f

clearing [klírɪŋ] N (terrain) claro m; (of checks) compensación f; **— house** banco de compensación m

cleats [klits] N (projection) tacos m pl, tapones m pl; (shoes) zapatos con tacos m pl

cleavage [klívɪʤ] N (cut) hendidura f; (in dress) escote m

cleave [kliv] VT hender[se]; **to — to** adherirse a

cleaver [klívə] N cuchilla f

clef [klɛf] N clave f

cleft [klɛft] N hendidura f; ADJ hendido, partido; **— lip** labio leporino m; **— palate** paladar hendido m

clemency [klémənsi] N clemencia f

clench [klɛntʃ] VT agarrar, asir; (teeth, fist) apretar

clergy [klɝʤi] N clero m, clerecía f; **—man**

clérigo m, pastor m; **—woman** pastora f

clerical [klérɪkəł] ADJ (of the clergy) clerical, eclesiástico; (of office personnel) de oficina; **— error** error de copia m; **— work** trabajo de escritorio m

clerk [klɝk] N (sales) dependiente -ta mf; (office) empleado -da de oficina mf; (court) escribiente mf, actuario -ria mf; VI trabajar como actuario -ria

clever [klévə] ADJ (ingenious) ingenioso; (smart) listo, vivo; (dexterous) habilidoso

cleverness [klévə·nis] N (ingenuity) ingenio m; (intelligence) inteligencia f, viveza f; (dexterity) habilidad f

cliché [kliʃé] N cliché m, muletilla f; Sp tópico m

click [klɪk] N (sound) clic m, chasquido m; (sound of heels) taconeo m; (on a computer) clic m, pulsación f; VI chascar; (on a computer) hacer clic, oprimir, pulsar; (heels) taconear; VT chascar, chasquear; **— and drag** pulsar y arrastrar

clickable image [klíkəbəłímɪʤ] N imagen en donde se puede pulsar f

client [kláɪənt] N (of professional or store) cliente -ta mf; (of social service) beneficiario -ria mf

clientele [klaɪəntéł] N clientela f

cliff [klɪf] N precipicio m, despeñadero m; (by the sea) acantilado m

climate [kláɪmɪt] N clima m

climatic [klaɪmǽDɪk] ADJ climático

climax [kláɪmæks] N clímax m, punto culminante m; VI culminar, alcanzar el clímax

climb [klaɪm] N (ascent) subida f; (in alpinism) escalada f; VI/VT (ascend) subir; (ascend with effort) trepar[se] [a], encaramar[se] [a]; VT (a mountain, wall) escalar; **to — down** bajar

climber [kláɪmə] N (in alpinism) escalador -ora mf; (plant) trepadora f

clinch [klɪntʃ] VT (resolve) rematar; (hammer down) remachar; (hug, in boxing) trabar; (secure) sujetar; (finalize) cerrar; N (nail) remache m; (embrace) abrazo m; (in boxing) clinch m

cling [klɪŋ] VI (to stick to) pegarse; (to hold onto) aferrarse

clinic [klínɪk] N clínica f; (workshop) taller m

clinical [klínɪkəł] ADJ clínico; **— trial** ensayo clínico m

clink [klɪŋk] N tintín m; VI tintinear

clip [klɪp] VT (cut) cortar; (trim) recortar; (shear) esquilar; (shorten) acortar; (hit) tocar; (fasten) abrochar; (attach paper) sujetar con un clip; N (fastener) gancho m; (for paper) clip m; (of cartridge) cargador m; (brooch) broche m; **—board** portapapeles m sg

clipper [klípə] N (shearer) esquilador -ra mf; **—s** (scissors) tijeras f pl; (hair trimmer) maquinilla *f*

clipping [klípɪŋ] N recorte *m*

clique [klɪk] N (political) camarilla *f*; (in school) pandilla *f*

cloak [klok] N capa *f*; (military) capote *m*; **—room** guardarropa *m*; VT (put a cloak on) vestirse con una capa; (hide) encubrir

clock [klak] N reloj *m*; **—-making** relojería *f*; **— radio** radio reloj *f*; **—work** maquinaria de reloj *f*; **like —work** con precisión, sin falta; VT **you swim and I'll — you** tú nadas y yo te tomo el tiempo; **the police —ed him at 90 mph** la policía lo pescó haciendo noventa millas por hora

clockwise [klákwaɪz] ADV en el sentido de las manecillas de reloj

clod [klad] N (piece of dirt) terrón *m*, pelotón *m*; (dolt) tonto -ta *mf*, necio -cia *mf*

clog [klag] VI/VT obstruir[se], tapar[se]; N (shoe) zueco *m*; **— dance** baile zapateado *m*

cloister [klɔ́ɪstə] N claustro *m*; (monastery) monasterio *m*; VT enclaustrar

clone [klon] N clon *m*; VT clonar

cloning [klónɪŋ] N clonaje *m*, clonación *f*

close[1] [kloz] VI/VT cerrar[se]; VT (a hole) tapar; **to — an account** cerrar una cuenta; **to — a meeting** levantar una sesión; **to — down a store** clausurar una tienda; **to — in upon** (oppress) oprimir; (approach) cercar a uno; **to — out** liquidar; N fin *m*; (act of closing) cierre *m*; **at the —** al cierre

close[2] [klos] ADJ (near) cercano; (dense) tupido; (intimate) íntimo, entrañable; **— attention** mucha atención *f*; **— by** cercano, *Am* aquí nomás; **—-fought** reñido; **—-knit** muy unido; **— translation** traducción fiel *f*; **at — range** de cerca; **that was a — call** nos salvamos por poco; N **—up** primer plano *m*; ADV cerca

closed [klozd] ADJ cerrado; **— circuit** circuito cerrado *m*; **—-minded** cerrado; **—-mindedness** cerrazón *f*

closely [klósli] ADV (examine) de cerca; (resemble) mucho; (study) detenidamente; (work) estrechamente

closeness [klósnɪs] N (of location) cercanía *f*; (of friendship) intimidad *f*; (correctness) fidelidad *f*

closer [klózə] N (baseball) relevista de cierre *mf*, cerrador -ora *mf*

closet [klázɪt] N ropero *m*, armario *m*; VI enclaustrarse; ADJ a escondidas

closure [klóʒə] N (conclusion) cierre *m*; (sense of completeness) clausura *f*

clot [klat] VI/VT coagular[se]; N coágulo *m*, cuajarón *m*

cloth [klɔθ] N tela *f*, tejido *m*; (wool) paño *m*; ADJ de tela; **— bound** encuadernado en tela; **man of the —** clérigo *m*

clothe [kloð] VT vestir; N **—s** ropa *f*; **—sline** tendedero *m*; **—spin** pinza *f*

clothier [klóðjə] N comerciante en ropa o paño *mf*

clothing [klóðɪŋ] N ropa *f*

clotting [klátɪŋ] N coagulación *f*

cloud [klaʊd] N nube *f*; **—burst** chaparrón *m*, aguacero *m*; VT nublar, anublar; (make indistinct, place under suspicion) enturbiar; **to — up** nublarse, anublarse; **to be on — nine** estar en el séptimo cielo; **under a —** bajo sospecha

cloudiness [kláʊdɪnɪs] N nebulosidad *f*, nubosidad *f*

cloudless [kláʊdlɪs] ADJ despejado

cloudy [kláʊdi] ADJ nublado; *Sp* nuboso; (gloomy) sombrío

clout [klaʊt] N influencia *f*

clove [klov] N clavo *f*; **— of garlic** diente de ajo *m*

cloven [klóvən] ADJ hendido; **—-hoofed** patihendido

clover [klóvə] N trébol *m*; **—leaf** trébol *m*; **to be in —** vivir en el lujo

clown [klaʊn] N payaso *m*; VI payasear, bufonear

cloy [klɔɪ] VI/VT (satiate) hastiar; (to be too sweet for) repugnar

club [klʌb] N (society, nightclub) club *m*; (stick) porra *f*, garrote *m*; (suit of cards) basto *m*; **—foot** pie zambo *m*; **—house** casa de club *f*; VT aporrear

cluck [klʌk] VI cloquear; N cloqueo *m*

clue [klu] N pista *f*, indicio *m*; **to have no —** no tener ni noción

clueless [klúlɪs] ADJ (absent-minded) despistado; (uninformed) en ayunas

clump [klʌmp] N (of bushes) matorral *m*; (of trees) arboleda *f*; VI/VT apiñar[se]

clumsiness [klʌ́mzɪnɪs] N torpeza *f*

clumsy [klʌ́mzi] ADJ torpe, desmañado, chambón; *Sp* patoso

clung [klʌŋ] *see* cling

clunker [klʌ́ŋkə] N cacharro *m*

cluster [klʌ́stə] N grupo *m*; (of grapes) racimo *m*; VI/VT agrupar[se], arracimar[se]

clutch [klʌtʃ] N (in a car) embrague *m*; **— pedal** pedal del embrague *m*; **to step on the —** pisar el embrague; **—es** garras *f pl*; VT (seize) asir; (hold) apretar

clutter [klʌ́tə] N desparramo *m*, desorden *m*, confusión *f*; VT **books —ed her desk** tenía libros desparramados por todo el escritorio

coach [kotʃ] N (carriage) coche *m*, carruaje *m*, carroza *f*; (bus) autobús *m*; (in sports) entrenador -ra *mf*; (in soccer) técnico -ca *mf*, director -ora técnico -ca *mf*; (in air travel) clase turista *f*; (tutor) profesor -ra particular *mf*; **—man** cochero *m*; VI/VT entrenar

coagulant [koǽgjələnt] ADJ & N coagulante *m*

coagulate [koǽgjələt] VI/VT coagular[se]
coagulation [koægjəléʃən] N coagulación f
coal [koɫ] N carbón m; — **bin** carbonera f; — **tar** alquitrán m
coalition [koəlíʃən] N coalición f
coarse [kɔrs] ADJ (fabric) burdo, basto; (sand) grueso; (manners, language) grosero, tosco, rudo
coarseness [kórsnıs] N (fabric) bastedad f; (language, manners) tosquedad f, rudeza f; (of a joke) chocarrería f
coast [kost] N costa f; — **Guard** Guardia Costera f; — **line** costa f; ADJ & ADV — **to** — de costa a costa; VI (on a sled) deslizar[se]; (in a car, on a bike) tirarse por una bajada; **he —ed through medical school** la Facultad de Medicina le resultó muy fácil
coastal [kóstl] ADJ costero
coat [kot] N abrigo m; (of paint) capa f, mano f; (on animals) pelaje m; — **of arms** escudo de armas m, blasón m; — **rack** percha f, perchero m; —**tail** faldón m; VT cubrir; (with paint) recubrir, dar una mano a; (with grease) engrasar; (with soap) enjabonar; (with sugar) bañar
coax [koks] VT persuadir con halagos, engatusar
coaxial cable [koæksiəlkébəɫ] N cable coaxial m
cob [kab] N mazorca f, panoja f; —**web** telaraña f
cobalt [kóbɔɫt] N cobalto m
cobbler [káblɚ] N (person who repairs shoes) zapatero -ra mf, remendón -ona mf; (dessert) budín de bizcocho y fruta m
cobblestone [kábəɫston] N adoquín m
cobra [kóbrə] N cobra f
cocaine [kokén] N cocaína f
coccyx [káksıks] N cóccix m
cock [kak] N (rooster) gallo m; (male bird) macho de ave de corral m; (faucet) llave f; (gun part) martillo m; —**fight** riña de gallos f; —**pit** (for cockfights) gallera f; (in an airplane) cabina f; —**scomb** cresta de gallo f; ADJ —**sure** gallito; VT (a gun) amartillar; (one's head) ladear
cock-a-doodle-doo [kákədudɫdú] INTERJ quiquiriquí
cockatoo [kákətu] N cacatúa f
cocker spaniel [kákɚspǽnjəɫ] N cócker m
cockroach [kákrotʃ] N cucaracha f
cocktail [káktéɫ] N cóctel m; — **party** cóctel m
cocky [káki] ADJ gallito, valentón
cocoa [kóko] N (powder) cacao m; (drink) chocolate m
coconut [kókənʌt] N coco m
cocoon [kəkún] N capullo m
cod [kad] N Sp abadejo m; Am bacalao m; —**-liver oil** aceite de hígado de bacalao m
coddle [kádɫ] VT mimar
code [kod] N código m; — **switching** alternancia de códigos f; VT codificar

codeine [kódin] N codeína f
codger [kádʒɚ] N vejete m, vejancón m
codify [kádəfaı] VT codificar
coding [kódıŋ] N codificación f
coed [kóed] ADJ mixto; N alumna universitaria f
coefficient [koəfíʃənt] N coeficiente m
coerce [koɚs] VT forzar, obligar
coercion [koɚʃən] N coacción f
coexist [koıgzíst] VI coexistir, convivir
coexistence [koıgzístəns] N coexistencia f, convivencia f
coffee [kɔ́fi] N café m; (with a little milk) cortado m; — **bean** grano de café m; — **break** descanso para tomar el café m; — **bush** cafeto m; — **maker** máquina de café f, cafetera f; —**pot** cafetera f; — **shop** (for coffee) café m; (for coffee and light meals) cafetería f; — **table** mesa baja f
coffer [kɔ́fɚ] N cofre m
coffin [kɔ́fın] N ataúd m, féretro m
cog [kag] N diente m; —**wheel** rueda dentada f
cogent [kódʒənt] ADJ convincente
cognac [kónjæk] N coñac m
cognate [kágnet] ADJ & N cognado m
cognitive [kágnıDıv] ADJ cognitivo
cohabitate [kohǽbıtet] VI cohabitar, convivir
cohabitation [kohæbıtéʃən] N cohabitación f, convivencia f
coherent [kohírənt] ADJ coherente; (sticking together) cohesivo
cohesion [kohíʒən] N cohesión f
coiffure [kwafjúr] N peinado m
coil [kɔıɫ] VI/VT arrollar[se], enrollar[se]; (snake) enroscar[se]; N (roll) rollo m; (spiral) tirabuzón m; (electric) bobina f; — **spring** muelle en espiral m
coin [kɔın] N moneda f; ADJ —**-operated** de monedas; VT acuñar (also words)
coinage [kɔ́ınıdʒ] N acuñación f (also of words)
coincide [koınsáıd] VI coincidir
coincidence [koínsıDəns] N coincidencia f, casualidad f
coitus [kóıDəs] N coito m
coke [kok] N (coal) cok m, coque m; (cocaine) fam coca f
cola [kólə] N gaseosa f
colander [kálændɚ] N colador m
cold [koɫd] ADJ frío; — **cream** cold cream m; — **cuts** fiambres m pl; — **fish** fam témpano m; — **snap** ola de frío f; — **sore** herpes m sg; — **war** guerra fría f; **to be** — tener frío; **to be out** — quedar seco; **it is — today** hace frío hoy; **he gave me the — shoulder** me hizo el vacío; **he quit — turkey** dejó de un día para otro; **he got — feet** se acobardó; N frío m; (illness) resfrío m, resfriado m, catarro m; **to catch a —** resfriarse
coldness [kóɫdnıs] N frialdad f
colic [kálık] N cólico m

colicky [kálıki] ADJ que sufre de cólico

coliseum [kɑlɪsíəm] N coliseo m

collaborate [kəlǽbəret] VI colaborar

collaboration [kəlæbəréʃən] N colaboración f

collaborator [kəlǽbəreDə] N colaborador -ora mf

collage [kəláʒ] N collage m

collagen [kúlədʒən] N colágeno m

collapse [kəlǽps] VI (fold into sections) plegarse; (cave in) hundirse, derrumbarse; (fail) fracasar; (faint) desmayarse; (empty of air, decline in value) colapsar[se]; N (falling in) derrumbe m, derrumbamiento m, desplome m; (breakdown) colapso m

collar [kúlə] N (for restraining dogs, necklace) collar m; (of a shirt) cuello m; **—bone** clavícula f; VT acollarar; (grab by the neck) agarrar por el cuello; **I was —ed by the boss** el jefe me agarró de charla

collate [kólet] VT (put in order) colacionar; (compare) cotejar

collateral [kəlǽDəəl] ADJ (on the side) colateral; (auxiliary) subsidiario; N garantía subsidiaria f; **— damage** daño colateral m

colleague [kálig] N colega mf

collect [kəlékt] VT (gather) recoger; (build a collection) coleccionar; (receive taxes) recaudar; VI/VT (receive payment) cobrar, percibir; (assemble) reunir[se]; (accumulate) acumular[se]; **to — oneself** calmarse; N — **call** llamada de cobro revertido f, llamada por/a cobrar f; **— on delivery** pago contra reembolso m

collection [kəlékʃən] N (set of collectibles, clothes) colección f; (for charity) colecta f; (of taxes) recaudación f, cobranza f, cobro m; (of data, fruit) recolección f; (of texts) recopilación f; (of water) captación f

collective [kəléktɪv] ADJ colectivo; — **bargaining** convenio colectivo m; N colectivo m, colectividad f

collector [kəléktə] N (of taxes) recaudador -ora mf; (of collectibles) coleccionista mf; (of other things) colector -ora mf

college [kálıdʒ] N (institution) universidad f; (university division) facultad f; (association) colegio m; **let's give it the old — try** esforcémonos al máximo

collegial [kəlídʒəl] ADJ cooperador

collegiate [kəlídʒɪt] ADJ universitario

collide [kəláɪd] VI/VT chocar

collie [káli] N collie m

collision [kəlíʒən] N colisión f, choque m

colloid [kálɔɪd] N coloide m

colloquial [kəlókwiəl] ADJ coloquial; — **expression** frase familiar f

colloquium [kəlókwiəm] N coloquio m, jornada f

collusion [kəlúʒən] N confabulación f

cologne [kəlón] N colonia f

Colombia [kəlámbiə] N Colombia f

Colombian [kəlámbiən] ADJ & N colombiano -na mf

colon¹ [kólən] N (punctuation) dos puntos m pl; (bowels) colon m

colon² [kəlón] (currency of El Salvador and Costa Rica) colón m

colonel [kɝnl] N coronel m

colonial [kəlóniəl] ADJ colonial

colonist [kálənɪst] N (settler) colono m; (colonizer) colonizador -ra mf

colonization [kalənɪzéʃən] N colonización f

colonize [kálənaɪz] VT colonizar

colonoscopy [kolənáskəpi] N colonoscopia f

colony [káləni] N colonia f

color [kálə] N color m; (colorfulness) colorido m; **— blindness** ceguera cromática f; **— monitor** monitor [a] color m; **— scanner** escáner color m; **the —s** la bandera; **he showed his true —s** se mostró tal cual era; **persons of —** gente de color f; **a — TV** un televisor en/a color; ADJ **—-blind** daltónico; **—-fast** de colores firmes; VT (give color) colorear; (make colorful) dar colorido; (influence) influir; (blush) ruborizarse

colorectal cancer [kolərɛ́ktl kǽnsə] N cáncer de colon m

colored [kálə-d] ADJ coloreado; (biased) sesgado

colorful [kálə-fəl] ADJ (full of color) colorido; (animals, plants) pintado; (eccentric) pintoresco

coloring [kálə-ɪŋ] N (tone) colorido m; (action) coloración f; (substance) colorante m

colorless [kálə-lɪs] ADJ (without color) incoloro; (bleached) descolorido

colossal [kəlásəl] ADJ colosal

colostomy [kəlástəmi] N colostomía f

colt [kolt] N potro m

column [káləm] N columna f

columnist [káləmnɪst] N columnista mf

coma [kómə] N coma m

comatose [kómətos] ADJ comatoso

comb [kom] N (for hair) peine m; (of a rooster) cresta f; (for wool) carda f; (for horses) almohaza f; (of honey) panal m; VT (hair) peinar; (wool) cardar; (search an area) peinar, batir; **to — one's hair** peinarse

combat¹ [kámbæt] N combate m

combat² [kəmbǽt] VI/VT combatir

combatant [kəmbǽtn̩t] ADJ & N combatiente mf

combative [kəmbǽDɪv] ADJ combativo

combination [kambənéʃən] N combinación f; — **lock** cerradura de combinación f

combine¹ [kəmbáın] VI/VT combinar[se]

combine² [kámbaın] N cosechadora f

combo [kámbo] N combo m

combustible [kəmbástəbəl] ADJ & N combustible m

combustion [kəmbástʃən] N combustión f

come [kʌm] VI venir; **an idea came to me** se me ocurrió una idea; **Christmas is coming** llega la Navidad; **milk —s from cows** la leche se saca de las vacas; **no harm will — to you** no te va a pasar nada; **the dress —s to her knees** el vestido le llega a las rodillas; **to — about** suceder; **to — across** (find) encontrar; (make an impression) parecer; **to — along** (accompany) acompañar; (appear) surgir; **how's your paper coming along?** ¿cómo va tu trabajo? **to — again** volver, volver a venir; **to — back** volver; **to make a —back** resurgir; (in sports) recuperarse; **to — down with a cold** cogerse un resfriado; **to — downstairs** bajar; **to — from** ser de; **to — in** entrar; **to — out** salir; **to — over** venir para acá; **to — to** volver en sí; **to — together** (meet) juntarse, unirse; (reach agreement) ponerse de acuerdo; **to — up** subir; **your name came up** tu nombre vino a colación; **to — up short** quedarse corto; N **—back** (reply) réplica f; (in sports) remontada f, recuperación f

comedian [kəmíðian] N cómico -ca mf, comediante mf

comedy [kámədi] N (genre) comedia f; (profession) humorismo m

comet [kámɪt] N cometa m

comfort [kámfɚt] VT reconfortar; N (feeling of ease) comodidad f, confort m, holgura f; (solace) consuelo m

comfortable [kámfɚɖəbəl] ADJ cómodo, confortable; **— life** vida holgada/desahogada f

comforter [kámfɚɖɚ] N edredón m

comic [kámɪk] ADJ cómico, chistoso, gracioso; **— book** revista de historietas f, cómic m; **—s** tiras cómicas f pl, historietas f pl; **— strip** tira cómica f

comical [kámɪkəl] ADJ cómico, gracioso

coming [kámɪŋ] N venida f; **— of Christ** advenimiento de Cristo m; **— from** proveniente de, originario de; **—s and goings** idas y venidas f pl; ADJ que viene, próximo

comma [kámə] N coma f

command [kəmǽnd] VT (order) mandar; (have authority over) comandar; **to — respect** inspirar respeto, imponerse; N (order) mandato m, orden f; (post) comandancia f; (dominance) dominio m; (on a computer) comando m; **— key** tecla de comando f; **he has a good — of English** domina bien el inglés; **to be in — of** estar al mando de; **to be under the — of** estar al mando de; **at your — a** sus órdenes

commandeer [kamǝndír] VT apoderarse de; (for the military) requisar

commander [kǝmǽndɚ] N (leader) jefe -fa mf;

(army officer) comandante mf; (navy officer) capitán -ana de fragata mf; **— in chief** comandante en jefe mf

commandment [kǝmǽndmǝnt] N mandamiento m

commemorate [kǝmémǝret] VT conmemorar

commemoration [kǝmemǝréʃǝn] N conmemoración f

commence [kǝméns] VI/VT comenzar, principiar

commencement [kǝménsmǝnt] N (beginning) comienzo m; (graduation) graduación f, colación f

commend [kǝménd] VT (praise) alabar; (entrust) encomendar

commendation [kamǝndéʃǝn] N (praise) alabanza f; (mention) mención de honor f

commensurate [kǝménsɚɪt] ADJ proporcional, acorde

comment [kámɛnt] N comentario m; **no —** sin comentarios; VI/VT comentar

commentary [kámɛnteri] N comentario m

commentator [kámǝnteɖɚ] N (person who comments) comentador -ra mf; (talking head) comentarista mf

commerce [kámɚs] N comercio m

commercial [kǝmɚ́ʃǝl] ADJ comercial; N (on radio or television) anuncio m

commercialize [kǝmɚ́ʃǝlaɪz] VT comercializar

commiserate [kǝmízɚet] VI/VT compadecerse de

commiseration [kǝmɪzɚéʃǝn] N conmiseración f

commissary [kámɪseri] N economato m

commission [kǝmíʃǝn] N (act, committee, payment) comisión f; (of a broker) corretaje m; (charge) encargo m; (mission) misión f; (title) nombramiento m; **to be in —** estar en servicio; **to be out of —** estar fuera de servicio; **to put out of —** (object) inutilizar; (person) retirar de servicio; VT (authorize) comisionar; (order) encargar; (appoint) nombrar; (get ready) poner en servicio; **—ed officer** oficial m

commissioner [kǝmíʃǝnɚ] N comisario -ria mf

commit [kǝmít] VT (perpetrate) cometer; (entrust) encargar; (direct) destinar; **to — an error** cometer un error; **to — a foul** cometer/hacer falta; **to — oneself to** comprometerse a/con; **to — to an asylum** internar; **to — to memory** aprender de memoria

commitment [kǝmítmǝnt] N compromiso m

committed [kǝmíɖɪd] ADJ (to a cause) comprometido

committee [kǝmíɖi] N comité m, comisión f

commode [kǝmód] N wáter m, inodoro m

commodity [kǝmáɖɪti] N (product) mercancía f, artículo m, producto m; (raw material) materia prima *f*

common [kámən] ADJ (shared, frequent) común; (general) general; (vulgar) ordinario; (unremarkable) simple; **— cold** resfriado *m*; **— denominator** denominador común *m*; **— law** derecho consuetudinario *m*; **— sense** sentido común *m*, sensatez *f*; **— soldier** soldado raso *m*; **— stock** acciones ordinarias *f pl*; **—wealth** (state) estado *m*; (republic) república *f*; ADJ **—place** trivial; N **—s** (land) ejido *m*

commotion [kəmóʃən] N conmoción *f*, revuelo *m*

communal [kəmjún] ADJ comunitario

commune[1] [kəmjún] VI (communicate) comunicarse, departir; (take communion) comulgar

commune[2] [kámjun] N comuna *f*

communicable [kəmjúnɪkəbəl] ADJ comunicable; (disease) transmisible

communicate [kəmjúnɪket] VI/VT comunicar[se]; (disease) transmitir[se]

communication [kəmjunɪkéʃən] N comunicación *f*

communicative [kəmjúnɪkəDɪv] ADJ comunicativo

communion [kəmjúnjən] N comunión *f*

communiqué [kəmjunɪké] N comunicado *m*

communism [kámjənɪzəm] N comunismo *m*

communist [kámjənɪst] N & ADJ comunista *mf*

community [kəmjúnɪDɪ] N comunidad *f*, colectividad *f*; **— spirit** espíritu comunitario *m*

commute [kəmjút] VT (reduce a sentence) conmutar; VI viajar diariamente al trabajo

commuter [kəmjúbə-] N persona que viaja diariamente al trabajo *f*

Comoros [káməroz] N Comoras *f pl*

compact[1] [kámpækt, kəmpǽkt] ADJ compacto; (dense) tupido, apretado; (concise) conciso; (make denser) tupir

compact[2] [kámpækt] N (agreement) pacto *m*; (case for powder) polvera *f*; **— disk** disco compacto *m*; VT compactar

compactness [kɑmpǽktnɪs] N densidad *f*; (conciseness) concisión *f*

companion [kəmpǽnjən] N (comrade, partner) compañero -ra *mf*; (caregiver) acompañante *mf*

companionship [kəmpǽnjənʃɪp] N compañía *f*

company [kámpəni] N compañía *f*; **to keep — with** codearse con, frecuentar

comparable [kámpə-bəl] ADJ comparable

comparative [kəmpǽrəDɪv] ADJ comparativo

compare [kəmpér] VI/VT comparar[se]; **beyond —** incomparable, sin parangón

comparison [kəmpǽrɪsən] N comparación *f*; **in — with** comparado con

compartment [kəmpártmənt] N

compartimiento *m*

compass [kámpəs] N (for drawing) compás *m*; (for directions) brújula *f*

compassion [kəmpǽʃən] N compasión *f*

compassionate [kəmpǽʃənɪt] ADJ compasivo

compatibility [kəmpæDəbílɪDi] N compatibilidad *f*

compatible [kəmpǽDəbəl] ADJ compatible (also of computers)

compatriot [kəmpétriət] N compatriota *mf*

compel [kəmpɛ́l] VT (force) obligar; (demand) exigir

compelling [kəmpɛ́lɪŋ] ADJ (argument) convincente; (story) emocionante

compensate [kámpənset] VT (make up for) compensar, resarcir; (pay) remunerar

compensation [kampənséʃən] N (making up for) compensación *f*; (remuneration) remuneración *f*

compete [kəmpít] VI/VT competir

competence [kámpɪDəns] N competencia *f*

competent [kámpɪDənt] ADJ competente

competition [kampɪtíʃən] N competencia *f*; (sports match) competición *f*, contienda *f*

competitive [kəmpɛ́DIDIV] ADJ competitivo; **— examination** *Sp* oposición *f*; *Am* concurso *m*; **— sports** deportes de competición *m pl*

competitiveness [kəmpɛ́DITIVNIs] N competitividad *f*

competitor [kəmpɛ́DIDə] N (business) competidor -ora *mf*; (sports) atleta *mf*

compilation [kampɪléʃən] N recopilación *f*

compile [kəmpáɪl] VT recopilar, compilar

compiler [kəmpáɪlə] N compilador *m*; **— language** lenguaje compilador *m*

complacency [kəmplésənsi] N confianza infundada *f*

complacent [kəmplésənt] ADJ confiado

complain [kəmplén] VI quejarse

complainant [kəmplénənt] ADJ & N recurrente *mf*

complaint [kəmplént] N queja *f*; (official) reclamo *m*; (civil charge) demanda *f*; (ailment) dolencia *f*

complement[1] [kámpləmənt] N complemento *m*; (of staff) dotación *f*

complement[2] [kámpləmɛnt] VT complementar

complementary [kamplǝméntri] ADJ complementario

complete [kəmplít] ADJ completo, pleno; **a — stranger** un perfecto desconocido; VT completar; **to — a pass** completar un pase

completion [kəmplíʃən] N finalización *f*, terminación *f*; **she brought the project to —** completó el proyecto

complex[1] [kəmplɛ́ks] ADJ complejo

complex[2] [kámpleks] N complejo *m*

complexion [kəmplɛ́kʃən] N (skin) cutis *m*; (color) tez *f*; (perspective) cariz *m*

complexity [kəmpléksɪDi] N complejidad f
compliance [kəmpláɪəns] N (obedience)
conformidad f, acatamiento m; (polite
reverence) pleitesía f; **in — with** en
conformidad con
complicate [kámplɪket] VT complicar
complicated [kámplɪkeDɪd] ADJ complicado
complication [kamplɪkéʃən] N complicación f
complicity [kəmplísɪDi] N complicidad f
compliment [kámpləmənt] N cumplido, halago
m; (on looks) piropo m; (from a suitor)
galantería f; **to pay someone a —** hacerle un
cumplido a alguien; **to send one's —s** enviar
saludos; VI/VT elogiar, halagar
comply [kəmpláɪ] VI obedecer; **to — with**
cumplir con, acatar
component [kəmpónənt] ADJ & N componente m
compose [kəmpóz] VI/VT componer; **to —
oneself** sosegarse
composed [kəmpózd] ADJ sosegado; **to be — of**
estar compuesto de, componerse de, constar
de
composer [kəmpózɚ] N compositor -ra mf
composite [kəmpázɪt] ADJ compuesto; N
amalgama f
composition [kampəzíʃən] N (make-up, musical
piece) composición f; (aggregate material)
compuesto m; (school essay) composición f,
redacción f
composure [kəmpóʒɚ] N compostura f
compound[1] [kámpaʊnd] ADJ & N compuesto m;
— fracture fractura expuesta f; **— interest**
interés compuesto m
compound[2] [kampáʊnd] VT (combine)
combinar; (worsen) empeorar
comprehend [kamprɪhénd] VT comprender
comprehensible [kamprɪhénsəbəl] ADJ
comprensible
comprehension [kamprɪhénʃən] N
comprensión f
comprehensive [kamprɪhénsɪv] ADJ
exhaustivo; **— insurance** seguro contra
todo riesgo m
compress[1] [kəmprés] VT comprimir; **—ed disk**
disco comprimido m; **—ed file** archivo
comprimido m
compress[2] [kámpres] N compresa f
compression [kəmpréʃən] N compresión f
comprise [kəmpráɪz] VT comprender, incluir;
to be —d of comprender, incluir
compromise [kámprəmaɪz] N (arrangement)
arreglo por concesiones mutuas m,
compromiso m; (intermediate thing) cruce m,
término medio m; VI/VT (make agreement)
transigir; Am transar; (jeopardize)
comprometer
comptroller [kəntrólɚ] N controlador -ra mf;
Am contralor -ora mf
compulsion [kəmpálʃən] N (impulse)

compulsión f, coacción f; (coercion) coerción f
compulsive [kəmpálsɪv] ADJ compulsivo
compulsory [kəmpálsəri] ADJ obligatorio,
obligado
computation [kampjutéʃən] N cómputo m,
cálculo m
compute [kəmpjút] VI/VT computar, calcular
computer [kəmpjúDɚ] N Am computadora f; Sp
ordenador m; **— engineer** ingeniero -ra en
computación mf, ingeniero -ra informático
-ca mf; **— graphics** gráficos por
computadora/ordenador m pl; **— literacy**
(process) alfabetización digital f; (result)
alfabetismo digital m; **— science** informática
f; **— virus** virus de computadora/
ordenador m
computerization [kəmpjuDɚɪzéʃən] N Sp
ordenación f, Am computarización f
computerize [kəmpjúDɚaɪz] VI/VT
informatizar, computarizar
computing [kəmpjúDɪŋ] N informática f; ADJ
informático
comrade [kámræd] N camarada mf
concave [kánkev] ADJ cóncavo
conceal [kənsíl] VT encubrir, ocultar, disimular
concealment [kənsílmənt] N encubrimiento m,
disimulo m
concede [kənsíd] VI/VT (recognize) conceder,
reconocer; (allow) conceder
conceit [kənsít] N (vanity) vanidad f; (literary
device) concepto m
conceited [kənsíDɪd] ADJ engreído, presumido
conceivable [kənsívəbəl] ADJ imaginable,
concebible
conceive [kənsív] VI/VT concebir; (a plan)
concebir, idear
concentrate [kánsəntret] VI/VT concentrar[se]
concentration [kansəntréʃən] N concentración
f; **— camp** campo de concentración m
concept [kánsept] N concepto m
conception [kənsépʃən] N concepción f
conceptual [kənséptʃuəl] ADJ conceptual
concern [kənsɚn] VT (be of interest) concernir,
atañer; (worry) preocupar; **to — oneself
with** ocuparse de; **to whom it may — a**
quien corresponda; N (interest) interés m;
(matter) asunto m; (worry) preocupación f;
(company) compañía f; **to be of no —** no
tener consecuencia
concerned [kənsɚnd] ADJ (involved)
involucrado; (anxious) preocupado; **as far as
I am —** en lo que a mí respecta; **to be —
about** preocuparse por
concerning [kənsɚnɪŋ] PREP tocante a,
respecto a
concert[1] [kánsɚt] N concierto m
concert[2] [kənsɚt] VT concertar
concession [kənséʃən] N concesión f
conciliate [kənsíliet] VI/VT (make compatible)

conciliar; (appease) aplacar
conciliation [kənsɪliéʃən] N conciliación f
concise [kənsáɪs] ADJ conciso, sucinto
conciseness [kənsáɪsnɪs] N concisión f
conclude [kənklúd] VI/VT concluir
conclusion [kənklúʒən] N conclusión f
conclusive [kənklúsɪv] ADJ concluyente
concoct [kənkákt] VT (contrive) fabricar, urdir; (prepare by cooking) preparar
concoction [kənkákʃən] N mejunje m
concord [kánkɔrd] N (peace) concordia f; (agreement) convenio m, acuerdo m
concrete¹ [kankrít] ADJ concreto
concrete² [kánkrit] N hormigón m; (made of concrete) de hormigón
concubine [káŋkjəbaɪn] N concubina f
concur [kənkɔ̀] VI estar de acuerdo
concussion [kənkáʃən] N (brain injury) conmoción cerebral f; (shock) concusión f
condemn [kəndém] VT condenar; (acquire public ownership) expropiar; (declare unsafe) declarar ruinoso
condemnation [kandemnéʃən] N condenación f, condena f
condensation [kandenséʃən] N condensación f; (of a book) compendio m
condense [kəndéns] VI/VT condensar[se]
condescend [kandəsénd] VI condescender a
condescension [kandəsénʃən] N condescendencia f
condiment [kándəmənt] N condimento m, aliño m
condition [kəndíʃən] N condición f; **he's got a heart —** sufre del corazón, tiene una afección cardíaca; **he's in good physical —** está en buen estado físico; **the patient is in critical —** el paciente está en estado crítico; **on — that** a condición de que; VT (restrict on a condition, establish a conditioned response) condicionar; (accustom oneself) acostumbrarse
conditional [kəndíʃənl] ADJ & N condicional m
conditioning [kəndíʃənɪŋ] N condicionamiento m
condolences [kəndólənsɪz] N pésame m, condolencias f; **to express one's —** dar las condolencias
condominium [kandəmíniəm] N condominio m
condone [kəndón] VT tolerar
conducive [kəndúsɪv] ADJ conducente
conduct¹ [kándʌkt] N conducta f, comportamiento m
conduct² [kəndʌkt] VI/VT (behave) conducirse, comportarse; (carry out) llevar a cabo; (direct, lead) dirigir; (serve as channel for) conducir
conduction [kəndákʃən] N conducción f
conductor [kəndáktə] N (substance that

conducts) conductor m; (of an orchestra) director -ora mf; (of a train) revisor -ora mf
conduit [kánduɪt] N conducto m
cone [kon] N cono m; (container) cucurucho m
confection [kənfékʃən] N (of clothes) confección f; (of candy) confitura f
confectionery [kənfékʃəneri] N confitería f; (shop) dulcería f; (candies) dulces m pl
confederacy [kənfɛ́dəəsi] N confederación f
confederate¹ [kənfɛ́dəɪt] ADJ & N confederado -da mf
confederate² [kənfɛ́dəret] VI/VT confederar[se]
confederation [kənfɛdəréʃən] N confederación f
confer [kənfɔ̀] VT (grant) conferir, atribuir; (consult) consultar; (negotiate) conferenciar
conference [kánfəəns] N (consultation) consulta f; (professional meeting) congreso m; (legislative) asamblea general f; (sports league) liga f; **— call** llamada en conferencia f
confess [kənfés] VI/VT confesar[se]
confession [kənféʃən] N confesión f
confessional [kənféʃənl] N confesionario m
confessor [kənfésə] N confesor m
confidant [kánfɪdant] N confidente mf
confide [kənfáɪd] VI/VT (entrust) confiar; VI (tell secrets to) hacer confidencias a
confidence [kánfɪdəns] N confianza f; (certainty) seguridad f; (secret communication) confidencia f; **— game** timo m; **— man** timador m, embaucador m; **in —** en confianza
confident [kánfɪdənt] ADJ seguro; **he's a — person** tiene mucha confianza
confidential [kanfɪdénʃəl] ADJ confidencial; (secretary, etc.) de confianza
configuration [kanfɪgjəréʃən] N configuración f (also for computers)
configure [kənfígjə] VT configurar
confine¹ [kənfáɪn] VT confinar, recluir; **to — oneself to** limitarse a
confine² [kánfaɪn] N confín m
confinement [kənfáɪnmənt] N confinamiento m
confirm [kənfɔ̀m] VT confirmar
confirmation [kanfəméʃən] N confirmación f
confiscate [kánfɪsket] VT confiscar
confiscation [kanfɪskéʃən] N confiscación f
conflagration [kanfləgréʃən] N incendio m
conflict¹ [kánflɪkt] N conflicto m, contienda f; **— of interest** conflicto de intereses m
conflict² [kənflíkt] VI oponerse
confluence [kánfluəns] N confluencia f
conform [kənfɔ̀rm] VI/VT conformar[se]
conformity [kənfɔ̀rmɪdi] N (agreement) conformidad f; (passive acquiescence) conformismo m
confound [kənfáʊnd] VT (bewilder) desconcertar; (confuse) confundir; **— it!** fam ¡caramba!
confront [kənfránt] VT (set face to face, fight)

confrontar; (face up to) enfrentarse a

confrontation [kʌnfrəntéʃən] N confrontación f, enfrentamiento m

confuse [kənfjúz] VT confundir

confused [kənfjúzd] ADJ (person) confundido; (situation) confuso; **to become —** confundirse

confusing [kənfjúzɪŋ] ADJ confuso

confusion [kənfjúʒən] N confusión f

congeal [kəndʒíł] VI/VT cuajar[se]

congenial [kəndʒínjəł] ADJ agradable, simpático

congenital [kəndʒénɪdł] ADJ congénito

congestion [kəndʒéstʃən] N congestión f

congestive heart failure [kəndʒéstɪv hárt feljə] ADJ insuficiencia cardíaca congestiva f

conglomeration [kʌnglaməréʃən] N (unit) conglomeración f; (mass) conglomerado m

Congo [káŋgo] N Congo m

Congolese [kaŋgəlíz] ADJ & N congoleño -ña mf

congratulate [kəngrǽtʃəlet] VT felicitar

congratulation [kəngrætʃəléʃən] N felicitación f, parabién m; **—s!** ¡enhorabuena! ¡albricias!

congregate [káŋgrɪget] VI/VT congregar[se]

congregation [kaŋgrɪgéʃən] N (worshipers) fieles m pl, feligreses m pl; (act of congregating, committee of cardinals) congregación f

congress [káŋgrɪs] N (professional) congreso m; (political) asamblea legislativa f; (US) congreso m; **—man** (US) congresista m; **—woman** (US) congresista f

congressional [kəngréʃənł] ADJ congresual

congruence [kəngrúəns] N congruencia f

conifer [kánəfə] N conífera f

conjecture [kəndʒéktʃə] N conjetura f; VI/VT conjeturar

conjugal [kándʒəgəł] ADJ conyugal

conjugate [kándʒəget] VI/VT conjugar[se]

conjugation [kandʒəgéʃən] N conjugación f

conjunction [kəndʒʌ́ŋkʃən] N conjunción f

conjunctivitis [kəndʒʌŋktəváɪDɪs] N conjuntivitis f

conjure [kándʒə] VT invocar; **to — up** evocar; VI hacer hechizos

connect [kənékt] VI/VT conectar[se], enlazar[se]; (buildings, callers) comunicar[se]; (concepts) relacionar[se]; (pipes) acoplar[se]; **—ing rod** biela f

connection [kənékʃən] N (act of connecting) conexión f, vinculación f; (of telephone) comunicación f, enganche m; (of concepts) relación f; (of pipes) acople m; (affinity) afinidad f; (supplier) contacto m; **—s** contactos m pl, enchufe m

connectivity [kanɛktívɪDi] N conectividad f

connive [kənáɪv] VI conspirar

connoisseur [kanəsúr] N conocedor -ora f

connotation [kanətéʃən] N connotación f

conquer [káŋkə] VT (win) conquistar; (overcome) vencer

conqueror [káŋkərə] N conquistador -ora mf; (one who overcomes) vencedor -ora mf

conquest [káŋkwest] N conquista f

conscience [kánʃəns] N conciencia f

conscientious [kanʃiéntʃəs] ADJ concienzudo

conscious [kánʃəs] ADJ consciente

consciousness [kánʃəsnɪs] N conciencia f; **to lose —** perder el conocimiento

conscript¹ [kənskrípt] VT reclutar

conscript² [kánskrɪpt] N recluta mf

conscription [kənskrípʃən] N reclutamiento m

consecrate [kánsɪkret] VT consagrar

consecration [kansɪkréʃən] N consagración f

consecutive [kənsékjəDɪv] ADJ consecutivo

consensus [kənsénsəs] N consenso m

consent [kənsént] N consentimiento m; VI consentir

consequence [kánsɪkwens] N consecuencia f; (negative) secuela f

consequent [kánsɪkwənt] ADJ consiguiente, resultante; N (in mathematics) consecuente m; (in logic) consiguiente m

consequently [kánsɪkwəntli] ADV por consiguiente, en consecuencia

conservation [kansə-véʃən] N conservación f, presérvación f

conservatism [kənsə́-vətɪzəm] N conservadurismo m

conservative [kənsə́-vəDɪv] ADJ & N conservador -ora mf

conservatory [kənsə́-vətɔri] N conservatorio m

conserve¹ [kənsə́-v] VT conservar, preservar

conserve² [kánsə-v] N confitura m

consider [kənsídə] VT considerar

considerable [kənsídə-əbəł] ADJ considerable

considerate [kənsídə-ɪt] ADJ considerado

consideration [kənsɪdəréʃən] N consideración f; (respect) miramiento m; (payment) remuneración f

considering [kənsídə-ɪŋ] PREP en vista de, teniendo en cuenta; **she cooks well, —** para ser ella, cocina bien

consign [kənsáɪn] VT consignar

consignee [kansaɪní] N consignatario -ria mf

consignment [kənsáɪnmənt] N consignación f; **on —** a/en consignación

consist [kənsíst] VI consistir [en]

consistency [kənsístənsi] N (adherence to principles) coherencia f, consecuencia f; (density) consistencia f

consistent [kənsístənt] ADJ (adherent to principles) consecuente, coherente; (cohering) consistente

consolation [kansəléʃən] N consuelo m, consolación f

console¹ [kənsół] VT consolar

console² [kánsoł] N consola f

consolidate [kənsálɪdet] VI/VT consolidar[se]

consolidation [kənsɑlɪdéʃən] N consolidación f
consonant [kɑ́nsənənt] N consonante f; ADJ consonante, conforme
consort¹ [kənsɔ́rt] VI **to — with** asociarse con
consort² [kɑ́nsɔrt] N consorte mf
consortium [kənsɔ́rʃiəm] N consorcio m
conspicuous [kənspíkjuəs] ADJ evidente
conspiracy [kənspírəsi] N conspiración f, conjura f
conspirator [kənspírədə-] N conspirador -ora mf, conjurado -da mf
conspire [kənspáɪr] VI conspirar, conjurar
constable [kɑ́nstəbəl] N oficial de policía mf; (keeper of fortress) condestable m
constancy [kɑ́nstənsi] N constancia f
constant [kɑ́nstənt] ADJ & N constante f
constellation [kɑnstəléʃən] N constelación f
consternation [kɑnstə-néʃən] N consternación f
constipate [kɑ́nstəpet] VT estreñir
constipated [kɑ́nstəpeDɪd] ADJ estreñido
constipation [kɑnstəpéʃən] N estreñimiento m
constituent [kənstítʃuənt] ADJ componente, constitutivo; N (component) componente m; (voter) votante mf; (part of a sentence) constituyente m
constitute [kɑ́nstɪtut] VT constituir
constitution [kɑnstɪtúʃən] N constitución f
constitutional [kɑnstɪtúʃən] ADJ constitucional; N caminata f
constrain [kənstrén] VT constreñir, restringir
constraint [kənstrént] N constreñimiento m
constrict [kənstríkt] VT constreñir
constriction [kənstríkʃən] N (action) constricción f; (place) estrechamiento m
construct¹ [kənstrákt] VT construir
construct² [kɑ́nstrakt] N invención f
construction [kənstrákʃən] N construcción f; — **company** constructora f
constructive [kənstráktɪv] ADJ constructivo
construe [kənstrú] VT interpretar
consul [kɑ́nsəl] N cónsul mf
consulate [kɑ́nsəlɪt] N consulado m
consult [kənsʌ́lt] VI/VT consultar; VI (serve as a consultant) asesorar
consultant [kənsʌ́ltənt] N asesor -ora mf
consultation [kɑnsəltéʃən] N consulta f
consultative [kənsʌ́ltəDɪv] ADJ consultivo
consulting [kənsʌ́ltɪŋ] N asesoramiento m, consultoría f; ADJ consultor; — **firm** firma consultora f
consumable [kənsúməbəl] ADJ — **goods** bienes consumibles m pl
consume [kənsúm] VI/VT consumir
consumer [kənsúmə-] N consumidor -ora mf; — **confidence index** índice de confianza del consumidor m; — **credit** crédito al consumidor m; — **protection** protección al consumidor f
consumerism [kənsúmərɪzəm] N

consumismo m
consuming [kənsúmɪŋ] ADJ (need) imperioso; (drive) abrasador
consummate¹ [kɑ́nsəmet] VT consumar
consummate² [kɑ́nsəmɪt] ADJ consumado
consumption [kənsʌ́mpʃən] N (using up) consumo m; (wasting of the body) consunción f; (tuberculosis) tisis f
consumptive [kənsʌ́mptɪv] ADJ tísico
contact [kɑ́ntækt] N contacto m; — **lens** lente de contacto mf; VI/VT (touch) tocar; (communicate with) contactar
contagion [kəntédʒən] N (spread) contagio m; (disease spread) enfermedad contagiosa f
contagious [kəntédʒəs] ADJ contagioso
contain [kəntén] VI/VT contener
container [kənténə-] N recipiente m; (on a ship) contenedor m; —**ship** buque portacontenedores m
containerize [kənténəraɪz] VT contenedorizar
containment [kənténmənt] N contención f
contaminate [kəntǽmənet] VT contaminar
contamination [kəntæmənéʃən] N contaminación f
contemplate [kɑ́ntəmplet] VT (observe) contemplar; (consider) considerar
contemplation [kɑntəmpléʃən] N (observation) contemplación f; (consideration) consideración f
contemporary [kəntémpəreri] ADJ contemporáneo
contempt [kəntémpt] N desprecio m, menosprecio m; — **of court** desacato al tribunal m
contemptible [kəntémptəbəl] ADJ despreciable, rastrero
contemptuous [kəntémptʃuəs] ADJ desdeñoso
contend [kənténd] VI (struggle) contender, lidiar; (argue) disputar; VT afirmar
content¹ [kəntént] ADJ (happy) contento; (resigned) conforme; N **to one's heart's** — a discreción
content², **contents** [kɑ́ntent[s]] N contenido m
contented [kənténtɪd] ADJ contento, satisfecho
contention [kənténʃən] N (opinion) opinión f; **in** — (disputed) en discusión; (still eligible) con posibilidades
contentious [kənténʃəs] ADJ conflictivo
contentment [kənténtmənt] N contento m
contest¹ [kɑ́ntest] N (competition) concurso m, certamen m; (struggle) contienda f
contest² [kəntést] VT (compete) contender; (dispute) disputar; (challenge) impugnar
contestant [kəntéstənt] N concursante mf, participante mf
context [kɑ́ntɛkst] N contexto m
contiguous [kəntígjuəs] ADJ contiguo, pegado
continent [kɑ́ntənənt] N (landmass) continente m; ADJ (sexually abstinent) continente; (of

bodily functions) capaz de controlar los esfínteres
continental [kɑntɪnéntl] ADJ continental
contingency [kəntíndʒənsi] N contingencia *f*; — **fund** fondo de contingencia *m*; — **planning** planificación para contingencias *f*
contingent [kəntíndʒənt] ADJ & N contingente *m*
continual [kəntínjuəl] ADJ continuo
continuance [kəntínjuəns] N continuación *f*; (delay) aplazamiento *m*
continuation [kəntɪnjuéʃən] N continuación *f*
continue [kəntínju] VI/VT continuar
continuing [kəntínjuɪŋ] ADJ continuado; — **education** educación para adultos *f*
continuity [kɑntɪnúɪdi] N continuidad *f*
continuous [kəntínjuəs] ADJ (uninterrupted in time) continuo; (uninterrupted in space) ininterrumpido
contortion [kəntɔ́rʃən] N contorsión *f*
contour [kántur] N contorno *m*
contra account [kántrə əkaʊnt] N cuenta de contrapartida *f*
contraband [kántrəbænd] N contrabando *m*
contraception [kɑntrəsépʃən] N anticoncepción *f*
contraceptive [kɑntrəséptɪv] ADJ & N anticonceptivo *m*
contract¹ [kántrækt] N contrato *m*; — **killer** asesino -na a sueldo *mf*; **by —** por contrato
contract² [kəntrǽkt] VI/VT contraer[se]; (assign by contract) contratar; **to — out** subcontratar
contraction [kəntrǽkʃən] N contracción *f*; (in childbirth) contracción *f*, pujo *m*
contractor [kántræktə] N contratista *mf*
contractual agreement [kəntrǽktʃuəlǝgrímənt] N acuerdo contractual *m*
contradict [kɑntrədíkt] VI/VT contradecir
contradiction [kɑntrədíkʃən] N contradicción *f*
contradictory [kɑntrədíktəri] ADJ contradictorio
contraption [kəntrǽpʃən] N chisme *m*, cosa *m*
contrary [kántreri] ADJ contrario, opuesto; (obstinate) testarudo; N lo contrario; **on the —** al contrario
contrast¹ [kántræst] N contraste *m*
contrast² [kəntrǽst] VI/VT contrastar
contravene [kɑntrəvín] VT contravenir
contribute [kəntríbjut] VI contribuir; (to a newspaper) colaborar; VT contribuir con, aportar
contribution [kɑntrəbjúʃən] N (donation, article) contribución *f*; (scientific) aporte *m*, aportación *f*
contributor [kəntríbjədə] N colaborador -ra *mf*
contrite [kəntráit] ADJ contrito
contrivance [kəntráivəns] N artefacto *m*
contrive [kəntráiv] VI/VT ingeniar; **he —d to get their money** se las ingenió para sacarles el dinero

contrived [kəntráivd] ADJ artificioso
control [kəntróⱡ] VI/VT controlar; N control *m*; (of a machine) mando *m*; **who's in —?** ¿quién manda? **under —** bajo control; — **freak** mandón -ona *mf*; — **key** tecla de control/ mando *f*; — **panel** panel de control *m*; — **tower** torre de control *f*
controller [kəntrólə] N (comptroller) controlador -ora *mf*; *Am* contralor *m*; (device) regulador *m*
controversial [kɑntrəvə́ʃəl] ADJ controvertido
controversy [kántrəvə·si] N controversia *f*, polémica *f*
contusion [kəntúʒən] N contusión *f*, magulladura *f*
conundrum [kənándrəm] N (riddle) adivinanza *f*, acertijo *m*; (mystery) enigma *m*
convalesce [kɑnvəlés] VI convalecer
convalescence [kɑnvəlésəns] N convalecencia *f*
convalescent [kɑnvəlésənt] ADJ & N convaleciente *mf*
convection [kənvékʃən] N convección *f*
convene [kənvín] VT convocar; VI reunirse
convenience [kənvínjəns] N (practicality) conveniencia *f*; (appliance) comodidad *f*; — **store** autoservicio *m*; **at your —** cuando le venga bien
convenient [kənvínjənt] ADJ conveniente, oportuno; (at hand) accesible
convent [kánvent] N convento *m*
convention [kənvénʃən] N (political assembly) convención *f*; (professional assembly) congreso *m*; (pact) convenio *m*; (international agreement, acceptable usage) convención *f*
conventional [kənvénʃənl] ADJ (not original) convencional; (traditional) clásico; — **loan** préstamo convencional *m*
conventioneer [kənvenʃənír] N congresista *mf*
converge [kənvə́dʒ] VI converger
convergence [kənvə́dʒəns] N convergencia *f*
conversant [kənvə́sənt] ADJ — **with** versado en
conversation [kɑnvə·séʃən] N conversación *f*; — **piece** tema de conversación *m*
converse [kənvə́s] VI conversar
conversion [kənvə́ʒən] N conversión *f*
convert¹ [kənvə́t] VI/VT convertir[se]
convert² [kánvə·t] N converso -sa *mf*
converter [kənvə́də·] N convertidor *m*
convertible [kənvə́dəbəⱡ] ADJ convertible; (car) descapotable; — **assets** activo convertible *m*; N (car) descapotable *m*
convex [kánveks] ADJ convexo
convey [kənvé] VT (carry) llevar; (transfer) transferir; (transmit) transmitir; (communicate) comunicar
conveyance [kənvéəns] N (vehicle) vehículo *m*; (transfer of property) transferencia *f*; (document) escritura de traspaso *f*
conveyer, conveyor [kənvéə·] N transmisor

-ora *mf;* — **belt** cinta transportadora *f*
convict[1] [kánvɪkt] N convicto -ta *mf*
convict[2] [kənvíkt] VI/VT declarar culpable
conviction [kənvíkʃən] N (belief) convicción *f*, convencimiento *m;* (act of convicting) declaración de culpabilidad *f;* (on one's record) condena *f*
convince [kənvíns] VT convencer
convincing [kənvínsɪŋ] ADJ convincente, contundente
convocation [kanvəkéʃən] N (act) convocación *f;* (group of people) asamblea *f*
convoke [kənvók] VT convocar
convoluted [kánvəlúdɪd] ADJ retorcido
convoy [kánvɔɪ] N convoy *m;* VT convoyar
convulse [kənváls] VI/VT convulsionar[se]
convulsion [kənválʃən] N convulsión *f*
coo [ku] VI arrullar; N arrullo *m*
cook [kʊk] N cocinero -ra *mf;* —**book** libro de cocina *m;* VT cocinar, guisar; **to — the books** falsificar los libros de contabilidad; **to — up a plan** urdir un plan; **her —ing is outstanding** cocina muy bien; **now we're —ing!** ahora sí
cookery [kúkəri] N cocina *f*
cookie [kúki] N (sweet food) galletita dulce *f;* (computer record) archivo cookie *m*
cool [kuɫ] ADJ (not hot) fresco; (indifferent) frío, indiferente; (calm) tranquilo; (good) excelente; *Carib* chévere; *RP* macanudo; *Sp* guay; **that's not —** eso no se hace; **—ing-off period** tregua *f;* N (cold) fresco *m;* (composure) tranquilidad *f;* VT (make cooler) enfriar; (air condition) refrigerar; **to — off** (get cold) enfriarse; (get cooler) refrescar[se]; (calm down) calmarse
coolant [kúlənt] N refrigerante *m*
cooler [kúlə-] N (room) cámara frigorífica *f;* (container) nevera portátil *f*
coolness [kúlnɪs] N (cold weather) fresco *m*, frescor *m;* (indifference) frialdad *f*, indiferencia *f*
coon [kun] N (raccoon) mapache *m;* **a —'s age** una eternidad
co-op [kóap] N cooperativa *f*
coop [kup] N jaula *f;* (for chickens) gallinero *m;* VT enjaular; **to — up** encerrar
cooperate [koápəret] VI cooperar
cooperation [koɑpəréʃən] N cooperación *f*
cooperative [koápə-əDɪv] ADJ (helpful) cooperativo; (relative to a cooperative) cooperativista; N cooperativa *f*
coordinate[1] [koórdṇɪt] ADJ coordinado; N coordenada *f;* —**s** (clothes) conjunto *m*
coordinate[2] [koórdṇet] VI/VT coordinar
coordinating [koórdṇeDɪŋ] ADJ coordinador
coordination [koórdṇéʃən] N coordinación *f*
coordinator [koórdṇeDə-] N coordinador -ora *mf*
cop [kap] N *fam* poli *mf*, polizonte *m;* VI **to — out**

zafarse
copayment [kópemənt] N copago *m*
cope [kop] VI **to — with** arreglárselas con; **I cannot — with this** no puedo con esto
copious [kópiəs] ADJ copioso
copper [kápə-] N cobre *m;* (cop) *fam* poli *mf;* ADJ de cobre
copulate [kápjəlet] VI copular
copulation [kapjəléʃən] N copulación *f*
copy [kápi] N (reproduction) copia *f;* (specimen, example) ejemplar *m;* (news story) texto *m;* —**cat** copión -ona *mf;* — **machine** copiadora *f;* — **protection** protección contra copias *f;* —**right** copyright *m*, derechos de autor *m pl;* **this material is —righted** reservados todos los derechos; VT copiar; **to —right** registrar los derechos
coquette [kokét] N coqueta *f*
coral [kórəɫ] N coral *m;* ADJ (related to coral) coralino; (made of coral) de coral; — **reef** arrecife de coral *m*
cord [kɔrd] N (thread) cuerda *f;* (for shoes) cordón *m;* (firewood measure) medida de leña *f;* —**s** pantalones de pana *m pl*
cordial [kórdʒəɫ] ADJ cordial; N licor *m*
cordless [kórdlɪs] ADJ inalámbrico
corduroy [kórdərɔɪ] N pana *f;* —**s** pantalones de pana *m pl*
core [kor] N (of fruit) corazón *m;* (of a problem) meollo *m;* (of a magnet, reactor) núcleo *m;* — **business** negocio principal *m;* — **inflation** inflación básica *f;* VT despepitar
cork [kɔrk] N (woody material) corcho *m;* (stopper, buoy) tapón *m;* —**screw** sacacorchos *m sg*, tirabuzón *m;* — **tree** alcornoque *m;* VT tapar con un corcho
corn [kɔrn] N (plant) maíz *m;* (painful growth) callo *m;* —**bread** pan de maíz *m;* —**cob** mazorca *f; Sp* zuro *m;* — **on the cob** choclo *m; Mex* elote *m;* —**ed beef** corned beef *m;* —**field** maizal *m; Mex* milpa *f;* —**flakes** copos de maíz *m pl;* —**meal** harina de maíz *f;* —**starch** Maicena™ *f*
corner [kórnə-] N (angle) ángulo *m;* (of a space) rincón *m;* (of two streets) esquina *f;* —**back** (football) esquinero *m;* — **kick** (soccer) saque/tiro de esquina *m*, córner *m;* —**stone** piedra angular *f;* — **table** mesa rinconera *f;* VT (trap) arrinconar, acorralar; (monopolize) monopolizar; VI doblar, *Sp* girar; — **the market** acaparar el mercado
cornered [kórnə-d] ADJ (animal) acorralado; (person) arrinconado
cornet [kɔrnét] N corneta *f*
cornice [kórnɪs] N cornisa *f*
corny [kórni] ADJ sensiblero; (joke) viejo
corollary [kórəlɛri] N corolario *m*
coronary [kórənɛri] ADJ coronario; — **bypass** puente cardiopulmonar *m;* — **care unit**

unidad de cuidado coronario *f*; **— failure** insuficiencia coronaria *f*; **— thrombosis** trombosis coronaria *f*

coronation [kɔrənéʃən] N coronación *f*

coroner [kɔ́rənə] N médico -ca forense *mf*

corporal [kɔ́rpəəl] ADJ corporal; N (rank) cabo *m*

corporate [kɔ́rpəɪt] ADJ corporativo; **— backing** patrocinio empresarial *m*; **— officers** ejecutivos -vas de empresa *mf pl*

corporation [kɔrpəréʃən] N sociedad anónima *f*

corps [kor] N cuerpo *m*

corpse [kɔrps] N cadáver *m*

corpulent [kɔ́rpjələnt] ADJ corpulento

corpus [kɔ́rpəs] N corpus *m*

corpuscle [kɔ́rpʌsəl] N corpúsculo *m*; (of blood) glóbulo *m*

corral [kərǽl] N corral *m*; VT acorralar

correct [kərɛ́kt] VT corregir; ADJ correcto; **that is —** es cierto

correction [kərɛ́kʃən] N corrección *f*; (for glasses) graduación *f*

correctness [kərɛ́ktnɪs] N corrección *f*

corrector [kərɛ́ktə] N corrector -ora *mf*

correlate[1] [kɔ́rəlet] VI/VT correlacionar

correlate[2] [kɔ́rəlɪt] N correlato *m*

correlation [kɔrəléʃən] N correlación *f*

correspond [kɔrɪspánd] VI (be in agreement) corresponder, responder; (exchange letters) cartearse, escribirse

correspondence [kɔrɪspándəns] N correspondencia *f*

correspondent [kɔrɪspándənt] ADJ correspondiente; N (writer of letters) correspondiente *mf*; (news gatherer) corresponsal *mf*, enviado -da *mf*

corresponding [kɔrɪspándɪŋ] ADJ correspondiente; (secretary) encargado de la correspondencia

corridor [kɔ́rɪdɔr] N corredor *m*, pasillo *m*

corroborate [kərábəret] VT corroborar

corrode [kəród] VI/VT corroer[se]

corrosion [kəróʒən] N corrosión *f*

corrupt [kərʌ́pt] ADJ (dishonest) corrupto; (rotten) corrompido; **to become —** corromperse; VT corromper, viciar; **—ed file** archivo corrupto *m*

corruption [kərʌ́pʃən] N corrupción *f*

corset [kɔ́rsɪt] N corsé *m*

cortex [kɔ́rteks] N córtex *m*, corteza cerebral *f*

corticosteriod [kɔrdɪkostérɔɪd] N corticoesteroide *m*

cortisone [kɔ́rdɪzon] N cortisona *f*

cosigner [kósaɪnə] N cosignatario -ria *mf*

cosmetic [kazmédɪk] ADJ & N cosmético *m*; **— surgery** cirugía estética *f*

cosmic [kázmɪk] ADJ cósmico

cosmology [kazmálədʒi] N cosmología *f*

cosmonaut [kázmənɔt] N cosmonauta *mf*

cosmopolitan [kazməpálɪtn̩] ADJ cosmopolita

cosmos [kázmos] N cosmos *m*

cost [kɔst] N costo *m*; Sp coste *m*; **—s** (in court) costas *f pl*; **at —** al costo/costo; **at all —s** a toda costa; **— of living** costo/coste de vida *m*; **to sell at —** vender al costo / al coste; VT costar; **how much does this —?** ¿cuánto vale/cuesta esto? ADJ **-benefit analysis** análisis costo-beneficio *m*; **— effective** económico

costar [kóstar] N coprotagonista *mf*, oponente *mf*

Costa Rica [kóstəríkə] N Costa Rica *f*

Costa Rican [kóstəríkən] ADJ & N costarricense *mf*, costarriqueño -ña *mf*

costly [kɔ́stli] ADJ costoso, caro

costume [kástum] N (style of clothing) vestimenta *f*; (in the theater) vestuario *m*; (disguise) disfraz *m*; **— jewelry** bisutería *f*

cot [kat] N catre *m*

cottage [kádɪdʒ] N (small house) casita *f*; (vacation house) cabaña *f*, chalé *m*; **— cheese** requesón *m*

cotter pin [kádəpɪn] N chaveta *f*

cotton [katn̩] N algodón *m*; **— candy** algodón de azúcar *m*; **— gin** desmontadora de algodón *f*; **—seed** semilla de algodón *f*; **—wood** álamo [de Virginia] *m*

couch [kautʃ] N sofá *m*; (psychiatrist's) diván *m*; **— potato** telebobo -ba *mf*; VT expresar

cougar [kúgə] N puma *f*

cough [kɔf] VI toser; **to — up** (spit) expectorar; (hand over) soltar, largar; N tos *f*; **—drop** pastilla para la tos *f*; **— syrup** jarabe para la tos *m*

could [kʊd] V AUX I **— do it if I wanted** podría hacerlo si quisiera; **— you arrive early?** ¿podrías llegar temprano? **— I leave early?** ¿puedo salir temprano? **you — be right** quizá tengas razón

council [káunsəl] N (religious) concilio *m*; (advisory) consejo *m*, junta *f*; (provincial) diputación *f*; (municipal) concejo *m*; **—man** concejal *m*; **—woman** concejal *f*, concejala *f*

councilor [káunsələ] N concejal *m*

counsel [káunsəl] N (advice) consejo *m*; (lawyer) abogado -da *mf*; VI/VT (give advice) aconsejar

counseling [káunsəlɪŋ] N (academic) asesoramiento *m*, orientación *f*; (psychological, marriage) terapia *f*

counselor [káunsələ] N consejero -ra *mf*; (lawyer) abogado -da *mf*

count [kaunt] VI/VT contar; **to — in** incluir; **to — on** contar con; **to — oneself lucky** considerarse dichoso; **to — out** excluir; N (reckoning) cuenta *f*; (charge) cargo *m*; (noble) conde *m*; (in baseball) conteo *m*; **—down** cuenta regresiva *f*

countenance [káuntn̩əns] N (expression) semblante *m*; (face) cara *f*; VT (tolerate) tolerar; (approve) aprobar

counter [káʊntə-] N (in a kitchen) *Sp* encimera *f*; *Am* mostrador *m*; (in a store) mostrador *m*; (in a bar) barra *f*; (in board games) tablero *m*; (counting device) contador *m*; **over the —** sin receta; ADJ contrario, opuesto; ADV **— to** contra; **to run — to** ser contrario a; VT (an argument) retrucar (a blow), devolver; VI/VT (reply) replicar

counteract [kaʊntə-ǽkt] VT contrarrestar

counterattack [káʊntə-ətæk] N contraataque *m*; VI/VT contraatacar

counterbalance[1] [kaʊntə-bǽləns] VI/VT contrapesar

counterbalance[2] [káʊntə-bæləns] N contrapeso *m*

counterclockwise [kaʊntə-klákwaɪz] ADV en el sentido opuesto al de las manecillas del reloj

counterculture [káʊntə-kʌltʃə-] N contracultura *f*

counterespionage [kaʊntə-éspiɑnɑʒ] N contraespionaje *m*

counterexample [káʊntə-ɪgzæmpəl] N contraejemplo *m*

counterfeit [káʊntə-fɪt] N falsificación *f*; ADJ falso; **— money** moneda falsa *f*; VT falsificar

countermand[1] [kaʊntə-mǽnd] VT contramandar

countermand[2] [káʊntə-mænd] N contraorden *f*

countermeasure [káʊntə-meʒə-] N contramedida *f*

counteroffer [káʊntə-ɔfə-] N contraoferta *f*

counterpart [káʊntə-part] N homólogo -ga *mf*

counterproductive [kaʊntə-prədáktɪv] ADJ contraproducente

counterrevolution [kaʊntə-revəlúʃən] N contrarrevolución *f*

countersign [káʊntə-saɪn] N contraseña *f*; VT refrendar

countess [káʊntɪs] N condesa *f*

countless [káʊntlɪs] ADJ incontables, innumerables

country [kántri] N (nation) país *m*; (territory) territorio *m*; (homeland) patria *f*; (rural area) campo *m*; ADJ (of the countryside) rural; (uncouth) rústico; **— club** club campestre *m*; **— code** código de país *m*; **—man** compatriota *m*; **— music** música country *f*; **— of origin** país de origen *m*; **—side** (rural area) campo *m*; (scenery) paisaje *m*; **—woman** compatriota *f*

county [káʊnti] N condado *m*; **— fair** feria [de ganado] *f*; **— seat** capital de condado *f*

coup [ku] N (success) golpe maestro *m*; (putsch) golpe de estado *m*; **— d'état** golpe de estado *m*

coupe [kup] N cupé *m*

couple [kápəl] N (of times, of forces, of people) par *m*; (romantic) pareja *f*; VI/VT (pair up)

formar parejas; VT (connect) acoplar; VI (copulate) copular

couplet [káplɪt] N pareado *m*

coupling [káplɪŋ] N (mechanical action) acoplamiento *m*, enganche *m*; (device) acople *m*, enganche *m*; (mating) cópula *f*

coupon [kjúpɑn] N cupón *m*

courage [kɛ́ɪdʒ] N valentía *f*, valor *m*, coraje *m*

courageous [kə-rédʒəs] ADJ valiente

courier [kúriə-] N mensajero -ra *mf*

course [kɔrs] N (of a river, of study, of a disease) curso *m*; (of a road, route) trayecto *m*; (of a ship, plane) derrotero *m*; (progression of time) marcha *f*; (dish) plato *m*; **— of action** línea de conducta *f*, proceder *m*; **in the — of a year** en el transcurso de un año; **in due —** a la larga; INTERJ **of —** claro, por supuesto, naturalmente; VI correr, fluir

court [kɔrt] N (courtyard) patio *m*; (atrium) patio interior *m*; (in sports) cancha *f*, pista *f*; (in a city) plazuela *f*, plazoleta *f*; (lower tribunal) juzgado *m*; (higher tribunal) tribunal *m*; (session) audiencia *f*; (royal residence, retinue) corte *f*; **—-martial** consejo de guerra *m*; **— of law** tribunal de justicia *m*; **— order** orden judicial *f*; **— reporter** estenotipista *mf*; **— room** tribunal *m*; **—yard** patio *m*; **to settle out of —** llegar a un arreglo extrajudicial; **to pay — to** cortejar; VT cortejar, galantear; **to — danger** tentar a la suerte; **to —-martial** someter a consejo de guerra; VI estar de novios

courteous [kɛ́ɪtiəs] ADJ cortés

courtesy [kɛ́ɪtɪsi] N (attitude) cortesía *f*; (act) fineza *f*, atención *f*

courtier [kɔ́rDiə-] N (member of the court) cortesano -na *mf*; (sycophant) adulador -ora *mf*

courtship [kɔ́rtʃɪp] N cortejo *m*

cousin [kázən] N primo -ma *mf*; **first —** primo -ma hermano -na *mf*

cove [kov] N ensenada *f*

covenant [kávənənt] N pacto *m*; (religious) alianza *f*

cover [kávə-] VI/VT cubrir, recubrir; (with lid, screen) tapar; (replace) sustituir; (include, deal with) comprender; (traverse) recorrer; (sing) hacer una versión; **—ed losses** pérdidas cubiertas *f pl*; **to — up** (wrap up) tapar bien; (hide) ocultar; N (lid) tapa *f*; (book) cubierta *f*, tapa *f*; (blanket) manta *f*; (for appliances, furniture) funda *f*; (front for activity) tapadera *f*, pantalla *f*; (shelter) resguardo *m*, abrigo *m*; **—all** mono *m*; **— charge** entrada *f*; **— girl** modelo de portada *f*; **— letter** carta con anexos *f*, carta de remisión *f*; **—-up** encubrimiento *m*; **to send under separate —** enviar por separado; **to take —** resguardarse; **under —** de incógnito;

under — of dark bajo el manto de la noche

coverage [kávəɪʤ] N cobertura f; **— level** nivel de cobertura m

covert [kovэ́t] ADJ encubierto

covet [kávɪt] VT (desire wrongly) codiciar; (want) ansiar

covetous [kávэdəs] ADJ codicioso

cow [kau] N (bovine female) vaca f; (female of other animals) hembra f; **—bell** cencerro m, esquila f; **—boy** vaquero m; **—hide** cuero de vaca m, vaqueta f; **—lick** remolino m; **—pox** vacuna f; **—shed** vaquería f, vaqueriza f; **to have a** — tener una pataleta; VT intimidar

coward [káuэd] N cobarde mf

cowardice [káuэdɪs] N cobardía f

cowardly [káuэdli] ADJ cobarde

cower [káuэr] VI achicarse

cowl [kaul] N capucha f

coy [kɔɪ] ADJ (coquettish) remilgado; (evasive) esquivo

coyote [kaɪódi, káɪot] N coyote m

cozy [kózi] ADJ (warm) acogedor; (beneficial) conveniente; VT **to — up to** adular

CPA [certified public accountant] [sípié] N contador -ora público -ca con licencia mf

CPI [consumer price index] [sípiáɪ] N índice de precios al consumidor m

CPR [cardiopulmonary resuscitation] [sípiár] N reanimación cardiopulmonar f

CPU [central processing unit] [sípijú] N UCP f

crab [kræb] N cangrejo m; (mechanism) carro corredizo m; (grouch) cascarrabias mf sg; **— apple** manzana silvestre f; **—s** (parasites) ladillas f pl; VI (fish) pescar cangrejos; (complain) quejarse

crack [kræk] VI (single fissure) rajarse; (multiple fissures) resquebrajarse, agrietarse; (psychological breakdown) sufrir un ataque de nervios; (of voice) quebrarse; VT (knuckles) hacer un chasquido con, chascar, chasquear; (nuts) cascar; (jokes) contar; (a prisoner) quebrar; (a case) resolver; (a code) descifrar; (a door) entreabrir; **to — down on** reprimir; **that —s me up** eso me hace desternillar de risa; N (fissure) rajadura f, grieta f, resquebrajadura f; (sound) chasquido m; (joke) pulla f, chanza f; **— cocaine** crack m; **—down** represión f; **—house** fumadero m; **—pot** excéntrico -ca mf; **at the — of dawn** al romper el alba; **I'd like a — at the championship** me gustaría poder participar en el campeonato

cracked [krækt] ADJ rajado, quebrado; (crazy) chiflado; **it's not all it's — up to be** no es para tanto

cracker [krǽkэr] N galleta f

crackle [krǽkэl] N (of paper) crujido m; (of fire) crepitación f; VI crujir, crepitar

cradle [krédl] N cuna f

craft [kræft] N (skill) destreza f; (cunning) astucia f; (occupation) arte m, oficio m; (boat) embarcación f; **—sman** artesano m; **—swoman** artesana f; VT fabricar

crafty [krǽfti] ADJ astuto, taimado

crag [kræg] N risco m, peñasco m, peñón m

craggy [krǽgi] ADJ peñascoso

cram [kræm] VT (pack in) embutir; VI (study intensely) memorizar; Sp empollar; **the bar was —med with people** el bar estaba atestado

cramp [kræmp] N (spasm) calambre m; (staple) grapa f; VI/VT (to suffer a spasm) acalambrar[se]; VT (to staple) engrapar; **you're —ing my style** me estorbas

cranberry [krǽnbɛri] N arándano rojo m

crane [kren] N (bird) grulla f; (machine) grúa f; VT **to — one's neck** estirar el cuello

cranium [kréniəm] N cráneo m

crank [kræŋk] N (mechanism) manivela f; (grouch) cascarrabias mf sg; (overzealous advocate) fanático -ca mf; **—case** cárter superior del aceite m; **—shaft** cigüeñal m; VI/VT arrancar con manivela

cranky [krǽŋki] ADJ (irritable) irritable; (eccentric) excéntrico

cranny [krǽni] N (crevice) rendija f; (corner) recoveco m

crash [kræʃ] VI (collide) estrellarse; (market) quebrar; (stay overnight with someone) quedarse a dormir; (hang up, as with a computer) bloquearse, caerse; (sleep) dormir; VT **to — a party** colarse en una fiesta; N (noise) estallido m; (collision) choque m; (financial collapse) quiebra f, colapso m; (computer failure) bloqueo m, caída f; **— landing** aterrizaje forzoso m

crass [kræs] ADJ craso

crate [kret] N cajón m, guacal m; VT poner en cajones

crater [krédэr] N cráter m

cravat [krəvǽt] N corbata f

crave [krev] VT anhelar; **I — chocolate** me muero por un chocolate

craving [krévɪŋ] N antojo m

crawl [krɔl] VI (on hands and knees) gatear; (on the belly) arrastrarse, reptar; (proceed slowly) avanzar a paso de tortuga; **to be —ing with** hormiguear de; N (swimming stroke) crol m; **traffic is going at a —** el tráfico va a paso de tortuga

crayon [kréan] N lápiz de color m, Crayola™ f

craze [krez] N (fad) moda pasajera f; VI/VT enloquecer[se]

craziness [krézɪnɪs] N locura f, chifladura f

crazy [krézi] ADJ & N loco -ca mf; **I'm — about you** estoy loco por ti; **that's —!** ¡qué locura! **to go —** volverse loco, enloquecerse

creak [krik] N (of wooden floor) crujido m; (of a

hinge) rechinamiento *m*; vi (a wooden floor) crujir; (a hinge) rechinar

cream [krim] N (milk product) crema *f*; *Sp* nata *f*; (medicament) crema *f*; — **cheese** queso de untar *m*, queso crema *m*; — **of tomato soup** sopa crema de tomate *f*; **the — of the crop** la flor y nata; vt (decream) desnatar; (butter, sugar) batir; (vegetables) preparar con salsa blanca; (defeat) aplastar

creamy [krimi] ADJ cremoso

crease [kris] N (in trousers) raya *f*, repliegue *m*; (wrinkle) arruga *f*; vt (trousers) planchar la raya; (wrinkle) arrugar

create [kriét] vi/vt crear

creation [kriéʃən] N creación *f*

creationism [kriéʃənɪzəm] N creacionismo *m*

creative [kriédɪv] ADJ creativo

creativity [kriətívɪdi] N creatividad *f*

creator [kriédə] N creador -ra *mf*

creature [krítʃə] N (being) ser *m*; (animal) animal *m*; **a — of your imagination** un producto de tu imaginación

credence [krídn̩s] N crédito *m*

credentials [krɪdéntʃəlz] N credenciales *f pl*

credibility [krɛDɪbílɪDi] N credibilidad *f*

credible [krɛDəbəl] ADJ creíble

credit [krɛDɪt] N crédito *m*; (commendation) reconocimiento *m*; — **approval** aprobación de crédito *f*; — **card** tarjeta de crédito *f*; — **counseling** asesoramiento de crédito *m*; — **line** línea de crédito *f*; — **history** historial de crédito *m*; — **rating** calificación crediticia *f*; — **report** informe de crédito *m*; —**s** créditos *m pl*; — **underwriters** aseguradores de crédito *m pl*; — **union** banco cooperativo *m*; **on** — a crédito; **to give** — **to** (believe) dar crédito; (ascribe) acreditar; ADJ —**worthy** solvente; vt (believe) creer; (enter as credit) acreditar; (attribute) atribuir; — **an account** abonar/acreditar a una cuenta

creditor [krɛDɪDə] N acreedor -ora *mf*

credulous [krɛdʒələs] ADJ crédulo

creed [krid] N credo *m*

creek [krik] N arroyo *m*, quebrada *f*

creep [krip] vi (crawl on belly) arrastrarse; (crawl on all fours) gatear; (grow upward) trepar; (go slowly) andar a paso de tortuga; **to — up on** acercarse furtivamente a; N (obnoxious person) *pej* persona repulsiva *f*, sinvergüenza *mf*; **that gives me the —s** eso me da asco; *Sp* eso me da grima

creeper [krípə] N enredadera *f*, planta trepadora *f*

creepy [krípi] ADJ repulsivo

cremate [krímet] vt cremar

Creole [kríoł] ADJ & N criollo -lla *mf*

creosote [kríəsot] N creosota *f*

crepe [krep] N (fabric) crespón *m*; (band of fabric) crespón negro *m*

crept [krɛpt] *see* creep

crescent [krɛsənt] N media luna *f*; ADJ creciente

crest [krɛst] N (of a wave, rooster) cresta *f*; (of feathers) penacho *m*, copete *m*; (of mountain) cima *f*, cumbre *f*; (of heraldic arms) timbre *m*; —**fallen** alicaído, cabizbajo; vi **the river —ed at two meters above flood level** el río creció hasta dos metros por encima de lo normal

crevice [krɛvɪs] N grieta *f*

crew [kru] N (for ships, etc.) tripulación *f*; (of workers) cuadrilla *f*; — **member** tripulante *mf*

crib [krɪb] N (bed) cuna *f*; (manger) pesebre *m*; (bin for grain) granero *m*; (cheat notes) hoja para copiar *f*; — **death** síndrome de muerte súbita infantil *m*; vi copiar

cricket [krɪkɪt] N (insect) grillo *m*; (game) críquet *m*

crime [kraɪm] N (illegal act) delito *m*; (act of violence against people) crimen *m*; (criminal activity) delincuencia *f*, criminalidad *f*

criminal [krímənəł] ADJ & N delincuente *mf*, malhechor -ora *mf*; (perpetrator of violent crimes) criminal *mf*; — **record** antecedentes delictivos *m pl*

crimp [krɪmp] vt rizar; N rizo *m*

crimson [krímzən] ADJ & N carmesí *m*, carmín *m*

cringe [krɪndʒ] vi **it makes me—** me da vergüenza ajena

cripple [krípəł] N *offensive* tullido -da *mf*; (in the legs) *pey* cojo -ja *mf*; (in the arms) *offensive* manco -ca *mf*; vt tullir

crisis [kráɪsɪs] N crisis *f*

crisp [krɪsp] ADJ (apple, bacon) crocante, crujiente; (weather) fresco y despejado; (hair) crespo; vi/vt volver crujiente

crispy [kríspi] ADJ crocante, crujiente

criterion [kraɪtíriən] N criterio *m*

critic [krídɪk] N crítico -ca *mf*

critical [krídɪkəł] ADJ crítico; — **stage** punto culminante *m*

criticism [krídɪsɪzəm] N crítica *f*

criticize [krídɪsaɪz] vt criticar

croak [krok] vi (make the sound of a frog) croar; (make the sound of a crow) graznar; (die) *fam* espichar; N (sound made by frogs) canto de rana *m*; (sound made by crows) graznido *m*

Croatia [kroéʃə] N Croacia *f*

Croatian [kroéʃən] ADJ & N croata *mf*

crochet [kroʃé] N ganchillo *m*, croché *m*, crochet *m*; — **hook** aguja de croché *f*; vi hacer ganchillo, hacer croché

crock [krak] N (pot) vasija *f*; (lies) pamplinas *f pl*

crockery [krákəri] N loza *f*

crocodile [krákədaɪł] N cocodrilo *m*

croissant [krəsánt] N cruasán *m*, croissant *m*

crony [króni] N compinche *mf*, compadre *m*, comadre *f*

cronyism [króniizəm] N amiguismo *m*

crook [krʊk] N (criminal) delincuente *mf*; (curve) curva *f*; (hook) gancho *m*; (staff) cayado *m*

crooked [krʊkɪd] ADJ (bent) torcido; Am chueco; (dishonest) deshonesto

crop [krɑp] N (harvest) cosecha *f*; (group of contemporaries) promoción *f*; (of a bird) buche *m*; (horse whip) fusta *f*; — **rotation** rotación de cultivos *f*; VT (graze) pastar, pacer; (trim) recortar; **to — up** surgir

croquet [kroké] N cróquet *m*

cross [krɔs] N (symbol) cruz *f*; (street intersection) cruce *m*; (soccer) pase cruzado *m*; (act of mixing) cruzamiento *m*; (in boxing) cruzado *m*; —**bar** (soccer) travesaño *m*, larguero *m*; (in gymnastics) barra *f*; (in high jump) listón *m*; (of a door) tranca *f*; —**-check** verificación *f*; —**court shot** golpe cruzado *m*; —**-fertilization** fecundación cruzada *f*; —**piece** cruceta *f*; —**-reference** referencia cruzada *f*; —**road** encrucijada *f*; — **section** corte transversal *m*; —**walk** cruce peatonal *m*, cebra *f*; —**word puzzle** crucigrama *m*; **to bear one's** — cargar la cruz; VI/VT (intersect, form a cross, breed, meet) cruzar[se]; (make sign of the cross) santiguarse; **to —-check** verificar; VT (betray) traicionar; (move to other side) cruzar; **to — examine** interrogar; **to — out** tachar; **to — over** (change allegiance) cambiar de bando; (go to the other side) traspasar; **to —-reference** hacer una referencia cruzada; **you've —ed the line** te pasaste de la raya; ADJ (transverse) transversal; (angry) enojado; —**-country** a campo traviesa; —**-cultural** transcultural; —**-eyed** bizco; **to be —-eyed** bizquear

crossing [krɔsɪŋ] N (street or railroad intersection, pedestrian path) cruce *m*; (hybridization, act of mixing) cruzamiento *m*; (of ocean) travesía *f*; (of a border) paso *m*; (of a river) vado *m*

crotch [krɑtʃ] N entrepierna *f*

crotchety [krɑtʃIdi] ADJ cascarrabias *inv*

crouch [kraʊtʃ] VI (stoop) agacharse; (prepare to spring) agazaparse

croup [krup] N tos *f*, croup *m*

crow [kro] N (bird) cuervo *m*; (sound of rooster) canto del gallo *m*; —**bar** alzaprima *f*; —**'s-foot** pata de gallo *f*; **to eat** — comerse sus propias palabras; VI cantar; (gloat, brag) jactarse

crowd [kraʊd] N (group of people) muchedumbre *f*, gentío *m*, aglomeración *f*; (at a performance) público *m*; (clique) pandilla *f*; VI (push forward) agolparse; VI/VT (gather in large numbers) apiñar[se], amontonar[se], aglomerar[se]; (gather in a confined space) hacinar[se]

crowded [kraʊdɪd] ADJ **it is — in here** hay demasiada gente aquí; **the restaurant is —** el restaurante está lleno

crown [kraʊn] N corona *f*; (of head) coronilla *f*, crisma *f*; (of a hat) copa *f*; — **jewels** joyas de la corona *f pl*; VT coronar; (hit on head) dar un coscorrón

crucial [krúʃəl] ADJ (element) fundamental; (moment) crucial

crucible [krúsəbəl] N crisol *m*

crucifix [krúsəfɪks] N crucifijo *m*

crucify [krúsəfaɪ] VT crucificar

crud [krʌd] N (filth) mugre *f*; (worthless thing, sickness, despicable person) *fam* porquería *f*

crude [krud] ADJ (vulgar, unpolished) basto, tosco; — **oil** petróleo crudo *m*

cruel [krúəl] ADJ cruel

cruelty [krúəlti] N crueldad *f*

cruise [kruz] VI (take a cruise) tomar un crucero; (patrol) patrullar; — **control** control de crucero *m*; **cruising speed** velocidad de crucero *f*; N crucero *m*; — **missile** misil crucero *m*

cruiser [krúzə-] N crucero *m*

crumb [krʌm] N (small) miga *f*, migaja *f*; (large) mendrugo *m*; VT (break into crumbs) desmigajar; (remove crumbs) sacar las migas

crumble [krámbəl] VI/VT (bread) desmigajar[se]; (clods of dirt) desmenuzar[se]; (house) desmoronar[se]

crummy [krámi] ADJ (place) *fam* de mala muerte; (object) *fam* de porquería; (show) flojo

crumple [krámpəl] VI/VT (crush) arrugar[se]; VI (collapse) aplastarse

crunch [krʌntʃ] VI/VT (eat noisily) mascar; N (sound) crujido *m*; (shortage) crisis *f*; —**es** abdominales *m pl*

crunchy [krántʃi] ADJ crocante, crujiente

crusade [kruséd] N cruzada *f*; VI (engage in a campaign) hacer una campaña

crusader [krusédə-] N cruzado -da *mf*; **a — for human rights** un paladín de los derechos humanos

crush [krʌʃ] VI/VT aplastar, machacar; (stone) demoler; N (act of crushing) aplastamiento *m*; (crowd) tumulto *m*; (infatuation) enamoramiento *m*; —**ing victory** victoria contundente *f*

crust [krʌst] N (of bread, earth) corteza *f*; (of bread) costra *f*; (of pie) tapa *f*

crusty [krásti] ADJ (with a crust) costroso; (grouchy) irascible

crutch [krʌtʃ] N muleta *f*

cry [kraɪ] N (shout) grito *m*; (weeping) llanto *m*; (call of a bird) reclamo *m*; —**baby** llorón -ona *mf*; **a far — from** muy distante de, muy lejos de; VI (shout) gritar; (weep) llorar; **to — over spilt milk** hacer como la lechera; **to — for**

attention reclamar atención; **to — for help** pedir socorro; **to — out** vocear

cryogenic [kraɪədʒénɪk] ADJ criogénico

crystal [krístļ] N cristal m; **— ball** bola de cristal f; **— clear** cristalino

crystalline [krístļɪn] ADJ cristalino

crystallize [krístļaɪz] VI/VT cristalizar[se]

cub [kʌb] N (lion) cachorro m; (bear) osezno m; (whale) ballenato m; (wolf) lobato m, lobezno m; **— reporter** reportero -ra novato -ta mf

Cuba [kjúbə] N Cuba f

Cuban [kjúbən] ADJ & N cubano -na mf

cubbyhole [kábɪhoʊl] N casilla f

cube [kjúb] N cubo m; **— root** raíz cúbica f; VT (cut) cortar en cubos; (raise to the third power) elevar al cubo

cubic [kjúbɪk] ADJ cúbico

cubicle [kjúbɪkəl] N cubículo m

cubism [kjúbɪzəm] N cubismo m

cuckold [kákəld] N cornudo m, cabrón m; VT poner los cuernos a

cuckoo [kúku] N cuclillo m, cuco m; **— clock** reloj de cucú m; ADJ & N chiflado -da mf; INTERJ cucú

cucumber [kjúkʌmbɚ] N pepino m

cud [kʌd] N **to chew the —** rumiar

cuddle [kádļ] VI/VT hacer[se] mimos; N mimo m

cuddly [kádli] ADJ mimoso

cudgel [kádʒəl] N porra f; VT aporrear

cue [kju] N (in theater) pie m; (psychological stimulus) estímulo m; **— ball** bola blanca f; **— stick** taco de billar m; VT dar pie, dar la señal

cuff [kʌf] N (of sleeve, glove) puño m; (of pants) bajo m; (blow) bofetada f; **hand—s** esposas f pl; VT (in making pants) hacer los bajos; (put on handcuffs) esposar; (hit) abofetear

cuisine [kwɪzín] N cocina f

cul-de-sac [káldəsæk] N callejón sin salida m

culinary [kjúlənɛri, kálənɛri] ADJ culinario

cull [kʌl] VT (choose) seleccionar, entresacar; (collect) recoger

culminate [kálmənet] VI/VT culminar

culmination [kʌlmənéʃən] N culminación f

culprit [kálprɪt] N culpable mf

cult [kʌlt] N (sect) secta religiosa f; (worship) culto m

cultivable [káltəvəbəl] ADJ cultivable

cultivate [káltəvet] VT cultivar

cultivated [káltəvedɪd] ADJ (land) cultivado; (plant) de cultivo; (person) culto

cultivation [kʌltəvéʃən] N (tillage) cultivo m; (education) cultura f

cultivator [káltəvedɚ] N (person) cultivador -ora mf; (implement) cultivadora f

cultural [káltʃəəl] ADJ cultural

culture [káltʃɚ] N cultura f; (microorganisms) cultivo m; **— shock** choque cultural m; VT (microorganisms) cultivar

cultured [káltʃəd] ADJ (person) culto; (pearl) cultivado, de cultivo

cumbersome [kámbɚsəm] ADJ (bulky) voluminoso; (unwieldy) incómodo

cumulative [kjúmjələtɪv] ADJ acumulativo

cumulus [kjúmjələs] N cúmulo m

cunning [kánɪŋ] ADJ (sly) astuto, zorro; N astucia f, maña f

cup [kʌp] N (with handle) taza f, pocillo m; (without handle) vaso m; (measure) taza f; (trophy, brassiere part) copa f; **—board** armario m, aparador m

cur [kɚ] N (dog) perro m; (villain) pej villano -na mf

curable [kjúrəbəl] ADJ curable

curator [kjúredɚ] N conservador -ora mf

curb [kɚb] N (of a street) Sp bordillo m; Mex borde m; RP cordón m; (of a well) brocal m; (restraint) freno m, restricción f; VT (emotions) refrenar; (spending) limitar

curd [kɚd] N cuajada f; VI/VT cuajar[se], coagular[se]

curdle [kɚdļ] VI/VT cuajar[se], coagular[se]; **my blood —d** se me heló la sangre

cure [kjur] N (healing, preserving meat) cura f, curación f; (method) tratamiento m; VI/VT curar[se]; **—all** sanalotodo m

curfew [kɚfju] N toque de queda m, queda f

curio [kjúrio] N curiosidad f

curiosity [kjuriásɪdi] N curiosidad f

curious [kjúriəs] ADJ curioso

curl [kɚl] VI/VT (form ringlets) rizar[se], ensortijar[se]; (coil) enroscar[se]; (smoke) alzarse en espirales; **to — up** ovillar[se]; N (of hair) rizo m, bucle m; (of smoke) espiral f

curler [kɚlɚ] N Sp rulo m; Mex tubo m; RP rulero m

curly [kɚli] ADJ rizado

currant [kɚənt] N (fruit) grosella f; (tree) grosellero m

currency [kɚənsi] N (money) moneda f, divisa f; (acceptance) aceptación f; **— exchange** mercado de divisas m; **— unit** unidad monetaria f

current [kɚənt] ADJ (commonly used) corriente; (prevalent) actual; **the — issue of a magazine** el último número de una revista; **— year** año en curso m; N (of river, electricity, air) corriente f

currently [kɚəntli] ADV actualmente

curriculum [kəríkjələm] N plan de estudios m, currículo m

curry [kɚri] N curry m

curse [kɚs] N (ill wish) maldición f; (swear word) palabrota f; VI/VT (wish ill) maldecir; (swear) decir palabrotas

cursive [kɚsɪv] ADJ cursivo; N cursiva f

cursor [kɚsɚ] N cursor m

curt [kɚt] ADJ (abrupt) seco, brusco; (brief) breve

curtail [kɚtél] VT restringir, cercenar

curtain [kɝ́tn̩] N cortina *f*; (theater) telón *m*; VT ponerle cortinas a

curvature [kɝ́vətʃʊr] N curvatura *f*; (of the spine) desviación *f*

curve [kɝv] N (also in baseball) curva *f*; **he threw me a — me** agarró desprevenido; VI/VT encorvar[se]; (road) torcer[se], desviar[se]

curved [kɝvd] ADJ curvo

cushion [kúʃən] N (pad) almohadilla *f*; (emergency resources, pad of air) colchón *m*; (pillow) almohadón *m*; (decorative pillow) cojín *m*; VT (put pads) poner almohadones; (soften a blow) amortiguar

cuspid [kʌ́spɪd] N colmillo *m*

cuss [kʌs] VI decir palabrotas; N **—word** *fam* palabrota *f*; **strange old —** *fam* bicho raro *m*

custard [kʌ́stəd] N flan *m*, natilla[s] *f sg or pl*

custodian [kʌstóɔbiən] N (caretaker) cuidador -ora *mf*; (guardian) custodio -dia *mf*

custody [kʌ́stədi] N custodia *f*; **to take into —** detener

custom [kʌ́stəm] N costumbre *f*, uso *m*; **—s** (government department) aduana *f*; (taxes) derechos de aduana *m pl*; **—[s]house** aduana *f*; ADJ **—-built** construido por encargo; **—-made** hecho a medida

customary [kʌ́stəmeri] ADJ acostumbrado

customer [kʌ́stəmɚ] N cliente -ta *mf*; **— base** clientela *f*; **— care** atención al cliente *f*; **— rights** derechos del cliente *m pl*; ADJ **— oriented** orientado al cliente

customize [kʌ́stəmaɪz] VT adaptar por encargo

cut [kʌt] VI/VT cortar; (shorten) acortar; (harvest) talar; (lower) rebajar; **—!** ¡corte[n]! **to — a deal** llegar a un arreglo; **to — across** (take a shortcut) cortar por; (transcend) trascender; **to — and paste** cortar y pegar; **to — back** reducir; **to — class** faltar a clase; **to — costs** reducir costos; **to — down on** reducir; **to — in** (interrupt) interrumpir; (in traffic) atravesarse; **to — prices** bajar los precios; **may I — in?** ¿me permite? **to — off** (interrupt) interrumpir; (intercept) interceptar; **to — out** omitir; **to be — out for** estar hecho para; **to — up** (divide) trozar; (misbehave) portarse mal; N corte *m*; (in salary) recorte *m*, reducción *f*; (of prices) rebaja *f*; (of a suit) hechura *f*, corte *m*; (insult) desaire *f*; **—back** recorte *m*; **— glass** cristal labrado *m*; **—off date** fecha límite *f*; ADJ **—and-dried** predeterminado; **—-rate** de rebajas; **—throat** despiadado

cutaneous [kjuténiəs] ADJ cutáneo

cute [kjut] ADJ mono, rico; **to act —** ser afectado, ser melindroso

cuticle [kjúɔtɪkəl] N cutícula *f*

cutlery [kʌ́tləri] N (knives, knife store) cuchillería *f*; (eating utensils) cubiertos *m pl*

cutlet [kʌ́tlɪt] N filete *m*

cutter [kʌ́dɚ] N (person) cortador -ora *mf*; (device) cortadora *f*; (sleigh) trineo *m*; **Coast Guard —** guardacostas *m sg*

cutting [kʌ́dɪŋ] ADJ (sharp) cortante; (cold) penetrante; (sarcastic) mordaz, sarcástico; **— board** tabla de cortar *f*; **— edge** filo *m*; **—-edge technology** tecnología de punta *f*; N (action) cortado *m*

CV [**curriculum vitae**] [síví] N currículo *m*, currículum vitae *m*

cyanide [sáɪənaɪd] N cianuro *m*

cybercafe [saɪbɚkafé] N cibercafé *m*

cybernetics [saɪbɚnɛ́dɪks] N cibernética *f*

cyberpunk [sáɪbɚpʌnk] N ciberpunk *m*

cyberspace [sáɪbɚspes] N ciberespacio *m*

cyborg [sáɪbɔrg] N cyborg *m*

cycle [sáɪkəl] N ciclo *m*

cyclical [síklɪkəl] ADJ cíclico

cyclone [sáɪklon] N ciclón *m*

cyclotron [sáɪklətran] N ciclotrón *m*

cylinder [sílɪndɚ] N cilindro *m*; (of a gun) tambor *m*; **— head** culata *f*

cylindrical [sɪlíndrɪkəl] ADJ cilíndrico

cymbal [símbəl] N címbalo *m*, platillo *m*

cynic [sínɪk] N cínico -ca *mf*

cynical [sínɪkəl] ADJ cínico

cynicism [sínɪsɪzəm] N cinismo *m*

cypress [sáɪprɪs] N ciprés *m*

Cypriot, Cypriote [sípriət] ADJ & N chipriota *mf*

Cyprus [sáɪprəs] N Chipre *m*

cyst [sɪst] N quiste *m*

cystic [sístɪk] ADJ cístico; **— fibrosis** fibrosis cística *f*

cytology [saɪtáləɔɡi] N citología *f*

czar [zar] N zar *m*

Czech [tʃɛk] ADJ & N checo -ca *mf*; **— Republic** República Checa *f*

Dd

dab [dæb] VT (pat) dar toques; (apply) aplicar con golpecitos; N toque *m*

dabble [dǽbəl] VI (splash) chapotear; (be interested superficially) ser aficionado a

dachshund [dáksənd] N perro salchicha *m*

dad [dæd] N papá *m*

daddy [dǽɔi] N papaíto *m*, papito *m*, papacito *m*

daffodil [dǽfədɪl] N narciso *m*

dagger [dǽɡɚ] N daga *f*, puñal *m*

dahlia [dǽljə] N dalia *f*

daily [déli] ADJ diario; **— planner** agenda *f*; **— wage** jornal *m*, salario *m*; N (newspaper) diario *m*

dainty [dénti] ADJ (delicate) delicado, exquisito; (finicky) remilgado

dairy [déri] N (milk) lechería *f*; (cheese) quesería

f; ADJ (industry) lechero; (product) lácteo; N producto lácteo *m*

daisy [dézi] N margarita *f*; **to be pushing up daisies** *fam* estar criando malvas

dale [deł] N valle *m*

dally [dǽli] VI (flirt) coquetear; (risk danger) jugar con fuego; (waste time) remolonear

dam [dæm] N presa *f*, represa *f*; VT represar

damage [dǽmɪʤ] N daño *m*, destrozo *m*; **— control** control de daños *m*; **—s** daños y perjuicios *m pl*; **to pay —s** indemnizar *m*; VI/VT dañar[se]

damaging [dǽmɪʤɪŋ] ADJ perjudicial

dame [dem] N (noblewoman) dama *f*; (woman) *pej* tipa *f*

damn [dæm] VT condenar

damnation [dæmnéʃən] N condenación *f*, perdición *f*

damned [dæmd] ADJ condenado

damp [dæmp] ADJ húmedo; N humedad *f*; VT (wet) humedecer; (deaden) amortiguar; (extinguish) apagar

dampen [dǽmpən] VT (wet) humedecer; (deaden) amortiguar; (depress) deprimir

dampness [dǽmpnɪs] N humedad *f*

damsel [dǽmzəl] N damisela *f*

dance [dæns] N (act of dancing, party, activity) baile *m*; (artistic activity, animal courtship movements) danza *f*; **— music** música bailable *f*; VI/VT (at a party) bailar; (in ballet, of animals) danzar; **she —d her way to stardom** llegó al estrellato bailando

dancer [dǽnsɚ] N bailarín -ina *mf*, danzante *mf*

dancercise [dǽnsɚsaɪz] N baile aeróbico *m*

dandelion [dǽndəlaɪən] N diente de león *m*

dandruff [dǽndrəf] N caspa *f*

dandy [dǽndi] N dandi *m*, señorito *m*; ADJ estupendo

Dane [den] N danés -esa *mf*

danger [déndʒɚ] N peligro *m*

dangerous [déndʒɚəs] ADJ peligroso

dangle [dǽŋgəł] VI/VT (hang) colgar; (sway) bambolear[se]; **her legs were dangling off the bench** sus piernas pendían del banco

Danish [déniʃ] ADJ danés; N bollo dulce *m*

dapple, dappled [dǽpəl[d]] ADJ pinto, moteado

dare [der] VI/VT (be brave) atreverse [a], osar; (challenge) desafiar; **how — you?** ¿cómo te atreves? N desafío *m*; **—devil** temerario -ria *mf*

daring [dérɪŋ] N atrevimiento *m*, osadía *f*; ADJ atrevido, osado, arriesgado

dark [dark] ADJ (in color) oscuro; (of hair) moreno, morocho, trigueño; (gloomy) sombrío, tenebroso; (evil, ignorant) oscuro; (shameful) turbio; **— Ages** [Alta] Edad Media *f*; **—room** cuarto oscuro *m*; **—-skinned** moreno; N oscuridad *f*; **after —** después de que oscurece

darken [dárkən] VI/VT oscurecer

darkness [dárknɪs] N (complete) oscuridad *f*, tinieblas *f pl*; (partial) penumbra *f*

darling [dárlɪŋ] ADJ & N amado -da *mf*, querido -da *mf*; **my —** vida mía, amor mío

darn [darn] VT zurcir, remendar; **—ing needle** aguja de zurcir *f*; N zurcido *m*; **it is not worth a —** no vale un comino; INTERJ ¡caramba! ¡caracoles!

dart [dart] N (missile) dardo *m*; (tuck) pinza *f*; (swift movement) movimiento rápido *m*; **—board** diana *f*; **to play —s** jugar a los dardos; VI disparar; **to — out** salir disparado

dash [dæʃ] VI/VT (of waves, porcelain) estrellar[se]; VT (plans) frustrar; VI (hopes) desplomarse; **to — by** pasar corriendo; **to — off/out** salir disparado; **to — off a letter** escribir de prisa una carta; N (line) raya *f*; (run) corrida *f*; (race) carrera *f*; (small amount) pizca *f*; (splash) salpicadura *f*; **the one-hundred-meter —** la carrera de los cien metros llanos/planos; **—board** tablero *m*, salpicadero *m*

data [déDə, dǽDə] N datos *m pl*; **—base** base de datos *f*; **—bank** banco de datos *m*; **— encryption** cifrado de datos *m*; **— file** archivo de datos *m*; **— input** entrada de datos *f*; **— management** gestión de datos *f*; **— processing** procesamiento de datos *m*, fichero de datos *m*; **— recovery** recuperación de datos *f*; **— storage** almacenamiento de datos *m*

date [det] N (time) fecha *f*; (appointment) cita *f*; (person) acompañante *mf*; (fruit) dátil *m*; **— due** fecha de vencimiento *f*; **out of —** anticuado; **to —** hasta ahora; **up to —** al día; VI (be dated) estar fechado; (go out socially) salir; VT (write the date) fechar; (show to be old-fashioned) delatar la edad; (go out socially) salir con; **to — from** datar de, remontarse a

dated [débɪd] ADJ (having a date) fechado; (old-fashioned) anticuado

daub [dɔb] VT (smear) embarrar, embadurnar; (apply unskillfully) pintarrajear

daughter [dɔ́Dɚ] N hija *f*; **—-in-law** nuera *f*

daunt [dɔnt] VT (intimidate) intimidar; (dishearten) desanimar

dauntless [dɔ́ntlɪs] ADJ intrépido

davenport [dǽvənport] N sofá grande *m*

dawn [dɔn] N alba *f*, amanecer *m*, aurora *f*; **the — of civilization** los albores de la civilización; VI amanecer, aclarar; **it just —ed on me that** caí en [la] cuenta de que

day [de] N día *m*; **— after tomorrow** pasado mañana *m*; **— before yesterday** anteayer *m*; **—break** amanecer *m*; **at —break** al amanecer; **—care** guardería *f*; **—dream** fantasía *f*; **— laborer** jornalero -ra *mf*;

—light luz del día *f*; **—light saving time** adelanto de la hora en verano *m*; **—time** día *m*; **—time activity** actividad diurna *f*; **—-to- —** día a día; **by —** de día; **by the —** por día; **eight-hour —** jornada de ocho horas *f*; **in my —** en mis tiempos; **in the old —s** antaño; **make my —** dame el gusto; **New Year's —** Año Nuevo *m*; ADJ diurno; VI **to —dream** soñar despierto

daze [dez] VT aturdir; N **to be in a —** estar aturdido

dazzle [dǽzəł] VI/VT deslumbrar

deacidify [diəsídɪfaɪ] VT neutralizar la acidez

deacon [díkən] N diácono *m*

deactivate [diǽktɪvet] VI/VT desactivar

deactivation [diæktɪvéʃən] N desactivación *f*

dead [ded] ADJ muerto; **he's a — duck** está muerto; **—-end job** puesto sin perspectivas *m*; **— sure** completamente seguro; **— tired** muerto de cansancio; N **— air** aire viciado *m*; **—beat** moroso -sa *mf*; **—bolt** pestillo *m*; **— end** callejón sin salida *m*; **— letter** letra muerta *f*; **—line** fecha límite *f*; **— link** enlace muerto *m*; **—lock** punto muerto *m*; **—pan** de palo; **— ringer** fiel retrato *m*; **—wood** (person) persona inútil *f*; (thing) cosa inútil *f*; **the —** los muertos; **in the — of the night** en el silencio de la noche; **in the — of winter** en pleno invierno; VI **to —lock** trancarse

deaden [dédn̩] VT amortiguar

deadly [dédli] ADJ (enemy) mortal; (poison) letal; (weapon) mortífero; ADV mortalmente; **— dull** sumamente aburrido

deaf [def] ADJ sordo; **—-mute** ADJ & N sordomudo -da *mf*

deafen [défən] VT (make deaf) ensordecer; (deaden) amortiguar

deafening [défənɪŋ] ADJ ensordecedor, atronador

deafness [défnɪs] N sordera *f*

deal [dił] VT (cards) dar, repartir; (drugs) vender; (a blow) dar, asestar; **to — in** comerciar en; **biology —s with the study of life** la biología se ocupa del estudio de la vida; **I have to — with all kinds of people** tengo que vérmelas con todo tipo de gente; N (business transaction) trato *m*, negocio *m*; (shady transaction) componenda *f*; (act of dealing cards) reparto *m*; **a great — of** una gran cantidad de; **it's a —** ¡trato hecho! **I got a raw —** me clavaron

dealer [dílə·] N (in cars, antiques) comerciante *mf*; (in drugs, arms) traficante *mf*; (of cards) el/la que reparte *mf*

dealership [dílə·ʃɪp] N concesionario *m*

dealings [dílɪŋz] N trato *m*, relaciones *f pl*; (business) negocios *m pl*

dealt [dɛłt] *see* deal

dean [din] N (of university, professional group) decano -na *mf*; (in church) deán *m*

dear [dɪr] ADJ (beloved) querido; (expensive) caro; (cherished) apreciado; **— Sir/Madam** Estimado señor / Estimada señora; **my —est wish** mi deseo más ferviente; N **he's such a —!** ¡es un amor! **my —** querido mío *m* / querida mía *f*; ADV caro; **that cost me —** eso me costó caro; **— me!** ¡Dios mío! **oh —!** ¡Dios mío!

dearth [dɚθ] N escasez *f*

death [deθ] N muerte *f*; **—bed** lecho de muerte *m*; **— benefits** beneficios por fallecimiento *m*; **— certificate** partida de defunción *f*; **— penalty** pena de muerte *f*; **— rate** tasa de mortalidad *f*; **— row** pabellón de los condenados a muerte *m*; **he's on — row** está condenado a muerte *m*; **— squad** escuadrón de la muerte *m*; **— toll** mortandad *f*; **—trap** trampa mortal *f*; **— wish** instinto suicida *m*; **to put to —** ejecutar; **we have discussed this to —** hemos discutido esto hasta el hartazgo; **I'm sick to — of this job** estoy harto de este trabajo

debacle [dɪbákəł] N debacle *f*

debase [dɪbés] VT degradar, envilecer

debatable [dɪbépəbəł] ADJ discutible

debate [dɪbét] N debate *m*; VI/VT (discuss) debatir, discutir; (weigh a decision) considerar

debilitate [dɪbílɪtet] VT debilitar

debilitating [dɪbílɪteɪŋ] ADJ debilitante

debit [débɪt] N débito *m*, adeudo *m*; (column in an account) debe *m*; (total sum owed) pasivo *m*; **— card** tarjeta de débito *f*; VT adeudar; **to — an account** adeudar una cuenta

debriefing [dibrífɪŋ] N informe *m*

debris [dəbrí] N (ruins) escombros *m pl*; (detritus) detritus *m* [pl]

debt [dɛt] N deuda *f*; **— relief** alivio de la deuda *m*; **bad —** cuenta incobrable *f*; **to get into —** endeudarse; ADJ **—-ridden** sobreendeudado

debtor [détə·] N deudor -ora *mf*

debug [dibʌ́g] VT depurar

debugger [dibʌ́gə·] N depurador *m*

debugging [dibʌ́gɪŋ] N depuración *f*

debunk [dibʌ́ŋk] VT (ideas, beliefs) desacreditar; (myths) desmitificar

debut [debjú] N (of a play or film) estreno *m*; (in society) presentación en sociedad *f*; **to make a —** (an actor) debutar; (in society) presentarse en sociedad; VI/VT (a film) estrenar[se]; (a product) lanzar[se] al mercado

decade [déked] N década *f*, decenio *m*

decadence [dékədəns] N decadencia *f*

decadent [dékədənt] ADJ decadente

decaffeinated [dikǽfinéɪd] ADJ descafeinado

decal [díkæl] N calcomanía *f*, autoadhesivo *m*

decalcification [dikælsɪfɪkéʃən] N

descalcificación f

decanter [dɪkǽntə-] N garrafa f

decapitate [dɪkǽpɪtet] VT decapitar

decathlon [dɪkǽθlɑn] N decatlón m

decay [dɪkéʹ] VI/VT (biological matter) descomponer[se]; (teeth) cariar[se]; VI (health) deteriorarse; (radioactive matter) desintegrarse; N (moral) decadencia f; (biological) descomposición f; (nuclear) desintegración f; (tooth) caries f

decayed [dɪkéd] ADJ (flesh) putrefacto; (tooth) cariado

decease [dɪsís] N muerte f, fallecimiento m; VI morir, fallecer

deceased [dɪsíst] ADJ & N difunto -ta mf

deceit [dɪsít] N engaño m, trampa f

deceitful [dɪsítfəl] ADJ tramposo, engañoso

deceive [dɪsív] VI/VT engañar

decelerate [diséləret] VI desacelerar

December [dɪsémbə-] N diciembre m

decency [dísənsi] N decencia f

decent [dísənt] ADJ decente

decentralization [disɛntrəlɪzéʃən] N descentralización f

deception [dɪsépʃən] N engaño m

deceptive [dɪséptɪv] ADJ engañoso; — **practice** práctica comercial desleal f

decibel [désəbəl] N decibelio m

decide [dɪsáɪd] VT (make a decision) decidir; (award victory) fallar; **what —d you to come?** ¿qué te motivó a venir?

decided [dɪsáɪdɪd] ADJ (resolute) decidido; (clear) claro

deciduous [dɪsíʤuəs] ADJ deciduo, caduco; — **tooth** diente de la primera dentición m

decimal [désəməl] ADJ decimal

decimate [désəmet] VT diezmar

decipher [dɪsáɪfə-] VT descifrar

decision [dɪsíʒən] N decisión f; (in court) fallo m

decisive [dɪsáɪsɪv] ADJ decisivo

deck [dɛk] N (of a boat) cubierta f; (of a house) terraza f; (of playing cards) baraja f; **hit the —!** ¡cuerpo a tierra! VT (knock down) tumbar; (decorate) decorar; **to — oneself out** emperifollarse

declaration [dɛkləréʃən] N declaración f, pronunciamiento m

declare [dɪklér] VI/VT declarar, afirmar

decline [dɪkláɪn] N (deterioration) decadencia f; (slope) declive m; (reduction in prices) baja f; VI/VT declinar; (an offer) rechazar; **to — to do something** negarse a hacer algo

decode [dikód] VT descodificar

decompose [dikəmpóz] VT/VI descomponer[se]

decompress [dikəmprés] VT descomprimir

decongest [dikənʤést] VT descongestionar

decongestant [dikənʤéstənt] N descongestionante m

decontaminate [dikəntǽmɪnet] VT

descontaminar

decontamination [dikəntǽmɪnéʃən] N descontaminación f

decorate [dékəret] VT decorar; (award medals) condecorar

decoration [dɛkəréʃən] N (embellishment) adorno m; (interior decorating) decoración f; (medal of honor) condecoración f

decorative [dékə-əDɪV] ADJ decorativo

decorous [dékə-əs] ADJ decoroso

decorum [dɪkórəm] N decoro m

decoy [díkɔɪ] N (artifact) señuelo m, reclamo m; (live animal or person) cimbel m; VT atraer con señuelo/cimbel

decrease¹ [díkris] N disminución f, merma f

decrease² [díkris] VI/VI disminuir, mermar

decree [dɪkrí] N decreto m; VI/VT decretar

decrepit [dɪkrépɪt] ADJ decrépito

decrepitude [dɪkrépɪtud] N decrepitud f

decry [dɪkráɪ] VT condenar

decrypt [dikrípt] VT descifrar

decryption [dikrípʃən] N descifrado m, descodificación f

dedicate [déDɪket] VI/VT dedicar[se]; VT (a highway) inaugurar

dedication [deDɪkéʃən] N (act of dedicating) dedicación f; (in a book) dedicatoria f; (of a highway, etc.) inauguración f

deduce [dɪdús] VT deducir

deduct [dɪdʌ́kt] VT deducir

deductible [dɪdʌ́ktəbəl] ADJ deducible, desgravable; N deducible m

deduction [dɪdʌ́kʃən] N deducción f

deed [did] N (action) acción f; (exploit) hazaña f; (certificate of ownership) escritura f

deem [dim] VT considerar

deep [dip] ADJ (extending down) hondo, profundo; (dark) oscuro; (of a voice) grave; — **in debt** cargado de deudas; — **in thought** absorto; —-**sea** de altura; **he's got — pockets** es un ricachón; **he went off the — end with his hobby** se le fue la mano con el pasatiempo; **she went — into the woods** se adentró en el bosque; **ten meters —** de diez metros de profundidad; N — **freeze** congelador m; **the —** el piélago, el abismo; ADV **to dive —** bucear en las profundidades; VT **to —-six** hacer desaparecer

deepen [dípən] VI/VT ahondar, profundizar

deer [dir] N ciervo m, venado m; —**skin** gamuza f

deface [dɪfés] VT (disfigure) desfigurar; (smear with paint) pintarrajear; (mutilate) mutilar

defame [dɪfém] VT difamar

default [dɪfɔ́lt] N (negligence) negligencia f; (failure to pay) incumplimiento m; (failure to appear in court) rebeldía f; (computer setting) opción por defecto f; **in —** en mora; **by —** por defecto, por omisión; (in sports) por abandono de los contrincantes; VI (on a loan) incumplir, no pagar; (in a sports match) no comparecer

defeat [dɪfit] VT vencer, derrotar; N derrota *f*

defecate [défiket] VI defecar, evacuar

defect[1] [dífekt] N defecto *m*

defect[2] [dífekt] VI desertar

defection [dɪfékʃən] N defección *f*

defective [dɪféktɪv] ADJ defectuoso

defend [dɪfénd] VI/VT defender

defendant [dɪféndənt] N (criminal) acusado -da *mf*, reo -a *mf*; (civil) demandado -da *mf*

defender [dɪféndə] N defensor -ora *mf*; (sports) defensa *mf*

defense [dɪféns] N defensa *f*

defenseless [dɪfénslɪs] ADJ indefenso

defensible [dɪfénsəbəl] ADJ defendible

defensive [dɪfénsɪv] ADJ defensivo; — **medicine** medicina defensiva *f*; N **on the —** a la defensiva

defer [dɪfɚ] VT (a meeting) diferir, posponer; (a payment) prorrogar; (an appointment) dilatar; (from military service) eximir; **to — to another's opinion** remitirse a la opinión de otro

deference [défəəns] N deferencia *f*

deferral [dɪfɚəl] N aplazamiento *m*

defiance [dɪfáɪəns] N (challenge) desafío *m*; (resistance to authority) rebeldía *f*; **in —** of en abierta oposición a

defiant [dɪfáɪənt] ADJ desafiante

defibrillate [dɪfíbrəlet] VT desfibrilar

defibrillation [dɪfɪbrɪléʃən] N desfibrilación *f*

defibrillator [dɪfbrɪləDɚ] N desfibrilador *m*

deficiency [dɪfíʃənsi] N deficiencia *f*

deficient [dɪfíʃənt] ADJ deficiente

deficit [défɪsɪt] N déficit *m*; — **spending** gastos deficitarios *m pl*

defile [dɪfáɪl] VT (violate) mancillar; (desecrate) profanar; (to make dirty) ensuciar

define [dɪfáɪn] VI/VT definir

defining [dɪfáɪnɪŋ] ADJ decisivo

definite [défənɪt] ADJ (clearly defined) definido, determinado; (certain) seguro; **she was — in her demands** ella fue terminante es sus exigencias; — **article** artículo definido *m*

definitely [défənɪtli] ADV sin duda, definitivamente

definition [defəníʃən] N definición *f*

definitive [dɪfínɪDɪv] ADJ (final) definitivo; (authoritative) de mayor autoridad

deflate [dɪflét] VI/VT desinflar[se]

deflation [dɪfléʃən] N deflación *f*

deflect [dɪflékt] VI/VT desviar[se]

deforestation [dɪfɔrɪstéʃən] N deforestación *f*

deform [dɪfɔrm] VI/VT deformar[se]

deformed [dɪfɔrmd] ADJ deforme

deformity [dɪfɔrmɪDi] N (body part) deformidad *f*; (act or result of deforming) deformación *f*

defraud [dɪfrɔd] VT defraudar

defray [dɪfré] VT sufragar, costear

defrost [dɪfrɔst] VI/VT descongelar[se]

deft [dɛft] ADJ diestro, habilidoso

defunct [dɪfʌŋkt] ADJ caduco; **the Whig party is now —** el partido de los whigs se disolvió

defuse [dɪfjúz] VT (bomb) desactivar; (situation) distender

defy [dɪfáɪ] VT (challenge) desafiar; (resist) resistir

degenerate[1] [dɪdʒénəˌɪt] ADJ & N degenerado -da *mf*

degenerate[2] [dɪdʒénəret] VI degenerar[se]

degenerative [dɪdʒénəətɪv] ADJ degenerativo; — **joint disease** artrosis *f*, enfermedad degenerativa articular *f*

degradation [degrədéʃən] N degradación *f*

degrade [dɪgréd] VI/VT degradar[se]

degree [dɪgrí] N (stage) grado *m*; (academic) título *m*; **by —s** gradualmente; **to a —** hasta cierto punto; **to get a —** graduarse

dehumanize [dihjúmənaɪz] VI/VT deshumanizar

dehumidifier [dihjumíDɪfaɪɚ] N deshumidificador *m*

dehydrate [diháɪdret] VI/VT deshidratar[se]

deign [den] VI dignarse

deity [díɪDi] N deidad *f*

déjà vu [deʒavú] N deja vu *m*

dejected [dɪdʒéktɪd] ADJ abatido, desconsolado

dejection [dɪdʒékʃən] N abatimiento *m*, desconsuelo *m*

delay [dɪlé] N demora *f*, retraso *m*; VT demorar, retrasar; VI demorar, retrasarse

delectable [dɪléktəbəl] ADJ delicioso; N delicia *f*

delegate[1] [délɪgɪt] N delegado -da *mf*

delegate[2] [délɪget] VT delegar

delegation [delɪgéʃən] N delegación *f*, representación *f*

delete [dɪlít] VT (omit) suprimir; (cross out) tachar; — **key** tecla de borrado *f*

deleterious [delɪtíriəs] ADJ nocivo

deletion [dɪlíʃən] N supresión *f*

deliberate[1] [dɪlíbə⋅ɪt] ADJ (intentional) deliberado; (careful) cuidadoso

deliberate[2] [dɪlíbəret] VI/VT deliberar

deliberately [dɪlíbə⋅ɪtli] ADV a propósito, deliberadamente

deliberation [dɪlɪbəréʃən] N deliberación *f*

delicacy [délɪkəsi] N (fineness, precision, sensitivity) delicadeza *f*; (food) manjar *m*, delicatessen *f pl*, golleria *f*; (breakability) fragilidad *f*

delicate [délɪkɪt] ADJ delicado, tenue; (breakable) frágil; (acute) fino

delicatessen [delɪkatésən] N (store) tienda de fiambres *f*, charcutería *f*; RP rotisería *f*; (foods) delicatessen *f pl*

delicious [dɪlíʃəs] ADJ delicioso, rico

delight [dɪláɪt] N (pleasure) deleite *m*, regalo *m*;

(source of pleasure) delicia f; VI/VT deleitar[se]
delighted [dɪláɪdɪd] ADJ encantado; **to be — to** alegrarse de; **I'm — to meet you** me alegro de conocerla; **I'd be — to dance with you** me encantaría bailar contigo
delightful [dɪláɪtfəl] ADJ encantador
delimit [dɪlímɪt] VT delimitar
delineate [dɪlíniet] VT delinear
delinquent [dɪlíŋkwənt] ADJ & N (debtor) moroso -sa mf; (wrongdoer) delincuente mf; (juvenile) delincuente juvenil mf
delirious [dɪlírias] ADJ (hysterical) delirante; (happy) contentísimo; **to be —** delirar
delirium [dɪlíriəm] N delirio m
deliver [dɪlívə-] VT (hand over) entregar; (hand out) repartir; (liberate) liberar; (pronounce a speech) pronunciar; (administer a blow) dar; (have a baby) dar a luz; (assist a birth) atender en un parto; **to — the goods** cumplir con lo prometido
deliverance [dɪlívə-əns] N liberación f
delivery [dɪlívəri] N (handing out) entrega f, expedición f; (things to be delivered) pedido m; (birth) parto m; (speaking) ejecución f, expresión oral f; **on —** a la entrega; **— service** servicio de entrega m; **— truck** camión de reparto m; **to take —** aceptar entrega
dell [dɛl] N hondonada f
deltoids [déltɔɪdz] N deltoides m sg
delude [dɪlúd] VT engañar
deluge [déljuʤ] N diluvio m; VT abrumar
delusion [dɪlúʒən] N (act of deluding, state of being deluded) engaño m; **—s of grandeur** delirios de grandeza m pl
deluxe [dɪláks] ADJ de lujo
demagogue, demagog [déməgag] N demagogo -ga mf
demand [dɪmænd] VT (ask for) exigir; (require) requerir, exigir; N exigencia f, reivindicación f; **on —** por demanda
demanding [dɪmændɪŋ] ADJ exigente
demarcate [dɪmárket] VT demarcar
demean [dɪmín] VT menospreciar
demeanor [dɪmínə-] N conducta f, comportamiento m
demented [dɪméntɪd] ADJ demente
dementia [dɪménʃə] N demencia f
demijohn [démiʤan] N damajuana f
demise [dɪmáɪz] N fallecimiento m, desaparición f
demo [démo] N demostración f
demobilize [dimóbəlaɪz] VT desmovilizar
democracy [dɪmákrəsi] N democracia f
democrat [déməkræt] N demócrata mf
democratic [deməkrǽdɪk] ADJ democrático
democratization [dɪmakrədɪzéʃən] N democratización f
demographics [deməgrǽfɪks] N demografía f

demolish [dɪmálɪʃ] VT demoler, derrumbar
demon [dímən] N demonio m
demonstrate [démənstret] VT (prove) demostrar; (show a product) hacer una demostración; VI manifestar
demonstration [demənstréʃən] N (proof, exhibition) demostración f; (protest) manifestación f, concentración f
demonstrative [dɪmánstrəDɪv] ADJ demostrativo
demonstrator [démənstreDə-] N manifestante mf
demoralize [dɪmɔrəlaɪz] VT desmoralizar
demote [dɪmót] VT degradar, bajar de categoría
den [dɛn] N (of an animal) guarida f; (room in a house) cuarto de estar m; (cave) cueva f; **— of iniquity** antro de perdición m
dengue fever [déŋgi fívə-] N dengue m
denial [dɪnáɪəl] N (assertion that an allegation is false) desmentido m; (refusal to approve) denegación f, negativa f; (refusal to recognize) negación f; **he is in —** no lo quiere aceptar
denigrate [dénɪgret] VT denigrar
denim [dénɪm] N tela de vaquero f
Denmark [dénmark] N Dinamarca f
denomination [dɪnamənéʃən] N (name, monetary value) denominación f; (sect) secta religiosa f
denominator [dɪnámɪneDə-] N denominador m
denotation [dinotéʃən] N denotación f
denote [dɪnót] VT denotar
denounce [dɪnáuns] VT denunciar
dense [dɛns] ADJ (compacted) denso, tupido, cerrado; (stupid) fam burro, duro de entenderas
density [dénsɪDi] N densidad f
dent [dɛnt] N abolladura f; **to make a — in a task** hacer mella en una tarea; VI/VT abollar[se]
dental [déntl] ADJ dental; **— care** cuidado dental m; **— floss** hilo dental m; **— hygienist** higienista dental mf; **— implant** implante dental m; **— plaque** placa dental f; **— school** facultad de odontología f
dentifrice [déntəfrɪs] N dentífrico m, pasta dental f
dentist [déntɪst] N dentista mf
dentistry [déntɪstri] N odontología f
dentures [déntʃə-z] N dientes postizos m pl
denunciation [dɪnansiéʃən] N denuncia f, acusación f
deny [dɪnáɪ] VT (state that something is false) negar, desmentir; (refuse to approve) rechazar; **to — oneself** abstenerse
deodorant [dióDə-ənt] N desodorante m
deodorize [dióDəraɪz] VT desodorizar
deoxidize [diáksɪdaɪz] VT desoxidar
depart [dɪpárt] VI (leave) salir, partir; (deviate)

desviarse, apartarse; (die) fallecer, dejar de existir

departed [dɪpárDɪd] ADJ & N difunto -ta *mf*

department [dɪpártmənt] N (of company, school, country) departamento *m*; (of government) ministerio *m*; (of a store) sección *f*; (of knowledge, expertise) especialidad *f*; — **head** jefe -fa de departamento *mf*; — **store** gran almacén *m*

departure [dɪpártʃə-] N (scheduled) salida *f*; (not scheduled) partida *f*; (deviation) desviación *f*

depend [dɪpénd] VI depender; **to — on** (rely on) contar con; (be conditioned by) depender de; —**ing on the number of guests** dependiendo de la cantidad de invitados

dependable [dɪpéndəbəl] ADJ confiable, fiable

dependence [dɪpéndəns] N dependencia *f*

dependency [dɪpéndənsi] N dependencia *f*

dependent [dɪpéndənt] ADJ dependiente; **success is — on perseverance** el éxito depende de la perseverancia; N familiar a cargo *mf*

depict [dɪpíkt] VT (verbally) describir; (visually) representar

depilate [dépəlet] VT depilar[se]

depilatory [dɪpílətɔri] ADJ & N depilatorio *m*

deplane [diplén] VI desembarcar

deplete [dɪplít] VT agotar

depletion [dɪplíʃən] N agotamiento *m*

deplorable [dɪplɔ́rəbəl] ADJ deplorable

deplore [dɪplɔ́r] VT deplorar

deploy [dɪplɔ́i] VT desplegar

deport [dɪpɔ́rt] VT deportar; VI comportarse

deportment [dɪpɔ́rtmənt] N comportamiento *m*, conducta *f*

depose [dɪpóz] VT (overthrow) deponer, derrocar; (testify) declarar; (take testimony) tomar declaración

deposit [dɪpázɪt] VT (add to an account) depositar; *Sp* ingresar; (place) colocar; N (amount added to an account) depósito *m*; *Sp* ingreso *m*; (of a mineral) yacimiento *m*; (earnest money) señal *f*, anticipo *m*; — **slip** hoja de depósito *f*

deposition [dɛpəzíʃən] N (removal from office) deposición *f*; (testimony) declaración *f*

depositor [dɪpázɪtə-] N depositante *mf*

depot [dípo] N (of trains) estación *f*; (of buses) terminal *mf*; (for storage) almacén *m*, depósito *m*; (for military training) cuartel *m*

depraved [dɪprévd] ADJ depravado

deprecate [déprɪket] VT despreciar

depreciate [dɪpríʃiet] VT (currency) depreciar[se]; (goods) desvalorizar[se], amortizar[se]

depreciation [dɪpriʃiéʃən] N (of currency) depreciación *f*; (of goods) amortización *f*

depress [dɪprés] VT deprimir

depressed [dɪprést] ADJ deprimido

depressing [dɪprésɪŋ] ADJ deprimente

depression [dɪpréʃən] N depresión *f*

deprive [dɪpráiv] VT privar

depth [dɛpθ] N (of hole, feeling) profundidad *f*, hondura *f*; (of the voice) gravedad *f*; **in the —s** en las profundidades; **in — a fondo**; **what is the — of that bookshelf?** ¿cuánto miden estos estantes de fondo? **he has sunk to such —s** ha caído muy bajo; **in the — of the night** bien entrada la noche; **in the — of winter** en lo más crudo del invierno

deputation [dɛpjətéʃən] N delegación *f*

deputy [dépjəbi] N (elected official) diputado -da *mf*; (substitute) suplente *mf*

derail [dɪrél] VI/VT descarrilar[se]

deranged [dɪréndʒd] ADJ trastornado, demente

derby [dɝ́bi] N (hat) sombrero hongo *m*; (race) derby *m*

deregulate [dirégjələt] VT desregular

derelict [dérəlikt] ADJ (deserted) abandonado; (negligent) negligente; N (ship) buque abandonado *m*; (person) vagabundo -da *mf*

dereliction [dɛrəlíkʃən] N — **of duties** abandono de funciones *m*

deride [dɪráid] VT escarnecer, ridiculizar

derision [dɪríʒən] N escarnio *m*

derivation [dɛrəvéʃən] N derivación *f*

derivative [dɪrívəDɪv] ADJ & N derivado *m*

derive [dɪráiv] VI/VT derivar[se]; **to — pleasure from** disfrutar de

dermabrasion [dɝ́məbreʒən] N abrasión cutánea *f*, dermabrasión *f*

dermatologist [dɝmətá: ́ləʤɪst] N dermatólogo -ga *mf*

dermatology [dɝmətáːləʤi] N dermatología *f*

derogatory [dɪrágətɔri] ADJ despectivo

derrick [dérɪk] N torre de perforación *f*

descend [dɪsénd] VI/VT descender; —**ing sort** clasificación descendiente *f*; **to — upon** caer sobre

descendant [dɪséndənt] ADJ & N descendiente *mf*

descent [dɪsént] N (act of descending, decline) descenso *m*; (slope) bajada *f*; (lineage) descendencia *f*

describe [dɪskráib] VT describir

description [dɪskrípʃən] N descripción *f*, caracterización *f*; **of all —s** de todas clases

descriptive [dɪskríptɪv] ADJ descriptivo

desecrate [désɪkret] VT profanar

desecration [dɛsɪkréʃən] N profanación *f*

desegregate [diségrɪget] VI/VT eliminar la segregación racial

deselect [disɪlékt] VT anular [una selección previa]

desensitize [disénsɪtaɪz] VT insensibilizar

desert[1] [dézɚt] ADJ (barren, empty) desierto; (of the desert) desértico; N desierto *m*

desert[2] [dɪzɝ́t] VI/VT (a person, place)

abandonar; (military service) desertar

deserter [dɪzɔ́ːDɚ] N desertor -ora *mf*

desertion [dɪzɔ́ːʃən] N (of a person or place) abandono *m*; (from the military) deserción *f*

deserve [dɪzɔ́ːv] VT merecer

deserving [dɪzɔ́ːvɪŋ] ADJ merecedor

desiccate [désɪket] VI/VT desecar[se]

design [dɪzáɪn] VI/VT (prepare a sketch of) diseñar, trazar; (plan) planear, idear; N (model, pattern) diseño *m*; (sketch) esbozo *m*; **he has —s on her** le ha echado el ojo

designate [dézɪgnet] VT designar, denominar; **—d hitter** bateador -ora designado -da *mf*

designation [dezɪgnéʃən] N denominación *f*, designación *f*

designer [dɪzáɪnɚ] N diseñador -ora *mf*; **— drugs** drogas de diseño *f pl*

desirability [dɪzaɪrəbílɪDi] N deseabilidad *f*, conveniencia *f*

desirable [dɪzáɪrəbəl] ADJ deseable

desire [dɪzáɪr] VT desear; **I — your cooperation** requiero tu cooperación; N deseo *m*

desirous [dɪzáɪrəs] ADJ deseoso

desist [dɪsíst] VI desistir

desk [desk] N escritorio *m*; (school) pupitre *m*; **—top computer** *Am* computadora de escritorio *f*, *Sp* ordenador de sobremesa *m*; **—top publishing** edición de sobremesa *f*, autoedición *f*

desolate[1] [désəlɪt] ADJ (barren) desolado

desolate[2] [désəlet] VT desolar, asolar

desolation [desəléʃən] N desolación *f*, asolamiento *m*

despair [dɪspér] N desesperanza *f*; VI desesperarse, perder la esperanza

despairing [dɪspérɪŋ] ADJ de desesperación

desperate [déspɚɪt] ADJ desesperado

desperately [déspɚɪtli] ADV desesperadamente; **— ill** gravemente enfermo; **he's — looking for funds** está desesperado buscando financiación

desperation [despɚéʃən] N desesperación *f*

despicable [dɪspíkəbəl] ADJ despreciable, deleznable

despise [dɪspáɪz] VT despreciar, menospreciar

despite [dɪspáɪt] N despecho *m*; PREP a pesar de

despoil [dɪspɔ́ɪl] VT despojar

despondency [dɪspándənsi] N abatimiento *m*, desaliento *m*

despondent [dɪspándənt] ADJ abatido, desalentado

despot [déspət] N déspota *mf*

despotic [dɪspáDɪk] ADJ despótico

despotism [déspəʊɪzəm] N despotismo *m*

dessert [dɪzɔ́ːt] N postre *m*

destabilize [distébəlaɪz] VT desestabilizar

destination [destənéʃən] N destino *m*

destine [déstɪn] VT destinar; **she's —d for**

greatness promete grandes cosas

destiny [déstəni] N destino *m*

destitute [déstɪtut] ADJ menesteroso, indigente; **— of** falto de, desprovisto de

destroy [dɪstrɔ́ɪ] VT (demolish) destruir, deshacer; (kill an animal) sacrificar; (ruin a reputation) arruinar

destroyer [dɪstrɔ́ɪɚ] N (person who destroys) destructor -ora *mf*; (ship) destructor *m*

destructible [dɪstráktəbəl] ADJ destructible

destruction [dɪstrákʃən] N (act of demolishing) destrucción *f*; (act of killing) matanza *f*; (act of ruining a reputation) ruina *f*

destructive [dɪstráktɪv] ADJ destructivo, destructor

detach [dɪtǽtʃ] VT separar, desprender; (troops) destacar

detachment [dɪtǽtʃmənt] N (physical) separación *f*; (emotional) desapego *m*; (of troops) destacamento *m*; (of the retina) desprendimiento *m*

detail[1] [dítel] N detalle *m*, pormenor *m*; (military) destacamento *m*; **to go into —** detallar, pormenorizar

detail[2] [dítél] VT detallar, pormenorizar; (assign duties) destacar

detain [dɪtén] VT detener

detect [dɪtékt] VT detectar

detection [dɪtékʃən] N detección *f*

detective [dɪtéktɪv] N detective *mf*; **— novel** novela policial *f*

detector [dɪtéktɚ] N detector *m*

detention [dɪténʃən] N (in jail) detención *f*; (in school) castigo *m*

deter [dɪtɔ́ː] VT (dissuade) disuadir; (prevent) prevenir

detergent [dɪtɔ́ːdʒənt] N detergente *m*

deteriorate [dɪtíriəret] VI deteriorar[se]

deterioration [dɪtiriəréʃən] N deterioro *m*

determination [dɪtɚmənéʃən] N (act of determining) determinación *f*; (resolution) resolución *f*; (persistence) tesón *m*, perseverancia *f*

determine [dɪtɔ́ːmɪn] VT determinar; **to — to do something** decidirse a hacer algo

determined [dɪtɔ́ːmɪnd] ADJ (resolute) decidido, resuelto; (persistent) tesonero

determiner [dɪtɔ́ːmɪnɚ] N (grammatical) determinante *m*

determining [dɪtɔ́ːmɪnɪŋ] ADJ determinante

detest [dɪtést] VT detestar, abominar de

detestable [dɪtéstəbəl] ADJ detestable

dethrone [diθrón] VT destronar

detonate [détnet] VI/VT detonar

detonation [detnéʃən] N detonación *f*

detour [dítur] N desvío *m*; VI/VT desviar[se]

detoxification [dituksəfɪkéʃən] N destoxificación *f*

detract [dɪtrǽkt] VT distraer; VI **to — from**

disminuir

detrimental [detrəméntl] ADJ perjudicial

deuce [dus] N (in tennis) deuce *m*, cuarenta iguales

devaluation [divæljuéʃən] N devaluación *f*

devastate [dévəstet] VT devastar, asolar

devastating [dévəsteDɪŋ] ADJ devastador

develop [dɪvéləp] VI/VT (mature, elaborate) desarrollar[se]; (build houses on) construir, edificar; (treat film) revelar; **she —ed an allergy** le vino una alergia; **—ing country** país en desarrollo *m*

developer [dɪvéləpə] N (of computer programs) desarrollador -ora *mf*; (of real estate) promotor -ora *mf*; **a late —** persona de maduración tardía *f*

development [dɪvéləpmənt] N (evolution) desarrollo *m*; (buildings) urbanización *f*, colonia *f*; (of a photograph) revelado *m*

developmental [dɪveləpméntl] ADJ relativo al desarrollo

deviate [dívíet] VI/VT desviar[se]

deviation [diviéʃən] N desviación *f*

device [dɪváɪs] N (gadget) dispositivo *m*; (literary convention) recurso *m*; (emblem) divisa *f*; **they left me to my own —s** me dejaron que me las arreglara sola

devil [dévəl] N diablo *m*; **lucky —!** ¡suertudo! **what the — are you saying?** ¿qué diablos dices? **—'s advocate** abogado del diablo *m*

devilish [dévəlɪʃ] ADJ (evil) diabólico; (extreme) endiablado, endemoniado

deviltry [dévəltri] N (mischief) diablura *f*; (witchcraft) brujería *f*

devious [dívəs] ADJ (roundabout) sinuoso, tortuoso; (crafty) taimado, retorcido

devise [dɪváɪz] VT idear, urdir

devoid [dɪvɔ́ɪd] ADJ **— of** falto de, desprovisto de

devolution [devəlúʃən] N devolución *f*

devote [dɪvót] VT dedicar; (consecrate) consagrar

devoted [dɪvóDɪd] ADJ (friend) leal; (parent) dedicado; (worshiper) devoto

devotion [dɪvóʃən] N devoción *f*

devour [dɪváʊr] VT devorar

devout [dɪváʊt] ADJ devoto

dew [du] N rocío *m*; **—drop** gota de rocío *f*; **—point** punto de condensación *m*

dexterity [dekstériDi] N destreza *f*

dextrose [dékstros] N dextrosa *f*

diabetes [daɪəbíbiz] N diabetes *f*

diabolic [daɪəbálɪk] ADJ diabólico

diacritic [daɪəkrídɪk] ADJ & N diacrítico *m*

diagnose [daɪəgnós] VT diagnosticar

diagnosis [daɪəgnósɪs] N diagnóstico *m*, diagnosis *f*

diagnostic [daɪəgnástɪk] ADJ diagnóstico

diagonal [daɪǽgənl] ADJ & N diagonal *f*

diagram [dáɪəgræm] N diagrama *m*

dial [dáɪəl] N (of a watch, clock) esfera *f*; (of

radio) dial *m*; **— tone** *Sp* señal de marcar *f*; *Am* tono de discar *m*; VI/VT (a telephone number) *Sp* marcar; *Am* discar

dialect [dáɪəlekt] N dialecto *m*

dialectic [daɪəléktɪk] ADJ dialéctico; N dialéctica *f*

dialectology [daɪəlektáləʤi] N dialectología *f*

dialogue, dialog [dáɪəlɑg] N diálogo *m*; VI dialogar

dialysis [daɪǽlɪsɪs] N diálisis *f*

diameter [daɪǽmɪDə] N diámetro *m*

diamond [dáɪəmənd] N (stone) diamante *m*; (shape) rombo *m*

diaper [dáɪpə] N pañal *m*; VT poner pañales

diaphragm [dáɪəfræm] N diafragma *m*

diarrhea [daɪəriə] N diarrea *f*

diary [dáɪəri] N diario *m*

diastolic [daɪəstálɪk] ADJ diastólico

diatribe [dáɪətraɪb] N diatriba *f*

dice [daɪs] N PL dados *m pl*; VT cortar en cubos; **no —!** (impossibility) no hay forma, *Am* ¡ni modo! (refusal) de ninguna manera

dichotomy [daɪkáDəmi] N dicotomía *f*

dicker [díkə] VI regatear

dictate [díktet] VI/VT dictar; N dictado *m*, precepto *m*

dictation [dɪktéʃən] N dictado *m*; **to take —** escribir al dictado

dictator [díkteDə] N dictador -ora *mf*

dictatorship [dɪktéDəʃɪp] N dictadura *f*

diction [díkʃən] N dicción *f*

dictionary [díkʃəneri] N diccionario *m*

did [dɪd] *see* do

didactic [daɪdǽktɪk] ADJ didáctico

die [daɪ] VI morir[se]; **to — down/away** disminuir; **to — off** irse muriendo; **to — out** morirse, extinguirse; **my car —d** se me murió el coche; N (game piece) dado *m*; (press) molde *m*; (stamp) cuño *m*, troquel *m*; **—hard** intransigente *mf*

diesel [dízəl] N diesel *m*; **— engine** motor diesel *m*

diet [dáɪɪt] N (food) dieta *f*; (controlled intake of food) dieta *f*, régimen *m*; **to be/go on a —** estar a dieta/régimen; **to put on a —** poner a dieta; VI estar a dieta, hacer dieta

dietary [dáɪɪteri] ADJ dietético

dietitian [daɪɪtíʃən] N dietista *mf*

differ [dífə] VI diferir; **to — with** disentir, no estar de acuerdo con; **to — from** ser diferente de

difference [dífərəns] N diferencia *f*; **it makes no —** no importa, da igual

different [dífərənt] ADJ diferente, distinto

differential [dɪfərénʃəl] ADJ & N (difference, car part) diferencial *m*; **— equation** ecuación diferencial *f*

differentiate [dɪfərénʃiet] VI/VT diferenciar[se], distinguir[se]

differentiation [dɪfərenʃiéʃən] N diferenciación *f*

differently [dífəəntli] ADV de manera

diferente; **they act** — no se comportan igual
difficult [dífɪkəlt] ADJ difícil
difficulty [dífɪkʌlti] N dificultad f; **with** — con dificultad, dificilmente
diffident [dífɪdənt] ADJ tímido
diffuse¹ [dɪfjúz] VI/VT difundir
diffuse² [dɪfjús] ADJ difuso
diffusion [dɪfjúʒən] N difusión f
dig [dɪg] VI/VT cavar; (by machine) excavar; (superficially) escarbar; **to — in the files** escarbar en los archivos; **to — under** socavar; **to — up** desenterrar; **he dug his heels into the ground** clavó los talones en el suelo; **I — your new shoes** están muy buenos tus zapatos nuevos; N (archaeological site) excavación f; (sarcastic remark) pulla f; **a — in the ribs** un codazo
digest¹ [dɪdʒést] VI/VT digerir
digest² [dáɪdʒest] N (summary) compendio m; (legal) digesto m
digestible [dɪdʒéstəbəl] ADJ digerible, digestible
digestion [dɪdʒéstʃən] N digestión f
digestive [dɪdʒéstɪv] ADJ digestivo
digit [dídʒɪt] N dígito m
digital [dídʒɪd̬l] ADJ digital; — **camera** cámara digital f; — **computer** Am computadora digital f, Sp ordenador digital m; — **photography** fotografía digital f
digitalize [dídʒɪd̬laɪz] VT digitalizar
digitize [dídʒɪtaɪz] VT digitalizar
dignified [dígnəfaɪd] ADJ digno
dignitary [dígnɪteri] N dignatario -ria mf
dignity [dígnɪd̬i] N dignidad f
digress [dɪgrés] VI divagar
digression [dɪgréʃən] N digresión f
dike [daɪk] N dique m
dilapidated [dɪlǽpɪdeɪd̬ɪd] ADJ (machine) destartalado; (furniture) desvencijado; (house) derruido, venido abajo
dilate [dáɪleɪt] VI/VT dilatar[se]
dilation [daɪléʃən] N dilatación f
dilemma [dɪlémə] N dilema m
dilettante [dílɪtɑnt] N diletante mf
diligence [dílədʒəns] N diligencia f
diligent [dílədʒənt] ADJ diligente, hacendoso
dill [dɪl] N eneldo m; — **pickle** pepinillo en vinagre con eneldo m
dilute [dɪlút] VI/VT diluir[se]; ADJ diluido
dim [dɪm] ADJ (light) tenue; (outline) difuso; (room) oscuro, en penumbras; (person) fam de pocas luces; —**wit** fam tonto, bobo; VI/VT (make less bright) atenuar; VT (switch to low beam) bajar
dime [daɪm] N moneda de diez centavos f; **unskilled workers are a — a dozen** sobran los obreros no cualificados
dimension [dɪménʃən] N dimensión f
diminish [dɪmínɪʃ] VI/VT disminuir, menguar; **the law of —ing returns** la ley de los rendimientos decrecientes
diminution [dɪmənúʃən] N disminución f, mengua f
diminutive [dɪmínjəd̬ɪv] ADJ diminuto; N diminutivo m
dimmer [dímə] N regulador de voltaje m
dimness [dímnɪs] N oscuridad f, penumbra f
dimple [dímpəl] N hoyuelo m; VT formar hoyuelos
din [dɪn] N estruendo m, estrépito m
dine [daɪn] VI cenar; **to — out** cenar afuera
diner [dáɪnə] N (restaurant) cafetería f; (on a train) coche comedor m; (person) comensal mf
ding-a-ling [díŋəlɪŋ] N (silly person) ganso -sa mf; (eccentric person) excéntrico -ca mf; (sound) tilín m
dingy [díndʒi] ADJ deslucido
dining [dáɪnɪŋ] ADJ — **car** coche comedor m; — **room** comedor m
dinner [dínə] N (main meal) comida f; (at midday) almuerzo m; (in the evening) cena f; — **jacket** smoking m; —**time** hora de la comida f
dinosaur [dáɪnəsɔr] N dinosaurio m
dint [dɪnt] ADV LOC **by** — **of** a fuerza de
dip [dɪp] VT (make wet) mojar; (scoop) sacar; (immerse) sumergir; (immerse in insecticide) bañar; (immerse in sauce, coffee) pringar, mojar; VI (sun) hundirse; (stocks) bajar; (road) hacer una bajada; (airplane) descender súbitamente; N (act of wetting) mojada f; (portion of ice-cream) bola f, cucharada f; (sauce) mojo m; (reduction in sales) disminución f; (low place in a road) declive m; (low place in the land) hondonada f; (swim) baño m; (airplane maneuver) descenso rápido m; (irritating person) pej pesado -da mf
diphtheria [dɪpθíriə] N difteria f
diphthong [dífθɔŋ] N diptongo m
diploma [dɪplómə] N diploma m
diplomacy [dɪplóməsi] N diplomacia f
diplomat [dípləmæt] N diplomático -ca mf
diplomatic [dɪpləmǽd̬ɪk] ADJ diplomático
dipper [dípə] N cucharón m, cazo m
dire [daɪr] ADJ terrible, espantoso; — **need** necesidad acuciante f; — **predictions** predicciones funestas f pl; — **situation** situación extrema f
direct [dɪrékt] ADJ directo; — **current** corriente continua f; — **object** complemento directo m; — **quotation** cita textual f; ADV directamente; VI/VT dirigir; **he —ed me to leave** me mandó irme
direction [dɪrékʃən] N dirección f; —**s** indicaciones f pl; **I'm thinking in that** — me inclino por eso
directive [dɪréktɪv] ADJ directivo; N directiva f
director [dɪréktə] N (theater, movies) director

-ra *mf*; (film, TV) realizador -ora *mf*
directory [dɪréktəri] N directorio *m*
dirigible [dəríʤəbəl] ADJ & N dirigible *m*
dirt [dɚt] N (filth) suciedad *f*; (foul substance)
mugre *f*; (earth) tierra *f*; — **bag** *offensive*
porquería *f*; **I've got some — on him** le
conozco los trapos sucios; ADJ — **cheap**
baratísimo; —-**poor** pobrísimo
dirty [dɚ́di] ADJ sucio, mugriento; — **joke** chiste
verde *m*; — **look** mirada asesina *f*; — **money**
dinero sucio *m*; — **shame** pena horrible *f*; —
trick trampa *f*; — **word** palabrota *f*; *Sp* taco
m; — **work** trabajo sucio *m*; VI/VT ensuciar;
ADV **to talk** — decir cosas obscenas
disability [dɪsəbílɪɾi] N incapacidad *f*,
discapacidad *f*, minusvalía *f*; — **insurance**
seguro de discapacidad *m*
disable [dɪsébəl] VT (person) incapacitar;
(device) desactivar
disabled [dɪsébəld] ADJ discapacitado,
minusválido
disabuse [dɪsəbjúz] VT desengañar
disadvantage [dɪsədvǽntɪʤ] N desventaja *f*; **to**
be at a — estar en desventaja
disadvantaged [dɪsɪdvǽntɪʤd] ADJ carenciado
disagree [dɪsəgrí] VI (differ in opinion) disentir,
no estar de acuerdo; (differ) diferir; **pizza—s**
with me no me cae bien la pizza
disagreeable [dɪsəgríəbəl] ADJ desagradable
disagreement [dɪsəgrímənt] N (lack of
agreement, argument) desacuerdo *m*;
(discrepancy) discrepancia *f*
disallow [dɪsəláu] VT desaprobar; (in sports)
anular
disappear [dɪsəpír] VI desaparecer
disappearance [dɪsəpírəns] N desaparición *f*
disappoint [dɪsəpɔ́int] VI/VT decepcionar,
desilusionar; **to be —ed** estar desilusionado
disappointing [dɪsəpɔ́intɪŋ] ADJ decepcionante
disappointment [dɪsəpɔ́intmənt] N decepción
f, desilusión *f*
disapproval [dɪsəprúvəl] N desaprobación *f*
disapprove [dɪsəprúv] VI/VT desaprobar
disarm [dɪsárm] VI/VT desarmar[se]
disarmament [dɪsárməmənt] N desarme *m*
disarray [dɪsəré] N desordenar; N confusión *f*,
desorden *m*; **in** — en desorden
disaster [dɪzǽstɚ] N desastre *m*
disastrous [dɪzǽstrəs] ADJ desastroso
disavow [dɪsəváu] VT negar
disband [dɪsbǽnd] VT disolver; VI desbandarse
disbelief [dɪsbɪlíf] N incredulidad *f*
disbelieve [dɪsbɪlív] VI/VT descreer de
disburse [dɪsbɝ́s] VT desembolsar
disbursement [dɪsbɝ́smənt] N desembolso *m*
discard[1] [dɪskárd] VT (a card) descartar;
(garbage) desechar
discard[2] [dɪskárd] N (card) descarte *m*; (garbage)
desecho *m*

discern [dɪsɚ́n] VT (distinguish mentally)
discernir; (perceive) percibir
discernment [dɪsɚ́nmənt] N discernimiento *m*
discharge[1] [dɪstʃárʤ] VI/VT (battery, load,
firearm) descargar[se]; (obligation) cumplir;
(prisoner) poner en libertad, soltar; (odor)
despedir; (soldier) dar de baja; (patient) dar
de alta; (a debt) pagar; (pus) supurar
discharge[2] [dɪstʃárʤ] N (of a battery, load,
firearm) descarga *f*; (of an obligation)
cumplimiento *m*; (of a prisoner) puesta en
libertad *f*; (of an odor) emisión *f*; (of a soldier)
baja *f*; (of a patient) alta *f*; (of a debt) pago *m*;
(of oil) pérdida *f*; (of pus) supuración *f*;
(uterine, vaginal) flujo *m*; (from a job)
despido *m*
disciple [dɪsáɪpəl] N discípulo -la *m*
discipline [dísəplɪn] N disciplina *f*; VT
disciplinar
disclaimer [dɪskléma] N descargo de
responsabilidad *m*
disclose [dɪsklóz] VT revelar
disco [dísko] N discoteca *f*
discolor [dɪskʌ́lə] VI/VT decolorar[se]
discomfort [dɪskʌ́mfɚt] N malestar *m*
disconcert [dɪskənsɚ́t] VT desconcertar
disconnect [dɪskənɛ́kt] VI/VT desconectar; N
desconexión *f*
disconnected [dɪskənɛ́ktɪd] ADJ (broken)
desconectado; (incoherent) inconexo
disconsolate [dɪskánsəlɪt] ADJ desconsolado
discontent [dɪskəntɛ́nt] N descontento *m*
discontinue [dɪskəntínju] VT suspender,
interrumpir
discontinuous [dɪskəntínjuəs] ADJ discontinuo
discord [dískɔrd] N (lack of concord) discordia *f*,
desavenencia *f*; (dissonance) disonancia *f*,
discordancia *f*
discotheque [dískotek] N discoteca *f*
discount [dískaunt] VT (deduct from a charge,
take into account in advance) descontar; (sell
at a reduced price) rebajar; (disregard)
ignorar; N descuento *m*; **at a** — con
descuento, con rebaja
discourage [dɪskɝ́ɪʤ] VT desanimar, desalentar;
to — from disuadir de
discouragement [dɪskɝ́ɪʤmənt] N desánimo
m, desaliento *m*
discourse[1] [dískɔrs] N (conversation, talk)
discurso *m*; (treatise) disertación *f*
discourse[2] [dískɔrs] VI (talk) discurrir; (treat a
subject) disertar
discourteous [dɪskɝ́ɾiəs] ADJ descortés
discourtesy [dɪskɝ́ɾɪsi] N descortesía *f*
discover [dɪskʌ́vɚ] VT descubrir
discoverer [dɪskʌ́vərɚ] N descubridor -ora *mf*
discovery [dɪskʌ́vəri] N descubrimiento *m*
discredit [dɪskrɛ́dɪt] VT (injure the reputation
of) desacreditar; (give no credence to) no

creer; N descrédito *m*
discreet [dɪskrít] ADJ discreto
discrepancy [dɪskrépənsi] N discrepancia *f*
discrete [dɪskrít] ADJ (separate) separado; (en matemáticas) discreto
discretion [dɪskréʃən] N discreción *f*; **at your own** — a discreción; **at the judge's** — al arbitrio del juez
discretionary [dɪskréʃəneri] ADJ discrecional; **— income** ingresos discrecionales *m pl*
discriminate [dɪskrímənet] VI/VT distinguir; **to — against** discriminar a
discrimination [dɪskrɪmɪnéʃən] N discriminación *f*
discuss [dɪskʌ́s] VT discutir
discussion [dɪskʌ́ʃən] N discusión *f*
disdain [dɪsdén] N desdén *m*, desprecio *m*; VT (treat with contempt) desdeñar; (think unworthy of a response) no dignarse a
disdainful [dɪsdénfəl] ADJ desdeñoso
disease [dɪzíz] N enfermedad *f*
diseased [dɪzízd] ADJ enfermo
disembark [dɪsɪmbárk] VI/VT desembarcar
disenfranchise [dɪsɪnfrǽntʃaɪz] VT (politician) proscribir; (minorities) privar de derechos, desheredar
disengage [dɪsɪngédʒ] VI/VT (a clutch) soltar[se]; (from a situation) distanciar[se]
disentangle [dɪsɪntǽŋgəl] VI/VT desenredar[se], desenmarañar[se]
disfavor [dɪsfévər] VT mirar con malos ojos; N **to fall into** — (a person) caer en desgracia; (a fashion) caer en desuso
disfigure [dɪsfígjər] VT desfigurar
disgrace [dɪsgrés] N (dishonor) deshonra *f*; (shame) vergüenza *f*; **to fall into** — caer en desgracia; VT deshonrar
disgraceful [dɪsgrésfəl] ADJ vergonzoso
disgruntled [dɪsgrántld] ADJ descontento, resentido
disguise [dɪsgáɪz] VT disfrazar[se]; N disfraz *m*
disgust [dɪsgʌ́st] VT (repel) asquear, repugnar; (displease) disgustar; N asco *m*, repugnancia *f*
disgusted [dɪsgʌ́stɪd] ADJ asqueado, repugnado
disgusting [dɪsgʌ́stɪŋ] ADJ asqueroso, repugnante
dish [dɪʃ] N (plate, food, quantity) plato *m*; (serving container) fuente *f*; (attractive person) *fam* bombón *m*; **—es** vajilla *f*; **—cloth/towel** paño de cocina *m*, repasador *m*; **—washer** lavaplatos *m sg*, lavavajillas *m sg*; **—water** agua de fregar *f*; VI/VT (serve food) servir; **to — out** repartir
dishearten [dɪshártn̩] VT desanimar, descorazonar, desalentar
disheartening [dɪshártnɪŋ] ADJ descorazonador, desalentador
dishevel [dɪʃévəl] VT desgreñar
disheveled [dɪʃévəld] ADJ (hair) desgreñado,

revuelto; (clothes) desaliñado
dishonest [dɪsánɪst] ADJ deshonesto
dishonesty [dɪsánɪsti] N deshonestidad *f*
dishonor [dɪsánər] N deshonra *f*; VT deshonrar; (a check) no pagar
dishonorable [dɪsánəəbəl] ADJ deshonroso
disillusion [dɪsɪlúʒən] N desilusión *f*, desencanto *m*; VT desilusionar, desencantar
disinfect [dɪsɪnfékt] VT desinfectar
disinfectant [dɪsɪnféktənt] N desinfectante *m*
disinfection [dɪsɪnfékʃən] N desinfección *f*
disinfestation [dɪsɪnfɛstéʃən] N desinfestación *f*
disinformation [dɪsɪnfəméʃən] N desinformación *f*
disinherit [dɪsɪnhérɪt] VT desheredar
disintegrate [dɪsíntɪgret] VI/VT desintegrar[se]
disintegration [dɪsɪntɪgréʃən] N desintegración *f*
disinterested [dɪsíntrɪstɪd] ADJ desinteresado
disjointed [dɪsdʒɔ́ɪntɪd] ADJ desarticulado
disk, disc [dɪsk] N disco *m*; (game piece) tejo *m*; (in a computer) disco *m*, disquete *m*; **— brake** freno de disco *m*; **— capacity** capacidad de almacenamiento de disco *f*; **— drive** disquetera *f*; **— jockey** pinchadiscos *mf sg*
diskette [dɪskét] N disquete *m*; **— drive** unidad de disquete *f*
dislike [dɪsláɪk] N aversión *f*, tirria *f*; VT **I — parties** no me gustan las fiestas
dislocate [dɪslóket] VT dislocar, descoyuntar
dislocation [dɪslokéʃən] N dislocación *f*, luxación *f*
dislodge [dɪsládʒ] VT (force out) desatascar; (displace) desprender
disloyal [dɪslɔ́ɪəl] ADJ desleal
dismal [dízməl] ADJ pésimo; **a — failure** un fracaso rotundo
dismantle [dɪsmǽntl] VT (a factory) desmantelar; (a car, watch) desmontar
dismay [dɪsmé] VT (disappoint) consternar; (daunt) desalentar; (alarm) alarmar; N (disappointment) consternación *f*; (loss of courage) desaliento *m*; (alarm) alarma *f*
dismember [dɪsmémbər] VT desmembrar
dismiss [dɪsmís] VT (fire a private employee) despedir; (fire a public employee) destituir, cesar; (reject a possibility) desechar, descartar; (discharge from military service) dar de baja; (reject a claim) desestimar; (ignore a person) ningunear; **class —ed!** ¡pueden retirarse!
dismissal [dɪsmísəl] N (firing) destitución *f*, despido *m*; (of a possibility) rechazo *m*; (from military service) baja *f*; (of a claim) desestimación *f*; (of a person) ninguneo *m*
dismount [dɪsmáʊnt] VI (get off a horse) desmontarse, apearse; (take apart) desarmar; N bajada *f*
disobedience [dɪsəbídɪəns] N desobediencia *f*

disobedient [dɪsəbídiənt] ADJ desobediente

disobey [dɪsəbé] VI/VT desobedecer

disorder [dɪsɔ́rdə-] N (confusion) desorden *m*; (public disturbance) desorden público *m*; (illness) trastorno *m*, desarreglo *m*

disorderly [dɪsɔ́rdə-li] ADJ (untidy) desordenado; (unruly) revoltoso; — **conduct** alteración del orden público *f*

disorganization [dɪsɔrgənizéʃən] N desorganización *f*

disorganized [dɪsɔ́rgənaɪzd] ADJ desorganizado

disown [dɪsón] VT repudiar

disparage [dɪspǽrɪdʒ] VT denigrar

disparate [díspə-ɪt] ADJ dispar

dispassionate [dɪspǽʃənɪt] ADJ desapasionado

dispatch [dɪspǽtʃ] VT despachar; N (sending off) envío *m*; (putting to death) ejecución *f*; (news story, official communication) despacho *m*; (promptness) prontitud *f*

dispel [dɪspél] VT disipar

dispensable [dɪspénsəbəl] ADJ prescindible

dispensary [dɪspénsəri] N dispensario *m*

dispensation [dɪspenséʃən] N (relaxation of law) dispensa *f*; (act of handing out) dispensación *f*

dispense [dɪspéns] VT (goods) dispensar; (justice) administrar; **to — from an obligation** eximir de una obligación; **to — with** prescindir de

dispersal [dɪspə́rsəl] N dispersión *f*

disperse [dɪspə́rs] VI/VT dispersar[se]; ADJ disperso

dispersed [dɪspə́rst] ADJ disperso

displace [dɪsplés] VT (evict) desalojar; (take up space, remove from office) desplazar; **—d person** (domestic) desplazado -da *mf*; (foreign) expatriado -da *mf*

displacement [dɪsplésmənt] N (of refugees, of a ship) desplazamiento *m*; (of an engine) cilindrada *f*

display [dɪsplé] VT (exhibit) exhibir, exponer; (unfold) desplegar; (flaunt) ostentar; (show on a computer screen) visualizar; N (of wares, etc.) exhibición *f*, despliegue *m*; (advertisement) cartel *m*; (flaunting) ostentación *f*; (computer screen) pantalla *f*, visualizador *m*, display *m*

displease [dɪsplíz] VT contrariar, desagradar, descontentar; VI molestar

displeasure [dɪspléʒə-] N disgusto *m*, desagrado *m*

disposable [dɪspózəbəl] ADJ — **income** ingresos disponibles *m pl*

disposal [dɪspózəl] N (arrangement) disposición *f*; (elimination) eliminación *f*

dispose [dɪspóz] VT (give inclination) predisponer; (set in order, make ready) disponer; **to — of** descartar, eliminar

disposition [dɪspəzíʃən] N (attitude)

temperamento *m*; (inclination) inclinación *f*, tendencia *f*; (arrangement, disposal) disposición *f*

dispossess [dɪspəzés] VT desposeer

disproportionate [dɪsprəpórʃənɪt] ADJ desproporcionado

disprove [dɪsprúv] VT refutar

dispute [dɪspjút] N disputa *f*; VT discutir, impugnar

disqualify [dɪskwáləfaɪ] VT (deprive of rights) inhabilitar; (exclude from a sport event) descalificar

disregard [dɪsrɪgárd] VT hacer caso omiso de, ignorar; N (neglect) descuido *m*; (disrespect) falta de respeto *f*

disrepair [dɪsrɪpér] N mal estado *m*; **in —** deteriorado

disreputable [dɪsrépjəbəbəl] ADJ (of bad reputation) de mala reputación; (shabby) de mala muerte

disrespect [dɪsrɪspékt] N desacato *m*, falta de respeto *f*; VT faltar el respeto

disrespectful [dɪsrɪspéktfəl] ADJ irrespetuoso

disrobe [dɪsrób] VI/VT desvestir[se]

disrupt [dɪsrápt] VT (cause disorder) trastornar, trastocar; (interrupt) interrumpir

dissatisfied [dɪssǽdɪsfaɪd] ADJ insatisfecho, disconforme

dissatisfy [dɪssǽdɪsfaɪ] VT no satisfacer

dissect [daɪsékt] VT (cut apart) disecar; (analyze argument) analizar minuciosamente

dissemble [dɪsémbəl] VI/VT (hide) disimular; (feign) fingir

disseminate [dɪsémənet] VT (spread out) diseminar, propagar; (publicize) divulgar

dissemination [dɪsemənéʃən] N (spreading out) diseminación *f*; (publicizing) divulgación *f*

dissension [dɪsénʃən] N disensión *f*, disenso *m*

dissent [dɪsént] VI disentir; N disenso *m*

dissertation [dɪsə-téʃən] N (formal discourse) disertación *f*; (doctoral treatise) tesis de doctorado *f*

dissident [dísɪdənt] N disidente *mf*

dissimilar [dɪssímələ-] ADJ diferente

dissimulation [dɪsɪmjəléʃən] N disimulo *m*

dissipate [dísəpet] VI/VT disipar[se]

dissipation [dɪsəpéʃən] N disipación *f*

dissolute [dísəlut] ADJ disoluto, vicioso

dissolution [dɪsəlúʃən] N disolución *f*

dissolve [dɪzálv] VI/VT disolver[se]

dissuade [dɪswéd] VT disuadir

distance [dístəns] N distancia *f*, recorrido *m*; — **learning** educación a distancia *f*; **in the —** a lo lejos, en la lejanía; VT distanciarse de, distanciar

distant [dístənt] ADJ (far away, aloof) distante; (remote) lejano, remoto; **to be — from** distar de

distaste [dɪstést] N aversión *f*

distasteful [dɪstéstfəɬ] ADJ desagradable

distemper [dɪstémpɚ] N moquillo m

distend [dɪsténd] VI/VT distender[se]

distill [dɪstíɬ] VI/VT destilar[se]

distillation [dɪstəléʃən] N destilación f

distillery [dɪstíləri] N destilería f

distinct [dɪstíŋkt] ADJ (different) distinto; (clear) bien delineado, neto

distinction [dɪstíŋkʃən] N (honor) distinción f; (differentiation) distinción f, diferenciación f; **he passed with —** aprobó con sobresaliente

distinctive [dɪstíŋktɪv] ADJ distintivo

distinguish [dɪstíŋgwɪʃ] VI/VT distinguir

distinguished [dɪstíŋgwɪʃt] ADJ distinguido

distinguishing [dɪstíŋgwɪʃɪŋ] ADJ distintivo

distort [dɪstórt] VT (an object) deformar; (reports, sound) distorsionar

distortion [dɪstórʃən] N (object) deformación f; (image, sound) distorsión f; (of a statement) tergiversación f

distract [dɪstrǽkt] VT distraer, entretener

distracted [dɪstrǽktɪd] ADJ distraído, disperso

distraction [dɪstrǽkʃən] N distracción f; **to drive to —** volver loco

distraught [dɪstrɔ́t] ADJ angustiado

distress [dɪstrés] N (anxiety) angustia f; (pain) dolor m, congoja f; **to be in —** (a person) estar en apuros; (a ship, plane) estar en peligro; VT (cause anxiety) angustiar, atribular; (cause pain) acongojar, afligir

distressing [dɪstrésɪŋ] ADJ inquietante

distribute [dɪstríbjut] VT distribuir, repartir

distribution [dɪstrəbjúʃən] N distribución f, reparto m

distributor [dɪstríbjədɚ] N distribuidor m

district [dístrɪkt] N distrito m, comarca f; **— attorney** fiscal de distrito mf

District of Columbia [dístrɪktəvkəlʌ́mbiə] N Distrito de Columbia m

distrust [dɪstrʌ́st] N desconfianza f; VT desconfiar de

distrustful [dɪstrʌ́stfəɬ] ADJ desconfiado

disturb [dɪstɚ́b] VI/VT (interrupt, interfere, perplex) perturbar; (trouble) turbar, perturbar, trastornar; (mess up) desarreglar; **do not —** se ruega no molestar

disturbance [dɪstɚ́bəns] N disturbio m; (weather) perturbación f

disuse [dɪsjús] N desuso m; **to fall into —** caer en desuso

ditch [dɪtʃ] N (trench) zanja f; (roadside) cuneta f; (for irrigation) acequia f; VT (make ditches) abrir zanjas; (get rid of) deshacerse de; (crash-land an airplane on water) hacer un amarizaje

dither [dídɚ] VI (hesitate) titubear; N **it threw her into a —** se puso muy nerviosa

ditsy [dítsi] ADJ atolondrado, cabeza de chorlito

ditto [dído] PRON & ADV ídem

diuretic [daɪərɛ́dɪk] ADJ & N diurético m

diurnal [daɪɚ́nl] ADJ diurno

divan [dɪvǽn] N diván m, canapé m

dive [daɪv] VI (into water) zambullirse, chapuzar, Am tirarse un clavado; (into an activity) zambullirse; (with scuba equipment) bucear; (airplane) bajar en picado -da; (submarine) sumergirse; N (of a person) zambullida f, chapuz m; (of an airplane) picado -da mf; (cheap bar) antro m

diver [dáɪvɚ] N saltador -ora mf; (high-dive) clavadista mf; (scuba) buzo mf

diverge [dɪvɚ́dʒ] VI (branch off, differ in opinion) divergir; VI/VT (deviate) desviar

divergence [dɪvɚ́dʒəns] N (separation, difference in opinion) divergencia f; (deviation) desviación f

diverse [dɪvɚ́s] ADJ (of various kinds) diverso; (different) diferente

diversify [dɪvɚ́səfaɪ] VI/VT diversificar[se]

diversion [dɪvɚ́ʒən] N (entertainment) entretenimiento m; (distraction) distracción f; (military) diversión f; (turning aside) desvío m, desviación f

diversity [dɪvɚ́sɪdi] N diversidad f

divert [dɪvɚ́t] VI/VT (turn aside) desviar, distraer; (distract) entretener

diverticulitis [dɪvɚtɪkjəláɪdɪs] N diverticulitis f

divest [dɪvɛ́st] VT (strip) despojar; (get rid of) deshacerse de

divide [dɪváɪd] VI/VT dividir[se]; (classify) clasificar[se]; N línea divisoria f

dividend [dívɪdɛnd] N dividendo m

divine [dɪváɪn] ADJ divino; VI/VT adivinar

divinity [dɪvínɪdi] N (godhead, state or quality of being divine) divinidad f; (theology) teología f

division [dɪvíʒən] N división f

divorce [dɪvórs] N divorcio m; VI/VT divorciar[se]

divot [dívət] N (golf) chuleta f

divulge [dɪvʌ́ldʒ] VT divulgar, publicar

dizziness [dízinɪs] N mareo m

dizzy [dízi] ADJ (person) mareado; (height) vertigoso; (speed) vertiginoso; **— spell** vahído m

DJ [disc jockey] [dídʒe] N pinchadiscos mf sg

Djibouti [dʒɪbúti] N Yibuti m

Djiboutian [jɪbúdiən] ADJ & N yibutiano -na mf

DNA [deoxyribonucleic acid] [diéné] N ADN m

do [du] VI/VT hacer; **to — away with** eliminar; **to — one's hair** arreglarse el pelo; **to — the dishes** lavar los platos; **to — drugs** tomar drogas; **to — in** matar; **to — time** cumplir una condena; **to — well** prosperar; **to — without** prescindir de; **we were —ing 100 kph** íbamos a cien kph; **to have nothing to — with** no tener nada que ver con; **that will —** basta; **that won't —** eso no sirve; **I'm —ing well** estoy bien; **this will have to —**

habrá que conformarse con esto; **—-it-yourself** hágalo usted mismo; V AUX **I feel as you** — pienso igual que tú; **how — you —?** ¿cómo estás? **— you hear me?** ¿me oyes? **yes, I** — sí; **— come again** vuelve por favor; N (hairstyle) peinado m; (party) fiesta f

DOA [dead on arrival] [dióé] ADJ muerto -ta antes de ingresar al hospital

docile [dásəl] ADJ dócil

dock [dɑk] N (pier) muelle m; (for landing) desembarcadero m, atracadero m; (water between piers) dique m, dársena f; **—worker** trabajador -ora portuario -ria mf; **dry —** dique seco m; VI/VT (a boat) atracar; (a space ship) acoplar[se]; (wages) descontar

doctor [dáktə] N (physician) médico -ca mf; (PhD, scholar) doctor -ora mf; (expert) especialista mf; VT (treat) atender; (cure) curar; (restore) restaurar; (counterfeit) alterar; **I —ed up this recipe** le hice unos retoques a esta receta

doctorate [dáktə‑ɪt] N doctorado m

doctrine [dáktrɪn] N doctrina f

document[1] [dákjəmənt] N documento m

document[2] [dákjəmɛnt] VT documentar

documentary [dakjəméntəri] N documental m

documentation [dakjəmɪntéʃən] N documentación f

dodder [dádə‑] VI (stumble along) tambalearse, titubear; (shake) temblequear

dodge [dɑdʒ] VT esquivar, sortear; VI (be evasive) dar rodeos; (move sideways) apartarse, echarse a un lado; N evasiva f

doe [do] N cierva f; (female of various animals) hembra f

dog [dɔg] N perro m, perra f; **—catcher** perrero -ra mf; **— collar** collar de perro m; **—fight** (dogs) pelea de perros f; (aircraft) combate aéreo m; (people) reyerta f; **—house** casilla de perro f; Sp caseta f; **to be in the —house** haber caído en desgracia, estar en capilla; **— paddle** natación estilo perrito m; **—sled** trineo para perros m; **— tag** placa de identificación f; **—wood** cornejo m; **to go to the —s** venirse abajo; ADJ **—-eared** sobado, muy gastado; **—gone** maldito; VT (follow) seguir la pista de; (harass) hostigar; **to —-paddle** nadar estilo perrito

doggy [dɔ́gi] N perrito -ta mf; **— bag** bolsa para las sobras f

dogma [dɔ́gmə] N dogma m

dogmatic [dɔgmǽdɪk] ADJ dogmático

doily [dɔ́ɪli] N mantelito m

doings [dúɪŋz] N actividades f pl

dole [doł] N (alms) limosna f; **to be on the —** estar cobrando el seguro de desempleo/paro; **to — out** repartir

doleful [dółfəł] ADJ apesadumbrado, triste

doll [dɑł] N (toy) muñeco -ca mf; (attractive female) muñeca f; **—house** casa de muñecas f; VI **to get —ed up** emperifollarse, empaquetarse

dollar [dálə] N dólar m; **— diplomacy** diplomacia del dólar f; **— sign** signo del dólar m

dolly [dáli] N (doll) muñeca f; (cart) carretilla f

dolphin [dɔ́łfɪn] N (mammal) delfín m; (fish) dorado m

dolt [dołt] N zopenco -ca mf

domain [domén] N dominio m

dome [dom] N (roof) cúpula f, domo m; (head) coco m, pelada f

domestic [dəmɛ́stɪk] ADJ (appliance, pet, chore) doméstico; (devoted to homemaking) hogareño; (home-loving) casero; (of a country) interno, nacional; **— violence** violencia doméstica f; N doméstico -ca mf

domesticate [dəmɛ́stɪket] VI/VT (animals) domesticar; (plants) aclimatar

domicile [dáməsaɪł] N domicilio m

dominant [dámənənt] ADJ dominante

dominate [dámənet] VI/VT dominar; VI señorear

domination [dɑmənéʃən] N (act of dominating) dominación f; (rule) dominio m

domineer [dɑmənír] VI/VT dominar, mandonear

domineering [dɑmənírɪŋ] ADJ tiránico, mandón

Dominica [dəmínɪkə] N Dominica f

Dominican [dəmínɪkən] ADJ & N (of Dominica) dominiqués -esa mf; (of the Dominican Republic) dominicano -na mf

Dominican Republic [dəmínɪkənrɪpáblɪk] N República Dominicana f

dominion [dəmínjən] N dominio m, señorío m

domino [dámənо] N (game, costume) dominó m; (piece) ficha f

don [dɑn] N (title, form of address, mafia boss) don m; (lecturer) profesor -ora universitario -ria mf; VT ponerse, vestirse

donate [dónet] VI/VT donar

donation [donéʃən] N donación f

done [dʌn] see do

done [dʌn] ADJ terminado, acabado; **when you are** — cuando termines; **to be all — in** estar muerto de cansancio; **the meat is well** — está bien asada la carne; **that sort of thing just isn't** — eso no se hace

donkey [dáŋki] N burro m, asno m, borrico m

donor [dónə] N donante mf, donador -ora mf

doodad [dúdæd] N (trinket) chuchería f; (device) chisme m, coso m

doohickey [dúhɪki] N chisme m, coso m

doom [dum] N perdición f; **—sday** día del juicio final m; VT condenar; **to be —ed to failure** estar condenado al fracaso

door [dɔr] N puerta f; **—bell** timbre m;

—keeper portero -ra *mf*; **—knob** pomo *m*;
—man portero *m*; **—mat** felpudo *m*; **—step**
umbral *m*; **—way** puerta *f*, portal *m*; **I
showed him the —** lo eché; ADJ **-to-—** de
puerta a puerta
dopamine [dópəmin] N dopamina *f*
dope [dop] N (narcotic) droga *f*; (stimulant)
estimulante *m*; (information) chismes *m pl*;
(moron) *fam* zopenco; VT dopar; **to —
oneself up** medicarse en exceso
dork [dɔrk] N *fam* idiota *mf*, tarambana *mf*
dorky [dɔ́rki] ADJ **that's a — dress** *fam* pareces
una tonta con ese vestido
dormant [dɔ́rmənt] ADJ latente
dormitory [dɔ́rmɪtɔri] N residencia estudiantil *f*
DOS [Disk Operating System] [das] N DOS *m*
dose [dos] N dosis *f*; VT dosificar
dossier [dɔ́sie] N expediente *m*
dot [dɑt] N punto *m*; (on a tie) pinta *f*; **—-com**
punto com; **—-matrix printer** impresora
de matriz de puntos *f*; **—ted eighth note**
corchea con puntillo *f*; **on the —** en punto;
VT marcar con puntos
dotage [dódɪdʒ] N chochez *f*, chochera *f*; **to be in
one's —** chochear, estar chocho
dote [dot] VI **to — on** estar chocho con
double [dʌ́bəl] ADJ doble; **— agent** doble agente
mf; **—-barreled** de doble caño; **— bass**
contrabajo *m*; **— bed** cama doble *f*; **—-blind
test** prueba de doble incógnita *f*; **— bind**
dilema *m*; **— boiler** baño de María *m*; **—-
breasted** cruzado; **— chin** papada *f*; **—-
cross** traición *f*; **— click** doble pulsación *f*; **—
dealing** duplicidad *f*; **— entry** entrada por
partida doble *f*; **— fault** doble falta *f*; **—
indemnity** doble indemnización *f*; **— play**
doble matanza *f*; **— sided** de dos caras; **—
shift** turno doble *m*; **— standard** trato
discriminatorio *m*; **— vision** doble visión *f*;
to do a — take quedar atónito; ADV **to sleep
— dormir de a dos**; N (in baseball) doble *m*,
doblete *m*; (in tennis) **—s** *m pl*, juego
de dobles *m*; VI/VT duplicar[se]; (an effort)
redoblar[se]; (fold, be twice as old, challenge
a bid) doblar[se]; **to — up** (bend over)
doblarse; (crowd) amontonarse; **to —-check**
verificar; **to —-click** pulsar dos veces; **to —-
cross** traicionar; **to —-date** salir dos parejas
juntas; **to —-talk** salirse con evasivas; **this
sofa —s as a bed** este sofá sirve también de
cama
doubt [daʊt] VI/VT dudar; (not trust) desconfiar;
N duda *f*; **beyond a —** indudablemente; **in —**
en duda; **no —!** ¡sin duda!
doubtful [dáʊtfəl] ADJ dudoso
doubtless [dáʊtlɪs] ADV (certainly) sin duda;
(probably) probablemente
dough [do] N pasta *f*, masa *f*; (money) pasta *f*,
mosca *f*; **—nut** rosquilla *f*; *Mex* dona *f*; *Sp*

donut *m*
douse [daʊs] VI/VT empapar; (a flame) apagar
[con agua]
dove [dʌv] N paloma *f*
dove [dov] *see* dive
dowdy [dáʊdi] ADJ (article of clothing) pasado de
moda; (person) sin gracia
dowel [dáʊəl] N clavija *f*
down [daʊn] ADV abajo; **— and dirty** sucio; **—
and out** tirado; **to be — with** estar de
acuerdo con; **to come — with a cold** caer
con gripe, *Sp* cogerse un resfriado; **to fall —**
caerse; **to get — to work** aplicarse al trabajo;
to go/come — bajar; **to lie —** acostarse,
echarse; **to put someone —** denigrar a
alguien; **to turn — the volume** bajar el
volumen; **to water — a drink** rebajar una
bebida con agua; **to write —** anotar; **two
blocks —** dos calles más abajo; **slow —!**
¡anda más despacio! **the wind died —**
amainó el viento; **one — and two to go**
hicimos uno y nos quedan dos por hacer;
prices are — han bajado los precios; **the
system is —** se cayó el sistema; **they're —
on me** están mal conmigo; PREP **— the
street** calle abajo; ADJ (depressed) abatido; N
(turn for the worse) revés *m*; (feathers)
plumón *m*; VT (knock, shoot) derribar; (drink
quickly) despachar de un solo trago; (defeat)
vencer; (football play) oportunidad *f*
downcast [dáʊnkæst] ADJ abatido, cabizbajo
downfall [dáʊnfɔl] N ruina *f*
downgrade [dáʊngred] N declive *m*, pendiente
f; VT quitarle importancia a
downhill[1] [dáʊnhɪl] ADV cuesta abajo; **his
health is going —** su salud se deteriora
downhill[2] [dáʊnhɪl] ADJ **a — slope** una
pendiente; N bajada contra-reloj *f*
download [dáʊnlod] VT descargar; N descarga *f*
down payment [dáʊnpémənt] N entrega inicial
f, entrada *f*
downplay [dáʊnple] VT quitar la importancia a
downpour [dáʊnpor] N aguacero *m*
downright [dáʊnraɪt] ADJ absoluto; **—
foolishness** reverenda tontería *f*; **he was —
angry** echaba chispas
downshift [dáʊnshɪft] VI rebajar [el cambio]
downside [dáʊnsaɪd] N inconveniente *m*
downsize [dáʊnsaɪz] VI (personnel) hacer
reducción; VT (an object or organization)
reducir el tamaño de; (one's lifestyle)
simplificar; **he got —d** perdió el trabajo
cuando hicieron reducción de personal
downstairs[1] [dáʊnstérz] ADV abajo; (in the
apartment one floor lower) en el piso de abajo
downstairs[2] [dáʊnsterz] ADJ de abajo; N planta
baja *f*
downstream [dáʊnstrím] ADV río abajo
downtime [dáʊntaɪm] N (of a machine) tiempo

de inactividad *m*; (of a person) horas de ocio *f pl*

down-to-earth [dáuntəɨ̇θ] ADJ sensato, práctico

downtown [dáuntáun] ADV (toward) al centro; (in) en el centro; ADJ del centro, céntrico; N centro *m*

downturn [dáuntɚn] N tendencia a la baja *f*

down under [dáunándə] ADV en/a Australia

downward [dáunwəd] ADJ descendente; — **mobility** descenso social *m*; —**s** hacia abajo

downwind [dáunwínd] ADV en la dirección del viento

downy [dáuni] ADJ sedoso, suave

dowry [dáuri] N dote *f*

doze [doz] VI dormitar; N siesta *f*

dozen [dázən] N docena *f*

drab [dræb] ADJ triste; N pardo *m*

draft [dræft] N (of air) corriente *f*; (drink) trago *m*; (bank) giro *m*; (outline) esbozo *m*; (military) conscripción *f*, quinta *f*; (of a ship) calado *m*; — **beer** cerveza de barril *f*; — **horse** caballo de tiro *m*; —**sman** dibujante *m*; VT (to sketch) esbozar; (to compose) redactar; (to select for military service) conscribir

drag [dræg] VI/VT (haul slowly) arrastrar[se]; (search a body of water) dragar; **don't — me into this** no me metas en esto; **to —-and-drop/release** arrastrar y soltar; **to — on and on** eternizarse; **to — out** estirar; N (dredge) draga *f*; (boring person) pesado -da *mf*; (hassle) lata *f*; (counterforce) resistencia *f*; (on a cigarette) pitada *f*; — **race** carrera de dragsters *f*; — **strip** pista de dragsters *f*

dragon [drǽgən] N dragón *m*; —**fly** libélula *f*

drain [dren] N (channel) desagüe *m*, sumidero *m*; (depletion of resources) sangría *f*, fuga *f*; —**pipe** desaguadero *m*, desagüe *m*; **to go down the** — irse por la borda; VI/VT (empty a sink) desagotar[se], desaguar[se]; (exhaust) agotar[se]; VT (wetlands) drenar, sanear; VI (a battery) descargarse

drainage [drénɪdʒ] N (act of draining) desagüe *m*, drenaje *m*; (system for draining) drenaje *m*; — **pipe** tubo de desagüe *m*

drake [drek] N pato [macho] *m*

drama [drámə] N drama *m*

dramatic [drəmǽdɪk] ADJ dramático

dramatically [drəmǽdɪkli] ADV (changing) de forma fundamental, fundamentalmente; (presenting) de manera dramática/teatral

dramatist [drámətɪst] N dramaturgo -ga *mf*

dramatize [drámətaɪz] VI/VT dramatizar

drank [dræŋk] *see* drink

drape [drep] VI (hang in folds) colgar, drapear; VT (cover) cubrir; N cortina *f*

drapery [drépəri] N cortinado *m*, colgadura *f*

drastic [drǽstɪk] ADJ drástico

draw [drɔ] VT (a picture) dibujar; (lines, shapes) trazar; (a cart) tirar de; (a curtain) correr; (cards, blood, water, conclusion, strength) sacar; (a crowd) atraer; (comparison, distinction) hacer; (a sword) desenvainar; VI (of a boat) tener calado; (of a fireplace) tirar; (in sports, have the same score) empatar; (receive money) cobrar; (withdraw money) retirar, sacar; **to — aside** apartar[se]; **to — away** separar[se]; **to — a breath** aspirar, tomar aliento; **to — a blank** quedarse en blanco; **to — in** involucrar; **to — lots/straws** echar a la suerte, sortear; **to — near** acercarse; **to — off** irse, retirarse; **to — on** (be based on) basarse en; (have recourse to) recurrir a; **to — out** (remove) sacar; (prolong) alargar, prolongar; **to — up** (approach) acercar[se]; (write) redactar; (shrink) encoger; N (in sports, tie game) empate *m*; (lot) número sorteado *m*; (attraction) atracción *f*; —**back** inconveniente *m*; —**bridge** puente levadizo *m*

drawer [drɔə] N cajón *m*; (small) gaveta *f*; —**s** calzones *m pl*

drawing [drɔ́ɪŋ] N (picture) dibujo *m*; (raffle) sorteo *m*; — **room** sala [de recibo] *f*

drawn [drɔn] ADJ demacrado; —-**out** interminable

drawn [drɔn] *see* draw

dread [dred] N pavor *m*, terror *m*, espanto *m*; VT **I — going to the dentist** me aterra ir al dentista

dreadful [drédfəl] ADJ horrendo, espantoso, temible

dream [drim] N sueño *m* (also aspiration); (reverie) ensueño *m*, ensoñación *f*; (fancy) ilusión *f*; —**land** tierra del ensueño *f*; — **team** equipo de estrellas *m*; — **world** mundo de ensueño *m*; VI/VT soñar; **to — of** soñar con; **I wouldn't — of stealing** no se me ocurriría robar; **to — that** soñar que; **to — up** imaginar; ADJ **a — holiday** unas vacaciones perfectas

dreamer [drímə] N (impractical person) soñador -ora *mf*; (visionary) visionario -ria *mf*

dreamt [dremt] *see* dream

dreary [dríri] ADJ sombrío, deprimente

dredge [dredʒ] N draga *f*; VT (a river) dragar; (facts) desenterrar, sacar a luz

dregs [dregz] N heces *f pl*, poso *m*; — **of society** escoria de la sociedad *f*

drench [drentʃ] VT empapar, calar; —**ed in blood** bañado en sangre

dress [dres] N (article of clothing for women) vestido *m*; (attire) ropa *f*; (formal) traje de etiqueta *m*, ropa de etiqueta *f*; (costume) vestimenta *f*; —**maker** modista *mf*; — **rehearsal** ensayo general *m*; — **shirt**

camisa para traje *f*; **what's the — code?**
¿cómo hay que ir vestido? VI/VT vestir; VT
(store window) arreglar; (slaughtered
animals) limpiar; (salad) aderezar; (hides)
adobar; (a wound) vendar; **to — down**
(scold) regañar; (wear casual clothes) ponerse
ropa informal; **to — up** (wear fine clothes)
vestirse de gala; (make more appealing)
embellecer

dresser [drésə-] N cómoda *f*; **she is a good —** se
viste con elegancia

dressing [drésɪŋ] N (act, result) vestir *m*; (for
salad) aderezo *m*; (for fowl) relleno *m*; (for
wounds) gasa *f*, vendaje *m*; **—-down** regaño
m; **— gown** bata *f*; **— room** (in a theater)
camerino *m*; (in a store) probador *m*; **— table**
tocador *m*

drew [dru] *see* draw

dribble [drɪbəl] VI (trickle) gotear; (drool)
babear; VT (a ball) driblar, regatear; (liquid)
rociar; N (trickle) goteo *m*; (small quantity)
chorrito *m*; (of a ball) drible *m*, regate *m*

dried [draɪd] ADJ seco; **— fig** higo paso/seco *m*;
—-up (without water) seco; (wizened)
arrugado

drift [drɪft] N (direction) deriva *f*; (current)
corriente *f*; (meaning) sentido *m*, tenor *m*;
(pile) montón *m*, acumulación *f*; **—wood**
madera flotante *f*; **do you get my —?** ¿me
captas la onda? VI (float) flotar; (be adrift) ir a
la deriva; (wander) errar; **he —ed off** se
durmió; VI/VT (deviate) desviar[se];
(accumulate) amontonar[se], acumular[se]

drifter [drɪftə-] N (wanderer) vagabundo -da *mf*;
(of a worker) itinerante *mf*

drill [drɪl] N (tool) taladro *m*; (dental) fresa *f*;
(training) ejercicios *m pl*; (procedure)
procedimiento *m*; (rehearsal) simulacro *m*;
(cloth) dril *m*; VI/VT (make a hole) taladrar,
perforar, barrenar; (train) entrenar[se],
adiestrar[se]; VI (train) hacer ejercicios;
(practice) practicar; VT hacer practicar

drink [drɪŋk] VI/VT (person) beber; (animal)
abrevar; (absorb, take in) absorber; **to — up**
apurar el trago; **to — to someone's health**
brindar por alguien; N bebida *f* (also
alcoholic); (a measure of beverage) trago *m*

drinkable [drɪŋkəbəl] ADJ potable

drinking [drɪŋkɪŋ] ADJ **— water** agua potable *f*;
he has a — problem tiene problemas con el
alcohol

drip [drɪp] N goteo *m*; (a bore) plasta *mf*; VI
gotear

drive [draɪv] VI/VT (a car) conducir, manejar; (an
animal) arrear; VI (go in a vehicle) ir en coche;
VT (move forth) impulsar, impeler; (convey)
llevar [en coche]; (force) forzar; (a nail)
clavar; (a ball) tirar, golpear; **to — a hard
bargain** regatear mucho; **to — away**

ahuyentar; **to — someone mad** volver loco
a alguien; **what are you driving at?** ¿qué
quieres decir con eso? N (ride) paseo [en coche]
m; (of an animal) arreo *m*; (urge) impulso *m*,
(of a computer) unidad *f*; (military offensive)
ofensiva *f*; (road) carretera *f*; (driveway)
camino *m*; (campaign) campaña *f*; (energy)
empuje *m*; (propulsion system) propulsión *f*;
(of a ball) tiro *m*; (in tennis and golf) drive *m*;
—-by shooting tiroteo desde un coche *m*; **—
-in** drive-in *m*, establecimiento en que el
cliente es atendido en el coche *m*; **—-in
movie theater** autocine *m*; **—way** camino
de entrada *m*, entrada de coches *f*; **front
wheel —** tracción delantera *f*

drivel [drɪvəl] N (saliva) baba *f*; (idiocy) tontería
f; VI babearse

driveling [drɪvəlɪŋ] ADJ baboso; **he's a — idiot**
es un oligofrénico

driven [drɪvən] *see* drive

driver [draɪvə-] N (chauffeur) chofer *mf*,
conductor -ra *mf*; (of animals) arriero -ra *mf*;
(golf club) driver *m*; (in a computer)
controlador *m*

driving [draɪvɪŋ] ADJ **— force** impulso *m*; **—
rain** lluvia torrencial *f*; **— school**
autoescuela *f*

drizzle [drɪzəl] VI lloviznar; N llovizna *f*

drone [dron] N (male bee, idler) zángano *m*;
(remote-controlled vehicle) vehículo
teledirigido *f*; (drudge) esclavo *m*; (sound)
zumbido *m*; VI/VT (make a sound) zumbar;
(talk) hablar monótonamente

drool [drul] N baba *f*; VI babearse

droop [drup] VI (sag) colgarse; (flag)
languidecer; (wither) marchitarse; **his
shoulders —** tiene los hombros caídos;
—ing ears orejas gachas *f pl*

drop [drɑp] N (liquid quantity) gota *f*; (descent)
caída *f*; (incline) declive *m*; (in value) baja *f*;
(in prices) caída *f*; (cologne) pastilla *f*; (of
mail, etc.) buzón *m*, punto de recolección *m*;
(of supplies) lanzamiento *m*; **—out** (student)
desertor -ora escolar *mf*; (marginalized
person) marginado -da *mf*; **— shot** dejada de
volea *f*; VI caer; (let fall) dejar caer, descargar;
(in golf) dropar; **to — a line** mandar unas
líneas; **to — from sight** desaparecer; **to —
in** caer de sorpresa; **to — out** (sports)
retirarse; (school) abandonar; **why don't
you — by?** ¿por qué no pasas por aquí? VI/VT
(a course) abandonar; (a curtain) bajar; ADJ
—-dead beautiful hermosísima

dropper [drɑpə-] N gotero *m*

drought [draʊt] N sequía *f*

drove [drov] N tropel *m*

drove [drov] *see* drive

drown [draʊn] VI/VT ahogar[se]

drowning [draʊnɪŋ] N ahogamiento *m*

drowse [drauz] vi (be half-asleep) dormitar; (feel drowsy) estar amodorrado

drowsiness [dráuzinis] N modorra f, somnolencia f

drowsy [dráuzi] ADJ amodorrado, somnoliento; **to become** — amodorrarse

drudge [drʌʤ] N esclavo del trabajo m, fregona f; vi trabajar como un esclavo

drug [drʌg] N (chemical substance, narcotic) droga f; (medicine) medicamento m; **—ged** drogado, endrogado; **— abuse** abuso de drogas m; **— addict** drogadicto -ta mf; **—store** (drugs) farmacia f; (non-drug items) droguería f; perfumería f; **— trafficker** narcotraficante mf; vt (stupefy with drugs) drogar; (mix with a drug) adulterar con droga

druggist [drʌ́gist] N farmacéutico -ca mf, droguero -ra mf

drum [drʌm] N (musical instrument) tambor m; (of ear) tímpano m; (receptacle for storing liquids) barril m; **—head** parche m; **—stick** (music) palillo de tambor m; (fowl) pata f; vi (play a drum) tocar el tambor; (beat rhythmically) tamborilear; **to — out** expulsar; **to — up** fomentar; **I'm trying to — this idea into his head** le estoy repitiendo esta idea con insistencia

drummer [drʌ́mə] N (classical) tambor m; (folk) tamborilero -ra mf; (rock & roll) baterista mf

drunk [drʌŋk] ADJ & N borracho -cha mf; fam mamado -da mf; **to get** — emborracharse

drunk [drʌŋk] see drink

drunkard [drʌ́ŋkəd] N borracho -cha mf, borrachín -ina mf

drunken [drʌ́ŋkən] ADJ borracho, embriagado

drunkenness [drʌ́ŋkənnis] N borrachera f, embriaguez f

dry [drai] ADJ seco; (sober) sobrio; (topic, book) árido, aburrido; **— land** tierra firme f; **— cleaner** (business) tintorería f; (owner of business) tintorero -ra mf; **— cleaning** limpieza en seco f; **— county** condado seco m; **— wit** humor agudo m; **— goods** géneros m pl; **— measure** medida para áridos f; **— run** prueba f; **— ice** hielo seco m; **— dock** dique seco m, varadero m; vi/vt (wet clothes) secar[se]; (leather) resecar[se]; **to — up** secarse, resecarse; **to — out** desintoxicar[se]

dryer [dráiə] N (hair) secador m; (clothes) secadora f

dryness [dráinis] N (skin) sequedad f; (land, lecture) aridez f

dual [dúəl] ADJ (function) doble; (ownership) compartido

dub [dʌb] vt (translate a film) doblar; (give a nickname) apodar

dubious [dúbiəs] ADJ dudoso

duchess [dʌ́tʃis] N duquesa f

duck [dʌk] N (bird) pato m; (downward dodge)

agachada f; vi/vt (plunge under water) hundir[se]; (bend down) agachar[se]; vt (avoid) esquivar

duckling [dʌ́kliŋ] N patito m

duct [dʌkt] N conducto m; **— tape** cinta aislante f

ductile [dʌ́ktl] ADJ dúctil

dud [dʌd] N (disappointing thing) chasco m; (useless person) inútil m; (unexploded bomb) bomba que no estalla f; **—s** (clothes) ropa f, fam trapos m pl; (belongings) pertenencias f pl

dude [dud] N (dandy) chulo m; (fellow) tipo m

due [du] ADJ (payable) pagadero; (immediately owed) vencido; (fitting, rightful) debido; (adequate) suficiente; **— date** fecha de vencimiento f; **— diligence** diligencia debida f; **in — time/course** a su debido tiempo; **the train is — at two o'clock** se supone que el tren llega a las dos; ADV **— east** hacia el este; N (punishment) merecido m; **give Mary her —; she's honest** tienes que reconocer que María es honrada; **—s** cuotas f pl

duel [dúəl] N duelo m; vi/vt batirse en/a duelo [con alguien]

duet [duét] N (played) dúo m; (sung) dueto m

dug [dʌg] see dig

dugout [dʌ́gaut] N (canoe) piragua f; (underground refuge) trinchera f

DUI [driving under the influence] [díjúái] N delito de conducir en estado de ebriedad m

duke [duk] N duque m; **to put up one's —s** levantar los puños; vt **to — it out** arreglarlo con los puños

dukedom [dúkdəm] N ducado m

dull [dʌl] ADJ (lackluster) opaco; (listless, muted) apagado; (boring) aburrido, soso, desanimado; (blunt) romo, desafilado; (sluggish, stupid) lento; (pain) sordo; vi/vt (a knife) desafilar[se]; (color) opacar[se]; (sound, impact) amortiguar[se]; (pain) aliviar[se]; (senses) embotar[se], entorpecer[se]

duly [dúli] ADV debidamente

dumb [dʌm] ADJ (mute) mudo; (dull) tonto; **—bell** (handweight) mancuerna f; (stupid person) bobo -ba mf; **—founded** patitieso, atónito; vt **to — down** simplificar demasiado

dumbness [dʌ́mnis] N (muteness) mudez f; (foolishness) estupidez f

dummy [dʌ́mi] N (figure) muñeco m; (fool) tonto -ta mf; (front) hombre de paja m; ADJ (fake) falso; **a — president** un títere

dump [dʌmp] vt (unload) descargar; (empty) botar; (transfer computer data) vaciar; (dismiss) echar, despedir; (discard waste) tirar la basura, descargar desechos; (flood a market) hacer dumping; (abandon) plantar; **to — on** (criticize) criticar; (unload problems) descargarse; N (place for waste) vertedero m, basural *m*, basurero *m*; (of weapons) depósito *m*; (act of discarding) vertido *m*; **—truck** camión volteador *m*, volquete *m*, *Am* volqueta *f*; **to be in the —s** estar deprimido, estar depre

dumping [dámpɪŋ] N vertido *m*

dunce [dʌns] N burro -rra *mf*, tonto -ta de capirote *mf*

dune [dun] N duna *f*, médano *m*

dung [dʌŋ] N boñiga *f*, bosta *f*; **—hill** estercolero *m*

dungeon [dánʤən] N mazmorra *f*

dunk [dʌŋk] VT (a donut) remojar; (a basketball) volcar, enterrar; (a person) sumergir

duodenum [duədínəm] N duodeno *m*

dupe [dup] N (gullible person) ingenuo -nua *mf*, inocente *mf*; *Sp* primo -ma *mf*; (manipulated person) títere *m*; VT embaucar

duplex [dúplɛks] N & ADJ dúplex *m*

duplicate¹ [dúplɪkɪt] ADJ & N duplicado *m*; **in —** por duplicado

duplicate² [dúplɪket] VT duplicar[se]

duplicity [duplísɪDi] N duplicidad *f*

durability [dʊrəbílɪDi] N durabilidad *f*

durable [dúrəbəł] ADJ (long-lasting) duradero; (serviceable) sufrido

duration [dʊréʃən] N duración *f*

duress [dʊrɛs] N coacción *f*

during [dúrɪŋ] PREP durante

dusk [dʌsk] N atardecer *m*, anochecer *m*; **at —** al atardecer

dusky [dáski] ADJ (dark) oscuro; (gloomy) sombrío

dust [dʌst] N polvo *m*; **—pan** pala *f*; **to bite the — (die)** *fam* espichar; (lose) morder el polvo de la derrota; **cloud of —** polvareda *f*; VI/VT (remove dust) quitar/sacudir el polvo [a]; VT (sprinkle with powder) espolvorear; VI (become dusty) empolvarse; **to — off** desempolvar

duster [dásta‑] N plumero *m*

dusty [dásti] ADJ polvoriento

Dutch [dʌtʃ] ADJ & N holandés -esa *mf*; (language) holandés *m*; **to go —** pagar a escote

Dutchman [dátʃmən] N holandés *m*

duty [dúpi] N deber *m*, obligación *f*; (tax on imports) derechos aduaneros *m pl*; (any tax) impuesto *m*; **to be on —** estar de guardia; **to be off —** no estar de guardia; ADJ **-free** libre de impuestos

DVD [digital versatile disc] [dívidí] N DVD *m*

dwarf [dwɔrf] ADJ & N enano -na *mf*; VT hacer parecer pequeño

dwarfism [dwɔ́rfɪzəm] N enanismo *m*

dwell [dwɛł] VI morar, habitar; **to — on a subject** dilatarse en un asunto

dweller [dwélə‑] N habitante *mf*, morador -ora *mf*

dwelling [dwélɪŋ] N vivienda *f*, domicilio *m*

dwelt [dwɛłt] *see* dwell

DWI [driving while intoxicated] [dídʌbəłjuáɪ] N delito de conducir en estado de ebriedad *m*

dwindle [dwíndł] VI/VT menguar, mermar

dye [daɪ] N tinte *m*, tintura *f*; VT teñir

dying [dáɪɪŋ] ADJ moribundo

dynamic [daɪnǽmɪk] ADJ dinámico; N dinámica *f*

dynamite [dáɪnəmaɪt] N dinamita *f*; VT dinamitar; ADJ fabuloso

dynamo [dáɪnəmo] N dínamo *m*

dynasty [dáɪnəsti] N dinastía *f*

dysentery [dísənteri] N disentería *f*

dysfunction [dɪsfʌ́ŋkʃən] N disfunción *f*

dyslexia [dɪsléksiə] N dislexia *f*

Ee

each [itʃ] ADJ cada; **— person** cada persona; PRON cada uno; **— receives a prize** cada uno recibe un premio; **they looked at — other** se miraron el uno al otro

eager [ígə‑] ADJ (enthusiastic) ansioso; (avid) ávido

eagerness [ígə‑nɪs] N (enthusiasm) ansia *f*, afán *m*; (strong desire) avidez *f*

eagle [ígəł] N águila *f*; **--eye** ojo de lince *m*

eaglet [ígłɪt] N aguilucho *m*

ear [ir] N (outer organ) oreja *f*; (inner organ, sense of hearing, musical aptitude) oído *m*; (of corn) mazorca *f*; *Am* elote *m*; **--ache** dolor de oídos *m*; **--drops** gotas para los oídos *f pl*; **--drum** tímpano *m*; **--lobe** lóbulo de la oreja *m*; **--muff** orejera *f*; **--phone** audífono *m*, auricular *m*; **--plug** tapón del oído *m*; **--ring** pendiente *m*, zarcillo *m*, arete *m*; **by —** de oído; **within —shot** al alcance del oído; **he has the — of the governor** el gobernador le presta mucha atención; VT **to --mark** asignar

earful [írfʊł] N **I got an —** (scolding) me echó un rapapolvo; (gossip) me dio la lata

early [ɝ́li] ADJ temprano; **— detection** diagnóstico precoz *m*; **— man** hombre primitivo *m*; **— retirement** jubilación anticipada *f*; **— riser/bird** madrugador -ora *mf*, mañanero -ra *mf*; **the — bird gets the worm** al que madruga, Dios lo ayuda

earn [ɝn] VI/VT (money, admiration, etc.) ganar; (salary) cobrar, ganar; (interest) devengar; **—ed run** carrera limpia *f*; **—ed run average** promedio de carreras limpias permitidas *m*; **to — a living** ganarse la vida

earnest [ɝ́nɪst] ADJ (sincere) serio, formal;

(grave) grave; **in** — en serio; — **money** señal
f; *Mex* enganche m
earnestness [ɘ́rnɪstnɪs] N (sincerity) seriedad f,
formalidad f; (gravity) gravedad f; **in all** —
con toda sinceridad
earnings [ɘ́rnɪŋz] N (of a person) ingresos m pl;
(of a business) ganancias f pl
earth [ɜθ] N tierra f; —**mover** excavadora f;
—**quake** terremoto m, temblor de tierra m;
—**worm** lombriz f; **the** — la Tierra; ADJ
—**shaking** revolucionario
earthen [ɘ́θɘn] ADJ (wall) de tierra; (pot) de
barro; —**ware** vajilla de barro f, cerámica f
earthly [ɘ́θli] ADJ terrenal; — **possessions**
bienes terrenales m pl; **to be of no** — **use** no
servir para nada
earthy [ɘ́θi] ADJ natural; (person) campechano;
(sense of humor, joke) basto; — **smell** olor a
tierra m
ease [iz] N (facility) facilidad f; (unaffectedness)
soltura f, desparpajo m; (comfort) comodidad
f; (lack of worry) tranquilidad f; (fullness of a
garment) holgura f; **at** — (military) en
descanso; (comfortable) tranquilo, a gusto; **a
life of** — una vida desahogada; **ill at** —
incómodo; VT (make easier) facilitar; VI/VT
(relieve pain) aliviar[se]; (release from
tension) aflojar[se]; (relieve anxiety)
tranquilizar[se]; **to** — **up** aflojar
easel [ízɘl] N caballete m
east [ist] N este m, oriente m; ADJ del este,
oriental; ADV — **of here** al este [de aquí]; **to
go** — ir al / hacia el este; **back** — en el este
Easter [ístɘr] N Pascua f; — **egg** huevo de Pascua
m; — **Sunday** Domingo de Pascua m
eastern [ístɘrn] ADJ oriental, del este
eastward [ístwɘrd] ADV & ADJ hacia el este
easy [ízi] ADJ (simple) fácil, sencillo; (compliant)
fácil; (comfortable) cómodo; (informal)
desenvuelto; (unworried) tranquilo; — **chair**
poltrona f; —**going** calmoso; — **terms**
facilidades de pago f pl; — **does it** despacito;
take it — cálmate; **he's on** — **street** vive en
la abundancia; **within** — **reach** al alcance de
la mano; ADV **go** — **on me** sea bueno
eat [it] VI/VT comer[se]; VT (costs) absorber; **to** —
away corroer, comer; **to** — **breakfast**
desayunar[se]; **to** — **dinner** (midday) comer;
(evening) cenar; **to** — **lunch** comer,
almorzar; **to** — **one's heart out** morirse de
envidia; **to** — **one's words** tragarse las
palabras; **to** — **supper** cenar; **to** — **up**
comerse todo; **what's** —**ing you?** ¿qué
bicho te picó?
eaten [ítn] *see* eat
eating [ídɪŋ] N (act) comer m; (food) comida f; —
disorder trastorno de la alimentación m; —
utensils cubiertos m pl; — **apples**
manzanas para comer f pl

eaves [ivz] N PL alero m; **to** —**drop** escuchar
furtivamente
e-banking [íbæŋkɪŋ] N banca electrónica f
ebb [ɛb] N (flowing back) reflujo m; (decay)
decadencia f; — **tide** reflujo m; **to be at a
low** — estar en un punto bajo; VI (tide) bajar;
(energy) decaer
ebony [ɛ́bɘni] N ébano m
e-book [íbʊk] N libro electrónico m
e-business [íbɪznɪs] N comercio electrónico m
eccentric [ɛkséntrɪk] ADJ & N excéntrico -ca mf
ecclesiastic [ɪkliziǽstɪk] ADJ & N eclesiástico m
echelon [ɛ́ʃɘlɑn] N (military formation) escalón
m; (rank) nivel m, estrato m
echo [ɛ́ko] N eco m; VI hacer eco; **the gym** —**ed
with laughter** el gimnasio resonó de risas;
VT repetir
echocardiogram [ɛkokárdɪɘgræm] N
ecocardiograma m
eclectic [ɪkléktɪk] ADJ ecléctico
eclipse [ɪklíps] N eclipse m; VT eclipsar
eco-friendly [ikofréndli] ADJ ecológico
ecological [ikolɑ́dʒɪkɘl] ADJ ecológico
ecology [ɪkɑ́lɘdʒi] N ecología f
e-commerce [íkɑmɘrs] N comercio electrónico m
economic [ɛkɘnɑ́mɪk] ADJ económico; N —**s**
economía f
economical [ɛkɘnɑ́mɪkɘl] ADJ económico
economist [ɪkɑ́nɘmɪst] N economista mf
economize [ɪkɑ́nɘmaɪz] VI economizar
economy [ɪkɑ́nɘmi] N economía f (also thrift);
ADJ — **car** coche económico m; — **class** clase
turista f
ecosystem [íkosɪstɘm] N ecosistema m
ecstasy [ɛ́kstɘsi] N éxtasis m (also drug)
Ecuador [ɛ́kwɘdɔr] N Ecuador m
Ecuadorian [ɛkwɘdɔ́riɘn] ADJ & N ecuatoriano
-na mf
ecumenical [ɛkjɘménɪkɘl] ADJ ecuménico
eczema [ɛ́gzɘmɘ] N eccema m
eddy [ɛ́di] N remolino m; VI arremolinarse
edge [ɛdʒ] N borde m, canto m; (of a knife) filo m;
(of a block) arista f; **to be on** — estar
nervioso; **her voice has an** — **to it** tiene la
voz penetrante; **a competitive** — una
ventaja sobre la competencia; VT (make an
edge) hacerle el borde; (sharpen) afilar;
(move sideways) meterse de costado; **to** —
out ganar por un pelito; **to** — **up**
aproximarse; ADV —**wise** de costado
edgy [ɛ́dʒi] ADJ nervioso
edible [ɛ́dɘbɘl] ADJ & N comestible m
edict [ídɪkt] N edicto m, bando m
edifice [ɛ́dɘfɪs] N edificio m
edify [ɛ́dɘfaɪ] VT edificar
edit [ɛ́dɪt] VT (revise, correct) corregir; (serve as
editor) editar; (revise a film) montar; **to** —
out eliminar; N corrección f
edition [ɪdíʃɘn] N edición f

editor [édɪtə] N (director of a publication) redactor -ora *mf*; (compiler, radio or film worker) editor -ora *mf*; (proofreader) corrector -ora *mf*

editorial [edɪtóriəł] ADJ editorial; N editorial *f*

editorialize [edɪtóriəlaɪz] VI editorializar

educate [édʒəket] VT educar

education [edʒəkéʃən] N educación *f*, enseñanza *f*; (academic subject) pedagogía *f*; **school of —** escuela normal *f*

educational [edʒəkéʃənł] ADJ educativo

educator [édʒəkedə] N educador -ora *mf*

EEG [electroencephalogram] [íidʒí] N electroencefalograma *m*

eel [ił] N anguila *f*

eerie [íri] ADJ misterioso

effect [ɪfékt] N efecto *m*; **to go into —** entrar en vigencia, ponerse en operación; **in —** vigente, operativo; **I wrote a letter to that —** escribí una carta en ese sentido; **personal —s** efectos personales *m pl*; VT efectuar

effective [ɪféktɪv] ADJ efectivo, eficaz; (a law) vigente; **— date** fecha de vigencia *f*

effectively [ɪféktɪvli] ADV (well) eficazmente; (in fact) de hecho, en efecto

effectiveness [ɪféktɪvnɪs] N efectividad *f*, eficacia *f*

effectual [ɪféktʃuəł] ADJ eficaz

effeminate [ɪfémənɪt] ADJ afeminado

efficacy [éfɪkəsi] N eficacia *f*

efficiency [ɪfíʃənsi] N eficiencia *f*; **— apartment** estudio *m*

efficient [ɪfíʃənt] ADJ eficiente; (motor) económico

effigy [éfədʒi] N efigie *f*; **to burn in —** quemar en efigie

effort [éfət] N (exertion) esfuerzo *m*; (work of art) obra *f*; (campaign) campaña *f*

effrontery [ɪfrʌ́ntəri] N descaro *m*

effusive [ɪfjúsɪv] ADJ efusivo

egg [ɛg] N huevo *m*; (female gamete) óvulo *m*; (fellow) tipo *m*; **—beater** batidor de huevos *m*; **—head** empollón -na *mf*; **—nog** rompopo *m*, rompope *m*, ponche de huevo *m*; **—plant** berenjena *f*; **—shell** cáscara de huevo *f*; **—white** clara de huevo *f*; **— yolk** yema de huevo *f*; **to have — on one's face** estar avergonzado, quedar mal; **to lay an —** (of a hen) poner un huevo; (fail) fracasar; **to walk on —shells** ir pisando huevos; ADJ **—-shaped** ovoide; VT **to — on** incitar

ego [ígo] N (self) yo *m*, ego *m*; (vanity) ego *m*; (self-esteem) amor propio *m*; **winning the prize was an — trip for him** ganar el premio le aceitó el ego

egocentric [igosέntrɪk] ADJ egocéntrico

egotism [ígatɪzəm] N egotismo *m*

Egypt [ídʒɪpt] N Egipto *m*

Egyptian [ɪdʒípʃən] ADJ & N egipcio -cia *mf*

eight [et] NUM ocho; **— hundred** ochocientos

eighteen [ettín] NUM dieciocho

eighth [etθ] ADJ, N & ADV octavo *m*; **— note** corchea *f*

eighty [édi] NUM ochenta

either [íðə] ADJ & PRON **— will do** cualquiera de los dos está bien; **choose — suit** elige uno de los dos trajes; **choose —** elige uno [u otro] de los dos; **there were flowers on — side of the road** había flores a ambos lados de la carretera; ADV **if you don't, I won't —** si tú no lo haces, yo tampoco; **I'll go — by bus or by car** voy [o] en autobús o en auto

ejaculate [ɪdʒǽkjələt] VI/VT eyacular; (exclaim) exclamar

eject [ɪdʒékt] VT (throw out) echar, expulsar; VI/VT (throw from a plane) eyectar[se]

ejection [ɪdʒékʃən] N expulsión *f*

EKG [electrocardiogam] [íkédʒí] N electrocardiograma *m*

elaborate¹ [ɪlǽbə-ɪt] ADJ (ornate) elaborado; (detailed) detallado

elaborate² [ɪlǽbəret] VI/VT (create) elaborar; (develop) desarrollar

elapse [ɪlǽps] VI transcurrir, pasar

elastic [ɪlǽstɪk] ADJ elástico; N elástico *m*; (rubber band) goma elástica *f*

elasticity [ɪlæstísɪdi] N elasticidad *f*

elated [ɪlédɪd] ADJ eufórico

elbow [éłbo] N codo *m*; VI/VT codear, dar codazos; **to — one's way through** abrirse paso a codazos

elder [éłdə] ADJ (older) mayor; N (older person) mayor *mf*; (old person) anciano -na *mf*; (in a church) miembro del consejo de una iglesia *m*; **our —s** nuestros mayores *m pl*

elderly [éłdə-li] ADJ anciano

e-learning [ilɜ-nɪŋ] N educación en línea *f*

elect [ɪlékt] ADJ (elected) electo; (chosen by God) elegido; VI/VT elegir

election [ɪlékʃən] N elección *f*

elector [ɪléktə] N elector -ora *mf*

electoral [ɪléktə-əł] ADJ electoral

electric [ɪléktrɪk] ADJ eléctrico; (exciting) electrizante; (excited) electrizado; **— chair** silla eléctrica *f*; **— eel** anguila eléctrica *f*; **— eye** célula fotoeléctrica *f*; **— meter** contador eléctrico *m*; **— storm** tormenta eléctrica *f*

electrical [ɪléktrɪkəł] ADJ eléctrico; **— engineer** ingeniero -ra electricista *mf*; **— engineering** ingeniería eléctrica *f*; **— tape** cinta aislante *f*

electrician [ɪlεktríʃən] N electricista *mf*

electricity [ɪlεktrísɪdi] N electricidad *f*

electrify [ɪléktrəfaɪ] VT (apply electricity) electrificar; (thrill) electrizar

electrocardiogram [ɪlεktrokárdiəgræm] N electrocardiograma *m*

electrocute [ɪléktrəkjut] VT electrocutar

electrode [ɪléktrod] N electrodo *m*

electroencephalogram [ɪlɛktroɛnsɛ́fələgræm] N electroencefalograma *m*
electrolysis [ɪlɛktrɑ́lɪsɪs] N electrólisis *f*
electromagnet [ɪlɛktromǽgnɪt] N electroimán *m*
electromagnetic [ɪlɛktromægnɛ́ᴅɪk] ADJ electromagnético
electron [ɪlɛ́ktrɑn] N electrón *m*; — **microscope** microscopio electrónico *m*
electronic [ɪlɛktrɑ́nɪk] ADJ electrónico; — **banking** banca electrónica *f*; — **mail** correo electrónico *m*; —**s** electrónica *f*; — **signature** firma electrónica *f*
elegance [ɛ́lɪgəns] N elegancia *f*, gallardía *f*
elegant [ɛ́lɪgənt] ADJ elegante, gallardo; (gift) de lujo
element [ɛ́ləmənt] N elemento *m*; (component part) componente *m*, pieza *f*; (for heating) resistencia *f*; **the —s** los elementos
elemental [ɛləmɛ́ntl̩] ADJ elemental; — **forces** fuerzas de la naturaleza *f pl*
elementary [ɛləméntri] ADJ elemental; — **school** escuela primaria *f*
elephant [ɛ́ləfənt] N elefante -ta *mf*
elevate [ɛ́ləvet] VT elevar
elevation [ɛləvéʃən] N (action of elevating, elevated place) elevación *f*; (altitude) altura *f*
elevator [ɛ́ləveᴅɚ] N ascensor *m*; *Am* elevador *m*; (for grain) elevador *m*
eleven [ɪlɛ́vən] NUM once
elf [ɛɫf] N elfo *m*; (mischievous person) pillo -lla *mf*
elicit [ɪlísɪt] VT provocar; **to — admiration** despertar admiración
eligibility [ɛlɪʤəbílɪᴅi] N elegibilidad *f*
eligible [ɛ́lɪʤəbəɫ] ADJ elegible; **an — bachelor** un buen partido; **you are — for a scholarship** tienes derecho a solicitar una beca
eliminate [ɪlímənet] VT eliminar
elimination [ɪlɪmənéʃən] N eliminación *f*
elite [ɪlít] N elite *f*, élite *f*
elitist [ɪlíᴅɪst] ADJ & N elitista *mf*
elk [ɛɫk] N alce *m*
elliptical [ɪlíptɪkəɫ] ADJ elíptico
elm [ɛɫm] N olmo *m*
elongate [ɪlɔ́ŋget] VI/VT alargar[se]
elope [ɪlóp] VI fugarse para casarse a escondidas
eloquence [ɛ́ləkwəns] N elocuencia *f*
eloquent [ɛ́ləkwənt] ADJ elocuente
El Salvador [ɛɫsǽɫvədɔr] N El Salvador *m*
else [ɛɫs] ADJ & ADV **who — was there?** ¿quién más estaba? **someone —'s son** el hijo de otro; **somebody —** [algún] otro; **or —** si no; **leave town or —** vete del pueblo o sufre las consecuencias / o verás lo que es bueno; **nobody —** nadie más; **nothing —** nada más; **how —?** ¿de qué otra forma? ADV **—where** (location) en otra parte / en otro lado; (movement) a otra parte / a otro sitio
elucidate [ɪlúsɪdet] VI/VT elucidar, dilucidar, esclarecer
elucidation [ɪlusɪdéʃən] N elucidación *f*, dilucidación *f*
elude [ɪlúd] VT eludir
elusive [ɪlúsɪv] ADJ (slippery) escurridizo; (evasive) esquivo; (difficult to understand) difícil de entender
emaciated [ɪméʃieᴅɪd] ADJ escuálido, descarnado
e-mail [ímeɫ] N correo electrónico *m*; — **address** dirección de correo electrónico *f*
emanate [ɛ́mənet] VI/VT emanar
emanation [ɛmənéʃən] N emanación *f*
emancipate [ɪmǽnsəpet] VT emancipar
emancipation [ɪmænsəpéʃən] N emancipación *f*
emasculate [ɪmǽskjəlet] VT castrar; (remove testicles) castrar, emascular
embalm [ɪmbɑ́m] VT (the body of a deceased person) preparar; (a mummy) embalsamar
embalming [ɪmbɑ́mɪŋ] N preparación del cuerpo *f*
embankment [ɪmbǽŋkmənt] N terraplén *m*
embargo [ɪmbɑ́rgo] N embargo *m*; VT imponer un embargo a/contra
embark [ɪmbɑ́rk] VI/VT embarcar[se]
embarrass [ɪmbǽrəs] VT (cause shame) hacerle pasar vergüenza a; (cause discomfit, financial difficulties) poner en aprietos; **—ed** avergonzado, en aprietos; **I'm —ed about my teeth** me dan vergüenza mis dientes; **I'm —ed to tell you** me da vergüenza decírtelo
embarrassing [ɪmbǽrəsɪŋ] ADJ (shameful) vergonzoso, penoso; (hindering) embarazoso
embarrassment [ɪmbǽrəsmənt] N (shame) vergüenza *f*, bochorno *m*, pena *f*; (act of embarrassing) vergüenza *f*; (financial difficulty) aprieto *m*; **he's an — to the company** hace quedar mal a la compañía; **we have an — of riches** nadamos en la abundancia
embassy [ɛ́mbəsi] N embajada *f*
embattled [ɪmbǽdl̩d] ADJ hostigado, agobiado
embed [ɪmbɛ́d] VT incrustar
embedded [ɪmbɛ́ᴅɪd] ADJ incrustado
embellish [ɪmbɛ́lɪʃ] VT adornar, ornamentar
ember [ɛ́mbɚ] N ascua *f*, brasa *f*
embezzle [ɪmbɛ́zəɫ] VT desfalcar, malversar
embezzlement [ɪmbɛ́zəɫmənt] N desfalco *m*, peculado *m*, malversación *f*
embitter [ɪmbíᴅɚ] VT amargar
emblem [ɛ́mbləm] N emblema *m*, divisa *f*
embody [ɪmbɑ́ᴅi] VT (personify) personificar; (to provide with a body) encarnar
embolism [ɛ́mbəlɪzəm] N embolia *f*
embrace [ɪmbrés] VI/VT (hug, adopt) abrazar[se]; (include) abarcar; N abrazo *m*

embroider [ɪmbrɔ́ɪDə-] VI/VT bordar, recamar

embroidery [ɪmbrɔ́ɪDəri] N bordado *m*

embroil [ɪmbrɔ́ɪɫ] VT (involve in a conflict) meter en un lío; (throw into confusion) embrollar

embryo [émbrio] N embrión *m*

embryonic [embriáník] ADJ embriónico, embrionario

emerald [émə-əld] N esmeralda *f*

emerge [ɪmɔ́-ʤ] VI (come into view) emerger; (arise, as a question, problem) surgir

emergency [ɪmɔ́-ʤənsi] N emergencia *f*; — **brake** freno de emergencia *m*; — **exit** salida de emergencia *f*; — **room** urgencias *f pl*

emergent [ɪmɔ́-ʤənt] ADJ emergente

emerging [ɪmɔ́-ʤɪŋ] ADJ emergente

emigrant [émɪgrənt] ADJ & N emigrante *mf*

emigrate [émɪgret] VI emigrar

emigration [emɪgréʃən] N emigración *f*

eminence [émənəns] N eminencia *f*

eminent [émənənt] ADJ eminente

emissary [émɪseri] N emisario -ria *mf*

emission [ɪmíʃən] N emisión *f*

emit [ɪmít] VT (light, sound) emitir; (smells) despedir; (sparks) echar

emoticon [ɪmóDɪkan] N emoticón *m*, emoticono *m*

emotion [ɪmóʃən] N emoción *f*

emotional [ɪmóʃənɫ] ADJ (of the emotions) emocional; (arousing or expressing emotions) emotivo; (easily moved) sensible

empathy [émpəθi] N empatía *f*

emperor [émpərə-] N emperador *m*; — **penguin** pingüino emperador *m*

emphasis [émfəsɪs] N énfasis *m*, hincapié *m*

emphasize [émfəsaɪz] VT enfatizar, hacer hincapié en, subrayar

emphatic [ɪmfǽDɪk] ADJ enfático

emphysema [emfɪsímə] N enfisema *m*

empire [émpaɪr] N imperio *m*

empirical [ɪmpírɪkəɫ] ADJ empírico

employ [ɪmplɔ́ɪ] VT emplear; (hire) emplear, ocupar; N empleo *m*; **to be in someone's —** trabajar a las órdenes de alguien

employee [ɪmplɔ́ɪi] N empleado -da *mf*

employer [ɪmplɔ́ɪə-] N patrón -na *mf*; **—s'** patronal

employment [ɪmplɔ́ɪmənt] N empleo *m*; (occupation) ocupación *f*; — **bureau** agencia de empleo *f*; — **opportunities** oportunidades laborales *f pl*; **place of —** lugar de trabajo

empower [ɪmpáʊə-] VT (authorize) autorizar; (give strength) potenciar

empress [émprɪs] N emperatriz *f*

emptiness [émptɪnɪs] N vacío *m*

empty [émpti] ADJ (devoid of content) vacío; (devoid of activity) desocupado; **—-handed** con las manos vacías; VI/VT vaciar[se],

volcar[se]; (flow into) desembocar; N **to run on —** (of a car, person) quedarse sin combustible

emulate [émjəlet] VT emular (also computer term)

enable [ɪnébəɫ] VT permitir

enact [ɪnǽkt] VT (a law) promulgar; (a role) desempeñar

enamel [ɪnǽməɫ] N esmalte *m*; VT esmaltar

enamor [ɪnǽmə-] VT enamorar; **to be —ed of** estar enamorado de

encamp [ɪnkémp] VI acampar

encephalitis [ɪnsefəláɪDɪs] N encefalitis *f*

enchant [ɪntʃǽnt] VT (bewitch) hechizar; (delight) encantar

enchanting [ɪntʃǽntɪŋ] ADJ encantador

enchantment [ɪntʃǽntmənt] N encantamiento *m*, encanto *m*, hechicería *f*

encircle [ɪnsɔ́-kəɫ] VT cercar, ceñir

enclave [ánklev] N enclave *m*

enclose [ɪnklóz] VT (confine someone or something) encerrar; (fence in) cercar; (put in the same envelope) adjuntar, anexar

enclosure [ɪnklóʒə-] N (wall or fence) cerca *f*; (enclosed area) cercado *m*, recinto *m*; (enclosed document) documento adjunto *m*; (act of enclosing) encierro *m*

encode [ɪnkód] VT codificar

encoding [ɪŋkóDɪŋ] N codificación *f*

encompass [ɪnkámpəs] VT (include) abarcar, englobar; (surround) circundar

encore [ánkɔr] N bis *m*; INTERJ ¡otra!

encounter [ɪnkáʊntə-] VI/VT encontrar[se]; **they —ed the enemy army** se enfrentaron con el ejército enemigo; N (meeting, athletic event) encuentro *m*; (battle) enfrentamiento *m*

encourage [ɪnkɔ́-ɪʤ] VT (inspire with confidence) alentar, animar; (promote) fomentar, estimular

encouragement [ɪnkɔ́-ɪʤmənt] N (inspiration) aliento *m*, ánimo *m*; (promotion) estímulo *m*, fomento *m*

encouraging [ɪŋkɔ́-əʤɪŋ] ADJ alentador

encroach [ɪnkróʧ] VT **to — upon** (liberties) cercenar; (territory) usurpar; (time) quitar

encrypt [ɪnkrípt] VT codificar, cifrar

encryption [ɪŋkrípʃən] N cifrado *m*

encumber [ɪnkámbə-] VT (block) impedir; (burden) agobiar; (charge an account) gravar

encumbrance [ɪŋkámbrəns] N gravamen *m*

encyclopedia [ɪnsaɪkləpídiə] N enciclopedia *f*

end [end] N (temporal) fin *m*, término *m*; (limit, boundary) final *m*, extremo *m*; (tip) cabo *m*; (aim) fin *m*; (in football) exterior *m*; — **key** tecla [de] fin *f*; **—-of-life care** cuidado terminal *m*; — **table** mesa pequeña *f*; — **zone** zona de ensayo *f*, zona de anotación *f*; **at the — of the movie** al final de la película; **the north — of town** el barrio norte; **no —**

of things un sinfín de cosas; **at the — of the day** al fin y al cabo; **on —** de punta; **for days on —** día tras día; **to put an — to** poner fin a; VI/VT terminar; (a street) morir; **he —ed his life** puso fin a su vida; **a prayer —s the class** la clase termina con una oración; **a war to — all wars** una guerra que supera a todas las anteriores; ADV **— to —** uno tras otro

endanger [ɪndéndʒə] VT poner en peligro; **—ed species** especie en peligro de extinción f

endear [ɪndír] VI **to — oneself** congraciarse; **his humor —ed him to her** se ganó la simpatía de ella gracias a su humor

endearing [ɪndírɪŋ] ADJ entrañable

endeavor [ɪndévə] VT (try) tratar de, intentar, procurar; VI (strive) esforzarse por; N esfuerzo m

endemic [ɪndémɪk] ADJ endémico

ending [éndɪŋ] N final m; (of a story) desenlace m; (derivational, inflectional) terminación f; (inflectional) desinencia f

endless [éndlɪs] ADJ (having no end) interminable; (continuous) sin fin; (infinite) eterno

endocrine [éndəkrɪn] ADJ endocrino

endocrinology [ɛndəkrɪnálədʒi] N endocrinología f

endoderm [éndodəm] N endodermo m

endorphin [ɪndɔ́rfɪn] N endorfina f

endorse [ɪndɔ́rs] VT (sign a check) endosar; (support) respaldar; (authorize a document) refrendar, visar

endorsement [ɪndɔ́rsmənt] N (signature) endoso m; (backing) respaldo m; (authorization) refrendo m

endorser [ɪndɔ́rsə] N (check signer) endosante mf; (supporter) partidario -ria mf; (authorizer) refrendario -ria mf

endow [ɪndáʊ] VT (grant funds) hacer un legado; (furnish powers) dotar

endowment [ɪndáʊmənt] N (funds granted) legado m, dotación f; (power) dote f; **— annuity** anualidad dotal f; **— fund** fondo de un legado m

endurance [ɪndúrəns] N (stamina) resistencia f; (ability to bear pain) aguante m

endure [ɪndúr, ɪndjúr] VT (undergo) sobrellevar, soportar, pasar; VI (live on) durar; (bear up) aguantar

enema [énəmə] N enema m, lavativa f

enemy [énəmi] N enemigo -ga mf

energetic [ɛnədʒɛ́tɪk] ADJ enérgico

energy [énədʒi] N energía f; **— policy** política energética f

enervate [énəvet] VT enervar, debilitar

enforce [ɪnfɔ́rs] VT hacer cumplir

enforcement [ɪnfɔ́rsmənt] N **the sheriff is responsible for the — of the law** el

alguacil es responsable de hacer cumplir la ley

engage [ɪngédʒ] VT (hire) contratar; (attract) captar, atraer; (interlock) engranar; **to — the brake** poner el freno; **to — someone in conversation** trabar conversación con alguien; **to — in battle** trabar batalla; **to be —d in something** estar ocupado en algo; **to be —d to be married** estar comprometido [para casarse], estar prometido

engaged [ɪngédʒd] ADJ comprometido

engagement [ɪngédʒmənt] N (commitment) compromiso m; (betrothal) compromiso m, noviazgo m; (employment) empleo m; (battle) batalla f; (gear interlocking) engranaje m

engender [ɪndʒéndə] VT engendrar

engine [éndʒɪn] N (machine) máquina f; (in a vehicle) motor m; (locomotive) locomotora f; **— block** bloque del motor m

engineer [ɛndʒənír] N ingeniero -ra mf; (of locomotive) maquinista mf; VT (create) idear; (plot) maquinar

engineering [ɛndʒəníriŋ] N ingeniería f

English [íŋglɪʃ] ADJ inglés; N (spin) efecto m; **the —** los ingleses; **—man, —woman** inglés -esa mf

engrave [ɪngrév] VI/VT grabar

engraver [ɪngrévə] N grabador -ora mf

engraving [ɪngréviŋ] N grabado m

engross [ɪngrós] VT absorber

engrossed [ɪngróst] ADJ absorto

engulf [ɪngʌ́lf] VT (swallow) tragar; (overwhelm) abrumar

enhance [ɪnhǽns] VT (intensify) realzar; (improve) mejorar

enigma [ɪnígmə] N enigma m

enjoin [ɪndʒɔ́ɪn] VT instar; **to — from** prohibir

enjoy [ɪndʒɔ́ɪ] VI/VT (take pleasure) disfrutar [de], gozar [de]; (benefit from) gozar [de]; **—!** ¡que lo disfrutes! **to — oneself** divertirse; **to — the use of** usufructuar

enjoyable [ɪndʒɔ́ɪəbəl] ADJ (pleasant) agradable, gozoso; (fun) ameno

enjoyment [ɪndʒɔ́ɪmənt] N (act of enjoying) goce m, disfrute m; (right of use) usufructo m; (pleasure) placer m, gozo m

enlarge [ɪnlárdʒ] VI/VT agrandar[se]; VT (blow up a photo) ampliar; VI **to — upon** explayarse sobre, extenderse sobre

enlargement [ɪnlárdʒmənt] N (photo, building) ampliación f; (act of enlarging) agrandamiento m; (temporary swelling) dilatación f

enlighten [ɪnláɪtn] VT (morally) iluminar; (intellectually) explicar, ilustrar

enlightenment [ɪnláɪtnmənt] N (moral) iluminación f; (intellectual) explicación f; **the — la Ilustración**

enlist [ɪnlíst] VI/VT (for the army) alistar[se]; (for a campaign) conseguir el apoyo de

enlistment [ɪnlístmənt] N alistamiento *m*

enliven [ɪnláɪvən] VT animar, avivar

enmity [énmɪDi] N enemistad *f*

ennoble [ɪnnóbəl] VT ennoblecer

enormous [ɪnɔ́rməs] ADJ enorme, descomunal

enough [ɪnʌ́f] ADJ suficiente; ADV **he's tall —** tiene altura suficiente; N lo suficiente; **we have — to live comfortably** tenemos lo suficiente como para vivir cómodamente; **that is —** con eso basta; **more than —** bastante; INTERJ ¡basta!

enrage [ɪnréʤ] VT enfurecer

enrapture [ɪnrǽptʃə] VT embelesar

enrich [ɪnrítʃ] VT enriquecer

enrichment [ɪnrítʃmənt] N enriquecimiento *m*

enroll [ɪnróɫ] VI/VT matricular[se], inscribir[se]

enrollment [ɪnróɫmənt] N matrícula *f*, inscripción *f*; **what is your —?** ¿cuántos alumnos tienes matriculados?

ensemble [ɑnsámbəl] N conjunto *m*

ensign [énsɪn] N (naval rank) alférez de fragata *mf*; (flag) enseña *f*; (badge) insignia *f*

enslave [ɪnslév] VT esclavizar

ensnare [ɪnsnér] VT atrapar, coger en una trampa

ensue [ɪnsú] VI (follow) ocurrir después, suceder; (result from) resultar; **the ensuing events** los sucesos subsiguientes

ensure [ɪnʃʊ́r] VT asegurar

entail [ɪntél] VT implicar, conllevar

entangle [ɪntǽŋgəl] VT enredar

enter [éntə] VT (go in) entrar en/a; (join) ingresar en/a; (write) escribir; (put data in a computer) dar entrada a; (put data in account books) asentar; (start negotiations) iniciar; VI/VT (register for a competition) inscribir[se]; VI salir / entrar a escena; **to — into** (make an agreement) concertar; (form part of) figurar en

enterprise [éntə̩praɪz] N empresa *f*

enterprising [éntə̩praɪzɪŋ] ADJ emprendedor

entertain [entə̩tén] VI/VT (amuse) divertir, recrear; (host) invitar; **we — a lot** tenemos invitados muy a menudo; (consider) contemplar; (harbor) abrigar

entertainer [entə̩ténə̩] N artista *mf*

entertaining [entə̩ténɪŋ] ADJ (fun) divertido; (serving as pastime) entretenido; (pleasant) ameno

entertainment [entə̩ténmənt] N (source of fun) diversión *f*; (pastime) entretenimiento *m*; (of guests) agasajo *m*

enthrall [ɪnθrɔ́l] VT (captivate) cautivar, hechizar; (make a slave of) esclavizar

enthusiasm [ɪnθúziæzəm] N entusiasmo *m*

enthusiast [ɪnθúzɪəst] N entusiasta *mf*

enthusiastic [ɪnθuziǽstɪk] ADJ entusiasta; **I'm very — about the trip** estoy muy entusiasmado con el viaje

entice [ɪntáɪs] VI/VT (attract) atraer; (lure) tentar; (seduce) seducir

entire [ɪntáɪr] ADJ (unbroken) entero; (complete) completo; **the — crew** toda la tripulación, la tripulación entera

entirety [ɪntáɪrɪDi] N totalidad *f*

entitle [ɪntáɪɖl] VT (give a title) titular, intitular; (give a right) dar derecho

entitlement [ɪntáɪɖlmənt] N derecho *m*

entity [éntɪDi] N (institution) entidad *f*; (being) ente *m*, ser *m*

entomology [entəmáləʤi] N entomología *f*

entourage [ántʊraʤ] N séquito *m*, cortejo *m*

entrails [éntrelz] N entrañas *f pl*

entrance¹ [éntrəns] N (act, point of entering) entrada *f*; (permission to enter) ingreso *m*; **— examination** examen de ingreso *m*

entrance² [ɪntrǽns] VT embelesar

entrant [éntrənt] N participante *mf*; **—s in the law profession** abogados recién recibidos *m pl*

entrap [ɪntrǽp] VT (ensnare) coger con una trampa; (deceive) embaucar

entreaty [ɪntríDi] N súplica *f*, ruego *m*

entrench [ɪntréntʃ] VI (establish) afianzar[se]; (dig trenches) atrincherar; **a deeply —ed habit** un hábito muy arraigado

entrepreneur [antrəprənúr] N empresario -ria *mf*

entrepreneurship [antrəprənúrʃɪp] N espíritu emprendedor *m*

entropy [éntrəpi] N entropía *f*

entrust [ɪntrʌ́st] VT confiar, encomendar

entry [éntri] N (act, point of entry) entrada *f*; (permission to enter) ingreso *m*; (record) anotación *f*; (contestant) participante *mf*; (dictionary definition) entrada *f*, artículo *m*; (computer) entrada *f*; (in bookkeeping) asiento *m*; **double — accounting** contabilidad por partida doble *f*; ADJ **—-level** que no requiere experiencia

enumerate [ɪnúməret] VT enumerar

enunciate [ɪnʌ́nsiet] VI/VT (pronounce) articular; (state a theory) enunciar; (proclaim) proclamar

envelop [ɪnvéləp] VT envolver

envelope [énvəlop] N sobre *m*

enviable [énviəbəl] ADJ envidiable

envious [énviəs] ADJ envidioso

environment [ɪnváɪə̩nmənt] N ambiente *m*, medio ambiente *m*; (biological) medio ambiente *m*, ecología *f*; (in computers) entorno *m*; ADJ ambiental; (biological) medioambiental, ecológico

environmental [ɪnvaɪə̩nméntɫ] ADJ ambiental; (biological) medioambiental, ecológico; **— impact study** estudio del impacto ambiental *m*

environmentalist [ɪnvaɪə̩nméntɫɪst] N

ecologista *mf*

envisage [ɪnvízɪʤ] VT anticipar, prever

envision [ɪnvíʒən] VT imaginar

envoy [ánvɔɪ] N enviado -da *mf*

envy [énvi] N envidia *f*; VI/VT envidiar

enzyme [énzaɪm] N enzima *f*

ephemeral [ɪfémə·əl] ADJ efímero

epic [épɪk] ADJ épico; N (poem) epopeya *f*; (genre) épica *f*

epicenter [épɪsɛntə·] N epicentro *m*

epidemic [ɛpɪdémɪk] ADJ epidémico; N epidemia *f*

epidermis [ɛpɪdə́·mɪs] N epidermis *f*

epiglottis [ɛpɪɡlɑtɪs] N epiglotis *f*

epilepsy [épələpsi] N epilepsia *f*

epileptic [ɛpəléptɪk] ADJ epiléptico

epilogue, epilog [épəlɔɡ] N epílogo *m*

epiphany [ɪpífəni] N epifanía *f*

episode [épɪsod] N episodio *m*

episodic [ɛpɪsɑ́dɪk] ADJ (sporadic) episódico; (serial) en episodios

epitaph [épɪtæf] N epitafio *m*

epitome [ɪpítəmi] N epítome *m*

epoch [épək] N época *f*; **—-making** trascendental

Epsom salt [épsəmsɔ́lt] N sal de Epsom *f*

equal [íkwəl] ADJ igual; **— rights** igualdad de derechos *f*; **an — contest** una competición pareja; **to be — to a task** ser capaz de cumplir una tarea; N igual *m*; **— sign** signo de igual *m*; VT igualar

equality [ɪkwáliti] N igualdad *f*

equalize [íkwəlaɪz] VT igualar; (electronically) ecualizar

equalizer [íkwəlaɪzə·] N (in soccer) gol del empate *m*

equally [íkwəli] ADV igualmente

equate [ɪkwét] VT equiparar

equation [ɪkwéʒən] N ecuación *f*

equator [ɪkwédə·] N ecuador *m*

Equatorial Guinea [ɛkwətɔ́riəlgíni] N Guinea Ecuatorial *f*

equidistant [ikwɪdístənt] ADJ equidistante

equilibrium [ikwəlíbriəm] N equilibrio *m*

equine [íkwaɪn] ADJ & N equino *m*

equinox [íkwənɑks] N equinoccio *m*

equip [ɪkwíp] VT equipar

equipment [ɪkwípmənt] N (supplies) equipo *m*; (act of equipping) equipamiento *m*

equitable [ékwɪdəbəl] ADJ equitativo, justo

equity [ékwɪdi] N equidad *f*, valor libre de hipoteca de una propiedad *m*; **equities** acciones *f pl*

equivalent [ɪkwívələnt] ADJ & N equivalente *m*

equivocal [ɪkwívəkəl] ADJ equívoco

era [írə] N era *f*

eradicate [ɪrǽdɪket] VT (extirpate) erradicar; (pull up by roots) arrancar

eradication [ɪrædɪkéʃən] N erradicación *f*

erase [ɪrés] VI/VT borrar[se]

eraser [ɪrésə·] N (pencil) goma de borrar *f*; (blackboard) borrador *m*

erasure [ɪréʃə·] N (act of erasing) borrado *m*; (smudge) borrón *m*

erect [ɪrékt] ADJ erecto; (of the body) erguido; VT erigir

ergonomic [ɚɡənámɪk] ADJ ergonómico

ergonomics [ɚɡənámɪks] N ergonomía *f*

Eritrea [ɛrɪtríə] N Eritrea *f*

Eritrean [ɛrɪtríən] ADJ & N eritreo -a *mf*

ermine [ɚ́mɪn] N armiño *m*

erode [ɪród] VI/VT erosionar[se]

erogenous [ɪráʤənəs] ADJ erógeno

erosion [ɪróʒən] N erosión *f*

err [ɛr] VI errar

errand [érənd] N mandado *m*, recado *m*; **— boy** mandadero *m*

errant [érənt] ADJ errante

erratic [ɪrǽdɪk] ADJ (unpredictable) irregular, errático; (eccentric) excéntrico; (wandering) errante

erroneous [ɪróniəs] ADJ erróneo, errado

error [érə·] N (also in baseball) error *m*; **to be in —** estar errado; **— message** mensaje de error *m*

erudite [érjədaɪt] ADJ erudito

erudition [ɛrjədíʃən] N erudición *f*

erupt [ɪrápt] VI (volcano) hacer erupción; (angry person) estallar; (pimples) salir

eruption [ɪrápʃən] N erupción *f*

escalate [éskəlet] VI (prices) aumentar; (violence) intensificarse, aumentar

escalator [éskəleDə·] N escalera mecánica *f*

escapade [éskəped] N (adventure) aventura *f*; (prank) travesura *f*

escape [ɪskép] N (of gas) escape *m*; (from reality) escape *m*, evasión *f*; (of prisoners) fuga *f*, evasión *f*; (means of escaping) escapatoria *f*; **— key** tecla de escape *f*; VI escapar[se], evadirse; VT (elude) eludir; **his name —s me** no me acuerdo de su nombre

escort[1] [éskɔrt] N (people who accompany) escolta *mf*; (male companion) acompañante *m*; (paid female companion) señorita de compañía *f*

escort[2] [ɪskɔ́rt] VT (protect) escoltar; (accompany) acompañar

escrow [éskro] N **— account** cuenta de depósito en garantía *f*; ADV LOC **in —** en custodia

escudo [ɪskúdo] N escudo *m*

Eskimo [éskəmo] N esquimal *mf*

esophagus [ɪsáfəgəs] N esófago *m*

esoteric [ɛsətérɪk] ADJ esotérico

especial [ɪspéʃəl] ADJ especial

especially [ɪspéʃəli] ADV (above all) especialmente; (mainly) sobre todo; **he's — tired today** hoy está más cansado que de costumbre

espionage [éspiənɑʒ] N espionaje *m*
esplanade [ésplənəd] N explanada *f*
espouse [ıspáuz] VT defender, abrazar
essay¹ [ése] N ensayo *m*
essay² [esé] VT ensayar
essence [ésəns] N esencia *f*; time is of the — el tiempo apremia
essential [ısénʃəl] ADJ esencial
establish [ıstǽblıʃ] VT (cause to be accepted, prove the validity of) establecer; (found) fundar
establishment [ıstǽblıʃmənt] N (action or fact) establecimiento *m*, conformación *f*; (authority) establishment *m*; (of a custom, system) implantación *f*; (of a regime) instauración *f*
estate [ıstét] N (piece of land) hacienda *f*; (possessions) bienes *m pl*; (property) propiedades *f pl*; (of a deceased person) testamentaria *f*; — tax impuesto de sucesión *m*
esteem [ıstím] VT (regard highly) estimar; (consider) considerar; N estima *f*
estimate¹ [éstəmet] VT estimar, evaluar; VI hacer una estimación
estimate² [éstəmıt] N (calculation) estimación *f*; (approximate charge) presupuesto *m*
estimation [estəméʃən] N (opinion) juicio *m*; (esteem) estima *f*; (estimate) estimación *f*; in my — a mi juicio
Estonia [estóniə] N Estonia *f*
Estonian [estónian] ADJ & N estonio -nia *mf*
estrange [ıstréndʒ] VT (alienate) enajenar; to become —d separarse
estrogen [éstrədʒən] N estrógeno *m*
estuary [éstʃueri] N estuario *m*
et cetera, etc. [etsétrə] ADV etcétera, etc.
etch [etʃ] VI/VT (engrave) grabar; (outline) perfilar[se]
etching [étʃıŋ] N grabado *m*
eternal [ıtɝ́nl] ADJ eterno
eternity [ıtɝ́nıDi] N eternidad *f*
ethanol [éθənɑl] N etanol *m*
ether [íθɚ] N éter *m*
ethernet [íθɚnet] N ethernet *m*
ethical [éθıkəl] ADJ ético
ethics [éθıks] N ética *f*
Ethiopia [iθiópiə] N Etiopía *f*
Ethiopian [iθiópian] ADJ & N etíope *mf*
ethnic [éθnık] ADJ étnico; (dances, clothes) tradicional; — Chinese de ascendencia china; — cleansing limpieza étnica *f*
ethnicity [eθnísıDi] N etnicidad *f*; (group) grupo étnico *m*
ethnography [eθnágrəfi] N etnografía *f*
ethnology [eθnálədʒi] N etnología *f*
ethyl alcohol [éθəlǽlkəhɑl] N alcohol etílico *m*
etiquette [éDıkıt] N etiqueta *f*
etymology [eDəmálədʒi] N etimología *f*

EU [European Union] [íjú] N UE *f*
eucalyptus [jukəlíptəs] N eucalipto *m*
eulogy [júlədʒi] N (praise) elogio *m*; (at a funeral) panegírico *m*
eunuch [júnək] N eunuco *m*
euphemism [júfəmızəm] N eufemismo *m*
euphoria [jufɔ́riə] N euforia *f*
euro [júro] N euro *m*
Europe [júrəp] N Europa *f*
European [jurəpían] ADJ & N europeo -a *mf*; — Union Unión Europea *f*; — Union budget presupuesto comunitario *m*
Eustachian tube [justéʃən] N trompa de Eustaquio *f*
euthanasia [juθənéʒə] N eutanasia *f*
evacuate [ıvǽkjuet] VI/VT (remove due to danger, defecate) evacuar; (empty a building) desalojar
evade [ıvéd] VT (taxes, responsibilities) evadir, burlar; (questions) eludir
evaluate [ıvǽljuet] VT (assess) evaluar; (appraise) avaluar, tasar
evaluation [ıvæljuéʃən] N evaluación *f*
evangelical [ıvændʒélıkəl] ADJ evangélico
evaporate [ıvǽpəret] VI/VT evaporar[se]; VI (vanish) esfumarse
evaporation [ıvæpəréʃən] N evaporación *f*
evasion [ıvéʒən] N (escape) evasión *f*; (subterfuge) evasiva *f*
evasive [ıvésıv] ADJ evasivo
eve [iv] N (day before) víspera *f*; (evening) atardecer *m*; on the — of en vísperas de
even [ívən] ADJ (flat) plano, llano; (smooth) liso; (parallel) paralelo; (without fluctuation) parejo; (equal) igual; (divisible by two) par; (placid) tranquilo; —handed imparcial; —-tempered apacible; an — dozen una docena exacta; to be — with someone estar a mano con alguien; to get — with someone desquitarse de alguien; ADV (still, yet) aun; (for extreme case) hasta, inclusive, incluso; — if/though aun cuando; — my mother went hasta mi madre fue; — so aun así; it's — more expensive es aun más caro; not — ni siquiera; VI/VT (make a surface even) nivelar[se]; (make accounts even) emparejar
evening [ívnıŋ] N tarde *f*; (dusk) atardecer *m*; — gown vestido de fiesta *m*, vestido de noche *m*; — party velada *f*; — star lucero de la tarde *m*; good —! ¡buenas noches!
event [ıvént] N (happening) hecho *m*, evento *m*; (of importance) acontecimiento *m*, suceso *m*; in any — en todo caso; in the — of en caso de
eventful [ıvéntfəl] ADJ agitado, movido
eventual [ıvéntʃuəl] ADJ (later) posterior; (final) final
eventuality [ıventʃuǽlıDi] N eventualidad *f*

eventually [ɪvéntʃuəli] ADV a la larga
ever [évə-] ADV alguna vez; **—more** para
siempre; **— since** desde entonces; **have you
— studied French?** ¿alguna vez has
estudiado francés? **how did you — do this?**
¿cómo pudiste hacer esto? **for — and —** por/
para siempre jamás; **hardly —** casi nunca; **if
—** si alguna vez; **more than —** más que
nunca; **the best friend I — had** el mejor
amigo que he tenido jamás; **for —more**
para/por siempre jamás; ADJ **—green** [planta]
perenne f; **—lasting** eterno
every [évri] ADJ (each) cada; **— child is
different** cada niño es diferente; (all)
todo[s]; **— once in a while** de vez en
cuando; **— other day** cada dos días, un día sí
y otro no; **—where** (location) por/en todas
partes; (direction) a todas partes; **we go —
Friday** vamos todos los viernes; PRON
—body todos -das mf pl, todo el mundo m; **—
day** todos los días; **—one** todos -das mf pl,
todo el mundo m; **—thing** todo; **you are
—thing to me** eres todo para mí; ADJ **—day**
(of clothes) de diario, de todos los días; (of
occurrences) cotidiano
evict [ɪvíkt] VT desalojar
evidence [évɪdəns] N evidencia f; (data in court)
prueba f; **to be in —** ser evidente; VI/VT
evidenciar[se], demostrar[se]
evident [évɪdənt] ADJ evidente
evil [ívəl] ADJ (wicked) malo, malvado; (harmful)
maligno; N (force of nature) mal m; (human
wickedness) maldad f; **—doer** malhechor
-ora mf; **— eye** mal de ojo m; **the lesser of
two —s** el mal menor
evocation [ɛvəkéʃən] N evocación f
evoke [ɪvók] VT (call up) evocar; (elicit) provocar
evolution [ɛvəlúʃən] N evolución f
evolutionary [ɛvəlúʃəneri] ADJ evolutivo
evolve [ɪválv] VI/VT desarrollar[se]; VI
evolucionar
ewe [ju] N oveja f
ex [ɛks] N ex mf
exacerbate [ɪgzǽsə-bet] VI/VT exacerbar
exact [ɪgzǽkt] ADJ exacto; VT exigir
exacting [ɪgzǽktɪŋ] ADJ exigente
exactly [ɪgzǽktli] ADV exactamente,
precisamente; **he's not — a genius** no es un
genio ni mucho menos / no es ningún genio
que digamos; **they arrived — at three**
llegaron exactamente a las tres
exaggerate [ɪgzǽdʒəret] VT exagerar
exalt [ɪgzɔ́lt] VT exaltar
exam [ɪgzǽm] N examen m
examination [ɪgzæmənéʃən] N examen m (also
medical)
examine [ɪgzǽmɪn] VT (inspect) examinar;
(analyze) analizar
example [ɪgzǽmpəl] N ejemplo m

exasperate [ɪgzǽspəret] VT exasperar
excavate [ékskəvet] VT excavar
excavator [ékskəveɒə-] N (person) excavador
-ora mf; (machine) excavadora f
exceed [ɪksíd] VT (go beyond) exceder, rebasar;
(be superior to) superar, sobrepasar
exceeding [ɪksíɒɪŋ] N superación f
exceedingly [ɪksíɒɪŋli] ADV sumamente,
extremadamente
excel [ɪksél] VI sobresalir, lucirse, descollar
excellence [éksələns] N excelencia f
excellent [éksələnt] ADJ excelente
except [ɪksépt] PREP excepto, menos; **all the
students — Pam** todos los estudiantes
menos Pam; CONJ excepto, salvo; **the cars
are identical — that one is older** los
coches son idénticos salvo que uno es más
viejo; **we would go to the beach, — for
the inclement weather** iríamos a la playa
si no fuera por el mal tiempo; VT exceptuar
excepting [ɪkséptɪŋ] PREP exceptuando
exception [ɪksépʃən] N excepción f; **with the —
of** con/a excepción de; **to take —** (object)
objetar; (resent) ofenderse
exceptional [ɪksépʃənl] ADJ (unusual)
excepcional; (gifted) superdotado;
(handicapped) con necesidades especiales
excerpt[1] [éksə-pt] N fragmento m
excerpt[2] [éksə-pt, ɪksə́pt] VT seleccionar
fragmentos
excess [ékses] N exceso m, hartazgo m; **—
baggage** exceso de equipaje m; **— profits
tax** impuesto sobre ganancias excesivas m; **—
weight** exceso de peso m; **in — of twenty
pounds** más de veinte libras; **to drink to —**
beber en exceso
excessive [ɪksésɪv] ADJ excesivo, desmedido
exchange [ɪkstʃéndʒ] VT (replace with
something similar) cambiar; (give mutually)
intercambiar; (trade political prisoners,
books, CDs) canjear; (barter) permutar; **to —
greetings** saludarse; N (replacement)
cambio m; (interchange) intercambio m;
(barter) permuta f; (of prisoners, books) canje
m; (for stock trading) bolsa f; (for commodity
trading) lonja f; (telephone) central de
teléfonos f; **— student** estudiante de
intercambio mf; **rate of —** tipo de cambio m,
tasa de cambio f
excise [éksaɪz] N impuesto sobre bienes de
consumo m
excite [ɪksáɪt] VT (agitate, arouse) excitar,
alborotar; (enthuse) entusiasmar
excited [ɪksáɪɒɪd] ADJ (agitated, aroused)
excitado; (enthusiastic) entusiasmado,
ilusionado; **to get —** (aroused) excitarse;
(enthused) entusiasmarse
excitement [ɪksáɪtmənt] N (arousal) excitación
f; (enthusiasm) entusiasmo m

exciting [ɪksáɪDɪŋ] ADJ (stimulating) excitante; (thrilling) emocionante, apasionante

exclaim [ɪksklém] VI exclamar

exclamation [ɛkskləméʃən] N exclamación *f*; — **point** signo de admiración *m*

exclude [ɪksklúd] VT excluir

exclusion [ɪksklúʒən] N exclusión *f*

exclusive [ɪksklúsɪv] ADJ exclusivo; — **of** sin incluir

excommunicate [ɛkskəmjúnɪket] VT excomulgar

excrement [ɛ́kskrəmənt] N excremento *m*

excrescence [ɪkskrésəns] N excrecencia *f*

excrete [ɪkskrít] VI/VT excretar

excretion [ɪkskríʃən] N excreción *f*

excruciating [ɪkskrúʃieDɪŋ] ADJ insoportable, atroz

excursion [ɪkskɚ́ʒən] N excursión *f*

excusable [ɪkskjúzəbəl] ADJ excusable, disculpable

excuse¹ [ɪkskjúz] VT (release from a duty, seek exemption) excusar, eximir; (forgive) disculpar, perdonar; — **me!** (forgive me) disculpe; (let me pass) con permiso; (excuse me?) ¿cómo? ¿perdón? *Mex* ¿mande?

excuse² [ɪkskjús] N excusa *f*, disculpa *f*; **it's a poor — for a car** no merece llamarse un coche

executable [ɛgzəkjúDəbəl] ADJ ejecutable

execute [ɛ́ksɪkjut] VT ejecutar (also computer term); (by firing squad) fusilar

execution [ɛksɪkjúʃən] N ejecución *f*; (by firing squad) fusilamiento *m*; — **wall** paredón *m*

executioner [ɛksɪkjúʃənɚ] N verdugo *mf*

executive [ɪgzɛ́kjəDɪv] ADJ ejecutivo; N (person) ejecutivo -va *mf*; (branch of government) poder ejecutivo *m*

executor [ɪgzɛ́kjəDɚ] N albacea *mf*

exemplary [ɪgzɛ́mpləri] ADJ ejemplar

exemplify [ɪgzɛ́mpləfaɪ] VT ejemplificar

exempt [ɪgzɛ́mpt] VT eximir, dispensar; ADJ exento, libre

exemption [ɪgzɛ́mpʃən] N exención *f*, franquicia *f*

exercise [ɛ́ksɚsaɪz] N ejercicio *m*; —**s** ceremonia *f*; VT ejercer; VI hacer ejercicio; — **electrocardiogram** prueba de esfuerzo máximo *f*; **to be** —**d about something** estar disgustado por algo

exert [ɪgzɚ́t] VT ejercer; **to** — **oneself** esforzarse, empeñarse

exertion [ɪgzɚ́ʃən] N (use of powers, faculties) ejercicio *m*; (vigorous action) esfuerzo *m*, empeño *m*

exfoliation [ɪksfoliéʃən] N exfoliación *f*

exhale [ɛkshél] VT exhalar; VI espirar

exhaust [ɪgzɔ́st] VT agotar, desmadejar; (a topic) tratar exhaustivamente; N (from a car) escape *m*

exhausted [ɪgzɔ́stɪd] ADJ rendido, agotado

exhausting [ɪgzɔ́stɪŋ] ADJ agotador

exhaustion [ɪgzɔ́stʃən] N (act or process of exhausting) agotamiento *m*; (weakness, tiredness) fatiga *f*

exhaustive [ɪgzɔ́stɪv] ADJ exhaustivo

exhibit [ɪgzíbɪt] VI/VT (manifest) exhibir; (put on view) exponer; N exposición *f*

exhibition [ɛksəbíʃən] N (manifestation, show of skills) exhibición *f*; (public display of objects) exposición *f*

exhibitionism [ɛksɪbíʃənɪzəm] N exhibicionismo *m*

exhilarated [ɪgzíləreDɪd] ADJ exultante

exhort [ɪgzɔ́rt] VT exhortar

exhumation [ɛgzjuméʃən] N exhumación *f*

exile [ɛ́gzaɪl] N exilio *m*, destierro *m*; (person exiled) exiliado -da *mf*, desterrado -da *mf*; VT exiliar

exist [ɪgzíst] VI existir

existence [ɪgzístəns] N existencia *f*

existential [ɛgzɪsténʃəl] ADJ existencial

existing [ɪgzístɪŋ] ADJ existente

exit [ɛ́gzɪt] N salida *f*; VI/VT salir [de]; (theater) hacer mutis; — **interview** entrevista de salida *f*; — **strategy** estrategia de salida *f*; VI salir; **he** —**ed the building** salió del edificio

exodus [ɛ́ksədəs] N éxodo *m*

exonerate [ɪgzánəret] VT exonerar

exorbitant [ɪgzɔ́rbɪDənt] ADJ exorbitante

exorcise [ɛ́ksɔrsaɪz] VT exorcisar

exorcism [ɛ́ksɔrsɪzəm] N exorcismo *m*

exotic [ɪgzáDɪk] ADJ exótico

expand [ɪkspǽnd] VI/VT expandir[se], ampliar[se]; (an equation, an idea) desarrollar[se]; (through heat) dilatar[se]; —**ed memory** memoria expandida *f*

expanse [ɪkspǽns] N extensión *f*

expansion [ɪkspǽnʃən] N expansión *f*; (of an equation, of an idea) desarrollo *m*; (through heat) dilatación *f*; — **slot** ranura para accesorios *f*

expansive [ɪkspǽnsɪv] ADJ expansivo

expatriate¹ [ɛkspétriet] VI/VT expatriar[se]

expatriate² [ɛkspétriit] N expatriado -da *mf*

expect [ɪkspɛ́kt] VT esperar; **we** — **guests** esperamos visita[s]; **I** — **you to be on time** cuento con que vengas puntualmente; **I'm** —**ed to work fifty hours a week** tengo que trabajar cincuenta horas por semana; **I** — **you're tired** estarás cansado; **she's** —**ing** está embarazada/encinta

expectation [ɛkspɛktéʃən] N (anticipation) expectación *f*; (expected thing) expectativa *f*; **he has great** —**s** tiene grandes expectativas

expectorant [ɪkspɛ́ktɚənt] ADJ & N expectorante *m*

expectorate [ɪkspɛ́ktəret] VI/VT expectorar

expedient [ɪkspídiənt] ADJ conveniente,

expeditivo

expedite [ékspɪdaɪt] VT (facilitate) agilizar; (deal with promptly) despachar

expedition [ekspɪdíʃən] N expedición f

expeditionary [ekspɪdíʃəneɪ] ADJ expedicionario

expel [ɪkspél] VT (discharge) expeler; (throw out) expulsar

expend [ɪkspénd] VT gastar, agotar

expenditure [ɪkspéndɪtʃə-] N gasto m

expense [ɪkspéns] N gasto m; — **account** cuenta de gastos f; **they had fun at my** — se divirtieron a mi costa

expensive [ɪkspénsɪv] ADJ caro

experience [ɪkspírians] N experiencia f; VT experimentar; —**d** experimentado

experiment [ɪkspérəmənt] N experimento m; VI experimentar

experimental [ɪkspérəméntl] ADJ experimental

experimentation [ɪkspɛrɪməntéʃən] N experimentación f

expert [ékspɜt] N experto -ta mf; ADJ experto, idóneo, perito; — **system** sistema experto m

expertise [ekspə-tíz] N pericia f

expiration [ekspəréʃən] N (of a contract) vencimiento m, caducidad f; (breathing out) espiración f

expire [ɪkspáɪr] VI (die, terminate) expirar; (breathe out) espirar; (lapse) vencer, caducar

explain [ɪksplén] VT explicar; **he tried to** — **away his absence** trató de justificar su ausencia

explainable [ɪksplénəbəl] ADJ explicable

explanation [eksplənéʃən] N explicación f

explanatory [ɪksplǽnətɔri] ADJ explicativo

expletive [éksplɪdɪv] N palabrota f

explicable [ɪksplíkəbəl] ADJ explicable

explicit [ɪksplísɪt] ADJ explícito

explode [ɪksplód] VI/VT estallar, hacer explosión, explotar; VT (a theory) hacer añicos; VI (population) disparar se

exploit[1] [éksplɔɪt] N hazaña f, proeza f

exploit[2] [ɪksplɔ́ɪt] VT explotar

exploitation [eksplɔɪtéʃən] N explotación f

exploration [ekspləréʃən] N exploración f

exploratory [ɪksplɔ́rətɔri] ADJ exploratorio

explore [ɪksplɔ́r] VI/VT explorar; (a topic) bucear

explorer [ɪksplɔ́rə-] N explorador -ora mf

explosion [ɪksplóʒən] N explosión f, estallido m

explosive [ɪksplósɪv] ADJ & N explosivo m

exponent [ɪkspónənt] N exponente m

export[1] [ɪkspórt] VI/VT exportar

export[2] [éksport] N exportación f

exportation [eksportéʃən] N exportación f

exporter [ɪkspórdə-] N exportador -ora mf

exporting [ɪkspórdɪŋ] N exportación f; — **firm** empresa exportadora f

expose [ɪkspóz] VT (to lay open to danger, exhibit, subject to light) exponer; (to make known) revelar; (to unmask) desenmascarar

exposition [ekspəzíʃən] N exposición f

exposure [ɪkspóʒə-] N (to danger, to light, act of exposing) exposición f; (disclosure) revelación f; **to die of** — morir de frío

expound [ɪkspáund] VI/VT exponer, explicar

express [ɪksprés] VT expresar; (send by mail) enviar por correo expreso; (squeeze out) exprimir; ADJ (clearly indicated) expreso; — **delivery** envío rápido m; — **train** tren expreso m; ADV por expreso; N (train) expreso m

expression [ɪkspréʃən] N expresión f

expressive [ɪksprésɪv] ADJ expresivo

expressiveness [ɪksprésɪvnɪs] N expresividad f

expropriate [ekspróʊpriet] VT expropiar

expulsion [ɪkspʌ́lʃən] N expulsión f

exquisite [ekskwízɪt] ADJ exquisito, primoroso; (pain) penetrante

extant [ékstənt] ADJ existente

extemporaneous [ɪkstɛmpəréniəs] ADJ improvisado

extend [ɪksténd] VI/VT extender[se]; (a street) ampliar[se]; **he —ed his hand to her** le tendió la mano

extended [ɪksténdɪd] ADJ (extensive) extenso; (prolonged) prolongado; (folded out) extendido; — **coverage** cobertura extendida f; — **care facility** centro de atención médica prolongada m

extension [ɪksténʃən] N extensión f (also phone line); (of a deadline) prórroga f; (addition) anexo m, ampliación f; — **cord** extensión f

extensive [ɪksténsɪv] ADJ extenso; (agriculture) extensivo

extent [ɪkstént] N extensión f; **to a great** — en alto grado; **to such an** — **that** a tal grado que; **to the** — **that you are able** en la medida en que seas capaz; **to a certain** — hasta cierto punto

extenuate [ɪksténjuet] VT atenuar

exterior [ɪkstíriə] ADJ & N exterior m

exterminate [ɪkstɜ́mənet] VT exterminar

extermination [ɪkstɜmənéʃən] N exterminio m, exterminación f

external [ɪkstɜ́nl] ADJ externo; (concerned with foreign countries) exterior

extinct [ɪkstíŋkt] ADJ extinto

extinguish [ɪkstíŋgwɪʃ] VT apagar, extinguir

extol [ɪkstól] VT ensalzar, enaltecer

extort [ɪkstórt] VT extorsionar

extortion [ɪkstórʃən] N extorsión f

extra [ékstrə] ADJ de más, adicional; **make some** — **cakes** haz unos pasteles de más / adicionales / extras; N extra m (including newspaper, actor); ADV extra; **extrasensorial**; (soccer) — **time** tiempo suplementario m, tiempo de descuento m; ADJ —**marital** extramarital; —**ordinary** extraordinario;

—**sensory** extrasensorial
extract[1] [ékstrækt] N (something extracted)
extracto *m*; (passage from a book)
fragmento *m*
extract[2] [ɪkstrǽkt] VT extraer; (a secret) sonsacar
extraction [ɪkstrǽkʃən] N extracción *f*
extradite [ékstrədaɪt] VT extraditar
extradition [ekstrədíʃən] N extradición *f*
extraneous [ɪkstrénɪəs] ADJ superfluo
extrapolate [ɪkstrǽpəlet] VI/VT extrapolar
extravagance [ɪkstrǽvəgəns] N (unnecessary
expense) despilfarro *m*, derroche *m*; (excess)
exceso *m*; (oddity) extravagancia *f*
extravagant [ɪkstrǽvəgənt] ADJ (shopper)
gastador, derrochador; (price) exorbitante;
(praise, demand) excesivo
extreme [ɪkstrím] ADJ & N extremo *m*; **to go to
—s** exagerar, llegar a extremos; **to the —**
extremadamente, sumamente
extremely [ɪkstrímli] ADV extremadamente,
sumamente; **it's — cold** hace un frío que
pela; **she's — intelligent** es inteligentísima
extremity [ɪkstrémɪdi] N extremidad *f*
extricate [ékstrɪket] VT sacar; VI **to — oneself
from** conseguir salir de
extrovert [ékstrəvɚt] N extrovertido -da *mf*
extroverted [ékstrəvɚdɪd] ADJ extrovertido
exuberant [ɪgzúbɚənt] ADJ exuberante
exude [ɪgzúd] VI/VT (liquid) exudar;
(cheerfulness, confidence) emanar
exult [ɪgzʌ́lt] VI exultar
eye [aɪ] N ojo *m* (also of hurricane, needle, cube);
(look) mirada *f*; **—ball** globo ocular *m*;
—brow ceja *f*; **— chart** cartilla de examen de
vista *f*; **— contact** contacto visual *m*;
—dropper cuentagotas *m sg*; **— drops**
colirio *m*, gotas oftálmicas *f pl*; **—glass** (of a
telescope, microscope) ocular *m*; **—glasses**
anteojos *m pl*, lentes *m pl*; **— injury** lesión
ocular *f*; **—lash** pestaña *f*; **—lid** párpado *m*;
—liner delineador *m*; **—-opener** revelación
f; **—piece** ocular *m*; **—sight** vista *f*; **—sore**
monstruosidad *f*; **— shadow** sombra para
ojos *f*; **— socket** órbita *f*; **— strain** vista
cansada *f*; **—tooth** colmillo *m*; **—witness**
testigo ocular *mf*; **my —s are bad** tengo
mala vista; **in the twinkling of an —** en un
abrir y cerrar de ojos; **her dress caught his
—** su vestido le llamó la atención; **to keep an
— on** cuidar, vigilar; **to see — to —** estar de
acuerdo; **in the —s of the law** ante la ley; **to
give someone an —** hacerle ojito a
alguien; **to have —s for someone** estar
prendado de alguien; **to keep one's — open**
tener cuidado; VT mirar
eyeful [áɪfʊl] N **we got an —** vimos más que
suficiente
e-zine [ízin] N revista electrónica *f*

Ff

fable [fébəl] N fábula *f*
fabric [fǽbrɪk] N tela *f*, tejido *m*; (wool) paño *m*;
(of society) estructura *f*; **— softener**
suavizante *m*
fabricate [fǽbrɪket] VT (goods) fabricar; (a story)
inventar
fabulous [fǽbjələs] ADJ fabuloso
facade [fəsád] N fachada *f*
face [fes] N (of head, coin, cube, facial
expression) cara *f*; (of a building) frente *m*; (of
a watch) esfera *f*; (of the Earth) faz *f*; **—cloth**
toalla para la cara *f*; **—lift** lifting *m*; **— value**
valor nominal *m*; **about —!** ¡media vuelta!
left —! ¡a la izquierda! **on the — of it**
aparentemente; **she put on a brave —** se
comportó con entereza; **to make —s** hacer
muecas; **to lose —** quedar mal; **to save —**
quedar bien; **to show one's —** aparecerse;
ADJ **—-to—** cara a cara; ADV **in the — of**
ante, frente a; VT (stand opposite to) encarar;
(meet defiantly) enfrentar, enfrentarse con,
afrontar; (look forward) mirar a/hacia; (to
have the front toward) dar a/hacia; (to put on
facing) ribetear; **to — down** intimidar; **to —
the music** dar la cara; **to — with marble**
revestir de mármol
faceless [féslɪs] ADJ (anonymous) anónimo;
(without a face) sin cara
facet [fǽsɪt] N faceta *f*
facetious [fəsíʃəs] ADJ gracioso
facial [féʃəl] ADJ facial; N limpieza de cutis *f*
facilitate [fəsílɪtet] VT facilitar
facility [fəsílɪdi] N (skill) facilidad *f*; **facilities**
(of a building) instalaciones *f pl*; (restroom)
aseo *m*, servicio *m*
fact [fækt] N hecho *m*; **hard —s** datos concretos
m pl; **is that a —!** ¡no me digas! **as a matter
of —** de hecho; **in — de** hecho; **it's a — of
life** así son las cosas
faction [fǽkʃən] N facción *f*
factor [fǽktɚ] N factor *m*; VT descomponer en
factores; VI **to — in** tener en cuenta
factory [fǽktəri] N fábrica *f*
factual [fǽktʃuəl] ADJ (of facts) fáctico; (based on
facts) objetivo; **— error** error de hecho *m*
faculty [fǽkəlti] N (ability) facultad *f*; (in a
college) profesorado *m*, cuerpo docente *m*,
claustro *m*
fad [fæd] N moda pasajera *f*
fade [fed] VI/VT (cloth) decolorar[se],
desteñir[se]; (color) deslavar[se]; VI (strength)
disminuir; (lights) apagarse; (feelings, colors)
desvanecerse

fail [feɫ] vɪ (faculties, organs, machinery, structure) fallar; (experiment, plan) fracasar, frustrarse; (health) decaer; (business) quebrar, hacer bancarrota; vɪ/vᴛ (exam, student) suspender, reprobar; **he —ed to remember their anniversary** no se acordó de su aniversario; **don't — to come** no dejes de venir; **without —** sin falta

failure [féɫjə²] ɴ (of a plan, a person) fracaso *m*; (of organs) insuficiencia *f*; (of faculties) deterioro *m*; (of machinery) falla *f*, *Sp* fallo *m* (of business), quiebra *f*, bancarrota *f*; (in an exam) suspenso *m*; (to keep a promise, to reach a goal) incumplimiento *m*; **her — to respond puzzled me** su falta de respuesta me confundió

faint [fent] ADJ (sound) débil; (light) tenue; (image) vago; **to feel —** sentirse mareado; **—-hearted** timorato, cobarde; ɴ desmayo *m*, desfallecimiento *m*; vɪ desmayarse, desfallecer

faintness [féntnıs] ɴ (of sound) debilidad *f*; (of light) tenuidad *f*; (of an image) vaguedad *f*

fair [fɛr] ADJ (just) justo; (by the rules) limpio; (large) considerable; (of weather) bueno; (of sky) despejado; (of wind) propicio; (of complexion) blanco; **— market price** precio justo en el mercado *m*; **— play** juego limpio *m*; **— chance of success** buena probabilidad de éxito *f*; **the — sex** el sexo bello; **that's not —!** ¡no vale! ¡no es justo! ADV **to play —** jugar limpio, ɴ feria *f*; **—ground** real de la feria *m*; **—way** calle *f*, fairway *m*

fairly [férli] ADV (justly) justamente; (moderately) medianamente; **— difficult** bastante difícil

fairness [férnıs] ɴ (justice) justicia *f*; (whiteness) blancura *f*

fairy [féri] ɴ hada *f*; **— godmother** hada madrina *f*; **—land** país de las hadas *m*; **— tale** cuento de hadas *m*

faith [feθ] ɴ fe *f*; (fidelity) fidelidad *f*; **— healing** curanderismo *m*; **in good —** de buena fe; **to have — in someone** tener confianza en alguien; **to keep —** cumplir con la palabra

faithful [féθfəɫ] ADJ fiel

faithfulness [féθfəɫnıs] ɴ fidelidad *f*

faithless [féθlıs] ADJ (disloyal) desleal, falso; (lacking in faith, fidelity) infiel

fake [fek] ɴ (object) objeto falso *m*; (person who fakes) farsante *mf*; ADJ falso *m*; **— pearls** perlas de fantasía *f pl*; ɴ (in sports) amague *m*, finta *f*; vᴛ (render false, counterfeit) falsificar; **to — a foul** tirarse; vɪ/vᴛ (feign) fingir

falcon [fǽɫkən] ɴ halcón *m*

Falkland Islands [fɔ́kləndáıləndz] ɴ Islas Malvinas *f pl*

fall [fɔɫ] vɪ (drop) caer[se]; (slope downward) bajar; (be assigned to) tocar a, recaer sobre; **to — asleep** dormirse; **to — back** retroceder; **to — back on** recurrir a; **to — behind** atrasarse, retrasarse; **to — down** (drop) caerse; (fail) fallar; **to — in with** asociarse con; **to — in love** enamorarse; **to — off** disminuir; **to — out with** reñir con; **to — through** quedar en la nada; **he —s for blondes** se enamora de las rubias; **you — for it** te dejas engañar; ɴ (drop) caída *f*; (of a terrain) declive *m*; (season) otoño *m*; **— guy** cabeza de turco *mf*; **—ing out** desavenencia *f*, pique *m*; **—ing star** estrella fugaz *f*; **—s** catarata *f*, salto de agua *m*

fallacious [fəléʃəs] ADJ falaz

fallacy [fǽləsi] ɴ (false notion) falacia *f*; (false argument) sofisma *m*

fallen [fɔ́lən] *see* fall

fallible [fǽləbəɫ] ADJ falible

Fallopian tubes [fəlópiəntúbz] ADJ trompas de Falopio *f pl*

fallout [fɔ́laut] ɴ (particle-settling) precipitación radiactiva *f*; (consequences) repercusiones *f pl*

fallow [fǽlo] ADJ baldío, en barbecho; ɴ barbecho *m*; vᴛ dejar en barbecho

false [fɔɫs] ADJ falso; **to bear — witness** jurar en falso; **— advertising** publicidad engañosa *f*; **— alarm** falsa alarma *f*; **— arrest** detención ilegal *f*; **— pretense** estafa *f*; **— start** salida en falso *f*; **— step** paso en falso *m*; **— teeth** dentadura postiza *f*

falsehood [fɔ́lshʊd] ɴ falsedad *f*, mentira *f*

falseness [fɔ́lsnıs] ɴ falsedad *f*

falsify [fɔ́lsəfai] vᴛ falsificar, falsear

falter [fɔ́ltə²] vɪ (hesitate) vacilar, entrecortarse; (stutter) titubear

fame [fem] ɴ fama *f*

famed [femd] ADJ afamado

familiar [fəmíljə²] ADJ (generally known) familiar, conocido; (informal) familiar; (too friendly) confianzudo; (closely personal) íntimo; **to be — with a subject** conocer bien un tema

familiarity [fəmıljǽrıɪdi] ɴ familiaridad *f*

family [fǽmli] ɴ familia *f*; **— doctor** médico general *m*; **— man** hombre de familia *m*; **— name** apellido *m*; **— planning** planificación familiar *f*; **— practice** medicina familiar *f*; **— room** cuarto de estar *m*; **— tree** árbol genealógico *m*; **— values** valores tradicionales *m pl*

famine [fǽmın] ɴ (lack of food) hambruna *f*, hambre *f*; (scarcity) escasez *f*

famished [fǽmıʃt] ADJ hambriento, muerto de hambre; **to be —** morirse de hambre

famous [féməs] ADJ famoso

fan [fæn] ɴ (handheld) abanico *m*; (electrical) ventilador *m*; (for cleaning grain) aventadora *f*; (of sports) aficionado -da *mf*, hincha *mf*; (of a person) admirador -ora *mf*; **— belt** correa del ventilador *f*; — **mail** correo de admiradores *m*; VT (blow air) abanicar; (enliven) avivar; **to — out** abrirse en abanico

fanatic [fənǽDɪk] ADJ & N fanático -ca *mf*

fanaticism [fənǽDɪsɪzəm] N fanatismo *m*

fanciful [fǽnsɪfəl] ADJ (whimsical) caprichoso; (imaginary) imaginario; (given to fantasy) fantasioso

fancy [fǽnsi] N fantasía *f*; (whim) capricho *m*; **to strike one's —** gustarle a alguien; **to take a — to** aficionarse a; **he took a — to his teacher** se enamoró de su maestra; ADJ (luxurious) de lujo; (elaborate) elaborado; (strange) estrafalario; **— free** despreocupado; **— work** bordado fino *m*; VT imaginar[se]; **he fancies himself an artist** se cree artista; **just — the idea!** ¡figúrate!

fanfare [fǽnfer] N fanfarria *f*; **with great —** con bombo y platillo

fang [fæŋ] N colmillo *m*

fantasize [fǽntəsaɪz] VI fantasear

fantastic [fæntǽstɪk] ADJ fantástico

fantasy [fǽntəsi] N fantasía *f*

FAQ [frequently asked questions] [fæk] N preguntas frecuentes *f pl*

far [far] ADV lejos; **— and away** sin duda; **and wide** por todas partes; **— away/off** lejos, lejano; **— be it from me to complain** no es mi intención quejarme; **— more money** mucho más dinero; **— off we could see land** a lo lejos divisábamos tierra; **as — as I know** que yo sepa; **as — as I'm concerned** en lo que a mí respecta; **by —** con mucho; **how — do I need to walk?** ¿cuánto tengo que caminar? **how — is the church?** ¿a cuánto queda la iglesia? **so — hasta** ahora; **we talked — into the night** hablamos hasta entrada la noche; **we traveled as — as Chicago** viajamos hasta Chicago; ADJ lejano; **—fetched** (implausible) inverosímil, peregrino; (forced) traído por los cabellos; **—-flung** remoto; **—-off** distante; **—-out** radical, poco convencional; **—-reaching** de gran alcance; **—sighted** (with defective vision) présbita, hipermétrope; (seeing the future) con visión de futuro; **the — corner** la esquina de más allá; **it is a — cry from what you said** dista mucho de lo que dijiste

farce [fɑrs] N farsa *f*

fare [fer] N (ticket) billete *m*; (ticket price) pasaje *m*; (price of transport) tarifa *f*; (food) comida *f*; (taxi patron) pasajero -ra *mf*; **—well** despedida *f*; **to bid —well to** despedirse de; **—well!** ¡adiós! VI I **—d well in the course** me fue bien en el curso

farm [fɑrm] N (large) hacienda *f*; (small) granja *f*; **—hand** labrador -ora *mf*, peón *m*; **—house** alquería *f*, caserío *m*; **—land** tierra de cultivo

f; **— produce** productos agrícolas *m pl*; **—yard** (enclosed) corral *m*; (open) patio *m*; VI/VT cultivar; **to — out** (lease) dar en arriendo; (distribute) repartir; (subcontract) subcontratar

farmer [fɑ́rmɚ] N agricultor -ora *mf*; (small) granjero -ra *mf*; (large) hacendado -da *mf*

farming [fɑ́rmɪŋ] N agricultura *f*; ADJ agrícola *mf*

farther [fɑ́rðɚ] ADV más lejos; **it's an even — distance** es una distancia mayor todavía; **the concept was extended —** el concepto se extendió más; **— on** más adelante; ADJ más lejano

farthest [fɑ́rðɪst] ADJ el más lejano; ADV lo más lejos

fascinate [fǽsənet] VI/VT fascinar, alucinar

fascinating [fǽsəneDɪŋ] ADJ fascinante

fascination [fæsənéʃən] N fascinación *f*

fascism [fǽʃɪzəm] N fascismo *m*

fascist [fǽʃɪst] N fascista *mf*

fashion [fǽʃən] N (style) moda *f*; (way) manera *f*, modo *m*; **— plate** figurín *m*; **after a —** más o menos; **to be in —** estar de moda; VT hacer; (with metal) forjar; (with putty) moldear; (character) formar

fashionable [fǽʃənəbəl] ADJ de moda

fast [fæst] ADJ (quick) rápido, veloz; (ahead of a watch) adelantado; (firm, permanent) firme; (closed) atrancado; (loyal) fiel; (dissolute) disipado; **—ball** recta *f*; **— break** contraataque *m*; **— food** comida rápida *f*; **life in the — lane** vida loca *f*; **— money** dinero mal habido *m*; ADV (quickly) rápido, rápidamente; (firmly) firmemente; **— asleep** profundamente dormido; N ayuno *m*; VI ayunar; VI/VT **to —-forward** avanzar

fasten [fǽsən] VT (with buckles, buttons, hooks) abrochar[se], prender; (with ribbon, thread) atar; (door) atrancar

fastener [fǽsənɚ] N cierre *m*

fastidious [fæstídiəs] ADJ (hard to please) maniático; (painstaking) minucioso

fasting [fǽstɪŋ] N ayuno *m*

fat [fæt] ADJ gordo; **— cat** pez gordo *m*; **— cell** célula adiposa *f*; **— chance** ¡ni soñar! **—head** idiota *mf*; **— job** trabajo lucrativo *m*; **— profits** pingües ganancias *f pl*; **to get —** engordar; N (oily substance) grasa *f*; (animal tissue) gordura *f*, sebo *m*; **the — of the land** la abundancia de la tierra

fatal [fédl] ADJ letal

fatality [fətǽlɪDi] N víctima fatal *f*; **— rate** índice de mortalidad *m*

fate [fet] N (lot) destino *m*, fatalidad *f*, hado *m*; (outcome) suerte *f*; VT destinar

father [fɑ́ðɚ] N padre *m*; **— figure** figura paterna *f*; **—-in-law** suegro *m*; **—land** patria *f*; VT engendrar

fatherhood [fáðə‧hʊd] N paternidad f

fatherly [fáðə‧li] ADV paternal

fathom [fǽðəm] N braza f; VT (measure) sondear; (understand) comprender

fatigue [fətíg] N fatiga f; **—s** ropa de faena f; VI/ VT fatigar[se], rendir[se]

fatness [fǽtnɪs] N gordura f

fatso [fǽtso] N pej gordinflón m, tonel m

fatten [fǽtn̩] VT engordar, cebar

fatty [fǽɾi] ADJ adiposo, graso; **— acids** ácidos grasos m pl; N (insult for fat people) pej gordo -da mf

faucet [fɔ́sɪt] N grifo m, llave f

fault [fɔlt] N (defect, misdeed) falta f; (responsibility) culpa f; (geological) falla f; **—finder** criticón -ona mf; **no-—** sin culpa; **careful to a —** demasiado cuidadoso; **to be at —** ser culpable; **to find — with** criticar a

faultless [fɔ́ltlɪs] ADJ perfecto

faulty [fɔ́lti] ADJ defectuoso; (grammar) vicioso

fauna [fɔ́nə] N fauna f

faux pas [fopá] N gaffe f, metedura de pata f

favor [févə‧] N (kind act, goodwill) favor m, gracia f; (popularity) popularidad f; (party gift) sorpresa f; VT (give help, show preference) favorecer; (foster) propiciar; (approve of) estar a favor de; **they are —ed to win** son los favoritos; **she —s her mother** se parece a su madre; **he's out of —** ha caído en desgracia

favorable [févə‧əbəl] ADJ favorable

favorite [févə‧ɪt] ADJ & N preferido -da mf, favorito -ta mf, predilecto -ta mf

favoritism [févə‧ɪtɪzəm] N favoritismo m

fawn [fɔn] N cervatillo m; VI **to — over** adular

fax [fæks] N fax m, facsímil m; VT faxear, enviar por fax

FBI [**Federal Bureau of Investigation**] [ɛfbíáɪ] N FBI m

fear [fir] N miedo m, temor m; **— of God** temor de Dios m; VI/VT (be afraid of) temer, tenerle miedo a; (suspect) temerse; **to — for** temer por

fearful [fírfəl] ADJ (causing fear) terrible, espantoso; (showing fear) temeroso, miedoso, medroso

fearless [fírlɪs] ADJ intrépido

fearlessness [fírlɪsnɪs] N intrepidez f

feasible [fízəbəl] ADJ factible

feast [fist] N (party, religious celebration) fiesta f; (abundant meal) festín m, banquete m; VI **to — on** darse un festín de; **to — one's eyes on** deleitarse la vista con

feat [fit] N (heroic act) hazaña f; (achievement) logro m

feather [féðə‧] N pluma f; **a — in one's cap** un triunfo personal; **—weight** peso pluma m; **birds of a — flock together** Dios los cría y ellos se juntan; VI/VT (grow feathers, cover

with feathers) emplumar; (change blade angle) poner horizontal

feature [fítʃə‧] N (characteristic) aspecto m, característica f; (newspaper article) reportaje m; (facial) facción f, fisonomía f, rasgo m; **— article** artículo principal m; **— film** largometraje m; VT (give prominence to) destacar; (depict) mostrar; **this film —s John Smith** esta película cuenta con la actuación de John Smith; **— that!** ¡imagínate! VI figurar

February [fébjuɛri] N febrero m

fecal [fíkəl] ADJ fecal

feces [físiz] N PL heces f pl

fed [fɛd] see feed

federal [fédə‧əl] ADJ federal

federation [fɛdə‧réʃən] N federación f

fee [fi] N (professional) honorarios m pl; (artist) cachet m; (admission) derecho de admisión m; **—s** (university) matrícula f

feeble [fíbəl] ADJ (person) débil, endeble; (sound, light) tenue; **—-minded** (retarded) pej retrasado; (stupid) tonto

feed [fid] VI/VT (supply with food, materials) alimentar[se]; (prompt lines) apuntar; (broadcast) transmitir; **he —s sugar cubes to his horse** le da terrones de azúcar a su caballo; **I fed him a lie** le dije una mentira; **to be fed up** estar harto, estar hasta la coronilla; VI **to — into** desembocar en; N (fodder) pienso m, cebo m; (transmission) transmisión f; **—back** (electronic, mechanical) retroalimentación f; (critical) respuesta f, reacción f

feeding [fídɪŋ] N alimentación f; **—ing frenzy** (of the press) escándalo periodístico m; (of sharks, etc.) carnicería f; **— tube** sonda de alimentación f

feel [fil] VI/VT (perceive, experience) sentir[se]; (examine with the hands) palpar; (suffer) sufrir; (have an opinion) creer; VI (grope, check out) tantear; (seem) parecer; **to — one's way** tantear el camino, andar a tientas; **I — for you** te compadezco; **it —s soft** está suave al tacto; **I — like a coffee** tengo ganas de tomar un café; **to — up to something** sentirse capaz de algo; N (feeling) sensación f; (sense) tacto m; (ability) don m; (groping) manoseo m, toqueteo m

feeler [fílə‧] N (of insects) antena f; (of snails) cuerno m; (person who feels) persona emotiva f; **to put out —s** tantear el terreno

feeling [fílɪŋ] N (sense of touch) tacto m; (instance of physical perception) sensación f; (emotion) sentimiento m; (opinion) opinión f; (compassion) compasión f; **a — of sadness** un sentimiento de tristeza; **with —** con sentimiento; **to hurt someone's —s** herirle los sentimientos a alguien; ADJ sensible

feign [fen] VI/VT fingir, simular, aparentar

feisty [fáɪsti] ADJ (aggressive) pugnaz, belicoso; (energetic) vivaz

feline [fílaɪn] ADJ felino

fell [fɛl] VT (an animal) derribar; (a tree) talar; N (pelt) piel de animal f; **in one — swoop** de un golpe

fell [fɛl] *see* fall

fellow [félo] N (member) miembro m; (scholar) becario -ria mf; (man or boy) tipo m; **— citizen** conciudadano -na mf; **— man** prójimo m; **— student** compañero -ra de clase mf

fellowship [félofɪp] N (friendly relations) amistad f; (community of interest) confraternidad f; (scholarship) beca f

felony [féləni] N delito grave m

felt [fɛlt] N fieltro m; ADJ de fieltro

felt [fɛlt] *see* feel

female [fímeł] N (animal) hembra f; (person) mujer f; ADJ (animal, fastener) hembra; (person) femenino

feminine [fémənɪn] ADJ femenino

femininity [fémənínɪti] N feminidad f

feminism [fémənɪzəm] N feminismo m

feminist [fémɪnɪst] ADJ & N feminista mf

femur [fímⱸ] N fémur m

fence [fɛns] N (barrier) cerca f, cerco m, valla f; (person who deals in stolen goods) Am reducidor -ora mf, Sp perista mf; (store for stolen goods) tienda de artículos robados f; **to be sitting on the —** estar indeciso; VT (enclose) cercar, vallar; **to — in** cercar; **to — off** dividir con una cerca; VI (sport) practicar esgrima

fencing [fénsɪŋ] N (dealing in stolen goods) tráfico en artículos robados m; (barrier) cerca f; (construction of barrier) cerco m; (sport) esgrima f

fender [féndⱸ] N guardabarro[s] m sg, guardafango m; **— bender** choquecito m

ferment¹ [fɚmɛnt] N fermento m

ferment² [fⱸmɛnt] VI/VT fermentar[se]

fermentation [fⱸmɛntéʃən] N fermentación f

fern [fⱸn] N helecho m

ferocious [fəróʃəs] ADJ feroz, fiero

ferocity [fəɾásɪDi] N ferocidad f, fiereza f

ferret [féɾɪt] N hurón m; VI **to — out** hurgar

Ferris wheel [férɪshwił] N rueda gigante f

ferry [féɾi] N ferry m, transbordador m; **— boat** ferry m; VT transportar de una orilla a otra; VI viajar en ferry

fertile [fⱸdł] ADJ fértil, fecundo

fertility [fⱸtílɪDi] N fertilidad f

fertilization [fⱸdlɪzéʃən] N fertilización f, fecundación f

fertilize [fⱸdlaɪz] VT fertilizar; (female, egg) fecundar; (land) abonar

fertilizer [fⱸdlaɪzⱸ] N fertilizante m, abono m

fervent [fⱸvənt] ADJ ferviente

fervor [fⱸvⱸ] N fervor m

fester [féstⱸ] VI (form pus) supurar; (rankle) enconarse

festival [féstəvəl] N festival m

festive [féstɪv] ADJ festivo

festivity [festívɪDi] N festividad f

fetal [fídl] ADJ fetal; **— position** posición fetal f; **— monitoring** monitorización fetal f

fetch [fɛtʃ] VT Sp ir a por; Am ir a buscar; **the ring —ed a fancy price** nos dieron una buena suma por el anillo; VI/VT (dog) buscar

fetching [fétʃɪŋ] ADJ atractivo

fetish [fédɪʃ] N fetiche m

fetter [fédⱸ] N grillete m; VT engrillar

fetus [fíDəs] N feto m

feud [fjud] N enemistad hereditaria f; VI pelear

feudal [fjúdl] ADJ feudal

fever [fívⱸ] N fiebre f, calentura f; **— blister** herpes febril m; **— pitch** punto álgido m

feverish [fívⱸɪʃ] ADJ (related to fever) febril; (having a fever) afiebrado, destemplado

few [fju] ADJ & PRON pocos; **—er than expected** menos de los que se esperaba; **a —** unos pocos, algunos; **the —** una minoría

fiancé [fiansé] N novio m, prometido m; **—e** novia f, prometida f

fiasco [fiǽsko] N fiasco m

fib [fɪb] N mentirilla f; VI decir mentirillas

fiber [fáɪbⱸ] N (textile) fibra f; (animal, vegetable) hebra f; **—optic** de fibra óptica; **—glass** fibra de vidrio f

fibrous [fáɪbrəs] ADJ fibroso

fickle [fɪkł] ADJ veleidoso, mudable

fiction [fíkʃən] N ficción f

fictional [fíkʃənł] ADJ novelesco

fictitious [fɪktíʃəs] ADJ ficticio

fiddle [fídł] N violín m; VI (play the violin) tocar el violín; **to — around** perder el tiempo; **to — with** juguetear con; **they like to — with the computer** siempre juguetean con la computadora

fidelity [fɪdélɪDi] N fidelidad f; **high —** alta fidelidad f

fidget [fɪdʒɪt] VI estar inquieto; **stop —ing!** ¡deja de moverte!

fiduciary [fɪdúʃieri] ADJ & N fiduciario -ria mf

field [fiłd] N (land, computers, heraldry, optics) campo m; (in sports) campo m; Am cancha f; (of oil) yacimiento m; (group of competitors) participantes mf pl; (of knowledge) campo m, terreno m; **— artillery** artillería de campaña f; **— day** (day for outdoor activity) día de campo m; (for military maneuvers) día de maniobras m; (unrestrained enjoyment) festín m; **— glasses** binoculares m pl; **— goal** gol de campo m; **— mouse** ratón de campo m; **— trip** (in school) paseo escolar m; (in science) viaje de estudio m; **—work** trabajo de campo *m*; VT (a baseball) atrapar, fildear; (questions) contestar

fielding [fíldɪŋ] N (of questions) contestación *f*; (of baseballs) fildeo *m*

fiend [find] N (devil) demonio *m*, diablo *m*; (fanatic) fanático -ca *mf*

fierce [fɪrs] ADJ (animals) feroz, fiero; (illness) espantoso; (storms, etc.) furioso, espantoso; (competition, debate) intenso, encarnizado; (look) torvo

fierceness [fírsnɪs] N ferocidad *f*, bravura *f*

fiery [fáɪəri] ADJ (passionate) fogoso; (hot, causing burning sensation) ardiente

fife [faɪf] N pífano *m*

fifteen [fíftín] NUM quince

fifth [fɪfθ] ADJ & N quinto *m*; (measure of liquor) tres cuartos de un litro *m pl*

fifty [fífti] NUM cincuenta; ADV **to go —— —** ir a medias; ADJ **a —— —— chance** un cincuenta por ciento de probabilidades

fig [fɪg] N higo *m*; — **leaf** hoja de higuera *f*; — **tree** higuera *f*; **it's not worth a —** no vale ni un pepino/pito

fight [faɪt] N (combat) lucha *f*, combate *m*; **the — against AIDS** la lucha contra el SIDA; (argument) pelea *f*, riña *f*; VI/VT (combat) luchar [con], pelear [con]; VI (argue) pelear, reñir; **to — a duel** batirse a duelo; **to — back** (to hold back) contener; (resist) resistir; **to — it out** arreglarlo a los golpes; **to — off** rechazar; **to — one's way through** abrirse camino a la fuerza

fighter [fáɪDə] N (boxer) boxeador -ora *mf*; (someone who fights) luchador -ora *mf*; (dog, cock) animal de pelea/riña *m*; — **airplane** avión caza *m*

fighting [fáɪDɪŋ] N (fight) lucha *f*; ADJ combativo; — **chance** posibilidad remota *f*; — **words** palabras incendiarias *f pl*

figurative [fíɡjəɚDɪV] ADJ (art) figurativo; (language) figurado

figure [fíɡjɚ] N (number, amount) cifra *f*; (form, bodily shape, representation, dance move, syllogism) figura *f*; (character) personaje *m*; —**head** figurón de proa *m*; — **of speech** figura retórica *f*; —**s** (written symbols) números *m pl*; — **skating** patinaje artístico *m*; **to cut a poor —** dar una mala impresión; VI (appear) figurar; VI/VT (think) imaginar[se], figurar[se]; **to — in** tener en cuenta; **to — on** contar con; **to — out** (solve) resolver; (calculate) calcular; **it —s!** no me extraña, era de esperar; VT calcular

Fijian [fíʤiən] N fijiano -na *mf*

Fiji Islands [fíʤiáɪləndz] N Islas Fiji *f pl*

filament [fíləmənt] N filamento *m*

file [faɪl] N (documents) archivo *m*; (for computers) archivo *m*, fichero *m*; (official report) expediente *m*, legajo *m*; (line) fila *f*;

(tool) lima *f*; — **compression** compresión de archivos *f*; — **format** formato de archivo/ fichero *m*; —**name** nombre de archivo *m*; — **server** servidor *m*; **on —** archivado; **filing cabinet** fichero *m*, archivador *m*; VT (papers) archivar; (news story) entregar; (tax return, claim, etc.) presentar; **to — a suit** entablar una demanda, querellarse; VI (for a job) presentarse; (walk in a line) desfilar; VI/VT (smooth) limar

filial [fíliəl] ADJ filial

filiation [fɪliéʃən] N filiación *f*

filibuster [fíləbʌstə] VI/VT practicar obstrucción parlamentaria; N filibusterismo *m*, obstrucción *f*

filigree [fíləɡri] N filigrana *f*

fill [fɪl] VI/VT (glass, container) llenar[se]; (a hole, a pastry, land) rellenar; **the smell —ed the room** la habitación se llenó del olor; **the airline —ed the position** la compañía aérea llenó el cargo; **the new employee —ed the vacancy** el nuevo empleado ocupó el cargo vacante; VT (a tooth) empastar; (prescription, order) despachar; (a need) satisfacer; VI (sails) hinchar; **to — out** llenar; **to — in** (inform) informar; (fill out a form) llenar; (replace) sustituir; **to — up** llenarse hasta el tope

fillet¹ [fɪlé] N filete *m*; VT filetear

fillet² [fílɪt] N cinta *f*

filling [fílɪŋ] N (act) rellenado *m*; (filler) relleno *m*; (of a tooth) empaste *m*; — **station** estación de servicio *f*, gasolinera *f*

filly [fíli] N potranca *f*

film [fɪlm] N (video) película *f*, filme *m*; (celluloid) película *f*, cinta *f*; (thin coating) película *f*; —**industry** industria cinematográfica *f*; —**maker** cineasta *mf*; VI/ VT filmar, cinematografiar

filming [fílmɪŋ] N filmación *f*

filter [fíltə] N filtro *m*; VI/VT filtrar[se]

filtering [fíltəɪŋ] N filtración *f*

filth [fɪlθ] N (dirt, despicable person) mugre *f*, suciedad *f*; (moral impurity) porquería *f*; (vulgar material) obscenidades *f pl*

filthiness [fílθinɪs] N suciedad *f*

filthy [fílθi] ADJ (dirty) cochino, mugriento; (vile) puerco, cochino; Sp guarro; (obscene) obsceno; — **rich** riquísimo

filtration [fɪltréʃən] N filtración *f*

fin [fɪn] N aleta *f*

final [fáɪnl] ADJ (result, conclusion) final; (last) último; (conclusive) definitivo; — **score** resultado final *m*; — **stretch** recta final *f*; N (in sports) final *f*; (exam) examen final *m*

finalist [fáɪnlɪst] N finalista *mf*

finalize [fáɪnlaɪz] VT completar, ultimar

finally [fáɪnli] ADV (at last) finalmente, por fin; (lastly) finalmente, por último

finance [fáinæns] N finanza f; **—s** finanzas f pl; VI/VT (to fund) financiar; (to purchase on credit) comprar financiado

financial [finǽnʃəl] ADJ financiero; **— disclosure** divulgación financiera f

financier [finænsír] N financiero -ra mf

financing [fáinænsiŋ] N financiamiento m; Am financiación f

find [faind] VT hallar, encontrar; (discover) descubrir; (determine innocence or guilt) declarar; VI (determine officially) fallar; **to — fault with** criticar a, censurar a; **to — out** (discover) descubrir; (verify) averiguar; N hallazgo m

finding [fáindiŋ] N fallo m; **—s** resultados m pl

fine [fain] ADJ (wine, sand, hair, precious metal) fino; (thread) delgado; (cloth) delicado; (artist, athlete) consumado; (manners) refinado; (good-looking person) atractivo, guapo; (weather) bueno; (distinction) sutil; **— arts** bellas artes f pl; **— print** letra pequeña f, letra chica f; **I'm —** estoy bien; **to feel —** sentirse muy bien de salud; **to have a — time** pasarlo bien; N multa f; VT multar; **to — -tune** (a receiver) sintonizar; (an engine) ajustar; (a plan) afinar

finery [fáinəri] N galas f pl

finesse [finés] N (subtlety) sutileza f; (tact) diplomacia f; VI usar artimañas; VT conseguir por artimañas

finger [fíŋgɚ] N dedo m; **— food** canapé m, aperitivo m; **—nail** uña f; **—print** huella dactilar/digital f; **—tip** punta del dedo f; **at one's —tips** al alcance de la mano; **little —** dedo meñique m; **middle —** dedo del corazón m; **to give someone the —** hacerle un gesto obsceno a alguien; **I'll keep my —s crossed** cruzo los dedos; **to wrap someone around one's —** meterse a alguien en el bolsillo; **I can't put my — on it** no sabría decir lo que es; VT (play a guitar) tañer; (squeal on) delatar

finicky [fíniki] ADJ melindroso, dengoso

finish [fíniʃ] VI/VT (end) terminar[se], finalizar[se]; VT (polish) pulir; (varnish) barnizar; (kill) liquidar; **to — off** acabar con, rematar; **to — up** terminar; N (ending) final m; (decisive end) fin m; (polish, treatment) acabado m; (varnish) barniz m; (coat of paint) última mano f; **— line** meta f; **with a rough —** sin pulir

finished [fíniʃt] ADJ (doomed) acabado; (polished) pulido

finite [fáinait] ADJ finito

Finland [fínlənd] N finlandia f

Finn [fin] N finlandés -esa mf, finés -esa mf

Finnish [fíniʃ] ADJ finlandés, finés

fir [fɚ] N abeto m

fire [fair] N (flame) fuego m; (conflagration) incendio m; (passion) ardor m; (for cigarettes, hearths) lumbre f; **— alarm** alarma contra incendios f; **—cracker** triquitraque m; **— drill** simulacro de incendio m; **— department** cuerpo de bomberos m; **— engine** coche de bomberos m, autobomba f; **— escape** escalera de incendios f; **— extinguisher** extinguidor [de incendios] m, extintor m; **— fighter** bombero -ra mf; **—fly** luciérnaga f; **— hydrant** boca de incendio f; **— insurance** seguro contra incendios m; **—man** (who extinguishes) bombero m; (who stokes) fogonero m; **—place** hogar m, chimenea f; **—proof** ininflamable, a prueba de incendio; **— sale** venta de liquidación f; **—side** hogar m; **— station** estación de bomberos f; **— trap** edificio sin medios de escape en caso de incendio m; **—wall** cortafuegos m sg; **—wood** leña f; **—works** fuegos artificiales m pl; **when he finds out, there will be —works** cuando se entere, se va a armar la gorda; **to be on —** estar quemándose; **to catch —** incendiarse, prenderse fuego; **to set — to** prender fuego a, incendiar; **under —** bajo fuego; **to play with —** jugar con fuego; **firing pin** percutor m; **firing squad** pelotón de fusilamiento m; VT (pottery) cocer; (an employee) despedir; (a projectile) lanzar; **to —proof** hacer incombustible, ignifugar; VI/VT (a gun) disparar; **to — up** entusiasmar; **to — off** (gun) disparar; (letter) despachar

firm [fɚm] ADJ (solid, unwavering) firme; (fixed) fijo; (not fluctuating, as prices) estable; VI/VT **to — up** (finalize) concretar; (harden) endurecer; N firma f; **—ware** programas almacenados en circuitos integrados m pl

firmly [fɚmli] ADV con firmeza, firmemente

firmness [fɚmnis] N firmeza f

first [fɚst] ADJ primero; **— aid** primeros auxilios m pl; **— base** primera base f, inicial f; **— baseman** primera base mf, inicialista mf; **to get to — base** comenzar con éxito; **—born** primogénito -ta mf; **— chapter** capítulo primero m, primer capítulo m; **— class** primera clase f; **—-class** de primera clase; **— cousin** primo hermano; **—-degree** (burn) de primer grado; (murder) en primer grado; **— floor** (ground floor) planta baja f; **for the — time** por primera vez; **— half** primer tiempo m; **—hand** de primera mano; **— lady** primera dama f; **— name** nombre de pila m; **— person** primera persona f; **—-rate** de primera clase; ADV (before anything else) primero; **I'd die —** antes la muerte; **at —** al principio; **— off** al principio; N (first in series) primero -ra mf; (low gear) primera f

fiscal [fískəl] ADJ fiscal; **— period** año fiscal m

fish [fiʃ] N (in water) pez m; (out of water)

pescado *m*; — **farm** piscifactoría *f*; —**hook** anzuelo *m*; — **market** pescadería *f*; — **story** patraña *f*; **like a — out of water** como sapo de otro pozo; **neither — nor fowl** ni chicha ni limonada; **I have other — to fry** tengo otras cosas mejores que hacer; VI/VT pescar; **to — out** sacar, rebuscar; **to — for compliments** buscar cumplidos; **to —tail** colear

fisherman [fíʃəmən] N pescador *m*

fishery [fíʃəri] N (for breeding) piscifactoría *f*; (for fishing) pesquería *f*; (industry) industria pesquera *f*

fishing [fíʃɪŋ] N pesca *f*; — **pole/rod** caña de pescar *f*; — **tackle** aparejos de pescar *m pl*; **to go**— ir de pesca

fishy [fíʃi] ADJ (of smell, taste) a pescado; (suspicious) sospechoso

fissure [fíʃə] N fisura *f*

fist [fɪst] N puño *m*; —**fight** pelea a puñetazos *f*

fistula [fístʃələ] N fístula *f*

fit [fɪt] ADJ (suited) apto; (healthy) en buen estado físico; **are you — for driving?** ¿estás en condiciones de manejar? ADV **he didn't see — to greet her** no se dignó a saludarla; N (process of fitting) prueba *f*; (mechanical union) encaje *m*; (attack of a disease) ataque *m*; (sudden outburst) rapto *m*; (of anger, coughing) acceso *m*; **to throw a —** tener una pataleta; **by —s and starts** a trompicones; **that suit is a good —** ese traje le queda bien; VT (be suitable for) adecuarse a; (be in agreement with) cuadrar con, ajustarse a; (measure for clothes) tomarle las medidas a; (make suitable) capacitar, preparar; **to — in with** acomodarse a; **I tried to — you in** traté de incluirte; VI (conform to contours of a person) quedarle bien a alguien; (conform to the contours of a mechanism) encajar

fitness [fítnɪs] N (suitability) aptitud *f*; (health) buen estado físico *m*

fitting [fítɪŋ] ADJ apropiado; N ajuste *m*; (trying on) prueba *f*

five [faɪv] NUM cinco; — **hundred** quinientos

fix [fɪks] VT (repair, arrange) arreglar; (place permanently, determine) fijar; (prepare food) preparar; **to — up** arreglar, aviar; **to get an animal —ed** castrar a un animal; **I was —ing to call** estaba a punto de llamar; **I'll — you!** ¡ya te arreglo! N (predicament) apuro *m*, aprieto *m*; (temporary repair) arreglo provisorio *m*; (narcotic injection) chute *m*; **to get a — on** localizar

fixed [fɪkst] ADJ (stationary) fijo; (arranged in advance) arreglado; — **term** a plazo fijo; —**rate mortgage** hipoteca de tasa fija *f*

fixture [fíkstʃə] N (bath, kitchen component) instalaciones *f pl*; **she's a permanent — in this office** está siempre en la oficina

fizzle [fízəl] VI (fail) fracasar; **to — [out]** (make a noise) apagarse chisporroteando; (interest) esfumarse

flabby [flǽbi] ADJ flácido/fláccido

flaccid [flǽsɪd] ADJ flácido/fláccido

flag [flæg] N (also in golf) bandera *f*; —**pole** mástil *m*; —**staff** mástil *m*; —**stone** losa *f*, baldosa *f*; VT (adorn with flags) embanderar; (mark with flags) marcar con banderas; (for attention) marcar, identificar; **to — [down]** hacer parar; VI (diminish) menguar

flagrant [flégrənt] ADV flagrante

flair [fler] N (aptitude) aptitud *f*, facilidad *f*; (style) estilo *m*

flak [flæk] N (antiartillery fire) fuego antiaéreo *m*; (criticism) crítica *f*

flake [flek] N (snow) copo *m*; (small thin piece) escama *f*; (eccentric person) chiflado -da *mf*; VI descascararse

flamboyant [flæmbóɪənt] ADJ (clothes) llamativo; (behavior) extravagante

flame [flem] N llama *f*; — **thrower** lanzallamas *m sg*; **old** — viejo amor *m*; VI llamear, flamear, encenderse

flaming [flémɪŋ] ADJ (emitting flames) llameante; (like a flame) flamígero; (ardent) ardiente; — **red** rojo encendido

flammable [flǽməbəl] ADJ inflamable

flank [flæŋk] N (of a bastion or army) flanco *m*; (of an animal) ijar *m*; VT flanquear

flannel [flǽnl] N franela *f*, lanilla *f*

flap [flæp] VI (wings) aletear; (flag) flamear; VT (wings) batir; (arms) sacudir; N (of a jacket, pocket) cartera *f*; (of a saddle, table) hoja *f*; (of an airplane) alerón *m*; (action of flapping) aleteo *m*

flare [fler] VI (burn unsteadily) llamear; (become wider) ensancharse; **to — up** (fire) avivarse; (activity, illness) recrudecer; VT (a skirt) levantar; (a flame) avivar; (a pipe) abocinar; (signal by flare) señalar con bengala; N (flaring light, burst of flame) llamarada *f*; (signal light) bengala *f*; (sudden emotional outburst) arranque *m*; (outward curvature) vuelo *m*; —**up** recrudecimiento *m*

flash [flæʃ] N (of light) destello *m*, ráfaga *f*; (of explosion) fogonazo *m*; (news, camera, vision, computer memory) flash *m*; —**back** flashback *m*, escena retrospectiva *f*; —**bulb** flash *m*; — **flood** riada *f*; —**light** linterna *f*; — **of hope** rayo de esperanza *m*; — **of lightning** relampagueo *m*, rayo *m*; **in a —** en un instante; VI/VT (shine) destellar [sobre]; (expose oneself) exhibir[se]; VI (gleam) relucir, fulgurar, relampaguear; (appear) aparecer; VT (display) ostentar; **to — by** pasar como un relámpago

flashing [flǽʃɪŋ] ADJ destellante

flashy [flǽʃi] ADJ (colorful) llamativo;

(ostentatious) ostentoso; (tasteless) chillón, de mal gusto

flask [flæsk] N (glass container) frasco m; (in a laboratory) matraz m, redoma f; (for alcoholic beverages) petaca f

flat [flæt] ADJ (surface) plano; (land) llano; (skin) liso; (spatial orientation) horizontal, acostado; (city) arrasado, aplastado; (shoes, nose) chato; (tire) desinflado, pinchado; (color) apagado; (beer, tonic water) sin gas; (mood) soso; (paint) mate; (denial) terminante; (photo) sin contraste; (pitch) demasiado grave; (musical note) bemol; **—footed** con pie plano; **— rate** tarifa fija f; **— tax** impuesto de tasa única m; **trading was —** hubo poco movimiento bursátil; **to be — broke** estar completamente pelado; **to fall —** (of a body) caer de plano/redondo; (of a joke) caer mal; (of a plan) fracasar; N (shoe) zapato sin tacón m; (flat tire) desinflado m, pinchadura f, pinchazo m; (wooden box) caja para plantas f; (musical note) bemol m; **—iron** plancha f; ADV **—out** (directly) absolutamente; (at full speed) a toda velocidad; **in two minutes —** en dos minutos exactos

flatten [flǽtn̩] VI/VT (make flat) achatar[se], aplanar[se]; VT (knock down) tumbar, voltear; (raze) arrasar

flatter [flǽtə-] VI/VT (manipulate) lisonjear, adular; (praise) halagar; **this picture —s you** esta foto te favorece; **I was —ed by his attentions** me halagaron sus atenciones

flatterer [flǽdərə-] N lisonjero -ra mf, adulador -ora mf

flattering [flǽdə-ɪŋ] ADJ (comment) lisonjero, halagüeño; (person) adulón

flattery [flǽdəri] N lisonja f, adulación f, halago m

flatulence [flǽtʃələns] N flatulencia f

flaunt [flɔnt] VI/VT ostentar, lucir[se]

flavor [flévə-] N (taste, quality) sabor m; (flavoring) condimento m; VT sazonar

flavorless [flévə-lɪs] ADJ insípido

flaw [flɔ] N (in character, in construction) defecto m; (in an argument) falla f

flawless [flɔ́lɪs] ADJ (logic) impecable; (behavior) intachable, irreprochable; (appearance) perfecto

flax [flæks] N lino m

flea [fli] N pulga f; **— collar** collar antipulgas m; **— market** Sp rastro m; Am mercado de [las] pulgas m

fled [flɛd] see flee

flee [fli] VI huir; VT huir de

fleece [flis] N vellón m; VT (shear) trasquilar, esquilar; (defraud) estafar; (in card games) pelar, desplumar

fleet [flit] N (of boats, buses) flota f; (of cars)

parque m; ADJ veloz

fleeting [flídɪŋ] ADJ fugaz, efímero, pasajero

flemish [flémɪʃ] ADJ & N flamenco -ca mf

flesh [flɛʃ] N carne f; (of a fruit) pulpa f; **— and blood** carne y hueso; **of my own — and blood** de mi propia sangre; **in the —** en persona; VI/VT **to — out** (a character) dar cuerpo a; (an argument) desarrollar

fleshy [fléʃi] ADJ (succulent) carnoso; (fat) metido en carnes

flew [flu] see fly

flexibility [flɛksəbílɪɾi] N flexibilidad f

flexible [flɛ́ksəbəl] ADJ flexible

flicker [flíkə-] VI (stars) titilar; (candle) parpadear; N (of light) parpadeo m, titilación f; (of hope) rayo m

flier [fláɪə-] N (one who flies) volador -ora mf; (aviator) aviador -ora mf; (leaflet) volante m

flight [flaɪt] N (act of flying) vuelo m; (trajectory) trayectoria f; (flock of birds) bandada f; (group of military aircraft) escuadrilla f; (escape) fuga f, huida f; **— attendant** auxiliar de vuelo mf; **— plan** plan de vuelo m; **— school** escuela de aviación f; **— recorder** caja negra f; **— simulator** simulador de vuelo m, registrador de vuelo m; **a — of fancy** una fantasía; **— of stairs** tramo de escalera m; **to put to —** poner en fuga; **to take —** darse a la fuga

flimsy [flímzi] ADJ (structure, argument) endeble; (excuse) flojo, pobre

flinch [flɪntʃ] VI pestañear

fling [flɪŋ] VT arrojar, lanzar; **she flung herself at the attacker** se le tiró arriba al atacante; **he flung himself into his work** se dedicó de lleno a su trabajo; **he flung open the door** abrió la puerta de golpe; N (act of flinging) lanzamiento m; (sexual affair) aventura f

flint [flɪnt] N pedernal m

flip [flɪp] VT (a coin) tirar; (a switch on) levantar; (a switch off) bajar; (a pancake) dar vuelta; VI (go head over heels) dar una voltereta; (get excited, go crazy) volverse loco; **to — through** hojear; **—-flop** (reversal of opinion) giro de 180 grados m; (backward somersault) voltereta para atrás f; (slipper) chancleta f; **— side** la otra cara de la moneda

flippant [flípənt] ADJ (frivolous) frívolo, displicente; (impudent) impertinente

flipper [flípə-] N aleta f

flirt [flɜt] VI coquetear; N coqueto -ta mf

flirtation [flɜtéʃən] N coquetería f, coqueteo m

flit [flɪt] VI revolotear; **a smile —s across her face** una sonrisa le cruza la cara

float [flot] VI (rest on water, air, fluctuate freely) flotar; (in soup) sobrenadar; (drift) errar, ir a la deriva; **she —ed down the stairs** se deslizó por la escalera; VT (set afloat) poner a flote; (start a company, scheme) lanzar; (issue shares) emitir; (let fluctuate) dejar flotar; (try out an idea) proponer; N (thing that floats) flotador *m*; (on a line) corcho *m*, boya *f*; (in a parade) carro alegórico *m*, carroza *f*; (with soda) gaseosa con helado *f*

flock [flɑk] N (birds, children) bandada *f*; (sheep) rebaño *m*; (worshipers) grey *f*; (people) muchedumbre *f*; VI acudir en masa, afluir; **to — around someone** rodear a alguien; **to — together** andar juntos

flog [flɑg] VT azotar

flood [flʌd] N inundación *f*; (of tides) creciente *f*; **—gate** (of a dam) compuerta *f*; (of a canal lock) esclusa *f*; **— insurance** seguro contra inundaciones *m*; **—light** reflector *m*; **— of tears** torrente de lágrimas *m*; **the —** el Diluvio Universal; VI/VT inundar[se], anegar[se]; (car) ahogar[se], emborrachar[se]

floor [flɔr] N (surface of a room, vehicle) suelo *m*, piso *m*; (story) piso *m*; (of sea) fondo *m*; (for dancing) pista *f*; (minimum level) mínimo *m*; **to have the —** tener la palabra; VT (knock down) tumbar, derribar; (stun, surprise) asombrar; **— it!** ¡acelera! *Sp* ¡mete caña!

flooring [flɔrɪŋ] N revestimiento *m*

flop [flɑp] VI (flail) zarandearse; (fish) dar coletazos; (drop) dejarse caer; (fail) fracasar; **to — down** dejarse caer, desplomarse; **to — over** voltear[se] flojamente; N (failure) fracaso *m*; (sound) ruido sordo *m*

floppy [flɑpi] ADJ caído; **— disk** disquete *m*, floppy *m*

flora [flɔrə] N flora *f*

florist [flɔrɪst] N florista *mf*; **—'s shop** florería *f*

floss [flɔs] N (silk fibers) seda floja *f*; (for embroidery) hilo de seda *m*; (dental) hilo dental *m*; VI/VT pasar hilo dental [por]

flounder [flaʊndɚ] VI (in mud, etc.) andar/moverse con dificultades; (for an answer) quedarse sin saber qué decir, perder pie; N platija *f*

flour [flaʊr] N harina *f*

flourish [flɝɪʃ] VI (prosper) florecer, prosperar; VT (brandish) blandir; N (ornament, florid language, brandishing) floreo *m*; (of music) floritura *f*; (of a signature) rúbrica *f*; **in full —** en plena eclosión

flow [flo] VI (run) fluir, correr; (issue forth) surgir, brotar; (come and go) circular; (fall loosely) caer; (abound) abundar; (rise) crecer; **to — into** desembocar en, afluir a; N (of liquid) flujo *m*; (of electricity) corriente *f*; (of traffic, blood, air) circulación *f*; **—chart** diagrama de flujo *m*, organigrama *m*; **— of words** torrente de palabras *m*

flower [flaʊɚ] N flor *f*; (paragon) flor y nata *f*; **in — en flor; — bed** *Mex, Sp* arriate *m*; *RP*

cantero *m*; **—pot** maceta *f*, tiesto *m*; **— vase** florero *m*; VI florecer

flowery [flaʊɚi] ADJ (of a garden, language) florido; (of a pattern) floreado; (of a fragrance) floral

flowing [flóɪŋ] ADJ (liquid) fluyente; (clothing) suelto

flown [flon] *see* fly

flu [flu] N gripe *f*, *Am* gripa *f*

fluctuate [flʌ́ktʃuet] VI fluctuar

fluctuation [flʌktʃuéʃən] N fluctuación *f*

fluency [flúənsi] N fluidez *f*

fluent [flúənt] ADJ fluido; **he is — in French** habla francés con fluidez/soltura

fluff [flʌf] VT mullir; (blunder) pifiar; N pelusa *f*; (blunder) pifia *f*; **this book is pure —** este libro es insustancial

fluffy [flʌ́fi] ADJ (airy) mullido; (covered with fluff) peludo

fluid [flúɪd] ADJ & N fluido *m*, líquido *m*; **— ounce** onza líquida [29.42 milliliters] *f*; **— retention** retención de líquido *f*

fluke [fluk] N (of whale) aleta *f*; (chance) chiripa *f*; **by a —** por chiripa

flung [flʌŋ] *see* fling

flunk [flʌŋk] VI/VT *Am* reprobar, *Sp* suspender; VI **to — out** *Am* salir reprobado, *Sp* salir suspendido

flunky [flʌ́ŋki] N (lackey, servant) lacayo *m*; (yes-man) adulón *m*

fluorescent [flʊrésənt] ADJ fluorescente; **— light** tubo fluorescente *m*

fluoride [flɔ́raɪd] N (chemical) fluoruro *m*; (dental aid) flúor *m*

fluorine [flɔ́rin] N flúor *m*

flurry [flɝi] N (of snow) nevisca *f*; (of activity) frenesí *m*

flush [flʌʃ] N (rosy glow, heat) rubor *m*; (of anger) arranque *m*; (of youth, color) resplandor *m*; (of embarrassment) sonrojo *m*; (in poker) color *m*; **did you hear the — of the toilet?** ¿oíste el sonido de la cisterna? ADJ (well supplied, rich) forrado; (ruddy, reddish) rubicundo; (full) rebosante; **— with** a[l] ras de; **— against** pegado a; VI/VT (make or turn red) sonrojar[se], ruborizar[se]; (activate toilet) tirar la cadena; (rinse) baldear

fluster [flʌ́stɚ] VI/VT agitar[se], poner[se] nervioso

flute [flut] N (musical instrument) flauta *f*; (of a column) estría *f*; VT estriar

flutter [flʌ́dɚ] VI (wings) aletear; (butterfly) revolotear; (flag) tremolar; (heart) palpitar; VT (agitate) agitar; N (of wings) aleteo *m*; (of excitement) agitación *f*; (of a fly) tremolar *m*; (of the heart) palpitación *f*

flux [flʌks] N fluxión *m*; **a state of —** un estado de cambio continuo

fly [flaɪ] VI (through air) volar; (from danger)

huir; (flag) ondear; (kite) remontar; VT (aircraft) pilotar; (air cargo) transportar en avión; **to — away** volarse; **to — into a rage** montar en cólera; **to — off the handle** perder los estribos; **to — open [shut]** abrirse [cerrarse] de un golpe; **to — out of a room** salir disparado de un cuarto; **that idea won't —** esa idea no va a ser aceptada; **he flew the coop** se escapó; N (insect) mosca *f*; (over a zipper) bragueta *f*; **— ball** (in baseball) volea *f*, bombo *m*, elevado *m*, palomita *f*; **—catcher** papamoscas *m sg*; **—swatter** matamoscas *m sg*; **—wheel** volante *m*; **on the —** al vuelo

flying [fláɪŋ] ADJ (passing through the air) volador; (fluttering) ondeante; **with — colors** con distinción; **— saucer** platillo volador *m*; N **I hate —** no me gusta viajar en avión

foam [fom] N (suds, padding) espuma *f*; **— rubber** goma espuma *f*; VI hacer espuma; **to — at the mouth** echar espuma por la boca

focus [fókəs] N foco *m*; VI/VT (bring into or be in focus) enfocar[se]; (concentrate) centrarse; **to — on** fijarse en

fodder [fɑ́dɚ] N forraje *m*

foe [fo] N enemigo -ga *mf*

fog [fɑg] N niebla *f*; **to be in a —** estar confundido; **—horn** sirena de niebla *f*; VI/VT (confuse) ofuscar; (spray with insecticide) fumigar; (become faded) velar[se]; **to — up** (window) empañar[se]; (one's sight) nublar[se]; **the airport was —ged in** el aeropuerto estaba cerrado por niebla

foggy [fɑ́gi] ADJ (weather) brumoso, nebuloso; (window) empañado; (confused) confuso; (blurred, as a photograph) borroso

foil [fɔɪl] N (any metal) hoja de metal *f*; (aluminum) papel de aluminio *m*; (on mirrors) azogue *m*; (rapier) florete *m*; (thing contrasted) contraste *m*; VT frustrar

fold [fotɬ] VI/VT (sheets) doblar[se]; (paper, folding chairs) plegar[se]; (wings, flag) replegar[se]; (in cards) abandonar; (close a business) cerrar[se]; (end a performance) bajar de cartel; **to — one's arms** cruzarse de brazos; N (pleat, hollow) pliegue *m*; (crease) doblez *m*; (enclosure) redil *m*, aprisco *m*; (sheep) rebaño *m*; (congregation) grey *f*; **to rejoin the —** volver al redil; **three —** tres veces

folder [fótdɚ] N (file) carpeta *f*; (instrument for folding) plegadera *f*

folding [fótdɪŋ] ADJ plegadizo, plegable; **— chair** silla plegadiza *f*; **— screen** biombo *m*; N doblado *m*

foliage [fóliɪʤ] N follaje *m*, fronda *f*, ramaje *m*

folic acid [fólɪkǽsɪd] N ácido fólico *m*

folio [fólio] N (page) folio *m*; (book) libro en folio *m*

folk [fok] N (people) gente *f*; (nation) pueblo *m*; ADJ popular; **— dance** baile folclórico/folklórico *m*; **—lore** folclore/folklore *m*; (traditional stories) leyendas tradicionales *f pl*; **— medicine** medicina tradicional *f*; **— music** música folclórica/folklórica *f*; **— song** canción tradicional *f*; **— tale** cuento folclórico/folklórico *m*; **old —s** los viejos; **—s** (relatives) parientes *m pl*; *fam* (parents) padres *m pl*, viejos *m pl*

folkloric [foklórɪk] ADJ folclórico/folklórico

follicle [fálɪkəl] N folículo *m*

folliculitis [fəlɪkjəláɪdɪs] N foliculitis *f*

follow [fálo] VI/VT seguir; (be a consequence) seguirse; (come next) ir a continuación; **to — suit** seguir el ejemplo, secundar; **to — through** llevar a cabo; **to — up [on]** (pursue) obtener más detalles [sobre]; (develop) desarrollar; N **—through** (in sports) acompañamiento *m*, continuación *f*; **—up** seguimiento *m*

follower [fáloɚ] N seguidor -ora *mf*

following [fáloɪŋ] N seguidores -oras *mf pl*; **the — lo** siguiente; ADJ siguiente

foment [fomént] VT fomentar

fond [fɑnd] ADJ **I'm — of cats** soy amigo de los gatos, me encantan los gatos; **I'm — of Chinese food** me gusta la comida china; **I'm — of John** le tengo cariño a Juan; **— hopes** ilusión *f*; **to become — of** encariñarse de

fondle [fándl] VI/VT acariciar

fondness [fándnɪs] N (affection) cariño *m*, afecto *m*; (liking or weakness) afición *f*

font [fɑnt] N (of water) pila *f*; (of characters) tipo de letra *m*

food [fud] N comida *f*, alimento *m*; **— chain** cadena alimenticia *f*; **— poisoning** intoxicación por alimentos *f*; **— stamps** cupones para alimentos *m pl*; **—stuff** producto alimenticio *m*; **— for thought** algo para reflexionar

fool [ful] N (foolish person) tonto -ta *mf*, bobo -ba *mf*, necio -cia *mf*; (jester) bufón *m*; **—proof** (plan) infalible, a prueba de fallos; (device) a prueba de tontos; **to make a — of** hacer quedar como un tonto; **to play the —** hacer el tonto; **I'm a card-playing —** soy loco por los naipes; VI bromear; **to — around** tontear; VT engañar

foolish [fúlɪʃ] ADJ tonto, necio

foolishness [fúlɪʃnɪs] N tontería *f*, bobería *f*, sandez *f*

foot [fʊt] N pie *m*; (of an animal) pata *f*; **— -and-mouth disease** fiebre aftosa *f*; **—ball** (American) fútbol americano *m*; (soccer) fútbol *m*; (ball) balón [de fútbol] *m*, pelota [de fútbol] *f*; **— fault** falta de pie *f*; **—hill** pie de la montaña *m*; **—hold** punto de apoyo *m*;

—lights candilejas *f pl*; **—man** lacayo *m*; **—note** nota al pie de página *f*, llamada *f*; **—path** senda *f*; **—print** huella *f*, pisada *f*; **—race** carrera a pie *f*; **— soldier** soldado de infantería *m*; **—step** pisada *f*, paso *m*; **—print** huella *f*, pisada *f*; **—stool** taburete *m*; **—wear** calzado *m*; **—work** (in sports) juego de piernas *m*; **to follow in the —steps of** seguir los pasos de; **he has a —hold in the computer business** ha logrado establecerse en el negocio de la informática; **it'll take some pretty fancy —work to get out of this** va a ser difícil zafarse de esto; **on —** a pie; **to put one's — in it** meter la pata; VI **to — it** andar a pie; VT **to — the bill** pagar la cuenta

footing [fʊ́dɪŋ] N (basis) base *f*; (foothold) punto de apoyo *m*; **to be on a friendly — with** tener relaciones amistosas con; **to lose one's — perder pie

for [fɔr] PREP para, por; **this gift is — John** este regalo es para John; **we're headed — the beach** vamos para la playa; **this is a device — sorting letters** este es un aparato para clasificar cartas; **they gave me enough food — three people** me dieron comida [como] para tres personas; **she's studying — the bar** está estudiando para el examen de abogacía; **the party is planned — Saturday** la fiesta está organizada para el sábado; **he has a good eye — talent** tiene buen ojo para descubrir talento; **he works — IBM** trabaja para IBM; **smoking is bad — your health** fumar es perjudicial para la salud; **he's mature — his age** es maduro para su edad; **I've come — the money** he venido por el dinero; **she asked — you** preguntó por ti; **I walk to work — the exercise** voy al trabajo andando por el ejercicio; **we went to Spain — a month** fuimos a España por un mes; **she did it — the first time** lo hizo por primera vez; **my wife signed — me** mi esposa firmó por mí; **mothers feel love — their children** las madres sienten amor por sus hijos; **they fired him — arriving late** lo echaron por llegar tarde; **run — your life!** ¡corre por tu vida! **she took me — a fool** me tomó por tonto; **thanks — the help** gracias por la ayuda; **I paid ten dollars — the book** pagué diez dólares por el libro; **I'm — gun control** estoy por el control de armas; **— all her intelligence** a pesar de su inteligencia; **that's not — you to decide** a ti no te toca decidir esto; **as — him** en cuanto a él; **it's time — me to go** es hora de que me vaya; **to know — a fact** saber a ciencia cierta; CONJ porque, pues; **I wish to eat, — I'm hungry** quiero comer, pues tengo hambre

forage [fɔ́rɪdʒ] N (feed) forraje *m*; (searching) recolección *f*; VI (gather food) forrajear; VT (feed) dar forraje a; (collect) recolectar

foray [fɔ́re] N incursión *f*, correría *f*; VI (explore) incursionar; (maraud) saquear

forbade [fɔrbéd] *see* forbid

forbear [fɔrbér] VT abstenerse de; VI contenerse

forbid [fərbíd] VT prohibir

forbidden [fərbídn] ADJ prohibido

forbidden [fɔrbídn] *see* forbid

forbidding [fərbídɪŋ] ADJ (strict) severo; (daunting) imponente

force [fɔrs] N fuerza *f*; **— out** (baseball) out forzado *m*; **in —** (effective) en vigor, vigente; (in large numbers) en masa; **armed —s** fuerzas armadas *f pl*; VT (oblige, compel) obligar; (rape, break open) forzar; **she —d a laugh** soltó una risa forzada; **to — upon** imponer; **to — one's way** abrirse paso a la fuerza; **to — out** (from a place) echar a la fuerza; (in baseball) forzar out

forced [fɔrst] ADJ forzado, obligado; (of a landing) forzoso; **— page break** salto de página forzado *m*

forceful [fɔ́rsfəl] ADJ (of personality) fuerte; (of arguments) convincente, contundente; (of behavior) enérgico

forceps [fɔ́rsəps] N (in obstetrics) fórceps *m*; (in dentistry) tenazas *f pl*, gatillo *m*

forcible [fɔ́rsəbəl] ADJ (done by force) forzoso; (effective) convincente; **— entry** allanamiento de morada *m*

ford [fɔrd] N vado *m*; VT vadear

fore [fɔr] ADJ delantero; (of a ship) de proa; N **to come to the —** ponerse en evidencia; INTERJ (in golf) ¡cuidado!

forearm [fɔ́rɑrm] N antebrazo *m*

forebear [fɔ́rber] N antepasado -da *mf*

forebode [fɔrbód] VT (foretell) presagiar; (have a presentiment) presentir

foreboding [fɔrbódɪŋ] N (omen) presagio *m*; (presentiment) presentimiento *m*

forecast [fɔ́rkæst] N pronóstico *m*; VI/VT pronosticar

foreclose [fɔrklóz] VI ejecutar una hipoteca

foreclosure [fɔrklóʒə] N ejecución *f*

forefather [fɔ́rfɑðə] N antepasado *m*

forefront [fɔ́rfrʌnt] ADV LOC **at the —** a la cabeza, a la vanguardia

forego, forgo [fɔrgó] VT abstenerse de

foregone [fɔrgɔn] ADJ **it's a — conclusion** eso es de cajón

foreground [fɔ́rgraund] N primer plano *m*

forehand [fɔ́rhænd] N (in tennis) derecha *f*, golpe de derecha *m*

forehead [fɔ́rɪd] N frente *f*

foreign [fɔ́rɪn] ADJ (from another country) extranjero; (not local) foráneo; (alien) ajeno; **— affairs** relaciones exteriores *f pl*; **— aid**

ayuda exterior f; **— body** cuerpo extraño m; **—-born** nacido en el extranjero; **— currency** divisa f; **— debt** deuda exterior f; **— exchange** cambio de divisas m; **— exchange system** sistema cambiario m; **— matter** materia extraña f; **— policy** política exterior f; **— trade** comercio exterior m

foreigner [fɔ́rənə] N extranjero -ra mf

foreman [fɔ́rmən] N (in a factory) capataz m, sobrestante m; (of a jury) presidente m

foremost [fɔ́rmost] ADJ principal, preeminente

forensic [fərɛ́nzɪk] ADJ forense

forerunner [fɔ́rɪanə] N (precursor) precursor -ora mf; (omen) presagio m; (harbinger) mensajero -ra mf

foresaw [fɔrsɔ́] see foresee

foresee [fɔrsí] VT prever, prevenir

foreseeable [fɔrsíabəl] ADJ previsible

foreseen [fɔrsín] see foresee

foresight [fɔ́rsaɪt] N previsión f

foreskin [fɔ́rskɪn] N prepucio m

forest [fɔ́rɪst] N (temperate) bosque m; (tropical) selva f; **— fire** incendio forestal m; **— ranger** guardabosque[s] m sg

forestall [fɔrstɔ́l] VT bloquear

forester [fɔ́rɪstə] N (forest ranger) guardabosque[s] m sg

forestry [fɔ́rɪstri] N silvicultura f; **— division** división forestal f

foretell [fɔrtɛ́l] VT predecir, vaticinar

foretold [fɔrtɔ́ld] see foretell

forever [fɔrɛ́və] ADV para siempre; **I'm — having to pick up after him** siempre tengo que estar juntando sus cosas; **we can't go on like this** — no podemos seguir así por toda la vida

foreword [fɔ́rwəd] N prólogo m

forfeit [fɔ́rfɪt] VT perder; N (fine) multa f; (loss) pérdida f

forfeiture [fɔ́rfɪtʃə] N confiscación f, pérdida f

forgave [fɔrgév] see forgive

forge [fɔ́rdʒ] N fragua f, forja f; VT (plans) fraguar; (metal, agreement) forjar, fraguar; VI/VT (signature, legal document) falsificar; **to — ahead** abrirse paso

forgery [fɔ́rdʒəri] N falsificación f

forget [fəgɛ́t] VI/VT olvidar, olvidarse de; **I forgot my keys** se me olvidaron las llaves; **to — oneself** meter la pata; N **—-me-not** nomeolvides mf

forgetful [fəgɛ́tfəl] ADJ olvidadizo; **— of** negligente de

forgetfulness [fəgɛ́tfəlnɪs] N falta de memoria f

forgive [fəgív] VI/VT perdonar; (a debt) perdonar, disculpar

forgiven [fəgívən] see forgive

forgiveness [fəgívnɪs] N perdón m

forgiving [fəgívɪŋ] ADJ clemente

forgo [fɔrgó] see forego

forgot [fɔrgát] see forget

forgotten [fɔrgátn] see forget

fork [fɔrk] N (for eating) tenedor m; (for hay) horca f, trinche m; (for tuning) diapasón m; (in a road) bifurcación f; **—lift** montacargas de horquilla m sg; VI bifurcarse; **to — over** soltar

forlorn [fɔrlɔ́rn] ADJ desamparado, abandonado

form [fɔrm] N forma f; (type) modalidad f; (physical condition) condiciones físicas f pl; (document to be filled in) formulario m; VI/VT formar[se]

formal [fɔ́rməl] ADJ formal; **— attire** ropa de etiqueta f; **— dance** baile de etiqueta m

formaldehyde [fɔrmǽldɪhaɪd] N formaldehído m

formality [fɔrmǽlɪdi] N (conventionality) formalidad f; (rigidity) formalismo m; (legal step) trámite m

format [fɔ́rmæt] N formato m; VT formatear

formation [fɔrméʃən] N formación f

formative [fɔ́rmədɪv] ADJ formativo

formatting [fɔ́rmædɪŋ] N formateo m

former [fɔ́rmə] ADJ **the — capital** la antigua capital; **my — husband** mi ex-marido; **the — president** el ex-presidente; **in — times** antiguamente; PRON aquel [aquella, etc.], ese [esa, etc.]

formerly [fɔ́rməli] ADV antes, anteriormente

formidable [fɔ́rmɪDəbəl] ADJ formidable

formula [fɔ́rmjələ] N fórmula f, formulación f; (for babies) preparado para biberón m

formulate [fɔ́rmjələt] VT formular

formulation [fɔrmjəléʃən] N formulación f

fornicate [fɔ́rnɪket] VI fornicar

forsake [fɔrsék] VT abandonar, desamparar

forsaken [fɔrsékən] see forsake

forsook [fɔrsúk] see forsake

fort [fɔrt] N fuerte m, fortaleza f; **to hold [down] the —** quedar de guardián

forth [fɔrθ] ADV (time) en adelante; (space) hacia adelante; **to go —** irse; **and so —** etcétera, y así sucesivamente

forthcoming [fɔrθkámɪŋ] ADJ (approaching) venidero, próximo; (available) disponible; (frank, friendly) abierto; (soon to be published) de próxima aparición

forthright [fɔ́rθraɪt] ADJ directo

forthwith [fɔrθwíθ] ADV en seguida, al punto

fortification [fɔrDəfɪkéʃən] N fortificación f

fortify [fɔ́rDəfaɪ] VT (building, body) fortificar; (food) enriquecer; (hair, mind) fortalecer; (argument) reforzar

fortitude [fɔ́rDɪtud] N fortaleza f, entereza f

fortress [fɔ́rtrɪs] N fortaleza f

fortuitous [fɔrtúɪDəs] ADJ (coincidental) fortuito; (lucky) afortunado

fortunate [fɔ́rtʃənɪt] ADJ afortunado

fortunately [fɔ́rtʃənɪtli] ADV afortunadamente

fortune [fɔ́rtʃən] N fortuna f; — **teller** adivino -na mf; **it cost me a** — me costó un dineral; **to tell someone's** — decirle la buenaventura a alguien

forty [fɔ́rɖi] NUM cuarenta; — **love** (in tennis) quince a nada

forum [fɔ́rəm] N foro m

forward [fɔ́rwəd] ADJ (toward the front) hacia adelante; (leading, in the front) delantero; (pushy) descarado; ADV adelante, en adelante; **to bring** — presentar; VT reexpedir; N (in sports) delantero -ra mf; (in basketball) alero -ra mf

fossil [fásəl] N fósil m; (old fogey) carcamal m, carca mf; — **fuel** combustible fósil m

foster [fɔ́stə] VT (promote) fomentar, promover; (bring up) criar; — **family** familia de acogida f

fought [fɔt] see fight

foul [faʊl] ADJ (dirty, illicit) sucio; (disgusting) asqueroso; (of a smell) fétido; (of weather) inclemente; (of winds) adverso; (morally offensive) vil; (of air) viciado; —**mouthed** mal hablado; **the police suspect** — **play** la policía sospecha que fue un crimen; N (in sports) falta f, faul m; —-**up** desastre m; VT (make dirty) ensuciar; (pollute) viciar; (tarnish) manchar; VI cometer una falta; **to** — **up** estropear

found [faʊnd] VT (establish) fundar; (build) cimentar

found [faʊnd] see find

foundation [faʊndéʃən] N (establishment, institution) fundación f; (of a building) cimiento m; (of an argument) fundamento m; (cosmetic) base f

founder [fáʊndə] N (establisher) fundador -ora mf; (smith) fundidor -ora mf; VI (sink) zozobrar, irse a pique; (fail) fracasar

foundry [fáʊndri] N fundición f

fountain [fáʊntn̩] N fuente f; — **pen** pluma fuente f

four [fɔr] NUM cuatro; — **hundred** cuatrocientos; —**score** ochenta; N —-**eyes** fam cuatro ojos mf sg; —-**letter word** palabrota f; —**some** grupo de cuatro m

fourteen [fɔrtín] NUM catorce

fourth [fɔrθ] ADJ cuarto; N cuarta parte f; **the Fourth of July** el cuatro de julio

fowl [faʊl] N (domestic) ave de corral m; (wild) ave m

fox [faks] N zorro m, zorra f; (crafty person) persona astuta f; (attractive person) guapetón -ona mf; —**hole** madriguera f; (military) trinchera f

foxy [fáksi] ADJ (crafty) zorro; (attractive) sexy

foyer [fɔ́iə] N vestíbulo m

fraction [frǽkʃən] N fracción f, quebrado m

fracture [frǽktʃə] N fractura f; VI/VT

fracturar[se]

fragile [frǽdʒəl] ADJ frágil

fragment[1] [frǽgmənt] N fragmento m

fragment[2] [frægmént] VI/VT fragmentar[se]

fragmentation [frægməntéʃən] N fragmentación f

fragrance [frégrəns] N fragancia f

fragrant [frégrənt] ADJ fragante

frail [frel] ADJ frágil, débil

frailty [fréłti] N fragilidad f, debilidad f

frame [frem] N (of a building, airplane, furniture) armazón m; (of eyeglasses) montura f, armadura f; (of a car) chasis m; (of a person's body) estatura f; (of a picture, door) marco m; (for embroidery) bastidor m; (on a strip of film) imagen f; — **of mind** disposición f; —**work** (of a house, structure) armazón m; (of reference) marco m, esquema m; VT (a document) forjar; (a question, plan) formular; (a picture) enmarcar; (a person) tenderle una trampa

franc [fræŋk] N franco m

France [fræns] N Francia f

franchise [frǽntʃaɪz] N (license) concesión f, franquicia f; (voting privilege) derecho al voto m; VT conceder en franquicia, dar la concesión para

frank [fræŋk] ADJ franco, abierto; VT franquear; N salchicha alemana f

frankfurter [frǽŋkfɔ́rtə] N salchicha alemana f

frankness [frǽŋknɪs] N franqueza f

frantic [frǽntɪk] ADJ (wild) frenético; (desperate) desesperado

fraternal [frətɔ́rnl̩] ADJ fraternal, fraterno

fraternity [frətɔ́rnɪɖi] N (relationship) fraternidad f, confraternidad f; (student association) asociación estudiantil f

fraternize [frǽɖərnaɪz] VI confraternizar, fraternizar

fraud [frɔd] N (deceit) fraude m; (impostor) farsante mf, impostor -ora mf

fraudulent [frɔ́dʒələnt] ADJ (of a business, etc.) fraudulento; (of a person) engañoso

fray [fre] N (fight) reyerta f, riña f; (harsh debate) refriega f; VI/VT (rub, wear out) desgastar[se], deshilachar[se]; (strain) crispar[se]

freak [frik] N (anomaly) anomalía f; (monster) monstruo m, anormal mf; (enthusiast) fanático -ca mf; (pervert) pervertido -da mf; ADJ (unusual) insólito; VI chiflar, flipar; **to** — **out** chiflar[se], flipar[se]

freakish [fríkɪʃ] ADJ insólito

freckle [frékəl] N peca f; VI/VT cubrir[se] de pecas

freckled [frékəld] ADJ pecoso

free [fri] ADJ (having liberty, unrestricted, loose, uncombined chemically, independent) libre; (unobstructed, unoccupied) libre, despejado; (without charge) gratis, gratuito; (generous) generoso; (unstinted) sin límites,

descontrolado; (frank) franco, abierto; —
and clear libre de gravámenes; — **and easy**
despreocupado; — **delivery** entrega gratuita
f; — **enterprise** empresa libre *f*; — **fall** caída
libre *f*; —-**for-all** rifirrafe *m*; — **kick** tiro
libre *m*; —**lance** freelance *m*; — **lunch/ride**
algo gratis *m*; — **market** mercado libre *m*; —
radical radical libre *m*; — **speech** libertad
de expresión *f*; — **spirit** espíritu fuerte *m*;
—**style** estilo libre *m*, crol *m*; —**thinker**
libre pensador -ora *mf*; — **throw** tiro libre *m*;
— **trade** libre comercio *m*; — **verse** verso
libre *m*; —**way** autopista *f*, autovía *f*; — **will**
libre albedrío *m*; **to give someone a—
hand** dar rienda suelta a alguien; **to set—**
poner en libertad; **sugar-**— sin azúcar; ADV
libremente; — **lance** por cuenta propia; **for**
— gratis; VT (liberate) liberar; (deliver, rid)
librar; (untie a knot) desenredar; (drain)
desatascar; **to —load** gorronear; **to — up**
(time) dejar libre
freebie [fríbi] N yapa *f*
freedom [frídəm] N libertad *f*; — **of speech**
libertad de expresión *f*; **we all want — from
fear** todos queremos vivir libres de miedo; **I
want — from having to go to work every
day** no quiero tener que ir a trabajar todos los
días
freeze [friz] VI/VT (food, water) congelar[se];
(accounts) bloquear[se], congelar[se]; **to —-
dry** liofilizar; **he froze to death** murió
congelado; **my computer froze up** se me
colgó la computadora / el ordenador; VI (of
temperature) helar; N (action or state of being
frozen) congelación *f*; (cold snap) helada *f*
freezer [frízə˞] N congelador *m*
freezing [frízɪŋ] ADJ helado; — **cold** frío glacial
m; — **point** punto de congelación *m*
freight [fret] N (load) carga *f*; (charge) flete *m*,
porte *m*; — **train** tren de carga *m*, tren de
mercancías *m*
freighter [frédə˞] N buque de carga *m*
French [frɛntʃ] ADJ francés; — **dressing** salsa
francesa *f*; — **fries** *Am* papas fritas *f pl*; *Sp*
patatas fritas *f pl*; — **horn** corno francés *m*;
—**man** francés *m*; —**woman** francesa *f*; N
(language) francés; **the** — los franceses
frenzy [frénzi] N frenesí *m*; **he worked
himself into a** — se puso histérico
frequency [fríkwənsi] N frecuencia *f*
frequent [fríkwənt] ADJ frecuente; VT frecuentar
frequently [fríkwəntli] ADV con frecuencia, a
menudo; — **asked questions** preguntas
frecuentes *f pl*
fresh [frɛʃ] ADJ (pure, cool, not stale, not frozen,
not tired) fresco; (new) nuevo; (bold)
impertinente, atrevido; (healthy) lozano; —
paint pintura fresca *f*; — **water** agua dulce *f*;
ADV — **out of school** recién salido de la

escuela; **we're — out of ideas** se nos
acabaron las ideas
freshen [fréʃən] VI/VT refrescar[se]; **to — up**
arreglarse, lavarse
freshman [fréʃmən] N (student) estudiante de
primer año *mf*; (novice) novato -ta *mf*
freshness [fréʃnɪs] N (of food, of temperature)
frescor *m*, frescura *f*; (of skin, flowers, youth
lozanía *f*; (of an idea) originalidad *f*;
(impudence) descaro *m*
fret [frɛt] VI/VT (worry) preocupar[se]; (irritate)
irritar[se]; N traste *m*
fretful [frétfəl] ADJ ansioso, inquieto
friar [fráɪə˞] N fraile *m*
friction [fríkʃən] N fricción *f*, rozamiento *m*
Friday [fráɪde] N viernes *m*
fried [fraɪd] ADJ frito
friend [frɛnd] N amigo -ga *mf*
friendliness [fréndlinɪs] N afabilidad *f*,
simpatía *f*
friendly [fréndli] ADJ amistoso, simpático,
amigable; — **advice** consejo de amigo *m*;
user-— fácil de usar
friendship [fréndʃɪp] N amistad *f*
frigate [frígɪt] N fragata *f*
fright [fraɪt] N (fear) espanto *m*, susto *m*;
(grotesque thing or person) espantajo *m*,
esperpento *m*; **to take** — asustarse
frighten [fráɪtn̩] VI/VT espantar[se], asustar[se];
to — away ahuyentar, espantar
frightened [fráɪtnd] ADJ asustado, espantado;
to get — espantarse
frightful [fráɪtfəl] ADJ espantoso, pavoroso; **we
had a — time** lo pasamos horrible; **he's a —
flatterer** es un adulón espantoso
frigid [frídʒɪd] ADJ (of weather) gélido; (of
personal relations) frío
frill [frɪl] N (trimming) volante *m*; (something
superfluous) adorno *m*; **no-**—**s** sin lujos
fringe [frɪndʒ] N (of a rug) fleco *m*, orla *f*; (of a
city) periferia *f*; (of a political party) extremo
m; (of society) margen *m*; — **benefits**
prestaciones *f pl*, complementos *m pl*; VT
orlar, poner un fleco
Frisbee® [frízbi] N disco volador *m*
frisk [frɪsk] VI/VT (frolic) retozar, triscar;
(search) cachear
frisky [fríski] ADJ retozón
fritter [frídə˞] VI/VT desmenuzar[se]; VI irse
gastando de poco a poco; **to — away**
malgastar; N buñuelo *m*, churro *m*
frivolity [frɪvɑ́lɪdi] N frivolidad *f*
frivolous [frívələs] ADJ frívolo
fro [fro] ADV **to and** — de aquí para allá
frock [frɑk] N (dress) vestido *m*; (habit) hábito *m*
frog [frag] N (animal) rana *f*; (fastener) alamar *m*
(of a hoof) ranilla *f*; (French person) *pej*
franchute -ta *mf*; **to have a — in one's
throat** tener gallos en la garganta; —**man**

hombre rana *m*

rolic [frálɪk] N retozo *m*; VI retozar

rom [frʌm, frəm] PREP desde, de, por; — **here
to there** desde aquí hasta allá; — **two to
four** de las dos a las cuatro; — **what I can
tell** por lo que yo veo; **four hours — now**
de aquí a cuatro horas, dentro de cuatro
horas; **different — the other one** diferente
del otro; **to come — Minnesota** ser de
Minesota; **death — starvation** muerte por
inanición *f*

ront [frʌnt] N frente *m*; (cover for illegal
activity) pantalla *f*; —**runner** favorito -ta
mf; —**wheel drive** tracción delantera *f*; **in
— of** en frente de, delante de; ADJ delantero;
VI/VT (face) dar a; (cover up) servir de pantalla

rontal [frʌ́ntl] ADJ frontal

rontier [frʌntír] N frontera *f*; ADJ fronterizo; —
spirit espíritu pionero *m*; — **town** pueblo
fronterizo *m*

rost [frɔst] N helada *f*, escarcha *f*; VI/VT helar,
escarchar; VT (a cake) bañar; (glass) esmerilar;
(hair) hacer rayitos/reflejos; —**bite** necrosis
por congelación *f*

rosting [frɔ́stɪŋ] N (of a cake) baño *m*; (for glass)
esmerilado *m*; (of hair) rayos *m pl*, reflejos *m
pl*

rosty [frɔ́sti] ADJ (cold, unfriendly) helado;
(covered with frost) escarchado

roth [frɔθ] N espuma *f*; VI echar espuma; VT
batir

rown [fraʊn] VI fruncir el ceño; **to — on**
desaprobar; N ceño *m*

roze [froz] *see* freeze

rozen [frózən] ADJ congelado

rozen [frózən] *see* freeze

ructose [frúktos] N fructosa *f*

rugal [frúgəl] ADJ (economical) económico,
ahorrativo; (meager) frugal

ruit [frut] N (food) fruta *f*; (plant part, product
of labor) fruto *m*; —**cake** (food) torta de
frutas secas *f*; (crazy person) *fam* chiflado -da
mf

ruitful [frútfəl] ADJ fructífero

ruitless [frútlɪs] ADJ infructuoso

rumpy [frʌ́mpi] ADJ matrona

rustrate [frʌ́stret] VT frustrar; **to get —d**
frustrar[se]

rustration [frʌstréʃən] N frustración *f*

ry [fraɪ] VI/VT (cook, also execute by
electrocution) freír[se]; —**ing pan** sartén *f*; N
(fried potato) papa/patata frita *f*; (gathering
with fried food) fiesta con comida frita *f*;
(young fish) alevín *m*; **small —** gente
menuda *f*

udge [fʌʤ] N turrón blando de chocolate *m*; VI
(cheat) hacer trampa; (avoid an issue) dar
rodeos

uel [fjúəl] N (combustible) combustible *m*,

carburante *m*; (topic) tema *m*; — **injection**
inyección *f*; — **oil** fuel *m*; VT (a vehicle) llenar
el tanque, cargar de combustible; (fire,
debate) avivar

fugitive [fjúʤɪtɪv] ADJ (fleeing) fugitivo;
(transitory) fugaz; N fugitivo -va *mf*, prófugo
-ga *mf*

fulfill [fʊlfíl] VT (promise, order) cumplir;
(need) satisfacer; **she doesn't feel —ed** no
se siente realizada

fulfillment [fʊlfílmənt] N (of a promise, order)
cumplimiento *m*; (of a need) satisfacción *f*; (of
a person) realización *f*; (of a dream)
culminación *f*

full [fʊl] ADJ (completely filled) lleno; (complete)
completo; (a dress) amplio; (a person's figure)
relleno; (sated) harto; —**-blooded** de raza;
—**-blown** (of disease) declarado; (complete)
auténtico; —**-bodied** con cuerpo; —**-
fledged** verdadero; —**-grown** adulto; —
house full *m*; —**-length** (movie) de
largometraje; (mirror) de cuerpo entero; —
moon luna llena *f*; — **name** nombre
completo *m*; —**-scale** (model) de tamaño
natural; (war) total; (investigation)
exhaustivo; —**-service** de servicio completo;
—**-size** (bed) de matrimonio; (model) de
tamaño natural; —**-term** a término; — **time**
tiempo completo *m*, de tiempo completo; **to
pay in —** pagar el total de la deuda; ADV **you
know — well** sabes perfectamente; **it hit
him — in the chest** le pegó en pleno pecho

fully [fʊ́li] ADV (entirely) completamente,
plenamente; (at least) al menos

fumble [fʌ́mbəl] N pérdida de balón *f*; VI (search
for) buscar a tientas; (move clumsily) andar a
tientas; (blunder) meter la pata; (football)
perder el balón; **he —d his way into the
living room** entró a tientas a la sala

fume [fjum] VI (be angry) rabiar; (emit vapors,
smoke) emitir humo; N —**s** gases *m pl*,
vapores *m pl*, tufo *m*

fumigate [fjúmɪget] VT fumigar

fun [fʌn] N diversión *f*; **for —** por gusto; **to
make — of** burlarse de; **to have —**
divertirse; ADJ divertido

function [fʌ́ŋkʃən] N función *f*; — **key** tecla de
función *f*; VI (work) funcionar; (serve) oficiar

functional [fʌ́ŋkʃənl] ADJ funcional

fund [fʌnd] N (of money) fondo *m*; (of
knowledge) acervo *m*; —**-raising**
recaudación de fondos *f*; VT financiar

fundamental [fʌndəméntl] ADJ fundamental; N
fundamento *m*

fundamentalism [fʌndəméntlɪzəm] N
fundamentalismo *m*

fundamentally [fʌndəméntli] ADV
fundamentalmente

funding [fʌ́ndɪŋ] N financiamiento *m*,

financiación f

funeral [fjúnəɹəl] N funeral m, entierro m, exequias f pl; — **director** director -ora de pompas fúnebres mf; — **home** casa de pompas fúnebres f, funeraria f; — **service** funeral m; **it's your —** te estás cavando tu propia tumba; ADJ (march, procession) fúnebre; (pyre) funerario; (expenses) de entierro

funereal [fjunírıəl] ADJ lúgubre

fungible [fʌ́ndʒıbəl] ADJ fungible

fungicide [fʌ́ndʒısaɪd] N fungicida m

fungus [fʌ́ŋgəs] N hongo m

funky [fʌ́ŋki] ADJ (of music) funky; (strange) estrafalario, raro; (smelly) hediondo

funnel [fʌ́nl] N (for liquids) embudo m; (in a chimney) humero m; VT canalizar, encauzar

funny [fʌ́ni] ADJ (amusing) cómico, chistoso, gracioso; (strange) raro; — **farm** fam loquero m, loquería f; **that's not —** eso no tiene gracia; **don't get — with me** no te pases de listo; N **funnies** historietas f pl, tiras cómicas f pl; ADV raro

fur [fɝ] N (hair) pelo m; (coat) pelaje m; (hide) piel f; — **store** peletería f; VT forrar de piel

furious [fjúrıəs] ADJ (person) furioso, sañudo, rabioso; (fight, storm) feroz; (activity) febril

furlough [fɝlo] N licencia f, permiso m; VT dar licencia

furnace [fɝnıs] N (for heating) caldera f; (in industry) horno m

furnish [fɝnıʃ] VT (put in furniture) amueblar; (equip) equipar; (provide) proporcionar, suministrar, facilitar

furniture [fɝnıtʃə] N muebles m pl, mobiliario m; — **store** mueblería f

furrow [fɝo] N surco m; VT (soil) arar; (face) fruncir

furry [fɝi] ADJ peludo

further [fɝðə] ADV **we want to go —** queremos ir más lejos; **I refuse to discuss this —** me niego a seguir discutiendo esto; (additionally) [lo que] es más; ADJ (more distant) más lejano; (additional) adicional; VT (promote) promover; ADV **—more** además

furthest [fɝðıst] ADJ [el] más lejano, [el] más remoto; ADV más lejos

furtive [fɝdıv] ADJ (stealthy) furtivo; (shifty) sospechoso

fury [fjúri] N furia f, furor m, saña f

fuse [fjuz] N (in an explosive) mecha f; (in a circuit) fusible m; **he has a short —** tiene pocas pulgas; **he blew a —** estalló; VT (to join) fusionar; VI/VT (to merge) fusionar[se]; (to blend metals) fundir[se]

fuselage [fjúsəlɑʒ] N fuselaje m

fusion [fjúʒən] N fusión f

fuss [fʌs] N (bustle) alboroto m, bulla f; (uproar) escándalo m; (argument) discusión f; VI

(worry about trifles) preocuparse por naderías; (complain) quejarse

fussiness [fʌ́sınıs] N remilgo m, ñoñería f

fussy [fʌ́si] ADJ (particular) quisquilloso, remilgado; (whiny) quejica, cargoso

futile [fjúdl] ADJ inútil

futility [fjutílıdi] N inutilidad f

future [fjútʃə] N futuro m, porvenir m; **—s** futuros m pl; ADJ futuro

fuzz [fʌz] N (fluff) pelusa f; (fine hair) vello fino m; (on the lip) bozo m

fuzzy [fʌ́zi] ADJ (fluffy) cubierto de pelusa; (hairy) velloso; (blurred) borroso; (muddled) confuso

FYI [for your information] [éfwáɪáɪ] ADV para su información

Gg

gab [gæb] VI parlotear, charlar; N parloteo m, charla f; **gift of —** labia f, facundia f

gable [gébəl] N hastial m; — **roof** tejado de dos aguas m; — **window** buhardilla f

Gabon, Gabun [gəbón] N Gabón m

Gabonese [gæbəníz] ADJ & N gabonés -esa mf

gad [gæd] VI **to — about** callejear

gadget [gǽdʒıt] N coso m, chisme m

gaffe [gæf] N gaffe f, metedura de pata f

gag [gæg] VT (stop up mouth, silence) amordazar; (cause to choke) dar arcadas; VI tener arcadas N (thing stuffed into mouth) mordaza f; (joke) gag m, burla f; — **order** orden de supresión de la libertad de expresión f

gaiety [géɪdi] N alegría f; **gaieties** festejos m pl

gain [gen] VT ganar; VI **to — on** irse acercando a VI/VT (watch) adelantar; N (profit, act of gaining) ganancia f; (in weight) aumento m

gainful [génfəl] ADJ remunerado

gait [get] N marcha f, paso m

galaxy [gǽləksi] N galaxia f

gale [gel] N ventarrón m, vendaval m; **—-force winds** vientos huracanados m pl; — **of laughter** risotada f

Galicia [gəlíʃə] N Galicia f

Galician [gəlíʃən] ADJ & N gallego -ga mf

gall [gɔl] N (bile, bitterness) hiel f; (impudence) morro m; (of a plant) agalla f; — **bladder** vesícula f [biliar] f; **—nut** agalla f; **—stone** cálculo biliar m; VT (irritate) irritar

gallant¹ [gǽlənt] ADJ (brave) valiente; (attentive to women) galante

gallant² [gəlánt] N galán m

gallantry [gǽləntri] N (courage) valentía f, bizarría f; (chivalrous attention) galantería f

gallery [gǽləri] N (art, shopping) galería f;

(theater) paraíso *m*, gallinero *m*; (golf) público *m*

galley [gǽli] N (kitchen) cocina *f*; (boat) galera *f*; **— proof** galerada *f*

gallium [gǽliəm] N galio *m*

gallon [gǽlən] N galón [3.7853 liters] *m*

gallop [gǽləp] VI galopar; N galope *m*

gallows [gǽloz] N horca *f*, cadalso *m*

galore [gəlɔ́r] ADV en abundancia

galoshes [gəlɑ́ʃɪz] N chanclos *m pl*

galvanize [gǽlvənaɪz] VT (metals) galvanizar; (a crowd) electrizar

Gambia [gǽmbiə] N Gambia *f*

Gambian [gǽmbiən] ADJ & N gambiano -na *mf*

gamble [gǽmbəl] VI jugar; VT jugarse; **I'll — my whole fortune on this venture** voy a jugarme todo en este negocio; **to — away** perder en el juego; N (risk) riesgo *m*; (bet) apuesta *f*

gambler [gǽmblə▪] N apostador -ora *mf*, tahúr *m*

gambling [gǽmblɪŋ] N juego [de apuestas] *m*

game [gem] N juego *m*; (match of chess, etc.) partida *f*; (sports match) partido *m*; (wild animals and their meat) caza *f*; **— console** consola de juegos *f*; **— plan** (deporte) plan de juego *m*; (negocios) estrategia *f*; **— point** punto de juego *m*; **— room** sala recreativa *f*; **— show** programa concurso *m*; **to be fair —** ser blanco legítimo; ADJ **I'm — for some tennis** me apunto para jugar al tenis; **he has a — knee** tiene la rodilla lisiada

gamut [gǽmət] N gama *f*

gander [gǽndə▪] N ganso [macho] *m*; **to take a — at** echarle un vistazo a

gang [gǽŋ] N (of youths, thieves, etc.) pandilla *f*, gavilla *f*, banda *f*; (group of friends) grupo *m*; **—plank** pasarela *f*; **—way** (passage way) pasillo *m*; (on a ship) pasamano *m*; **—way!** ¡abran cancha! VI **to — up on** conspirar contra, conspirar en masa

gangrene [gǽŋgrin] N gangrena *f*; VI/VT gangrenar[se]

gangster [gǽŋstə▪] N gángster *m*, maleante *m*

gap [gǽp] N (breach) brecha *f*, hueco *m*; (of memory) laguna *f*; (of time) intervalo *m*; **she has a — between her teeth** tiene los dientes separados; VT espaciar [correctamente]

gape [gep] VI mirar boquiabierto

garage [gərɑ́ʒ] N (for parking) garaje *m*; (for repairing) taller mecánico *m*; **— sale** venta de garaje *f*; VT estacionar en un garaje

garb [garb] N vestimenta *f*, atavío *m*; VT vestir, ataviar

garbage [gɑ́rbɪʤ] N basura *f*; **— can** bote de basura *m*; **— disposal unit** trituradora *f*; **—man** basurero *m*; **— truck** camión de la basura *m*; **what a load of —!** ¡qué montón de mentiras!

garden [gɑ́rdn̩] N jardín *m*; **— of Eden** jardín del Edén *m*; VI cultivar un jardín

gardener [gɑ́rdnə▪] N jardinero -ra *mf*

gargle [gɑ́rgəɫ] VI hacer gárgaras; VT hacer gárgaras con; N (liquid) gargarismo *m*; (sound) gárgara *f*

garland [gɑ́rlənd] N guirnalda *f*

garlic [gɑ́rlɪk] N ajo *m*

garment [gɑ́rmənt] N prenda *f*

garner [gɑ́rnə▪] VT cosechar

garnet [gɑ́rnɪt] N granate *m*

garnish [gɑ́rnɪʃ] VT (decorate) decorar; (decorate food) aderezar, guarnecer; (withhold wages) retener; N (decoration) adorno *m*, decoración *f*

garret [gǽrɪt] N desván *m*, buhardilla *f*

garrison [gǽrɪsən] N guarnición *f*; VT guarnecer

garrulous [gǽrələs] ADJ locuaz, gárrulo

garter [gɑ́rdə▪] N liga *f*; **— belt** liguero *m*, portaligas *m sg*; **— snake** culebra de jaretas *f*; VT sujetar con ligas

gas [gǽs] N (vapor) gas *m*; (fuel) gasolina *f*; (flatulence) gases *m pl*; **— chamber** cámara de gas *f*; **— mask** máscara de gas *f*; **— pedal** acelerador *m*; **— station** gasolinera *f*; **to step on the —** acelerar; **we had a —** lo pasamos bomba; VT asfixiar con gas, matar en la cámara de gas; **to — up** llenar el tanque

gaseous [gǽʃəs] ADJ gaseoso

gash [gǽʃ] N tajo *m*; VT hacer un tajo en

gasket [gǽskɪt] N junta [de culata] *f*

gasoline [gǽsəlin] N gasolina *f*, nafta *f*

gasp [gǽsp] N (cry) grito sofocado *m*; (pant) jadeo *m*, boqueada *f*; VI (cry out) dar un grito sofocado; (in surprise) quedar boquiabierto; (for breath) jadear, boquear

gastric [gǽstrɪk] ADJ gástrico; **— ulcer** úlcera gástrica *f*

gastritis [gæstrɑ́ɪdɪs] N gastritis *f*

gastroenteritis [gæstroentərɑ́ɪdɪs] N gastroenteritis *f*

gastrointestinal [gæstrointéstinl̩] ADJ gastrointestinal; **— tract** tubo digestivo *m*

gastronomy [gæstrɑ́nəmi] N gastronomía *f*

gate [get] N (to a garden) portón *m*; (to a city) puerta *f*; (at an airport) puerta de embarque *f*; **—way** (entrance, access) puerta [de entrada] *f*; (in computers) portal *m*

gather [gǽðə▪] VT (bring together) reunir, allegar; (pick) recolectar; (deduce) deducir, colegir; (sew) fruncir; VI (come together) reunirse; (collect) juntarse; (contract into folds) fruncirse; **to — dust** juntar polvo/ tierra; **to — speed** acelerar; N frunce *m*

gathering [gǽðə▪ɪŋ] N (meeting) asamblea *f*; (social) tertulia *f*; (assemblage of people) concurrencia *f*, reunión *f*; (act of gathering fruit, etc.) recolección *f*

gaudy [gɔ́di] ADJ (of bright color) chillón; (ostentatious) llamativo

gauge [geʤ] VT (measure) medir; (estimate) estimar; (calibrate) calibrar; N (measurement standard) medida *f*; (caliber) calibre *m*; (measuring device) medidor *m*; (track width) entrevía *f*

gaunt [gɔnt] ADJ demacrado

gauntlet [gɔ́ntlɪt] N (glove) guante *m*; (mailed glove) guantelete *m*; **to throw down the —** retar, desafiar; **to run the —** sufrir acosos

gauze [gɔz] N gasa *f*

gave [gev] *see* give

gavel [gǽvəl] N martillo *m*

gawk [gɔk] VT mirar boquiabierto

gawky [gɔ́ki] ADJ torpe, desgarbado

gay [ge] ADJ (happy) alegre, festivo; (homosexual) gay, homosexual; N *fam* gay *m*, homosexual *m*

gaze [gez] VI mirar fijamente, contemplar; N mirada fija *f*

gazelle [gəzɛ́l] N gacela *f*

gazette [gəzɛ́t] N gaceta *f*

gear [gir] N (equipment) equipo *m*; (cog) rueda dentada *f*; (assembly of cogs) engranaje *m*; (transmission speed) marcha *f*, cambio *m*; (personal property) pertenencias *f pl*; **—box** caja de cambios *f*; **—shift lever** palanca de cambios *f*; **to be in —** estar engranado; **to change —s** cambiar de marcha, poner el cambio; **to put into —** engranar; **to put out of —** desengranar; VI **to — up** prepararse

gearing [gírɪŋ] N engranaje *m*

gecko [gɛ́ko] N geco *m*

geek [gik] N persona que tiene exagerada pasión por la informática *f*

Geiger counter [gáɪgə-káʊntə-] N contador Geiger *m*

gel [ʤɛl] VI/VT cuajar[se]

gelatin [ʤɛ́lətn] N gelatina *f*

gem [ʤɛm] N (precious stone) gema *f*; (valuable person) joya *f*; **—stone** piedra preciosa *f*

gender [ʤɛ́ndə-] N género *m*; **— discrimination** discriminación de género *f*; **— gap** diferencias entre los sexos *f pl*; **—- specific** propio de un solo sexo

gene [ʤin] N gen *m*; **— marker** marcador genético *m*; N **— pool** conjunto de genes de una población *m*; **— splicing** empalme genético *m*; **— therapy** terapia genética *f*

genealogy [ʤiniálaʤi] N genealogía *f*

general [ʤɛ́nə-əł] ADJ & N general *mf*; **in—** por lo general; **— practitioner** médico -ca general *mf*

generality [ʤɛnə-ǽlɪDi] N generalidad *f*

generalization [ʤɛnə-əlizéʃən] N generalización *f*

generalize [ʤɛ́nə-əlaiz] VI/VT generalizar

generally [ʤɛ́nə-əli] ADV generalmente

generate [ʤɛ́nə-et] VT generar

generation [ʤɛnə-éʃən] N generación *f*; **— gap** brecha generacional *f*, abismo generacional *m*

generator [ʤɛ́nə-eDə-] N generador *m*

generic [ʤɛnɛ́rɪk] ADJ genérico; **— brand** marca genérica *f*

generosity [ʤɛnə-rásɪDi] N generosidad *f*, larguez a *f*

generous [ʤɛ́nə-əs] ADJ generoso

genetic [ʤənɛ́Dɪk] ADJ genético; **— code** código genético *m*; **— engineering** ingeniería genética *f*; **— fingerprinting** identificación genética *f*; **— marker** marcador genético *m*; N **—s** genética *f*

genetically [ʤənɛ́Dɪkli] ADV **— modified** transgénico

genial [ʤínjəł] ADJ afable, de buen genio

genital [ʤɛ́nɪdl] ADJ genital

genius [ʤínjəs] N genio *m*

genocide [ʤɛ́nəsaɪd] N genocidio *m*

genome [ʤínom] N genoma *m*

genre [ʒánrə] N género *m*

genteel [ʤɛntíł] ADJ refinado

gentile [ʤɛ́ntaɪł] ADJ & N gentil *mf*

gentle [ʤɛ́ntł] ADJ (kindly) amable; (mild, slow, gradual) suave; (tame) manso

gentleman [ʤɛ́ntłmən] N caballero *m*

gentlemanly [ʤɛ́ntłmənli] ADJ caballeroso

gentleness [ʤɛ́ntłnɪs] N (kindness) amabilidad *f*; (mildness) suavidad *f*; (tameness) mansedumbre *f*

gently [ʤɛ́ntli] ADV (smoothly) suavemente; (tactfully) con mucho tacto

genuine [ʤɛ́njuɪn] ADJ genuino

genus [ʤínəs] N género *m*

geocentric [ʤiosɛ́ntrɪk] ADJ geocéntrico

geographical [ʤiəgrǽfɪkəł] ADJ geográfico

geography [ʤiágrəfi] N geografía *f*

geological [ʤiəláʤɪkəł] ADJ geológico

geology [ʤiáləʤi] N geología *f*

geometric [ʤiəmɛ́trɪk] ADJ geométrico

geometry [ʤiámɪtri] N geometría *f*

geophysics [ʤiofízɪks] N geofísica *f*

geopolitical [ʤiopəlíDɪkəł] ADJ geopolítico

Georgia [ʤɔ́rʤə] N Georgia *f*

Georgian [ʤɔ́rʤən] ADJ & N georgiano -na *mf*

geostationary [ʤiostéʃəneri] ADJ geoestacionario

geothermal [ʤioθ*ə*məł] ADJ geotérmico

geranium [ʤə-réniəm] N geranio *m*

geriatric [ʤɛ-riǽtrɪk] ADJ geriátrico; N **—s** geriatría *f*

germ [ʤ*ə*m] N (microorganism) microbio *m*, germen *m*; (bud, embryo, rudiment) germen *m*; **— warfare** guerra biológica *f*

German [ʤ*ə*mən] ADJ & N alemán -na *mf*; **— measles** rubeola, rubéola *f*; **— shepherd** pastor alemán *m*

germane [ʤ*ə*mén] ADJ pertinente, relacionado

Germanic [ʤə-mǽnɪk] ADJ germánico -ca

Germany [ʤ*ə́*məni] N Alemania *f*

germinate [dʒɔ́·mənet] VI germinar; VT hacer germinar

gerund [dʒérənd] N gerundio *m*

gestate [dʒéstet] VI/VT gestar[se]

gestation [dʒestéʃən] N gestación *f*

gesticulate [dʒestíkjəlet] VI gesticular

gesture [dʒéstʃɚ] N gesto *m*, ademán *m*; (token) muestra *f*; VI gesticular

gesundheit [gəzúnthaɪt] INTERJ (after a sneeze) ¡salud! *Sp* ¡Jesús!

get [gɛt] VT (receive, earn) recibir; (obtain) obtener; (reach by phone) comunicarse con; (hear, understand) entender; (seize) agarrar; *Sp* coger; (prevail) conseguir, lograr; (affect) afectar; (catch disease) pescar; *Sp* coger; **to — across** comunicar; **to — ahead** prosperar; **to — along [with]** llevarse bien [con]; **to — angry** enojarse; **to — around** (skirt) esquivar, evitar; (go out) salir mucho; **to — away** escapar[se]; **to — away with** quedar impune; **to — back** (return) volver; (recover something) recuperar; **to — back at** vengarse de; **to be —ting on in years** ponerse viejo; **to — by** (go past) pasar; (survive) ir tirando; **to — dark** oscurecer; **to — down** (lower oneself) bajar; (depress) deprimir; (swallow) tragar; **to — down to business / brass tacks** ir al grano; **to — going** ponerse en marcha; **to — in** (enter) entrar; (arrive) llegar; (a vehicle) subir a; **to — it** captar, entender; **to — married** casarse; **to — nowhere** no llegar a ningún lado; **to — off** (dismount, get down) bajar; (not receive punishment) salir impune; (leave work) salir; **to — off on** enloquecerse por; **to — off someone's back** dejar de fastidiar; **to — old** envejecer; **to — on** montarse a; **to — out** (take out) sacar; (exit) salir; **to — over** (recuperate) recuperarse, sobreponerse a; (forgive) olvidar; **to — ready** preparar[se]; **to — rich** enriquecerse; **to — rid of** deshacerse de; **to — sick** enfermarse; **to — somewhere** tener resultado; **to — through** (survive an ordeal) sobrevivir; (reach by phone, be understood) comunicarse; (complete) lograr terminar; **to — to someone** afectar a alguien; **to — together** reunirse; **to — up** (arise) levantarse; (prepare) montar; **I got him to do it** conseguí/logré que lo hiciera; **I have got to do it** tengo que hacerlo; **we got our house painted** nos pintaron la casa; **he got a year in jail** le dieron un año de cárcel; **we — to stay up late in summer** en el verano nos dejan quedarnos despiertos hasta tarde; **that —s my goat** eso me fastidia; N —**away** (escape) escape *m*; (vacation) escapada *f*; —**together** reunión *f*; —**up** disfraz *m*, atuendo *m*; **from the —-go** desde el principio

geyser [gáɪzɚ] N géiser *m*

Ghana [gúnə] N Ghana *f*

Ghanaian [gúniən] ADJ & N ghanés -esa *mf*

ghastly [gǽstli] ADJ (horrible) horrendo, espantoso; (cadaverous) cadavérico

ghetto [gɛ́do] N gueto *m*

ghost [gost] N fantasma *m*; — **town** pueblo fantasma *m*; —**writer** colaborador -ora anónimo -ma *mf*; **not a — of a chance** ni la menor posibilidad

ghostly [góstli] ADJ fantasmagórico

ghoul [guł] N fantasma *m*

giant [dʒáɪənt] N & ADJ gigante -ta *mf*

gibberish [dʒíbɚɪʃ] N jerigonza *f*

gibbon [dʒíbən] N gibón *m*

Gibraltar [dʒɪbrɔ́łtɚ] N Gibraltar *m*

Gibraltarian [dʒɪbrɔłtériən] ADJ & N gibraltareño -ña *mf*

giddy [gídi] ADJ (dizzy) mareado; (of heights) vertigoso; (of speed) vertiginoso

gift [gɪft] N (thing given, act of giving) regalo *m*, presente *m*; (special ability) don *m*; — **certificate** vale por un regalo *m*; — **tax** impuesto sobre las donaciones *m*; —**-wrap** envolver para regalo; VT regalar

gifted [gíftɪd] ADJ (artist) talentoso; (child) superdotado

gigabyte [gígəbaɪt] N gigabyte *m*

gigahertz [gígəhɚts] N gigahercio *m*

gigantic [dʒaɪɡǽntɪk] ADJ gigantesco, gigante

giggle [gígəł] VI reír tontamente; N risita tonta *f*

gild [gɪłd] VT dorar

gill [gɪł] N agalla *f*

gilt [gɪłt] ADJ & N dorado *m*

gimmick [gímɪk] N treta *f*, estratagema *f*

gin [dʒɪn] N (liquor) ginebra *f*; — **rummy** gin rummy *m*

ginger [dʒíndʒɚ] N jengibre *m*; — **ale** ginger ale *m*; —**bread** pan de jengibre *m*

gingham [gíŋəm] N guingán *m*

gingivitis [dʒɪndʒəváɪdɪs] N gingivitis *f*

giraffe [dʒəræf] N jirafa *f*

gird [gɚd] VT ceñir; **to — oneself** prepararse

girder [gɚdɚ] N viga *f*

girdle [gɚdł] N faja *f*; VT rodear

girl [gɚł] N (female child) niña *f*; (young female) muchacha *f*, joven *f*, chica *f*; (servant) muchacha *f*, chacha *f*; —**friend** novia *f*

girlhood [gɚłhʊd] N niñez *f*

girlish [gɚ́lɪʃ] ADJ de niña

girth [gɚθ] N (of things) circunferencia *f*; (of persons) contorno *m*; (of horses) cincha *f*; VT cinchar

gist [dʒɪst] N esencia *f*, lo esencial

GI [gastrointestinal] tract [dʒiáɪ] N tubo digestivo *m*

give [gɪv] VT dar; (a gift) regalar; (a party) organizar; (a name) poner; (a donation) donar; **I don't — a hoot** me importa un

comino; VI dar; (yield) ceder; (break)
romperse; **to — away** (a gift) regalar, donar;
(the bride) entregar; (a secret) revelar; **to —
back** devolver; **to — in** (acknowledge defeat)
rendirse; **to — off** emitir, despedir,
desprender; **to — out** (announce) anunciar;
(distribute) repartir; (become exhausted)
rendirse; (run out) acabarse; **to — over**
entregar; **to — up** (surrender) darse por
vencido; (stop) dejar [de]; **we'll work on
this two years, — or take a month** vamos
a trabajar en esto dos años, un mes más, un
mes menos; N elasticidad f; **— and take** toma
y daca m

given [gívən] ADJ (stated, fixed) dado;
(bestowed) regalado; **— name** nombre de
pila m; **— that she's not here** dado que ella
no está; **— to** propenso a; N premisa f

given [gívən] see give

giver [gívə] N dador -ora mf, donador -ora mf

gizmo [gízmo] N coso m, chisme m

glacial [gléʃəl] ADJ glacial

glacier [gléʃə] N glaciar m

glad [glæd] ADJ contento; **I'm — to see you** me
alegro de verte; **I'd be — to help** sería un
placer ayudarle

gladden [glædn] VT alegrar, regocijar, alborozar

gladiator [glǽbiedə] N gladiador m

glamorous [glǽmərəs] ADJ glamoroso,
encantador

glamour [glǽmə] N (charm) glamour f, encanto
m; (excitement) atractivo m

glance [glæns] VI echar un vistazo; **to — off**
rebotar con efecto; N (look) vistazo m;
(bounce) rebote oblicuo m

gland [glænd] N glándula f

glandular [glǽndʒələ] ADJ glandular

glare [glɛr] N (bright light) relumbre m; (stare)
mirada furiosa f; VI (shine) relumbrar; (stare
fiercely) lanzar una mirada hostil

glaring [glérɪŋ] ADJ (blinding) deslumbrante;
(obvious) evidente; (hostile) hostil

glass [glæs] N (substance) vidrio m; (window
pane) vidrio m, cristal m; (tumbler) vaso [de
vidrio] m; (mirror) espejo m; (glassware)
cristalería f; (magnifier) lupa f; **—blowing**
soplado de vidrio m; **— ceiling** techo de
cristal m; **— cutter** cortavidrio m; **—es**
anteojos m pl, lentes m pl, gafas f pl; **— eye** ojo
de vidrio m; **—maker** vidriero -ra mf;
—ware cristalería f

glassy [glǽsi] ADJ vidrioso

glaucoma [glɔkómə] N glaucoma m

glaze [glez] VT (windows) poner vidrios a;
(ceramics) vidriar; (food) glasear; (wood)
barnizar; VI vidriarse; N (pottery) vidriado m,
barniz m; (food) glaseado m

glazier [gléʒə] N vidriero -ra mf

gleam [glim] N reflejo m, brillo m; **a — of hope**

un rayo de esperanza; VI brillar, relucir

glean [glin] VT (grain) espigar; (information)
extraer, deducir

glee [gli] N regocijo m, júbilo m; **— club** coro m

glib [glɪb] ADJ (fluent) de mucha labia;
(superficial) simplista, superficial

glide [glaɪd] VI (slide) deslizarse; (fly) planear; N
(sliding movement) deslizamiento m; (flight)
planeo m

glider [gláɪdə] N planeador m

glimmer [glímə] N luz trémula f; **a — of hope**
un destello de esperanza; **the — of an idea** el
atisbo de una idea; VI guiñar, emitir una luz
trémula

glimpse [glɪmps] N (look) ojeada f, vistazo m;
(hint) atisbo m; VT ojear

glint [glɪnt] N destello m; VI destellar

glisten [glísən] VI brillar, relucir

glitch [glɪtʃ] N fallo m, problema técnico m

glitter [glíbə] VI destellar; N (light) destello m;
(showiness) brillo m; (sparkling powder)
brillantina f

gloat [glot] VI regodearse; N regodeo m

glob [glɑb] N pegote m

global [glóbəl] ADJ global, mundial; **— backup**
respaldo global m; **— positioning system**
sistema mundial de posicionamiento m; **—
warming** calentamiento global m

globalization [globəlɪzéʃən] N globalización f

globe [glob] N globo m; (map of the Earth) globo
terráqueo m

globule [glábjuł] N glóbulo m

globulin [glábjəlɪn] N globulina f

gloom [glum] N (darkness) oscuridad f;
(melancholy) melancolía f, tristeza f

gloomy [glúmi] ADJ (dark, depressing) sombrío,
lúgubre, tenebroso; (melancholic)
melancólico, deprimido

glorify [glórəfaɪ] VT glorificar

glorious [glóriəs] ADJ (wonderful) magnífico,
excelente; (related to glory) glorioso

glory [glóri] N gloria f; VI **to — in** regocijarse con

gloss [glɔs] N (shine, cosmetic) brillo m;
(marginal note) glosa f; (in a dictionary)
acepción f; VT (polish) lustrar, dar brillo a;
(explain) glosar; **to — over** disfrazar,
encubrir

glossary [glósəri] N glosario m

glossy [glósi] ADJ lustroso; (paper) glaseado

glottal [glɑdl] ADJ (cancer) glótico; (phonetic)
glotal

glottis [glɑDɪs] N glotis f

glove [glʌv] N guante m; (baseball) guante m,
manopla f; **— compartment** guantera f

glow [glo] N incandescencia f; (of cheeks) rubor
m; (of emotion) calor m; VI resplandecer; (of
metal) estar al rojo vivo; (of cheeks)
ruborizarse; **to — with health** estar
rebosante de salud; **—worm** luciérnaga f

glowing [glóɪŋ] ADJ (with light) incandescente; (colors) vivo; (with health) rebosante; (report) favorable

glucose [glúkos] N glucosa *f*

glue [glu] N cola *f*, pegamento *m*; VT (put glue on) engomar; (stick together) pegar; (stick wood together) encolar; **she's —d to the television** está pegada al televisor

glum [glʌm] ADJ tristón

glut [glʌt] VI/VT (with food) hartar[se]; VT (with products) saturar; N superabundancia *f*

gluten [glútn̩] N gluten *m*

glutton [glʌ́tn̩] N glotón -ona *mf*

gluttonous [glʌ́tnəs] ADJ glotón

gluttony [glʌ́tni] N glotonería *f*, gula *f*

glycerin [glísəɪn] N glicerina *f*

gnarled [nɑrld] ADJ (knotty) nudoso, sarmentoso; (twisted) retorcido

gnash [næʃ] VI/VT rechinar

gnat [næt] N jején *m*

gnaw [nɔ] VI/VT (bite, corrode) roer; (torment) remorder; **to — a hole** hacer un agujero a mordiscos

GNP [gross national product] [ʤiénpí] N PNB *m*

gnu [nu] N ñu *m*

go [go] VI (move) ir; (function) andar, marchar; **—ing price** precio vigente *m*; **to — against** oponerse a; **to — ahead** seguir adelante; **to — all out** dar todo de sí; **to — along** conformarse; **to — around** (circumvent) dar la vuelta a; (circulate) circular; (be sufficient) alcanzar; **to — around with** andar con; **to — away** irse; **to — back** volver; **to — back on one's word** faltar a la palabra; **to — beyond** traspasar; **to — by** (pass) pasar; (be guided by) guiarse por; **to — by another name** usar otro nombre; **to — crazy** enloquecerse; **to — down** (descend) bajar; (fall) caer, estrellarse; (lose) perder; (be accepted) gustar; **to — for it** atreverse; **— for it!** ¡adelante! ¡atrévete! **to — in with** participar; **to — it alone** tirarse solo; **to — off** (explode) estallar; (happen) suceder; (leave) irse; **to — off on** regañar; **to — on** (happen) pasar; (continue) seguir; **to — out** (extinguish) apagarse; (socialize) salir; **to — over** (review) repasar, revisar; (read) leer; (cross) cruzar; **to — through** (suffer) sufrir; (examine) examinar; (be approved) ser aprobado; (spend) gastar; **to — through with** llevar a cabo; **to — to sleep** dormirse; **to — under** (go bankrupt) quebrar; (sink) hundirse; **to — up** (building) levantarse; (prices) subir; **pizza to —** pizza para llevar; **to let —** soltar[se]; **the car went for a good price** el coche se vendió a un buen precio; **he's smart, as dogs —** para ser perro, es inteligente; **that old couch has got to —**

hay que deshacerse de ese sofá viejo; **cows — "moo"** las vacas hacen "mu"; **they — straight for the pizza** se van derechito a la pizza; **she's —ing to buy a house** va a comprar una casa; **anything —es** todo vale; **what I say —es** lo que yo digo, vale; **don't — to any trouble** no te molestes; **— figure!** ¡vaya a saber uno! **I've got to — [to the bathroom]** tengo que ir [al baño]; N (energy) energía *f*; (attempt) intento *m*; **— ahead** visto bueno *m*; **—-between** intermediario -ria *mf*; **—-cart** kart *m*; **in one — de una vez; on the —** a las corridas; **at the first —** de primera; **they made a — of it** tuvieron éxito; **it's a —** ¡trato hecho! **from the word —** desde el vamos

goad [god] N aguijada *f*; VT aguijonear

goal [gol] N (objective) meta *f*; (score) gol *m*; **— area** área de penales *f*; **—keeper** portero -ra *mf*, arquero -ra *mf*; **— kick** saque de meta *m*, saque de puerta *m*; **— line** línea de meta *f*; **— post** palo *m*, poste *m*

goalie [góli] N guardameta *mf*

goat [got] N cabra *f*; **—herd** cabrero -ra *mf*; **he gets my —** me saca de quicio

goatee [gotí] N perilla *f*

gobble [gábəl] VI/VT (devour) engullir; VI (turkey) gluglutear; **to — up** engullir

gobbledygook [gábəldiguk] N jerigonza *f*

gobbler [gáblə-] N pavo *m*

goblet [gáblɪt] N copa *f*

goblin [gáblɪn] N duende *m*

god, God [gɑd] N dios *m*, Dios *m*; **— bless you!** (blessing) ¡que Dios te bendiga! (after a sneeze) ¡salud! ¡Jesús! **—child** ahijado -da *mf*; **—father** padrino *m*; **—forsaken** de mala muerte; **—given** divino; **—mother** madrina *f*; **—send** bendición *f*; **— willing** si Dios quiere; **by —** por Dios; **my —!** ¡Dios mío!

goddess [gádɪs] N diosa *f*

godless [gádlɪs] ADJ impío

godly [gádli] ADJ piadoso

goggles [gágəlz] N gafas protectoras *f pl*, antiparras *f pl*

going [góɪŋ] ADJ que marcha bien; **—s-on** tejemanejes *m pl*

goiter [gɔ́ɪɾə-] N bocio *m*

gold [gold] N oro *m*; **— bullion** oro en lingotes *m*; **— digger** mujer cazafortunas *f*; **—finch** jilguero *m*; **—fish** pez dorado *m*; **— medal** medalla de oro *f*; **—smith** orfebre *m*; **a heart of —** un corazón de oro

golden [góldən] ADJ (made of gold) de oro, áureo; (of gold color) dorado; **— eagle** águila dorada *f*; **— parachute** paracaídas dorado *m sg*; **— retriever** golden retriever *m*; **— rule** regla de oro *f*

golf [gɑlf] N golf *m*; **— bag** bolsa de golf *f*; **— ball** pelota de golf *f*; **— cart** coche/cochecito de golf *m*; — **club** (stick) palo de golf *m*; (place) club de golf *m*; — **course** campo de golf *m*

gonad [gónæd] N gónada *f*

gondola [gándələ] N (boat, basket under a balloon) góndola *f*; (cable car) cabina *f*

gone [gɔn] ADJ **my computer is** — desapareció mi computadora; **the candy is all** — se acabaron los dulces

gone [gɔn] *see* go

gong [gɑŋ] N batintín *m*, gong *m*

gonorrhea [gɑnərɪə] N gonorrea *f*

good [gud] ADJ bueno; (valid) válido; — **faith** buena fe *f*; —**-for-nothing** inútil, zanguango; — **for two burritos** vale por dos burritos; —**-looking** guapo, apuesto; —**natured** apacible, bonachón, de buen genio; —**will** buena voluntad *f*; **for** — para siempre; **a** — **hour** una hora larga; **a** — **many** muchos; **to have a** — **time** divertirse; **to make** — cumplir; **to smell** — oler bien; N (moral act, benefit) bien *m*; **for your own** — por tu propio bien; INTERJ ¡bien! — **afternoon** buenas tardes; —**bye** adiós; — **day** buenos días; — **evening** buenas noches; — **morning** buenos días; — **night** buenas noches; N —**s** mercancías *f pl*; —**s and services** bienes y servicios *m pl*; **to deliver the** —**s** cumplir lo prometido

goodly [gúdli] ADJ (considerable) considerable; (of fine appearance) de buen aspecto

goodness [gúdnɪs] N bondad *f*; (of food) calidad *f*; INTERJ ¡Dios mío!

goody [gúdi] N golosina *f*; —— santurrón -ona *mf*; INTERJ ¡qué bien!

goof [guf] VI pifiar; **to** — **off** perder el tiempo; **to** — **up** pifiarla; N pifia *f*

goofy [gúfi] ADJ (person) bobalicón; (idea) tonto

goose [gus] N (bird, fool) ganso -sa *mf*; —**berry** (berry) grosella espinosa *f*; (bush) grosellero *m*; —**bumps** carne de gallina *f*; — **egg** cero *m*; VT **to** — **someone** sorprender a alguien tocándole entre las nalgas

GOP [Grand Old Party] [dʒiópi] N Partido Republicano *m*

gopher [gófɚ] N ardilla de tierra *f*

gore [gɔr] N sangre derramada *f*; VT cornear

gorge [gɔrdʒ] N (body part) garganta *f*; (ravine) garganta *f*, tajo *m*; VI **to** — **one's self [on]** atracarse [de], darse un atracón [de]

gorgeous [gɔrdʒəs] ADJ (woman, outfit) precioso; (weather) espléndido

gorilla [gərílə] N gorila *mf*; (thug) matón *m*

gory [gɔri] ADJ (of a battle) sangriento; (of a surface) ensangrentado

gospel [gáspəl] N evangelio *m*; (music) gospel *m*; — **truth** pura verdad *f*

gossip [gásəp] N (rumor) chismorreo *m*, murmuración *f*, habladurías *f pl*; (person) chismoso -sa *mf*; (woman) comadre *f*; **a piece of** — un chisme *m*; VI chismear, murmurar

gossipy [gásəpi] ADJ chismoso, lenguaraz

got [gɑt] *see* get

Gothic [gáθɪk] ADJ gótico; N (language) gótico *m*, godo *m*; (style) estilo gótico *m*

gotten [gɑtn] *see* get

gouge [gaudʒ] N gubia *f*; VT (scoop) sacar con gubia; (overcharge) cobrar de más; **to** — **someone's eyes out** arrancarle los ojos a alguien

gourd [gɔrd] N calabaza *f*

gourmet [gɔrmé] N & ADJ gourmet *mf*; — **cheese** queso fino *m*

gout [gaut] N gota *f*

govern [gávɚn] VI/VT gobernar, regir; VT (in grammar) regir

governability [gʌvɚnəbílɪdi] N gobernabilidad *f*

governess [gávɚnɪs] N institutriz *f*

governing [gávɚnɪŋ] N gobernación *f*; — **principle** principio rector *m*

government [gávɚnmənt] N gobierno *m*; (in grammar) rección *f*; — **agency** agencia gubernamental *f*; —**-backed** respaldado por el gobierno

governmental [gʌvɚnméntl] ADJ gubernamental, gubernativo

governor [gávɚnɚ] N (leader) gobernador -ora *mf*; (of an engine) regulador *m*

gown [gaun] N (woman's dress) vestido *m*; (for sleeping) camisón *m*; (in hospital) bata *f*; (for graduation) toga *f*

grab [græb] VT agarrar, prender; **how does that idea** — **you?** ¿qué te parece esa idea? VI **to** — **at** tratar de agarrar; N agarrón *m*; **up for** —**s** a la rebatiña

grace [gres] N gracia *f*; (of movement) garbo *m*; (of expression) donaire *m*; **to say** — dar la oración; **to be in the good** —**s of someone** gozar del favor de alguien, disfrutar de la gracia de alguien; VT (adorn) adornar; (honor) honrar, agraciar

graceful [grésfəl] ADJ (of movement) grácil, garboso; (of behavior) donoso

gracefulness [grésfəlnɪs] N gracia *f*, donaire *m*

gracious [gréʃəs] ADJ (kind) gentil, cortés; (elegant) elegante; (merciful) misericordioso; —! ¡válgame Dios!

graciousness [gréʃəsnɪs] N gentileza *f*

gradation [gredéʃən] N gradación *f*

grade [gred] N (rank) grado *m*; (category) calidad *f*; (year in school) año *m*, curso *m*; (marks) nota *f*, calificación *f*; (slope) declive *m*; **to make the** — alcanzar el nivel deseado; — **point average** promedio de notas *m*; VT (classify) clasificar; (assign grades) calificar, corregir; (level) nivelar

gradual [grædʒuəl] ADJ gradual

graduate¹ [grædʒuɪt] N (advanced student)

estudiante de posgrado *mf*; (degree-holder) graduado -da *mf*, egresado -da *mf*; ADJ de posgrado; — **school** programa de posgrado *m*

graduate² [grǽdʒuet] VI graduarse, titularse; VT (confer a degree) dar un diploma a; (mark a scale) graduar

graduation [grædʒuéʃən] N graduación *f*

graffiti [grəfídi] N grafiti *m*, pintada *f*

graft [græft] N (of plant, tissue) injerto *m*; (corruption) concusión *f*, corrupción *f*; VI/VT injertar[se]

grain [gren] N (cereal, seed) grano *m*, mies *f*; (photographic texture) grano *m*; (of gold) pepita *f*; (of wood, meat, stone) veta *f*; (texture) textura *f*; (small amount) pizca *f*; **against the** — a/al redopelo, a contrapelo

gram [græm] N gramo *m*

grammar [grǽmə] N gramática *f*

grammatical [grəmǽDIkəł] ADJ gramatical

granary [grénəri] N granero *m*, troje *m*

grand [grænd] ADJ (splendid) grandioso, espléndido; (lofty) elevado; (impressive) impresionante; **—child** nieto -ta *mf*; **—children** nietos *m pl*; **—daughter** nieta *f*; **—father** abuelo *m*; **—fathered** eximido por la cláusula del abuelo; — **jury** jurado de acusación *m*; **—mother** abuela *f*; **—ma** abuelita *f*; **—pa** abuelito *m*; **—parent** abuelo *m*; **—parents** abuelos *m pl*; — **piano** piano de cola *m*; **—son** nieto *m*; **—stand** tribuna *f*; **a — old man** un gran señor; **the — total** el total

grandeur [grǽndʒə] N grandiosidad *f*

grandiose [grǽndios] ADJ (complex) complejo; (of speech) grandilocuente, rimbombante; (imposing) grandioso

granite [grǽnɪt] N granito *m*

grant [grænt] VT (give) conceder, otorgar, dispensar; (accept) admitir; (transfer) ceder; **to take for —ed** (an assumption) dar por sentado; (a person) no valorar; N (something granted) concesión *f*; (act of granting) concesión *f*, otorgamiento *m*; (subsidy, e.g., for scientists) subvención *f*

granular [grǽnjələ] ADJ granuloso

granulate [grǽnjələt] VI/VT granular[se]

grape [grep] N uva *f*; **—fruit** pomelo *m*, toronja *f*; **—vine** vid *f*; (ornamental) parra *f*; **I heard it through the —vine** me lo contó un pajarito

graph [græf] N (curve) gráfica *f*; — **paper** papel cuadriculado *m*; VT grafiar

graphic [grǽfɪk] ADJ gráfico; — **design** diseño gráfico *m*; N gráfico *m*; **—s** gráfica *f*; **—s card** tarjeta gráfica *f*

graphite [grǽfaɪt] N grafito *m*

grapple [grǽpəł] VI/VT (hold) aferrar; (struggle) luchar, lidiar

grasp [græsp] VT (seize) agarrar, asir, aferrar; (understand) comprender; VI **to — at/for** tratar de agarrar; N (hold) agarre *m*, asidero *m*; (comprehension) comprensión *f*; **within one's** — al alcance; **to have a good — of a subject** dominar una materia

grass [græs] N (plant) hierba *f*; (lawn) césped *m*; (pasture) pasto *m*; (in tennis) césped *m*, hierba *f*; **—hopper** saltamontes *m sg*, saltón *m*; **—land** pradera *f*, pastizal *m*; — **roots** las bases *f pl*

grassy [grǽsi] ADJ herboso

grate [gret] N (of a fireplace) parrilla *f*; (partition, guard) reja *f*, verja *f*; VT (install a grate) enrejar; (mince) rallar; (rub teeth together) crujir, rechinar; VI **to — on** rechinar

grateful [grétfəł] ADJ agradecido

grater [grépə] N rallador *m*

gratification [grædəfikéʃən] N gratificación *f*

gratify [grǽDəfaɪ] VT complacer, gratificar

grating [grépɪŋ] N reja *f*, enrejado *m*, rejilla *f*; ADJ (discordant) rechinante; (irritating) irritante

gratitude [grǽDɪtud] N gratitud *f*

gratuitous [grətúɪDəs] ADJ gratuito

gratuity [grətúɪDi] N propina *f*

grave [grev] ADJ grave; N fosa *f*, sepultura *f*; **—digger** sepulturero *m*; **—stone** lápida *f*; **—yard** cementerio *m*; **—yard shift** turno de la noche *m*; **to have one foot in the —** *fam* estar por reventar

gravel [grǽvəł] N grava *f*; VT cubrir con grava

gravitation [grævɪtéʃən] N gravitación *f*

gravitational [grævɪtéʃənəł] ADJ gravitatorio

gravity [grǽvɪDi] N gravedad *f* (also seriousness)

gravy [grévi] N jugo de carne *m*; **the rest is —** el resto es fácil

gray [gre] ADJ gris; (hair) canoso; (horse) rucio; — **area** zona gris *f*; **-haired** cano, canoso; — **matter** materia gris *f*; N gris *m*; VI/VT agrisar; (hair) encanecer

grayish [gréɪʃ] ADJ grisáceo

graze [grez] VI/VT (feed) pacer, pastar, apacentar; (brush) rozar; N roce *m*

grease [gris] N grasa *f*; VT engrasar; **to — someone's palm** untarle la mano a alguien, engrasar a alguien

greasy [grísi, grízi] ADJ (covered with grease) grasiento; (impregnated with grease) grasoso; (hair) graso

great [gret] ADJ (large, numerous) grande; (good, excellent, considerable) gran; **—aunt** tía abuela *f*; **-grandchild** bisnieto -ta *mf*; **-grandfather** bisabuelo *m*; **-grandmother** bisabuela *f*; **----grandchild** tataranieto -ta *mf*; **a — tree blocked the path** un árbol grande bloqueaba el camino; **she's a — friend** es una gran amiga; **a — while** un largo rato;

she's — at tennis juega muy bien al tenis; **a — deal of** mucho; ADV muy bien, excelente; **she did —** le fue muy bien; N **the —s** los/las grandes *mf*; **they occur in —er numbers** son más numerosos; **he's the —est** es el mejor; INTERJ ¡qué bien!

greatly [grétli] ADV **it's — improved** lo han mejorado mucho / está mucho mejor; **we're — interested** estamos muy interesados

greatness [grétnɪs] N grandeza *f*

Greece [gris] N Grecia *f*

greed [grid] N codicia *f*

greedy [grídi] ADJ (covetous) codicioso; (voracious) voraz; (eager) ávido

Greek [grik] ADJ & N griego -ga *mf*; **that's — to me** para mí es chino

green [grin] ADJ (green in color, verdant, unripe, inexperienced, nauseated, environmentally conscious) verde; **—back** dólar *m*; **— bean** *Sp* judía verde *f*; *Mex* ejote *m*; *RP* chaucha *f*; *Carib* habichuela; **— card** tarjeta verde *f*; **—horn** novato -ta *mf*; **—house** invernadero *m*; **—house effect** efecto invernadero *m*; **— light** luz verde *f*; **— pepper** pimiento verde *m*; N (color) verde *m*; (lawn) césped *m*; (pasture) prado *m*; (in golf) green *m*; (commons) ejido *m*; **—s** verduras de hoja verde *f pl*

greenish [grínɪʃ] ADJ verdoso

greenness [grínnɪs] N verdor *m*

greet [grit] VT (say hello) saludar; (welcome) dar la bienvenida; (receive) recibir

greeting [grídɪŋ] N saludo *m*; **— card** tarjeta de felicitación *f*; **—s!** ¡saludos!

gregarious [grɪgérias] ADJ (person) sociable; (animal) gregario

gremlin [grémlɪn] N duende *m*

Grenada [grənédə] N Granada *f*

grenade [grənéd] N granada *f*

Grenadian [grənédiən] ADJ & N granadino -na *mf*

grew [gru] *see* grow

greyhound [gréhaʊnd] N galgo *m*

griddle [grídl] N plancha *f*

gridlock [grídlak] N paralización *f*; VI paralizarse

grief [grif] N congoja *f*, pesar *m*, pesadumbre *f*; **to come to —** sufrir una desgracia; **to give someone —** meterse con alguien, jorobar a alguien; **good —!** ¡caramba! ADJ **—-stricken** acongojado, desconsolado

grievance [grívəns] N (complaint) queja *f*; (cause for complaint) motivo de queja *m*

grieve [griv] VI estar de duelo; **to — for/over** llorar, lamentar [la muerte de alguien]; **he's grieving over the loss of his dog** lamenta la muerte de su perro; VT **that —s me** eso me apena

grieved [grivd] ADJ apenado

grievous [grívəs] ADJ (painful) doloroso, penoso; (atrocious) grave, atroz; (sorrowful) dolido

grill [grɪl] N (metal grid, restaurant fixture) parrilla *f*; (food) parrillada *f*; VI/VT asar a la parrilla; (interrogate) interrogar

grille [grɪl] N parrilla *f*

grim [grɪm] ADJ (news, situation) desalentador; (war) cruento; (joke) macabro

grimace [grímɪs] N mueca *f*, mohín *m*; VI hacer muecas

grime [graɪm] N mugre *f*, suciedad *f*

grimy [gráɪmi] ADJ mugriento, sucio; **to make — percudir; to get —** percudirse

grin [grɪn] VI sonreír; N sonrisa *f*; **wipe that — off your face** deja de reírte

grind [graɪnd] VI/VT (mill finely) moler; (mill coarsely) triturar; (make shiny) pulir; (rub harshly) rechinar; (study hard) estudiar mucho; *Sp* empollar; **to — to a halt** pararse con un chirrido; VT (drudgery) trabajo pesado *m*; (overzealous student) empollón -ona *mf*; **—stone** muela *f*; **the daily —** la lucha diaria; **to keep one's nose to the —stone** matarse trabajando/estudiando

grinder [gráɪndɚ] N (for coffee, pepper) molinillo *m*; (for meat) picadora *f*; (for sharpening tools) afilador *m*

grip [grɪp] N (hold) agarre *m*; (control) control *m*; (handle) mango *m*; (on a baseball bat, golf club) agarre *m*, empuñadura *f*; **he had a firm — on the tool** tenía bien agarrada la herramienta; **get a — on yourself** contrólate, cálmate; VT (seize) agarrar, asir; (take hold, interest) atrapar

gripe [graɪp] VI quejarse, rezongar, renegar; N queja *f*

grisly [grízli] ADJ cruento, espantoso

gristle [grísəl] N cartílago *m*

grit [grɪt] N (sand) arena *f*; (pluck) firmeza *f*; **—s** sémola de maíz *f*; VT **to — one's teeth** apretar los dientes

gritty [gríɾi] ADJ (sandy) arenoso; (plucky) resuelto

grizzly [grízli] ADJ (grayish) grisáceo; **— bear** oso pardo *m*

groan [gron] N quejido *m*, gemido *m*; VI quejarse, gemir; (creak) crujir

grocer [grósɚ] N tendero -ra *mf*; *Mex* abarrotero -ra *mf*; *Carib* bodeguero -ra *mf*; *RP* almacenero -ra *mf*

grocery [grósəri] N tienda de comestibles *f*; *Mex* tienda de abarrotes *f*; *Carib* bodega *f*; *RP* almacén *m*; **groceries** comestibles *m pl*

groin [grɔɪn] N ingle *f*

groom [grum] N (in a wedding) novio *m*; (in a stable) mozo de cuadra *m*, caballerizo *m*; VT (a horse) almohazar; (prepare for a position) preparar; **to — oneself** arreglarse; **well-**

—**ed** bien arreglado

groove [gruv] N (narrow cut) estría f, ranura f; (on a record, road) surco m; (routine) rutina f; VT estriar, acanalar

grope [grop] VI (feel one's way) andar a tientas; (search) buscar a tientas; N toqueteo m

gross [gros] ADJ (before deductions) bruto; (flagrant) flagrante; (indecent) grosero; (overall) general; (disgusting) asqueroso; — **domestic product** producto interno bruto m; — **income** ingreso bruto m; — **pay** salario bruto m; N gruesa f; VT recaudar en bruto; **to** — **out** dar asco, asquear

grotesque [grotésk] ADJ grotesco

grotto [grádo] N gruta f

grouch [grautʃ] N cascarrabias mf sg, refunfuñón -ona mf, rezongón -ona mf; VI refunfuñar

grouchy [gráutʃi] ADJ cascarrabias, refunfuñón

ground [graUnd] N (land, electrical cable) tierra f; (soil) suelo m; (basis) fundamento m; — **ball** (in baseball) roletazo m; — **floor** planta baja f; —**hog** marmota f; —**s** (reason) motivo m; (dregs) borra f, poso m; (tract of land) terreno m; **to gain/lose** — ganar/perder terreno; **to stand one's** — ponerse firme; **from the** — **up** de piso a techo; VT (a wire) conectar a tierra; (a ship) hacer encallar; (punish) poner en penitencia; **the 747 was** —**ed** se prohibió volar en el 747

ground [graUnd] see grind

groundless [gráundlɪs] ADJ infundado

group [grup] N grupo m; — **discount** descuento por grupo m; — **therapy** terapia de grupo f; VI/VT agrupar[se]

grouper [grúpə-] N mero m

groupie [grúpi] N admiradora f

grouping [grúpɪŋ] N agrupamiento m

grove [grov] N arboleda f, plantío m; **orange** — naranjal m

grovel [grávəl] VI arrastrarse, humillarse

grow [gro] VI (naturally increase in size) crecer; (increase) aumentar, acrecentarse; (expand) desarrollarse; VT (crops) cultivar; (beard) dejarse crecer; **to** — **old** envejecer; **to** — **up** madurar; **Thai food** —**s on you** la comida tailandesa acaba gustándote

growing [gróɪŋ] N cultivo m; — **pains** (physical symptom) dolores del crecimiento m pl; (troubles) dificultades iniciales f pl; **he's a** — **boy** es un muchacho en crecimiento

growl [grauł] VI gruñir; (of thunder) retumbar; (of stomach) rugir; N gruñido m

grown [gron] ADJ adulto; — **man** hombre hecho y derecho m; N —**-up** adulto m; ADJ —- **up** para adultos

grown [gron] see grow

growth [groθ] N (increase in size) crecimiento m; (increase in number) aumento m, acrecentamiento m; (tumor) bulto m;

(expansion) desarrollo m; — **hormone** hormona del crecimiento f; **a** — **industry** una industria en expansión

grudge [grʌdʒ] N resentimiento m

grueling [grúlɪŋ] ADJ arduo

gruesome [grúsəm] ADJ cruento, truculento

gruff [grʌf] ADJ (manner) bronco; (voice) ronco

grumble [grámbəl] VI/VT refunfuñar, rezongar; N refunfuño m, gruñido m

grumpy [grámpi] ADJ refunfuñón, gruñón, rezongón

grunt [grʌnt] VI/VT gruñir; N gruñido m

guarantee [gærəntí] N (promise, pledge) garantía f; (guaranty) fianza f; VT (promise, pledge) garantizar; (warrant) dar fianza, avalar; —**d loan** préstamo garantizado m

guarantor [gærəntɔr] N fiador -ora mf

guaranty [gǽrənti] N (guarantee) garantía f; (thing taken as security) fianza f; (guarantor) fiador -ora mf

guard [gard] VT custodiar; (watch over) vigilar; (protect) proteger; VI **to** — **against** guardarse de; N (person that guards) guardia mf, guarda mf; (of a machine) dispositivo protector m; **to be on** — estar alerta / estar en guardia; — **dog** perro guardián m; —**rail** baranda f, pasamano m

guardian [gárdiən] N guardián -ana mf; (legal) tutor -ora mf; — **angel** ángel de la guarda m

guardianship [gárdiənʃɪp] N tutela f

Guatemala [gwɑDəmálə] N Guatemala f

Guatemalan [gwɑDəmálən] ADJ & N guatemalteco -ca f

guava [gwávə] N guayaba f

guerrilla [gərílə] N — **army** guerrilla f

guess [ges] VT (hazard, conjecture) adivinar; (suppose) suponer; VI (conjecture) conjetura f; (supposition) suposición f; **I'll give you three** —**es** te doy tres oportunidades para adivinar

guest [gest] N (to a party, function) invitado -da mf; (at a restaurant) cliente mf; (overnight) huésped mf

guffaw [gəfɔ́] N carcajada f, risotada f

guidance [gáɪdɪns] N (act of guiding) dirección f; (counsel) orientación f; (in a missile) teledirección f

guide [gaɪd] VT (serve as a guide) guiar; (direct the course of) dirigir; (counsel) orientar; —**d missile** misil guiado m; N (person) guía mf; (publication, mechanism) guía f; —**book** guía f; — **dog** perro guía m; —**lines** directivas f pl, pautas f pl, directrices f pl

guild [gɪłd] N gremio m, corporación f

guile [gaɪł] N astucia f

guilt [gɪłt] N culpa f; — **trip** manipulación por acusaciones falsas f

guiltless [gíłtlɪs] ADJ inocente

guilty [gíłti] ADJ culpable; **we find the**

defendant not — hallamos al acusado inocente

Guinea [gíni] N Guinea f; **— pig** conejillo de Indias m; **—-Bissau** Guinea-Bissau f

Guinean [gínɪən] ADJ & N guineano -na mf

guise [gaɪz] ADV LOC **under the — of** so/bajo pretexto de; **in the — of** a manera de

guitar [gɪtár] N guitarra f

gulf [gʌlf] N (body of water) golfo m; (abyss, gap) abismo m; **— Stream** Corriente del Golfo f

gull [gʌl] N (bird) gaviota f; (dupe) crédulo -la mf; Sp primo -ma mf

gullet [gʌlɪt] N gaznate m

gullible [gʌləbəl] ADJ crédulo, ingenuo

gully [gʌli] N barranco m, barranca f; (gutter) alcantarilla f

gulp [gʌlp] VT tragar saliva; N trago m

gum [gʌm] N goma f; (for chewing) chicle m; **—s** encías f pl; VT **to — up** (ruin) jorobar; (stick) pegotear

gumption [gámpʃən] N (initiative) iniciativa f, arranque m; (courage) agallas f pl

gun [gʌn] N (firearm) arma de fuego f; (revolver) revólver m; (rifle) rifle m; (shotgun) escopeta f; (cannon) cañón m; (for painting, nailing) pistola f; VT (an engine) acelerar; **—boat** cañonero m; **—fire** tiroteo m; **—man** pistolero m; **—powder** pólvora f; **—shot** disparo m; **—shot wound** herida de bala f; **at —point** a mano armada; **to stick to one's —s** mantenerse firme; **don't jump the —** no te precipites; **to be under the —** estar bajo mucha presión; VT **to — down** matar a tiros; **to — for** andar a la caza de

gung-ho [gʌnhó] ADJ fanático, entusiasta

gunner [gánə] N (shooting artillery) artillero -ra mf; (shooting a machine gun) ametrallador -ora mf

gurgle [gə́gəl] VI (water) borbotar; (baby) gorjear; N (of water) borboteo m; (of a baby) gorjeo m

gush [gʌʃ] VI (liquids) chorrear, brotar; (talk effusively) hablar con efusividad

gust [gʌst] N ráfaga f; **— of wind** racha/ráfaga de viento f, ventolera f; VI soplar en ráfagas

gusto [gásto] N (pleasure) placer m; (enthusiasm) entusiasmo m

gut [gʌt] N tripa f; (belly) barriga f; **— feeling** corazonada f; **—s** (intestines) entrañas f pl; VT (eviscerate) destripar; (destroy the insides of) destrozar el interior de; (strip) desmantelar

gutter [gʌdə] N (in the street) alcantarilla f; (on the roof) canaleta f, desagüe m; (squalor) miseria f

guy [gaɪ] N (man) tipo m; Sp tío m; **you —s** ustedes; Sp vosotros/vosotras; **— wire** cable m

Guyana [gaɪánə] N Guyana f

Guyanese [gaɪəníz] ADJ & N guyanés -esa mf

gym [dʒɪm] N gimnasio m

gymnasium [dʒɪmnéziəm] N gimnasio m

gymnastics [dʒɪmnǽstɪks] N gimnasia f

gynecologist [gaɪnəkáləʤɪst] N ginecólogo -ga mf

gynecology [gaɪnəkáləʤi] N ginecología f

gyp [dʒɪp] VT estafar, timar; N estafa f, timo m

gypsum [dʒípsəm] N yeso m

gypsy [dʒípsi] N & ADJ gitano -na mf

gyrate [dʒáɪret] VI girar

gyroscope [dʒáɪrəskop] N giroscopio m

Hh

habit [hǽbɪt] N (custom) hábito m, costumbre f; (clerical dress) hábito m; (vice) vicio m; **—-forming** adictivo

habitat [hǽbɪtæt] N hábitat m

habitual [həbítʃuəl] ADJ habitual

hack [hæk] N (cut) tajo m, machetazo m; (cough) tos seca f; (horse for hire) caballo de alquiler m; (nag) jamelgo m; (writer) escritor -ora mercenario -ria mf; **—saw** sierra para metales f; VI/VT tajar, cortar a machetazos; VI toser con tos seca

hacker [hǽkə] N pirata informático -ca mf

had [hæd] see have

hag [hæg] N (witch) bruja f; (ugly old woman) vieja fea f

haggard [hǽgəd] ADJ demacrado

haggle [hǽgəl] VI regatear

hail [hel] N (precipitation) granizo m; (greeting) saludo m; (shout) llamada f; **— Mary** Ave María f; **—storm** granizada f; VI (precipitate) granizar; VT (greet) saludar; (call out) llamar; (acclaim) aclamar; **to — from** ser oriundo de

hair [her] N pelo m; (of the head only) cabello m; (of the body only) vello m; (on plants) pelusa f; **—brush** cepillo para el cabello m; **—cut** corte de pelo m; **to get a —cut** cortarse el pelo; **—do** peinado m; **—dresser** peluquero -ra mf, peinador -ora mf; **—follicle** folículo capilar m; **—line** nacimiento del pelo f; **—line fracture** fractura fina f; **—piece** postizo m; **—pin** horquilla f; **—-raising** horripilante, espeluznante; **—spray** fijador m

hairless [hérlɪs] ADJ (deprived of hair) pelado; (growing no hair) lampiño

hairy [héri] ADJ (including head) peludo; (body only) velludo

Haiti [hébi] N Haití m

Haitian [héʃən] ADJ & N haitiano -na mf

hake [hek] N merluza f

half [hæf] N mitad f; **— an apple** media

manzana f; ADJ medio; —-**baked** (not fully cooked) a medio cocer; (not fully developed) mal concebido; —-**breed** mestizo -za mf; — **brother** medio hermano m; —-**cocked** mal preparado; **he went off** —-**cocked** actuó precipitadamente; —-**cooked** a medio cocer; —-**dozen** media docena f; —-**hearted** desganado; —-**hour** media hora f; —-**life** vida media f; —-**moon** media luna f; —-**note** blanca f; —-**open** entreabierto, entornado; — **past one** la una y media; —**time** medio tiempo m, descanso m; —-**truth** verdad a medias f; — **volley** media volea f; —**way** a medio camino; —**way house** casa de rehabilitación f; —**way measures** medidas parciales f pl; —**way point** punto medio m; —-**wit** pej imbécil mf, papamoscas mf; **at** —-**mast** a media asta; **to do something** —**way** hacer algo a medias; **to go halves** ir a medias

halibut [hǽləbət] N hipogloso m
halitosis [hælɪtósɪs] N halitosis f
hall [hɔl] N (corridor) corredor m, pasillo m; (large room) salón m, sala f; (building) edificio m; —**mark** distintivo m; —**way** (corridor) corredor m, pasillo m; (entrance) zaguán m, vestíbulo m
Halloween [hæləwín] N víspera del día de Todos los Santos f, noche de brujas f
hallucinate [həlúsənet] VI alucinar
hallucination [həlusənéʃən] N alucinación f
hallucinogen [həlúsənədʒən] N alucinógeno m
halo [hélo] N halo m, aureola f
halogen [hǽlədʒən] ADJ halógeno
halt [hɔlt] N **to come to a** — detenerse; VI/VT parar, detener[se]; —! ¡alto!
halter [hɔ́ltɚ] N cabestro m
halting [hɔ́ltɪŋ] ADJ vacilante
halve [hæv] VT partir por la mitad
ham [hæm] N (meat) jamón m; (attention getter) payaso m; —**string** (human) ligamento de la corva m; (horse) tendón del jarrete m; **to — it up** sobreactuar, exagerar
hamburger [hǽmbɚɡɚ] N (meat) carne picada de vaca/res f; (sandwich, patty) hamburguesa f
hamlet [hǽmlɪt] N aldea f, poblado m, caserío m
hammer [hǽmɚ] N martillo m; VI/VT martillar, amartillar; **to — out** (an agreement) forjar; (differences) negociar
hammock [hǽmək] N hamaca f
hamper [hǽmpɚ] N canasto m, cesto m; VT impedir, embarazar
hamster [hǽmstɚ] N hámster m
hand [hænd] N mano f; (of a clock) aguja f, manecilla f; (farm helper) peón m; —**bag** (purse) bolsa f, cartera f; (valise) maletín m; —**ball** (American game) pelota f, frontón m; (European game) balonmano m; (in soccer)

mano f; —**bill** volante m; —**cuffs** esposas f pl; — **grenade** granada de mano f, bomba de piña f; —**gun** revólver m; — **in** — [cogidos] de la mano; —**kerchief** pañuelo m; —**out** (notes) repartido m, ejemplario m; (alms) limosna f; —**saw** serrucho m; **the** —**shake** apretón de manos m; —**stand** pino m, paro de manos m; —**work** trabajo manual m; —**writing** letra f; **at** — (within reach) al alcance; (about to happen) cerca; **in** — (under control) bajo control; (available) disponible, en mano; **on** — disponible, a mano; **on the other** — en cambio, por otra parte; **to have one's** —s **full** estar ocupadísimo; ADJ —**held** de mano; —**made** hecho a mano; —-**picked** cuidadosamente seleccionado; —s-**on** práctico; VT entregar, dar; **to** —**cuff** esposar; **to** — **down** (a thing) pasar; (a judgment) pronunciar; **to** — **in** entregar; **to** — **over** entregar
handful [hǽndfʊl] N manojo m, puñado m
handicap [hǽndikæp] N (physical disability) impedimento m, minusvalía f; (mental disability) retardo m; (disadvantage) desventaja f; (in golf) hándicap m; — **race** carrera de hándicap f; VT (hinder) perjudicar, handicapar; (injure) lisiar; **physically** —**ped** minusválido físico
handiwork [hǽndiwɚk] N labor f
handle [hǽndl] N (straight) mango m; (curved) asa f; (of a drawer) manija f; (of a knife) empuñadura f, puño m; —**bar** manubrio m; VT (manage) manejar; (touch) manipular, tocar; (deal in) comerciar en; **the car** —s **easily** el coche tiene buena maniobrabilidad
handling [hǽndlɪŋ] N (dealing) manejo m; (touching) manipulación f; (charge) porte m; (of a car) maniobrabilidad f; — **charges** cargos de tramitación m pl
handsome [hǽnsəm] ADJ guapo, bien parecido; **a** — **sum** una suma considerable
handy [hǽndi] ADJ (near) a [la] mano; (practical) práctico; (skillful) hábil, diestro; N —**man** hombre habilidoso m
hang [hæŋ] VI/VT colgar, suspender; VT (door) colocar; (one's head) inclinar; (a condemned person) ahorcar; VI pender; — **in there!** ¡ánimo! **to** — **around** quedarse por ahí, rondar; **to** — **on** (hold tight) agarrarse bien; (persevere) aguantar; (wait) esperar; **to** — **out** (be outside) estar fuera; (socialize with) andar [con]; **to** — **over** sobresalir; **to** — **paper on a wall** empapelar una pared; **to** — **up** colgar; **sentenced to** — condenado a la horca; N caída f; — **glider** ala delta f; —**man** verdugo m; —**nail** padrastro m, uña encarnada f, uñero m; —**out** sitio frecuentado m; —**over** resaca f; —-**up** complejo m; **to get the** — **of something** agarrarle la onda a

algo

hangar [hǽŋə] N hangar m

hanger [hǽŋə] N colgadero m; (for clothes) percha f

hanging [hǽŋɪŋ] N muerte en la horca f; **—s** colgaduras f pl, tapiz m; ADJ colgante

hanky-panky [hǽŋkipǽŋki] N (deceit) tejemaneje m; (illicit sexual activity) aventuras f pl

haphazard [hæphǽzəd] ADV a la buena de Dios; ADJ irregular

happen [hǽpən] VI suceder, pasar, acontecer; **I — to know** da la casualidad de que sé; **to — to pass by** acertar a pasar; **to — upon** encontrarse con, toparse con

happening [hǽpənɪŋ] N acontecimiento m, suceso m

happily [hǽpɪli] ADV (in a state of happiness) felizmente; (luckily) afortunadamente; **they lived — ever after** vivieron felices y comieron perdices

happiness [hǽpɪnɪs] N felicidad f, dicha f

happy [hǽpi] ADJ (satisfied) feliz, dichoso; (pleased) contento; (lucky) afortunado; **— ending** final feliz m; **to be — to** hacer algo de buena gana

harangue [hərǽŋ] N arenga f; VT arengar

harass [hərǽs] VT acosar, hostigar

harassment [hərǽsmənt] N acoso m, hostigamiento m

harbor [hárbə] N (for ships) puerto m; (refuge) refugio m; **— authority** autoridad portuaria; VT (refugees, criminals, suspicions) albergar; (hopes) abrigar

hard [hard] ADJ (firm) duro; (difficult) difícil; (arduous) arduo; **to play —ball** ser despiadado; **—-boiled egg** huevo duro m; **— cash** dinero contante y sonante m; **— coal** antracita f; **— copy** copia en papel f, copia impresa f; **— core** núcleo resistente m; **—-core** radical; **— disk** disco duro m; **— disk drive** unidad de disco duro f; **— feelings** resentimiento m; **— hat** casco m; **—headed** testarudo; **—-hearted** duro de corazón; **— liquor** bebida alcohólica fuerte f; **— luck** mala suerte f; **— of hearing** medio sordo; **— page break** salto de página forzado m; **— palate** paladar óseo m; **—-pressed** en aprietos; **— return** salto de línea forzado m; **—ware** (metal articles) ferretería f; (computer) hardware m; **—ware store** ferretería f; **—wood** madera noble f; **— water** agua dura f; **— winter** invierno crudo m; **—-wired** programado; **—-working** trabajador; ADV (fall, push) con fuerza; (work) duro, con ahínco

harden [hárdn] VI/VT (make or become hard) endurecer[se]; (make or become experienced) curtir[se]

hardening [hárdnɪŋ] N endurecimiento m

hardly [hárdli] ADV (scarcely) apenas, difícilmente; (at all) en absoluto; **— anyone** casi nadie; **— surprising** nada sorprendente

hardness [hárdnɪs] N dureza f

hardship [hárdʃɪp] N penuria f, penalidad f

hardy [hárdi] ADJ robusto

hare [hɛr] N liebre f; **—brained** descabellado; **—lip** labio leporino m; **—lipped** con labio leporino, labihendido

harem [hérəm] N harén m

harm [harm] N daño m, mal m, perjuicio m; VT (object) dañar; (person) hacer daño; (chances) perjudicar

harmful [hármfəl] ADJ perjudicial, dañino, nocivo

harmless [hármlɪs] ADJ inocuo, inofensivo

harmonic [harmánɪk] ADJ & N armónico m

harmonious [harmóniəs] ADJ armonioso

harmonize [hármənaɪz] VI/VT armonizar

harmony [hárməni] N armonía f

harness [hárnɪs] N arnés m, jaez m, guarnición f; VT (put on a harness) enjaezar; (utilize) aprovechar

harp [harp] N arpa f; VI (play the harp) tocar el arpa; (insist) machacar; **to — on** insistir sobre

harpoon [harpún] N arpón m; VT arponear

harpsichord [hárpsɪkɔrd] N clavicémbalo m

harrowing [hǽroɪŋ] ADJ angustioso; **— adventure** aventura espeluznante f

harry [hǽri] VT acosar, hostigar

harsh [harʃ] ADJ (words) duro; (surface) áspero; (character, discipline) severo, férreo; (winter) crudo, riguroso

harshness [hárʃnɪs] N (of words) dureza f; (of a surface) aspereza f; (of character, discipline) severidad f; (of a winter) rigor m

harvest [hárvɪst] N cosecha f; (of sugar) zafra f; VT cosechar

has [hæz] see have

hash [hæʃ] N guisado m, picadillo m

hashish [hǽʃɪʃ] N hachís m

hassle [hǽsəl] N rollo m, lío m; VT jorobar

haste [hest] N prisa f; **in —** de prisa; **to make —** darse prisa, apresurarse; Am apurarse

hasten [hésən] VI apresurarse; Am apurarse; VT acelerar, adelantar

hasty [hésti] ADJ apresurado, precipitado, presuroso; Am apurado; **to be —** precipitarse, apresurarse

hat [hæt] N sombrero m

hatch [hæʧ] VI/VT (chicks) empollar; (plot, scheme) fraguar, maquinar; N (chicks) nidada f; (opening) escotilla f; **— way** escotilla f

hatchet [hǽʧɪt] N hacha f; **— job** crítica feroz f; **— man** sicario m; **to bury the —** hacer las paces

hate [het] N odio m; VI/VT odiar; **I — to admit it** me molesta admitirlo; **I — eating leftovers**

detesto comer restos
hateful [hétfəl] ADJ odioso, aborrecible
hatred [hétrɪd] N odio m
haughtiness [hɔ́dɪnɪs] N altivez f, altanería f, soberbia f
haughty [hɔ́di] ADJ altivo, altanero, soberbio
haul [hɔl] VT (transport) transportar; (drag) arrastrar; (pull) jalar [de], tirar [de]; N (quantity transported) carga f; (tug) tirón m; (catch of fish) redada f; (stolen goods) botín m; **long — distancia larga** f
haunch [hɔntʃ] N anca f
haunt [hɔnt] VI/VT (frequent) frecuentar, rondar; (enchant) embrujar; **that idea —s me** me obsesiona esa idea; **—ed house** casa embrujada f; N (of animals, criminals) guarida f; (of people socializing) sitio frecuentado m
have [hæv] V AUX haber; VT tener; **to — to** tener que; **to — a baby** dar a luz; **to — a look at** echar una mirada a; **to — a suit made** mandarse hacer un traje; **— him come later** dile que venga más tarde; **what did she — on?** ¿qué tenía puesto? **we've been had** nos estafaron
haven [hévən] N abrigo m, refugio m
havoc [hévək] N estrago m; **to wreak —** hacer estragos
hawk [hɔk] N gavilán m; VT pregonar
hay [he] N heno m; **— fever** alergia al polen f; **— loft** henil m; **—seed** paleto -ta mf; **—stack** almiar m; **to look for a needle in a —stack** buscar una aguja en un pajar
hazard [hǽzəd] N (chance) azar m; (danger) peligro m; VT arriesgar, aventurar
hazardous [hǽzədəs] ADJ peligroso; **— substance** sustancia peligrosa f
haze [hez] N neblina f, calina f; VT atormentar [como parte de un rito de iniciación]
hazel [hézəl] N avellano m; **—nut** avellana f; ADJ de avellano
hazy [hézi] ADJ (weather) brumoso; (idea) confuso, vago
HDL [high density lipoprotein] [étʃdiél] N LAD f
he [hi] PRON él; **—-goat** macho cabrío m; **— who** el que, quien
head [hɛd] N (of body) cabeza f; (of bed) cabecera f; (chief) jefe -fa mf; **—ache** dolor de cabeza m; **— coach** entrenador -ora en jefe mf; **— cold** resfrío m; **—count** recuento de personas m; **—dress** tocado m, adorno para la cabeza m; **—gear** (hat) sombrero m; (helmet) casco m; (for a horse) cabezada f; **—hunter** cazatalentos mf sg; **—land** cabo m, promontorio m; **—light** faro delantero m; **—line** titular m; **—long** (head first) de cabeza; (hastily) precipitadamente; **— of hair** cabellera f; **— of state** mandatario -ria

mf; **—phone** audífono m, auricular m; **—quarters** (military) cuartel general m; (police) jefatura f; (corporation) oficina central f; **—rest** reposacabezas m sg; **—set** auriculares m pl; **—s or tails** cara o cruz; **I can't make —s or tails of it** esto no tiene ni pies ni cabeza; **— start** ventaja f; **—stone** lápida f; **—strong** testarudo; **—way** avance m; **—word** voz f; **to make —way** avanzar, progresar; **it went to his —** se le fue a la cabeza; **to be out of one's —** desvariar; **to come to a —** (a crisis) precipitarse; (an abscess) supurar; **to keep one's —** mantener la calma; VT (lead) encabezar; (steer) dirigir; (in soccer) cabecear; VI dirigirse; **to — up** liderar; **to — off** atajar; ADV **-on** de frente, frontal
header [hɛdə-] N (in soccer) cabezazo m, pase de cabeza m; (in text) cabecera f, encabezado m
heading [hɛdɪŋ] N encabezamiento m
heal [hil] VT curar; VI (get well) sanar, curarse; (form a scar) cicatrizar
health [hɛlθ] N salud f; **— care** asistencia médica f; **— care system** sistema de asistencia de salud m; **— care provider** profesional de la salud mf; **— food** comida macrobiótica f; **— insurance** seguro de salud m
healthful [hɛlθfəl] ADJ saludable, sano
healthy [hɛlθi] ADJ sano, saludable
heap [hip] N montón m, pila f; VT amontonar, apilar; VI **to — up** amontonarse
hear [hir] VI/VT (perceive) oír; VT (listen) escuchar; **to — about/of someone/ something** oír hablar de alguien/algo; **to — from someone** tener noticias de alguien; **I won't — of your leaving** no quiero saber de que te vayas
heard [hɜd] see hear
hearer [hírə-] N oyente mf
hearing [hírɪŋ] N (sense) oído m; (trial) audiencia f; **within —** al alcance del oído; **— aid** audífono m; ADJ **—-impaired** sordo
hearsay [hírse] N testimonio de oídas m; **by —** de oídas
hearse [hɜs] N coche fúnebre m, carroza f
heart [hɑrt] N (organ) corazón m; (spirit) ánimo m; **—ache** angustia f; **— attack** ataque cardíaco m; **—beat** latido m; **I would do it in a —beat** lo haría sin pestañear; **—burn** acidez de estómago f; **— disease** enfermedad coronaria f; **— murmur** soplo cardíaco m; **at —** en realidad, en el fondo; **from the bottom of one's —** de corazón, con toda el alma; **to learn by —** aprender de memoria; **to take —** cobrar ánimo; **to take to —** tomar a pecho; ADJ **—broken** inconsolable; **—felt** sincero, sentido; **my —felt sympathy** mi más sentido pésame; **—-warming** reconfortante

hearten [hártn̩] VT animar

hearth [harθ] N hogar *m*

heartless [hártlɪs] ADJ despiadado, desalmado

hearty [hárdi] ADJ (cordial) cordial; (strong) fuerte; — **appetite** apetito saludable *m*; a — **laugh** una risa desbordante; — **meal** una comida abundante

heat [hit] N (warmth) calor *m*; (passion) ardor *m*; (estrus) celo *m*; (source of heat) calefacción *f*; (preliminary race) eliminatoria *f*; — **exchange** equilibrio térmico *m*; —**stroke** insolación *f*; VI/VT calentar[se]; **to — up** acalorarse

heater [hídə] N calentador *m*

heating [hídɪŋ] N calefacción *f*; — **pad** almohadilla eléctrica *f*

heave [hiv] VT (raise) levantar; (throw) arrojar, lanzar; (sigh) exhalar; (pull) jalar; VI (pant) jadear; (vomit) hacer arcadas; N (throw) lanzamiento *m*; (pull) tirón *m*

heaven [hévən] N cielo *m*

heavenly [hévənli] ADJ celestial; — **bodies** cuerpos celestes *m pl*; **it was** — estuvo divino

heavily [hévəli] ADV (fall) pesadamente; (drink) mucho; **he's breathing** — está jadeando; **he's — indebted** está muy endeudado / tiene muchas deudas

heaviness [hévinɪs] N pesadez *f*

heavy [hévi] ADJ (weighty) pesado; (thick) grueso, pesado; (dense) denso; (oppressive) opresivo; — **artillery** artillería pesada *f*; — **breathing** jadeos *m pl*; —**duty** de servicio pesado; —**handed** severo, autoritario; **with a — heart** abatido; — **rain** lluvia fuerte *f*; — **schedule** agenda cargada *f*; —**weight** peso pesado *m*; N villano -na *mf*

Hebrew [híbru] N & ADJ hebreo -a *mf*; (language) hebreo *m*

heck [hɛk] INTERJ ¡caramba! **what the — are you doing?** ¿qué demonios haces? **that was a — of a good game** fue un partidazo

hectare [héktɛr] N hectárea *f*

hectic [héktɪk] ADJ febril, agitado

hedge [hɛdʒ] N (row of bushes) seto *m*; (precaution) precaución *f*; — **fund** fondo especulativo *m*; —**hog** erizo *m*; VI/VT (a bet) cubrir[se]; VT (a question) evadir

hedonism [hídṇɪzəm] N hedonismo *m*

heebie-jeebies [híbidʒíbiz] N **it gives me the** — me pone los pelos de punta

heed [hid] VT atender; N atención *f*, cuidado *m*; **to pay — to** prestar atención a

heel [hil] N (of foot or sock) talón *m*; (of shoe) tacón *m*; **to kick up one's —s** tirar la chancleta, soltarse el pelo; VT poner tacón a; VI/VT seguir de cerca

hegemony [hɪdʒéməni] N hegemonía *f*

heifer [héfə] N novilla *f*, vaquilla *f*

height [haɪt] N (of a building, mountain) altura *f*; (of a person) estatura *f*; (utmost point) colmo *m*

heighten [háɪtn̩] VI/VT (increase) aumentar[se]; (intensify) realzar

Heimlich maneuver [háɪmlɪkmənúvə-] N maniobra de Heimlich *f*

heinous [hénəs] ADJ aborrecible

heir [ɛr] N heredero -ra *mf*; — **apparent** presunto heredero *m*, presunta heredera *f*; —**s and assigns** herederos y cesionarios *m pl*

heiress [ɛ́rɪs] N heredera *f*

held [hɛld] *see* hold

helicopter [hélɪkɑptə-] N helicóptero *m*

helium [híliəm] N helio *m*

helix [hílɪks] N hélice *f*

hell [hɛl] N infierno *m*

hello [helóʊ] INTERJ ¡hola! (on the telephone) hola; *Sp* diga; *Mex* bueno

helm [hɛlm] N timón *m*

helmet [hélmɪt] N (for bikes, etc.) casco *m*; (armor) yelmo *m*

help [hɛlp] N (aid) ayuda *f*; (rescue) auxilio *m*; (remedy) remedio *m*; (employee) empleado -da *mf*; — **desk** servicio de ayuda al usuario *m*; INTERJ ¡auxilio! ¡socorro! VI/VT (aid) ayudar, asistir; (rescue) auxiliar, socorrer; — **yourself** sírvete; **he cannot — it** no puede evitarlo; **he cannot — but come** no puede menos que venir; **may I — you?** ¿en qué le puedo servir?

helper [hélpə-] N ayudante *mf*, asistente *mf*

helpful [hélpfəl] ADJ (useful) útil; (willing to help) servicial

helping [hélpɪŋ] N porción *f*

helpless [hélplɪs] ADJ desamparado, desvalido

helplessness [hélplɪsnɪs] N desamparo *m*, desvalimiento *m*

hem [hɛm] N dobladillo *m*, *Am* ruedo *m*; VT hacer dobladillos en, orillar; **to — in** arrinconar; **to — and haw** vacilar

hematoma [himətómə] N hematoma *m*

hemisphere [hémɪsfɪr] N hemisferio *m*

hemlock [hémlak] N cicuta *f*

hemoglobin [híməglobɪn] N hemoglobina *f*

hemophilia [himəfíliə] N hemofilia *f*

hemorrhage [hémərɪdʒ] N hemorragia *f*

hemorrhoids [hémərɔɪdz] N hemorroides *f pl*

hemp [hɛmp] N cáñamo *m*

hen [hɛn] N (chicken) gallina *f*; (female bird) ave hembra *f*; ADJ —**pecked** dominado por su mujer

hence [hɛns] ADV de ahí; —**forth** de aquí en adelante, de hoy en adelante; **a week** — de aquí a una semana

hepatitis [hɛpətáɪdɪs] N hepatitis *f*

her [hɚ] PRON **I see** — la veo; **I talk to** — le hablo [a ella]; **I went with** — fui con ella; POSS ADJ **this is** — **dog** este es su perro, este es el perro de ella

herald [hérəld] N heraldo *m*; VT anunciar, proclamar

herb [ɜb] N hierba *f*

herbal [ɜ́bəl] ADJ de hierbas; — **tea** tisana *f*

herbicide [hɜ́bɪsaɪd] N herbicida *m*

herbivore [hɜ́bəvɔr] N herbívoro *m*

herbivorous [hɜbívərəs] ADJ herbívoro

herd [hɜd] N (of animals) manada *f*; (of goats) hato *m*; (of sheep) rebaño *m*; (of horses, donkeys) recua *f*; **the — common** — el populacho, la chusma; **—sman** pastor *m*; VT arrear; VI ir en manada

here [hir] ADV aquí, acá; — **it is** aquí está; **—after** en adelante; **the —after** el más allá; **—by** (in writing) por la presente; **I —by pronounce you husband and wife** los declaro marido y mujer; **—in** en el presente; **—'s to you!** ¡a tu salud! **—tofore** hasta ahora; **—with** (hereby) por la presente; (attached) adjunto; **come —!** ¡ven acá! **the — and now** el presente; **that is neither — nor there** eso no viene al caso

hereditary [hərédɪteri] ADJ hereditario

heredity [hərédɪti] N herencia *f*

heresy [hérɪsi] N herejía *f*

heretic [hérɪtɪk] N hereje *mf*

heritage [hérɪtɪdʒ] N herencia *f*, patrimonio *m*

hermaphrodite [hə-mǽfrədaɪt] N hermafrodita *mf*

hermetic [hɜmédɪk] ADJ hermético

hermit [hɜ́mɪt] N ermitaño -ña *mf*; — **crab** ermitaño *m*

hernia [hɜ́niə] N hernia *f*; **—ted** herniado; **—ted disk** hernia de disco *f*

hero [híro] N (brave man) héroe *m*; (main character) protagonista *m*

heroic [hɪróɪk] ADJ heroico

heroin [héroɪn] N heroína *f*

heroine [héroɪn] N heroína *f*

heroism [héroɪzəm] N heroísmo *m*

heron [hérən] N garza *f*

herpes [hɜ́piz] N herpes *m*

herring [hérɪŋ] N arenque *m*

hers [hɜz] PRON **this book is** — este libro es suyo / de ella; **these things are** — estas cosas son suyas; — **is bigger** el suyo / la suya es más grande; **a friend of** — un amigo suyo / de ella

herself [hɜsélf] PRON ella misma; **she's not — today** hoy no es la misma de siempre; **she was sitting by** — estaba sentada sola; **she — did it** lo hizo sola, lo hizo ella misma; **she talks to** — ella habla para sí, habla consigo misma; **she looked at** — **in the mirror** se miró en el espejo; **she bought** — **a house** se compró una casa

hesitant [hézɪtənt] ADJ vacilante

hesitate [hézɪtet] VI (pause) vacilar; (stutter) titubear; (doubt) dudar

hesitating [hézɪtedɪŋ] ADJ vacilante

hesitation [hɛzɪtéʃən] N (pause) vacilación *f*; (stammer) titubeo *m*; (doubt) duda *f*

heterogeneous [hɛDəədʒíniəs] ADJ heterogéneo

heterosexual [hɛDərosékʃuəl] ADJ heterosexual

hexagon [héksəgən] N hexágono *m*

hey [he] INTERJ ¡oiga!

heyday [héde] N auge *m*

hi [haɪ] INTERJ hola; **say — to your sister for me** dale recuerdos a tu hermana de mi parte

hiatus [haɪéDəs] N hiato *m*

hibernate [háɪbə-net] VI hibernar

hiccup, hiccough [híkʌp] N hipo *m*; VI hipar, tener hipo

hick [hɪk] N & ADJ paleto -ta *mf*

hickory [híkəri] N nogal americano *m*

hid, hidden [hɪd, hídn] *see* hide

hidden [hídn] ADJ (out of sight) oculto; (illegal) clandestino; — **agenda** intereses ocultos *m pl*

hide [haɪd] VI/VT ocultar[se], esconder[se]; — **and seek** escondite *m*, escondidas *f pl*; **—out** escondite *m*; N cuero *m*, piel *f*, pellejo *m*

hideous [hídiəs] ADJ horrendo, espantoso

hierarchy [háɪərɑrki] N jerarquía *f*

hieroglyphic [haɪrəglífɪk] ADJ & N jeroglífico *m*

high [haɪ] ADJ alto; (intoxicated) ebrio; (on drugs) volado; — **altitude sickness** enfermedad de altura *f*; — **and dry** (ship) en seco; (person) colgado; — **blood pressure** hipertensión *f*; **—brow** culto; **—class** de clase; — **contrast** alto contraste *m*; — **definition television** televisión de alta definición *f*; — **density** alta densidad *f*; **—er-up** superior; **—er education** educación superior *f*; — **explosive** explosivo de alta potencia *m*; — **fever** fiebre elevada *f*; — **fidelity** alta fidelidad *f*; — **finance** altas finanzas *f pl*; **—grade** de calidad superior; **—handed** arbitrario; — **jump** salto alto *m*; **—lands** tierras altas *f pl*; **—level** de alto nivel; **—light** lo más destacado; **—lighting** (on a computer) selección de texto *f*; **—lights** (in hair) claritos *m pl*, mechas *f pl*; **—minded** idealista; **—octane gasoline** súper *m*; **—pitched** agudo; — **point** culminación *f*; **—powered** de alta potencia; **—pressure** estresante, intenso; **—priced** caro; **—quality** de alta calidad; **—return** de alta rentabilidad; **—rise** de muchos pisos; **—risk** de alto riesgo; **—risk behavior** conducta de alto riesgo *f*; **—risk patient** paciente con alto riesgo *mf*; — **school** escuela secundaria *f*, colegio *m*; Sp instituto *m*; — **seas** alta mar *f*; **—sounding** altisonante; **—speed** de alta velocidad; — **spirits** buen ánimo *m*; **—strung** nervioso; **—tech** alta tecnología *f*; — **temperature** temperatura máxima *f*; — **tide** pleamar *f*; **—way** carretera *f*, ruta *f*; **— wind** ventarrón *m*; **in — gear** a toda marcha; **two feet** — dos pies de altura; **it is — time that** ya era hora de que; **to look — and low** buscar por todas partes; N flash *m*, subida *f*; VT **to —light** (emphasize) destacar, resaltar

highly [háɪlɪ] ADV **— amusing** sumamente divertido; **— paid** muy bien pagado; **— qualified** altamente cualificado; **he spoke — of her** habló muy bien de ella

highness [háɪnɪs] N alteza *f*

hijack [háɪdʒæk] VT secuestrar [un vehículo]

hike [haɪk] N caminata *f*; **take a —!** ¡ve a freír espárragos! VI salir a caminar

hilarious [hɪlérɪəs] ADJ graciosísimo, para morirse de risa

hill [hɪl] N (elevated area) colina *f*, cerro *m*; (pile) montón *m*; **—billy** paleto -ta *mf*; **—side** ladera *f*; **—top** cumbre *f*, cima *f*

hillock [hílək] N otero *m*

hilly [hílɪ] ADJ accidentado

hilt [hɪlt] N empuñadura *f*; **to the —** al máximo

him [hɪm] PRON **I see —** lo veo; *Sp* le veo; **I talk to —** le hablo; **I went with —** fui con él

himself [hɪmsélf] PRON él mismo; **he — wrote the letter** él mismo escribió la carta; **he's not — today** hoy no es el mismo de siempre; **he was sitting by —** estaba sentado solo; **he talks to —** él habla para sí, habla consigo mismo; **he looked at — in the mirror** se miró en el espejo; **he bought — a house** se compró una casa

hind [haɪnd] ADJ trasero; **—most** último; **in —sight** a posteriori; N cierva *f*

hinder [híndər] VT impedir, entorpecer, estorbar

Hindi [híndi] N hindi *m*

hindrance [híndrəns] N obstáculo *m*, impedimento *m*, traba *f*

Hindu [híndu] ADJ & N hindú *mf*

hinge [hɪndʒ] N gozne *m*, quicio *m*; VT engoznar, poner goznes; VI **to — on** depender de

hint [hɪnt] N (clue) indirecta *f*, pista *f*; (trace) dejo *m*; **to take the —** darse por enterado; VT insinuar

hip [hɪp] N cadera *f*; **— replacement** (operation) sustitución protésica de la cadera *f*; (prosthesis) prótesis de cadera *f*

Hippocratic oath [hɪpəkrǽɔɪkóθ] N juramento hipocrático

hippopotamus [hɪpəpádəməs] N hipopótamo *m*

hire [haɪr] VT (engage for work) contratar; VI/VT (rent) alquilar[se]; **— and fire** contratar y despedir; **to — out** dar en alquiler, alquilar; N (engagement) contratación *f*; (employee) nuevo -va empleado -da *mf*; (rent) alquiler *m*

his [hɪz] POSS ADJ **this is — dog** este es su perro / el perro de él; PRON **these things are —** estas cosas son suyas; **— is right here** el suyo / la suya está aquí; **a friend of —** un

amigo suyo / una amiga suya

Hispanic [hɪspǽnɪk] ADJ hispánico, hispano; N hispano -na *mf*

hiss [hɪs] VI sisear; (to boo) silbar; N siseo *m*

histamine [hístəmin] N histamina *f*

historian [hɪstórɪən] N historiador -ra *mf*

historic [hɪstórɪk] ADJ histórico

historical [hɪstórɪkəl] ADJ histórico

history [hístərɪ] N historia *f*

histrionics [hɪstriánɪks] N histrionismo *m*

hit [hɪt] VT (a target) dar en; (a car) chocar con; (a key) pulsar, tocar; (a baseball) batear; **to — a homerun** batear un jonrón, pegar un cuadrangular; **to — it off** llevarse bien desde el principio; **to — the mark** acertar, dar en el blanco; **to — upon an idea** dar con una idea; **to — on a person** tratar de ligar con alguien; N (blow) golpe *m*; (success) éxito *m*; (dose) dosis *f*; **that was a — with me** me encantó; **—man** sicario *m*; **—s** (on a website) visitas *f pl*; ADJ **—-and-run** que se da a la fuga después de atropellar a alguien; **—-or-miss** al azar

hitch [hɪtʃ] VT atar, amarrar; (pants) levantar; (yoke) uncir, enganchar; **to get —ed** casarse; **to —hike** *Sp* hacer autostop; *Am* hacer dedo; N (knot) nudo *m*; (difficulty) dificultad *f*; (period) período *m*

hither [híðə] ADV acá; **— and thither** acá y allá; **—to** hasta ahora

HIV [human immunodeficiency virus] [étʃáɪví] N VIH *m*

hive [haɪv] N (shelter for bees) colmena *f*; (colony of bees) enjambre *m*; **—s** urticaria *f*

HMO [health maintenance organization] [étʃémó] N organización de mantenimiento de salud *f*

hoard [hɔrd] N reserva *f*; VI/VT acaparar

hoarse [hɔrs] ADJ ronco; (like alcoholics) aguardentoso

hoarseness [hórsnɪs] N ronquera *f*

hoax [hoks] N engaño *m*

hobble [hábəl] VI (limp) cojear; VT (tie to impede walking) manear; (hinder) trabar; N cojera *f*; (rope) traba *f*, manea *f*

hobby [hábɪ] N hobby *m*

hobo [hóbo] N vagabundo *m*

hockey [háki] N hockey *m*

hodgepodge [hádʒpadʒ] N mezcolanza *f*, batiburrillo *m*

hoe [ho] N azada *f*, azadón *m*; VI/VT limpiar con azadón

hog [hag] N puerco *m*, cerdo *m*, marrano *m*; *Am* chancho *m*; **—wash** pamplinas *f pl*; **to live high on the —** vivir en la abundancia; VT acaparar, adueñarse de

hoist [hɔɪst] VT izar; N torno *m*, guinche *m*

hokey [hóki] ADJ sensiblero

hold [hold] VT (bear) llevar, sujetar; (contain)

contener; (detain) detener; (decide legally, sustain a note) sostener; (opine) opinar; **to — back** detener; **to — down** sujetar; **to — forth** perorar; **to — hands** tomarse de la mano; **to — in place** sujetar; **to — a meeting** celebrar una reunión; **to — someone responsible** hacerle a uno responsable; **to — someone to his word** obligar a uno a cumplir con su palabra; **to — oneself erect** ponerse derecho; **to — one's own tongue** defenderse; **to — one's tongue** callarse, morderse la lengua; **— the pickles on that burger!** una hamburguesa sin pepinillos, por favor; VI (remain fast) aguantar, resistir; (occupy a position) ocupar; (be valid) ser válido; **to — off** mantener[se] a distancia; **to — off doing something** abstenerse de hacer algo; **to — liable** responsabilizar; **to — on** (not let go) agarrar[se], sujetar[se]; (stop) esperar; (persist) persistir; **to — out** aguantar; **to — still** quedarse/estarse quieto; **to — tight** agarrarse; **to — to one's promise** cumplir con la palabra; **to — up** (raise) alzar; (detain) detener; (rob) atracar, asaltar; (persevere) aguantar; **how much does it — ?** ¿Qué capacidad tiene? N (grip) agarro m; (thing to grasp) asidero m; (dominion) dominio m; (wrestling move) llave f; (in music) calderón m; (of a ship) bodega f; **—up** golpe m, atraco m; **to get — of** agarrar; **to take — of** Sp coger, agarrar; **to have a good — on something** agarrarse bien de algo

holder [hóld♦] N (person) tenedor -ora mf, poseedor -ora mf; (device) receptáculo m

holding [hóldɪŋ] N propiedad f; **— company** holding m; **—s** (financial) valores en cartera m pl; (of a library) fondos m pl

hole [hoł] N agujero m; (in a wall) boquete m; (of an animal) madriguera f; (in the ground, in golf) hoyo m; **to be in a —** hallarse/estar en un apuro/aprieto; **—in-one** hoyo en uno m

holiday [hálɪde] N día de fiesta m; **—s** vacaciones f pl

holiness [hólɪnɪs] N santidad f

holistic [holístɪk] ADJ holístico

Holland [hálənd] N Holanda f

hollow [hálo] ADJ (empty) hueco; (concave) cóncavo; (sunken) hundido; (insincere) falso; N (cavity) hueco m, concavidad f; (valley) hondonada f, hondo m; VT **to — out** ahuecar, vaciar

holly [háli] N acebo m

holocaust [háləkɔst] N holocausto m

holster [hółst♦] N pistolera f, funda de pistola f

holy [hóli] ADJ santo, sagrado; **— Bible** Santa Biblia f; **— cow/Moses/mackerel!** ¡que increíble! Sp ¡jobar! **— Ghost** Espíritu Santo m; **— Spirit** Espíritu Santo m; **— war** guerra

santa f; **— water** agua bendita f

homage [hámɪdʒ] N homenaje m; **to pay —** rendir homenaje, honrar

home [hom] N casa f, hogar m; (for old people, orphans) asilo m, hogar m; **—boy** amigo del barrio m; **— economics** economía doméstica f; **— delivery** entrega a domicilio f; **— equity loan** préstamo garantizado por el valor residual de la vivienda m; **— game** partido en casa m; **—land** patria f; **—less** sin techo; **— office** (headquarters) oficina central f; (at home) oficina en el hogar f; **—owner** propietario -ria de vivienda mf; **—owners' association** asociación de propietarios de vivienda f; **— page** página de inicio f; **— plate** goma f, plato m; **— rule** autonomía f; **— run** jonrón m, cuadrangular m; **at —** en casa; **to be —sick** echar de menos / extrañar [a la familia]; **—sickness** morriña f, añoranza f; **— stretch** último trecho m; **—work** tarea domiciliaria f, deber m; ADJ doméstico; ADV (direction) a casa; (location) en casa; **to strike —** dar en el blanco; ADJ **—made** casero

homely [hómli] ADJ (ugly) feo; (familiar) familiar, doméstico

homeopathic [homiopǽθɪk] ADJ homeopático

homeopathy [homiápəθi] N homeopatía f

homestead [hómstɛd] N heredad f, casa de la familia f

homeward [hómw♦d] ADV a casa; **— bound** camino a casa

homicide [hámɪsaɪd] N homicidio m

homogeneous [homədʒíniəs] ADJ homogéneo

homogenize [homádʒənaɪz] VT homogeneizar

homonym [hámənɪm] N homónimo m

homophobia [homəfóbiə] N homofobia f

homophobic [homəfóbɪk] ADJ homofóbico

homosexual [homosékʃuəł] ADJ & N homosexual mf

Honduran [hɑndúrən] ADJ & N hondureño -ña mf

Honduras [hɑndúrəs] N Honduras f

hone [hon] VT afilar; **to — one's skills** desarrollar las destrezas; N piedra de afilar f

honest [ánɪst] ADJ honrado, honesto; **I'll be — with you** voy a ser franco contigo; **—!** ¡de veras!

honesty [ánɪsti] N (integrity) honradez f, honestidad f; (sincerity) franqueza f

honey [háni] N (sweet substance) miel f; (endearment) querido -da mf; **—bee** abeja f; **—comb** panal m; **—suckle** madreselva f

honeymoon [hánɪmun] N luna de miel f; VI pasar la luna de miel

honk [hɑŋk] N (of a car) bocinazo m, pitazo m; (of a goose) graznido m; VI/VT (car) tocar la bocina; VI (goose) graznar

honor [án♦] N (respect, privilege) honor m;

(good reputation) honra *f;* **with —s** con honores; **your —** su señoría; VT (revere) honrar; (accept invitation, check) aceptar; **to — a promise** cumplir [con] una promesa

honorable [ánəəbəl] ADJ honorable

honorary [ánəreri] ADJ honorario

hood [hʊd] N (of a coat) capucha *f,* caperuza *f;* (of a car) capó *m; Am* tapa *f;* VT encapuchar

hoodlum [húdləm] N maleante *mf,* gamberro -rra *mf*

hoof [hʊf] N casco *m,* pezuña *f;* VI **to — it** ir andando

hook [hʊk] N (for lifting) gancho *m,* garfio *m;* (for fishing) anzuelo *m;* **— and eye** alamar *m,* macho y hembra *m;* **by — or by crook** por las buenas o por las malas; **—up** conexión *f,* enganche *m;* VT (snag) enganchar; (a dress) abrochar; **to — up** conectar, enganchar

hooked [hʊkt] ADJ (shaped like a hook) ganchudo; (addicted) enganchado

hooky [húki] N **to play —** hacer novillos

hooligan [húlɪɡən] N *Sp* gamberro -rra *mf, Am* patotero -ra *mf*

hoop [hup] N (also in basketball) aro *m*

hoot [hut] VI/VT (of owl) ulular; (in derision) abuchear; N (of an owl) ululato *m;* (cry of derision) abucheo *m;* **I don't give a —** no me importa un comino; **it's a —** es para morirse de risa

hop [hɑp] VI saltar, brincar; **to — on** subirse a montar; N (short jump) saltito *m,* brinco *m;* (dance) bailongo *m;* **—s** lúpulo *m*

hope [hop] N esperanza *f;* VI/VT esperar; **to — for** esperar; **to — against —** esperar lo imposible

hopeful [hópfəl] ADJ (having hopes) esperanzado; (giving hopes) esperanzador, alentador

hopefully [hópfəli] ADV **— she'll come** ojalá [que] venga

hopeless [hóplɪs] ADJ (without hope) desesperanzado; (with no solution) irremediable; (unattainable) inalcanzable; **— cause** causa perdida *f;* **it is —** no tiene remedio; **the new secretary is — with numbers** el nuevo secretario es un desastre con los números

hopelessness [hóplɪsnɪs] N desesperanza *f*

horde [hɔrd] N (of people) horda *f;* (of animals) plaga *f*

horizon [həráɪzən] N horizonte *m*

horizontal [hɔrɪzántl] ADJ horizontal

hormone [hórmon] N hormona *f;* **— therapy** terapia hormonal *f*

horn [hɔrn] N (of an animal, substance) cuerno *m,* asta *f;* (of an automobile) bocina *f,* claxon *m;* (musical) corno *m,* trompa *f;* **— of plenty** cuerno de la abundancia *m;* **to toot one's own —** darse autobombo; VI **to — in**

entrometerse

hornet [hórnɪt] N avispón *m;* **—'s nest** avispero *m*

horny [hórni] ADJ calloso

horoscope [hórəskop] N horóscopo *m*

horrendous [həréndəs] ADJ horrendo

horrible [hórəbəl] ADJ horrible

horrid [hórɪd] ADJ horrendo

horrify [hórəfaɪ] VT horrorizar

horror [hórə] N horror *m*

hors d'oeuvre [ɔrdɹ́v] N entremés *m*

horse [hɔrs] N caballo *m;* **—back** lomo de caballo *m;* **to ride —back** montar a caballo, cabalgar; **—fly** tábano *m;* **—laugh** carcajada *f;* **—man** jinete *m;* **—manship** equitación *f;* **—play** payasadas *f pl;* **—power** caballo de fuerza *m;* **— race** carrera de caballos *f;* **—radish** rábano picante *m;* **— sense** sentido común *m;* **—shoe** herradura *f;* **hold your —s!** ¡para el carro! VI **to — around** payasear

horticulture [hórtɪkʌltʃə] N horticultura *f*

hose [hoz] N (for legs) medias *f pl;* (for liquids) manguera *f,* manga *f*

hosiery [hóʒəri] N (stockings) medias *f pl;* (shop for stockings) calcetería *f*

hospice [háspɪs] N (inn) hospicio *m;* (hospital) hospital para enfermos terminales *m*

hospitable [haspídəbəl] ADJ hospitalario, acogedor

hospital [háspɪdl] N hospital *m*

hospitality [haspɪtǽlɪdi] N hospitalidad *f*

hospitalize [háspɪdlaɪz] VT internar

host [host] N (also computer) anfitrión *m;* (in a home or hotel, for a parasite) huésped *m;* (on television) presentador -ora *mf;* (army) hueste *f;* (multitude) multitud *f,* cúmulo *m;* (wafer) hostia *f*

hostage [hástɪdʒ] N rehén *mf*

hostel [hástl] N hostal *m*

hostelry [hástlri] N hostería *f*

hostess [hóstɪs] N anfitriona *f*

hostile [hástl] ADJ hostil; **— takeover** compra hostil *f*

hostility [hastílɪDi] N hostilidad *f*

hot [hat] ADJ (at high temperature) caliente; (sweltering) caluroso; (spicy) picante; (sexy) bueno; (stolen) robado; (recent) de último momento; (popular) popular; **— and heavy** apasionado, apasionadamente; **—bed** semillero *m;* **— dog** perro caliente *m;* **—headed** impetuoso, exaltado; **—house** invernadero *m;* **— potato** patata caliente *f;* **— seat** situación embarazosa *f;* **—shot** estrella *f;* **—tub** jacuzzi *m;* **it is — today** hace calor hoy; **— under the collar** enojado; VT **to —wire** hacerle un puente a

hotel [hotɫ́] N hotel *m;* **—keeper** hotelero -ra *mf*

hound [haʊnd] N perro de caza *m,* sabueso *m;* VT

acosar, perseguir

hour [auɾ] N hora *f*; — **hand** horario *m*; **his finest** — su mejor momento *m*

hourly [áurli] ADV (on the hour) cada hora; (by the hour) por horas; — **wages** salario por hora *m*

house[1] [haus] N (residence) casa *f*; (legislature) cámara legislativa *f*; — **arrest** detención domiciliaria *f*; —**boat** casa flotante *f*; —**cleaning** limpieza de la casa *f*; —**hold** casa *f*, familia *f*; —**keeper** (in a house) ama de llaves *f*; (in a home) encargado -da de limpieza *mf*; —**keeping** mantenimiento del hogar *m*; —**top** techo *m*, tejado *m*; —**wife** ama de casa *f*; —**work** trabajo de casa *m*, quehaceres domésticos *m pl*; **in-** — interno; **on the** — la casa paga; **to keep** — cuidar la casa; —**hold expenses** gastos del hogar *m pl*; —-**to-** — puerta a puerta

house[2] [haus] VI/VT alojar

housing [háuzɪŋ] N (place to live) vivienda *f*; (protective covering) caja *f*

hovel [hávəł] N (hut) choza *f*, cabaña *f*, tugurio *m*; (open shed) cobertizo *m*

hover [hávə-] VI (bird) cernerse; (hang in air) estar suspendido; (linger) rondar; —**craft** aerodeslizador *m*

how [hau] ADV cómo; — **about your mom?** ¿y tu mamá? — **beautiful!** ¡qué hermoso! — **come?** ¿por qué? — **early [late, soon]?** ¿cuándo? ¿a qué hora? — **far is it?** ¿a qué distancia está? ¿cuánto dista de aquí? — **long?** ¿cuánto tiempo? — **many?** ¿cuántos? — **much is it?** ¿cuánto vale? — **old are you?** ¿cuántos años tienes? **no matter** — **much it rains** por mucho que llueva; **he knows** — **difficult it is** él sabe lo difícil que es

however [hauévə-] CONJ sin embargo, no obstante; ADV — **you want it** como quieras; — **difficult it may be** por muy difícil que sea; — **much it rains** por mucho que llueva

howl [hauł] VI aullar; (wind) ulular; (with laughter) reír a carcajadas; N aullido *m*, alarido *m*

HQ [headquarters] [étʃkjú] N oficina central *f*, sede central *f*

HR [human resources] [etʃár] N recursos humanos *m pl*

HTML [HyperText Markup Language] [etʃtiéméł] N HTML *m*

hub [hʌb] N (center of wheel) cubo *m*; (center of activity) núcleo *m*; —**cap** tapacubos *m sg*

hubbub [hábʌb] N alboroto *m*, barullo *m*

huckster [hákstə-] N (peddler) vendedor ambulante *m*; (promoter) mercachifle *m*

huddle [hádł] VI/VT (form a group) apiñar[se]; (curl up) acurrucar[se]; (consult) conferenciar; N tropel *m*; (group meeting for

consultation) reunión *f*; **to be in a** — estar agrupados; **to get in a** — agruparse

hue [hju] N matiz *m*

huff [hʌf] N **to get into a** — enojarse; VI **to** — **and puff** resoplar

hug [hʌg] VI/VT abrazar[se]; **to** — **the coast** costear; N abrazo *m*

huge [hjudʒ] ADJ enorme, fiero

hull [hʌl] N (of a ship, airplane) casco *m*; (of beans, peas) vaina *f*; (of fruits, nuts) cáscara *f*; VT (beans, peas) desvainar; (nuts) cascar

hum [hʌm] VI/VT (person) tararear; (insect, machine) zumbar; (place of activity) hervir; **to** — **to sleep** arrullar; N (of voice) tarareo *m*; (of insect, machine) zumbido *m*

human [hjúmən] ADJ & N humano *m*; — **being** ser humano *m*; — **immunodeficiency virus** virus de inmunodeficiencia humana *m*

humane [hjumén] ADJ humano, humanitario

humanism [hjúmənɪzəm] N humanismo *m*

humanitarian [hjumænɪtériən] ADJ humanitario

humanity [hjumænɪDi] N humanidad *f*; **humanities** humanidades *f pl*

humble [hámbəł] ADJ humilde; VT humillar

humid [hjúmɪd] ADJ húmedo

humidify [hjumíɾəfaɪ] VT humidificar

humidity [hjumíDɪDi] N humedad *f*

humiliate [hjumíliet] VT humillar, vejar

humiliation [hjumɪliéʃən] N humillación *f*

humility [hjumíłɪDi] N humildad *f*

hummingbird [hámɪŋbə-d] N colibrí *m*

humor [hjúmə-] N humor *m*, humorismo *m*; **out of** — de mal humor, malhumorado; VT complacer a

humorous [hjúmə-əs] ADJ gracioso, chistoso

hump [hʌmp] N joroba *f*, giba *f*, corcova *f*; **we're over the** — ya pasamos lo peor; —**back** jorobado -da *mf*; —**back whale** ballena jorobada *f*, yubarta *f*

hunch [hʌntʃ] N presentimiento *m*, corazonada *f*; —**back** (person) jorobado -da *mf*; (hump) corcova *f*; VI encorvar

hundred [hándrid] NUM cien[to]; **a** — **people** cien personas; **a** — **and fifty people** ciento cincuenta personas; N cien/ciento *m*; —**s** centenares *m pl*, cientos *m pl*

hundredth [hándrɪdθ] ADJ centésimo

hung [hʌŋ] *see* hang 'ahorcar'

Hungarian [hʌŋgériən] ADJ & N húngaro -ra *mf*

Hungary [hángəri] N Hungría *f*

hunger [hángə-] N hambre *f*; VI pasar hambre; **to** — **for** ansiar, anhelar

hungry [hángri] ADJ hambriento; **to be** — tener hambre; **to go** — pasar hambre

hunk [hʌŋk] N pedazo *m*, cacho *m*; **he's a real** — es un cacho de hombre, es un papacito

hunt [hʌnt] VI/VT (seek prey) cazar; **to** — **down** dar caza a; **to** — **for** buscar; N (activity of hunting) caza *f*; (instance of hunting) cacería *f*; (search) búsqueda *f*

hunter [hántə·] N (who captures game) cazador -ora *mf*; (seeker) buscador -ora *mf*; (dog) perro de caza *m*

hunting [hántɪŋ] N caza *f*; — **knife** cuchillo de caza *m*

huntsman [hántsmən] N cazador *m*

hurdle [hɜ́dl] N (impediment) obstáculo *m*; (in races) valla *f*; VT saltar

hurl [hɜ·l] VI/VT arrojar, lanzar, precipitar

hurrah [həráĵ] INTERJ ¡hurra!

hurricane [hɜ́ɪkən] N huracán *m*

hurried [hɜ́id] ADJ apresurado; *Am* apurado

hurry [hɜ́i] VI darse prisa, apresurarse; **to — in [out]** entrar [salir] de prisa; **to — up** apresurar[se], dar[se] prisa; *Am* apurar[se]; VT apresurar; *Am* apurar; N prisa *f*; *Am* apuro *m*; **to be in a —** tener prisa; *Am* estar apurado

hurt [hɜ·t] VI/VT (to injure) lastimar[se], hacer[se] daño; (damage) dañar[se]; (harm) perjudicar[se]; **to — someone's feelings** lastimar/herir a alguien; VI (suffer pain) doler; **my tooth —s** me duele la muela / el diente; N (damage) daño *m*; (wound) herida *f*, lastimadura *f*; ADJ (physically) lastimado, herido; (emotionally) herido; **to get —** lastimarse

hurtful [hɜ́tfəl] ADJ hiriente

husband [házbənd] N marido *m*, esposo *m*; VT administrar

hush [hʌʃ] VI/VT aquietar[se], callar[se]; —! ¡chitón! ¡silencio! **to — up a scandal** encubrir un escándalo; N silencio *m*; **he gave her — money** compró su silencio

husk [hʌsk] N (shell) cáscara *f*; (pod) vaina *f*; (of corn) *Am* chala *f*; *Sp* farfolla *f*; VT (corn) quitar la chala/farfolla a; (beans, peas) desvainar

husky [háski] ADJ (build) ronco; (strong) recio; N (breed of dog) husky *m*, perro esquimal *m*

hustle [hásəl] VI (work energetically) afanarse; (swindle) estafar; VT (hurry along) empujar; N (bustle) ajetreo *m*; (scheme) timo *m*; — **and bustle** ajetreo *m*, trajín *f*

hut [hʌt] N choza *f*, cabaña *f*

hyacinth [háɪəsɪnθ] N jacinto *m*

hybrid [háɪbrɪd] ADJ híbrido

hybridization [haɪbrɪdɪzéʃən] N hibridación *f*

hydrate [háɪdret] N hidrato *m*; VI/VT hidratar[se]

hydraulic [haɪdrɔ́lɪk] ADJ hidráulico

hydrocarbon [háɪdrəkarbən] N hidrocarburo *m*

hydroelectric [haɪdroɪléktrɪk] ADJ hidroeléctrico

hydrogen [háɪdrədʒən] N hidrógeno *m*; — **bomb** bomba de hidrógeno *f*; — **peroxide** peróxido de hidrógeno *m*, agua oxigenada *f*

hydrophobia [haɪdrəfóbiə] N hidrofobia *f*

hydroplane [háɪdrəplen] N hidroavión *m*

hyena [haɪínə] N hiena *f*

hygiene [háɪdʒin] N higiene *f*

hygienic [haɪdʒénɪk] ADJ higiénico

hygienist [haɪdʒínɪst] N higienista *mf*

hymen [háɪmən] N himen *m*

hymn [hɪm] N himno *m*

hype [háɪp] N exageración *f*; VT promocionar [exageradamente]

hyper [háɪpə·] ADJ hiperactivo

hyperactive [haɪpəæktɪv] ADJ hiperactivo

hyperbaric chamber [haɪpə·bǽrɪk tʃémbə·] N cámara hiperbárica *f*

hyperdocument [haɪpə·dákjəmənt] N hiperdocumento *m*

hyperlink [háɪpə·lɪŋk] N hiperenlace *m*, hipervínculo *m*

hypermedia [haɪpə·mídiə] N hipermedia *m*

hypersensitive [haɪpə·sénsɪtɪv] ADJ hipersensible

hypertension [haɪpə·ténʃən] N hipertensión *f*, presión arterial alta *f*

hyperventilate [haɪpə·véntlet] VI hiperventilar

hyphen [háɪfən] N guión *m*

hypnosis [hɪpnósɪs] N hipnosis *f*

hypnotherapy [hɪpnoθérəpi] N hipnoterapia *f*

hypnotize [hípnətaɪz] VT hipnotizar

hypoallergenic [haɪpoæləʤénɪk] ADJ hipoalérgico

hypochondriac [haɪpokándriæk] N hipocondríaco *mf*, hipocondriaco *mf*

hypocrisy [hɪpákrɪsi] N hipocresía *f*

hypocrite [hípəkrɪt] N hipócrita *mf*

hypocritical [hɪpəkrídɪkəl] ADJ hipócrita, doblado

hypodermic needle [haɪpədɜ́·mɪk nídl] N aguja hipodérmica *f*

hypoglycemia [haɪpoglaɪsímiə] N hipoglucemia *f*

hypothesis [haɪpáθɪsɪs] N hipótesis *f*

hypothyroidism [haɪpoθáɪrɔɪdɪzəm] N hipotiroidismo *m*

hysterectomy [hɪstəréktəmi] N histerectomía *f*

hysterical [hɪstérɪkəl] ADJ (out of control) histérico; (funny) desternillante

Ii

I [aɪ] PRON yo

I-beam [áɪbim] N viga doble *f*

Iberian [aɪbíriən] ADJ ibérico

Ibero-American [aɪbiroəmérɪkən] ADJ iberoamericano -na

ibuprofen [aɪbjuprófɪn] N ibuprofeno *m*

ice [aɪs] N hielo *m*; — **age** periodo glaciar *m*; —**berg** iceberg *m*; —**box** nevera *f*;

refrigerador *m*; — **cream** helado *m*; —
cream cone cucurucho de helado *m*; —-
cream parlor heladería *f*; — **hockey**
hockey sobre hielo *m*; — **skates** patines de
cuchilla *m pl*; — **water** agua helada *f*; **to
break the** — romper el hielo; **on** — en
suspenso; VI/VT (freeze) helar[se]; (cover with
ice) cubrir[se] de hielo; VT (cover with icing)
bañar; (insure a deal) cerrar; **to** —**-skate**
patinar sobre hielo; —**d tea** té helado *m*

Iceland [áɪslənd] N Islandia *f*

Icelander [áɪsləndə-] N islandés -esa *mf*

Icelandic [aɪslǽndɪk] ADJ islandés

icicle [áɪsɪkəɬ] N carámbano *m*

icing [áɪsɪŋ] N (frosting) baño *m*; (formation of
ice) formación de hielo *f*

icon [áɪkɑn] N icono *m*, ícono *m* (also computer
term)

ICU [intensive care unit] [áɪsíjú] N unidad de
cuidados intensivos *f*

icy [áɪsɪ] ADJ helado

ID [identification card] [áɪdí] N tarjeta de
identidad *m*

idea [aɪdíə] N idea *f*

ideal [aɪdíəɬ] N ideal *m*; ADJ ideal, idóneo

idealism [aɪdíəlɪzəm] N idealismo *m*

idealist [aɪdíəlɪst] N idealista *mf*

idealistic [aɪdɪəlístɪk] ADJ idealista

identical [aɪdéntɪkəɬ] ADJ idéntico; — **twins**
gemelos *m pl*, gemelas *f pl*

identification [aɪdɛntəfɪkéʃən] N identificación
f; — **card** tarjeta de identidad *m*, cédula de
identidad *f*

identify [aɪdéntəfaɪ] VI/VT identificar[se]

identity [aɪdéntɪɖi] N identidad *f*; — **theft** robo
de identidad *m*

ideological [aɪdɪəládʒɪkəɬ] ADJ ideológico

ideology [aɪdɪálədʒɪ] N ideología *f*

idiocy [ídɪəsɪ] N idiotez *f*

idiom [ídɪəm] N modismo *m*

idiosyncrasy [ɪdɪosínkrəsɪ] N idiosincrasia *f*

idiot [ídɪət] N idiota *mf*

idiotic [ɪdɪádɪk] ADJ idiota

idle [áɪdɬ] ADJ (not active) ocioso; (lazy) perezoso,
holgazán; (of a machine, worker) parado; (of
an engine) en ralentí; (meaningless) vacío; VI
(person) holgazanear; (motor) girar en vacío;
VT (cause to be idle) dejar parado/desocupado

idleness [áɪdɬnɪs] N (inactivity) ociosidad *f*, ocio
m, holganza *f*; (sloth) pereza *f*

idler [áɪdlə-] N holgazán -ana *mf*, zanguango -ga
mf

idol [áɪdɬ] N ídolo *m*

idolatry [aɪdálətrɪ] N idolatría *f*

idolize [áɪdlaɪz] VT idolatrar

idyll [áɪdɬ] N idilio *m*

if [ɪf] CONJ si; — **I were you** en tu lugar / yo que
tú; — **only I had known** de haber sabido /
ojalá hubiera sabido; **he's tall,** — **a bit**

stooped es alto, aunque un poco encorvado;
N —**s** condiciones *f pl*; **no** —**s, ands, or buts**
no hay pero que valga

igloo [íglu] N iglú *m*

ignite [ɪgnáɪt] VI/VT encender[se], prender fuego
[a]

ignition [ɪgníʃən] N ignición *f*, encendido *m*; —
switch llave de contacto *f*

ignoble [ɪgnóbəɬ] ADJ innoble

ignorance [ígnərəns] N ignorancia *f*

ignorant [ígnərənt] ADJ ignorante

ignore [ɪgnór] VT ignorar

ilk [ɪɬk] N ralea *f*, calaña *f*

ill [ɪɬ] ADJ enfermo, malo; — **fortune** mala
suerte *f*; — **nature** mal genio *m*, mala índole
f; — **repute** mala fama *f*; — **will** mala
voluntad *f*; N (sickness) enfermedad *f*;
(calamity) calamidad *f*; ADJ —**-advised**
imprudente; — **at ease** incómodo; —**-bred**
maleducado; —**-fated** fatídico, funesto,
desastrado; —**-gotten** mal adquirido; —**-
humored** malhumorado; —**-mannered**
maleducado, grosero; —**-natured** de mal
genio; ADV **we can** — **afford to stop now**
no podemos darnos el lujo de detenernos
ahora

illegal [ɪlígəɬ] ADJ ilegal

illegitimate [ɪlɪdʒídəmɪt] ADJ ilegítimo

illicit [ɪlísɪt] ADJ ilícito

illiteracy [ɪlídərəsɪ] N analfabetismo *m*

illiterate [ɪlídərɪt] ADJ & N analfabeto -ta *mf*

illness [ɪ́lnɪs] N enfermedad *f*

illuminate [ɪlúmənət] VI/VT iluminar[se]

illumination [ɪlumənéʃən] N iluminación *f*

illusion [ɪlúʒən] N ilusión *f*

illusory [ɪlúʒərɪ] ADJ ilusorio

illustrate [íləstret] VI/VT ilustrar

illustration [ɪləstréʃən] N ilustración *f*, estampa *f*

illustrator [íləstredə-] N ilustrador -ra *mf*,
dibujante *mf*

illustrious [ɪlʌ́strɪəs] ADJ ilustre, eximio

image [ímɪdʒ] N imagen *f*

imagery [ímɪdʒri] N conjunto de imágenes *m*

imaginary [ɪmǽdʒəneri] ADJ imaginario,
fabuloso

imagination [ɪmædʒənéʃən] N imaginación *f*,
fantasía *f*

imaginative [ɪmǽdʒənədɪv] ADJ imaginativo,
fantasioso

imagine [ɪmǽdʒɪn] VI/VT imaginar[se]; — **that!**
¡figúrate!

imbalance [ɪmbǽləns] N desequilibrio *m*

imbecile [ímbəsəɬ] N imbécil *mf*

imbibe [ɪmbáɪb] VI/VT beber

imbue [ɪmbjú] VT imbuir, infundir

IMF [International Monetary Fund] [áɪémɛ́f]
N FMI *m*

imitate [ímɪtet] VT imitar

imitation [ɪmɪtéʃən] N imitación *f*; — **leather**

imitación de cuero *f*

imitator [ímɪtedə·] N imitador -ora *mf*

immaculate [ɪmǽkjəlɪt] ADJ inmaculado

immaterial [ɪmətíriəł] ADJ inmaterial; **it is —
to me** me es indiferente

immature [ɪmətʃúr] ADJ inmaduro

immediate [ɪmídiɪt] ADJ inmediato

immediately [ɪmídiɪtli] ADV inmediatamente,
enseguida

immense [ɪméns] ADJ inmenso

immensity [ɪménsɪDi] N inmensidad *f*

immerse [ɪmɔ́·s] VT (submerge) sumergir;
(absorb) sumir

immersed [ɪmɔ́·st] ADJ inmerso

immigrant [ímɪgrənt] ADJ & N inmigrante *mf*

immigrate [ímɪgret] VI inmigrar

immigration [ɪmɪgréʃən] N inmigración *f*

imminent [ímənənt] ADJ inminente

immobile [ɪmóbəł] ADJ inmóvil

immobilize [ɪmóbəlaɪz] VT inmovilizar

immodest [ɪmádɪst] ADJ inmodesto

immodesty [ɪmádɪsti] N inmodestia *f*

immoral [ɪmɔ́rəł] ADJ inmoral

immorality [ɪmɔrǽlɪDi] N inmoralidad *f*

immortal [ɪmɔ́rdl] ADJ & N inmortal *mf*

immortality [ɪmɔrtǽlɪDi] N inmortalidad *f*

immovable [ɪmúvəbəł] ADJ inamovible

immune [ɪmjun] ADJ inmune; — **system**
sistema inmune *m*

immunity [ɪmjúnɪDi] N inmunidad *f*

immunodeficiency [ɪmjənodɪfíʃənsi] N
inmunodeficiencia *f*

immutable [ɪmjúDəbəł] ADJ inmutable

impact [ímpækt] N impacto *m*; VI/VT repercutir
[sobre]; **—ed molar** muela impactada *f*

impair [ɪmpér] VT dañar, deteriorar,
menoscabar; **—ed** con las facultades
disminuidas

impairment [ɪmpérmənt] N daño *m*, deterioro
m, menoscabo *m*

impala [ɪmpálə] N impala *m*

impale [ɪmpéł] VT empalar

impart [ɪmpárt] VT (bestow knowledge)
impartir; (reveal) revelar

impartial [ɪmpárʃəł] ADJ imparcial

impartiality [ɪmparʃíælɪDi] N imparcialidad *f*

impasse [ímpæs] N impasse *m*

impassioned [ɪmpǽʃənd] ADJ apasionado

impassive [ɪmpǽsɪv] ADJ impasible

impatience [ɪmpéʃəns] N impaciencia *f*

impatient [ɪmpéʃənt] ADJ impaciente

impeach [ɪmpítʃ] VT acusar formalmente; **to —
a person's honor** poner en tela de juicio el
honor de uno

impeachment [ɪmpítʃmənt] N impeachment *m*

impede [ɪmpíd] VT obstaculizar, estorbar, trabar

impediment [ɪmpéDəmənt] N impedimento *m*,
obstáculo *m*; (of speech) defecto *m*

impel [ɪmpéł] VT impeler

impending [ɪmpéndɪŋ] ADJ inminente

impenetrable [ɪmpénɪtrəbəł] ADJ impenetrable

imperative [ɪmpérəDɪv] ADJ (like a command)
imperativo; (necessary) imperioso; N
(command, grammatical mood) imperativo
m; (obligation) obligación *f*

imperceptible [ɪmpə·séptəbəł] ADJ
imperceptible

imperfect [ɪmpɔ́·fɪkt] ADJ & N imperfecto *m*

imperial [ɪmpíriəł] ADJ imperial

imperialism [ɪmpíriəlɪzəm] N imperialismo *m*

imperil [ɪmpérəł] VT poner en peligro

imperious [ɪmpíriəs] ADJ imperioso

impersonal [ɪmpɔ́·sən̩l] ADJ impersonal

impersonate [ɪmpɔ́·sənet] VT (assume traits of)
hacerse pasar por; (mimic) imitar

impersonator [ɪmpɔ́·sənedə·] N imitador -ora
mf

impertinence [ɪmpɔ́·tn̩əns] N impertinencia *f*

impertinent [ɪmpɔ́·tn̩ənt] ADJ impertinente

impervious [ɪmpɔ́·viəs] ADJ impermeable; (to
reason) refractario

impetigo [ɪmpɪtáigo] N impétigo *m*

impetuous [ɪmpétʃuəs] ADJ impetuoso

impetus [ímpəDəs] N ímpetu *m*, empuje *m*

impious [ímpiəs] ADJ impío

implacable [ɪmplǽkəbəł] ADJ implacable

implant¹ [ɪmplǽnt] VT implantar

implant² [ímplænt] N implante *m*

implantation [ɪmplæntéʃən] N implantación *f*

implement¹ [ímpləmənt] N implemento *m*,
utensilio *m*

implement² [ímpləmɛnt] VT implementar,
instrumentar

implementation [ɪmpləmɪntéʃən] N
implementación *f*

implicate [ímplɪket] VT implicar, involucrar

implication [ɪmplɪkéʃən] N implicación *f*; **by —**
implícitamente

implicit [ɪmplísɪt] ADJ implícito

implore [ɪmplɔ́r] VI/VT implorar

imply [ɪmpláɪ] VT dar a entender

impolite [ɪmpəláɪt] ADJ descortés

import¹ [ɪmpɔ́rt] VT (bring in) importar

import² [ímpɔrt] N (act of importing, thing
imported) importación *f*; (significance)
significado *m*; **—export company**
compañía de importación y exportación *f*

importance [ɪmpɔ́rtn̩s] N importancia *f*,
relevancia *f*

important [ɪmpɔ́rtn̩t] ADJ importante,
relevante

impose [ɪmpóz] VT imponer; **to — [upon]**
abusar [de]

imposing [ɪmpózɪŋ] ADJ imponente,
impresionante

imposition [ɪmpəzíʃən] N (act of imposing,
burden) imposición *f*; (abuse) abuso *m*

impossibility [ɪmpasəbílɪDi] N imposibilidad *f*

impossible [ɪmpásəbəl] ADJ (not possible) imposible; (unbearable) insoportable; **to make** — imposibilitar

impostor [ɪmpástə] N impostor -ora *mf*

impotence [ímpətəns] N impotencia *f*

impotent [ímpətənt] ADJ impotente

impoverish [ɪmpávə·ɪʃ] VT empobrecer

impregnate [ɪmprégnet] VT (cause to be permeated) impregnar; (make pregnant) fecundar, preñar

impress [ɪmprés] VT (make a mark by pressing) estampar; VI/VT (affect deeply) impresionar

impression [ɪmpréʃən] N impresión *f*; (feeling) impresión *f*, sensación *f*

impressive [ɪmprésɪv] ADJ impresionante

imprint¹ [ímprɪnt] N (indentation) impresión *f*, marca *f*; (printer's mark) pie de imprenta *m*

imprint² [ɪmprínt] VT (impress on) imprimir; (fix firmly in mind) grabar

imprison [ɪmprízən] VT (in jail) encarcelar; (anywhere) apresar

imprisonment [ɪmprízənmənt] N encarcelamiento *m*

improbable [ɪmprábəbəl] ADJ improbable

impromptu [ɪmprámptu] ADJ improvisado; **he gave the speech** — improvisó el discurso; N impromptu *m*

improper [ɪmprápə·] ADJ indecoroso, inconveniente

improve [ɪmprúv] VI/VT mejorar[se]; **to — upon** mejorar

improvement [ɪmprúvmənt] N (of a plan) mejora *f*; (in health) mejoría *f*

improvisation [ɪmpravɪzéʃən] N improvisación *f*

improvise [ímprəvaɪz] VI/VT improvisar

imprudent [ɪmprúdņt] ADJ imprudente, desatinado

impudence [ímpjədəns] N impertinencia *f*, descaro *m*, desparpajo *m*

impudent [ímpjədənt] ADJ impertinente, descarado

impulse [ímpʌls] N impulso *m*; **to act on —** obrar impulsivamente

impulsive [ɪmpʌ́lsɪv] ADJ impulsivo

impunity [ɪmpjúnɪDi] N impunidad *f*

impure [ɪmpjúr] ADJ impuro

impurity [ɪmpjúrɪDi] N impureza *f*

in [ɪn] PREP en; (in tennis) buena, dentro; — **London** en Londres; — **haste** de prisa; — **the morning** por/en la mañana; — **writing** por escrito; **she was walking** — **the street** andaba por la calle; **to arrive** — **London** llegar a Londres; **the books** — **the box** los libros de la caja; **at two** — **the morning** a las dos de la mañana; **dressed** — **white** vestido de blanco; **the tallest** — **his class** el más alto de su clase; **to come** — **a week** venir dentro de una semana; ADV adentro, dentro; **is she** — **or out?** ¿está adentro o

afuera? **to be all** — estar rendido; **to be — with someone** estar bien con alguien; **to come** — entrar; **to have it** — **for someone** tenerle ojeriza a una persona; **to put** — meter; **the doctor is** — el doctor está; **hats are** — los sombreros están de moda; — **field** cuadro interior *m*; N — **patient** paciente internado -da *mf*; — **patient care** internación *f*; — **seam** entrepierna *f*; — **step** empeine *m*; ADJ **the** — **place to eat** el restaurante de moda; **an** — **joke** una broma para un grupo selecto

inability [ɪnəbílɪDi] N inhabilidad *f*, incapacidad *f*

inaccessible [ɪnæksésəbəl] ADJ inaccesible, inasequible

inaccurate [ɪnǽkjə·ɪt] ADJ (not precise) inexacto, impreciso; (wrong) incorrecto

inactive [ɪnǽktɪv] ADJ inactivo

inactivity [ɪnæktívɪDi] N inactividad *f*

inadequate [ɪnǽDɪkwɪt] ADJ (insufficient) insuficiente; (unacceptable) inaceptable

inadmissible [ɪnədmísəbəl] ADJ inadmisible

inadvertent [ɪnədvɝ́tņt] ADJ (unintentional) involuntario; (careless) descuidado, negligente

inadvisable [ɪnədváɪzəbəl] ADJ desaconsejable

inane [ɪnén] ADJ necio

inanimate [ɪnǽnəmɪt] ADJ inanimado

inasmuch as [ɪnəzmátʃæz] CONJ puesto que

inattentive [ɪnəténtɪv] ADJ desatento

inaudible [ɪnɔ́Dəbəl] ADJ inaudible

inaugurate [ɪnɔ́gjəret] VT (initiate) inaugurar; (induct into office) investir de un cargo

inauguration [ɪnɔgjəréʃən] N (initiation) inauguración *f*; (induction) investidura *f*

inboard [ínbɔrd] ADJ dentro del casco

inborn [ínbɔ́rn] ADJ innato

Inca [íŋkə] ADJ & N inca *mf*

incandescence [ɪŋkændésəns] N incandescencia *f*

incandescent [ɪŋkændésənt] ADJ incandescente

incantation [ɪŋkæntéʃən] N conjuro *m*

incapable [ɪnképəbəl] ADJ incapaz

incapacitate [ɪnkəpǽsɪtet] VT incapacitar

incarcerate [ɪnkársəret] VT encarcelar

incarnation [ɪnkarnéʃən] N encarnación *f*

incendiary [ɪnséndɪeri] ADJ & N incendiario -ria *mf*; — **bomb** bomba incendiaria *f*

incense¹ [ínsɛns] N incienso *m*

incense² [ínsɛns] VT encolerizar

incentive [ɪnséntɪv] N incentivo *m*, acicate *m*

inception [ɪnsépʃən] N comienzo *m*

incessant [ɪnsésənt] ADJ incesante

incest [ínsɛst] N incesto *m*

incestuous [ɪnséstʃuəs] ADJ incestuoso

inch [ɪntʃ] N pulgada [2.54 centímetros] *f*; **to be within an** — **of** estar a un punto de; VI avanzar poco a poco

incidence [ínsɪdəns] N incidencia f

incident [ínsɪdənt] N incidente m, lance m; (crime, accident) suceso m

incidental [ɪnsɪdéntl] ADJ (happening in accordance with) accesorio; — **music** música incidental f; N —**s** gastos menores m pl

incidentally [ɪnsɪdéntli] ADV a propósito

incinerate [ɪnsínərɛt] VT incinerar

incipient [ɪnsípiənt] ADJ incipiente, naciente

incision [ɪnsíʒən] N incisión f

incisive [ɪnsáɪsɪv] ADJ incisivo

incisor [ɪnsáɪzə-] N (tooth) incisivo m

incite [ɪnsáɪt] VT incitar

inclement [ɪnklémənt] ADJ inclemente

inclination [ɪnklənéʃən] N (slope) inclinación f; (tendency) afición f, inclinación f

incline[1] [ɪnkláɪn] VI/VT inclinar[se]

incline[2] [ɪnkláɪn] N declive m, pendiente f

include [ɪnklúd] VT incluir

including [ɪŋklúdɪŋ] ADJ **it costs a thousand dollars, not — air travel** cuesta mil dólares, sin incluir el vuelo; **that whole week, — Saturday** toda esa semana, incluyendo el sábado / el sábado inclusive; — **you, there are four of us** incluyéndote a ti, somos cuatro

inclusion [ɪŋklúʒən] N (acceptance) inclusión f; (addition) incorporación f

inclusive [ɪnklúsɪv] ADJ inclusivo; **from Monday to Friday** — de lunes a viernes inclusive

incoherent [ɪnkohírənt] ADJ incoherente

income [ínkʌm] N Sp renta f; Am ingreso m; — **tax** Sp impuesto sobre la renta m; Am impuesto sobre ingresos m; — **tax return** declaración de impuestos sobre la renta / los ingresos f

incoming [ínkʌmɪŋ] ADJ entrante

incomparable [ɪnkámpə-ə-bəl] ADJ incomparable, sin parangón

incompatible [ɪnkəmpǽDəbəl] ADJ incompatible

incompetent [ɪnkámpɪtənt] ADJ incompetente

incomplete [ɪnkəmplít] ADJ incompleto

incomprehensible [ɪnkamprɪhénsəbəl] ADJ incomprensible

inconceivable [ɪnkənsívəbəl] ADJ inconcebible

inconclusive [ɪnkənklúsɪv] ADJ no concluyente

inconsiderate [ɪnkənsíDə-ɪt] ADJ desconsiderado

inconsistency [ɪnkənsístənsi] N (condition) inconsecuencia f; (instance) incoherencia f

inconsistent [ɪnkənsístənt] ADJ inconsecuente

inconspicuous [ɪnkənspíkjuəs] ADJ poco llamativo; **to be** — pasar inadvertido

inconstancy [ɪnkánstənsi] N inconstancia f

inconstant [ɪnkánstənt] ADJ inconstante

incontinent [ɪnkántənənt] ADJ incontinente

incontrovertible [ɪnkɑntrəvə́-Dəbəl] ADJ incontrovertible

inconvenience [ɪnkənvínjəns] N (state of being inconvenient) inconveniencia f; (thing that is inconvenient) molestia f, inconveniente m; VT incomodar, molestar

inconvenient [ɪnkənvínjənt] ADJ (bothersome) incómodo; (untimely) inoportuno

incorporate [ɪnkɔ́rpərɛt] VI/VT (include) incorporar[se]; (form a corporation) constituir[se] en sociedad

incorporation [ɪŋkɔrpəréʃən] N (inclusion) incorporación f; (integration) integración f

incorrect [ɪnkərékt] ADJ incorrecto

incorrigible [ɪnkɔ́rɪdʒəbəl] ADJ incorregible

increase[1] [ɪnkrís] VI/VT aumentar[se], incrementar[se]

increase[2] [ínkris] N aumento m, incremento m

increasingly [ɪnkrísɪŋli] ADV cada vez más

incredible [ɪnkrédəbəl] ADJ increíble

incredulous [ɪnkrédʒələs] ADJ incrédulo

increment [ínkrəmənt] N incremento m

incriminate [ɪnkrímənɛt] VT incriminar

incubator [íŋkjəbeɪDə-] N incubadora f

inculcate [ɪnkʌ́lket] VT inculcar

incumbent [ɪnkʌ́mbənt] ADJ **a duty — upon me** un deber que me incumbe; N titular m

incur [ɪnkə́-] VT (an expense) incurrir en; (a debt) contraer

incurable [ɪŋkjúrəbəl] ADJ incurable

indebted [ɪndɛ́Dɪd] ADJ endeudado, en deuda

indebtedness [ɪndɛ́Dɪdnɪs] N endeudamiento m, adeudo m

indecency [ɪndísənsi] N indecencia f

indecent [ɪndísənt] ADJ indecente; — **exposure** delito de exhibicionismo m

indecision [ɪndɪsíʒən] N indecisión f

indeed [ɪndíd] ADV de verdad; INTERJ (ironically) ¡no me digas! (sincerely) ¡tienes razón! ¡efectivamente!

indefensible [ɪndɪfɛ́nsəbəl] ADJ indefendible

indefinite [ɪndɛ́fənɪt] ADJ indefinido

indelible [ɪndɛ́ləbəl] ADJ indeleble

indelicate [ɪndɛ́lɪkɪt] ADJ (tactless) indelicado; (offensive) indecoroso

indemnify [ɪndɛ́mnəfaɪ] VT indemnizar

indemnity [ɪndɛ́mnɪDi] N indemnización f

indent [ɪndɛ́nt] VI/VT sangrar

indentation [ɪndəntéʃən] N (notch) muesca f; (blank space) sangría f

independence [ɪndɪpɛ́ndəns] N independencia f

independent [ɪndɪpɛ́ndənt] ADJ independiente, autónomo

indestructible [ɪndɪstrʌ́ktəbəl] ADJ indestructible

indeterminate [ɪndɪtə́-mənɪt] ADJ indeterminado

index [índɛks] N índice m; — **card** ficha f; — **finger** índice m; VT (incorporate into an index) poner en el índice; (make the index)

poner/hacer un índice; (adjust wages) indexar
indexing [índɛksɪŋ] N indexación f
India [índiə] N India f
Indian [índiən] ADJ & N indio -a mf; — **Ocean** Océano Indico m
indicate [índɪkét] VT indicar
indication [ɪndɪkéʃən] N indicación f
indicative [ɪndíkəDɪv] ADJ & N indicativo m
indicator [índɪkèDə] N indicador m
indict [ɪndáɪt] VT acusar
indictment [ɪndáɪtmənt] N acusación f
indifference [ɪndífrəns] N indiferencia f
indifferent [ɪndífrənt] ADJ indiferente
indigenous [ɪndíʤənəs] ADJ (person) indígena; (plant, animal) autóctono
indigent [índɪʤənt] ADJ & N indigente mf
indigestion [ɪndɪʤéstʃən] N indigestión f
indignant [ɪndígnənt] ADJ indignado
indignation [ɪndɪgnéʃən] N indignación f
indignity [ɪndígnɪDi] N ultraje m, afrenta f
indigo [índɪgo] N índigo m, añil m; — **blue** azul añil m
indirect [ɪndɪrékt] ADJ indirecto; — **object** complemento/objeto indirecto m
indiscreet [ɪndɪskrít] ADJ indiscreto
indiscretion [ɪndɪskréʃən] N indiscreción f
indispensable [ɪndɪspénsəbəl] ADJ indispensable, imprescindible
indispose [ɪndɪspóz] VT indisponer
indisposed [ɪndɪspózd] ADJ indispuesto; **to become** — indisponerse
indistinct [ɪndɪstíŋkt] ADJ indistinto
individual [ɪndəvíʤuəl] ADJ individual; N individuo m, persona f; pej sujeto m, individuo m
individualism [ɪndəvíʤuəlɪzəm] N individualismo m
individualist [ɪndəvíʤuəlɪst] N individualista mf
individuality [ɪndəvɪʤuǽlɪDi] N individualidad f
indivisible [ɪndəvízəbəl] ADJ indivisible
indoctrinate [ɪndáktrɪnét] VT adoctrinar
indolence [índələns] N indolencia f, desidia f
indolent [índələnt] ADJ indolente, haragán
indomitable [ɪndámɪDəbəl] ADJ indomable
Indonesia [ɪndəníʒə] N Indonesia f
Indonesian [ɪndəníʒən] ADJ & N indonesio -sia mf
indoor [índɔr] ADJ interior
indoors [índɔrz] ADV dentro; **to go** — entrar, ir para adentro
induce [ɪndús] VT inducir
inducement [ɪndúsmənt] N aliciente m, incentivo m
induct [ɪndʌ́kt] VT (initiate) admitir, iniciar; (draft) reclutar
induction [ɪndʌ́kʃən] N (philosophical, electrical) inducción f; (into an organization)

admisión f, iniciación f
indulge [ɪndʌ́lʤ] VT mimar, consentir; VI **to** — **in** darse a, entregarse a; **to** — **oneself** [**in**] darse el gusto [de]
indulgence [ɪndʌ́lʤəns] N (act or state of indulging, religious) indulgencia f; (thing indulged in) exceso m, lujo m
indulgent [ɪndʌ́lʤənt] ADJ indulgente; (toward a child) complaciente
industrial [ɪndʌ́striəl] ADJ industrial
industrialist [ɪndʌ́striəlɪst] N industrial mf
industrialization [ɪndʌstriəlɪzéʃən] N industrialización f
industrious [ɪndʌ́striəs] ADJ (student) aplicado, diligente; (worker) industrioso
industry [índəstri] N (manufacturing) industria f; (hard work) diligencia f; — **standards** normas industriales f pl
inebriated [ɪníbrieDɪd] ADJ ebrio
inedible [ɪnédəbəl] ADJ incomestible, incomible
ineffable [ɪnéfəbəl] ADJ inefable
ineffective [ɪnɪféktɪv] ADJ ineficaz, ineficiente
ineffectual [ɪnɪféktʃuəl] ADJ ineficaz
inefficient [ɪnɪfíʃənt] ADJ ineficiente
ineligible [ɪnélɪʤəbəl] ADJ inelegible
inept [ɪnépt] ADJ inepto
inequality [ɪnɪkwálɪDi] N desigualdad f
inert [ɪnɜ́t] ADJ inerte
inertia [ɪnɜ́ʃə] N inercia f
inescapable [ɪnɪsképəbəl] ADJ inevitable, ineludible
inestimable [ɪnéstəməbəl] ADJ inestimable
inevitable [ɪnévɪDəbəl] ADJ inevitable
inexcusable [ɪnɪkskjúzəbəl] ADJ inexcusable
inexhaustible [ɪnɪgzɔ́stəbəl] ADJ inagotable
inexorable [ɪnéksəəbəl] ADJ inexorable
inexpensive [ɪnɪkspénsɪv] ADJ económico, barato
inexperienced [ɪnɪkspírɪənst] ADJ no experimentado, inexperto
inexplicable [ɪnɪksplíkəbəl] ADJ inexplicable
infallible [ɪnfǽləbəl] ADJ infalible
infamous [ínfəməs] ADJ infame, de mala fama
infamy [ínfəmi] N infamia f
infancy [ínfənsi] N primera infancia f
infant [ínfənt] N bebé mf
infantile [ínfəntaɪl] ADJ infantil
infantry [ínfəntri] N infantería f; —**man** infante m
infatuated [ɪnfǽtʃueDɪd] ADJ enamorado
infect [ɪnfékt] VT (cause disease) infectar; (spread a mood) contagiar
infection [ɪnfékʃən] N infección f
infectious [ɪnfékʃəs] ADJ (disease) infeccioso, contagioso; (mood) contagioso
infer [ɪnfɜ́] VT inferir, deducir
inference [ínfəəns] N inferencia f, deducción f
inferior [ɪnfíriə] ADJ inferior
inferiority [ɪnfiriórɪDi] N inferioridad f; —

complex complejo de inferioridad *m*
infernal [ɪnfɝ́nl] ADJ infernal
inferno [ɪnfɝ́no] N (fire) incendio *m*; (hot place) infierno *m*
infertility [ɪnfɚtíɫɪɾi] N infertilidad *f*
infest [ɪnfɛ́st] VT infestar, plagar
infestation [ɪnfɛstéʃən] N infestación *f*
infiltrate [ɪnfíɫtret] VI/VT infiltrar[se]; **to — an organization** infiltrarse en una organización
infinite [ínfənɪt] ADJ & N infinito *m*
infinitive [ɪnfínɪɾɪv] ADJ & N infinitivo *m*
infinity [ɪnfínɪɾi] N (large number) infinidad *f*; (space) infinito *m*
infirm [ɪnfɝ́m] ADJ enfermizo, achacoso
infirmary [ɪnfɝ́məri] N enfermería *f*
infirmity [ɪnfɝ́mɪɾi] N enfermedad *f*, achaque *m*
inflame [ɪnflém] VT (with infection) inflamar[se]; (with passion) enardecer[se]; (with fire) encender[se]
inflammation [ɪnfləméʃən] N inflamación *f*
inflate [ɪnflét] VI/VT (fill with air) inflar[se], hincharse; (exaggerate) exagerar
inflation [ɪnfléʃən] N (rise in prices) inflación *f*; (introduction of air) inflado *m*
inflexible [ɪnfléksəbəɫ] ADJ inflexible
inflict [ɪnflíkt] VT (impose on) infligir; **to — a blow** asestar un golpe
influence [ínfluəns] N influencia *f*, influjo *m*; VT influir en/sobre, incidir en; **— peddling** tráfico de influencias *m*
influential [ɪnfluénʃəɫ] ADJ influyente
influenza [ɪnfluénzə] N gripe *f*
influx [ínflʌks] N (of fluid, goods) entrada *f*; (of people) afluencia *f*
infomercial [ínfoməʃəɫ] N infomercial *m*, publirreportaje *m*
inform [ɪnfɝ́m] VI/VT (give knowledge) informar[se]; VT (inspire) inspirar; **to — against/on** delatar a, denunciar a
informal [ɪnfɝ́məɫ] ADJ informal
informant [ɪnfɝ́rmənt] N informante *mf*
information [ɪnfɚméʃən] N (news, data, details, act of informing) información *f*; (details) informes *m pl*; **— superhighway** autopista de la información *f*
informative [ɪnfɝ́məɾɪv] ADJ informativo
informer [ɪnfɝ́mɚ] N informante *mf*, delator -ora *mf*, *pej* soplón -ona *mf*
infotainment [ɪnfoténmənt] N entretenimiento informativo *m*
infraction [ɪnfrǽkʃən] N infracción *f*
infrared [ɪnfrəréd] ADJ & N infrarrojo *m*
infrastructure [ínfrəstrʌktʃɚ] N infraestructura *f*
infringe [ɪnfríndʒ] VT infringir; VI **to — upon** violar
infringement [ɪnfríndʒmənt] N infracción *f*, violación *f*

infuriate [ɪnfjúriet] VT enfurecer, sublevar
infuse [ɪnfjúz] VT infundir
ingenious [ɪndʒínjəs] ADJ ingenioso
ingenuity [ɪndʒənúɪɾi] N ingenio *m*, inventiva *f*
ingenuous [ɪndʒénjuəs] ADJ ingenuo *f*
ingenuousness [ɪndʒénjuəsnɪs] N ingenuidad *f*
ingest [ɪndʒɛ́st] VI/VT ingerir
ingrate [íngret] N ingrato -ta *mf*
ingratitude [ɪngrǽdɪtud] N ingratitud *f*
ingredient [ɪngrídiənt] N ingrediente *m*
ingrown [íngron] ADJ encarnado
inhabit [ɪnhǽbɪt] VT habitar
inhabitant [ɪnhǽbɪtənt] N habitante *mf*
inhale [ɪnhéɫ] VI/VT inhalar, aspirar
inherent [ɪnhérənt] ADJ inherente
inherit [ɪnhérɪt] VI/VT heredar
inheritance [ɪnhérɪɾəns] N herencia *f*; **— tax** impuesto a la herencia *m*
inherited [ɪnhérɪɾɪd] ADJ patrimonial
inhibit [ɪnhíbɪt] VT inhibir, cohibir
inhibiting [ɪnhíbɪɾɪŋ] ADJ inhibidor
inhibition [ɪnɪbíʃən] N inhibición *f*, cohibición *f*
inhibitor [ɪnhíbɪɾɚ] N inhibidor *m*
inhospitable [ɪnhɑspíɾəbət] ADJ (person) inhospitalario; (place) inhóspito
inhuman [ɪnhjúmən] ADJ inhumano
inimitable [ɪnímɪɾəbət] ADJ inimitable
initial [ɪníʃəɫ] ADJ & N inicial *f*; VT firmar las iniciales
initialize [ɪníʃəlaɪz] VT inicializar
initially [ɪníʃəli] ADV al comienzo, inicialmente
initiate [ɪníʃiet] VT iniciar
initiative [ɪníʃəɾɪv] N iniciativa *f*
inject [ɪndʒɛ́kt] VI/VT inyectar[se], pinchar[se]
injection [ɪndʒɛ́kʃən] N inyección *f*
injunction [ɪndʒʌ́ŋkʃən] N mandato judicial *m*, orden judicial *f*
injure [índʒɚ] VI/VT herir[se]; (sports) lesionar[se]
injurious [ɪndʒúriəs] ADJ (harmful) perjudicial; (defamatory) injurioso
injury [índʒəri] N herida *f*, lesión *f*; **— time** (soccer) descuento *m*
injustice [ɪndʒʌ́stɪs] N injusticia *f*
ink [ɪŋk] N tinta *f*; VT (mark with ink) entintar; (sign) firmar; **— cartridge** cartucho de tinta *m*; **—-jet printer** impresora de inyección de tinta *f*; **—pad** almohadilla *f*; **—well** tintero *m*
inkling [íŋklɪŋ] N idea *f*
inlaid [ínled] ADJ incrustado; **— work** incrustación *f*
inland [ínlənd] ADJ interior; ADV tierra adentro
inlay[1] [ínlé] VT incrustar
inlay[2] [ínle] N incrustación *f*
inmate [ínmet] N (in a prison) preso -sa *mf*, recluso -sa *mf*; (in an asylum) internado -da *mf*; (in a hospital) paciente *mf*
inn [ɪn] N posada *f*, fonda *f*; **—keeper** posadero -ra *mf*, fondista *mf*

innate [ínét] ADJ innato

inner [ínə-] ADJ (inside) interior; (intimate) íntimo; — **city** zona céntrica empobrecida f; — **ear** oído interno m; —**most** más recóndito; — **tube** cámara f

inning [ínɪŋ] N entrada f

innocence [ínəsəns] N (absence of guilt) inocencia f; (naiveté) candidez f, candor m

innocent [ínəsənt] ADJ & N inocente mf

innocuous [ínákjuəs] ADJ innocuo, inocuo

innovate [ínəvet] VI innovar

innovating [ínəveDɪŋ] ADJ innovador, renovador

innovation [ínəvéʃən] N innovación f

innovative [ínəveDIV] ADJ innovador

innovator [ínəveDə-] N innovador -ora mf

innuendo [ɪnjuéndo] N insinuación f

innumerable [ɪnúmə-əbəl] ADJ innumerables

inoculate [ɪnákjəlet] VI/VT inocular[se]

inoffensive [ɪnəfénsɪv] ADJ inofensivo

inoperable [ɪnápə-əbəl] ADJ inoperable

inopportune [ɪnapə-tún] ADJ inoportuno

inordinate [ɪnɔ́rdnɪt] ADJ desmesurado

inorganic [ɪnɔrgǽnɪk] ADJ inorgánico; — **chemistry** química inorgánica f

input [ínput] N (electric, computer) entrada f; (opinion) opinión f; VT ingresar/entrar datos

inquire [ɪŋkwáɪr] VI/VT inquirir, preguntar; — **about/after** preguntar por; **to — into** indagar, investigar

inquiry [íŋkwəri] N (scientific) investigación f; (police) pesquisa f; **we made inquiries about hotels** hicimos averiguaciones acerca de hoteles

inquisition [ɪŋkwɪzíʃən] N inquisición f

inquisitive [ɪnkwízɪDIV] ADJ (curious) inquisitivo, curioso; (asking many questions) preguntón

insane [ɪnsén] ADJ demente, loco; — **asylum** manicomio m

insanity [ɪnsǽnɪDi] N locura f, demencia f

insatiable [ɪnséʃəbəl] ADJ insaciable

inscribe [ɪnskráɪb] VT (mark) inscribir; (engrave) grabar; (dedicate) dedicar

inscription [ɪnskrípʃən] N (marks, engraving) inscripción f; (dedication) dedicatoria f

inscrutable [ɪnskrúDəbəl] ADJ inescrutable

insect [ínsɛkt] N insecto m

insecticide [ɪnsɛ́ktɪsaɪd] N insecticida m

insectivorous [ɪnsɛktívə-əs] ADJ insectívoro

insecure [ɪnsɪkjúr] ADJ inseguro

insecurity [ɪnsɪkjúrɪDi] N inseguridad f

insemination [ɪnsɛmɪnéʃən] N inseminación f

insensible [ɪnsɛ́nsəbəl] ADJ insensible

insensitive [ɪnsɛ́nsɪDIV] ADJ insensible

inseparable [ɪnsɛ́pə-əbəl] ADJ inseparable

insert[1] [ɪnsɚ́t] VT insertar, introducir; (into a text) intercalar

insert[2] [ínsɚt] N encarte m

insertion [ɪnsɚ́ʃən] N inserción f; (into a text) intercalación f

inside[1] [ɪnsáɪd] PREP dentro de; ADV dentro, adentro

inside[2] [ínsaɪd] N interior m; — **job** delito cometido por un empleado m; —**s** entrañas f pl; — **track** pista interior f; **to turn — out** volver del revés; **he passed me on the —** me pasó por la derecha; ADJ (interior) interior

insider [ɪnsáɪDə-] N privilegiado -da mf; — **trading** abuso de información privilegiada m

insidious [ɪnsídiəs] ADJ insidioso

insight [ínsaɪt] N (intuition) perspicacia f; (discernment) discernimiento m

insignia [ɪnsígniə] N insignia f

insignificant [ɪnsɪgnífɪkənt] ADJ insignificante, menudo, nimio

insincere [ɪnsɪnsír] ADJ insincero

insinuate [ɪnsínjuet] VT insinuar

insinuation [ɪnsɪnjuéʃən] N insinuación f

insipid [ɪnsípɪd] ADJ insípido, soso

insist [ɪnsíst] VI/VT insistir; **to — on** insistir en

insistence [ɪnsístəns] N insistencia f

insistent [ɪnsístənt] ADJ insistente

insole [ínsoɫ] N plantilla f

insolence [ínsələns] N insolencia f

insolent [ínsəlant] ADJ insolente, atrevido

insoluble [ɪnsáljəbəl] ADJ insoluble

insolvent [ɪnsáɫvənt] ADJ insolvente

insomnia [ɪnsámniə] N insomnio m

inspect [ɪnspɛ́kt] VT inspeccionar; **to — the troops** pasar revista a la tropa, revistar la tropa

inspection [ɪnspɛ́kʃən] N inspección f; (of troops) revista f

inspector [ɪnspɛ́ktə-] N inspector -ora mf

inspiration [ɪnspəréʃən] N inspiración f

inspire [ɪnspáɪr] VI/VT inspirar

instability [ɪnstəbílɪDi] N inestabilidad f

install [ɪnstɔ́ɫ] VT instalar; — **program** programa instalador m

installation [ɪnstəléʃən] N instalación f

installment [ɪnstɔ́ɫmənt] N (payment of debt) cuota f; (of a book) entrega f, fascículo m; **to pay in —s** pagar a plazos

instance [ínstəns] N ejemplo m; **for —** por ejemplo; **court of first —** tribunal de primera instancia m

instant [ínstənt] N instante m; **this —** ahora mismo; ADJ inmediato; — **coffee** café instantáneo m; — **messaging** mensajería instantánea f

instantaneous [ɪnstənténiəs] ADJ instantáneo

instead [ɪnstéd] ADV — **of** en lugar de, en vez de; **she didn't want a desk, so she ordered a chair** — no quería un escritorio, así que pidió una silla en su lugar

instigate [ínstɪget] VT instigar

instigator [ínstɪgeɪdə] N (of a crime) instigador -ora *mf*; (of an event) causante *mf*
instill [ɪnstɪ́l] VT inculcar
instinct [ínstɪŋkt] N instinto *m*
instinctive [ɪnstɪ́ŋktɪv] ADJ instintivo
institute [ínstɪtut] N instituto *m*; VT instituir
institution [ɪnstɪtúʃən] N institución *f*
institutional [ɪnstɪtúʃənəl] ADJ institucional
instruct [ɪnstrʌ́kt] VT (teach) instruir; (command, advise) dar instrucciones; (command) mandar
instruction [ɪnstrʌ́kʃən] N instrucción *f*; **—s** (orders) órdenes *f pl*; (information) instrucciones *f pl*, indicaciones *f pl*
instructive [ɪnstrʌ́ktɪv] ADJ instructivo
instructor [ɪnstrʌ́ktə] N (of skills) instructor -ora *mf*; (of knowledge) profesor -ora *mf*
instrument [ínstrəmənt] N instrumento *m*; **— panel** salpicadero *m*, tablero *m*
instrumental [ɪnstrəméntl] ADJ instrumental; **to be — in** ser fundamental para
insubordinate [ɪnsəbɔ́rdnɪt] ADJ insubordinado
insufferable [ɪnsʌ́fəəbəl] ADJ insufrible
insufficiency [ɪnsəfíʃənsi] N insuficiencia *f*
insufficient [ɪnsəfíʃənt] ADJ insuficiente
insulate [ínsəlet] VT aislar
insulation [ɪnsəléʃən] N aislamiento *m*
insulator [ínsəlepə] N (material) aislante *m*; (device) aislador *m*
insulin [ínsəlɪn] N insulina *f*; **— shock** choque insulínico *m*
insult[1] [ɪnsʌ́lt] VT insultar, injuriar
insult[2] [ínsʌlt] N insulto *m*, injuria *f*
insulting [ɪnsʌ́ltɪŋ] ADJ insultante, injurioso
insuperable [ɪnsúpəəbəl] ADJ insuperable
insurable [ɪnʃúrəbəl] ADJ asegurable
insurance [ɪnʃúrəns] N seguro *m*; **— agent** agente de seguros *mf*; **— company** compañía de seguros *f*; **— policy** póliza de seguro *f*
insure [ɪnʃúr] VI/VT asegurar[se]
insurgent [ɪnsɜ́dʒənt] N alzado -da *mf*
insurmountable [ɪnsəmáʊntəbəl] ADJ insuperable
insurrection [ɪnsərékʃən] N insurrección *f*
intact [ɪntǽkt] ADJ intacto
intangible [ɪntǽndʒəbəl] ADJ intangible
integer [íntɪdʒə] N (número) entero *m*
integral [íntɪgrəl] ADJ (complete) integral; (forming part of) integrante; **— calculus** cálculo integral *m*; N integral *f*
integrate [íntɪgret] VT integrar; VI integrarse a
integration [ɪntɪgréʃən] N integración *f*
integrity [ɪntégrɪDi] N integridad *f*
intellect [íntlɛkt] N intelecto *m*
intellectual [ɪntlɛ́ktʃuəl] ADJ & N intelectual *mf*
intelligence [ɪntélɪdʒəns] N inteligencia *f* (also secret information); **— quotient** coeficiente intelectual / de inteligencia *m*
intelligent [ɪntélɪdʒənt] ADJ inteligente

intelligible [ɪntélɪdʒəbəl] ADJ inteligible
intend [ɪnténd] VT pensar; **to — to do something** pensar hacer algo; **a book —ed for children** un libro destinado/dirigido a los niños
intense [ɪnténs] ADJ intenso
intensify [ɪnténsɪfaɪ] VI/VT intensificar[se]
intensity [ɪnténsɪDi] N intensidad *f*
intensive [ɪnténsɪv] ADJ intensivo; **— care unit** sala de cuidados intensivos *f*
intent [ɪntént] N intención *f*, propósito *m*; **to/ for all —s and purposes** en la práctica; ADJ atento; **— on** resuelto a
intention [ɪnténʃən] N intención *f*
intentional [ɪnténʃənəl] ADJ intencional; **— base on balls** base por bolas intencional *f*
intentionally [ɪnténʃənəli] ADV a propósito
inter [ɪntɜ́] VT sepultar
interact [ɪntəǽkt] VI interactuar
interaction [ɪntəǽkʃən] N interacción *f*
interactive [ɪntəǽktɪv] ADJ interactivo
intercede [ɪntəsíd] VI interceder
intercept [ɪntəsépt] VT interceptar
interception [ɪntəsépʃən] N interceptación *f*
intercession [ɪntəséʃən] N intercesión *f*
interchange[1] [íntətʃendʒ] N cambio *m*; (on road) enlace *m*; Sp intercambiador *m*
interchange[2] [ɪntətʃéndʒ] VI/VT cambiar, intercambiar
intercourse [íntəkɔrs] N comunicación *f*, trato *m*
interest [íntrɪst] N interés *m*; (financial) interés *m*, rédito *m*; (share in a business) participación *f*; **—-bearing** que devenga intereses; **—-free** libre de intereses, sin intereses; **— rate** tasa de interés *f*; **mining —s** los negocios mineros; VT interesar; **may I — you in a cookie?** ¿te puedo ofrecer una galleta?
interested [íntrɪstɪd] ADJ interesado; **— party** parte interesada *f*; **to be/become — in** interesarse en/por
interesting [íntrɪstɪŋ] ADJ interesante
interface [íntəfes] N interface *mf*, interfaz *f*
interfere [ɪntəfír] VI interferir; (meddle) entrometerse; **to — with** interferir en
interference [ɪntəfírəns] N interferencia *f*, injerencia *f*
interferon [ɪntəfírɑn] N interferón *m*
interim [íntəɪm] N ínterin *m*; ADJ (person) interino; (decision) provisional
interior [ɪntíriə] ADJ & N interior *m*; **— decoration** decoración de interiores *f*; **— design** diseño de interiores *m*
interjection [ɪntədʒékʃən] N interjección *f*, exclamación *f*
interlace [ɪntəlés] VI/VT entrelazar[se]
interlinear [ɪntəlíniə] ADJ interlineal
interlock [ɪntəlák] VI/VT (gears) engranar[se];

(branches, etc.) entrelazar[se]; N interlock m

interlocking [ɪntə-lákɪŋ] ADJ (gears) engranado; (branches) entrelazado

interlude [ɪntə-lud] N (interval) intervalo m; (musical) interludio m; (theatrical) entremés m

intermediary [ɪntə-míDieri] ADJ intermediario

intermediate [ɪntə-míDiɪt] ADJ intermedio

interment [ɪntɜ́-mənt] N entierro m

interminable [ɪntɜ́-mənəbəl] ADJ interminable

intermingle [ɪntə-míŋgəl] VI/VT entremezclar[se]

intermission [ɪntə-míʃən] N entreacto m, intervalo m

intermittent [ɪntə-mítnt] ADJ intermitente

intern [ɪ́ntɜ-n] VT internar, confinar; N (prisoner, doctor) interno -na mf

internal [ɪntɜ́-nl] ADJ interno, interior; —- **combustion engine** motor de combustión interna m; — **hard disk** disco duro interno m; — **revenue** rentas internas f pl; — **Revenue Service** Hacienda f

internalize [ɪntɜ́-nəlaɪz] VT interiorizar, internalizar

international [ɪntə-nǽʃən] ADJ internacional; — **law** derecho internacional m

Internet [ɪ́ntə-net] N internet m, red f, web f; — **access** acceso a internet m; — **access provider** proveedor de acceso a internet m; — **banking** banca por internet f; — **community** comunidad internauta f; — **user** internauta mf

internist [ɪntɜ́-nist] N internista mf

internship [ɪ́ntə-nʃɪp] N (medical) internado m; (student) práctica f

interpersonal [ɪntə-pɜ́-sənl] ADJ interpersonal

interpose [ɪntə-póz] VI/VT interponer[se]

interpret [ɪntɜ́-prɪt] VI/VT interpretar

interpretation [ɪntə-prɪtéʃən] N interpretación f

interpreter [ɪntɜ́-prɪDə-] N intérprete mf

interracial [ɪntə-réʃəl] ADJ interracial

interrelated [ɪntə-rɪlédɪd] ADJ interrelacionado

interrogate [ɪntɛ́rəget] VI/VT interrogar

interrogation [ɪntɛrəgéʃən] N interrogación f, interrogatorio m

interrogative [ɪntə-rágəDɪv] ADJ interrogativo; N palabra/oración interrogativa f

interrupt [ɪntə-rʌ́pt] VI/VT interrumpir

interruption [ɪntə-rʌ́pʃən] N interrupción f

intersect [ɪntə-sɛ́kt] VI/VT (math) intersecar[se]; (road) cruzar[se]

intersection [ɪ́ntə-sɛkʃən] N (math) intersección f; (street) cruce m, intersección f

intersperse [ɪntə-spɜ́-s] VT (scatter) esparcir; (intermingle) entremezclar, entreverar; (spice up) salpicar

interstate [ɪ́ntə-stet] ADJ interestatal; — **highway** autopista interestatal f

interstellar [ɪntə-stélə-] ADJ interestelar

interstice [ɪntɜ́-stɪs] N intersticio m

intertwine [ɪntə-twáɪn] VI/VT entrelazar[se]

interval [ɪ́ntə-vəl] N intervalo m

intervene [ɪntə-vín] VI intervenir; (mediate) interponerse, mediar

intervening [ɪntə-vínɪŋ] ADJ interventor

intervention [ɪntə-vénʃən] N intervención f; (mediation) mediación f

interview [ɪ́ntə-vju] N entrevista f; (for entertainment) Sp interviú f; VT entrevistar; VI entrevistarse

intestinal [ɪntéstənl] ADJ intestinal; — **flora** flora intestinal f; — **obstruction** obstrucción intestinal f

intestine [ɪntéstɪn] ADJ & N intestino m; **small** — intestino delgado m; **large** — intestino grueso m

intimacy [ɪ́ntəməsi] N intimidad f

intimate[1] [ɪ́ntəmɪt] ADJ íntimo, entrañable; (knowledge) profundo

intimate[2] [ɪ́ntəmet] VT insinuar, dar a entender

intimation [ɪntəméʃən] N insinuación f

intimidate [ɪntímɪdet] VT intimidar, acobardar

into [ɪ́ntu] PREP **she came** — **the room** entró en/a la habitación; **he put it** — **the box** lo metió en la caja; **he translated it** — **German** lo tradujo al alemán; **he ran** — **a tree** chocó contra un árbol; **it fell** — **oblivion** cayó en el olvido; **he went** — **medicine** entró a medicina; **I'm really** — **pop music** me ha dado por la música pop

intolerable [ɪntálə-əbəl] ADJ intolerable

intolerance [ɪntálə-əns] N intolerancia f

intolerant [ɪntálə-ənt] ADJ intolerante

intonation [ɪntənéʃən] N entonación f

intoxicate [ɪntáksɪket] VI/VT embriagar (also exhilarate); (poison) intoxicar

intoxication [ɪntaksɪkéʃən] N (drunkenness) embriaguez f; (poisoning) intoxicación f

intransigent [ɪntrǽnzɪdʒənt] ADJ intransigente

intransitive [ɪntrǽnzɪDɪv] ADJ intransitivo

intrauterine device [ɪntrəjúDə-rɪndɪváɪs] N dispositivo intrauterino m

intravenous [ɪntrəvínəs] ADJ intravenoso; — **feeding** alimentación intravenosa f

intrepid [ɪntrépɪd] ADJ intrépido

intricate [ɪ́ntrɪkɪt] ADJ intrincado

intrigue[1] [ɪntríg] VI/VT intrigar

intrigue[2] [ɪ́ntrig] N intriga f

intrinsic [ɪntrínzɪk] ADJ intrínseco

introduce [ɪntrədús] VT (put in, bring) introducir; (make acquainted) presentar

introduction [ɪntrədákʃən] N (of a book) introducción f; (of a custom or system) introducción f, implantación f; (to a person) presentación f

introspection [ɪntrəspékʃən] N introspección f

introvert [ɪ́ntrəvə-t] N introvertido -da mf

introverted [ɪ́ntrəvɜ-Dɪd] ADJ introvertido

intrude [ɪntrúd] VI/VT interrumpir; (penetrate, of rock) penetrar

intruder [ɪntrúdə·] N intruso -sa *mf*

intrusion [ɪntrúʒən] N (interruption) interrupción *f*; (penetration) intrusión *f*

intrusive [ɪntrúsɪv] ADJ (rock) intrusivo; (people) entrometido

intubation [ɪntjubéʃən] N intubación *f*

intuition [ɪntuíʃən] N intuición *f*

intuitive [ɪntúɪDɪv] ADJ intuitivo

inundate [ínəndet] VT inundar

invade [ɪnvéd] VI/VT invadir

invader [ɪnvédə·] N invasor -ora *mf*

invalid[1] [ínvəlɪd] ADJ & N (infirm) inválido -da *mf*

invalid[2] [ɪnvǽlɪd] ADJ (not valid) nulo

invaluable [ɪnvǽljuəbəl] ADJ invalorable, inestimable

invariable [ɪnvériəbəl] ADJ invariable

invariably [ɪnvériəbli] ADV siempre

invasion [ɪnvéʒən] N invasión *f*

invasive [ɪnvésɪv] ADJ invasivo

invent [ɪnvént] VT inventar

invention [ɪnvénʃən] N (act of inventing, thing invented) invención *f*, invento *m*; (falsehood) invención *f*

inventive [ɪnvéntɪv] ADJ inventivo

inventor [ɪnvéntə·] N inventor -ora *mf*

inventory [ínvəntɔri] N inventario *m*; VT inventariar

inverse [ɪnvɝs] ADJ & N inverso *m*

inversion [ɪnvɝʒən] N inversión *f*

invert [ɪnvɝt] VT invertir

invest [ɪnvést] VI/VT (money) invertir; (a rank upon someone) investir

investigate [ɪnvéstɪget] VI/VT investigar, indagar

investigation [ɪnvestɪgéʃən] N investigación *f*

investigator [ɪnvéstɪgeDə·] N investigador -ora *mf*

investment [ɪnvéstmənt] N (of money) inversión *f*; (of rank) investidura *f*; — **broker** corredor -ora de bolsa *mf*

investor [ɪnvéstə·] N inversionista *mf*, inversor -ora *mf*

invigorate [ɪnvígəret] VT vigorizar

invincible [ɪnvínsəbəl] ADJ invencible

invisible [ɪnvízəbəl] ADJ invisible

invitation [ɪnvɪtéʃən] N invitación *f*

invite[1] [ɪnváɪt] VI/VT invitar; **to — trouble** buscarse problemas

invite[2] [ínvaɪt] N *fam* invitación *f*

inviting [ɪnváɪDɪŋ] ADJ atractivo, seductor

in vitro fertilization [ɪnvítrof·dlɪzéʃən] N fertilización in vitro *f*

invocation [ɪnvəkéʃən] N invocación *f*

invoice [ínvɔɪs] N factura *f*; VT facturar

invoke [ɪnvók] VT invocar

involuntary [ɪnválənteri] ADJ involuntario

involve [ɪnválv] VT (take, last) suponer; **how much time will this —?** ¿cuánto tiempo supone esto?; (consist of, entail) consistir en, involucrar; **what does your work —?** ¿en qué consiste tu trabajo?; (be in question) ser cuestión de; **national security is —d!** ¡es una cuestión de seguridad nacional!; (implicate) implicar; **they tried to —** her trataron de implicarla; (wrapped up in) estar metido; **he's very —d in the family business** está muy metido en el negocio familiar; (have a liaison) enredarse; **she got —d with a married man** se enredó con un hombre casado

involved [ɪnválvd] ADJ complicado, enrevesado

involvement [ɪnvɔ́lvmənt] N (in a crime) implicación *f*; (in a project) participación *f*; (with a person) relación *f*

inward [ínwəd] ADV hacia dentro; ADJ interior

iodide [áɪdaɪd] N yoduro *m*

iodine [áɪdaɪn] N yodo *m*

ion [áɪɑn] N ión *m*

ionize [áɪənaɪz] VT ionizar

ipecac syrup [ípɪkæksɪrəp] N jarabe de ipecacuana *m*

IPO [initial public offering] [áɪpíó] N oferta pública inicial *f*

IQ [intelligence quotient] [áɪkjú] N coeficiente de inteligencia *m*

Iran [ɪrán] N Irán *m*

Iranian [ɪréniən] ADJ & N iraní *mf*

Iraq [ɪrǽk] N Irak *m*

Iraqi [ɪrǽki] ADJ & N iraquí *mf*

irascible [ɪrǽsəbəl] ADJ irascible

irate [aɪrét] ADJ airado

ire [aɪr] N ira *f*

Ireland [áɪrlənd] N Irlanda *f*

iridescent [ɪrɪdésənt] ADJ iridiscente, tornasolado

iridium [ɪrídiəm] N iridio *m*

iris [áɪrɪs] N (part of eye) iris *m*; (plant, flower) lirio *m*; (rainbow) arco iris *m*

Irish [áɪrɪʃ] ADJ irlandés; N (language) irlandés *m*; **the —** los irlandeses

irk [ɝk] VT fastidiar; **—ed** fastidiado

irksome [ɝksəm] ADJ engorroso, molesto

iron [áɪə·n] N (element, golf club) hierro *m*; (appliance) plancha *f*; **in —s** en grilletes; — **deficiency anemia** anemia por deficiencia de hierro *f*; **—work** herrajes *m pl*; **—works** fundición *f*; ADJ férreo, de hierro; VI/VT planchar; **to — out a difficulty** allanar una dificultad

ironic [aɪránɪk] ADJ irónico

ironing [áɪə·nɪŋ] N planchado *m*

irony [áɪroni] N ironía *f*; (mockery) ironía *f*, sorna *f*

irradiate [ɪrédiet] VT irradiar

irrational [ɪrǽʃənl] ADJ irracional

irrefutable [ɪrɪfjúDəbəl] ADJ irrefutable
irregular [ɪrégjələ-] ADJ irregular
irregularity [ɪregjəlǽrɪDi] N irregularidad *f*
irrelevant [ɪrɛ́ləvənt] ADJ no pertinente; **your age is** — tu edad no viene al caso
irreparable [ɪrɛ́pə-əbəl] ADJ irreparable
irreplaceable [ɪrɪplésəbəl] ADJ irreemplazable
irreproachable [ɪrɪprótʃəbəl] ADJ irreprochable
irresistible [ɪrɪzístəbəl] ADJ irresistible
irresponsibility [ɪrɪspɑnsəbílɪDi] N irresponsabilidad *f*
irresponsible [ɪrɪspɑ́nsəbəl] ADJ irresponsable
irretrievable [ɪrɪtrívəbəl] ADJ irrecuperable
irreverent [ɪrɛ́və-ənt] ADJ irreverente
irreversible [ɪrɪvɝ́səbəl] ADJ irreversible
irrevocable [ɪrɛ́vəkəbəl] ADJ irrevocable
irrigate [ɪ́rɪget] VI/VT (a garden) irrigar, regar; (the eyes) irrigar
irrigation [ɪrɪgéʃən] N riego *m*, irrigación *f*; — **ditch** acequia *f*
irritable [ɪ́rɪDəbəl] ADJ irritable, colérico
irritate [ɪ́rɪtet] VI/VT irritar
irritating [ɪ́rɪteDɪŋ] ADJ irritante
irritation [ɪrɪtéʃən] N irritación *f*
IRS [**Internal Revenue Service**] [áɪɑrɛ́s] N Hacienda *f*
is [ɪz] *see* be
Islam [ɪzlɑm] N islamismo *m*, islam *m*
Islamic [ɪzlɑ́mɪk] ADJ islámico
island [áɪlənd] N isla *f*
islander [áɪləndə-] N isleño -ña *mf*
isle [aɪl] N isla *f*
isobar [áɪsəbɑr] N isobara *f*
isolate [áɪsəlet] VT aislar
isolation [aɪsəléʃən] N aislamiento *m*, marginación *f*
isolationism [aɪsəléʃənɪzəm] N aislacionismo *m*
isometric [aɪsəmétrɪk] ADJ isométrico
isotope [áɪsətop] N isótopo *m*, isotopo *m*
Israel [ɪ́zriəl] N Israel *m*
Israeli [ɪzréli] ADJ & N israelí *mf*
issue [ɪ́ʃu] N (of printed matter) tirada *f*; (of stock, bonds) emisión *f*; (copy of a magazine) número *m*, entrega *f*; (of a fluid) flujo *m*; (problem) problema *m*, tema *m*; (progeny) descendencia *f*; **he's got** —**s** es muy acomplejado; **to take** — **with** discrepar de; VT (written material) publicar; (a decree) promulgar; (a permit, document) expedir; (shares) emitir; (to flow) brotar; (to come out of) salir de; (to descend from) descender de
isthmus [ɪ́sməs] N istmo *m*
it [ɪt] PRON — **all started yesterday** todo empezó ayer; — **is necessary** es necesario; — **is raining** llueve, está lloviendo; — **is said that** se dice que; — **is two o'clock** son las dos; — **was broken** estaba roto; **who is** —? ¿quién es? **if** — **weren't five o'clock** si no fueran las cinco; **I saw** — lo/la vi; **he**

talked about — habló de eso; **what time is** —? ¿qué hora es? **how is** — **going?** ¿qué tal? **I don't get** — no entiendo; **you're** —! ¡tú la traes!
IT [**information technology**] [áɪti] N informática *f*
Italian [ɪtǽljən] ADJ & N italiano -na *mf*
italic [ɪtǽlɪk] ADJ itálico; N —**s** letra bastardilla/ cursiva *f*
italicize [ɪtǽlɪsaɪz] VT poner en bastardilla/ cursiva
Italy [ɪdli] N Italia *f*
itch [ɪtʃ] VI/VT picar; **to be** —**ing to** tener ganas de; N (sensation) comezón *f*, picazón *f*; (longing) ansia *f*
itching [ɪ́tʃɪŋ] N comezón *f*, picazón *f*
itchy [ɪ́tʃi] ADJ que pica; **it feels** — me pica
item [áɪDəm] N (piece of news) artículo *m*; (topic of gossip) tema de conversación *m*; (unit) ítem *m*; (couple) pareja *f*
itemize [áɪDəmaɪz] VT (list) enumerar; (break down) desglosar; —**d invoice** factura detallada *f*
itinerant [aɪtínə-ənt] ADJ itinerante, ambulante
itinerary [aɪtínəreri] N (schedule) itinerario *m*; (guidebook) guía de viajeros *f*
its [ɪts] POSS ADJ su/sus, de él, de ella, de ello
itself [ɪtsɛ́lf] PRON **this story wrote** — esta historia se escribió sola; **the bike was standing by** — la bici estaba parada sola; **the dog bit** — el perro se mordió [a sí mismo]; **the fox found** — **a hole** la zorra se encontró una guarida
IUD [**intrauterine device**] [áɪjúdí] N DIU *m*
IV [**intravenous**] [áɪví] ADJ intravenoso
Ivorian [aɪvóriən] ADJ & N marfileño -ña *mf*
ivory [áɪvri] N marfil *m*; — **tower** torre de marfil *f*
Ivory Coast [áɪvrikóst] N Costa de Marfil *f*
ivy [áɪvi] N hiedra *f*

Jj

jab [dʒæb] VI/VT (hit) golpear; (hit with elbow) codear; N (blow) golpe *m*; (blow with elbow) codazo *m*; (in boxing) jab *m*, puñetazo directo *m*
jabber [dʒǽbə-] VI (unintelligibly) farfullar; (incessantly) charlotear; N (unintelligible) farfulla *f*; charloteo *m*
jack [dʒæk] N (tool) gato *m*; (card) sota *f*; (plug-in) hembra *f*, toma *f*; (flag) bandera de proa *f*; —**ass** asno *m*, burro *m* (also person); —**hammer** martillo neumático *m*; —**knife** navaja *f*; — **of all trades** hombre orquesta

m; —**pot** premio gordo *m*; —**rabbit** liebre americana *f*; **you don't know** — no sabes ni un comino; VT **to** — **up** (a car) alzar con gato; (prices) subir

jackal [ʤǽkəɫ] N chacal *m*

jacket [ʤǽkɪt] N (clothing) chaqueta *f*; (of a book) forro *m*; (of a potato) piel *f*

jade [ʤed] N jade *m*

jaded [ʤédɪd] ADJ (disenchanted) de vuelta; (sated) hastiado

jagged [ʤǽgɪd] ADJ recortado, desigual

jaguar [ʤǽgwar] N jaguar *m*

jail [ʤeɫ] N cárcel *f*; —**break** fuga *f*; VT encarcelar

jailer [ʤélə·] N carcelero -ra *mf*

jalopy [ʤəlápi] N cacharro *m*

jam [ʤæm] VT (stuff) embutir; (block) atestar; (immobilize) trabar; (make unworkable) obstruir, atascar, atorar; (stop radio signals) interferir; VI (become stuck or unworkable) atascarse; (crowd in) apiñarse; **to** — **on the brakes** frenar de golpe; **to** — **one's fingers** pillarse los dedos; N (jelly) mermelada *f*, dulce *m*; (difficult situation) aprieto *m*; (traffic) embotellamiento *m*; — **session** jam *m*

Jamaica [ʤəmékə] N Jamaica *f*

Jamaican [ʤəmékən] ADJ & N jamaicano -na *mf*, jamaiquino -na *mf*

janitor [ʤǽnɪdə·] N conserje *m*

January [ʤǽnjueri] N enero *m*

Japan [ʤəpǽn] N Japón *m*

Japanese [ʤæpəníz] ADJ & N japonés -esa *mf*

jar [ʤɑr] VI/VT (shake) sacudir[se]; (clash) chocar; **to** — **one's nerves** ponerle a uno los nervios de punta; N (container) tarro *m*, frasco *m*, pote *m*; (large earthen container) tinaja *f*; (collision) choque *m*; (shake) sacudida *f*

jargon [ʤárgən] N jerga *f*

jasmine [ʤǽzmɪn] N jazmín *m*

jasper [ʤǽspə·] N jaspe *m*

jaundice [ʤɔ́ndɪs] N ictericia *f*

jaundiced [ʤɔ́ndɪst] ADJ ictérico

jaunt [ʤɔnt] N excursión *f*; VI pasear

javelin [ʤǽvlɪn] N jabalina *f*

jaw [ʤɔ] N (of animal) quijada *f*; (of human) mandíbula *f*; (of mammals) fauces *f pl*; —**bone** mandíbula *f*, maxilar *m*

jay [ʤe] N arrendajo *m*

jazz [ʤæz] N jazz *m*; VI **to** — **up** animar

jealous [ʤɛ́ləs] ADJ (possessive) celoso; (envious) envidioso; (protective) protector

jealousy [ʤɛ́ləsi] N celos *m pl*

jeans [ʤinz] N jeans *m pl*, vaqueros *m pl*

jeer [ʤɪr] VI/VT (mock) mofarse [de], burlarse [de]; (boo) abuchear, befar; N (act of mockery) mofa *f*, burla *f*; (boos) abucheo *m*, befa *f*

jelly [ʤɛ́li] N jalea *f*; —**fish** medusa *f*

jeopardize [ʤépə·daɪz] VT comprometer, poner

en peligro

jeopardy [ʤépə·di] ADV LOC **in** — en peligro

jerk [ʤɝk] N (quick pull) tirón *m*; (muscular contraction) espasmo *m*; (idiot) *pej* pelmazo *m*; VI/VT tironear; **to** — **around** manipular

jerky [ʤɝki] ADJ espasmódico; N tasajo *m*

jersey [ʤɝzi] N jersey *m*

jest [ʤest] N broma *f*, chanza *f*; **in** — en broma; VI bromear

jester [ʤéstə·] N bufón *m*

Jesuit [ʤézuɪt] N jesuita *m*

jet [ʤet] N (stream) chorro *m*; (spout) surtidor *m*; (stone) azabache *m*; —**[air]plane** avión a reacción *m*; — **engine** motor a reacción *m*; — **lag** jet lag *m*; —**liner** avión a reacción de pasajero *m*; — **propulsion** propulsión a chorro *f*; — **set** jet set *m*, jet-set *m*; — **stream** (of air) corriente en chorro *f*; (of a jet) chorro *m*; ADJ —-**black** negro como el azabache; VI (stream out) salir a chorros; (travel) volar en avión a reacción; VT (spew out) lanzar a chorros; (transport) transportar en avión a reacción

jettison [ʤédɪsən] VT echar por la borda

Jew [ʤu] N judío -a *mf*

jewel [ʤúəɫ] N (ornament, prized person) joya *f*, alhaja *f*; (stone) gema *f*; (watch jewel) rubí *m*; — **box** joyero *m*

jeweler [ʤúələ·] N joyero -ra *mf*; —**'s shop** joyería *f*

jewelry [ʤúəɫri] N joyas *f pl*, alhajas *f pl*; — **box** alhajero *m*; — **store** joyería *f*

Jewish [ʤúɪʃ] ADJ judío

jiffy [ʤɪfi] ADV LOC **in a** — en un santiamén

jig [ʤɪg] N (dance) giga *f*; —**saw** sierra de vaivén *f*; —**saw puzzle** rompecabezas *m sg*; VI (dance) bailotear

jiggle [ʤígəɫ] VI/VT zangolotear[se], zarandear[se]; N zangoloteo *m*, zarandeo *m*

jilt [ʤɪlt] VT dejar plantado

jingle [ʤíŋgəɫ] VI tintinear; VT agitar; N retintín *m*; (short song) jingle *m*

jinx [ʤɪŋks] N persona que trae mala suerte *f*; VT traer mala suerte

job [ʤab] N (task) tarea *f*; (position) trabajo *m*, empleo *m*; (theft) golpe *m*; **to be out of a** — estar sin trabajo; *Sp* estar en [el] paro; **by the** — a destajo; **to do a good** — hacer buen trabajo; VI trabajar a destajo; **on-the--training** capacitación en el lugar de trabajo *f*

jobber [ʤábə·] N (day-worker) trabajador -ora a destajo *mf*; (wholesaler) vendedor -ora mayorista *mf*

jobless [ʤáblɪs] ADJ sin trabajo; *Sp* en paro

jock [ʤak] N deportista *mf*; — **[strap]** suspensorio *m*

jockey [ʤáki] N jockey *m*; VI **to** — **for position** disputarse la posición

jocular [ʤákjələ·] ADJ jocoso

jog [ʤag] VI (run) correr, trotar; VT (refresh) refrescar; N trote *m*; **to go for a —** salir a correr

jogging [ʤágɪŋ] N jogging *m*, footing *m*

join [ʤɔɪn] VI/VT juntar[se]; (pipes) acoplar[se], unir[se]; (bones) articular[se]; (a club) asociarse [a]; (the navy, etc.) alistarse [en]

joint [ʤɔɪnt] N (point of contact) juntura *f*, junta *f*; (connection between bones) articulación *f*, coyuntura *f*; (nodule on a plant) nudo *m*; (dive, bar) antro *m*; **out of —** descoyuntado; ADJ (shared) común; **— account** cuenta conjunta *f*; **— action** acción colectiva *f*; **— custody** custodia compartida *f*; **— owner** copropietario -ria *mf*; **— session** sesión plena *f*; **— venture** joint venture *m*

jointly [ʤɔɪntli] ADV conjuntamente

joke [ʤok] N broma *f*, chiste *m*; VI bromear

joker [ʤókɚ] N (person who jokes) bromista *mf*, guasón -ona *mf*; (card) comodín *m*

jokingly [ʤókɪŋli] ADV en broma

jolly [ʤáli] ADJ jovial

jolt [ʤolt] N sacudida *f*; VT sacudir; **to — along** avanzar a los tumbos

Jordan [ʤɔrdn] N Jordania *f*

Jordanian [ʤɔrdénian] ADJ & N jordano -na *mf*

jostle [ʤásəl] VI/VT codear[se], dar empujones [a]; N empujón *m*

jot [ʤat] VT **to — down** apuntar; N pizca *f*

journal [ʤɝnl] N (diary) diario *m*; (periodical) revista *f*; (logbook) cuaderno de bitácora *m*

journalism [ʤɝnəlɪzəm] N periodismo *m*

journalist [ʤɝnəlɪst] N periodista *mf*

journalistic [ʤɝnəlístɪk] ADJ periodístico

journey [ʤɝni] N viaje *m*; VI viajar

joust [ʤaʊst] N justa *f*

jowl [ʤaʊl] N carrillo *m*, moflete *m*

joy [ʤɔɪ] N (delight) alegría *f*, regocijo *m*, alborozo *m*; (source of delight) deleite *m*; **—ride** paseo en coche robado *m*; **—stick** joystick *m*, palanca de mando *f*

joyful [ʤɔɪfəl] ADJ alborozado

joyous [ʤɔɪəs] ADJ jubiloso, alegre

jubilant [ʤúbələnt] ADJ jubiloso

jubilee [ʤubəlí] N jubileo *m*

Judaism [ʤúdiɪzəm] N judaísmo *m*

judge [ʤʌʤ] N juez -eza *mf*; (in tennis) juez -eza de silla *mf*; **to be a good — of character** saber juzgar a la gente; VI/VT juzgar; (estimate) calcular

judgment [ʤʌʤmənt] N juicio *m*; (in court) fallo *m*; **— day** día del juicio final *m*

judicial [ʤudíʃəl] ADJ judicial

judicious [ʤudíʃəs] ADJ juicioso, sensato

judo [ʤúdo] N judo *m*, yudo *m*

jug [ʤʌg] N (pitcher) jarro *m*, jarra *f*; (storage jar) pote *m*

juggle [ʤʌgəl] VI/VT hacer juegos malabares [con], hacer malabarismo [con]; **to — the accounts** manipular las cuentas

juggler [ʤʌglɚ] N malabarista *mf*

jugular [ʤʌgjələ] N yugular *f*

juice [ʤus] N jugo *m*; (fruit only) Sp zumo *m*

juicer [ʤúsɚ] N exprimidor *m*

juicy [ʤúsi] ADJ jugoso; **a — story** un cuento sabroso

juke [ʤuk] N (in sports) amague *m*, finta *f*; **—box** juke-box *m*

July [ʤulái] N julio *m*

jumble [ʤʌmbəl] VI/VT revolver[se] *m*; N revoltijo *m*

jumbo [ʤʌmbo] ADJ jumbo, gigantesco; **— jet** jumbo *m*

jump [ʤʌmp] VI (spring) saltar; (increase, as temperature, prices) dar un salto; VT (capture in checkers) comer; (ride a horse over barrier) hacer saltar; (mug) asaltar; (cross a river, mountains, etc.) salvar; **to — at** abalanzarse sobre; **to — over** saltar; **to —-start** hacer un puente; **to — the track** descarrilarse; **to — to conclusions** hacer deducciones precipitadas; N salto *m*; (in prices) subida repentina *f*; **—rope** cuerda de saltar *f*; **—shot** tiro en suspensión *m*; **—suit** mono *m*

jumper [ʤʌmpɚ] N (person who jumps) saltador -ora *mf*; (dress) jumper *m*; Sp pichi *m*; **— cable** puente *m*

jumpy [ʤʌmpi] ADJ nervioso, asustadizo

junction [ʤʌŋkʃən] N (act or state of joining) unión *f*; (joining of two rivers) confluencia *f*; (of two railways) empalme *m*, entronque *m*; (of roads) cruce *m*

juncture [ʤʌŋktʃɚ] N (point where joined) juntura *f*; **at this —** en esta coyuntura

June [ʤun] N junio *m*

jungle [ʤʌŋgəl] N selva *f*, jungla *f*; **the law of the —** la ley de la selva

junior [ʤúnjɚ] ADJ (younger) menor; (more recent) más nuevo, de menos antigüedad; **— college** institución para los dos primeros años de la licenciatura *f*; **John Smith Jr.** John Smith, hijo; N estudiante del tercer año *mf*

juniper [ʤúnəpɚ] N enebro *m*

junk [ʤʌŋk] N (useless articles) trastos viejos *m pl*; (metal) chatarra *f*; (Chinese boat) junco *m*; **— dealer** chatarrero -ra *mf*; **— food** comida basura *f*, porquerías *f pl*; **— mail** publicidad por correo *f*; **— e-mail** correo electrónico basura *m*; **—yard** chatarrería *f*; VT desechar, echar a la basura

junkie [ʤʌŋki] N *fam* drogata *mf*, drogota *mf*

jurisdiction [ʤʊrɪsdíkʃən] N jurisdicción *f*

jurisprudence [ʤʊrɪsprúdns] N jurisprudencia *f*

juror [ʤúrɚ] N miembro de un jurado *m*, jurado -da *mf*

jury [ʤúri] N jurado *m*; **— box** banco de jurado *m*; VT **to —-rig** chapucear

just [dʒʌst] ADJ justo; ADV (exactly) exactamente, precisamente; (only) solo; **— like that** Am así nomás; **he — left** acaba de salir; **she is — a little girl** no es más que una niña; **you'll — have to wait** tendrás que esperar; **— barely** apenas; **the meeting is — starting** la reunión apenas comienza; **that is — what I wanted to talk to you about** precisamente de eso te quería hablar

justice [dʒʌstɪs] N (fairness) justicia f; (judge) juez -eza mf; **to bring to —** enjuiciar; **the painting doesn't do him —** el retrato no le favorece

justification [dʒʌstəfɪkéʃən] N justificación f

justify [dʒʌstəfaɪ] VT justificar

jut [dʒʌt] VI sobresalir, proyectarse

juvenile [dʒúvənaɪl] ADJ juvenil; **— delinquent** delincuente juvenil mf

juxtapose [dʒʌkstəpoz] VT yuxtaponer

Kk

kangaroo [kæŋgərú] N canguro m

karat, carat [kǽrət] N quilate m

kayak [káɪæk] N kayak m

Kazak, Kazakh [kəzǽk] ADJ & N kazako -ka mf

Kazakhstan [kɑzúkstɑn] N Kazajstán m

keel [kil] N quilla f; VI/VT volcar[se]; **to — over** (ship) volcar[se]; (person) caer de cabeza, desplomarse

keen [kin] ADJ (edge) afilado; (perception) fino; (mind) agudo, penetrante

keenness [kínnɪs] N (of a blade) lo afilado; (of perception) fineza f; (of mind) agudeza f

keep [kip] VI (continue) seguir; (not spoil) aguantar; VT (retain) guardar; (maintain) mantener; (employ) tener; (look after) cuidar; **to — a diary** llevar un diario; **to — a secret** guardar un secreto; **to — at it** persistir; **to — away** mantener[se] alejado; **to — back** (stay away) tener a raya; (restrain) contener; **to — bad company** andar en mala compañía; **to — from** (prevent) impedir; (protect) proteger contra; **to — [on] talking** seguir hablando; **to — the door open** mantener la puerta abierta; **to — off the grass** no pisar el césped; **to — up** (perform as well) seguir el tren; (stay informed) mantenerse al tanto; **to — one's hands off** no tocar; **to — someone posted** mantener al corriente a alguien; **to — quiet** estarse callado; **to — to the right** mantenerse a la derecha; **to — track of** (do accounts) llevar la cuenta de; (consider) no perder de vista; **to — watch** vigilar; **he —s a maid** tiene una criada; **she kept me on the**

phone me [re]tuvo en el teléfono; N **for —s** (forever) para siempre; (for real) en serio; **—sake** recuerdo m

keeper [kípə] N (of people) guardián m; (of things) custodio m

keeping [kípɪŋ] N custodia f; **in — with** en armonía con

keg [kɛg] N barril m

Kegel exercises [kégəl ɛksəsaɪzɪz] N ejercicios de Kegel m pl

kennel [kénl] N residencia de perros f

Kenya [kénjə] N Kenia f

Kenyan [kénjən] ADJ & N keniata mf

kept [kɛpt] see keep

kernel [kʰnl] N (seed) semilla f, grano m; (essence) meollo m

kerosene [kérəsin] N queroseno m

kestrel [késtrəl] N cernícalo m

ketchup [kétʃəp] N salsa de tomate f, cátsup m

kettle [kédl] N caldera f, hervidor m; (for tea) tetera f; **—drum** tímpano m, timbal m; **that's another — of fish** es harina de otro costal

key [ki] N (for locks) llave f; (secret, book of answers) clave f; (for winding) clavija f; (on keyboard) tecla f; (island) cayo m; (music) clave f; **—board** teclado m; **—hole** ojo de la cerradura m; **— indicator** indicador clave m; **—note** tónica f; **—note address** discurso de apertura m; **—pad** teclado numérico m; **—ring** llavero m; **— signature** armadura f; **—stone** piedra angular f; **—stroke** pulsación [de la tecla] f; **—word** palabra clave f; **—word search** búsqueda por palabra clave f; **to sing on —** cantar a tono; ADJ clave; VT (scratch) rayar; **to be —ed up** estar sobreexcitado

kg [kíləgræm] see kilogram

khaki [kǽki] N kaki m, caqui m

kick [kɪk] VI/VT (person) patear; (horse) dar coces [a], cocear; VI (gun) dar un culatazo, retroceder; **to — around** (discuss) discutir; (to mistreat) dar por la cabeza; **to — at** dar patadas; **to — out** echar a patadas; **to — start** arrancar; **to — the bucket** estirar la pata; **to — up a lot of dust** levantar una polvareda; **to — a habit** dejar un vicio; N (by a person) patada f, puntapié m; (by a soccer player) patada f; (of a horse) coz f; Am patada f; (of a gun) culatazo m; (in the air) pataleo m; **this whisky has a —** este whisky es fuerte; **I get a — out of swimming** me encanta nadar; **—back** comisión ilegal f; Mex mordida f; **—off** (football) saque de inicio m; (soccer) saque inicial m; **—stand** soporte m

kid [kɪd] N (young goat) cabrito m, chivo m; (leather) cabritilla f; (child) niño -ña mf; (young person) chico -ca mf; **— stuff** juego de niños m; VI bromear, embromar, tomar el pelo

kidnap [kídnæp] VT secuestrar, raptar

kidnapper [kídnæpɚ] N secuestrador -ora *mf*

kidnapping [kídnæpɪŋ] N secuestro *m*, rapto *m*

kidney [kídni] N riñón *m*; — **bean** judía *f*; — **failure** insuficiencia renal *f*; — **stone** cálculo renal *m*

kill [kɪl] VI/VT matar; (drink completely) terminar; (turn off) apagar; **that comedian —s me** ese cómico me mata de risa; N (animal killed) caza *f*; (slaughter) matanza *f*; —**joy** aguafiestas *mf sg*

killer [kílɚ] N asesino -na *mf*; — **bee** abeja asesina *f*; — **whale** orca *f*; **a — game** un partidazo

killing [kílɪŋ] N (slaughter) matanza *f*; (murder) asesinato *m*; (animal killed) caza *f*; **to make a —** llenarse de oro

kilo [kílo] N kilo *m*, quilo *m*

kilobyte [kíləbait] N kilobyte *m*

kilogram [kíləgræm] N kilogramo *m*

kilometer [kɪlámɪDɚ] N kilómetro *m*

kilowatt [kíləwɑt] N kilovatio *m*; —**-hour** kilovatio-hora *f*

kin [kɪn] N parentela *f*, parientes *m pl*; —**sman** pariente *m*; —**swoman** parienta *f*; **next of —** deudos *m pl*

kind [kaind] ADJ (benevolent) bondadoso, bueno; (words) amable; **to be — to animals** ser cariñoso con los animales; —**hearted** de buen corazón; — **of tired** algo cansado; N clase *f*, tipo *m*, género *m*; **to pay in —** (without money) pagar en especie; (retaliate) pagar con la misma moneda

kindergarten [kíndɚgɑrtn] N jardín infantil / de niños *m*; Sp parvulario *m*

kindle [kíndl] VT (fire) prender; (interest) despertar, provocar; VI encenderse

kindling [kíndlɪŋ] N leña ligera *f*, astillas *f pl*

kindly [káindli] ADJ bondadoso, bueno; ADV (with kindness) amablemente; (please) por favor; **we thank you —** le agradecemos mucho; **not to take — to criticism** no aceptar de buen grado las críticas

kindness [káindnɪs] N (state) bondad *f*, amabilidad *f*; (act) favor *m*

kindred [kíndrɪd] ADJ emparentado; — **spirits** espíritus afines *m pl*, almas gemelas *f pl*

kinesiology [kənizɪálədʒi] N quinesiología *f*

kinesthesia [kɪnɪsθíʒə] N cinestesia *f*

king [kɪŋ] N rey *m* (also in chess, cards); (in checkers) dama *f*; —**fisher** martín pescador *m*; —**pin** (in a mechanism) pivote central *m*; (in bowling) bolo central *m*; (person) figura central *f*; ADJ —**-sized** extra grande

kingdom [kíŋdəm] N reino *m*

kingly [kíŋli] ADJ real

kink [kɪŋk] N (bend) doblez *m*; (pain) tortícolis *f*

kinky [kíŋki] ADJ crespo

kinship [kínʃɪp] N (family connection) parentesco *m*; (likeness) afinidad *f*

kiosk [kíask] N quiosco *m*

Kiribati [kirəbádi] N Kiribati *m*

kiss [kɪs] VI/VT besar[se]; N beso *m*

kit [kɪt] N (of tools) caja *f*; (of first aid) botiquín *m*; (of sewing notions) costurero *m*

kitchen [kítʃɪn] N cocina *f*; —**ware** utensilios de cocina *m pl*

kite [kait] N (toy) cometa *f*; (bird) milano *m*

kitten [kítn] N gatito *m*

kitty [kídi] N (young cat) gatito *m*, minino *m*; (petty cash) caja chica *f*, fondo *m*

kleptomania [klɛptəméniə] N cleptomanía *f*

kleptomaniac [klɛptəméniæk] N cleptómano -na *mf*

knack [næk] N buena mano *f*, maña *f*; **once you get the —** una vez que le agarras la vuelta/onda

knapsack [nǽpsæk] N mochila *f*

knave [nev] N (in cards) sota *f*

knead [nid] VT amasar, sobar

knee [ni] N rodilla *f*; —**cap** rótula *f*; —**-deep** hasta las rodillas; —**-jerk liberal** liberal fanático *m*; —**-jerk reaction** reacción visceral *f*; VT dar un rodillazo

kneel [nil] VI arrodillarse

knell [nɛl] N doble *m*; VI doblar

knelt [nɛlt] *see* kneel

knew [nu] *see* know

knickknack [níknæk] N chuchería *f*, baratija *f*

knife [naif] N cuchillo *m*; (big) cuchilla *f*; (folding) navaja *f*; (for carving) trinchante *m*; VT acuchillar; **at —point** a punta de cuchillo

knight [nait] N caballero *m*; (in chess) caballo *m*; — **errant** caballero andante *m*; VT armar caballero

knighthood [náithud] N (all knights) caballería *f*; (title) orden de la caballería *f*

knit [nit] VI/VT tejer; **to — one's brow** fruncir el entrecejo / el ceño

knitting [nídɪŋ] N tejido *m*; — **needle** aguja de punto *f*

knob [nɑb] N (on a door) pomo *m*, perilla *f*, tirador *m*; (protuberance) protuberancia *f*

knock [nɑk] VI (hit) golpear; (precombust) golpetear; (call at the door) llamar, tocar; VT (criticize) criticar; **to — a hole in the wall** hacer un agujero en la pared a golpes; **to — down** derribar, echar abajo, tumbar; **to — off** (stop working) terminar; (reduce) rebajar; (make fall) tirar; (kill) liquidar; — **it off!** ¡basta! **to — into** golpearse contra; **to — out** noquear; **to — over** voltear, revolcar; N (pounding) golpe *m*, toque *m*; (criticism) crítica *f*; (in a motor) golpeteo *m*; —**out** (boxing) nocaut *m*; (attractive person) bomba *f*; ADJ —**-kneed** patizambo, zambo

knocker [nákɚ] N llamador *m*, aldaba *f*

knoll [noɫ] N morro *m*, loma *f*

knot [nat] N nudo *m* (also in wood, unit of speed); (of people) grupo *m*; (swelling) chichón *m*; VI/VT anudar[se]

knotty [nádi] ADJ (full of knots) nudoso; (difficult) dificultoso, enredado

know [no] VI/VT (to have knowledge of, to know how to) saber; VT (to be acquainted with, have sexual intercourse with) conocer; (to recognize) reconocer; (distinguish) distinguir; **to — how to swim** saber nadar; **to — of** estar enterado de; N **to be in the —** estar al tanto; **—-how** pericia *f*; **—-it-all** sabelotodo *mf*

knowing [nóiŋ] ADJ (complicitous) cómplice; (astute) astuto

knowingly [nóiŋli] ADV a sabiendas

knowledge [nálɪdʒ] N (awareness) conocimiento *m*; (information known) saber *m*, conocimientos *m pl*; **not to my —** no que yo sepa

known [non] ADJ **little —** poco conocido; **well — ** bien conocido; **he's — for his cooking** se le conoce por su cocina; **the truth wasn't — until last year** no se supo la verdad hasta el año pasado

known [non] *see* know

knuckle [nákəɫ] N nudillo *m*; **—ball** bola de nudillos *f*; **—head** tarambana *mf*; VI **to — down** arremangarse, aplicarse con empeño; **to — under** someterse

Korea [kɔríə] Corea *f*

Korean [kɔríən] ADJ & N coreano -na *mf*

kosher [kóʃə] ADJ kosher

Kuwait [kuwét] N Kuwait *m*

Kuwaiti [kuwédi] ADJ & N kuwaití *mf*

Kyrgyzstan [kírgistən] N Kirguistán *m*

Ll

lab [læb] *see* laboratory

label [lébəɫ] N (sticker) etiqueta *f*, rótulo *m*; (characterization) calificativo *m*; (brand) marca *f*; (of recording companies) sello *m*; VT etiquetar, rotular

labor [lébə] N trabajo *m*, labor *f*; (body of workers) mano de obra *f*; (working class) clase obrera *f*; (uterine contractions) trabajo de parto *m*; **—-intensive** que requiere mucha mano de obra; **— pains** dolores de parto *m pl*; **— union** sindicato *m*; **to be in —** estar de parto; ADJ laboral; VI (work) trabajar; (dedicate oneself) afanarse; **to — under a disadvantage** sufrir una desventaja

laboratory [lǽbrətɔri] N laboratorio *m*

laborer [lébərə] N jornalero -ra *mf*; (unskilled)

peón -ona *mf*

laborious [ləbóriəs] ADJ (industrious) laborioso; (difficult) trabajoso

labrador [lǽbrədɔr] N (dog) labrador *m*

labyrinth [lǽbərɪnθ] N laberinto *m*

lace [les] N (cloth) encaje *m*; (cord) cordón *m*; VT (to adorn with lace) bordar con encaje; (to insert laces into) poner cordones a; (to spike) echar alcohol; VI atarse

lack [læk] N falta *f*, carencia *f*; VI/VT carecer de, faltarle a uno; **he —s courage** le falta valentía; **—luster** mediocre

lackey [lǽki] N lacayo *m*

lacking [lǽkɪŋ] ADJ (deficient) deficiente; **good bars are — in this town** faltan buenos bares en este pueblo; **— in** falto de, carente de

laconic [ləkánɪk] ADJ lacónico

lacquer [lǽkə] N laca *f*; VT lacar, laquear

lactation [læktéʃən] N lactancia *f*

lactic acid [lǽktɪkǽsɪd] N ácido láctico *m*

lactose [lǽktos] N lactosa *f*; **— intolerance** intolerancia a la lactosa *f*

ladder [lǽdə] N escalera *f*

laden [lédn] ADJ cargado

ladle [lédɫ] N cucharón *m*, cazo *m*; VT servir con cucharón

lady [lédi] N señora *f*, dama *f*; **—bug** mariquita *f*; **—like** muy fina; **—love** amada *f*; **ladies' room** *Sp* aseo de damas *m*, *Am* servicio de damas *m*

lag [læg] VI (fall behind) quedarse atrás, rezagarse; (flag) disminuir; N retardo *m*, retraso *m*

lagoon [ləgún] N laguna *f*

laid [led] *see* lay

laid-back [ledbǽk] ADJ apacible, tranquilo

lain [len] *see* lie 'estar situado'

lair [lɛr] N guarida *f*

lake [lek] N lago *m*

lamb [læm] N cordero *m*; (yearling) borrego *m*

lame [lem] ADJ cojo; *Am* rengo; **—brained** idiota; **— duck** funcionario -ria cesante *mf*; **— excuse** pretexto tonto *m*; VT dejar cojo

lament [ləmént] N lamento *m*; VI lamentar[se]; VT llorar

lamentable [ləméntəbəɫ] ADJ lamentable

lamentation [læməntéʃən] N lamentación *f*, lamento *m*

laminate [lǽmənet] VT laminar

lamp [læmp] N lámpara *f*; (on a street) farol *m*; **—post** farol *m*; **—shade** pantalla *f*

LAN [local area network] [læn] N red [de área] local *f*

lance [læns] N lanza *f*; (lancet) lanceta *f*; VT lancear; (a wound) abrir con una lanceta

lancet [lǽnsɪt] N lanceta *f*

land [lænd] N tierra *f*; (lot) terreno *m*; (country) país *m*, tierra *f*; **—fill** vertedero *m*; **— grant university** universidad con terrenos concedidos por el estado *f*; —**lady** casera *f*, propietaria *f*; —**lord** casero *m*, propietario *m*; —**mark** (marker) hito *m*, mojón *m*; (historical) hito *m*; — **mine** mina *f*; —**owner** hacendado -da *mf*; —**scape** (terrain) paisaje *m*; (in printing) orientación horizontal *f*; —**scape architecture** paisajismo *m*; —**slide** (mass of land) derrumbe *m*, desprendimiento *m*; (election) victoria aplastante *f*; — **use** ordenamiento territorial *m*; VI/VT (a ship) atracar; (an airplane) aterrizar; **you'll — in jail** terminarás en la cárcel; VT (a fish) *Sp* coger; *Am* pescar; (a job) conseguir

landing [lǽndɪŋ] N (of a ship) desembarco *m*; (of cargo) desembarque *m*; (of an airplane) aterrizaje *m*; (place) desembarcadero *m*; (on stairs) descansillo *m*; — **field** campo de aterrizaje *m*; — **gear** tren de aterrizaje *m*; — **strip** pista de aterrizaje *f*

lane [len] N (country road) sendero *m*; (road division) carril *m*; (for ships) ruta *f*

language [lǽŋgwɪdʒ] N lengua *f*, idioma *m*; (faculty of speech, computer code) lenguaje *m*

languid [lǽŋgwɪd] ADJ lánguido

languish [lǽŋgwɪʃ] VI languidecer

languor [lǽŋgəʳ] N languidez *f*

lanky [lǽŋki] ADJ larguirucho, zancudo

lanolin [lǽnəlɪn] N lanolina *f*

lantern [lǽntəʳn] N farol *m*; (of a lighthouse) faro *m*, linterna *f*

Laos [léas] N Laos *m*

Laotian [leóʃən] ADJ & N laosiano -na *mf*

lap [læp] N (part of body) regazo *m*; (part of a race) vuelta *f*; —**dog** perro faldero *m*; —**top computer** *Am* computadora portátil *f*, *Sp* ordenador portátil *m*; **to live in the — of luxury** vivir en la abundancia; VI/VT lamer

lapel [ləpél] N solapa *f*

lapidary [lǽpɪderi] ADJ & N lapidario -ria *mf*

lapse [læps] N (period of time) lapso *m*; (linguistic error) lapsus *m*; (defect in memory) fallo *m*; (fall) caída *f*; (termination) caducidad *f*; VI (fall) caer; (decline) decaer; (end) caducar, vencer

larceny [lársəni] N latrocinio *m*, hurto *m*

lard [lɑrd] N manteca *f*; VT enmantecar; (with bacon) mechar

large [lɑrdʒ] ADJ grande; —-**scale** a gran escala; **a — company** una gran compañía / una compañía grande; **at —** (not in jail) suelto, libre; N tamaño grande *m*

largely [lárdʒli] ADV (in the greatest number) en su mayoría; (to the greatest degree) en gran parte

lariat [lǽriət] N reata *f*

lark [lɑrk] N (bird) alondra *f*; (bit of fun) diversión *f*; **to go on a —** ir de jarana

larva [lárvə] N larva *f*

laryngeal [ləríndʒəl] ADJ laríngeo; — **angina** angina laríngea *f*

laryngitis [lǽrəndʒáɪdɪs] N laringitis *f*

larynx [lǽrɪŋks] N laringe *f*

lascivious [ləsívɪəs] ADJ lascivo

laser [lézəʳ] N láser *m*; — **beam** rayo láser *m*; — **printer** impresora láser *f*

lash [læʃ] N (blow with a whip, tail, etc.) azote *m*, latigazo *m*; (blow of waves) embate *m*; (part of eye) pestaña *f*; VT (whip) azotar; (tie) amarrar; **to — out** fustigar

lasso [lǽso] N lazo *m*, reata *f*; VT lazar; *Am* enlazar

last [læst] ADJ (in a series) último; (definitive) final; —-**ditch** desesperado; — **minute** de último momento; — **name** apellido *m*; — **night** anoche; — **rites** extrema unción *f*, viático *m*; — **straw** colmo *m*; — **word** última palabra *f*; — **year** el año pasado; **next to the** — penúltimo; ADV último; **to arrive** — ser el último en llegar; **when — seen** cuando se lo vio por última vez; **at** — finalmente; N el último; (of a shoe) horma *f*; VI durar; (live on) perdurar

lasting [lǽstɪŋ] ADJ duradero, perdurable

lastly [lǽstli] ADV por último

latch [lætʃ] N pestillo *m*, picaporte *m*, cierre *m*; VI cerrar con el pestillo; **to — on** agarrarse de; **to — onto** pegarse a

late [let] ADJ (tardy) tardío; (hour) avanzada; (recent) reciente, último; (recently deceased) finado; — **afternoon** atardecer *m*; —**comer** rezagado -da *mf*; — **fee** recargo por mora *m*; ADV tarde; — **in the night** a una hora avanzada de la noche; — **into the night** hasta cualquier hora de la noche; — **in the week** a finales de la semana; **it is —** ya es tarde; **of** — últimamente; **to be** — llegar tarde; **to work** — trabajar hasta tarde; **the train was ten minutes** — el tren llegó con diez minutos de retraso

lately [létli] ADV últimamente

lateness [létnɪs] N tardanza *f*

latent [létnt] ADJ latente

later [létəʳ] ADJ posterior; ADV más tarde, con posterioridad; **see you** — hasta luego; — **on** más tarde

lateral [lǽdəəl] ADJ lateral

latest [léDɪst] ADJ último; **the — fashion** la última moda; **the — news** las últimas novedades; N **at the** — a más tardar

latex [léteks] N látex *m*

lathe [leð] N torno *m*

lather [lǽðəʳ] N (foam) espuma *f*; (sweat) sudor *m*; **he got into a** — se puso histérico; VT enjabonar; VI hacer espuma

Latin [lǽtn] ADJ latino; — **America** América Latina *f*, Latinoamérica *f*; — **American** latinoamericano -na *mf*; N (language) latín *m*

latitude [lǽDItud] N latitud *f*; (freedom) flexibilidad *f*

latrine [lətrín] N letrina *f*

latter [lǽDɚ] ADJ último; **in the — days of the Roman Republic** en los últimos días de la República Romana; **toward the — part of the week** a finales de la semana; **the —** este *m*, esta *f*

lattice [lǽDIs] N enrejado *m*, entramado *m*; (of a window) celosía *f*

Latvia [lǽtvɪə] N Letonia *f*

Latvian [lǽtvɪən] ADJ & N letón -ona *mf*

laud [lɔd] VT loar

laudable [lɔ́Dəbəł] ADJ laudable, loable

laugh [lǽf] VI reír[se]; **to — at** reírse de; **to — loudly** reírse a carcajadas; **to — up/in one's sleeve** reírse para sus adentros; **she —ed in his face** se rió en su cara; N risa *f*; **we did it for —s** lo hicimos por diversión

laughable [lǽfəbəł] ADJ risible

laughingstock [lǽfɪŋstɑk] N hazmerreír *m*

laughter [lǽftɚ] N risa *f*

launch [lɔntʃ] VT (a boat) botar; (a rocket, new product) lanzar; (software) iniciar; **to — forth/out** lanzarse; N lancha *f*; (act of launching a boat) botadura *f*; (act of launching a rocket) lanzamiento *m*

launder [lɔ́ndɚ] VI/VT (clothes) lavar; (money) blanquear, lavar; (wash and iron clothes) lavar y planchar

Laundromat™ [lɔ́ndrəmæt] N lavadero automático *m*

laundry [lɔ́ndri] N (business establishment) lavandería *f*, lavadero *m*; (room in house) cuarto de lavado *m*, lavadero *m*; (clothes to be washed) ropa sucia *f*; (washed clothes) ropa limpia *f*

laurel [lɔ́rəł] N laurel *m* (also honor); **to rest on one's —s** dormirse sobre los laureles

lava [lávə] N lava *f*

lavatory [lǽvətɔri] N (basin) lavabo *m*; (bathroom) baño *m*, retrete *m*

lavender [lǽvəndɚ] N espliego *m*, lavanda *f*; ADJ lavanda

lavish [lǽvɪʃ] ADJ (generous) pródigo, espléndido; (abundant) abundante, copioso; VT prodigar; **to — praise upon** colmar de alabanzas a

law [lɔ] N ley *f*; (discipline) derecho *m*, jurisprudencia *f*; (police) policía *f*; **— and order** orden público *m*; **—breaker** infractor -ora *mf*, transgresor -ora *mf*; **—maker** legislador -ora *mf*; **— of diminishing returns** ley de [los] rendimientos decrecientes *f*; **— student** estudiante de derecho *mf*; **—suit** pleito *m*, litigio *m*; **to practice —** ejercer la abogacía; **to take the — into one's hands** hacer justicia por mano propia; ADJ **—-abiding** respetuoso de las leyes

lawful [lɔ́fəł] ADJ (in accordance with the law) legal; (allowed by law) lícito; (recognized by law) legítimo

lawless [lɔ́lɪs] ADJ (anarchic) anárquico; (illegal) ilegal

lawn [lɔn] N césped *m*, grama *f*; **— mower** cortadora de césped *f*

lawyer [lɔ́jɚ] N abogado -da *mf*

lax [læks] ADJ laxo

laxative [lǽksəDIV] ADJ & N laxante *m*, purgante *m*

laxity [lǽksIDi] N flojedad *f*, laxitud *f*

lay [le] VT colocar; (eggs) poner; (a cable) tender; **to — aside** (abandon) dejar de lado; (save) guardar; **to — a wager** apostar; **to — bare** poner al descubierto; **to — bricks** poner ladrillos; **to — down arms** rendir las armas; **to — down the law** imponerse; **to — hold of** asir, agarrar; **to — into** atacar; **to — off a workman** despedir temporalmente a un obrero; **to — one's head on a pillow** recostar la cabeza sobre una almohada; **to — open** exponer; **to — out a plan** trazar un plan; **to — up** almacenar; **to be laid up** estar en cama; **to — waste to** asolar; N situación *f*, orientación *f*; **—man** (nonexpert) lego *m*; (clergy) laico *m*; **—out** despido temporal de un empleado *m*; **—out** diseño/trazado de página *m*; ADJ lego, laico

lay [le] *see* lie 'estar situado'

layer [léɚ] N capa *f*; (geological) estrato *m*; (hen) gallina ponedora *f*; **— cake** tarta de capas *f*

laziness [lézɪns] N pereza *f*, holgazanería *f*, flojera *f*

lazy [lézi] ADJ perezoso, holgazán, flojo

LBO [leveraged buyout] [ɛ́łbíó] N compra apalancada *f*

LDL [low density lipoprotein] [ɛ́łdíɛ́ł] N LBD *f*

lead¹ [lɛd] N (metal) plomo *m*; (graphite) mina *f*; **— poisoning** intoxicación con plomo *f*

lead² [lid] VT (guide) guiar; (guide a horse) llevar de la rienda; (induce, take) llevar, inducir; (be in charge, be first) encabezar, liderar; (direct) dirigir; (be superior to) estar a la cabeza de; **to — a life of ease** llevar una vida fácil; **to — the way** mostrar el camino; VI (provide passage to, result in) llevar a; (be first) estar a la cabeza; **to — astray** llevar por mal camino; N (first position) delantera *f*, primer lugar *m*; (clue) indicio *m*; (most important role) papel principal *m*, liderazgo *m*; **—off** comienzo; **— story** noticia principal *f*; **to take the —** (in sports) ponerse por delante en el marcador

leaden [lɛ́dn̩] ADJ (of lead) de plomo; (color) plomizo; (oppressive, slow) pesado

leader [lídɚ] N (in politics) líder *mf*, caudillo *m*; (in a race) líder *mf*; (in music) director -ora *mf*; (as a guide) guía *mf*

leadership [lídəʃip] N dirección *f*, liderazgo *m*

leading [lídɪŋ] ADJ (most important) principal; (arriving first) delantero; **— indicators** indicadores anticipados *m pl*; **— man** actor principal *m*

leaf [lif] N hoja *f*; VI echar hojas; **to — through a book** hojear un libro

leafless [líflɪs] ADJ sin hojas, deshojado

leaflet [líflɪt] N (small leaf) foliolo *m*; (printed matter) volante *m*; (folded printed matter) pliego *m*

leafy [lifi] ADJ (with foliage) frondoso; (in the form of leaves) de hoja

league [lig] N (alliance) liga *f*; (unit of distance) legua *f*; VI/VT aliar[se]

leak [lik] N (in a roof) gotera *f*; (in a boat, bucket, etc.) agujero *m*; (of information) filtración *f*; (of gas, steam, electricity) escape *m*, fuga *f*; VI (roof) gotear[se]; (boat) hacer agua; (gas) salirse, escaparse; (information) filtrarse; VT revelar información interna confidencial

leaky [liki] ADJ (roof) que tiene goteras; (boat) que hace agua; (gas, electricity) que pierde

lean [lin] VI/VT (incline) inclinar[se]; (support) apoyar[se], reclinar[se], recostar[se]; **to — on** presionar; ADJ magro; **— year** mal año *m*

leap [lip] VI/VT saltar; **to — at a chance** aprovechar una oportunidad; **to — to mind** ocurrírsele a uno; N salto *m*; **—frog** pídola *f*; **— year** año bisiesto *m*

leapt [lɛpt] *see* leap

learn [lɜrn] VI/VT aprender; (find out) enterarse de

learned [lɜ́rnɪd] ADJ erudito, letrado

learner [lɜ́rnə] N estudiante *mf*; (driver) aprendiz *-iza mf*

learning [lɜ́rnɪŋ] N (result) erudición *f*, saber *m*; (process) aprendizaje *m*; **— disability** problema de aprendizaje *m*

learnt [lɜrnt] *see* learn

lease [lis] N (action) arrendamiento *m*; (contract) contrato de arrendamiento *m*; (period) período de arrendamiento *m*; **for —** se arrienda; **to have a new — on life** nacer de nuevo; VI/VT arrendar

leash [liʃ] N traílla *f*, correa *f*

least [list] ADJ **he doesn't have the — chance** no tiene la más mínima posibilidad; **the — amount of money** la menor cantidad de dinero; **— common denominator** mínimo común denominador *m*; ADV menos; **the — important** el/la menos importante; **at —** al menos, por lo menos; N **I received the — of anyone** yo fui el que recibió menos de todos

leather [lɛ́ðə] N cuero *m*; ADJ de cuero; **— strap** correa *f*

leave [liv] VT (a person, thing) dejar; (a place) salir de, irse de; VI salir, partir; **to — off**

(stop) parar de; (omit) omitir; **to — out** omitir; **I have two books left** me quedan dos libros; N permiso *m*; **to be on — of** estar de licencia; **— of absence** licencia *f*; **to take — of** despedirse de

leaven [lɛ́vən] N levadura *f*; VT leudar

leavings [lívɪŋz] N (leftovers) sobras *f pl*; (refuse) desperdicios *m pl*

Lebanese [lɛbəníz] ADJ & N libanés *-esa mf*

Lebanon [lɛ́bənən] N Líbano *m*

lecherous [lɛ́tʃəəs] ADJ lujurioso

lecture [lɛ́ktʃə] N (presentation) conferencia *f*, disertación *f*; (sermon) sermón *m*; (long-winded speech) perorata *f*; VI (present) dar una conferencia, disertar; VT (scold) sermonear

lecturer [lɛ́ktʃəə] N conferenciante *mf*; (academic rank) profesor *-ora mf*

led [lɛd] *see* lead

LED [light-emitting diode] [ɛ́ɬídí] N LED *m*

ledge [lɛdʒ] N cornisa *f*

ledger [lɛ́dʒə] N libro mayor *m*

leech [litʃ] N sanguijuela *f*

leer [lɪr] VT (sideways) mirar de soslayo; (lecherously) mirar con lujuria; N (sideways) mirada de soslayo *f*; (lecherous) mirada lujuriosa *f*

leeway [líwe] N margen de maniobra *m*; (of a ship) deriva *f*

left [lɛft] ADJ izquierdo; **—-click** presionar el botón izquierdo del ratón; **—-handed** zurdo; **—-handed compliment** alabanza irónica *f*; **—-handed tool** herramienta para zurdos *f*; **— justification** alineación a la izquierda *f*; **—-wing** de izquierdas; N izquierda *f*; **at / on/to/toward the —** a/hacia la izquierda; **to make a —** doblar/girar a la izquierda

left [lɛft] *see* leave

leftist [lɛ́ftɪst] N & ADJ izquierdista *mf*

leg [lɛg] N (human) pierna *f*; (animal, furniture) pata *f*; (wading bird) zanca *f*; (of a journey) etapa *f*; **to be on one's last —s** estar en las últimas; **to pull someone's —** tomarle el pelo a alguien; **to stretch one's —s** estirar las piernas

legacy [lɛ́gəsi] N legado *m*

legal [lígəɬ] ADJ (in accordance with the law) legal; (permitted by law) lícito; (recognized by law) legítimo; (having to do with the law) jurídico; **— age** mayoría de edad *f*; **— code** ordenamiento *m pl*; **— fees** honorarios del abogado *m pl*; **— holiday** día feriado *m*; **— procedure** procedimiento jurídico *m*; **— tender** moneda de curso legal *f*

legality [lɪgǽlɪDi] N legalidad *f*

legalization [ligəlɪzéʃən] N legalización *f*

legalize [lígəlaɪz] VT legalizar

legation [lɪgéʃən] N legación *f*

legend [lɛ́dʒənd] N leyenda *f* (also inscription);

(of a map) clave f

legendary [léʤǝnderi] ADJ legendario

leggings [légɪŋz] N (ankle to knee) polainas f pl; (trousers) leggings m pl

legible [léʤǝbǝł] ADJ legible

legion [líʤǝn] N legión f

legionnaire [liʤǝnér] N legionario m; **—'s disease** enfermedad del legionario f, legionelosis f

legislate [léʤɪslet] VI/VT legislar

legislation [léʤɪsléʃǝn] N legislación f

legislative [léʤɪsleDIV] ADJ legislativo

legislator [léʤɪsleDǝ] N legislador -ora mf

legislature [léʤɪsletʃǝ] N legislatura f

legitimacy [lǝʤídǝmǝsi] N legitimidad f

legitimate [lɪʤídǝmɪt] ADJ legítimo

legitimize [lǝʤídǝmaɪz] VT legitimar

legume [légjum] N legumbre f

leisure [líʒǝ] N ocio m, holgura f; **— activities** actividades recreativas f pl; **— hours** horas de ocio f pl, tiempo libre m; **to be at —** estar desocupado; **do it at your —** hazlo cuando te convenga

leisurely [líʒǝli] ADJ lento, deliberado; ADV sin prisa

lemon [lémǝn] N limón m; ADJ de limón; **— tree** limonero m

lemonade [lemǝnéd] N limonada f

lend [lend] VI/VT prestar; **to — a hand** dar una mano

lender [léndǝ] N (person who lends) prestador -ora mf; (professional) prestamista mf

length [leŋkθ] N (of an object, road) largo m, largura f, longitud f; (of a movie) duración f; (of a book) extensión f; **at —** (in detail) pormenorizadamente; (finally) finalmente; **by two —s** por dos cuerpos; **two meters in — dos** metros de largo; **to go to any —s** hacer lo imposible

lengthen [léŋkθǝn] VI/VT alargar[se]

lengthwise [léŋkθwaɪz] ADV & ADJ a lo largo

lengthy [léŋkθi] ADJ largo, prolongado

lenient [líniǝnt] ADJ indulgente

lens [lenz] N lente m; (of the eye) cristalino m

Lent [lent] N Cuaresma f

lent [lent] see lend

lentil [léntl] N lenteja f

Leon [león] N León m

Leonese [liǝníz] ADJ leonés

leopard [lépǝd] N leopardo m

leprosy [léprǝsi] N lepra f

lesbian [lézbiǝn] ADJ lesbiano; N lesbiana f

lesion [líʒǝn] N lesión f

Lesotho [lǝsóto] N Lesoto m

less [les] ADJ, ADV & PREP menos; **I have — than you do** tengo menos que tú; **— and —** cada vez menos

lessen [lésǝn] VI/VT disminuir, aminorar

lessening [lésǝnɪŋ] N disminución f

lesser [lésǝ] ADJ menor

lesson [lésǝn] N lección f

lest [lest] CONJ no sea que; **— you should think I'm teasing** para que no vayas a creer que estoy bromeando

let [let] VT (permit) dejar, permitir; (rent) alquilar; **— him come** que venga; **—'s do it** hagámoslo; **to — be** dejar en paz; **to — down** (lower) bajar; (disappoint) decepcionar; **to — go** soltar; **to — in** dejar entrar; **to — know** hacer saber; **to — off** (not punish) dejar ir; (allow to get off) dejar bajar; **to — through** dejar pasar; **to — up** (permit to stand) dejar incorporarse; (cease) disminuir; N (in tennis) repetición f; **—down** desilusión f; **—up** tregua f

lethal [líθǝł] ADJ letal

lethargic [lǝθárʤɪk] ADJ aletargado, letárgico

lethargy [léθǝʤi] N letargo m; **to fall into a —** aletargarse

letter [léDǝ] N (of alphabet) letra f; (missive) carta f; **— carrier** cartero -ra mf; **—head** membrete m; **—head paper** papel membretado m; **—-spacing** espacio entre caracteres m; **—s** letras f pl; **the — of the law** la letra de la ley f; **to the —** al pie de la letra; VT grabar

lettuce [léDɪs] N lechuga f

leukemia [lukímiǝ] N leucemia f

levee [lévi] N dique m

level [lévǝł] ADJ llano, plano; **—-headed** sensato; **— playing field** terreno de juego parejo m; **— with** a nivel de; **a — tablespoon** una cucharada al ras; N nivel m (also tool); **on the —** en serio; VT (make level) nivelar, igualar; (to demolish) arrasar, allanar; (to knock down a person) tumbar; (to aim criticism) dirigir; (to aim a gun) apuntar; **to — off** quedar paralelo al suelo; **to — with** hablar en serio con/a

lever [lévǝ] N palanca f

leverage [lévǝɪʤ] N (influence) palanca f; (physical, financial) apalancamiento m

levity [lévɪDi] N ligereza f

levy [lévi] N (of taxes) recaudación f; (of troops) leva f; VT (taxes) recaudar; (troops) reclutar, hacer una leva de

lewd [lud] ADJ lascivo

lewdness [lúdnɪs] N lascivia f

lexical [léksɪkǝł] ADJ léxico

lexicography [leksɪkágrǝfi] N lexicografía f

lexicon [léksɪkǝn] N léxico m

liability [laɪǝbílɪDi] N (disadvantage) desventaja f; (debit) pasivo m; (debts) deudas f pl; (responsibility) responsabilidad legal f; **— insurance** seguro contra daños a terceros m; **liabilities** obligaciones f pl

liable [láɪǝbǝł] ADJ responsable; **— to** propenso a; **she's — to get angry** es probable que se enoje

liaison [liézɑn] N (connection) enlace *m*; (illicit love affair) aventura *f*

liar [láIə-] N mentiroso -sa *mf*, embustero -ra *mf*

libel [láIbəl] N libelo *m*, difamación *f*; VT difamar

liberal [líbə-əl] ADJ & N liberal *mf*

liberalism [líbə-əlɪzəm] N liberalismo *m*

liberality [lìbə-ǽlɪDi] N (generosity) liberalidad *f*; (tolerance) tolerancia *f*

liberalization [lìbə-əlizéʃən] N liberalización *f*

liberalize [líbə-əlaɪz] VI/VT liberalizar[se]

liberate [líbə-et] VT (give freedom to) libertar, liberar; (release from obligation) librar; (give off) desprender

liberation [lìbə-éʃən] N liberación *f*

liberator [líbə-eDə-] N libertador -ora *mf*

Liberia [laɪbíriə] N Liberia *f*

Liberian [laɪbírian] ADJ & N liberiano -na *mf*

libertine [líbə-tin] ADJ & N libertino -na *mf*, calavera *m*

liberty [líbə-Di] N libertad *f*; **at** — autorizado

libidinous [lɪbídnəs] ADJ libidinoso

libido [lɪbíDo] N libido *f*

librarian [laɪbríriən] N bibliotecario -ria *mf*

library [láɪbreri] N biblioteca *f*

libretto [lɪbréDo] N libreto *m*

Libya [líbjə] N Libia *f*

Libyan [líbjən] ADJ & N libio -bia *mf*

license [láɪsəns] N (permission) permiso *m*; (driver's permit, poetic freedom) licencia *f*; — **plate** placa *f*, matrícula *f*; VT (issue license to) otorgar una licencia; (give permission) autorizar

licensing authority [láɪsənsɪŋ əθɔ́rɪDi] N autoridad para otorgar licencias *f*

licentious [laɪsénʃəs] ADJ licencioso

lick [lɪk] VT (touch with tongue) lamer (also waves); (thrash) dar una paliza; (defeat) derrotar; N lamida *f*, lengüetazo *m*; (blow) golpe *m*; **not to do a — of work** no mover un dedo

lickety-split [lɪkɪDisplít] ADV en un santiamén

licking [líkɪŋ] N paliza *f*

licorice [líkə-ɪʃ] N regaliz *m*

lid [lɪd] N (of a container) tapadera *f*, tapa *f*; (of eye) párpado *m*; (on prices) tope *m*

lie [laɪ] N (falsehood) mentira *f*, embuste *m*; (orientation of an object) orientación *f*; — **detector** detector de mentiras *m*; **to give the — to** desmentir; VI mentir; **to — one's way out of a situation** salirse de una situación a mentiras; (be buried) yacer; (to be on a flat surface) estar; (to be situated) estar situado; (be horizontal) tumbarse, acostarse; **he's lying in bed** está acostado en la cama; **to — back** recostarse; **to — down** acostarse, tumbarse; **to — in wait** acechar

Liechtenstein [líktənstaɪn] N Liechtenstein *m*

Liechtensteiner [líktənstaɪnə-] N

liechtensteiniano -na *mf*

lien [lin] N gravamen *m*, carga *f*

lieu [lu] ADV LOC **in — of** en vez de

lieutenant [luténənt] N teniente *mf*; — **colonel** teniente coronel *mf*; — **governor** vicegobernador -ora *mf*

life [laɪf] N vida *f*; —**-and-death** de vida o muerte; —**boat** bote de salvamento *m*; — **cycle** ciclo vital *m*; — **expectancy** expectativa de vida *f*; —**guard** salvavidas *mf sg*; — **imprisonment** prisión perpetua *f*; — **insurance** seguro de vida *m*; — **jacket** salvavidas *m sg*; — **of the party** alma de la fiesta *f*; — **preserver** salvavidas *m sg*; — **raft** balsa salvavidas *f*; — **savings** ahorros de toda la vida *m pl*; — **span** duración de la vida *f*; —**style** estilo de vida *m*; —**-support system** (in space) equipo de vida *m*; (in a hospital) máquina corazón-pulmón *f*; —**time** vida *f*; ADJ (relative to life) vital; (for duration of life) vitalicio; ADJ —**like** natural, que parece vivo; —**long** de toda la vida; —**-sized** de tamaño natural

lifeless [láɪflɪs] ADJ (without living things) sin vida; (dead) muerto, sin vida; (fainted) desfallecido; (without liveliness) sin animación

lifer [láɪfə-] N (prisoner) condenado -da a cadena perpetua *mf*; (soldier) militar de carrera *m*

lift [lɪft] VT (hoist) levantar; (steal) robar; (plagiarize) copiar; VI (disperse) disiparse; (go up) elevarse; N (upward force) empuje *m*; (feeling) mejoría de ánimo *f*; (device for lifting) montacargas *m sg*; **to give someone a —** llevar en coche; *Mex* dar un aventón; —**off** despegue *m*

ligament [lígəmənt] N ligamento *m*

ligature [lígətʃə-] N ligadura *f*

light [laɪt] N (luminescence) luz *f*; (device) luz *f*, lámpara *f*; (for traffic) semáforo *m*; (perspective) perspectiva *f*; (for cigarettes) fuego *m*; —**-emitting diode** diodo electroluminiscente *m*; —**house** faro *m*; —**-year** año luz *m*; ADJ (well-lighted) claro; (of little weight) ligero, leve; (of clothes) fresco; *Am* liviano; — **blue** azul claro *m*; —**-headed** mareado; —**hearted** alegre; — **rain** lluvia fina *f*; —**-skinned** de tez blanca; — **touch** mano delicada *f*; —**weight** de peso ligero; **to make — of** restar importancia a; VI/VT (turn on, ignite) encender[se], prender[se]; (provide light, brighten) iluminar[se]; (land on) posarse en; **to — up** (cigarette) prender, encender; (face) iluminarse; **to — upon** caer sobre

lighten [láɪtn] VI/VT (make / become lighter) aligerar[se], aliviar[se]; (brighten) iluminar[se]; — **up!** ¡no tomes las cosas a la tremenda!

lighter [láɪdɚ] N encendedor m
lighting [láɪdɪŋ] N iluminación f; (in the street) alumbrado m
lightly [láɪtli] ADV (toast) ligeramente; (touch) levemente, suavemente; **I don't take your criticism —** no tomo tus críticas a la ligera
lightness [láɪtnɪs] N (little weight) ligereza f, levedad f; (brightness) claridad f
lightning [láɪtnɪŋ] N relámpago m; — **bug** luciérnaga f; — **rod** pararrayos m sg; **it happened at — speed** pasó como rayo; VI relampaguear
likable [láɪkəbəl] ADJ agradable, simpático
like [laɪk] ADV & PREP como; **to feel — going** tener ganas de ir; **to look — someone** parecerse a alguien; **it looks — rain** parece que va a llover; ADJ semejante, parecido; **in — manner** del mismo modo; —-**minded** del mismo parecer; N —**s gustos** m pl, preferencias f pl; VT gustarle a uno; **he —s dogs** le gustan los perros; **do whatever you —** haz lo que quieras; CONJ **he talked — he was crazy** hablaba como si estuviera loco; **she came — you predicted she would** vino, tal como tú pronosticaste; **I'm —, "you're crazy"** yo pensé/dije, "estás loco"; INTERJ **he was, —, way too old** era como que demasiado viejo
likelihood [láɪklihʊd] N probabilidad f; **in all — he came** lo más probable es que haya venido
likely [láɪkli] ADJ (probable) probable; (believable) creíble; (promising) prometedor; **John is — to win** es probable que gane Juan; ADV probablemente
liken [láɪkən] VT comparar
likeness [láɪknɪs] N (similarity) parecido m; (portrait) retrato m
likewise [láɪkwaɪz] ADV (the same thing) lo mismo; **we did —** hicimos lo mismo; (similarly) asimismo; (also) también
liking [láɪkɪŋ] N preferencia f, gusto m
lilac [láɪlək] N lila f; ADJ lila
lily [líli] N lirio m, azucena f; ADJ —-**white** (very white) blanquísimo; (pure) puro; (for whites only) exclusivamente para blancos
limb [lɪm] N (branch) rama f; (appendage) miembro m
limber [límbɚ] ADJ flexible; VT hacer flexible; VI **to — up** estirarse
lime [laɪm] N (mineral) cal f; (fruit, color) lima f; —**light** candilejas f pl; **in the —light** en el candelero; —**stone** piedra caliza f; — **tree** limero m
limit [límɪt] N límite m; **to the —** al máximo; VT limitar
limitation [lɪmɪtéʃən] N limitación f
limitless [límɪtlɪs] ADJ ilimitado
limousine [líməzin] N limusina f
limp [lɪmp] N cojera f, renguera f; VI cojear,

renguear, renquear; ADJ (body) flácido; (plants) mustio
limpid [límpɪd] ADJ límpido
line [laɪn] N (bus route, telephone connection) línea f; (of words) renglón m, línea f; (row) raya f, hilera f; (cord) cuerda f; (persons waiting) cola f, fila f; (business) ramo m; (wrinkle) arruga f; (boundary) límite m; — **drive** (baseball) línea f; — **of credit** línea de crédito f; — **of scrimmage** línea de golpeo f; —**s** (in a play) parte f; —**sman** juez -eza de línea m f; —**up** hilera de personas f; (sports) alineación f; **drop me a —** escríbeme unas líneas; **out of —** irrespetuoso; **to get in —** hacer cola; VI/VT (border) alinear, bordear; (put in a lining) forrar; **to — up** alinear[se]; ADJ **off-—** fuera de línea; **on-—** en línea
lineage [líniɪʤ] N linaje m, estirpe f
linear [líniɚ] ADJ lineal
lined [laɪnd] ADJ (with lines) rayado; (with a lining) forrado
linen [línɪn] N (fabric) lino m; (bedclothes) ropa blanca f
liner [láɪnɚ] N (ocean) transatlántico m; (air) avión comercial m; (eye) delineador m
linger [líŋgɚ] VI (stay) quedarse, demorarse; (persist) persistir; (saunter) rezagarse; (contemplate) detenerse; (delay death) aguantar
lingerie [lɑnʒəré] N lencería f
linguist [líŋgwɪst] N lingüista m f
linguistics [lɪŋgwístɪks] N lingüística f
liniment [línəmənt] N linimento m
lining [láɪnɪŋ] N forro m; **every cloud has a silver —** no hay mal que por bien no venga
link [lɪŋk] N (of a chain) eslabón m; (bond, tie) vínculo m; (rail, radio connection) enlace m; (computer) enlace m, vínculo m; VI/VT enlazar[se], conectar[se]; (on a computer) vincular
linnet [línɪt] N pardillo m
linoleum [lɪnóliəm] N linóleo m
linseed [línsid] N linaza f; — **oil** aceite de linaza m
lint [lɪnt] N pelusa f
lion [láɪən] N león m; —**'s share** la parte del león
lioness [láɪənɪs] N leona f
lip [lɪp] N labio m; (of a pitcher) borde m; — **balm** crema para labios f; —**stick** lápiz de labios m, carmín m; **don't give me no —!** no me contestes; VI **to — read** leer los labios
liposuction [láɪposʌkʃən] N liposucción f
liqueur [lɪkɜ́] N licor m
liquid [líkwɪd] ADJ líquido; — **assets** activo líquido m; — **measure** medida para líquidos f; N líquido m
liquidate [líkwɪdet] VI/VT liquidar
liquidation [lɪkwɪdéʃən] N liquidación f
liquidity [lɪkwídɪdi] N liquidez f

liquor [líkɚ] N bebida espirituosa f

lira [líɾə] N lira f

lisp [lɪsp] N ceceo m; VI cecear

list [lɪst] N (series of items) lista f; (of a ship) escora f; — **price** precio de lista m; — **server** servidor de lista m; VT (make a list) hacer una lista de; VI (lean) escorar; **this chair —s for two hundred dollars** esta silla está a doscientos dólares

listen [lísən] VI/VT (hear) escuchar, oír; (heed) escuchar, prestar atención; **to — in** (on radio) sintonizar; (eavesdrop) escuchar a hurtadillas

listener [lísənɚ] N oyente mf; **radio —** radioescucha mf, oyente mf

listing [lístɪŋ] N listado m

listless [lístlɪs] ADJ lánguido

lit [lɪt] ADJ (provided with light) iluminado; (tipsy) alegre, alumbrado

lit [lɪt] see **light**

literacy [líɾəsi] N (action of making literate) alfabetización f; (rate) alfabetismo m

literal [líɾəɾḷ] ADJ literal

literary [líɾəɾeɾi] ADJ literario

literate [líɾəɾt] ADJ (who can read and write) alfabeto; (erudite) erudito, letrado; **he's barely —** apenas sabe leer y escribir

literature [líɾəɾtʃɚ] N literatura f; (handbills) impresos m pl, folletos m pl; **the scientific —** la literatura científica

lithium [líθiəm] N litio m; **—-ion battery** batería de iones de litio f

Lithuania [lɪθuéniə] N Lituania f

Lithuanian [lɪθuénián] ADJ & N lituano -na mf

litigant [líɾɪɡənt] N litigante mf

litigation [lɪɾɪɡéʃən] N litigio m, pleito m

litter [líɾɚ] N (young animals) camada f, cría f; (stretcher) camilla f; (straw) cama de paja para animales f; (trash) basura f; (for cats) arena higiénica f; VI/VT (dirty) ensuciar; (strew) esparcir; VI (give birth) parir

little [líɾḷ] ADJ (small) pequeño, chico; (not much) poco; — **brother** hermano menor m, hermanito m; — **finger** [dedo] meñique m; — **pig** puerquito m; **a — coffee** un poco de café; **a — while** un ratito, un poco; ADV & N poco; — **by —** poco a poco

livable [lívəbəl] ADJ funcional

live¹ [lɪv] VI/VT vivir; **to — together** convivir; **to — up to** cumplir; **to — it up** tirar la casa por la ventana; **long — the king!** ¡viva el rey! ADJ **all the — long day** todo el santo día

live² [laɪv] ADJ vivo; (ammunition) cargado; — **coal** ascua encendida f; — **oak** roble de Virginia m; **—stock** ganado m, ganadería f; — **wire** (electric) cable cargado m; (person) persona vivaz f; **before a — audience** en vivo; **—-in** con cama; ADV en vivo y en directo

livelihood [láɪvlihʊd] N sustento m

liveliness [láɪvlinɪs] N viveza f, animación f

lively [láɪvli] ADJ (party) animado; (person) vivaz, avispado; ADV con animación

liver [lívɚ] N hígado m

livid [lívɪd] ADJ (pallid, bluish) lívido; (angry) furibundo

living [lívɪŋ] N (life) vida f; — **expenses** gastos de subsistencia m pl; — **room** sala f, living m; — **together** cohabitación f; — **wage** salario de subsistencia m; — **will** documento de instrucciones previas m, documento de voluntad anticipada m; **to earn/make a —** ganarse la vida; **the —** los vivos; ADJ vivo, viviente

lizard [lízɚd] N lagartija f

llama [lámə] N llama f

load [lod] N (supported mass) carga f; (weight) peso m; (ship cargo) cargamento m; **no-fund** fondo sin comisión de entrada m; **—s of** montones de; VI/VT cargar; **to — down** colmar; **to — oneself down** agobiarse

loaf [lof] N hogaza de pan f, pan m; VI holgar, holgazanear, haraganear

loafer [lófɚ] N (idler) holgazán -ana mf, haragán -ana mf, gandul -la mf; (shoe) mocasín m

loan [lon] N préstamo m; (to a government) empréstito m; — **application** solicitud de préstamo f; — **guarantee** garantía de préstamo f; — **officer** funcionario -ria de préstamos mf; — **shark** usurero -ra mf; **—word** préstamo m; VI/VT prestar

loath [loθ] ADJ renuente; **to be — to** ser renuente a

loathe [loð] VT aborrecer

loathsome [lóðsəm] ADJ repugnante, abominable

lob [lab] VT tirar por lo alto; N (tennis) globo m

lobby [lábi] N (vestibule) vestíbulo m; (special interest) grupo de presión m, lobby m; VI/VT (influence) presionar

lobbyist [lábiıst] N representante de un grupo de presión mf

lobe [lob] N lóbulo m

lobotomy [labáɾəmi] N lobotomía f

lobster [lábstɚ] N langosta f

local [lókəl] ADJ local; — **bus** (computer) vía de transmisión local f; — **printer** impresora local f; — **train** tren de cercanías m

localize [lókalaɪz] VT localizar

locate [lóket] VI/VT (establish in a place) situar, ubicar; (find) localizar; VI (settle) radicarse, establecerse

location [lokéʃən] N (position) ubicación f, emplazamiento m; (finding) localización f; **on —** en exteriores

lock [lak] N (door) cerradura f; (canal) esclusa f; (firearms, wrestling) llave f; (of hair) mecha f, mechón m; **—jaw** tétanos m sg; **—-out** cierre patronal m; **—smith** cerrajero -ra mf; **to**

have a — on the award tener asegurado el premio; VI/VT cerrar con llave; (make immovable) trabar[se]; **to — in** encerrar; **to — out** dejar afuera; **to — up** (door) cerrar con llave; (animal) encerrar; (prisoner) encarcelar; (valuables) poner bajo llave

locker [lókɚ] N (for athletic equipment) casillero m; (for frozen food) cámara frigorífica f; **— room** vestuario m

locket [lákɪt] N relicario m, guardapelo m

locomotive [lokəmóDɪv] N locomotora f

locust [lókəst] N langosta f; **— tree** algarrobo m

lodge [lɑdʒ] N (of fraternal organization) logia f; (cabin) cabaña f; (hotel) posada f, mesón m; VI/VT alojar[se], hospedar[se]; **to — a complaint** presentar una queja

lodger [ládʒɚ] N inquilino -na mf

lodging [lάdʒɪŋ] N alojamiento m, hospedaje m, albergue m

loft [lɔft] N (attic) desván m; (for choir) coro m; (for hay) pajar m; VT tirar por lo alto

lofty [lɔ́fti] ADJ elevado, encumbrado

log [lɑg] N (wood) leño m, madero m, rollizo m; (ship record) cuaderno de bitácora m; (record of activity) diario m; (on a computer) registro m; **— cabin** cabaña de troncos f; VI/VT (cut trees) cortar; **—-in name** nombre de acceso m; VT (write down) anotar; **to — in** ingresar al sistema; **to — off/out** finalizar una sesión; VT registrar una acción

logarithm [lógərɪðəm] N logaritmo m

logic [lάdʒɪk] N lógica f; **— board** placa lógica f

logical [lάdʒɪkəl] ADJ lógico

logically [lάdʒɪkli] ADV lógicamente

logistics [lədʒístɪks] N logística f

loin [lɔɪn] N ijada f; (in animals) ijar m; (cut of meat) lomo m; **—s** entrañas f pl

loiter [lɔ́ɪDɚ] VI (idly) holgazanear; (with ill intent) merodear; **to — behind** rezagarse

loll [lɑl] VI arrellanarse

lollipop [lálipap] N Sp pirulí m; Mex paleta f; RP chupetín m

lone [lon] ADJ (solitary) solitario; (only) único

loneliness [lónlinɪs] N soledad f

lonely [lónli] ADJ solo

lonesome [lónsəm] ADJ solo

long [lɑŋ] ADJ largo; **a — way from home** lejos de casa; **to work — hours** trabajar muchas horas; **— distance** de larga distancia; **— division** división de más de una cifra f; **—-hand** letra manuscrita f; **— johns** calzoncillos largos m pl; **— jump** salto largo m; **—-lasting** duradero, perdurable; **—-lived** (batteries) duradero; (people) longevo; **—-range** (missiles) de largo alcance; (plans) a largo plazo; **—shoreman** estibador m; **—-suffering** sufrido; **—-term** a largo plazo; **—-term care** atención médica a largo plazo f; **—time friend** viejo amigo; **— underwear**

calzoncillo largo m; **—-winded** verborrágico, palabrero; **it's a — shot** es muy improbable; **— time** mucho, mucho tiempo; **— ago** hace mucho tiempo; **— before** mucho antes; **—live ... !** ¡viva ... ! **all winter** — todo el invierno; **how — did he stay?** ¿cuánto tiempo se quedó? **not for** — no por mucho tiempo; **so — !** ¡hasta luego! **to be — in coming** tardar en venir; **three meters** — tres metros de largo; **will you be —?** ¿tardarás mucho? **the whole day** — todo el santo día; VI **to — for** anhelar

longer [lɔ́ŋgɚ] ADJ más largo; ADV más; **no** — ya no; **how much —?** ¿hasta cuándo?

longevity [lɑndʒévɪdi] N longevidad f

longing [lɔ́ŋɪŋ] N anhelo m; ADJ anhelante

longitude [lάndʒɪtud] N longitud f

look [lʊk] VI (see) mirar; (seem) parecer; **it —s good on you** te queda bien, te luce; **to — after** atender, cuidar; **to — alike** parecerse; **to — down on someone** despreciar a alguien; **to — for** (search for) buscar; (anticipate) esperar; **I — forward to it** lo espero con ansia, me da mucha ilusión; **to — into** investigar; **she —s her age** aparenta la edad que tiene; **to — out on** dar a, tener vista a; **to — out of** asomarse a; **— out!** ¡cuidado! **to — over** dar un vistazo a; **to — up** (upward) levantar la vista; (in a directory) buscar; **to — up to** admirar; N (gaze) mirada f; (examination) vistazo m; **—-alike** doble mf; **—out** (person) vigía mf; (place) mirador m, vigía f; **to be on the —out** estar alerta; **—s** aspecto m, pinta f; **good —s** belleza f

looking glass [lʊ́kɪŋglæs] N espejo m

loom [lum] N telar m; VI (appear indistinctly) dibujarse; (threaten) cernerse

loon [lun] N (bird) somorgujo m; (person) chiflado -da mf

loony [lúni] ADJ chiflado

loop [lup] N (for fastening) presilla f; (in a rope) lazo m; (of a flight) rizo m; (electric) circuito cerrado m; (computer programming, ice-skating) bucle m; **—hole** escapatoria f; **in the** — al corriente, al tanto de lo que pasa; VI (make a loop) hacer un lazo; (curve around) serpentear; (loop the loop) rizar el rizo; VT enlazar

loose [lus] ADJ (free) suelto; (not tight) flojo; (approximate) libre; (unfettered) desatado; (immoral) disoluto; (promiscuous) fácil; **— cannon** mono con una metralleta m; **— change** suelto m, cambio m; **— end** cabo suelto m; **—-fitting** holgado; **—-jointed** de articulaciones flexibles; **—-leaf** [de] hojas sueltas; **to let** — soltar; VT desatar, soltar

loosen [lúsən] VI/VT (untie) soltar[se], desatar; (make/become less tight/dense/strict) aflojar[se]

looseness [lúsnɪs] N (of skin) flojedad *f*; (of morals) relajamiento *m*; (of clothing) holgura *f*; (of soil) friabilidad *f*; (of translation) lo libre

loot [lut] N botín *m*; VI/VT saquear

lop [lap] VT (cut) recortar; (eliminate) eliminar; VI caer[se]; ADJ —**sided** (leaning to one side) ladeado; (unbalanced) desequilibrado; (listing) escorado

lope [lop] VI correr a pasos largos

loquacious [lokwéʃəs] ADJ locuaz

loquat [lókwɑt] N níspero *m*

lord [lɔrd] N señor *m*; (God) Señor *m*; (British title) lord *m*; —**'s Prayer** Padrenuestro *m*; **my**—! ¡Dios mío! VI **to**— **it over someone** tratarle a alguien con arrogancia

lordly [lɔ́rdli] ADJ (kingly) señorial; (haughty) altivo

lordship [lɔ́rdʃɪp] N (title) señoría *f*; (power) señorío *m*

lore [lɔr] N saber *m*

lose [luz] VI/VT perder; (a pursuer) dejar atrás; **to** — **sight of** perder de vista; **to** — **oneself in thought** ensimismarse

loser [lúzɚ] N perdedor -ora *mf*

loss [lɔs] N (destruction) pérdida *f*; (misplacement) pérdida *f*, extravío *m*; (sports) derrota *f*; **to be at a** — no saber qué hacer; **to sell at a** — vender con pérdida; —**es** bajas *f pl*

lost [lɔst] ADJ perdido; — **cause** caso perdido *m*; — **in thought** absorto; **to get** — perderse, extraviarse

lost [lɔst] *see* lose

lot [lɑt] N (parcel) lote *m*; (fate) suerte *f*, destino *m*; (piece of land) solar *m*, terreno *m*; **the** — todo; **a** — **of** /—**s of** mucho[s]; **a** — **of money** mucho dinero; **by** — al azar; **to draw** — a echar suertes; **to fall to one's** — caerle en suerte a uno; ADV **a** — **better** mucho mejor

lotion [lóʃən] N loción *f*

lottery [lɑ́dəri] N lotería *f*

loud [laud] ADJ (noisy) ruidoso; (strong) fuerte; (ostentatious) chillón; —**speaker** altavoz *m*, altoparlante *m*; —**mouth** bocazas *mf sg*; ADV fuerte, alto

Lou Gehrig's disease [lugérɪgz dɪzíz] N enfermedad de Lou Gehrig *f*

lounge [laundʒ] VI repantigarse, arrellanarse; N (waiting room) sala de espera *f*; (room in bar) salón *m*; (divan) diván *m*; — **chair** diván *m*

louse [laus] N piojo *m*

lousy [láuzi] ADJ (infested with lice) piojoso; (contemptible) despreciable; (poorly done) pésimo

lout [laut] N bruto *m*

lovable [lʌ́vəbəl] ADJ adorable

love [lʌv] N (affection) amor *m*; (fondness) afición *f*; (in tennis) nada *f*; — **affair** aventura *f*, amorío *m*; — **at first sight** amor a primera vista *m*, flechazo *m*; — **life** vida sentimental *f*; — **seat** confidente *m*; **books were her great** — los libros fueron su gran pasión; **to be in** — estar enamorado; **to fall in** — **with** enamorarse de; **to make** — to hacerle el amor a; VI/VT amar, querer; **I** — **to eat apples** me encanta comer manzanas

loveliness [lʌ́vlinɪs] N (beauty) hermosura *f*; (charm) encanto *m*

lovely [lʌ́vli] ADJ (beautiful) hermoso; (charming) encantador; (pleasant) ameno

lover [lʌ́vɚ] N (sexually involved) amante *mf*; (in love) enamorado -da *mf*, amante *mf*; (interested in) aficionado -da *mf*

loving [lʌ́vɪŋ] ADJ cariñoso, afectuoso

low [lo] ADJ (not high) bajo; (base) vil; (humble) humilde; (downcast) abatido; (deep in pitch) grave; — **beam** luces cortas *f pl*; —**brow** poco culto; —**budget** de bajo presupuesto; —**cal** de bajas calorías; —**cost** de bajo precio; —**down** verdad *f*; —**end** de baja calidad; — **gear** primera marcha *f*; —**grade** (inferior) inferior; (low) bajo; —**income** de bajos ingresos; —**key** tranquilo; —**land** tierra baja *f*; —**level** de bajo nivel; —**life** canalla *f*; — **quality** baja calidad *f*; —**tech** sencillo; — **tide** bajamar *f*, marea baja *f*; **dress with a** — **neck** vestido escotado *m*; **to be** — **on something** estar escaso de algo; **to be in** — **spirits** estar abatido/desanimado; ADV bajo; **to buy** — comprar barato; N (sound of a cow) mugido *m*; VI mugir

lower [lóɚ] VI/VT bajar; (prices) rebajar; (flag, sail) arriar; ADJ más bajo, inferior; —**case** minúscula *f*; — **house** cámara de diputados *f*

lowliness [lólinɪs] N humildad *f*

lowly [lóli] ADJ humilde

loyal [lɔ́iəl] ADJ leal

loyalty [lɔ́iəlti] N lealtad *f*

LSD [**lysergic acid diethylamide**] [ɛ́lɛsdí] N LSD *m*

lubricant [lúbrɪkənt] ADJ & N lubricante *m*

lubricate [lúbrɪket] VI/VT lubricar

lucid [lúsɪd] ADJ lúcido

lucidity [lusídɪdi] N lucidez *f*

luck [lʌk] N suerte *f*; **in** — de suerte; **to be out of** — estar de mala suerte; VI **to** — **into** conseguir por un golpe de suerte; **to** — **out** tener suerte

luckily [lʌ́kɪli] ADV afortunadamente

lucky [lʌ́ki] ADJ afortunado; — **charm** amuleto de la suerte *m*; **to be** — tener suerte

lucrative [lúkrədɪv] ADJ lucrativo

ludicrous [lúdɪkrəs] ADJ ridículo

lug [lʌg] VT acarrear

luggage [lʌ́gɪdʒ] N equipaje *m*; — **rack** rejilla *f*

lukewarm [lúkwɔ́rm] ADJ (not warm or cold) tibio; (indifferent) indiferente

lull [lʌl] VT (put to sleep) arrullar; VI/VT (soothe)

calmar[se]; N (calm) calma f, tregua f; (sound) arrullo m

lullaby [lʌ́ləbaɪ] N canción de cuna f, nana f

lumbago [lʌmbégo] N lumbago m

lumbar [lʌ́mbɑr] ADJ lumbar

lumber [lʌ́mbə-] N madera f; —**jack** leñador m; —**man** maderero m; — **mill** aserradero m; —**yard** almacén de maderas m; VI/VT (cut trees) talar; (move heavily) moverse pesadamente; (make a low noise) tronar

luminous [lúmənəs] ADJ luminoso

lump [lʌmp] N (in breast) bulto m; (in sauce) grumo m; (in throat) nudo m; (of coal) trozo m; (of food) plasta f; (on head) chichón m; (of sugar) terrón m; **to take one's —s** recibir palos; — **sum** pago global m; VT juntar; VI agrumarse

lumpectomy [lʌmpéktəmi] N tumorectomía f

lumpy [lʌ́mpi] ADJ grumoso

lunar [lúnə-] ADJ lunar; —**eclipse** eclipse lunar m

lunatic [lúnətɪk] ADJ & N lunático -ca mf, loco -ca mf; — **fringe** extremistas mf pl

lunch [lʌntʃ] N comida f, almuerzo m; —**time** hora de comer/almorzar f; **out to** — (having lunch) almorzando; (crazy) en la luna; VI comer, almorzar

lung [lʌŋ] N pulmón m

lunge [lʌndʒ] N arremetida f; VI arremeter, abalanzarse; **to** — **at** arremeter contra, abalanzarse sobre

lupus [lúpəs] N lupus m

lurch [lə-tʃ] N tambaleo m; **to give a** — tambalearse; **to leave someone in the** — dejar a alguien en la estacada; VI tambalearse, dar barquinazos

lure [lʊr] N (thing that attracts) atractivo m, gancho m; (in hunting) señuelo m; (in fishing) cebo m; VT atraer, seducir

lurid [lúrɪd] ADJ (gruesome) sangriento; (shocking) escabroso

lurk [lə-k] VI (lie in wait) estar en acecho, acechar; (move furtively) moverse furtivamente

luscious [lʌ́ʃəs] ADJ (delicious) exquisito, delicioso; (sexy) voluptuoso

lust [lʌst] N (sexual desire) lujuria f, lascivia f; (craving) deseo m, ansia f; VI desear; **to** — **after** codiciar

luster [lʌ́stə-] N lustre m, brillo m

lustful [lʌ́stfəl] ADJ lujurioso

lusty [lʌ́sti] ADJ (robust) robusto; (full of lust) lujurioso

Luxembourg [lʌ́ksəmbə-g] N Luxemburgo m

Luxembourger [lʌ́ksəmbə-gə-] N luxemburgués -esa mf

Luxembourgian [lʌksəmbə́-giən] ADJ luxemburgués

luxurious [lʌgʒúriəs] ADJ (characterized by luxury) lujoso; (luxuriant) exuberante

luxury [lʌ́gʒəri] N lujo m; — **tax** impuesto suntuario m; ADJ de lujo

lye [laɪ] N lejía f

lying [láɪɪŋ] ADJ mentiroso

Lyme disease [láɪm dɪzɪz] N enfermedad de Lyme f

lymph [lɪmf] N linfa f; — **node** nodo linfático m

lymphocyte [lɪ́mfəsaɪt] N linfocito m

lymphoma [lɪmfómə] N linfoma m

lynch [lɪntʃ] VT linchar

lynx [lɪŋks] N lince m

lyre [laɪr] N lira f

lyric [lírɪk] N poema lírico m; — **poetry** lírica f; —**s** letra f; ADJ lírico

lyrical [lírɪkəl] ADJ lírico

lyricism [lírɪsɪzəm] N lirismo m

Mm

ma'am [mæm] N señora f

Macao [məkáU] N Macao m

macaroni [mækəróni] N macarrones m pl

Macedonia [mæsɪdóniə] N Macedonia f

Macedonian [mæsɪdóniən] ADJ & N macedonio -nia mf

machine [məʃín] N máquina f; (of government) maquinaria f, aparato m; — **gun** (not portable) ametralladora f; (portable) metralleta f; — **language** lenguaje de máquina m, lenguaje máquina m; ADJ —-**made** hecho a máquina; VT trabajar a máquina

machinery [məʃínəri] N maquinaria f

machinist [məʃínɪst] N maquinista mf, operario -ria mf

mackerel [mǽkə-əl] N caballa f

macro [mǽkro] N serie de instrucciones f

mad [mæd] ADJ (crazy) loco; (angry) rabioso, enojado; (hydrophobic) rabioso; — **cow disease** encefalopatía espongiforme bovina f, enfermedad de las vacas locas f; —**man** loco m; **to be** — **about someone** estar loco por alguien; **to drive** — enloquecer, volver loco; **to get** — enojarse; **to go** — volverse loco, enloquecerse; **like** — como loco

Madagascan [mædəgǽskən] ADJ & N malgache mf

Madagascar [mædəgǽskɑr] N Madagascar m

madam [mǽdəm] N (title) señora f

maddening [mǽdn̩ɪŋ] ADJ enloquecedor

made [med] ADJ —-**to-measure** hecho a la medida; —-**to-order** hecho por encargo; —-**up** (invented) inventado, falso; (wearing makeup) maquillado; **to be** — **of** ser de; **to have something** — mandar hacer algo; **I'm**

a — man estoy hecho; **to have it** — estar hecho

made [med] *see* make

madness [mǽdnɪs] N (insanity) locura *f*; (anger) rabia *f*

Mafia [mɑ́fiə] N mafia *f*

mafioso [mɑfióso] N mafioso *m*

magazine [mǽgəzin] N (publication) revista *f*; (room for ammunition) polvorín *m*; (part of gun) cargador *m*

magic [mǽdʒɪk] N magia *f*; ADJ mágico; — **bullet** panacea *f*; — **wand** varita mágica *f*

magical [mǽdʒɪkəl] ADJ mágico

magician [mədʒíʃən] N (person adept at magic) mágico -ca *mf*; (person adept at finances) mago -ga *mf*

magistrate [mǽdʒɪstret] N magistrado -da *mf*

magma [mǽgmə] N magma *m*

magnanimous [mægnǽnəməs] ADJ magnánimo

magnate [mǽgnet] N magnate *m*

magnesia [mægníʒə] N magnesia *f*

magnesium [mægníziəm] N magnesio *m*

magnet [mǽgnɪt] N imán *m*

magnetic [mægnédɪk] ADJ magnético; — **pole** polo magnético *m*; — **resonance imaging** imagen por resonancia magnética *f*; — **tape** cinta magnetofónica *f*

magnetism [mǽgnɪtɪzəm] N magnetismo *m*

magnetize [mǽgnɪtaɪz] VT magnetizar, imantar

magnificence [mægnífɪsəns] N magnificencia *f*

magnificent [mægnífɪsənt] ADJ magnífico

magnify [mǽgnɪfaɪ] VT (to make larger) aumentar; (to make louder) amplificar; (to exaggerate) exagerar, magnificar

magnitude [mǽgnɪtud] N magnitud *f*

magnolia [mægnóljə] N (flower) magnolia *f*; (tree) magnolio *m*

magpie [mǽgpaɪ] N urraca *f* (also hoarder)

mahogany [məhágəni] N caoba *f*

maid [med] N criada *f*, sirvienta *f*; (in hotel) camarera *f*; — **of honor** dama de honor *f*

maiden [médn] N *lit* doncella *f*, virgen *f*; — **voyage** primer viaje *m*; — **name** nombre de soltera *m*

mail [mel] N correo *m*; (electronic) mensaje *m*; (of metal) malla *f*; —**bag** cartera *f*; —**box** buzón *m*; —**man** cartero *m*; — **order** pedido por correo *m*; — **order business** negocio de ventas por correo *m*; VT echar al correo; —**ing list** lista de correo *f*

maim [mem] VT mutilar

main [men] ADJ principal; — **office** oficina central *f*; N (pipe) cañería principal *f*; (sea) alta mar *f*; —**frame** *Sp* ordenador central *m*, *Am* computadora central *f*; —**land** continente *m*; —**spring** muelle real *m*; —**stream** tendencia mayoritaria *f*; —**stream engineering** ingeniería conforme a la corriente dominante *f*; —**stay** pilar *m*, puntal *m*; — **street** calle principal *f*

mainly [ménli] ADV principalmente, fundamentalmente

maintain [mentén] VT (repair, support) mantener; (assert) afirmar

maintenance [méntnəns] N (repairs) mantenimiento *m*; (monetary support) manutención *f*; — **cost** costo de mantenimiento *m*

maize [mez] N maíz *m*

majestic [mədʒéstɪk] ADJ majestuoso

majesty [mǽdʒɪsti] N majestad *f*; **Your** — Su Majestad

major [médʒɚ] ADJ (greater) mayor, más grande; (large) grande; — **key** mayor *m*; N (military rank) comandante *m*; (field of study) especialidad *f*, carrera *f*; — **league** liga mayor *f*; VI especializarse

majority [mədʒɔ́rɪdi] N (greater number) mayoría *f*; (age) mayoría de edad *f*; — **ownership** propiedad mayoritaria *f*; **the** — el grueso

make [mek] VT (do) hacer; (create) fabricar; (cause) causar; (earn) ganar; (a speech) pronunciar; **to — a clean breast of** sacarse del pecho; **to — a decision** tomar una decisión; **to — a living** ganarse la vida; **to — a train** llegar a tiempo para tomar un tren; **to — a turn** girar, doblar; **to — away with** fugarse con; **to — believe** hacer de cuenta que; **to — out** (see) vislumbrar, divisar; (read) descifrar; (kiss) *Sp* morrear; *Am* besuquearse; **to — possible** posibilitar; **to — too much of** exagerar; **to — up** (a story) inventar; (after a quarrel) hacer las paces; (a loss) recuperar; (one's face) maquillarse; (one's mind) decidirse; **to — up for** compensar; **two plus two —s four** dos y dos son cuatro; **what do you — of that?** ¿cómo interpretas eso? **I'll — it up to you** te voy a compensar por eso; **you'll — a good teacher** vas a ser un buen profesor; N (brand) marca *f*; —**up** (composition) composición *f*; (character) carácter *m*; (cosmetics) maquillaje *m*; ADJ —**shift** provisional

maker [mékɚ] N (creator) creador -ora *mf*, hacedor -ora *mf*; (manufacturer) fabricante *m*

makings [mékɪŋz] N (potential) potencial *m*; (ingredients) ingredientes *m pl*

maladjusted [mælədʒʌ́stɪd] ADJ inadaptado

malady [mǽlədi] N mal *m*

malaise [məléz] N malestar *m*

malaria [məlériə] N malaria *f*, paludismo *m*

Malawi [məláwi] N Malawi *m*

Malawian [məláwiən] ADJ & N malawiano -na *mf*

Malaysia [məlézə] N Malasia *f*

Malaysian [məléʒən] ADJ & N malasio -sia *mf*

malcontent [mǽɬkəntɛnt] ADJ & N descontento -ta *mf*

Maldives [mɔ́ɬdaɪvz] N Maldivas *f pl*

Maldivian [mɔɬdívian] ADJ & N maldivo -va *mf*

male [mel] ADJ (animal, plant) macho; (person) varón; (trait) masculino; N (animal, plant) macho *m*; (person) varón *m*

malevolent [məlévələnt] ADJ malévolo

malformation [mǽɬfɔrméʃən] N malformación *f*

malfunction [mǽɬfʌ́ŋkʃən] N funcionamiento defectuoso *m*; VI funcionar mal

Mali [máli] N Malí *m*

Malian [málian] ADJ & N malí *mf*

malice [mǽlɪs] N malicia *f*; **with — aforethought** con premeditación y alevosía

malicious [məlíʃəs] ADJ malicioso

malign [məláɪn] VT calumniar, difamar

malignancy [məlígnənsi] N (quality) malignidad *f*; (tumor) tumor maligno *m*

malignant [məlígnənt] ADJ maligno

mall [mɔl] N (closed street) paseo *m*; (enclosed shopping area) galería *f*, centro comercial *m*

mallet [mǽlɪt] N mazo *m*

malnourished [mǽɬnɔ́rɪʃt] ADJ desnutrido

malnutrition [mǽɬnutríʃən] N desnutrición *f*

malpractice [mǽɬprǽktɪs] N negligencia *f*, mala práctica *f*

malt [mɔlt] N malta *f*; **—ed milk** leche malteada *f*

Malta [mɔ́ɬtə] N Malta *f*

Maltese [mɔɬtíz] ADJ & N maltés -esa *mf*

mama, mamma [mámə] N mamá *f*; **—'s boy** nene de mamá *m*

mammal [mǽməl] N mamífero *m*

mammary [mǽməri] ADJ mamario

mammography [mæmágrəfi] N mamografía *f*

mammoth [mǽməθ] ADJ enorme; N mamut *m*

man [mæn] N hombre *m*; (servant) criado *m*; (in games) pieza *f*, ficha *f*; **— and wife** marido y mujer; **—hunt** persecución *f*; **—kind** humanidad *f*; **—-of-war** (ship) buque de guerra *m*; (jellyfish) medusa *f*; **—power** (for work) mano de obra *f*; **—slaughter** (accidental) homicidio culposo *m*, homicidio involuntario *m*; (unpremeditated) homicidio sin premeditación *m*; **—-to-— defense** defensa al hombre *f*, defensa de asignación *f*, defensa individual *f*; **every — for himself** cada cual para sí; **to a —** unánimemente; ADJ **—-eating** que come carne humana; **—-made** (fiber) sintético; (lake) artificial; INTERJ ¡hombre! VT (a fort) guarnecer; (a ship) tripular; **to —handle** violentar

manage [mǽnɪdʒ] VT (succeed in) conseguir, lograr; (direct) dirigir, administrar, gestionar; (maneuver) manejar; VI **to — without help** arreglárselas sin ayuda

manageable [mǽnɪdʒəbəl] ADJ manejable; (hair) dócil

managed [mǽnɪdʒd] ADJ **— care** plan de salud administrado *m*; **— funds** fondos administrados *m pl*

management [mǽnɪdʒmənt] N (act of managing) dirección *f*, gestión *f*; (persons controlling a business) gerencia *f*, patronal *f*, gestión *f*; (area of study) empresariales *f pl*

manager [mǽnɪdʒɚ] N (of a store) gerente -ta *mf*; (of a company) director -ora *mf*

mandate [mǽndet] N mandato *m*; VT decretar

mandatory [mǽndətɔri] ADJ obligatorio

mandolin [mǽndəlɪn] N mandolina *f*

mane [men] N (of a lion) melena *f*; (of a horse) crin *f*

maneuver [mənúvɚ] N maniobra *f*; VI/VT maniobrar

manganese [mǽŋgəniz] N manganeso *m*

mange [mendʒ] N sarna *f*, roña *f*

manger [méndʒɚ] N pesebre *m*

mangle [mǽŋgəl] VT (mutilate) magullar, mutilar; (ruin) estropear

mango [mǽŋgo] N mango *m*

mangrove [mǽŋgrov] N mangle *m*

mangy [méndʒi] ADJ sarnoso

manhood [mǽnhʊd] N virilidad *f*; (men collectively) hombres *m pl*; (adult age) edad adulta *f*

mania [ménia] N manía *f*

maniac [méniæk] N maníaco -ca *mf*, maniaco -ca *mf*

maniacal [mənáɪəkəl] ADJ maníaco

manic-depressive [mǽnɪkdɪprésɪv] ADJ maniaco-depresivo

manicure [mǽnɪkjur] N manicura *f*; VT manicurar

manifest [mǽnəfɛst] ADJ manifiesto; N (list of cargo) manifiesto *m*, hoja de ruta *f*; VT (show) manifestar, poner de manifiesto; (express) declarar

manifestation [mǽnəfɛstéʃən] N manifestación *f*

manifesto [mǽnɪfɛ́sto] N manifiesto *m*

manifold [mǽnəfold] ADJ diverso; N (on a motor) colector *m*

manila [mənílə] N abacá *m*; **— envelope** sobre manila *m*

manioc [mǽniɑk] N mandioca *f*, yuca *f*

manipulate [mənípjələt] VT manipular

manipulation [mənɪpjəléʃən] N manipulación *f*

manlike [mǽnlaɪk] ADJ (manly) varonil; (mannish) hombruna; (resembling a human) de hombre

manliness [mǽnlinɪs] N virilidad *f*

manly [mǽnli] ADJ varonil, viril

manner [mǽnɚ] N (way) manera *f*, modo *m*, forma *f*; (type) tipo *m*; (outward bearing) aire *m*, ademán *m*, porte *m*; **—s** modales *m pl*, crianza *f*; **in the — of** a la manera de

mannerism [mǽnərɪzəm] N peculiaridad f
mannish [mǽnɪʃ] ADJ hombruno, varonil
manor [mǽnə] N feudo m, solar m; — **house** casa solariega f
mansion [mǽnʃən] N mansión f
mantel [mǽntl] N repisa de chimenea f
mantle [mǽntl] N manto m
mantra [mǽntrə] N mantra f
manual [mǽnjuəl] ADJ & N manual m; — **labor** trabajo manual m
manufacture [mænjəfǽktʃə] VT fabricar, manufacturar; (clothes, shoes) confeccionar; N fabricación f, manufactura f; (of clothes, shoes) confección f
manufacturer [mænjəfǽktʃərə] N fabricante m; —**'s suggested retail price** precio sugerido por el fabricante m
manufacturing [mænjəfǽktʃərɪŋ] N fabricación f, manufactura f; ADJ fabril, manufacturero; — **empire** imperio industrial m
manure [mənúr] N estiércol m; VT estercolar, abonar
manuscript [mǽnjəskrɪpt] ADJ & N manuscrito m
many [méni] ADJ muchos; — **apples** muchas manzanas; — **came** vinieron muchos; — **a time** muchas veces; **a great** — muchísimos; **as** — **as** tantos como; **as** — **as five** cinco; **how** —? ¿cuántos? **three books too** — tres libros de más; **too** — demasiados
map [mæp] N (geographical) mapa m; (of streets) plano m; VT trazar un mapa de; **to** — **out** planear
maple [mépəl] N Sp arce m; Am maple m; — **syrup** miel de arce/maple f
mar [mɑr] VT estropear
marathon [mǽrəθən] N maratón mf
marble [mɑ́rbəl] N mármol m; (toy) canica f, bola f; **to play** —**s** jugar a las canicas; ADJ de mármol, marmóreo
march [mɑrtʃ] N marcha f; VI marchar; (leave) marcharse; **to** — **in** entrar; **to** — **out** marcharse; VT hacer marchar
March [mɑrtʃ] N marzo m
mare [mer] N yegua f
margarine [mɑ́rdʒərɪn] N margarina f
margin [mɑ́rdʒɪn] N margen m; — **of error** margen de error m; — **of safety** margen de seguridad m; **on** — comprado en cuenta de margen
marginal [mɑ́rdʒən] ADJ marginal
marginalization [mɑrdʒənɪzéʃən] N marginación f
marginalize [mɑ́rdʒənaɪz] VT marginar
marigold [mǽrɪgold] N caléndula f, maravilla f
marijuana, marihuana [mærəwɑ́nə] N marihuana f, mariguana f
marinate [mǽrənet] VT marinar
marine [mərín] ADJ (of the sea) marino;

(maritime) marítimo; — **corps** infantería de marina f; N soldado de infantería de marina m
marionette [mærɪənét] N marioneta f
marital [mǽrɪtl] ADJ conyugal, matrimonial; — **status** estado civil m
maritime [mǽrɪtaɪm] ADJ marítimo
mark [mɑrk] N marca f, seña f; (token) señal f; (indication) seña f; (grade) nota f, calificación f; (former German currency) marco m; —**down** rebaja de precio f; —**sman** tirador m; **he's a good** —**sman** tiene muy buena puntería / muy buen tino; —**up** (amount above wholesale price) margen de ganancia m; **the halfway** — el punto medio, la mitad; **to hit the** — dar en el blanco; **on your** —, **get set, go!** ¡en sus marcas, listos y ya! ¡en sus marcas, listos, fuera! **to make one's** — distinguirse; **to miss the** — errar el tiro; **easy** — blanco fácil m; VT (write on) marcar; (indicate) señalar; (observe) observar, notar; (grade) calificar; —**ed for greatness** destinado a la grandeza; — **my words!** ¡ya verás! **to** — **down prices** rebajar los precios; **to** — **off** acotar, deslindar; **to** — **up prices** subir los precios
marker [mɑ́rkə] N marcador m
market [mɑ́rkɪt] N mercado m; —**analysis** análisis de mercado m; —**place** mercado m; — **price** precio de mercado m; — **share** sector del mercado m; **I'm in the** — **for** estoy buscando; VT comercializar, mercadear
marketable [mɑ́rkɪdəbəl] ADJ vendible
marketing [mɑ́rkɪdɪŋ] N (field of study) mercadotecnia f, marketing m; (selling) comercialización f
marmalade [mɑ́rməled] N mermelada de naranja f
maroon [mərún] ADJ & N bordó/bordeaux m; VT abandonar
marquis [mɑrkí] N marqués m
marquise [mɑrkíz] N marquesa f
marriage [mǽrɪdʒ] N matrimonio m; (combination) combinación f; — **license** licencia de matrimonio f
marriageable [mǽrɪdʒəbəl] ADJ casadero
married [mǽrid] ADJ (united in marriage) casado; (relation to marriage) conyugal; — **couple** matrimonio m; **to get** — casarse
marrow [mǽro] N (in the bones) médula f; (food) tuétano m; (essential part) meollo m
marry [mǽri] VT (to marry off) casar; (to get married) casarse con; VI casarse
marsh [mɑrʃ] N pantano m, ciénaga f
marshal [mɑ́rʃəl] N (military) mariscal m; (police chief) alguacil m; (of a parade) maestro de ceremonia m; VT (facts, forces) reunir; (troops) formar
Marshallese [mɑrʃəlíz] ADJ & N marshalés -esa mf

Marshall Islands [márʃəláɪləndz] N Islas
Marshall f pl
marshmallow [márʃmɛlo] N malvavisco m
marshy [márʃi] ADJ pantanoso, cenagoso
martial [márʃəɫ] ADJ marcial; — **arts** artes
marciales f pl; — **law** ley marcial f
martin [mártn̩] N avión m
martini [martíni] N martini m
martyr [márdɚ] N mártir m; VT martirizar
martyrdom [márdɚdəm] N martirio m
marvel [márvəɫ] N maravilla f; VI maravillarse
marvelous [márvələs] ADJ maravilloso
Marxism [márksɪzəm] N marxismo m
mascara [mæskǽrə] N rímel m
mascot [mǽskat] N mascota f
masculine [mǽskjəlɪn] ADJ masculino
mash [mæʃ] VT aplastar, pisar; —**ed potatoes**
puré de papas/patatas m; N (pulpy mass) puré
m; (food for livestock) afrecho m; (malt) malta
remojada f
mask [mæsk] N máscara f, careta f; VT
enmascarar; —**ed ball** baile de máscaras m
masochism [mǽsəkɪzəm] N masoquismo m
mason [mésən] N (builder) albañil m;
(Freemason) masón m
masonry [mésənri] N (bricklaying) albañilería f;
(fraternal order) masonería f
masquerade [mæskəréd] N mascarada f; VI **to**
— **as** hacerse pasar por
mass [mæs] N masa f; (in church) misa f; —
communication comunicación de masas f;
— **marketing** comercialización masiva f; —
media medios de comunicación [de masas] m
pl; — **production** fabricación en masa f; —
storage almacenamiento masivo m; —
transit transporte público m; —
unemployment desempleo/paro masivo m;
the —**es** las masas f pl; VI/VT juntar[se] en
masa; (troops) concentrar[se]
massacre [mǽsəkɚ] N masacre m; VT masacrar
massage [məsáʒ] N masaje m; — **parlor** salón
de masajes m; VT (give a massage) masajear;
(change data) manipular
masseur [məsɚ́] N masajista m
masseuse [məsús] N masajista f
massive [mǽsɪv] ADJ (severe) masivo; (solid)
macizo; (large) enorme
mast [mæst] N mástil m, árbol m
mastectomy [mæstéktəmi] N mastectomía f
master [mǽstɚ] N (person in control) amo -a mf,
señor -ora mf; (owner of slave or animal) amo
-a mf; (best representative, skilled laborer)
maestro m; (young boy) señorito m; (tape or
disk) original m; —**'s degree** maestría f; ADJ
(dominant) dominante; — **bedroom**
dormitorio principal m; — **key** llave maestra
f; —**mind** cerebro m; —**piece** obra maestra
f; VT dominar; **to** —**mind** planificar y dirigir
masterful [mǽstɚfəɫ] ADJ magistral

masterly [mǽstɚli] ADJ magistral
mastery [mǽstɚi] N dominio m
mastiff [mǽstɪf] N mastín m, alano m
masturbate [mǽstɚbet] VI/VT masturbar[se]
mat [mæt] N (floor covering) estera f; (for wiping
feet) felpudo m; (in gymnastics) colchoneta f;
(of hair) maraña f; VI enmarañarse
match [mætʃ] N (pair) pareja f; (chess game)
partida f; (tennis, golf game) partido m;
(boxing encounter) combate m; (device for
fire) fósforo m, cerilla f; —**ball** bola de
partido f; —**box** cajita de fósforos f; —**maker**
casamentero -ra mf; —**point** punto de
partido m; **he has no** — no tiene igual; **he is
a good** — es un buen partido; **the hat and
coat are a good** — el abrigo y el sombrero
hacen juego; VI/VT hacer juego [con]; VI (to
correspond) estar de acuerdo; **the colors
don't** — los colores no combinan; VT (equal)
igualar; (come to correspond) poner de
acuerdo; (form pairs) parear
matching [mǽtʃɪŋ] ADJ emparejados; — **colors**
colores que combinan m pl; — **pair** pareja f;
— **shoes** zapatos del mismo par m pl
matchless [mǽtʃlɪs] ADJ sin par
mate [met] N (one of a pair) pareja f; (friend)
compañero -ra mf; (on a ship) oficial m; (in
chess) mate m; VI/VT aparear[se]
material [mətíriəɫ] ADJ (made of matter)
material; (pertinent) pertinente; N
(substance) material m; (fabric) tejido m,
género m
materialism [mətíriəlɪzəm] N materialismo m
materialize [mətíriəlaɪz] VI/VT materializar[se],
plasmarse
maternal [mətɚ́nl̩] ADJ (motherly) maternal;
(on mother's side of family) materno
maternity [mətɚ́nɪdi] N maternidad f; — **leave**
licencia por maternidad f
math [mæθ] N matemática[s] f [pl]
mathematical [mæθəmǽdɪkəɫ] ADJ
matemático
mathematician [mæθəmətíʃən] N matemático
-ca mf
mathematics [mæθəmǽdɪks] N matemática[s] f
[pl]
matinee [mætn̩é] N matiné f
mating [médɪŋ] N (copulation) cópula f;
(reproduction) reproducción f
matriarch [métriɑrk] N matriarca f
matriculate [mətríkjəlet] VI/VT matricular[se]
matriculation [mətrɪkjəléʃən] N matriculación
f, matrícula f
matrilineal [mætrəlíniəɫ] ADJ matrilineal
matrimony [mǽtrəmoni] N matrimonio m
matrix [métrɪks] N matriz f
matron [métrən] N (married woman or widow)
matrona f; (in a hospital) jefa de enfermeras f
matter [mǽdɚ] N (substance, pus) materia f;

(affair) asunto m; (printed) impreso m; (reading) material de lectura m; — for **complaint** motivo de queja m; **a — of two minutes** cosa de dos minutos f; **as a — of fact** de hecho, precisamente; **it is of no —** no tiene importancia; **no — what you say** no importa lo que digas; **as a — of course** por rutina; **what is the —?** ¿qué pasa? VI importar; **it doesn't —** no importa

mattress [mǽtrɪs] N colchón m

maturation [mætʃəréʃən] N maduración f

mature [mətʃúr] ADJ maduro; **a — note** un pagaré vencido/pagadero m; **for — audiences** para adultos; VI/VT madurar[se]; (a savings bond) vencer[se]

maturing [mətʃúrɪŋ] N maduración f

maturity [mətʃúrɪdi] N madurez f; (of a debt) vencimiento m

maul [mɔl] VT atacar, herir gravemente

Mauritania [mɔrɪténiə] N Mauritania f

Mauritanian [mɔrɪténiən] ADJ & N mauritano -na mf

Mauritian [mɔríʃən] ADJ & N mauriciano -na mf

Mauritius [mɔríʃəs] N Mauricio m

maverick [mǽvərɪk] N cimarrón m; (person) inconformista mf, cimarrón -ona mf

maxim [mǽksɪm] N máxima f, sentencia f

maximize [mǽksəmaɪz] VT maximizar

maximum [mǽksəməm] ADJ & N máximo m

may [me] V AUX **— I sit down?** ¿puedo sentarme? **— you have a merry Christmas** que pases una feliz Navidad; **it — be that** puede ser que; **it — rain** puede [ser] que llueva, tal vez llueva; **she — have been late** puede [ser] que haya llegado tarde; **be that as it —** sea como fuere

May [me] N mayo m; **— Day** primero de mayo m; **—pole** mayo m

Maya [máɪə] N & ADJ maya mf

Mayan [máɪən] N & ADJ maya mf

maybe [mébi] ADV quizá[s], tal vez

mayonnaise [méənez] N mayonesa f, mahonesa f

mayor [méər] N alcalde m

mayoralty [méərəlti] N alcaldía f

maze [mez] N laberinto m

MBA [master of business administration] [émbié] N máster en administración de empresas m, maestría en administración de empresas f

MD [medicine doctor] [émdí] N doctor -ora en medicina mf

me [mi] PRON **she sees —** me ve; **he talks to —** me habla; **he comes with —** viene conmigo; **he did it for —** lo hizo para mí

meadow [médo] N pradera f, prado m; **—lark** alondra f

meager [mígə] ADJ escaso, exiguo

meal [mil] N (repast) comida f; (flour) harina f;

—time hora de comer f

mean [min] ADJ (unkind) cruel; (petty) vil; (humble) humilde; (stingy) mezquino; (difficult) de mal genio; (middle) medio; **— spirited** mezquino; **I make a — lasagna** me sale muy rica la lasagna; N (average) media f, promedio m; **—s** medios m pl; **the ends justify the —s** el fin justifica los medios; **a man of —s** un hombre adinerado; **by —s of** por medio de; **—s of transport** medios de transporte m pl; **—s test** prueba de ingresos f; **by all —s** (of course) por supuesto; (using all resources) por todos los medios; **by no —s** de ningún modo; VT (intend) querer, tener intenciones de; (signify) querer decir, significar; **he —s well** tiene buenas intenciones; **winning —s everything to them** lo que más les importa es ganar; **they are meant for each other** son el uno para el otro

meander [miǽndə] VI (be winding) serpentear; (to wander) vagar

meaning [mínɪŋ] N (sense) significado m, sentido m; (purpose) sentido m; ADJ **well-— bien intencionado

meaningful [mínɪŋfəl] ADJ (result, event) significativo, trascendente; (sentence) coherente

meaningless [mínɪŋlɪs] ADJ sin sentido

meanness [mínnɪs] N (cruelty) crueldad f; (pettiness) mezquindad f

meant [mɛnt] see mean

meantime [míntaɪm] ADV LOC **in the —** mientras tanto

meanwhile [mínhwaɪl] ADV mientras tanto

measles [mízəlz] N sarampión m

measurable [méʒərəbəl] ADJ medible, mensurable

measure [méʒə] N (dimension) medida f; (criterion) criterio m; (in musical bar) compás m; (bill) proyecto de ley m; **beyond —** sobremanera; **dry —** medida de áridos f; **in large —** en gran parte; **—s** medidas f pl; VI/VT medir; **to — up** compararse con; **measuring tape** cinta de medir f, metro m

measured [méʒəd] ADJ (rhythmical) acompasado; (moderate) moderado, mesurado

measurement [méʒəmənt] N (act of measuring) medición f; (dimension) medida f, dimensión f

meat [mit] N carne f; (essential point) meollo m; **—ball** albóndiga f; **—loaf** pan/pastel de carne m

meaty [mídi] ADJ (with meat) con mucha carne; (substantial) sustancioso

mechanic [mɪkǽnɪk] ADJ & N mecánico m; N **—s** mecánica f

mechanical [mɪkǽnɪkəl] ADJ mecánico

mechanism [mékənizəm] N mecanismo *m*

medal [médl] N medalla *f*; VT ganar una medalla

meddle [médl] VI entrometerse, inmiscuirse

meddler [médlə] N entrometido -da *mf*

meddlesome [médlsəm] ADJ entrometido

media [mídiə] N (communication) medios *m pl*, media *m pl*, medios de comunicación masiva *m pl*; (cables) cables del ordenador/ de la computadora *m pl*

median [mídiən] ADJ mediano; N (middle value, line) mediana *f*

mediate [mídiet] VI/VT mediar

mediation [midiéʃən] N mediación *f*

mediator [mídieDə] N mediador -ora *mf*

medical [médɪkəl] ADJ médico; — **chart** hoja clínica *f*; — **exam** examen médico *m*; — **examiner** médico -ca forense *mf*; — **history** historia clínica *f*; — **record** expediente médico *m*; — **school** facultad de medicina *f*

medicate [médɪket] VT medicar

medication [medɪkéʃən] N medicación *f*

medicine [médɪsɪn] N (profession) medicina *f*; (drug) medicamento *m*, fármaco *m*; — **ball** balón medicinal *m*; — **cabinet** botiquín *m*; — **man** curandero *m*

medieval [mɪdívəl] ADJ medieval

mediocre [mibiókə] ADJ mediocre

mediocrity [mibiákrɪDi] N mediocridad *f*

meditate [médɪtet] VI meditar

meditation [medɪtéʃən] N meditación *f*, recogimiento *m*

Mediterranean [medɪtərénɪən] ADJ mediterráneo

medium [mídiəm] N (substance, agency) medio *m*; (person who contacts spirits) médium *mf*; — **of exchange** medio de cambio *m*; ADJ mediano; ADV término medio

medley [médli] N (music) popurrí *m*; (mixture) mezcla *f*

meek [mik] ADJ manso

meekness [míknɪs] N mansedumbre *f*

meet [mit] VT (encounter) encontrarse con; (make acquaintance) conocer; (face in conflict) enfrentar; (satisfy) satisfacer; (pay) pagar; **to — a deadline** cumplir el plazo; **to — expenses** sufragar los gastos; **to — halfway** partir la diferencia; **to — a train** esperar un tren; **I will — you at the station** nos encontramos/vemos en la estación; **have you met my brother?** ¿conoces a mi hermano? **we were met with disapproval** se nos recibió con desaprobación; VI (encounter) encontrarse; (make acquaintance) conocerse; (have a meeting) reunirse; (cross) cruzarse; **to — in battle** trabar batalla; **to — with** (intentional) reunirse con; (unintentional) tropezar con; N encuentro deportivo *m*, competición *f*

meeting [míDɪŋ] N reunión *f*, junta *f*; (political) mitin *m*; (crossing of roads) cruce *m*

megabyte [mégəbaɪt] N megabyte *m*

megahertz [mégəhɚtz] N megahertz *m*, megahercio *m*

megalomania [megəloméniə] N megalomanía *f*

megaphone [mégəfon] N megáfono *m*, bocina *f*

melancholy [mélənkɑli] N melancolía *f*; ADJ melancólico

melanoma [melənómə] N melanoma *m*

meld [meld] VT fusionar

melee [méle] N reyerta *f*, tumulto *m*

mellow [mélo] ADJ (soft) dulce, suave; (gentle) tranquilo; VI/VT suavizar[se]

melodic [məlɑdɪk] ADJ melódico

melodious [məlódiəs] ADJ melodioso, melódico

melodrama [mélodrɑmə] N melodrama *m*

melody [mélədi] N melodía *f*

melon [mélən] N melón *m*

melt [melt] VI/VT (liquefy) derretir[se]; (dissolve) disolver[se]; — **ing pot** crisol *m*; N —**down** (fusion) catástrofe por fusión nuclear incontrolada *f*; (any developing disaster) catástrofe *f*

member [mémbə] N miembro *m* (also body part)

membership [mémbəʃɪp] N (number) número de miembros/socios *m*; (state) calidad de miembro/socio *f*

membrane [mémbren] N membrana *f*

memento [məménto] N recuerdo *m*

memoir [mémwar] N memoria *f*; —**s** memorias *f pl*, autobiografía *f*

memorable [mémərəbəl] ADJ memorable

memorandum [meməréndəm] N memorándum *m*

memorial [məmóriəl] N (monument) monumento conmemorativo *m*; (petition) memorial *m*; ADJ conmemorativo

memorize [méməraɪz] VI/VT memorizar

memory [méməri] N (faculty) memoria *f*; (recollection) recuerdo *m*; — **cache** caché de memoria *f*; — **map** mapa de memoria *m*

menace [ménɪs] N amenaza *f*; VI/VT amenazar

mend [mend] VT remendar; **to — matters** enmendar la situación; **to — one's ways** enmendarse, reformarse; (bones) soldarse; N remiendo *m*; **to be on the —** ir mejorando

menial [míniəl] ADJ (lowly) bajo; (job) servil; N criado -da *mf*

meningitis [menɪndʒaɪDɪs] N meningitis *f*

menopause [ménəpɔz] N menopausia *f*

menstruate [ménstruet] VI menstruar

menstruation [menstruéʃən] N menstruación *f*

mental [méntl] ADJ mental; (insane) *fam* chiflado; — **health** salud mental *f*; — **illness** enfermedad mental *f*; — **retardation** retraso mental *m*

mentality [mɛntǽlɪDi] N mentalidad *f*

mention [mɛ́nʃən] VT mencionar; **don't — it** no hay de qué; N mención *f*

mentor [mɛ́ntɔr] N mentor -ora *mf*

menu [mɛ́nju] N (list of dishes) carta *f*, menú *m*; (computer) menú *m*; **— bar** (computer) barra de menú *f*

meow [mjau] INTERJ miau

mercantile [mɝ́kəntil] ADJ mercantil

mercenary [mɝ́sənɛri] ADJ mercenario

merchandise[1] [mɝ́tʃəndaɪs] N mercancía *f*, mercadería *f*

merchandise[2] [mɝ́tʃəndaɪz] VT comercializar

merchandising [mɝ́tʃəndaɪzɪŋ] N mercadeo *m*, comercialización *f*

merchant [mɝ́tʃənt] N (trader) comerciante *m*, mercader *m*; ADJ mercante; **— marine** marina mercante *f*

merciful [mɝ́sɪfəl] ADJ misericordioso

merciless [mɝ́sɪlɪs] ADJ despiadado

mercury [mɝ́kjəri] N mercurio *m*; (on a mirror) azogue *m*

mercy [mɝ́si] N (compassion) misericordia *f*, clemencia *f*, piedad *f*; **to be at the — of** estar a merced de; **— killing** eutanasia *f*

mere [mir] ADJ mero, simple; **a — trifle** una nonada

merely [mírli] ADV (only) solo, solamente; (simply) simplemente

merge [mɝdʒ] VI/VT (forces) unir[se]; (colors) fundir[se]; (companies) fusionar[se]; (data files) fusionar; N fusión *f*

merger [mɝ́dʒɚ] N fusión *f*; **—s and acquisitions** fusiones y adquisiciones *f pl*

meridian [mərídiən] ADJ & N meridiano *m*

merit [mɛ́rɪt] N mérito *m*; **— pay** paga por mérito *f*; **— raise** aumento por mérito *m*; VT merecer

meritorious [mɛrɪtɔ́riəs] ADJ meritorio

mermaid [mɝ́med] N sirena *f*

merriment [mɛ́rɪmənt] N alegría *f*, algazara *f*

merry [mɛ́ri] ADJ alegre; **—-go-round** tiovivo *m*; **—maker** fiestero -ra *mf*, juerguista *mf*; **—making** fiesta *f*, juerga *f*; **to make —** divertirse; INTERJ **— Christmas** Feliz Navidad *f*, Felices Pascuas

mesa [mésə] N mesa *f*

mesh [mɛʃ] N (of metal) malla *f*; (of fiber) red *f*; (of gears) engranaje *m*; VI engranar

mesmerize [mɛ́zmɚaɪz] VI/VT hipnotizar

mess [mɛs] N (state of confusion) desorden *m*, desarreglo *m*; (disorderly person) desordenado -da *mf*, mugriento -ta *mf*; (confused person) desastre *m*; (difficult situation) lío *m*, jaleo *m*; (food for soldiers) rancho *m*; (cafeteria) cantina *f*; **— hall** cantina *f*; **— of fish** plato de pescado *m*; **to make a — of** (a room) ensuciar, desordenar; (a project) estropear; VI/VT **to — around**

(waste time) perder el tiempo; (philander) correr detrás de las mujeres; **to — up** (a room) alborotar, desordenar; (clothes, hair) desarreglar; (a project) estropear; **to — with** meterse con

message [mɛ́sɪdʒ] N mensaje *m*, recado *m*; **I get the —** ya caí en cuenta

messenger [mɛ́səndʒɚ] N mensajero -ra *mf*

messy [mɛ́si] ADJ (chaotic) desordenado; (embarrassing) embarazoso

met [mɛt] *see* meet

metabolic [mɛDəbálɪk] ADJ metabólico

metabolism [mətǽbəlɪzəm] N metabolismo *m*

metal [mɛ́dl] N metal *m*; **— detector** detector de metales *m*; ADJ de metal, metálico

metallic [mətǽlɪk] ADJ metálico

metallurgy [mɛ́dlɚdʒi] N metalurgia *f*

metamorphosis [mɛDəmɔ́rfəsɪs] N metamorfosis *f*

metaphor [mɛ́Dəfɔr] N metáfora *f*

metaphysical [mɛDəfízɪkəl] ADJ metafísico

metaphysics [mɛDəfízɪks] N metafísica *f*

metastasis [mətǽstəsɪs] N metástasis *f*

metastasize [mətǽstəsaɪz] VI metastatizar

meteor [mídiɚ] N meteoro *m*; **— shower** lluvia de meteoritos *f*

meteorite [mídiəraɪt] N meteorito *m*

meteorological [mɪDiɚəláḏʒɪkəl] ADJ meteorológico

meteorology [mɪDiɚáləḏʒi] N meteorología *f*

meter [míDɚ] N (unit of length) metro *m*; (measuring device) contador *m*, medidor *m*

methane [mɛ́θen] N metano *m*

method [mɛ́θəd] N método *m*

methodical [məθádɪkəl] ADJ metódico

methodology [mɛθədáləḏʒi] N metodología *f*

meticulous [mətíkjələs] ADJ detallista

metric [mɛ́trɪk] ADJ métrico

metro [mɛ́tro] N metro *m*

metronome [mɛ́trənom] N metrónomo *m*

metropolis [mətrápəlɪs] N metrópoli *f*, urbe *f*

metropolitan [mɛtrəpálɪDən] ADJ metropolitano

mettle [mɛ́dl] N temple *m*, valor *m*

mew [mju] N maullido *m*; VI maullar

Mexican [mɛ́ksɪkən] ADJ & N mexicano -na *mf*

Mexico [mɛ́ksɪko] N México *m*

mezzanine [mɛ́zənin] N entrepiso *m*, entresuelo *m*

mickey mouse [míkimáus] ADJ poco serio, informal

microbe [máɪkrob] N microbio *m*

microbiology [maɪkrobaɪáləḏʒi] N microbiología *f*

microcomputer [maɪkrokəmpjúDɚ] N *Am* microcomputadora *f*; *Sp* microordenador *m*

microeconomics [maɪkroɛkənámɪks] N microeconomía *f*

microfiche [máɪkrofiʃ] N microficha *f*

microfilm [máɪkrofɪlm] N microfilme *m*

micromanage [maɪkromǽnɪʤ] VI/VT administrar con excesivo control

micron [máɪkrɑn] N micrón *m*, micrómetro *m*

Micronesia [maɪkroníʒə] N Micronesia *f*

Micronesian [maɪkrəníʒən] ADJ & N micronesio -sia *mf*

microorganism [maɪkroórgənɪzəm] N microorganismo *m*

microphone [máɪkrafon] N micrófono *m*

microprocessor [maɪkroprásesə] N microprocesador *m*

microscope [máɪkrəskop] N microscopio *m*

microscopic [maɪkrəskápɪk] ADJ microscópico

microsurgery [maɪkrosə́ʤəri] N microcirujía *f*

microwave [máɪkrowev] N microonda *f*; — **oven** [horno] microondas *m sg*

mid [mɪd] ADJ medio; —**air** en el aire; —**day** [del] mediodía *m*; —**field player** (soccer) centrocampista *m*; —**life** madurez *f*; —**life crisis** crisis de la edad madura *f*; —**night** [de] medianoche *f*; —**shipman** guardiamarina *m*; **in** —**stream** (of a river) en medio del río; (of a task) en plena actividad; —**summer** pleno verano *m*; —**term examination** examen a mitad del curso *m*; —**way** a medio camino, a mitad del camino; —**wife** partera *f*, comadre *f*

middle [mɪ́dl] ADJ (average) medio, mediano; (intermediate) intermedio; (central) central; —-**aged** de mediana edad; — **Ages** Edad Media *f*; — **class** clase media *f*, burguesía *f*; —-**class neighborhood** barrio de clase media; — **ear** oído medio *m*; — **finger** dedo mayor *m*, dedo del corazón *m*; —**man** intermediario *m*, revendedor *m*; — **management** administración intermedia *f*; — **name** segundo nombre *m*; —- **of-the-road** moderado; —**sized** [de] tamaño mediano; N medio *m*; (waist) cintura *f*; **in the** — **of** en el medio de; **I'm in the** — **of something** estoy ocupado haciendo algo; **toward the** — **of the month** a mediados del mes

midget [mɪ́ʤɪt] N enano -na *mf*

MIDI [musical instrument digital interface] [mɪ́di] N interfaz digital de instrumentos musicales *f*

midst [mɪdst] ADV LOC medio *m*, centro *m*; **in the** — **of** en medio de, entre; **in our** — entre nosotros

mien [min] N porte *m*

might [maɪt] V AUX **it** — **be that** podría ser que; **he said it** — **rain tomorrow** dijo que tal vez lloviera mañana; **she** — **have been late** puede ser que haya llegado tarde; N poder *m*, poderío *m*

mighty [máɪdi] ADJ (strong) poderoso, potente; (large) imponente; ADV muy

migraine [máɪgren] N migraña *f*, jaqueca *f*

migrant [máɪgrənt] ADJ migratorio, migrante; N trabajador -ora itinerante *mf*, bracero -ra *mf*

migrate [máɪgret] VI (also computers) migrar

migration [maɪgréʃən] N migración *f*

migratory [máɪgrətɔri] ADJ migratorio

mild [maɪld] ADJ (gentle) suave; (moderate) moderado; (not serious) leve

mildew [mɪ́ldu] N moho *m*

mildness [máɪldnɪs] N (gentleness) suavidad *f*; (lack of gravity) levedad *f*

mile [maɪl] N milla *f*; —**stone** hito *m*

mileage [máɪlɪʤ] N (distance, odometer reading) millaje *m*, kilometraje *m*; **this car gets good** — este coche es económico; **what kind of** — **are you getting?** ¿cuántos kilómetros por litro hace tu coche?

milieu [mɪljú] N ambiente *m*

militance [mɪ́lɪtəns] N militancia *f*

militancy [mɪ́lɪtənsi] N militancia *f*

militant [mɪ́lɪtənt] ADJ & N (fanatic) militante *mf*; (combatant) combatiente *mf*

military [mɪ́lɪteri] ADJ militar; N **the** — (armed forces) el ejército; (military personnel) los militares

militia [məlíʃə] N milicia *f*

milk [mɪlk] N leche *f*; — **chocolate** chocolate con leche *m*; —**maid** lechera *f*; —**man** lechero *m*; — **shake** batido *m*; VT ordeñar; (exploit) exprimir; **he's** —**ing it for all it's worth** le está sacando todo el jugo

milky [mɪ́lki] ADJ (consistency) lechoso; (product) lácteo; — **Way** Vía Láctea *f*

mill [mɪl] N (building) molino *m*; (factory) fábrica *f*; (for sugar) trapiche *m*, ingenio *m*; (rotating tool) fresa *f*; (small grinder) molinillo *m*; —**stone** muela de molino *f*; a —**stone around your neck** una piedra al cuello; VT (grind grain) moler; (cut wood) aserrar; (cut grooves on coins) acordonar; (machine) fresar; **to** — **around** dar vueltas

millennium [məlɪ́niəm] N milenio *m*

miller [mɪ́lə] N (person who mills) molinero -ra *mf*; (machine for milling) fresadora *f*; (moth) mariposa nocturna *f*

milligram [mɪ́lɪgræm] N miligramo *m*

milliliter [mɪ́lɪlidə] N mililitro *m*

millimeter [mɪ́lɪmidə] N milímetro *m*

milliner [mɪ́lənə] N sombrerero -ra *mf*

millinery [mɪ́lənɛri] N (shop) sombrerería *f*; (hats) sombreros de señora *m pl*

million [mɪ́ljən] N millón *m*; **a** — **dollars** un millón de dólares

millionaire [mɪljənɛ́r] N millonario -ria *mf*

millionth [mɪ́ljənθ] ADJ & N millonésimo *m*

mime [maɪm] N (actor) mimo *m*; (technique, performance) pantomima *f*; VI hacer la mímica

mimic [mɪ́mɪk] VT imitar, remedar; N mono -na

mf, remedador -ora *mf*

mince [mɪns] VT picar, desmenuzar; **not to —
words** no tener pelos en la lengua; **—meat**
picadillo *m*; **I'm going to make —meat of
you** te voy a hacer picadillo

mind [maɪnd] N (thinking process) mente *f*;
(person of intellect) inteligencia *f*; (opinion)
parecer *m*, opinión *f*; **— games**
manipulación psicológica *f*; **— over matter**
el espíritu sobre la materia; **—set** actitud *f*,
forma de pensar *f*; **to be out of one's —** estar
loco; **to bear in —** tener en cuenta; **to
change one's —** cambiar de parecer/
opinión; **to give someone a piece of one's**
— cantarle a alguien las cuarenta; **I have a —
to** me dan ganas de; **to make up one's —**
decidirse; **to my —** a mi modo de ver; **to
speak one's —** freely hablar con toda
franqueza; **what do you have in —?** ¿qué
tienes en mente? **to call to —** recordar; **to
keep one's — on one's work** concentrarse
en el trabajo; ADJ **—altering** alucinógeno;
VT (take care of) cuidar; (pay attention to)
atender a; (obey) obedecer; **I don't —** no
tengo inconveniente en ello; **— what you
say** cuidado con lo que dices; **to — one's
own business** no meterse en lo ajeno

mindful [máɪndfəl] ADJ atento

mine [maɪn] PRON **this book is —** este libro es
mío; **these things are —** estas cosas son
mías; **— is bigger** el mío / la mía es más
grande; **a friend of —** un amigo mío / una
amiga mía; N mina *f* (also explosive device);
—field campo minado *m*; **— sweeper**
dragaminas *m sg*, barreminas *m sg*; VT (plant
explosives) minar; (dig out minerals) extraer;
(exploit an area for minerals) explotar; VI (lay
mines) sembrar minas; (dig a mine) cavar una
mina; **to — for** extraer

miner [máɪnə] N mina -ra *mf*

mineral [mínəɹəl] ADJ & N mineral *m*; **— rights**
derechos mineros *m pl*; **— water** agua
mineral *f*

mingle [míngəl] VI mezclarse; (sounds)
confundirse; VT mezclar

miniature [mínɪətʃə] N miniatura *f*; ADJ en
miniatura

minicomputer [mɪnɪkəmpjúᴅə] N *Am*
minicomputadora *f*; *Sp* miniordenador *m*

minimal [mínəməl] ADJ mínimo

minimize [mínəmaɪz] VT minimizar

minimum [mínəməm] ADJ & N mínimo *m*; **—
wage** salario mínimo *m*

mining [máɪnɪŋ] N (exploitation of mines)
minería *f*; (act of mining) minado *m*; ADJ
minero; **open —** minería a cielo abierto *f*

miniskirt [mínɪskət] N minifalda *f*

minister [mínɪstə] N (official) ministro -tra *mf*;
(pastor) pastor -ora *mf*, clérigo *m*; VI **to — to**

atender a

ministerial [mɪnɪstíɹiəl] ADJ ministerial

ministry [mínɪstri] N (government agency)
ministerio *m*; (functions of pastor) clerecía *f*

minivan [mínɪvæn] N camioneta *f*

mink [mɪŋk] N visón *m*

minnow [míno] N pececillo *m*

minor [máɪnə] ADJ (smaller) menor, más
pequeño; (of secondary importance) menor;
— key tono menor *m*; **— league** liga menor
f; N (young person) menor de edad *mf*;
(musical interval) tono menor *m*; (subfield)
asignatura secundaria *f*; VI tener como
segunda especialización

minority [mənɔ́ɹɪdi] N (smaller part or group)
minoría *f*; (state of being underage)
minoridad *f*; (member of a minority)
miembro de una minoría *m*; ADJ minoritario;
— partner socio -cia minoritario -tia *mf*

mint [mɪnt] N (flavor) menta *f*, hierbabuena *f*;
(candy) pastilla de menta *f*; (money) casa de la
moneda *f*; VT acuñar

minus [máɪnəs] PREP **seven — four** siete menos
cuatro; **we came — my brother** vinimos
sin mi hermano; N signo de menos *m*; ADJ
negativo

minuscule [mínəskjul] ADJ minúsculo

minute[1] [mínɪt] N minuto *m*; **— hand** minutero
m; **—s** actas *f pl*

minute[2] [maɪnút] ADJ (small) diminuto;
(detailed) detallado, minucioso

miracle [mírəkəl] N milagro *m*

miraculous [mɪrǽkjələs] ADJ milagroso

mirage [mɪráʒ] N espejismo *m*

mire [maɪr] N (mud) cieno *m*, fango *m*; (muddy
place) ciénaga *f*; VI/VT (bog down) atascar[se]
en el fango; (be or get covered with mud)
enlodar[se]

mirror [mírə] N espejo *m*; (large) luna *f*; **—
image** imagen especular *f*; VT reflejar

mirth [mɜθ] N risa *f*, hilaridad *f*

mirthful [mɜ́θfəl] ADJ risueño

miry [máɪri] ADJ cenagoso, fangoso

misanthropy [mɪsǽnθɹəpi] N misantropía *f*

misappropriation [mɪsəpropriéʃən] N
malversación *f*

misbehave [mɪsbɪhév] VI portarse mal

miscalculate [mɪskǽlkjəlet] VI/VT (in math)
calcular mal; (in situations) equivocarse

miscarriage [mɪskǽrɪdʒ] N aborto espontáneo
m, malparto *m*; **— of justice** injusticia *f*

miscarry [mɪskǽri] VI (abort) abortar
espontáneamente; (fail) malograrse,
frustrarse

miscellaneous [mɪsəlénɪəs] ADJ diverso; (texts)
misceláneo; **— expenses** gastos varios *mf*

mischief [místʃɪf] N travesura *f*, diablura *f*,
picardía *f*; (serious prank) barrabasada *f*,
bellaquería *f*; **this will come to —** va a

suceder una desgracia

mischievous [mɪstʃəvəs] ADJ travieso, pícaro

misconception [mɪskənsépʃən] N concepto erróneo *m*

misconduct[1] [mɪskándʌkt] N (bad behavior) mala conducta *f*; (malfeasance) mala administración *f*

misconduct[2] [mɪskəndákt] VT administrar mal; **to — oneself** portarse mal

miscue [mɪskjú] N pifia *f*; VI/VT pifiar

misdeed [mɪsdíd] N fechoría *f*

misdemeanor [mɪsdimínə] N delito menor *m*

miser [máɪzə] N avaro -ra *mf*, tacaño -ña *mf*

miserable [mízəəbəl] ADJ infeliz, dichado; **a — day** un día asqueroso; **a — failure** un fracaso rotundo

miserly [máɪzə·li] ADJ avariento, tacaño

misery [mízəri] N (wretchedness) desgracia *f*; (poverty) miseria *f*; (unhappiness) infelicidad *f*

misfit [mɪsfɪt] N inadaptado -da *mf*

misfortune [mɪsfɔ́rtʃən] N desgracia *f*, desdicha *f*, desventura *f*

misgivings [mɪsgívɪŋz] N aprensión *f*, recelo *m*

misguided [mɪsgáɪdɪd] ADJ mal aconsejado, poco feliz

mishap [míshæp] N contratiempo *m*, percance *m*

misinform [mɪsɪnfɔ́rm] VT desinformar, dar información errónea

misjudge [mɪsʤʌ́ʤ] VT juzgar mal

mislay [mɪslé] VT (keys, etc.) extraviar, perder; (a document) traspapelar; (lay wrong) colocar mal

mislead [mɪslíd] VT (in the wrong direction) guiar por mal camino; (into error) engañar, confundir

misleading [mɪslídɪŋ] ADJ engañoso

mismanage [mɪsmǽnɪʤ] VT administrar mal

misogyny [mɪsáʤəni] N misoginia *f*

misplace [mɪsplés] VT (lose keys, etc.) extraviar; (lose a document) traspapelar; (place wrong) colocar mal; **she —d her trust** confió en la persona equivocada

misprint [mísprɪnt] N errata *f*, error de imprenta *m*

misrepresent [mɪsreprɪzɛ́nt] VT distorsionar, tergiversar

misrepresentation [mɪsreprɪzəntéʃən] N distorsión *f*, tergiversación *f*

miss [mɪs] VI (fail to hit) errar; (misfire) fallar; VT (fail to hit) errar, no acertar; (fail to be on time for) perder; (fail to attend) faltar a; (feel absence of) echar de menos; *Am* extrañar; **he just —ed being killed** por poco se mata; **he** (of a target) tiro errado *m*; (in a motor) falla *f*; (from class) falta *f*; (young woman) señorita *f*; **— Smith** la señorita Smith

misshapen [mɪsʃépən] ADJ deforme

missile [mísəl] N (projectile) proyectil *m*;

(guided weapon) misil *m*

missing [mísɪŋ] ADJ (not present) ausente; (lost) perdido; **— link** eslabón perdido *m*; **one book is —** falta un libro

mission [míʃən] N misión *f*; **— statement** declaración de la misión *f*

missionary [míʃəneri] ADJ & N misionero -ra *mf*

misspell [mɪsspɛ́l] VT (written) escribir mal; (oral) deletrear mal

misstatement [mɪsstétmənt] N declaración errónea/falsa *f*

misstep [místɛp] N paso en falso *m*

mist [mɪst] N (of water droplets) neblina *f*, bruma *f*; (of perfume) rocío *m*; VI lloviznar; VT rociar

mistake [mɪsték] N error *m*, equivocación *f*; (orthographical) falta *f*; **to make a — equivocarse**; VI/VT equivocar[se]; **I — my sister for my mother** confundo a mi hermana con mi madre

mistaken [mɪstékən] ADJ equivocado; **to be — estar** equivocado, equivocarse; **unless I'm — si** no me equivoco

mistaken [mɪstékən] *see* mistake

mister [místə] N señor *m*

mistletoe [mísəltò] N muérdago *m*

mistook [mɪstúk] *see* mistake

mistreat [mɪstrít] VT maltratar

mistreatment [mɪstrítmənt] N maltrato *m*

mistress [místrɪs] N (of a household) señora *f*; (employing servants, animal owner) ama *f*; (lover) amante *f*

mistrial [místraɪl] N proceso viciado de nulidad *m*

mistrust [mɪstrást] N desconfianza *f*; VT desconfiar de

mistrustful [mɪstrástfəl] ADJ desconfiado, receloso

misty [místi] ADJ (foggy) neblinoso, brumoso; (in tears) nublado; (blurry) empañado

misunderstand [mɪsʌndəstǽnd] VT comprender mal, malinterpretar

misunderstanding [mɪsʌndəstǽndɪŋ] N (confusion) malentendido *m*; (failure to understand) equivocación *f*, mala inteligencia *f*; (argument) desavenencia *f*

misuse[1] [mɪsjús] N (of drugs) abuso *m*; (of a word) mal uso *m*; (of funds) malversación *f*

misuse[2] [mɪsjúz] VT (drugs) abusar de; (a friend) maltratar; (a word) emplear mal; (funds) malversar

mite [maɪt] N ácaro *m*; ADV **a — greedy** un poquito codicioso

mitigate [mídɪget] VT mitigar

mitochondria [maɪdokándriə] N mitocondria *f*

mitten [mɪtn̩] N manopla *f*

mix [mɪks] VI/VT mezclar[se]; **to — up** confundir; N mezcla *f*; (for baking) preparado *m*; **—-up** (confusion) confusión *f*; (fight) pelea f

mixed [mɪkst] ADJ mixto; — **bag** grupo heterogéneo m; — **doubles** dobles mixtos m pl; — **drink** cóctel m; — **-up** confundido

mixer [mɪksə·] N (appliance) batidora f; (party) fiesta f; (soda) refresco m; (sound technician) mezclador -ora mf; (sound device) mezcladora f

mixture [mɪkstʃə·] N mezcla f

moan [mon] N quejido m, gemido m; VI gemir, quejarse; VI/VT lamentar

moat [mot] N foso m

mob [mab] N (disorderly crowd) tumulto m, turba f; (crowd) muchedumbre f, populacho m; (mafia) mafia f; VT (attack) asaltar; (crowd) atestar

mobile [móbəl] ADJ móvil; (personnel) que tiene movilidad; — **home** casa prefabricada f; — **Internet** internet móvil m; — **phone** [teléfono] móvil m, [teléfono] celular m

mobility [mobílɪDi] N movilidad f

mobilization [mobəlɪzéʃən] N movilización f

mobilize [móbəlaɪz] VI/VT movilizar[se]

moccasin [mákəsɪn] N mocasín m (also snake)

mock [mak] VI (ridicule) burlar[se]; VT (imitate) remedar; ADJ de práctica; — **battle** simulacro de batalla m; N —**-up** maqueta f, modelo m

mockery [mákəri] N (ridicule) burla f; (imitation) remedo m; (travesty) farsa f

mockingbird [mákɪŋbə·d] N sinsonte m

mode [mod] N modo m; — **of delivery** modo de entrega m; — **of payment** forma de pago f

model [mádl] N (guide) modelo m; (person) modelo mf, maniquí mf; ADJ modelo, ejemplar; — **school** escuela modelo f; VI/VT modelar; (display clothes) lucir

modem [módəm] N módem m

moderate¹ [mádə·ɪt] ADJ (not excessive) moderado, mesurado; (person) comedido; (weather) templado; (price) módico; N moderado -da mf

moderate² [mádə·ret] VI/VT moderar[se] (also preside at meetings)

moderation [mɑDə·réʃən] N moderación f, mesura f

modern [mádə·n] ADJ moderno; — **age** modernidad f

modernism [mádə·nɪzəm] N modernismo m

modernity [mədə́·nɪDi] N modernismo m

modernization [mɑDə·nɪzéʃən] N modernización f

modernize [mádə·naɪz] VI/VT modernizar[se], innovar

modernness [mádə·nnɪs] N modernismo m

modest [mádɪst] ADJ (humble) modesto; (chaste) recatado, honesto

modesty [mádɪsti] N (humility) modestia f; (chastity) recato m, pudor m, honestidad f

modification [mɑDəfɪkéʃən] N modificación f

modify [mádəfaɪ] VT modificar

modulate [mádʒəlet] VI/VT modular[se]

modulation [mɑdʒəléʃən] N modulación f

module [mádʒul] N módulo m

mohair [móhɛr] N mohair m

moist [mɔɪst] ADJ húmedo

moisten [mɔ́ɪsən] VI/VT humedecer[se]

moisture [mɔ́ɪstʃə·] N humedad f

moisturizer [mɔ́ɪstʃə·raɪzə·] N [crema] hidrante/ humectante f

molar [mólə·] ADJ molar; N muela f, molar m

molasses [mələ́sɪz] N melaza f

mold [mold] N (form) molde m; (fungi) moho m; (mettle) temple m; VT (shape) moldear, plasmar; (adapt) amoldar; (fuse) fundir; VI/VT (become moldy) enmohecer[se]

molder [móldə·] VI/VT descomponerse; (paper) enmohecerse

molding [móldɪŋ] N (adornment) moldura f; (action of molding) moldeado m

Moldova [mɔldóvə] N Moldavia f

Moldovan [mɔłdóvən] ADJ & N moldavo -va mf

moldy [móldi] ADJ mohoso

mole [mol] N (blemish) lunar m; (animal, spy) topo m; (breakwater) rompeolas m sg

molecular [məlékjələ·] ADJ molecular

molecule [málɪkjul] N molécula f

molest [məlést] VT abusar sexualmente de

mollify [máləfaɪ] VT apaciguar, aplacar

mollusk [máləsk] N molusco m

molt [molt] VI (birds) mudar la pluma; (snakes) mudar la piel; N muda f

molten [móltn] ADJ fundido

molybdenum [məlíbdənəm] N molibdeno m

mom [mam] N mamá f; — **and pop store** tienda familiar f

moment [mómənt] N momento m; **being a parent has its —s** ser padre/madre tiene sus momentos de recompensa

momentary [móməntɛri] ADJ momentáneo

momentous [mómɛntəs] ADJ importante, trascendental

momentum [mómɛntəm] N (in physics) momento m; (in politics, sports) empuje m

mommy [mámi] N mami f

Monaco [mánəko] N Mónaco m

monarch [mánɑrk] N monarca mf

monarchical [mənárkɪkəl] ADJ monárquico

monarchist [mánə·kɪst] N monárquico -ca f

monarchy [mánə·ki] N monarquía f

monastery [mánəstɛri] N monasterio m

Monday [mánde] N lunes m

Monegasque [mɑnɪgásk] ADJ & N monegasco -ca mf

monetary [mánɪtɛri] ADJ monetario

money [máni] N dinero m; —**-back guarantee** garantía de devolución de dinero f; — **belt** faltriquera en forma de cinturón f; —

changer cambista *mf*; **— laundering** lavado de dinero *m*; **— machine** cajero automático *m*; **— market** mercado de valores *m*; **— market account** cuenta de mercado monetario *f*; **— order** giro postal *m*; **to get one's —'s worth** sacar jugo al dinero; ADJ **—-grubbing** codicioso; **—-making** lucrativo, rentable

moneyed [mánid] ADJ adinerado

Mongolia [maŋgóliə] N Mongolia *f*

Mongolian [maŋgóliən] ADJ & N mongol -ola *mf*

mongoloid [máŋgəlɔid] ADJ mongoloide

mongoose [máŋgus] N mangosta *f*

mongrel [máŋgrəl] ADJ & N mestizo *m*

monitor [mánitə] N monitor *m*; (in a school) celador -ora *mf*; **— lizard** varano *m*; VT monitorear

monitoring [mánitəiŋ] N monitoreo *m*, monitorización *f*

monk [mʌŋk] N monje *m*, religioso *m*

monkey [máŋki] N mono *m*, mico *m*; **— bars** jaula de los monos *f*; **— business** (mischief) picardía *f*; (trickery) chanchullo *m*; **— wrench** llave inglesa *f*; **to have a — on one's back** estar adicto; VI **to — around** bobear, payasear; **to — with** bobear con

monogamy [mənágami] N monogamia *f*

monologue, monolog [mánəbg] N monólogo *m*

mononucleosis [manonukliósis] N mononucleosis *f*

monopolize [mənápəlaiz] VT monopolizar

monopoly [mənápəli] N monopolio *m*

monotonous [mənátṇəs] ADJ monótono

monotony [mənátṇi] N monotonía *f*

monsignor [mansínjər] N monseñor *m*

monster [mánstə] N monstruo *m*; ADJ enorme, monstruo *inv*

monstrosity [manstrásIDi] N monstruosidad *f*

monstrous [mánstrəs] ADJ monstruoso

month [mʌnθ] N mes *m*

monthly [mánθli] ADJ mensual; **— installment** mensualidad *f*; N publicación mensual *f*, mensuario *m*; ADV mensualmente

monument [mánjəmənt] N monumento *m*

monumental [manjəmέntḷ] ADJ monumental

moo [mu] N mugido *m*; VI mugir

mooch [mutʃ] VI/VT gorronear; N pedigüeño -ña *mf*

mood [mud] N (emotional state) humor *m*, vena *f*, ánimo *m*; (grammatical category) modo *m*; **to be in a good —** estar de buen humor; **to be in the — to** tener ganas de

moody [múdi] ADJ (sullen) malhumorado; (changing) voluble

moon [mun] N luna *f*; **—beam** rayo de luna *m*; **—light** claro de la luna *m*, luz de la luna *f*; **—lighting** pluriempleo *m*; **—shine** bebida alcohólica destilada sin licencia *f*; **once in a blue —** de Pascuas a Ramos

moor [mur] VI/VT amarrar; N páramo *m*

Moor [mur] N moro -ra *mf*

Moorish [múriʃ] ADJ morisco, moro

moose [mus] N alce *m*

moot [mut] ADJ **it became a — point** dejó de tener importancia

mop [map] N (for floors) *Sp* fregona *f*, *Sp* mopa *f*; *Mex* trapeador *m*; (for dust) plumero *m*; (of hair) greña *f*; **—-up** (of an enemy) limpieza *f*; (of a task) remate *m*; VI/VT pasar la mopa [sobre]; *Am* trapear; **to — one's brow** enjugarse la frente; **to — up** (a spill) limpiar; (an enemy) acabar con; (a task) rematar

mope [mop] VI andar abatido

moped [móped] N ciclomotor *m*, scooter *m*

moral [mɔrəl] ADJ moral; N moraleja *f*; **—s** moral *f*

morale [mərǽl] N moral *f*

moralist [mɔrəlist] N moralista *mf*

morality [mərǽlIDi] N moralidad *f*

moralize [mɔrəlaiz] VI/VT moralizar

morbid [mɔrbid] ADJ mórbido, morboso

morbidity [mɔrbíDIDi] N (predisposition to illness) morbilidad *f*; (producing illness) morbosidad *f*

more [mɔr] ADJ & ADV más; **— and —** cada vez más; **— or less** más o menos; **there is no —** no hay más; **—over** además

morgue [mɔrg] N depósito de cadáveres *m*, morgue *f*

moribund [mɔrəband] ADJ moribundo

morning [mɔrniŋ] N mañana *f*; **— glory** dondiego de día *m*; **— sickness** náuseas *f pl*; **— star** lucero del alba *m*; **good —!** ¡buenos días! **tomorrow —** mañana por la mañana; ADJ de la mañana, matutino

Moroccan [mərákən] ADJ & N marroquí *mf*

Morocco [məráko] N Marruecos *m*

moron [mɔran] N imbécil *m*

morphine [mɔrfin] N morfina *f*

morsel [mɔrsəl] N bocado *m*

mortal [mɔrdḷ] ADJ & N mortal *mf*; **— sin** pecado mortal *m*

mortality [mɔrtǽlIDi] N (rate) mortalidad *f*; (toll) mortandad *f*

mortar [mɔrdə] N (for pounding) mortero *m* (also ballistics); (for bricks) argamasa *f*, mezcla *f*; **—board** birrete *m*

mortgage [mɔrgidʒ] N hipoteca *f*; VT hipotecar; ADJ hipotecario; **—-backed securities** valores respaldados por hipoteca *m pl*

mortgagor [mɔrgidʒə] N deudor -ora hipotecario -ria *mf*

mortification [mɔrdəfikéʃən] N mortificación *f*

mortify [mɔrdəfai] VI/VT mortificar[se]

mortuary [mɔrtʃueri] N mortuorio *m*

mosaic [mozéik] N mosaico *m*

Moslem [mázləm] ADJ & N musulmán -ana *mf*

mosque [mask] N mezquita *f*

mosquito [məskíᴅo] N mosquito m; — **net** mosquitero m

moss [mɔs] N musgo m

mossy [mɔ́si] ADJ musgoso

most [most] ADJ — **children are good** la mayoría de los niños son buenos; — **people** la mayoría de la gente; **the — money** más dinero m; **the — votes** el mayor número de votos; **for the — part** generalmente; PRON **the — that I can do** lo más que puedo hacer; **we ate the —** comimos más que nadie; — **of the guests are here** ha llegado la mayoría de los invitados; ADV **the — ambitious** el más ambicioso; **a — pleasant day** un día de lo más agradable

mostly [móstli] ADV generalmente

motel [motél] N motel m

moth [mɔθ] N (pest) polilla f; (nocturnal insect) mariposa nocturna f; —**ball** bolita de naftalina f; —**eaten** apolillado

mother [máðə] N madre f; —**board** placa madre f; — **country** madre patria f; —-**in-law** suegra f; —-**of-pearl** madreperla f; — **tongue** lengua materna f; VT mimar a, cuidar de/a

motherhood [máðəʰud] N maternidad f

motherly [máðəli] ADJ maternal

motif [motíf] N motivo m

motion [móʃən] N (movement) movimiento m; (signal) ademán m; (proposal) moción f; — **picture** película de cine f; —-**picture industry** industria cinematográfica f; — **sickness** mareo m; VI/VT hacer un ademán

motionless [móʃənlɪs] ADJ inmóvil

motivate [móᴅəvet] VT motivar

motivation [moᴅəvéʃən] N motivación f

motive [móᴅɪv] N motivo m; ADJ motriz

motley [mátli] ADJ abigarrado

motor [móᴅə] N motor m; —**bike** motocicleta pequeña f; —**boat** lancha a motor f; —**cycle** motocicleta f; —**cyclist** motociclista mf; — **home** casa rodante f, caravana f; — **scooter** scooter m; — **vehicle** vehículo motorizado m; VI pasear en coche

motorist [móᴅə·ɪst] N automovilista mf

motto [máᴅo] N lema f

mound [maund] N montículo m; **burial** — túmulo m; — **of laundry** pila de ropa f

mount [maunt] VI/VT (get on) montar; VI (increase) subir; VT (assemble) armar; N (mountain) monte m; (getting on a horse) montar f; (animal for riding) montura f

mountain [mauntn] N montaña f; — **bike** bicicleta de montaña f; — **climber** alpinista mf; — **climbing** alpinismo m, montañismo m; — **goat** cabra montés f; — **lion** puma f, gato montés m; — **range** (large) cordillera f; (small) sierra f; —**side** ladera [de una montaña] f; —**top** cumbre [de una montaña]

f; ADJ (animal, person) montañés; (thing) de montaña

mountaineer [mauntnír] N alpinista mf

mountainous [máuntnəs] ADJ montañoso

mourn [mɔrn] VI estar de duelo/luto; VT llorar; **to — for** llorar a

mourner [mɔ́rnə] N doliente mf

mournful [mɔ́rnfəl] ADJ lúgubre, triste

mourning [mɔ́rnɪŋ] N luto m, duelo m; **to be in** — estar de luto/duelo; ADJ de luto

mouse [maus] N ratón m (also computer); — **pad** alfombrilla [de ratón] f; — **port** puerto de ratón m; —**trap** ratonera f

mouth[1] [mauθ] N boca f; (of a cave) abertura f; (of a river) desembocadura f; — **piece** (part of a trumpet) boquilla f; (spokesman) portavoz mf; —-**to-mouth resuscitation** respiración boca a boca f; —**wash** enjuague bucal m; ADJ —-**watering** delicioso

mouth[2] [mauð] VT articular silenciosamente una palabra; VI **to — off** contestar

mouthful [máuθful] N (of food) bocado m; (of liquid) bocanada f, buche m

movable [múvəbəl] ADJ movible, móvil

move [muv] VI (change position) mover[se] (also board games); (change residence) mudar[se] de casa; (sell) venderse; **to — away** (distance oneself) apartarse; (change residence) irse; **to — forward** avanzar; **to — on** seguir adelante; **to — out** mudarse de casa; VT (propose) proponer; (affect emotionally) conmover; N (act of changing position) movimiento m; (change of residence) mudanza f; (action toward a goal) paso m; (play, in games) jugada f; **get a — on there!** ¡date prisa! **he made the first —** dio el primer paso

movement [múvmənt] N (motion, part of a watch) movimiento m; (of troops) desplazamiento m; **to have a bowel —** mover el vientre

mover [múvə] N compañía de mudanzas f; —**s and shakers** la plana mayor

movie [múvi] N película f, filme m; —**s** cine m; —**making** cinematografía f

moving [múvɪŋ] ADJ (target) móvil; (car) en movimiento; (company) de mudanzas; (story) conmovedor; — **picture** película f; — **van** camión de mudanzas m

mow [mo] VT cortar; (harvest) segar

mower [móə] N (for lawns) cortadora de césped f, cortacésped m; (farm implement) segadora f; (farmworker) segador -ora mf

mown [mon] see mow

Mozambican [mozæmbíkən] ADJ & N mozambiqueño -ña mf

Mozambique [mozæmbík] N Mozambique m

Mozarabic [mozǽrəbɪk] ADJ mozárabe

Mr. [místə] N Sr. m

MRI [magnetic resonance imaging] [émárái] N IRM f

Mrs. [mísiz] N Sra. f

Ms. [miz] N Sra. f

much [mʌtʃ] ADJ & ADV mucho; — **the same** casi lo mismo; — **like the others** muy parecido a los demás; **as — as** tanto como; **how — ?** ¿cuánto? **too —** demasiado; **very —** muchísimo; **to make — of** dar mucha importancia a; — **as I'd like, I won't do it** aunque me gustaría, no lo voy a hacer; **that's not — of a book** ese libro no es gran cosa; **she cried so —** lloró tanto; **they need water, — as they need sun** necesitan agua, del mismo modo que necesitan sol

muck [mʌk] N (manure) estiércol m; (mire) cieno m, lodo m; (filth) porquería f

mucous [mjúkəs] ADJ mucoso

mucus [mjúkəs] N mucosidad f

mud [mʌd] N lodo m, barro m; — **slinging** difamación f

muddle [mʌdḷ] VT (confuse) confundir; (make turbid) enturbiar; VI **to — along** ir tirando; **to — through** salir del paso; N (confusion) confusión f; (confused situation) embrollo m

muddy [mʌ́di] ADJ (path) lodoso, barroso; (shoes) embarrado; (vague) confuso; VT (cover with mud) enlodar, embarrar; (make unclear) enturbiar

muff [mʌf] N manguito m; VT estropear

muffin [mʌ́fin] N mollete m

muffle [mʌ́fəl] VT amortiguar

muffler [mʌ́flə] N (scarf) bufanda f; (exhaust device) silenciador m

mug [mʌg] N (ceramic) tazón m; (glass) jarra f; (face) jeta f; VT atracar

mugger [mʌ́gə] N asaltante mf; atracador -ora mf

muggy [mʌ́gi] ADJ bochornoso

mulatto [muládo] ADJ & N mulato -ta mf

mulberry [mʌ́lbɛri] N mora f; — **tree** moral m

mule [mjuł] N mulo -la mf (also in drug trafficking)

mull [mʌl] VI/VT rumiar

multicultural [mʌltikʌ́ltʃərəl] ADJ multicultural

multilateral [mʌltilə́dəəl] ADJ multilateral

multimedia [mʌltimídiə] N & ADJ INV multimedia m

multiple [mʌ́ltəpəl] N múltiplo m; ADJ múltiple; — -**choice** de opción múltiple; — **personality disorder** trastorno de personalidad múltiple m; — **sclerosis** esclerosis múltiple f

multiplication [mʌltəplikéʃən] N multiplicación f; — **sign** signo de multiplicación m; — **table** tabla de multiplicar f

multiplicity [mʌltəplísidi] N multiplicidad f

multiply [mʌ́ltəplai] VI/VT multiplicar[se]

multiscreen [mʌ́ltiskrin] ADJ multipantalla

multitasking [mʌ́ltitæskiŋ] N multitarea f

multitude [mʌ́ltitud] N multitud f

multiuser [mʌltijúzə] N multiusuario -ria mf

multi-year [mʌ́ltijír] ADJ multianual

mum [mʌm] ADJ callado; **to keep —** callarse la boca

mumble [mʌ́mbəl] VI/VT mascullar; N refunfuño m

mumbo jumbo [mʌmbodʒámbo] N jerigonza f

mummy [mʌ́mi] N momia f

mumps [mʌmps] N paperas f pl

munch [mʌntʃ] VT mascar

mundane [mʌndén] ADJ mundano

municipal [mjunísəpəl] ADJ municipal; — **council** concejo m

municipality [mjunisəpǽlidi] N municipio m, municipalidad m

munition [mjuníʃən] N munición f

mural [mjúrəl] ADJ & N mural m

murder [mɝ́də] N asesinato m, homicidio m; **to get away with —** salirse con la suya; **that exam was —** ese examen fue matador; VI/VT asesinar

murderer [mɝ́dərə] N asesino mf, homicida mf

murderous [mɝ́dəəs] ADJ asesino, homicida

murky [mɝ́ki] ADJ (of water, matter) turbio; (of sky) oscuro

murmur [mɝ́mə] N (noise) murmullo m, susurro m; (complaint) queja f; VI/VT (make noise) murmurar, susurrar; (complain) quejarse

muscle [mʌ́səl] N músculo m; — **relaxant** relajante muscular m; — **strain** distensión muscular f; — **tone** tonicidad muscular f, tono muscular m

muscular [mʌ́skjələ] ADJ (relative to muscles) muscular; (endowed with muscles) musculoso; — **dystrophy** distrofia muscular f

muse [mjuz] VI meditar; VT cavilar; N musa f

museum [mjuzíəm] N museo m

mushroom [mʌ́frum] N seta f, hongo m, champiñón m

mushy [mʌ́ʃi] ADJ (soft) fofo; (sentimental) sensiblero

music [mjúzik] N música f; — **stand** atril m; — **video** Am video musical m; Sp vídeo musical m

musical [mjúzikəl] ADJ (pertaining to music) musical; (fond of music) aficionado a la música, melómano; — **comedy** comedia musical f

musician [mjuzíʃən] N músico -ca mf

muskrat [mʌ́skræt] N ratón almizclero m

Muslim [mázləm] ADJ & N musulmán -ana mf

muslin [mázlin] N muselina f

muss [mʌs] VT revolver, alborotar; N revoltijo m

mussel [mʌ́səł] N mejillón *m*

must [mʌst] V AUX **you — arrive before nine** debes llegar antes de las nueve; **you really — eat at that restaurant** tienes que comer en ese restaurante; **you — be his son** debes [de] / has de ser su hijo; **they — have seen me** deben [de] haberme visto

mustache, moustache [mʌ́stæʃ] N bigote *m*; (large) mostacho *m*

mustard [mʌ́stə-d] N mostaza *f*; **— gas** gas mostaza *m*

muster [mʌ́stə-] VT (troops) formar; (courage) juntar, reunir; VI (assemble for inspection) formar; (come together) reunirse; **to — out** dar de baja; **to — up one's courage** juntar valor; N revista *f*; **to pass** — ser aceptable

musty [mʌ́sti] ADJ (stale smelling) con olor a encierro/humedad; (antiquated) anticuado

mutant [mjútṇt] ADJ & N mutante *mf*

mutation [mjutéʃən] N mutación *f*

mute [mjut] ADJ mudo; N (mute person) mudo -da *mf*; (for musical instruments) sordina *f*

mutilate [mjúdḷet] VT mutilar

mutiny [mjútṇi] N motín *m*; VI amotinarse

mutter [mʌ́də-] VI/VT refunfuñar, musitar; N refunfuño *m*

mutton [mʌ́tṇ] N carne de cordero *f*

mutual [mjútʃuəł] ADJ mutuo; **— fund** fondo mutuo/mutual *m*

muzzle [mʌ́zəł] N (snout) hocico *m*; (mouthguard) bozal *m*; (gun opening) boca *f*; VT (a dog) abozalar, poner bozal a; (critics) amordazar, silenciar

my [mai] POSS ADJ mi; **these are — friends** estos son mis amigos; **oh —**! ¡Dios mío! **— foot!** ¡ni lo pienses!

Myanmar [mjɑnmɑ́r] N Myanmar *m*

myocardial infarction [maɪoʊkɑ́rdiəł ɪnfɑ́rkʃən] N infarto del miocardio *m*

myopia [maɪóʊpiə] N miopía *f*

myriad [mɪ́riəd] N miríada *f*, sinfín *m*; **— problems** un sinfín de problemas

myrtle [mɝ́dḷ] N mirto *m*, arrayán *m*

myself [maɪsɛ́łf] PRON **I — wrote the letters** yo mismo escribí las cartas; **I'm not — today** hoy no soy la misma de siempre; **I was sitting by —** estaba sentado solo; **I talk to —** hablo solo; **I looked at — in the mirror** me miré en el espejo; **I bought — a house** me compré una casa

mysterious [mɪstíriəs] ADJ misterioso

mystery [mɪ́stəri] N misterio *m*

mystic [mɪ́stɪk] ADJ & N místico -ca *mf*

mystical [mɪ́stɪkəł] ADJ místico

myth [mɪθ] N mito *m*

mythic [mɪ́θɪk] ADJ mítico

mythical [mɪ́θɪkəł] ADJ mítico

mythological [mɪθəlɑ́dʒɪkəł] ADJ mitológico

mythology [mɪθɑ́lədʒi] N mitología *f*

Nn

nab [næb] VT pescar; *Sp* coger

nag [næg] N (horse) jaca *f*, rocín *m*, penco *m*; (complainer) quejica *mf*; VI/VT regañar, criticar

nail [neł] N (for wood) clavo *m*; (of finger, toe) uña *f*; **—-biter** situación angustiante *f*; **— file** lima *f*; **— polish** esmalte para uñas *m*; **to hit the — on the head** dar en el clavo; VT (fasten) clavar; (nab) pescar; *Sp* coger

naive [naɪ́v] ADJ ingenuo, cándido, bonachón

naiveté [naɪvté] N ingenuidad *f*

naked [nékɪd] ADJ desnudo

nakedness [nékɪdnɪs] N desnudez *f*

name [nem] N nombre *m*; **—-brand** marca comercial *f*; **—plate** placa *f*; **—sake** tocayo *m*; **—tag** etiqueta de identificación *f*; **— of the game** lo esencial *m*; **to call someone —s** motejar a alguien; **to make a — for oneself** hacerse un nombre; **what is your —?** ¿cómo te llamas? VT nombrar; **— your price** haz una oferta

nameless [némlɪs] ADJ anónimo

namely [némli] ADV a saber, en concreto

Namibia [nəmíbiə] N Namibia *f*

Namibian [nəmíbiən] ADJ & N namibio -bia *mf*

nanny [næni] N niñera *f*

nanosecond [nǽnoʊsɛkənd] N nanosegundo *m*

nanotechnology [nǽnoʊteknálədʒi] N nanotecnología *f*

nap [næp] N (sleep) siesta *f*; (fibers) pelo *m*; **to take a —** echar/dormir una siesta; VI echar/dormir una siesta

napalm [népɑłm] N napalm *m*

nape [nep] N nuca *f*

napkin [nǽpkɪn] N servilleta *f*

narcissism [nɑ́rsɪsɪzəm] N narcisismo *m*

narcissus [nɑrsɪ́səs] N narciso *m*

narcolepsy [nɑ́rkəlɛpsi] N narcolepsia *f*

narcotic [nɑrkɑ́dɪk] ADJ & N narcótico *m*, estupefaciente *m*

narcotrafficking [nɑrkotrǽfɪkɪŋ] N narcotráfico *m*

narrate [nǽret] VI/VT narrar

narration [næréʃən] N narración *f*

narrative [nǽrəɪv] ADJ narrativo; N narrativa *f*

narrator [nǽrədə-] N narrador -ora *mf*

narrow [nǽro] ADJ (of little width) estrecho, angosto; (limited in scope) limitado; (intolerant) intolerante; **to have a — escape** salvarse por poco; **— gauge** de vía angosta/ estrecha; **—-minded** intolerante; N **—s** desfiladero *m*, estrecho *m*, angostura *f*; VI/VT angostar[se], estrechar[se]; **to — down**

reducir

narrowness [nǽrɔnɪs] N (quality of being narrow) estrechez f, angostura f

nasal [nézəł] ADJ nasal

nastiness [nǽstɪnɪs] N (filth) suciedad f; (stinkiness) asquerosidad f; (rudeness, obscenity) grosería f

nasturtium [nəstə́ɾʃəm] N capuchina f

nasty [nǽsti] ADJ (mess) sucio; (smell) asqueroso; (comment) hiriente; (accident) feo; (word) grosero; (disposition) malo

natal [nédł] ADJ natal

nation [néʃən] N nación f; ADJ **—wide** a escala nacional

national [nǽʃənł] ADJ nacional; **— park** parque nacional m; **— team** seleccionado nacional m; N ciudadano -na mf, nacional mf

nationalism [nǽʃənəlɪzəm] N nacionalismo m

nationalist [nǽʃənəlɪst] N & ADJ nacionalista MF

nationality [nǽʃənǽlɪɾi] N nacionalidad f; **adjective of —** gentilicio m

nationalize [nǽʃənəlaɪz] VT nacionalizar

native [néɾɪv] ADJ nativo; **— language** lengua nativa f; **— plants** flora nativa f; **my — Italy** mi Italia natal f; (innate) innato; N (person born in a place) natural m; (member of a tribal group) indígena mf, nativo -va mf; **he's a — of Italy** es oriundo de Italia

nativity [nətívɪɾi] N nacimiento m; **— scene** pesebre m; **the —** la Natividad

NATO [North Atlantic Treaty Organization] [néɾo] N OTAN f

natural [nǽtʃəəł] ADJ natural; (inborn) innato; **— childbirth** parto natural m; **— gas** gas natural m; **— resources** recursos naturales m pl; **— selection** selección natural f; N (musical sign) becuadro m; **he is a — for that job** tiene aptitud natural para ese puesto

naturalist [nǽtʃəəlɪst] N naturalista mf

naturalization [nǽtʃəəlɪzéʃən] N naturalización f

naturalize [nǽtʃəəlaɪz] VI/VT naturalizar[se]

naturally [nǽtʃəəli] ADV (of course) naturalmente; **I have — curly hair** tengo rizos naturales

naturalness [nǽtʃəəłnɪs] N naturalidad f

nature [nétʃə] N naturaleza f; (disposition) genio m, natural m

naught [nɔt] N (zero) cero m; (nothing) nada f

naughtiness [nɔ́dɪnɪs] N travesuras f pl

naughty [nɔ́di] ADJ (child) travieso, pícaro, pillo; **— word** picardía f

Nauru [naúru] N Nauru m

Nauruan [naúruən] ADJ & N nauruano -na mf

nausea [nɔ́ziə] N náuseas f pl, mareo m

nauseate [nɔ́ziet] VT dar náuseas; **to be —d** tener náuseas

nauseating [nɔ́zieɾɪŋ] ADJ nauseabundo, nauseoso

nauseous [nɔ́ʃəs] ADJ (feeling nausea) mareado, nauseoso; (causing nausea) nauseabundo, nauseoso

nautical [nɔ́dɪkəł] ADJ náutico

naval [névəł] ADJ naval; **— officer** oficial de marina m

Navarrese [nævəríz] ADJ & N navarro -rra mf

nave [nev] N nave f

navel [névəł] N ombligo m; **— orange** naranja de ombligo f

navigable [nǽvɪgəbəł] ADJ navegable

navigate [nǽvɪget] VI/VT navegar

navigation [nævɪgéʃən] N navegación f; (science) náutica f

navigator [nǽvɪgeɾə] N navegante mf

navy [névi] N marina [de guerra] f, armada f; **— bean** judía blanca f; **— blue** azul marino m

nay [ne] N (refusal) no m; (negative vote) voto negativo m

Nazi [nátsi] N nazi mf

near [nɪr] ADV cerca; **— at hand** cerca, a la mano; **to come/go/draw —** acercarse; PREP cerca de; **— the end of the month** hacia fines del mes; **to be — death** estar a punto de morir; ADJ cercano, próximo; **— East** Cercano Oriente m, Oriente Próximo m; **—sighted** miope; **I had a — miss** por poco me sucede un accidente; VI/VT acercarse [a]

nearby [nírbái] ADV cerca; ADJ cercano, próximo

nearly [nírli] ADV casi, cerca de; **I — did it** casi lo hago

nearness [nírnɪs] N cercanía f, proximidad f

neat [nit] ADJ (clean) limpio, pulcro; (ordered) ordenado; (cool) bueno

neatness [nítnɪs] N (cleanness) limpieza f, pulcritud f; (order) orden m

nebulous [nébjələs] ADJ nebuloso

nebulousness [nébjələsnɪs] N nubosidad f

necessary [nésɪsɛri] ADJ (needed) necesario; (involuntary) forzoso

necessitate [nəsésɪtet] VT requerir

necessity [nəsésɪɾi] N necesidad f; **out of —** por necesidad

neck [nɛk] N (of a human) cuello m; (of an animal) pescuezo m; (of clothes) escote m; (throat) garganta f; **— and —** parejos; **—lace** collar m; **—line** escote m; **— of land** istmo m; **—tie** corbata f

necrology [nəkrálədʒi] N necrología f

necrosis [nəkrósis] N necrosis f

nectar [nɛ́ktə] N néctar m

nectarine [nɛktərín] N nectarina f

need [nid] N (lack) necesidad f; (poverty) carencia f; **in —** en aprietos; **if — be** en caso de necesidad; VT necesitar, precisar; **you — to come at four** tienes que venir a las cuatro

needle [nídł] N aguja f; **—point** bordado m; **—work** (embroidery) bordado m; (sewing) costura f; VT pinchar

needless [nídlıs] ADJ innecesario; — **to say** huelga decir

needy [nídi] ADJ necesitado, menesteroso

ne'er-do-well [nérduwɛl] N inútil *mf*

negate [nıgét] VT negar

negation [nıgéʃən] N negación *f*

negative [négəDıv] ADJ negativo; **the search proved** — la búsqueda no dio resultado; N negativa *f*; (photographic) negativo *m*; **this plan has one** — este plan tiene una contra; INTERJ ¡negativo!

neglect [nıglékt] VT (fail to heed) postergar; (fail to care for) descuidar; (fail to carry out) desatender; **you're** — **ing your friends** tienes abandonados a tus amigos; **to** — **to** olvidarse de; N negligencia *f*, descuido *m*

neglectful [nıgléktfəl] ADJ negligente, descuidado

negligence [néglıdʒəns] N negligencia *f*

negligent [néglıdʒənt] ADJ negligente, descuidado

negligible [néglıdʒəbəl] ADJ despreciable, minúsculo

negotiate [nıgóʃiet] VI/VT (a contract) negociar, gestionar; (an obstacle) salvar

negotiating [nıgóʃieDıŋ] ADJ negociador

negotiation [nıgóʃiéʃən] N negociación *f*, gestión *f*

negotiator [nıgóʃieDə] N negociador -ora *mf*

Negro [nígro] ADJ & N negro -gra *mf*

neigh [ne] N relincho *m*; VI relinchar

neighbor [nébə] N (person who lives near) vecino -na *mf*; (fellow human) prójimo -ma *mf*; ADJ vecino; VI **to** — **with** lindar con

neighborhood [nébəhud] N vecindario *m*, barrio *m*; **in the** — **of a hundred dollars** alrededor de cien dólares

neighboring [nébərıŋ] ADJ vecino, colindante

neither [níðə] PRON ninguno de los dos, ni [el] uno ni [el] otro; — **of the two** ninguno de los dos; ADJ ninguno de los dos; — **one of us** ninguno de nosotros dos; CONJ ni; — **hot nor cold** ni caliente ni frío; — **will I** yo tampoco

nemesis [némısıs] N némesis *f*

neologism [niálədʒızəm] N neologismo *m*

neon [nían] N neón *m*

neonatal [nionédl] ADJ neonatal

Nepal [nəpɔ́l] N Nepal *m*

Nepali [nəpóli] ADJ & N nepalés -esa *mf*, nepalí *mf*

nephew [néfju] N sobrino *m*

nephritis [nəfráıdıs] N nefritis *f*

nepotism [népətızəm] N nepotismo *m*

nerd [nɜd] N (technological adept) persona aficionada a las computadoras / los ordenadores *f*; (socially inept person) persona socialmente inepta *f*

nerve [nɜv] N (anatomy) nervio *m*; (courage) valor *m*; (impertinence) descaro *m*, morro *m*; — **cell** neurona *f*; — **gas** gas nervioso *m*; —-

[w]racking angustiante; **he gets on my** —**s** me saca de quicio

nervous [nɜ́vəs] ADJ nervioso; — **breakdown** ataque de nervios *m*

nervousness [nɜ́vəsnıs] N nerviosismo *m*

nest [nɛst] N nido *m*; (brood) nidada *f*; — **egg** ahorros *m pl*; — **of thieves** guarida de ladrones *f*; VI/VT anidar; (fit together) encajarse

nestle [nésəl] VI acurrucarse; VT apoyar, recostar

net [nɛt] N (fishing, network, tennis) red *f*; (in hair) redecilla *f*; —**work** red *f*; —**working** (social) relaciones profesionales *f pl*; (computer) diseño de redes y comunicaciones *m*; VT (catch a fish) pescar con red; (cover with a net) cubrir con una red; (catch a criminal) atrapar; (hit the tennis net) dar en la red; (make money after expenses) producir/ganar neto; ADJ neto; — **price** precio neto *m*; — **profit** ganancia neta *f*; — **assets** activo neto *m*; — **income** ingreso neto *m*; — **worth** patrimonio neto *m*

Netherlander [néðələndə] N holandés -esa *mf*

Netherlands [néðələndz] N Países Bajos *m pl*

nettle [nédl] N ortiga *f*

neural [núrəl] ADJ neural

neuralgia [nurǽldʒə] N neuralgia *f*

neurasthenia [nurəsθíniə] N neurastenia *f*

neurologist [nurálədʒıst] N neurólogo -ga *mf*

neuron [núran] N neurona *f*

neurosis [nurósıs] N neurosis *f*

neurosurgeon [núrosɝdʒən] N neurocirujano -na *mf*

neurosurgery [núrosɝdʒəri] N neurocirugía *f*

neurotic [nurádık] ADJ & N neurótico -ca *mf*

neurotransmitter [nurotrǽnzmıDə] N neurotransmisor *m*

neuter [núDə] ADJ neutro; VT castrar

neutral [nútrəl] ADJ neutral, imparcial; (of colors) neutro; N punto muerto *m*

neutrality [nutrǽlıDi] N neutralidad *f*

neutralize [nútrəlaız] VI/VT neutralizar[se]

neutron [nútran] N neutrón *m*; — **bomb** bomba de neutrones *f*

never [névə] ADV nunca, jamás; — **mind** no te preocupes; **this will** — **do** esto no va a funcionar; —**ending** interminable

nevertheless [nɛvəðəlés] ADV & CONJ sin embargo, no obstante

new [nu] ADJ (not old) nuevo; (fresh) otro; **a** — **sheet of paper** otra hoja de papel; — **age [music]** [música] nueva era *f*; —**born baby** recién nacido -da *mf*; —**comer** recién llegado -da *mf*; —**fangled** moderno, recién inventado; —**found** nuevo; — **year** año nuevo *m*; — **Year's Eve** fin de año *m*; *Sp* nochevieja *f*

newly [núli] ADV recientemente; — **arrived** recién llegado; —**wed** recién casado

newness [núnis] N novedad *f*

news [nuz] N (item) noticias *f pl*; (latest gossip) novedades *f pl*; (newspaper) periódico *m*; **it is — to me** recién me entero; **— broadcast/ bulletin** noticiero *m*, noticiario *m*; **—cast** noticiero *m*, noticiario *m*, informativo *m*; **— clipping** recorte de diario *m*; **—letter** boletín informativo *m*; **—paper** periódico *m*, diario *m*; **—print** papel de periódico *m*; **—room** sala de redacción *f*; **—stand** quiosco *m*; **piece of —** noticia *f*; ADJ **—worthy** de interés periodístico

newt [nut] N tritón *m*

New Zealand [nuzíland] N Nueva Zelanda *f*

New Zealander [nuzíləndə-] N neozelandés -esa *mf*

next [nekst] ADJ (future) próximo, entrante; (following) siguiente; (contiguous) contiguo, de al lado; **—-door** de al lado; **who's —?** ¿quién sigue? ADV después, luego; **— best** segundo en calidad; **when — we meet** cuando nos volvamos a ver; PREP **— of kin** familiares *m pl*; **— to** junto a, al lado de

nibble [níbəl] VI/VT (bite) mordiscar, mordisquear; (eat) picotear; (of fish) picar; N (bite) mordisco *m*; (act of nibbling) mordisqueo *m*

Nicaragua [nɪkəɾágwə] N Nicaragua *f*

Nicaraguan [nɪkəɾágwən] ADJ & N nicaragüense *mf*

nice [naɪs] ADJ (kind) amable, simpático; (agreeable) *Am* lindo, *Sp* majo; **it's — and hot** está bien calentito

nicety [náɪsɪDi] N (subtlety) sutileza *f*; (detail) detalle *m*

niche [nɪtʃ] N (also environmental) nicho *m*; **— marketing** mercadeo de nicho *m*; **I've found my —** he encontrado mi lugar

nick [nɪk] N (chip) muesca *f*; (cut) corte *m*; **in the — of time** justo a tiempo; VT (chip) hacer muescas; (cut) cortar; **—name** apodo *m*, mote *m*, sobrenombre *m*; **to —name** apodar

nickel [níkəl] N (metal) níquel *m*; (coin) moneda de cinco centavos *f*; **—-plated** niquelado

nicotine [níkətin] N nicotina *f*

niece [nis] N sobrina *f*

Niger [náɪdʒə-] N Níger *m*

Nigeria [naɪdʒíɾiə] N Nigeria *f*

Nigerian [naɪdʒíɾiən] ADJ & N nigeriano -na *mf*

Nigerien [naɪdʒíɾien] ADJ & N nigerino -na *mf*

niggardly [nígə-dli] ADJ mezquino

night [naɪt] N noche *f*; ADJ nocturno, de noche; **—club** club nocturno *m*; **—fall** anochecer *m*, atardecer *m*; **—gown** camisón *m*; **—life** vida nocturna *f*; *Sp* marcha *f*; **—light** lamparilla *f*; **—mare** pesadilla *f*; **— owl** trasnochador -ora *mf*; **— shift** turno de la noche *m*; **—stand** veladora *f*, mesilla de noche *f*; **—time** noche *f*; **— watchman** celador *m*

nightingale [náɪtŋɡeł] N ruiseñor *m*

nightly [náɪtli] ADV todas las noches; ADJ nocturno

nihilism [náɪəlɪzəm] N nihilismo *m*

nil [nɪł] ADJ nulo

nimble [nímbəł] ADJ ágil

nincompoop [nínkəmpup] N *fam* tarambana *mf*, bobalicón -ona *mf*

nine [naɪn] NUM nueve; **— hundred** novecientos

nineteen [naɪntín] NUM diecinueve

ninety [náɪnti] NUM noventa

ninth [náɪnθ] ADJ & N noveno *m*

nip [nɪp] VT (pinch) pellizcar; (bite) mordiscar, mordisquear; (cause frostbite) helar; **to — in the bud** cortar de raíz; **to — off** despuntar; VI (drink in sips) dar sorbitos; N (pinch) pellizco *m*; (bite) mordisco *m*; (sip) traguito *m*, sorbito *m*; (cold) frío *m*; **it's going to be — and tuck** va a ser muy reñido

nipple [nípəł] N (on female breast) pezón *m*; (on male breast) tetilla *f*; (on bottle) tetina *f*

nitpick [nítpɪk] VI criticar detalles insignificantes

nitrate [náɪtret] N nitrato *m*

nitric acid [náɪtrɪkǽsɪd] N ácido nítrico *m*

nitrogen [náɪtrədʒən] N nitrógeno *m*

nitroglycerin [naɪtroglísə-ɪn] N nitroglicerina *f*

nitty-gritty [níDigríDi] N **to get down to the — ir** al grano

no [no] ADV no; **— longer** ya no; **— man's land** tierra de nadie *f*; **— matter how much** por mucho que; **— one** ninguno, nadie; **— smoking** se prohíbe fumar; **—where** (location) en ninguna parte / ningún lado; (direction) a ninguna parte / ningún lado; **he was a —-show** no se presentó; **a —-win situation** una situación insoluble; **there is — more** no hay más; ADJ ningun[o]; **I have — friends** no tengo amigos; **it's a —-brainer** la respuesta es obvia; **— friend of mine will go hungry** ningún amigo mío pasará hambre; **of — use** inútil; N (refusal) no *m*; (negative vote) voto negativo *m*; ADJ **—-frills** básico, sin lujos

nobility [nobílɪti] N nobleza *f*, hidalguía *f*

noble [nóbəł] ADJ & N noble *mf*; **—man** hidalgo *m*

nobody [nóbaɒi] PRON nadie, ninguno; N don nadie, pelagatos *mf sg*

nocturnal [nakt͡ɛ́nł] ADJ nocturno

nod [nad] VI/VT (signal affirmation) asentir con la cabeza; VI (doze) cabecear, dar cabezadas; **to — off** dormirse; N (as signal) inclinación de cabeza *f*, saludo con la cabeza *m*; (from sleepiness) cabezada *f*

node [nod] N (of cells) nódulo *m*; (in plants) nudo *m*; (in physics) nodo *m*

noise [nɔɪz] N ruido *m*; **— pollution**

contaminación sonora *f*; vi **it is being —d about that** corre el rumor que

noiseless [nɔ́izlɪs] ADJ silencioso

noisy [nɔ́izi] ADJ ruidoso

nomad [nómæd] N nómada *mf*

nomenclature [nóminkletʃə-] N nomenclatura *f*

nominal [námən] ADJ nominal

nominate [námənet] VT nominar

nomination [namənéʃən] N nominación *f*

nominee [naməní] N candidato -ta *mf*

nonchalant [nɑnʃəlánt] ADJ despreocupado

noncollectible [nɑnkəléktəbəl] ADJ incobrable

noncommercial [nɑnkəmɔ́ʃəl] ADJ no comercial

noncommissioned officer [nɑnkəmíʃənd ɔ́fisə-] N suboficial *m*

nonconforming [nɑnkənfɔ́rmɪŋ] ADJ no conforme

nonconformist [nɑnkənfɔ́rmɪst] ADJ & N inconformista *mf*

none [nʌn] PRON ninguno; **I want — of that** no me quiero meter en eso; **that is — of your business** no es asunto tuyo; ADV **— too soon** al último momento; **—theless** sin embargo

nonentity [nɑnéntɪdi] N nulidad *f*

nonessential [nɑnisénʃəl] ADJ no esencial

nonexistent [nɑnigzístənt] ADJ inexistente

nonfiction [nɑnfíkʃən] N no ficción *f*

nongovernmental [nɑngʌvə-nméntl] ADJ no gubernamental

nonnegotiable [nɑnnɪgóʃəbəl] ADJ no negociable

nonpartisan [nɑnpárdɪzən] ADJ (neutral) imparcial; (not affiliated) sin afiliación política

nonperformance [nɑnpə-fɔ́rmɑns] N incumplimiento *m*

nonproductive [nɑnprədʌ́ktɪv] ADJ improductivo

nonprofit [nɑnpráfɪt] ADJ sin fines de lucro; N organización sin fines de lucro *f*

nonrefundable [nɑnrɪfándəbəl] ADJ no reembolsable

nonresident [nɑnrézɪdənt] ADJ & N no residente *mf*

nonsense [nánsɛns] N tonterías *f pl*, monsergas *f pl*, estupideces *f pl*; **to talk —** decir barbaridades/disparates

nonstop [nánstáp] ADJ sin escala, directo; ADV sin parar

nontaxable [nɑntǽksəbəl] ADJ no tributable

nonvoting [nɑnvódɪŋ] ADJ sin derecho a voto

noodle [núdl] N fideo *m*, tallarín *m*

nook [nʊk] N rincón *m*

noon [nun] N mediodía *m*; **— hour** mediodía *m*, hora de comer; **—time** mediodía *m*

noose [nus] N soga *f*, lazo *m*; **with a — around his neck** con la soga al cuello; VT (catch with a rope) enlazar; (make a loop in) hacer un lazo corredizo en

nope [nop] ADV no

nor [nɔr] CONJ ni; **we have neither eggs — flour** no tenemos ni huevos ni harina

Nordic [nɔ́rdɪk] ADJ nórdico

norm [nɔrm] N norma *f*, normativa *f*

normal [nɔ́rməl] ADJ normal; (perpendicular) normal; **to return to —** volver a la normalidad; (perpendicular line) línea perpendicular *f*

normalcy [nɔ́rməlsi] N normalidad *f*

normality [nɔrmǽlɪDi] N normalidad *f*

normalize [nɔ́rməlaɪz] VI/VT normalizar[se]

normally [nɔ́rməli] ADV (in a normal way) de manera normal, con toda normalidad *f*; (usually) normalmente

north [nɔrθ] N norte *m*; **—east** noreste, hacia el noreste; **—west** noroeste *m*, hacia el noroeste; ADJ (in the north) norte, norteño; (from the north) del norte; **— America** América del Norte *f*; **— American** norteamericano -na *mf*; **—eastern** del noreste; **— Korea** Corea del Norte *f*; **— Korean** norcoreano -na; **— Pole** Polo Norte *m*; **— wind** cierzo *m*, viento norte *m*; **the — entrance** la entrada norte; ADV al norte, hacia el norte

northern [nɔ́rðə-n] ADJ del norte; (from the north) norteño; (in the north) septentrional; **— lights** aurora boreal *f*

northerner [nɔ́rðə-nə-] N norteño -ña *mf*

northward [nɔ́rθwə-d] ADV hacia el norte

Norway [nɔ́rwe] N Noruega *f*

Norwegian [nɔrwídʒən] ADJ & N noruego -ga *mf*

nose [noz] N nariz *f*, (of an airplane) morro *m*; (of an animal) hocico *m*; (perspicacity) olfato *m*; **—bleed** hemorragia nasal *f*; **—dive** caída en picado *f*; **—job** rinoplastia *f*; **keep your — clean** no te metas en líos; **on the —** exactamente; **to pick one's —** hurgarse las narices; VI/VT (move forward) entrar de punta; (muzzle) hocicar; **to — around** husmear

nostalgia [nɑstǽldʒə] N nostalgia *f*

nostalgic [nɑstǽldʒɪk] ADJ nostálgico

nostrils [nástrəlz] N narices *f pl*, ventanillas de la nariz *f pl*

nosy, nosey [nózi] ADJ entrometido

not [nɑt] ADV no; **I'm — your friend** no soy tu amigo; **— at all** (no way) de ningún modo; (you're welcome) de nada; **— at all sure** nada seguro; **— even a word** ni una palabra

notable [nódəbəl] ADJ notable, destacable

notably [nódəbli] ADV notablemente

notarize [nódəraɪz] VT notariar

notary [nódəri] N notario -ria *mf*; **— public** notario -ria público -ca *mf*

notation [notéʃən] N (system of signs) notación

f; (act of writing) anotación *f*; (short note) anotación *f*, apunte *m*

notch [nɑtʃ] N (nick) muesca *f*, mella *f*; (degree) grado *m*; **a — above the rest** mejor que los demás; VT hacer una muesca; **he —ed another win** se anotó otra victoria

note [not] N (written) nota *f*, anotación *f*; (musical) nota *f*; (touch) toque *m*; (financial) pagaré *m*; (currency) billete *m*; **—book** cuaderno *m*; (small) libreta *f*; **—s** apuntes *m pl*; **of—** de renombre / de nota; **to take — of** notar; ADJ **—worthy** notable; VT (notice) notar; (write down) anotar, apuntar

noted [nódɪd] ADJ célebre

nothing [nʌ́θɪŋ] PRON nada *f*; (score) cero, nada; N (insignificant person) don nadie *m*; (insignificant thing) nadería *f*; **— to it** no tiene ciencia; ADV **it was — like that** no fue así para nada; **we did it for —** (free) lo hicimos gratis; (fruitlessly) lo hicimos en balde

notice [nódɪs] N (information) aviso *m*; (warning) advertencia *f*; (attention) atención *f*; **a week's —** una semana de plazo; **to give — renunciar; to take —** hacer caso; VT (perceive) notar, advertir, percatarse [de]; (pay attention to) fijarse [en], reparar [en]

noticeable [nódɪsəbəl] ADJ perceptible, apreciable

noticeably [nódɪsəbli] ADV notablemente

notification [noɖəfɪkéʃən] N notificación *f*

notify [nóɖəfaɪ] VT notificar

notion [nóʃən] N noción *f*, idea *f*; (whim) capricho *m*; **—s** mercería *f*

notorious [notɔ́rias] ADJ de mala fama; **he's a — liar** tiene fama de mentiroso

nougat [núgət] N turrón *m*

noun [naʊn] N sustantivo *m*

nourish [nɚ́ɪʃ] VT (a person) nutrir, alimentar; (a hope) abrigar

nourishing [nɚ́ɪʃɪŋ] ADJ nutritivo

nourishment [nɚ́ɪʃmənt] N (food) alimento *m*; (act of nourishing) alimentación *f*

novel [návəl] N novela *f*; ADJ novedoso

novelist [návəlɪst] N novelista *mf*

novelty [návəlti] N novedad *f*; **the — soon wore off** se pasó la novedad; **novelties** chucherías *f pl*

November [novémbɚ] N noviembre *m*

novice [návɪs] N novato -ta *mf*, pipiolo -la *mf*; (religious) novicio -cia *mf*

novocaine [nóvəken] N novocaína *f*

now [naʊ] ADV ahora; **— and then** de vez en cuando; **— that** ahora que; **he left just — salió hace poco, recién salió; —, —, calm down!** bueno, bueno, ¡cálmate!

nowadays [náʊədez] ADV hoy [en] día

noxious [nákʃəs] ADJ nocivo

nuance [núɑns] N matiz *m*

nuclear [núkliɚ] ADJ nuclear; **— energy** energía nuclear *f*; **— family** familia nuclear *f*; **— fission** fisión nuclear *f*; **— fusion** fusión nuclear *f*; **— physics** física nuclear *f*; **— weapon** arma nuclear *f*

nucleus [núkliəs] N núcleo *m*

nude [nud] ADJ & N desnudo *m*

nudge [nʌʤ] VI/VT codear; N golpe suave con el codo *m*

nugget [nágɪt] N (of gold) pepita *f*; (of chicken) pedacito *m*; (of wisdom) perla *f*

nuisance [núsəns] N molestia *f*; *Sp* pesadez *f*; (legal) perjuicio *m*; **you're such a —!** ¡qué pesado eres tú! **— tax** impuesto de consumo *m*

nuke [nuk] N arma nuclear *f*; VT (bomb) bombardear con armas nucleares; (cook) calentar en microondas

null [nʌl] ADJ nulo; **— and void** nulo

nullify [nʌ́ləfaɪ] VT anular

numb [nʌm] ADJ entumecido; **to get — entumecerse;** VT entumecer

number [nʌ́mbɚ] N número *m*; **— one** uno mismo *m*; **—-crunching** procesamiento de datos numéricos complejos *m*; VI (total) ascender a; **I — him among my friends** lo cuento entre mis amigos; VT numerar

numberless [nʌ́mbɚlɪs] ADJ sin número

numbskull, numskull [nʌ́mskʌl] N zopenco -ca *mf*

numeral [númɚəl] N número *m*; ADJ numeral

numerical [numɛ́rɪkəl] ADJ numérico

numerous [númɚəs] ADJ numeroso

nun [nʌn] N monja *f*, religiosa *f*

nuptial [nʌ́pʃəl] ADJ nupcial; N **—s** nupcias *f pl*

nurse [nɚs] N (for the sick) enfermero -ra *mf*; (for children) niñera *f*; VT (give milk) amamantar, lactar; (tend to a sick person) cuidar; **to — a grudge** guardar rencor; **to — a cup of coffee** tomar una taza de café a sorbitos; **to — a cold** cuidarse durante un resfrío; VI (drink milk) mamar

nursery [nɚ́sri] N (children's room) cuarto para niños *m*; (day-care center) guardería *f*; (place for growing plants) almáciga *f*, vivero *m*, plantel *m*; **— rhyme** canción infantil *f*, ronda *f*; **— school** preescolar *m*; *Sp* parvulario *m*; *Am* jardín infantil *m*

nursing [nɚ́sɪŋ] N (profession) enfermería *f*; (care) cuidado *m*; **— home** (for old people) hogar de ancianos *m*; (for sick people) casa de salud *f*

nurture [nɚ́tʃɚ] VT (rear) criar; (feed) nutrir, alimentar; (encourage) fomentar; N (rearing) crianza *f*; (feeding) alimentación *f*

nut [nʌt] N (fruit) fruto seco *m*; (device) tuerca *f*; (person) excéntrico -ca *mf*; **—cracker** cascanueces *m sg*; **—meg** nuez moscada *f*; **—s** ADJ crazy; **—s and bolts** los fundamentos;

—**shell** cáscara de fruto seco *f*; **in a —shell** en pocas palabras
nutrient [nútriant] N nutriente *m*
nutrition [nutríʃən] N nutrición *f*, alimentación *f*
nutritious [nutríʃəs] ADJ nutritivo, alimenticio
nylon [náilɑn] N nilón *m*, nailon *m*

Oo

oak [ok] N roble *m*, encina *f*; — **grove** robledal *m*
oar [ɔr] N remo *m*; VI/VT remar, bogar; —**lock** tolete *m*
OAS [Organization of American States] [óéés] N OEA *f*
oasis [oésɪs] N oasis *m*
oat [ot] N avena *f*; —**meal** (flour) harina de avena *f*; (breakfast food) gachas de avena *f pl*; —**s** avena *f*
oath [oθ] N (pledge) juramento *m*; (curse) maldición *f*; (swear word) palabrota *f*, taco *m*; **to take an** — prestar juramento
obedience [obíDiəns] N obediencia *f*
obedient [obíDiənt] ADJ obediente
obese [obís] ADJ obeso
obesity [obísiDi] N obesidad *f*
obey [obé] VI/VT obedecer
obituary [obítʃueri] N nota necrológica *f*, obituario *m*
object[1] [ábdʒɪkt] N objeto *m*; (of a verb) complemento *m*
object[2] [əbdʒékt] VI/VT objetar
objection [əbdʒékʃən] N objeción *f*
objectionable [əbdʒékʃənəbəl] ADJ objetable
objective [əbdʒéktɪv] ADJ objetivo; N objetivo *m*, finalidad *f*
objectivity [ɑbdʒektívɪDi] N objetividad *f*
obligate [ábləget] VT obligar
obligated [ábligeDid] ADJ obligado, comprometido
obligation [ɑbligéʃən] N obligación *f*; **under no** — **to buy** sin compromiso de compra
obligatory [əblígətɔri] ADJ obligatorio, obligado
oblige [əbláiʤ] VT (make obliged) obligar; VI/VT (do a favor for) complacer; VI (obey an order) obedecer; **much —d!** ¡muchas gracias! ¡muy agradecido!
obliging [əbláiʤiŋ] ADJ complaciente; *Am* comedido
oblique [oblík] ADJ oblicuo
obliterate [əblíDəret] VT (blot out) tachar; (destroy) arrasar, destruir
oblivion [əblíviən] N olvido *m*
oblivious [əblívias] ADJ inconsciente; — **to the danger** ajeno al peligro
obnoxious [əbnákʃəs] ADJ (remark, behavior) ofensivo; (person) odioso
oboe [óbo] N oboe *m*
obscene [əbsín] ADJ obsceno; **his salary is** — lo que gana es escandaloso
obscenity [əbsénɪDi] N obscenidad *f*
obscure [əbskjúr] ADJ oscuro; VT oscurecer
obscurity [əbskjúrɪDi] N oscuridad *f*
obsequious [əbsíkwiəs] ADJ obsequioso
observance [əbzɝvəns] N observancia *f*
observant [əbzɝvənt] ADJ observador
observation [ɑbzɚvéʃən] N observación *f*
observatory [əbzɝvatɔri] N observatorio *m*
observe [əbzɝv] VT observar; (holidays, rituals) guardar
observer [əbzɝvɚ] N observador -ora *mf*; (of elections) interventor -ora *mf*
obsess [əbsés] VI/VT obsesionar[se]; **he's —ing over it** está obsesionado con eso
obsession [əbséʃən] N obsesión *f*
obsessive-compulsive [əbsésɪvkəmpʌ́lsɪv] ADJ obsesivo-compulsivo
obsolescence [absəlésəns] N desuso *m*
obsolete [ɑbsəlít] ADJ anticuado, desusado
obstacle [ábstəkəl] N obstáculo *m*
obstetrician [ɑbstətríʃən] N obstetra *mf*
obstetrics [ɑbstétrɪks] N obstetricia *f*
obstinacy [ábstənəsi] N obstinación *f*, terquedad *f*, porfía *f*
obstinate [ábstənɪt] ADJ obstinado, terco, recalcitrante; **to be** — obstinarse
obstruct [əbstrʌ́kt] VI/VT obstruir; (traffic) atascar, obstruir
obstruction [əbstrʌ́kʃən] N obstrucción *f*
obtain [əbtén] VT obtener, procurar; VI prevalecer
obtainable [əbténəbəl] ADJ conseguible
obviate [ábviet] VT obviar
obvious [ábviəs] ADJ obvio, evidente
obviously [ábviəsli] ADV & INTERJ evidentemente, obviamente
occasion [əkéʒən] N (moment) ocasión *f*; (chance) oportunidad *f*, ocasión *f*; (cause) motivo *m*; (event) acontecimiento *m*, ocasión *f*; VT ocasionar
occasional [əkéʒənl] ADJ ocasional
occasionally [əkéʒənli] ADV de vez en cuando, ocasionalmente
occidental [ɑksɪdéntl] ADJ & N occidental *mf*
occlusion [əklúʒən] N obstrucción *f*, oclusión *f*
occult [əkʌ́lt] ADJ oculto; N ocultismo *m*, ciencias ocultas *f pl*; VT ocultar
occupancy [ákjəpənsi] N ocupación *f*; — **rate** tasa de ocupación *f*
occupant [ákjəpənt] N ocupante *mf*
occupation [akjəpéʃən] N ocupación *f*
occupational [akjəpéʃənl] ADJ ocupacional; — **hazard/risk** riesgo ocupacional *m*; — **therapy** laborterapia *f*, terapia ocupacional *f*
occupy [ákjəpaɪ] VI/VT ocupar

occur [əkə́r] VI ocurrir, suceder; **it —red to me** se me ocurrió

occurrence [əkə́rəns] N suceso m, acontecimiento m

ocean [óʃən] N océano m

oceanic [oʃiǽnɪk] ADJ oceánico

oceanography [oʃənágrəfi] N oceanografía f

ocelot [ásəlɑt] N ocelote m

o'clock [əklák] ADV **it is one** — es la una; **it is two** — son las dos

octagon [áktəgən] N octágono m, octógono m

octane [ákten] N octano m

octave [áktɪv] N octava f

October [aktóbə] N octubre m

octopus [áktəpəs] N pulpo m

oculist [ákjəlɪst] N oculista mf

OD [overdose] [ódí] N sobredosis f; VI tomar una sobredosis

odd [ad] ADJ (unusual) extraño; (not even) impar, non; **—ball** excéntrico -ca mf; **— change** suelto m, cambio m; **— job** trabajo ocasional m; **— shoe** zapato sin compañero m; ADV **thirty-—** treinta y tantos

oddity [ádɪti] N rareza f; (person) excéntrico -ca mf

odds [adz] N (probabilities) probabilidades f pl; **— and ends** cachivaches m pl; **the — are against me** llevo las de perder; **to be at —** estar en desacuerdo; ADJ **—-on favorite** favorito m

ode [od] N oda f

odious [ódiəs] ADJ odioso

odor [ódə] N olor m; (bad) hedor m

odorless [ódəlɪs] ADJ inodoro

odorous [ódəəs] ADJ oloroso

of [əv] PREP de; **— course** por supuesto, desde luego; **a quarter — five** las cinco menos cuarto; **doctor — medicine** doctor -ora en medicina mf; **the smell — paint** el olor a pintura; **a friend — mine** un amigo mío

off [ɔf] ADV **— and on** de vez en cuando; **— the record** extraoficialmente; **ten cents —** rebaja de diez centavos f; **ten miles —** a diez millas de distancia; **to take a day —** tomarse un día libre; ADJ **— chance** posibilidad remota f; **—-color** verde; **— season** temporada baja f; **— year** de producción decreciente; **our deal is —** se canceló nuestro plan; **prices are —** los precios han caído; **you're — by a mile** estás equivocadísimo; **he's a little —** está tocadito; **with his hat —** sin el sombrero; **the electricity is —** está apagada la electricidad; **to be — to war** haberse ido a la guerra; **to be well —** tener mucho dinero; PREP **— course** fuera de curso; **he drove — the road** se salió de la carretera; **I bought it — a gypsy** se lo compré a un gitano; **he's — playing golf** se fue a jugar al golf; VT

liquidar

off-duty [ɔ́fdúdi] ADJ **to be —** no estar de turno

offend [əfénd] VI/VT (insult) ofender, afrentar; (affect disagreeably) desagradar

offender [əféndə] N delincuente mf

offense[1] [əféns] N (sin, insult) ofensa f; (misdemeanor) delito m; **no — was meant** no te lo tomes a mal

offense[2] [áfɛns] (in sports) ofensiva f

offensive [əfénsɪv] ADJ ofensivo; **— line** línea ofensiva f; **— series** serie ofensiva f, ataque m; N ofensiva f

offer [ɔ́fə] VT ofrecer; **to —** ofrecerse a; N oferta f; **make an —** hacer una oferta

offering [ɔ́fəɪŋ] N (thing given in worship) ofrenda f; (thing presented for sale) oferta f; (action of offering) ofrecimiento m

offhand [ɔ́fhǽnd] ADV **he remarked —** mencionó al descuido; ADJ **an — remark** un comentario descuidado

office [ɔ́fɪs] N (function) cargo m, función f; (place) oficina f, despacho m; (headquarters) oficinas f pl; **— boy** mandadero de oficina m; **— building** edificio para oficinas m; **— suite** (furniture) juego ofimático m; (rooms) suite f; (software) paquete de programas de productividad m; **through the —s of** por la intervención de

officer [ɔ́fɪsə] N (military) oficial m; (police) agente de policía mf; (of an organization) directivo -va mf

official [əfíʃəl] ADJ oficial; N funcionario -ria mf

officiate [əfíʃiet] VI oficiar; (in sports) arbitrar

officious [əfíʃəs] ADJ oficioso

off-key [ɔ́fkí] ADJ desafinado

off-limits [ɔ́flímɪts] ADJ vedado, de acceso prohibido

off-line [ɔ́flám] ADV fuera de línea

off-season [ɔ́fsizən] N temporada baja f; ADJ de temporada baja

offset[1] [ɔ́fsɛt] N offset m

offset[2] [ɔ́fsɛt, ɔfsɛ́t] VT compensar

offshore [ɔ́fʃór] ADJ & ADV cerca de la costa; **— account** cuenta en un paraíso fiscal f; **— drilling** explotación petrolífera en el fondo del mar f

offside [ɔ́fsáid] ADV fuera de juego

offspring [ɔ́fsprɪŋ] N prole m

offstage [ɔ́fstédʒ] ADV & ADJ entre bastidores, fuera de escena

off-the-record [ɔ́fθərékəd] ADJ oficioso

often [ɔ́fən] ADV a menudo; **how —?** ¿con qué frecuencia? ¿cada cuánto?

ogre [ógə] N ogro m

oh [o] INTERJ **— no!** ¡ay no! **— really?** ¿de veras? **— well** está bien, vale; **— yeah?** (not true) ¡qué va! (really?) ¿de veras?

ohm [om] N ohmio m

oil [ɔɪł] N (for cars, cooking) aceite m; (crude)

petróleo m; —**can** alcuza f, aceitera f; —**cloth**
hule m, tela de hule f; —**factory** aceitera f; —
field campo petrolífero m; —**industry**
industria petrolera f; —**lamp** quinqué m; —
painting pintura al óleo f, óleo m; —**pan**
cárter m; —**pipeline** oleoducto m; —**rig**
plataforma petrolífera f; —**slick** mancha de
petróleo f; —**spill** vertido de petróleo m; —
tanker barco petrolero m; —**well** pozo de
petróleo m; ADJ —**bearing** petrolífero; —-
exporting exportador de petróleo; —-
producing petrolífero; VT (apply oil)
aceitar; (bribe) untar

oily [ɔ́ili] ADJ (food) aceitoso; (liquid) oleoso;
(hair) graso; (person) untuoso

oink [ɔ́ɪŋk] VI gruñir; N gruñido m

ointment [ɔ́ɪntmənt] N ungüento m

OK/okay [oké] ADJ bien; **he's an —** guy es un
buen tipo; **his work is just —** su trabajo no
es nada del otro mundo; ADV bien; **it's —**
(fine) está bien; (adequate) es regular; N **to
give one's —** dar el visto bueno; VT dar el
visto bueno, aprobar; INTERJ bien, Sp vale

okra [ókrə] N quingombó m

old [old] ADJ viejo; (objects only) antiguo; (wine)
añejo; —**age** vejez f, ancianidad f; —-**boy
network** red favoritista entre hombres f; —-
fashioned (unfashionable) pasado de moda;
(antiquated) anticuado; (morally prudish)
chapado a la antigua; —**fogey** carcamal m,
carca m; —**hat** pasado de moda; —**maid**
solterona f; —-**time** antiguo, viejo; —-
timer (longtime member) miembro de la
vieja guardia m; (oldster) viejo m; —**wives'
tale** superstición f; —**world** viejo mundo m;
days of — antaño; **how — are you?**
¿cuántos años tienes? —**man** (husband)
marido m; (father) fam viejo m; **I'm not —
enough to drive** soy muy joven para
conducir; **to be an — hand at** ser ducho en

olden [óldn] ADJ **in — days** antaño

oldie [óldi] N viejo éxito m

oleander [óliændə] N adelfa f

olfactory [ɔlfǽktəri] ADJ olfatorio

olive [áliv] N (tree) olivo m; (fruit) aceituna f,
oliva f; —**branch** ramo de olivo m; —**grove**
olivar m; —**oil** aceite de oliva m; —**wood**
madera de olivo m; ADJ verde oliva

Olympiad [olímpiæd] N Olimpiada f,
Olimpíada f

Olympic [olímpik] ADJ olímpico; —**Games**
Olimpiadas f pl, Olimpíadas f pl, Juegos
Olímpicos m pl

Oman [omán] N Omán m

Omani [ománi] ADJ & N omaní mf

omelet [ámlɪt] N tortilla francesa f

omen [ómən] N agüero m, presagio m

ominous [ámənəs] ADJ (threatening)
amenazador; (like an omen) agorero

omission [omíʃən] N omisión f

omit [omít] VT omitir

omnipotence [ɑmnípətəns] N omnipotencia f

omnipotent [ɑmnípətənt] ADJ omnipotente

omniscience [ɑmníʃəns] N omnisciencia f

omniscient [ɑmníʃənt] ADJ omnisciente

omnivorous [ɑmnívəəs] ADJ omnívoro

on [ɑn] PREP en, sobre, encima de; —**the table**
en / sobre / encima de la mesa; —**all sides**
por todos lados; —**arriving** al llegar; —-
board a bordo; —**call** de guardia; —**credit**
al fiado; —**drugs** drogado; —**horseback** a
caballo; —**Monday** el lunes; —**purpose** a
propósito; —**screen** en la pantalla; —**the
house** la casa paga; —**time** a tiempo; **a
book —stamps** un libro sobre sellos; **do
you have any cigarettes — you?** ¿tienes
cigarros? **drunk —beer** borracho de
cerveza; **to talk —the phone** hablar por
teléfono; ADJ —**line** en línea; —**line
banking** banca en línea f; —**line help**
ayuda en línea f; ADV —**and —** dale que dale;
his hat is — lleva puesto el sombrero; **the
light is —** está encendida la luz; **there's a
war —** estamos en guerra; **you're —**
(broadcasting) estás en el aire; (acceptance) te
acepto la propuesta

once [wʌns] ADV (in the past, a single time) una
vez; (if ever) si alguna vez; —**and for all** una
vez por todas, definitivamente; —**in a while**
de vez en cuando; —**upon a time** érase una
vez; **at —** de inmediato, enseguida; **just this
—** sólo por esta vez; CONJ una vez que,
cuando; N una vez; —-**over** vistazo m

oncology [ɑnkálədʒi] N oncología f

one [wʌn] NUM uno; —**book** un libro; —
hundred cien; —**hundred and one** ciento
uno; —**thousand** mil; —-**armed** manco;
—-**armed bandit** tragaperras m/sg; —-
eyed tuerto; —**John Smith** un tal John
Smith; —-**man band** hombre orquesta m; —
on — mano a mano; —-**sided fight** pelea
desigual f; —-**upmanship** competitividad f;
—-**way street** calle de sentido único f; **his
—chance** su única oportunidad; **the —and
only** el único; **this is —smart dog** es un
perro muy listo; N & PRON uno m; —**at a
time** de a uno; —**by —** uno por uno; **love —
another** amaos los unos a los otros; **the —
who** el/la que; **the green —** el verde; **this —
** este/esta

oneself [wʌnsɛ́lf] PRON **to be —** ser uno mismo;
to sit by — estar sentado solo; **to talk to —**
hablar para sí; **to look at — in the mirror**
mirarse en el espejo; **to buy —a house**
comprarse una casa

ongoing [ángoɪŋ] ADJ continuo

onion [ánjən] N cebolla f; —**patch** cebollar m

onlooker [ánlʊkə] N espectador -ora *mf*, mirón -ona *mf*

only [ónli] ADJ único; ADV solo, solamente; **I — just caught the train** por poco pierdo el tren; CONJ solo que, pero

onomatopoeia [anəmɑɒəpíə] N onomatopeya *f*

onset [ánset] N comienzo *m*

on-side kick [ɔnsaɪd kík] N patada lateral *f*

onto [ántu] PREP en, sobre, encima de; **she got — the plane late** subió tarde al avión; **he dropped it — the table** lo dejó caer en la mesa; **I'm — your plot** conozco tu plan

onward [ánwəd] ADV hacia adelante

onyx [ániks] N ónix *m*

oops [ʊps] INTERJ ¡huy!

ooze [uz] VI/VT rezumar[se]; N cieno *m*

opal [ópəl] N ópalo *m*

opaque [opék] ADJ opaco

OPEC [Organization of Petroleum Exporting Countries] [ópɛk] N OPEP *f*

open [ópən] VI/VT abrir[se]; **to — into** comunicarse con; **to — one's way** abrirse paso; **to — onto** dar a; **to — up** abrirse; ADJ abierto; **— and shut** claro, evidente; **— code** código abierto *m*; **— door policy** política de acceso libre *f*; **--ended** sin restricciones; **--heart surgery** cirujía de corazón abierto *f*; **--minded** de amplias miras; **--mouthed** boquiabierto; **— question** cuestión discutible *f*; **— season** temporada de caza *f*; **— source software** software de fuente abierta *m*; **to criticism** expuesto a la crítica; N (outdoors) aire libre *m*; (tournament) abierto *m*

opener [ópənə] N abridor *m*; (in sports) primer partido *m*; **for —s** para empezar

opening [ópəniŋ] N (open space) abertura *f*; (act of making or becoming open, ceremony) apertura *f*; (beginning) comienzo *m*; (clearing) claro *m*; (vacancy) vacante *m*, apertura *f*; (pretext) oportunidad *f*; **— bid** oferta de apertura *f*; **— ceremony** ceremonia de apertura *f*; **— night** estreno *m*; **at the — a/en la apertura**

openness [ópənnɪs] N franqueza *f*, transparencia *f*, apertura *f*

opera [ápərə] N ópera *f*; **— glasses** gemelos *m pl*; **— house** ópera *f*

operable [ápərəbəl] ADJ operable

operate [ápəret] VI (function) funcionar; (intervene surgically) operar; **to — on a person** operar a una persona; VT (run a machine) manejar; (administrate) dirigir; (make function) accionar

operating [ápərɛdɪŋ] N **— costs** costos de operación *m pl*; **— room** sala de operaciones *f*, quirófano *m*; **— system** sistema operativo *m*

operation [ɑpəréʃən] N (surgical intervention, mission, math function) operación *f*; (function) funcionamiento *m*; (use of a machine) manejo *m*; **to be in —** (law) estar vigente; (machine) estar funcionando

operative [ápəɹəɒɪv] ADJ (law) vigente; (contract provision) pertinente; (word) clave, operativo; N (machine worker) operario -ria *mf*; (spy) agente *mf*

operator [ápəretə] N (telephone, math) operador -ora *mf*; (machine) operario -ria *mf*; (stock) especulador -ora *mf*; **he's a smooth — es un astuto**

ophthalmologist [ɑfθæʌmáɫədʒɪst] N oftalmólogo -ga *mf*

opiate [ópiət] N opiáceo *m*

opinion [əpínjən] N opinión *f*

opium [ópiəm] N opio *m*

opossum [əpásəm] N zarigüeya *f*

opponent [əpónənt] N opositor -ora *mf*, contrincante *mf*, adversario -ria *mf*, oponente *mf*

opportune [ɑpə-tún] ADJ oportuno

opportunistic [ɑpə-tunístɪk] ADJ oportunista, aprovechado

opportunity [ɑpə-túnɪɾi] N oportunidad *f*, ocasión *f*

oppose [əpóz] VI/VT oponer[se]

opposing [əpózɪŋ] ADJ opuesto, contrario; **— thumb** pulgar oponible *m*

opposite [ápəzɪt] ADJ (contrary) opuesto, contrario; **— to** frente a; PREP frente a, en frente de; N contrario *m*, opuesto *m*; ADV en frente

opposition [ɑpəzíʃən] N oposición *f*; **they met with little —** encontraron poca resistencia

oppress [əprés] VT oprimir

oppression [əpréʃən] N opresión *f*

oppressive [əprésɪv] ADJ (regime) opresivo; (heat) bochornoso, sofocante

oppressor [əprésə] N opresor -ora *mf*

optic [áptɪk] ADJ óptico; N **—s** óptica *f*

optical [áptɪkəl] ADJ óptico; **— character recognition** sistema de reconocimiento óptico de caracteres *m*; **— fiber** fibra óptica *f*; **— illusion** ilusión óptica *f*; **— resolution** resolución óptica *f*

optician [aptíʃən] N óptico -ca *mf*

optimal [áptəməl] ADJ óptimo

optimism [áptəmizəm] N optimismo *m*

optimist [áptəmɪst] N optimista *mf*

optimistic [aptəmístɪk] ADJ optimista

optimize [áptəmaɪz] VT optimizar

option [ápʃən] N opción *f* (also financial); (feature) extra *m*; **to leave one's —s open** no descartar posibilidades

optional [ápʃənl] ADJ opcional, optativo

optometrist [aptámɪtrɪst] N optometrista *mf*

optometry [aptámɪtri] N optometría *f*

opulence [ápjələns] N opulencia *f*

opulent [ápjələnt] ADJ opulento

or [ɔr] CONJ o; **seven — eight** siete u ocho

OR [operating room] [óár] N quirófano *m*, sala de operaciones *f*

oracle [ɔ́rəkəl] N oráculo *m*

oral [ɔ́rəl] ADJ oral; (hygiene) bucal

orange [ɔ́rɪndʒ] N naranja *f*; **— blossom** azahar *m*; **— grove** naranjal *m*; **— tree** naranjo *m*; ADJ & N anaranjado *m*

orangutan [ərǽŋətæn] N orangután *m*

orator [ɔ́rədə] N orador -ora *mf*

oratory [ɔ́rətɔri] N (skill in speaking) oratoria *f*; (place for prayer) oratorio *m*

orbit [ɔ́rbɪt] N órbita *f*; VI/VT orbitar

orbital [ɔ́rbɪdl] ADJ orbital

orbiter [ɔ́rbɪdə] N orbitador *m*

orchard [ɔ́rtʃəd] N huerto *m*; (large) huerta *f*

orchestra [ɔ́rkɪstrə] N orquesta *f*

orchestrate [ɔ́rkɪstret] VT orquestar

orchid [ɔ́rkɪd] N orquídea *f*

ordain [ɔrdén] VT (as minister) ordenar; (with an edict) decretar

ordeal [ɔrdíl] N suplicio *m*, tortura *f*; **— by fire** ordalía de fuego *f*

order [ɔ́rdə] N (command) orden *f*, mandato *m*; (request, commission) pedido *m*; (sequence, obedience to law) orden *m*; **holy —s** órdenes sagradas *f pl*; **an apology is in —** corresponde una disculpa; **in — to** para; **in working —** en buen estado; **in — that** para que, a fin de que; **on —** encargado; **out of —** no funciona; **to put in —** ordenar; VI/VT (command, arrange) ordenar, mandar; (place an order) pedir

ordering [ɔ́rdə-ɪŋ] N (putting in order) ordenación *f*, ordenamiento *m*

orderly [ɔ́rdə-li] ADJ ordenado; N (military) ordenanza *m*; (hospital) camillero *m*

ordinal [ɔ́rdnəl] ADJ ordinal

ordinance [ɔ́rdnəns] N ordenanza *f*

ordinary [ɔ́rdneri] ADJ común, corriente, ordinario; **do it the — way** hazlo de la forma habitual

ordination [ɔrdnéʃən] N ordenación *f*

ore [ɔr] N mineral *m*

oregano [ərégəno] N orégano *m*

organ [ɔ́rgən] N órgano *m* (also musical instrument)

organic [ɔrgǽnɪk] ADJ orgánico; **— chemistry** química orgánica *f*

organism [ɔ́rgənɪzəm] N organismo *m*

organist [ɔ́rgənɪst] N organista *mf*

organization [ɔrgənɪzéʃən] N organización *f*, planificación *f*

organizational [ɔrgənɪzéʃənl] ADJ organizativo; **— chart** organigrama *m*

organize [ɔ́rgənaɪz] VI/VT organizar[se]

organized [ɔ́rgənaɪzd] ADJ organizado

organizer [ɔ́rgənaɪzə] N organizador -ora *mf*

organizing [ɔ́rgənaɪzɪŋ] ADJ organizativo

orgy [ɔ́rdʒi] N orgía *f*

orient[1] [ɔ́riant] N oriente *m*

orient[2] [ɔ́rient] VT orientar

oriental [ɔriéntl] ADJ & N oriental *mf*

orientate [ɔ́rientet] VT orientar

orientation [ɔrientéʃən] N (guidance) orientación *f*; (tendency, leaning) tendencia *f*

orifice [ɔ́rəfɪs] N orificio *m*

origin [ɔ́rədʒɪn] N origen *m*, procedencia *f*; (of a river) naciente *f*, nacimiento *m*

original [ərídʒənl] ADJ original, originario; N original *m*

originality [ərɪdʒənǽlɪdi] N originalidad *f*

originate [ərídʒənet] VI/VT originar[se]

oriole [ɔ́riol] N oropéndola *f*

Orlon™ [ɔ́rlan] N orlón *m*

ornament[1] [ɔ́rnəmənt] N adorno *m*, ornamento *m*

ornament[2] [ɔ́rnəmənt] VT adornar, ornamentar

ornamental [ɔrnəméntl] ADJ ornamental

ornamentation [ɔrnəmɪntéʃən] N ornamentación *f*

ornate [ɔrnét] ADJ adornado en exceso; **— style** estilo rebuscado *m*

ornithology [ɔrnəθálədʒi] N ornitología *f*

orphan [ɔ́rfən] ADJ & N huérfano -na *mf*; VT dejar huérfano a

orphanage [ɔ́rfənɪdʒ] N orfanato *m*, hospicio *m*

orthodontics [ɔrθədántɪks] N ortodoncia *f*

orthodox [ɔ́rθədaks] ADJ ortodoxo

orthography [ɔrθágrəfi] N ortografía *f*

oscillate [ásəlet] VI oscilar; VT hacer oscilar

oscillation [asəléʃən] N oscilación *f*

osmosis [azmósɪs] N ósmosis *f*

osprey [áspre] N águila pescadora *f*

ossify [ásəfaɪ] VI osificarse

ostensible [asténsəbəl] ADJ supuesto

ostentation [astɪntéʃən] N ostentación *f*

ostentatious [astɪntéʃəs] ADJ ostentoso

osteoarthritis [astioarθráɪdɪs] N osteoartritis *f*

osteoporosis [astiopərósɪs] N osteoporosis *f*

ostracize [ástrəsaɪz] VT aislar

ostrich [ástrɪtʃ] N avestruz *m*

OTC [over-the-counter] [ótísí] ADJ extrabursátil

other [Áðə] ADJ, PRON, & N otro -tra *mf*; **— than Bob** salvo Bob; **every — day** cada dos días, un día sí y otro no; **— wise** de otro modo; **—worldly** fantástico

otter [Áðə] N nutria *f*

ouch [autʃ] INTERJ ¡ay!

ought [ɔt] V AUX **you — to sit down** deberías sentarte; **we — to get up early** deberíamos levantarnos más temprano

ounce [auns] N onza *f*

our [aur] POSS ADJ nuestro

ours [aurz] ADJ nuestro; **this book is —** este libro es nuestro; **these things are —** estas cosas son nuestras; PRON el nuestro / la nuestra; — **is bigger** el nuestro / la nuestra es más grande; **a friend of** — un amigo nuestro

ourselves [aʊrsélvz] PRON **we made the cake** — nosotros mismos hicimos la torta; **we were sitting by** — estábamos sentados solos; **we look at** — **in the mirror** nos miramos en el espejo; **we bought** — **a house** nos compramos una casa

oust [aʊst] VT echar, expulsar

out [aʊt] ADV (outside) fuera; ADJ (turned off, extinguished) apagado; (tennis) fuera; (baseball) out; —**-of-date** pasado de moda, anticuado; N (way out) escape m; (baseball) out m; PREP **she ran** — **the door** salió corriendo por la puerta; **they locked me** — me dejaron fuera; —**-and**— **criminal** criminal empedernido m; —**-and**— **refusal** una negativa rotunda; — **of bounds** (golf) fuera de límites; — **of commission/ order** fuera de servicio; — **of fashion** pasado de moda; — **of fear** por miedo; **he's really** — **of it** está ido, está despistado; — **of joint** dislocado; — **of money** sin dinero; — **of print/stock** agotado; — **of touch with** desconectado de; — **of tune** desentonado; — **of work** desempleado; — **to lunch** *fam* chiflado; **made** — **of** hecho de; **miniskirts are on the way** — las minifaldas se están dejando de usar; **I had it** — **with him** me peleé con él; **you were** — no estabas; **before the week is** — antes de que termine la semana; **the book is just** — acaba de publicarse el libro; **the secret is** — se ha divulgado el secreto; **we had some, but now we're** — teníamos, pero se nos acabó; **I'm** — **$10** perdí $10; INTERJ ¡fuera! VT (expel) expulsar; (expose) descubrir; VI **the truth will** — se descubrirá la verdad

outage [áʊdɪdʒ] N apagón m

outbreak [áʊtbrek] N (of pimples) erupción f; (of war) comienzo m; (of disease) brote m

outburst [áʊtbɜst] N (emotional) arrebato m; (of tears) ataque m; (of violence) motín m, explosión f

outcast [áʊtkæst] ADJ & N marginado -da mf

outcome [áʊtkʌm] N resultado m, desenlace m

outcry [áʊtkraɪ] N clamor m, protesta f

outdated [aʊtdéɪdɪd] ADJ anticuado

outdo [aʊtdú] VT superar

outdoor [áʊtdɔr] ADJ al aire libre; — **advertising** publicidad exterior f

outdoors [aʊtdɔrz] ADV al aire libre, afuera

outer [áʊdə] ADJ exterior; — **ear** oído externo m; — **space** espacio exterior m

outfield [áʊtfild] N jardín m

outfielder [áʊtfildə] N jardinero -ra mf

outfit [áʊtfɪt] N (gear) equipo m; (clothes)

conjunto m; (soldiers) unidad f; VI/VT equipar, habilitar

outfox [aʊtfáks] VT ser más listo que

outgoing[1] [áʊtgoɪŋ] ADJ (leaving) saliente

outgoing[2] [áʊtgoɪŋ] ADJ (extrovert) extrovertido

outgrow [aʊtgró] VT **she will** — **her clothes** la ropa le quedará pequeña; **she will** — **her epilepsy** la epilepsia se le irá con la edad

outing [áʊdɪŋ] N excursión f, paseo m

outlandish [aʊtlǽndɪʃ] ADJ estrafalario

outlast [aʊtlǽst] VT (last longer than) durar más que; (live longer than) sobrevivir a

outlaw [áʊtlɔ] N bandido -da mf, forajido -da mf; VT prohibir

outlay[1] [áʊtle] N gasto m, desembolso m

outlay[2] [aʊtlé] VT gastar, desembolsar

outlet [áʊtlɪt] N (exit) salida f; (stream) desagüe m, emisario m; (store) tienda f; (electric connection) toma de corriente f; **she needs an** — **for her talent** necesita canalizar su talento

outline [áʊtlaɪn] N (abstract) bosquejo m, esbozo m, trazado m; (boundary) contorno m; VT (summarize) bosquejar, esbozar; (draw) delinear; (plan) trazar

outlook [áʊtluk] N perspectiva f, panorama m

outlying [áʊtlaɪŋ] ADJ (marginal) periférico; (distant) remoto

outpatient [áʊtpeʃənt] N paciente ambulatorio -ria mf, paciente externo -na mf

output [áʊtpʊt] N (production) rendimiento m; (computer information) salida f; — **device** dispositivo de salida m

outrage [áʊtredʒ] N (offense) ultraje m, agravio m, atropello m; (indignation) indignación f; VT (offend) ultrajar, agraviar; (enrage) indignar

outrageous [aʊtrédʒəs] ADJ (offensive) ultrajante; (exorbitant) exorbitante; (extravagant) extravagante

outreach[1] [áʊtritʃ] N extensión f

outreach[2] [aʊtrítʃ] VT exceder

outright[1] [aʊtráɪt] ADV completamente; **he bought it** — lo compró al contado; **he rejected it** — lo rechazó categóricamente

outright[2] [áʊtraɪt] ADJ — **denial** negativa rotunda f; — **lie** mentira descarada f

outset [áʊtset] N comienzo m, principio m

outshine [aʊtʃáɪn] VT eclipsar

outside[1] [aʊtsáɪd] ADV fuera, afuera; PREP fuera de

outside[2] [áʊtsaɪd] ADJ (external) exterior; (foreign) foráneo; N exterior m; — **chance** posibilidad remota f; — **interference** interferencia externa f; **in a week, at the** — en una semana, a lo sumo; **to close on the** — cerrar por fuera

outsider [aʊtsáɪdə] N forastero -ra mf

outskirts [áʊtskɜts] N alrededores m pl, afueras

f pl

outsourcing [áutsɔrsɪŋ] N contratación externa *f*

outspoken [autspókən] ADJ franco

outstanding [autstǽndɪŋ] ADJ (excellent) sobresaliente, destacado; (pending) pendiente

outstretched [autstrétʃt] ADJ extendido

outward [áutwəd] ADJ exterior, externo; — **appearances** apariencias *f pl*; ADV hacia fuera; — **bound** que sale

outweigh [autwé] VT (weigh more) pesar más que; (be more important) sobreponerse a, valer más que

outwit [autwít] VT ser más listo que

oval [óvəl] ADJ oval, ovalado; N óvalo *m*

ovarian [ovérian] ADJ ovárico

ovary [óvari] N ovario *m*

ovation [ovéʃən] N ovación *f*

oven [Ávən] N horno *m*

over [óvə] PREP — **here** acá; — **in Japan** allá en Japón; — **many years** durante muchos años; — **the counter** (medicine) sin receta; (stocks) extrabursátil; — **the sea** al otro lado del mar; — **the hill** viejo; — **there** allá; **an umbrella** — **his head** un paraguas sobre la cabeza; **I heard it** — **the radio** lo oí por la radio; **he jumped** — **the fence** saltó por encima de la cerca; **he is** — **her in the hierarchy** él está por encima de ella en la jerarquía; **not** — **one year** no más de un año; **he hit him** — **the head with a rock** le golpeó en la cabeza con una piedra; **all** — **the city** por toda la ciudad; **I'm** — **it** (recovered) me he recuperado; (no longer interested) ya no me interesa; ADV — **again** de nuevo, otra vez; — **against** en contraste con; — **and** — una y otra vez; — **generous** demasiado generoso; **do it** — hazlo de nuevo, hazlo otra vez; **the world** — por todo el mundo; **it is** — **with** se acabó; INTERJ — **and out** cambio y fuera

overachiever [ovəətʃívə] N (bookish) empollón -ona *mf*; (successful) persona muy exitosa *f*

overactive [ovəǽktɪv] ADJ hiperactivo, demasiado activo

overall [óvəɔl] ADJ global, total; N —**s** mono *m*, overol *m*

overbearing [ovəbérɪŋ] ADJ mandón -ona, dominante

overboard [óvəbɔrd] ADV (into the water) al agua; **she went** — **on her project** se le fue la mano con su proyecto

overcast [óvəkæst] ADJ nublado, encapotado; **to become** — nublarse, encapotarse

overcharge[1] [ovətʃárdʒ] VI/VT cobrar demasiado, cobrar de más

overcharge[2] [óvətʃardʒ] N cobro excesivo *m*

overcoat [óvəkot] N sobretodo *m*, gabán *m*

overcome [ovəkám] VI/VT (to get the better of)

superar; (to overwhelm) embargar; **to be** — **by weariness** estar agobiado

overcompensate [ovəkámpɪnset] VI sobrecompensar

overcorrection [ovəkərékʃən] N sobrecorrección *f*

overdose [óvədos] N sobredosis *f*; VI tomar una sobredosis

overdraft [óvədræft] N sobregiro *m*, descubierto *m*

overdraw [ovədrɔ́] VI/VT sobregirar[se]

overdrawn [ovədrɔ́n] ADJ en descubierto, sobregirado

overdrive [óvədraɪv] N superdirecta *f*

overdue [ovədú] ADJ (borrowed item) atrasado; (bill) vencido

overeat [ovəít] VI comer en exceso

overestimate [ovəéstɪmet] VT sobreestimar

overexcite [ovərɪksáɪt] VT sobreexcitar

overextended [ovərɪksténdɪd] ADJ sobreextendido

overflow[1] [ovəfló] VI desbordar, rebosar

overflow[2] [óvəflo] N desborde *m*

overgrown [ovəgrón] ADJ cubierto, crecido; — **boy** muchacho demasiado crecido para su edad *m*

overhang[1] [ovəhǽŋ] VI (jut) proyectarse; (hang over) estar suspendido

overhang[2] [óvəhæŋ] N saliente *m*

overhaul[1] [óvəhɔl] VT revisar

overhaul[2] [óvəhɔl] N revisión *f*

overhead[1] [óvəhed] N gastos generales *m pl*; ADJ elevado; — **projector** retroproyector *m*

overhead[2] [óvəhéd] ADV en lo alto

overhear [ovəhír] VT oír por casualidad

overjoyed [ovədʒóɪd] ADJ rebosante de alegría

overkill [óvəkɪl] N exageración *f*

overland [óvəlænd] ADV & ADJ por tierra

overlap[1] [ovəlǽp] VI/VT solapar[se], superponer[se]

overlap[2] [óvəlæp] N traslapo *m*

overlay[1] [ovəlé] VT cubrir; (with gold, etc.) incrustar

overlay[2] [óvəle] N cubierta *f*; (with metal, wood) revestimiento *m*, chapa *f*

overload[1] [ovəlód] VT sobrecargar, recargar, saturar

overload[2] [óvəlod] N sobrecarga *f*

overlook[1] [ovəlúk] VT (fail to mention) pasar por alto, omitir; (pardon) perdonar; (look from above) mirar desde arriba; (afford a view of) dar a, tener vista a

overlook[2] [óvəluk] N mirador *m*

overly [óvəli] ADV excesivamente

overnight[1] [óvənaɪt] ADJ — **delivery** entrega al otro día *f*; — **guest** invitado -da a dormir *mf*

overnight[2] [ovənáɪt] ADV **he succeeded** — tuvo éxito de la noche a la mañana

overpass [óvəpæs] N paso elevado *m*

overpower [ovə·páuə·] VT abrumar

overpowering [ovə·páuə·ɪŋ] ADJ abrumador

overpriced [ovə·práɪst] ADJ demasiado caro

overproduction [ovə·prədákʃən] N superproducción f

overqualified [ovə·kwálifaɪd] ADJ sobrecalificado

overreach [ovə·ríʧ] VI **to — oneself** abarcar demasiado

overreact [ovə·riǽkt] VI reaccionar exageradamente

override [ovə·ráɪd] VT anular

overrule [ovə·rúl] VT anular

overrun[1] [ovə·rán] VT (overflow) desbordar; (exceed) exceder; (invade) infestar

overrun[2] [óvə·rʌn] N exceso de costos m

overseas [ovə·síz] ADV (beyond the sea) en ultramar; (abroad) en el extranjero

oversee [ovə·sí] VI (workers) dirigir, supervisar; (accounts) fiscalizar

overseer [óvə·sir] N capataz -za mf, supervisor -ora mf

overshadow [ovə·ʃǽdo] VT eclipsar, opacar

overshoe [óvə·ʃu] N chanclo m

oversight [óvə·saɪt] N (mistake) descuido m; (act of overseeing workers) supervisión f; (act of overseeing accounts) fiscalización f

overstep [ovə·stép] VT excederse en

overstrike [óvə·straɪk] VT imprimir un carácter directamente encima de otro

overt [ovə́t] ADJ evidente

overtake [ovə·ték] VT (pass someone) pasar, rebasar; (befall) abatirse sobre

overtax [ovə·tǽks] VT (tax too much) gravar excesivamente; (demand too much) exigir demasiado

overthrow[1] [ovə·θró] VT derrocar, derribar

overthrow[2] [óvə·θro] N derrocamiento m

overtime [óvə·taɪm] N (in a game) prórroga f, tiempo suplementario m; (at work) horas extras f pl; **to work —** hacer horas extras

overture [óvə·ʧə·] N (musical composition) obertura f; (initial move) propuesta f

overturn [ovə·tə́n] VI/VT volcar(se); VT (a decision) anular; (a government) derrocar

overview [óvə·vju] N vista global f, panorama m

overweight[1] [ovə·wét] ADJ **he's —** pesa demasiado

overweight[2] [óvə·wet] N sobrepeso m

overwhelm [ovə·hwélm] VT abrumar, agobiar

overwhelming [ovə·hwélmɪŋ] ADJ (responsibility, task) abrumador, agobiante; (victory) arrollador

overwork[1] [ovə·wə́k] VI trabajar demasiado; VT hacer trabajar demasiado

overwork[2] [óvə·wə·k] N exceso de trabajo m

overwrite mode [óvə·raɪtmod] VT modo de reescritura m

ovulate [ávjəlet] VI ovular

ovulation [αvjəléʃən] N ovulación f

owe [o] VI/VT deber; (a sum) adeudar, deber

owing [óɪŋ] ADJ debido; **— to** debido a

owl [aʊl] N lechuza f, búho m

own [on] ADJ & PRON propio; **— goal** autogol m, gol en contra m; **a house of his —** una casa suya; **to be on one's —** ser independiente; **to come into one's —** conseguir lo que uno se merece; **to hold one's —** mantenerse firme; VT poseer; **to — up [to]** confesar

owner [ónə·] N dueño -ña mf, propietario -ria mf; **— financing** financiamiento por el propietario m

ownership [ónə·ʃɪp] N propiedad f

ox [aks] N buey m

oxidation [aksidéʃən] N oxidación f

oxidize [áksidaɪz] VI/VT oxidar[se]

oxygen [áksɪʤən] N oxígeno m; **— tent** cámara de oxígeno f

oyster [óɪstə·] N ostra f; (large) ostión m

ozone [ózon] N ozono m; **— layer** capa de ozono f

Pp

pace [pes] N paso m; **—maker** marcapasos m sg; VT (traverse) ir y venir por; (set the tempo) marcar al paso; (measure) medir a pasos

pacific [pəsífɪk] ADJ pacífico; **— Ocean** Océano Pacífico m

pacification [pæsifikéʃən] N pacificación f

pacifier [pǽsəfaɪə·] N chupete m

pacifism [pǽsəfɪzəm] N pacifismo m

pacify [pǽsəfaɪ] VT (a country) pacificar; (a person) apaciguar

pack [pæk] N (of wolves) manada f; (of dogs) jauría f; (of cigarettes) cajilla f, cajetilla f; (of cloth) compresa f; (of cards) baraja f; (of cyclists) pelotón m; **— animal** acémila f, bestia de carga f; **—rat** rata urraca f; (person who saves everything) urraca f; **a — of lies** una sarta de mentiras f; VT empacar, empaquetar; (carry a gun) portar; (crowd) atestar; (load) cargar; **to — off** despachar; **to — one's bags** hacer las maletas

package [pǽkɪʤ] N paquete m (also organized vacation); **— deal** (agreement) acuerdo global m; (tourism, travel) paquete turístico m; VT (gift) empaquetar; (food) envasar

packaging [pǽkɪʤɪŋ] N embalaje m, empaque m

packer [pǽkə·] N empacador -ora mf, embalador -ora mf

packet [pǽkɪt] N paquete m

packing [pǽkɪŋ] N embalaje m

pact [pækt] N pacto m

pad [pæd] N (cushion) almohadilla f (also for ink); (block of paper) bloc m; (for aircraft) pista f; (for spacecraft) plataforma de lanzamiento f; VT (stuff with padding) acolchar; (add to dishonestly) rellenar

padding [pǽdɪŋ] N relleno m; (cotton) guata f; (of a speech) ripio m

paddle [pǽdl] N (for rowing) pala f, remo m; (for mixing, beating, ping-pong) paleta f; — **wheel** rueda de paleta f; VI (row) remar; VT hacer avanzar remando; (hit) dar una paletada

paddock [pǽdək] N (field) prado m; (enclosure at racetrack) paddock m

padlock [pǽdlɑk] N candado m; VT cerrar con candado

pagan [pégən] ADJ & N pagano -na mf

paganism [pégənɪzəm] N paganismo m

page [pedʒ] N (sheet) hoja f, página f; (boy servant) paje m; (hotel employee) botones m sg; — **break** salto de página m; VT (number pages) paginar; (call) llamar por altavoz; *Mex* vocear; **to — through** hojear

pageant [pǽdʒənt] N (parade) desfile m; (show) espectáculo m

pager [pédʒə˞] N buscapersonas m sg

paid [ped] ADJ pagado; —-**up** liberado, totalmente pagado, pagado

paid [ped] *see* pay

pail [pel] N balde m, cubeta f

pain [pen] N dolor m; (suffering) sufrimiento m; —**killer** analgésico m; **on — of** so pena de; **to take —s** esmerarse; **he's a** — es un chinche; ADJ —**staking** esmerado; VT (physical) doler; (mental) apenar

painful [pénfəl] ADJ (hurting) doloroso; (distressing) penoso; (difficult) arduo

painless [pénlɪs] ADJ sin dolor, indoloro

paint [pent] N (substance) pintura f; (spotted horse) pinto m; —**brush** (for art) pincel m; (for a house) brocha f; VI/VT pintar; **to — the town red** irse de juerga

painter [péntə˞] N pintor -ora mf

painting [péntɪŋ] N pintura f

pair [per] N par m; (married couple) pareja f; **a — of scissors** unas tijeras, una tijera; VI/VT aparear[se], emparejar[se]; **to — off** aparearse

pajamas [pədʒǽməz] N pijama/piyama mf

Pakistan [pǽkɪstæn] N Paquistán m

Pakistani [pækɪstǽni] ADJ & N paquistano -na mf

pal [pæl] N compañero -ra mf, compadre m, comadre f

palace [pǽlɪs] N palacio m

palate [pǽlɪt] N paladar m

palatial [pəléʃəl] ADJ suntuoso

Palau [pɑláu] N Paláu m

pale [pel] ADJ pálido, macilento; N **beyond the — inaceptable**; VI palidecer

paleness [pélnɪs] N palidez f

paleontology [peliɑntálɑdʒi] N paleontología f

Palestine [pǽlɪstaɪn] N Palestina f

Palestinian [pæləstínɪən] ADJ palestino; N palestino -na mf

palette [pǽlɪt] N paleta f

palisade [pælɪséd] N empalizada f; —**s** acantilados m pl

pall [pɔl] VT (cover with a cloth) cubrir con un paño mortuorio; (satiate) hartar; VI (tire) cansar; N paño mortuorio m; —**bearer** portador del féretro m; **to cast a — on** empañar

palliative [pǽliədɪv] N paliativo m

pallid [pǽlɪd] ADJ pálido

pallor [pǽlə˞] N palidez f

palm [pɑm] N (part of hand) palma f; (tree) palmera f, palma f; — **Sunday** Domingo de Ramos m; —**top computer** *Am* computadora de mano f, *Sp* ordenador de mano m; VT (hide in palm) escamotear; **to — something off on someone** encajar algo a alguien

palpable [pǽlpəbəl] ADJ (perceptible) palpable; (tangible) tangible

palpitate [pǽlpɪtet] VI palpitar

palpitation [pælpɪtéʃən] N palpitación f

palsy [pálzi] N parálisis f

paltry [pɔ́ltri] ADJ miserable, despreciable

pamper [pǽmpə˞] VT mimar, consentir

pamphlet [pǽmflɪt] N (informative) folleto m; (political) panfleto m

pan [pæn] N (for boiling) cazuela f, cacerola f, cazo m; (for frying) sartén f; (for baking) molde m; —**handle** mango de sartén m; —**handler** pordiosero -ra mf; VT criticar duramente; VI **to — for gold** extraer oro; **to — out** dar buen resultado; **to —handle** mendigar, pordiosear

panacea [pænəsíə] N panacea f

Panama [pǽnəmɑ] N Panamá f

Panamanian [pænəménɪən] ADJ & N panameño -ña mf

Pan-American [pænəmérɪkən] ADJ panamericano

pancake [pǽnkek] N panqueque m; **flat as a — chato** como una tabla

pancreas [pǽnkriəs] N páncreas m

panda [pǽndə] N panda m

pandemic [pændémɪk] ADJ pandémico m; N pandemia f

pander [pǽndə˞] VI consentir

pane [pen] N vidrio m, cristal m

panel [pǽnl] N (wall) revestimiento m; (group of experts) panel m; (of instruments) tablero m; VT revestir con paneles

paneling [pǽnlɪŋ] N (wall) panel m

pang [pæŋ] N (sharp pain, hunger) punzada f; (anguish) remordimientos m pl

panic [pǽnɪk] ADJ & N pánico *m*; ADJ —-
stricken sobrecogido de pánico
panorama [pænərǽmə] N panorama *m*
panoramic [pænərǽmɪk] ADJ panorámico
pansy [pǽnzi] N pensamiento *m*
pant [pænt] VI jadear
panther [pǽnθə·] N pantera *f*
panties [pǽntiz] N *Sp* bragas *f pl*; *Mex* pantaletas
f pl; *RP* bombacha *f*
pantomime [pǽntəmaɪm] N pantomima *f*
pantry [pǽntri] N despensa *f*, alacena *f*
pants [pænts] N pantalones *m pl*, pantalón *m*
pantyhose [pǽntihoz] N panty *m*
papa [pápə] N papá *m*
papacy [pépəsi] N papado *m*
papal [pépəl] ADJ papal
papaya [pəpáɪə] N papaya *f*; *Cuba* fruta bomba *f*
paper [pépə·] N (material) papel *m*; (newspaper)
periódico *m*; (assignment) trabajo *m*; (oral
contribution) comunicación *f*; (written
contribution) artículo *m*; —**back** libro en
rústica *m*; — **clip** clip *m*, sujetapapeles *m sg*;
— **cutter** guillotina *f*; — **feeder** alimentador
de hojas *m*; — **money** papel moneda *m*; —**s**
papeles *m pl*; — **shredder** trituradora *f*;
—**weight** pisapapeles *m sg*; —**work** (forms)
papeleo *m*; (procedures) trámites *m pl*; on —
por escrito; VI/VT empapelar
paprika [pæpríka] N pimentón *m*, páprika *f*
pap smear [pæp smir] N citología *f*
Papua New Guinea [pǽpjuənugíni] N Papúa
Nueva Guinea *f*
Papua New Guinean [pǽpjuənugínɪən] ADJ &
N papú *mf*
par [pɑr] N (financial) paridad *f*; (in golf) par *m*;
— **value** valor nominal *m*; **at** — a la par;
below — bajo par; **to be on a** — **with** estar
en pie de igualdad con; **to feel above** —
sentirse mejor que lo normal; VT hacer el par
parachute [pǽrəʃut] N paracaídas *m sg*
parachuting [pǽrəʃutɪŋ] N paracaidismo *m*
parachutist [pǽrəʃudɪst] N paracaidista *mf*
parade [pəréd] N (procession) desfile *m*;
(military review) parada *f*; — **ground** campo
de maniobras *m*; VI desfilar; VT hacer
ostentación de
paradigm [pǽrədaɪm] N paradigma *m*
paradise [pǽrədaɪs] N paraíso *m*
paradox [pǽrədɑks] N paradoja *f*
paradoxical [pærədɑ́ksɪkəl] ADJ paradójico
paraffin [pǽrəfɪn] N parafina *f*
paragraph [pǽrəgræf] N párrafo *m*; VT dividir
en párrafos
Paraguay [pǽrəgwaɪ] N Paraguay *m*
Paraguayan [pærəgwáɪən] ADJ & N paraguayo
-ya *mf*
parakeet [pǽrəkit] N perico *m*, periquito *m*
parallel [pǽrəlɛl] ADJ & N paralelo *m*;
(geometry) paralela *f*; — **port** puerto paralelo

m; VT (run equidistant from) correr paralelo
a; (compare) comparar
paralysis [pərǽləsɪs] N (of the body) parálisis *f*;
(of a transportation system) paralización *f*
paralytic [pærəlíDɪk] ADJ paralítico -ca
paralyze [pǽrəlaɪz] VT paralizar
paramedic [pærəmédɪk] ADJ & N paramédico -ca
mf
parameter [pərǽmɪDə·] N parámetro *m*
paramilitary [pærəmílɪteri] ADJ & N
paramilitar *mf*
paramount [pǽrəmaʊnt] ADJ supremo, sumo
paranoia [pærənɔ́ɪə] N paranoia *f*
paranoid [pǽrənɔɪd] ADJ & N paranoico -ca *mf*;
— **delusion** delirio paranoico *m*
paranormal [pærənɔ́rməl] ADJ paranormal
paraphernalia [pærəfənéljə] N parafernalia *f*
paraphrase [pǽrəfrez] N paráfrasis *f*; VI/VT
parafrasear
paraplegic [pærəplídʒɪk] ADJ N parapléjico -ca
mf
parapsychology [pærəsaɪkáləʤi] N
parapsicología *f*
parasite [pǽrəsaɪt] N parásito *m*
parasitic [pærəsíDɪk] ADJ parasítico; — **disease**
enfermedad parasitaria *f*
parasol [pǽrəsɔl] N parasol *m*, sombrilla *f*
paratroops [pǽrətrups] N tropas paracaidistas *f*
pl
parcel [pɑ́rsəl] N (package) paquete *m*; (lot)
partida *f*; (land) parcela *f*; — **post** paquete
postal *m*; VT (land) parcelar; **to** — **out**
repartir
parch [pɑrtʃ] VT secar; **I'm** —**ed** estoy muerto de
sed
parchment [pɑ́rtʃmənt] N pergamino *m*
pardon [pɑ́rdn] N perdón *m*, gracia *f*; (legal)
indulto *m*; **I beg your** — perdone; VT
perdonar, disculpar; (legally) indultar
pare [per] VT mondar, pelar; **to** — **down**
expenditures reducir gastos
parent [pérənt] N padre *m*, madre *f*; —
directory directorio padre *m*; —**s** padres *m*
pl
parental [pəréntl] ADJ parental; — **control**
control paternal *m*
parenthesis [pərénθəsɪs] N paréntesis *m*
parenting [pérəntɪŋ] N — **guide** guía para
padres *f*; — **skill** habilidad para educar a los
hijos *f*; **good** — buena crianza de los hijos *f*
pariah [pəráɪə] N paria *mf*
parish [pǽrɪʃ] N parroquia *f*; — **priest** [cura]
párroco *m*
parishioner [pəríʃənə·] N feligrés -esa *mf*,
parroquiano -na *mf*
parity [pǽrɪDi] N paridad *f*
park [pɑrk] N parque *m*; (for baseball) estadio de
béisbol *m*; VI/VT estacionar, aparcar
parking [pɑ́rkɪŋ] N estacionamiento *m*,

aparcamiento *m*; **— lot** estacionamiento *m*, aparcamiento *m*; **— place** lugar de estacionamiento/aparcamiento *m*

Parkinson's disease [párkɪnsənzdɪzɪz] N enfermedad de Parkinson *f*

parlance [párləns] N habla *f*

parley [párli] N (peace negotiation) parlamento *m*; (discussion) discusión *f*; VI parlamentar

parliament [párləmənt] N parlamento *m*

parliamentary [parləméntri] ADJ parlamentario

parlor [párlə] N sala *f*, salón *m*; **— game** juego de salón *m*; **beauty —** salón de belleza *m*

parochial [pərókiəl] ADJ (of a parish) parroquial; (provincial) pueblerino

parody [pǽrədi] N parodia *f*; VT parodiar

parole [pəról] N libertad condicional *f*; VT poner en libertad condicional

parrot [pǽrət] N loro *m*, papagayo *m*; VT repetir como loro

parry [pǽri] VT (a blow) parar; (a remark) eludir; N parada *f*

parse [pars] VT analizar

parser [pársə] N analizador *m*

parsing [pársɪŋ] N análisis *m*

parsley [pársli] N perejil *m*

parsnip [pársnɪp] N chirivía *f*

parson [pársən] N pastor -ora *mf*

part [part] N (component) parte *f*; (role) papel *m*; (in hair) raya *f*; **— and parcel** parte esencial *f*; **— time** tiempo parcial *m*; **in foreign —s** en el extranjero; **spare —s** piezas de repuesto *f pl*, repuestos *m pl*; ADJ **—-time** a tiempo parcial; VI/VT (cut into parts) partir[se]; (divide into parts) dividir[se]; (separate, leave) separar[se]; **to — company** separarse; **to — one's hair** hacerse la raya; **to — with** desprenderse de

partake [parték] VI **to — in** participar; **to — of** (share) compartir; (eat) comer

partial [párʃəl] ADJ parcial

participant [partísəpənt] ADJ & N participante *mf*, partícipe *mf*

participate [partísəpet] VI participar

participation [partɪsəpéʃən] N participación *f*

participle [párdɪsɪpəl] N participio *m*

particle [párdɪkəl] N partícula *f*; **— board** aglomerado *m*

particular [pətíkjələ] ADJ particular; (fussy) quisquilloso; N **in — en** particular; **—s** particulares *m pl*

parting [párdɪŋ] N (farewell) despedida *f*; (separation) separación *f*; **— of the ways** encrucijada *f*

partisan [párdɪzən] N (supporter) partidario -ria *mf*, partidista *mf*; (guerrilla) partisano -na *mf*; ADJ (of supporters) partidario, partidista; (of guerrillas) de partisanos

partition [partíʃən] N (distribution) reparto *m*; (division) división *f*, partición *f*; (wall) tabique *m*, mampara *f*; VT (distribute) repartir; (divide) dividir; (divide with a wall) tabicar

partly [pártli] ADV en parte

partner [pártnə] N (in business) socio -cia *mf*; (in an activity) compañero -ra *mf*; (in dancing, sports, marriage) pareja *f*

partnership [pártnəʃɪp] N (business) sociedad *f*; (relationship) asociación *f*

partridge [pártrɪdʒ] N perdiz *f*

party [párdi] N (get-together) fiesta *f*; (political group) partido *m*; (group of people) partida *f*; (litigant) parte *f*; **— of four** mesa para cuatro *f*; **— animal** fiestero -ra *mf*, parrandero -ra *mf*; VI ir de juerga

pass [pæs] VI (to go by) pasar; **to — a kidney stone** expulsar un cálculo renal; **to — away** fallecer; **to — for** pasar por; **to — in review** pasar revista; **to — on** (die) fallecer; (approve) aceptar; (refuse) no querer; **to — out** desmayarse; **to — over** pasar por alto; **to — up an opportunity** dejar pasar una oportunidad; VT (a ball) pasar; (a law) aprobar; (an exam, test) aprobar; **to — judgment** juzgar; **to — oneself off as** hacerse pasar por; **— me the salt** pásame la sal, alcánzame la sal; N (road through mountains) paso *m*; (motion, permission) pase *m*; (for transportation) abono *m*; (over a surface) pasada *f*; (on an exam) aprobación *f*; (of a ball) pase *m*; **—key** llave maestra *f*; **—port** pasaporte *m*; **—word** contraseña *f*, clave de seguridad *f*; **—word protected** protegido por contraseña; **he made a — at her** trató de ligar con ella

passable [pǽsəbəl] ADJ (penetrable) transitable; (mediocre) pasable

passage [pǽsɪdʒ] N (fare, musical or textual phrase, alley) pasaje *m*; (passing of time) paso *m*, transcurso *m*; (hallway in a house) pasillo *m*; (secret pathway) pasadizo *m*; (crossing) travesía *f*; (approval of a bill) aprobación *f*; **—way** (corridor) corredor *m*, pasillo *m*; (alley) pasaje *m*

passenger [pǽsəndʒə] N pasajero -ra *mf*

passerby [pǽsəbai] N transeúnte *mf*, viandante *mf*

passing [pǽsɪŋ] N fallecimiento *m*; ADJ **each — day** cada día que pasa; **— grade** nota de aprobado *f*; **— fancy** capricho pasajero *m*; **— mention** mención al pasar *f*; **— shot** pasante *m*

passion [pǽʃən] N pasión *f*

passionate [pǽʃənit] ADJ apasionado

passive [pǽsiv] ADJ pasivo; N pasiva *f*

past [pæst] ADJ pasado; **— due** en mora, vencido; **— participle** participio pasado *m*; **— perfect** pluscuamperfecto *m*; **— peformance** rendimiento previo *m*; **—**

precedents precedentes anteriores *m pl;* —
tense tiempo pretérito *m;* **the — president**
el expresidente; PREP **— hope** más allá de
toda esperanza; **— noon** después de
mediodía; **the house — the store** la casa
pasando la tienda; **we went — the tower**
pasamos al lado de la torre; **half — two** las
dos y media; **a woman — forty** una mujer
de más de cuarenta años; ADV **for some
time** — desde hace algún tiempo; **they
drove** — pasaron en coche; N (time) pasado
m; (tense) pretérito *m*

pasta [pástə] N pasta *f*

paste [pest] N (soft material, puree) pasta *f;*
(glue) engrudo *m;* **—board** cartón *m;* VT
pegar

pastel [pæstéł] ADJ & N pastel *m*

pasteurize [pǽstʃəraɪz] VT pasterizar/
pasteurizar

pastime [pǽstaɪm] N pasatiempo *m*

pastor [pǽstə] N pastor -ora *mf*

pastoral [pǽstə-əł] ADJ (literary) pastoril;
(ecclesiastical) pastoral; N pastoral *f;* (literary
work) égloga *f*

pastry [péstri] N (in general) pastelería *f;*
(specific) pastel *m;* **— cook** pastelero -ra *mf,*
repostero -ra *mf;* **— shop** pastelería *f,*
repostería *f*

pasture [pǽstʃə] N (grassland) prado *m;* (grass)
pasto *m;* (for horses) potrero *m;* VI/VT pastar,
pacer, apacentar

pasty [pésti] ADJ pastoso

pat [pæt] ADJ banal; **down** — al dedillo; **to
stand** — mantenerse firme; VT dar
palmaditas [a]; N palmadita *f;* N — **of butter**
porción de mantequilla *f*

patch [pætʃ] N (piece of cloth to repair clothes)
remiendo *m,* parche N (also for eye,
computer); (spot or area, as of ice) tramo [con
hielo] *m;* (plot) parcela *f;* VT (repair)
remendar; **to — up a quarrel** hacer las paces

patent [pǽtnt] ADJ (evident) patente; (protected
by patent) patentado; **— leather** charol *m;* N
patente *f;* **— pending** patente en trámite; VT
patentar

paternal [pətɜ́-nl] ADJ (fatherly) paternal; (of the
father's lineage) paterno

paternity [pətɜ́-nɪdi] N paternidad *f;* **— test**
prueba de paternidad *f*

path [pæθ] N (walkway) senda *f,* sendero *m;* (on a
computer) ruta *f;* (of a projectile, storm)
trayectoria *f;* **—way** senda *f,* sendero *m*

pathetic [pəθéDɪk] ADJ (moving) patético;
(contemptible) lamentable

pathogen [pǽθədʒən] N patógeno *m*

pathology [pæθáləʤi] N patología *f*

pathos [péθas] N patetismo *m*

patience [péʃəns] N paciencia *f*

patient [péʃənt] ADJ & N paciente *mf*

patiently [péʃəntli] ADJ con paciencia

patriarch [pétriɑrk] N patriarca *m*

patriarchal [petriɑ́rkəł] ADJ patriarcal

patrimonial [pǽtrɪmóniəł] ADJ patrimonial

patrimony [pǽtrəmoni] N patrimonio *m*

patriot [pétriət] N patriota *mf*

patriotic [petriáDɪk] ADJ patriótico

patriotism [pétriətɪzəm] N patriotismo *m*

patrol [pətrół] VI/VT patrullar, rondar; N
patrulla *f,* ronda *f;* **— car** patrullero *m;*
—man patrullero *m*

patron [pétrən] N (customer) cliente -ta *mf;*
(benefactor) benefactor -ora *mf,* mecenas *mf;*
(saint) patrono *m*

patronage [pétrənɪʤ] N (support of an artist)
mecenazgo *m;* (clientele) clientela *f;*
(political) clientelismo *m;* **we appreciate
your** — agradecemos su preferencia

patronize [pétrənaɪz] VT (be condescending)
tratar con condescendencia; (do business
with) frecuentar

patter [pǽDə] VI (strike lightly) golpetear;
(chatter) parlotear; N (small blows) golpeteo
m; (chatter) parloteo *m*

pattern [pǽDə-n] N (for sewing) molde *m;* (for
drawing) plantilla *f;* (of behavior) patrón *m;*
VI/VT **to — something after** modelar algo a
imitación de, basarse en el modelo de; **to —
oneself after** seguir el ejemplo de

paucity [pósɪdi] N escasez *f*

paunch [pɔntʃ] N panza *f,* barriga *f*

pause [pɔz] N pausa *f;* VI (while talking) hacer
pausa; (while moving) detenerse

pave [pev] VT (with asphalt) pavimentar; (with
bricks) enladrillar; (with flagstones) enlosar;
to — the way for preparar el camino para

pavement [pévmənt] N (roadway) calzada *f;* (of
asphalt) pavimento *m;* (of bricks) enladrillado
m; (of flagstones) enlosado *m*

pavilion [pəvíljən] N pabellón *m*

paw [pɔ] N pata *f;* (with claws) garra *f;* VT (touch
with paw) tocar con la pata; (touch with
claws) dar zarpazos; (grope) manosear

pawn [pɔn] N (object left in deposit) prenda *f;*
(chess piece) peón *m;* (puppet) títere *m;*
—broker prestamista *mf;* **—shop** casa de
empeños *f,* monte de piedad *m;* **in** — en
prenda; VT empeñar, dejar en prenda

pay [pe] VT (remit) pagar; VI (be profitable) ser
provechoso, convenir; (be worthwhile) valer
la pena; **to — attention** prestar atención,
fijarse en; **to — back** (return) restituir;
(retaliate) vengarse; **to — a compliment**
hacer un cumplido; **to — homage** rendir
homenaje; **to — one's respects** saludar; **to
— off a debt** cancelar una deuda, amortizar
una deuda; **to — out** desembolsar, pagar; **to
— a visit** hacer una visita; **to — through
the nose** pagar demasiado; **I will — for**

your meal te pago la comida; N (payment) pago m; (wages) paga f, salario m; **—back** (payment) restitución f; (revenge) venganza f; **—check** cheque del sueldo m; **— cut** recorte salarial m; **—day** día de pago m; **— freeze** congelación salarial f; **—load** carga útil f; **—off** (pay) pago m; (reward) recompensa f; (bribe) soborno m; **— phone** teléfono público m; **— raise** aumento salarial / de sueldo m; **—roll** nómina f, planilla f; **— scale** escala salarial f; **to hit —dirt** encontrar una mina de oro

payable [péəbəl] ADJ pagadero

payee [peí] N tenedor -ora mf, beneficiario -ria mf

payment [pémənt] N pago m, abono m; **— in full** liquidación f; **car —s** cuotas del coche f pl

payola [peólə] N soborno m

PC [písí] N (personal computer) PC m; (political correctness) lo políticamente correcto; ADJ (politically correct) políticamente correcto

pea [pi] N guisante m; Am arveja f; **—nut** Sp cacahuete m; Mex cacahuate m; Am maní m; **—nut butter** Sp crema de cacahuete f; Mex crema de cacahuate f; Am manteca/mantequilla de maní f

peace [pis] N paz f; **— officer** oficial de policía m; **— of mind** serenidad f; **at —** en paz; **to keep the —** mantener el orden público; **to hold one's —** callar

peaceful [písfəl] ADJ pacífico, tranquilo

peach [pitʃ] N durazno m; Sp melocotón m; (nice thing or person) delicia f, monada f; **— tree** durazno m, duraznero m, Sp melocotonero m

peacock [píkɑk] N pavo real m, pavón m

peak [pik] N (of a mountain) pico m, cumbre f; (of production, of one's abilities) punto máximo m; (of one's career) punto culminante m; **— load** carga máxima f; **— season** temporada alta f; **— time** hora punta f

peal [pil] N (of bells) repique m; (of laughter) carcajada f; VI/VT repicar

pear [pɛr] N pera f; **— tree** peral m

pearl [pɝl] N perla f; **— necklace** collar de perlas m

pearly [pɝli] ADJ (color) nacarado, perlado; (with pearls) perlado; **the — gates** las puertas del cielo

peasant [pézənt] ADJ & N campesino -na mf

peat [pit] N turba f

pebble [pébəl] N guijarro m, piedrecilla f; (smooth) canto m

pecan [pɪkán] N pacana f

peccary [pékəri] N pecarí/pécari m

peck [pɛk] VI/VT (strike with beak) picar; (eat bit by bit) picotear; (kiss) dar un besito; **—ing order** jerarquía f; **to — a hole** agujerear a picotazos; N (quick stroke) picotazo m; (kiss)

besito m; (measure) medida de áridos [9 litros] f; **you're in a — of trouble** estás metido en un lío

pectoral [péktə-əl] ADJ & N pectoral m

peculiar [pɪkjúljə] ADJ peculiar, particular

peculiarity [pɪkjuljǽrɪDi] N peculiaridad f

pedagogical [pɛDəgádʒɪkəl] ADJ pedagógico

pedagogue [péDəgɑg] N pedagogo -ga mf

pedagogy [péDəgɑdʒi] N pedagogía f

pedal [pédl] N pedal m; VI/VT pedalear

pedant [pédnt] N pedante mf

pedantic [pədǽntɪk] ADJ pedante

peddle [pédl] VI/VT ir vendiendo de puerta en puerta; **to — gossip** repartir chismes

peddler [pédlə] N buhonero -ra mf, mercachifle m

pederast [péDəræst] N pederasta m

pederasty [péDəræsti] N pederastia f

pedestal [pédɪstl] N pedestal m

pedestrian [pədéstriən] N peatón -ona mf; ADJ pedestre

pediatrician [piDiətríʃən] N pediatra mf

pediatrics [piDiǽtrɪks] N pediatría f

pedigree [péDəgri] N (of persons) linaje m; (of animals) pedigrí m

pedophile [péDəfaɪl] N pedófilo -la mf

pedophilia [pɛDəfíliə] N pedofilia f

pee [pi] VI fam hacer pipí; N fam pipí m

peek [pik] VI atisbar; N atisbo m

peel [pil] VI/VT (fruit, tree) pelar[se], descortezar[se]; (paint) descascarar[se]; **to keep one's eyes —ed** mantener los ojos abiertos; N cáscara f

peeler [pílə] N pelador m

peep [pip] VI/VT (begin to appear) asomar[se]; VI (make sound of chicks) piar; **to — at** atisbar; N (look) atisbo m; (sound of chicks) pío m; **—hole** mirilla f

peer [pir] N par m (also nobleman); **— group** grupo paritario m; VI (look attentively) escudriñar; (peep out) asomar

peerless [pírlɪs] ADJ incomparable, sin par

peeve [piv] VT irritar; **to get —d** ponerse de mal humor; N cosa que irrita f

peevish [pívɪʃ] ADJ malhumorado

peg [pɛg] N percha f; (on violin) clavija f; **to take a person down a —** bajarle los humos a alguien; VT (fix with pegs) clavar, clavetear; (set a price) fijar

pejorative [pɪdʒɔ́rəDɪv] ADJ peyorativo, despectivo

pelican [pélɪkən] N pelícano m

pellet [pélɪt] N (ball) bola f, bolita f; (shot) perdigón m

pell-mell [pélmɛl] ADJ confuso, tumultuoso; ADV a troche y moche

pelt [pɛlt] N piel f, pellejo m; VI/VT acribillar; **to — with stones** apedrear

pelvis [pélvɪs] N pelvis f

pen [pɛn] N (fountain) pluma f; (ballpoint) bolígrafo m; (for pigs) pocilga f; (for sheep) redil m; (for cows) corral m; **— holder** mango de pluma m, portaplumas m sg; **— name** seudónimo m; VT (write) escribir; (shut in) acorralar, encerrar; **— computer** Am bolígrafo-computadora portátil f, Sp bolígrafo-ordenador portátil m

penal [pínl] ADJ penal

penalize [pénəlaɪz] VT penar; (in sports) penalizar

penalty [pénlti] N (punishment) pena f, castigo m; (forfeiture) multa f; (in sports) penalidad f, infracción f; **— area** (in soccer) área de penales f; **— kick** (in soccer) tiro de penalidad f, penalti m; **— shootout** (in soccer) definición por penales f; **— stroke** (in golf) golpe de penalidad m

penance [pénəns] N penitencia f

pencil [pénsəl] N (writing instrument) lápiz m; (beam of light) haz m; **— sharpener** sacapuntas m sg

pendant [péndənt] ADJ pendiente

pendent [péndənt] ADJ pendiente

pending [péndɪŋ] ADJ pendiente; PREP **— his arrival** hasta que llegue, mientras no llegue

pendulum [péndʒələm] N péndulo m

penetrate [pénɪtret] VT penetrar

penetrating [pénɪtredɪŋ] ADJ penetrante

penetration [pénɪtréʃən] N penetración f

penguin [péŋgwɪn] N pingüino m

penicillin [pɛnɪsílɪn] N penicilina f

peninsula [pənínsələ] N península f

penis [pínɪs] N pene m

penitent [pénɪtənt] ADJ & N penitente mf

penitentiary [pɛnɪténʃəri] N penitenciaría f, penal m

penmanship [pénmənʃɪp] N escritura f, caligrafía f

pennant [pénənt] N banderín m, gallardete m

penniless [pénɪlɪs] ADJ pobre, sin dinero

penny [péni] N centavo m; **—-pincher** tacaño -ña mf; **to cost a pretty —** costar un dineral

pension [pénʃən] N (paid to a worker) jubilación f; (paid to a worker's survivors) pensión f; **— fund** caja de jubilaciones f; VT jubilar, pensionar

pensioner [pénʃənə] N pensionista mf

pensive [pénsɪv] ADJ pensativo

pent [pɛnt] ADJ encerrado; **—-up** acumulado

pentagon [péntəgɑn] N pentágono m

penthouse [pénthaʊs] N penthouse m

penultimate [pɪnʌ́ltəmɪt] ADJ penúltimo

people [pípəl] N gente f; (national group) pueblo m; VT poblar

pep [pɛp] N energía f; VI **to — up** animar

pepper [pépə] N (black) pimienta f; (green) pimiento m; (plant, shaker) pimentero m; **—mint** menta f; VT pimentar; **to — with**

bullets acribillar a balazos

peptic ulcer [péptɪk ʌ́lsə] N úlcera péptica f

per [pə] PREP (for each) por; (according to) según; **— capita** per capita; **—cent** por ciento; **— diem** Am viático m, Sp dieta f

percale [pəkél] N percal m

perceive [pəsív] VT percibir

percentage [pəséntɪdʒ] N porcentaje m

percentile [pəséntaɪl] N percentil m

perceptible [pəséptəbəl] ADJ perceptible

perception [pəsépʃən] N percepción f

perceptive [pəséptɪv] ADJ (pertaining to perception) perceptivo; (having keen perception) perspicaz

perch [pətʃ] N (rod for birds) percha f; (type of fish) perca f; VT (alight) posarse; VI/VT (set) encaramar[se]

percolate [pə́kəlet] VI/VT filtrar[se]

percussion [pəkʌ́ʃən] N percusión f

perdition [pədíʃən] N perdición f

perennial [pəréniəl] ADJ perenne; **— plant** planta perenne f

perfect¹ [pə́fɪkt] ADJ perfecto; **a — stranger** un completo desconocido

perfect² [pəfékt] VT perfeccionar

perfection [pəfékʃən] N perfección f

perfectionist [pəfékʃənɪst] N perfeccionista mf

perfectly [pə́fiktli] ADV (completely) totalmente; (without error) a la perfección, perfectamente; **stand — still** no te muevas

perforate [pə́fəret] VI/VT perforar[se]; VT calar

perforation [pə́fəréʃən] N perforación f

perform [pəfɔ́rm] VT (a task) ejecutar, realizar; (a rite, ceremony) celebrar; (a contract) cumplir; (a play) representar; VI (give a performance) actuar; (play music) interpretar; (function) funcionar; (do well) rendir; **to — simultaneously** simultanear

performance [pəfɔ́rməns] N (of a task) ejecución f; (of a ceremony) celebración f; (of a contract) cumplimiento m; (of a device) desempeño m, rendimiento m; (of a play) representación f; (of an actor) actuación f; (of music) interpretación f; **— review** evaluación del rendimiento f

performer [pəfɔ́rmə] N (drama) artista mf, actor m, actriz f; (music) artista mf, intérprete mf

perfume¹ [pə́fjum] N perfume m

perfume² [pəfjúm] VT perfumar

perfumery [pəfjúməri] N (store) perfumería f; (collection) perfumes m pl

perhaps [pəhǽps] ADV tal vez, quizá[s], acaso

peril [pérəl] N peligro m

perilous [pérələs] ADJ peligroso

perimeter [pərímɪdə] N perímetro m

period [píriəd] N período m; (historical) época f; (punctuation) punto m; (menstruation) período m, regla f; **you can't go, —!** no

puedes ir, y sanseacabó; **within a — of ten days** en el término de diez días
periodic [pɪriádɪk] ADJ periódico; — **table** tabla periódica *f*
periodical [pɪriádɪkəł] ADJ periódico; N revista *f*
peripheral [parífəəł] ADJ & N periférico *m*; — **vision** visión periférica *f*
periphery [pərífəri] N periferia *f*
periscope [pérɪskop] N periscopio *m*
perish [pérɪʃ] VI perecer
perishable [pérɪʃəbəł] ADJ perecedero
peritonitis [perɪtnáɪDɪs] N peritonitis *f*
perjure [pɔ́dʒɚ] VI **to — oneself** perjurarse, jurar en falso
perjury [pɔ́dʒɚi] N perjurio *m*
perks [pɔ˞ks] N beneficios adicionales *m pl*
permanence [pɔ́mənəns] N permanencia *f*
permanent [pɔ́mənənt] ADJ permanente; (of a position) titular
permeable [pɔ́miəbəł] ADJ permeable
permeate [pɔ́miet] VI/VT permear
permissible [pəmísəbəł] ADJ permisible, lícito
permission [pəmíʃən] N permiso *m*
permissive [pəmísɪv] ADJ permisivo
permit[1] [pɔ́mɪt] VI/VT (allow) permitir; (make possible) posibilitar
permit[2] [pɔ́mɪt] N permiso *m*
permutation [pɔmjutéʃən] N permutación *f*
pernicious [pəníʃəs] ADJ pernicioso
peroxide [pəráksaɪd] N peróxido *m*
perpendicular [pɔpɪndíkjələ˞] ADJ & N perpendicular *f*
perpetrate [pɔ́pɪtret] VT perpetrar
perpetual [pəpétʃuəł] ADJ perpetuo
perpetuate [pəpétʃuet] VT perpetuar
perplex [pəpléks] VT confundir, dejar perplejo; —**ed** perplejo
perplexity [pəpléksɪDi] N perplejidad *f*
persecute [pɔ́sɪkjut] VT perseguir
persecution [pɔsɪkjúʃən] N persecución *f*
persecutor [pɔ́sɪkjuDə˞] N perseguidor -ora *mf*
perseverance [pɔsəvírəns] N perseverancia *f*
persevere [pɔsəvír] VI perseverar, persistir
Persia [pɔ́ʒə] N Persia *f*
Persian [pɔ́ʒən] ADJ & N persa *mf*
persist [pəsíst] VI (continue, endure) persistir; (to be insistent) insistir
persistence [pəsístəns] N (endurance) persistencia *f*; (insistence) insistencia *f*
persistent [pəsístənt] ADJ (lasting) persistente; (insisting) insistente, machacón
person [pɔ́sən] N persona *f*
personable [pɔ́sənəbəł] ADJ agradable
personage [pɔ́sənɪdʒ] N personaje *m*
personal [pɔ́sən] ADJ personal; — **computer** *Sp* ordenador personal *m*; *Am* computadora personal *f*; — **effects** efectos personales *m pl*; — **foul** falta personal *f*; — **identification number** número de identificación personal

m; — **pronoun** pronombre personal *m*; — **property** bienes muebles *m pl*; **to make a — appearance** presentarse en persona
personality [pɔsənǽlɪDi] N personalidad *f*; — **disorder** trastorno de la personalidad *m*
personally [pɔ́sənəli] ADV personalmente; **don't take it** — no lo tomes a pecho / a mal
personify [pəsánəfaɪ] VT personificar
personnel [pɔsənɛ́ł] N personal *m*
perspective [pəspɛ́ktɪv] N perspectiva *f*
perspicacious [pɔspɪkéʃəs] ADJ perspicaz
perspiration [pɔspəréʃən] N transpiración *f*
perspire [pəspáɪr] VI transpirar
persuade [pəswéd] VT persuadir, convencer
persuasion [pəswéʒən] N persuasión *f*; (belief) convicción *f*
persuasive [pəswésɪv] ADJ persuasivo, convincente
pert [pɔ˞t] ADJ (insolent) insolente; (lively) vivaz
pertain [pətén] VI atañer, corresponder
pertinent [pɔ́tnənt] ADJ pertinente
perturb [pətɔ́b] VT perturbar
Peru [pərú] N Perú *m*
perusal [pərúzəł] N lectura *f*
peruse [pərúz] VT (read carefully) leer con cuidado; (read carelessly) hojear
Peruvian [pərúvian] ADJ & N peruano -na *mf*
pervade [pəvéd] VT difundirse por
perverse [pəvɔ́s] ADJ perverso
perversion [pəvɔ́ʒən] N perversión *f*
perversity [pəvɔ́sɪDi] N perversidad *f*
pervert[1] [pəvɔ́t] VT pervertir; (misconstrue) desvirtuar
pervert[2] [pɔ́vɔt] N pervertido -da *mf*
peso [péso] N peso *m*
pessimism [pésəmɪzəm] N pesimismo *m*
pessimist [pésəmɪst] N pesimista *mf*
pest [pest] N (insect, disease) peste *f*, plaga *f*; (person) pesado -da *mf*
pester [péstə˞] VT molestar
pesticide [péstɪsaɪd] N pesticida *m*
pestilence [péstələns] N pestilencia *f*
pet [pet] N (animal) mascota *f*; (favorite) favorito -ta *mf*, preferido -da *mf*; ADJ predilecto; — **name** apodo cariñoso *m*; VT (caress) acariciar; (pat) dar palmaditas a
petal [pédł] N pétalo *m*
petition [pətíʃən] N petición *f*, solicitud *f*; VI/VT peticionar, solicitar
petrify [pétrəfaɪ] VI/VT petrificar[se]
petroleum [pətróliəm] N petróleo *m*; — **products** productos petrolíferos *m pl*; — **jelly** vaselina *f*
petticoat [pédikot] N enaguas *f pl*
petty [pédi] ADJ (trivial) trivial; (mean) mezquino; — **cash** caja chica *f*; — **larceny** ratería *f*; — **officer** suboficial de marina *m*
petunia [pɪtúnjə] N petunia *f*
pew [pju] N banco *m* / banca *f* de iglesia

pewter [pjúɖə] N peltre *m*
peyote [peóɖi] N peyote *m*
phantom [fǽntəm] N fantasma *m*
pharmaceutical [farməsúɖıkəl] ADJ farmacéutico; N producto farmacéutico *m*, fármaco *m*
pharmacist [fárməsıst] N farmacéutico -ca *mf*
pharmacology [farməkáləʤı] N farmacología *f*
pharmacy [fárməsı] N farmacia *f*
pharynx [fǽrıŋks] N faringe *f*
phase [fez] N fase *f*; VI **to — out** retirar por etapas; **to — in** incorporar paulatinamente
pheasant [fézənt] N faisán *m*
phenomenon [fınámənan] N fenómeno *m*
philanthropy [fılǽnθrəpi] N filantropía *f*
philharmonic [fılharmánık] ADJ filarmónico; N filarmónica *f*
Philippine [fíləpin] ADJ & N filipino -na *mf*
Philippines [fíləpinz] N filipinas *f pl*
philosopher [fılásəfə-] N filósofo -fa *mf*
philosophical [fıləsáfıkəl] ADJ filosófico
philosophy [fılásəfi] N filosofía *f*
phishing [fíʃıŋ] N phishing *m*
phlegm [flɛm] N flema *f*
phobia [fóbiə] N fobia *f*
phone [fon] N teléfono *m*; — **card** tarjeta telefónica *f*; VI/VT telefonear
phonetic [fənɛ́dık] ADJ fonético
phonetics [fənɛ́dıks] N fonética *f*
phonograph [fónəgræf] N fonógrafo *m*
phonology [fənáləʤı] N fonología *f*
phony [fóni] ADJ falso
phosphate [fásfet] N fosfato *m*
phosphorus [fásfə-əs] N fósforo *m*
photo [fóɖo] N foto *f*; — **finish** final muy reñido *m*
photocopier [fóɖəkapiə-] N fotocopiadora *f*
photocopy [fóɖəkapi] N fotocopia *f*; VI/VT fotocopiar
photoelectric [foɖoıléktrık] ADJ fotoeléctrico
photogenic [foɖəʤɛ́nık] ADJ fotogénico
photograph [fóɖəgræf] N fotografía *f*; VT fotografiar
photographer [fətágrəfə-] N fotógrafo -fa *mf*
photography [fətágrəfi] N fotografía *f*
photon [fótan] N fotón *m*
photosynthesis [foɖosínθəsıs] N fotosíntesis *f*
phrase [frez] N frase *f*; VI/VT expresar; (musical) frasear
phylum [fáıləm] N filo *m*
physical [fízıkəl] ADJ físico; — **education** educación física *f*; — **geography** geografía física *f*; — **science** ciencia física *f*; — **therapy** fisioterapia *f*
physician [fızíʃən] N médico -ca *mf*; —'s **assistant** ayudante médico -ca sanitario -ria *mf*
physicist [fízısıst] N físico -ca *mf*
physics [fízıks] N física *f*

physiological [fıziəláʤıkəl] ADJ fisiológico
physiology [fıziáləʤi] N fisiología *f*
physique [fızík] N físico *m*
pianist [piǽnıst] N pianista *mf*
piano [piǽno] N piano *m*; — **bench** banqueta de piano *f*; — **hammer** martinete *m*; — **player** pianista *mf*; — **stool** taburete de piano *m*
picaresque [pıkərésk] ADJ picaresco
piccolo [píkəlo] N flautín *m*, pícolo *m*
pick [pık] VT (choose) escoger, elegir; (gather flowers) juntar; (play a guitar) puntear; (clean teeth) mondarse; (eat with the bill) picotear; (provoke a fight) armar, entablar; VI picar; **to — at** picotear; **to — apart** criticar; **to — a lock** violar una cerradura con ganzúa; **to — on** meterse con; **to — out** (choose) escoger; (distinguish) distinguir; **to — pockets** ratear; **to — up** (gather) recoger; (lift) levantar; (learn) aprender; (order) ordenar; (improve) mejorar; **to — up speed** acelerar la marcha; N (tool) pico *m*; (of a guitar) púa *f*; (act of selecting) selección *f*; (thing or person selected) elección *f*; (the best) lo selecto, lo mejor; —**ax[e]** zapapico *m*; —**lock** ganzúa *f*; —**pocket** ratero -ra *mf*, carterista *mf*; —**up** (taking on freight) recolección *f*; (improvement in business) recuperación *f*; (acceleration) aceleración *f*; —**up truck** camioneta *f*; ADJ —**-proof** a prueba de ladrones
picket [píkıt] N piquete *m* (also union worker); — **fence** cerca de piquetes *f*; VT (fence) vallar; (block with workers) bloquear, *Am* piquetear
pickle [píkəl] N pepinillo en vinagre *m*, curtido *m*; **to be in a** — hallarse en un aprieto; VT encurtir, escabechar; —**d fish** pescado al/en escabeche *m*, pescado adobado *m*
picnic [píknık] N picnic *m*; — **area** merendero *m*; VI hacer un picnic
pictorial [pıktɔ́riəl] ADJ pictórico
picture [píktʃə-] N (image) imagen *f*; (drawing) dibujo *m*; (photo) fotografía *f*; (situation) panorama *m*; (movie) película *f*; — **frame** marco *m*; — **gallery** galería de pinturas *f*; — **tube** tubo de imagen *m*; **she is the — of unhappiness** es la imagen de la infelicidad; VT (describe) describir; (imagine) imaginar
picturesque [pıktʃərésk] ADJ pintoresco
pie [paı] N pastel *m*, tarta *f*; — **chart** diagrama de pastel *m*; — **graph** gráfica de pastel *f*; — **in the sky** castillos en el aire *m pl*; **it's as easy as** — es pan comido
piece [pis] N (of music, in a board game, of furniture) pieza *f*; (of wood, rock, pie) pedazo *m*, trozo *m*; —**meal** por partes; — **of advice** consejo *m*; — **of cake** pan comido *m*; — **of land** parcela *f*, terreno *m*; — **of one's mind** regaño *m*; — **of news** noticia *f*; —**work** trabajo a destajo *m*; **to go to —s**

descomponerse; VI **to — together**
(assemble) armar; (make sense of) atar cabos

pier [pɪr] N muelle *m*, embarcadero *m*;
(breakwater) rompeolas *m sg*

pierce [pɪrs] VI/VT (make a hole in) agujerear,
perforar; (penetrate) penetrar; (cause a sharp
pain) punzar

piercing [pírsɪŋ] ADJ (glance, sound)
penetrante; (pain) punzante; N perforación *f*

piety [páɪɪDi] N piedad *f*

pig [pɪg] N puerco *m*, cerdo *m*, cochino *m*; Sp
guarro *m*; **-headed** testarudo, cabezón;
—-iron hierro en lingotes *m*; **— Latin**
jerigonza *f*; **—pen** pocilga *f*; **—tail** coleta *f*

pigeon [pídʒən] N paloma *f*; (young) pichón *m*;
—hole casilla *f*; **— loft** palomar *m*; VT **to
—hole** encasillar

piggy [pígi] N cerdito *m*; **—bank** alcancía *f*; Sp
hucha *f*; ADV **—back** a hombros, a cuestas

pigment [pígmənt] N pigmento *m*

pike [paɪk] N (weapon) pica *f*; (fish) lucio *m*

pile [paɪł] N (ordered stack) pila *f*; (chaotic group)
montón *m*, amontonamiento *m*; (surface of a
carpet) pelo *m*; (post) pilote *m*; **— driver**
martinete *m*; **—s** almorranas *f pl*; **—-up**
accidente múltiple *m*; VI/VT apilar[se],
amontonar[se]

pilfer [pílfɚ] VI/VT ratear, sisar

pilferage [pílfɚɪdʒ] N ratería *f*

pilgrim [pílgrəm] N peregrino -na *mf*, romero
-ra *mf*

pilgrimage [pílgrəmɪdʒ] N peregrinación *f*,
romería *f*

pill [pɪl] N píldora *f*, pastilla *f*; (naughty child)
pesado -da *mf*

pillage [pílɪdʒ] N pillaje *m*, saqueo *m*, rapiña *f*;
VI/VT pillar, saquear

pillar [pílɚ] N pilar *m*, columna *f*

pillow [pílo] N almohada *f*; **—case** funda *f*

pilot [páɪłət] N piloto *m* (also test, light); (of a
boat) timonel *m*, piloto *m*; VT pilotar,
comandar

pimple [pímpəł] N grano *m*, barro *m*

pin [pɪn] N (sewing implement) alfiler *m*;
(ornament) prendedor *m*; (rod) pasador *m*,
perno *m*; (bowling) bolo *m*; (electric) pata *f*,
clavija *f*; **—cushion** alfiletero *m*; **—wheel**
molinete *m*, remolino *m*; **to be on —s and
needles** estar en ascuas; VT (affix with pins)
prender; (in wrestling) inmovilizar; **to —
someone down** (hold down) inmovilizar;
(force to act) hacer que concrete detalles; **to
— one's hopes on** poner sus esperanzas en;
to —point localizar con precisión; **to — up**
sujetar con alfileres

PIN [personal identification number] [pɪn]
N PIN *m*

pincers [pínsɚz] N (of lobsters) pinzas *f pl*; (tool)
tenazas *f pl*

pinch [pɪntʃ] VT (squeeze with fingers) pellizcar;
(squeeze tightly, hamper) apretar; (steal)
birlar; (arrest) prender; VI (be too tight)
apretar; (economize) economizar; **—ed
nerve** nervio pellizcado *m*, nervio pinzado
m; N (act of pinching) pellizco *m*; (small
amount) pizca *f*; (trying circumstances)
aprieto *m*, apuro *m*; **— hitter** bateador -ora
emergente *mf*; **— runner** corredor
emergente *m*

pine [paɪn] N pino *m*; **—apple** piña *f*, ananá[s] *m*;
— cone piña *f*; **— grove** pinar *m*; **— nut**
piñón *m*; VI **to — away** languidecer; **to — for**
anhelar, suspirar por

pingpong [píŋpɑŋ] N ping-pong *m*, tenis de
mesa *m*

pinion [pínjən] N piñón *m*

pink [pɪŋk] N rosado *m*, rosa *m*; **—eye**
conjuntivitis *f*; **— slip** notificación de despido
f; **in the —** rebosante de salud; ADJ rosado,
rosa

pinnacle [pínəkəł] N pináculo *m*

pint [paɪnt] N pinta *f*; ADJ **-sized** diminuto

pinto bean [píntobɪn] N judía pinta *f*

pioneer [paɪənír] N pionero -ra *mf*; VI ser el
primero en hacer algo; VT promover

pious [páɪəs] ADJ (religious) pío, piadoso;
(hypocritical) beato

pipe [paɪp] N (for smoking) pipa *f*; (for water)
tubo *m*, caño *m*; (of an organ) tubo *m*; (flute)
caramillo *m*, flauta *f*; **— dream** ilusiones *f pl*;
—line (for oil) oleoducto *m*; (for gas)
gasoducto *m*; (for water) tubería *f*; **in the
—line** en trámite; **— wrench** llave inglesa *f*;
VT (convey water) conducir por cañerías;
(make music) tocar la flauta; VI chillar; **to —
down** callarse

piping [páɪpɪŋ] N (many pipes) cañería *f*, tubería
f; (border on clothes) ribete *m*; (sound of
pipes) sonido de la gaita/flauta *m*; ADJ **— hot**
hirviendo

pipsqueak [pípskwik] N chisgarabís *m*,
mequetrefe *m*

piracy [páɪrəsi] N piratería *f*

pirate [páɪrɪt] N pirata *mf*; VT piratear

pistol [pístł] N pistola *f*, revólver *m*; VT **to —-
whip** dar culatazos

piston [pístn̩] N pistón *m*, émbolo *m*; **— ring**
segmento de compresión *m*; **— rod** eje del
pistón *m*

pit [pɪt] N (hole) hoyo *m*, pozo *m*; (in a garage,
theater) foso *m*; (trap) trampa *f*; (seed) hueso
m; (part of a racetrack) box *m*, paddock *m*;
(part of the stomach) boca *f*; **—fall** (trap)
trampa *f*; (difficulty) dificultad *f*; **this is the
—s** esto es lo peor; VI/VT (make holes)
picarse; VT **to — against** oponer, enfrentar

pitch [pɪtʃ] VT (throw) tirar, lanzar; (try to sell)
pregonar; **to — a tent** armar una tienda; VI

(plane, ship) cabecear; **to — in** colaborar; N (throw) tiro *m*, lanzamiento *m*; (in music) tono *m*; (in printing) espaciado *m*; (slope) grado de inclinación *m*; (tar) brea *f*, pez *f*; **— dark** oscuro como boca del lobo; **—fork** horca *f*, horquilla *f*

pitcher [pítʃə-] N (vessel) cántaro *m*, jarro *m*, jarra *f*; (in baseball) lanzador -ora *mf*; **—'s mound** montículo *m*

pith [pɪθ] N (in plants, feathers) médula *f*; (essence) meollo *m*

pithy [píθi] ADJ sustancial

pitiful [pídɪfəl] ADJ (deserving pity) lastimoso; (deserving contempt) despreciable

pitiless [pídɪlɪs] ADJ despiadado

pituitary [pɪtúɪtɛri] ADJ pituitario; **— gland** glándula pituitaria *f*

pity [pídi] N compasión *f*, lástima *f*; **what a —!** ¡qué lástima! VT compadecerse [de]

pivot [pívət] N pivote *m*; VI pivotar

pixel [píksəl] N píxel *m*

pizza [pítsə] N pizza *f*

placard [plǽkə-d] N cartel *m*

placate [plékét] VT apaciguar

place [ples] N (site) lugar *m*, sitio *m*; (position) puesto *m*; **— mat** mantel individual *m*; **— of birth** lugar de nacimiento *m*; **— of business** oficina *f*; **— of worship** templo *m*; **— setting** cubierto para una persona *m*; **in — of** en lugar de; **it is not my — to do it** no me corresponde a mí hacerlo; VT (put) colocar; (identify) situar, ubicar; **to — an order** hacer un pedido; **to — an ad** poner un anuncio; VI (in sports) clasificarse

placebo [pləsíbo] N placebo *m*

placement [plésmənt] N (in levels, categories) colocación *f*, posicionamiento *m*; (in space) emplazamiento *m*

placenta [pləsɛ́ntə] N placenta *f*

placid [plǽsɪd] ADJ plácido

plagiarism [pléʤərɪzəm] N plagio *m*

plague [pleg] N plaga *f*, peste *f*; VT atormentar, apestar

plaid [plæd] N tela escocesa *f*

plain [plen] ADJ (without embellishment) sencillo, llano; (clear) claro; (downright, unadulterated) puro; (ordinary) común; (unattractive) poco atractivo; **in — sight** en plena vista; **—clothesman** policía en traje de civil *m*; **—Jane** sencillo; ADV completamente; N llano *m*, llanura *f*

plaintiff [pléntɪf] N demandante *mf*, querellante *mf*

plan [plæn] N plan *m*; (drawing, sketch, map, outline) plano *m*; VI/VT planear, planificar; (diagram) hacer el plano de; **—ned parenthood** planificación familiar *f*

plane [plen] N (airplane) avión *m*; (surface) plano *m*; (tool) cepillo *m*; **— tree** plátano *m*; ADJ

plano; **— geometry** geometría plana *f*; VI (glide, hover) planear; VT (smooth) cepillar, planear

planet [plǽnɪt] N planeta *m*

planetarium [plænɪtɛ́riəm] N planetario *m*

plank [plæŋk] N (board) tabla *f*, tablón *m*; (tenet) principio *m*, base *f*; VT entarimar

plankton [plǽŋktən] N plancton *m*

planning [plǽnɪŋ] N planeamiento *m*, planificación *f*

plant [plænt] N (vegetation) planta *f*; (industrial installation) fábrica *f*, planta *f*; (mole, spy) topo *m*; VT (plants) plantar; (ideas) sembrar; (a spy, evidence) colocar

plantain [plǽntən] N plátano *m*

plantation [plæntéʃən] N plantación *f*

plaque [plæk] N placa *f*; (on teeth) sarro *m*, placa *f*

plasma [plǽzmə] N plasma *m*, gas ionizado *m*

plaster [plǽstə-] N (substance) yeso *m*; (preparation applied to body) emplasto *m*; **— of Paris** yeso *m*; VT (cover with plaster) revocar; (apply a preparation) emplastar; (cover with posters) cubrir, empapelar; (defeat) aplastar; **to — down one's hair** achatarse el pelo; **to get —ed** emborracharse

plastic [plǽstɪk] ADJ plástico; **— surgery** cirugía plástica/estética *f*

plate [plet] N (for food) plato *m*; (for collections) bandeja *f*; (metal) plancha *f*, lámina *f*; (license) placa *f*; **— glass** vidrio cilindrado *m*; **— tectonics** tectónica de placas *f*; VT (apply metal covering) chapar, enchapar; (apply armor) blindar

plateau [plætó] N meseta *f*, macizo *m*

platform [plǽtfɔrm] N plataforma *f* (also in politics, computers); (railway) andén *m*; (mobile) tarima *f*, tinglado *m*

platinum [plǽtnəm] N platino *m*

platitude [plǽtɪtud] N lugar común *m*, perogrullada *f*

platter [plǽdə-] N fuente *f*

plausible [plɔ́zəbəl] ADJ plausible

play [ple] VT (game) jugar; (an opponent) jugar contra; (an instrument) tocar; (a drama) representar; (a role) desempeñar; (bet on) apostar; **to — a joke** gastar una broma; **to — cards** jugar a los naipes; **to — havoc** hacer estragos; **to — tennis** jugar al tenis; **to — the fool** hacerse el tonto; VI (divert oneself, gamble) jugar; (kid) bromear; (make music) tocar; **to — along** seguir la corriente; **to — down** minimizar; **to be all —ed out** estar agotado; N (recreational activity, looseness) juego *m*; (instance of playing) jugada *f*; (theater work) obra de teatro *f*; **— on words** juego de palabras *m*; **—boy** playboy *m*; **—ground** recreo *m*, patio *m*; **—ing card** naipe *m*; **—mate** compañero -ra de juego *mf*; **—off [game]** [partido de] desempate *m*; **the**

—offs las eliminatorias *f pl*; **—thing** juguete *m*

player [pléə] N (one who plays, gambler) jugador -ora *mf*; (musician) músico -ca *mf*; (influential person) persona influyente *f*; (womanizer) mujeriego *m*; (actor) actor *m*, actriz *f*; (participant) participante *mf*; — **piano** pianola *f*

playful [pléfəl] ADJ juguetón

playwright [pléraɪt] N dramaturgo -ga *mf*

plea [pli] N (entreaty) súplica *f*, ruego *m*; (allegation) alegato *m*; **to enter a — of guilty** declararse culpable

plead [plid] VI/VT (entreat) suplicar, rogar; (defend) abogar, defender; **to — guilty** declararse culpable

pleasant [plézənt] ADJ agradable, grato, placentero

pleasantry [plézəntri] N cortesía *f*

please [pliz] ADV por favor; VI/VT agradar, complacer; **as you —** como quieras; **to be —d to** tener el gusto de, tener gusto en; **to be —d with** estar satisfecho con

pleasing [plízɪŋ] ADJ agradable

pleasure [pléʒə] N placer *m*, gusto *m*, agrado *m*; **— trip** viaje de placer *m*

pleat [plit] N (pleat, fold) pliegue *m*, tabla *f*; (wide) tabla *f*; VT plisar; (wide) tablear

pled [plɛd] *see* plead

pledge [plɛdʒ] N (promise) promesa *f*; (security deposit) prenda *f*; (in a fraternity) miembro provisorio *m*; **as a — of** en prenda de; VI/VT (promise) prometer; VT (give as a deposit) empeñar; **to — one's word** dar la palabra; **to — to secrecy** exigir promesa de discreción

plenary [plénəri] ADJ & N plenario *m*

plentiful [pléntɪfəl] ADJ abundante, copioso

plenty [plénti] N abundancia *f*, **— of time** suficiente tiempo *m*; **that's —** con eso basta

pliable [pláɪəbəl] ADJ (flexible) flexible; (docile) dócil

pliant [plaɪənt] ADJ (flexible) flexible; (docile) dócil

pliers [pláɪəz] N alicates *m pl*, tenazas *f pl*

plight [plaɪt] N aprieto *m*

plod [plɑd] VI (walk) caminar trabajosamente; (work) trabajar laboriosamente

plop [plɑp] VI hacer plaf; VT dejar caer; N plaf *m*

plot [plɑt] N (storyline) trama *f*, argumento *m*; (conspiracy) complot *m*, conspiración *f*; (land) parcela *f*, era *f*; (floor plan) plano *m*; VI/VT (plan secretly) tramar, conspirar, maquinar; VT (make a graph) hacer un gráfico; **to — a course** trazar un curso

plotter [plɑtə] N (one who plots) conspirador -ora *mf*; (device) trazador de gráficos *m*

plover [plóvə] N chorlito *m*

plow [plaʊ] N arado *m*; **—share** reja de arado *f*; VI/VT arar; (uncultivated area) roturar; **to — through** abrirse paso

plowing [pláʊɪŋ] N labranza *f*

pluck [plʌk] VT (a feather, flower) arrancar; (bird) desplumar; (guitar) puntear, pulsar; **to — out/off** desprender; **to — up courage** animarse, cobrar ánimo; N (act of plucking) tirón *m*; (courage) valor *m*

plug [plʌg] N (stopper) tapón *m*; (horse) *pej* penco *m*; (electric) enchufe *m*; (advertisement) mención favorable *f*; (tobacco) rollo *m*; **—-in** (electrical) enchufe *m*; (computer accessory) plug-in *m*; VT (close) tapar; (advertise) hacer una mención favorable de; VI **to — along** no parar; **to — in** enchufar; **to — up** tapar

plum [plʌm] N (fruit) ciruela *f*; **— tree** ciruelo *m*; **that job is a real —** ese trabajo es estupendo

plumage [plúmɪdʒ] N plumaje *m*

plumb [plʌm] N (lead weight) plomada *f*; **— bob** plomada *f*; **to be out of —** no estar a plomo; ADJ (perpendicular) a plomo; ADV (in a vertical direction) a plomo; (completely) completamente; VT (measure depth) sondear; (test for verticality) aplomar; (examine) examinar

plumber [plámə] N plomero -ra *mf*; *Sp* fontanero -ra *mf*

plumbing [plámɪŋ] N (work and trade) plomería *f*; *Sp* fontanería *f*; (system of pipes) cañerías *f pl*

plume [plum] N penacho *m*; VT adornar con plumas

plummet [plámɪt] VI precipitarse; N plomada *f*

plump [plʌmp] ADJ rechoncho, regordete, rollizo; VI/VT **to — down** dejar[se] caer

plunder [plándə] N (act of plundering) pillaje *m*, saqueo *m*; (loot) botín *m*; VI/VT pillar, saquear

plunge [plʌndʒ] VI/VT (into water) zambullir[se], sumergir[se]; (into something solid) hundir[se]; VI (fall) precipitarse; (slope downward) bajar repentinamente; **to — headlong** echarse de cabeza; N zambullida *f*; (rush) salto *m*

plunger [plándʒə] N (for a toilet) desatascador *m*; (of a pump) émbolo *m*

pluperfect [plupə́fɪkt] N pluscuamperfecto *m*

plural [plúrəl] ADJ & N plural *m*

plurality [plurǽlɪdi] N pluralidad *f*

plus [plʌs] PREP más; N (advantage) ventaja *f*; **two — three** dos más tres *m*; **on the — side** en el lado positivo; **— sign** signo de más *m*

plush [plʌʃ] N felpa *f*; ADJ (fabric) afelpado; (hotel) lujoso

plutonium [plutóniəm] N plutonio *m*

ply [plaɪ] VT (use) manejar; (assail with questions) acosar; (navigate a body of water) surcar; VI (travel regularly) recorrer con regularidad; (work steadily) aplicarse; **to — a trade** ejercer un oficio; N (layer of cloth, rubber) capa *f*; (layer of plywood) chapa *f*; **—wood**

madera compensada *f*, contrachapado *m*

pneumatic [numǽbɪk] ADJ neumático

pneumonia [numónjə] N pulmonía *f*

poach [potʃ] VT (eggs) escalfar; VI/VT (game) cazar furtivamente

pocket [pákɪt] N (in clothes) bolsillo *m*; (vein of ore) filón *m*; (on a pool table) tronera *f*; (of air) bache *m*; (of poverty) bolsa *f*; **—book** cartera *f*, Sp bolso *m*; **— book** libro de bolsillo *m*; **—knife** navaja *f*; **— of resistance** foco de resistencia *m*; VT meterse en el bolsillo; (appropriate) embolsar; (knock in a billiard ball) meter en la tronera

pod [pad] N (seed vessel) vaina *f*; (herd of cetaceans) manada *f*

podiatrist [pədáɪətrɪst] N podólogo -ga *mf*

podiatry [pədáɪətri] N podiatría *f*

podium [pódiəm] N podio *m*

poem [póəm] N poema *m*, poesía *f*

poet [póɪt] N poeta *mf*

poetic [poétɪk] ADJ poético; **— justice** justicia divina *f*; N **—s** poética *f*

poetry [pótri] N poesía *f*

poignant [póɪnjant] ADJ conmovedor

poinsettia [pɔɪnsέɾɪə] N flor de Pascua *f*

point [pɔɪnt] N (place) punto *m*; (score, in sports) punto *m*, anotación *f*; (sharp end) punta *f*; **— after touchdown** punto extra *m*; **— guard** (basketball) base *mf*, conductor -ora *mf*, guardia *mf*; **— of origin** punto de origen *m*; **— of view** punto de vista *m*; **it is not to the —** no viene al caso; **I don't see the —** no le veo el sentido; **on the — of** a punto de; ADV **—-blank** a quemarropa; VT (direct finger at) apuntar con, señalar con; (indicate) señalar; **to — at** (with finger) señalar; (with a gun) apuntar hacia; **to — out** señalar, indicar; **to — up** enfatizar

pointed [pɔ́ɪntɪd] ADJ (having a point) puntiagudo; (piercing) agudo; **— arch** arco ojival *m*

pointer [pɔ́ɪntɚ] N (stick) puntero *m*; (on a scale) indicador *m*; (dog) perro de muestra *m*; (advice) consejo *m*

pointless [pɔ́ɪntlɪs] ADJ inútil

poise [pɔɪz] N (balance, steadiness) equilibrio *m*; (dignified bearing) aplomo *m*; **to be —d to** estar listo para; VI/VT equilibrar[se]

poison [pɔ́ɪzən] N veneno *m*, ponzoña *f*; **— ivy** hiedra venenosa *f*; VT envenenar, emponzoñar

poisoning [pɔ́ɪzənɪŋ] N (accidental) intoxicación *f*; (intentional) envenenamiento *m*

poisonous [pɔ́ɪzənəs] ADJ venenoso, ponzoñoso

poke [pok] VT (jab) clavar, pinchar; (stir a fire) atizar; (thrust out, as one's head) asomar; **to — out an eye** sacar un ojo; VI **to — along** andar perezosamente; **to — around** husmear; **to — fun at** burlarse de; **to — into**

meterse en; **to — out** (project) sobresalir; N pinchazo *m*

Poland [pólənd] N Polonia *f*

polar [pólɚ] ADJ polar; **— bear** oso polar *m*

polarity [polǽrɪɾi] N polaridad *f*

polarization [polɚɪzéʃən] N polarización *f*

polarize [póləraɪz] VI/VT polarizar[se]

pole [pol] N (long piece of wood, metal) poste *m*; (for a flag) asta *f*; (for vaulting) pértiga *f*, garrocha *f*; (earth's axis) polo *m*; (for skiing) bastón *m*; **— vault** salto con pértiga *m*

Pole [pol] N polaco -ca *mf*

polemic [polémɪk] ADJ polémico *m*; N polémica *f*

police [polís] N policía *f*; **— car** patrullero *m*; **— dog** perro policía *m*; **— force** cuerpo de policía *m*; **—man** policía *m*; **— officer** oficial de policía *mf*, Am carabinero -ra *mf*; **— operation** Am operativo policial *m*; **— report** parte policial *m*; **— state** estado policíaco *m*; **— station** comisaría de policía *f*; **—woman** policía *f*; VT patrullar

policy [pálɪsi] N (procedure) política *f*; (for insurance) póliza *f*

polio [pólio] N polio *f*

Polish [pólɪʃ] ADJ & N polaco -ca *mf*

polish [pálɪʃ] N (sheen) lustre *m*, refinamiento *m*; (refinement) urbanidad *f*, cultura *f*; (substance for furniture) cera *f*; (substance for shoes) betún *m*; VT (a speech) pulir; (a metal) sacar brillo; (a car) encerar; (shoes) lustrar, embetunar; **to — off** despachar; **to — up** (metal) sacar brillo; (speech) pulir

polite [polátt] ADJ cortés

politeness [poláttnɪs] N cortesía *f*

politic [pálɪtɪk] ADJ diplomático, político

political [políɾɪkəl] ADJ político; **— prisoner** preso -sa político -ca *mf*; **— science** ciencias políticas *f pl*

politically correct [políɾɪklikɚékt] ADJ políticamente correcto

politician [polɪtíʃən] N político -ca *mf*

politics [pálɪtɪks] N política *f*

polka [pótkə] N polca *f*; **— dot** lunar *m*

poll [pol] N (survey) encuesta *f*; **—s** (elections) comicios *m pl*; (voting place) urna *f*; VT (survey) encuestar; (receive votes) obtener; (record vote of) registrar

pollen [pálən] N polen *m*

pollinate [pálənet] VT polinizar

pollute [polút] VI/VT contaminar

pollution [polúʃən] N contaminación *f*

polo [pólo] N polo *m*

polyester [paliéstɚ] N poliéster *m*

polygamy [palígami] N poligamia *f*

polyglot [páliglat] ADJ & N políglota *mf*

polygraph [páligræf] N polígrafo *m*

polymer [páləmɚ] N polímero *m*

polyp [pálɪp] N pólipo *m*

polyunsaturated [paliʌnsǽtʃəreɾɪd] ADJ

poliinsaturado

polyurethane [pɑlijúrəθen] N poliuretano m

pomegranate [pámɪɡrænɪt] N granada f; — **tree** granado m

pomp [pɑmp] N pompa f, boato m, aparato m

pompous [pámpəs] ADJ pomposo, aparatoso

pond [pɑnd] N (natural) charca f; (artificial) estanque m; (for irrigation) balsa f

ponder [pándə-] VI meditar; VT considerar

ponderous [pándə-əs] ADJ enorme

pontoon [pantún] N (on a bridge) pontón m; (on an airplane) flotador m

pony [póni] N póney m; —**tail** colita f, cola de caballo f; VI **to — up** soltar

Ponzi scheme [pánzi skím] N timo en pirámide m pl

poodle [púdl] N caniche m

pool [puɫ] N (puddle of water, blood, etc.) charco m; (swimming place) piscina f, Mex alberca f; (association of competitors) pool m; (game) pool m, billar m; (bets) pozo m; — **table** billar m; — **hall** billar m; VI acumularse; VT combinar fondos

poop [pup] N (part of ship) popa f; (excrement) fam caca f; VI fam hacer caca

poor [pʊr] ADJ (lacking money) pobre; (deficient) malo; **I'm a — cook** no sé cocinar; —**house** asilo para los pobres m; — **little thing** pobrecito -ta mf; N **the** — los pobres

pop [pɑp] VI (balloon) reventar, estallar; (eyes, cork) saltar; **to — in** entrar de paso; VT (make explode) hacer reventar; (take out cork) hacer saltar; (put) meter; (take, as pills) tomar; **to — a question** espetar una pregunta; **to — corn** hacer palomitas; N estallido m, detonación f; —**corn** palomitas f pl; — **music** música popular f; — **quiz** prueba sorpresa f; — **of a cork** taponazo m; —**-up menu** menú emergente m

pope [pop] N papa m

poplar [páplə-] N álamo m, chopo m; — **grove** alameda f

poppy [pápi] N amapola f

popular [pápjələ-] ADJ popular; **he's very — with the ladies** tiene mucho éxito con las mujeres

popularity [pɑpjəlǽɪ ɪDi] N popularidad f

populate [pápjəlet] VT poblar

population [pɑpjəlé fən] N población f

populous [pápjələs] ADJ populoso

porcelain [pɔ́rsəlɪn] N porcelana f

porch [pɔ́rt ʃ] N porche m

porcupine [pɔ́rkjəpaɪn] N puercoespín m

pore [pɔr] N poro m; VI **to — over a book** estudiar detenidamente un libro

pork [pɔrk] N carne de cerdo f; — **chop** chuleta de cerdo f

porn [pɔrn] N porno m

pornography [pɔrnáɡrəfi] N pornografía f

porous [pɔ́rəs] ADJ poroso

porpoise [pɔ́rpəs] N marsopa f

port [pɔrt] N (harbor, computer) puerto m; (wine) oporto m; (left side of ship) babor m; — **city** ciudad portuaria f; —**hole** ojo de buey m; — **of entry** puerto de entrada m

portable [pɔ́rDəbəɫ] ADJ portátil

portal [pɔ́rdl] N portal m (also of Internet)

portent [pɔ́rtɛnt] N (omen) presagio m, agüero m; (marvel, prodigy) portento m

portentous [pɔrtɛ́ntəs] ADJ (ominous) de mal agüero; (prodigious) portentoso

porter [pɔ́rDə-] N mozo -za mf

portfolio [pɔrtfólio] N cartera f

portion [pɔ́rʃən] N porción f; VI **to — out** repartir

portly [pɔ́rtli] ADJ grueso

portrait [pɔ́rtrɪt] N (likeness) retrato m; (printing orientation) orientación vertical f

portray [pɔrtré] VT (draw, describe) retratar; (in a drama) representar

portrayal [pɔrtréəɫ] N (portrait) retrato m; (act of portraying) representación f, caracterización f

Portugal [pɔ́rtʃəɡəɫ] N Portugal m

Portuguese [pɔ́rtʃəɡiz] ADJ & N portugués -esa mf

pose [poz] N (posture) pose f, postura f; (affected attitude) afectación f; VI (sit as a model) posar; (act affectedly) afectar una actitud; VT (to make sit as model) hacer posar; (to present) plantear; **to — as** hacerse pasar por

position [pəzíʃən] N (place) posición f; (job) puesto m, colocación f; (political stance) posicionamiento m; VI situar, colocar; **to — oneself** posicionarse

positive [pázɪDɪv] ADJ positivo; — **proof** prueba certera f; **I am —** estoy seguro

possess [pəzɛ́s] VT poseer

possessed [pəzɛ́st] ADJ (by a spirit) poseído; (by an idea) obsesionado

possession [pəzɛ́ʃən] N posesión f; **to take —** tomar posesión

possessive [pəzɛ́sɪv] ADJ & N posesivo m

possessor [pəzɛ́sə-] N poseedor -ora f

possibility [pɑsəbílɪDi] N posibilidad f

possible [pásəbəɫ] ADJ posible, eventual

post [post] N (pole) poste m; (position) puesto m; (mail) correo m; —**card** tarjeta postal f; —**haste** a la brevedad; —**man** cartero m; —**mark** matasellos m; —**master** director de correos m; —**office** oficina de correos f, casa de correos f; —**-office box** apartado postal m; ADJ — **paid** porte pagado; VT (affix) fijar; (announce) anunciar; (list) poner en lista; (place) apostar, situar; (mail) echar al correo; **keep me —ed** mantenme al tanto

postage [póstɪdʒ] N franqueo m; — **meter** franqueadora f; — **stamp** Sp sello m; Am estampilla f; Mex timbre m

postal [póstl] ADJ postal; **to go** — perpetrar un ataque homicida, volverse loco

postdate [posdét] VT posfechar

poster [póstə] N cartel m, póster m, afiche m; — **child** modelo perfecto m

posterior [pastíriə] ADJ posterior; N trasero m

posterity [pastériti] N posteridad f

postgraduate [postgrǽdʒuit] ADJ de posgrado; N posgrado -da mf

posthumous [pástʃəməs] ADJ póstumo

postnasal [postnézəl] ADJ postnasal

postnatal [postnédl] ADJ posparto; — **care** cuidado posparto m inv

postpartum [postpártəm] ADJ posparto m

postpone [postpón] VT posponer, aplazar

postponement [postpónmənt] N aplazamiento m

postscript [póstskrɪpt] N posdata f

postulate[1] [pástʃəlet] VT postular

postulate[2] [pástʃəlɪt] N postulado m

posture [pástʃə] N (carriage, attitude) postura f; (affectation) afectación f; VI darse aires

postwar period [póstwár pírɪəd] N posguerra f

posy [pózi] N ramillete m

pot [pat] N (vessel) olla f, marmita f; (marijuana) marihuana f; —**hole** bache m; ADJ — **-bellied** panzudo, barrigón

potable [pódəbəl] ADJ potable

potassium [pətǽsiəm] N potasio m

potato [pətédo] N Sp patata f; Am papa f; — **chip** patata/papa frita [a la inglesa] f, chip m

potency [pótnsi] N potencia f

potent [pótnt] ADJ potente

potentate [pótntet] N potentado -da mf

potential [pəténʃəl] ADJ & N potencial m

potion [póʃən] N poción f

potter [pádə] N alfarero -ra mf

pottery [pádəri] N (craft, shop) alfarería f; (objects) cerámica f, objetos de alfarería m pl

pouch [pautʃ] N bolsa f; (for mail) valija f; (for tobacco) petaca f

poultry [póltri] N aves de corral f pl

pounce [pauns] VI saltar; **to** — **upon/on** abalanzarse sobre; **to** — **on an opportunity** no dejar pasar una oportunidad; N salto m

pound [paund] N (unit of weight, British currency) libra f; (place for stray dogs) perrera f; VT (on a door) golpear; (seeds) machacar; (a military target) bombardear; VI (beat) latir con fuerza

pour [pɔr] VT verter; VI (leave en masse) salir en tropel; (rain) llover a cántaros; **to** — **out one's feelings** desahogarse

pout [paut] VI hacer pucheros; N puchero m

poverty [pávə·ɖi] N pobreza f, penuria f; ADJ — **-stricken** indigente

powder [páudə·] N polvo m; (for the face) polvos m pl; (for guns) pólvora f; — **compact** polvera f; — **puff** borla f; **to take a** — poner pies en polvorosa; VI/VT (use powder) empolvar[se]; (pulverize) pulverizar[se]

power [páuə·] N (control, military might) poder m, poderío m; (in physics, in math) potencia f; (physical strength) fuerza f; (energy) energía f; — **of attorney** poder m; — **plant** central eléctrica f; —**-save mode** modo de ahorro de energía m; — **steering** dirección asistida f; — **supply** suministro de energía m; — **surge** sobrecarga de voltaje f; **in** — oficialista; **legislative** —**s** atribuciones legislativas f pl; VI —**ed by gas** movido por gas; **to** — **down** apagar; **to** — **on/up** encender

powerful [páuə·fəl] ADJ poderoso, potente

powerless [páuə·lɪs] ADJ impotente

PR [**public relations**] [piár] N relaciones públicas f pl

practical [prǽktɪkəl] ADJ práctico; — **joke** broma pesada f, chasco m; — **nurse** enfermero -ra sin título mf

practically [prǽktɪkli] ADV prácticamente

practice [prǽktɪs] N (repeated exercise) práctica f; (habit) costumbre f; (doctor's office) consultorio m; (lawyer's office) bufete m; VI/VT practicar; VT (a profession) ejercer; **in** — en la práctica, prácticamente

practiced [prǽktɪst] ADJ experto, perito

practitioner [prǽktíʃənə·] N practicante mf; **general** — médico -ca general mf

pragmatic [prægmǽdɪk] ADJ pragmático

prairie [préri] N pradera f, llanura f

praise [prez] N alabanza f, elogio m; VT alabar, elogiar; —**worthy** loable, encomiable

prance [præns] VI cabriolar, hacer cabriolas; N cabriola f

prank [præŋk] N travesura f, chasco m; **to play** —**s** hacer travesuras

prawn [prɔn] N langostino m; Sp gamba pequeña f

pray [pre] VI/VT (religious) rezar, orar; (beg) rogar, suplicar

prayer [prɛr] N (devout petition to God) oración f, rezo m; (entreaty) ruego m, súplica f

praying mantis [préɪŋmǽntɪs] N mantis religiosa f

preach [pritʃ] VI/VT predicar; (moralize) sermonear

preacher [prítʃə·] N predicador -ora mf

preamble [príæmbəl] N preámbulo m

preapproved [priəprúvd] ADJ preaprobado

precancerous [prikǽnsə·əs] ADJ precanceroso

precarious [prɪkériəs] ADJ precario

precaution [prɪkóʃən] N precaución f

precautionary [prɪkóʃəneri] ADJ preventivo

precede [prisíd] VI/VT preceder

precedence [présɪdəns] N precedencia f, prioridad f

preceding [prisídɪŋ] ADJ precedente, anterior

precept [prísɛpt] N precepto *m*

precinct [prísɪŋkt] N distrito *m*; (police station) comisaría *f*; —**s** límites *m pl*

precious [préʃəs] ADJ precioso; (overly refined) preciosista; — **little** muy poco; — **metal** metal precioso *m*; — **stone** piedra preciosa *f*

precipice [présəpɪs] N precipicio *m*, derrumbadero *m*

precipitate[1] [prɪsípɪtet] VI/VT precipitar[se]

precipitate[2] [prɪsípɪtɪt] ADJ & N precipitado *m*

precipitation [prɪsɪpɪtéʃən] N precipitación *f*

precipitous [prɪsípɪDəs] ADJ (steep) escarpado; (hasty) precipitado

precise [prɪsáɪs] ADJ preciso, exacto

precisely [prɪsáɪsli] ADV & INT precisamente, exactamente

precision [prɪsíʒən] N precisión *f*, exactitud *f*; (of expression) propiedad *f*

preclude [prɪklúd] VT excluir; **that doesn't — our considering your application** esto no obsta para que tengamos en cuenta su solicitud

precocious [prɪkóʃəs] ADJ precoz

precursor [prɪksɚ] N precursor *m*

predator [préDətɚ] N depredador *m*

predatory [préDətɔri] ADJ (animal) depredador; (persona) rapaz

predecessor [prédɪsɛsɚ] N predecesor -ora *mf*, antecesor -ora *mf*

predestine [pridéstɪn] VT predestinar

predetermined [priditɝmɪnd] ADJ predeterminado

predicament [prɪdíkəmənt] N aprieto *m*

predicate[1] [prédɪkɪt] ADJ & N predicado *m*

predicate[2] [prédɪket] VT basar

predict [prɪdíkt] VT predecir

prediction [prɪdíkʃən] N predicción *f*, vaticinio *m*

predilection [prɛdɪlékʃən] N predilección *f*

predispose [pridɪspóz] VI/VT predisponer

predisposition [pridɪspəzíʃən] N predisposición *f*

predominance [prɪdámənəns] N predominio *m*

predominant [prɪdámənənt] ADJ predominante

predominate [prɪdámənet] VI/VT predominar, preponderar

preeclampsia [priìklæmpsiə] N preeclampsia *f*

preexisting [priɪgzístɪŋ] ADJ preexistente

preface [préfɪs] N prefacio *m*, prólogo *m*; VT hacer una introducción; (a book) prologar

prefer [prɪfɝ] VT preferir; **to — a claim** presentar una demanda

preferable [préfɚəbəl] ADJ preferible

preference [préfɚəns] N preferencia *f*

preferential [prɛfɚénʃəl] ADJ preferente

preferred [prɪfɝd] ADJ preferido; — **stocks** acciones preferentes *f pl*

prefix [prífɪks] N prefijo *m*; VT poner un prefijo

pregnancy [prégnənsi] N embarazo *m*; (of an animal) preñez *f*; — **test** prueba de embarazo *f*

pregnant [prégnənt] ADJ (person) embarazada, encinta; (animal) preñada; (full of meaning, rain) preñado, cargado

prehensile [prihénsəl] ADJ prensil

prehistoric [prihɪstɔ́rɪk] ADJ prehistórico

prejudge [pridʒʌ́dʒ] VT prejuzgar

prejudice [prédʒəDɪs] N (bias) prejuicio *m*; (harm) perjuicio *m*; VT (cause bias against) predisponer en contra; (harm) perjudicar

preliminary [prɪlímənɛri] ADJ & N preliminar *m*

prelude [prélud] N preludio *m*; VI/VT preludiar

premarital [primérɪdl] ADJ prematrimonial

premature [primətʃúr] ADJ prematuro; — **birth** parto prematuro *m*

premeditated [priméDɪteDɪd] ADJ premeditado

premenstrual [priménstruəl] ADJ premenstrual

premier [primír] N primer ministro *m*; primera ministra *f*; ADJ principal

premiere [prɪmír] N estreno *m*, première *f*

premise [prémɪs] N premisa *f*; —**s** local *m*

premium [prímiəm] N (bonus) premio *m*; (insurance) prima *f*; (surcharge) recargo *m*; **at a** — muy escaso; ADJ superior

premonition [prɛməníʃən] N premonición *f*

prenatal [prinédl] ADJ prenatal; — **care** atención prenatal *f*, cuidado prenatal *m*

prenuptial [prɪnʌ́pʃəl] ADJ prenupcial; — **agreement** capitulaciones matrimoniales *f pl*

preoccupy [priákjəpaɪ] VT absorber

preowned [priónd] ADJ de segunda mano

prepacked [pripǽkt] ADJ preempacado

prepaid [pripéd] ADJ pagado de antemano; **to send** — enviar porte pagado

preparation [prɛpəréʃən] N (act of preparing) preparación *f*; (substance) preparado *m*; (for a trip) preparativos *m pl*

preparatory [prépɚətɔri] ADJ preparatorio, preparativo

prepare [prɪpér] VI/VT preparar[se]

preponderance [prɪpándəəns] N preponderancia *f*

preponderant [prɪpándəənt] ADJ preponderante

preposition [prɛpəzíʃən] N preposición *f*

preposterous [prɪpástɚəs] ADJ absurdo

prerecorded [pririkɔ́rDɪd] ADJ pregrabado

prerequisite [prirékwəzɪt] N prerequisito *m*

prerogative [prɪrágəDɪv] N prerrogativa *f*

prescribe [prɪskráɪb] VT (order) prescribir; (medicine) recetar

prescription [prɪskrípʃən] N (order) prescripción *f*; (of medicine) receta *f*

presence [prézəns] N presencia *f*; — **of mind** aplomo *m*, presencia de ánimo *f*

present[1] [prézənt] N (time) presente *m*; (gift)

regalo *m*, presente *m*; **at**— ahora; **for the**— por ahora; ADJ (at a place) present; (at this time) actual; — **company excepted** con perdón de los presentes; — **participle** gerundio *m*; — **perfect** pretérito perfecto *m*; —**-day** actual

present² [prɪzént] VT presentar, entregar
presentable [prɪzéntəbəɫ] ADJ presentable
presentation [prɛzəntéʃən] N (act of presenting) presentación *f*, entrega *f*; (speech) ponencia *f*; (exposition) planteamiento *m*
presentiment [prɪzéntəmənt] N presentimiento *m*
presently [prézəntli] ADV (soon) pronto; (now) actualmente
preservation [prɛzɚvéʃən] N preservación *f*, conservación *f*
preservative [prɪzɚ́vədɪv] N conservante *m*
preserve [prɪzɚ́v] VI/VT (protect) preservar; (keep food fresh) conservar; N (for game) coto *m*; (for animals) reserva *f*; —**s** mermelada *f*, dulce *m*
preset [prisét] ADJ preestablecido
preside [prɪzáɪd] VI presidir; **to**— **over a meeting** presidir una reunión
presidency [prézɪDənsi] N presidencia *f*
president [prézɪDənt] N presidente -ta *mf*
presidential [prɛzɪdénʃəɫ] ADJ presidencial
press [prɛs] VI/VT (bear down, squeeze) apretar, oprimir; (a computer key) oprimir, presionar; (iron) planchar; (force) presionar; (extract juice) prensar; (put under pressure) apremiar; **to**— **on** avanzar; **to**— **one's point** insistir en un argumento; **to**— **through** abrirse paso; N (newspapers) prensa *f*; (printing machine) imprenta *f*; (crowding) empuje *m*; — **conference** conferencia de prensa *f*; — **corps** cuerpo de prensa *m*; — **release** comunicado de prensa *m*
pressing [prɛ́sɪŋ] ADJ apremiante, urgente
pressure [prɛ́ʃɚ] N presión *f*; — **cooker** olla a presión *f*; — **gauge** manómetro *m*; — **group** grupo de presión *m*; VT apremiar, presionar
prestige [prɛstíʒ] N prestigio *m*
prestigious [prɛstíʤəs] ADJ prestigioso
presumably [prɪzúməbli] ADV — **he is already prepared** es de suponer que ya esté preparado
presume [prɪzúm] VI (be presumptuous) presumir; VT (suppose) suponer; (dare) atreverse a
presumption [prɪzámpʃən] N presunción *f*
presumptuous [prɪzámptʃuəs] ADJ presuntuoso, presumido
presuppose [prisəpóz] VT presuponer
pretax [priténs] ADJ antes de impuestos
preteen [prɪtín] ADJ & N preadolescente *mf*
pretend [prɪténd] VI/VT (make believe) hacer de cuenta que; (feign) fingir; VT (claim)

pretender; **to**— **to the throne** pretender el trono
pretense [prítɛns] N (faked action or belief) engaño *m*; (false show) apariencia *f*; **under**— **of** so pretexto de
pretension [prɪténʃən] N pretensión *f*; (pretext) pretexto *m*
pretentious [prɪténʃəs] ADJ (full of pretension) pretencioso; (showy) ostentoso
pretext [prítɛkst] N pretexto *m*
pretrial [pritráɫ] ADJ anterior al juicio
pretty [príɾi] ADJ (human only) *Sp* guapo; ADV bastante; — **well** bastante bien, francamente bien; VI/VT **to**— **up** embellecer
prevail [prɪvéɫ] VI (win) prevalecer; (be widespread, dominant) preponderar, imperar; **to**— **on/upon** persuadir
prevailing [prɪvéɫɪŋ] ADJ (opinion) predominante; (feeling) reinante, imperante; — **winds** vientos predominantes
prevalent [prévələnt] ADJ prevaleciente, preponderante
prevent [prɪvént] VT (keep from occurring) prevenir; VI/VT (impede) impedir
prevention [prɪvénʃən] N prevención *f*; (of a disease) prevención *f*, profilaxis *f*
preventive [prɪvéntɪv] ADJ preventivo, cautelar
preview [prívju] N preestreno *m*
previewing [prívjuwɪŋ] N previsualización *f*
previous [prívjəs] ADJ previo, anterior
previously [prívjəsli] ADV previamente, anteriormente
prey [pre] N (animal) presa *f*; VI **to**— **on** (animals) alimentarse de; (people) explotar; **it**—**s upon my mind** me tiene preocupado
price [praɪs] N precio *m*; **at any**— a toda costa; — **control** control de precios *m*; — **fixing** fijación de precios *f*; — **index** índice de precios *m*; — **tag** etiqueta de precio *f*; VT (set price) poner precio a; (ask price) averiguar el precio de
priceless [práɪslɪs] ADJ (without price) invalorable; (amusing) divertidísimo
pricey [práɪsi] ADJ caro
pricing [práɪsɪŋ] N fijación de precios *f*
prick [prɪk] N (puncture) pinchazo *m*; (sharp point) púa *f*; VI/VT pinchar, punzar; **to**— **up one's ears** parar las orejas
prickly [príkli] ADJ espinoso; — **heat** sarpullido causado por el calor *m*; — **pear** tuna *f*, nopal *m*
pride [praɪd] N orgullo *m*; (excessive) soberbia *f*; VI **to**— **oneself on** enorgullecerse de
priest [prist] N sacerdote *m*; (Catholic only) cura *m*
priesthood [prísthʊd] N sacerdocio *m*
prim [prɪm] ADJ remilgado
primarily [praɪmérɪli] ADV principalmente, más que nada

primary [práɪmɛri] N elección primaria *f*; ADJ primario; (main) fundamental, principal; — **care** atención primaria *f*; — **colors** colores primarios *m pl*; — **election** elección primaria *f*; — **school** escuela primaria *f*

primate [práɪmet] N primate *m*

prime [praɪm] ADJ (principal) fundamental; (of a number) primo; (select) de primera; — **minister** primer ministro *m*, primera ministra *f*; N (number) número primo *m*; **to be in one's** — estar en la flor de la edad, estar en la plenitud de la vida; — **rate** tasa prima *f*; VT preparar; (a pump) cebar

primer¹ [prímɚ] N (first book) manual elemental *m*

primer² [práɪmɚ] N (pump part) cebador *m*

primitive [prímɪtɪv] ADJ & N primitivo -va *mf*

prince [prɪns] N príncipe *m*

princely [prínsli] ADJ noble, principesco; **a — sum** una suma muy grande

princess [prínsɛs] N princesa *f*

principal [prínsəpəl] ADJ principal; N (money invested) capital *m*; (giver of power of attorney) poderdante *mf*, mandante *mf*; (head of a school) director -ora *mf*

principle [prínsəpəl] N principio *m*

print [prɪnt] VI/VT imprimir; (write in block letters) escribir en letra de molde; **to — out** imprimir; N (type) letra de imprenta *f*; (of art) lámina *f*; (of photographs) copia *f*; (of finger) huella digital *f*; (on cloth) estampado *m*; **—out** versión impresa *f*; **in —** publicado, en venta; **out of —** agotado

printer [prínta] N (person) impresor -ora *mf*, gráfico -ca *mf*; (machine) impresora *f*; — **driver** controlador de impresora *m*; — **feeder** alimentador de impresora *m*

printing [príntɪŋ] N (art, trade) imprenta *f*; (process) impresión *f*, tipografía *f*; (block letters) letra de molde *f*, letra de imprenta *f*; — **press** imprenta *f*; **this book is in its second —** este libro está en su segunda tirada

prior [práɪɚ] ADJ previo; — **to** anterior a

priority [praɪóɾɪdi] N prioridad *f*; **having —** prioritario

prism [prízəm] N prisma *m*

prison [prízən] N prisión *f*, cárcel *f*, presidio *m*

prisoner [prízənɚ] N (captive) prisionero -ra *mf*; (in jail) preso -sa *mf*, presidiario -ria *mf*; — **of war** prisionero -ra de guerra *mf*

pristine [prɪstín] ADJ (immaculate) puro; (perfect) perfecto

privacy [práɪvasi] N privacidad *f*; — **statement** declaración sobre la privacidad *f*

private [práɪvɪt] ADJ (not public) privado; (individual) particular; — **enterprise** empresa privada *f*; — **eye** detective privado -da *mf*; — **parts** partes pudendas *f pl*; — **property** propiedad privada *f*; **—s** partes pudendas *f pl*; — **school** escuela privada *f*; — **sector** sector privado *m*; **a — citizen** un particular; **in —** en privado; N soldado raso *m*

privation [praɪvéʃən] N privación *f*

privatization [praɪvəbɪzéʃən] N privatización *f*

privatize [práɪvətaɪz] VT privatizar

privilege [prívəlɪdʒ] N privilegio *m*

privileged [prívlɪdʒd] ADJ privilegiado

privy [prívi] ADJ **to be —** estar enterado de; N retrete *m*

prize [praɪz] N (reward) premio *m*; (booty) botín *m*; — **fight** pelea de boxeo profesional *f*; — **fighter** boxeador -ora *mf*, pugilista *mf*; VT apreciar

pro [pro] N profesional *mf*

probability [prabəbílɪdi] N probabilidad *f*

probable [prábəbəl] ADJ probable

probate [próbet] N legalización de una validación testamentaria *f*

probation [probéʃən] N libertad condicional *f*

probationary [probéʃəneri] ADJ probatorio; — **period** período de prueba *m*

probe [prob] VI/VT (explore with a probe) sondear; (examine) examinar; N sonda *f* (also in space); (investigation) indagación *f*

problem [prábləm] N problema *m*; **—s** problemática *f*

procedure [prəsídʒɚ] N procedimiento *m*; (legal) trámite *m*

proceed [prəsíd] VI (originate) proceder; (continue) proseguir, continuar; **to — against** demandar a; **to — to** proceder a

proceeds [prósidz] N ganancia *f*, lo recaudado

proceedings [prəsídɪŋz] N (events) acontecimientos *m pl*; (record of a conference) actas *f pl*, memoria *f*; (legal action) procedimiento *m*

process [práses] N proceso *m*; **in the — of** en vías de

processing [prásesɪŋ] N (of applications) tramitación *f*; (of data, substances) procesamiento *m*; — **power** potencia procesadora *f*

procession [prəséʃən] N procesión *f*

processor [prásesɚ] N procesador *m*

pro-choice [protʃóɪs] ADJ pro-elección

proclaim [proklém] VT proclamar

proclamation [prakləméʃən] N proclamación *f*, proclama *f*

procrastinate [prəkrǽstənet] VI/VT dejar para último momento

procreate [prókriet] VI/VT procrear, engendrar

proctology [praktálədʒi] N proctología *f*

procure [prəkjúr] VT procurar, obtener

prod [prad] VT aguijonear; **they —ded me into going / to go** insistieron en que fuera

prodigal [prádɪgəl] ADJ & N pródigo -ga *mf*

prodigious [prədídʒəs] ADJ prodigioso

prodigy [prádədʒi] N prodigio *m*

produce¹ [pródus] N (vegetables) verduras *f pl*, hortalizas *f pl*

produce² [pradús] VI/VT producir; VT (present) presentar

producer [pradúsə-] N productor -ora *mf*; (of a movie) realizador -ora *mf*

product [prádəkt] N producto *m*

production [pradákʃən] N producción *f*; (TV, radio) producción *f*, realización *f*; (exaggerated situation) teatro *m*

productive [pradáktɪv] ADJ productivo

productivity [pradʌktívɪdi] N productividad *f*

profane [profén] ADJ profano; (vulgar) grosero; VT profanar

profanity [prafǽnɪdi] N groserías *f pl*, palabrotas *f pl*

profess [prafés] VI (publicly accept, take vows) profesar; VT (state) afirmar; (claim) pretender

profession [praféʃən] N profesión *f*

professional [praféʃənəl] ADJ & N profesional *mf*

professor [prafésə-] N profesor -ora universitario -ria *mf*; (full) catedrático -ca *mf*

proffer [práfə-] VT ofrecer; N oferta *f*

proficiency [prafíʃənsi] N competencia *f*

proficient [prafíʃənt] ADJ competente

profile [prófaɪl] N (contour) perfil *m*; **a high-case** un caso muy sonado

profit [práfɪt] N (gain) ganancia *f*; **— and loss** ganancias y pérdidas *f pl*; **— margin** margen de ganancia *m*; **— sharing** participación en las ganancias de una empresa *f*; **at a —** con ganancia; **to turn a —** dar ganancia; **not for —** sin fines de lucro; VI salir ganando; **to — from** (benefit) aprovechar, sacar provecho de; (use to get an advantage) aprovecharse de; VT servir

profitability [prafɪtabílɪdi] N rentabilidad *f*

profitable [práfɪdəbəl] ADJ (beneficial) provechoso; (lucrative) lucrativo, rentable

profound [prafáund] ADJ profundo

profundity [prafándɪdi] N profundidad *f*

profuse [prafjús] ADJ profuso, pródigo

progesterone [prodʒéstəron] N progesterona *f*

prognosis [pragnósɪs] N pronóstico *m*

program [prógræm] N programa *m*; VI/VT programar

programmable [prógræməbəl] ADJ programable

programmer [prógræmə-] N programador -ora *mf*

programming [prógræmɪŋ] N programación *f*; **— language** lenguaje de programación *m*

progress¹ [prágrɛs] N progreso *m*

progress² [pragrés] VI progresar

progression [pragréʃən] N progresión *f*

progressive [pragrésɪv] ADJ (advancing) progresivo; ADJ & N (liberal) progresista *mf*, progresivo -va *mf*

prohibit [prohíbɪt] VT prohibir, vedar

prohibition [proəbíʃən] N prohibición *f*

project¹ [prádʒɛkt] N proyecto *m*

project² [pradʒékt] VI/VT (plan) proyectar[se]; VI (jut out) sobresalir

projectile [pradʒéktaɪl] N proyectil *m*; ADJ arrojadizo

projection [pradʒékʃən] N (plan) proyección *f*; (jut) saliente *f*

projector [pradʒéktə-] N proyector *m*

proletariat [prolɪtériət] N proletariado *m*

pro-life [prolíf] ADJ antiaborto

proliferation [prolɪfəréʃən] N proliferación *f*

prolific [prolífɪk] ADJ prolífico

prologue [prólɔg] N prólogo *m*

prolong [prolɔ́ŋ] VT prolongar

prolongation [prolɔŋéʃən] N prolongación *f*

promenade [pramənéd] N paseo *m*; (dance) baile *m*; VI/VT pasear[se]

prominent [prámənənt] ADJ prominente

promiscuous [pramískjuəs] ADJ promiscuo, liviano

promise [prámɪs] N promesa *f*; **he showed —** prometía mucho; VI/VT prometer

promising [prámɪsɪŋ] ADJ prometedor

promissory [prámɪsɔri] ADJ promisorio; **— note** pagaré *m*

promontory [práməntɔri] N promontorio *m*

promote [pramót] VT (foster) promover, fomentar; (advance in rank) ascender; (in school) pasar de año, promover; (advertise) promocionar

promoter [pramódə-] N (fomenter) propulsor -ora *mf*; (organizer) promotor -ora *mf*

promotion [pramóʃən] N (act of promoting) promoción *f*; (advance in rank) ascenso *m*

promotional [pramóʃənl] ADJ promocional

prompt [prampt] ADJ (quick) rápido; (punctual) puntual; VT (cause) inducir; (in theater) apuntar; **to give someone a —** apuntarle a alguien

promptly [prámptli] ADV (soon) pronto; (punctually) puntualmente

promulgate [práməlget] VT promulgar

prone [pron] ADJ (disposed) propenso, proclive; (face down) boca abajo; (prostrate) postrado

prong [prɔŋ] N púa *f*, diente *m*

pronoun [prónaun] N pronombre *m*

pronounce [pranáuns] VT (enunciate) pronunciar; (declare) declarar

pronounced [pranáunst] ADJ pronunciado

pronouncement [pranáunsmənt] N pronunciamiento *m*

pronunciation [prənʌnsiéʃən] N pronunciación *f*

proof [pruf] N (evidence, test, trial printing) prueba *f*; (of alcohol) graduación *f*, grado *m*; **— of purchase** comprobante de compra *m*; **—reader** corrector -ora de pruebas *mf*, revisor -ora de pruebas *mf*; **fifty —**

veinticinco por ciento de graduación alcohólica; **fire—** a prueba de incendios; **water—** impermeable; **bullet—** a prueba de balas

prop [prɑp] N (pole) puntal *m*; (in theater) accesorio *m*; (propeller) hélice *f*; (support) sostén *m*, apoyo *m*; (of a plant) tutor *m*; VT **to — against** apoyar en, sostener en; **to — up** apuntalar, sostener

propaganda [prɑpəɡǽndə] N propaganda *f*

propagate [prɑ́pəɡet] VI/VT propagar[se]

propagation [prɑpəɡéʃən] N propagación *f*

propane [própen] N propano *m*

propel [prəpɛ́l] VT propulsar, impulsar

propeller [prəpɛ́lə] N hélice *f*

propensity [prəpɛ́nsɪDi] N propensión *f*

proper [prɑ́pə] ADJ (appropriate) apropiado; (decorous) decoroso; (genuine) como Dios manda; (correct) correcto; (in math, grammar) propio; **to be — to** ser propio de

properly [prɑ́pə-li] ADV (appropriately) apropiadamente; (correctly) correctamente; (decorously) decorosamente

property [prɑ́pə-Di] N (characteristic) propiedad *f*; (real estate) propiedad *f*, finca *f*; (assets) bienes *m pl*; **— damage** daños materiales *m pl*

prophecy [prɑ́fɪsi] N profecía *f*

prophesy [prɑ́fɪsaɪ] VI/VT profetizar

prophet [prɑ́fɪt] N profeta -tisa *mf*

prophetic [prəfɛ́Dɪk] ADJ profético

propitious [prəpíʃəs] ADJ propicio

proponent [prəpónənt] N (person who proposes) proponente *mf*; (adherent) defensor -ora *mf*

proportion [prəpɔ́rʃən] N proporción *f*; **out of —** desproporcionado; VT proporcionar; **well —ed** bien proporcionado

proportional [prəpɔ́rʃənl] ADJ proporcional

proportionate [prəpɔ́rʃənɪt] ADJ proporcional

proposal [prəpózəl] N (suggestion) propuesta *f*; (of marriage, dishonest) proposición *f*

propose [prəpóz] VI/VT (suggest) proponer; VI (ask in marriage) declararse, hacer una propuesta de matrimonio; **to — to do something** proponerse hacer algo

proposition [prɑpəzíʃən] N proposición *f*; VT hacer proposiciones deshonestas

proprietor [prəpráɪIDə] N propietario -ria *mf*

propriety [prəpráɪIDi] N decoro *m*

propulsion [prəpʌ́lʃən] N propulsión *f*

prorate [prorét] VT prorratear

prosaic [prozéɪk] ADJ prosaico

prose [proz] N prosa *f*

prosecute [prɑ́sɪkjut] VI/VT (take to court) procesar, enjuiciar; VT (pursue) llevar adelante

prosecution [prɑsɪkjúʃən] N (act of prosecuting) procesamiento *m*; (officials who prosecute) ministerio público *m*, fiscalía *f*

prosecutor [prɑ́sɪkjuDə] N fiscal *mf*

proselytize [prɑ́səlɪtaɪz] VT convertir; VI buscar ganar prosélitos

prospect [prɑ́spɛkt] N (outlook, possibility) perspectiva *f*, expectativa *f*; (candidate) candidato -ta *mf*; (possible client) posible cliente -ta *mf*; VT prospectar; VI **to — for** buscar

prospective [prəspɛ́ktɪv] ADJ posible, potencial

prospector [prɑ́spɛktə] N prospector -ora *mf*

prosper [prɑ́spə] VI prosperar

prosperity [prɑspɛ́rɪDi] N prosperidad *f*, bonanza *f*

prosperous [prɑ́spərəs] ADJ próspero

prostate [prɑ́stet] N próstata *f*; **— gland** próstata *f*

prosthesis [prɑsθísɪs] N prótesis *f*

prostitute [prɑ́stɪtut] N prostituto -ta *mf*; VT prostituir

prostitution [prɑstɪtúʃən] N prostitución *f*

prostrate [prɑ́stret] VT postrar; ADJ (lying flat, overcome) postrado; (lying face down) boca abajo

protagonist [protǽɡənɪst] N protagonista *mf*

protect [prətɛ́kt] VI/VT proteger, amparar

protection [prətɛ́kʃən] N protección *f*

protectionist [prətɛ́kʃənɪst] ADJ & N proteccionista *mf*

protective [prətɛ́ktɪv] ADJ protector

protector [prətɛ́ktə] N protector -ora *mf*

protectorate [prətɛ́ktərɪt] N protectorado *m*

protégé, protégée [próDəʒe] N protegido -da *mf*

protein [prótin] N proteína *f*

protest¹ [prótɛst] N protesta *f*, reclamación *f*

protest² [prətɛ́st] VI/VT protestar, reclamar

Protestant [prɑ́dɪstənt] ADJ & N protestante *mf*

protestation [protəstéʃən] N declaración *f*

protocol [próDəkɔl] N protocolo *m*

proton [prótɑn] N protón *m*

protoplasm [próDəplæzəm] N protoplasma *m*

prototype [próDətaɪp] N prototipo *m*

protozoan [proDəzóən] N protozoario *m*

protract [protrǽkt] VT prolongar

protrude [protrúd] VI sobresalir, proyectarse

protuberance [prətúbərəns] N protuberancia *f*

proud [praud] ADJ orgulloso; (haughty) soberbio; **to be — of** enorgullecerse de, ufanarse de

prove [pruv] VT (demonstrate, verify) probar, demostrar; VI resultar; **events have —d me right** los hechos me han dado la razón

proverb [právɚb] N proverbio *m*, refrán *m*

provide [prəváɪd] VT (furnish) proveer, proporcionar; (supply) abastecer, aportar; (stipulate) estipular, prevenir; VI **to — for** (support) mantener; (stipulate) estipular; **to — with** proveer de, proporcionar; CONJ **—d [that]** con tal [de] que, siempre que

providence [práviɒəns] N providencia f
provider [prəváiɒə] N (supplier) proveedor -ora
mf; (breadwinner) sostén m
province [právins] N (area) provincia f;
(competence) competencia f
provincial [prəvínʃəl] ADJ (of a province)
provincial; (rustic) provinciano, pueblerino;
N provinciano -na mf
provision [prəvíʒən] N (act of providing, thing
provided) provisión f, suministro m,
prestación f; (precaution) medida f,
precaución f; (clause) estipulación f,
prevención f; —s provisiones f pl, víveres m
pl, bastimentos m pl, suministros m
provisional [prəvíʒənl] ADJ provisional
proviso [prəváizo] N condición f, estipulación f
provocation [pravəkéʃən] N provocación f
provoke [prəvók] VT provocar
provost [próvost] N vicerrector -ora mf
prow [prau] N proa f
prowess [práuis] N valentía f
prowl [praul] VI/VT rondar en acecho
proximity [praksímiɒi] N proximidad f
proxy [práksi] N (person) apoderado -da mf;
(power of attorney) poder m; **by —** por poder
prude [prud] N mojigato -ta mf, gazmoño -ña mf
prudence [prúdns] N prudencia f
prudent [prúdnt] ADJ prudente
prudery [prúdəri] N mojigatería f, gazmoñería f
prudish [prúdiʃ] ADJ mojigato, gazmoño
prune [prun] N ciruela pasa f; VI/VT podar
pry [prai] VT curiosear; **to — into** entrometerse;
to — open abrir por la fuerza; **to — a secret
out** extraer/arrancar un secreto
pseudonym [súdṇim] N pseudónimo/
seudónimo m
psoriasis [səráiəsis] N psoriasis/soriasis f
psych [saik] VT **to — out** intimidar
psicológicamente
psychedelic [saikədélik] ADJ psicodélico/
sicodélico
psychiatrist [saikáiətrist] N psiquiatra/siquiatra
mf
psychiatry [saikáiətri] N psiquiatría/siquiatría f
psychic [sáikik] ADJ psíquico/síquico; N médium
mf, psíquico -ca / síquico -ca mf
psychoanalysis [saikoénəlaiz] N psicoanálisis/
sicoanálisis m
psychological [saikəládʒikəl] ADJ psicológico/
sicológico
psychologist [saikáləʤist] N psicólogo -ga /
sicólogo -ga mf
psychology [saikáləʤi] N psicología/sicología f
psychopath [sáikəpæθ] N psicópata/sicópata mf
psychosis [saikósis] N psicosis/sicosis f
psychosomatic [saikosəmæɒik] ADJ
psicosomático/sicosomático
psychotherapy [saikoθérəpi] N psicoterapia/
sicoterapia f

psychotic [saikáɒik] ADJ psicótico/sicótico
puberty [pjúbə-ɒi] N pubertad f
pubic [pjúbik] ADJ púbico; **— hair** pelo púbico m
public [páblik] ADJ público; **— domain** dominio
público m; **— health** salud pública f; **—
relations** relaciones públicas f pl; **— school**
escuela pública f; **— service** servicio público
m; **to go —** proceder a la venta pública de
acciones, salir a bolsa; N público m
publication [pablikéʃən] N publicación f
publicity [pablísiɒi] N publicidad f, propaganda
f; **— campaign** campaña publicitaria f
publicize [páblisaiz] VT promocionar
publish [pábliʃ] VI/VT publicar, editar; **—ing
house** [casa] editorial f
publisher [pábliʃə-] N editor -ora mf
puck [pʌk] N puck m
pucker [pákə-] VI/VT fruncir[se]; N frunce m
pudding [púdiŋ] N budín m, pudín m
puddle [pádḷ] N charco m
pudendum [pjudéndəm] N partes pudendas f pl
Puerto Rican [pɔrdəríkən] ADJ & N
puertorriqueño -ña f
Puerto Rico [pɔrdəríko] N Puerto Rico m
puff [pʌf] N (air) resoplido m, soplo m; (smoke)
bocanada f; (on a cigarette) pitada f, chupada
f; (of a sleeve) bullón m; **— pastry** masa de
hojaldre f; VI (blow) resoplar; (breathe hard)
jadear; (smoke a cigarette) echar bocanadas;
to — up hincharse; **to — up with pride**
henchirse de orgullo
pug [pʌg] N dogo m; **— nose** nariz chata f
puke [pjuk] VI/VT vomitar, lanzar; N vómito m
pull [pul] VI/VT (tug) tirar, jalar; (extract)
arrancar, extraer; (stretch) estirar; (injure)
desgarrar; **to — apart** destrozar; **to — down**
(demolish) demoler; (earn) sacar; **to — for**
hinchar por; **to — off** conseguir; **to —
oneself together** calmarse; **to — over**
parar; **to — up** parar; **to — through**
salvarse; **to — strings** mover palancas; **to —
out** (leave a place) salir; (back out) retirarse;
the train —ed into the station el tren
entró a la estación; N (act of pulling) tirón m;
(force) fuerza f; (influence) influencia f;
(injury) desgarro m; **—-down menu** menú
abatible m
pullet [púlit] N polla f
pulley [púli] N polea f, carrucha f
pulmonary [pálmənɛri] ADJ pulmonar
pulp [pʌlp] N (of paper, wood, fruit) pulpa f; (of
grape, sugarcane, olive, etc.) bagazo m
pulpit [púlpit] N púlpito m
pulsar [pálsɑr] N púlsar m
pulsate [pálset] VI latir
pulse [pʌls] N pulso m; (single pulsation, act of
pulsing) pulsación f
pulverize [pálvəraiz] VT pulverizar[se]
puma [pjúmə] N puma f

pumice [pʌ́mɪs] N piedra pómez f

pump [pʌmp] N bomba f; (shoe) zapatilla f, zapato escotado m; (for gasoline) surtidor m; VI/VT bombear; (inflate) inflar; **to — someone for information** sonsacar [información] a alguien

pumpkin [pʌ́mpkɪn] N calabaza f

pun [pʌn] N juego de palabras m, retruécano m; VI hacer juegos de palabras

punch [pʌntʃ] N (blow) puñetazo m; (drink) ponche m; (drill) sacabocados m sg; (force) fuerza f, empuje m; **— bowl** ponchera f; **— line** remate de un chiste m; VI/VT (hit) dar un puñetazo; VT (drive cattle) arriar; (make a hole) agujerear; **to — in/out** marcar tarjeta

punctual [pʌ́ŋktʃuəl] ADJ puntual

punctuality [pʌŋktʃuǽlɪDi] N puntualidad f

punctuate [pʌ́ŋktʃuet] VI/VT puntuar; (interrupt) interrumpir; (accentuate) salpicar

punctuation [pʌŋktʃuéʃən] N puntuación f

puncture [pʌ́ŋktʃɚ] VI/VT pinchar[se]; Mex ponchar[se]; **—d tire** neumático pinchado m; N (action of perforating) perforación f; (hole) pinchazo m; **— wound** herida perforada f

pundit [pʌ́ndɪt] N experto -ta mf

pungent [pʌ́ndʒənt] ADJ (acrid) acre; (sarcastic) mordaz

punish [pʌ́nɪʃ] VT castigar, penar

punishment [pʌ́nɪʃmənt] N castigo m

punitive [pjúnɪDɪv] ADJ punitivo; **— damages** daños punitivos m pl

punk [pʌŋk] N (inexperienced boy) mocoso m; (hoodlum) gamberro m; (rock) punk m; (punker) punkero -ra mf

punt [pʌnt] N (kick) patada de despeje f; (boat) balsa f; VI/VT despejar; VI andar en balsa

punter [pʌ́ntɚ] N despejador m

puny [pjúni] ADJ endeble

pupil [pjúpəl] N (student) escolar mf; (part of eye) pupila f, niña f

puppet [pʌ́pɪt] N títere m, monigote m; **— show** teatro de títeres m

puppy [pʌ́pi] N cachorro m

purchase [pɝ́tʃəs] VI/VT comprar, adquirir; N compra f; (hold) asidero m; **— order** orden de compra f; **— price** precio de compra m

purchaser [pɝ́tʃəsɚ] N comprador mf

purchasing [pɝ́tʃəsɪŋ] N compra f; **— agent** agente de compras mf; **— power** poder adquisitivo m

pure [pjʊr] ADJ puro; ADJ & N **—bred** purasangre m

puree [pjuré] N puré m

purgative [pɝ́gəDɪv] ADJ & N purgante m

purgatory [pɝ́gətɔri] N purgatorio m

purge [pɝdʒ] VI/VT purgar[se]; N purga f

purify [pjúrəfaɪ] VI/VT purificar[se], depurar[se]

purist [pjúrɪst] N purista mf

puritanical [pjʊrɪtǽnɪkəl] ADJ puritano

purity [pjúrɪDi] N pureza f

purple [pɝ́pəl] N morado m, púrpura f; ADJ morado, púrpura

purport¹ [pɝ́pɔrt] N (meaning) significado m; (purpose) propósito m

purport² [pɚpórt] VT pretender

purpose [pɝ́pəs] N propósito m, objetivo m; **on — adrede**, a propósito

purr [pɝ] N ronroneo m (also motors); VI ronronear

purse [pɝs] N bolso m, cartera f; VT **to — one's lips** fruncir los labios

pursuant [pɚsúənt] ADV LOC **— to** conforme a, de acuerdo con

pursue [pɚsú] VT (follow) perseguir; (strive) dedicarse a; (continue) continuar con; (practice a profession) ejercer

pursuer [pɚsúɚ] N perseguidor -ora mf

pursuit [pɚsút] N (chase) persecución f, seguimiento m, acoso m; (striving for) búsqueda f; (pastime) pasatiempo m; (practice) ejercicio m; **in — of** (chasing) detrás de; (striving for) en busca de

pus [pʌs] N pus m

push [pʊʃ] VI/VT (shove) empujar; VT (pressure) presionar, promover; (sell drugs) camellear; **to — a button** apretar un botón; VI (in childbirth) pujar; **to — aside/away** apartar; **to — forward** abrirse paso, avanzar; **to — open** abrir de un empujón; **to — through** hacer pasar; N empujón m; (military) ofensiva f; **—up** lagartija f; ADJ **—-button** de botones

pusher [pʊ́ʃɚ] N camello mf

pushy [pʊ́ʃi] ADJ insistente

pussy [pʊ́si] N minino m, gatito m; **— willow** sauce m

put [pʊt] VT poner, colocar; **to — a question** plantear una pregunta; **to — across** expresar; **to — away** guardar; **to — down** (write down) apuntar; (suppress) sofocar; (attribute) atribuir; (humiliate) humillar; (make a down payment) hacer un depósito; (a pet) sacrificar; **to — into** meter; **to — into words** expresar, decir; **to — in writing** poner por escrito; **to — off** (postpone) aplazar, posponer; (perturb) desagradar; (dissuade) disuadir; **to — on** ponerse; **to — on airs** darse tono; **to — on weight** engordar; **to — out** (extinguish) apagar, extinguir; (annoy) molestar; **to — the blame** echar la culpa; **to — to sea** echar al mar; **to — to sleep** sacrificar; **to — up** (construct) levantar; (lodge) alojar; **to — up for sale** poner a la venta; **to — up with** aguantar; **I felt —upon** sentí que se habían aprovechado de mí; N **—option** opción de venta f; **—-down** insulto m

putrid [pjútrɪd] ADJ putrefacto

putt [pʌt] VI/VT potear; N pat
putter [pʌ́də] VI entretenerse; N (golf) putter m
putty [pʌ́di] N masilla f; VT rellenar con masilla
puzzle [pʌ́zəl] N (jigsaw) rompecabezas m sg; (riddle) acertijo m; (problem) enigma m; (crossword) crucigrama m; VT dejar perplejo, desconcertar; VI **to — out** desentrañar; **to — over** meditar sobre; **to be —d** estar perplejo
pygmy [pígmi] N pigmeo -a mf
pylon [páɪlan] N pilón m
pyramid [pírəmɪd] N pirámide f
pyromania [paɪroméniə] N piromanía f
pyromaniac [paɪroméniæk] N pirómano -na mf
pyrotechnics [paɪrətéknɪks] N pirotecnia f
python [páɪθan] N pitón mf

Qq

Qatar [kətár] N Qatar m
Qatari [kətári] ADJ & N catarí mf
quack [kwæk] N (sound of duck) graznido m; (charlatan) matasanos mf, charlatán -ana mf; ADJ charlatán; VI graznar
quadrilateral [kwadrəlǽDəəɫ] ADJ & N cuadrilátero m
quadriplegic [kwadrəplídʒɪk] ADJ & N tetraplégico -ca mf
quadruped [kwádrəped] ADJ & N cuadrúpedo m
quadruplet [kwadrúplɪt] N cuatrillizo -za mf
quagmire [kwǽgmaɪr] N (bog) cenagal m, atascadero m; (crisis) atolladero m, atascadero m
quail [kweɫ] N codorniz f
quaint [kwent] ADJ pintoresco
quake [kwek] N (instance of quaking) temblor m; (earthquake) terremoto m; VI temblar
qualification [kwaləfɪkéʃən] N (for a race) clasificación f; (requirement) requisito m; **without —** sin reservas
qualify [kwáləfaɪ] VT (characterize) calificar; (moderate) moderar; (provide with credentials) capacitar; VI (for a race) clasificarse; (for a position) estar capacitado
qualifying [kwáləfaɪɪŋ] ADJ calificativo
qualitative [kwáliteDɪv] ADJ cualitativo
quality [kwáliDi] N (characteristic) cualidad f; (excellence) calidad f; **— control** control de calidad m
qualm [kwɑm] N escrúpulo m
quantify [kwántəfaɪ] VT cuantificar
quantitative [kwántiteDɪv] ADJ cuantitativo
quantity [kwántiDi] N cantidad f
quantum mechanics [kwántəmmək kǽnɪks] N mecánica cuántica f
quarantine [kwárəntin] N cuarentena f; VT poner en cuarentena

quarrel [kwórəl] N riña f, rencilla f; VI reñir, pelear
quarrelsome [kwórəlsəm] ADJ pendenciero
quarry [kwóri] N (stone) cantera f; (game) presa f; VT explotar
quart [kwort] N cuarto de galón [0.9463 litros] m
quarter [kwórDə] N (one-fourth) cuarto m, cuarta parte f; (coin) moneda de 25 centavos f; (of a sporting match) tiempo m; (of a calendar or school year) trimestre m; (district) barrio m; **—back** mariscal de campo m; **—master general** intendente mf; **— note** negra f; **—s** alojamiento m; **from all —s** de todas partes; **to give no — to the enemy** no dar cuartel al enemigo; ADJ cuarto; VT (divide) cuartear, dividir en cuartos; (execute) descuartizar; (lodge troops) acuartelar, acantonar
quarterly [kwórDəli] ADV trimestralmente; ADJ trimestral; N publicación trimestral f
quartet [kwortét] N cuarteto m
quartz [kworts] N cuarzo m
quasar [kwézar] N cuásar m, quásar m
quash [kwaʃ] VT (a rebellion) sofocar; (a decision) anular
quaver [kwévə] VI temblar; N temblor m; (in music) trémolo m
queasy [kwízi] ADJ nauseoso
queen [kwin] N reina f
queer [kwir] ADJ (strange) raro; (eccentric) excéntrico; **to feel —** sentirse raro; VT comprometer
quell [kwel] VT (suppress) reprimir, sofocar; (calm) calmar
quench [kwentʃ] VT (flames, thirst) apagar; (passions) aplacar, apagar
query [kwíri] N (question) pregunta f; (question mark) signo de interrogación m; (doubt) duda f; VT (ask) preguntar; (question) expresar dudas; (mark with a question mark) marcar con signo de interrogación
quest [kwest] N búsqueda f
question [kwéstʃən] N (thing asked) pregunta f; (issue) cuestión f; **— mark** signo de interrogación m; **beyond —** fuera de duda; **that is out of the —** ¡ni pensarlo! VT (ask) preguntar; (interrogate) interrogar; (call into doubt) dudar, cuestionar
questionable [kwéstʃənəbəl] ADJ (doubtful) cuestionable, discutible; (morally dubious) equívoco
questioner [kwéstʃənə] N interrogador -ora mf
questioning [kwéstʃənɪŋ] N interrogatorio m; ADJ (asking) interrogador; (doubting) cuestionador
questionnaire [kwestʃənér] N cuestionario m
queue [kju] N cola f, fila f; VT poner en la cola
quibble [kwíbəl] VI (split hairs) sutilizar; (evade) evadir; (argue) andar en dimes y diretes; N

(hairsplitting) sutileza *f*; (evasion) evasiva *f*

quiche [kiʃ] N quiche *f*

quick [kwɪk] ADJ rápido, pronto; **—-tempered** irascible, geniudo; **—-witted** agudo; ADV rápido; N (flesh under nails) carne viva *f*; (the living) los vivos; **to cut to the —** herir en lo vivo; **—sand** arena movediza *f*; **—silver** mercurio *m*, azogue *m*

quicken [kwíkən] VI/VT (speed up) acelerar[se], aligerar[se]; (liven) avivar[se]

quickly [kwíkli] ADV deprisa, de prisa

quickness [kwíknɪs] N (speed) rapidez *f*; (of wit) agudeza *f*

quiet [kwáɪt] ADJ (not noisy) silencioso; (not talking) callado; (restrained) tranquilo; (peaceful, still) reposado; **be —!** ¡silencio! ¡cállate! N (freedom from noise) silencio *m*; (tranquility) tranquilidad *f*, sosiego *m*; VT (make quiet) acallar; (make tranquil) sosegar, tranquilizar, serenar; VI **to — down** calmarse

quietly [kwáɪtli] ADV (talk) en voz baja; (walk) silenciosamente; **they — went about buying up shares** fueron comprando acciones sin llamar la atención

quill [kwɪl] N (feather) pluma *f*; (hollow base of feather) cañón *m*; (spine on a porcupine) púa *f*

quilt [kwɪlt] N colcha de retazos *f*; VI/VT hacer una colcha de retazos

quinine [kwáɪnaɪn] N quinina *f*

quip [kwɪp] N ocurrencia *f*; VI decir ocurrencias

quirk [kwɝk] N excentricidad *f*

quit [kwɪt] VT (a competition) abandonar; (a place) irse de, salir de; (a job) dejar; (a computer program) salir; **to call it —s** abandonar; **to — smoking** dejar de fumar; VI (withdraw) abandonar; (stop) parar; (resign) renunciar

quite [kwaɪt] ADV (very) bastante; (entirely) del todo, enteramente; **— a person** una persona admirable; **— a lot** bastante; **it's — the fashion** está muy de moda

quiver [kwívɚ] VI temblar; N (shake) temblor *m*; (sheath for arrows) carcaj *m*, aljaba *f*

quiz [kwɪz] N (test) prueba *f*; (show) concurso *m*; VI (give a quiz) examinar, poner una prueba; (interrogate) interrogar

quota [kwóɾə] N cuota *f*

quotation [kwotéʃən] N cita *f*; (of a price) cotización *f*; **— marks** comillas *f pl*

quote [kwot] VI/VT (words) citar; (prices) cotizar; **to — from** citar a; N (of words) cita *f*; (of a price) cotización *f*; **in —s** entre comillas

quotient [kwóʃənt] N cociente *m*

Rr

R & D [research and development] [árndí] N ID *mf*

rabbi [ræbaɪ] N rabino *m*

rabbit [ræbɪt] N conejo *m*

rabble [ræbəl] N chusma *f*, plebe *f*, gentuza *f*

rabid [ræbɪd] ADJ rabioso

rabies [rébiz] N rabia *f*

raccoon [rækún] N mapache *m*

race [res] N (lineage) raza *f*; (competition) carrera *f*; **—horse** caballo de carreras *m*; **—track** (for runners) pista *f*; (for horses) hipódromo *m*; VI (participate in competition) correr, competir en una carrera; (hurry) ir corriendo; (of heart) latir rápido; (of a motor) acelerar; VT (a horse) hacer correr; (an engine) acelerar; **I'll — you** te echo una carrera

racer [résɚ] N corredor -ora *mf*; (horse) caballo de carreras *m*

racial [réʃəl] ADJ racial

racism [résɪzəm] N racismo *m*

rack [ræk] N (for clothes) perchero *m*; (for luggage) baca *f*; (for spices) especiero *m*; (for towels) toallero *m*; (for torture) potro de tormento *m*; **— and pinion** cremallera *fy* piñón *m*; VT **to be —ed with pain** estar transido de dolor; **to — one's brain** devanarse los sesos; **to — up** acumular

racket [rækɪt] N (sports) raqueta *f*; (noise of an impact) estrépito *m*, estruendo *m*; (noise of voices and movement) barahúnda *f*, batahola *f*; (swindle) estafa *f*; (extortion) extorsión *f*

racketeer [rækitír] N (swindler) trapacero -ra *mf*, estafador -ora *mf*; (extortionist) extorsionista *mf*; VI (swindle) estafar; (extort) extorsionar

radar [réɖar] N radar *m*

radial [rédiəl] ADJ radial

radiance [rédiəns] N resplandor *m*, fulgor *m*

radiant [rédiənt] ADJ radiante, resplandeciente

radiate [rédiet] VI/VT irradiar, radiar

radiation [rediéʃən] N radiación *f*; **— sickness** enfermedad por radiación *f*; **— therapy** radioterapia *f*

radiator [rédieɖɚ] N radiador *m*

radical [ræɖɪkəl] ADJ & N radical *mf*

radicalism [rædikəlɪzəm] N radicalismo *m*

radio [rédio] N (device, system of communication) radio *f*; **— announcer** locutor -ora *mf*; **— listener** radioescucha *mf*; **— station** radiodifusora *f*; **— telescope** radiotelescopio *m*; **— transmitter** radiotransmisor *m*; **by —** por radio; ADJ **—active** radiactivo, radioactivo; VT (broadcast) transmitir por radio; VI/VT (call) llamar por radio

radiologist [reDiálə₃Ist] N radiólogo -ga *mf*

radiology [reDiálə₃i] N radiología *f*

radish [rǽDIʃ] N rábano *m*

radium [rédiəm] N radio *m*

radius [rédiəs] N radio *m*

radon [rédan] N radón *m*

raffle [rǽfəl] N rifa *f*, sorteo *m*; VI rifar, sortear

raft [ræft] N balsa *f*

rafter [rǽftɚ] N viga *f*

rag [ræg] N (piece of cloth) trapo *m*, guiñapo *m*; (on clothes) harapo *m*, andrajo *m*; — **doll** muñeca de trapo *f*

rage [red₃] N ira *f*, rabia *f*, cólera *f*; **to be all the** — estar de moda; VI enfurecerse; **to** — **with anger** bramar de ira

ragged [rǽgɪd] ADJ (ill-clothed) andrajoso, harapiento, desharrapado; (voice) ronco, roto; (on an edge) irregular, desigual; **to be on the** — **edge** estar al borde

raid [red] N (military) incursión *f*; (by police) allanamiento *m*, redada *f*; (by air) bombardeo aéreo *m*; VI/VT hacer una incursión; VT (attack) atacar; (rob) asaltar; (carry out a police operation on) allanar

raider [rédɚ] N empresa tiburón *f*

rail [rel] N (of a railroad track) riel *m*, carril *m*; (on a balcony) baranda *f*, barandilla *f*; — **fence** barrera *f*; —**road** ferrocarril *m*; —**road company** empresa ferroviaria *f*; —**road crossing** cruce de ferrocarril *m*; —**road employee** ferroviario -ria *mf*; —**way** ferrocarril *m*; **by** — por ferrocarril; VT **to** —**road** (goods) transportar por ferrocarril; (laws) hacer aprobar apresuradamente; (a person) condenar injustamente

railing [rélɪŋ] N (barrier) baranda *f*; (on a bridge) pretil *m*; (on a stairway) pasamano *m*

rain [ren] N lluvia *f*; —**bow** arco iris *m*; —**coat** impermeable *m*; —**drop** gota de lluvia *f*; —**fall** precipitación *f*; — **forest** selva tropical *f*; — **gauge** pluviómetro *f*; —**storm** temporal de lluvia *f*; — **water** agua llovediza *f*; VI/VT llover; — **or shine** llueva o truene; **to** — **cats and dogs** llover a cántaros

rainy [réni] ADJ lluvioso

raise [rez] VI/VT (voice, hand, a house, spirits) levantar[se]; VT (an alarm) dar; (funds) recaudar, captar; (a salary) aumentar; (a flag) izar; (crops) cultivar; (animals, children) criar; (money) recabar, recaudar; **to** — **a question** plantear una pregunta; **to** — **a racket** armar un alboroto; N aumento *m*

raisin [rézɪn] N pasa [de uva] *f*

rake [rek] N rastrillo *m*; VI/VT rastrillar; **to** — **in money** amasar dinero

rally [rǽli] VI/VT (reorganize troops) reunir[se],

juntar[se]; (inspire) reanimar; VI (demonstrate) concentrarse; (recuperate) recuperarse; (reinvigorate) recobrar ánimo; (rise in value) repuntar; (in tennis) pelotear; **to** — **around someone** apoyar a alguien; N (demonstration) concentración *f*; (recovery) recuperación *f*; (rise in prices) subida *f*; (in tennis) peloteo *m*

RAM [random-access memory] [ræm] N RAM *m*

ram [ræm] N (male sheep) carnero *m*; (tool for battering) ariete *m*; (part of a ship) espolón *m*; VT chocar contra; **to** — **a boat** embestir un buque con el espolón

ramble [rǽmbəl] VI vagar; **to** — **on** divagar; N paseo *m*

ramp [ræmp] N rampa *f*

rampage [rǽmped₃] N **to go on a** — andar destrozando todo; VI andar destrozando todo

rampant [rǽmpənt] ADJ desenfrenado

ran [ræn] *see* run

ranch [ræntʃ] N hacienda *f*; *Mex* rancho *m*

rancid [rǽnsɪd] ADJ rancio

rancor [rǽŋkɚ] N rencor *m*

random [rǽndəm] ADJ aleatorio, azaroso; **at** — al azar; — **access memory** memoria de acceso directo *f*

randomize [rǽndəmaɪz] VT aleatorizar

rang [ræŋ] *see* ring

range [rend₃] N (of types) gama *f*; (of a gun) alcance *m*; (of variation) fluctuación *f*; (of mountains) cadena *f*; (for shooting) campo de tiro *m*; (of an aircraft) autonomía *f*; (grazing place) campo abierto *m*; (stove) cocina *f*; estufa *f*; — **finder** telémetro *m*; — **of vision** alcance visual *m*; VT (align) alinear; (of a gun) tener alcance; VI (vary) oscilar; (be found in an area) extenderse; **his children** — **in age between 2 and 10** sus hijos van en edad entre 2 y 10

ranger [rénd₃ɚ] N (in a park) guardabosque[s] *mf*; (soldier) guardia de asalto *m*

rank [ræŋk] N (in a hierarchy) rango *m*, grado *m*; (line) fila *f*; — **and file** (of an army) tropa *f sg*; **the** —**s** (soldiers) la tropa; (union members) bases *f pl*; **a sculptor of the first** — un escultor de primer orden; VT (arrange) poner en orden de importancia; VI (rate) figurar; **to** — **high** tener alto rango; **to** — **second** estar clasificado en el segundo lugar; ADJ (smelly) hediondo; (growing vigorously) exuberante

ranking [rǽŋkɪŋ] N ránking *m*

ransack [rǽnsæk] VT saquear, desvalijar

ransom [rǽnsəm] N rescate *m*; VT rescatar

rant [rænt] VI/VT despotricar

rap [ræp] VI/VT (strike) golpear; (chat) charlar; VI (in music) rapear, cantar rap; N (blow) golpe *m*; (accusation) cargo *m*; **to take the** — ser el cabeza de turco; — **music** música rap *f*

rapacious [rəpéʃəs] ADJ rapaz

rape [rep] N (violation) violación f; (statutory) estupro m; (plant) colza f; (grape pulp) orujo m; VT violar

rapid [rǽpɪd] ADJ rápido; N —s rápidos m pl

rapidity [rəpídɪti] N rapidez f

rapport [rəpór] N relación f

rapt [ræpt] ADJ extasiado

rapture [rǽptʃə] N éxtasis m, embeleso m; **to go into a** — arrobarse

rare [rɛr] ADJ (infrequent) raro, poco frecuente; extraño; (of gas, earth) raro; (thin, of air) enrarecido; (excellent) excepcional; (not well cooked) crudo; — **earths** tierras raras f pl

rarely [rɛ́rli] ADV raramente, raras veces

rarity [rɛ́rɪti] N rareza f; (of air) enrarecimiento m

rascal [rǽskəl] N bribón m, bellaco m, pícaro m; Sp golfo m; **you little** —! ¡bandido! ¡sinvergüenza!

rash [ræʃ] ADJ (thoughtless) precipitado, temerario; N (on skin) sarpullido m

raspberry [rǽzbɛri] N frambuesa f; — **bush** frambueso m

raspy [rǽspi] ADJ ronco, áspero

rat [ræt] N rata f; **I smell a** — aquí hay gato encerrado; VT (one's hair) cardar; VI **to** — **on** delatar

ratchet [rǽtʃɪt] N trinquete m

rate [ret] N (charge) tarifa f; (unit charge for insurance) prima f; (pace) paso m, ritmo m; — **of exchange** tipo de cambio m; — **of interest** tasa de interés f; **at any** — en todo caso; **at this** — a este ritmo; **at the** — **of** a razón de; VT (estimate) valorar, estimar; (esteem) considerar; **he** —**s as the best** se le considera como el mejor; **he** —**s high** se le tiene en alta estima

rather [rǽðə] ADV (somewhat) bastante; (more precisely) más bien; — **than** en vez de; **I would** — **die than** antes la muerte que; **I would** — **not go** prefiero no ir

ratification [ræðɪfɪkéʃən] N ratificación f

ratify [rǽðəfaɪ] VT ratificar

rating [rédɪŋ] N (act of adjudging) calificación f; (for credit) clasificación f; (TV quotient) rating televisivo m, índice de audiencia m

ratio [réʃio] N razón f, proporción f

ration [rǽʃən] N ración f; VT racionar

rational [rǽʃənl] ADJ racional

rationale [ræʃənǽl] N motivo m

rationalize [rǽʃənlaɪz] VI/VT racionalizar

rationing [rǽʃənɪŋ] N racionamiento m

rattle [rǽdl] VI (bang) golpetear; (move noisily) traquetear; **to** — **on** parlotear; VT hacer sonar, sacudir; **to** — **off** recitar; N (banging) golpeteo m; (movement) traqueteo m; (toy) sonaja f, sonajero m; (of a rattlesnake) cascabel m; (of death) estertor m; —**snake**

víbora de cascabel f

raucous [rókəs] ADJ (loud) estridente; (rowdy) escandaloso

ravage [rǽvɪʤ] VI/VT asolar, arruinar; N estrago m

rave [rev] VI (rant) desvariar, delirar; VI/VT (roar) bramar; **to** — **about** deshacerse en elogios; N (theater review) crítica muy favorable f

raven [révən] N cuervo m; ADJ azabache

ravenous [rǽvənəs] ADJ voraz, famélico; **to be** — tener un hambre canina

ravine [rəvín] N quebrada f, barranco m, cañada f

raving [révɪŋ] ADJ delirante; (extraordinary) extraordinario; — **mad** loco de remate; N desvarío m

ravish [rǽvɪʃ] VT (kidnap) raptar, secuestrar; (rape) violar

raw [rɔ] ADJ (uncooked, unprocessed, damp and cold) crudo; (of vegetables) fresco, crudo; (unadorned) descarnado; — **flesh** carne viva f; — **material** materia prima f; — **sugar** azúcar bruto m; N —**hide** cuero crudo m

ray [re] N (beam) rayo m; (stingray) raya f

rayon [réɑn] N rayón m

raze [rez] VT arrasar, asolar

razor [rézə] N (device with blade) maquinilla de afeitar f, rasuradora f; (barber's tool) navaja f; (electric) rasuradora electrica f; — **blade** hoja de afeitar f; **safety** — navaja de seguridad f

reach [ritʃ] VI/VT (extend) alcanzar; **to** — **for** tratar de agarrar; Sp tratar de coger; **to** — **into** meter la mano en; VT (arrive at) llegar a; (contact) ponerse en contacto con; **to** — **out one's hand** alargar la mano; N alcance m; **beyond his** — fuera de su alcance; **within his** — a su alcance; **far** —**es** zona remota f

react [riǽkt] VI reaccionar

reaction [riǽkʃən] N reacción f

reactionary [riǽkʃənɛri] ADJ & N reaccionario -ria mf

reactor [riǽktə] N reactor m

read [rid] VI/VT leer; VT (interpret) interpretar; (give as a reading, indicate) decir, indicar, marcar; **it** —**s easily** es fácil de leer; N lectura f; — **protect** protección contra lectura f; —/**write file** archivo de lectura/escritura m

readable [rídəbəl] ADJ (legible) legible; (nice to read) ameno

reader [rídə] N (person who reads) lector -ora mf; (schoolbook) libro de lectura m, cartilla f; (anthology) antología f

readership [rídəʃɪp] N lectores m pl

readily [rédli] ADV fácilmente

readiness [rédɪnɪs] N estado de preparación m; (willingness) buena disposición f; **to be in** — estar preparado, estar listo

reading [rídɪŋ] N lectura f; (interpretation) interpretación f; — **room** sala de lectura f

readjust [riəʤʌ́st] VI/VT (improve fit) reajustar; (acclimate) readaptar

readjustment [riəʤʌ́stmənt] N (fitting) reajuste *m*; (acclimation) readaptación *f*

ready [rɛ́Di] ADJ (prepared) listo, preparado, pronto; (willing) dispuesto; (available) disponible; (quick) rápido; —**made** de confección

reaffirm [riəfɝ́m] VT reafirmar

reagent [riéʤənt] ADJ & N reactivo *m*

real [ril] ADJ real, verdadero; — **estate** bienes raíces *m pl*, bienes inmuebles *m pl*; — **time** tiempo real *m*

realism [ríəlizəm] N realismo *m*

realist [ríəlɪst] N realista *mf*

realistic [riəlístɪk] ADJ realista

reality [riǽlɪɖi] N realidad *f*; — **check** ajuste de perspectiva *m*

realization [riəlɪzéʃən] N (making real) realización *f*; (understanding) comprensión *f*

realize [ríəlaɪz] VT (achieve) realizar; (comprehend) darse cuenta [de], comprobar, percatarse [de]

really [rili] ADV (extremely) realmente; (truly) verdaderamente; (as question) ¿de veras? ¿verdad? **he's not — a lawyer** en realidad, no es abogado / no es abogado de verdad; **it's — hot in Seville** hace mucho calor en Sevilla; **she's a — good colleague** es una colega superbuena / es una buenísima colega

realm [rɛlm] N (kingdom) reino *m*; (domain) terreno *m*, esfera *f*

realtor™ [ríəltɚ] N agente inmobiliario -ria *mf*

reap [rip] VI/VT (cut with sickle) segar; (harvest) cosechar; **to — a benefit** obtener beneficio, sacar provecho

reaper [rípɚ] N (person) segador -ora *mf*; (machine) segadora *f*; (death) la Parca, la Muerte

reappear [riəpír] VI reaparecer

rear [rir] ADJ trasero, posterior; —**guard** retaguardia *f*; N (space at the back) parte de atrás *f*, fondo *m*; (backside) trasero *m*, posaderas *f pl*; — **end** trasero *m*; —**view mirror** espejo retrovisor *m*; VT (raise) criar; VI (rise on back legs) encabritarse, empinarse

reason [rízən] N (faculty) razón *f*; (cause) motivo *m*, razón *f*; **by — of** por causa de; **it stands to — es** lógico; VT razonar; **to — out** resolver por medio de la razón; **to — with** hacer entrar en razón

reasonable [rízənəbəl] ADJ razonable; (in price) módico, moderado

reasoning [rízənɪŋ] N razonamiento *m*, raciocinio *m*; ADJ racional

reassert [riəsɝ́t] VT reafirmar

reassure [riəʃúr] VT tranquilizar

rebate [ríbet] N reembolso *m*, reintegro *m*; VT reembolsar, reintegrar

rebel[1] [rɛ́bəl] ADJ & N rebelde *mf*, insurrecto -ta *mf*

rebel[2] [rɪbɛ́l] VI rebelarse

rebellion [rɪbɛ́ljən] N rebelión *f*

rebellious [rɪbɛ́ljəs] ADJ rebelde, insurrecto

rebelliousness [rɪbɛ́ljəsnɪs] N rebeldía *f*

reboot [ribut] VT reiniciar

rebound[1] [rɪbáʊnd] VI (bounce) rebotar; (catch a rebound) rebotear; (recover) recuperarse

rebound[2] [ríbaʊnd] N (bounce) rebote *m*; (recovery) recuperación *f*; **on the —** de rebote

rebuff [rɪbʌ́f] N desaire *m*, repulsa *f*; VT desairar, rechazar

rebuild [ribíld] VI/VT reconstruir, reedificar; (car engine) reacondicionar

rebuke [rɪbjúk] VT reprender, reprochar; N reproche *m*, reprimenda *f*

recall[1] [rɪkɔ́l] VT (remember) recordar; (call back) retirar; (remove from office) destituir

recall[2] [ríkɔl] N (memory) memoria *f*; (of a diplomat, product) retirada *f*; (from office) destitución *f*

recapitulate [rikəpítʃəlet] VI/VT recapitular

recast [rikǽst] VT refundir

recede [rɪsíd] VI retroceder; (of hairline) tener entradas

receipt [rɪsít] N recibo *m*; **upon — of** al recibo de; —**s** entradas *f pl*, ingresos *m pl*

receivable [rɪsívəbəl] ADJ a cobrar

receive [rɪsív] VI/VT recibir; (suggestions) acoger, recibir; (a broadcast) captar, recibir

receiver [rɪsívɚ] N recibidor -ora *mf*; (of a telephone) auricular *m*; (of a television or radio, in football) receptor *m*; (in tennis) restador -ora *mf*; (of a bankrupt business) síndico *m*

recent [rísənt] ADJ reciente

receptacle [rɪsɛ́ptəkəl] N receptáculo *m*

reception [rɪsɛ́pʃən] N (hotel, social event, TV) recepción *f*; (act of receiving) recibimiento *m*, acogida *f*; — **room** recibidor *m*

recess [ríses] N (niche) nicho *m*; (pause) descanso *m*; (playtime) recreo *m*; **in the —es of** en lo más recóndito de; VI/VT (a meeting) interrumpir; VT (a wall) hacer un nicho en

recession [rɪsɛ́ʃən] N (act of receding) retroceso *m*; (economic) recesión *f*

recessive gene [rɪsɛ́sɪvʤín] N gen recesivo *m*

recidivism [rɪsídəvɪzəm] N reincidencia *f*

recipe [rɛ́səpi] N receta *f*

recipient [rɪsípiənt] N destinatario -ria *mf*

reciprocal [rɪsíprəkəl] ADJ recíproco

reciprocate [rɪsíprəket] VI/VT corresponder [a], *Am* reciprocar

recital [rɪsáɪɖl] N recital *m*

recitation [resɪtéʃən] N recitación *f*

recite [rɪsáɪt] VI/VT recitar

reckless [rɛ́klɪs] ADJ (driver) temerario,

imprudente; (speed) desenfrenado

recklessness [réklisnis] N temeridad f, imprudencia f

reckon [rékən] VI/VT (calculate) calcular; (consider) considerar; (think) suponer

reckoning [rékənɪŋ] N (computation) cálculo m; (settlement of accounts) ajuste de cuentas m; **the day of —** el día del juicio m

reclaim [rɪklém] VT (win back, recover) recuperar; (make land usable) ganar, sanear

recline [rɪkláɪn] VI/VT reclinar[se], recostar[se]

recluse [réklus] ADJ & N solitario -ria mf, ermitaño -ña mf

recognition [rekəgníʃən] N reconocimiento m

recognizable [rekəgnáɪzəbəl] ADJ reconocible

recognize [rékəgnaɪz] VT reconocer

recoil[1] [rɪkóɪl] VI (firearm) dar un culatazo; (move back) retroceder

recoil[2] [rɪkóɪl] N (of a gun) culatazo m; (move back) retroceso m

recollect [rekəlékt] VI/VT recordar

recollection [rekəlékʃən] N recuerdo m

recommend [rekəménd] VI/VT recomendar

recommendation [rekəmendéʃən] N recomendación f

recompense [rékəmpens] VI/VT recompensar; N recompensa f

reconcile [rékənsaɪl] VT (persons) reconciliar; (statements) conciliar; **to —oneself to** resignarse a, conformarse con

reconciliation [rekənsɪliéʃən] N reconciliación f

reconnoiter [rikənóɪdə] VT reconocer; VI hacer un reconocimiento

reconsider [rikənsídə] VI/VT reconsiderar

reconstruct [rikənstrákt] VT reconstruir

reconstruction [rikənstrákʃən] N reconstrucción f

record[1] [rékəd] N (account) registro m, asiento m; (account of a meeting) acta f; (of criminal acts) antecedentes m pl; (of past activities) historial m, hoja de servicios f; (phonographic) disco m; (best performance) récord m, plusmarca f; **— player** tocadiscos m sg; **off the —** extraoficialmente

record[2] [rɪkórd] VI/VT (write down) registrar, apuntar; (cut a recording) grabar

recorder [rɪkórdə] N (archivist) archivero -ra mf; (sound device) grabadora f; (musical instrument) flauta dulce f

recording [rɪkórdɪŋ] N grabación f; **— company** grabadora f

recount[1] [rɪkáʊnt] VT (tell) narrar, relatar

recount[2] [rikáʊnt] VT (count again) recontar

recoup [rɪkúp] VI/VT recuperar

recourse [ríkɔrs] N recurso m; **to have — to** recurrir a

recover [rɪkávə] VI/VT recobrar[se], recuperar[se]; VI (lost health) restablecerse; VT (lost time, property) recuperar; (damages)

obtener indemnización

recovery [rɪkávəri] N (from an illness) recuperación f; (of investments) amortización f; (through a lawsuit) indemnización f; **— room** sala de recuperación f

recreation [rekriéʃən] N recreación f, recreo m, esparcimiento m

recreational [rekriéʃənəl] ADJ recreativo, de recreo; **— vehicle** caravana f

recriminate [rɪkrímənet] VI/VT recriminar

recruit [rɪkrút] N recluta mf; VI/VT reclutar

recruitment [rɪkrútmənt] N reclutamiento m, recluta f

rectangle [réktæŋgəl] N rectángulo m

rectangular [rektæŋgjələ] ADJ rectangular

rectify [réktəfaɪ] VT rectificar

rector [réktə] N rector -ora mf

rectum [réktəm] N recto m

recuperate [rɪkúpəret] VI/VT recuperar[se], recobrar[se]

recur [rɪkɚ] VI volver a ocurrir, repetirse

recurring [rɪkɚɪŋ] ADJ recurrente

recycle [risáɪkəl] VI/VT reciclar

recycling [risáɪklɪŋ] N reciclaje m

red [red] ADJ & N rojo m, colorado m; **— blood cell** glóbulo rojo m; **— card** tarjeta roja f; **--handed** fam in fraganti; **—headed** pelirrojo; **—-hot** candente, al rojo vivo; **— light** luz roja f; **—neck** granjero -ra blanco -ca pobre mf; **— pepper** pimienta de cayena f; **— prawn** carabinero m; **— snapper** pargo m; **— tape** trámites m pl; **— wine** vino tinto m; **—wood** secoya/secuoya f; **in the —** en números rojos; **to see —** enfurecerse

redden [rédŋ] VI/VT enrojecer, ruborizar[se]

reddish [rédɪʃ] ADJ rojizo, bermejo

redeem [rɪdím] VT (deliver from sin) redimir; (pay off a mortgage) cancelar; (buy back from pawnshop) desempeñar; (exchange) canjear; (fulfill) cumplir

redemption [rɪdémpʃən] N redención f; (of something pawned) desempeño m

redevelopment [ridɪvéləpmənt] N remodelación f

redness [rédnɪs] N rojez f; (inflammation) inflamación f

redress[1] [rídrɛs] N reparación f, desagravio m

redress[2] [rídrés] VT reparar, desagraviar

reduce [rɪdús] VI/VT reducir[se]; **she was —d to tears** se echó a llorar

reduction [rɪdákʃən] N reducción f

redundant [rɪdándənt] ADJ (repetitive) redundante; (superfluous) superfluo

reed [rid] N caña f, junco m, carrizo m; (of a musical instrument) lengüeta f

reef [rif] N (underwater ridge) escollo m; (of coral) arrecife m

reek [rik] VI heder, apestar; N hedor m

reel [ril] N carrete m, bobina f; VT (on a spool)

bobinar; VI tambalearse; **to — off** recitar; **to — in a fish** sacar un pez del agua

reelect [riilékt] VT reelegir

reelection [riilékʃən] N reelección f

reemployment [riimplɔ́imənt] N reinserción laboral f

reestablish [riistǽbliʃ] VT restablecer

refer [rifɚ] VI/VT referir; (direct to a source of information) remitir; (direct to a doctor) mandar; (mention) referirse a, aludir a

referee [refəri] N árbitro m; VT (a game) arbitrar; (a submission) hacer el referato

reference [réfərəns] N (mention) referencia f; — **book** libro de consulta m; **with — to** con respecto a, respecto de

referendum [refəréndəm] N referéndum m

referral [rifɚəl] N **he gave me a — to a specialist** me mandó con/a un especialista

refill¹ [rifil] VI/VT rellenar

refill² [rifil] N (for a pen) repuesto m; (for a lighter) carga f; **may I have a —?** ¿me sirve más?

refinance [rifáinæns] VI/VT refinanciar

refine [rifáin] VT (purify) refinar; (polish) refinar, pulir

refined [rifáind] ADJ refinado

refinement [rifáinmənt] N (of manners) refinamiento m, pulimento m; (of oil) refinación f

refinery [rifáinəri] N (of oil) refinería f; (of sugar) ingenio m

reflect [riflékt] VI/VT (mirror) reflejar; VI (ponder) reflexionar; **to — poorly on** desacreditar

reflection [riflékʃən] N (image) reflejo m; (consideration) reflexión f; (unfavorable observation) tacha f; **on —** pensándolo bien

reflector [riflékta] N reflector m

reflex [rífleks] ADJ & N reflejo m

reflexive [rifléksiv] ADJ reflexivo

reflux [ríflaks] N reflujo m

reform [rifɔ́rm] VI/VT reformar[se]; N reforma f

reformation [refəméʃən] N reforma f

reformatory [rifɔ́rmətɔri] N reformatorio m

reformer [rifɔ́rmə] N reformador -ora mf, reformista mf

refraction [rifrǽkʃən] N refracción f

refractory [rifrǽktəri] ADJ (not malleable) refractario; (rebellious) rebelde

refrain [rifrén] VI abstenerse; N (of a song) estribillo m

refresh [rifréʃ] VI/VT refrescar[se]; (computer screen) actualizar, refrescar

refreshing [rifréʃiŋ] ADJ (drink) refrescante; (sleep) reparador; (honesty) agradable

refreshment [rifréʃmənt] N (drink) refresco m; (food) refrigerio m

refrigerate [rifríʤəret] VT refrigerar

refrigeration [rifriʤəréʃən] N refrigeración f

refrigerator [rifríʤəreɾə] N frigorífico m, nevera f, refrigerador m; RP heladera f

refuge [réfjuʤ] N refugio m; **to give —** dar albergue

refugee [refjudʒí] N refugiado -da mf

refund¹ [rifand] N reembolso m

refund² [rifánd] VT reembolsar

refurbish [rifɚbiʃ] VT restaurar

refusal [rifjúzəl] N negativa f, rechazo m; **first — option** f

refuse¹ [rifjúz] VI/VT (deny a request) negar[se] [a]; **to —** rehusarse a, negarse a; VT (decline to accept) rechazar, no aceptar

refuse² [réfjus] N desechos m pl, desperdicios m pl

refute [rifjút] VT refutar, rebatir

regain [rigén] VT (recover) recobrar; (get back to) volver a

regal [rígəl] ADJ regio, real

regard [rigárd] VT (consider) considerar; (esteem) estimar; N (consideration) consideración f; (esteem) respeto m, estima f; **—s** recuerdos m pl, saludos m pl; **as —s** en cuanto a; **with — to** con respecto a

regarding [rigárdiŋ] PREP con respecto a

regardless [rigárdlis] ADV LOC **— of** independientemente de

regenerate [riʤénəret] VI/VT regenerar[se]

regent [ríʤənt] N regente -ta mf

reggae [rége] N reggae m

regime [riʒím] N régimen m

regiment [réʤəmənt] N regimiento m

region [ríʤən] N región f

regional [ríʤənl] ADJ regional

register [réʤistɚ] N (recording, range of voice) registro m; (entry) asiento m; VI/VT (enter into a list) registrar[se]; (enroll) matricular[se], inscribir[se]; VT (indicate) indicar, registrar; (a letter) certificar; VI (appear) aparecer; **that didn't —** no cayó en la cuenta

registered [réʤistɚd] ADJ registrado; **— mail** correo certificado m; **— nurse** enfermero -ra titulado -da mf; **— trademark** marca registrada f

registrar [réʤistrɑr] N secretario -ria de admisiones mf

registration [reʤistréʃən] N (of a car) matrícula f; (of a student) inscripción f

regret [rigrét] VT (feel sorry) lamentar; (feel rueful) arrepentirse de; N arrepentimiento m; **to send —s** enviar sus excusas

regretful [rigrétfəl] ADJ lleno de remordimientos

regrettable [rigrétəbəl] ADJ lamentable

regroup [rigrúp] VT reagrupar; VI reorganizarse

regular [régjələ] ADJ (symmetrical, uniform) regular; (normal) normal; (habitual) habitual; **a — fool** un verdadero necio; **a —**

guy un buen tipo; (habitual customer) parroquiano -na *mf*; (soldier) soldado de línea *m*

regularity [rɛgjəlǽrɪɾi] N regularidad *f*

regulate [rɛ́gjəlet] VT (control) regular; (make regular) regularizar

regulation [rɛgjəléʃən] N (act of regulating) regulación *f*; **—s** reglamento *m*, reglamentación *f*

regulator [rɛ́gjəleɾɚ] N regulador *m*

regurgitate [rɪgɝ́dʒɪtet] VI/VT regurgitar

rehabilitate [rihəbílɪtet] VI/VT rehabilitar[se]

rehabilitation [riəbɪlɪtéʃən] N rehabilitación *f*

rehearsal [rɪhɝ́səl] N ensayo *m*

rehearse [rɪhɝ́s] VI/VT ensayar

reign [ren] N reino *m*, reinado *m*; VI reinar

reimburse [rimbɝ́s] VI/VT reembolsar

reimbursement [rimbɝ́smənt] N reembolso *m*

rein [ren] N rienda *f* (also control); VI **to — in** dominar, refrenar

reincarnation [rinkarnéʃən] N reencarnación *f*

reindeer [réndɪr] N reno *m*

reinforce [rinfɔ́rs] VT reforzar

reinforcement [rinfɔ́rsmənt] N refuerzo *m*, reforzado *m*

reinsertion [rinsɝ́ʃən] N reinserción *f*

reinstate [rinstét] VT reinstaurar

reiterate [riíɾəret] VT reiterar

reject¹ [rɪdʒékt] VT rechazar

reject² [rɪ́dʒekt] N (thing) cosa rechazada *f*, desecho *m*; (person) rechazado -da *mf*

rejoice [rɪdʒɔ́ɪs] VI regocijarse

rejoicing [rɪdʒɔ́ɪsɪŋ] N regocijo *m*

rejoin [rɪdʒɔ́ɪn] VT (come again into a group) reincorporarse a; VI/VT (reunite) volver a unir[se]

rejuvenate [rɪdʒúvənet] VI/VT rejuvenecer

relapse¹ [rɪlǽps] VI (into bad health) recaer; (into crime) reincidir

relapse² [rílæps] N (into bad health) recaída *f*, recidiva *f*; (into crime) reincidencia *f*

relate [rɪlét] VT (tell) relatar, narrar; (connect) relacionar; VI **to —** to relacionarse con

related [rɪléɾɪd] ADJ (connected) relacionado; (kin) emparentado

relation [rɪléʃən] N (association) relación *f*; (act of narrating) narración *f*; (kinship) parentesco *m*; (relative) pariente -ta *mf*; **with — to** con respecto a

relationship [rɪléʃənʃɪp] N relación *f*

relative [rélaɾɪv] ADJ relativo; N pariente -ta *mf*, allegado -da *mf*; **— to** relativo a, referente a

relativity [relatívɪɾi] N relatividad *f*

relax [rɪlǽks] VI/VT relajar[se], distender[se]; VT (grip) aflojar

relaxation [rilækséʃən] N (recreation) esparcimiento *m*, recreo *m*; (loosening) relajamiento *m*, relajación *f*

relay¹ [ríle] N relevo *m*, posta *f*; (electrical) relé

m; **— race** carrera de relevos/postas *f*

relay² [ríle, rɪlé] VT transmitir; **to — a broadcast** transmitir un programa

release [rɪlís] VT (let go) soltar; (free prisoners) librar, poner en libertad; (energy) liberar; (news) divulgar; (discharge from hospital) dar de alta; N (liberation) liberación *f*; (permission) permiso *m*; (of film) estreno *m*; (of gas) escape *m*; (of energy) desprendimiento *m*

relegate [réliget] VT relegar

relent [rɪlént] VI aplacarse

relentless [rɪléntlɪs] ADJ implacable

relevant [rélovant] ADJ pertinente

reliability [rɪlaɪəbílɪɾi] N fiabilidad *f*, confiabilidad *f*

reliable [rɪláɪəbəɫ] ADJ fiable, confiable; (a person) formal

reliance [rɪláɪəns] N (dependency) dependencia *f*; (trust) confianza *f*

relic [rélɪk] N reliquia *f*

relief [rɪlíf] N (ease) alivio *m*; (aid) ayuda *f*; (projection) relieve *m*; (soldier) relevo *m*; (in golf) alivio *m*; **in —** en relieve; **— map** mapa en relieve *m*

relieve [rɪlív] VT (alleviate) aliviar; (free) liberar; (replace) relevar; VI **to — oneself** orinar

reliever [rɪlívɚ] N (baseball) relevista *mf*

religion [rɪlídʒən] N religión *f*

religious [rɪlídʒəs] ADJ religioso

relinquish [rɪlíŋkwɪʃ] VT (give up) renunciar; (let go) soltar

relish [rélɪʃ] VT (to like the taste) saborear, paladear; (enjoy) disfrutar; N (enjoyment) gusto *m*; (condiment) condimento de pepinillos en vinagre *m*

relocate [rilóket] VI/VT trasladar[se]

reluctance [rɪláktəns] N renuencia *f*

reluctant [rɪláktənt] ADJ renuente, reacio

rely [rɪláɪ] VI **to — on** (trust) confiar en; (depend on) depender de

REM [rapid eye movement] [áriém] N REM *m*, MOR *m pl*

remain [rɪmén] VI (continue to be) seguir siendo; (stay) quedar[se], permanecer; (to be left) quedar, restar; (to be left over) sobrar; N **—s** restos *m pl*

remainder [rɪméndɚ] N (extra) sobrante; (other) restante

remake¹ [rimék] VT rehacer; (film) hacer de nuevo

remake² [rímek] N nueva versión *f*

remark [rɪmárk] VT (comment) comentar, observar; (notice) notar, observar; **to — on** comentar; N observación *f*, comentario *m*

remarkable [rɪmárkəbəɫ] ADJ notable

remedial [rɪmídiəɫ] ADJ (rehabilitative) rehabilitador; (to improve skills) de recuperación

remedy [rémɪdɪ] N (solution) remedio *m*; (cure) cura *f*; VT (solve) remediar, subsanar; (heal) curar

remember [rɪmémbə] VI/VT recordar, acordarse [de]; — **me to him** mándale saludos míos

remind [rɪmáɪnd] VT recordar

reminder [rɪmáɪndə] N (of a date, deadline) recordatorio *m*; (warning) advertencia *f*

reminiscence [remənísəns] N reminiscencia *f*, recuerdo *m*

remiss [rɪmís] ADJ negligente

remission [rɪmíʃən] N remisión *f*

remit [rɪmít] VI/VT remitir

remittance [rɪmítns] N remesa *f*, giro *m*

remnant [rémnənt] N (remainder) resto *m*; (of fabric) retazo *m*, retal *m*; (vestige) vestigio *m*

remodel [rimádl] VI/VT remodelar

remodeling [rimádlɪŋ] N remodelación *f*

remorse [rimórs] N remordimiento *m*

remote [rimót] ADJ (far away) remoto, recóndito; (aloof) distante; (in kinship) lejano; — **access** acceso remoto *m*; — **control** control remoto *m*, mando a distancia *m*; — **login** acceso remoto *m*; — **server** servidor remoto *m*

removal [rimúvəl] N (dismissal) deposición *f*, alejamiento *m*; (elimination) eliminación *f*; (extirpation) extirpación *f*

remove [rimúv] VT (an obstacle) remover; (take away, take off) quitar; (dismiss) deponer; (eliminate) eliminar; (extirpate) extirpar; **to — from office** separar/apartar del cargo

remunerate [rimjúnəret] VT remunerar *f*, retribuir *f*

remuneration [rimjunəréʃən] N remuneración *f*, retribución *f*

renaissance [rénɪsəns] N renacimiento *m*; — **architecture** arquitectura renacentista *f*

renal [rínl] ADJ renal; — **failure** insuficiencia renal *f*

rend [rend] VI/VT desgarrar[se], rajar[se]

render [réndə] VT (give) dar; (cause to become) dejar; (depict) representar; (translate) traducir; (give homage, account) rendir; (provide services, assistance) prestar; (melt down fat) derretir; (deliver a verdict) pronunciar; **to — useless** inutilizar

rendition [rendíʃən] N (translation) traducción *f*; (interpretation) interpretación *f*, versión *f*

renegade [rénɪged] N renegado -da *mf*

renegotiate [rinɪgóʃiet] VI/VT renegociar

renegue [riníg] VI incumplir

renew [rinú] VT (vows, contract) renovar; (furniture) restaurar; (friendship, effort) reanudar; (a loan) prorrogar

renewable [rinúəbəl] ADJ renovable

renewal [rinúəl] N (of vows, contract) renovación *f*; (of furniture) restauración *f*; (of a city) remodelación *f*; (of friendship, effort) reanudación *f*; (of loan) prórroga *f*

renounce [rɪnáuns] VT (give up) renunciar a; (repudiate) repudiar, renegar de

renovate [rénəvet] VT renovar

renown [rɪnáun] N renombre *m*

renowned [rɪnáund] ADJ renombrado

rent [rent] N (monthly payment) alquiler *m*, arrendamiento *m*; **for —** se alquila, se arrienda; (fissure) rajadura *f*, hendidura *f*; (tear) rasgadura *f*; VI/VT (lease) alquilar, arrendar

rent [rent] *see* rend

rental [réntl] ADJ de alquiler; — **agreement** contrato de alquiler *m*; N alquiler *m*, arrendamiento *m*

renter [réntə] N inquilino -na *mf*

renunciation [rɪnʌnsiéʃən] N renuncia *f*

reopen [riópən] VI/VT (doors) reabrir[se]; (negotiations) reanudar[se]

reorganization [riɔrgənɪzéʃən] N reorganización *f*

reorganize [riɔ́rgənaɪz] VI/VT reorganizar[se]

repaginate [ripǽdʒɪnet] VT repaginar

repair [rɪpér] VT (fix) reparar, arreglar, componer; (shoes) remendar; **to — to** acudir a; N (fixing) reparación *f*; (of shoes) remiendo *m*, compostura *f*; **in good —** en buen estado; — **man** técnico en reparaciones *m*

reparation [repəréʃən] N reparación *f*, indemnización *f*

repay [rɪpé] VT (return money, favor) devolver; (pay off) pagar

repayment [rɪpémənt] N (of a sum) reembolso *m*; (of a loan) pago *m*

repeal [rɪpíl] VT derogar, revocar, abrogar; N derogación *f*, revocación *f*, abrogación *f*

repeat[1] [rɪpít] VI/VT repetir; N repetición *f*

repeat[2] [rɪpít] N repetición *f*

repeated [rɪpítɪd] ADJ repetido

repel [rɪpél] VI/VT repeler; (an attack) rechazar

repellent [rɪpélənt] ADJ & N repelente *m*

repent [rɪpént] VI/VT arrepentirse [de]

repentance [rɪpéntəns] N arrepentimiento *m*

repentant [rɪpéntənt] ADJ arrepentido, pesaroso

repercussion [repəkáʃən] N repercusión *f*; **to have —s** repercutir

repertoire [répətwar] N repertorio *m*

repetition [repɪtíʃən] N repetición *f*

replace [rɪplés] VT (place again) volver a colocar; (substitute for) sustituir, reemplazar; (provide a substitute for) reponer

replaceable [rɪplésəbəl] ADJ reemplazable, sustituible

replacement [rɪplésmənt] N (substitute, substitution) sustitución *m*, reemplazo *m*; (making up for) reposición *f*; — **parts** piezas de repuesto *f pl*

replenish [rɪplénɪʃ] VI/VT (supply) reabastecer;

(fill again) rellenar

replete [rɪplít] ADJ repleto

replica [réplɪkə] N réplica f

replicate [réplɪket] VT reproducir, replicar

replication [replɪkéʃən] N reproducción f, replicación f

reply [rɪplái] VI replicar, contestar; N réplica f, contestación f

report [rɪpórt] VT (recount) relatar; (make a crime known, denounce) denunciar; (make an accident known) dar parte de; VI hacer un informe, informar; **to — for duty** presentarse; **to — on** hacer un informe sobre; **to — sick** dar parte de enfermo, reportarse enfermo; **it is —ed that** se dice que; N informe m, comunicado m; (rumor) rumor m; (loud noise) estallido m; **— card** boletín de calificaciones m

reportedly [rɪpórdɪdlɪ] ADV según se informa

reporter [rɪpórdɚ] N (news) reportero -ra mf; (sports) cronista mf

repose [rɪpóz] VI/VT reposar, descansar; N reposo m, descanso m

repository [rɪpázɪtɔri] N (object) depósito m; (person) depositario -ria mf

repossess [ripəzés] VT retomar posesión de

represent [reprizént] VT representar

representation [reprizentéʃən] N representación f

representative [reprizéntədɪv] ADJ representativo; N representante mf

repress [rɪprés] VI/VT reprimir

repression [rɪpréʃən] N represión f

repressive [rɪprésɪv] ADJ represivo

reprieve [rɪprív] VT (pardon) indultar; (commute) conmutar; (delay) aplazar; N (pardon) indulto m; (commutation) conmutación f; (delay) aplazamiento m

reprimand [réprəmænd] N reprimenda f, regaño m; VT reprender, regañar

reprint¹ [rɪprínt] VI/VT reimprimir

reprint² [rɪprínt] N (action, result) reimpresión f; (offprint) separata f

reprisal [rɪpráɪzəl] N represalia f

reproach [rɪprótʃ] VT reprochar; N reproche m

reproduce [riprədús] VI/VT reproducir[se]

reproduction [riprədákʃən] N reproducción f

reproof [rɪprúf] N reprobación f

reprove [rɪprúv] VT reprobar

reptile [réptaɪl] N reptil m

republic [rɪpáblɪk] N república f

republican [rɪpáblɪkən] ADJ & N republicano -na mf

repudiate [rɪpjúdiet] VT repudiar

repugnance [rɪpágnəns] N repugnancia f

repugnant [rɪpágnənt] ADJ repugnante

repulse [rɪpáls] VT repeler, rechazar; N repulsa f, rechazo m

repulsive [rɪpálsɪv] ADJ repulsivo

reputable [répjədəbəl] ADJ reputado

reputation [repjətéʃən] N reputación f, fama f

request [rɪkwést] N solicitud f, petición f, requerimiento m; **at the — of** a solicitud de, a instancias de; VT solicitar, pedir

require [rɪkwáɪr] VI/VT (need) requerir; (demand) exigir

requirement [rɪkwáɪrmənt] N (demand) requisito m; (need) necesidad f

requisite [rékwɪzɪt] ADJ requerido, necesario; N requisito m

requisition [rekwɪzíʃən] N (taking over) requisa f; (order) pedido m; VT (take over) requisar; (order) pedir

rerun [rírʌn] N refrito m

rescind [rɪsínd] VT rescindir

rescue [réskju] VT rescatar, salvar; N rescate m, salvamento m; **to go to the — of** acudir al socorro de, salir al quite de

research¹ [rísɚtʃ] N investigación f

research² [rísɚtʃ] VI/VT investigar

researcher [rísɚtʃɚ] N investigador -ora mf

resell [risél] VT revender

resemblance [rɪzémbləns] N semejanza f, parecido m

resemble [rɪzémbəl] VT semejar, asemejarse a, parecerse a

resent [rɪzént] VT resentirse de

resentful [rɪzéntfəl] ADJ resentido, rencoroso

resentment [rɪzéntmənt] N resentimiento m

reservation [rezɚvéʃən] N reserva f; Am reservación f; **to have one's —s** tener reservas

reserve [rɪzɚ́v] VT reservar; N reserva f; (shyness) pudor m

reserved [rɪzɚ́vd] ADJ reservado

reservoir [rézɚvwɑr] N (tank) depósito m, alberca f; (artificial lake) embalse m, represa f

reset [risét] VT (computer, machine) reiniciar; **— key** tecla de reinicio f

reside [rɪzáɪd] VI residir

residence [rézɪDəns] N residencia f

resident [rézɪDənt] ADJ & N residente mf; (of a neighborhood) vecino -na mf

residential [rezɪDéntʃəl] ADJ residencial

residue [rézɪdu] N residuo m

resign [rɪzáɪn] VI/VT renunciar [a], dimitir [de]; **to — oneself to** resignarse a

resignation [rezɪgnéʃən] N (act of resigning an office) renuncia f, dimisión f; (accepting attitude) resignación f; **— letter** carta de renuncia f

resilience [rɪzíljəns] N (elasticity) elasticidad f; (adaptability) adaptabilidad f

resilient [rɪzíljənt] ADJ (elastic) elástico; (adaptable) adaptable

resin [rézɪn] N resina f

resist [rɪzíst] VT (a temptation) resistir; VI/VT (tyranny) resistirse [a]

resistance [rɪzístəns] N resistencia *f*
resistant [rɪzístənt] ADJ resistente
resolute [rézəlut] ADJ resuelto, decidido
resolution [rezəlúʃən] N resolución *f*
resolve [rɪzálv] VI/VT resolver[se]; **to — into** convertirse en; **to — to** decidir, resolver; N resolución *f*
resonance [rézənəns] N resonancia *f*
resonate [rézənet] VI/VT resonar
resort [rɪzɔ́rt] N (seaside) centro de veraneo *m*; (for skiing) estación de esquí *f*; **as a last —** como último recurso; VI **to — to** recurrir a
resound [rɪzáund] VI/VT resonar; **—ing victory** victoria contundente *f*
resource [rísɔrs] N recurso *m*
resourceful [rɪzɔ́rsfəl] ADJ ingenioso
respect [rɪspékt] VT respetar; N (esteem) respeto *m*; (detail) aspecto *m*; **with — to** [con] respecto a, respecto de
respectable [rɪspéktəbəl] ADJ respetable
respectful [rɪspéktfəl] ADJ respetuoso
respective [rɪspéktɪv] ADJ respectivo
respiration [respəréʃən] N respiración *f*
respiratory [réspərətɔri] ADJ respiratorio; **— failure** insuficiencia respiratoria *f*
respite [réspɪt] N (pause) respiro *f*, tregua *m*; (postponement) prórroga *f*
resplendent [rɪspléndənt] ADJ resplandeciente, refulgente
respond [rɪspánd] VI/VT responder
respondent [rɪspándənt] N (to a lawsuit) demandado -da *mf*; (to a poll) encuestado -da *mf*
response [rɪspáns] N respuesta *f*
responsibility [rɪspansəbílɪɾi] N responsabilidad *f*, reivindicación *f*
responsible [rɪspánsəbəl] ADJ responsable
rest [rest] N (repose) descanso *m*, reposo *m*; (musical) pausa *f*; (support) apoyo *m*; (remainder) resto *m*; **— home** (for convalescents) casa de reposo *f*; (for the aged) casa de ancianos *f*; **— room** servicio *m*; *Sp* aseo *m*; **an object at —** un objeto en reposo; **to — on** depender de; **let it —** déjalo en paz
restaurant [réstərənt] N restaurante *m*; *Am* restorán *m*
restitution [restɪtúʃən] N restitución *f*
restless [réstlɪs] ADJ (worried) inquieto; (fidgety) movedizo
restlessness [réstlɪsnɪs] N inquietud *f*, desasosiego *m*
restoration [restəréʃən] N restauración *f*
restore [rɪstɔ́r] VT restaurar
restrain [rɪstrén] VT (hold back) refrenar, contener, moderar; (bring under control) reducir; **—ing order** medida cautelar *f*

restraint [rɪstrént] N (self-control) compostura *f*, moderación *f*; (device) seguro *m*; **under —** bajo control
restrict [rɪstríkt] VT restringir; (someone's liberty) coartar
restriction [rɪstríkʃən] N restricción *f*
restructuring [ristrʌ́ktʃəɪŋ] N reestructuración *f*
result [rɪzʌ́lt] VI resultar; **to — from** resultar de; **to — in** dar por resultado; N resultado *m*; **as a —** de resultas, como resultado
resume [rɪzúm] VI/VT (take up again) reasumir, volver a asumir; (continue) reanudar
résumé [rézume] N currículum *m*, historial personal *m*
resurrection [rezərékʃən] N resurrección *f*
resuscitate [rɪsʌ́sɪtet] VI/VT resucitar
resuscitation [rɪsasɪtéʃən] N resucitación *f*
retail [rítel] N venta al por menor *f*; **— store** tienda minorista *f*; **— trade** comercio minorista *m*; VI/VT vender al por menor; **at —** al por menor, al menudeo
retailer [rítelə] N minorista *mf*, detallista *mf*
retain [rɪtén] VT (recall, confine, detain) retener; (keep) conservar, quedarse con; (hire) contratar
retainer [rɪténə] N (device that holds back) retén *m*; (payment) honorarios pagados por adelantado *m pl*
retaliate [rɪtáliet] VI vengarse
retaliation [rɪtæliéʃən] N venganza *f*
retard [rɪtárd] VI/VT retardar
retarded [rɪtárdɪd] ADJ retrasado
retention [rɪténʃən] N retención *f*
reticence [réɾɪsəns] N reserva *f*
retina [rétnə] N retina *f*
retinue [rétnu] N séquito *m*, comitiva *f*
retire [rɪtáɪr] VI/VT (stop working) retirar[se], jubilar[se]; (withdraw) retirar[se]; (go to bed) acostarse; (withdraw money, troops, machines) retirar
retiree [rɪtaɪrí] N jubilado -da *mf*
retirement [rɪtáɪrmənt] N retiro *m*, jubilación *f*; **— of debt** retiro de deuda *m*
retort [rɪtɔ́rt] N (reply) réplica *f*; (vessel) retorta *f*
retouch [rɪtʌ́tʃ] VT retocar; N retoque *m*
retrace [ritrés] VT (mental steps) repasar; (one's route) volver sobre
retract [rɪtrǽkt] VT (a statement) retractar; (claws) retraer[se]; VI desdecirse, retractarse
retreat [rɪtrít] N (place of refuge, period of meditation) retiro *m*, refugio *m*; (military) retirada *f*, repliegue *m*; (bugle call) retreta *f*; VI batirse en retirada, retroceder, replegarse
retrench [rɪtréntʃ] VI economizar
retrieval [rɪtrívəl] N recuperación *f*
retrieve [rɪtrív] VT (game animals) cobrar; (something lost) recuperar
retriever [rɪtrívə] N perro cobrador *m*
retro [rétro] ADJ retro

retroactive [rɛtroǽktɪv] ADJ retroactivo

retrospect [rɛ́trəspɛkt] ADV LOC **in** — mirando para atrás

retrovirus [rɛ́trovaɪrəs] N retrovirus *m*

return [rɪtɚ́n] VI (come back) volver, regresar; VT (put back) devolver, retornar; (deliver a verdict) fallar; — **to sender** devolver al remitente; N (to a place) vuelta *f*, regreso *m*; (of a thing) devolución *f*; (of profit) ganancia *f*; (on a typewriter) retorno de carro *m*; (on a computer) retroceso *m*, salto de línea *m*; — **address** señas del remitente *f pl*; — **game** revancha *f*; — **key** tecla de retorno *f*, tecla de retroceso *f*; — **of service** (tennis) resto *m*; — **ticket** billete de vuelta *m*; **by** — **mail** a vuelta de correo; **election** —**s** resultados electorales *m pl*; **in** — a cambio; **in** — **for** a cambio de; **income tax** — *Sp* declaración de la renta *f*; *Am* declaración de impuestos *f*

reunification [rijunɪfɪkéʃən] N reunificación *f*

reunion [rijúnjən] N reunión *f*

reunite [rijunáɪt] VI/VT reunir[se]

rev [rɛv] VI/VT acelerar en vacío

reveal [rɪvíl] VT revelar

revealing [rɪvílɪŋ] ADJ revelador; (neckline) atrevido

revel [rɛ́vəl] VI (enjoy) deleitarse, gozar; (party) parrandear; N parranda *f*

revelation [rɛvəléʃən] N revelación *f*; (book in Bible) Apocalipsis *m sg*

revelry [rɛ́vəlri] N parranda *f*, jarana *f*

revenge [rɪvɛ́ndʒ] N venganza *f*, revancha *f*

revengeful [rɪvɛ́ndʒfəl] ADJ vengativo

revenue [rɛ́vənu] N (of a government) rentas públicas *f pl*; (of a person) ingresos *m pl*; — **stamp** sello fiscal *m*

reverberate [rɪvɚ́bəret] VI reverberar; VT hacer reverberar

revere [rɪvír] VT reverenciar

reverence [rɛ́vərəns] N reverencia *f*, veneración *f*; VT venerar

reverend [rɛ́vərənd] ADJ & N reverendo -da *mf*

reverent [rɛ́vərənt] ADJ reverente

reverie, revery [rɛ́vəri] N ensueño *m*, ensoñación *f*

reverse [rɪvɚ́s] ADJ inverso, opuesto; **the** — **side** el revés; N (opposite) lo opuesto; (back of clothing, mishap) revés *m*; (back of a coin, medal) reverso *m*; (gear) marcha atrás *f*; (back of a piece of paper) dorso *m*; VI/VT invertir[se]; VT (a policy, a vehicle) dar marcha atrás; (a verdict) revocar

revert [rɪvɚ́t] VI revertir

review [rɪvjú] N (inspection of a military unit, periodical publication) revista *f*; (repetition of studied material) repaso *m*; (critique of a book, drama) reseña *f*, crítica *f*; (examination of a judicial case) revisión *f*; VI/VT (examine) repasar, revisar; VT (reexamine) revisar,

examinar; (inspect troops) pasar revista a; (write a critique of) reseñar

revile [rɪváɪl] VT vilipendiar, denostar

revise [rɪváɪz] VT corregir, enmendar

revision [rɪvíʒən] N (action of revising) corrección *f*; (revised version) versión corregida *f*

revitalize [rɪváɪdlaɪz] VT revitalizar

revival [rɪváɪvəl] N (of customs) retorno *m*; (of religious feeling) resurgimiento *m*, despertar *m*; (from unconsciousness) resucitación *f*; (of a play) reposición *f*, revisión *f*; (evangelical meeting) asamblea evangelística *f*

revive [rɪváɪv] VT (an unconscious person) reavivar, reanimar; (an apparently dead person) resucitar; (an old play) reponer; (a custom) restablecer; VI revivir, reanimarse; (be reestablished) restablecerse

revocation [rɛvəkéʃən] N revocación *f*

revoke [rɪvók] VT revocar

revolt [rɪvólt] N revuelta *f*, sublevación *f*; VI rebelarse, sublevarse; **it** —**s me** me da asco

revolting [rɪvóltɪŋ] ADJ repugnante, asqueroso

revolution [rɛvəlúʃən] N revolución *f*

revolutionary [rɛvəlúʃəneri] ADJ & N revolucionario -ria *mf*

revolve [rɪválv] VI/VT girar

revolver [rɪválvɚ] N revólver *m*

revolving credit [rɪválvɪŋ] N crédito rotativo *m*

revue [rɪvjú] N revista *f*

revulsion [rɪvʌ́lʃən] N repugnancia *f*, asco *m*

reward [rɪwɔ́rd] N recompensa *f*; VT recompensar

rewind [riwáɪnd] VI/VT rebobinar

rewrite[1] [riráɪt] VI/VT reescribir

rewrite[2] [rírait] N corrección *f*

rhea [ríə] N ñandú *m*

rhetoric [rɛ́dəɪk] N retórica *f*

rheumatic [rumǽdɪk] ADJ reumático; — **fever** fiebre reumática *f*

rheumatism [rúmətɪzəm] N reumatismo *m*, reuma *m*

rheumatoid [rúmətɔɪd] ADJ reumatoide

Rh factor [árétʃfæktɚ] N factor Rh *m*

rhinoceros [raɪnásərəs] N rinoceronte *m*

rhinoplasty [ráɪnoplæsti] N rinoplastia *f*

rhinovirus [ráɪnovaɪrəs] N rinovirus *m*

rhododendron [roɪdədéndrən] N rododendro *m*

rhubarb [rúbarb] N (vegetable) ruibarbo *m*; (brawl) reyerta *f*

rhyme [raɪm] N rima *f*; **without** — **or reason** sin ton ni son; VI/VT rimar

rhythm [ríðəm] N ritmo *m*

rhythmical [ríðmɪkəl] ADJ rítmico; (breathing) acompasado

rib [rɪb] N (of person, animal) costilla *f*; (of umbrella) varilla *f*; (in garment) canalé *m*, cordoncillo *m*; — **cage** caja torácica *f*; VT burlarse de

ribbon [ríbən] N (of cloth) cinta f; (of land) franja f, faja f

rice [raɪs] N arroz m; — **field** arrozal m

rich [rɪtʃ] ADJ rico; (tasty) sabroso; (buttery) mantecoso; (colorful) vivo; — **text format** formato de texto enriquecido m; N —**es** riquezas f pl

rickety [ríkɪdi] ADJ (shaky) desvencijado; (affected with rickets) raquítico

ricochet [ríkəʃe] N rebote m; VI rebotar

rid [rɪd] VT librar, desembarazar; **to get — of** librarse de, deshacerse de

ridden [rídn] see ride

riddle [rídl] N (puzzle) acertijo m, adivinanza f; (something puzzling) enigma m; VI hablar en enigmas; VT acribillar, perforar; **to be —d with graft** estar plagado de corrupción

ride [raɪd] VI (on a horse) cabalgar, jinetear; (on a bicycle) montar; (in a vehicle) andar/viajar/ir en; **this car —s well** este coche anda bien; **his hopes are riding on that** tiene las esperanzas puestas en eso; **just let it —** déjalo tranquilo; VT (travel on horse, bicycle) montar; (travel on bus) andar en; (harass) hostigar; **to — away** irse; **to — by** pasar; **to — out** capear; **to — up** subirse; N (in a vehicle) paseo m, viaje m; (at an amusement park) aparato m; **to give someone a —** llevar/acercar en coche; **to go on a —** dar un paseo

rider [ráɪdə] N (on a horse) jinete m; (on a bicycle) ciclista mf; (on an insurance policy) cláusula añadida f; (law) anexo m

ridge [rɪdʒ] N (back of an animal) espinazo m, lomo m; (chain of hills) cadena f; (of a roof) caballete m; (of cloth) cordoncillo m

ridicule [rídɪkjul] N burla f, mofa f; VT ridiculizar, poner en ridículo

ridiculous [rɪdíkjələs] ADJ ridículo

riffraff [rífræf] N pej gentuza f, chusma f

rifle [ráɪfəl] N rifle m, fusil m; VT robar; **to — through** revolver

rift [rɪft] N (opening) grieta f, hendidura f; (disagreement) desavenencia f

rig [rɪg] VT (sails) aparejar, equipar; (an election) amañar; **to — up** armar; N (on a ship) aparejo m, equipo m; (apparatus) aparato m; (truck) camión m

rigging [rígɪŋ] N jarcia f

right [raɪt] ADJ (not left) derecho; (not wrong) correcto, acertado; (suitable) adecuado; — **angle** ángulo recto m; —**-hand** derecho; —**-hand man** brazo derecho m; —**-handed** diestro; — **justification** alineación a la derecha f; —**-to-life** antiaborto, pro vida; — **triangle** triángulo recto m; — **wing** derechista, de derecha; **at the — moment** en el momento justo; **the — people** la gente indicada; **to be — tener razón; to be all —**

estar bien; **he's not in his — mind** no está en sus cabales; **to turn out —** salir bien; ADV (straight) derecho, directamente; (correctly) correctamente; (to the right) a la derecha; — **after** justo después de; — **face** media vuelta a la derecha; — **now** ahora mismo, ahorita; — **there** allí mismo; **it is — where you left it** está exactamente donde lo dejaste; **to hit — in the eye** darle de lleno en el ojo; — **click** pulsación en el botón derecho del ratón f; N (just claim) derecho m; (moral good) bien m; (direction, political persuasion) derecha f; — **of way** prioridad f, preferencia f; — **to work** derecho al trabajo m; **make a — at the corner** gira/dobla a la derecha; **to the —** a la derecha; **to be in the —** tener razón; VI/ VT (make upright) enderezar[se]; **to — click** pulsar el botón derecho del ratón; VT (correct) corregir

righteous [ráɪtʃəs] ADJ recto, justo; — **anger** rabia justificada f

righteousness [ráɪtʃəsnɪs] N rectitud f, superioridad moral f

rightful [ráɪtfəl] ADJ legítimo

rightist [ráɪdɪst] N derechista mf

rightly [ráɪtli] ADV con razón

rigid [rídʒɪd] ADJ rígido

rigidity [rɪdʒídɪti] N rigidez f

rigor [rígə] N rigor m

rigorous [rígəəs] ADJ riguroso

rim [rɪm] N (edge) borde m; (on a car) llanta f; Am rin m; (on a bicycle) aro m; (on a plate) filete m; (of glasses) montura f

rind [raɪnd] N (cheese) corteza f; (fruit) cáscara f

ring [rɪŋ] N (on finger, of smoke) anillo m; (for women only) sortija f; (under the eyes) ojeras f pl; (in the nose) argolla f; (circle) círculo m, redondel m, ruedo m; (in a circus) pista f; (for bullfights) plaza de toros f; (for boxing) cuadrilátero m; (for gymnastics) anillas f pl; (of criminals) banda f; (undertone) tono m; (sound of telephone) timbrazo m, telefonazo m; (sound of bells) retintín m, repique m; — **finger** anular m; — **leader** cabecilla mf; —**worm** tiña f; VT (surround) cercar; (make doorbell sound) tocar; (make bell sound) tañer; VI (of ears) zumbar; (make sound of a doorbell) sonar; (make sound of a bell) repicar, repiquetear; **to — the nose of an animal** ponerle una argolla en la nariz a un animal; **to — the hour** dar la hora; **to — true** parecer verdad; **to — up the sale** marcar la venta

ringlet [rínlɪt] N (curl) rizo m, bucle m, sortija f; (small ring) sortija pequeña f

rink [rɪŋk] N pista de patinaje f

rinkydink [rínkidɪŋk] ADJ de pacotilla

rinse [rɪns] VI/VT enjuagar, aclarar; N enjuague m, aclarado m

riot [ráɪət] N (uprising) motín *m*, tumulto *m*;
(excess) exceso *m*; **he's a —** es un cómico; VI
amotinarse

riotous [ráɪədəs] ADJ (wanton) desenfrenado;
(funny) graciosísimo

rip [rɪp] VI/VT rasgar[se], rajar[se]; VT (something
sewn) descoser; **to — away** desprender; **to —
into** asaltar; **to — off** robar; **to — out a
seam** descoser una costura; N rasgadura *f*,
rajadura *f*; **— cord** cordón de apertura *m*;
—off robo *m*

ripe [raɪp] ADJ maduro; **to be — for** estar
preparado/listo para; **— old age** edad
avanzada *f*

ripen [ráɪpən] VI/VT madurar[se], sazonar[se]

ripeness [ráɪpnɪs] N madurez *f*

ripening [ráɪpənɪŋ] N maduración *f*

ripple [rípəl] VI/VT (water) rizar[se]; (grass)
agitar[se]; N ondulación *f*, rizo *m*

rise [raɪz] VI (go up) subir; (increase) aumentar;
(get up, stand up) levantarse; (slope up)
elevarse; (arise) surgir; (of mist) levantarse;
(of the sun, moon) salir; (of dough) crecer,
leudar; **to — up in rebellion** sublevarse,
alzarse; **to — above** superar; **to — to the
challenge** aceptar el desafío y triunfar; N (of
prices, volume) subida *f*, aumento *m*; (of an
empire, talent) surgimiento *m*; (slope
upward) elevación *f*; **to get a — out of
someone** provocar a alguien; **to give — to**
ocasionar

risen [rízən] *see* rise

risk [rɪsk] N riesgo *m*; **— factors** factores de
riesgo *m pl*; **at —** a riesgo; **— -free** sin
riesgo; VT arriesgar, aventurar; **to — defeat**
correr el riesgo de perder, exponerse a perder

risky [rɪski] ADJ arriesgado, aventurado

risqué [rɪské] ADJ subido de tono, atrevido,
picante

Ritalin hydrochloride [rídəlɪnhaɪdrəklóraɪd]
N clorhidrato de Ritalina *m*

rite [raɪt] N rito *m*

ritual [rítʃuəl] ADJ & N ritual *m*

ritzy [rítsi] ADJ elegante

rival [ráɪvəl] ADJ & N rival *mf*; VT rivalizar con,
competir con

rivalry [ráɪvəlri] N rivalidad *f*

river [rívə-] N río *m*; **—bank** orilla *f*, ribera *f*; **—
transport** transporte fluvial *m*

rivet [rívɪt] N remache *m*; VT (put rivets)
remachar; (fix) fijar, clavar

riveting [rívɪdɪŋ] N (action) remache *m*; ADJ
(fascinating) fascinante

RNA [**ribonucleic acid**] [árɛné] N ARN *m*

roach [rotʃ] N cucaracha *f*

road [rod] N (in the country) camino *m*;
(highway) carretera *f*; **on the — to recovery**
en vías de recuperación; **— map** mapa
carretero *m*; **— rage** ira caminera *f*; **—side**

borde del camino *m*; **—way** camino *m*

roam [rom] VI/VT vagar [por], errar [por], rodar
[por]; VI vagabundear

roar [rɔr] VI/VT rugir, bramar; **to — with
laughter** reír a carcajadas; N rugido *m*,
bramido *m*; **— of laughter** risotada *f*,
carcajada *f*

roast [rost] VI/VT (meat, potatoes) asar[se];
(coffee, nuts) tostar, torrar; (criticize) criticar;
N (meat) asado *m*; (party) barbacoa *f*; **— beef**
rosbif *m*

rob [rab] VI/VT robar; **to — someone of
something** robarle algo a alguien

robber [rábə-] N ladrón -ona *mf*

robbery [rábəri] N robo *m*

robe [rob] N manto *m*, traje talar *m*, túnica *f*;
(ceremonial dress) toga *f*; (bath wrap) bata *f*

robin [rábɪn] N petirrojo *m*

robot [róbət] N robot *m*

robotics [robádɪks] N robótica *f*

robust [robást] ADJ (strong) robusto; (hearty)
saludable; (solid) sólido

rock [rak] N roca *f*; (crag) peñasco *m*, peñón *m*;
(diamond) diamante *m*; (music style) rock *m*;
— crystal cristal de roca *m*; **— salt** sal de
piedra *f*, sal gema/mineral *f*; **on the —** en las
rocas; **to go on the —s** tropezar en un
escollo; *Am* escollar; **to hit —-bottom** tocar
fondo; VI/VT (move to and fro) mecer[se];
(stagger) sacudir, estremecer; **to — to sleep**
arrullar

rocker [rákə-] N (chair) mecedora *f*; (fan or
performer of rock music) roquero -ra *mf*

rocket [rákɪt] N cohete *m*

rocketry [rákɪtri] N cohetería *f*

rocking [rákɪŋ] N **— chair** mecedora *f*; **—
horse** caballito de madera *m*, caballito
mecedor *m*

rocky [ráki] ADJ (with rocks) rocoso; (difficult)
difícil

rod [rad] N (stick) vara *f*, varilla *f*; (in engine)
vástago *m*; (measure of length)
aproximadamente 5 metros *f*

rode [rod] *see* ride

rodent [ródənt] N roedor *m*

rodeo [ródio] N rodeo *m*

rogue [rog] N pícaro -ra *mf*, bribón -ona *mf*; ADJ
solitario y bravo

roguish [rógɪʃ] ADJ (rascally) pícaro, bribón;
(mischievous) travieso

role [rol] N (in a drama) papel *m*, rol *m*; **—
model** modelo ejemplar *m*; **—-playing**
improvisación *f*

roll [rol] VI (move on wheels, rotate) rodar;
(rotate one's eyes) revolear; (sway)
balancearse, bambolearse; (reverberate)
retumbar; (flow as waves) ondular; VT (steel)
aplanar; (cigarettes) liar; (a drum) redoblar;
(one's r's) pronunciar la erre; **to — over in**

the snow revolcarse en la nieve; **to— up** arrollar, enrollar; **to— around** llegar; **to— back** reducir, rebajar; **to— by** pasar; **to— out** (products) lanzar; **to— over** (physically) volcar, darse vuelta; (investments) reinvertir; **to get—ing** ponerse en marcha; N (of paper, fabric, etc.) rollo m; (of coins) cartucho m; (of a ship) balanceo m; (of thunder) retumbo m; (of a drum) redoble m; (of members) lista f; (of waves) ondulación f; (of a typewriter) carro m; (of bread) bollo m, panecillo m; (of dice) tiro m; ADJ **—-on** de bolita

roller [rólə] N (for painting, moving things) rodillo m; (hair) rulo m, rulero m; **— coaster** montaña rusa f; **— skate** patín de ruedas m

rolling [rólɪŋ] ADJ (countryside) ondulado; (wheel) rodante; **— pin** rodillo m, palote m

roly-poly [rólipóli] ADJ rechoncho

ROM [read-only memory] [rɑm] N ROM f, memoria de ROM f, memoria de sólo lectura f

Roman [rómən] ADJ & N romano -na mf; **— numeral** número romano m

romance [rómæns] N (love affair, story) romance m; (romantic atmosphere) romanticismo m; VT cortejar; ADJ (linguistic) romance, románico

romanesque [romənésk] ADJ románico

Romania [roméniə] N Rumania f

Romanian [roméniən] ADJ & N rumano -na mf

romantic [románṭɪk] ADJ romántico

romanticism [romántəsɪzəm] N romanticismo m

romp [rɑmp] VI (frolic) retozar, brincar; (win easily) arrasar; N (frolic) retozo m; (victory) victoria fácil f

roof [ruf] N (ceiling) techo m, tejado m; (flat roof) azotea f; **— of the mouth** paladar m; **to hit the —** poner el grito en el cielo; VT techar

rookie [rúki] N novato -ta mf

room [rum] N (in building) cuarto m; (large) sala f; (in a hotel) habitación f; (space) lugar m, sitio m; **— and board** pensión completa f; **—mate** compañero -ra de cuarto mf; **— service** servicio a la habitación f; **to take up —** ocupar espacio; **the whole— laughed** todos los presentes se rieron; VI hospedarse, alojarse

roomy [rúmi] ADJ espacioso, amplio

roost [rust] N vara f; VI posarse [para dormir]

rooster [rústə] N gallo m

root [rut] N raíz f; **— canal** (part of tooth) canal radicular m, tratamiento de conducto m; **— directory** directorio de raíz m, directorio raíz m; **to take —** (a plant) echar raíces, prender; (an idea) arraigar[se]; VI (grow roots) arraigar[se], echar raíces, (dig) hozar; **to— for** animar; **to— out/up** (uproot) arrancar de raíz; (eradicate) erradicar

rope [rop] N (cord) soga f, cuerda f; (lasso) reata f,

lazo m; (on a ship) cabo m; (thick) maroma f; **to be at the end of one's —** no dar más; **to know the —s** conocer el paño, sabérselas todas; VT enlazar; **to— off** acordonar; **to— someone in** agarrar a alguien

Rorschach test [rórʃɑk test] N prueba de Rorschach f

rosary [rózəri] N rosario m

rose [roz] N rosa f; (color) rosa m; **—bud** capullo de rosa m, pimpollo de rosa m; **—bush** rosal m; ADJ **—-colored** de color rosa

rose [roz] see **rise**

rosemary [rózmɛri] N romero m

roseola [rozíələ] N roséola f

roster [rústə] N lista f

rostrum [rástrəm] N tribuna f

rosy [rózi] ADJ (pink) rosado, color de rosa; (of cheeks) sonrosado; **— future** porvenir halagüeño m

rot [rɑt] VI/VT pudrir[se]; N podredumbre f

rotary [róḍəri] ADJ rotatorio, rotativo

rotate [rótet] VI/VT rotar

rotation [rotéʃən] N rotación f, giro m

rotor [róḍə] N rotor m

rotten [rátn] ADJ (decomposing) podrido; (stinking) hediondo; (morally corrupt) corrupto; (despicable) odioso

rotund [roṭánd] ADJ rollizo

rouge [ruʒ] N colorete m

rough [rʌf] ADJ (coarse) áspero, rugoso; (violent) violento; (rude) tosco; (approximate) aproximado; (bumpy) desigual, irregular; (rugged) agreste, bronco; (stormy) picado, revuelto; **— diamond** diamante en bruto m; **— draft** borrador m; **— estimate** aproximación f; **— weather** mal tiempo m; **he had a — time** le fue mal; VI **to— it** vivir sin lujos ni comodidades

roughly [rʌfli] ADV (not smoothly) ásperamente; (rudely) groseramente, rudamente; (approximately) aproximadamente; **to estimate —** tantear

roughness [rʌfnɪs] N (lack of smoothness) aspereza f; (rudeness) rudeza f; (unevenness) desigualdad f; **the — of the sea** lo picado del mar

roulette [rulét] N ruleta f

round [raʊnd] ADJ redondo; **— number** número redondo m; **— trip** viaje de ida y vuelta m; N (of talks, drinks, dance) ronda f; (of cheese) rodaja f; (in cards, sports) vuelta f; (in boxing) round m, asalto m; (of golf) partido m, ronda f; (canon) canon m; **— of ammunition** carga de municiones f; **— of applause** aplauso m; **—up** (of cattle) rodeo m; (of criminals) redada f; **to make the—s** hacer la ronda; PREP & ADV **—about** indirecto; **—-the-clock** veinticuatro horas al día; **all year —** todo el año; **to come—**

pasar; **to go — a corner** doblar una esquina; VT (a corner) doblar; (an edge, a number) redondear; **to — off/out** redondear; **to — up** juntar, reunir; **to — up cattle** juntar el ganado

roundness [ráundnɪs] N redondez f

rouse [rauz] VI/VT (wake) despertar[se]; VT (instigate) incitar

rout [raut] N (defeat) derrota aplastante f; (flight) huida en desbandada f; VT (defeat) derrotar, destrozar; (cause to flee) poner en fuga

route [raut, rut] N ruta f, trayecto m, recorrido m; (of newspaper delivery) reparto m; VT dirigir

routine [rutín] N rutina f

rove [rov] VI/VT vagar [por], errar [por]

rover [róvɚ] N vagabundo -da mf

row[1] [rau] N (fight) riña f, pelea f, bronca f

row[2] [ro] N (line) fila f, hilera f, ringlera f; **four times in a —** cuatro veces seguidas; VI/VT (propel with oars) remar, bogar; **—boat** bote de remos m, barca f

rowdy [ráudɪ] ADJ (person) alborotador; (party) bullicioso; N camorrista mf

rower [róɚ] N remero -ra mf

royal [róɪəl] ADJ real; **— blue** azul marino m; **— flush** escalera real f

royalty [róɪəlti] N (group) realeza f; (person) miembro de la realeza m; **royalties** derechos m pl, regalías f pl

RSVP [**répondez s'il vous plaît**] [áɾésvípí] LOC S.R.C.

rub [rʌb] VI/VT (apply friction) frotar[se]; (massage) friccionar; (spread on) aplicar frotando; (make sore) rozar; **to — off** quitar[se] frotando; **to — out** borrar; **to — shoulders with** codearse con; **to — the wrong way** peinar a contrapelo; **don't — it in!** ¡no me lo refriegues por la cara! N (act of rubbing) fricción f; (difficulty) dificultad f; (abraded area) roce m, frote m

rubber [rʌ́bɚ] N caucho m, goma f; **— band** goma elástica f; **—s** chanclos m pl; **— stamp** sello de goma m; **— tree** gomero m; VT **to —- stamp** autorizar automáticamente

rubbing alcohol [rʌ́bɪŋ ǽlkəhɔl] N alcohol para fricciones m

rubbish [rʌ́bɪʃ] N (trash) basura f; (nonsense) pamplinas f pl

rubble [rʌ́bəl] N (debris) escombros m pl; (stone fragments) ripios m pl, cascote m

rubella [rubélə] N rubéola/rubeola f, sarampión alemán m

rubric [rúbrɪk] N rúbrica f

ruby [rúbi] N rubí m

ruckus [rʌ́kəs] N barahúnda f, jaleo m

rudder [rʌ́dɚ] N timón m

ruddy [rʌ́di] ADJ rubicundo

rude [rud] ADJ (impolite) grosero; (uncouth, crude, simple) tosco; (harsh) rudo

rudeness [rúdnɪs] N (impoliteness) grosería f; (crudeness) tosquedad f; (harshness) rudeza f

rueful [rúfəl] ADJ (inspiring pity) triste; (repentant) arrepentido

ruffian [rʌ́fiən] N rufián m

ruffle [rʌ́fəl] VI/VT (gather cloth) fruncir[se]; (raise feathers) erizar[se]; (ripple water) agitar[se], rizar[se]; (muss hair) desgreñar[se]; (bother a person) molestar[se], fastidiar[se]; N (frill on clothes) volante m; (gathering in cloth) frunce m, pliegue m; (ripples in water) ondulación f, rizo m

rug [rʌg] N alfombra f; (hairpiece) peluquín m

rugby [rʌ́gbi] N rugby m

rugged [rʌ́gɪd] ADJ (terrain) escarpado, áspero, fragoso; (face) recio; (manners) tosco; (way of life) duro; (man) robusto

ruin [rúɪn] N ruina f; **to go to —** arruinarse, venirse abajo; VI/VT arruinar[se], estropear[se]; (spoil) echar[se] a perder

ruinous [rúɪnəs] ADJ ruinoso

rule [rul] N (principle) regla f; (line separating newspaper columns) filete m; (government) mando m, gobierno m; **—s and regulations** reglamentos y disposiciones administrativas m pl; **the — of law** el imperio de la ley; **as a — of thumb** por regla general, a ojo de buen cubero; VI/VT (govern) reinar, gobernar; (decree) fallar, dictaminar, sentenciar; (put lines on paper) rayar, poner renglones; **to — out** excluir; **to — over** reinar, gobernar

ruler [rúlɚ] N (governor) gobernante mf; (measuring instrument) regla f

ruling [rúlɪŋ] N (decision) fallo m, sentencia f, dictamen m; (line on paper) renglón m; ADJ (governing) gobernante, reinante

rum [rʌm] N ron m

rumba [rʌ́mbə] N rumba m; VI rumbear

rumble [rʌ́mbəl] VI (as thunder) retumbar; (as a stomach) hacer ruido; (fight) pelear; N (roar) retumbo m; (growl) ruido m; (fight) pelea f

ruminate [rúmənet] VI rumiar

rummage [rʌ́mɪʤ] VI/VT rebuscar, hurgar; N cachivaches m pl; **— sale** venta de beneficencia f

rumor [rúmɚ] N rumor m; VT murmurar; **it is —ed that** se rumorea que, corre la voz que

rump [rʌmp] N (of quadruped) anca f, grupa f; (of bird) rabadilla f; (of person) trasero m

run [rʌn] VI (person, tears, water) correr; (stockings, dyes) correrse; (machines) funcionar; (faucet) chorrear; (candidate) presentarse como candidato; (sore) supurar; VT (a mile, a risk) correr; (one object through another) pasar; (a business) manejar; (a red light) comerse; (a news story) publicar; (a sum of money) costar; (a computer program) ejecutar; (a fever) tener; **— along**

now! ¡vete! **to — across someone**
encontrarse con alguien; **to — after**
perseguir; **to — around with** andar con; **to
— away** fugarse, escaparse; **to — down**
(stop working) dejar de funcionar; (capture)
aprehender; (criticize) hablar mal de; (run
over) atropellar; (tire) cansar; **to — dry**
secarse; **to — into** (encounter) tropezarse
con, encontrarse con; (collide) chocar con; **to
— out** salir corriendo; **to — out of money**
quedarse sin dinero; **to — over** (spill)
derramarse; (run down) atropellar, arrollar;
(move along a surface) deslizar por; **to —
through** (stab) atravesar; (squander)
despilfarrar; **to — up** acumular; **the play
ran for three months** la obra estuvo en
cartel durante tres meses; **it —s in the
family** es un rasgo de familia; N (act of
running) carrera f, corrida f; (point in
baseball) carrera f, anotación f; (defect in
stockings) carrera f, corrida f; (routine trip)
recorrido m; (of newspapers) tirada f; (of a
play) temporada en cartel f; (on a bank)
pánico m, corrida f; **—away** fugitivo -va mf;
—away horse caballo desbocado m; **—
batted in** carrera impulsada f; **— of good
luck** racha de buena suerte f; **— of the mill**
del montón; **—way** (for planes) pista f; (for
models) pasarela f; **to be on the —** estar
huyendo; **in the long —** a la larga; **he gave
me the —around** contestó con evasivas;
she gave us a —down nos hizo un
resumen; ADJ **—down** desvencijado
rung [rʌŋ] N (of a chair) barrote m; (of a ladder)
peldaño m
rung [rʌŋ] *see* ring
runner [rʌnɚ] N (one who runs) corredor -ora
mf; (on a table) tapete m; (on a sled) patín m;
(on a skate) cuchilla f; (on a plant) estolón m;
(of drugs, contraband) contrabandista mf; **—
up** segundo -da mf
running [rʌnɪŋ] N (of a race) corrida f, carrera f;
(of a business) manejo m, dirección f; (of
water) flujo m; (of machines) funcionamiento
m; (of a car) rodaje m; **to be out of the —**
estar fuera de combate; **— board** estribo m;
ADJ (sore) supurante; **— water** agua
corriente f; **in — condition** en buen estado;
for ten days — durante diez días seguidos
runt [rʌnt] N (animal) animal más pequeño de la
camada m; (person) *pej* mequetrefe m
rupture [rʌptʃɚ] N (of relations, internal organ)
ruptura f; (of a tire) rotura f; (hernia) hernia f;
VI/VT romper[se], reventar[se]
rural [rúrəl] ADJ rural
rush [rʌʃ] VI/VT (hurry) apresurar[se]; *Am*
apurar[se]; VT (a parcel) llevar con prisa,
llevar rápido; (an enemy) precipitarse,
abalanzarse sobre; **to — by/past** pasar

corriendo; **to — out** salir corriendo; N (haste)
prisa f; *Am* apuro m; (attack) acometida f;
(hurried activity) bullicio m; (plant) junco m;
— hour hora punta f; **— of air** ráfaga f; **— of
people** tumulto m; **— of water** torrente m;
— order pedido urgente m
Russia [rʌʃə] N Rusia f
Russian [rʌʃən] ADJ & N ruso -sa mf
rust [rʌst] N (oxidation) herrumbre f, orín m;
(disease) tizón m; ADJ **—colored** color
herrumbre; **—proof** inoxidable; VI/VT
herrumbrar[se]
rustic [rʌstɪk] ADJ rústico; N campesino -na mf,
paleto -ta mf
rusting [rʌstɪŋ] N oxidación f
rustle [rʌsəl] VI susurrar, crujir; VT hacer
susurrar, hacer crujir; **to — cattle** robar
ganado; N susurro m, crujido m
rusty [rʌsti] ADJ (oxidized) herrumbrado,
oxidado; (rust-colored) color herrumbre; (out
of practice) falto de práctica; **my German is
—** se me ha olvidado el alemán
rut [rʌt] N (furrow) surco m; (of a wheel) rodada
f; (routine) rutina f; (heat) celo m; **to be in a
—** ser esclavo de la rutina; VI estar en celo
ruthless [rúθlɪs] ADJ despiadado
ruthlessness [rúθlɪsnɪs] N crueldad f
Rwanda [ruándə] N Ruanda f
Rwandan [ruándən] ADJ & N ruandés -esa mf
rye [raɪ] N centeno m; **— bread** pan de centeno m

Ss

saber [sébɚ] N sable m
sabotage [sǽbətɑʒ] N sabotaje m; VT sabotear
sac [sæk] N bolsa f, saco m
saccharine [sǽkɚɪn] ADJ empalagoso; N
sacarina f
sack [sæk] N (bag) saco m, bolso m; (looting)
saqueo m; (in football) captura f; **in the —** en
la cama; VT (bag) embolsar, ensacar; (loot)
saquear; (fire) despedir
sacrament [sǽkrəmənt] N sacramento m
sacred [sékrɪd] ADJ sagrado
sacrifice [sǽkrəfaɪs] N (also in baseball)
sacrificio m; **at a —** con pérdida; VT sacrificar
sacrilege [sǽkrəlɪdʒ] N sacrilegio m
sacrilegious [sækrəlídʒəs] ADJ sacrílego
sacrum [sékrəm] N sacro m
sad [sæd] ADJ triste
sadden [sǽdn̩] VI/VT entristecer[se]; VT pesar
saddle [sǽdl̩] N (for horse) silla de montar f,
montura f; (for bicycle) sillín m; **—bag** alforja
f; **— horse** caballo de silla m; **— pad** carona f;
— tree arzón m; VT ensillar; **to — up**
ensillar; **to — someone with**

responsibilities cargar a alguien de responsabilidades

sadism [sédɪzəm] N sadismo *m*

sadistic [sədístɪk] ADJ sádico

sadness [sǽdnɪs] N tristeza *f*

safari [səfóri] N safari *m*

safe [sef] ADJ (secure) seguro, salvo; (trustworthy) digno de confianza; (careful) precavido, prudente; — **and sound** sano y salvo; — **deposit box** caja de seguridad *f*; —**guard** salvaguarda *f*; —**keeping** custodia *f*; — **mode** modo a prueba de fallos/errores *m*; N caja fuerte *f*; —**conduct** salvoconducto *m*; ADV (in baseball) safe; VT **to —guard** salvaguardar

safely [séfli] ADV (without danger) sin peligro; (without incident) sin percances; **I can — say** puedo decir con toda seguridad

safety [séfti] N seguridad *f*; — **belt** cinturón de seguridad *m*; — **device** mecanismo de seguridad *m*, seguro *m*; — **glass** vidrio inastillable *m*; — **net** red *f*; — **pin** imperdible *m*

saffron [sǽfrən] N (spice) azafrán *m*; (color) color azafrán *m*

sag [sæg] VI/VT (wall) combar[se], pandear[se]; VI (stock market, breast) caer; (spirits) decaer; (rope) aflojarse; (pants) abolsarse; **his shoulders** — tiene las espaldas caídas; N (of a wall) pandeo *m*, comba *f*; (in prices) caída *f*

sage [sedʒ] ADJ sabio; N (wise person) sabio -bia *mf*; (plant) salvia *f*

said [sed] *see* say

sail [sel] N (part of a boat) vela *f*; (trip) viaje en barco *m*; —**boat** velero *m*; —**fish** pez vela *m*; **under full** — a toda vela; **to set** — zarpar; VI/VT (travel by boat) navegar; (set sail) zarpar; **to — along** deslizarse, navegar; **to — along the coast** costear; **to — through an exam** aprobar un examen con facilidad

sailor [sélæ] N marinero -ra *mf*

saint [sent] N santo -ta *mf*; — **John** San Juan

saintly [séntli] ADJ santo, piadoso

sake [sek] N **for the — of** por; **for my** — por mí; **for pity's** — por el amor de Dios; **for brevity's** — para ser breve; **for the — of argument** por vía de argumento; **art for art's** — el arte por el arte

salad [sǽləd] N ensalada *f*; — **dressing** aderezo *m*

salamander [sǽləmændæ] N salamandra *f*

salary [sǽləri] N sueldo *m*, retribución *f*; — **bracket** categoría salarial *f*; — **range** escala de sueldos *f*, escala salarial *f*

sale [sel] N (act of selling) venta *f*; (special sales event) liquidación *f*, saldo *m*; —**s clerk** dependiente -ta *mf*; —**s force** personal de ventas *m*; —**sperson** dependiente -ta *mf*; —**s tax** impuesto sobre las ventas *m*; **for** — en

venta; **on** — con rebaja, rebajado

salient [séliənt] ADJ & N saliente *m*

saline [sélin] ADJ salino; — **solution** solución salina *f*

saliva [səláivə] N saliva *f*

sally [sǽli] N (sortie) salida *f*; (excursion) excursión *f*; VI salir, hacer una salida; **to — forth** salir

salmon [sǽmən] N salmón *m*

salmonella [sælmənélə] N salmonela *f*

salon [səlán] N salón *m*; (beauty parlor) salón de belleza *m*, peluquería *f*

saloon [səlún] N salón *m*, taberna *f*, bar *m*

salt [sɔlt] N sal *f*; (for smelling) sales *f pl*; —**cellar** salero *m*; — **lick** salegar *m*; — **mine** salina *f*; —**peter** salitre *m*; —**shaker** salero *m*; —**water** agua salada *f*; **old** — lobo de mar *m*; **the** — **of the earth** la sal de la tierra; VT salar; **to — away** ahorrar

salty [sɔlti] ADJ (food, water) salado; (soil, water) salobre

salutation [sæljətéʃən] N saludo *m*

salute [səlút] N saludo *m*; (of guns) salva *f*; VI/VT (greet) saludar; (acknowledge) reconocer

Salvadoran, Salvadorian [sælvədɔ́r(i)ən] ADJ & N salvadoreño -ña *mf*

salvage [sǽlvɪdʒ] N (recovery) salvamento *m*; (objects recovered) objetos salvados *m pl*; VT salvar

salvation [sælvéʃən] N salvación *f*

salve [sæv] N ungüento *m*, pomada *f*

salvo [sǽlvo] N salva *f*

same [sem] ADJ (identical) mismo; (similar) igual; —**day delivery** entrega el mismo día *f*; **it is all the** — **to me** me da igual, me da lo mismo; **the** — **to you** igualmente; **all the** — de todos modos

Samoa [səmóə] N Samoa *f*

Samoan [səmóən] ADJ & N samoano -na *mf*

sample [sǽmpəl] N muestra *f*; VT (try) probar; (take samples) muestrear

sampling [sǽmplɪŋ] N muestreo *m*

sanatorium [sænətóriəm] N sanatorio *m*

sanctify [sǽŋktəfaɪ] VT santificar

sanction [sǽŋkʃən] N sanción *f*; VT sancionar

sanctity [sǽŋktɪti] N santidad *f*

sanctuary [sǽŋktʃueri] N (church auditorium, place of refuge) santuario *m*; (game preserve) reserva *f*

sand [sænd] N arena *f*; —**box** arenero *m*; —**dollar** erizo de mar plano *m*; —**paper** papel de lija *m*; **to** —**paper** lijar; —**stone** arenisca *f*; —**storm** tormenta de arena *f*; —**trap** trampa de arena *f*; VT lijar, pulir

sandal [sǽndl] N sandalia *f*

sandwich [sǽndwɪtʃ] N bocadillo *m*, emparedado *m*; VT intercalar; **to be —ed between** quedar apretado entre

sandy [sǽndi] ADJ (full of sand) arenoso,

arenisco; (yellowish red) rubio

sane [sen] ADJ cuerdo

sang [sæŋ] *see* sing

sanitary [sǽnɪteri] ADJ sanitario; — **napkin** paño higiénico *m*

sanitation [sænɪtéʃən] N (sewers) saneamiento *m*; (hygiene) salubridad *f*

sanity [sǽnɪdi] N cordura *f*

sank [sæŋk] *see* sink

San Marinese [sænmærəníz] ADJ & N sanmarinense *mf*, sanmarinés -esa *mf*

San Marino [sænməríno] N San Marino *m*

Sanskrit [sǽnskrɪt] N sánscrito *f*

Santa Claus [sǽntəklɔz] N Papá Noel *m*, Santa Claus *m*

São Tomean [sautoméán] ADJ & N santotomense *mf*

São Tome and Principe [sautoméǽndprínsipe] N Santo Tomé y Príncipe *m*

sap [sæp] N (juice) savia *f*; (fool) tonto -ta *mf*; VT (exhaust) agotar

sapling [sǽplɪŋ] N (tree) árbol joven *m*; (person) jovenzuelo -la *mf*

sapphire [sǽfaɪr] N zafiro *m*

sarcasm [sárkæzəm] N sarcasmo *m*, socarronería *f*

sarcastic [sarkǽstɪk] ADJ sarcástico, socarrón

sarcoma [sarkómə] N sarcoma *m*

sarcophagus [sarkáfəgəs] N sarcófago *m*

sardine [sardín] N sardina *f*

sardonic [sardánɪk] ADJ sardónico

sash [sæʃ] N (around waist) faja *f*; (around shoulder) banda *f*; (on window) marco *m*, bastidor *m*

sassy [sǽsi] ADJ insolente

sat [sæt] *see* sit

satanic [sətǽnɪk] ADJ satánico

satchel [sǽtʃəl] N cartera *f*

satellite [sǽdlaɪt] N satélite *m*; — **dish** [antena] parabólica *f*

satiate [séʃiet] VT saciar, hartar

satin [sǽtn] N raso *m*, satén *m*

satire [sǽtaɪr] N sátira *f*

satirical [sətírɪkəl] ADJ satírico

satirize [sǽdəraɪz] VT satirizar

satisfaction [sædɪsfǽkʃən] N satisfacción *f*

satisfactory [sædɪsfǽktəri] ADJ satisfactorio

satisfied [sǽdɪsfaɪd] ADJ satisfecho

satisfy [sǽdɪsfaɪ] VI/VT satisfacer

saturate [sǽtʃəret] VI/VT (impregnate) saturar[se]; (soak) empapar[se]; **—d fat** grasa saturada *f*

Saturday [sǽdə-De] N sábado *m*

sauce [sɔs] N salsa *f*; —**pan** cacerola *f*; VT aderezar con salsa

saucer [sɔ́sə-] N platillo *m*

saucy [sɔ́si] ADJ (insolent) fresco, descarado, insolente; (who talks back) respondón

Saudi Arabia [sɔ́diərébiə] N Arabia Saudí *f*, Arabia Saudita *f*

Saudi Arabian [sɔ́diərébiən] ADJ & N saudí *mf*, saudita *mf*

saunter [sɔ́ntə-] VI pasearse, deambular

sausage [sɔ́sɪdʒ] N (thick) chorizo *m*; (thin) salchicha *f*; (cured) longaniza *f*; —**-making** charcutería *f*

savage [sǽvɪdʒ] ADJ (uncivilized) salvaje; (furious) rabioso; (rugged) agreste; N salvaje *m*; VT hacer trizas de

savagery [sǽvɪdʒri] N salvajismo *m*, barbarie *f*

savannah [səvǽnə] N sabana *f*

save [sev] VT (a sinner, a person in danger) salvar; (furniture) salvaguardar, proteger; (money, time, energy) ahorrar, economizar; (data) guardar; VI (lay up money, be economical) ahorrar; (protect) salvaguardar; **to — from** librar de; **— as** (on a computer) almacenar como, guardar como; **to — one's eyes** cuidarse la vista; N (in baseball) salvado *m*; PREP salvo, menos

savings [sévɪŋz] N ahorros *m pl*; — **account** cuenta de ahorros *f*; — **bank** caja de ahorros *f*

savior [sévjə-] N salvador -ora *mf*

savor [sévə-] N (taste) sabor *m*; (trace) dejo *m*; VT saborear

savory [sévəri] ADJ (delicious) sabroso; (not sweet) salado

savvy [sǽvi] N astucia *f*; ADJ astuto

saw [sɔ] N sierra *f*; —**horse** caballete *m*; VI/VT aserrar[se]; —**dust** aserrín *m*, serrín *m*; —**mill** aserradero *m*

saw [sɔ] *see* see

sawn [sɔn] *see* saw

saxophone [sǽksəfən] N saxofón *m*

say [se] VT (something interesting) decir; (a prayer) rezar; VI (a clock) marcar; (a sign) rezar, decir; —**!** ¡oye! **that is to —** es decir; — **I bought it** supongamos que yo lo comprara; **it goes without —ing** huelga decir[lo]; **there's a lot to be said for** es muy recomendable; **when all is said and done** al fin y al cabo; **you can — that again** tú lo has dicho; N **the final —** la última palabra; **to have one's —** dar su opinión; ADV **you could earn, —, a million dollars** podrías ganar, pongamos, un millón de dólares

saying [séɪŋ] N dicho *m*, refrán *m*

scab [skæb] N (of a wound) costra *f*; (on plants) roña *f*; (strikebreaker) esquirol *m*, amarillo -lla *mf*; VI (wound) formar una costra; (break a strike) ser esquirol

scabby [skǽbi] ADJ (wound) costroso; (plant) roñoso

scaffold [skǽfəld] N (in construction) andamio *m*; (of a gallows) patíbulo *m*

scald [skɔld] VI/VT escaldar[se]; N escaldadura *f*

scale [skel] N (progression) escala *f*; (for weighing) balanza *f*; (heavy-duty) báscula *f*;

(on fish, reptiles, human skin) escama *f*; **pair of —s** balanza *f*; VT (climb) escalar; (remove scales) escamar; VI/VT (adjust proportionately) graduar, escalar; **to — down** rebajar proporcionalmente

scallion [skǽljən] N cebollino *m*

scallop [skǽləp] N (mollusk) vieira *f*; (of beef) escalope *m*; (of fabric) festón *m*; VT festonear

scalp [skælp] N cuero cabelludo *m*; VT (to skin) arrancar la cabellera; (to resell) revender

scalpel [skǽlpəl] N bisturí *m*

scalper [skǽlpə-] N revendedor -ora *mf*

scam [skæm] N timo *m*, estafa *f*

scamp [skæmp] N pícaro -ra *mf*, tunante -ta *mf*, pillo -lla *mf*

scamper [skǽmpə-] VI (run) escabullirse, escaparse; (caper) cabriolar

scan [skæn] VT (horizon) escudriñar, escrutar; (brain) hacer una tomografía; (page) echar un vistazo a; (verse) escandir; (digitalize for computer) escanear; N tomografía *f*

scandal [skǽndl] N escándalo *m*

scandalize [skǽndlaɪz] VT escandalizar

scandalous [skǽndləs] ADJ escandaloso

scanner [skǽnə-] N escáner *m*

scanning [skǽnɪŋ] N escaneado *m*

scant [skænt] ADJ escaso

scanty [skǽnti] ADJ (provisions) escaso; (skirt) muy corto; (bikini) breve

scapegoat [sképgot] N chivo expiatorio *m*, cabeza de turco *m*

scapula [skǽpjələ] N escápula *f*, omóplato *m*

scar [skar] N cicatriz *f*, lacra *f*; VT dejar una cicatriz

scarce [skɛrs] ADJ escaso; **to be —** escasear

scarcely [skérsli] ADV (barely) apenas; **he's — a genius** no es un genio ni mucho menos

scarcity [skérsɪdi] N escasez *f*, pobreza *f*, carestía *f*

scare [skɛr] VI/VT espantar[se], asustar[se]; **to — away** ahuyentar; **to — up** reunir; N susto *m*, sobresalto *m*; (of war, of a heart attack) amago *m*; **—crow** espantapájaros *m sg*

scared [skɛrd] ADJ asustado; **I'm — of spiders** tengo miedo de las arañas / las arañas me dan miedo

scarf [skarf] N (woolen) bufanda *f*; (silk, cotton) pañuelo *m*; VI **to — up** engullir

scarlet [skárlɪt] N escarlata *m*, grana *f*; **— fever** escarlatina *f*

scary [skéri] ADJ (causing fright) de miedo; (easily frightened) asustadizo

scat [skæt] INTERJ ¡fuera!

scatter [skǽɖə-] VI/VT (seeds) esparcir[se], desparramar[se], desperdigar[se]; (crowd) dispersar[se]; **—brained** atolondrado; N **—brain** cabeza de chorlito *m*

scattered [skǽɖə-d] ADJ disperso

scavenge [skǽvɪndʒ] VT recoger, rescatar; VI

hurgar

scenario [sɪnério] N guión *m*; **worst-case —** el peor de los casos

scene [sin] N escena *f*; (sphere of activity) ambiente *m*, ámbito *m*; **to make a —** montar una escena; **behind the —s** entre bastidores

scenery [sínəri] N paisaje *m*; (on a stage) decorado *m*

scenic [sínɪk] ADJ panorámico

scent [sɛnt] N (smell) olor *m*; (fragrance) perfume *m*; (trace) pista *f*, rastro *m*; (sense of smell) olfato *m*; VI/VT (perceive through smell) olfatear; (intuit) presentir; (give fragrance to) perfumar

schedule [skɛ́dʒʊɫ] N (plan) calendario *m*; (timetable) horario *m*; (appendix) apéndice *m*; (list) lista *f*; **on —** al día, a la hora prevista; **ahead of —** adelantado; VT programar, fijar

scheme [skim] N (plan) plan *m*, proyecto *m*; (plot) ardid *m*, trama *f*; (of colors) combinación *f*; VI/VT maquinar, intrigar, tramar

schemer [skímə-] N maquinador -ora *mf*, intrigante *mf*

scheming [skímɪŋ] ADJ intrigante; N maquinación *f*

schizophrenia [skɪtsəfréniə] N esquizofrenia *f*

scholar [skálə-] N (student) alumno -na *mf*; (fellow) becario -ria *mf*; (erudite person) erudito -ta *mf*, estudioso -sa *mf*

scholarly [skálə-li] ADJ erudito

scholarship [skálə-ʃɪp] N (erudition) erudición *f*; (award) beca *f*

school [skuɫ] N (primary) escuela *f*, colegio *m*; (secondary) secundaria *f*; Sp instituto *m*; (university) universidad *f*; (of law, etc.) facultad *f*; (of language, driving) academia *f*; (of thought) escuela *f*; (of fish) banco *m*, cardumen *m*; **—boy** escolar *m*; **—girl** escolar *f*; **—house** escuela *f*; **—master** maestro -tra *mf*; **—mate** compañero -ra de escuela *mf*; **—room** aula *f*, sala de clase *f*; **—teacher** maestro -tra *mf*; **— year** año lectivo *m*; VT instruir, entrenar

schooling [skúlɪŋ] N instrucción *f*

schooner [skúnə-] N goleta *f*

sciatic nerve [saɪǽdɪknɜ-v] N nervio ciático *m*

science [sáɪəns] N ciencia *f*; **— fiction** ciencia ficción *f*

scientific [saɪəntífɪk] ADJ científico; **— method** método científico *m*

scientist [sáɪəntɪst] N científico -ca *mf*

scintillate [síntlet] VI (diamonds) centellear, destellar; (stars) titilar

scissor [sízə-z] VT cortar con tijera; N **—s** tijera *f*, tijeras *f pl*; **— kick** tijera *f*, tijereta *f*

sclerosis [sklərósɪs] N esclerosis *f*

scoff [skaf] N mofa *f*, burla *f*; VI mofarse; **to — at** mofarse de, burlarse de

scold [skołd] VI/VT reprender, regañar, reñir; N regañón -ona *mf*

scolding [skółdɪŋ] N regaño *m*, reprimenda *f*

scoliosis [skoliósɪs] N escoliosis *f*

scoop [skup] N (ladle) cucharón *m*; (spoon for ice cream) cuchara *f*; (shovel) pala *f*; (news item) primicia *f*; VT sacar con cuchara; (report first) adelantarse a; **to — in a good profit** sacar buena ganancia; **to — out** (water) achicar; (a hole) cavar; **to — up** recoger

scoot [skut] VI (go fast) correr; (go away) largarse

scooter [skúdə-] N (with motor) scooter *m*; (toy) monopatín *m*, patinete *m*

scope [skop] N (range) alcance *m*, ámbito *m*; (sphere) esfera *f*; VT observar

scorch [skɔrtʃ] VI/VT chamuscar[se], quemar[se]; N chamuscadura *f*; Am quemadura *f*

score [skor] N (partial result) tanteo *m*; (total result) resultado *m*; (on a test) calificación *f*; (scratch) arañazo *m*; (twenty) veintena *f*; (of music) partitura *f*; **—board** marcador *m*; **on that —** a ese respecto; **to keep —** llevar la cuenta; **to settle old —s** ajustar cuentas; **what is the —?** ¿cómo va el marcador? VT (grade) calificar; (orchestrate) orquestar; (scratch) arañar; VI/VT (make points) marcar, tantear; (hook up with someone) ligar; **to — a goal** marcar/meter un gol

scorn [skɔrn] N desdén *m*, menosprecio *m*; VI/VT desdeñar, menospreciar

scornful [skɔ́rnfəł] ADJ desdeñoso

scorpion [skɔ́rpiən] N escorpión *m*, alacrán *m*

Scotch [skatʃ] ADJ escocés; **— whisky** whisky escocés *m*

Scotland [skátlənd] N Escocia *f*

Scotsman [skátsmən] N escocés *m*

Scotswoman [skátswᴜmən] N escocesa *f*

Scottish [skádɪʃ] ADJ escocés

scoundrel [skáᴜndrəł] N bellaco *m*, infame *m*, truhán *m*

scour [skaᴜr] VT (clean) fregar, restregar; (search an area) inspeccionar

scourge [skɜdʒ] N (affliction, means of affliction) azote *m*; VT azotar

scout [skaᴜt] N (military) explorador -ora *mf*; (child explorer) explorador -ora *mf*, scout *mf*; (for talent) cazatalentos *mf sg*; **a good —** una buena persona; VI/VT explorar; VI **to — for** buscar

scowl [skaᴜł] N ceño fruncido *m*; VI fruncir el ceño

scram [skræm] VI largarse

scramble [skrǽmbəł] VI (climb) subir a gatas; **to — for** pelearse por; **to — up** subir a gatas; VT (eggs) revolver; (numbers) mezclar; **—d eggs** huevos revueltos *m pl*; VI (difficult climb) subida difícil *f*; (struggle for possession) arrebatiña *f*

scrap [skræp] N (fragment) fragmento *m*,

pedacito *m*; (of truth) ápice *m*; (fight) riña *f*, reyerta *f*; **—book** álbum de recortes *m*; **— iron** chatarra *f*; **— paper** papel borrador *m*; **—s** sobras *f pl*, desperdicios *m pl*; VT (break apart) desguazar; (discard) desechar; VI (fight) pelearse, reñir

scrape [skrep] VI/VT (rub) raspar; (damage) arañar; **to — along** ir tirando, ir pasándola; **to — by** arreglárselas; **to — together** reunir; **to bow and —** ser muy servil; N (act of scraping) raspado *m*; (injury) raspón *m*, raspadura *f*; (sound) chirrido *m*; (fight) pelea *f*; (difficult situation) aprieto *m*

scraper [skrépə-] N raspador *m*

scratch [skrætʃ] VI/VT (mark) arañar, rasguñar; (relieve itching) rascar[se]; (cancel from a race) retirar[se]; (cause itching) picar; VI (to dig, as a hen) escarbar; **to — out** (words) tachar; (eyes) sacar; N (injury) arañazo *m*, rasguño *m*; (sound) chirrido *m*; **to start from —** empezar de cero; **— test** examen dérmico de alergias *m*

scrawny [skrɔ́ni] ADJ esmirriado

scream [skrim] N grito *m*, alarido *m*; **he's a —** es un payaso; VI/VT gritar

screech [skritʃ] N (of brakes) chirrido *m*; (of voice) chillido *m*; **— owl** lechuza *f*; VI (of brakes) chirriar; (of voice) chillar

screen [skrin] N (movie, computer) pantalla *f*; (divider) biombo *m*; (on window) mosquitero *m*; (sifter) tamiz *m*; **— door** puerta con mosquitero *f*; **—ing test** prueba de detección *f*; **—pass** pase pantalla *m*; **—play** guión *m*; **— saver** protector de pantalla *m*, salvapantallas *m sg*; **—writer** guionista *mf*; VT (conceal) tapar; (sift) tamizar; (project) proyectar; (select) seleccionar

screw [skru] N (device) tornillo *m*; (one turn) vuelta *f*; (propeller) hélice *f*; **—driver** destornillador *m* (also cocktail); **to — on** enroscar; **to — up one's courage** cobrar ánimo; **to — around** perder tiempo

scribble [skríbəł] VI/VT garabatear, garrapatear; N garabato *m*

scrimp [skrɪmp] VI hacer economías

script [skrɪpt] N (writing) escritura *f*; (screenplay) guión *m*

scripture [skríptʃə-] N escritura sagrada *f*

scroll [skroł] N (roll) rollo *m*; (adornment) voluta *f*; VI **to — down** bajar el cursor

scrub [skrʌb] VI/VT (rub) fregar, restregar; **to — up** lavarse las manos; VT (cancel) cancelar; N (cleaning) friega *f*, fregada *f*; (bushes) maleza *f*; (rough terrain) breña *f*; **— pine** pino achaparrado *m*; **— team** equipo suplente *m*; **—woman** fregona *f*

scruple [skrúpəł] N escrúpulo *m*

scrupulous [skrúpjələs] ADJ escrupuloso

scrutinize [skrútnaɪz] VI/VT escrutar,

escudriñar

scrutiny [skrútn̩i] N escrutinio *m*, examen minucioso *m*

scuba [skúbə] N escafandra *f*; VI **to — -dive** bucear

scuff [skʌf] VT (shoes) rayar; (floor) marcar; N (on shoes) raya *f*; (on floor) marca *f*

scuffle [skʌ́fəl] N refriega *f*, riña *f*; VI (fight) pelear, reñir; (shuffle) arrastrar los pies

sculptor [skʌ́lptə] N escultor -ora *mf*

sculpture [skʌ́lptʃə] N escultura *f*; VI/VT esculpir

scum [skʌm] N (in a glass) capa de suciedad *f*; (on a pond) verdín *m*; (people) *pej* escoria *f*; (vile person) *pej* canalla *mf*; **—bag** *pej* canalla *mf*; VI cubrirse de espuma; VT espumar

scurrilous [skɜ́ələs] ADJ (coarse) grosero

scurry [skɜ́i] VI correr; **to — away/off** escabullirse

scurvy [skɜ́vi] N escorbuto *m*

scuttle [skʌ́dl̩] VI (run) correr; **to — away/off** escabullirse; VT (sink a ship) hundir; (abandon a plane) abandonar

scythe [saɪð] N guadaña *f*

sea [si] N mar *mf*; **—battle** batalla naval *f*; **—board** costa *f*, litoral *m*; **—coast** costa *f*, litoral *m*; **— cow** vaca marina *f*; **— current** corriente marina *f*; **—food** frutos del mar *m pl*; **— green** verdemar *m*; **—gull** gaviota *f*; **—horse** caballito de mar *m*; **—level** nivel del mar *m*; **—lion** león marino *m*; **—man** marino *m*, marinero *m*; **—plane** hidroavión *m*; **—port** puerto de mar *m*; **—power** potencia naval *f*; **—shore** costa *f*, **—sickness** mareo *m*; **—side** costa *f*, litoral *m*; **—turtle** tortuga marina *f*; **—urchin** erizo de mar *m*; **—weed** alga [marina] *f*; **at —** (on the ocean) en el mar; (confused) perdido; **by —** por barco; **to put to —** hacerse a la mar; **on the high —s** en alta mar; ADJ marino; **—faring** marinero; **—sick** mareado; **to get —sick** marearse; **—worthy** marinero

seal [sil] N (stamp) sello *m*; (on a jar) precinto *m*; (animal) foca *f*; **to set one's — to** sellar; VT (put a seal on) sellar; (close with a seal) precintar; **—ing wax** lacre *m*; **to — one's fate** determinar el destino de uno; **to — off** acordonar; **to — in** cerrar herméticamente; **to — with wax** lacrar

seam [sim] N (sewing) costura *f*; (in rock) grieta *f*; (in ore deposits) veta *f*; VT coser

seamstress [símstrɪs] N costurera *f*

seamy [sími] ADJ sórdido

sear [sɪr] VT chamuscar

search [sɜtʃ] VI/VT (an area) rastrear, requisar; (a suitcase) registrar; (a person) cachear; **— me!** ¡a mí que me registren! ¡yo que sé! **to — for** buscar; N (for something) búsqueda *f*; (of

baggage, ships) registro *m*; (of an area) rastreo *m*; **— and replace** buscar y reemplazar; **— engine** motor de búsqueda *m*, máquina de búsqueda *f*; **— function** función de búsqueda *f*; **— light** reflector *m*; **— warrant** orden de registro *m*; **in — of** en busca de

season [sízən] N (of the year) estación *f*; (period of time) temporada *f*, época *f*; (sports schedule) temporada *f*; **in —** en temporada/época; **— ticket** billete de abono *m*; **open —** temporada de caza/pesca *f*; **out of —** fuera de temporada/época; VT (to spice) sazonar, aderezar; VI (wood) secarse; **a —ed pilot** un piloto experimentado

seasonal [sízənəl] ADJ estacional

seasoning [sízənɪŋ] N condimento *m*, aliño *m*

seat [sit] N (furniture) asiento *m*; (of bicycle) sillín *m*; (in parliament) escaño *m*; (of government) sede *f*; (in the theater) localidad *f*; (buttocks) asentaderas *f pl*; (of clothes) fondillos *m pl*; **to take a —** sentarse, tomar asiento; **— belt** cinturón de seguridad *m*; VT (cause to sit) sentar; (accommodate with seats) tener capacidad para; (place) colocar; **to — oneself** sentarse

seborrhea [sɛbəriə] N seborrea *f*

seclude [sɪklúd] VT aislar; **to — oneself from** recluirse de, aislarse de

secluded [sɪklúdɪd] ADJ apartado, aislado, recogido

seclusion [sɪklúʒən] N recogimiento *m*, aislamiento *m*

second [sékənd] ADJ segundo; **— base** segunda base *mf*, intermedia *f*; **— baseman** segunda base *mf*, camarero -ra *mf*, intermediarista *mf*; **— child** segundón -ona *mf*; **— cousin** primo -ma segundo -da *mf*; **— fiddle** segundón -ona *mf*; **— floor** primer piso *m*; **— half** (sports) segundo tiempo *m*; **—hand** de segunda mano; **— lieutenant** subteniente *mf*; **— mortgage** segunda hipoteca *f*; **— nature** automático; **—rate** mediocre, de segunda; **to get —s** repetir, servirse por segunda vez; **— serve** segundo servicio *m*; **on — thought** pensándolo bien; N (part of a minute) segundo *m*; (helper in a duel) padrino *m*; **—s** (inferior wares) artículos de segunda *m pl*; (additional helping) segunda ración *f*; **in a —** ahorita; **may I have —s?** ¿puedo repetir? VT (support) secundar, apoyar; (assist in duels) apadrinar; (support a motion) apoyar; **to — -guess** cuestionar

secondary [sékəndɛri] ADJ secundario; **— school** escuela secundaria *f*

secondly [sékəndli] ADV en segundo lugar

secrecy [síkrɪsi] N secreto *m*

secret [síkrɪt] ADJ & N secreto *m*

secretariat [sɛkrɪtǽriət] N secretaría *f*

secretary [sékrɪtɛri] N (assistant) secretario -ria *mf*; (government) ministro -tra *mf*; (furniture) escritorio *m*

secrete [sɪkrít] VT (discharge) secretar, segregar; (hide) ocultar

secretion [sɪkríʃən] N secreción *f*

secretive [síkrɪDɪv] ADJ hermético

sect [sɛkt] N secta *f*

section [sékʃən] N (component) sección *f*; (of a chapter) apartado *m*; (of a text) trozo *m*; (of a city) sector *m*; (incision) corte *m*; (of orange) gajo *m*; VT seccionar

sector [séktə] N sector *m*

sectorial [sɛktɔ́riəl] ADJ sectorial

secular [sékjələ] ADJ secular; N (person) seglar *mf*, lego -ga *mf*

secure [sɪkjúr] ADJ (certain, safe) seguro; (firm) firme; VT (make certain, guarantee) asegurar, afianzar; (make firm) afirmar, cimentar; (obtain) obtener; (protect) proteger; (lock) cerrar con llave; (capture) capturar; (tie) amarrar

security [sɪkjúrɪDi] N (safety, freedom from worry) seguridad *f*; (guarantee) fianza *f*, garantía *f*; (guarantor) fiador -ora *mf*; **— deposit** depósito de garantía *m*; **securities** valores *m pl*

sedan [sɪdǽn] N sedán *m*

sedate [sɪdét] ADJ sosegado, tranquilo; VT sedar

sedation [sɪdéʃən] N sedación *f*

sedative [sédətɪv] ADJ & N calmante *m*, sedante *m*

sedentary [sédṇteri] ADJ sedentario

sediment [sédəmənt] N sedimento *m*; (dregs) heces *f pl*

sedition [sɪdíʃən] N sedición *f*

seduce [sɪdús] VI/VT seducir [a]

seduction [sɪdʌ́kʃən] N seducción *f*

see [si] VI/VT (perceive, find out, meet, visit) ver; (understand) entender; (make sure) fijarse, asegurarse; (date) salir con; **—ing-eye dog** perro guía *m*; **let me —** a ver; **to — to** encargarse de, atender; **to — off** despedir; **to — through someone** calar a alguien; **to — about** ocuparse de; **to — out** acompañar a la puerta; N sede *f*

seed [sid] N (grains) semilla *f*; (in tennis) cabeza de serie *f*; **to go to —** echarse a perder; **— bed** semillero *m*; VI/VT (sow) sembrar; VT (remove seeds) despepitar, quitar las semillas; (player) clasificar; VI producir semillas

seedy [sídi] ADJ sórdido

seek [sik] VT (search for) buscar; (ask for) pedir; **to — after** buscar; **to — to** tratar de, esforzarse por

seem [sim] VI parecer; **they — to be here** parece que están aquí; **it —s to me** me parece

seemingly [símɪŋli] ADV aparentemente

seen [sin] *see* see

seep [sip] VI/VT rezumar[se]

seer [sir] N vidente *mf*

seesaw [sísɔ] N balancín *m*, subibaja *m*; VI oscilar

seethe [sið] VI bullir, hervir; **he was seething** hervía de rabia

segment [ségmənt] N segmento *m*

segregate [ségrɪget] VI/VT segregar

seismic [sáɪzmɪk] ADJ sísmico

seize [siz] VT (grab) asir, agarrar; (take possession) apoderarse de; (take advantage of) aprovecharse de; (confiscate) embargar, incautarse de, secuestrar; **to — upon** asir; VI **to — [up]** (mechanism, motor) agarrotarse; **to — upon** valerse de

seizure [síʒə] N (of power) toma *f*; (of property) confiscación *f*; (of drugs, guns) incautación *f*, secuestro *m*; (epileptic) ataque *m*

seldom [séldəm] ADV rara vez, raramente

select [sɪlékt] ADJ selecto; VI/VT elegir, seleccionar

selection [sɪlékʃən] N selección *f*, elección *f*

selective [sɪléktɪv] ADJ selectivo

self [sɛlf] N (ego) yo *m*; **—-assurance** desenvoltura *f*; **—-control** autocontrol *m*; **—-defense** defensa propia *f*; (juridical term) legítima defensa *f*; **—-denial** abnegación *f*; **—-determination** autodeterminación *f*; **—-discipline** autodisciplina *f*; **—-esteem** autoestima *f*; **—-government** autogobierno *m*; **—-help** autoayuda *f*; **—-image** autoimagen *f*; **—-improvement** mejora personal *f*; **—-interest** interés personal *m*; **—-made man** hombre que debe su éxito a sus propios esfuerzos *m*; **—-pity** autocompasión *f*; **—-reliance** independencia *f*, autosuficiencia *f*; **—-respect** amor propio *m*; **—-sacrifice** sacrificio *m*; **—-satisfaction** autosatisfacción *f*; **his better —** su lado bueno *m*; **his former —** lo que era antes; ADJ **—-assured** desenvuelto; **—-centered** egocéntrico; **—-composed** tranquilo; **—-confident** con confianza de sí mismo; **—-conscious** (shy) cohibido; (with complexes) acomplejado; **—-destructive** autodestructivo; **—-employed** que trabaja por cuenta propia; **—-evident** evidente; **—-explanatory** claro, fácil de entender; **—-propelled** autopropulsado; **—-righteous** que afecta superioridad moral; **—-satisfied** pagado de sí, satisfecho de sí; **—-service** autoservicio; **—-serving** interesado; **—-sufficient** autosuficiente

selfish [sélfɪʃ] ADJ egoísta

selfishness [sélfɪʃnɪs] N egoísmo *m*

selfless [sélflɪs] ADJ desinteresado, generoso

sell [sɛl] VI/VT vender[se]; **his books — well** se venden bien sus libros; **to be sold on** estar entusiasmado con; **to — off** liquidar; **to — out** (dispose of) liquidar; (betray) traicionar,

vender; (run out) agotarse; N **—off**
(liquidation) liquidación f; (decline) baja f;
—out traición f
seller [sélə] N vendedor -ora mf
selling [sélɪŋ] N venta f
semantics [sɪmǽntɪks] N semántica f
semblance [sémbləns] N apariencia f
semester [səméstə] N semestre m
semicircle [sémɪsɚkəɫ] N semicírculo m
semicolon [sémɪkolən] N punto y coma m
semiconductor [semikəndáktə] N
semiconductor m
semifinal [sémifaɪn] ADJ & N semifinal f
seminar [sémɑnɑr] N seminario m
seminary [sémɑneri] N seminario m
Semitic [səmíɾɪk] ADJ semítico
senate [sénɪt] N senado m
senator [sénəɾə] N senador -ora mf
send [sɛnd] VT enviar, mandar; **that sent chills
down my spine** me dio escalofríos; **to —
away** hacer salir; **to — back** devolver; **to —
for** mandar buscar a; **to — in** remitir; **to —
out for** encargar; **to — word** mandar decir
sender [séndə] N remitente m
Senegal [sénɪgɔl] N Senegal m
Senegalese [senɪgəlíz] ADJ & N senegalés -esa mf
senile [sínaɪɫ] ADJ senil, chocho
senility [sɪnílɪɾi] N senilidad f, chochera f,
chochez f
senior [sínjə] ADJ (with more seniority) más
antiguo; (in school) de cuarto año; (for the
elderly) para ancianos; **John Smith —** John
Smith padre; N (person of higher rank)
superior mf; (fourth-year student) estudiante
de cuarto año mf; (elderly person) persona de
la tercera edad f; **to be somebody's —** ser
mayor que alguien; **— citizen** persona de la
tercera edad f; **— partner** socio -cia principal
mf
seniority [sinjórɪɾi] N antigüedad f
sensation [senséʃən] N sensación f
sensational [senséʃənɫ] ADJ sensacional
sense [sɛns] N (of humor, honor, direction)
sentido m; (of pain, insecurity) sensación f;
(meaning) significado m, sentido m; **— of
hearing** sentido del oído m; **— of humor**
sentido del humor m; **— of sight** sentido de
la vista m; **— of smell** sentido del olfato m; **—
of taste** sentido del gusto m; **— of touch**
sentido del tacto m; **to make —** tener
sentido; **to make — of something**
entender algo; **in a —** en cierto sentido; **to
take leave of one's —s** volverse loco; **to
come to one's —s** (wake up) volver en sí; (be
reasonable) recobrar el juicio; VT (perceive)
percibir, sentir; (intuit) intuir
senseless [sénslɪs] ADJ (meaningless) sin
sentido; (unconscious) inconsciente
sensibility [sensəbílɪɾi] N sensibilidad f

sensible [sénsəbəɫ] ADJ sensato, razonable,
juicioso
sensitive [sénsɪɾɪv] ADJ (to emotions) sensible;
(to stimuli) sensitivo
sensitivity [sensɪtívɪɾi] N sensibilidad f
sensitize [sénsɪtaɪz] VT sensibilizar
sensor [sénsɔr] N sensor m
sensory [sénsəri] ADJ sensorial; **— overload**
sobrecarga sensorial f
sensual [sénʃuəɫ] ADJ sensual
sensuality [senʃuǽlɪɾi] N sensualidad f
sensuous [sénʃuəs] ADJ sensual
sent [sent] see send
sentence [séntəns] N (to prison) sentencia f,
condena f; (phrase) oración f; VT condenar,
sentenciar
sentiment [séntəmənt] N sentimiento m
sentimental [sentəméntɫ] ADJ sentimental;
(excessively) sensiblero
sentimentality [sentəmentǽlɪɾi] N
sentimentalismo m; (excessive) sensiblería f
sentinel [séntɪnəɫ] N centinela m
sentry [séntri] N centinela m; **— box** garita f
separate[1] [séprɪt] ADJ (apart) separado
separate[2] [sépəret] VI/VT separar[se]
separation [sepəréʃən] N separación f
Sephardi [səfárdi] N sefardí mf, sefardita mf
September [septémbə] N septiembre m,
setiembre m
sequel [síkwəɫ] N continuación f
sequence [síkwəns] N secuencia f; (of events)
serie f; **in —** en orden; VT secuenciar
Serb [sɚb] N (person) serbio -bia mf
Serbian [sɚbiən] ADJ serbio; N (language) serbio
m; (person) serbio -bia mf
serenade [serənéd] N serenata f, ronda f; VI/VT
dar [una] serenata [a], rondar [a]
serene [sərín] ADJ sereno
serenity [sérénɪɾi] N serenidad f
sergeant [sárdʒənt] N sargento m
serial [síriəɫ] N (novel) novela por entregas f; ADJ
(published in installments) por entregas;
(murder) en serie; **— bus** bus en serie m; **—
connector** conector en serie m; **— killer**
asesino -na en serie mf; **— mouse** ratón en
serie m; **— number** número de serie m; **—
port** puerto serie/serial m; **— printer**
impresora en serie f
series [síriz] N serie f
serious [síriəs] ADJ serio; (illness) grave
seriously [síriəsli] ADV (consider) en serio;
(injure) gravemente; **—, what do you
want?** hablando en serio, ¿qué es lo que
quieres?
seriousness [síriəsnɪs] N seriedad f; (of an
illness) gravedad f
sermon [sɚmən] N sermón m
serpent [sɚpənt] N sierpe f, serpiente f
serrated [séreɪd] ADJ serrado

serum [sírəm] N suero *m*

servant [sɜ́vənt] N sirviente -ta *mf*, criado -da *mf*

serve [sɜv] VI/VT (in a restaurant, in a store) servir, atender; (in tennis) sacar; **to — a term in prison** cumplir una condena; **to — a warrant** entregar una orden judicial; **to — as** servir de; **to — notice** advertir; **to — one's purpose** resultarle útil a alguien; **it —s me right** me lo merezco; N (in tennis) saque *m*; **— and volley** saque y volea *m*

server [sɜ́və] N (one who serves) servidor -ora *mf*; (in a restaurant) camarero -ra *mf*; (for pie) utensilio para servir *m*; (computer) servidor *m*; (tennis player) sacador -ora *mf*

service [sɜ́vɪs] N servicio *m*; (in tennis) saque *m*, servicio *m*; (of a warrant) entrega *f*; **— break** rotura de servicio *f*; **— entrance** entrada de servicio *f*; **—man** (soldier) militar *m*; (for repairs) reparador *m*; **— station** gasolinera *f*, estación de servicio *f*; **at your —** a su servicio; VT (a car) revisar; (an industry) atender, servir; (a debt) pagar; **in — training** capacitación para empleados; **out of —** (broken) averiado, fuera de servicio

serviceable [sɜ́vɪsəbəl] ADJ (practical) práctico; (durable) duradero

servile [sɜ́vaɪl] ADJ servil

servitude [sɜ́vɪtud] N servidumbre *f*

sesame [sésəmi] N sésamo *m*, ajonjolí *m*

session [séʃən] N (meeting) sesión *f*; (semester) semestre *m*; (of Congress) período de sesiones *m*

set [sɛt] VT (place) colocar; (fix) fijar, establecer; (sic) azuzar; (print) componer; VI (cement) fraguar; (jelly) cuajar; (sun) ponerse; (glue) endurecerse; **to — a bone** reducir un hueso dislocado; **to — a diamond** engastar un diamante; **to — an example** dar ejemplo; **to — a poem to music** ponerle música a un poema; **to — a precedent** establecer un precedente; **to — a trap** tender una trampa; **to — a watch** poner el reloj en hora; **to — about** disponerse a; **to — aside** (move an object) apartar; (money) ahorrar; (a claim) rechazar; (a verdict) anular; **to — back** (hinder, make earlier) atrasar; (cost) costar; (a clock) retrasar; **to — forth** exponer; **to — forth on a journey** ponerse en camino; **to — free** librar; **to — off** (make explode) hacer estallar; (start on a journey) ponerse en camino; (intensify) resaltar; **to — one's heart on** tener la esperanza puesta en; **to — one's mind on** resolverse a; **to — out for** partir para; **to — out to** proponerse; **to — right** rectificar; **to — the table** poner la mesa; **to — up** (assemble) armar; (set a trap for) tender; (establish) establecer; (a computer program) instalar; **to — upon someone** acometer a alguien; ADJ (fixed)

fijo; (ready) listo; (hard) duro; N (ensemble) juego *m*; (group) conjunto *m*; (TV) aparato *m*; (scenery) escenario *m*; (of tennis) set *m*, manga *f*; **—back** revés *m*; **— of teeth** dentadura *f*; **— point** punto de set/manga *m*; **—up** (arrangement) arreglo *m*; (assembly) montaje *m*; (installation) instalación *f*; (trap) tongo *m*, timo *m*; **—up program** programa de instalación *m*

setter [sɛ́də] N sétter *m*

setting [sɛ́dɪŋ] N (act of putting down) colocación *f*; (jewel) engaste *m*; (in theater) escenario *m*; (of sun, moon) puesta *f*; (of dial) posición *f*; **— sun** sol poniente *m*

settle [sɛ́dl] VT (a territory) colonizar, poblar; (affairs) arreglar; (argument) zanjar; (lawsuit) arreglar; (an estate) liquidar; (a bill) saldar, solventar; (one's nerves) calmar; VI (end a dispute) llegar a un arreglo; (take up residence) establecerse; (alight) posarse; (sink to bottom) depositarse; **to — down** (get married) casarse; (mend one's ways) sentar cabeza; (take up residence) instalarse; (become calm) calmarse; **to — on a date** fijar/señalar una fecha; **to — for** conformarse con; **to — up** pagar

settlement [sɛ́dlmənt] N (community) colonia *f*, población *f*; (act of establishing) asentamiento *m*; (agreement) acuerdo *m*; (of a lawsuit) arreglo *m*; (of a bill) pago *m*, finiquito *m*; (final disposition) liquidación *f*

settler [sɛ́tlə] N colono -na *mf*, poblador -ora *mf*

settling [sɛ́dlɪŋ] N asentamiento *m*

seven [sévən] NUM siete; **— hundred** setecientos

seventeen [sɛvəntín] NUM diecisiete

seventh [sévənθ] ADJ séptimo

seventy [sévənti] NUM setenta

sever [sévə] VT (an arm) cortar; (relations) romper

several [sévəəl] ADJ varios

severance pay [sévəənspe] N indemnización por despido *f*

severe [səvír] ADJ (criticism, standards) severo; (winter, test) duro; (storm, heat) intenso; (illness) grave

severity [səvɛ́rɪdi] N (of criticism, standards) severidad *f*; (of water, test) dureza *f*; (of storm, heat) intensidad *f*; (of illness) gravedad *f*

Sevillian [səvíljən] ADJ & N sevillano -na; **— dances** sevillanas *f pl*

sew [so] VI/VT coser

sewage [súɪdʒ] N aguas negras *f pl*; **— system** alcantarillado *m*

sewer [súə] N alcantarilla *f*, cloaca *f*, colector *m*

sewing [sóɪŋ] N costura *f*; **— machine** máquina de coser *f*

sewn [son] *see* sew

sex [sɛks] N sexo *m*; — **appeal** atractivo sexual *m*; — **symbol** símbolo sexual *m*; VT sexar

sexism [séksɪzəm] N sexismo *m*

sexist [séksɪst] ADJ & N sexista *mf*

sexton [sékstən] N sacristán *m*

sexual [sékʃuəl] ADJ sexual; — **assault** violación *f*; — **discrimination** discriminación sexual *f*; — **harassment** acoso sexual *m*

sexuality [sɛkʃuælɪDi] N sexualidad *f*

sexy [séksi] ADJ sexy, morboso

Seychelles [seʃéł] N Seychelles *f pl*

shabby [ʃǽbi] ADJ (worn) gastado; (slovenly) andrajoso; (tawdry) sórdido; (mean) mezquino; **not too** — no está mal

shack [ʃæk] N casucha *f*, choza *f*

shackle [ʃǽkəł] N grillete *m*; —**s** cadenas *f pl*, grillos *m pl*; VT (put in chains) engrillar; (impede) estorbar

shad [ʃæd] N sábalo *m*

shade [ʃed] N (shadow) sombra *f*; (nuance) matiz *m*; (for windows) persiana *f*; (phantom) espectro *m*; (of a lamp) pantalla *f*; **a** — **longer** un poco más largo; **in the** — a la sombra; —**s** (sunglasses) *Am* lentes negros/oscuros *m pl*; *Sp* gafas de sol *f pl*; VT (protect from sun) sombrear, dar sombra

shadow [ʃǽdo] N (dark image, shade) sombra *f*; (phantom) espectro *m*; **in the** — **of** a la sombra de; **without a** — **of doubt** sin sombra de duda; VT (darken) sombrear; (make gloomy) ensombrecer; **to** — **someone** seguirle la pista a alguien

shady [ʃédi] ADJ sombreado, umbrío; — **character** sospechoso -sa *mf*; — **dealings** negocios turbios *m pl*

shaft [ʃæft] N (of a mine) pozo *m*; (of a feather) cañón *m*; (of an elevator) hueco *m*; (of an arrow) asta *f*

shaggy [ʃǽgi] ADJ peludo, lanudo

shake [ʃek] VI (tremble) temblar; VI/VT (move back and forth) sacudir[se]; (in order to mix) agitar[se]; (elude) deshacerse de; **to** — **hands** darse la mano; **to** — **one's head** menear la cabeza; **to** — **with cold** tiritar; **to** — **with fear** temblar de miedo; **to** — **off** (a cold, disappointment, etc.) deshacerse de; (depression) librarse de; **to** — **up** (a liquid) agitar; (a person) trastornar; N (violent) sacudida *f*; (of milk) batido *m*; **hand**— apretón de manos *m*; **the** —**s** escalofríos *m pl*; —**-up** reorganización *f*

shaken [ʃékən] *see* shake

shaky [ʃéki] ADJ (hand) tembloroso; (start) vacilante

shall [ʃæł] V AUX I — **come** vendré; — **I help you?** ¿te ayudo? **thou shalt not steal** no robarás

shallow [ʃǽlo] ADJ (plate) llano; (water) poco profundo; (breathing) superficial; (explanation) superficial, somero

shallowness [ʃǽlonɪs] N (of plate) lo llano; (of water) poca profundidad *f*; (of person) superficialidad *f*

sham [ʃæm] N (hoax) farsa *f*; (impostor) impostor -ora *mf*; — **battle** simulacro de batalla *m*

shambles [ʃǽmbəłz] N desorden *m*, caos *m*

shame [ʃem] N (embarrassment) vergüenza *f*; (dishonor) deshonra *f*; (pity) lástima *f*; — **on you!** ¡qué vergüenza! **to bring** — **upon** deshonrar; VT avergonzar

shameful [ʃémfəł] ADJ vergonzoso

shameless [ʃémlɪs] ADJ desvergonzado, descarado

shamelessness [ʃémlɪsnɪs] N desvergüenza *f*

shampoo [ʃæmpú] N (product) champú *m*; (act of washing) lavado del cabello *m*; VI/VT lavar con champú

shamrock [ʃǽmrɑk] N trébol *m*

shank [ʃæŋk] N (part of leg) canilla *f*, espinilla *f*; (cut of meat) pierna *f*, pata *f*

shanty [ʃǽnti] N casucha *f*; *Sp* chabola *f*; —**town** suburbio *m*

shape [ʃep] N (form) forma *f*; (condition) condición *f*; (silhouette) bulto *m*; **to be in bad** — andar mal; **to get in** — ponerse en forma; **to take** — configurarse; VT plasmar, dar forma a; **to** — **up** reformarse

shapeless [ʃéplɪs] ADJ informe

share [ʃɛr] N (portion) parte *f*, porción *f*; (stock) acción *f*; —**cropper** aparcero *m*; —**holder** accionista *mf*; VI/VT compartir; **to** — **in** participar en

shark [ʃɑrk] N (fish) tiburón *m*; (swindler) estafador -ora *mf*

sharp [ʃɑrp] ADJ (blade) afilado, filoso; (needle) puntiagudo; (curve) cerrado; (contrast) marcado, nítido; (smell) acre; (wind) cortante; (pain) punzante; (remark) mordaz, agudo; (mind) perspicaz; (musical note) sostenido; (dresser) elegante; (cheese) picante; (ear) fino; — **eye** vista aguzada *f*; —**shooter** tirador -ora de primera *mf*; —**-tongued** mordaz; —**-witted** agudo; N (in music) sostenido *m*

sharpen [ʃɑrpən] VI/VT (knife) afilar[se]; VT (pencil) sacar punta a; (skill) afinar

sharply [ʃɑrpli] ADV (contrast) marcadamente; (respond) bruscamente, con aspereza; (turn) bruscamente

sharpness [ʃɑrpnɪs] N (of a blade) lo afilado; (of a needle) lo puntiagudo; (of a curve) lo cerrado; (of a contrast) nitidez *f*; (of a smell) acritud *f*; (of pain) intensidad *f*; (of a remark) mordacidad *f*; (of a mind) perspicacia *f*, agudeza *f*; (of cheese) lo picante

shatter [ʃǽDɚ] VI/VT (glass) astillar[se], hacer[se] añicos; (nerves) destrozar[se]; (health)

quebrantar[se]; (hopes) frustrar
shave [ʃev] VI/VT (remove hair) afeitar[se],
rasurar[se]; VT (cut thin slices) cepillar;
(graze) rozar; **to — off** rapar; N afeitado *m*,
rasurado *m*; **he had a close —** se salvó por
poco
shaven [ʃévən] *see* shave
shaver [ʃévɚ] N afeitadora *f*
shavings [ʃévɪŋz] N virutas *f pl*
shawl [ʃɔl] N mantón *m*, chal *m*
she [ʃi] PRON ella; **— who** la que, quien; N —-
bear osa *f*
sheaf [ʃif] N (of corn) gavilla *f*; (of arrows) haz *m*;
(of paper) fajo *m*
shear [ʃir] VT esquilar, trasquilar; N **—s** (for
sheep) tijeras para esquilar *f pl*; (for plants)
tijeras para podar *f pl*; (for metal) cizallas *f pl*;
(for hair) tijeras de peluquero *f pl*
shearing [ʃírɪŋ] N esquila *f*, esquileo *m*
sheath [ʃiθ] N (of sword, peas) vaina *f*; (of knife,
umbrella) funda *f*
sheathe [ʃið] VT (a sword) envainar; (a knife)
enfundar
shed [ʃɛd] N cobertizo *m*, tinglado *m*, *Am* galpón
m; VT (tears) derramar; (light) arrojar;
(leaves) perder; (skin, hair) mudar, perder; VI
(be waterproof) ser impermeable; (lose hair)
pelechar; (lose leaves) deshojarse; (lose skin)
mudar la piel
sheen [ʃin] N brillo *m*
sheep [ʃip] N oveja *f*; **—dog** perro pastor *m*,
ovejero *m*; **—skin** (hide) piel de oveja *f*;
(leather) badana *f*; (parchment) pergamino *m*;
(diploma) diploma *m*
sheepish [ʃípɪʃ] ADJ vergonzoso, tímido
sheer [ʃir] ADJ (absolute) puro, total; (fine) fino;
(vertical) vertical, acantilado
sheet [ʃit] N (bedding) sábana *f*; (of ice) capa *f*; (of
paper) hoja *f*; (of glass) lámina *f*; (of rain)
cortina *f*; **— metal** chapa de metal *f*; **—
music** música en hojas de partitura *f*
shelf [ʃɛlf] N estante *m*, repisa *f*, anaquel *m*; (of
rock) saliente *f*
shell [ʃɛl] N (turtles, snail) caparazón *f*; (of
mollusk) concha *f*; (of egg, nut) cáscara *f*; (of
peas) vaina *f*; (of a ship) casco *m*; (of a
building) armazón *m*; (of artillery) proyectil
m; (of a rifle) cartucho *m*; **—fish** mariscos *m
pl*; VT (nuts, eggs) pelar; (peas) desgranar;
(military target) bombardear
shelter [ʃɛltɚ] N (refuge) refugio *m*, resguardo
m, abrigo *m*; **to take —** refugiarse,
guarecerse; VI/VT (take or give refuge)
refugiar[se], resguardar[se], abrigar[se]
shelve [ʃɛlv] VT (place on a shelf) colocar en un
estante; (defer) archivar
shepherd [ʃépɚd] N pastor *m*; (dog) perro
pastor *m*
sherbet [ʃɚbɪt] N sorbete *m*

sheriff [ʃérɪf] N alguacil *m*
sherry [ʃéri] N jerez *m*
shield [ʃild] N escudo *m*; VI/VT (protect)
escudar[se]; VT (conceal) ocultar
shift [ʃɪft] VI/VT (gears) cambiar; **to — for
oneself** arreglárselas solo; **to — the blame**
echar la culpa a otro; N (of gears, of wind)
cambio *m*; (dress) vestido suelto *m*; (of
workers) turno *m*; **— key** tecla de [cambio a]
mayúsculas *f*
shiftless [ʃíftlɪs] ADJ holgazán
shimmer [ʃímɚ] VI titilar; N titileo *m*
shin [ʃɪn] N espinilla *f*, canilla *f*; VI **to — up**
trepar
shine [ʃaɪn] VI brillar, relucir; VT (shoes) limpiar,
lustrar; (furniture) lustrar; N brillo *m*,
resplandor *m*; (of shoes) lustre *m*
shingle [ʃíŋɡəl] N (on roof) teja *f*; (sign) chapa *f*;
—s (skin disorder) culebrilla *f*, zona *f*; **to
hang out one's —** abrir un consultorio; VT
cubrir con tejas
shiny [ʃáɪni] ADJ (bright) brillante; (worn)
brilloso
ship [ʃɪp] N (on water) buque *m*, navío *m*; (in air)
avión *m*; **—builder** constructor -ora naval
mf; **—mate** camarada de a bordo *mf*;
—wreck naufragio *m*; **—yard** astillero *m*;
ADJ **—shape** ordenado; VT transportar; **to —
off** sacarse de encima; VI **to —wreck**
naufragar
shipment [ʃípmənt] N cargamento *m*, remesa *f*
shipper [ʃípɚ] N (sender) expedidor -ora *mf*;
(carrier) transportista *mf*
shipping [ʃípɪŋ] N envío *m*; **— charges** gastos
de envío *m pl*; **— and handling** gastos de
envío *m pl*
shirk [ʃɚk] VT evadir, esquivar, rehuir
shirt [ʃɚt] N camisa *f*; **in —sleeves** en mangas
de camisa; **—tail** faldón *m*
shiver [ʃívɚ] VI (from cold) tiritar; (from cold,
fear, etc.) temblar; N temblor *m*; **—s**
escalofríos *m pl*
shoal [ʃol] N (sandbank) bajío *m*, banco de arena
m; (school of fish) banco *m*, bandada *f*
shock [ʃak] N (impact, disturbance) choque *m*;
(of electricity) sacudida *f*; (of wheat) hacina *f*;
(physical convulsion) shock *m*, choque *m*; **—
absorber** amortiguador *m*; **— of hair**
guedeja *f*; **— therapy** terapia de electroshock
f, terapia electroconvulsiva *f*; **— troops**
tropas de choque *f pl*; **— wave** onda
expansiva *f*; VT (bewilder) chocar, horrorizar;
(discharge electricity) dar una descarga
eléctrica; (make bundles of grain) hacinar,
hacer gavillas de
shocking [ʃákɪŋ] ADJ chocante, escandaloso
shod [ʃad] *see* shoe
shoddy [ʃádi] ADJ chapucero
shoe [ʃu] N zapato *m*; (for brakes) zapata *f*; (for

horses) herradura *f*; —**horn** calzador *m*;
—**lace** cordón *m*; —**maker** zapatero -ra *mf*;
— **polish** betún *m*; — **repairman** zapatero
-ra remendón -ona *mf*; — **store** zapatería *f*;
—**string** cordón *m*; **to live on a —string**
vivir con poco dinero; **to tie one's —s** atarse
los zapatos; VT (a person) calzar; (a horse)
herrar

shone [ʃon] *see* shine

shoo-in [ʃúɪn] N favorito -ta *mf*

shook [ʃʊk] *see* shake

shoot [ʃut] VT (wound with a bullet) pegar un
tiro; (discharge a firearm) disparar; (film a
movie) rodar; (hit a soccer ball) chutar; VI
(discharge bullet, arrow) disparar, tirar; (be
discharged) dispararse; (hunt with a gun)
cazar; (germinate) brotar; (throw) lanzar;
(take a photo) fotografiar; (film) filmar; (try
to score, in soccer) chutar; (try to score, in
basketball) tirar; **to — at** disparar a, tirar a; **to
— at goal** patear al arco; **to — by** pasar
rápidamente; **to — down** (plane) derribar;
(argument) refutar; **to — forth** brotar; **to —
up** (grow) crecer rápidamente; (damage by
shooting) tirotear; (inject drugs) chutar; N
(new growth) yema *f*, retoño *m*, vástago *m*;
(filming) rodaje *m*

shooter [ʃúɚ] N (of guns) tirador -ora *mf*; (of
balls, soccer) goleador -ora *mf*

shooting [ʃúɪŋ] N (discharge of a gun) tiro *m*,
disparo *m*; (exchange of shots) tiroteo *m*;
(filming) filmación *f*; — **guard** escolta *mf*; —
match concurso de tiro *m*; — **pain** punzada
f; —**star** estrella fugaz *f*

shop [ʃɑp] N (store) tienda *f*; (artisan's place of
business, carpentry course) taller *m*;
(business) planta *f*; —**keeper** tendero -ra *mf*;
—**lifter** ladrón -ona de tiendas *mf*; —**lifting**
hurto en las tiendas *m*; — **window**
escaparate *m*, vitrina *f*; **to talk —** hablar de
negocios; VI ir de compras; **to — for** ir a
comprar; **to —lift** hurtar [en las tiendas]

shopper [ʃápɚ] N cliente -ta *mf*, comprador -ora
mf

shopping [ʃápɪŋ] N **to go —** ir de compras; —
center centro comercial *m*

shore [ʃɔr] N costa *f*, ribera *f*; (of a lake) orilla *f*;
VT **to — up** apuntalar

shorn [ʃɔrn] *see* shear

short [ʃɔrt] ADJ (not long in duration) corto,
breve; (not long in length) corto; (not tall)
bajo; (scanty) escaso; (curt) brusco; — **circuit**
cortocircuito *m*; —**comings** limitaciones *f pl*;
—**cut** atajo *m*, cortada *f*; —**fall** déficit *m*,
insuficiencia *f*; —**hand** taquigrafía *f*; —-
handed escaso de personal; —-**legged**
pernicorto; —**sighted** miope, corto de vista;
— **stop** torpedero -ra *mf*, campocorto *mf*; —
story cuento *m*; —**wave** onda corta *f*; **in the**

— **run/haul/term** a corto plazo; **for —** para
abreviar; **in —** en resumen, en suma; **in —
order** rápidamente; **to be — on** estar escaso
de, estar alcanzado de; **to be — on
something** faltarle a uno algo; **to cut —**
interrumpir; **I'm running — on sugar** se
me está acabando el azúcar; ADV **to stop —**
parar de repente, parar en seco; **to come up
—** quedarse corto; N (circuit) cortocircuito *m*;
—**s** short *m*, pantalón corto *m*; VI/VT (a
circuit) cortocircuitar[se]; (change) dar de
menos; **to —change** dar de menos; **to — out**
fundir

shortage [ʃɔrdɪdʒ] N escasez *f*, penuria *f*

shorten [ʃɔrtn] VI/VT acortar[se]; VT recortar

shortening [ʃɔrtnɪŋ] N (lard) manteca *f*;
(abbreviation) acortamiento *m*

shortly [ʃɔrtli] ADJ (soon) en breve, pronto;
(curtly) bruscamente, secamente

shortness [ʃɔrtnɪs] N (of length, height)
cortedad *f*; (of time) brevedad *f*; (of breath)
falta *f*; (of a reply) brusquedad *f*

shot [ʃɑt] N (discharge) tiro *m*, disparo *m*;
(photograph) foto *f*; (pellet) perdigón *m*,
plomo *m*; (ball in shot-putting) bala *f*;
(injection) inyección *f*; (swallow) trago *m*;
(throw) tirada *f*; (in soccer) tiro *m*, disparo *m*;
—**gun** escopeta *f*; — **put** lanzamiento de bala
m; **not by a long —** ni con mucho; **he is a
good —** tiene buena puntería; **to take a —**
disparar; **to take a — at** intentar

shot [ʃɑt] *see* shoot

should [ʃʊd] V AUX **I — think so** ya lo creo; **you
— arrive before nine** deberías llegar antes
de las nueve; **you — eat less** tendrías que
comer menos; **you — have seen her**
tendrías que haberla visto; **were he to
come, I — be pleased** si viniera, me
alegraría

shoulder [ʃóldɚ] N (of a person, coat) hombro
m; (cut of meat) paletilla *f*; (of a road) arcén *m*;
— **blade** (person) homóplato *m*; (animal)
paletilla *f*; — **pad** hombrera *f*; **to turn a cold
— to** hacerle el vacío a; **the responsibility
is on your —s** tú tienes la responsabilidad;
VT (a load) cargar al hombro; (a task, an
expense) cargar con, asumir; (a door)
empujar con el hombro

shout [ʃaʊt] VI/VT gritar; N grito *m*

shove [ʃʌv] VI/VT empujar; **to — aside** echar a
un lado; **to — off** (go away) largarse; (push
off) desatracar; N empujón *m*, empellón *m*

shovel [ʃʌvəl] N pala *f*; VT echar con la pala

show [ʃo] VT (exhibit) mostrar, manifestar;
(prove) demostrar; (indicate) indicar, marcar;
(a film, a TV program) dar; VI (be visible)
verse, asomar; (make an appearance)
aparecerse; — **him** in hazle entrar; **to —case**
presentar; **to — mercy** tener piedad; **to —**

off hacer alarde, aparentar; **to — up** aparecer; **to — someone up** poner a alguien en evidencia; **to — the way** señalar el camino; N (exhibition) exposición f; (display) demostración f; (ostentation) ostentación f, alarde m; (performance) espectáculo m; (showing) función f; (on TV) programa m; (movie theater) cine m; — **business** farándula f; **—case** vitrina f; **—down** confrontación f; **—-off** fanfarrón -ona mf; **to go to the —** ir al cine; **for —** para impresionar

shower [ʃáʊɚ] N (rain) aguacero m, chubasco m; (bath) ducha f; (for brides) fiesta para novias f; (of sparks, blows) lluvia f; VI (bathe) ducharse; (rain) llover; VT (with gifts) inundar; (with praise) colmar

shown [ʃon] see show

showy [ʃói] ADJ ostentoso; (attractive) vistoso

shrank [ʃræŋk] see shrink

shred [ʃrɛd] N (of paper) tira f; (of evidence) pizca f; **to be in —s** estar hecho jirones; **to tear to —s** hacer trizas; VI/VT (documents) triturar; (vegetables) rallar

shrew [ʃru] N (animal) musaraña f; (woman) arpía f

shrewd [ʃrud] ADJ astuto, sagaz

shriek [ʃrik] VI/VT chillar; N chillido m

shrill [ʃrɪl] ADJ chillón

shrimp [ʃrɪmp] N (animal) camarón m; (small person) renacuajo m; VI pescar camarones

shrine [ʃraɪn] N (chapel) capilla f; (altar) altar m

shrink [ʃrɪŋk] VI/VT (in size) encoger; VI (in value) reducirse; **to — from** retroceder; N (psychiatrist) fam loquero -ra mf; **—wrap** envoltura de plástico transparente f

shrinkage [ʃríŋkɪdʒ] N (of clothes) encogimiento m; (of value) reducción f

shrivel [ʃrívəl] VI/VT secar[se], marchitar[se]

shroud [ʃraʊd] N mortaja f; VT (to wrap for burial) amortajar; (to hide) cubrir

shrub [ʃrʌb] N arbusto m

shrug [ʃrʌg] VI encogerse de hombros; VT encogerse de; **to — off** minimizar, ignorar; N encogimiento de hombros m

shrunk [ʃrʌŋk] see shrink

shrunken [ʃrʌŋkən] see shrink

shudder [ʃʌdɚ] VI (from cold) tiritar; (from fear) temblar, estremecerse; N temblor m, estremecimiento m

shuffle [ʃʌfəl] VI/VT (cards) barajar; VT (mix) mezclar; VI (walk) arrastrar los pies; (dance) bailar arrastrando los pies; **to — along** N arrastrando los pies; N (of cards) barajadura f; (of feet) arrastrapiés m sg

shun [ʃʌn] VT rehuir, evitar

shut [ʃʌt] VI/VT cerrar[se]; **to — down** cerrar; **to — off** cortar; **to — out** impedir la entrada de; **to — up** (close) cerrar bien; (lock up)

encerrar; (be quiet) callarse; N **—-down** cese de actividades m; **—-eye** sueño m; **—-in** enfermo -ma confinado -da a la casa mf

shutter [ʃʌdɚ] N (of a window) postigo m, contraventana f; (of a camera) obturador m

shuttle [ʃʌdl] N (in loom) lanzadera f; (spaceship) transbordador espacial m; (airplane) puente aéreo m; (bus, train) servicio regular m; VI ir y venir; VT llevar y traer

shy [ʃaɪ] ADJ tímido, retraído; (wary) esquivo; (lacking) escaso; VI asustarse, respingar; **to — away** (start) asustarse, respingar; (avoid) esquivar

shyness [ʃáɪnɪs] N timidez f, retraimiento m

shyster [ʃáɪstɚ] N fam picapleitos m sg

sibling [síblɪŋ] N hermano m; hermana f; **— rivalry** rivalidad entre hermanos f

sic [sɪk] VT azuzar

sick [sɪk] ADJ (ill) enfermo; (deranged) enfermizo, morboso; (at heart) angustiado; **— and tired** harto; **to be —** estar harto de; **to be — to one's stomach** tener náuseas; **to make —** (disgust) dar asco; (anger) dar rabia, enfermar; **— leave** licencia por enfermedad f

sicken [síkən] VI/VT (with illness) enfermar[se], poner[se] enfermo; (with disgust) dar asco; (with anger) dar rabia, enfermar

sickening [síkənɪŋ] ADJ repugnante

sickle [síkəl] N hoz f; **— cell anemia** anemia falciforme f

sickly [síkli] ADJ enfermizo, enclenque

sickness [síknɪs] N enfermedad f

side [saɪd] N (of a coin, piece of paper) cara f; (of a person) costado m; (of a hill) ladera f; (of beef) media res f; (of a boat) banda f; (team) equipo m; (garnish) acompañamiento m; **—arm** arma de mano f; **—bar** ladillo m; **—board** aparador m; **—burns** patillas f pl; **—-glance** mirada de soslayo/reojo f; **—light** (illumination) luz lateral f; (detail) detalle incidental m; **—line** (in sports) banda f, línea de banda f; (in business) negocio suplementario m; **to sit on the —lines** no intervenir; **—walk** acera f; Carib andén m; Am vereda f; Mex banqueta f; **—wall** flanco m; **—ways** (walk) de costado; (glance) de soslayo; **— by —** uno al lado del otro; **by his —** a su lado; **by the —of** al lado de; **on all —s** por todos lados; ADJ (on the side) lateral; (secondary) secundario; VI **to —step** evitar, esquivar; **to —track** (a train) desviar; (attention) distraer; **to — with** ponerse del lado de

siding [sáɪdɪŋ] N revestimiento m

SIDS [sudden infant death syndrome] [sídz] N síndrome de muerte súbita infantil m

siege [sidʒ] N sitio m, asedio m, cerco m; **to lay — to** sitiar

Sierra Leone [siérəlión] N Sierra Leona *f*

sieve [sɪv] N tamiz *m*, cedazo *m*

sift [sɪft] VT cerner, tamizar; **to — through** revisar

sigh [saɪ] VI suspirar; N suspiro *m*

sight [saɪt] N (sense) vista *f*; (attraction) punto de interés *m*; (ridiculous thing or person) adefesio *m*, mamarracho *m*; (on a gun) mira *f*; **—seeing** turismo *m*; **in —** a la vista; **on —** en el acto; **he is out of —** ya no se ve; **at first —** a primera vista; **to catch — of** divisar; **to lose — of** perder de vista; **you're a — for sore eyes** dichosos los ojos que te ven; VT (a ship) avistar, divisar; (a gun) apuntar

sign [saɪn] N (gesture) seña *f*, señal *f*; (indication) muestra *f*, señal *f*, indicio *m*; (placard) letrero *m*; (omen) agüero *m*, presagio *m*; (astrological, mathematical) signo *m*; (on road) cartel *m*, letrero *m*; **— language** lenguaje de signos *m*; VI/VT (write name) firmar; (signal) hacer señas [de]; VT (hire) contratar; (use sign language) hablar por señas; **to — off on** aprobar; **to — over property** ceder una propiedad; **to — up** (in a club) anotarse; (in the army) alistarse

signal [sígn̩l] N señal *f*; VI/VT señalar, hacer señas [a]; ADJ notable

signature [sígnətʃə] N firma *f*

signer [sáɪnə] N firmante *mf*, signatario -ria *mf*

significance [sɪgnífɪkəns] N significación *f*

significant [sɪgnífɪkənt] ADJ significativo; **my — other** mi media naranja *f*

significantly [sɪgnífɪkəntli] ADV (considerably) apreciablemente, considerablemente; **he looked at me —** me dio una mirada significativa/expresiva

signify [sígnəfaɪ] VT significar

silence [sáɪləns] N silencio *m*; VT (child, fears) acallar; (criticism) silenciar, enmudecer

silencer [sáɪlənsə] N silenciador *m*

silent [sáɪlənt] ADJ (machine) silencioso; (person) callado, silencioso; **— agreement** acuerdo tácito *m*; **— film** película muda *f*

silhouette [sɪluét] N silueta *f*; VT **to be —d against** perfilarse contra

silicon [sɪ́lɪkən] N silicio *m*; **— chip** chip de silicio *m*

silk [sɪlk] N seda *f*; **— industry** industria sedera *f*; **—worm** gusano de seda *m*

silken [sɪ́lkən] ADJ (of silk) de seda; (like silk) sedoso

silky [sɪ́lki] ADJ sedoso

sill [sɪl] N alféizar *m*, antepecho *m*

silly [sɪ́li] ADJ necio, bobo, lelo

silo [sáɪlo] N silo *m*

silt [sɪlt] N cieno *m*, limo *m*

silver [sɪ́lvə] N (metal, color) plata *f*; (tableware) cubiertos de plata *m pl*; ADJ (of silver) de plata; (silver-colored) plateado; **— anniversary** las bodas de plata *f pl*; **—-plated** bañado en plata; **—-plating** plateado *m*; **—smith** platero -ra *mf*; **—ware** cubiertos de plata *m pl*; VT platear; (a mirror) azogar

similar [sɪ́mələ] ADJ semejante, similar

similarity [sɪmælǽrɪɾi] N semejanza *f*, similitud *f*

similarly [sɪ́mɪlə-li] ADV de manera similar; **—, a mile is longer than a kilometer** del mismo modo, una milla es más larga que un kilómetro; **they were — surprised** quedaron igualmente sorprendidos

simile [sɪ́məli] N símil *m*

simmer [sɪ́mə] VI/VT hervir a fuego lento; **to — down** calmarse

simple [sɪ́mpəl] ADJ (uncomplicated) simple, sencillo; (naive) simple; **—minded** simple, simplón

simpleton [sɪ́mpəltən] N simplón -ona *mf*, mentecato -ta *mf*

simplicity [sɪmplísɪɾi] N (lack of complication) sencillez *f*, simplicidad *f*; (naiveté) simpleza *f*

simplify [sɪ́mpləfaɪ] VI/VT simplificar

simplistic [sɪmplístɪk] ADJ simplista

simply [sɪ́mpli] ADV (in a simple manner) con sencillez; (merely) simplemente; **it is — ridiculous** francamente, es ridículo

simulate [sɪ́mjəlet] VI/VT simular

simulation [sɪmjəléʃən] N simulación *f*

simultaneous [saɪməltténias] ADJ simultáneo

sin [sɪn] N pecado *m*; VI pecar

since [sɪns] CONJ (continuously) desde que; (inasmuch as) puesto que, ya que; PREP (continuously) desde; (from a past time) a partir de; **we have been here — five** estamos aquí desde las cinco; ADV desde entonces; **ever —** desde entonces; **he died long —** murió hace mucho tiempo; **she has — agreed** después de eso consintió

sincere [sɪnsír] ADJ sincero

sincerity [sɪnsérɪɾi] N sinceridad *f*

sine [saɪn] N seno *m*

sinew [sɪ́nju] N tendón *m*

sinewy [sɪ́njui] ADJ (full of tendons) nervudo; (robust) membrudo; (chewy) estropajoso

sinful [sɪ́nfəl] ADJ (act) pecaminoso; (person) pecador

sing [sɪŋ] VI/VT cantar; N **—song** sonsonete *m*

Singapore [sɪ́ŋəpɔr] N Singapur *m*

Singaporean [sɪŋəpɔ́riən] ADJ & N singapurense *mf*

singe [sɪndʒ] VT chamuscar, socarrar; N chamusquina *f*, socarrina *f*

singer [sɪ́ŋə] N cantante *mf*; intérprete *mf*

single [sɪ́ŋgəl] ADJ (only one) solo, único; (for one person) individual; (unmarried) soltero; **— bed** cama de una plaza *f*; **—-entry bookkeeping** teneduría por partida simple *f*; **—-family home** vivienda unifamiliar *f*; **—**

file fila india *f*; **—-handed** solo, sin ayuda; **—-minded** resuelto; **—-spacing** sencillo *m*; **every — one** cada uno; **not a — word** ni una sola palabra; N (bill) billete de uno *m*; (unmarried person) soltero -ra *mf*; (record) disco sencillo *m*; (in baseball) sencillo *m*; **—s** (in tennis) individuales *m pl*; VT **to — out** elegir

singular [síŋgjələ] ADJ & N singular *m*

sinister [sínɪstə] ADJ siniestro

sink [sɪŋk] VI/VT sentar[se]; (ship) hundir[se]; VT (money) invertir; (a well) cavar; (a pipeline) enterrar; **it finally sank in** finalmente nos dimos cuenta de eso; **to — one's teeth into** clavar los dientes en; **to — to one's knees** caer de rodillas; **sunk in thought** absorto; **my heart sank** se me fue el alma al piso; **the sun was —ing** se iba poniendo el sol; N (in the kitchen) fregadero *m*; (in bathroom) lavabo *m*; (pond for sewage) pozo negro *m*; **—hole** socavón *m*, sumidero *m*

sinner [sínə] N pecador -ora *mf*

sinuous [sínjuəs] ADJ sinuoso

sinus [sáɪnəs] N seno *m*

sinusitis [saɪnəsáɪdɪs] N sinusitis *f*

sip [sɪp] VI/VT sorber; N sorbo *m*

siphon [sáɪfən] N sifón *m*; VI/VT (liquid) sacar con sifón; (money) desviar

sir [sɚ] N señor *m*

siren [sáɪrən] N sirena *f*

sirloin [sɚ́lɔɪn] N solomillo *m*

sister [sístə] N hermana *f*; **—-in-law** cuñada *f*; **— Mary** Sor María *f*

sit [sɪt] VI sentar[se]; (pose) posar; (be seated) estar sentado; (be located) estar situado; **to — down** sentarse; **to — in on a class** ir de oyente a una clase; **to — on** posponer; **to — out a dance** saltearse una pieza; **to — still** estarse quieto; **to — tight** mantenerse firme en su puesto; **to — up** incorporarse; **to — up all night** quedarse en vela; **to — well** caer bien; N **—-in** sentada *f*; **—-up** abdominal *m*

sitcom [sítkɑm] N comedia de situación *f*

site [saɪt] N (for construction) terreno *m*, solar *m*; (on the Internet) sitio *m*; **— license** licencia de sitio *f*; **on-— training** capacitación en el lugar de trabajo

sitter [sítə] N niñera *f*, Sp canguro *mf*

sitting [sídɪŋ] N sesión *f*; **in one —** de una sentada, de un tirón; ADJ **— duck** blanco fácil *m*; **— room** cuarto de estar *m*

situated [sítʃueɪdɪd] ADJ situado, ubicado

situation [sítʃuéʃən] N situación *f*

Sitz bath [síts bæθ] N baño de asiento *m*

six [sɪks] NUM seis; **— hundred** seiscientos; N **—-pack** paquete de seis *m*; **—-shooter** revólver de seis tiros *m*

sixteen [sɪkstín] NUM dieciséis

sixth [sɪksθ] ADV & N sexto *m*

sixty [síksti] NUM sesenta

size [saɪz] N tamaño *m*; (of clothing) talla *f*; VT clasificar según el tamaño; **to — up** juzgar

sizable, sizeable [sáɪzəbəl] ADJ de tamaño considerable

sizzle [sízəl] VI chisporrotear; N chisporroteo *m*

skate [sket] N patín *m*; **—board** monopatín *m*; VI/VT patinar

skein [sken] N madeja *f*

skeletal [skélɪdl] ADJ esquelético

skeleton [skélɪtən] N esqueleto *m*, osamenta *f*; (of a building) armazón *m*; **— key** llave maestra *f*

skeptic, sceptic [sképtɪk] N escéptico -ca *mf*

skeptical [sképtɪkəl] ADJ escéptico

skepticism [sképtɪsɪzəm] N escepticismo *m*

sketch [skɛtʃ] N (drawing) boceto *m*, croquis *m*; (outline) esbozo *m*, bosquejo *m*; (skit) sketch *m*; VI/VT (draw) dibujar; (outline) bosquejar

skew [skju] VT (cloth) sesgar; (data) tergiversar

skewer [skjúə] N brocheta *f*

ski [ski] N esquí *m*; **— jump** (sport) salto con esquís *m*; (course) pista de saltos *f*; **— lift** telesquí *m*; VI/VT esquiar [en]

skid [skɪd] N patinazo *m*; VI patinar

skiing [skíɪŋ] N esquí *m*

skill [skɪl] N destreza *f*, habilidad *f*, maña *f*

skilled [skɪld] ADJ diestro, habilidoso; **— worker** obrero -ra calificado -da *mf*

skillet [skílɪt] N sartén *f*

skillful, skilful [skílfəl] ADJ diestro, habilidoso

skim [skɪm] VT (milk) desnatar; (a broth) espumar; (pass near surface) rozar; VI/VT (read) leer por encima, repasar; **to — over** rozar; N **— milk** Sp leche desnatada *f*; Am leche descremada *f*

skimp [skɪmp] VI escatimar; **to — on** escatimar

skimpy [skímpi] ADJ (funds) escaso; (dress) corto; (bikini) pequeño

skin [skɪn] N piel *f* (also of animal, sausage, potato); (of the face) cutis *m*, tez *f*; (for carrying wine) pellejo *m*; (of boiled milk) nata *f*; (of grapes) hollejo *m*; **—-deep** superficial; **—-diving** natación submarina *f*; **—flint** roña *mf*; **—head** cabeza rapada *mf*; **to save one's —** salvar el pellejo; **to be saved by the — of one's teeth** salvarse por un pelo; VT (animal) despellejar, desollar; (fruit) pelar; (a person) quitarle a uno el dinero

skinny [skíni] ADJ flaco; **to —-dip** nadar desnudo

skip [skɪp] VI (jump) brincar, ir dando saltos; (omit) saltarse; (bounce) rebotar; VT (a page) saltar[se]; (class) faltar a; (a stone) hacer rebotar; **to — out** escaparse; N salto *m*, brinco *m*

skipper [skípə] N (captain) patrón -ona *mf*, capitán -ana *mf*; (jumper) saltador -ora *mf*

skirmish [skɚ́mɪʃ] N escaramuza *f*; VI

escaramuzar

skirt [skɚt] N falda f; VT bordear; **to — an issue** evitar un tema

skit [skɪt] N sketch m

skull [skʌl] N cráneo m, calavera f; **— and crossbones** calavera f

skunk [skʌŋk] N mofeta f; Am zorrillo m

sky [skaɪ] N cielo m; **— blue** azul celeste m; **—diving** paracaidismo extremo m; **—high** muy alto; **—lark** alondra f; **—light** clarabaya f; **—line** horizonte m; **—scraper** rascacielos m sg; VI **to —rocket** subir vertiginosamente

slab [slæb] N (of wood) trozo m; (of stone) losa f, laja f; (of meat) tajada f

slack [slæk] ADJ (not taut) flojo; (careless) descuidado; (sluggish) lento; **— season** temporada baja f; **to take up the —** llenar el vacío; **—s** pantalones m pl; VI holgazanear; **to — off** holgazanear

slag [slæg] N escoria f

slain [slen] see slay

slalom [slάləm] N slalom m

slam [slæm] VI/VT cerrar[se] de un golpe; VI (hit) chocar; VT (throw down) hacer golpear; (criticize) criticar; **to — on the brakes** dar un frenazo; **to — the door** dar un portazo; N (blow) golpazo m; (criticism) crítica f; (of a door) portazo m; **—-dunk** (easy decision) éxito seguro m

slander [slǽndɚ] N calumnia f, difamación f; VT calumniar, difamar

slanderous [slǽndɚəs] ADJ calumnioso, difamatorio

slang [slæŋ] N (jargon) jerga f; (argot) argot m

slant [slænt] N (orientation, bias) sesgo m; (of a roof) inclinación f; VI/VT (bias) sesgar; (slope) inclinar[se], ladear[se]

slap [slæp] N (to the body) palmada f; (to the face) bofetada f, torta f, cachetada f; (with a glove) guantada f; **—-happy** aturdido; **—stick** de golpe y porrazo; **a — in the face** un desaire; **a — on the wrist** un tirón de orejas; **a — on the back** una palmadita en la espalda; VT abofetear; **to — down** reprimir

slash [slæʃ] VI/VT (cut) acuchillar; Am tajear; VT (whip) azotar; (reduce) reducir, rebajar; N (sweeping stroke, wound) cuchillada f, tajo m; (typographical sign) barra f

slat [slæt] N tablilla f

slate [slet] N (rock, roofing) pizarra f; (color) color pizarra m; (list of candidates) lista de candidatos f; VT empizarrar; **this building is —d for destruction** se ha programado la demolición de este edificio

slaughter [slɔ́tɚ] N matanza f; **—house** matadero m; VT (animals) matar; (people, opponents) masacrar

slave [slev] N esclavo -va m f; **—driver** capataz de

esclavos m; **— labor** (workers) mano de obra esclava f; (work) trabajo de esclavos m; VI trabajar como esclavo -va

slavery [slévəri] N esclavitud f

Slavic [slάvɪk] ADJ eslavo

sleazy [slízi] ADJ (squalid) sórdido; (contemptible) despreciable

sled [slɛd] N trineo m

sledgehammer [slέdʒhæmɚ] N almádena f

sleek [slik] ADJ (hair) lustroso; (sports car) elegante

sleep [slip] VI/VT dormir; **it —s three** tiene espacio para que duerman tres personas; **to — around** ser promiscuo; **to — in** dormir hasta tarde; **to — it off** dormir la mona; **to — something off** dormir para que desaparezca algo; **to — over** dormir en casa ajena; **to — together** acostarse juntos; **to — with** acostarse con; **to — on it** consultarlo con la almohada; N sueño m; **— apnea** apnea obstructiva del sueño f; **— disorder** trastorno del sueño m; **— mode** modo de dormir m; **—walker** sonámbulo -la m f; **to go to —** dormirse; **to put to —** (put to bed) dormir a; (euthanize) sacrificar

sleeper [slípɚ] N (one who sleeps) persona que duerme f; (beam) durmiente m; (on a train) coche cama m; (unexpected success) éxito inesperado m; (sofa bed) sofá-cama m

sleepily [slípɪli] ADV con somnolencia

sleepiness [slípɪnɪs] N sueño m, somnolencia f

sleeping [slípɪŋ] N sueño m; ADJ dormido; **—bag** saco de dormir m; **— pill** píldora para dormir f, somnífero m; **— sickness** enfermedad del sueño f

sleepless [slíplɪs] ADJ (person) desvelado; (night) en blanco

sleepy [slípi] ADJ somnoliento, adormilado; **to be —** tener sueño

sleet [slit] N cellisca f; VI caer cellisca

sleeve [sliv] N manga f; **to have something up one's —** tener algo en la manga

sleigh [sle] N trineo m; **—bell** cascabel m; VI pasear en trineo

sleight of hand [sláɪd əvhǽnd] N prestidigitación f

slender [slέndɚ] ADJ delgado, esbelto

slept [slɛpt] see sleep

sleuth [sluθ] N sabueso -sa m f

slew [slu] see slay

slice [slaɪs] N (of bread, cheese) rebanada f; (of fruit) tajada f, raja f; (of meat) lonja f; (in tennis) cortado m, golpe cortado m; VT cortar, rebanar, tajar

slick [slɪk] ADJ (unctuous) untuoso; (sly) astuto; (slippery) resbaladizo

slicker [slíkɚ] N impermeable m

slid [slɪd] see slide

slide [slaɪd] VI/VT deslizar[se]; **to — in** cerrar[se] deslizando; **to — out** abrirse deslizando; **to let something —** dejar pasar algo; N deslizamiento *m*; (playground equipment) tobogán *m*; (of a trombone) vara corredera *f*; (photographic) diapositiva *f*; (for microscopes) portaobjeto *m*

slight [slaɪt] N desaire *m*; VT (snub) desairar; (neglect) descuidar; ADJ (slim) delgado; (delicate) delicado, tenue; (small in degree) leve, ligero

slightly [slaɪtli] ADV algo, un poco

slim [slɪm] ADJ delgado, esbelto; **a — chance** una posibilidad remota

slime [slaɪm] N (in rivers) limo *m*, fango *m*; (of snails) baba *f*; (despicable person) asqueroso -sa *mf*

slimy [slaɪmi] ADJ (muddy) fangoso; (slobbery) baboso, gomoso; (despicable) asqueroso

sling [slɪŋ] N (weapon) honda *f*; (for arm) cabestrillo *m*; **—shot** (toy) tirachinas *m sg*, tirador *m*; (weapon) honda *f*; VT lanzar; **to — a rifle over one's shoulder** ponerse el rifle en bandolera

slink [slɪŋk] VI (move furtively) andar furtivamente; (move provocatively) caminar provocativamente; **to — away** escurrirse

slip [slɪp] VI (slide) deslizarse; (slide accidentally) resbalar[se]; (fail to engage) patinar; (deteriorate) empeorar; VT (make slip) hacer resbalar; (put) meter; **to — away** escaparse, escabullirse; **to — by** correr; **to — in** meter[se]; **to — one's dress on** ponerse el vestido; **to — out** (leave) salir inadvertido; (say inadvertently) escapársele a uno algo; **to — up** meter la pata; **to let an opportunity — by** dejar pasar una oportunidad; **it —ped my mind** se me olvidó; **it —ped off** se zafó; N (act of slipping) resbalón *m*, traspié *m*; (mistake) equivocación *f*; (pillow cover) funda *f*; (underskirt) viso *m*; (piece of paper) papeleta *f*, tira de papel *f*; (space for boats) embarcadero *m*; **— of the tongue** lapsus [linguae] *m*; **—knot** nudo corredizo *m*; **Freudian —** acto fallido *m*

slipper [slípɚ] N zapatilla *f*, pantufla *f*

slippery [slípɚi] ADJ resbaloso, resbaladizo; (evasive) evasivo, escurridizo

slipshod [slípʃad] ADJ chapucero

slit [slɪt] VT cortar a lo largo; **to — someone's throat** degollar a alguien; **to — into strips** cortar en tiras; N raja *f*, hendidura *f*

slither [slíðɚ] VI serpentear, culebrear; N serpenteo *m*, culebreo *m*

sliver [slívɚ] N astilla *f*; VI/VT astillar[se]

slob [slab] N (unkempt) dejado -da *mf*; (uncouth) bruto -ta *mf*

slobber [slábɚ] N baba *f*; VI/VT babosear, babear[se]

slogan [slógən] N eslogan *m*, lema *m*

slop [slap] VT (splash) salpicar; (feed) dar de comer; N (pigswill) bazofia *f*; (mud) fango *m*

slope [slop] VI/VT inclinar[se]; N vertiente *f*, declive *m*, cuesta *f*, cortado *m*; (in math) pendiente *f*

sloppiness [slápɪnɪs] N chapucería *f*

sloppy [slópi] ADJ (muddy) fangoso; (splashed) salpicado; (slovenly) cochino; (poorly done) chapucero

slot [slat] N (for coins, letters) ranura *f*; (in a computer) bahía *f*, ranura *f*; (place in a series) casilla *f*; (job) puesto *m*; **— machine** tragamonedas *mf sg*, tragaperras *mf sg*; VT hacer una ranura

sloth [slɔθ] N (vice) pereza *f*; (animal) perezoso *m*

slouch [slaʊtʃ] N (posture) encorvamiento *m*; (inept person) torpe *mf*; (lazy person) holgazán -ana *mf*; VI/VT (crouch) andar agachado, encorvar[se]; (shuffle) andar caído de hombros

Slovakia [slováːkiə] N Eslovaquia *f*

Slovakian [slováːkiən] ADJ & N eslovaco -ca *mf*

Slovene [slovín] ADJ & N esloveno -na *mf*

Slovenia [slovíniə] N Eslovenia *f*

slovenliness [slávənlinɪs] N (of a person) desaseo *m*, desaliño *m*; (of work) descuido *m*

slovenly [slávənli] ADJ (unclean) desaseado; (unkempt) desaliñado; (poorly done) descuidado

slow [slo] ADJ (not fast) lento, tardo; (running behind) atrasado; (sluggish) lerdo, torpe, pesado; **in — motion** en cámara lenta; ADV lentamente, despacio; VI/VT **to — down/up** andar más despacio, frenar; N **—down** (in business) disminución de actividades *f*; (in labor disputes) huelga de celo *f*

slowly [slóli] ADV despacio, lento, lentamente; **— but surely** lenta pero seguramente

slowness [slónɪs] N (of speed) lentitud *f*; (of intelligence) torpeza *f*

slug [slʌɡ] N (bullet) bala *f*; (coin) moneda falsa *f*; (animal) babosa *f*; (swallow) trago *m*; (blow with fist) puñetazo *m*; VT aporrear; **to — it out** agarrarse a puñetazos

sluggard [slágɚd] N holgazán -ana *mf*

sluggish [slágɪʃ] ADJ (slow) lento; (torpid) aletargado, torpe

sluggishness [slágɪʃnɪs] N torpeza *f*

sluice [slus] N (channel with a gate) esclusa *f*; (channel) canal *m*; **— gate** compuerta *f*

slum [slʌm] N barrio bajo *m*; **—s** tugurios *m pl*; **—lord** propietario de tugurio *m*; VI visitar los barrios bajos; **to — it** divertirse en lugares de poca categoría

slumber [slámbɚ] VI dormir; N sueño *m*; **— party** fiesta de niñas que se quedan a dormir *f*

slump [slʌmp] VI (a person) desplomarse; (prices, markets) bajar repentinamente; N (in prices) baja repentina *f*; (in the economy) ralentización *f*; (in sports) mala racha *f*

slung [slʌŋ] *see* sling

slunk [slʌŋk] *see* slink

slur [slɚ] VT (pronounce indistinctly) pronunciar mal; (connect notes) ligar; N (connection of notes) ligado *m*; (insult) insulto *m*

slush [slʌʃ] N (melted snow) nieve a medio derretir *f*; (sludge) nieve fangosa *f*; (mud) fango *m*; (refuse) desperdicios *m pl*; — **fund** (illicit fund) cuenta para fines ilícitos *f*; (petty cash) caja chica *f*

sly [slaɪ] ADJ astuto, taimado; **on the —** a escondidas

smack [smæk] N (taste) dejo *m*; *Sp* deje *m*; (kiss) beso ruidoso *m*; (loud eating) chasquido *m*; (slap) palmada *f*, sopapo *m*; (heroin) *fam* caballo *m*; VT (kiss) dar un beso ruidoso; (eat loudly) chascar, chasquear; (slap) dar una palmada; **to — of** tener un dejo de

small [smɔl] ADJ (not large) pequeño, chico; (of build) menudo; (narrow) estrecho; (lowercase) minúsculo; (petty) mezquino; — **caps** versalillas *f pl*, versalitas *f pl*; — **change** cambio suelto *m*; — **fry** gente menuda *f*; — **intestine** intestino delgado *m*; — **pox** viruela *f*; — **talk** cháchara *f*; **to feel —** avergonzarse; N (size) pequeño *m*; — **of the back** baja espalda *f*

smallness [smɔlnɪs] N pequeñez *f*

smart [smart] ADJ (intelligent) listo, inteligente; (astute) astuto; (stylish) elegante; — **aleck/ alec** sabihondo -da *mf*; — **bomb** bomba inteligente *f*; — **card** tarjeta de circuito integrado *f*, tarjeta inteligente *f*; — **money** inversión inteligente *f*; — **remark** insolencia *f*; N (pain) escozor *m*; VI picar; **I'm —ing from his rude remarks** todavía me duelen sus groserías

smash [smæʃ] VT (destroy) estrellar, destrozar; (a rebellion) aplastar; **to — into** estrellarse contra; N (sound) estrépito *m*; (blow) choque violento *m*; (tennis shot) remate *m*; **a — hit** un exitazo

smear [smir] VT (daub) untar; (blur) correrse; (defeat) reventar; **to — with paint** pintorrear, pintarrajear; N (stain) mancha *f*; (culture) frotis *m*; — **campaign** campaña de difamación *f*

smell [smɛl] VI/VT oler; **to — of** oler a; **that —s** huele mal, apesta; **to — up** apestar; N (odor) olor *m*; (sense) olfato *m*; — **of** olor a

smelly [smɛli] ADJ hediondo, apestoso

smile [smaɪl] VI sonreír[se]; N sonrisa *f*

smiling [smaɪlɪŋ] ADJ risueño, sonriente

smirk [smɚk] N sonrisa suficiente *f*; VI sonreír con suficiencia

smith [smɪθ] N herrero -ra *mf*

smitten [smɪtn̩] *see* smite

smog [smag] N smog *m*

smoke [smok] N humo *m*; (cigarette) cigarro *m*, cigarrillo *m*; — **detector** detector de humo *m*, detector de incendios *m*; — **inhalation** inhalación de humo *f*; — **screen** cortina de humo *f*; —**stack** chimenea *f*; **to have a —** fumar; VI (put off smoke) echar humo; (go fast) volar; VT (tobacco) fumar; (ham, fish, glass) ahumar; **to — out** (drive out) ahuyentar con humo; (expose) poner al descubierto

smoker [smókɚ] N fumador -ora *mf*; (train car) vagón de fumar *m*

smoking [smókɪŋ] ADJ humeante; — **car** vagón de fumar *m*; — **gun** prueba irrefutable *f*; — **room** cuarto de fumar *m*; N (use of tobacco) tabaquismo *m*, fumar *m*

smoky [smóki] ADJ humoso

smolder, smoulder [smółdɚ] VI arder

smooth [smuð] ADJ (surface) liso; (skin) suave, terso; (tire) gastado; (sea) sereno, tranquilo; (manners) agradable, fino; (flatterer) zalamero; VT (make surface even) alisar; (make easy) allanar; **to — away** hacer desaparecer; **to — one's hair** atusarse el cabello; **to — over** limar asperezas

smoothness [smúðnɪs] N (of a surface) lisura *f*; (of skin) tersura *f*, suavidad *f*; (of sea) tranquilidad *f*; (of manners) fineza *f*; (of a flatterer) zalamería *f*

smote [smot] *see* smite

smother [smʌ́ðɚ] VT (stifle) ahogar[se], sofocar[se], asfixiar[se]; (envelop) cubrir; (overprotect) sobreproteger

smudge [smʌdʒ] N borrón *m*, mancha *f*; VI/VT borronear[se], manchar[se]

smug [smʌg] ADJ suficiente, petulante

smuggle [smʌ́gəl] VI/VT contrabandear, hacer contrabando; **to — in** entrar de contrabando; **to — out** sacar de contrabando

smuggler [smʌ́glɚ] N contrabandista *mf*

smut [smʌt] N (soot) hollín *m*; (pornography) pornografía *f*; (parasite) tizon *m*

snack [snæk] N tentempié *m*, bocadillo *m*; — **bar** cafetería *f*, tizón *m*

snafu [snæfú] N relajo *m*

snag [snæg] N (branch) gancho *m*; (in fabric) enganchón *m*; (any obstacle) pega *f*, obstáculo *m*, contrariedad *f*; **to hit a —** tropezar con un obstáculo; VI/VT enganchar[se]; VT (a ball) agarrar

snail [snel] N caracol *m*; — **mail** correo regular *m*; —**'s pace** paso de tortuga *m*

snake [snek] N serpiente *f*; —**bite** mordedura de serpiente *f*; — **in the grass** víbora *f*; —**skin** piel de serpiente *f*; VI serpentear

snap [snæp] VI (make sound) chasquear, dar un chasquido; (lose control) estallar, perder los estribos; VT (take a photograph) sacar; VI/VT (break) quebrar[se]; **to — at** (try to bite) tirar un mordiscón; (speak harshly) ladrar; **to — one's fingers** chasquear los dedos, castañetear con los dedos; **to — out of** recuperarse de; **to — shut** cerrar[se] de golpe; **to — together** abrochar; **to — up** llevarse; N (sound) chasquido m; (fastener) broche m; (bite) tarascada f; **it's a —** es pan comido; **— judgment** decisión atolondrada f; **—dragon** dragón m; **—shot** instantánea, foto f

snappy [snǽpi] ADJ (biting) mordedor; (elegant) elegante; **make it —!** ¡date prisa!

snare [sner] N (trap) trampa f; **— drum** tambor con bordón m; VT atrapar

snarl [snɑrɫ] VI/VT (growl) regañar; (tangle) enmarañar[se], enredar[se]; N (growl) gruñido m; (tangle) maraña f, enredo m

snatch [snætʃ] VT (seize) arrebatar; (kidnap) secuestrar; VI **to — at** dar manotazos; N (act of snatching) arrebato m; (fragment) fragmento m

snazzy [snǽzi] ADJ llamativo

sneak [snik] VI andar furtivamente; **to — in** entrar a escondidas; **to — out** salir a hurtadillas; VT **to — something in** meter algo a escondidas; **to — something out** sacar a escondidas; **to — a cigarette** fumar a escondidas; N persona solapada f

sneakers [snꞮ́kɚz] N zapatillas [deportivas] f pl, tenis m pl

sneer [snir] VI (smile) sonreír con sorna; **to — at** mofarse de; N expresión de sorna f

sneeze [sniz] VI estornudar; **that's nothing to — at** no es nada desdeñable; N estornudo m

snicker [snꞮ́kɚ] VI reírse burlonamente; N risita burlona f

snide [snaꞮd] ADJ malévolo

sniff [snꞮf] VI/VT husmear, olfatear; **to — at** husmear; (ridicule) menospreciar; N (act of sniffing) husmeo m, olfateo m; (smell) bocanada f

sniffle [snꞮ́fɫ] VI (with a cold) sorberse los mocos; (when crying) gimotear; N (when crying) gimoteo m; **the —s** un resfrío

snip [snꞮp] VT tijeretear; **to — off** cortar de un tijeretazo; N (act of snipping) tijeretada f, tijeretazo m; (piece cut off) pedacito m, recorte m; **— of conversation** retazo de conversación m

sniper [snaꞮ́pɚ] N francotirador -ora mf

snitch [snꞮtʃ] VI (tell on) chivar, chivatar; VT (rob) ratear; N soplón -ona mf, chivato -ta mf

snob [snɑb] N esnob mf

snoop [snup] VI fisgar, fisgonear; N fisgón -ona mf

snooze [snuz] VI dormitar; N siesta f; **to take a —** echar un sueñecito / un sueñito / una siesta

snore [snɔr] VI roncar; N ronquido m

snorkel [snɔ́rkɫ] N esnórquel m

snort [snɔrt] VI resoplar, bufar; VI/VT (drugs) esnifar; N resoplido m, bufido m; (drink) trago m

snout [snaꞷt] N hocico m, jeta f, morro m; (nose) fam napias f pl

snow [sno] N nieve f (also cocaine, heroin); **—ball** bola de nieve f; **—board** monopatín de nieve m; **—drift** ventisquero m; **—fall** nevada f; **—flake** copo de nieve m; **—man** muñeco de nieve m; **—mobile** motonieve f; **—plow** quitanieves m sg; **—shoe** raqueta f; **—storm** ventisca f; VI nevar; **the airport was —ed in** cerraron el aeropuerto por nieve; **to — under** (cover in snow) cubrir de nieve; (overwhelm) abrumar; **to —ball** aumentar rápidamente

snowy [snóꞮ] ADJ nevado; (white) níveo

snub [snʌb] VT volverle la cara a, desairar, despreciar; N desaire m, desprecio m; **—-nosed** chato; Am ñato

snuck [snʌk] see sneak

snuff [snʌf] VI **to — out** apagar, extinguir; N (tobacco product) rapé m; **to be up to —** dar la talla

snug [snʌg] ADJ (tight-fitting) ajustado; (comfortable) cómodo

so [so] ADV (in this way) así; (to this degree) tan; (so much) tanto; **— am I** yo también; **—-and-** fulano [de tal]; **— called** llamado; **— as to** para; **— far as I know** que yo sepa; **— many** tantos; **— much** tanto; **—-— regular; — much the better** tanto mejor; **— that** de modo que; **I was — a beauty queen!** ¡sí que fui reina de belleza! **— long!** ¡hasta luego! **— and — forth** etcetera, y así sucesivamente; **I believe —** creo que sí; **is that —?** ¿en serio? ¡no me digas! **ten minutes or —** unos diez minutos; INTERJ (upon discovering a secret) ajajá; CONJ (in order that) de modo que; (consequently) así que, entonces

soak [sok] VI/VT (immerse) remojar[se]; (drench) empapar[se]; **to — through** colarse por; **to — up** absorber, embeber; **to be —ed through** estar empapado, estar calado hasta los huesos; N remojón m

soap [sop] N jabón m; (television show) telenovela f; **— bubble** pompa de jabón f; **— dish** jabonera f; VT enjabonar

soapy [sópi] ADJ jabonoso

soar [sɔr] VI/VT (airplane) elevar[se]; (kite) remontar[se]; (hopes) aumentar[se]; (prices) disparar[se]; (glider) planear[se]; VI (bird) volar

sob [sɑb] VI sollozar, hipar; N sollozo m, hipo m

sober [sóbɚ] ADJ (not drunk) sobrio; (temperate) moderado; (serious, subdued) serio, sobrio; VI **to — up** (get over drunkenness) despejarse; (become more serious) sentar cabeza

sobriety [səbráııdi] N (not being drunk) sobriedad f; (moderation) moderación f; (seriousness) seriedad f

soccer [sákə] N fútbol m, balompié m; — **ball** esférico m; — **field** campo de juego m, cancha f; — **player** futbolista mf; — **World Cup** Campeonato Mundial de Fútbol m

sociable [sóʃəbəl] ADJ sociable

social [sóʃəl] ADJ (of society) social; (friendly) sociable; — **climber** arribista mf; — **science** ciencias sociales f pl; — **security** seguridad social f; — **welfare** asistencia social f; — **work** asistencia social f; N reunión social f

socialism [sóʃəlɪzəm] N socialismo m

socialist [sóʃəlɪst] ADJ & N socialista mf

socialize [sóʃəlaɪz] VT socializar; VI salir, tener trato social

society [səsáɪıdi] N sociedad f; (companionship) compañía f

socioeconomic [sosioɛkənámɪk] ADJ socioeconómico

sociology [sosiáləʤi] N sociología f

sociopath [sósiəpæθ] N sociópata mf

sock [sak] N (garment) calcetín m; (blow) puñetazo m, zumbido m; VT pegar, zumbar; **to — away** ahorrar

socket [sákıt] N (of eye) cuenca f; (electrical outlet) enchufe m; (for bulb) portalámparas m sg, casquillo m

sod [sad] N (lawn) césped m; (piece) tepe m; VT cubrir de césped

soda [sódə] N (drink) gaseosa f; (sodium hydroxide) soda f, sosa f; — **fountain** bar de bebidas sin alcohol m; — **pop** gaseosa f; — **water** agua con gas f

sodium [sódiəm] N sodio m

sodomy [sádəmi] N sodomía f

sofa [sófə] N sofá m; — **bed** sofá-cama m

soft [saft] ADJ (butter, bed, water, penalty) blando; (life) fácil, cómodo; (hair, skin) suave; (light) tenue; —**ball** softball m; —-**boiled eggs** huevos pasados por agua m pl; — **coal** carbón bituminoso m; — **drink** gaseosa f; — **page break** salto de página suave/automático m; — **palate** velo del paladar m; — **return** salto de línea suave m; —**ware** software m

soften [sɔfən] VI/VT ablandar[se]; (skin) suavizar[se]; VT (a blow) amortiguar; (voice) bajar

softly [sɔftli] ADV (talk) en voz baja; (walk) sin hacer ruido

softness [sɔftnıs] N (of butter) blandura f; (of hair, skin) suavidad f; (of light) tenuidad f

soggy [sági] ADJ (clothes) empapado; (day) húmedo

soil [sɔɪl] N suelo m, tierra f; VI/VT ensuciar[se], manchar[se]

solace [sálıs] N consuelo m; VT consolar

solar [sólə] ADJ solar; — **eclipse** eclipse de sol m; — **energy** energía solar f; — **plexus** plexo solar m; — **system** sistema solar m

sold [sold] see sell

solder [sádə] VI/VT soldar[se]; N soldadura f; —**ing iron** soldador m

soldier [sólʤə] N (of low rank) soldado m; (of any rank) militar m

sole [sol] ADJ solo, único; N (of a foot) planta f; (of a shoe) suela f; (fish) lenguado m

solely [sóli] ADV solamente; **you are — responsible** eres el único responsable

solemn [sáləm] ADJ solemne

solemnity [səlémnıdi] N solemnidad f

solenoid [sólənɔɪd] N solenoide m

solicit [səlísıt] VT (aid) pedir; (a prostitute) ofrecerse; VI (sell) vender, ofrecer productos

solicitor [səlísıdə] N abogado m; — **general** subsecretario -ria de justicia mf

solicitous [səlísıdəs] ADJ solícito

solid [sálıd] ADJ (firm) sólido; (dense) denso; — **blue** azul liso m; — **geometry** geometría del espacio f; — **gold** oro puro m; — **line** línea continua f; —-**state** de estado sólido; **for one — hour** por una hora entera; N sólido m

solidarity [salıdǽrıdi] N solidaridad f

solidify [səlídəfaɪ] VI/VT solidificar[se]

solidity [səlídıti] N solidez f

solitary [sálıteri] ADJ solitario; **to be in — confinement** estar incomunicado

solitude [sálıtud] N soledad f

solo [sólo] N (in music) solo m

soloist [sóloɪst] N solista mf

Solomon Islander [sáləmənáıləndə] N salomonense mf

Solomon Islands [sáləmənáıləndz] N Islas Salomón f pl

solstice [sólstıs] N solsticio m

soluble [sáljəbəl] ADJ soluble

solution [səlúʃən] N solución f

solve [salv] VT resolver, solucionar

solvent [sálvənt] N solvente m, disolvente m

Somalia [somáljə] N Somalia f

Somalian [somáljən] ADJ & N somalí mf

somber [sámbə] ADJ sombrío

some [sʌm] ADJ algún, alguno; **I worked for — time** trabajé un rato; **that is — dog!** ¡menudo perro! PRON algunos; **and then — y más todavía**; ADV — **twenty people** unas veinte personas; **I like it —** me gusta un poco

somebody [sámbadi] PRON alguien

someday [sámde] ADV algún día

somehow [sámhau] ADV de alguna manera; — **or other** de alguna manera u otra

someone [sámwan] PRON alguien, alguno

somersault [sámərsɔlt] N (on ground) voltereta f; (in air) salto mortal m; VI (on ground) dar una voltereta; (in air) dar un salto mortal

something [sámθɪŋ] PRON algo *m*; — **else** otra cosa; **thirty—** (age) treinta y tantos; (person) treintañero -ra *mf*

sometime [sámtaɪm] ADV algún día, en algún momento; **—s** a veces, de vez en cuando

somewhat [sámhwɑt] ADV algo

somewhere [sámhwer] ADV en alguna parte; — **else** en alguna otra parte

son [sʌn] N hijo *m*; **—-in-law** yerno *m*; — **of a gun** *fam* hijo de su madre *m*

sonar [sónɑr] N sonar *m*

song [sɔŋ] N canción *f*; (of a bird) canto *m*; — **and dance** cuento chino *m*; **—writer** compositor -ora *mf*; **—bird** ave canora *f*, pájaro cantor *m*; **to buy something for a —** comprar algo muy barato

sonic barrier [sánɪkbæriə-] N barrera del sonido *f*

sonnet [sánɪt] N soneto *m*

sonority [sənɔ́rɪdi] N sonoridad *f*

sonorous [sánə-əs] ADJ sonoro

soon [sun] ADV pronto; — **after nine** poco después de las nueve; **as — as** tan pronto como, en cuanto; **see you —** hasta pronto; **how — do you want it?** ¿para cuándo lo necesitas? **he arrived —er** llegó antes; **—er or later** tarde o temprano; **I'd —er stay here** prefiero quedarme aquí

soot [sʊt] N hollín *m*, tizne *m*

soothe [suð] VT calmar, aliviar

soothsayer [súθseə-] N agorero -ra *mf*

sooty [súdi] ADJ tiznado

sop [sɑp] VT empapar; **to — up** absorber; **to be —ping wet** estar empapado; N **—s** sopas *f pl*

sophisticated [səfístɪkeɪdɪd] ADJ sofisticado

sophomore [sáfəmɔr] N estudiante de segundo año *mf*

soprano [səprǽno] N soprano *m*

sorcerer [sɔ́rsərə-] N brujo *m*, hechicero *m*

sorceress [sɔ́rsə-ɪs] N hechicera *f*

sordid [sɔ́rdɪd] ADJ sórdido, escabroso

sore [sɔr] ADJ (painful) dolorido, doloroso; (grieved) dolorido; (angry) enojado; **—head** cascarrabias *mf*; **my arm is —** me duele el brazo; **to have a — throat** tener dolor de garganta; N llaga *f*, úlcera *f*

soreness [sɔ́rnɪs] N dolor *m*

sorority [sərɔ́rɪdi] N asociación femenina de estudiantes *f*

sorrow [sáro] N (sadness) pena *f*, pesar *m*, pesadumbre *f*; (cause of sadness) disgusto *m*

sorrowful [sárəfəl] ADJ triste, pesaroso

sorry [sári] ADJ **I am —** lo siento; **I am — about that** lo lamento; **I am — for her** la compadezco; **—?** ¿Cómo? **you'll be —** te arrepentirás; **he was in — shape** estaba en un estado lamentable

sort [sɔrt] N clase *f*, tipo *m*; **— of tired** algo cansado; **all —s of** toda clase de; **out of —s** (depressed) de mal humor; (ill) indispuesto;

— **key** tecla de ordenación *f*; — **order** orden de clasificación *m*; VT (classify) clasificar; (put in order) ordenar; **to — out** separar, apartar; **to — out a problem** resolver un problema

SOS [éso̱és] N SOS *m*

sought [sɔt] *see* seek

soul [sol] N alma *f*; — **music** música soul *f*; **not a — nadie**, ni un alma; **the — of tact** la imagen del tacto

sound [saʊnd] N sonido *m*; (inlet) brazo de mar *m*; — **barrier** barrera del sonido *f*; — **card** tarjeta de sonido *f*; —**proof** a prueba de sonido; —**track** banda sonora *f*; — **wave** onda sonora *f*; ADJ (healthy) sano; (sane) cuerdo; (well founded) bien fundado, lógico; — **advice** buen consejo *m*; — **sleep** sueño profundo *m*; **a — beating** una buena paliza; **of — mind** en su sano juicio; **safe and — sano** y salvo; VI sonar; VT (an alarm) tocar; (a channel) sondar; (opinion) sondear; **to — out** tantear, sondear

soup [sup] N sopa *f*; — **dish** plato sopero *m*; —**spoon** cuchara sopera *f*; — **tureen** sopera *f*

sour [saʊr] ADJ (acidic) agrio, ácido; (peevish) agrio, avinagrado; **to go —** (milk) cortarse, agriarse; (a relationship) estropearse; — **cream** *Sp* nata agria *f*; *Am* crema agria *f*; — **milk** leche cortada *f*; —**puss** cascarrabias *mf*, avinagrado -da *mf*; VI/VT agriar[se], avinagrar[se]; (milk) cortar[se]

source [sɔrs] N fuente *f*, origen *m*; — **code** código fuente *m*

sourness [sáʊrnɪs] N acidez *f*

souse [saʊs] VI/VT (plunge) zambullir[se]; (soak) empapar[se]; N borracho -cha *mf*, esponja *f*

south [saʊθ] N sur *m*, mediodía *f*; ADJ meridional, sureño; — **Africa** Sudáfrica *f*; — **African** sudafricano -na *mf*; — **America** América del Sur *f*, Sudamérica *f*; — **American** sudamericano -na *mf*; —**bound** con rumbo al sur; —**east** sureste, sudeste; —**eastern** sureste, sudeste; — **Korea** Corea del Sur *f*; — **Korean** surcoreano -na *mf*; —**paw** zurdo -da *mf*; — **pole** polo sur *m*; —**west** sudoeste, suroeste; —**western** sudoeste, suroeste; ADV hacia el sur

southern [sáðə-n] ADJ meridional, sureño

southerner [sáðə-nə-] N sureño -ña *mf*, meridional *mf*, habitante del sur *mf*

southward [sáʊθwə-d] ADV hacia el sur, rumbo al sur

souvenir [suvənír] N recuerdo *m*

sovereign [sávə-ɪn] ADJ & N soberano -na *mf*

sovereignty [sávə-ɪnti] N soberanía *f*

sow[1] [saʊ] N puerca *f*

sow[2] [so] VI/VT sembrar

sown [son] *see* sow[2]

soy [sɔɪ] N *Sp* soja *f*; *Am* soya *f*; —**bean** *Sp* semilla de soja f; Am semilla de soya f; — **sauce** Sp salsa de soja f; Am salsa de soya f

spa [spɑ] N balneario m

space [spes] N espacio m; —-**age** de la era espacial; —**bar** barra espaciadora f; —**craft** nave espacial f; —**ship** nave espacial f; — **shuttle** transbordador espacial m; — **station** estación espacial f; — **suit** traje espacial m; VT espaciar; **to** — **out** distraerse

spacious [spéʃəs] ADJ espacioso, amplio

spade [sped] N (shovel) pala f; (in cards) pica f; **to call a** — **a** — al pan, pan y al vino, vino

Spain [spen] N España f

spam [spæm] N correo electrónico basura m, spam m

span [spæn] N (of hand) palmo m; (of time) espacio m; (of attention) lapso m, período m; (of bridge) tramo m; (of wing) envergadura f; (of life) duración f; VT (time) abarcar; (a river) atravesar, salvar

Spaniard [spénjəd] N español -ola mf

Spanish [spænɪʃ] ADJ (of Spain) español; (Spanish-speaking) hispano; N (language) español m; — **America** Hispanoamérica f

spank [spæŋk] VT dar nalgadas; N palmada f, nalgada f

spanking [spǽŋkɪŋ] N zurra en las nalgas f; ADJ — **new** flamante

spare [spɛr] VT (embarrassment) ahorrar, evitar; (money) prestar; (an enemy) perdonar la vida a; (a worker) prescindir de; — **me!** ¡ten piedad de mí! **to** — **no expense** no escatimar gastos; **to have time to** — tener tiempo de sobra; ADJ (austere) austero; (extra) de sobra, de más; — **cash** dinero disponible m; — **parts** repuestos m pl; — **time** tiempo libre m; N (part) repuesto m; (tire) neumático de repuesto m

spark [spɑrk] N chispa f; — **plug** bujía f; VI chispear, echar chispas; VT (a riot) desencadenar; (interest, criticism) provocar

sparkle [spárkəl] VI (diamond) centellear; (sparkler) chispear; (eyes) brillar; N (flashing) brillo m, centelleo m; (spirit) viveza f, animación f

sparkling [spárklɪŋ] ADJ (diamond) centelleante; (eyes) brillante; — **water** agua con gas f; — **wine** vino espumoso m

sparrow [spǽro] N gorrión m

sparse [spɑrs] ADJ escaso; (hair) ralo

spasm [spǽzəm] N espasmo m

spasmodic [spæzmádɪk] ADJ espasmódico

spastic [spǽstɪk] ADJ espástico

spat [spæt] N riña f

spat [spæt] see spit

spatial [spéʃəl] ADJ espacial

spatter [spǽdə] VI/VT salpicar; N salpicadura f

spatula [spǽtʃələ] N espátula f

spawn [spɔn] VI desovar; VT engendrar; N (of

fish) huevas f pl; (of frogs) huevos m pl

spay [spe] VT esterilizar, castrar

speak [spik] VI hablar; VT (a language) hablar; (the truth) decir; (one's lines) recitar, decir; **so to** — por decirlo así, valga la expresión; **to** — **for** hablar en nombre de / a favor de; **to** — **one's mind** hablar sin rodeos; **to** — **out against** denunciar; **to** — **out for** defender; **to** — **up** hablar fuerte

speaker [spíkə] N orador -ora mf; (at a conference) conferenciante mf; (of a language) hablante mf; — **of the House** presidente -ta de la cámara de representantes mf; —**phone** teléfono con parlante m

spear [spir] N (weapon) lanza f; (for fishing) arpón m; (sprout) brote m; VT (a person, animal) alancear, herir con lanza; (a fish) arponear

spearmint [spírmɪnt] N mentaverde f

special [spéʃəl] ADJ especial; — **delivery** entrega inmediata f; — **education** educación especial f; — **effects** efectos especiales m pl; — **interest [group]** grupo de presión m; N (sale item) especialidad f; (TV program) especial m

specialist [spéʃəlɪst] N especialista m

specialization [spɛʃəlɪzéʃən] N especialización f, especialidad f

specialize [spéʃəlaɪz] VI/VT especializar[se]

specially [spéʃəli] ADV especialmente, específicamente

specialty [spéʃəlti] N especialidad f

species [spíʃiz] N especie f

specific [spɪsífɪk] ADJ específico, determinado; — **gravity** peso específico m; N —**s** detalles m pl

specifically [spɪsífɪkli] ADV concretamente, específicamente

specify [spésəfaɪ] VI/VT especificar

specimen [spésəmən] N (representative) espécimen m, ejemplar m; (sample) muestra f

speck [spɛk] N (small dot) mota f, manchita f; (small amount) pizca f

speckle [spékəl] N manchita f, mota f; VT salpicar, motear; —**d** moteado

spectacle [spéktəkəl] N espectáculo m; —**s** gafas f pl, anteojos m pl; **to make a** — **of oneself** dar un espectáculo, ponerse en ridículo

spectacular [spɛktǽkjələ] ADJ espectacular

spectator [spékteɪdə] N espectador -ora mf

spectrum [spéktrəm] N espectro m

speculate [spékjəlet] VI/VT especular

speculation [spɛkjəléʃən] N especulación f

speculative [spékjələdɪv] ADJ especulativo

speculator [spékjəledə] N especulador -ora mf

sped [spɛd] see speed

speech [spitʃ] N (faculty of speaking) habla f; (formal) discurso m; (in a play) parlamento m; — **defect** defecto de pronunciación m; —

recognition reconocimiento de habla *m*; — **synthesis** síntesis de habla *m*; **to make a —** pronunciar un discurso

speechless [spítʃlɪs] ADJ (dumb) mudo; (astonished) estupefacto

speed [spid] N (rapidity) velocidad *f*, rapidez *f*; (gear) velocidad *f*; (amphetamine) anfeta *f*; — **limit** límite de velocidad *m*; **at full —** a toda velocidad; VI (break speed limit) ir con exceso de velocidad; **to — by** pasar a toda velocidad; **to — off/away** irse a toda velocidad; **to — up** (a car, work) acelerar; (a delivery) hacer llegar a toda velocidad

speedometer [spɪdámɪtɚ] N velocímetro *m*

speedy [spídi] ADJ veloz, rápido

spell [spɛl] N (charm) hechizo *m*, sortilegio *m*, conjuro *m*; (period) temporada *f*; (sickness) ataque *m*; **to put under a —** hechizar; ADJ **—bound** hechizado; VT (spoken) deletrear; (written) escribir; (represent) significar, representar; **to —-check** comprobar la ortografía; **I —ed it out for him** se lo dije con todas las letras

spelling [spélɪŋ] N ortografía *f*; **— bee** concurso de ortografía *m*

spend [spɛnd] VT (money) gastar; (time) pasar; **—thrift** derrochador -ora *mf*, gastador -ora *mf*, pródigo -ga *mf*

spending [spéndɪŋ] N gastos *m pl*; **— cut** recorte de gastos *m*; **to go on a — spree** salir a gastar dinero a lo loco

spent [spɛnt] *see* spend

sperm [spɚm] N esperma *mf*; **— whale** cachalote *m*

spermicide [spɚ́məsaɪd] N espermicida *m*

sphere [sfɪr] N esfera *f*; **— of influence** esfera de influencia *f*

spherical [sférɪkəl] ADJ esférico

sphincter [sfíŋktɚ] N esfínter *m*

spice [spaɪs] N especia *f*; VT condimentar; **to — up** dar sal

spiciness [spáɪsɪnɪs] N lo picante

spick and span [spíkənspǽn] ADJ impecable

spicy [spáɪsi] ADJ picante

spider [spáɪdɚ] N araña *f*; **— monkey** mono araña *m*; **—'s web** telaraña *f*

spigot [spígət] N grifo *m*, espita *f*

spike [spaɪk] N (sprout) espiga *f*; (sharp object) púa *f*, pincho *m*; (on shoes) clavo *m*; **—s** zapatillas con clavos *f pl*; VT (impale) clavar; (add alcohol to) echar alcohol a; (hit a volleyball) picar

spill [spɪl] VI/VT volcar[se], derramar[se], verter[se]; VT (a rider) hacer caer; **to — the beans** descubrir el pastel; VI **to — over** (a liquid) desbordarse; (a conflict) extenderse; N (of water) derrame *m*; (of blood) derramamiento *m*; (fall) caída *f*

spilt [spɪlt] *see* spill

spin [spɪn] VT (wool) hilar; (a top, one's partner) hacer girar; VI dar vueltas, girar; **to — yarns** contar cuentos; N (turning) giro *m*, vuelta *f*; (of an airplane) barrena *f*; (political) sesgo *m*; **to take a —** dar una vuelta

spinach [spínɪtʃ] N espinaca *f*

spinal [spáɪnl] ADJ espinal, vertebral; **— column** columna vertebral *f*, espina dorsal *f*; **— cord** médula espinal *f*

spindle [spíndl] N (for weaving) huso *m*; (on machines) eje *m*

spine [spaɪn] N espina *f*, espinazo *m*

spinning [spínɪŋ] N (action) hilado *m*; (art) hilandería *f*; **— machine** máquina de hilar *f*; **— mill** hilandería *f*; **— top** trompo *m*, peonza *f*; **— wheel** rueca *f*

spinster [spínstɚ] N solterona *f*

spiral [spáɪrəl] ADJ & N espiral *m*; **— notebook** cuaderno de espiral *m*; **— staircase** escalera de caracol *f*

spire [spaɪr] N aguja *f*, chapitel *m*

spirit [spírɪt] N (ghost) espíritu *m*; (animation) ánimo *m*, brío *m*; (alcohol) alcohol *m*; **low —s** abatimiento *m*; **to be in good —s** estar de buen humor; VT **to — away** llevar como por arte de magia

spirited [spírɪtɪd] ADJ fogoso, brioso

spiritual [spírɪtʃuəl] ADJ & N espiritual *m*

spirituality [spɪrɪtʃuǽlɪti] N espiritualidad *f*

spit [spɪt] VI/VT escupir; N (saliva) escupitajo *m*; (for roasting) asador *m*, espeto *m*, espetón *m*; (of sand) banco *m*

spite [spaɪt] N despecho *m*, inquina *f*; **in — of** a pesar de; **out of —** por despecho; VT contrariar

spiteful [spáɪtfəl] ADJ malicioso

splash [splæʃ] VI/VT salpicar; VI chapotear, chapalear; N salpicadura *f*, chapoteo *m*; **to make a —** hacer olas

splatter [splǽdɚ] VI/VT salpicar; N salpicadura *f*

spleen [splin] N bazo *m*; (ill humor) mal humor *m*

splendid [spléndɪd] ADJ espléndido

splendor [spléndɚ] N esplendor *m*

splice [splaɪs] VT (tape, genes) empalmar, unir; N empalme *m*, unión *f*

splint [splɪnt] N tablilla *f*; VT entablillar

splinter [splíntɚ] N astilla *f*; VI/VT astillar[se]

split [splɪt] VI/VT (stone, wood) hender[se], rajar[se]; (candy bar) partir[se], dividir[se]; **to — hairs** hilar fino; **to — one's sides with laughter** desternillarse de risa; **to — the difference** partir la diferencia; ADJ (wood) partido, hendido; (a group) dividido; **—-level** en desnivel; **— personality** doble personalidad *f*; **— screen** pantalla dividida *f*; **— second** fracción de segundo *f*; N hendidura *f*, grieta *f*; (in a group) escisión *f*, división *f*

spoil [spɔɪɫ] VI (milk) cortar[se]; (food) echarse a perder; VT (vacation, performance) estropear, arruinar; (plans) desbaratar; (enjoyment) aguar; (child) malcriar, mimar demasiado; N —**s** botín *m*

spoiler [spɔ́ɪlə-] N alerón *m*

spoke [spok] N rayo *m*

spoke [spok] *see* speak

spoken [spókən] *see* speak

spokesperson [spókspɚsən] N portavoz *mf*, vocero -ra *mf*

sponge [spʌndʒ] N (animal, utensil) esponja *f*; (parasite) gorrón -ona *mf*; —**bath** baño de esponja *m*; —**cake** *Am* bizcochuelo *m*; *Sp* bizcocho *m*; VI **to**—**off** (clean) quitar con esponja; (take advantage of) gorronear; **to**—**up** absorber con una esponja

sponger [spʌ́ndʒə-] N gorrón -ona *mf*, parásito *m*

spongy [spʌ́ndʒi] ADJ esponjoso, esponjado

sponsor [spánsə-] N (of the arts) mecenas *mf*; (of sports, TV program) patrocinador -ora *mf*; (of a bill) proponente *mf*; VT (a child) apadrinar; (arts, sports, TV show) patrocinar; (bill) proponer

sponsorship [spánsə-ʃip] N patrocinio *m*

spontaneity [spantənéɪdi] N espontaneidad *f*

spontaneous [spʌnténiəs] ADJ espontáneo; —**abortion** aborto espontáneo *m*

spook [spuk] N (ghost) espectro *m*; (spy) espía *mf*

spool [spuɫ] N carrete *m*, carretel *m*; VT (wool) devanar; (tape) enrollar

spoon [spun] N cuchara *f*; VT cucharear, poner con una cuchara; **to**—**feed** dar de comer en la boca

spoonful [spúnfuɫ] N cucharada *f*

spore [spɔr] N espora *f*

sport [spɔrt] N deporte *m*; **to be a good**— tener espíritu deportivo; —**utility vehicle** vehículo utilitario deportivo *m*; —**s car** coche deportivo *m*; —**s jacket** saco de sport *m*, americana *f*; —**sman** (hunter) cazador *m*; (in sports) hombre de espíritu deportivo *m*; —**smanship** espíritu deportivo *m*, deportividad *f*; —**swriter** cronista deportivo -va *mf*; ADJ deportivo; VT lucir

sporty [spɔ́rdi] ADJ deportivo

spot [spat] N (stain) mancha *f*, mota *f*; (blemish) espinilla *f*; (insect bite) roncha *f*; (place) lugar *m*, paraje *m*; (difficult situation) aprieto *m*; **on the**— en el acto; —**check** inspección al azar *f*; —**light** (in theater) foco *m*; (outdoors) reflector *m*; **to be in the**—**light** ser el centro de atención; —**remover** quitamanchas *m sg*; VI/VT (stain) manchar, ensuciar; VT (see in the distance) divisar; (notice) notar; (give advantage) dar como ventaja

spotless [spátlɪs] ADJ inmaculado

spotted [spádɪd] ADJ manchado, moteado

spouse [spaʊs] N cónyuge *mf*; —**abuse** abuso conyugal *m*

spout [spaʊt] VT (throw) arrojar chorros de; (talk) soltar tonterías; VI (flow out) salir a chorros; (talk) perorar; N (of a fountain) caño *m*; (of a gutter) canalón *m*; (of a teapot) pico *m*

sprain [spren] VT torcerse; N torcedura *f*

sprang [spræŋ] *see* spring

sprawl [sprɔɫ] VI (spread limbs) despatarrarse; (extend) extenderse; (fall) tumbarse; N postura despatarrada *f*

spray [spre] VI/VT rociar[se]; N (of liquid) rociada *f*; (foam) espuma *f*; (of flowers) ramillete *m*; —**can** aerosol *m*; —**paint** pintura en aerosol *f*

spread [spred] VI/VT (arms, newspaper) extender[se]; (butter) untar[se]; (map) desdoblar[se]; (legs) abrir[se]; (seeds) esparcir[se]; (news) difundir[se], diseminar[se]; (odor) difundir[se], expandirse; (rumor) propalar; (panic) sembrar; VT (panic, news) sembrar; N (of ideas) difusión *f*; (of opinion) diseminación *f*; (of disease) propagación *f*; (of nuclear weapons) proliferación *f*; (for a bed) cubrecama *m*; (for bread) pasta *f*; (of food) festín *m*; (ranch) hacienda *f*; —**sheet** (paper) planilla de cálculo *f*; (program) planilla electrónica *f*

spree [spri] N parranda *f*, farra *f*; **to go on a**— ir de parranda/farra; **to go on a shopping**— gastar dinero desenfrenadamente

spring [sprɪŋ] VI saltar; **to**—**at** abalanzarse sobre; **to**—**from** nacer de; **to**—**open** abrir[se] de golpe; **to**—**to mind** venir a la mente; **to**—**up** surgir; VT **to**—**a leak** (boat) hacer agua; (pipe) comenzar a gotear; **to**—**news** dar una noticia de sopetón; N (season) primavera *f*; (coil) muelle *m*, resorte *m*; (elasticity) elasticidad *f*; (jump) salto *m*; (water) manantial *m*, fuente *f*; —**board** trampolín *m*; —**fever** fiebre de primavera *f*; —**mattress** colchón de muelles *m*; —**time** primavera *f*; —**water** agua de manantial *f*; **he's no**—**chicken** no se cuece en el primer hervor

sprinkle [spríŋkəɫ] VT (with sugar) espolvorear; (with droplets) salpicar, rociar; (rain) gotear, chispear

sprint [sprɪnt] VI (run) echarse una carrera; (run a competitive race) [e]sprintar; N (run) corrida corta *f*; (race) [e]sprint *m*

sprocket [sprákɪt] N piñón *m*, rueda dentada *f*

sprout [spraʊt] VI (leaf) brotar, salir; (plants) retoñar; (seeds) germinar; (houses) surgir; VT echar; **he**—**ed horns** le salieron cuernos; N retoño *m*, brote *m*, renuevo *m*

spruce [sprus] N picea *f*; VI **to**—**up** arreglarse

sprung [sprʌŋ] *see* spring

spun [spʌn] *see* spin

spunk [spʌŋk] N agallas *f pl*

spur [spɜr] N (on stirrups) espuela *f*; (stimulus) aguijón *m*; (of a rooster) espolón *m*; (of a mountain) estribación *f*; (of a railroad track) ramal *m*; **on the — of the moment** espontáneamente; VT espolear; **to — on** animar

spurious [spjúriəs] ADJ espurio

spurn [spɜrn] VT rechazar, desdeñar

spurt [spɜrt] VI salir a chorros; N (of water) chorro *m*; (of a runner) esfuerzo repentino *m*; **in —s** por rachas

sputter [spʌ́dɚ] VI (fire) chisporrotear; (person) refunfuñar; N (fire) chisporroteo *m*

sputum [spjúdəm] N esputo *m*

spy [spaɪ] N espía *mf*; **—glass** catalejo *m*; VI espiar; **to — on** espiar

squabble [skwábəl] VI reñir; N reyerta *f*

squad [skwad] N (of police) patrulla *f*; (for execution) pelotón *m*; (of athletes) equipo *m*; (for guarding) retén *m*; **— car** [coche] patrullero *m*

squadron [skwádrən] N (in navy) escuadra *f*; (in army) escuadrón *m*

squalid [skwálɪd] ADJ escuálido

squall [skwɔl] N (rain) chubasco *m*, borrasca *f*; (sound) berrido *m*; VI berrear

squalor [skwálɚ] N miseria *f*, escualidez *f*

squander [skwándɚ] VT despilfarrar, derrochar, disipar

squanderer [skwándərɚ] N derrochador -ora *mf*

square [skwɛr] N (shape) cuadrado *m*; (on a pattern) cuadro *m*; (plaza) plaza *f*, *Mex* zócalo *m*; (tool in carpentry) escuadra *f*; (on chessboard) casilla *f*; **— brackets** corchetes *m pl*; **— dance** cuadrilla *f*; **— knot** nudo de rizo *m*; **— meal** comida completa *f*; **— root** raíz cuadrada *f*; **he is a —** es muy conservador; VT (make square) cuadrar; (draw squares on) cuadricular; (multiply by itself) elevar al cuadrado; **to — one's shoulders** erguirse; ADJ (in shape) cuadrado; (at ninety degrees) en ángulo recto; (tied) empatado; (frank) franco; **to be — with someone** estar a mano con alguien; ADV **right — between the eyes** justo entre los ojos

squash [skwaʃ] N (gourd) calabaza *f*; (sport) squash *m*; VT (smash) aplastar, despachurrar

squat [skwat] VI (sit low) acuclillarse; (occupy) ocupar sin autorización; ADJ (sitting low) acuclillado; (thickset) rechoncho, achaparrado; N (nothing) nada; **he doesn't know—** no sabe un comino; **in a —** en cuclillas

squawk [skwɔk] VI (of chickens) cacarear; (complain) quejarse; N (of chickens) cacareo *m*; (complaint) quejido *m*

squeak [skwik] VI (door) rechinar, chirriar; (shoe) rechinar; (mouse) chillar; N (of door) rechinamiento *m*, chirrido *m*; (of shoe) rechinamiento *m*; (of mouse) chillido *m*

squeaky [skwíki] ADJ (door) chirriante; (shoes) rechinante

squeal [skwil] VI chillar; (complain) protestar; (snitch) chivatar, delatar; N chillido *m*

squeamish [skwímɪʃ] ADJ delicado

squeegee [skwídʒi] N escurridor de goma *m*, limpiavidrios *m sg*

squeeze [skwiz] VT apretar; (press very hard) estrujar; (an orange) estrujar, exprimir; (hug) abrazar; **to — into** meter[se] con dificultad en, encajar[se] en; **to — out** (an orange) exprimir; (a towel) escurrir; **to — through a crowd** abrirse paso entre la multitud; N (of hands) apretón *m*; (excessive squeeze) estrujón *m*; (hug) abrazo *m*; (lack) restricción *f*

squelch [skwɛltʃ] VT (revolt) aplastar, sofocar; (criticism) acallar

squid [skwɪd] N calamar *m*

squint [skwɪnt] VI (partially close eyes) entrecerrar los ojos; (look askance) mirar de soslayo; N (look with partially closed eyes) mirada con los ojos entrecerrados *f*; (side glance) mirada de soslayo *f*

squirm [skwɜrm] VI retorcerse; **to — out of a difficulty** zafarse de un aprieto

squirrel [skwɜrəl] N ardilla *f*

squirt [skwɜrt] VT echar un chisguete en; VI salir a chorritos; N chisguete *m*, chorrito *m*; **— gun** pistola lanzaagua *f*, pistola de agua *f*

Sri Lanka [srilánkə] N Sri Lanka *f*

Sri Lankan [srilánkən] ADJ & N cingalés -esa *mf*

stab [stæb] VI/VT apuñalar, acuchillar; **to — at** tirar puñaladas a; N (with a dagger) puñalada *f*; (with a knife) cuchillada *f*; (with a pocketknife) navajazo *m*; (of pain) punzada *f*, pinchazo *m*; **to take a — at** intentar; **— wound** cuchillada *f*

stability [stəbílɪdi] N estabilidad *f*

stabilization [stebəlɪzéʃən] N estabilización *f*

stable [stébəl] ADJ estable; N establo *m*, cuadra *f*; (for horses only) caballeriza *f*; VT poner en el establo

stack [stæk] N (ordered) pila *f*; (chaotic) montón *m*; (of a chimney) chimenea *f*; (in a library) estantería *f*; VT amontonar, apilar

stadium [stédiəm] N estadio *m*

staff [stæf] N (stick) cayado *m*; (of a flag) asta *f*; (personnel) personal *m*, plantel *m*; (of music) pentagrama *m*; **— of life** pan de cada día *m*; **— officer** oficial de estado mayor *m*; **editorial —** redacción *f*; **teaching —** cuerpo docente *m*; VT contratar personal para

stag [stæg] N (deer) venado *m*, ciervo *m*; (other animals) macho *m*; **— beetle** ciervo volante *m*; **— party** fiesta para hombres *f*

stage [steʤ] N (showplace) escenario *m*; (for popular entertainment) tablado *m*; (theater) teatro *m*, las tablas *f pl*; (period) etapa *f*, estadío *m*; (distance) etapa *f*; **—coach** diligencia *f*; **— fright** miedo al escenario *m*, fiebre de candilejas *f*; **—hand** tramoyista *mf*; **by —s** por etapas; VT (a play) poner en escena; (an attack) organizar

stagger [stǽgə] VI (totter) tambalearse, dar tumbos; VT (hit hard) hacer tambalear; (overwhelm) dejar azorado; (alternate) escalonar; N tambaleo *m*

stagnant [stǽgnənt] ADJ estancado

stagnate [stǽgnet] VI estancarse

stagnation [stægnéʃən] N estancamiento *m*

staid [sted] ADJ envarado

stain [sten] N (spot) mancha *f*; (color) tinte *m*, tintura *f*; VI/VT (spot) manchar[se]; (color) teñir[se]; **—ed-glass window** vitral *m*

stainless [sténlɪs] ADJ sin mancha; **— steel** acero inoxidable *m*

stair [ster] N peldaño *m*, escalón *m*; **—case** escalera *f*; **—s** escalera *f*; **—way** escalera *f*

stake [stek] N (pole) estaca *f*; (investment) interés *m*; (bet) apuesta *f*; **at —** en juego; **to die at the —** morir en la hoguera; VT estacar; **to — out** vigilar

stalactite [stəlǽktaɪt] N estalactita *f*

stalagmite [stəlǽgmaɪt] N estalagmita *f*

stale [stel] ADJ (bread) duro; (air) viciado; (joke) viejo; **—mate** punto muerto *m*

stalk [stɔk] N tallo *m*; VT acechar

stall [stɔl] N (at a market) puesto *m*; (at a fair) caseta *f*, barraca *f*; (in a stable) compartimiento *m*; VI (airplane) entrar en pérdida; (talks) llegar a un punto muerto; (motor) pararse; **he is —ing** está arrastrando los pies; VT (airplane) hacer entrar en pérdida; (talks) paralizar; (motor) parar

stallion [stǽljən] N semental *m*

stamina [stǽmənə] N resistencia *f*, aguante *m*

stammer [stǽmə] VI balbucear; N balbuceo *m*

stamp [stæmp] VT (a letter) sellar; *Mex* timbrar; *Am* estampillar; (an official document) sellar, timbrar; (a coin) acuñar; VT (with foot) pisotear, patalear; (with hoof) piafar; **to — out** eliminar; N (on a letter) *Sp* sello *m*; *Mex* timbre *m*; *Am* estampilla *f*; (on an official document) sello *m*, timbre *m*; (instrument, character) sello *m*; (on the ground) pisotón *m*; (sound) paso *m*; **— tax** timbre *m*

stampede [stæmpíd] N estampida *f*; VI huir en estampida; VT hacer huir en estampida

stance [stæns] N posición *f*, postura *f*; (political) posicionamiento *m*

stanch, staunch [stɔntʃ] VT restañar; ADJ (strong) firme; (loyal) fiel

stand [stænd] VI (take a standing position) ponerse de pie, levantarse; *Am* parar[se]; (to

be in a standing position) estar de pie; *Am* estar parado; (stop) detenerse; (withstand, tolerate) aguantar, tolerar, soportar; (remain valid) mantenerse; **to — aside** apartarse; **to — back** retroceder; **to — behind someone** respaldar a alguien; **to — by** (be uninvolved) mantenerse al margen; (be alert) estar alerta; (support) respaldar; **to — for** (denote) significar; (tolerate) tolerar; **to — one's ground** mantenerse firme; **to — out** destacarse, sobresalir; **to — up for** defender; **it —s to reason** es razonable; **it —s one meter tall** mide un metro de alto; **to — a chance of** tener posibilidad de; **where do you — on this issue?** ¿qué opinas al respecto? N (at a market) puesto *m*; (at a fair) caseta *f*; (of trees) bosque *m*; (opinion) posición *f*; (for music) atril *m*; (for taxis) parada *f*; **—by** recurso viejo *m*; **—by passenger** pasajero -ra en la lista de espera *mf*; **—off** empate *m*; **—point** punto de vista *m*; **to come to a —still** pararse; **to be at a —still** estar parado; ADJ **—alone** autónomo

standard [stǽndəd] N (of behavior) norma *f*; (of living, performance) nivel *m*; (of weights) patrón *m*; (banner) estandarte *m*; **gold —** patrón oro *m*; **—-bearer** portaestandarte *mf*; **— deviation** desviación estándar *f*; **— of living** nivel de vida *m*; **— time** hora oficial *f*; **to be up to —** satisfacer los requisitos; ADJ (normal) normal; (standardized) estándar

standardization [stændədɪzéʃən] N estandarización *f*

standardize [stǽndədaɪz] VT estandarizar, uniformar

standby [stǽndbaɪ] ADV **we're flying —** estamos volando standby

standing [stǽndɪŋ] N (position) posición *f*; (rank) rango *m*; (reputation) reputación *f*; ADJ (not seated) derecho, en pie; (permanent) permanente; (stagnant) estancado; **— order** pedido fijo *m*; **— ovation** ovación de pie *f*

stank [stæŋk] *see* stink

stanza [stǽnzə] N estrofa *f*

staple [stépəl] N (for paper) grapa *f*; (main product) producto principal *m*; (food) alimento básico *m*; ADJ (principal) principal; (basic) básico; VT engrapar

stapler [stéplə] N grapadora *f*

star [stɑr] N estrella *f* (also actor); (asterisk) asterisco *m*; **— attraction** atracción principal *f*; **—fish** estrella de mar *f*; **—light** luz de las estrellas *f*; **—-spangled** salpicado de estrellas; **a — student** un[a] estudiante sobresaliente; VT (act in) protagonizar; (put asterisk on) marcar con asterisco; (cover with stars) estrellar

starboard [stárbərd] N estribor *m*; ADV a estribor

starch [stɑrtʃ] N almidón *m* (also food); VT almidonar

stardom [stɑ́rDəm] N estrellato *m*

stare [ster] VI/VT mirar fijamente; N mirada fija *f*

stark [stɑrk] ADJ (landscape) yermo; (truth) descarnado, desnudo; (contrast) marcado; ADV — **naked** en cueros; — **raving mad** loco de remate

starling [stɑ́rlɪŋ] N estornino *m*

starry [stɑ́rɪ] ADJ estrellado

start [stɑrt] VI/VT (begin) comenzar, empezar; (a car) poner[se] en marcha, arrancar; VT (a fire) provocar; VI (jump) sobresaltarse; **to** — **off/out/up** empezar; **don't get him** —**ed** no le des cuerda; N (beginning) comienzo *m*, principio *m*; (of a race) salida *f*; (nervous jump) sobresalto *m*; (nervous jump of a horse) respingo *m*; —**-up** compañía recién establecida *f*; —**-up funds** capital inicial *m*; — **button** botón de inicio *m*; — **menu** menú de inicio *m*

starter [stɑ́rDɚ] N (on an automobile) arranque *m*; (for a race) juez de salida *mf*; **for** —**s** para empezar

startle [stɑ́rdl] VI/VT asustar[se], sobresaltar[se]

startling [stɑ́rdlɪŋ] ADJ asombroso, sorprendente

starvation [stɑrvéʃən] N inanición *f*

starve [stɑrv] VI/VT hambrear; VI morirse de hambre; VT matar de hambre; (for affection) privar de cariño

starving [stɑ́rvɪŋ] ADJ hambriento, muerto de hambre

stash [stæʃ] VI **to** — **away** ir ahorrando; N alijo *m*

state [stet] N estado *m*; — **of the art** con los últimos avances; —**room** (on a ship) camarote *m*; (on a train) compartimiento *m*; —**-run company** compañía estatal *f*; —**sman** estadista *m*; —**swoman** estadista *f*; VT (declare) declarar, aseverar, manifestar; (describe) exponer

stately [stétli] ADJ majestuoso, imponente

statement [stétmənt] N (declaration) declaración *f*, aseveración *f*; (bill) estado de cuentas *m*

static [stǽdɪk] ADJ estático; N interferencia *f*; — **electricity** electricidad estática *f*; **don't give me any** — no me compliques la vida

station [stéʃən] N estación *f*; (on the radio) emisora *f*; (on television) canal *m*; (social rank) condición *f*; — **wagon** camioneta *f*; VT (a sentry) apostar; (troops) estacionar

stationary [stéʃəneri] ADJ (not moving) estacionario; (stopped) detenido; (fixed) fijo

stationery [stéʃəneri] N (material) artículos de papelería *m pl*; (paper) papel de carta *m*

statistical [stətístɪkəl] ADJ estadístico

statistics [stətístɪks] N (science) estadística *f*; (data) estadísticas *f pl*

statue [stǽtʃu] N estatua *f*

stature [stǽtʃɚ] N (physical) estatura *f*; (moral) talla *f*

status [stǽDəs] N (prestige, rank) status *m*; (legal, financial) situación *f*; (marital) estado *m*; — **bar** (computer) barra de estado *f*; — **symbol** símbolo de status *m*

statute [stǽtʃut] N (bylaw) estatuto *m*; (law) ley *f*; — **of limitations** ley de prescripción *f*

statutory [stǽtʃətɔri] ADJ estatutario; — **rape** estupro *m*

stave [stev] N (of a barrel) duela *f*; VI **to** — **off** evitar

stay [ste] VI (remain) quedarse, permanecer; **to** — **away** mantenerse alejado; **to** — **in** quedarse en casa; **to** — **out of trouble** no meterse en líos; **to** — **up** quedarse levantado; VT **to** — **an execution** aplazar una ejecución; N (time spent) estancia *f*, estadía *f*, permanencia *f*; (support) sostén *m*, soporte *m*

stead [sted] N **in her** — en su lugar; **to stand one in good** — ser de provecho para uno

steadfast [stédfæst] ADJ fijo, firme

steadiness [stédinis] N (firmness) firmeza *f*; (of the hand) pulso *m*; (constancy) constancia *f*; (continuity) continuidad *f*

steady [stédi] ADJ (not shaky) firme; (constant) constante; (continuous) continuo; — **boyfriend** novio formal *m*; — **customer** cliente -ta asiduo -dua *mf*; — **income** ingreso fijo *m*; VI/VT (an object) asegurar; (nerves) calmar

steak [stek] N bistec *m*, churrasco *m*

steal [stil] VT (a thing, a base) robar, hurtar; (a girlfriend) soplar; VI **to** — **away/out** escabullirse, escaparse; N (bargain) ganga *f*

stealth [stelθ] N sigilo *m*; **by** — furtivamente

stealthy [stélθi] ADJ furtivo

steam [stim] N (evaporated water) vapor *m*; (arising from an object) vaho *m*; — **engine** máquina de vapor *f*; — **roller** apisonadora *f*, aplanadora *f*; — **ship** [buque de] vapor *m*; — **shovel** excavadora *f*; VT (cook) cocer al vapor; VI (give off steam) echar vapor; **to get** —**ed up** (angry) indignarse; (covered with vapor) empañarse

steamer [stímɚ] N buque de vapor *m*

steed [stid] N corcel *m*

steel [stil] N acero *m*; — **blue** azul acero *m*; — **industry** siderurgia *f*; — **mill** acería *f*; — **wool** lana de acero *f*; VT acerar; **to** — **oneself** prepararse

steep [stip] ADJ (hill) empinado, escarpado, acantilado; (decline) marcado; (price) excesivo; VT (tea) infusionar; VI (tea) estar en infusión, infusionarse

steeple [stípəl] N (spire) aguja *f*, chapitel *m*; (bell tower) campanario *m*

steer [stir] N (young bovine) novillo *m*; (grown

bovine) buey *m*; vi/vt (a car) conducir, manejar; (a ship) gobernar, timonear; vi (turn) girar, doblar; **to — clear of** evitar; **to — a conversation** desviar una conversación; **the car —s easily** el coche es fácil de conducir; **—ing** dirección *f*; **—ing wheel** volante *m*

stellar [stélə] ADJ estelar

stem [stɛm] N (of a plant) tallo *m*; (of a leaf) pedúnculo *m*, rabo *m*; (of a glass) pie *m*; (of a pipe) cañón *m*; **— cell** célula estaminal/ embrional *f*; vt detener, contener, estancar; **to — from** provenir de

stench [stɛntʃ] N hedor *m*, hediondez *f*, tufo *m*

stencil [sténsəl] N plantilla *f*, matriz *f*

stenographer [stənágrəfə] N taquígrafo -fa *mf*

step [stɛp] N (in walking, dancing) paso *m*; (on stairs) peldaño *m*, escalón *m*; (in music) tono *m*; **— by —** paso a paso; **—ladder** escalera *f*; **to take —s** (walk) dar pasos; vi dar un paso; **— this way** pase por aquí; **to — aside** hacerse a un lado; **to — back** retroceder; **to — down** (descend) bajar; (resign) renunciar; **to — off** bajar; **to — off a distance** medir a pasos una distancia; **to — on** pisar, pisotear; **to — on the gas** pisar el acelerador; **to — out** salir; (act) tomar medidas; **to — up** subir; **in — with the music** al compás de la música

stepbrother [stépbrʌðə] N hermanastro *m*

stepdaughter [stépdɔDə] N hijastra *f*

stepfather [stépfaðə] N padrastro *m*

stepmother [stépmʌðə] N madrastra *f*

steppe [stɛp] N estepa *f*

stepsister [stépsɪstə] N hermanastra *f*

stepson [stépsʌn] N hijastro *m*

stereo [stério] ADJ & N estéreo *m*

stereotype [stériotaɪp] N estereotipo *m*

sterile [stérəl] ADJ estéril

sterility [stərílɪDi] N esterilidad *f*

sterilize [stérəlaɪz] VT esterilizar

stern [stɚn] ADJ austero, severo, adusto; N (of a ship) popa *f*

sternum [stɚnəm] N esternón *m*

steroid [stérɔɪd] N esteroide *m*

stethoscope [stéθəskop] N estetoscopio *m*

stew [stu] VI/VT (cook) estofar[se], guisar[se]; VI (worry) preocuparse; N estofado *m*, guiso *m*; **to be in a —** estar preocupado

steward [stúəd] N (manager) administrador *m*; (on a ship) camarero *m*; (on an airplane) auxiliar de vuelo *m*

stewardess [stúə-DIS] N (on a ship) camarera *f*; (on an airplane) auxiliar de vuelo *f*, azafata *f*

stick [stɪk] N (of wood) palo *m*, vara *f*; (of firewood) raja *f*; (of dynamite) cartucho *m*; **—shift** palanca de cambios *f*; **—-up** atraco *m*, asalto *m*; VI/VT (adhere) pegar[se], adherir[se]; VT (place) poner, meter; (stab) clavar,

pinchar; VI (become jammed) atascarse; **— 'em up!** ¡arriba las manos! **to — out** salir, sobresalir; **to — out one's head** asomar la cabeza; **to — out one's tongue** sacar la lengua; **to — to a job** persistir en una tarea; **to — up** (point up) estar parado de punta; **to — up for** defender; **to — someone up** asaltar/atracar a alguien

sticker [stíkə] N (thistle) abrojo *m*; (adhesive) etiqueta adhesiva *f*

sticky [stíki] ADJ pegajoso

stiff [stɪf] ADJ (leather, cardboard) tieso, duro; (drink) fuerte, cargado; (shirt) almidonado; (back) entumecido; (test) difícil; (breeze) fuerte; (personality) envarado; (climb) arduo; (price) alto; **to get —** entumecerse; N (cadaver) *fam* fiambre *m*

stiffen [stífən] VI/VT (leather) endurecer[se]; (back) entumecer[se]; (shirt) almidonar[se]; **to — up** agarrotar[se]

stiffness [stífnɪs] N (of leather) dureza *f*, tiesura *f*; (of one's back) entumecimiento *m*; (of one's personality) envaramiento *m*; (of resistance) firmeza *f*

stifle [stáɪfəl] VI/VT ahogar[se], sofocar[se]; **to — a yawn** contener un bostezo

stigma [stígmə] N estigma *m*

stigmatize [stígmətaɪz] VI/VT estigmatizar

still [stɪl] ADJ (not moving) quieto; (quiet) silencioso; **—born** nacido muerto; **— life** naturaleza muerta *f*; VT acallar; ADV todavía, aún; **he's — here** todavía está [aquí]; CONJ de todos modos, en todo caso; **—, it's a good buy** en todo caso, es una ganga; N (for distilling) alambique *m*; (quiet) silencio *m*

stillness [stílnɪs] N (not moving) quietud *f*; (silence) silencio *m*

stilt [stɪlt] N (for walking) zanco *m*; (support) pilote *m*

stilted [stíltɪd] ADJ (personality) envarado; (style) afectado

stimulant [stímjələnt] ADJ & N estimulante *m*

stimulate [stímjəlet] VT estimular

stimulation [stɪmjəléʃən] N estimulación *f*

stimulus [stímjələs] N estímulo *m*

sting [stɪŋ] VI/VT (insects, thorns) picar; (insects) aguijonear; VT (shampoo) hacer picar; (rain) azotar; (cheat) timar; N (pain) picadura *f*; (stinger) aguijón *m*; (confidence game) golpe *m*; **— of remorse** punzada de remordimiento *f*; **—ray** manta raya *f*

stinger [stíŋə] N aguijón *m*

stinginess [stíndʒɪnɪs] N tacañería *f*, mezquindad *f*

stingy [stíndʒi] ADJ mezquino, tacaño

stink [stɪŋk] VI (smell bad) heder, apestar; **to — of** heder a; **to — up** dar mal olor a; **your performance —s** tu actuación es un desastre; N hedor *m*

stipend [stáɪpɪnd] N (fellowship) beca f; (salary) estipendio m

stipulate [stípjəlet] VT estipular

stipulation [stɪpjəléʃən] N estipulación f

stir [stɜ] VI (move) bullir, rebullir; (awaken) despertar; VT (mix) revolver; (move emotionally) conmover; (stoke) atizar; **to — up** (trouble) provocar, suscitar; (an old grudge) remover; **to — -fry** saltear; N **— - crazy** claustrofóbico; **to give something a** **— revolver algo; to cause a —** causar revuelo

stirring [stɜ́ɪŋ] ADJ (moving) conmovedor

stirrup [stɜ́rəp] N estribo m

stitch [stɪtʃ] N (in sewing) puntada f; (on a wound) punto m; **to be in —es** desternillarse de risa; VI/VT coser

St. Kitts and Nevis [sɛntkítsənnívɪs] N San Cristóbal y Nieves m

St. Lucia [sɛntlúʃə] N Santa Lucía f

St. Lucian [sɛntlúʃən] ADJ & N santalucense mf

stock [stak] N (selection) surtido m; (reserves) existencias f pl; (livestock) ganado m; (lineage) estirpe f; (shares) acciones f pl, valores m pl; (in grafting) patrón m; (broth) caldo m; **—broker** corredor -ora de bolsa mf, bolsista mf; **— company** sociedad anónima f; **— exchange** bolsa de valores f; **—holder** accionista mf; **—market** mercado de valores m, bolsa de valores f; **— market trends** tendencias bursátiles f pl; **— options** opciones f pl; **—pile** acopio m; **—room** depósito m; **— size** tamaño ordinario m; **—yard** corral m; **in —** en existencia; **out of —** agotado; VT (sell) vender; (fill shelves) abastecer; **to — up on** surtirse de, acumular; **to —pile** acopiar; ADJ (trite) trillado

stockade [stakéd] N (fence) estacada f, empalizada f; (prison) prisión militar f

stocking [stákɪŋ] N (hose) media f; (sock) calcetín m

stocky [stáki] ADJ robusto

stoic [stóik] ADJ & N estoico -ca mf

stoke [stok] VT (fire) atizar; (engine) alimentar

stole [stol] (fur) estola f

stole [stol] see steal

stolen [stólən] see steal

stomach [stʌ́mək] N (organ) estómago m; (belly) panza f, barriga f; **he has a big —** es barrigón; **to lie on one's —** estar panza abajo; VT (tolerate) aguantar

stomp [stamp] VI pisar fuerte; VT (crush) pisotear; (defeat) aplastar

stone [ston] N (rock, gem) piedra f; (in fruit) hueso m; (in kidneys) cálculo m; **within a —'s throw** a tiro de piedra; **— Age** Edad de Piedra f; ADJ **—deaf** sordo como una tapia; VT (a person) lapidar; (a fruit) deshuesar; **to —wall** bloquear, ignorar

stony [stóni] ADJ (made of stone) pétreo; (driveway) pedregoso; (silence) sepulcral

stood [stud] see stand

stool [stul] N (furniture) taburete m, banqueta f; (excrement) materia fecal f; **— pigeon** soplón -ona mf, chivato -ta mf

stoop [stup] VI (bend over) agacharse; (have bad posture) encorvarse; **to — to** rebajarse a; N (posture) encorvamiento m; (porch) entrada f, porche m; **to walk with a —** andar encorvado; ADJ **—-shouldered** encorvado, cargado de espaldas

stop [stap] VI (halt) parar, detenerse; (malfunction) parar[se]; VT (halt) parar, detener; (cancel) cancelar; (suspend) suspender; (plug) tapar; **to — at nothing** no tener escrúpulos; **to — by/in** visitar; **to — from** impedir; **to — over at** hacer escala en; **to — short** parar en seco; **to — up** tapar, atascar; **it —ped raining** paró/dejó de llover; N parada f, detención f; (on organ) registro m; **—gap** arreglo provisorio m; **—light** semáforo m; **—over** escala f; **— sign** Sp stop m; Am señal de pare f; Mex alto m; **—volley** (tennis) dejada de volea f; **—watch** cronómetro m; **to bring to a —** parar; **to make a —** parar

stoppage [stápɪdʒ] N interrupción f; (strike) huelga f

stopper [stápɚ] N tapón m

storage [stórɪdʒ] N almacenaje m, almacenamiento m; (of electronic data) almacenamiento m; **— battery** acumulador m; **— device** dispositivo de almacenamiento m; **to keep in —** almacenar

store [stɔr] N (shop) tienda f, almacén m; (supply) reserva f, provisión f; **—house** (warehouse) almacén m, depósito m; (source) mina f, fuente f; **—keeper** tendero -ra mf, almacenista mf; **—room** almacén m, depósito m; **what is in — for us?** ¿qué nos espera? VT (commercial goods) almacenar; (personal effects) guardar; **to — up** acumular

stork [stɔrk] N cigüeña f

storm [stɔrm] N (on land) tormenta f; (at sea) tempestad f, temporal m; (of protest) ola f; **— troops** tropas de asalto f pl; VT (attack) tomar por asalto; VI **to — in/out** entrar/salir en tromba

stormy [stórmi] ADJ tormentoso, tempestuoso

story [stóri] N (tale) cuento m, historia f; (newspaper article) artículo m; (lie) mentira f; (information) información f; (plot) argumento m, trama f; (floor) piso m

stout [staut] ADJ (fat) corpulento; (robust) robusto, fornido; (strong) fuerte; (courageous) valiente

stove [stov] N (for heating) estufa f; (for cooking) cocina f; estufa f

stow [sto] VT (keep) guardar; (hide) esconder;

(put in cargo hold) estibar; **to — away on a ship** viajar de polizón

stowaway [stóəwe] N polizón -ona *mf*

straddle [strǽdl] VI/VT estar a horcajadas; VT (a fence) ponerse a horcajadas; (one's legs) abrir; (not take sides) no comprometerse

strafe [stref] VT ametrallar

straggle [strǽgəl] VI **to — along/behind** rezagarse; **to — in** entrar de a pocos

straight [stret] ADJ (not curved) recto; (not tilted) derecho; (in succession) seguido; (hair) lacio, liso; (teeth) parejo; (frank) franco; (heterosexual) heterosexual; **— A's** sobresaliente en todo; **—edge** regla *f*; **— face** cara seria *f*; **— flush** escalera de color *f*; ADJ **—forward** (honest) honesto; (simple) sencillo, campechano; (clear) claro; ADV **— ahead** todo derecho, todo recto; **for two hours —** dos horas seguidas; **to come — home** volver derecho a casa; **to leave — after lunch** irse justo después de comer; **to set a person —** aclararle algo a alguien; **tell me —** dímelo francamente; **he can't think —** no puede pensar con claridad; N (of a racetrack) recta *f*

straighten [strétn] VI/VT enderezar[se]; (situation) arreglar[se]; VT (hair) alisar, RP laciar; **to — out a child** enderezar a un niño

straightness [strétnɪs] N derechura *f*

strain [stren] VI (pull) tironear; (try hard) esforzarse; VT (exhaust) agotar; (hurt voice) forzar; (injure a joint) torcer; (injure a muscle) sufrir un tirón en; (hurt a relationship) crear una tirantez en; VI/VT (filter) colar[se]; N (effort) esfuerzo *m*; (injury) torcedura *f*; (pressure) presión *f*; (trouble in a relationship) tirantez *f*; (lineage) cepa *f*

strainer [strénɚ] N colador *m*

strait [stret] N estrecho *m*; **in dire —s** en aprietos; **—jacket** camisa de fuerza *f*, chaleco de fuerza *m*; ADJ **—laced** puritano

strand [strænd] VI/VT (a ship) encallar, varar; VT (a person) dejar plantado; **to be — ed** (boat) estar encallado; (person) quedar plantado; N (beach) costa *f*, playa *f*; (of rope) ramal *m*; (of thread) hebra *f*; (of hair) mechón *m*

strange [strendʒ] ADJ (bizarre) extraño, raro; (unknown) desconocido

strangeness [strénd͡ʒnɪs] N (unusualness) lo extraño, rareza *f*; (unexpectedness) lo inesperado

stranger [stréndʒɚ] N (unknown person) extraño -ña *mf*, desconocido -da *mf*; (outsider) forastero -ra *mf*; **to be no — to something** tener experiencia con algo

strangle [strǽŋgəl] VI/VT estrangular[se]; (creativity) coartar; N **—hold** (in wrestling) llave al cuello *f*; (in markets) monopolio *m*

strap [stræp] N (leather band) correa *f*, tira *f*; (on

a dress) tirante *m*; VT atar con correa; **to — in** amarrar[se], abrochar[se]

stratagem [strǽɾədʒəm] N estratagema *f*

strategic [strətídʒɪk] ADJ estratégico

strategy [strǽɾədʒi] N estrategia *f*

stratosphere [strǽɾəsfir] N estratosfera *f*

stratum [strǽɾəm] N estrato *m*

straw [strɔ] N paja *f* (also for drinking); **—berry** fresa *f*; **— man** testaferro *m*; **— vote** votación de prueba *f*; ADJ **—-colored** pajizo

stray [stre] VI (deviate, digress) desviarse; (get lost) perderse; (wander) vagar; (sin) descarriarse, perderse; ADJ extraviado, perdido; N perro/gato mostrenco *m*

streak [strik] N (line) raya *f*; (vein) vena *f*; (of luck) racha *f*; (of light) rayo *m*; VI (run naked) correr desnudo; (get discolored) aclararse

stream [strim] N (jet) chorro *m*; (river) río *m*; (brook) arroyo *m*; ADJ **—lined** (vehículo) aerodinámico; (business) racionalizado; VI (water) correr, fluir; (blood) derramar; **to — out** brotar, manar; **to — in** entrar a raudales

streaming [strímɪŋ] N corriente *f*, flujo *m*; **— audio** flujo continuo de datos de audio *m*; **— video** flujo continuo de datos de vídeo *m*

street [strit] N calle *f*; **—car** tranvía *f*; **—lamp** farol *m*, poste de alumbrado *m*; **— sweeper** barrendero -ra *mf*

strength [strɛŋθ] N fuerza *f*; (spiritual) firmeza *f*; **on the — of** en base a

strengthen [strɛ́ŋθən] VI/VT fortalecer[se], reforzar[se]

strengthening [strɛ́ŋθənɪŋ] N fortalecimiento *m*

strenuous [strɛ́njuəs] ADJ arduo

strep throat [strɛ́prót] N infección por estreptococo *f*

stress [strɛs] N (tension) tensión *f*; (strain) estrés *m*; (pressure) esfuerzo *m*; (emphasis) énfasis *m*; (accent) acento *m*; **— test** prueba de esfuerzo *f*; VT (emphasize) enfatizar; (accentuate) acentuar; (exert force) someter a un esfuerzo; (put under pressure) estresar; **to — out** estresarse

stressful [strɛ́sfəl] ADJ estresante

stretch [strɛt͡ʃ] VI/VT (make or become longer) estirar[se], alargar[se]; (extend) extender[se]; (exaggerate) exagerar; **to — oneself** estirarse, desperezarse; **to — out** (lengthen) extender[se]; (lie) tumbarse, tenderse; N (act of stretching) desperezo *m*; (segment of road) trecho *m*, tramo *m*; (period of time) período *m*; (exaggeration) exageración *f*; **— mark** estría *f*

stretcher [strɛ́t͡ʃɚ] N camilla *f*

strew [stru] VT esparcir

strewn [strun] *see* strew

stricken [stríkən] ADJ (with disease) aquejado; (by a flood) afectado; (with fear) aterrado

stricken [stríkən] *see* strike

strict [strɪkt] ADJ estricto; **in — confidence** en absoluta confianza

stridden [strídn] see stride

stride [straɪd] VI caminar a paso largo, dar zancadas; IN (gait) paso m; (long step) zancada f, tranco m

strident [stráɪdənt] ADJ estridente

strife [straɪf] N conflictos m pl

strike [straɪk] VI/VT (hit) golpear, pegar; (stop work) hacer huelga [contra]; VT (find oil, etc.) dar con, encontrar; (occur to) ocurrírsele a uno; (cross out) tachar; (mark by chimes) dar; (light a match, etc.) encender; (make a coin) acuñar; **to — a compromise/deal** llegar a un acuerdo; **to — one's fancy** antojársele a uno; **to — out** (cross out) tachar; (set forth) encaminarse; (fail) fracasar; (in baseball) poncharse; **to — someone out** ponchar a alguien; **to — up a conversation** entablar conversación; **to — up a friendship** trabar amistad; **how does she — you?** ¿qué tal te parece? N (work stoppage) huelga f; (attack) ataque m; (finding of oil) descubrimiento m; (in baseball) strike m; **—breaker** esquirol m, rompehuelgas m sg; **—out** ponchado m, ponche m; **—through** tachado m; **— zone** zona de strike f; **called —** strike cantado m

striker [stráɪkə] N (person on strike) huelguista mf; (of a bell) badajo m; (in soccer) artillero -ra mf

striking [stráɪkɪŋ] ADJ (unusual, conspicuous) notable; (attractive) llamativo; (on strike) en huelga

string [strɪŋ] N (cord) cuerda f, cordel m; (of pearls, lies) sarta f; (of questions) serie f; (of data) secuencia f; (of beans) fibra f; (of garlic, peppers) ristra f; **— bean** habichuela f, judía verde f; **—s** (in an orchestra) cuerdas f pl; (on a tennis racket) cordaje m, encordado m; **no —s attached** sin condiciones; VT (beads) ensartar; (a musical instrument) encordar; **to — along** tener en ascuas; **to — out** extender[se], prolongar[se]; **to — up** colgar, ahorcar; **to be strung out** estar muy tenso

stringent [stríndʒənt] ADJ (law, need) riguroso; (time limit) estrecho, ajustado

strip [strɪp] VI/VT (make/get naked) desnudar[se]; VT (remove bark) descortezar; (remove leaves) deshojar; (remove sheets) deshacer; (remove varnish) quitar el barniz; (damage gears) estropear el engranaje; **to — search** registrar al desnudo; **to —-mine** explotar a cielo abierto; N (of a thing) tira f; (of land) faja f; **— mall** centro comercial m; **— search** registro al desnudo m

stripe [straɪp] N (band) raya f, lista f, banda f; (military insignia) galón m; (type) tipo m

striped [straɪpt, stráɪpɪd] ADJ listado, rayado

strive [straɪv] VI esforzarse por, luchar por

striven [strívən] see strive

strode [strod] see stride

stroke [strok] N (in golf, tennis, of luck, of genius) golpe m; (cerebral hemorrhage) derrame cerebral m; (movement in swimming) brazada f; (style in swimming) estilo m; (of a piston) carrera f; (of a painter's brush) pincelada f, trazo m; (of lightning) rayo m; **at the — of ten** al dar las diez; VT (pet) acariciar; (praise) halagar

stroll [strol] VI dar un paseo, pasearse; N paseo m, caminata f

stroller [strólə] N cochecito de bebé m

strong [strɔŋ] ADJ fuerte; (husky) recio; (eyesight, probability) bueno; (protest) enérgico; (views, faith, support) firme; (features, resemblance) marcado; (argument) sólido; **—hold** (fortress) fortaleza f; (center of activity) baluarte m; **—-willed** (resolute) resuelto, decidido; (stubborn) terco; ADV **to be going —** seguir activo; VT **to —-arm** intimidar

strongly [strɔ́ŋli] ADV (argue, object) enérgicamente; (pull) con fuerza

strove [strov] see strive

struck [strʌk] see strike

structural [strʌ́ktʃərəl] ADJ estructural

structure [strʌ́ktʃə] N (the way parts are arranged) estructura f; (thing constructed) construcción f; VT estructurar

structuring [strʌ́ktʃəɪŋ] N estructuración f

struggle [strʌ́gəl] VI (with difficulties) luchar, bregar; (with an assailant) forcejear; **she —s in math** la pasa mal en matemáticas; N lucha f; (of ideas) pugna f, lucha f; (fight) contienda f, forcejeo m; **it's a —** da mucho trabajo

strung [strʌŋ] see string

strut [strʌt] VI pavonearse; N pavoneo m; (support) tirante m, puntal m; (shock absorber) amortiguador m

strychnine [stríknaɪn] N estricnina f

stub [stʌb] N talón m; VT **to — one's toe** dar[se] un tropezón, reventarse el dedo

stubble [stʌ́bəl] N (of a crop) rastrojo m; (of a beard) barba de unos días f

stubborn [stʌ́bən] ADJ terco, testarudo

stubbornness [stʌ́bə-nnɪs] N terquedad f, testarudez f

stucco [stʌ́ko] N estuco m; VT estucar

stuck [stʌk] ADJ (unable to move) atascado; (adhering) pegado; **to be — on someone** estar loco por alguien; **—-up** estirado, presumido

stuck [stʌk] see stick

stud [stʌd] N (knob) tachuela f, tachón m; (earring) arete m; (cufflink) gemelo m; (on shirtfront) botón m; (horse, man) semental m; (horse) garañón m; VT tachonar

student [stúdnt] N alumno -na mf; (secondary,

university) estudiante *mf*; — **body** alumnado *m*; ADJ estudiantil
studio [stúdio] N estudio *m*, taller *m*; — **apartment** estudio *m*
studious [stúdiəs] ADJ estudioso
study [stʌ́di] N estudio *m*; VT estudiar
stuff [stʌf] N (material) materia *f*, material *m*; (things) trastos *m pl*, bártulos *m pl*; (cloth) paño *m*, tela *f*; (affair) cosa *f*; (junk) cachivaches *m pl*; VT (mattress) rellenar; (dead animal) embalsamar, disecar; **to — into** meter en; **I'm —ed** estoy lleno
stuffing [stʌ́fɪŋ] N relleno *m*
stuffy [stʌ́fi] ADJ (person) envarado; (air) viciado; (nose) tapado
stumble [stʌ́mbəl] VI (trip) tropezar, trastabillar, dar un traspié; (stutter) balbucear; **to — out** salir a tropezones; **to — upon** tropezar con; **stumbling block** obstáculo *m*; N tropezón *m*, tropiezo *m*, traspié *m*
stump [stʌmp] N (of a tree) tocón *m*, cepa *f*; (of a tooth) raigón *m*; (of a limb) muñón *m*; **to be on the —** hacer una campaña electoral; VT (baffle) dejar perplejo; (remove stumps) arrancar los tocones de; **to — the country** recorrer el país haciendo campaña
stun [stʌn] VT (shock, surprise) dejar atónito, pasmar; (render unconscious) dejar sin sentido; **— gun** pistola tranquilizante *f*
stung [stʌŋ] *see* sting
stunk [stʌŋk] *see* stink
stunning [stʌ́nɪŋ] ADJ (shocking) pasmoso; (beautiful) elegante, bellísimo
stunt [stʌnt] VT (stop growth) atrofiar; (do acrobatic tricks) hacer acrobacia; N (feat) acrobacia *f*; (for publicity) maniobra *f*; **—man** doble *m*; **—woman** doble *f*; **to pull a —** hacerse el listo
stupefy [stúpəfaɪ] VT (make lethargic) atontar, embrutecer; (astonish) dejar estupefacto, alelar
stupendous [stupéndəs] ADJ estupendo
stupid [stúpɪd] ADJ tonto, estúpido, majadero
stupidity [stupíDɪDi] N tontería *f*, estupidez *f*, majadería *f*
stupor [stúpɚ] N estupor *m*
sturdy [stɚ́di] ADJ (person) fornido, fuerte; (construction) sólido, robusto
stutter [stʌ́Dɚ] VI tartamudear, tartajear; VT decir tartamudeando; N (act of stuttering) tartamudeo *m*; (speech defect) tartamudez *f*
stutterer [stʌ́Dɚɚ] N tartamudo -da *mf*
stuttering [stʌ́Dɚɪŋ] ADJ tartamudo; N (act of stuttering) tartamudeo *m*; (speech defect) tartamudez *f*
St. Vincent and the Grenadines [sentvínsəntəndəgrénədinz] N San Vicente y las Granadinas *m*

sty [staɪ] N (for pigs) pocilga *f*; (in eye) orzuelo *m*
style [staɪɫ] N estilo *m*; (type) modelo *m*; — **sheet** página de estilo *f*; **out of —** fuera de moda; **like it's going out of —** como loco; VT (a book) intitular; (hair) peinar; **he —s himself Professor Smith** se hace llamar Profesor Smith
stylish [staɪlɪʃ] ADJ elegante, de moda
stylistic [staɪlístɪk] ADJ estilístico
stylistics [staɪlístɪks] N estilística *f*
stymie, stymy [stáɪmi] VT obstaculizar
Styrofoam™ [stáɪrəfom] N poliestireno *m*
suave [swɑv] ADJ urbano, educado
subcommittee [sʌ́bkəmɪDi] N subcomité *m*
subconscious [sʌbkánʃəs] ADJ subconsciente
subcontract [sʌbkántrækt] VT subcontratar
subdivide [sʌbdɪváɪd] VT subdividir
subdivision [sʌbdɪvíʒən] N subdivisión *f*; (of land) parcelación *f*
subdue [səbdú] VT (overcome, vanquish) sojuzgar, someter, rendir; (repress) reprimir; (attenuate) atenuar
subdued [səbdúd] ADJ (atmosphere) tranquilo; (mood) deprimido; (lighting, color) tenue
subject[1] [sʌ́bdʒɪkt] N (of a king) súbdito -ta *mf*; (of a sentence, in an experiment) sujeto *m*; (in school) asignatura *f*, materia *f*; — **matter** tema *m*; ADV LOC — **to** (changes, laws, conditions) sujeto a; (depression, earthquakes) propenso a
subject[2] [səbdʒékt] VT someter
subjection [səbdʒékʃən] N sometimiento *m*
subjective [səbdʒéktɪv] ADJ subjetivo
subjectivity [sʌbdʒɛktívɪDi] N subjetividad *f*
subjugate [sʌ́bdʒəget] VT sojuzgar, avasallar
subjunctive [səbdʒʌ́ŋktɪv] ADJ & N subjuntivo *m*
sublet [sʌblét] VI/VT subarrendar
sublime [səbláɪm] ADJ sublime
submarine [sʌbmərín, sʌ́bmərin] ADJ submarino; N submarino *m*
submerge [səbmɚ́dʒ] VI/VT sumergir[se]
submerged [səbmɚ́dʒd] ADJ inmerso, sumergido
submission [səbmíʃən] N (humility) sumisión *f*; (subjugation) sometimiento *m*, sumisión *f*; (sending) entrega *f*, envío *m*
submissive [səbmísɪv] ADJ sumiso
submit [səbmít] VI/VT someter[se]; (to a judge) elevar[se]; **to — a report** presentar un informe
subordinate[1] [səbɔ́rdn̩ɪt] ADJ & N subordinado -da *mf*, subalterno -na *mf*
subordinate[2] [səbɔ́rdn̩et] VT subordinar
subpar [sʌbpár] ADJ inferior
subpoena [səpínə] N citación *f*, orden de comparecencia *f*
subroutine [sʌ́brutin] N subrutina *f*
subscribe [səbskráɪb] VI (underwrite, sign) suscribir; (receive a magazine) abonarse,

suscribirse; (agree with) adherirse a

subscriber [səbskráɪbɚ] N (to shares) suscriptor -ora *mf*; (to services) abonado -da *mf*; (to a magazine) suscriptor -ora *mf*, abonado -da *mf*; (to an idea) partidario -ria *mf*

subscript [sʌ́bskrɪpt] N subíndice *m*

subscription [səbskrípʃən] N suscripción *f*, abono *m*

subsequent [sʌ́bsɪkwənt] ADJ subsiguiente

subsequently [sʌ́bsɪkwəntli] N posteriormente, con posterioridad *f*

subservient [səbsɚviənt] ADJ servil

subside [səbsáɪd] VI (sediment) hundirse; (water level) bajar; (volcano, storm, anger) calmarse, aquietarse

subsidiary [səbsídieri] ADJ subsidiario; N sucursal *f*, filial *f*

subsidize [sʌ́bsɪdaɪz] VT subvencionar, subsidiar

subsidy [sʌ́bsɪdi] N subvención *f*, subsidio *m*

substance [sʌ́bstəns] N sustancia *f*; — **abuse** abuso de sustancias *m*

substandard [sʌbstǽndɚd] ADJ de calidad inferior

substantial [səbstǽnʃəl] ADJ (changes) sustancial; (food, lecture) sustancioso; (furniture) sólido; (amount) considerable, importante; **to be in — agreement** estar básicamente de acuerdo

substantiate [səbstǽnʃiet] VT (verify) verificar; (prove) probar

substantive [sʌ́bstəntɪv] ADJ & N sustantivo *m*

substitute [sʌ́bstɪtut] VT sustituir, reemplazar; **I —d water for milk** usé agua en vez de leche, sustituí/reemplacé la leche por agua; VI **John —d for Mary** Juan sustituyó/ reemplazó a María; N (one who substitutes) sustituto *m*, reemplazo *m*; (teacher, athlete) suplente *mf*; (thing) sucedáneo *m*

substitution [sʌbstɪtúʃən] N sustitución *f*; **the — of water for milk** la sustitución de leche por agua

subterfuge [sʌ́btɚfjudʒ] N subterfugio *m*

subterranean [sʌbtəréniən] ADJ subterráneo

subtitle [sʌ́btaɪd̩l] N subtítulo *m*

subtle [sʌ́d̩l] ADJ sutil

subtlety [sʌ́d̩lti] N sutileza *f*

subtotal [sʌ́btod̩l] N subtotal *m*

subtract [səbtrǽkt] VT (deduct) restar; (take away) sustraer

subtraction [səbtrǽkʃən] N sustracción *f*, resta *f*

suburb [sʌ́bɚb] N barrio residencial periférico *m*

suburban [səbɚbən] ADJ (residential) residencial; (on the outskirts) periférico

subversive [səbvɚ́sɪv] ADJ subversivo

subway [sʌ́bwe] N metropolitano *m*, metro *m*, subterráneo *m*

succeed [səksíd] VI (be successful) tener éxito; (manage) lograr; **to — to** heredar; VT (follow) suceder a

success [səksés] N éxito *m*

successful [səksésfəl] ADJ (person) exitoso; (effort) productivo, satisfactorio; **to be —** tener éxito

succession [səkséʃən] N sucesión *f*

successive [səksésɪv] ADJ sucesivo

successor [səksésɚ] N sucesor -ora *mf*

succinct [səksíŋkt] ADJ sucinto, escueto

succor [sʌ́kɚ] N socorro *m*; VT socorrer

succumb [səkʌ́m] VI sucumbir

such [sʌtʃ] ADJ tal; — **as** tal como; **at — and — a place** en tal o cual lugar; **he's — an idiot!** ¡es tan idiota! **in — a case** en tal caso / en semejante caso; **there's no — thing** eso no existe; PRON **hobbies, pastimes, and —** hobbies, pasatiempos y cosas por el estilo; **a car — as yours** un coche como el tuyo; ADV **— nice neighbors** vecinos tan simpáticos

suck [sʌk] VI/VT chupar; (suckle) mamar; (vacuum, pump) aspirar; **to be —ed into** ser arrastrado a; VI; **to — in air** aspirar

sucker [sʌ́kɚ] N (gullible person) primo -ma *mf*; (lollipop) *Sp* pirulí *m*; *Mex* paleta *f*; *RP* chupetín *m*

sucrose [súkros] N sacarosa *f*

suction [sʌ́kʃən] N succión *f*, aspiración *f*

Sudan [sudǽn] N Sudán *m*

Sudanese [sudníz] ADJ & N sudanés -esa *mf*

sudden [sʌ́d̩n] ADJ súbito, repentino, brusco; — **death** (also in sports) muerte súbita *f*; — **infant death syndrome** síndrome de muerte infantil súbita *m*; **all of a —** de repente, de improviso

suddenly [sʌ́d̩nli] ADV de repente, repentinamente

suddenness [sʌ́d̩nnɪs] N brusquedad *f*, lo repentino

suds [sʌdz] N espuma *f*

sue [su] VI/VT demandar, poner pleito; **to — for** pedir, suplicar; **to — for damages** demandar por daños y perjuicios

suede [swed] N gamuza *f*, ante *m*

suffer [sʌ́fɚ] VI/VT (feel pain) sufrir, padecer; VT (tolerate) tolerar

sufferer [sʌ́fərɚ] N paciente *mf*

suffering [sʌ́fəɪŋ] N sufrimiento *m*, padecimiento *m*

suffice [səfáɪs] VI/VT bastar, ser suficiente

sufficient [səfíʃənt] ADJ suficiente, bastante

suffix [sʌ́fɪks] N sufijo *m*

suffocate [sʌ́fəket] VI/VT ahogar[se], sofocar[se]; (to die, kill) asfixiar[se]

suffocation [sʌfəkéʃən] N ahogo *m*, sofoco *m*

suffrage [sʌ́frɪdʒ] N sufragio *m*

sugar [ʃúgɚ] N azúcar *mf*; (endearment) cariño *m*; — **cane** caña de azúcar *f*; VT azucarar; **to — the pill** dorar la píldora

suggest [səgdʒést] VT (propose) sugerir; (hint) insinuar; **—ed retail price** precio sugerido m

suggestion [səgdʒéstʃən] N (proposal) sugerencia f; (in hypnosis) sugestión f

suggestive [səgdʒéstɪv] ADJ insinuante; **to be — of** evocar

suicide [súsaɪd] N (act) suicidio m; (person) suicida mf; **to commit —** suicidarse

suit [sut] N (clothes) traje m; (in cards) palo m, color m; (lawsuit) demanda f, pleito m, querella f; **—case** maleta f, valija f; VT (adapt) adaptar, ajustar; (satisfy) satisfacer; (look good) quedarle bien a, sentarle bien a; (be convenient, appropriate) convenir, venir bien; **— yourself** haz lo que te parezca

suitable [súːdəbəl] ADJ (appropriate) apropiado; (apt) apto

suitably [súːdəbli] ADV como corresponde

suite [swit] N (series) serie f; (series of rooms, musical composition) suite f; (furniture) juego m; (software) paquete de programas de productividad m

suitor [súːə-] N pretendiente m, galán m

sulfate, sulphate [sʌ́lfet] N sulfato m

sulfide, sulphide [sʌ́lfaɪd] N sulfuro m

sulfur, sulphur [sʌ́lfə-] N azufre m

sulfuric, sulphuric [sʌlfjúrɪk] ADJ sulfúrico

sulk [sʌlk] VI enfurruñarse; N **to be in a —** estar enfurruñado

sulky [sʌ́lki] ADJ malhumorado, enfurruñado

sullen [sʌ́lən] ADJ hosco, huraño

sully [sʌ́li] VT mancillar, ensuciar

sultry [sʌ́ltri] ADJ (hot) bochornoso, sofocante; (sensual) sensual

sum [sʌm] N suma f; **in —** en resumen; VI **to — up** resumir, recapitular

summarize [sʌ́məraɪz] VI/VT resumir

summary [sʌ́məri] N resumen m; ADJ sumario

summer [sʌ́mə-] N verano m, lit estío m; **— resort** balneario m, lugar de verano m; **— school** cursos de verano m pl; **—time** verano m; VI veranear

summit [sʌ́mɪt] N cumbre f, cima f

summon [sʌ́mən] VT (a witness) citar; (an employee, the police) llamar; N **—s** citación judicial f

sumptuous [sʌ́mptʃuəs] ADJ suntuoso

sun [sʌn] N sol m; **to —bathe** tomar el sol; **—beam** rayo de sol m; **—block** protector solar m; **—burn** quemadura de sol f; **—dial** reloj de sol m; **—down** puesta de[l] sol f; **—flower** girasol m; **—glasses** gafas de sol f pl, anteojos de sol m pl; **—lamp** lámpara solar f; **—light** luz del sol f; **—rise** salida de[l] sol f, amanecer m; **—screen** protector solar m; **—set** puesta de[l] sol f; **—shine** luz [del sol] f; **—spot** mancha solar f; **—stroke** insolación f; **—tan** bronceado m; **—up** salida del sol f; VI **to — oneself** tomar el sol; **to —burn** quemar[se] al sol

Sunday [sʌ́nde] N domingo m; **— school** escuela dominical f

sundry [sʌ́ndri] ADJ diversos

sung [sʌŋ] see sing

sunk [sʌŋk] see sink

sunny [sʌ́ni] ADJ (day, patio) soleado; (disposition) alegre

super [súpə-] N (of a building) conserje m, portero -ra mf; ADJ (wonderful) súper, bárbaro

superb [supə́b] ADJ excelente

supercharger [súpə-tʃardʒə-] N sobrealimentador m

supercomputer [súpə-kəmpjudə-] N Am supercomputadora f; Sp superordenador m

superego [supə-ígo] N superego m, superyó m

superficial [supə-fíʃəl] ADJ superficial

superfluous [supə́fluəs] ADJ superfluo

superhuman [supə-hjúmən] ADJ sobrehumano

superimpose [supə-ɪmpóz] VT superponer, sobreponer

superintendent [supə-ɪnténdənt] N (of work) superintendente mf, capataz mf; (of building) conserje mf, portero -ra mf

superior [supíriə-] ADJ & N superior mf

superiority [supiriɔ́rɪdi] N superioridad f

superlative [supə́lədɪv] ADJ & N superlativo m

supermarket [súpə-markɪt] N supermercado m, súper m

supernatural [supə-nǽtʃə-əl] ADJ sobrenatural

superpower [súpə-pauə-] N superpotencia f

superscript [súpə-skrɪpt] N superíndice m

supersede [supə-síd] VT reemplazar

supersonic [supə-sánɪk] ADJ supersónico

superstar [súpə-star] N superestrella f

superstition [supə-stíʃən] N superstición f

superstitious [supə-stíʃəs] ADJ supersticioso

superstore [súpə-stɔr] N hipermercado m

supervise [súpə-vaɪz] VI/VT supervisar, fiscalizar

supervision [supə-víʒən] N supervisión f, fiscalización f

supervisor [súpə-vaɪzə-] N supervisor -ora mf

supine [súpaɪn] ADJ supino

supper [sʌ́pə-] N cena f

supplant [səplǽnt] VT suplantar

supple [sʌ́pəl] ADJ (flexible) flexible, elástico; (agile) ágil, grácil

supplement¹ [sʌ́pləmənt] N (of a newspaper) suplemento m; (of a book) apéndice m; (of one's diet) complemento m

supplement² [sʌ́pləment] VT complementar, suplementar

supplemental [sʌpləméntəl] ADJ suplementario

supplier [səplaɪə-] N abastecedor -ora mf, proveedor -ora mf

supply [səplaɪ] VT abastecer, suministrar; N (act of supplying) abastecimiento m; **— and demand** oferta y demanda f; **in short —**

escaso; **supplies** suministros *m pl*,
provisiones *f pl*; **office supplies** artículos de
oficina *m pl*; **military supplies** pertrechos
m pl

support [səpórt] VT (keep from falling) sostener,
soportar; (encourage) apoyar; (facilitate)
potenciar; (corroborate) corroborar; (help
with computers) soportar; **to be —ed by**
fundamentarse en/sobre; N (of a structure)
sostén *m*, soporte *m*; (of a family) sustento *m*;
(of a candidate, idea) apoyo *m*; (of a theory)
respaldo *m*; (for a computer) soporte *m*; **—
group** grupo de apoyo *m*

supporter [səpórdɚ] N partidario -ria *mf*,
simpatizante *mf*; (in sports) hincha *mf*

supportive [səpórdɪv] ADJ solidario; **you've
always been very — of us** siempre nos has
apoyado

suppose [səpóz] VT suponer; **we are —d to go**
tenemos que ir

supposedly [səpózɪdli] ADV supuestamente

supposition [sʌpəzíʃən] N suposición *f*,
supuesto *m*

suppository [səpázɪtɔri] N supositorio *m*

suppress [səprés] VT (repress) reprimir;
(eliminate) suprimir; (a revolt) sofocar

suppression [səpréʃən] N (repression) represión
f; (elimination) supresión *f*; (of a revolt)
sofocación *f*

supremacy [suprémǝsi] N supremacía *f*

supreme [suprím] ADJ supremo

surcharge [sɝtʃɑrdʒ] N recargo *m*, prima *f*

sure [ʃur] ADJ seguro; (judgment) certero; (hand)
firme; **to make — of** asegurarse de; ADV **he
— drinks a lot** es una esponja; **may I sit
here? —!** ¡me pуedo sentar? ¡cómo no!

surely [ʃúrli] ADV seguramente, ciertamente; **—
you jest** no hablarás en serio; **he will —
come** seguramente vendrá

surf [sɝf] N (breaking waves) rompientes *mf pl*;
(foam) espuma *f*; (undertow) resaca *f*;
—board tabla de surf *f*; VI/VT (on water)
hacer surfing [en], surfear; (on the Internet)
navegar, surfear

surface [sɝfɪs] N superficie *f*; (of a solid) cara *f*; VI
(come to top) emerger; (turn up) salir a la luz;
VT (a submarine) sacar a la superficie; (a road)
revestir

surfeit [sɝfɪt] N (excess) exceso *m*; (feeling of
fullness) hartazgo *m*; VI/VT hartar[se]

surfing [sɝfɪŋ] N (on water) surfing *m*; (on the
Internet) navegación *f*

surge [sɝdʒ] N (of people, disgust) oleada *f*; (of
waves) oleaje *m*; (of electricity) sobrecarga de
voltaje *f*; **— protector** protector contra
sobrecargas de voltaje *m*; VI (people)
precipitarse; (current) subir

surgeon [sɝdʒən] N cirujano -na *mf*

surgery [sɝdʒəri] N cirujía *f*; (room) quirófano *m*

surgical [sɝdʒɪkəl] ADJ quirúrgico; **— dressing**
vendaje quirúrgico *m*; **— instruments**
instrumentos quirúrgicos *m pl*

Suriname, Surinam [súrɪnɑm] N Surinam *m*

Surinamese [surɪnɑmíz] ADJ & N surinamés
-esa *mf*

surly [sɝli] ADJ malhumorado, hosco, arisco

surmise [sɚmáɪz] VT conjeturar, suponer; N
conjetura *f*, suposición *f*

surmount [sɚmáʊnt] VT superar

surname [sɝnem] N apellido *m*

surpass [sɚpǽs] VT superar, sobrepujar

surpassing [sɚpǽsɪŋ] N superación *f*

surplus [sɝplʌs] N excedente *m*, sobrante *m*,
sobra *f*; (of funds) superávit *m*

surprise [sɚpráɪz] N sorpresa *f*; VT sorprender

surprising [sɚpráɪzɪŋ] ADJ sorprendente

surprisingly [sɚpráɪzɪŋli] ADV
sorprendentemente; **not —** como era de
esperar

surreal [sɚríəl] ADJ surrealista

surrealism [sɚríəlɪzəm] N surrealismo *m*

surrealist [sɚríəlɪst] N surrealista *mf*

surrealistic [sɚriəlístɪk] ADJ surrealista

surrender [sɚrɛ́ndɚ] VI (accept defeat)
rendir[se], darse por vencido; (give oneself
up) entregarse; VT entregar; N rendición *f*

surreptitious [sɚəptíʃəs] ADJ subrepticio

surrogate [sɝəgɪt] ADJ sustituto; **— mother**
madre de alquiler *f*

surround [sɚáʊnd] VT rodear, circundar; (a
city) sitiar

surrounding [sɚáʊndɪŋ] ADJ circundante; N
—s alrededores *m pl*, inmediaciones *f pl*,
entorno *m*

surtax [sɝtæks] N sobretasa *f*

surveillance [sɚvélɑns] N vigilancia *f*

survey[1] [sɚvé] VT (evaluate) evaluar; (measure)
medir; (contemplate) contemplar; (poll)
encuestar

survey[2] [sɝve] N (inspection) reconocimiento *m*,
inspección *f*; (measure) medición *f*;
(overview) panorama *m*; (poll) encuesta *f*,
sondeo *m*; **— course** curso general *m*

surveyor [sɚvéɚ] N agrimensor -ora *mf*

survival [sɚváɪvəl] N supervivencia *f*,
sobrevivencia *f*; (subsistence) subsistencia *f*;
the — of the fittest la supervivencia del
más apto

survive [sɚváɪv] VI/VT sobrevivir (also live
longer than); (subsist) subsistir

surviving [sɚváɪvɪŋ] ADJ superviviente

survivor [sɚváɪvɚ] N sobreviviente *mf*,
superviviente *mf*

susceptible [səséptəbəl] ADJ susceptible; **to be
— of proof** poderse demostrar; **to be — to
pneumonia** ser propenso a la pulmonía

suspect[1] [sáspɛkt] N sospechoso -sa *mf*

suspect[2] [səspékt] VT sospechar, recelar

suspend [səspénd] VT suspender

suspenders [səspéndəz] N tirantes *m pl*

suspense [səspéns] N (uncertainty) incertidumbre *f*; (in movie) suspenso *m*; *Sp* suspense *m*; **to keep in —** mantener en suspenso, tener en vilo

suspension [səspénʃən] N suspensión *f*; (of a ban) levantamiento *m*; **— bridge** puente colgante *m*

suspicion [səspíʃən] N sospecha *f*

suspicious [səspíʃəs] ADJ (causing suspicion) sospechoso; (experiencing suspicion) suspicaz, desconfiado

sustain [səstén] VT (weight) sostener, sustentar; (pretense, effort) mantener; (an injury) sufrir; (an objection) admitir; (a musical note) sostener

sustainable [səsténəbəł] ADJ sostenible, sustentable

sustenance [sástənəns] N sustento *m*, alimento *m*

suture [sútʃə] N sutura *f*

swab [swɑb] N bola de algodón *f*, *RP* hisopo *m*; VT pasar un hisopo sobre

swagger [swǽgə] VI (walk) pavonearse, contonearse; (boast) fanfarronear; N (walk) pavoneo *m*, contoneo *m*; (bluster) fanfarronería *f*

swallow [swálo] N (drink) trago *m*; (bird) golondrina *f*; VI/VT tragar; **to — up** consumir

swallowing [swáloɪŋ] N deglución *f*

swam [swæm] *see* swim

swamp [swɑmp] N pantano *m*, ciénaga *f*; **—land** cenagal *m*; VI/VT (flood) inundar[se]; (overwhelm) abrumar[se], agobiar[se]

swampy [swámpi] ADJ pantanoso, cenagoso

swan [swɑn] N cisne *m*; **— dive** salto del ángel *m*; **— song** canto de cisne *m*

swap [swɑp] VT cambiar, canjear; N cambio *m*, canje *m*

swarm [sworm] N enjambre *m*; VI (of bees) salir en enjambre; (of people, tourists) pulular, hormiguear; **to be —ing with** ser un hervidero de, abundar en

swarthy [swórði] ADJ trigueño, moreno

swat [swɑt] VT (a person) pegar; (flies) aplastar; **to — at** manotear; N manotazo *m*

sway [swe] VI/VT (move to and fro) balancear[se], bambolear[se]; (move hips) menear[se]; (influence) influir [en]; N (movement) balanceo *m*, vaivén *m*, bamboleo *m*; (influence) influencia *f*; **to hold — over** dominar

Swazi [swázi] N suazi *mf*

Swaziland [swázilænd] N Suazilandia *f*

swear [swɛr] VI/VT (vow) jurar; (use profanity) decir palabrotas; *Sp* soltar tacos; **to — in** (give oath) juramentar; (take oath) prestar juramento; **she —s by canned peaches**

para ella no hay nada como los duraznos enlatados; **to — off** renunciar a; **to — to** jurar por

sweat [swɛt] VI (perspire) sudar; (ooze) exudar, sudar; (worry) preocuparse; N sudor *m*; **— glands** glándulas sudoríparas *f pl*; **—shirt** sudadera *f*; **—suit** equipo deportivo *m*; *Sp* chándal *m*; **no —** no hay problema

sweater [swɛDə] N suéter *m*, jersey *m*

sweating [swɛDɪŋ] N sudor *m*, sudoración *f*, transpiración *f*

sweaty [swɛDi] ADJ sudoroso, sudado

Swede [swid] N sueco -ca *mf*

Sweden [swídn] N Suecia *f*

Swedish [swídɪʃ] ADJ sueco

sweep [swip] VI/VT (clean with broom, scan) barrer; (dredge) dragar; VT (touch) rozar; (search) rastrear; VI (spread) extenderse; **to — away** llevar, arrastrar; **to — down upon** caer sobre, asolar; **to — off** limpiar; **to — into** (enter majestically) entrar majestuosamente; (enter quickly) entrar rápidamente; **to — up** recoger; N (cleaning) barrida *f*; (extension) extensión *f*; (movement) barrido *m*; (search) rastreo *m*

sweeper [swípə] N (for cleaning) barredora *f*; (in soccer) líbero *m*

sweeping [swípɪŋ] ADJ (statement) [demasiado] general; (victory) aplastante

sweet [swit] ADJ (in flavor, personality) dulce; (in smell) bueno, fragante; **—-and-sour** agridulce; **—heart** querido -da *mf*; **— pea** *Sp* guisante de olor *m*; **— potato** batata *f*, boniato *m*; *Mex* camote *m*; **to have a — tooth** ser goloso; N dulce *m*, golosina *f*; **my — ** mi vida, mi alma; VT **to —-talk** halagar

sweeten [switn] VI/VT (a food) endulzar[se]; (an experience) dulcificar[se]

sweetener [switnə] N endulzante *m*, edulcorante *m*

sweetness [switnɪs] N (of personality) dulzura *f*; (of taste) dulzor *m*

swell [swɛł] VI/VT (limbs, with pride) hinchar[se], henchir[se]; VI (river) crecer; (population) crecer, engrosar[se]; VT (make grow) hacer crecer, hacer aumentar, engrosar; N (of ocean) oleaje *m*; ADJ regio, bárbaro

swelling [swɛlɪŋ] N hinchazón *f*

swelter [swɛłtə] VI sofocarse de calor

swept [swɛpt] *see* sweep

swerve [swɜv] VI/VT (in a car) virar; (from a goal) desviar[se]; N viraje *m*

swift [swɪft] ADJ ligero, veloz, raudo; N vencejo *m*

swiftness [swíftnɪs] N velocidad *f*, rapidez *f*

swim [swɪm] VI/VT nadar; (float) flotar; **to — across** atravesar nadando; **my head is —ming** me da vueltas la cabeza; **I love**

—ming me encanta nadar; N *Mex* alberca *f*;
—suit traje de baño *m*; **to take a —** ir a
nadar, dar una nadada

swimmer [swímə·] N nadador -ora *mf*; **—'s ear**
otitis externa *f*

swimming [swímɪŋ] N natación *f*; **— pool**
piscina *f*

swindle [swíndl̩] VT estafar; N estafa *f*,
trapacería *f*

swine [swaɪn] N puerco *m*, cerdo *m*; (person)
offensive puerco -ca *mf*, sinvergüenza *mf*

swing [swɪŋ] VI/VT (on a swing) columpiar[se];
(move to and fro) balancear[se];
bamboleaur[se]; (baseball, golf) dar un swing
[con]; VI (change) virar; **to — and miss**
abanicar; **to — around** dar vueltas; **to —
open** abrirse; VT (make turn) hacer girar;
(influence) influir sobre; **to — a deal**
concretar un negocio; **I can't — a new car**
no me puedo dar el lujo de comprar un auto
nuevo; N (playground toy) columpio *m*;
(oscillation) balanceo *m*, vaivén *m*, bamboleo
m; (in golf, baseball, music) swing *m*;
(change) cambio *m*; **— and a miss** abanico
m; **in full —** en su apogeo; **to get into the
— of things** agarrarle la onda a algo, cogerle
el tranquillo a algo

swipe [swaɪp] VT (steal) afanar, sisar; (slide)
deslizar; **to — a card** pasar una tarjeta por un
lector; N (insult) insulto *m*; **to take a — at
someone** (physical) tirarle un manotazo a
alguien; (verbal) insultar

swirl [swɝl] VI/VT arremolinar[se]; (dancers)
girar; N remolino *m*; (smoke) espiral *f*

Swiss [swɪs] ADJ & N suizo -za *mf*; **— cheese**
queso suizo *m*

switch [swɪtʃ] N (change) cambio *m*; (electrical)
interruptor *m*, llave *f*; (stick for whipping)
varilla *f*; (on railways) agujas *f pl*; **—blade**
navaja automática *f*; **—board** centralita *f*;
—man guardagujas *m sg*; **—-hitter** (in
baseball) bateador -ora ambidiestro *mf*; VI/VT
cambiar [de]; (train cars) desviar; **to — off**
(current) cortar; (light, TV) apagar; **to — on**
encender, prender

Switzerland [swítsə·lənd] N Suiza *f*

swivel [swívəl] N pivote *m*; **— chair** silla
giratoria *f*

swollen [swólən] ADJ hinchado

swollen [swólən] *see* swell

swoon [swun] VI desvanecerse, desmayarse; **to
— over someone** morirse por alguien; N
vahído *m*

swoop [swup] VI **to — down upon** abalanzarse
sobre; N descenso súbito *m*; **at one fell —** de
un tirón

sword [sɔrd] N espada *f*; **—fish** pez espada *m*

swore [swɔr] *see* swear

sworn [swɔrn] *see* swear

swum [swʌm] *see* swim

swung [swʌŋ] *see* swing

sycamore [síkəmɔr] N sicomoro *m*

syllable [síləbəl] N sílaba *f*

syllabus [síləbəs] N programa [de estudios] *m*

syllogism [síləʤɪzəm] N silogismo *m*

symbiosis [sɪmbiósɪs] N simbiosis *f*

symbol [símbəl] N símbolo *m*

symbolic [sɪmbálɪk] ADJ simbólico

symbolism [símbəlɪzəm] N simbolismo *m*

symbolize [símbəlaɪz] VT simbolizar

symmetrical [sɪmétrɪkəl] ADJ simétrico

symmetry [símɪtri] N simetría *f*

sympathetic [sɪmpəθétɪk] ADJ (compassionate)
compasivo; (understanding) comprensivo,
solidario; (favoring) favorable; (nervous
system) simpático

sympathize [símpəθaɪz] VI (be compassionate)
compadecer[se]; (be understanding)
comprender; (be in favor) favorecer; **to —
with** estar a favor de

sympathizer [símpəθaɪzə·] N simpatizante *mf*

sympathizing [símpəθaɪzɪŋ] ADJ
simpatizante

sympathy [símpəθi] N (compassion) compasión
f; (understanding) comprensión *f*;
(condolence) condolencia *f*, pésame *m*; **to
extend one's —** dar el pésame

symphony [símfəni] N sinfonía *f*; **— orchestra**
orquesta sinfónica *f*

symposium [sɪmpóziəm] N simposio *m*

symptom [símptəm] N síntoma *m*

synagogue [sínəgɑg] N sinagoga *f*

synchronize [síŋkrənaɪz] VI/VT sincronizar[se]

synchronous [síŋkrənəs] ADJ sincrónico

syndicate[1] [síndɪkɪt] N sindicato *m*

syndicate[2] [síndɪket] VI/VT (form a syndicate)
sindicar[se]; VT (sell rights) vender los
derechos de

syndrome [síndrom] N síndrome *m*

synergy [sínə·ʤi] N sinergia *f*

synonym [sínənɪm] N sinónimo *m*

synonymous [sɪnánəməs] ADJ sinónimo

synopsis [sɪnápsɪs] N sinopsis *f*

syntax [síntæks] N sintaxis *f*

synthesis [sínθəsɪs] N síntesis *f*

synthesize [sínθəsaɪz] VI/VT sintetizar

synthesizer [sínθəsaɪzə·] N sintetizador *m*

synthetic [sɪnθétɪk] ADJ sintético

syphilis [sífəlɪs] N sífilis *f*

Syria [síriə] N Siria *f*

Syrian [síriən] ADJ & N sirio -ria *mf*

syringe [sərínʤ] N jeringa *f*

syrup [sírəp] N (food) almíbar *m*, jarabe *m*;
(medicine) jarabe *m*

system [sístəm] N sistema *m*; **— crashes** caídas
del sistema *f pl*

systematic [sɪstəmædɪk] ADJ sistemático

systematize [sístəmətaɪz] VI/VT sistematizar

systemic [sɪstémɪk] ADJ sistémico
systolic [sɪstálɪk] ADJ sistólico

Tt

tab [tæb] N (on a keyboard) tabulador *m*; (on
index cards) pestaña *f*, ceja *f*; (bill) cuenta *f*; —
key tecla de tabulación *f*; VI tabular
table [tébəl] N (furniture) mesa *f*; (list) tabla *f*; —
lamp lámpara de mesa *f*; — **of contents**
tabla de contenido *f*, índice *m*; **at** — a la mesa;
VT posponer indefinidamente, dar carpetazo
a; —**cloth** mantel *m*; —**spoon** (spoon)
cuchara grande *f*; (measurement) cucharada *f*;
—**spoonful** cucharada *f*; — **tennis** tenis de
mesa *m*; —**ware** vajilla *f*, servicio de mesa *m*
tablet [tǽblɪt] N (pill) pastilla *f*, tableta *f*; (paper)
bloc *m*; (stone) tabla *f*, lápida *f*; (portable
writing surface) tablilla *f*
tabloid [tǽblɔɪd] N (paper size) tabloide *m*; (type
of press) prensa amarilla/sensacionalista *f*
taboo [tæbú] N tabú *m*
tabulate [tǽbjəlet] VT tabular
tachometer [tækámɪdə-] N tacómetro *m*
tacit [tǽsɪt] ADJ tácito
taciturn [tǽsɪtɚn] ADJ taciturno
tack [tæk] N (nail) tachuela *f*; (stitch) hilván *m*;
(heading of a boat) rumbo *m*; (course of
action) táctica *f*; (equipment for a horse)
arreos *m pl*; VT (to nail) clavar con tachuelas;
(to stitch) hilvanar; **to** — **on** agregar; VI virar,
cambiar de rumbo
tackle [tǽkəl] N (for fishing, hoisting) aparejo *m*;
(in rugby, football) placaje *m*, parada *f*;
(person) atajador *m*; VT (a problem)
enfrentar, abordar; (a task) emprender; (a
horse) poner arreos; VI/VT (rugby, American
football) placar, atajar
tacky [tǽki] ADJ (in bad taste) de mal gusto,
chabacano; *Sp* hortera; (sticky) pegajoso
tact [tækt] N tacto *m*
tactful [tǽktfəl] ADJ que tiene tacto
tactics [tǽktɪks] N táctica *f*
tactile [tǽktl] ADJ táctil
tactless [tǽktlɪs] ADJ falto de tacto
tag [tæg] N (label) etiqueta *f*; (question) coletilla
f; (nickname) apodo *m*; **to play** — jugar al
pillapilla; VT etiquetar; (in the game of tag)
pillar; **to** — **along** acompañar
tail [tel] N cola *f*, rabo *m*; (of a shirt) faldón *m*;
(pursuer) perseguidor -ora *mf*; —**bone**
rabadilla *f*; — **end** (of a concert) final *m*; (of a
procession) cola *f*; —**light** luz trasera *f*;
—**pipe** tubo de escape *m*; —**s** (of a coin) cruz
f; (of a tuxedo) frac *m*; —**spin** barrena *f*; **to**
—**gate** seguir demasiado de cerca [a otro

coche]
tailor [télɚ] N sastre *m*; — **shop** sastrería *f*; VT
hacer a medida; (adapt) adaptar
taint [tent] N (stain) mancha *f*; (contamination)
contaminación *f*; VI/VT (stain) manchar[se];
(contaminate) contaminar[se]
Taiwan [taɪwán] N Taiwán *m*
Taiwanese [taɪwɑníz] ADJ & N taiwanés -esa *mf*
Tajik [tɑdʒík] ADJ & N tayiko -ka *mf*
Tajikistan [tɑdʒíkɪstæn] N Tayikistán *m*
take [tek] VT (a load) llevar; (someone else's
property) robar, llevarse; (one number from
another) restar; (prisoner, medicine,
measures, a course) tomar; (one of a set)
elegir, coger; (a bribe) aceptar; (a prize)
recibir; (advice) seguir; (a walk) dar; (a
vacation) irse; (a trip) hacer; (a piece of news)
recibir; (a photo) sacar; **to** — **a bath** bañarse;
to — **after** parecerse a; **to** — **a look at** echar
un vistazo a; **to** — **a notion to** ocurrírsele a
uno; **to** — **apart** desarmar, desmontar; **to** —
aside apartar; **to** — **away** (carry away)
llevarse; (steal) sustraer; **to** — **back** devolver;
to — **back one's words** retractarse; **to** — **by
surprise** tomar desprevenido; **to** — **care of**
(a person) cuidar de; (a matter) atender a; **to**
— **charge of** encargarse de; **to** — **down in
writing** anotar, apuntar; **to** — **effect** entrar
en vigencia; **to** — **exercise** hacer ejercicio;
to — **in** (include) incluir; (observe) observar;
(deceive) embaucar; (provide shelter for)
albergar; (make smaller) tomar, achicar; **to** —
leave despedirse; **to** — **off** (remove)
quitar[se]; (conduct) llevar; (discount)
rebajar; (start flight) despegar; **to** — **offense**
ofenderse; **to** — **office** asumir un cargo; **to**
— **on** (accept) asumir; (hire) tomar,
contratar; (acquire) adquirir; **to** — **out**
(withdraw) sacar; (carry out [food], take on a
date) llevar; **to** — **over** hacerse cargo [de]; **to**
— **place** tener lugar; **to** — **revenge**
vengarse; **to** — **stock** hacer un balance; **to** —
stock in tener confianza en; **to** — **the floor**
tomar la palabra; **to** — **to heart** tomar a
pecho; **to** — **to one's heels** poner pies en
polvorosa; **to** — **to task** reprender, regañar;
to — **up a matter** tratar un asunto; **to** — **up
again** retomar; **to** — **up space** ocupar
espacio; **I** — **it that** supongo que; **it** —**s ten
minutes** lleva diez minutos; **the
vaccination didn't** — la vacuna no prendió;
N (profits) ingresos *m pl*; (of fish) pesca *f*,
captura *f*; (of a film production) toma *f*;
(opinion) opinión *f*; (approach) enfoque *m*;
—**off** (of an airplane) despegue *m*; (parody)
parodia *f*; —**over** (of a government) toma de
poder *f*; (of a company) adquisición *f*
taken [tékən] *see* take
talcum [tǽlkəm] N talco *m*; — **powder** polvo de

talco *m*

tale [teɪl] N (story) cuento *m*, relato *m*; (lie) mentira *f*

talent [tǽlənt] N talento *m*

talented [tǽləntɪd] ADJ talentoso

talk [tɔk] VI/VT hablar; (chat) charlar; VT (nonsense) decir; (a language) hablar; (politics) hablar de; **to — back** contestar con impertinencia; **to — down to** hablar con arrogancia a; **to — someone into something** convencer a alguien para que haga algo; **to — out of** disuadir de; **to — over** discutir; **to — up** alabar, hacer propaganda; N (formal speech) charla *f*; (gossip) habladurías *f pl*; (lingo) habla *f*; **— of the town** la comidilla del pueblo *f*; **— show** programa de entrevistas *m*

talkative [tɔ́kədɪv] ADJ hablador, parlanchín, charlatán

tall [tɔl] ADJ alto; **— order** misión imposible *f*; **— tale** cuento chino *m*, patraña *f*; **six feet —** de seis pies de altura; **how — are you?** ¿cuánto mides?

tallow [tǽlo] N sebo *m*

tally [tǽli] N (account) cuenta *f*; VT llevar la cuenta; **to — up** sumar; **to — with** concordar con

tambourine [tæmbərín] N pandereta *f*

tame [tem] ADJ (docile) manso, dócil; (domesticated) domesticado; (dull) aburrido; VT (make docile) amansar, domar; (domesticate) domesticar

tamper [tǽmpɚ] VI **to — with** (a jury) sobornar; (a lock) intentar forzar; (a document) alterar, amañar; ADJ **—-proof** a prueba de alteración

tampon [tǽmpɑn] N tampón *m*

tan [tæn] VI/VT (cure) curtir[se]; (darken skin) broncear[se], tostar[se]; VT (cure) adobar; (spank) zurrar; N color tostado *m*; (of skin) bronceado *m*; (car) color tostado *m*; (skin) bronceado, tostado

tandem [tǽndəm] N tándem *m*; **in — with** en colaboración con

tangent [tǽndʒənt] ADJ & N tangente *f*; **to go off on a —** salirse por la tangente

tangerine [tǽndʒərín] N mandarina *f*; Am tangerina *f*

tangible [tǽndʒəbəl] ADJ tangible

tangle [tǽŋɡəl] VI/VT enredar[se], enmarañar[se]; N enredo *m*, maraña *f*; (in hair) nudo *m*, enredijo *m*

tank [tæŋk] N tanque *m* (also military), depósito *m*; VT guardar en un tanque; VI **to — up** (with gasoline) llenar el tanque; (with alcohol) emborracharse

tannery [tǽnəri] N curtiduría *f*, tenería *f*; Am curtiembre *f*

tantalize [tǽntəlaɪz] VT atormentar con tentaciones

tantamount [tǽntəmaʊnt] ADJ **to be — to** equivaler a

tantrum [tǽntrəm] N berrinche *m*, perrera *f*, rabieta *f*

Tanzania [tænzəníə] N Tanzania *f*

Tanzanian [tænzéniən] ADJ & N tanzano -na *mf*

tap [tæp] N golpecito *m*; (repeated) golpeteo *m*; (with the hand) palmadita *f*; (faucet) llave *f*; Sp grifo *m*; **— dance** claqué *m*; **— water** agua de llave *f*; VI/VT (once) tocar; (repeatedly) golpetear; (with fingers) tamborilear; (utilize) explotar; (draw off liquid) extraer; **to — a tree** sangrar un árbol; **to — a telephone** intervenir un teléfono

tape [tep] N (adhesive, magnetic) cinta *f*; **— measure** cinta métrica *f*; **— recorder** grabadora *f*, grabador *m*; **— recording** grabación *f*; **—worm** lombriz *f*, solitaria *f*; VT (affix) atar con cinta; VI/VT (record) grabar; **to —-record** grabar

taper [tépɚ] N (diminished size) estrechamiento *m*; (candle) vela *f*, candela *f*; VI/VT afinar[se]; **to — off** (become smaller) afinar[se]; (diminish) ir disminuyendo

tapestry [tǽpɪstri] N (wall hanging) tapiz *m*; (art, industry) tapicería *f*

tapioca [tæpiókə] N tapioca *f*

tapir [tépɚ] N tapir *m*

tar [tɑr] N alquitrán *m*, brea *f*; VT alquitranar; **to — and feather** emplumar

tarantula [tərǽntʃələ] N tarántula *f*

tardy [tɑ́rdi] ADJ **to be —** llegar tarde

target [tɑ́rɡɪt] N blanco *m*; **— practice** tiro al blanco *m*

tariff [tǽrɪf] N tarifa *f*, arancel *m*

tarnish [tɑ́rnɪʃ] VI/VT (metal) deslustrar[se], empañar; (reputation) manchar[se]

tart [tɑrt] ADJ (fruit) agrio, ácido; (remark) mordaz; N (pie) tarta *f*

tartar [tɑ́rdɚ] N (in wine) tártaro *m*; (on teeth) sarro *m*; **— sauce** salsa tártara *f*

task [tæsk] N tarea *f*, labor *f*; **— bar** barra de tareas *f*; **— force** fuerza de tarea *f*; **—master** tirano -na *mf*; **to take to —** reprender, regañar

tassel [tǽsəl] N borla *f*

taste [test] VT (perceive) sentir el gusto/sabor de; (try) probar; (try wine) catar; VI **to — of onion** saber a cebolla; **it —s sour** tiene un sabor agrio; N (sense, aesthetic judgment) gusto *m*; (flavor) sabor *m*; (small amount of food) bocadito *m*; (small amount of drink) sorbo *m*; **— bud** papila gustativa *f*

tasteless [téstlɪs] ADJ (with no taste) soso, desabrido; (in bad taste) de mal gusto

tasty [tésti] ADJ sabroso

tatter [tǽdɚ] N andrajo *m*, harapo *m*, pingajo *m*

tattered [tǽdɚd] ADJ harapiento, andrajoso

tattle [tǽdl] VI acusar; **to — on** acusar a; N

—**tale** acusetas *mf sg*
tattoo [tætú] N tatuaje *m*; VI/VT tatuar[se]
taught [tɔt] *see* teach
taunt [tɔnt] VT provocar, burlarse de; N provocación *f*, pulla *f*
taut [tɔt] ADJ tenso, tirante
tavern [tævən] N taberna *f*, cantina *f*
tawdry [tɔ́dri] ADJ (affair) sórdido; (outfit) charro
tax [tæks] N impuesto *m*, contribución *f*, gravamen *m*; (burden) carga *f*; VT (a product) gravar; (a person) cobrar impuestos a; (patience, resources) poner a prueba; — **attorney/lawyer** abogado -da tributarista *mf*; — **code** código impositivo *m*; —**deductible** desgravable; — **deduction** deducción impositiva *f*; — **evasion** evasión de impuestos *f*; —**payer** contribuyente *mf*; — **return** declaración de impuestos *f*; — **shelter** abrigo impositivo *m*, refugio fiscal *m*; — **withholding** retención impositiva *f*; ADJ —**exempt** no gravable, exento de impuestos; —**free** libre de impuestos
taxable [tæksəbəl] ADJ imponible, tributable
taxation [tækséʃən] N (result of taxing) impuestos *m pl*; (act of taxing) imposición de contribuciones *f*
taxi [tæksi] N taxi *m*; VI ir en taxi; (an airplane) rodar por la pista; —**cab** taxi *m*
taxidermy [tæksɪdɚmi] N taxidermia *f*
taxonomy [tæksánəmi] N taxonomía *f*
tea [ti] N té *m*; — **bag** bolsita de té *f*; —**cup** taza de té *f*; —**kettle/pot** tetera *f*; — **party** té *m*; —**spoon** (spoon) cuchara *f*, cucharilla *f*; (measurement) cucharadita *f*; —**spoonful** cucharadita *f*; —**time** hora del té *f*
teach [titʃ] VI/VT enseñar; **to — a class** dar clase
teacher [títʃɚ] N (primary school) maestro -tra *mf*; (secondary school) profesor -ora *mf*; —**s college** [escuela] normal *f*
teaching [títʃɪŋ] N enseñanza *f*; —**s** enseñanzas *f pl*; — **activities** actividades pedagógicas *f pl*; — **profession** magisterio *m*
team [tim] N equipo *m*; (of yoked animals) yunta de bueyes *f*; (of horses) tiro *m*, enganche *m*; —**mate** compañero -ra de equipo *mf*; VI **to — up** unirse, formar un equipo
teamster [tímstɚ] N transportista *mf*, camionero -ra *mf*
tear[1] [tir] N lágrima *f*; —**drop** lágrima *f*; — **gas** gas lacrimógeno *m*; **to burst into —s** romper a llorar
tear[2] [tɛr] VI/VT (rip) rasgar[se]; (rip a hole) hacer[se] un siete; VT **to — along** ir a toda velocidad; **to — apart** (rip up) romper, destrozar; (separate) separar; **to — away** apartar[se]; **to — down** (a building) demoler, derribar; (a machine) desarmar, desmontar; (a person) denigrar; **to — one's hair**

arrancarse los cabellos; N desgarrón *m*, desgarradura *f*, rasgón *m*
tearful [tírfəł] ADJ (look) lloroso; (farewell) triste
tease [tiz] VT (make fun of a person) molestar, fastidiar; (tantalize sexually) provocar; (comb wool, hair) cardar; **to — out** sacar; N provocadora *f*
teat [tit] N teta *f*
techie [téki] N *fam* experto -ta en computación *mf*
technical [téknɪkəł] ADJ técnico; — **support** soporte técnico *m*
technician [tɛkníʃən] N técnico -ca *mf*, perito -ta *mf*
technique [tɛkník] N técnica *f*
technological [tɛknəládʒɪkəł] ADJ tecnológico
technology [tɛknáladʒi] N tecnología *f*, técnica *f*
tectonics [tɛktánɪks] N tectónica *f*
tedious [tídɪəs] ADJ tedioso, aburrido
tedium [tídɪəm] N hastío *m*
tee [ti] N (T-shirt) camiseta *f*; (golf ball support) tee *m*; (start of hole in golf) punto de salida *m*
teem [tim] VI **to — with** abundar en, estar lleno de
teen [tin] *see* teenager
teenager [tínedʒɚ] N adolescente *mf*
teens [tinz] N (teenage years) adolescencia *f*; (numbers 13–19) números de trece a diecinueve *m pl*
teethe [tið] VI **the baby is teething** al bebé le están saliendo los dientes
teetotaler [títódlɚ] N abstemio -mia *mf*
telecast [téləkæst] N teledifusión *f*
telecommunication [tɛlɪkəmjunikéʃən] N telecomunicación *f*; —**s** telecomunicaciones *f pl*
telecommuting [tɛlɪkəmjúDɪŋ] N teletrabajo *m*
teleconference [télɪkanfəəns] N teleconferencia *f*
telegram [téləgræm] N telegrama *m*
telegraph [téləgræf] N telégrafo *m*; VI/VT telegrafiar
telegraphic [tɛləgrǽfɪk] ADJ telegráfico
telemarketing [tɛləmárkɪDɪŋ] N telemercadeo *m*, telemarketing *m*
telepathy [təlépəθi] N telepatía *f*
telephone [téləfon] N teléfono *m*; — **book** guía telefónica *f*; — **booth** cabina telefónica *f*; — **number** número telefónico *m*; — **operator** telefonista *mf*; — **receiver** auricular *m*, tubo de teléfono *m*; VI/VT telefonear, llamar por teléfono
telescope [téləskop] N telescopio *m*; VI plegarse
televisable [tɛləváɪzəbəł] ADJ televisivo
televise [téləvaɪz] VT televisar
television [téləvɪʒən] N (medium) televisión *f*; (device) televisor *m*; — **program** programa televisivo *mf*; — **viewer** televidente *mf*
tell [tɛł] VI/VT (the truth) decir; (a story) contar;

to — apart distinguir; to — on someone acusar a alguien; to — someone off regañar a alguien; to — time decir la hora; I can't — if he's old or young no sé si es viejo o joven; his age is beginning to — se le comienza a notar la edad; ADJ a —tale sign una señal reveladora; he is a —tale es un acusica

teller [télə] N (narrator) narrador -ora mf; (in a bank) cajero -ra mf

temerity [təmérɪDi] N temeridad f

temp [tɛmp] N empleado -da temporal mf

temper [témpə] N (hardness) temple m; (bad humor) mal genio m; to keep one's — mantener la calma; to lose one's — perder los estribos, encolerizarse; VT templar

temperament [témpəəmənt] N temperamento m, genio m, talante m

temperance [témpəəns] N (moderation) templanza f, temperancia f; (abstinence from alcohol) abstinencia de bebidas alcohólicas f

temperate [témpəɪt] ADJ (weather) templado; (opinions, habits) moderado

temperature [témpəətʃur] N temperatura f; to have a — tener fiebre

tempest [témpɪst] N tempestad f

tempestuous [tɛmpéstʃuəs] ADJ tempestuoso

template [témplɪt] N plantilla f

temple [témpəl] N (church) templo m; (side of the forehead) sien f

temporal [témpəəl] ADJ temporal

temporary [témpəreri] ADJ temporal, eventual

tempt [tɛmpt] VT tentar

temptation [tɛmptéʃən] N tentación f

tempting [témptɪŋ] ADJ tentador

ten [tɛn] NUM diez; N —s of candidates decenas de candidatos f pl

tenacious [tənéʃəs] ADJ tenaz

tenacity [tənǽsɪDi] N tenacidad f

tenant [ténənt] N inquilino -na mf, arrendatario -ria mf

tend [tɛnd] VT (care for) cuidar; to — to (take care of) ocuparse de; (lean toward) tender, inclinarse

tendency [téndənsi] N tendencia f

tender [téndə] ADJ tierno; (painful) sensible; N (offer) oferta f; (legal currency) curso legal m; (person who tends) cuidador -ora mf, vigilante mf; VT presentar, ofrecer

tenderness [téndənɪs] N (of feeling) ternura f; (of meat) terneza f, ternura f; (sensitivity to pain) sensibilidad f

tendinitis [tɛndənáɪDɪs] N tendinitis f

tendon [téndən] N tendón m

tendril [téndrəl] N zarcillo m

tenement [ténəmənt] N casa de vecindad f

tenet [ténɪt] N principio m

tennis [ténɪs] N tenis m; — court cancha de tenis f, pista de tenis f; — elbow codo de tenista m; — player tenista mf; — shoes tenis m pl

tenor [ténə] N tenor m

tense [tɛns] ADJ tenso; N (grammatical) tiempo m

tension [ténʃən] N (stress) tensión f; (tautness) tirantez f

tent [tɛnt] N (camping) tienda de campaña f; (circus) carpa f; VI acampar

tentacle [téntəkəl] N tentáculo m

tentative [téntəDɪv] ADJ tentativo

tenth [tɛnθ] ADJ & N décimo m

tenuous [ténjuəs] ADJ (light, color, cloth) tenue; (peace) frágil

tenure [ténjə] N (of professorship) titularidad f; (of an office) ocupación f

tepid [tépɪd] ADJ tibio

terabyte [térəbaɪt] N terabyte m

term [tɝm] N (word, mathematical expression) término m; (period) período m; (time in office) mandato m; (semester) semestre m; (trimester) trimestre m; (set date for payment) plazo m; — life insurance seguro de vida a término m; — paper trabajo final m; —s condiciones f pl; at — a término; to be on good —s estar en buenas relaciones; not to be on speaking —s no hablarse; to come to —s aceptar; VT denominar

terminal [tɝmənl] ADJ terminal; N (of airport, computer) terminal mf; (electric) terminal m

terminate [tɝmənet] VI/VT terminar[se]

termination [tɝmənéʃən] N terminación f; (of an employee) despido m

terminology [tɝmənάlədʒi] N terminología f

termite [tɝmaɪt] N termita f

terrace [téris] N terraza f, escalón m; VT poner terrazas en, escalonar

terrain [tərén] N terreno m

terrestrial [təréstriəl] ADJ terrestre

terrible [térəbəl] ADJ terrible, tremendo

terrier [tériə] N terrier m

terrific [tərífɪk] ADJ estupendo

terrify [térəfaɪ] VT aterrar, aterrorizar, espeluznar

territory [térɪtɔri] N territorio m

terror [térə] N terror m

terrorism [térəɪzəm] N terrorismo m

terrorist [térəɪst] N terrorista mf

terrorize [térəaɪz] VT aterrorizar

terse [tɝs] ADJ lacónico

test [tɛst] N (trial, experiment) prueba f; (of intelligence, multiple choice) test m; (examination) examen m, prueba f; — market mercado de prueba m; — pilot piloto de pruebas m; — tube tubo de ensayo m, probeta f; —-tube baby bebé de probeta m; to undergo a — someterse a una prueba; to take a — dar un examen; to give a — poner un examen; to put to the — poner a prueba; VT (put to the test) probar, poner a prueba; (give an exam) poner una prueba, examinar; —ing pruebas f pl; to —-drive probar; VI **girls — better than boys** en los exámenes salen mejor las niñas que los niños

testament [téstəmənt] N testamento *m*; (testimony) testimonio *m*

testicle [téstɪkəl] N testículo *m*

testify [téstəfaɪ] VI (serve as witness) testificar; (confirm) dar fe

testimony [téstəmoni] N testimonio *m*

testosterone [testástərɒn] N testosterona *f*

tetanus [tétnəs] N tétano[s] *m*

tetracycline [tetrasáɪklɪn] N tetraciclina *f*

Teutonic [tutánɪk] ADJ teutónico

text [tɛkst] N texto *m*; **—book** libro de texto *m*; **— editor** editor de texto[s] *m*; **— message** mensaje de texto *m*; VT enviar mensajes de texto, *RP* textear

textile [tékstaɪl] ADJ textil; N textil *m*, tejido *m*; **— mill** fábrica de tejidos *f*

texture [tékst∫ə] N textura *f*

Thai [taɪ] ADJ & N (person) tailandés -esa *mf*; (language) tailandés *m*

Thailand [táɪlænd] N Tailandia *f*

than [ðæn] CONJ que; **I have more — you** tengo más que tú; **more — once** más de una vez

thank [θæŋk] VT dar las gracias, agradecer; **to have oneself to — for** tener la culpa de; INTERJ **— heaven!** ¡gracias a Dios! **— you** gracias; **—-you letter** carta de agradecimiento *f*; N **—s** gracias *f pl*

thankful [θǽŋkfəl] ADJ agradecido

thankfulness [θǽŋkfəlnɪs] N gratitud *f*, agradecimiento *m*

thankless [θǽŋklɪs] ADJ ingrato

thanksgiving [θæŋksgívɪŋ] N acción de gracias *f*; **— Day** día de acción de gracias *m*

that [ðæt] ADJ (something nearer the speaker) ese, esa; (something more remote from speaker) aquel, aquella; **— dog** ese/aquel perro *m*; **— one** (nearer) ese, esa; DEMON PRON (nearer to speaker) ese, esa; (more remote from speaker) aquel, aquella; (neuter) eso, aquello; **— is my daughter** esa/aquella es mi hija; **— was a nightmare** eso/aquello fue una pesadilla; REL PRON que; **the bike — disappeared** la bici que desapareció; **the pen — I was writing with** la lapicera con la que / la cual escribía; **— is** es decir; CONJ que; **she said — she would come** dijo que vendría; ADV tan; **it's not — far** no queda tan lejos; **— much** tanto; **she was — tall** era así de alta

thatch [θæt∫] N paja *f*; *Am* quincha *f*; VT techar con paja; *Am* quinchar; **—ed roof** techo de paja *m*; *Am* techo de quincha *m*

thaw [θɔ] VI/VT (food) descongelar[se]; (ice and snow) derretir[se]; (relations, refrigerator) deshelar[se]; N deshielo *m*

the [ðə, ðɪ] DEF ART (singular) el *m*, la *f*; **— boy** el chico *m*; (plural) los *m*, las *f*; **— girls** las

chicas *f pl*; **— good thing about that** lo bueno de eso; ADV **— more I work, — less I accomplish** cuanto más trabajo, menos consigo

theater, theatre [θíəⱱə-] N teatro *m*

theatrical [θiǽtrɪkəl] ADJ teatral

theft [θɛft] N hurto *m*, robo *m*

their [ðer] POSS ADJ **this is — dog** este es su perro, este es el perro de ellos

theirs [ðerz] PRON **this book is —** este libro es suyo, este libro es de ellos/ellas; **these things are —** estas cosas son suyas / de ellos / de ellas; **— is bigger** el suyo / la suya / el de ellos / la de ellos es más grande; **a friend of —** un amigo suyo, un amigo de ellos

them [ðem] PRON los *m pl*, las *f pl*; **I see —** los/las veo; **I talk to —** les hablo a ellos; **I went with —** fui con ellos/ellas

thematic [θɪmǽtɪk] ADJ temático

theme [θim] N (topic) tema *m*; (essay) ensayo *m*, redacción *f*; **— park** parque temático *m*; **— song** tema *m*

themselves [ðemsélvz] PRON **they — built their house** ellos mismos se construyeron la casa; **they are not — today** hoy no son los mismos de siempre; **they were sitting by —** estaban sentados solos; **they looked at — in the mirror** se miraron en el espejo; **they talk to —** hablan solos; **they bought — a yacht** se compraron un yate

then [ðen] ADV (at that time) entonces, en aquel tiempo; **it was cheaper —** era más barato en aquel tiempo; (after) luego, después; **from — on** a partir de entonces; **now and —** de vez en cuando; **until —** hasta entonces; **I ate, — I paid** comí, luego pagué; **now —** ahora bien; **are you sorry —?** ¿estás arrepentido pues? ADJ entonces; **the — president** el entonces presidente; CONJ entonces; **if not, — you should stay** si no, entonces deberías quedarte

theologian [θiəlóʤən] N teólogo -ga *mf*

theological [θiəláʤɪkəl] ADJ teológico

theology [θiáləʤi] N teología *f*

theoretical [θiərédɪkəl] ADJ teórico

theory [θíəri] N teoría *f*; **in —** en teoría

therapeutic [θerəpjúdɪk] ADJ terapéutico

therapist [θérəpɪst] N terapeuta *mf*; (psychologist) psicólogo -ga *mf*

therapy [θérəpi] N terapia *f*

there [ðer] ADV *Am* allí; *Am* allí; (more remote) allá; *Sp* allí; **—abouts** por ahí, más o menos; **—after** (later) después; (always subsequently) de allí en adelante; **—by** así, de ese modo; **— ensued a war** a continuación hubo una guerra; **—fore** por consiguiente, por lo tanto; **—in** en eso, allí; **— is/are** hay; **— goes the bus** ahí va el autobús; **— —**

bueno, bueno; —**of** de eso; —**on** (on that) encima; (later) luego, después; —**upon** (after) luego, después; (for this reason) por consiguiente; (upon that) encima; —**with** (with that) con eso; (after that) luego, en seguida; **who's** —? ¿quién es? **is Mary** —? ¿está María? **we got** — **at 5** llegamos a las 5

thermal [θɚ́məl] ADJ termal; — **energy** energía térmica f

thermal [θɚ́məl] ADJ térmico

thermodynamic [θɚmodaɪnǽmɪk] ADJ termodinámico

thermometer [θɚmámɪdɚ] N termómetro m

thermonuclear [θɚmonúkliɚ] ADJ termonuclear

thermos [θɚ́məs] N termo m

thermostat [θɚ́məstæt] N termostato m

thesaurus [θɪsɔ́rəs] N (synonym dictionary) diccionario de sinónimos m; (large dictionary) diccionario m

these [ðiz] ADJ & PRON estos, estas

thesis [θísɪs] N tesis f

they [ðe] PRON ellos, ellas

thick [θɪk] ADJ (slice) grueso; (fog, soup) espeso; (accent) marcado; (wit) torpe; **one inch** — una pulgada de espesor; — **as thieves** como carne y uña; ADJ —**headed** estúpido; —**set** grueso; —**skinned** insensible; N **the** — **of the fight** lo más reñido de la pelea; **through** — **and thin** pase lo que pase

thicken [θíkən] VI/VT espesar[se], trabar[se]; **the plot** —**s** la trama se complica

thicket [θíkɪt] N soto m, matorral m, boscaje m

thickness [θíknɪs] N (of paper, wood) espesor m, grosor m; (of soup) lo espeso; (of lips) lo grueso; (of a beard) lo tupido; (of hair) lo abundante

thief [θif] N ladrón -ona mf

thieve [θiv] VI/VT hurtar, robar

thigh [θaɪ] N muslo m

thimble [θímbəl] N dedal m

thin [θɪn] ADJ (ice, wire) delgado, fino; (person) flaco; (vegetation, beard, hair) ralo; (voice) tenue, fino; (air) enrarecido; (excuse) débil; (soup) aguado; VI/VT (paint, soup, sauce) diluir; (hair) entresacar; **to** — **out** (hair) ralear; (crowd) dispersarse

thing [θɪŋ] N cosa f; **there's no such** — eso no existe; **that is the** — **to do** eso es lo que hay que hacer; **the** — **about Mary** lo que pasa con María

thingamajig [θíŋəmədʒɪg] N chisme m, coso m

think [θɪŋk] VI/VT (reason) pensar, razonar; (believe) creer, opinar; **to** — **about** pensar en; **to** — **back** recordar; **to** — **it over/ through** pensarlo bien, reflexionar sobre; **I'm** —**ing of you** pienso en ti; **what do you** — **of Mary?** ¿qué piensas de María? **I thought of a plan** se me ocurrió un plan; **to**

— **up an excuse** inventar/elucubrar una excusa; **I don't** — **so** no creo; **who does he** — **he is?** ¿quién se cree que es? **to** — **well of** tener buena opinión de; **she** —**s nothing of spending $1000** no le importa nada gastar $1000

thinking [θíŋkɪŋ] N current — la opinión actual f; **to my way of** — a mi parecer; ADJ pensante

thinner [θínɚ] N disolvente m

thinness [θínnɪs] N (of ice, person) delgadez f, flacura f; (of hair) escasez f; (of air) enrarecimiento m; (of soup) fluidez f

third [θɚd] ADJ tercer[o]; — **base** tercera base f, antesala f; — **baseman** tercero m, antesalista m; — **chapter** capítulo tercero m, tercer capítulo m; — **person** tercera persona f; —**rate** de poca categoría; — **World** Tercer Mundo m; ADV tercero; N tercio m; (gear, musical interval) tercera f; **the** — **of March** el tres de marzo

thirst [θɚst] N sed f; VI tener sed; **to** — **for** tener sed de, estar sediento de

thirsty [θɚ́sti] ADJ sediento; **to be** — tener sed

thirteen [θɚtín] NUM trece

thirty [θɚ́Di] NUM treinta; ADJ & N —**something** treintañero -ra mf

this [ðɪs] ADJ & PRON este m, esta f, esto (neuter); — **dog** este perro; — **is a disaster** esto es un desastre

thistle [θísəl] N cardo m

thong [θɔŋ] N (strip of leather) correa f; (garment) tanga mf; (shoe) chancleta f

thorax [θɔ́ræks] N tórax m

thorn [θɔrn] N (sharp growth) espina f; (plant) espino m

thorny [θɔ́rni] ADJ espinoso, escabroso

thorough [θɚ́o] ADJ (exhaustive) exhaustivo, minucioso, detenido; (conscientious) concienzudo; —**bred** ADJ de pura sangre; N purasangre m

those [ðoz] ADJ & PRON (nearer) esos m, esas f; PRON (more remote) aquellos m, aquellas f; — **of you** los de vosotros/ustedes; — **that/who** los/las que

though [ðo] CONJ aunque; **as** — como si; ADV sin embargo

thought [θɔt] N (act, product of thinking) pensamiento m; (idea) idea f; (opinion) opinión f; (concern) consideración f; **to be lost in** — estar abstraído; **to give it no** — no darle importancia; **the very** — la mera idea; **at the** — **of** ante la idea de; **on second** — pensándolo bien; **my** —**s are with you** te acompaño en el sentimiento

thought [θɔt] see think

thoughtful [θɔ́tfəl] ADJ (considerate) considerado, atento; (well thought out) bien pensado; (reflective) pensativo, reflexivo

thoughtfulness [θɔ́tfəlnɪs] N consideración f
thoughtless [θɔ́tlɪs] ADJ (inconsiderate) desconsiderado; (careless) descuidado; (not reflective) irreflexivo
thoughtlessness [θɔ́tlɪsnɪs] N (lack of consideration) desconsideración f; (carelessness) descuido m; (lack of reflection) falta de reflexión f
thousand [θáʊzənd] NUM mil
thrash [θræʃ] VI/VT (whip, defeat) zurrar, vapulear, apalear; (thresh) trillar, desgranar; **to — around** revolverse, agitarse; **to — out a matter** ventilar un asunto
thread [θrɛd] N (in fabric) hilo m; (on a screw) rosca f; ADJ **—bare** raído; VT (a needle) enhebrar; (beads) ensartar; (a screw) enroscar; **to — one's way** abrirse paso
threat [θrɛt] N amenaza f
threaten [θrɛ́tn] VI/VT amenazar
threatening [θrɛ́tnɪŋ] ADJ amenazador, amenazante
three [θri] NUM tres; **— hundred** trescientos; ADJ **—-dimensional** tridimensional; **—-point basket** triple m; **—-point play** jugada de tres puntos f
thresh [θrɛʃ] VT trillar
threshold [θrɛ́ʃhold] N umbral m
threw [θru] see throw
thrift [θrɪft] N economía f
thrifty [θrɪ́fti] ADJ económico, ahorrativo
thrill [θrɪl] VI/VT emocionar[se], ilusionar[se]; N emoción f, ilusión f
thrive [θraɪv] VI (person, economy) prosperar, florecer; (plants) crecer mucho
throat [θrot] N garganta f
throb [θrɑb] VI latir, palpitar; N latido m, palpitación f
throes [θroz] ADV LOC **in the — of war** en plena guerra; **in the — of death** agonizando
throne [θron] N trono m
throng [θrɔŋ] N muchedumbre f, turbamulta f; VI apiñarse, llegar en tropel
throttle [θrádl] N (of a motor) válvula reguladora f, acelerador m; (of a motorcycle) puño giratorio del gas m; VT ahogar, estrangular
through [θru] PREP por, a través de; (as intermediary) por medio de; **Monday — Friday** de lunes a viernes; **all — the night** toda la noche; ADV (completely) de un lado a otro; (from beginning to end) de principio a fin, de cabo a rabo; **loyal — and —** leal a toda prueba; **he's an aristocrat — and —** es un aristócrata de pura cepa; **to carry —** llevar a cabo; ADJ (ticket, train) directo; **to be — (with a task) haber terminado; (in a profession) estar acabado; we're —! (with a boyfriend) ¡se acabó entre nosotros!
throughout [θruáʊt] PREP (all through) por

todo; (during) a lo largo de, durante; ADV (duration) de principio a fin; (space) por todas partes
throw [θro] VI/VT (a ball) tirar, lanzar; (a light, voice) arrojar; (a switch) conectar; (a pot on a wheel) modelar; (a punch) lanzar; (a wrestler) tumbar; (a game for a bribe) dejarse perder; (a rider) desmontar; (a party) dar, organizar; **that really threw me** eso me confundió; **to — away** (dispose of) tirar, arrojar; (squander) malgastar; **to — down** tirar al suelo; **to — in** añadir; **to — into gear** engranar; **to — in the clutch** embragar; **to — out** (garbage) tirar, arrojar; (unruly guest) echar; **to — up** vomitar, devolver; N (act or instance of throwing) tiro m; (of dice) tirada f; (shawl) chal m; (blanket) manta f; **—-in** (soccer) saque de banda m; ADJ **—away** desechable
thrown [θron] see throw
thrush [θrʌʃ] N tordo m, zorzal m
thrust [θrʌst] VT (stab) clavar; (shove) empujar; **to — oneself upon** meterse en; **to — a task upon someone** imponerle una tarea a alguien; **to — aside** echar a un lado; VI (push) dar un empujón; (stab at) lanzar una estocada; (push through) empujar para pasar; N (stab) estocada f; (force of a jet engine) empuje m; (shove) empujón m; (military assault) arremetida f, acometida f
thud [θʌd] N golpe sordo m; VI caer con un golpe sordo
thug [θʌg] N matón m
thumb [θʌm] N pulgar m; **—tack** chinche f, tachuela f; **under the — of** bajo la bota de; VT hojear; **to give a —s up** aprobar
thump [θʌmp] N golpe sordo m; VI hacer un ruido sordo
thunder [θʌ́ndər] N trueno m; **—bolt** rayo m; **—head** nubarrón m; **—storm** tormenta eléctrica f, tronada f; VI tronar
thunderous [θʌ́ndərəs] ADJ atronador, estruendoso
Thursday [θə́zde] N jueves m
thus [ðʌs] ADV así; **— far** (space) hasta aquí; (time) hasta ahora
thwart [θwɔrt] VT frustrar
thyme [taɪm] N tomillo m
thyroid [θáɪrɔɪd] N tiroides m sg
Tibet [tɪbét] N Tíbet m
Tibetan [tɪbétn] ADJ & N tibetano -na mf
tic [tɪk] N tic m, manía f
tick [tɪk] N (sound of a clock) tic tac m; (cover of a pillow) funda f; (checkmark) marca f; (insect) garrapata f; VI hacer tic tac; **to — off** (check off) marcar; (anger) enojar
ticket [tíkɪt] N billete m; Am boleto m; (slate of candidates) candidatura f; (summons) multa f; (tag) etiqueta f; **— office** taquilla f; VT (give passage) vender billetes; (give summons)

multar

tickle [tíkəɫ] VT (poke) cosquillear, hacer cosquillas; (amuse) dar ilusión; VI picar; N picazón f, cosquilleo m

ticklish [tíklɪʃ] ADJ (prone to tickling) cosquilloso; (delicate) delicado

tidal [táɪdl] ADJ — **wave** (tsunami) tsunami m, maremoto m; (large wave) marejada f

tidbit [tídbɪt] N (snack) golosina f; (gossip) chisme jugoso m

tide [taɪd] N marea f; (of opinion) corriente f; —**water** (water) agua de marea f; (land) marisma f; VT **to** — **over** cubrir

tidy [táɪdi] ADJ (orderly) ordenado; (large) considerable; VI/VT arreglar; **to** — **oneself up** arreglarse

tie [taɪ] VI (fasten) atarse; (make same score) empatar; VT (fasten) atar; (make a knot) hacer un nudo en; (make same score as) empatar con; **to** — **a record** empatar una marca; **to** — **down** atar; **to** — **in** cuadrar; **to** — **one on** emborracharse; **to** — **tight** atar fuerte; **to** — **up** (bind) atar; (hinder) bloquear; (occupy) ocupar; (moor a ship) amarrar; N (cord) cuerda f; (relations) lazo m, vínculo m; (cravat) corbata f; (railway) durmiente m, traviesa f; (score) empate m; —**-break** (in sports) desempate m; (in tennis) muerte súbita f

tier [tir] N nivel m

tiger [táɪgə] N tigre m

tight [taɪt] ADJ (knot, nut) apretado, ajustado; (clothes) ceñido, ajustado; (control) firme, estricto; (race) reñido; (stingy) tacaño, mezquino; (drunk) borracho; — **end** (football) receptor cerrado m; —**-fisted** agarrado; —**rope** cuerda floja f; —**wad** tacaño -ña mf; **to be in a** — **spot** estar en un aprieto; ADV bien, herméticamente; **to hold on** — agarrarse bien

tighten [táɪtn] VI/VT (knot, nut, belt) apretar[se]; (control) estrechar[se]

tightness [táɪtnɪs] N (narrowness) estrechez f; (stinginess) tacañería f

tilde [tíɫdə] N tilde f

tile [taɪl] N (on a roof) teja f; (on a floor) baldosa f; (on a wall) azulejo m; — **roof** tejado m; VT (roof) tejar; (floor) embaldosar; (wall) azulejar

till [tɪl] PREP hasta; CONJ hasta que; VI/VT (plow) labrar, arar; N (cash drawer) caja f

tilt [tɪɫt] VI/VT ladear[se], inclinar[se]; N (act or instance of tilting) ladeo m, inclinación f; (incline) declive m; (joust) justa f; **at full** — a toda velocidad

timber [tímbə] N (cut wood) madera [de construcción] f; (trees) árboles para madera m pl; (beam) viga f; —**line** límite de la vegetación arbórea m; — **wolf** lobo gris m

timbre [tímbə] N timbre m

time [taɪm] N (past, present, future) tiempo m; (on the clock) hora f; (occasion) vez f; (period) período m, momento m, época f; —**-and-a-half pay** paga de tiempo y medio f; —**bomb** bomba de tiempo f; — **frame** plazo aproximado de tiempo m; —**keeper** cronometrador -ora mf; — **limit** límite de tiempo m; —**out** descanso m; —**piece** reloj m; —**share** tiempo compartido m; —**signature** compás m; —**table** horario m; —**zone** huso horario m; **at** —**s** a veces; **at the same** — a la vez, al mismo tiempo; **at this** — en este momento; **behind** — atrasado; **lunch** — hora del almuerzo f; **from** — **to** — de vez en cuando; **for the** — **being** por el momento; **in** — a tiempo; **in no** — en seguida; **on** — ya era hora; **on** — puntual; **to buy on** — comprar a plazo; **after** — una vez tras otra; **to do** — cumplir una condena; **to have a good** — divertirse; **what** — **is it?** ¿qué hora es? VT (a race) cronometrar; (a test) fijar la duración de; (one's arrival) fijar la hora de; **to** — **an attack well** atacar en el momento oportuno

timeless [táɪmlɪs] ADJ eterno

timely [táɪmli] ADJ oportuno

timer [táɪmə] N (person) cronometrador -ora mf; (device) reloj m

timid [tímɪd] ADJ tímido, apocado

timidity [tɪmɪdɪdi] N timidez f, apocamiento m

timing [táɪmɪŋ] N (measurement) cronometraje m; (synchronization) sincronización f; **that was good** — lo hiciste en el momento oportuno

timorous [tíməəs] ADJ timorato

tin [tɪn] N (metal) estaño m; (tin plate) hojalata f; — **can** lata f; —**foil** papel de estaño m, papel de aluminio m; VT estañar

tincture [tíŋktʃə] N tintura f

tinder [tíndə] N yesca f

tinge [tɪndʒ] VT (tint) teñir; (affect slightly) matizar; N (of color) tinte m, matiz m; (of taste) dejo m; (of irony) matiz m

tingle [tíŋgəɫ] VI sentir hormigueo, hormiguear; **to** — **with excitement** estremecerse de entusiasmo; N hormigueo m

tinker [tíŋkə] VI ocuparse, entretenerse; **to** — **with** hacer ajustes

tinkle [tíŋkəɫ] VT (ring lightly) tintinear; (urinate) fam hacer pipí; N tintineo m

tinnitus [tɪnáɪɾəs] N tinitus m

tinsel [tínsəɫ] N (Christmas trim) espumillón m, guirnalda f; (tawdry decoration) oropel m

tint [tɪnt] N (hue) matiz m; (for hair) tinte m, tintura f; (for glass) coloreado m; VT (hair) teñir; (glasses) colorear

tiny [táɪni] ADJ diminuto, chiquito

tip [tɪp] N (point) punta f; (gratuity) propina f;

(piece of advice) consejo *m*; VI/VT (tilt) inclinar[se], ladear[se]; (give a gratuity) dar propina [a]; **to — a person off** advertir a alguien; **to — one's hat** sacarse/quitarse el sombrero; **to — over** volcar[se]

tipsy [típsi] ADJ alegre

tiptoe [típto] N punta del pie *f*; **on —s** de puntillas; VI andar de puntillas

tirade [táɪred] N diatriba *f*

tire [taɪr] N neumático *m*; *Mex* llanta *f*; *Am* goma *f*; VI/VT cansar[se], fatigar[se]; **to — out** cansar, fatigar

tired [taɪrd] ADJ cansado, fatigado; **— out** agotado; **I'm — of your complaining** estoy harto de tus quejas

tireless [táɪrlɪs] ADJ incansable

tiresome [táɪrsəm] ADJ aburrido, pesado, plasta

tissue [tíʃu] N (cell aggregate) tejido *m*; (handkerchief) pañuelo de papel *m*; **— paper** papel tisú *m*

tit [tɪt] N paro *m*

titanic [taɪténɪk] ADJ titánico

titanium [taɪténiəm] N titanio *m*

tithe [taɪð] N diezmo *m*; VI pagar el diezmo

titillate [tídlet] VT (sexually) excitar; (interest) despertar interés

title [táɪdl] N título *m*; (of a painting) rótulo *m*; **— deed** título de propiedad *m*; **— page** portada *f*

TNT [tíéntí] N TNT *m*

to [tu] PREP **I gave it — you** te lo di a ti; **to count — ten** contar hasta diez; **I called — find out** llamé para averiguar; **— my surprise** para mi sorpresa; **a quarter — five** las cinco menos cuarto; **bills — be paid** cuentas por pagar; **things — do** cosas que hacer; **frightened — death** muerto de susto; **from house — house** de casa en casa; ADV **— and fro** de acá para allá; **to come — volver en sí**

toad [tod] N sapo *m*; **—stool** seta *f*, hongo no comestible *m*

toast [tost] VI/VT (brown) tostar[se]; VT (congratulate) brindar por; N (bread) tostada *f*; (congratulation) brindis *m*

toaster [tóstɚ] N tostadora *f*; **— oven** horno tostador *m*

tobacco [təbǽko] N tabaco *m*

today [tədé] ADV hoy; (nowadays) hoy día

toddler [tádlɚ] N niño pequeño *m*, niña pequeña *f*

toe [to] N dedo del pie *m*; (of shoe, sock) punta *f*; **—nail** uña del dedo del pie *f*; VT (touch with toe) tocar con el dedo del pie; **to — the line** hacer buena letra, entrar en vereda

together [təgéðɚ] ADV (in union) juntos; (at the same time) al mismo tiempo; **— with** junto con; **all —** todos juntos

Togo [tógo] N Togo *m*

Togolese [togəlíz] ADJ & N togolés -esa *mf*

toil [tɔɪl] VI trabajar, esforzarse, bregar; N trabajo *m*, esfuerzo *m*

toilet [tɔ́ɪlɪt] N (bowl) inodoro *m*; (lavatory) aseo *m*, lavabo *m*; **— paper** papel higiénico *m*; **—trained** que ya no usa pañales

token [tókən] N (symbol) señal *f*; (keepsake) recuerdo *m*; (coinlike metal piece) ficha *f*; **— payment** pago nominal *m*; **as a — of friendship** en prenda de amistad

told [told] *see* tell

tolerance [tálɚəns] N tolerancia *f*

tolerant [tálɚənt] ADJ tolerante

tolerate [tálɚret] VT tolerar

toll [tol] N (of bells) tañido *m*; (payment) peaje *m*; (charges) tarifa *f*; (of victims) balance *m*; **— bridge** puente de peaje *m*; **— road** carretera de peaje *f*; ADJ **—free** libre de cargos; VI/VT tañer [a muerto]

tomato [təmédo] N tomate *m*

tomb [tum] N tumba *f*, sepulcro *m*, sepultura *f*; **—stone** lápida *f*

tomcat [támkæt] N gato macho *m*

tomorrow [təmóro] ADV & N mañana *f*; **— morning** mañana por la mañana *f*

ton [tʌn] N tonelada *f*

tone [ton] N (pitch) tono *m*; (of a voice, instrument) sonoridad *f*; (of a speech) tono *m*, tónica *f*; VI **to — down** moderar, matizar

toner [tónɚ] N tóner *m*; **— cartridge** cartucho de tóner *m*

Tonga [táŋgə] N Tonga *m*

Tongan [táŋgən] ADJ & N tongano -na *mf*

tongs [tɔŋz] N tenazas *f pl*

tongue [tʌŋ] N (body part, language, of a flame) lengua *f*; (of a shoe) lengüeta *f*; **— depressor** depresor de lengua *m*; **— in cheek** irónicamente; **— twister** trabalenguas *m sg*; **on the tip of my —** en la punta de la lengua; **to hold one's —** callarse la boca; VI tocar con la lengua; **to —-lash** reprender; **to be —-tied** tener trabada la lengua

tonic [tánɪk] ADJ tónico; N (medicine) tónico *m*; (water, key note) tónica *f*; **— water** agua tónica *f*

tonight [tənáɪt] ADV esta noche

tonsil [tánsəl] N amígdala *f*

tonsillitis [tɑnsəláɪdɪs] N amigdalitis *f*, anginas *f pl*

too [tu] ADV (in addition) también; (excessively) demasiado; **— bad!** ¡qué lástima! **— many** demasiados; **— much** demasiado

took [tuk] *see* take

tool [tul] N herramienta *f*; **—bar** barra de herramientas *f*; **—box/kit** caja de herramientas *f*; **—shed** cobertizo para herramientas *m*

toot [tut] VI/VT (horn) sonar; (whistle) pitar; (trumpet) tocar; **to — one's own horn** darse autobombo; N (of horn, trumpet) toque m; (of horn) bocinazo m; (of whistle) pitido m

tooth [tuθ] N (front) diente m; (back) muela f; **—ache** dolor de muelas m; **—brush** cepillo de dientes m; **— decay** caries [dental] f sg; **— fairy** ratoncito Pérez m; **— mark** dentellada f; **—paste** pasta dental f, pasta dentífrica f; **—pick** mondadientes m sg, palillo de dientes m; **to fight — and nail** luchar a brazo partido; **to have a sweet —** ser goloso

toothed [tuθt] ADJ dentado

toothless [túθlɪs] ADJ desdentado

top [tɑp] N (of a mountain) cumbre f, cima f; (of a page) parte superior f; (of a jar) tapa f; (of a convertible) capota f; (of a table) superficie f; (of a tree) copa f; (toy) trompo m, peonza f; (blouse) blusa f; **—coat** abrigo m; **— dollar** precio exorbitante m; **— hat** sombrero de copa m; **—spin** liftado m; **at — speed** a velocidad máxima; **to be — dog** ir a la cabeza; **to be at the — of the class** ser el mejor de la clase; **at the — of one's voice** a voz en cuello; **filled up to the —** lleno hasta el tope; **from — to bottom** de arriba abajo; **on — of** encima de; ADJ (officer, floor) superior; (shelf, step) más alto; **—-flight** de primera; **—heavy** desbalanceado; **—most** superior; **—-rated** de la más alta categoría; **—-secret** altamente confidencial; **—-notch** de primera; VT (a tree) desmochar; (a list) encabezar; (a performance) superar; (a level) exceder; **to — off** (an action) rematar; (a tank) llenar hasta el tope; **that —s everything!** ¡eso es el colmo!

topaz [tópæz] N topacio m

topic [tápɪk] N tema m, materia f, Am tópico m

topical [tápɪkəl] ADJ (of medicine) tópico; (current) de actualidad

topless [táplɪs] ADJ topless; **— swimsuit** monokini m

topple [tápəl] VT (knock over) derribar; (overthrow) derrocar; VI (fall) volcarse; (lose power) caer; **to — over** volcarse

topsy-turvy [tápsitˈɜ́vi] ADJ & ADV patas arriba

torch [tɔrtʃ] N antorcha f

tore [tɔr] see tear

torment¹ [tɔ́rment] N tormento m

torment² [tɔrmént] VT atormentar, martirizar

torn [tɔrn] see tear²

tornado [tɔrnédo] N tornado m

torpedo [tɔrpíɾo] N torpedo m; **— boat** torpedero m; VT torpedear

torpid [tɔ́rpɪd] ADJ torpe

torpor [tɔ́rpɚ] N letargo m, torpor m

torque [tɔrk] N par de torsión m

torrent [tɔ́rənt] N torrente m

torrential [tɔrénʃəl] ADJ torrencial

torrid [tɔ́rɪd] ADJ tórrido

torsion [tɔ́rʃən] N torsión f

torso [tɔ́rso] N torso m, tronco m

tortoise [tɔ́rDɪs] N tortuga f

tortuous [tɔ́rtʃuəs] ADJ tortuoso

torture [tɔ́rtʃɚ] N tortura f; VT torturar

torturous [tɔ́rtʃɚəs] ADJ torturante, torturador

toss [tɔs] VT (a ball, coin) tirar; (one's head) echar; (a salad) revolver; **to — aside** echar a un lado; VI (waves) cabecear; (a person in bed) dar vueltas; N (of coin, ball) tiro m; (of head) sacudida f

total [tódl] ADJ & N total m; **— amount** importe total m, montante m; **— loss** pérdidas totales f pl

totalitarian [totælɪtériən] ADJ totalitario

totter [tádɚ] VI tambalear[se], titubear

touch [tʌtʃ] VI/VT (have physical contact with) tocar; (move deeply) conmover, enternecer; (compare with) compararse con, igualar; (affect) afectar; **to — down** aterrizar; **to — off** provocar; **to — up** retocar; **to — upon** mencionar; N (contact) contacto m, roce m, toque m; (sense) tacto m; (knack) mano f; (slight amount) poquito m; ; **—down** anotación f; **—down pass** envío de anotación m, pase de anotación m; **— screen** pantalla táctil f; **—-sensitive display** pantalla táctil f; **—stone** piedra de toque f; **a woman's —** un toque femenino; **finishing —** toque final m; **to keep in —** mantenerse en contacto; ADJ **—-and-go** precario; **—-tone** de botones

touching [tʌ́tʃɪŋ] ADJ conmovedor

touchy [tʌ́tʃi] ADJ hipersensible

tough [tʌf] ADJ (leather) fuerte, resistente; (fighter) duro, fuerte; (steak) duro, correoso; (situation) difícil; (neighborhood) bravo

toughen [tʌ́fən] VI/VT (leather) curtir[se]; (meat) endurecer[se]; (person) endurecerse

toughness [tʌ́fnɪs] N (of leather) resistencia f; (of a fighter, steak) dureza f; (of a situation) dificultad f; (of a neighborhood) lo bravo

toupee [tupé] N peluquín m

tour [tur] N (professional, artistic) gira f; (touristic) tour m, excursión f; (of a building) visita f; VI/VT (artistic, political) hacer una gira [por]; (touristic) hacer un tour

tourism [túrɪzəm] N turismo m

tourist [túrɪst] N turista mf; **— attraction** atracción turística f; **— class** clase turista/turística f

tournament [tɝ́nəmənt] N torneo m

tourniquet [tɝ́nɪkɪt] N torniquete m

tow [to] VT remolcar; N (pull) remolque m; (fiber) estopa f; **—rope** cuerda de remolque f; **— truck** remolque m, grúa f, Am guinche m; **in — a cuestas**

toward, towards [təwɔ́rd(z)] PREP (in the direction of) hacia; (for) para; **— four o'clock** a eso de las cuatro; **to feel angry —**

estar enojado con

towel [táʊəl] N toalla f

tower [táʊə‑] N torre f; — **model** Am computadora torre f, Sp ordenador torre m; VI **to — over** elevarse sobre, dominar

towering [táʊə‑ɪŋ] ADJ (tall) elevado, muy alto; (excessive) desmedido

town [taʊn] N (large) ciudad f; (small) pueblo m, localidad f; (downtown) centro m; — **hall** ayuntamiento m; **out of —** de viaje

toxic [táksɪk] ADJ tóxico; — **shock syndrome** síndrome de choque tóxico m

toxin [táksɪn] N toxina f

toy [tɔɪ] N juguete m; — **poodle** caniche enano m; VI **to — with** (fiddle with) juguetear con; (consider) considerar

trace [tres] N (path, mark, footprint) huella f; (mark) rastro m, traza f; (vestige) vestigio m; VT (a plan) trazar; (history) examinar; (an image) calcar; (a criminal) rastrear

trachea [trékiə] N tráquea f

tracheotomy [trekiátəmi] N traqueotomía f

track [træk] N (of a heel, animal) huella f; (of a wheel) rodada f; (for racing) pista f; (path) senda f, sendero m; (of a railroad) vía f; (on a record) surco m; (on a CD) tema m, pista f; (of study) orientación f; — **and field** atletismo m; — **meet** encuentro de atletismo m; — **record** trayectoria f; **to be off the —** estar descarrilado; **to keep — of** seguir el hilo de; VI/VT (a criminal) rastrear, seguir la pista de; (an aircraft, a student, progress) seguir; VI (wheels) estar alineado; (stylus) seguir los surcos; **to — down** perseguir; **to — in mud** traer lodo en los pies

tract [trækt] N (of land) terreno m; (political) octavilla f; (digestive) tubo m

traction [trǽkʃən] N tracción f

tractor [trǽktə‑] N tractor m; —-**trailer** tractocamión m

trade [tred] N (buying and selling) comercio m, trato m; (industry) industria f; (swap) canje m, cambio m; (manual labor) oficio m; (profession) profesión f; (people in a business) gremio m; —-**in** entrega como parte de pago f; —-**off** compensación f; —-**mark** marca registrada f, marca de fábrica f; — **agreement** acuerdo comercial m; — **balance** balanza comercial f; — **barrier** barrera comercial f; — **name** (of product) nombre comercial m; (of company) razón social f; — **school** escuela industrial f; — **union** sindicato m; VI/VT (buy and sell) comerciar, negociar; (exchange) canjear; (traffic) traficar; **to — in** entregar

trader [trédə‑] N (dealer) comerciante mf; (at fairs) feriante mf; (of slaves) tratante mf

trading [trédɪŋ] N transacciones f pl, comercio m; — **partners** socios comerciales m pl

tradition [trədíʃən] N tradición f

traditional [trədíʃənəl] ADJ tradicional

traffic [trǽfɪk] N (of drugs) tráfico m; (of vehicles) tránsito m, tráfico m; — **accident** accidente de tránsito m; — **jam** atasco circulatorio m; — **light** semáforo m; VI traficar

tragedy [trǽdʒɪdi] N tragedia f

tragic [trǽdʒɪk] ADJ trágico

trail [trel] VI/VT (drag) arrastrar[se]; (follow in a race) ir detrás [de]; (track) seguir la pista [de], rastrear; VT (leave a trace) dejar una estela / un reguero de; VI **to — off** desvanecerse, apagarse; N (trace) rastro m, huella f; (path) trocha f, sendero m, senda f; (of smoke) estela f; (of blood) reguero m; — **bike** motocicleta de trail f

trailer [trélə‑] N (of a truck) remolque m; (of a film) sinopsis f, trailer m, avance m; (house) caravana f

train [tren] N (railroad) tren m; (part of a dress) cola f; — **of thought** hilo de pensamiento m; VI/VT (worker) capacitar[se]; (troops, athlete) adiestrar[se]; Am entrenar[se]; VT (an animal) amaestrar; (a child) educar, formar; (a cannon) apuntar; **to — on** (a camera, eye) enfocar

trainee [trení] N aprendiz -iza mf, practicante mf

trainer [trénə‑] N (of animals) amaestrador -ora mf; (of workers, troops, athletes) entrenador -ora mf

training [trénɪŋ] N (of animals) amaestramiento m; (of workers) capacitación f; (of troops, athletes) entrenamiento m, adiestramiento m; (of children) educación f

trait [tret] N rasgo m, seña f

traitor [trédə‑] N traidor -ora mf

trajectory [trədʒéktəri] N trayectoria f

tramp [træmp] VT (trample) pisar; VI andar con pasos pesados; (roam, as a hobo) vagabundear; N (hobo) vagabundo -da mf

trample [trǽmpəl] VT pisotear; **to — on/over** pisotear, atropellar; **to — out** apagar de un pisotón

trampoline [trǽmpəlín] N trampolín m, cama elástica f

trance [træns] N trance m

tranquil [trǽŋkwɪl] ADJ tranquilo

tranquilizer [trǽŋkwɪlaɪzə‑] N tranquilizante m

tranquillity [træŋkwɪ́lɪdi] N tranquilidad f

transact [trænzǽkt] VT llevar a cabo

transaction [trænzǽkʃən] N transacción f, negocio m; —**s** actas f pl

transatlantic [trænzɪtlǽntɪk] ADJ transatlántico

transcend [trænsénd] VI/VT trascender

transcendence [trænséndəns] N trascendencia f

transcendental [trænsendéntl] ADJ transcendental, trascendente

transcribe [trænskráɪb] VT transcribir
transcript [trænskrɪpt] N transcripción *f*
transfer [trænsfəʳ] VI/VT (on a bus, train)
trasbordar; (a prisoner, worker) trasladar[se];
VT (loyalty, rights, money, data) transferir;
(property) traspasar; N (on a bus, train)
trasbordo *m*; (of loyalty, rights, money, data)
transferencia *f*; (of a prisoner, worker)
traslado *m*; (of property) traspaso *m*; — **of**
ownership traspaso de propiedad *m*; —
rate velocidad de transferencia *f*
transferable [trænsfɚəbəl] ADJ transferible
transfix [trænsfíks] VT (impale) traspasar,
atravesar; (paralyze) paralizar
transform [trænsfɔ́rm] VI/VT transformar[se]
transformation [trænsfəméʃən] N
transformación *f*
transformer [trænsfɔ́rmə] N transformador *m*
transfusion [trænsfjúʒən] N transfusión *f*; **to**
give a — dar una transfusión de sangre,
poner sangre
transgress [trænzgrés] VT transgredir; **to —**
against pecar contra; **to — the bounds of**
traspasar los límites de
transgression [trænzgréʃən] N transgresión *f*,
pecado *m*
transient [trénziənt] ADJ transeúnte, pasajero;
N transeúnte *mf*, vagabundo -da *mf*
transistor [trænzístə] N transistor *m*
transit [trénzɪt] N tránsito *m*; **in —** en tránsito,
de paso
transition [trænzíʃən] N transición *f*
transitive [trénzɪDɪv] ADJ transitivo
transitory [trénzɪtɔri] ADJ transitorio, pasajero
translate [trénzlet] VI/VT traducir
translation [trænzléʃən] N (rendering in
different language) traducción *f*; (movement)
translación *f*
translator [trénzleDə] N traductor -ora *mf*
transmission [trænzmíʃən] N transmisión *f*
transmit [trænzmít] VI/VT transmitir
transmitter [trænzmíDə] N transmisor *m*
transnational [trænznǽʃənəl] ADJ
transnacional
transom [trénsəm] N travesaño *m*, montante *m*
transparency [trænzpérənsi] N transparencia *f*
transparent [trænspérənt] ADJ transparente; **to**
be — traslucirse
transpire [trænspáɪr] VI (happen) ocurrir;
(become known) descubrirse; VI/VT (perspire)
transpirar
transplant¹ [trénsplænt] VI/VT trasplantar
transplant² [trénsplænt] N trasplante *m*
transport¹ [trénspɔrt] VT transportar, acarrear
transport² [trénspɔrt] N (moving) transporte
m, acarreo *m*; (airplane) avión de transporte
m; (rapture) éxtasis *m*; (of freight) flete *m*
transportation [trænspɚtéʃən] N transporte *m*
transpose [trænspóz] VI/VT (letters) transponer;

(a song) transportar
transverse [trænsvɚ́s] ADJ transversal; (flute)
transverso
trap [træp] N trampa *f*; (for hunting) trampa *f*,
cepo *m*; (under a sink) sifón *m*; —**door**
trampilla *f*; VI/VT (to capture animals) cazar
con trampa, atrapar; VT (to pin) aprisionar
trapeze [trəpíz] N trapecio *m*
trapezoid [trépɪzɔɪd] N & ADJ trapezoide *m*
trash [træʃ] N basura *f*, desechos *m pl*; (people)
pej gentuza *f*; — **can** cubo de basura *m*
trashy [tréʃi] ADJ ordinario
trauma [trɔ́mə] N (physical) traumatismo *m*;
(psychological) trauma *m*
traumatic [trəmǽDɪk] ADJ traumático
travel [trévəl] VI/VT viajar [por]; VI (sound
waves) propagarse; (in basketball) caminar,
hacer pasos; N viaje *m*; — **agency** agencia de
viajes *f*; — **expenses** gastos de viaje *m pl*,
gastos de desplazamiento *m pl*; —**s** viajes *m pl*
traveler [trévələ] N viajero -ra *mf*; —**'s check**
cheque de viajero *m*
traverse [trəvɚ́s] VI/VT atravesar, cruzar;
(skiing) bajar en diagonal; N (crossbar)
travesaño *m*; (crossing) travesía *f*
travesty [trévɪsti] N farsa *f*
tray [tre] N bandeja *f*
treacherous [trétʃəəs] ADJ traicionero, alevoso
treachery [trétʃəri] N traición *f*, alevosía *f*
tread [trɛd] VI/VT (trample) pisar, pisotear; VI
(walk) andar, caminar; N (step) paso *m*; (on
tire) banda de rodadura/rodaje *f*; (on shoe)
dibujo *m*; —**mill** cinta rodante *f*
treason [trízən] N traición *f*
treasure [tréʒə] N tesoro *m*; — **hunt** búsqueda
del tesoro *f*; VT atesorar
treasurer [tréʒərə] N tesorero -ra *mf*
treasury [tréʒəri] N tesorería *f*, tesoro *m*;
secretary of the — ministro -tra de
hacienda *mf*
treat [trit] VI/VT (act toward, discuss in writing,
give medical aid) tratar; **I —ed myself to ice**
cream me di un festín de helado; N
(pleasure) placer *m*; (gift) regalo *m*; **my —** yo
invito
treatable [tríDəbəl] ADJ tratable
treatise [tríDɪs] N tratado *m*
treatment [trítmənt] N trato *m*, tratamiento *m*;
(artistic handling) interpretación *f*
treaty [tríDi] N tratado *m*
treble [trébəl] ADJ (triple) triple; (of higher clef)
de tiple; — **clef** clave de sol *f*; N tiple *m*; VI/VT
triplicar
tree [tri] N árbol *m*; — **hugger** ecologista *mf*;
—**top** copa de árbol *f*; **up a —** en aprietos
treeless [tríləs] ADJ pelado, sin árboles
trek [trɛk] N expedición *f*; VI viajar con dificultad
tremble [trémbəl] VI temblar; N temblor *m*
tremendous [trɪméndəs] ADJ tremendo

tremor [trémə-] N temblor *m*, sacudida *f*

tremulous [trémjələs] ADJ trémulo

trench [trentʃ] N (military) trinchera *f*; (for pipes) zanja *f*; (on sea floor) fosa *f*; — **coat** trinchera *f*, gabardina *f*

trend [trend] N tendencia *f*

trendy [tréndi] ADJ de moda

trespass [tréspæs] N (illegal entry) entrada ilegal *f*; (religious) deuda *f*; VI (enter illegally) entrar ilegalmente; **to — against** (violate) violar; (sin) pecar; **no —ing** prohibido el paso

triage [triáʒ] N triaje *m*, clasificación *f*

trial [tráɪəl] N (testing) ensayo *m*, prueba *f*; (attempt) tentativa *f*; (affliction) aflicción *f*; (in a court of law) juicio *m*, proceso *m*; — **balloon** globo sonda *m*; — **by fire** prueba de fuego *f*; — **flight** vuelo de prueba *m*; — **offer** oferta de prueba *f*; — **period** período de prueba *m*; — **run** ensayo *m*, prueba *f*; **by — and error** por ensayo y error

triangle [tráɪæŋgəl] N triángulo *m*

triangular [traɪǽŋgjələ-] ADJ triangular

tribe [traɪb] N tribu *f*

tribulation [trɪbjəléʃən] N tribulación *f*

tribunal [traɪbjúnəl] N tribunal *m*

tributary [trɪbjɔ́teri] ADJ & N tributario *m*, afluente *m*

tribute [trɪbjut] N (tax) tributo *m*; (testimonial) homenaje *m*

triceps [tráɪseps] N tríceps *m sg*

trick [trɪk] N (ruse) treta *f*, trampa *f*, trapisonda *f*; (magician's) truco *m*; (prank) broma *f*; (in cards) baza *f*; **to be up to one's old —s** hacer de las suyas; **to play a — on someone** gastarle una broma a alguien; VT hacer trampa, engañar; **to — someone into something** hacer que alguien haga algo por medio de artilugios

trickery [tríkəri] N engaños *m pl*, argucias *f pl*

trickle [tríkəl] VI gotear; **to — in [out]** llegar [irse] de a poco; N goteo *m*

trickster [tríkstə-] N embustero -ra *mf*

tricky [tríki] ADJ (artful) mañoso; (difficult) complicado

tricycle [tráɪsɪkəl] N triciclo *m*

trifle [tráɪfəl] N (worthless thing) fruslería *f*, nadería *f*, bobada *f*; (cheap purchase) bagatela *f*; (small sum) miseria *f*; VI **to — with** jugar con; **to — away** perder

trigger [trígə-] N gatillo *m*; VT desencadenar

trill [trɪl] VI/VT (bird) trinar; (musical instrument) tremolar; (the **r**sound) pronunciar con vibración; N (of birds, etc.) trino *m*; (of the **r**sound) vibración *f*

trillion [tríljən] N billón *m*

trilogy [trílədʒi] N trilogía *f*

trim [trɪm] VT (adorn) adornar, guarnecer; (an edge) bordear; (fingernails, hair, threads) recortar; (hedge) podar; (airplane) equilibrar; (a wick) despabilar; ADJ (neat) cuidado; (slim) delgado; (fit) en buen estado físico; N (embellishment) adorno *m*; (of sails) orientación *f*; (cutting of hair) recorte *m*; (cutting of hedge) poda *f*; (of an airplane) equilibrio *m*

trimming [trímɪŋ] N (act of cutting) recorte *m*; (on a uniform) orla *f*, ribete *m*; **—s** (embellishments) adornos *m pl*; (food) guarniciones *f pl*; (parts cut off) recortes *m pl*

Trinidad and Tobago [trínɪdædəntəbégo] N Trinidad y Tobago

Trinidadian [trínɪdǽdiən] ADJ & N trinitense *mf*

trinket [tríŋkɪt] N chuchería *f*, baratija *f*

trio [trío] N trío *m*

trip [trɪp] N (journey, drug-induced condition) viaje *m*; (experience) experiencia *f*; (accidental stumble) tropezón *m*; (making fall) zancadilla *f*; — **planner** planificador de rutas *m*; VT (cause to stumble) hacer una zancadilla a; (trip up) confundir; (release a catch) soltar; (blow a fuse) hacer saltar; VI (stumble) tropezar; (skip) andar con paso ligero; (make a mistake) equivocarse; (hallucinate) viajar; (blow a fuse) saltar

triphthong [trípθɔŋ] N triptongo *m*

triple [trípəl] ADJ & N (also in baseball) triple *m*; VI (in baseball) pegar un triple; VT (multiply by three) triplicar

triplet [tríplɪt] N trillizo *m*

tripod [tráɪpad] N trípode *m*

trite [traɪt] ADJ trivial, trillado

triumph [tráɪəmf] N triunfo *m*; VI triunfar

triumphant [traɪ́mfənt] ADJ triunfante, triunfador

trivial [trívɪəl] ADJ trivial, baladí, fútil

trod [trad] *see* tread

trodden [tradn] *see* tread

trolley [tráli] N (electric bus) trole *m*, trolebús *m*; (on tracks) tranvía *m*

trombone [trambón] N trombón *m*

troop [trup] N (of scouts) tropa *f*; (of soldiers) escuadrón *m*; (of tourists) horda *f*; **—s** tropas *f pl*

trophy [trófi] N trofeo *m*

tropic [trápɪk] N trópico *m*

tropical [trápɪkəl] ADJ tropical

trot [trat] VI trotar; VT hacer trotar; **to — out** sacar a relucir; N trote *m*

trouble [trábəl] VT (afflict) aquejar; (make turbid) enturbiar; VI/VT (bother) molestar[se]; (disturb) preocupar[se]; **to —shoot** solucionar problemas; N (problem) problema *m*; (difficulty) dificultad *f*, sinsabor *m*; (disturbance) disturbio *m*; (effort) molestia *f*; (ailment) enfermedad *f*, trastorno *m*; (mechanical breakdown) avería *f*, desperfecto *m*; **—maker** agitador -ora *mf*, revoltoso -sa

mf; **—shooter** solucionador -ora *mf*, localizador -ora de averías *mf*; **to be in —** estar en un aprieto; **it is not worth the —** no vale la pena; **to make —** causar problemas; **to take the —** tomarse la molestia; ADJ **—free** sin problemas

trough [trɔf] N (for food) pesebre *m*, comedero *m*; (for water) abrevadero *m*, bebedero *m*; (of weather, on ocean floor) depresión *f*

trousers [tráʊzɚz] N pantalones *m pl*

trousseau [trúso] N ajuar *m*

trout [traʊt] N trucha *f*

trowel [tráʊəl] N (for mortar) llana *f*, paleta *f*; (for digging) desplantador *m*

truant [trúənt] N alumno -na que falta a clase sin permiso *mf*

truce [trus] N tregua *f*

truck [trʌk] N (vehicle) camión *m*; *Mex* troca *f*; (dealings) trato *m*; (vegetables) hortalizas *f pl*; **— driver** camionero -ra *mf*; *Mex* troquero -ra *mf*; VI/VT transportar en camión; *Mex* transportar en troca

trudge [trʌdʒ] VI andar con dificultad

true [tru] ADJ verdadero; (story) verídico; (copy, translation) fiel; (well) a plomo; (wheel) alineado, centrado; VT **—blue** leal; **—false test** prueba de verdadero o falso *f*; **his dream came —** su sueño se hizo realidad

truly [trúli] ADV (surprisingly) verdaderamente; (sincerely) sinceramente; (actually) en realidad, realmente; (accurately) fielmente; **very — yours** su seguro servidor, atentamente

trumpet [trʌ́mpɪt] N trompeta *f*; VI/VT (musician) trompetear; (elephant) barritar

trunk [trʌŋk] N (of tree, body) tronco *m*; (receptacle) baúl *m*; (of elephant) trompa *f*; (of a car) maletero *m*, *Mex* cajuela *f*; **—s** traje de baño *m*

trust [trʌst] N (confidence) confianza *f*; (charge) cargo *m*; (firm) trust *m*; (fund) fondo fideicomiso *m*; VI/VT (rely on) confiar en, fiarse de; VT (believe) creer; (hope) esperar

trustee [trʌsti] N (person holding property of another) fideicomisario -ria *mf*; (administrator) administrador -ora *mf*

trusteeship [trʌstíʃɪp] N (position of holding property) fideicomiso *m*; (administrative position) cargo de administrador *m*

trustful [trʌ́stfəl] ADJ confiado

trusting [trʌ́stɪŋ] ADJ confiado

trustworthy [trʌ́stwɚði] ADJ fidedigno, digno de confianza

trusty [trʌ́sti] ADJ leal

truth [truθ] N verdad *f*

truthful [trúθfəl] ADJ (account) verídico; (person) veraz

truthfulness [trúθfəlnɪs] N veracidad *f*

try [traɪ] VT (attempt) tratar de, intentar; (test, taste) probar; (strain) poner a prueba; (put on trial) procesar, enjuiciar; **to — on** probarse; **to — one's luck** probar fortuna; **to — and** tratar de; **to — out** (test) probar; (for a team) presentarse para; N intento *m*, tentativa *f*; **—out** prueba *f*

trying [tráɪɪŋ] ADJ penoso

tryst [trɪst] N cita romántica *f*

T-shirt [tíʃɚt] N camiseta *f*

tub [tʌb] N (for bathing) bañera *f*; (for butter) envase *m*; (for washing) tina *f*

tuba [túbə] N tuba *f*

tube [tub] N tubo *m* (also electronic); (television) televisor *m*

tuberculosis [tʊbɚkjəlósɪs] N tuberculosis *f*

tubular [túbjələ] ADJ tubular

tuck [tʌk] VT (stick in) meter; (make fold) alforzar; **to — in one's shirt** meter la camisa dentro del pantalón; **to — into bed** arropar; **to — something under one's arm** meterse algo bajo el brazo; N alforza *f*

Tuesday [túzde] N martes *m*

tuft [tʌft] N (of feathers) penacho *m*; (of hair) mechón *m*, copete *m*; (of plants) mata *f*

tug [tʌg] VI/VT (pull) tirar, jalar; (drag) arrastrar; **to — at** tironear; N (pull) tirón *m*; (boat) remolcador *m*

tuition [tuíʃən] N matrícula *f*

tulip [túlɪp] N tulipán *m*

tumble [tʌ́mbəl] VI (fall) caer; (collapse) venirse abajo; (do handsprings, etc.) dar volteretas; **to — down** rodar; **to — dry** secar en la secadora; **to — over** tropezarse; N (fall) caída *f*; (gymnastic trick) voltereta *f*

tumbler [tʌ́mblə] N (glass) vaso *m*; (person) acróbata *mf*

tummy [tʌ́mi] N barriguita *f*

tumor [túmə] N tumor *m*

tumult [túmʌlt] N tumulto *m*

tumultuous [tumʌ́ltʃuəs] ADJ tumultuoso

tuna [túnə] N (fish) atún *m*, bonito *m*; (prickly pear) tuna *f*

tune [tun] N (melody) tonada *f*, aire *m*; (electronic adjustment) sintonía *f*; **—up** afinación *f*; **to be in —** (in pitch) estar afinado; (adjusted) sintonizado; **to be out of —** estar desafinado; VT (engine) afinar; (musical instrument) afinar, templar; (radio) sintonizar; **to — in** sintonizar; **to — out** ignorar

tuner [túnə] N afinador -ora *mf*; (electronic) sintonizador *m*

tungsten [tʌ́ŋstən] N tungsteno *m*

tunic [túnɪk] N túnica *f*

Tunisia [tuníʒə] N Túnez *m*

Tunisian [tuníʒən] ADJ & N tunesino -na *mf*

tunnel [tʌ́nəl] N túnel *m*; (for traffic) viaducto *m*; **— vision** visión en túnel *f*; VI cavar; VT hacer un túnel

turban [tɜ́·bən] N turbante *m*

turbine [tɜ́·baɪn] N turbina *f*

turbocharger [tɜ́·boʊʧɑɾdʒɚ] N turbocompresor *m*

turbojet [tɜ́·boʊdʒet] N turborreactor *m*

turbulence [tɜ́·bjələns] N turbulencia *f*

turbulent [tɜ́·bjələnt] ADJ turbulento

turf [tɜ˞f] N (lawn) césped *m*; (peat) turba *f*; (track for horse races) pista *f*; (territory) territorio *m*; VT cubrir con césped

Turk [tɜ˞k] N turco -ca *mf*

turkey [tɜ́·ki] N pavo *m*; **— vulture** buitre pavo *m*

Turkey [tɜ́·ki] N Turquía *f*

Turkish [tɜ́·kɪʃ] ADJ turco; **— bath** baño turco *m*

Turkmen [tɜ́·kmən] ADJ & N turcomano -na *mf*

Turkmenistan [tɜ·kmɛnɪstǽn] N Turkmenistán *m*

turmoil [tɜ́·mɔɪl] N confusión *f*, agitación *f*

turn [tɜ˞n] VT (corner) doblar, dar vuelta; (wheel, key) girar, dar vuelta; (page) dar vuelta; (soil) labrar; (stomach) revolver; (ankle) torcer[se]; (a river) desviar; VI (change color) cambiar de color; (become) ponerse; (rotate) girar; (change direction) girar, dar la vuelta; **to — against** volverse en contra de; **to — around** dar la vuelta, girar; **to — away** (face) volver; (eyes) apartar; (person) rechazar; **to — back** (return) volver; (a clock) atrasar; **to — down** (offer, request) rechazar; (radio) bajar; **to — in** (hand in/over) entregar; (go to bed) acostarse; **to — inside out** dar vuelta al revés; **to — into** convertir[se] en; **to — off** (light) apagar; (faucet) cerrar; (a road) salir de; (person in general sense) disgustar; (person in sexual sense) quitarle las ganas a alguien; **to — on** (light) encender, prender; (faucet) abrir; (person) excitar; **to — out** (light) apagar; (people) expulsar; (product) producir; **to — out well** salir bien; **to — over** (car) volcar[se]; (engine) arrancar; (thought, idea, etc.) dar vueltas a; (criminal, weapon, etc.) entregar; **— table** plato giratorio *m*; **to — to** (have recourse to) acudir a, recurrir a; (become) volver[se]; **to — up** aparecer; **to — up one's nose** desdeñar; **to — up one's sleeves** arremangarse; **to — upside down** dar vuelta; N (rotation) vuelta *f*, revolución *f*; (change of direction) giro *m*, vuelta *f*; (change in condition) cambio *m*; (curve) recodo *m*, curva *f*; (opportunity) turno *m*; **— of mind** actitud *f*; **—off** (disgusting thing) asco *m*; (road exit) salida *f*; **— of phrase** giro *m*; **—out** concurrencia *f*; **—over** (of employees) renovación *f*; (of merchandise) volumen *m*; (in football) pérdida de balón *f*; (pastry) empanada *f*, pastelito *m*; (of a ball) pérdida *f*; **—pike** autopista *f*; **—stile** torniquete *m*, molinete *m*;

— signal intermitente *m*; **at every —** a cada paso; **bad —** mala pasada *f*; **good —** favor *m*; **his bad teeth are a —off** sus feos dientes me dan asco / me repugnan; **his foreign accent is a —-on** su acento extranjero me excita; **it's my —** me toca a mí; **to take —s** turnarse

turnip [tɜ́·nɪp] N nabo *m*

turpentine [tɜ́·pəntaɪn] N trementina *f*, aguarrás *m*

turquoise [tɜ́·kɔɪz] N turquesa *f*

turret [tɜ́·ɪt] N (small tower, gun tower) torreta *f*; (on a ship) torre *f*

turtle [tɜ́·dl] N tortuga *f*; **—dove** tórtola *f*; **—neck** cuello vuelto *m*

tusk [tʌsk] N colmillo *m*

tutor [túdɚ] N profesor -ora particular *mf*; VI/VT dar clases particulares

tutorial [tutɔ́riəl] ADJ de tutoría; N (computer) tutorial *m*; (math, Spanish) cursillo *m*

Tuvalu [túvəlu] N Tuvalu *m*

Tuvaluan [tuvəlúən] ADJ & N tuvaluano -na *mf*

tuxedo [tʌksído] N esmoquin *m*

TV [**television**] [tívi] N *fam* tele *f*

twang [twæŋ] N (in music) tañido *m*; (of speech) nasalidad *f*; VI (vibrate) vibrar; VT hacer vibrar; VI/VT (speak nasally) ganguear

twangy [twǽŋi] ADJ gangoso

tweak [twik] VT (pinch) pellizcar; (adjust) ajustar; N (pinch) pellizco *m*; (adjustment) ajuste *m*

tweed [twid] N tweed *m*

tweezers [twízɚz] N pinzas *f pl*

twelve [twɛlv] NUM doce

twentieth [twɛ́ntiəθ] NUM vigésimo; **it's his — birthday** hoy cumple veinte años; **it's the — time I've told you** ya te lo dije veinte veces

twenty [twɛ́nti] NUM veinte; **—-five** veinticinco

twerp [twɚp] N idiota *mf*, papanatas *mf sg*

twice [twaɪs] ADV dos veces

twig [twɪg] N ramita *f*

twilight [twáɪlaɪt] N crepúsculo *m*, ocaso *m*; **— zone** zona gris *f*

twin [twɪn] ADJ & N (fraternal) mellizo -za *mf*; (identical) gemelo -la *mf*; **— bed** cama individual *f*

twine [twaɪn] N cuerda *f*; VI/VT (twist) enroscar[se]; (interlace) entrelazar[se]

twinge [twɪndʒ] N (of pain, remorse) punzada *f*

twinkle [twíŋkəl] VI (star) titilar, parpadear; (eyes) brillar; N (of stars) titileo *m*, parpadeo *m*; (of eyes) brillo *m*

twirl [twɚl] VI/VT girar, dar vueltas [a]; N giro *m*, vuelta *f*; (of ice cream) espiral *m*

twist [twɪst] VI/VT (wind, coil) torcer[se]; (distort) tergiversar[se]; (writhe) retorcer[se]; (coil) enroscar[se]; N (of an ankle) torcedura *f*; (distortion) tergiversación *f*; (in a road, coil) vuelta *f*; (unforeseen event) vuelta de tuerca *f*

twister [twístə] N tornado *m*

twitch [twɪtʃ] VI/VT crispar[se], mover[se]; N (tic) tic *m*; (pang) punzada *f*; (tug) tirón *m*

twitter [twídə] VI gorjear; N gorjeo *m*

two [tu] NUM dos; — **hundred** doscientos; —-**point conversion** conversión de dos puntos *f*; **my — cents' worth** mi opinión *f*; **to put — and — together** atar cabos; ADJ —-**bit** de chicha y nabo; —-**edged** de doble filo; —-**faced** (with two faces) de dos caras; (hypocritical) hipócrita, falso; —-**fisted** pendenciero; —-**way** de dos sentidos

tycoon [taɪkún] N magnate *mf*

type [taɪp] N tipo *m*, índole *f*; — **face** tipo de letra *m*; —**script** texto escrito a máquina *m*; —**writer** máquina de escribir *f*; —**writing** mecanografía *f*; VI/VT (a letter) escribir a máquina, mecanografiar, digitar, teclear, tipiar, tipear; VT (blood) determinar el grupo sanguíneo; **to — set** componer; **to —-write** escribir a máquina; ADJ —**written** escrito a máquina

typhoid [táɪfɔɪd] N tifoidea *f*; — **fever** fiebre tifoidea *f*, tifus *m*

typhoon [taɪfún] N tifón *m*

typhus [táɪfəs] N tifus *m*

typical [típɪkəl] ADJ típico

typist [táɪpɪst] N mecanógrafo -fa *mf*

typo [táɪpo] N error tipográfico *m*

typographical [taɪpəɡrǽfɪkəl] ADJ tipográfico; — **error** error de imprenta *m*, errata *f*

typology [taɪpáləʤi] N tipología *f*

tyrannical [tɪrǽnɪkəl] ADJ tiránico

tyranny [tírəni] N tiranía *f*

tyrant [táɪrənt] N tirano -na *mf*

Uu

ubiquitous [jubíkwɪdəs] ADJ ubicuo

U-boat [júbot] N submarino alemán *m*

udder [ʌ́də] N ubre *f*

UFO [unidentified flying object] [júéfó] N OVNI *m*

Uganda [jugǽndə] N Uganda *f*

Ugandan [jugǽndən] ADJ & N ugandés -esa *mf*

ugliness [ʌ́ɡlinis] N fealdad *f*

ugly [ʌ́ɡli] ADJ feo; (incident) deplorable; (mood) de perros

uh-huh [ʌ́hʌ́] INTERJ *fam* sí

Ukraine [jukrén] N Ucrania *f*

Ukrainian [jukrénian] ADJ & N ucraniano -na *mf*

ulcer [ʌ́lsə] N úlcera *f*

ulcerate [ʌ́lsəret] VI ulcerar

ulcerous [ʌ́lsə-əs] ADJ ulceroso

ulna [ʌ́lnə] N cúbito *m*

ulterior [ʌltíriə] ADJ ulterior; — **motive** segunda intención *f*

ultimate [ʌ́ltəmɪt] ADJ (destination) último, final; (authority) final, máximo; (principle) fundamental; (vacation) perfecto; N súmmum *m*

ultimately [ʌ́ltəmɪtli] ADV en última instancia

ultimatum [ʌltəméɖəm] N ultimátum *m*

ultralight [ʌ́ltralaɪt] ADJ & N ultraligero *m*

ultramodern [ʌltrəmádən] ADJ ultramoderno

ultrasound [ʌ́ltrəsaund] N ultrasonido *m*; — **imaging** imágenes por ultrasonido *f pl*

ultraviolet [ʌltrəváɪəlɪt] ADJ & N ultravioleta *m*

umbilical cord [ʌmbílɪkəlkɔrd] N cordón umbilical *m*

umbrella [ʌmbrélə] N paraguas *m sg*

umpire [ʌ́mpaɪr] N árbitro *m*; (in tennis) juez -eza de silla *mf*; VI/VT arbitrar

unable [ʌnébəl] ADJ **to be —** no poder

unabridged [ʌnəbríʤd] ADJ íntegro

unaccented [ʌnǽksentɪd] ADJ sin acento

unacceptable [ʌnɪkséptəbəl] ADJ inaceptable, inadmisible

unaccustomed [ʌnəkʌ́stəmd] ADJ (not used to) no acostumbrado; (uncommon) insólito

unadjusted [ʌnəʤʌ́stɪd] ADJ no ajustado

unadulterated [ʌnədʌ́ltəreɪɖɪd] ADJ puro

unaffected [ʌnəféktɪd] ADJ (not affected) no afectado; (sincere) natural, sincero; (unpretentious) sin afectación

unaffiliated [ʌnəfíliedɪd] ADJ no afiliado

unanimity [junəním̩ɪɖi] N unanimidad *f*

unanimous [junǽnəməs] ADJ unánime

unarmed [ʌnármd] ADJ desarmado

unassuming [ʌnəsúmɪŋ] ADJ modesto, sin pretensiones

unattached [ʌnətǽtʃt] ADJ (piece of paper) suelto; (person) soltero

unauthorized [ʌnɔ́θəraɪzd] ADJ no autorizado

unavailable [ʌnəvéiləbəl] ADJ no disponible

unavoidable [ʌnəvɔ́ɪdəbəl] ADJ inevitable, ineludible

unaware [ʌnəwér] ADJ inconsciente; ADV **to be — of** ignorar; —**s** sin darse cuenta

unbalanced [ʌnbǽlənst] ADJ desequilibrado

unbearable [ʌnbérəbəl] ADJ inaguantable, insoportable

unbeatable [ʌnbídəbəl] ADJ imbatible

unbeaten [ʌnbítn̩] ADJ invicto

unbecoming [ʌnbɪkámɪŋ] ADJ (behavior) impropio; (clothes) que no [le] luce

unbelief [ʌnbɪlíf] N incredulidad *f*, descreimiento *m*

unbelievable [ʌnbɪlívəbəl] ADJ increíble

unbeliever [ʌnbɪlívə] N descreído -da *mf*

unbending [ʌnbéndɪŋ] ADJ inflexible

unbiased [ʌnbáɪəst] ADJ imparcial

unbounded [ʌnbáʊndɪd] ADJ illimitado

unbridled [ʌnbráɪdld] ADJ desenfrenado

unbroken [ʌnbrókən] ADJ (intact) intacto; (not tamed) indomado; (uninterrupted) ininterrumpido

unbuckle [ʌnbʌkəl] VT desabrochar

unbutton [ʌnbʌtn] VI/VT desabotonar, desabrochar

uncalled-for [ʌnkɔ́ldfɔr] ADJ injustificado

uncanny [ʌnkǽni] ADJ inexplicable, misterioso

uncertain [ʌnsɝ́tn] ADJ incierto

uncertainty [ʌnsɝ́tnti] N incertidumbre f

unchanged [ʌntʃéndʒd] ADJ inalterado

uncharitable [ʌntʃǽrɪɾəbəl] ADJ duro, poco caritativo

uncivilized [ʌnsívəlaɪzd] ADJ incivilizado

uncle [ʌ́ŋkəl] N tío m; **to say** — darse por vencido

unclean [ʌnklín] ADJ (dirty) sucio; (impure) impuro

uncollectable [ʌnkəléktəbəl] ADJ incobrable

uncomfortable [ʌnkʌ́mfɚɾəbəl] ADJ incómodo

uncommon [ʌnkámən] ADJ (unusual) poco común; (extraordinary) extraordinario

uncompromising [ʌnkámprəmaɪzɪŋ] ADJ (intransigent) intransigente; (unfailing) incondicional

unconcerned [ʌnkənsɝ́nd] ADJ indiferente

unconditional [ʌnkəndíʃənəl] ADJ incondicional

unconfirmed [ʌnkənfɝ́md] ADJ no confirmado

unconscious [ʌnkánʃəs] ADJ inconsciente

unconstitutional [ʌnkanstɪtúʃənl] ADJ inconstitucional

uncontrollable [ʌnkantróləbəl] ADJ (movement) incontrolable; (urge, laughter) incontenible

unconventional [ʌnkənvénʃənəl] ADJ poco convencional

uncouth [ʌnkúθ] ADJ tosco

uncover [ʌnkʌ́vɚ] VI/VT descubrir[se]; VI (remove bedcovers) destaparse

uncovered [ʌnkʌ́vɚd] ADJ descubierto

unctuous [ʌ́ŋktʃuəs] ADJ untuoso, zalamero

uncultivated [ʌnkʌ́ltəveɪɾd] ADJ (person) inculto, no cultivado; (land) no cultivado

uncultured [ʌnkʌ́ltʃɚd] ADJ inculto

undaunted [ʌndɔ́ntɪd] ADJ impávido, intrépido

undecided [ʌndɪsáɪdɪd] ADJ indeciso

undeclared [ʌndɪklérd] ADJ no declarado

undefined [ʌndɪfáɪnd] ADJ indefinido

undelete utility [ʌndɪlít jutílɪɾi] N programa para recuperar datos borrados m

undeniable [ʌndɪnáɪəbəl] ADJ innegable, indudable

under [ʌ́ndɚ] PREP (below) bajo, debajo de, abajo de; (in a ranking) por debajo de; (less) menos de; — **the Democrats** durante el mandato de los Demócratas; — **a pseudonym** bajo un pseudónimo; — **cost** a menos del costo/coste,

por debajo del costo/coste; — **contract** bajo contrato; — **wraps** oculto; ADV (below) debajo, abajo; (less than) menos; **to be** — estar inconsciente

underage [ʌndɚéʤ] ADJ menor de edad; — **drinking** consumo de alcohol por menores de edad m

underarm [ʌ́ndɚɑrm] N axila f

underbrush [ʌ́ndɚbrʌʃ] N maleza f

undercharge [ʌndɚtʃárʤ] VI cobrar de menos

underclass [ʌ́ndɚklæs] N subproletariado m

undercover [ʌndɚkávɚ] ADJ clandestino, secreto

undercut [ʌndɚkʌ́t] VT (undermine) socavar; (sell for less) vender por menos que

underdeveloped [ʌndɚdɪvéləpt] ADJ subdesarrollado

underdog [ʌ́ndɚdɔg] N el de abajo m, la de abajo f

underemployed [ʌndɚɛmplɔ́ɪd] ADJ subempleado

underestimate [ʌndɚéstəmet] VT (person) subestimar; (price) subvaluar

underfed [ʌndɚféd] ADJ desnutrido

underfoot [ʌndɚfʊ́t] ADJ (beneath the feet) bajo los pies; (in the way) estorbando

undergird [ʌndɚgɝ́d] VT reforzar

undergo [ʌndɚgó] VT (an operation) someterse a; (a change) experimentar, sufrir

undergraduate [ʌndɚgrǽʤuɪt] N estudiante de pregrado mf; — **course** clase de pregrado f

underground¹ [ʌndɚgráʊnd] ADV (under the earth) bajo tierra; (secretly) en secreto

underground² [ʌ́ndɚgraʊnd] ADJ (under the earth) subterráneo; (secret) clandestino; N resistencia f, grupo clandestino m

underhanded [ʌndɚhǽndɪd] ADJ (secret) secreto, solapado; (illicit) ilícito

underlie [ʌndɚláɪ] VI/VT subyacer [a]

underline [ʌ́ndɚlaɪn] VT subrayar

underlying [ʌndɚláɪɪŋ] ADJ (inflation, racism) subyacente; (problems) de fondo

undermine [ʌndɚmáɪn] VT minar, menoscabar

underneath [ʌndɚníθ] PREP bajo, debajo de, abajo de; ADV debajo, abajo; N la parte inferior

undernourished [ʌndɚnɝ́ɪʃt] ADJ desnutrido

underpants [ʌ́ndɚpænts] N (for men) calzoncillos m pl; (for women) Sp bragas f pl; Mex pantaletas f pl; RP bombacha f

underrated [ʌndɚréɪɾd] ADJ infravalorado

underscore [ʌndɚskór] N subrayado m; VT subrayar

undersecretary [ʌndɚsékrəteri] N subsecretario -ria mf

undersell [ʌndɚsél] VT (to sell at a low price) malbaratar; (to sell cheaper) vender a menos precio

undershirt [ʌ́ndɚshɝt] N camiseta f

underside [ʌ́ndə-saɪd] N parte inferior *f*
undersigned [ʌ́ndə-sáɪnd] N abajo firmante *mf*, infrascrito -ta *mf*
underskirt [ʌ́ndə-skɜ-t] N enaguas *f pl*
understaffed [ʌ́ndə-stǽft] ADJ falto de personal
understand [ʌ́ndə-stǽnd] VI/VT comprender, entender; **I — you're leaving** tengo entendido que te vas; **to — about** saber de/ entender de
understandable [ʌ́ndə-stǽndəbəl] ADJ comprensible
understanding [ʌ́ndə-stǽndɪŋ] N (comprehension) comprensión *f*, entendimiento *m*; (tolerance) comprensión mutua *f*; (agreement) acuerdo *m*; ADJ comprensivo
understate [ʌ́ndə-stét] VT minimizar
understood [ʌ́ndə-stúd] ADJ entendido; (implicit) sobreentendido
understood [ʌ́ndə-stúd] *see* understand
understudy [ʌ́ndə-stʌ́di] N suplente *mf*, sobresaliente *mf*; VI/VT suplir [a], servir de sobresaliente [para]
undertake [ʌ́ndə-ték] VT emprender, acometer; **to — to** comprometerse a
undertaken [ʌ́ndə-tékən] *see* undertake
undertaker [ʌ́ndə-tekə-] N director -ora de funeraria / pompas fúnebres *mf*, funerario -ria *mf*
undertaking [ʌ́ndə-tékɪŋ] N empresa *f*
under-the-table [ʌ́ndə-ðətébəl] ADJ ilícito, bajo cuerda
undertone [ʌ́ndə-ton] N (low voice) voz baja *f*; (undercurrent) tónica *f*
undertook [ʌ́ndə-túk] *see* undertake
undertow [ʌ́ndə-to] N resaca *f*
undervalued [ʌ́ndə-vǽljud] ADJ infravalorado
underwater [ʌ́ndə-wɔtə-, ʌ́ndə-wótə-] ADJ submarino; ADV por debajo del agua
underwear [ʌ́ndə-wer] N ropa interior *f*
underweight [ʌ́ndə-wet] ADJ de peso insuficiente
underworld [ʌ́ndə-wɜ-ld] N (of criminals) hampa *f*; (netherworld) el más allá
underwrite [ʌ́ndə-raɪt] VI/VT (finance) financiar; (sign) suscribir; (insure) asegurar
underwriter [ʌ́ndə-raɪDə-] N (insurance) asegurador -ora *mf*; (stock exchange) suscriptor -ora *mf*
undesirable [ʌ́ndɪzáɪrəbəl] ADJ indeseable
undetermined [ʌ́ndɪtɜ́-mɪnd] ADJ indeterminado
undid [ʌ́ndíd] *see* undo
undisclosed [ʌ́ndɪsklózd] ADJ no divulgado
undisturbed [ʌ́ndɪstɜ́-bd] ADJ (unworried, uninterrupted) tranquilo; (unspoiled) virgen
undivided [ʌ́ndɪváɪDɪd] ADJ indiviso
undo [ʌ́ndú] VT (reverse an action) deshacer, anular; (unfasten) desabrochar, desabotonar;

(destroy) destruir; (loosen hair) soltar
undocumented [ʌ́ndákjəmɛntɪd] ADJ indocumentado
undoing [ʌ́ndúɪŋ] N (reversal) deshacer *m*; (destruction) destrucción *f*, perdición *f*; (of buttons) desabrochar *m*
undone [ʌ́ndʌ́n] ADJ (unfinished) sin terminar; (ruined) perdido; (unfastened) desabrochado; **to come —** (clothing) desabrocharse; (person) desquiciarse
undone [ʌ́ndʌ́n] *see* undo
undoubtedly [ʌ́ndáʊDIdli] ADV indudablemente, sin duda
undress [ʌ́ndrés] VI/VT desnudar[se], desvestir[se]
undue [ʌ́ndú] ADJ (inappropriate) indebido; (excessive) excesivo
undulate [ʌ́ndʒəlet] VI/VT ondular
undying [ʌ́ndáɪɪŋ] ADJ imperecedero, eterno
unearned [ʌ́nɜ́-nd] N inmerecido; **— run** (baseball) carrera sucia *f*
unearth [ʌ́nɜ́θ] VT desenterrar
uneasiness [ʌ́nízɪnɪs] N (feeling) inquietud *f*, desasosiego *m*, desazón *f*; Sp grima *f*; (of peace) precariedad *f*; (of silence, situation) incomodidad *f*; (of sleep) agitación *f*
uneasy [ʌ́nízi] ADJ (feeling) inquieto; (peace) precario; (silence) incómodo; (situation) molesto; (sleep) agitado
uneducated [ʌ́nédʒəkeDɪd] ADJ inculto, ignorante
unemployable [ʌ́nɪmplɔ́iəbəl] ADJ inempleable
unemployed [ʌ́nɪmplɔ́id] ADJ (jobless) desocupado, desempleado, Sp parado; (unused) ocioso
unemployment [ʌ́nɪmplɔ́imənt] N desocupación *f*, desempleo *m*, Sp paro *m*; **— compensation** seguro de paro *m*; Sp paro *m*; **— rate** Am tasa de desempleo *f*, Sp tasa de paro *f*
unending [ʌ́néndɪŋ] ADJ interminable
unequal [ʌ́níkwəl] ADJ desigual; **to be — to a task** no ser capaz de cumplir una tarea
unequivocal [ʌ́nɪkwívəkəl] ADJ inequívoco, tajante
unerase [ʌ́nɪrés] VT recuperar archivos borrados
unethical [ʌ́néθɪkəl] ADJ no ético
uneven [ʌ́nívən] ADJ (rough) irregular, accidentado; (inequitable) desigual; (not uniform) desparejo; (odd, of numbers) impar
uneventful [ʌ́nɪvéntfəl] ADJ sin incidente
unexpected [ʌ́nɪkspéktɪd] ADJ inesperado
unexpressive [ʌ́nɪksprésɪv] ADJ inexpresivo
unfailing [ʌ́nféɪlɪŋ] ADJ (inexhaustible) inagotable; (dependable) infalible
unfair [ʌ́nfér] ADJ (measure, price) injusto; (competition) injusto, desleal
unfaithful [ʌ́nféθfəl] ADJ infiel
unfamiliar [ʌ́nfəmíljə-] ADJ (unknown) poco

familiar, desconocido; (unacquainted) poco familiarizado

unfasten [ʌnfǽsən] VI/VT desabrochar[se], desprender[se]

unfavorable [ʌnféva·əbəl] ADJ desfavorable

unfeeling [ʌnfílɪŋ] ADJ insensible

unfettered [ʌnfɛ́da·d] ADJ (untied) desatado; (free) libre

unfinished [ʌnfínɪʃt] ADJ (matter) inacabado, inconcluso; (business) pendiente; (wood) sin terminar, sin barnizar; (task) inconcluso, sin terminar

unfit [ʌnfít] ADJ (unsuitable) no apto; (incapable) incapaz

unfold [ʌnfóld] VT (open out) desdoblar, desplegar; VI (happen) desarrollarse; (reveal) revelarse

unforced error [ʌ́nfɔrst ɛ́rə·] N (tennis) error no forzado m

unforeseen [ʌnfɔrsín] ADJ imprevisto

unforgettable [ʌnfa·gɛ́dəbəl] ADJ inolvidable

unfortunate [ʌnfɔ́rtʃənɪt] ADJ desgraciado, desafortunado, desventurado

unfortunately [ʌnfɔ́rtʃənətli] ADV desafortunadamente, lamentablemente

unfounded [ʌnfáʊndɪd] ADJ infundado

unfriendly [ʌnfréndli] ADJ (forces) hostil; (person) antipático

unfurl [ʌnfɹ́ɫ] VT desplegar[se]

unfurnished [ʌnfɹ́nɪʃt] ADJ sin amueblar, desamueblado

ungainly [ʌngénli] ADJ (ungraceful) desgarbado, desmadejado; (clumsy) torpe

ungrateful [ʌngrɛ́tfəl] ADJ ingrato, desagradecido

unguarded [ʌngárdɪd] ADJ (incautious) descuidado, desprevenido; (unattended) sin vigilancia; (defenseless) indefenso; **an — moment** un momento de descuido

unhappiness [ʌnhǽpɪnɪs] N infelicidad f

unhappy [ʌnhǽpi] ADJ (sad) infeliz, desdichado, desgraciado; (dissatisfied) insatisfecho; (infelicitous) poco afortunado

unharmed [ʌnhármd] ADJ ileso

unhealthy [ʌnhɛ́łθi] ADJ (climate, food, lifestyle) malsano, insalubre; (complexion, obsession) enfermizo

unheard-of [ʌnhɹ́ɁDʌv] ADJ inaudito, desconocido

unhinge [ʌnhíndʒ] VT desquiciar

unholy [ʌnhóli] ADJ (noise) infernal; (alliance) nefasto

unhook [ʌnhúk] VT (disentangle) desenganchar; (undo) desabrochar

unhurt [ʌnhɹ́t] ADJ ileso

uniform [júnəfɔrm] ADJ & N uniforme m

uniformity [junəfɔ́rmɪDi] N uniformidad f

unify [júnəfaɪ] VI/VT unificar[se]

unilateral [junəlǽdə·əɫ] ADJ unilateral

unimportant [ʌnɪmpɔ́rtn̩t] ADJ insignificante, sin importancia

uninhabited [ʌnɪnhǽbɪDɪd] ADJ deshabitado

uninhibited [ʌnɪnhíbɪDɪd] ADJ desinhibido, desenfadado

uninspired [ʌnɪnspáɪrd] ADJ poco inspirado

uninstall [ʌnɪnstáɫ] VT desinstalar

uninsured [ʌnɪnʃúrd] ADJ sin seguro médico

unintelligible [ʌnɪntɛ́lɪdʒəbəl] ADJ ininteligible

uninterrupted [ʌnɪntərʌ́ptɪd] ADJ ininterrumpido

union [júnjən] N unión f; (labor) sindicato m, gremio m; **— dues** cuotas sindicales f pl; **— labor** mano de obra sindicalizada/agremiada f; **— leader** dirigente sindical mf

unionize [júnjənaɪz] VI/VT sindicar[se], agremiar[se]

unique [juník] ADJ único, singular; **that feature is — to the South** ese rasgo es peculiar del sur

unisex [júnəsɛks] ADJ unisex

unison [júnəsən] ADV LOC **in —** al unísono

unit [júnɪt] N (part of a whole) unidad f; (part of a machine) módulo m

unitarian [junɪtérɪən] ADJ unitario

unitary [júnɪtɛri] ADJ unitario

unite [junáɪt] VI/VT unir[se]

United Arab Emirates [junáɪDɪdǽrəbémə·ɪts] N Emiratos Árabes Unidos m pl

United Kingdom [junáɪDɪdkíŋdəm] N Reino Unido m

United States [junáɪDɪdstéts] N Estados Unidos m pl

unity [júnɪDi] N unidad f; (concord) unión f

universal [junəvɹ́səɫ] ADJ universal; **— donor** donante universal mf; **— joint** acoplamiento universal de cardán m

universe [júnəvɹ·s] N universo m

university [junəvɹ́sɪDi] N universidad f; **— degree** título universitario m

unjust [ʌndʒʌ́st] ADJ injusto

unjustifiable [ʌndʒʌstəfáɪəbəl] ADJ injustificable

unkempt [ʌnkɛ́mpt] ADJ (uncombed) desgreñado, despeinado; (messy) desaliñado

unkind [ʌnkáɪnd] ADJ antipático, poco amable

unknown [ʌnnón] ADJ desconocido; **— quantity** incógnita f; **it is —** se ignora

unlawful [ʌnlɔ́fəl] ADJ ilegal

unleaded [ʌnlɛ́dɪd] ADJ sin plomo

unleash [ʌnlíʃ] VT desatar

unless [ənlɛ́s] CONJ a menos que, a no ser que

unlicensed [ʌnláɪsənst] ADJ (without permission) sin permiso, ilícito; (without credentials) no acreditado

unlike [ʌnláɪk] ADJ distinto, diferente; **he is — me** es diferente de mí; PREP a diferencia de; **how — you to forget!** ¡me extraña que te hayas olvidado!

unlikely [ʌnláɪkli] ADJ (improbable) improbable; (not realistic) inverosímil; (exotic) exótico; **I am — to come** es improbable que venga

unlimited [ʌnlímɪdɪd] ADJ ilimitado

unload [ʌnlód] VI/VT (take cargo from) descargar; VI (pour out one's feelings) desahogarse; (sell) liquidar

unlock [ʌnlák] VI/VT abrir con llave

unlucky [ʌnláki] ADJ (unfortunate) desafortunado; (ominous) aciago, funesto; **an — number** un número de mala suerte

unmanageable [ʌnmǽnɪʤəbəl] ADJ (crisis, situation) inmanejable; (person) rebelde

unmanned [ʌnmǽnd] ADJ (deprived of courage) achicado; (with no crew) no tripulado

unmarked [ʌnmárkt] ADJ sin marcar

unmarried [ʌnmǽrid] ADJ soltero

unmask [ʌnmǽsk] VI/VT desenmascarar[se]

unmistakable [ʌnmɪstékəbəl] ADJ inconfundible

unmitigated [ʌnmídɪgedɪd] ADJ absoluto

unmoved [ʌnmúvd] ADJ (unflinching) impasible; (indifferent) indiferente

unnatural [ʌnnǽʧəəl] ADJ (contrary to nature) no natural; (unloving) desnaturalizado; (monstrous) monstruoso; (affected) afectado

unnecessary [ʌnnésəseri] ADJ innecesario

unnoticed [ʌnnódɪst] ADJ inadvertido, desapercibido

unobserved [ʌnɑbzśvd] ADJ inadvertido

unobtrusive [ʌnəbtrúsɪv] ADJ discreto

unoccupied [ʌnákjəpaɪd] ADJ (house) desocupado; (territory) no ocupado

unofficial [ʌnəfíʃəl] ADJ extraoficial, no oficial

unoriginal [ʌnəríʤənəl] ADJ poco original

unorthodox [ʌnɔ́rθədɑks] ADJ heterodoxo

unpack [ʌnpǽk] VT (a suitcase) deshacer, desempacar; (a carton) desembalar

unpaid [ʌnpéd] ADJ (debt) impagado, por pagar; (work) no remunerado

unplayable [ʌnpléəbəl] ADJ (golf) injugable

unpleasant [ʌnplézənt] ADJ desagradable

unpleasantness [ʌnplézəntnɪs] N (quality or state of being unpleasant) lo desagradable; (unpleasant episode) desavenencia f, disgusto m

unplug [ʌnplág] VI/VT desenchufar

unpopular [ʌnpápjələ] ADJ (decision) impopular; **she was — in school** tenía pocos amigos en la escuela

unprecedented [ʌnprésɪdentɪd] ADJ sin precedente, inaudito

unpredictable [ʌnprɪdíktəbəl] ADJ impredecible, imprevisible

unpremeditated [ʌnpriméDɪteDɪd] ADJ impremeditado; (murder) sin premeditación

unprepared [ʌnprɪpérd] ADJ (surprised) desprevenido; (not ready) no preparado

unpretentious [ʌnprɪténʃəs] ADJ modesto, sin pretenciones

unprincipled [ʌnprínsəpəld] ADJ sin escrúpulos, falto de principios

unprintable [ʌnpríntəbəl] ADJ impublicable

unproductive [ʌnprədáktɪv] ADJ improductivo

unprofessional [ʌnprəféʃənəl] ADJ poco profesional

unprofitable [ʌnpráfɪdəbəl] ADJ no rentable

unpublished [ʌnpábliʃt] ADJ inédito, sin publicar

unpunished [ʌnpáníʃt] ADJ impune

unqualified [ʌnkwálɪfaɪd] ADJ (worker) Sp no cualificado; Am no calificado; (support) incondicional; (disaster) absoluto

unquestionable [ʌnkwéstʃənəbəl] ADJ incuestionable, indiscutible

unravel [ʌnrǽvəl] VI/VT (a rope) desenredar[se]; (a sweater) destejer[se]; (cloth) deshilachar[se]; (a plan) deshacer[se]; VT (a mystery) desentrañar

unreal [ʌnríəl] ADJ (not real) irreal; (unbelievable) increíble

unreasonable [ʌnrízənəbəl] ADJ (excessive) exagerado; (irrational) irracional, poco razonable

unrecognizable [ʌnrekəgnáɪzəbəl] ADJ irreconocible

unrefined [ʌnrɪfáɪnd] ADJ (oil, sugar) no refinado; (behavior) inculto, grosero

unrelated [ʌnrɪléDɪd] ADJ no relacionado

unreliable [ʌnrɪláɪəbəl] ADJ (person) informal; (machine, information) Sp poco fiable; Am poco confiable

unreported [ʌnrɪpórDɪd] ADJ sin declarar

unrest [ʌnrést] N malestar m, agitación f

unrestricted [ʌnrɪstríktɪd] ADJ no restringido

unroll [ʌnról] VI/VT desenrollar[se]

unruly [ʌnrúli] ADJ (student) indisciplinado, revoltoso, díscolo; (country) ingobernable; (hair) rebelde

unsafe [ʌnséf] ADJ (risky) arriesgado; (dangerous) peligroso

unsanitary [ʌnsǽniteri] ADJ (behavior) antihigiénico, insalubre; (place, climate) insalubre

unsatisfactory [ʌnsæDɪsfǽktəri] ADJ no satisfactorio, insatisfactorio

unscrew [ʌnskrú] VT desatornillar, destornillar

unscrupulous [ʌnskrúpjələs] ADJ sin escrúpulos

unseasonable [ʌnsízənəbəl] ADJ impropio de la estación

unseat [ʌnsít] VT derribar

unsecured [ʌnsɪkjúrd] ADJ sin garantía

unseen [ʌnsín] ADJ invisible, oculto

unselfish [ʌnsélfíʃ] ADJ desinteresado

unselfishness [ʌnsélfíʃnɪs] N desinterés m

unsettled [ʌnsédld] ADJ (situation)

desordenado; (wilderness) sin colonizar; (case) pendiente; (weather) variable

unsightly [ʌnsáɪtli] ADJ feo, antiestético

unskilled [ʌnskɪ́ld] ADJ (not trained) inexperto; (not qualified) *Sp* no cualificado; *Am* no calificado

unsolicited [ʌnsəlísɪDɪd] ADJ no solicitado

unsophisticated [ʌnsəfístɪkeDɪd] ADJ sencillo, no sofisticado

unsound [ʌnsáund] ADJ (argument) erróneo, falso; (body) enfermizo; (mind) demente; (foundation) poco sólido; (investment) poco seguro

unspeakable [ʌnspíkəbəl] ADJ indecible

unspecified [ʌnspésɪfaɪd] ADJ no especificado

unsportsmanlike [ʌnspórtsmənlaɪk] ADJ antideportivo

unstable [ʌnstébəl] ADJ inestable

unsteady [ʌnstéDi] ADJ (walk) inseguro, inestable; (flame) tembloroso; (pulse) irregular

unsuccessful [ʌnsəksésfəl] ADJ sin éxito, infructuoso

unsuitable [ʌnsúdəbəl] ADJ (person) no apto; (place) inadecuado, inapropiado

unsuspected [ʌnsəspéktɪd] ADJ insospechado

untenable [ʌnténəbəl] ADJ insostenible

unthinkable [ʌnθíŋkəbəl] ADJ impensable

untidy [ʌntáɪDi] ADJ (dress) desaliñado, desastrado; (room) desordenado

untie [ʌntáɪ] VI/VT desatar[se], destrabar[se]

until [əntíł] PREP hasta; CONJ hasta que

untimely [ʌntáɪmli] ADJ (ill-timed) inoportuno; (premature) prematuro

untiring [ʌntáɪrɪŋ] ADJ incansable, denodado

untold [ʌntółd] ADJ (riches) incalculable; (suffering) inaudito

untouched [ʌntátʃt] ADJ (not injured) ileso; (not affected) no afectado; **he left his dessert —** no tocó el postre

untrained [ʌntrénd] ADJ (worker) *Sp* no cualificado; *Am* no calificado; (animal) no amaestrado; (eye) inexperto

untried [ʌntráɪd] ADJ (untested) no probado, no ensayado; (not taken to trial) no juzgado

untrue [ʌntrú] ADJ (incorrect) falso; (unfaithful) infiel; (disloyal) desleal

untutored [ʌntúDəd] ADJ (unschooled) sin instrucción; (unsophisticated) inculto

untwist [ʌntwíst] VT desenroscar

unused [ʌnjúzd] ADJ (no used) sin usar; (unaccustomed) no habituado

unusual [ʌnjúʒuəł] ADJ (infrequent) desacostumbrado, raro; (highly abnormal) inusitado, insólito

unvarnished [ʌnvárnɪʃt] ADJ (without varnish) sin barnizar; (straightforward) puro

unveil [ʌnvéł] VT (remove a veil) quitar el velo a; (reveal) descubrir

unwarranted [ʌnwórəntɪd] ADJ injustificado

unwelcome [ʌnwéłkəm] ADJ (untimely) inoportuno; (unpleasant) desagradable; (poorly received) mal recibido

unwholesome [ʌnhółsəm] ADJ malsano

unwieldy [ʌnwíłdi] ADJ poco manejable, difícil de manejar

unwilling [ʌnwílɪŋ] ADJ **to be —** to no estar dispuesto a

unwise [ʌnwáɪz] ADJ imprudente

unwonted [ʌnwóntɪd] ADJ inusitado, inacostumbrado

unworthy [ʌnwɝ́ði] ADJ indigno

unwrap [ʌnrǽp] VT desenvolver

unwritten [ʌnrítn] ADJ no escrito; (agreement) de palabra

unzip [ʌnzíp] VT abrir la cremallera

up [ʌp] ADV (position) arriba; (direction) hacia arriba; **—-front** (paid in advance) inicial; (frank) franco; **— and down** de arriba para abajo; **— against** enfrentado con; **he's — for reelection** se presenta para la reelección; **I'm feeling —** me siento optimista; **I'm — for golf** tengo ganas de jugar al golf; **prices are —** los precios han subido; **that is — to you** queda en tus manos, es cosa tuya; **the children are already —** ya se levantaron los niños; **the moon is —** salió la luna; **the wheat is —** germinó el trigo; **time is —** se terminó el tiempo; **to be — on the news** estar al corriente de las noticias; **to be — to one's old tricks** hacer de las suyas; **what's —?** ¿qué pasa? **he — and went** agarró y se fue; PREP **— the current** contra la corriente; **— the river** río arriba; **— the street** calle arriba; **— to now** hasta ahora; N **—s and downs** altibajos *m pl*; VI; ADJ (assembled) armado; (finished) terminado, concluido; **—-and-coming** prometedor; **—-to-date** actualizado

upbeat [ʌ́pbit] ADJ optimista

upbringing [ʌ́pbrɪŋɪŋ] N crianza *f*

update [ʌpdét] VT actualizar; N actualización *f*

upend [ʌpénd] VI/VT (stand on end) poner[se] de punta; (defeat) derrotar

upgrade [ʌ́pgred] VT (facilities) mejorar; (computer) actualizar; N (facilities) mejora *f*; (computer) actualización *f*

upheaval [ʌphívəł] N trastorno *m*

upheld [ʌphéłd] *see* uphold

uphill[1] [ʌ́phíł] ADV cuesta arriba

uphill[2] [ʌ́phíł] ADJ penoso, arduo

uphold [ʌphółd] VT sostener, apoyar; (legal decision) refrendar

upholster [ʌphółstə] VT tapizar

upholstery [ʌphółstəri] N tapicería *f*

upkeep [ʌ́pkip] N mantenimiento *m*

uplift [ʌplíft] VT (physically) elevar; (spiritually)

edificar

upload [áplod] VT cargar, subir; N carga f

upon [əpán] PREP sobre, encima de; **— arriving** al llegar; **once — a time** érase una vez

upper [ápə] ADJ (higher) superior; (high) alto; **to have the — hand** dominar, llevar la ventaja; N (of shoe) pala f; (of berth) litera superior f; **— class** clase alta f; **— crust** flor y nata f; **—case** mayúsculo; **—cut** (in boxing) gancho al mentón m; **—most** (highest) de más arriba; (most important) mayor; **— respiratory infection** infección respiratoria alta f; **—s** dentadura postiza superior f

uppity [ápiDi] ADJ presumido

upright [áprait] ADJ (posture) erecto, erguido; (position) vertical; (character) íntegro, recto, cabal; **— piano** piano vertical m; N (column) montante m; (piano) piano vertical m; (post) poste m

uprightness [ápraitnis] N (physical) verticalidad f; (moral) rectitud f

uprising [ápraiziŋ] N alzamiento m, levantamiento m

uproar [ápror] N tumulto m, alboroto m, bulla f

uproarious [ápróriəs] ADJ (tumultuous) tumultuoso; (funny) graciosísimo

uproot [áprút] VT arrancar de raíz, desarraigar

upscale [ápskeł] ADJ de lujo

upset[1] [ápsét] VT/VI (overturn) volcar[se], tumbar; (distress) trastornar[se], perturbar[se], alterar[se]; VT (in sports) derrotar al favorito; ADJ (overturned) volcado; (ill) indispuesto; (distressed) disgustado, enojado

upset[2] [ápset] N (overturning) vuelco m; (unexpected defeat) derrota inesperada f; (emotional state) trastorno m, disgusto m; (illness) malestar m

upshot [ápʃət] N consecuencia f

upside [ápsaid] N (upper part) parte superior f; (positive prospect) lo bueno; ADJ & ADV **— down** al revés, patas arriba

upstage [ápstédʒ] VT eclipsar

upstairs[1] [ápstérz] ADV (location) arriba, en el piso de arriba; (movement) [para] arriba

upstairs[2] [ápsterz] ADJ de arriba; N piso de arriba m

upstart [ápstart] N advenedizo -za mf

uptake [áptek] N **quick on the —** listo; **slow on the —** duro de entendederas

uptight [áptáit] ADJ (nervous) nervioso; (conventional) estreñido

up-to-the-minute [áptəðəmínit] ADJ actualizado

upturn [áptɚn] N (prices) aumento m, subida f; (markets) tendencia alcista f

upward [ápwəd] ADV (toward a higher place) hacia arriba; **— of** más de; ADJ ascendente; **—**

mobility ascenso social m; **— trend** tendencia al alza f

uranium [juréniəm] N uranio m

urban [ə́bən] ADJ urbano; **— blight** tugurización f; **— legend** leyenda urbana f; **— renewal** renovación urbana f; **— sprawl** expansión urbana f

urbanism [ə́bənizəm] N urbanismo m

urchin [ə́tʃin] N pilluelo -la mf, guaje -ja mf

urethra [juríθrə] N uretra f

urge [ə́dʒ] VT (exhort) exhortar, urgir; (beg) rogar; (propose) propugnar; **to — on** animar; N impulso m, gana f

urgency [ə́dʒənsi] N urgencia f

urgent [ə́dʒənt] ADJ urgente

urinal [jurənl] N urinario m, mingitorio m

urinalysis [jurənǽlisis] N análisis de orina m

urinary [jurəneri] ADJ urinario; **— tract** vías urinarias f pl

urinate [júrinet] VI/VT orinar

urine [júrin] N orina f

URL [Uniform Resource Locator] [juárél] N URL m

urn [ɚn] N urna f

urologist [jurálədʒist] N urólogo -ga mf

Uruguay [júrəgwai] N Uruguay m

Uruguayan [jurəgwáiən] ADJ & N uruguayo -ya mf

us [ʌs] PRON nos; **she saw —** nos vio; **he came with —** vino con nosotros; **he gave it to —** nos lo dio [a nosotros]

USA [United States of America] [júéʃé] N EEUU m sg/pl

usable [júzəbəł] ADJ utilizable, aprovechable

usage [júsidʒ] N uso m, costumbre f

USB [Universal Serial Bus] [júésbí] N USB m; **— port** puerto USB m

use[1] [juz] VT usar, utilizar (also exploit); (consume) gastar; (take advantage of) aprovecharse de; VI **to — up** gastar, agotar

use[2] [jus] N (application) uso m; (utilization) empleo m, utilización f, aprovechamiento m; (usefulness) utilidad f; **it is of no —** es inútil; **out of —** en desuso; **to have no — for** no soportar; **to make — of** usar, utilizar; **to put to —** utilizar; **what is the — of it?** ¿para qué sirve?

used[1] [juzd] ADJ usado

used[2] [just] VI **to be — to** estar acostumbrado a; **it — to be green** antes era verde

useful [júsfəł] ADJ útil

usefulness [júsfəłnis] N utilidad f

useless [júsłis] ADJ inútil, inservible

uselessness [júsłisnis] N inutilidad f

user [júzə] N usuario -ria mf; **—-friendly** fácil de utilizar; **— group** grupo de usuarios m; **—name** nombre del usuario m

usher [ʌ́ʃə] N acomodador -ora mf; VT conducir, acompañar; **to — in** (a person) acompañar;

(an era) anunciar, marcar el comienzo de

usual [júʒuəl] ADJ (habitual) usual, habitual; (everyday) de todos los días; **as** — como siempre; **she wasn't her** — **self** no era la de siempre; **the** — **thing** lo normal; **more than** — más que de costumbre

usually [júʒuəli] ADV generalmente, normalmente; **he** — **doesn't mind** no suele importarle

usurp [jusɚp] VI/VT usurpar

usury [júʒəri] N usura f

utensil [juténsəl] N utensilio m, útil m

uterine [júDə‐ɪn] ADJ uterino

uterus [júDə‐əs] N útero m

UTI [**urinary tract infection**] [jútíáɪ] N infección del tracto urinario f

utilitarian [jutɪlɪtɛ́rɪən] ADJ utilitario

utility [jutɪlɪti] N (usefulness) utilidad f; (public service) empresa de servicio público f, empresa de agua o electricidad f; — **furniture** muebles prácticos m pl; — **program** programa utilitario m; — **room** lavadero m

utilization [judlɪzéʃən] N utilización f

utilize [júdlaɪz] VT utilizar

utmost [Átmost] ADJ (extreme) sumo, extremo; (farthest) más distante; N máximo m; **he did his** — hizo cuanto pudo; **to the** — al máximo

utopia [jutópiə] N utopía f

utter [ÁDɚ] VT (emit) dar, proferir; (say) decir, pronunciar; (make circulate) poner en circulación; ADJ absoluto, completo

utterance [ÁDə‐əns] N (of words) enunciado m; (of money) emisión f

uvula [júvjələ] N campanilla f, úvula f

Uzbek [úzbɛk] ADJ & N uzbeko -ka mf

Uzbekistan [uzbékɪstæn] N Uzbekistán m

Vv

vacancy [vékənsi] N (job) vacante f; (room in hotel) habitación libre f; **no** — completo

vacant [vékənt] ADJ (position) vacante; (expression) vacío; (seat, room) libre

vacate [véket] VI/VT (a room) desalojar, desocupar; (a contract) anular; (a position) dejar vacante

vacation [vekéʃən] N vacaciones f pl; **on** — de vacaciones

vaccinate [væksənet] VI/VT vacunar

vaccination [væksənéʃən] N vacunación f

vaccine [væksín] N vacuna f

vacillate [væsəlet] VI vacilar

vacuum [vækjum] N vacío m; — **cleaner** aspiradora f; — **tube** tubo de vacío m; ADJ —-

packed envasado al vacío; VI/VT pasar la aspiradora

vagabond [vǽgəbɑnd] ADJ & N vagabundo -da mf

vagina [vədʒáɪnə] N vagina f

vaginal [vǽdʒənl] ADJ vaginal; — **bleeding** hemorragia vaginal f; — **discharge** flujo vaginal m; — **itching** escozor vaginal m

vaginitis [vædʒɪnáɪtɪs] N vaginitis f

vagrancy [végrənsi] N vagancia f

vagrant [végrənt] ADJ & N vagabundo -da mf

vague [veg] ADJ vago, indistinto

vain [ven] ADJ (futile) vano, hueco; (proud of appearance) vanidoso; **in** — en vano

Valencian [vəlénsiən] ADJ & N valenciano -na

valentine [vǽləntaɪn] N (card) tarjeta del día de San Valentín f; (person) querido -da mf; —**'s Day** día de San Valentín m, día de los enamorados m

valet [vælé] N (manservant) criado m; (in a hotel) mozo de habitación m; (car parker) aparcacoches m sg

valiant [væljənt] ADJ valiente

valid [vælɪd] ADJ válido, valedero; **to be/ become** — tener efectividad

validity [vəlɪ́dɪti] N validez f

valise [vəlíz] N maleta f, valija f

valley [væli] N valle m

valor [vǽlɚ] N valor m, valentía f

valorize [vǽləraɪz] VT valorar

valorous [vǽləəs] ADJ valeroso, valiente

valuable [væljəbəl] ADJ valioso, preciado; N —**s** objetos de valor m pl

valuation [væljuéʃən] N (value) valoración f; (appraisal) tasación f, valuación f

value [vælju] N valor m; VT valorar

valve [vælv] N (for fluids) válvula f; (on mollusks) valva f

vamp [væmp] N vampiresa f; VT seducir

vampire [væmpaɪr] N vampiro m

van [væn] N camioneta f

vandal [vændl] N vándalo m

vane [ven] N (for weather) veleta f; (of a fan, windmill) aspa f; (of propeller) paleta f

vanilla [vənílə] N vainilla f

vanish [vænɪʃ] VI desaparecer, esfumarse

vanity [vænɪDi] N vanidad f; — **table** tocador m

vanquish [vǽnkwɪʃ] VT vencer

vantage point [vǽntɪdʒpɔɪnt] N mirador m

Vanuatu [vɑnuátu] N Vanuatu m

Vanuatuan [vɑnuátuən] ADJ & N vanuatuense m

vapor [vépɚ] N vapor m, humo m

vaporize [vépəaɪz] VI/VT vaporizar[se]

variable [vériəbəl] ADJ & N variable f; — **annuity** anualidad variable f

variance [vériəns] N discrepancia f, desacuerdo m; **to be at** — no concordar

variant [vériənt] N variante f, modalidad f

variation [veriéʃən] N variación f

varicose [vǽrɪkos] ADJ varicoso; — **veins** Sp

varices *f pl; Am* várices *f pl*

varied [vérɪd] ADJ variado, vario

variegated [vérɪɪɡedɪd] ADJ variopinto

variety [vəráɪɪDi] N variedad *f*

various [vérɪəs] ADJ vario

varnish [várnɪʃ] N barniz *m*, charol *m*; VT barnizar, charolar

varsity [vársɪDi] N equipo universitario *m*

vary [véri] VI/VT variar

vascular [væskjəlɚ] ADJ vascular

vase [ves] N jarrón *m*; (for flowers) florero *m*

vasectomy [vəséktəmi] N vasectomía *f*

Vaseline™ [væsəlín] N vaselina *f*

vast [væst] ADJ vasto, inmenso

vastly [væstli] ADV enormemente

vastness [væstnɪs] N inmensidad *f*

vat [væt] N tina *f*, barrica *f*

VAT [value-added tax] [viétí] N IVA *m*

Vatican City [vǽDɪkənsíDi] N Ciudad del Vaticano *f*

vaudeville [vódvɪl] N vodevil *m*

vault [vɔlt] N (arched structure) bóveda *f*; (burial chamber) panteón *m*; (place for valuables) cámara acorazada *f*; (jump) salto *m*; VT (cover with a vault) abovedar; VI/VT (jump) saltar

VCR [videocassette recorder] [vísíár] N *Am* video *m; Sp* vídeo *m*

veal [vil] N ternera *f*; — **cutlet** chuleta de ternera *f*

vector [vɛktɚ] N vector *m*

veer [vir] VI/VT virar; N virada *f*

vegan [vígən] ADJ & N vegan *mf*

vegetable [védʒtəbəl] N (food) verdura *f*, hortaliza *f*; (plant, comatose person) vegetal *m*; — **garden** huerto *m*; (large) huerta *f*; — **kingdom** reino vegetal *m*; — **oil** aceite vegetal *m*

vegetarian [vedʒɪtériən] ADJ & N vegetariano -na *mf*

vegetate [védʒɪtet] VI vegetar

vegetation [vedʒɪtéʃən] N vegetación *f*

vegetative [védʒɪtetɪv] ADJ vegetativo

vehemence [víəməns] N vehemencia *f*

vehement [víəmənt] ADJ vehemente

vehicle [víɪkəl] N vehículo *m*

veil [vel] N velo *m*; VT velar

vein [ven] N (blood vessel, style) vena *f*; (small deposit of ore) veta *f*; (large deposit of ore) filón *m*

veined [vend] ADJ (marble) veteado; (leaf) nervado

velocity [vəlásɪDi] N velocidad *f*

velvet [vélvɪt] N terciopelo *m*; ADJ (of velvet) de terciopelo; (like velvet) aterciopelado

velvety [vélvɪDi] ADJ aterciopelado

vendetta [vɛndéDə] N vendetta *f*

vending machine [véndɪŋməʃin] N expendedor automático *m*, máquina expendedora *f*

vendor [véndɚ] N vendedor -ora *mf*, proveedor

-ora *mf*; (in a stall) puestero -ra *mf*

veneer [vənír] N (layer of wood) chapa *f*; (outward appearance) barniz *m*; VT chapar, enchapar

venerable [vénəəbəl] ADJ venerable

venerate [vénəret] VT venerar

veneration [venəréʃən] N veneración *f*

venetian blind [vəníʃənbláɪnd] N veneciana *f*

Venezuela [venɪzwélə] N Venezuela *f*

Venezuelan [venɪzwélən] ADJ & N venezolano -na *mf*

vengeance [véndʒəns] N venganza *f*; **with a —** (violently) con furia; (energetically) con ganas

vengeful [véndʒfəl] ADJ vengativo

venison [vénəsən] N carne de venado *f*

venom [vénəm] N veneno *m*

venomous [vénəməs] ADJ venenoso

vent [vɛnt] N (outlet for air) ventilación *f*; (opening of a volcano) chimenea *f*; **to give — to anger** desahogar la ira; VI/VT desahogar[se], descargar[se]

ventilate [véntlet] VI/VT ventilar[se]

ventilation [ventléʃən] N ventilación *f*

ventilator [véntleDɚ] N ventilador *m*

ventricle [véntrɪkəl] N ventrículo *m*

venture [véntʃɚ] N (adventure) aventura *f*; (business enterprise) empresa *f*; — **capital** capital de riesgo *m*; VI/VT aventurar[se], arriesgar[se]

venue [vénju] N lugar *m*

veranda [vərǽndə] N porche *m*, terraza *f*

verb [vɚb] N verbo *m*

verbal [vɚbəl] ADJ (linguistic, related to verbs) verbal; (not written) oral

verbatim [vɚbéDəm] ADJ textual; ADV textualmente

verbiage [vɚbiɪdʒ] N palabrerío *m*

verbose [vɚbós] ADJ verboso

verdict [vɚdɪkt] N veredicto *m*

verdure [vɚdʒɚ] N *lit* verdura *f*

verge [vɚdʒ] ADV LOC **on the — of** al borde de, a punto de; VI **to — on** rayar en, lindar con

verification [verɪfɪkéʃən] N verificación *f*, comprobación *f*

verify [vérɪfaɪ] VT verificar, constatar, comprobar

veritable [vérɪDəbəl] ADJ verdadero

vermillion [vɚmíljən] ADJ & N bermellón *m*

vermin [vɚmɪn] N bichos *m pl*

vermouth [vɚmúθ] N vermú *m*

vernacular [vɚnǽkjəlɚ] ADJ vernáculo; N (plain language) lengua vernácula *f*

versatile [vɚsədl] ADJ versátil

verse [vɚs] N verso *m*; (stanza) estrofa *f*; (line of poem) verso *m*; (in Bible) versículo *m*

versed [vɚst] ADJ versado

version [vɚʒən] N versión *f*

versus [vɚsəs] PREP contra; (in sports) versus

vertebra [vɚ́dəbrə] N vértebra *f*
vertebrate [vɚ́dəbrɪt] ADJ vertebrado
vertical [vɚ́dɪkəl] ADJ vertical
vertigo [vɚ́dɪgo] N vértigo *m*
very [véri] ADV muy; — **many** muchísimos; — **much** muchísimo; **it is — cold today** hace mucho frío hoy; ADJ (same) mismo; (mere) mero
vessel [vésəl] N (container) vasija *f*; (duct) vaso *m*; (ship) nave *f*
vest [vest] N chaleco *m*; VT conferir; **—ed interests** intereses creados *m pl*
vestibule [véstɪbjuł] N vestíbulo *m*, zaguán *m*
vestige [véstɪʤ] N vestigio *m*
vet [vet] N (veterinarian) veterinario -ria *mf*; (veteran) veterano -na militar *mf*; VT evaluar
veteran [vέdərən] ADJ & N veterano -na *mf*
veterinarian [vɛdərənériən] N veterinario -ria *mf*
veterinary [vɛ́dərɛneri] ADJ veterinario; **— medicine** veterinaria *f*
veto [vído] N veto *m*; VT vetar
vex [veks] VT molestar, irritar
via [váiə, víə] PREP (by way of) vía; (by means of) por
viability [vaiəbílɪdi] N viabilidad *f*
viable [váiəbəl] ADJ viable
vial [váiəł] N ampolla *f*, frasco *m*
vibrate [váibret] VI/VT vibrar
vibration [vaibréʃən] N vibración *f*
vibrator [váibredɚ] N vibrador *m*
vicarious [vaikériəs] ADJ indirecto
vice [vais] N vicio *m*
vice president [váisprézIdənt] N vicepresidente -ta *mf*
viceroy [váisrɔi] N virrey *m*
viceroyalty [vaisróiəłti] N virreinato
vice versa [váisəvɚ́sə] ADV viceversa
vicinity [visínɪdi] N vecindad *f*, cercanías *f pl*, aledaños *m pl*
vicious [víʃəs] ADJ (violent) violento, sanguinario; (evil) maligno, perverso; (malicious) malicioso; **— circle** círculo vicioso *m*; **— dog** perro fiero *m*, perro bravo *m*
vicissitude [visísitud] N vicisitud *f*, peripecia *f*
victim [víktim] N víctima *f*
victimize [víktəmaiz] VT (make victim) victimizar; (dupe) estafar
victor [víktɚ] N vencedor -ora *mf*
victorious [viktóriəs] ADJ victorioso
victory [víktəri] N victoria *f*
video [vídio] N Am video *m*; Sp vídeo *m*; **—cassette** Am video *m*; Sp vídeo *m*; **—cassette recorder** videocasete *m*; **—conference** videoconferencia *f*; **— console** videoconsola *f*; **— game** videojuego *m*; **— portal** Am portal de videos *m*; Sp portal de vídeos *m*; **—tape** Am cinta de video *f*; Sp

cinta de vídeo *f*; **— clip** videoclip *m*
vie [vai] VI competir; **to — for power** disputarse el poder
Vietnam [vietnám] N Vietnam *m*
Vietnamese [viitnəmíz] ADJ & N vietnamita *mf*
view [vju] N (field of vision) vista *f*; (opinion) opinión *f*; (panorama) visión panorámica *f*; **—point** punto de vista *m*; **in — of** en vista de; **to be within —** estar a la vista; **with a — to** con el propósito de; VT (see) ver; (consider) enfocar
viewer [vjúɚ] N telespectador -ora *mf*, televidente *mf*
vigil [víʤəl] N vigilia *f*, vela *f*; **to keep —** velar
vigilance [víʤələns] N vigilancia *f*
vigilant [víʤələnt] ADJ vigilante
vigor [vígɚ] N vigor *m*, pujanza *f*, dinamismo *m*
vigorous [vígɚəs] ADJ vigoroso
vile [vail] ADJ (evil) vil, ruin; (foul, bad) pésimo
villa [vílə] N quinta *f*, casa de campo *f*
village [vílıʤ] N aldea *f*, villa *f*
villager [vílıʤɚ] N aldeano -na *mf*
villain [vílən] N villano -na *mf*
villainous [vílənəs] ADJ vil, villano
villainy [víləni] N villanía *f*, vileza *f*
vindicate [víndıket] VT reivindicar, vindicar
vindication [vindikéʃən] N reivindicación *f*, vindicación *f*
vindictive [vindíktiv] ADJ vengativo
vine [vain] N (grapevine) vid *f*; (decorative) parra *f*; (stem) sarmiento *m*; (climbing plant) enredadera *f*
vinegar [vínigɚ] N vinagre *m*
vineyard [vínjəd] N viña *f*, viñedo *m*
vintage [víntıʤ] N (act or season of gathering grapes) vendimia *f*; (harvest of grapes) cosecha *f*; (year) año *m*; ADJ (wine) añejo; (classic) excelente; (old) antiguo, de colección; (typical) típico
vinyl [váinł] N vinilo *m*
viola [vióla] N viola *f*
violate [váiəlet] VT violar; (a law) violar, quebrantar
violation [vaiəléʃən] N violación *f*; (traffic) infracción *f*
violence [váiələns] N violencia *f*
violent [váiələnt] ADJ violento
violet [váiəlit] N (flower) violeta *f*; (color) violeta *m*; ADJ violeta
violin [vaiəlín] N violín *m*
violinist [vaiəlínist] N violinista *mf*
VIP [very important person] [víáipí] N & ADJ VIP *m*
viper [váipɚ] N víbora *f*
viral [váirəł] ADJ viral
virgin [vɚ́ʤin] ADJ & N virgen *f*; (uninitiated) no iniciado -da *mf*; **— Islands** Islas Vírgenes *f pl*
virginal [vɚ́ʤənl] ADJ virginal
virile [vírəł] ADJ viril

virility [vərílIDi] N virilidad *f*

virology [vaIráləd͡ʒi] N virología *f*

virtual [vɜ́tʃuəl] ADJ virtual; — **community** comunidad virtual *f*; — **reality** realidad virtual *f*; — **stores** tiendas virtuales *f pl*

virtually [vɜ́tʃuəli] ADV (remotely) virtualmente; (almost) prácticamente

virtue [vɜ́tʃu] N virtud *f*

virtuosity [vɜtʃuásIDi] N virtuosismo *m*

virtuoso [vɜtʃuóso] ADJ & N virtuoso -sa *mf*

virtuous [vɜ́tʃuəs] ADJ virtuoso

virulent [vírələnt] ADJ virulento

virus [váIrəs] N virus *m*; — **-free** libre de virus; — **protection software** programas de protección contra virus *m pl*

visa [vízə] N Am visa *f*; Sp visado *m*

vis-à-vis [vízəvi] PREP con respecto a

visceral [vísərəl] ADJ visceral

viscous [vískəs] ADJ viscoso

vise [vaIs] N tornillo de banco *m*

visibility [vIzIbílIDi] N visibilidad *f*

visible [vízəbəl] ADJ visible

Visigoth [vízIgɔθ] N visigodo -da *mf*

vision [víʒən] N (sense, apparition) visión *f*; (eyesight) vista *f*

visionary [víʒɛneri] ADJ & N visionario -ria *mf*

visit [vízIt] VT visitar; (afflict) infligir; VI estar de visita; **to — with** charlar con; N (stay) visita *f*; (chat) charla *f*

visitation [vIzItéʃən] N (apparition) visitación *f*; (punishment) castigo *m*; (parental right) régimen de visita *m*

visiting [vízIDIŋ] ADJ (team) visitante

visitor [vízIDə] N visita *f*, visitante *mf*

visor [váIzə] N visera *f*

vista [vístə] N (visual) vista *f*; (mental) perspectiva *f*

visual [víʒuəl] ADJ visual; — **recognition** reconocimiento visual *m*

visualize [víʒuəlaIz] VT visualizar, imaginar

vital [váIdl] ADJ vital; — **signs** signos vitales *m pl*

vitality [vaItǽlIDi] N vitalidad *f*

vitamin [váIdəmIn] N vitamina *f*

vituperation [vaItupəréʃən] N vituperación *f*, vituperio *m*

vivacious [vaIvéʃəs] ADJ vivaz, vivaracho

vivacity [vaIvǽsIDi] N vivacidad *f*

vivid [vívId] ADJ vívido, vivo

vivisection [vIvIsɛkʃən] N vivisección *f*

vocabulary [vokǽbjəleri] N vocabulario *m*

vocal [vókəl] ADJ (musical) vocal; (outspoken) vociferante; — **cords** cuerdas vocales *f pl*

vocalic [vokǽlIk] ADJ vocálico

vocation [vokéʃən] N vocación *f*

vociferous [vosífɚəs] ADJ vociferante

vodka [vádkə] N vodka *m*

vogue [vog] N boga *f*, moda *f*; **in —** en boga, de moda

voice [vɔIs] N voz *f*; — **mail** correo de voz *m*,

contestador automático *m*; — **recognition** reconocimiento de voz *m*; — **synthesis** síntesis de voz *f*; VT expresar

voicing [vɔ́IsIŋ] N sonoridad *f*

void [vɔId] ADJ (devoid, empty) vacío; (not binding) nulo, inválido; — **of** desprovisto de; N vacío *m*; VT (bowels) evacuar; (a check) anular; — **ed check** cheque anulado *m*

volatile [válədl] ADJ (liquid) volátil; (political situation) explosivo, conflictivo; (stock market) voluble; (temperament) cambiante

volcanic [vɑlkǽnIk] ADJ volcánico

volcano [vɑlkéno] N volcán *m*

volition [volíʃən] N volición *f*; **of one's own —** por su propia voluntad

volley [váli] N (of firearms) descarga *f*; (of protests, arrows, stones) lluvia *f*; (of a tennis ball) volea *f*; — **ball** voleibol *m*, balonvolea *m*; VI/VT (shoot bullets) descargar; (hit tennis balls) volear

volt [volt] N voltio *m*

voltage [vóltId͡ʒ] N voltaje *m*

volume [váljəm] N volumen *m*, tomo *m*

voluminous [vəlúmInəs] ADJ voluminoso

voluntary [válənteri] ADJ voluntario

volunteer [valəntír] ADJ & N voluntario -ria *mf*; VI/VT (offer) ofrecer[se], brindar[se]; RP comedir[se]; VI (do volunteer work) trabajar de voluntario -ria

voluptuous [vəlʌ́ptʃuəs] ADJ voluptuoso

vomit [vámIt] N vómito *m*; VI/VT vomitar

voodoo [vúdu] N vudú *m*

voracious [vəréʃəs] ADJ voraz

vortex [vórtɛks] N vórtice *m*

vote [vot] N (right, ballot) voto *m*; (act of voting) votación *f*; VI votar; VT (a bill) aprobar; (a political party) votar a/por; **to — against** votar en contra; **to — in favor** votar a favor; **to — to do something** votar por hacer algo

voter [vódɚ] N votante *f*

voting [vódIŋ] N votación *f*

vouch [vautʃ] VI **to — for** dar fe de, salir de fiador a, fiar a; VT **to — that** dar fe de que

voucher [váutʃɚ] N (receipt) comprobante *m*; (coupon) vale *m*; (person) fiador -ora *mf*, garante *mf*

vow [vau] N voto *m*; **to take a —** prometer; VT jurar

vowel [váuəl] N vocal *f*

voyage [vɔIId͡ʒ] N (long trip) viaje *m*; (trip by sea) travesía *f*; VI viajar

voyeur [vɔIɜ́] N mirón -ona *mf*

VP [**vice president**] [vípí] N vice presidente -ta *mf*

vulgar [vʌ́lgɚ] ADJ (rude) ordinario, grosero, soez; (popular, vernacular) vulgar

vulgarity [vʌlgǽrIDi] N ordinariez *f*, vulgaridad *f*

vulnerable [vʌ́lnɚəbəl] ADJ vulnerable

vulture [vʌ́ltʃɚ] N buitre *m*

Ww

wacky [wǽki] ADJ (person) chiflado; (idea) descabellado

wad [wɑd] N (for artillery, for filling) taco *m*; (ball) pelota *f*, pelotón *m*; (of money) rollo *m*, fajo *m*; (of cotton) bola *f*; VI/VT (a firearm) atacar; (a piece of paper) hacer una pelota [con]

waddle [wɑ́dl] VT anadear, andar como un pato; N anadeo *m*

wade [wed] VI andar por el agua; **to — through a book** leer con dificultad un libro

wafer [wéfɚ] N (cookie) oblea *f*; (in Catholic ritual) hostia *f*; (computer) lámina/oblea de silicio *f*

waffle [wáfəl] ADJ Sp gofre *m*; Am wafle *m*; — **iron** Sp plancha para hacer gofres *f*; Am waflera *f*

waft [wæft] VI flotar; VT llevar por el aire; N (of air) ráfaga *f*; (of odor) ola *f*

wag [wæg] VI/VT menear[se], mover[se]; **to — the tail** colear; N (movement) meneo *m*, movimiento *m*; (joker) bromista *mf*

wage [wedʒ] N salario *m*; — **earner** asalariado -da *mf*; (paid daily) jornalero -ra *mf*; —**s** salario *m*; (daily) jornal *m*; — **scale** escala salarial *f*; VT (war) hacer; (battle) librar

wager [wédʒɚ] N apuesta *f*; VI/VT apostar

wagon [wǽgən] N (horsedrawn) carro *m*; (covered) carreta *f*; (toy) carrito *m*; **to fix someone's —** vengarse de alguien; **to be on the —** abstenerse de bebidas alcohólicas

wail [wel] VI lamentar; N lamento *m*

waist [west] N cintura *f*; (of garment) talle *m*; —**band** pretina *f*; —**coat** chaleco *m*; —**line** talle *m*, cintura *f*

wait [wet] VI/VT esperar; **to — for** esperar; **to — on** servir; **to — tables** trabajar de camarero -ra; N espera *f*; **to lie in — for** estar en/al acecho de

waiter [wéɾɚ] N camarero *m*, mozo *m*, mesero *m*

waiting [wéɾɪŋ] N espera *f*; — **list** lista de espera *f*; — **room** sala de espera *f*

waitress [wétrɪs] N camarera *f*, moza *f*, mesera *f*

waive [wev] VT (rights) renunciar a; (a rule) hacer una excepción

waiver [wévɚ] N (of rights) renuncia *f*; (of rules) excepción *f*

wake [wek] VI/VT despertar[se]; **to — up** despertar[se]; N (at death) velatorio *m*; (of a ship) estela *f*, surco *m*; —**up call** (in a hotel) llamada del servicio despertador *f*; (to action) llamada de atención *f*; **in the — of** después de, detrás de

wakeful [wékfəl] ADJ (awake) despierto;

(insomniac) insomne

waken [wékən] VI/VT despertar[se]

Wales [welz] N Gales *m sg*

walk [wɔk] VI andar, caminar; (to a place) ir a pie; (go away) marcharse; (in baseball) sacar una base por bolas *f*; **to — back** volver a pie; **to — down** bajar a pie; **to — in** entrar caminando; **to — out** (to go out) salir caminando; (to abandon) dejar; (to strike) declararse en huelga; **to — up** subir a pie; VT (to cause to walk) hacer caminar; (to trace on foot) recorrer; **to — the streets** callejear; **to — someone** (baseball) darle una base por bolas; N (period of walking) paseo *m*, caminata *f*; (pace) paso *m*; (gait) andar *m*; — **of life** condición *f*; —**out** huelga *f*; **to take a —** pasear, dar un paseo

walker [wɔ́kɚ] N (device to aid walking) andador *m*; (one who walks) caminante *mf*; (in sports) marchista *mf*

walking [wɔ́kɪŋ] ADJ andante; — **papers** despido *m*; — **stick** bastón *m*

wall [wɔl] N (interior) pared *f*; (garden) muro *m*, tapia *f*; (fort) muralla *f*; (of silence) barrera *f*; —**paper** papel de empapelar *m*; —**flower** alhelí *m*; —**to-** de pared a pared; **to have one's back to the —** estar entre la espada y la pared; **to drive someone up the —** sacar a alguien de quicio; **I was climbing the —s** me moría de aburrimiento; **she was a —flower** no la sacaban a bailar; VT **to —paper** empapelar

wallet [wálɪt] N cartera *f*, billetera *f*

wallow [wálo] VI (roll) revolcarse; (indulge oneself) regodearse

walnut [wɔ́lnʌt] N nuez *f*; — **tree** nogal *m*

walrus [wɔ́lrəs] N morsa *f*

waltz [wɔlts] N vals *m*; VI valsar

wand [wɑnd] N (rod) vara *f*; (magic) varita *f*

wander [wándɚ] VI/VT vagar [por], errar [por]; **to — away** perderse; **my mind —s easily** me distraigo fácilmente

wanderer [wándərɚ] N vagabundo -da *mf*

wane [wen] VI menguar, flaquear; N **to be on the —** ir menguando

wannabe [wánəbi] N aspirante *mf*

want [wɑnt] VI/VT (desire) querer; **he —s judgment** le falta juicio; **he's —ed in Texas** se lo busca en Texas; N (desire) deseo *m*; (lack) falta *f*; (scarcity) escasez *f*; **to be in —** estar necesitado; — **ad** [anuncio] clasificado *m*

wanting [wántɪŋ] ADJ (lacking) falto; (deficient) deficiente

wanton [wántən] ADJ (immoderate) desenfrenado; (immoral) lascivo; (senseless, unprovoked) gratuito

war [wɔr] N guerra *f*; — **crime** crimen de guerra *m*; —**fare** guerra *f*; — **games** juegos de guerra *m pl*, simulacro de batalla *m*; **—head** ojiva *f*; **—ship** acorazado *m*; VI guerrear, hacer la guerra; **—like** bélico *f*

warble [wɔ́rbəl] VI gorjear; N gorjeo *m*

warbler [wɔ́rblə-] N (European) curruca *f*; (American) arañero *m*

ward [wɔrd] N (district) distrito *m*; (of a hospital) pabellón *m*; (of a tutor) pupilo -la *mf*; VI **to — off** resguardarse de, conjurar

warden [wɔ́rdn̩] N (of prison) alcaide *m*

wardrobe [wɔ́rdrob] N (room) guardarropa *m*; (furniture) armario *m*, ropero *m*; (garments) vestuario *m*, guardarropa *m*

warehouse [wɛ́rhaʊs] N almacén *m*, depósito *m*

wares [wɛrz] N mercancías *f pl*

warm [wɔrm] ADJ (bath) caliente; (clothes) abrigado; (weather) caluroso; (colors, reception) cálido; **—-blooded** de sangre caliente; **—hearted** de buen corazón; **it is — today** hace calor hoy; N **—up** precalentamiento *m*; VI/VT calentar[se]; **to — over** recalentar; **to — up** calentar[se], templar[se]; **it —s my heart** me alegra el corazón; **she —ed to the idea** se entusiasmó con la idea

warmth [wɔrmθ] N calor *m*, tibieza *f*

warn [wɔrn] VI/VT (advise of danger) advertir; (urge to behave) amonestar

warning [wɔ́rnɪŋ] N (of danger) advertencia *f*; (of punishment) amonestación *f*

warp [wɔrp] N (yarn) urdimbre *f*; (curve) comba *f*, alabeo *m*; VI/VT (wood) combar[se], alabear[se]; (character) deformar[se]; **he has a —ed personality** tiene una personalidad retorcida

warrant [wɔ́rənt] N orden *f*; **a — for his arrest** una orden de arresto contra él; VT garantizar

warranty [wɔ́rənti] N garantía *f*; VT garantizar

warrior [wɔ́riə-] N guerrero -ra *mf*

wart [wɔrt] N verruga *f*

wary [wɛ́ri] ADJ cauteloso, cauto; **to be — of** desconfiar de

was [wɑz] *see* be

wash [wɑʃ] VI/VT lavar[se]; **to — out** (a bottle) lavar; (a substance) quitar lavando; (a creekbed) erosionar; **to — up** lavarse; **the bottle was —ed up on the shore** la botella fue traída por el mar; **he was —ed away by the waves** fue arrastrado por las olas; **his excuse won't —** su excusa no va a colar; N (act of washing) lavado *m*; (clothes to be washed) ropa para lavar *f*; (washed clothes) ropa lavada *f*; **—cloth** toallita para lavarse *f*; **—out** (erosion) derrubio *m*; (failure) fracaso *m*; **—room** lavabo *m*, lavatorio *m*; **—-and-wear** de lava y pon, de no planchar; **—ed-up** fracasado; **—ed-out** desteñido

washable [wɑ́ʃəbəl] ADJ lavable

washer [wɑ́ʃə-] N (washing machine) lavadora *f*,

máquina de lavar *f*; (metal ring) arandela *f*; **—woman** lavandera *f*

washing [wɑ́ʃɪŋ] N lavado *m*; **— machine** lavadora *f*, máquina de lavar *f*

wasp [wɑsp] N avispa *f*

WASP [White Anglo-Saxon Protestant] [wɑsp] N persona blanca, anglosajona y protestante *f*

waste [west] VI/VT (squander resources) malgastar, desperdiciar; **to — away** consumirse; VT (squander time) perder; (murder) liquidar; N (of resources) desperdicio *m*, malgasto *m*, derroche *m*; (of time) pérdida *f*; (refuse) desperdicios *m pl*, desechos *m pl*; (liquid refuse) vertido *m*; **—land** tierra yerma *f*, páramo *m*; **— of time** pérdida de tiempo *f*; **—paper basket** papelera *f*; **— products** productos de desecho *m pl*; **— treatment** tratamiento de residuos *m*; **to go to —** desperdiciarse; **to lay — to** asolar

wasted [wéstɪd] ADJ (squandered) desperdiciado; (debilitated) consumido; (drunk) borracho

wasteful [wéstfəl] ADJ (person) despilfarrador, gastador; (method) antieconómico

watch [wɑtʃ] VI (look) mirar; (be careful) cuidarse; (be vigilant) vigilar; VT (view) mirar, ver; (observe) observar; (tend) cuidar; **— out for the cars!** ¡cuidado con los coches! **to — for** estar a la espera de; **to — over** proteger; N (timepiece) reloj *m*; (period of wakefulness) vela *f*, vigilia *f*; (vigilant guard) guardia *mf*; (duty shift) guardia *f*; (lookout) centinela *m*; **—band** pulsera *f*; **—dog** (type of dog) perro guardián *m*; (organization) organismo de control *m*; **—maker** relojero -ra *mf*; **—making** relojería *f*; **—man** vigilante *m*, sereno *m*; **—tower** atalaya *f*, torre de vigilancia *f*; **—word** (password) contraseña *f*; (motto) consigna *f*, lema *m*; **to be on the —** estar alerta; **to keep — on/over** vigilar a

watchful [wɑ́tʃfəl] ADJ alerta, atento

water [wɔ́də-] N agua *f*; **—bed** cama de agua *f*; **—bird** ave acuática *f*; **— buffalo** búfalo de agua *m*; **—color** acuarela *f*; **—cress** berro *m*; **—fall** (small) cascada *f*; (large) catarata *f*; **—front** muelles *m pl*; **—fountain** fuente *f*, Mex, RP llave *f*; **— heater** calentador de agua *m*; **— lily** nenúfar *m*; **—melon** sandía *f*; **— pistol** pistola de agua *f*; **— power** energía hidráulica *f*; **—shed** vertiente *f*; **— ski** esquí acuático *m*; **— softener** ablandador de agua *m*; **— sports** deportes acuáticos *m pl*; **—spout** (pipe) tubo de desagüe *m*; (tornado) tromba *f*; **— supply** abastecimiento de agua *m*; **— table** capa freática *f*; **— vapor** vapor de agua *m*; **—way** vía navegable *f*; **my — broke** se me rompieron las aguas, se me rompió la fuente; ADJ **—logged** empapado; **—proof** (fabric) impermeable; (watch) sumergible; **—tight** hermético; VT (irrigate) regar; (dilute) aguar; VI/VT (animals) abrevar; **—ed-down** (with water) aguado; (simplified) simplificado; (softened) suavizado; **to —proof** impermeabilizar; **to —-ski** hacer esquí acuático; **my eyes are —ing** me lloran los ojos; **it makes my mouth** — se me hace agua la boca

watery [wóɖəi] ADJ (watered-down) aguado; (like water) acuoso; (boggy) húmedo

watt [wɑt] N vatio m

wattage [wɑ́DIdʒ] N vataje m

wave [wev] N (radio) onda f; (water, heat, fashion) ola f; (of disgust, of people) oleada f; (with the hand) saludo m; **—length** longitud de onda f; **on the same —length** en la misma onda, en sintonía; VI (flag) ondear; (hair) ondular[se]; VI (greet) saludar con la mano; **to — good-bye** decir adiós con la mano

waver [wévɚ] VI (hesitate) vacilar, titubear; (falter) flaquear

wavy [wévi] ADJ ondeado, ondulado

wax [wæks] N cera f; (for seals) lacre m; **— paper** papel encerado m; VT (cover with wax) encerar; (defeat) derrotar; VI (moon) crecer; **to —poetic** ponerse poético

way [we] N (road) camino m; (manner) modo m, manera f; **—farer** caminante mf; **— in** entrada f; **— out** salida f; **—s** costumbres f pl; **—side** borde del camino m; **— through** paso m, pasaje m; **a long — off** muy lejos; **by — of London** por Londres; **by — of comparison** a modo de comparación; **by the —** a propósito; **in no —** de ningún modo; **on the — to** rumbo a; **to get out of the —** apartarse; **to go out of one's — to** desvivirse por; **to look the other —** hacer la vista gorda; **to lead the —** ir a la cabeza; **to be in a bad —** hallarse mal de salud; **to give —** (yield) ceder; (break) quebrarse; **to get one's — salirse** con la suya; **to make — for** abrir paso para; ADJ **—-out** estrafalario; VT **to —lay** (wait in ambush) estar al acecho de; (attack) asaltar; (stop) detener

wayward [wéwɚd] ADJ (disobedient) desobediente; (willful) porfiado

we [wi] PRON nosotros -as mf

weak [wik] ADJ débil; (deficient) flojo; **— force** fuerza débil f; **—-kneed** achicado; **— sister** (coward) cobarde mf; **— link** parte más delgada del hilo f

weaken [wíkən] VI/VT debilitar[se], quebrantar[se]

weakling [wíkliŋ] N alfeñique m

weakness [wíknıs] N debilidad f, flaqueza f; (deficiency) flojedad f

wealth [wɛłθ] N riqueza f

wealthy [wɛ́łθi] ADJ rico, adinerado, pudiente

wean [win] VT destetar; **to — oneself of** quitarse el vicio de

weapon [wɛ́pən] N arma f

wear [wɛr] VT (have on) llevar, tener puesto; (dress in habitually) usar; VI/VT (waste away) desgastar[se]; **to — away** gastar[se], desgastar[se]; **to — down** (a person) agotar; (a pencil) desgastar; **to — off** perder efecto; **to — on** prolongarse; **to — out** (make unfit) gastar[se], degastar[se], sobar[se]; (expend) agotar; **it —s well** es duradero; N (use) gasto m; (clothes) ropa f; (durability) durabilidad f; (deterioration) desgaste m; **— and tear** desgaste m

weariness [wírinıs] N cansancio m, fatiga f

wearing [wɛ́riŋ] ADJ (causing wear) desgastante; (causing fatigue) cansado

wearisome [wírisəm] ADJ fastidioso

weary [wíri] ADJ cansado, fatigado; VI/VT cansar[se], fatigar[se]

weasel [wízəł] N comadreja f

weather [wɛ́ðɚ] N tiempo m; (storm) tempestad f; **—-beaten** desgastado/curtido por la intemperie; **— bureau** oficina meteorológica f; **— conditions** condiciones atmosféricas f pl; **—man** meteorólogo m; **— report** parte meteorológico m; **—vane** veleta f; **it is fine —** hace buen tiempo; **to be under the —** estar enfermo; ADJ **—proof** resistente a la intemperie; VI/VT (a surface) gastar[se]; (skin) curtir; (crisis, storm) capear

weave [wiv] VT (cloth, basket) tejer, entretejer; (to put together) urdir, tramar; **to — together/into** entretejer, entrelazar; **to — one's way** zigzaguear; N tejido m

weaver [wívɚ] N tejedor -ora mf

web [wɛb] N (of a spider) telaraña f; (of lies) sarta f; (membrane) membrana f; (Internet) web f; (animal) palmípedo m; **— browser** navegador [web] m; **—cast** transmisión por la web f; **—foot** pata palmada f; **— hosting** alojamiento web m; **—master** administrador -ora de un sitio web mf; **— page** página web f; **—site** sitio web m; VT; **—footed** palmípedo; VI/VT **to —cast** transmitir por la web

wed [wɛd] VI/VT casarse [con]; VT casar m

wedding [wɛ́DIŋ] N boda f, casamiento m; **— day** día de boda m; **— dress** traje de novia m; **— ring** anillo de boda m

wedge [wɛdʒ] N cuña f; **to drive a — between** separar; VT acuñar, meter cuñas entre; **to be —d between** estar apretado entre

Wednesday [wɛ́nzde] N miércoles m

wee [wi] ADJ chiquito, pequeñito

weed [wid] N mala hierba f; (marijuana) hierba f; **—killer** herbicida m; VT deshierbar, escardar; **to — out** eliminar

week [wik] N semana *f*; **—day** día de semana *m*; **—end** fin de semana *m*; **a — from today** de aquí en una semana

weekly [wíkli] ADJ semanal; ADV semanalmente; N semanario *m*

weep [wip] VI llorar, lagrimear

weeping [wípɪŋ] ADJ lloroso; **— willow** sauce llorón *m*; N llanto *m*

weevil [wívəl] N gorgojo *m*

weigh [we] VI/VT pesar; (consider) ponderar, sopesar, barajar; **to — anchor** levar anclas; **to — down** agobiar, abrumar; **to — on one's conscience** pesar en la conciencia de uno

weight [wet] N (heaviness, importance) peso *m*; (for clocks, scales, barbells) pesa *f*; **—lifting / —training** levantamiento de pesas *m*, halterofilia *f*; **—-watcher** persona a dieta *f*; **to put on —** engordar; **to lose —** adelgazar; VT (add weight) añadir peso; (in statistics) ponderar; **to — someone down** agobiarle a uno

weightless [wétlɪs] ADJ ingrávido

weighty [wédi] ADJ importante

weird [wɪrd] ADJ (strange) extraño; (supernatural) misterioso

weirdo [wírdo] N bicho raro *m*, ente *m*

welcome [wɛ́lkəm] N bienvenida *f*; ADJ bienvenido; **— mat** alfombrilla *f*, felpudo *m*; **— rest** descanso agradable *m*; **you are —** no hay de qué, de nada; **you are — here** estás en tu casa; **you are — to use it** a tus órdenes; VT dar la bienvenida a, acoger

weld [wɛld] VI/VT soldar[se]; N soldadura *f*

welfare [wɛ́lfɛr] N (good fortune) bienestar *m*; (public assistance) asistencia social *f*; **— state** estado de bienestar *m*

well [wɛl] ADV bien; **— then** pues bien; **—-being** bienestar *m*; **—-nigh** casi, muy cerca de; **he is — over fifty** tiene mucho más de cincuenta años; **all is —** todo está bien; INTERJ ¡bueno! ADJ (healthy) bien de salud, sano; N (of water, oil) pozo *m*; (of staircase) caja *f*; **—-spring** fuente *f*, manantial *m*; ADJ **—-bred** bien educado; **—-defined** bien definido; **—-done** (steak) bien cocido; (a task) bien hecho; **—-fed** bien alimentado; **—-founded** bien fundamentado; **—-groomed** bien arreglado, aseado; **—-heeled** adinerado; **—-informed** bien informado; **—-known** (of a fact) bien sabido; (of a person) bien conocido, notorio; **—-made** bien hecho; **—-meaning** bien intencionado; **—-off** adinerado, acomodado; **—-read** leído, educado; **—-rounded** completo; **—-spoken** bien hablado; **—-to-do** adinerado; VI **tears —ed up in his eyes** se le llenaron los ojos de lágrimas

wellness [wɛ́lnɪs] N (health) salud *f*; (health care) medicina preventiva *f*

welsh [wɛlʃ] VI **to — on** (a debt) no pagar; (a promise) no cumplir

Welsh [wɛlʃ] ADJ & N galés -esa *mf*

welt [wɛlt] N verdugón *m*

went [wɛnt] *see* go

wept [wɛpt] *see* weep

were [wɚ] *see* be

west [wɛst] N (cardinal point) oeste *m*; (hemisphere) occidente *m*; **— Berlin** Berlín occidental *m*; **— Indies** Antillas *f pl*; ADJ **— wind** viento del oeste *m*; ADV (direction) hacia el oeste; (location) al oeste

western [wɛ́stɚn] ADJ occidental, del oeste; N (movie genre) película del oeste *f*

westerner [wɛ́stɚnɚ] N occidental *mf*

westward [wɛ́stwɚd] ADV hacia el oeste; ADJ occidental

wet [wɛt] ADJ (drenched) mojado; (damp, rainy) húmedo; **— blanket** aguafiestas *mf sg*; **—land** humedal *m*; **— nurse** nodriza *f*; **— paint** pintura fresca *f*; **— suit** traje de buzo *m*; VI/VT (soak) mojar[se]; (dampen) humedecer[se]

wetness [wɛ́tnɪs] N humedad *f*

whack [hwæk] VI/VT (hit) golpear, pegar; (assassinate) *fam* liquidar; **to — off** (cut) cortar; N (blow) golpazo *m*; *Sp vulg* hostia *f*; **to take a — at** hacer un intento de; **out of —** descompuesto, averiado

whale [hwel] N ballena *f*; VI pescar ballenas

wharf [hwɔrf] N muelle *m*, embarcadero *m*

what [hwɑt] INTERR PRON & N qué; **— did you say?** ¿qué dijiste? **— for?** ¿para qué? **—'s the matter?** ¿qué pasa? **—'s the score?** ¿cómo va el marcador? **and —not** y demás; REL PRON lo que; **come — may** venga lo que venga; **anyplace —soever** en cualquier lugar; **so —?** y qué? **take — you need** toma lo que necesites; ADJ qué; **— books did you want?** ¿qué libros querías? **take — books you need** toma los libros que necesites; INTERJ cómo, qué; **— happy children!** ¡qué niños más felices! **— luck!** ¡qué buena suerte!

whatever [hwɑtévɚ] PRON lo que; **do it, — happens** hazlo, pase lo que pase; **— you may think** pienses lo que pienses; **— do you mean?** ¿qué demonios quieres decir? **take — you need** toma lo que necesites; ADJ any **— person —** una persona cualquiera / cualquier persona; **— no money —** nada de dinero; INTERJ (anything) ¡lo que sea! (I give up) ¡lo que tú digas!

wheat [hwit] N trigo *m*; **— germ** germen de trigo *m*

wheel [hwil] N (disc) rueda *f*; (of cheese) horma *f*; (for pottery) torno *m*; (for steering a car) volante *m*; (for steering a ship) timón *m*;

—barrow carretilla *f*; **—base** batalla *f*, paso *m*; **—chair** silla de ruedas *f*; **—s** (car) *fam* coche *m*; VT (a round object) hacer rodar; (a person, bicycle, wheelchair) empujar; VI **to — out** sacar rodando; **to — in** entrar rodando; **to — around** girar sobre los talones

wheeze [hwiz] N resuello ruidoso *m*; VI resollar

when [hwɛn] ADV & CONJ cuando; INTERJ, ADV, & N cuándo

whenever [hwɛnévɚ] CONJ **— I see him** (each time) cada vez que lo veo; ADV (at a future time) **— I see him** cuando lo vea

where [hwɛr] ADV, N, & INTERR PRON dónde *m*; (direction) adónde; CONJ donde; (direction) adonde

whereabouts [hwɛ́rəbaʊts] N paradero *m*; INTERR ADV dónde

whereas [hwɛrǽz] CONJ mientras que; (in preambles) visto que, considerando que

whereby [hwɛrbái] ADV por lo cual

wherefore [hwɛ́rfɔr] ADV por lo cual

wherein [hwɛrín] ADV en donde

whereof [hwɛráv] REL PRON de que; INTERR PRON de qué

whereupon [hwɛrəpán] ADV después de lo cual

wherever [hwɛrévɚ] ADV dondequiera que

wherewithal [hwɛ́rwɪðɔl] N medios *m pl*, fondos *m pl*

whet [hwɛt] VT (stimulate) estimular; (sharpen) afilar; **—stone** piedra de afilar *f*

whether [hwɛ́ðɚ] CONJ **— we like it or not** nos guste o no nos guste; **I doubt — we can do it** dudo [de] que lo podamos hacer; **he asked — I was coming** me preguntó si venía

which [hwɪtʃ] INTERR PRON cuál[es]; **— do you want?** ¿cuál[es] quieres? REL PRON que; **the apple, — I just bought** la manzana, que acabo de comprar; **the book of — I spoke** el libro del que / del cual hablé; **that — you don't know can hurt you** lo que no sabes puede hacerte daño; INTERR ADJ qué, cuál[es] de; **— house is it?** ¿qué casa es? ¿cuál de las casas es?

whichever [hwɪtʃévɚ] PRON & ADJ (no matter which) cualquiera [que]; **— you choose, you'll regret it later** elijas el que elijas, te arrepentirás después; (anyone that) el que / la que; **choose — you like** elije el que quieras

whiff [hwɪf] N (waft) soplo *m*; (odors, scandal) bocanada *f*, tufillo *m*; **to take a —** oler

while [hwaɪl] N rato *m*; **a short —** un ratito; **a short — ago** hace poco; CONJ (during) mientras; (whereas) mientras que; (even though) aunque; VT **to — away** pasar

whim [hwɪm] N capricho *m*, antojo *m*

whimper [hwímpɚ] VI/VT lloriquear, gimotear; N lloriqueo *m*, gimoteo *m*

whimsical [hwímzɪkəl] ADJ caprichoso, antojadizo

whine [hwaɪn] VI (whimper) gemir; (complain) quejarse; N (whimper) gemido *m*; (complaint) quejido *m*; **stop whining!** ¡deja de quejarte!

whiner [hwáɪnɚ] N llorón -ona *mf*, quejica *mf*

whiny [hwáɪni] ADJ quejoso, quejica

whip [hwɪp] N azote *m*, látigo *m*, rebenque *m*; VT (hit with a whip) azotar, fustigar; (spank) zurrar, dar una paliza; (beat to a froth) batir; (defeat) vencer; **to — out** sacar; **to — up** (prepare) preparar rápidamente; (incite) incitar

whipping [hwípɪŋ] N zurra *f*, paliza *f*; **— cream** crema para batir *f*

whir [hwɚ] VI zumbar; N zumbido *m*

whirl [hwɚl] VI girar; **to — around** arremolinarse; **my head —s** me da vueltas la cabeza; N (rotation) giro *m*; (of water) remolino *m*; **—pool** remolino *m*; **—pool bath** baño de remolino *m*; **—wind** torbellino *m*, remolino de viento *m*; **—wind tour** gira relámpago *f*; **my head is in a —** me da vueltas la cabeza; **to give it a —** probarlo

whisk [hwɪsk] VT (sweep) barrer; (beat) batir; **to — away** llevarse de prisa; VI **to — by** pasar rápidamente; N (broom) escobilla *f*; (beater) batidor *m*

whisker [hwískɚ] N (hair of beard) pelo de la barba *m*; (sideburn) patilla *f*; (of animals) bigote *m*

whiskey, whisky [hwíski] N whisky *m*

whisper [hwíspɚ] VI/VT (person) cuchichear, secretear; (leaves, water) susurrar; N (people) cuchicheo *m*; (leaves, water) susurro *m*; **to talk in a —** cuchichear

whistle [hwísəl] VI/VT silbar; (loud) chiflar; (in protest) rechiflar; VI (referee, train) pitar; **to — for someone** llamar a uno con un silbido; N (sound) silbido *m*; (loud sound) chiflido *m*; (of a referee) pitido *m*; (instrument) silbato *m*, pito *m*; **—-blower** acusador -ora *mf*

white [hwaɪt] ADJ (color, ethnicity) blanco; **— blood cell** glóbulo blanco *m*; **— bread** pan blanco *m*; **—caps** cabrillas *f pl*; **—-collar** administrativo, de cuello blanco; **— gold** oro blanco *m*; **— hair** cana *f*; **— lie** mentirilla *f*; **— noise** ruido blanco *m*; **—wash** (paint) lechada *f*; (cover-up) encubrimiento *m*; N blanco *m* (also ethnicity); (of egg) clara *f*; VT **to —wash** (paint) blanquear, enjalbegar; (cover up) encubrir

whiten [hwaɪtn] VI/VT blanquear[se], emblanquecer

whiteness [hwáɪtnɪs] N blancura *f*

whitish [hwáɪdɪʃ] ADJ blancuzco, blanquecino

whittle [hwídl] VI/VT tallar; **to — away** ir gastando; **to — down expenses** reducir los gastos

whiz [hwɪz] VI zumbar; **to — by** pasar zumbando; VT hacer zumbar; N (sound) zumbido *m*; (ace) as *m*; — **kid** niño -ña prodigio *mf*

who [hu] REL PRON quien[es]; INTERR PRON quién[es]; **he —** el que

WHO [World Health Organization] [dábə1juétʃó] N OMS *f*

whoa [hwo] INTERJ (to express amazement) ¡jo! (to stop a horse) ¡so!

whoever [huévə-] REL PRON (whatever person) quienquiera que, el/la que; INTERR PRON (who) quién

whole [hoł] ADJ (complete) completo, íntegro; (unbroken) entero; (uninjured) ileso; —- **grain** integral; **the — day** todo el día; **to go — hog** tirar la casa por la ventana; N todo *m*; (for amounts) totalidad *f*; —**sale** venta al por mayor *f*, mayoreo *m*; —**saler** comerciante al por mayor *mf*, mayorista *mf*, almacenista *mf*; **as a —** en su totalidad; **on the —** en general; ADV —**sale** al por mayor; VI/VT **to —sale** vender al por mayor

wholesome [hółsəm] ADJ sano

whom [hum] REL PRON a quien[es]; **for/to/ with —** para/a/con quien; INTERR PRON a quién[es]

whoop [hwup] N (shout) grito *m*; (gasp) respiración convulsiva *f*; VI (person) gritar; (owl) ulular; **to — it up** armar jaleo

whopper [hwápə-] N (large thing) cosa enorme *f*; (lie) mentira *f*, trola *f*

whopping [hwápɪŋ] ADJ enorme

whose [huz] REL PRON cuyo; **the man — son is here** el hombre cuyo hijo está aquí; INTERR PRON de quién; **— book is this?** ¿de quién es este libro?

why [hwaɪ] ADV & CONJ por qué; **that's the reason — he left** es por eso que se fue; N porqué *m*; INTERJ **—, of course!** ¡pero claro!

wick [wɪk] N mecha *f*, pabilo *m*

wicked [wɪkɪd] ADJ malvado, perverso

wickedness [wɪkɪdnɪs] N maldad *f*, perversidad *f*

wicker [wɪkə-] N mimbre *m*; **— chair** silla de mimbre *f*

wide [waɪd] ADJ (broad) ancho; (of great range) amplio; (spacious) vasto, extenso; **— apart** muy apartados; —-**awake** muy despierto, despabilado; **— body** avión de fuselaje ancho *m*; —-**eyed** ojiabierto, con los ojos bien abiertos; **— of the mark** lejos del blanco; —- **open** abierto de par en par; —**receiver** receptor abierto *m*; —**spread** (over a wide area) extendido; (among many people) generalizado; **to open —** (a door) abrir de par

en par; (one's mouth) abrir bien; **two feet —** dos pies de ancho

widely [wáɪdli] ADV **it is — known that** es bien sabido que; **he is a — known artist** es un artista muy conocido; **he is — read** es muy leído; **— different versions** versiones muy diferentes

widen [wáɪdn] VI/VT ensanchar[se], ampliar[se]

widow [wído] N viuda *f*

widower [wídoə] N viudo *m*

width [wɪdθ] N ancho *m*, anchura *f*

wield [wiłd] VT (power) ejercer; (tool) manejar; (weapon) blandir, esgrimir

wife [waɪf] N esposa *f*, señora *f*, *Sp* mujer *f*

wifi [wireless fidelity] [wáɪfaɪ] N wifi *f*

wig [wɪg] N peluca *f*

wiggle [wígəł] VI/VT (hips) menear[se]; (toes) mover[se]; N (of hips) meneo *m*; (of toes) movimiento *m*; **— room** flexibilidad *f*

wigwam [wígwɑm] N tienda indígena *f*

wild [waɪłd] ADJ (animal, savage) salvaje, bravío, bronco; (plant) silvestre; (party) desenfrenado; (conduct) alocado; (storm, temperament) violento; (hair) desordenado; (look) extraviado, desencajado; (enthusiasm) delirante; **— boar** jabalí *m*; **— card** comodín *m*; —**cat** gato montés *m*; —-**eyed** de mirada extraviada, con los ojos desencajados; —**fire** fuego arrasador *m*; —**flower** flor silvestre *f*; **— goose chase** búsqueda inútil *f*; —**life** fauna *f*; **I'm just — about Mary** estoy loco por María; **not in your —est dreams** ni lo pienses; **to drive someone —** volver loco a alguien; **to talk —** decir disparates; N **—s** regiones salvajes *f pl*

wilderness [wíłdə-nɪs] N (near mountains) monte *m*; (desert) desierto *m*; (jungle) jungla *f*

wile [waɪł] N artimaña *f*, treta *f*

will [wɪł] VT (use willpower) conseguir a fuerza de voluntad; (bequeath) legar, dejar; V AUX **if you —** si quieres; **she — come** va a venir, vendrá; **this motorcycle — go 100 mph** esta motocicleta puede hacer 100 millas por hora; **in spite of everything, he — not stop complaining** a pesar de todo, no deja de quejarse; **she — just sit for hours doing nothing** se pasa horas sentada sin hacer nada; **that — do** basta; N (wish) voluntad *f*; (testament) testamento *m*; —**power** fuerza de voluntad *f*; **at —** a discreción, a voluntad

willful [wíłfəł] ADJ testarudo, porfiado

willies [wíliz] N escalofríos *m pl*

willing [wílɪŋ] ADJ dispuesto, voluntarioso

willingly [wílɪŋli] ADV de buena gana, gustosamente

willingness [wílɪŋnɪs] N buena voluntad *f*, buena gana *f*

willow [wílo] N sauce *m*

wilt [wɪlt] VI/VT (plant) marchitar[se]; VI (person) languidecer

wily [wáɪli] ADJ astuto, artero

wimp [wɪmp] N pelele m

win [wɪn] VI/VT ganar; VT (support, fame, affection) ganarse; (victory) alcanzar, conseguir; **to — out** ganar, triunfar; **to — over** conquistar; **a —— situation** una situación beneficiosa para ambas partes; N victoria f

wince [wɪns] VI hacer una mueca; N mueca f

winch [wɪntʃ] N cabrestante m, torno m, Am guinche m

wind¹ [wɪnd] N (air) viento m; (gas) gases m pl; **—bag** charlatán -ana mf; **—breaker**™ cazadora f; **—fall** ganancia inesperada f; **— instrument** instrumento de viento m; **—mill** molino de viento m; **—pipe** tráquea f; **— power** energía eólica f; **—shield** parabrisas m sg; **—shield wiper** limpiaparabrisas m sg; **—sock** manga de viento f; **—surfing** windsurf m; **— tunnel** túnel aerodinámico m; **to get — of** enterarse de; **to break —** ventosear; **to catch one's —** recobrar el aliento; ADJ **—ward** de barlovento; ADV **—ward** hacia/a barlovento

wind² [waɪnd] VT enrollar; (watch) dar cuerda a; VI (take a bending course) serpentear; **to — around** enrollarse; **to — down** (relax) tranquilizarse; (come to a conclusion) irse terminando; **to — up** (string) enrollar; (a clock) dar cuerda; (a project) completar; (in jail) acabar; VI (turn) vuelta f; (bend) recodo m; **—up** conclusión f

winding [wáɪndɪŋ] ADJ sinuoso; **— staircase** escalera de caracol f

window [wíndo] N (in building, on screen) ventana f; (in building, large) ventanal m; (in car, plane) ventanilla f; (in a shop) escaparate m; Am vidriera f; **—pane** cristal m, vidrio m; **— shade** visillo m; **—sill** alféizar m

windy [wíndi] ADJ ventoso; **it is —** hace/hay viento

wine [waɪn] N vino m; **— cellar** bodega f; **—glass** copa f; **—grower** viticultor -ora mf, viñatero -ra mf; **— industry** industria vinícola f; **—skin** odre m; **— tasting** cata de vinos f

winery [wáɪnəri] N bodega f

wing [wɪŋ] N (of bird, plane, building, table) ala f; **— nut** tuerca [de] mariposa/palomilla f; **—span/—spread** envergadura f; **—tip** extremo del ala m; **in the —s** en los bastidores; **under one's —** al amparo de alguien; **to take —** levantar vuelo; VT volar; VT (wound slightly) herir en el ala/brazo; **to — it** improvisar

winger [wíŋə] N (in soccer) ala mf, extremo mf

wink [wɪŋk] VI/VT guiñar; **to — approval** guiñar en aprobación; **to — at** hacer la vista gorda; N guiño m, guiñada f; **I didn't sleep a — no** pegué un ojo

winner [wínə] N ganador -ora mf, triunfador -ora mf

winning [wínɪŋ] ADJ (successful) ganador, vencedor; (charming) atractivo; **—s** ganancias f pl

wino [wáɪno] N pej borracho -cha mf

winter [wíntə] N invierno m; **— weather** clima invernal m; VI invernar

wintry [wíntri] ADJ invernal

wipe [waɪp] VT (sweat, tears) enjugar; (wet surfaces) secar; (dry surface) limpiar; **to — away** enjugar; **to — off** limpiar; **to — out** aniquilar; **to — up** limpiar

wiper [wáɪpə] N limpiaparabrisas m sg

wire [waɪr] N (filament) alambre m; (telegram) telegrama m; **— fence** alambrado m; **—tap** intervención del teléfono f, pinchazo m; **— transfer** transferencia electrónica f; **by —** por telégrafo; VT (an appliance) alambrar; (a house) electrificar; VI/VT (a message) telegrafiar; (money) girar; **to — together** atar con alambre; **to —tap** intervenir un teléfono, pinchar un teléfono

wired [waɪrd] ADJ (installed) alambrado; (tied) atado con alambre; (electrified) electrificado; (enthusiastic) sobreexcitado

wireless [wáɪrlɪs] ADJ inalámbrico; **— Internet** internet inalámbrico m

wiring [wáɪrɪŋ] N cableado m

wiry [wáɪri] ADJ (skinny) nervudo; (like wire) crespo

wisdom [wízdəm] N (moral) sabiduría f; (scholarly) saber m; **— tooth** muela del juicio f

wise [waɪz] ADJ (discerning) sabio; (prudent) sensato, prudente; (erudite) erudito; **—crack** broma f, chiste m; **— guy** sabihondo m; **the Three — Men** los Tres Reyes Magos; N **in no — de** ningún modo; VI **to — up** avisparse

wish [wɪʃ] VT desear; **I — you were here** ojalá estuvieras aquí; **I — you the best** te deseo lo mejor; **to — for** pedir; **to — upon a star** pedir un deseo; N deseo m; **to make a —** pedir un deseo; **best —es** saludos

wishy-washy [wíʃiwɑʃi] ADJ indeciso

wistful [wístfəl] ADJ (pensive) pensativo; (nostalgic) nostálgico

wit [wɪt] N (intelligence) agudeza f, ingenio m; (verbal humor) gracejo m, sal f, chispa f; (person) persona aguda f, persona ingeniosa f; **to be at one's —s' end** no saber qué más hacer; **to live by one's —s** vivir de su ingenio; **to lose one's —s** perder el juicio; **to use one's —s** valerse de su ingenio

witch [wɪtʃ] N bruja f; **—craft** brujería f; **— hunt** cacería de brujas f

with [wɪθ, wɪð] PREP con; **rice — chicken** arroz con pollo *m*; **the man — glasses** el hombre de gafas; **I left my son — Mary** dejé a mi hijo al cuidado de María; **to be — it** está al día; **— me** conmigo; **— you** contigo, con usted

withdraw [wɪðdrɔ́] VI/VT retirar[se]

withdrawal [wɪðdrɔ́əł] N (of troops) retirada *f*; (from public office) alejamiento *m*; (from a bank) *Am* retiro *m*; *Sp* retirada *f*; **— [symptoms]** síndrome de abstinencia *m*

withdrawn [wɪθdrɔ́n] *see* withdraw

withdrew [wɪθdrú] *see* withdraw

wither [wɪ́ðɚ] VI/VT (of a plant) marchitar[se]; (of a person) consumir[se]; **she — ed him with a look** lo fulminó con la mirada

withheld [wɪθhéłd] *see* withhold

withhold [wɪθhółd] VT (approval) negar; (funds) retener; (truth) ocultar

withholding tax [wɪθhółdɪŋtæks] N impuesto deducido del salario *m*

within [wɪðín] PREP dentro de; **— five miles** a menos de cinco millas; ADV dentro, adentro

without [wɪðáut] PREP sin; **— my seeing him** sin que yo lo vea; ADV fuera, afuera

withstand [wɪθstǽnd] VI/VT resistir

withstood [wɪθstúd] *see* withstand

witness [wɪ́tnɪs] N (person) testigo *mf*; (testimony) testimonio *m*; **to bear —** atestiguar; VT (see) presenciar; (sign) firmar como testigo

witticism [wɪ́DɪsIzem] N ocurrencia *f*

witty [wɪ́Di] ADJ ocurrente, dicharachero

wizard [wɪ́zɚd] N (sorcerer) mago *m*, brujo *m*, hechicero *m*; (computer expert) experto -ta *mf*; (genius) genio *m*

wobble [wábəł] N tambaleo *m*, bamboleo *m*; VI/VT tambalear[se], bombolear[se]

woe [wo] N aflicción *f*; **— is me!** ¡pobre de mí!

woeful [wófəł] ADJ lamentable

wok [wak] N wok *m*

woke [wok] *see* wake

woken [wókən] *see* wake

wolf [wułf] N lobo *m*; **— spider** araña lobo *f*

woman [wúmən] N mujer *f*; *fam* tía *f*; **a — 's touch** un toque femenino; **women's lib[eration]** movimiento de liberación femenina *m*; **women's rights** derechos de la mujer *m pl*

womanhood [wúmənhud] N (condition) condición de mujer *f*; (all women) las mujeres *f pl*

womanizer [wúmənaɪzɚ] N mujeriego *m*

womankind [wúmənkaɪnd] N las mujeres *f pl*

womanly [wúmənli] ADJ femenino

womb [wum] N (uterus) útero *m*, matriz *f*; (insides of something) vientre *m*; (center) seno *m*

won [wʌn] *see* win

wonder [wándɚ] VI/VT preguntarse; **to — at** admirarse de, maravillarse de; **I — what time it is** ¿qué hora será? N (marvel) maravilla *f*; (surprise) asombro *m*; (miracle) milagro *m*; **it's a — that** es asombroso que; **it's no — that** no es de extrañar que

wonderful [wándɚfəł] ADJ maravilloso, estupendo

woo [wu] VI/VT cortejar

wood [wud] N (material, also golf club) madera *f*; (firewood) leña *f*; **— cutter** leñador -ora *mf*; **— louse** cochinilla *f*; **— pecker** pájaro carpintero *m*; **— s** bosque *m*; **— shaving** viruta *f*; **— shed** leñera *f*; **— sman** leñador *m*; **— winds** maderas *f pl*; **— work** carpintería *f*, maderaje *m*; **to come out of the — work** salir de la nada

wooded [wúdɪd] ADJ arbolado

wooden [wúdn̩] ADJ (of wood) de madera; (lifeless) inexpresivo

woody [wúdi] ADJ (with trees) arbolado; (like wood) leñoso

woof [wuf] N (of fabric) trama *f*; INTERJ (sound made by a dog) ¡guau!

wool [wuł] N lana *f*; **— sweater** suéter de lana *m*

woolen [wúlən] ADJ de lana; N **— s** (fabric) tejido de lana *m*; (clothes) ropa de lana *f*

woolly [wúli] ADJ lanudo

word [wɝd] N (lexical unit) vocablo *m*, palabra *f*; (promise) palabra *f*; (news) noticia *f*, aviso *m*; (order) mandato *m*, orden *m*; **— for —** palabra por palabra; **— processing** procesamiento de textos *m*; *Sp* tratamiento de texto[s] *m*; **— s [of a song]** letra [de una canción] *f*; **— spacing** espaciado de palabras *m*; **— wrap** retorno de línea automático *m*; **I found out by — of mouth** me lo dijeron; **may I have a — with you?** ¿podemos hablar? **to eat one's — s** tragarse/comerse las palabras; VT (oral) expresar; (written) formular

wording [wɝ́dɪŋ] N formulación *f*

wordy [wɝ́di] ADJ verboso, prolijo

wore [wɔr] *see* wear

work [wɝk] N (effort) trabajo *m*; (employment) empleo *m*, trabajo *m*; (artistic product, fortification) obra *f*; **— book** cuaderno/libro de trabajo *m*; **— day** día laborable *m*; **— environment** entorno de trabajo *m*; **— flow** flujo de trabajo *m*; **— force** mano de obra *f*; **— load** cantidad/carga de trabajo *f*; **— man** obrero *m*; **— of art** obra de arte *f*; **— out** sesión de ejercicio *f*; **— permit** permiso de trabajo *m*; **— place** lugar de trabajo *m*; **— schedule** horario de trabajo *m*; **— sheet** planilla *f*, hoja de ejercicios *f*; **— shop** taller *m*; **— station** estación de trabajo *f*; **— stoppage** huelga *f*, paro laboral *m*; **— s** fábrica *f*; **the — s** todo; **— week**

semana de trabajo *f*; **he's hard at** — está trabajando duro; ADJ —-**related** laboral; VI (labor) trabajar; (function) funcionar; VT (change) efectuar; (metal, land) trabajar; (a crowd) manipular; (a mine) explotar; (employees) hacer trabajar; **to** — **in[to]** introducir; **to** — **loose** soltar[se], aflojar[se]; **to** — **on** (repair) arreglar; (improve) tratar de mejorar; **to** — **one's way through college** pagarse los estudios trabajando; **to** — **one's way up** ascender a fuerza de trabajo; **to** — **out** (a plan) urdir; (a problem) resolver; **he** —**s out every day** hace ejercicio todos los días; **to** — **overtime** trabajar horas extras; **it all** —**ed out** al final todo salió bien; **to be all** —**ed up** estar sobreexcitado; **to get** —**ed up** agitarse

workaholic [wɜ˞kəhálɪk] N adicto -ta al trabajo *mf*

worker [wɜ˞kə˞] N trabajador -ora *mf*; (in a factory) obrero -ra *mf*; (in an office) oficinista *mf*

working [wɜ˞kɪŋ] N (act of someone who works, shaping of metals) trabajo *m*; (operation) funcionamiento *m*, operación *f*; (of a problem) cálculo *m*; (of a mine) explotación *f*; ADJ (class) obrero, trabajador; (majority) suficiente; — **class** clase obrera/trabajadora *f*; — **lunch** comida de trabajo *f*; —**man** obrero *m*

workmanship [wɜ˞kmənʃɪp] N (skill) habilidad *f*, destreza *f*; (quality of work) confección *f*

world [wɜ˞ld] N mundo *m*; — **Bank** Banco Mundial *m*; — **Cup** Copa del Mundo *f*; —**view** cosmovisión *f*; — **war** guerra mundial *f*; — **Wide Web** web *f*, red [mundial electrónica] *f*, ADJ —-**class** de categoría mundial; —-**famous** de fama mundial; —-**shaking** trascendental; —-**wide** mundial

worldly [wɜ˞ldli] ADJ (mundane) mundano, temporal; (sophisticated) de mundo, corrido; (material) material

worm [wɜ˞m] N gusano *m*; ADJ —-**eaten** comido por los gusanos, carcomido; VT desparasitar, quitar las lombrices; **to** — **a secret out of someone** extraerle/sonsacarle un secreto a alguien; **to** — **oneself into** insinuarse en

worn [wɔrn] ADJ desgastado, usado

worn [wɔrn] *see* wear

worrisome [wɜ˞isəm] ADJ preocupante, inquietante

worry [wɜ˞i] VI/VT preocupar[se], inquietar[se]; VT (harass) hostigar; VI **to** — **with** juguetear con; N preocupación *f*, inquietud *f*, zozobra *f*; —**wart** preocupón -ona *mf*

worse [wɜ˞s] ADJ & ADV peor; — **and** — cada vez peor; — **than ever** peor que nunca; **from bad to** — de mal en peor; **so much the** — tanto peor; **to be** — **off** estar peor que antes;

to change for the — empeorar[se]; **to get** — empeorar[se]

worship [wɜ˞ʃɪp] N (act of worshiping) adoración *f*; (ceremony) culto *m*; VT (revere) adorar, venerar; VI (attend services) asistir al culto

worshiper [wɜ˞ʃɪpə˞] N (one who worships) adorador -ora *mf*; —**s** fieles *mf pl*

worst [wɜ˞st] ADJ & ADV **the** — **one** el/la peor; **the** — **thing** lo peor; —-**case scenario** el peor de los casos; VT derrotar

worth [wɜ˞θ] ADJ **to be** — **a dollar** valer un dólar; **to be** — **hearing** ser digno de oírse; **to be** —**while** valer la pena; **it's** —-**doing** vale la pena hacerlo; VT valor *m*, valía *f*; **ten cents'** — **of** diez centavos de; **to get one's money's** — **out of** aprovechar al máximo

worthless [wɜ˞θlɪs] ADJ (useless) inútil; (despicable) despreciable; — **check** cheque sin fondos *m*

worthy [wɜ˞ði] ADJ (meritorious) digno, meritorio; (esteemed) benemérito; — **cause** causa noble *f*; — **of praise** digno de elogio; N persona ilustre *mf*

would [wʊd] V AUX I — **do it if I could** lo haría si pudiera; — **you please open the door?** ¿podrías abrir la puerta por favor? **he said he** — **do it** dijo que lo haría; **as a child, I** — **play all the time** de niño, jugaba todo el tiempo; — **that she were alive!** ¡ojalá estuviera viva!

wound[1] [wund] N herida *f*; VI/VT herir; (with an arrow) flechar

wound[2] [waund] *see* wind

wove [wov] *see* weave

woven [wóvən] *see* weave

wow [waʊ] VT impresionar; INTERJ ¡huy!

wrangle [ræŋgəl] VI/VT (quarrel) discutir; (obtain) agenciarse de; VT (herd) juntar; *Am* rodear; N riña *f*, pendencia *f*

wrangler [ræŋglə˞] N vaquero -ra *mf*

wrap [ræp] VT envolver; **to** — **up** (a present) envolver; (a baby) arropar; (a task) terminar; (against the cold) abrigar[se]; **to be** —**ped in** estar envuelto en; **to be** —**ped up in** estar absorto en; N (coat) abrigo *m*; (shawl) chal *m*; —-**up** (summary) resumen *m*; (end) final *m*; **keep under** —**s** mantener secreto

wrapper [ræpə˞] N envoltura *f*, envoltorio *m*

wrapping [ræpɪŋ] N envoltura *f*; — **paper** papel para envolver *m*

wrath [ræθ] N ira *f*, cólera *f*

wreak [rik] VT **to** — **havoc** hacer estragos

wreath [riθ] N corona *f*; — **of smoke** espiral de humo *f*

wreck [rɛk] N (building) ruina *f*; (car, plane) restos *m pl*; (a ship) pecio *m*; (shipwreck) naufragio *m*; (person) desastre *m*, ruina *f*; (accident) accidente *m*; VI tener un accidente; VT (a ship) naufragar; (a car, totally) destrozar; (a car, with minor damage) chocar; (a building) demoler

wreckage [rékɪʤ] N (of a building) escombros *m pl*; (of a car, plane) restos de un accidente *m pl*; (of a ship) pecio *m*

wrecker [rékɚ] N (tow truck) grúa *f*, camión de remolque *m*; (worker) obrero -ra de demolición *mf*

wrench [rentʃ] N (twist) torcedura *f*; (pull) tirón *m*; (tool) llave de tuercas *f*; VT torcer, retorcer; **to — off/out** arrancar de un tirón, arrebatar

wrest [rest] VT (pull) arrancar; (take away) arrebatar

wrestle [résəɫ] VI/VT luchar [con/contra]; N lucha *f*

wrestler [réslɚ] N luchador -ora *mf*

wrestling [réslɪŋ] N lucha libre *f*

wretch [retʃ] N miserable *mf*, infeliz *mf*

wretched [rétʃɪd] ADJ (unfortunate) desdichado, infeliz; (despicable) vil, miserable, arrastrado; (inferior) pésimo

wriggle [rígəɫ] VI culebrear, serpentear; **to — out of** escabullirse de; VT menear, retorcer

wring [rɪŋ] VT (twist) torcer, retorcer; (extract) arrancar; **to — one's hands** retorcerse las manos; **to — out** escurrir

wrinkle [rɪ́ŋkəɫ] N arruga *f*, surco *m*; (problem) problema *m*; VI/VT arrugar[se]

wrist [rɪst] N muñeca *f*; **—watch** reloj [de] pulsera *m*

writ [rɪt] N auto *m*, mandato *m*

write [raɪt] VI/VT escribir; (transfer data) grabar; **to — back** contestar; **to — down** apuntar; **to — off** cancelar; **to — out** escribir en forma completa; **to — -protect** proteger contra grabación; **to — up** hacer un reportaje sobre; **it's written all over his face** se le ve en la cara; **she —s for a living** es escritora; N **— -up** reportaje *m*; **— protection** protección contra grabación *f*

writer [ráɪɾɚ] N escritor -ora *mf*, literato -ta *mf*

writhe [raɪð] VI retorcerse

writing [ráɪɾɪŋ] N (act of writing) escritura *f*; (handwriting) letra *f*, escritura *f*; (style) estilo *m*; **— desk** escritorio *m*; **— paper** papel de escribir *m*; **—s** obra *f*; **to put in —** poner por escrito

written [rítn̩] *see* write

wrong [rɔŋ] ADJ (incorrect) incorrecto, equivocado; (improper) inapropiado; **what's — with you?** ¿qué te pasa? **you are —** estás equivocado; **the — side of a fabric** el revés de una tela; **— side out** con lo de adentro para afuera; **to be on the — side of the road** ir a contramano / en sentido contrario; **that is the — book** ese no es el libro; **it is in the — place** está fuera de lugar; ADV mal; **to go —** salir mal; N (evil) mal *m*; (injustice)

injusticia *f*; **to be in the —** (not be right) estar equivocado; (be to blame) tener la culpa; **to do —** hacer mal; VT perjudicar

wrongful [rɔ́nfəɫ] ADJ injusto, injustificado

wrongly [rɔ́ŋli] ADV (reported) incorrectamente; (accused) injustamente

wrote [rot] *see* write

wrought [rɔt] ADJ forjado; **— iron** hierro forjado *m*

wrung [rʌŋ] *see* wring

wry [raɪ] ADJ (smile) torcido; (remark, humor) irónico; **to make a — face** torcer la cara

WTO [World Trade Organization] [dʌ́bəʧutió] N OMT *f*

WWW [World Wide Web] [dʌ́bəʧudʌ́bəʧudʌ́bəʧu] N web *f*

Xx

xenophobia [zɛnəfóbiə] N xenofobia *f*

Xerox™ [zíraks] N fotocopia *f*; VI/VT fotocopiar

x-rated [éksreɪɾəd] ADJ pornográfico

x-ray [éksre] N rayos X *m pl*, radiografía *f*; VI/VT radiografiar

xylophone [záɪləfon] N xilofón *m*, xilófono *m*

Yy

yacht [jɑt] N yate *m*; VI navegar en yate

y'all [jɔɫ] PRON *Am* ustedes *mf*; *Sp* vosotros -as *mf*

Yankee [jǽŋki] ADJ & N estadounidense del norte del país *mf*

yard [jɑrd] N (measure) yarda [0.9144m] *f*; (spar) verga *f*; (courtyard) patio *m*; (grassy area) jardín *m*; **—stick** (stick) vara de medida [de una yarda] *f*; (criterion) patrón *m*, norma *f*

yarn [jɑrn] N (material) hilo *m*; (story) cuento *m*

yawn [jɔn] VI bostezar; N bostezo *m*

yeah [jéə] ADV *fam* sí; *fam* **— right!** ¡de eso, nada! ¡qué va!

year [jir] N año *m*; **—book** anuario *m*; ADJ **— -end** de fin de año; **—-round** de todo el año; **—-to-date** del año hasta la fecha

yearling [jírlɪŋ] N animal de un año *m*; (of cows) añojo -ja *mf*

yearly [jírli] ADJ anual; ADV anualmente

yearn [jɚn] VI anhelar, suspirar por

yearning [jɚ́nɪŋ] N anhelo *m*

yeast [jist] N levadura *f*

yell [jeɫ] VI/VT gritar; N grito *m*

yellow [jélo] ADJ (color) amarillo; (coward)

cobarde; **— card** (in soccer) tarjeta amarilla *f*; **— fever** fiebre amarilla *f*; **— jacket** avispa *f*; **— pages** páginas amarillas *f pl*; N amarillo *m*; VI/VT poner[se] amarillo, amarillear

yellowish [jέloɪʃ] ADJ amarillento

yelp [jɛłp] VI gañir, aullar; N gañido *m*, aullido *m*

Yemen [jémən] N Yemen *m*

Yemeni [jémənɪ] ADJ & N yemení *mf*

yen [jɛn] N (currency of Japan) yen *m*; (desire) anhelo *m*; VI anhelar

yes [jɛs] ADV sí; **— no question** pregunta de sí o no *f*

yesterday [jέstɚde] ADV & N ayer *m*; **the day before** — anteayer

yet [jɛt] ADV & CONJ **are they here —?** ¿ya llegaron? **they aren't here** — todavía no llegan, aún no han llegado; **— another** otro más; **ugly — charming** feo pero encantador; **as** — todavía, aún

yield [jiłd] VI/VT (surrender, give in) ceder; (produce) rendir, redituar; **to — 5 percent** dar un cinco por ciento de interés; N (production) rendimiento *m*, producción *f*; (of stocks) rédito *m*

yodel [jódł] VI cantar a la tirolesa; N canto tirolés *m*

yoga [jógə] N yoga *m*

yogurt [jógɚt] N yogur *m*

yoke [jok] N (crossbar) yugo *m*; (pair of animals) yunta *f*; (on a shirt) canesú *m*; VT uncir

yolk [jok] N yema *f*

yonder [jándɚ] ADJ aquel; ADV (location) allá; (direction) hacia allá

yore [jɔr] N **in days of** — antaño

you [ju] SUBJ PRON (sg informal) tú; *RP, Central Am* vos; (sg formal) usted; (pl informal) *Sp* vosotros; *Am* ustedes; (pl formal) ustedes; **I see** — (sg informal) te veo; (sg formal) lo veo; (pl informal) *Sp* os veo; *Am* los veo; (pl formal) los veo; **I talk to** — (sg informal) te hablo; (sg formal) le hablo; (pl informal) *Sp* os hablo; *Am* les hablo; (pl formal) les hablo; **I went with** — (sg informal) fui contigo; (sg formal) fui con usted; (pl informal) *Sp* fui con vosotros; *Am* fui con ustedes; (pl formal) fui con ustedes; **it's for** — (sg informal) es para ti; (sg informal) *RP, Central Am* es para vos; (sg formal) es para usted; (pl informal) *Sp* es para vosotros; *Am* es para ustedes; (pl formal) es para ustedes; **this is how** — **make bread** así se hace el pan

young [jʌŋ] ADJ joven; **— man** joven *m*; **— people** gente joven *f*; **— woman** joven *f*; N (offspring) cría *f*

youngster [jʌ́ŋstɚ] N muchacho -cha *mf*, jovencito -ta *mf*

your [jɔr] POSS ADJ **this is** — **dog** (sg informal) este es tu perro; (sg formal) este es su perro;

(pl informal) *Sp* este es vuestro perro, *Am* este es su perro; (pl formal) este es su perro

yours [jɔrz] PRON **this book is** — (sg informal) este libro es tuyo; (sg formal) este libro es suyo / de usted; (pl informal) *Sp* este libro es vuestro; *Am* este libro es suyo / de ustedes; (pl formal) este libro es suyo / de ustedes; **— is bigger** (sg informal) el tuyo / la tuya es más grande; (sg formal) el suyo / el de usted / la suya / la de usted es más grande; (pl informal) *Sp* el vuestro / la vuestra es más grande; *Am* el suyo / el de ustedes es más grande; (pl formal) el suyo / el de ustedes es más grande; **a friend of** — (sg informal) un amigo tuyo; (sg formal) un amigo suyo / de usted; (pl informal) *Sp* un amigo vuestro; *Am* un amigo suyo / de ustedes; **— truly** atentamente

yourself [jɔrsέłf] PRON **you — wrote the letter** (sg informal) tú mismo escribiste la carta; (sg formal) usted mismo escribió la carta; **you yourselves wrote the letter** (pl informal) *Sp* vosotros mismos escribisteis la carta; *Am* ustedes mismos escribieron la carta; (pl formal) ustedes mismos escribieron la carta; **you are not — today** (sg informal) hoy no eres el mismo de siempre; (sg formal) hoy no es el mismo de siempre; **you are not yourselves today** *Sp* hoy no sois los mismos de siempre; *Am* hoy no son los mismos de siempre; (pl formal) hoy no son los mismos de siempre; **you were sitting by** — (sg informal) tú estabas sentado solo; (sg formal) usted estaba sentado solo; **you were sitting by yourselves** (informal) *Sp* vosotros estabais sentados solos; *Am* ustedes estaban sentados solos; (pl formal) ustedes estaban sentados solos; **you look at — at the mirror** (sg informal) tú te miras en el espejo; (sg formal) usted se mira en el espejo; **you look at yourselves at the mirror** (pl informal) *Sp* vosotros os mirais en el espejo; *Am* ustedes se miran en el espejo; (pl formal) ustedes se miran en el espejo; **you bought — a house** (sg informal) te compraste una casa; (sg formal) usted se compró una casa; **you bought yourselves a house** (pl informal) *Sp* os comprasteis una casa; *Am* se compraron una casa; (pl formal) se compraron una casa

youth [juθ] N (person) joven *m*; (young age) juventud *m*

youthful [júθfəł] ADJ juvenil

yo-yo [jójo] N yo-yo *m*

yuan [juán] N yuan *m*

yucca [jákə] N yuca *f*

yuck [jʌk] INTERJ puaj, puaf

Yugoslavia [jugoslávɪə] N Yugoslavia *f*

Yugoslavian [jugoslávɪən] ADJ & N yugoslavo -va *mf*

Yuletide [júłtaɪd] N Navidad *f*

yummy [jámi] ADJ delicioso; INTERJ ¡qué rico!
yuppie [jápi] N yuppie *mf*

Zz

Zambia [zǽmbiə] N Zambia *f*
Zambian [zǽmbiən] ADJ & N zambiano -na *mf*
zany [zéni] ADJ loco, chiflado
zap [zæp] VT liquidar
zeal [ziɫ] N celo *m*, fervor *m*
zealot [zélət] N fanático -ca *mf*
zealous [zéləs] ADJ celoso, fervoroso
zebra [zíbrə] N cebra *f*
zenith [zíníθ] N cenit *m*
zephyr [zéfɚ] N céfiro *m*
zeppelin [zépəlɪn] N zepelín *m*, dirigible *m*
zero [ziro] NUM cero *m*; **there's — possibility that he'll come** las posibilidades de que venga son nulas
zest [zɛst] N entusiasmo *m*
zigzag [zígzæg] N zigzag *m*; ADJ & ADV en zigzag; VI zigzaguear, andar en zigzag; VT hacer zigzaguear
Zimbabwe [zɪmbábwe] N Zimbabue *m*
Zimbabwean [zɪmbábweən] ADJ & N zimbabuo -bua *mf*
zinc [zɪŋk] N cinc *m*, zinc *m*
zip [zɪp] VI/VT cerrar/abrir con cremallera; **to — by** pasar volando; **to — over** ir corriendo; N cero *m*; **— code** código postal *m*
zipper [zípɚ] N cremallera *f*, cierre [relámpago] *m*
zirconium [zɚkóniəm] N circonio *m*
zodiac [zódiæk] N zodíaco *m*
zombie [zámbi] N zombi *mf*
zone [zon] N zona *f*; **— defense** defensa en zonas *f*; VT dividir en zonas
zoning [zónɪŋ] N zonificación *f*
zoo [zu] N zoológico *m*; *Sp* zoo *m*; **—keeper** guardián -ana del zoológico *mf*
zoological [zoəládʒɪkəɫ] ADJ zoológico
zoology [zoáladʒi] N zoología *f*
zoom [zum] VI (make sound) zumbar; **to — in** ampliar una imagen; **to — off** salir zumbando; **to — out** achicar la imagen; N zumbido *m*; **— lens** teleobjetivo *m*, zoom *m*
zucchini [zukíni] N calabacín *m*
zygote [záɪgot] N cigoto *m*, zigoto *m*